SOCIAL MOVEMENTS

Readings on Their Emergence, Mobilization, and Dynamics

Doug McAdam

David A. Snow

University of Arizona

Roxbury Publishing Company

Library of Congress Cataloging-in-Publication Data

McAdam, Doug.
    Social movements: readings on their emergence, mobilization, and dynamics/
    Doug McAdam and David A. Snow
      p. cm.
    Includes bibliographical references and index
    ISBN 0-935732-86-1 (pbk.)
    1. Social movements. 2. Social movements—United States.
    I. Snow, David A., 1943- II. Title.
HN28.M33 1997   96-19081
303.48'4—dc20   CIP

SOCIAL MOVEMENTS: Readings on Their Emergence, Mobilization, and Dynamics

Cover photo credits (beginning in the upper left-hand corner, moving clockwise): (1) photo of Hare Krishna devotees furnished courtesy of the Iskcon World Review; (2) photo of an anti-tree-cutting demonstration provided courtesy of Earth First!; (3) photo of a street march against the mistreatment of animals provided by PETA (People for the Ethical Treatment of Animals); (4) photo of a pro-choice street demonstration provided courtesy of The Feminist Majority Foundation.

Publisher and Editor: Claude Teweles
Production Editors: Sacha A. Howells and Dawn VanDercreek
Assistant Editors: Joyce Rappaport, C. Max-Ryan
Production Assistant: James Ballinger
Typesetting: Synergistic Data Systems

Printed on acid-free paper that meets the standards of the Environmental Protection Agency.

ISBN 0-935732-86-1

ROXBURY PUBLISHING COMPANY
P.O. Box 491044
Los Angeles, California 90049-9044
Tel.: (213) 653-1068
Fax: (213) 653-4140
Email: roxbury@crl.com

Table of Contents

UNIT ONE: EMERGENCE: FACILITATING CONDITIONS   1

Part 1:
Conditions of Strain: Conflict and Breakdown

Part 2:
Conditions of Conduciveness: Political Opportunities

Part 3:
Conditions of Organization: Facilitative Contexts

UNIT TWO: PROCESSES OF MICROMOBILIZATION

Part 4:
Microstructural Factors: Social Networks

Part 5:
Motivational Factors I: Barriers to and Correlates of Participation

Part 10:
Movement Careers: Intra-Movement Dynamics

Part 11:

Outcomes and Consequences of
Social Movement Participation and Activity

Preface

The seeds for this book were sown in 1988 when the two of us and Debra Friedman discussed the compilation of a reader on social movements. For various reasons the project never moved beyond the drafting of a tentative outline. The idea remained dormant until early 1995, when Claude Teweles, the President and Publisher of Roxbury Publishing Company, called to inquire about the prospect of us putting together a reader on collective behavior and social movements. In the ensuing discussions, we both expressed frustration over the laborious and repetitive task of assembling readings and having them copied for the courses we teach on collective action and social movements. And we both relished the prospect of having a ready-made reader available for adoption in our undergraduate and graduate courses. Thus, the timing of Claude's invitation was right, the idea of nearly a decade ago was resuscitated, and we began to forge ahead. This book is the finished product, although not the final one—as we see the reader evolving and changing every several years as new work becomes available.

We believe that *Social Movements: Readings on Their Emergence, Mobilization, and Dynamics* is more than simply a compilation of readings on social movements and related collective action phenomena. We say this because the book includes a fairly lengthy introduction on the conceptualization of social movements. Also, each of the eleven chapters begins with an introduction that sketches the problem, issue, or process addressed and summarizes how the selections enhance understanding of the issue presented.

We wish to emphasize that this book has been a joint enterprise from its inception to its completion. We developed the organizational outline together, assembled the reading selections together, and each wrote the first drafts of half of the chapter introductions. One of us had to be listed first, so we agreed to do it alphabetically. Thus, the order of authorship should be read as nothing more than a formality.

Finally, we want to acknowledge and thank a number of people who assisted us in different ways in bringing this project to fruition: Claude Teweles for rekindling the idea and coaxing us to develop it; Brenda Wilhelm for helping us assemble clean copies of the selected readings; Barb McIntosh for lending her manuscript typing skills to various aspects of the enterprise; and the following eight reviewers—Steve Barkan, University of Maine, Orono; Debra Cornelius, Shippensburg University; William A. Gamson, Boston College; Robert Kleidman, Cleveland State University; Carol Mueller, Arizona State University, West; Nelson Pichardo, SUNY Albany; Verta Taylor, Ohio State University; and Ralph H. Turner, UCLA—for their helpful suggestions, many of which were incorporated into the book. ✦

Doug McAdam
David A. Snow

Alternative Uses of Selections

	Gender	Race and Ethnicity	Non-U.S.	Revolution	Culture	Collective Behavior	Cults and Religious Movements
Part 1							
1. Goldstone			X	X			
2. Bélanger and Pinard		X	X				
3. Useem						X	
Part 2							
4. Jenkins and Perrow		X					
5. Kriesi et al.			X				
6. Kurzman			X	X	X		X
Part 3							
7. Petras and Zetlin			X	X			
8. Morris		X					
9. McAdam		X					
Part 4							
10. Snow et al.							X
11. Gould			X	X			
12. McAdam and Paulsen		X			X		
13. Mueller	X						
Part 5							
14. Oegama and Klandermans			X				
15. Opp and Roehl			X	X			
16. Oliver						X	
17. Walsh and Warland						X	
Part 6							
18. Snow et al.					X		
19. Noonan	X		X	X	X		
20. Ellingson		X			X	X	
Part 7							
21. Loftland					X		X
22. Snow and Phillips					X		X
23. Hirsh					X	X	
24. Hall					X		X
Part 8							
25. Tarrow			X				
26. McAdam		X					
27. Gamson						X	
Part 9							
28. Koopmans			X				
29. Barkan		X					
30. Jasper and Poulsen					X		

	Gender	Race and Ethnicity	Non-U.S.	Revolution	Culture	Collective Behavior	Cults and Religious Movements
Part 10							
31. Taylor	X				X		
32. Staggenborg	X						
33. Haines		X					
34. Rochford						X	X
Part 11							
35. Taylor and Raeburn	X				X		
36. Meyer and Whittier	X						
37. Amenta et al.					X		

About the Contributors

Edwin Amenta is Associate Professor of Sociology at New York University. His interests and publications are in political sociology, comparative and historical sociology, social movements, and social policy. He is the coauthor of a number of papers dealing with the intersection of these topics, and the author of the forthcoming *Bold Relief: Institutional Politics and the Origins of U.S. Public Social Provision in Depression and War*.

Steven E. Barkan is Professor of Sociology at the University of Maine. He is the author of *Protestors on Trial: Criminal Justice in the Southern Civil Rights and Vietnam Antiwar Movements* (1985) and of several journal articles on political trials, rank-and-file feminist activism, racial prejudice and punitive attitudes toward criminals, and other topics. His most recent publication is *Criminology: A Sociological Understanding* (1997).

Sarah Bélanger worked as a graduate student under Maurice Pinard and is currently working as a research analyst with Status of Women Canada. She specializes in socioeconomic research and policy analysis on gender equality issues.

Robert D. Benford is Associate Professor of Sociology at the University of Nebraska-Lincoln. He has published numerous articles on framing processes and other social constructionist issues associated with social movements, nuclear politics, war museums, and environmental controversies. He is the editor of Twayne Publisher's Social Movements Past and Present series.

Bruce G. Carruthers is Associate Professor at Northwestern University. His research intersects both historical and economic foundations of capitalist markets. He has recently published *City of Capital: Politics and Markets in the English Financial Revolution* (1996) and is currently finishing a comparative political study of British and American bankruptcy law.

Karl Dieter-Opp is Professor of Sociology at the University of Leipzig. One of the leading proponents of a rational choice perspective on collective action, Opp has published extensively on the role of micro-attitudinal and meso-level structural factors on constraining individual activism.

Jan Willem Duyvendak received his Ph.D. in political science from the University of Amsterdam in 1993. His dissertation on new social movements in France was subsequently published as a book entitled *The Power of Politics: New Social Movements in France* (1995).

Sheldon Ekland-Olson is Professor of Sociology and Dean of the College of Liberal Arts at the University of Texas at Austin. He is coauthor of *Justice Under Pressure* (1993) and *The Rope, the Chair and the Needle: Capital Punishment in Texas, 1923-90* (1994).

Stephen Ellingson is a recent graduate of the University of Chicago. His dissertation examines how the processes of discursive innovation and contestation shaped the transformation of abolitionism and political action in the United States before the Civil War. His current research interests include the sociology of culture, religion and politics, social movements, and historical sociology.

William A. Gamson is Professor of Sociology at Boston College and codirects the Media Research and Action Project (MRAP). Gamson is the author of several books, including *Talking Politics* (1992) and *The Strategy of Social Protest* (1990). He is a former president of the American Sociological Association. His current interests focus on the media and public education strategies of groups mobilizing around issues of social justice.

Jack Goldstone is Professor of Sociology at the University of California at Davis and one of the foremost authorities on revolution. His book *Revolution and Rebellion in the Early Modern World* (1991) received the 1993 Distinguished Publication Award from the American Sociological Association.

Marco Giugni received his Ph.D. in political science from the University of Geneva. Along with Hanspeter Kriesi, Ruud Koopmans, and Jan Willem Duyvendak, he coauthored *The Politics of New Social Movements in Western Europe: A Comparative Analysis* (1995). His current research interests include the consequences of social movements and national migration policies in comparative perspective.

Roger Gould is Associate Professor of Sociology at the University of Chicago. He recently published *Insurgent Identities,* a study of urban conflict in 19th-century Paris, and is currently doing research on the network context of violence in honor societies.

Herbert H. Haines is Associate Professor of Sociology at the State University of New York, Cortland. He is the author of *Against Capital Punishment: The Anti-Death Penalty Movement in America, 1972-1994* (1996) and *Black Radicals and the Civil Rights Mainstream, 1954-1970 (1988). His research interests include constructionist theory, political contention of crime and criminal justice issues, and interpersonal and collective violence.*

John R. Hall is Professor of Sociology at the University of California, Davis. His work on countercultural social movements includes a study of utopian communal groups in the United States during the 1960s and '70s (*The Ways Out,* 1978), and a sociological and cultural history of Jim Jones and People's Temple (*Gone From the Promised Land,* 1987). His recent publications include essays on culture, stratification, and social movements. He is currently conducting research on the Solar Temple and Aum Shinrikyo in Japan.

Eric L. Hirsch is Associate Professor of Sociology at Providence College. He received his Ph.D. in Sociology from the University of Chicago and taught at Columbia University from 1982-1990. He authored *Urban Revolt: Ethnic Politics in the Nineteenth Century Chicago Labor Movement* (1990) and has published numerous articles on contemporary social movements, homelessness, and racism.

James M. Jasper is a sociologist who lives and writes in New York City. Educated at Harvard and the University of California at Berkeley, he has taught at Berkeley, Columbia, Princeton, and New York University. He is interested in the moral and cultural dimensions of political action and is currently writing a book about race, immigration, and the American character. His works include *Nuclear Politics* (1990), *The Animal Rights Crusade* (1992), and *The Art of Moral Protest* (1997).

J. Craig Jenkins is Professor of Sociology and Faculty Associate at the Mershon Center for International Security, Ohio State University. In addition to his work in social movement theory, he is coeditor with Bert Klandermans of *The Politics of Social Protest: Comparative Perspectives on States and Social Movements* and is working on the development of an early-warning system to forecast humanitarian disasters and refugee problems on a world-wide scale. He also continues his work on social movement philanthropy and the politics of economic policy in the United States.

Bert Klandermans is Professor of Applied Social Psychology at the Free University in Amsterdam, the Netherlands. His research focuses on mobilization and participation in social movements. He is currently studying the Farmers' Protest in the Netherlands and Spain, and (with Johan Olivier, University of Pretoria) the responses of movement and countermovement supporters to social and political transitions in South Africa. He is editor of a series on social movements, protest and contention with the University of Minnesota Press and is author of *Social Construction of Protest: Social Psychological Principles of Movement Participation* and coeditor (with Craig Jenkins) of *The Politics of Social Protest: Comparative Perspectives on States and Social Movements.*

Ruud Koopmans is a senior researcher at the Wissenschaftszentrum Berlin fur Sozialforschung (WZB). He is the author of *Democracy from Below, New Social Movements and the Political System in West Germany* (1995) and coauthor of both *Tussen verbeelding en macht. 25 jaar nieuwe sociale bewegingen in Nederland* (1992) and *New Social Movements in Western Europe: A Comparative Analysis* (1995). His current research focuses on the interplay between extreme right mobilization and the politics of immigration in Western Europe, particularly in Germany.

Hanspeter Kriesi is Professor of Political Science at the University of Geneva, Switzerland. He has taught political and social-cultural sciences at the University of Amsterdam and at the Institute for Sociology at the University of Zurich. He has participated in a number of studies on the motivation of social movements in Western Europe. His current research interests include right-wing extremism, the impact of information on political predispositions, and direct democracy.

Charles Kurzman is Assistant Professor at Georgia State University in Atlanta. Expanding from his doctoral research on the Iranian Revolution, he is currently editing a volume of works by liberal Islamic thinkers and writing a comparative-historical analysis of constitutional revolutions of the early 20th century.

John Lofland is Professor of Sociology at the University of California at Davis and has served as Chair of the Section of Collective Behavior and Social Movements of the American Sociological Association. His publications on social movements include *Social Movement Organizations: Guide to Research on Insurgent Realities* (1996), *Polite Protestors; The American Peace Movement of the 1980s* (1993), *Protest: Studies of Collective Behavior and Social Movements* (1986), and *Doomsday Cult* (Enlarged Edition, 1977). His publications on other topics include, with Lyn H. Lofland, *Analyzing Social Settings: A Guide to Qualitative Observation and Analysis* (Third Edition, 1995).

David S. Meyer is Assistant Professor in the Political Science Department at City College in New York. He has written extensively on peace activism in the United States and on the relationship between institutionalized politics and social movements. His book *A Winter of Discontent: The Nuclear Freeze and American Politics* (1990) brings these two emphases together in an analysis of the emergence and development of the nuclear freeze movement.

Aldon Morris is Professor of Sociology at Northwestern University. His primary research interests are in social movements, racial inequality, and social inequality. He has written extensively on the civil rights movement and is author of *The Origins of the Civil Rights Movements: Black Communities Organizing for Change* (1984). Morris believes that social change efforts should be informed by social scientific knowledge.

Carol Mueller is Associate Professor at the West Campus of Arizona State University. She is a graduate of the University of California at Berkeley (in American History) and of Rutgers and Cornell Universities (in Sociology). She has edited or coedited *Women's Movements of the U.S. and Western Europe* (with Mary Katzenstein); the *Politics of the Gender Gap*; and *Frontiers in Social Movement Theory* (with Aldon Morris). Her current interest is the challenge to social movement theory of non-western collective action, with specific reference to the popular movements that toppled the Honecker regime in the former German Democratic Republic.

Rita K. Noonan is a Ph.D. candidate at Indiana University. Her research focuses on Third World development, gender, social movements, and political sociology. She recently conducted research in Costa Rica under a Fulbright grant and is an American Association of University Women fellow. Her current interests include analyzing the ways in which national priorities for women's health organizatons are contested and reshaped in Costa Rica.

Dirk Oegema is a lecturer in the Department of Political Science at the Free University in Amsterdam, the Netherlands. He recently completed his dissertation on the decline of the Dutch peace movement. Currently he is conducting research in the field of communication and political participation, focusing on voting and participation in social movement organizations.

Pamela E. Oliver is Professor of Sociology at the University of Wisconsin at Madison. Long a major contributor to the field of social movement studies, Oliver is perhaps best known for her work, with Gerald Marwell, on the micro- and meso-level dynamics of mobilization.

Ronnelle Paulsen is Assistant Professor at the University of Texas at Austin. Her research and teaching interests focus on stratification in collective action with an emphasis on community empowerment. She has published a number of articles on these topics and is currently working on a book manuscript entitled *Being Shot At and Missed: Perceptions of Participation in Neighborhood Associations*.

Charles Perrow, Professor of Sociology at Yale University, has long been recognized as one of the leading organizational scholars in the world. His book *Complex Organizations: a Critical Essay* (1986) is a classic work in the field of organizational sociology. He has also conducted research on social movements and more recently contributed to our understanding of complex technological systems and the risks that accompany them with his book *Normal Accidents* (1984).

James Petras is Professor of Sociology at SUNY-Binghamton, and author and coauthor of 25 books. His latest books include *Empire or Re-*

public?: American Global Power and Domestic Decay (1995) and *Democracy and Poverty in Chile* (1993).

Cynthia L. Phillips currently teaches at Our Lady of the Lake University in San Antonio, Texas. She holds a Ph.D. in Sociology from the University of Texas at Austin and a J.D. from the University of Arizona and has taught previously at Cleveland State University and the University of Texas, Permian Basin. She is interested in criminology, the sociology of law, and social psychology.

Maurice Pinard is Professor of Sociology at McGill University. He has published extensively on various political movements and especially on ethnic conflict. He is currently writing on the Québec independence movement and on ethnic politics in comparative prospective.

Jane D. Poulsen is a Ph.D. candidate at New York University. Her research interests are in social movements, economic sociology, and sex and gender. Her dissertation, "The Politics of Institutional Decline," applies a social movement perspective to the decline of organized labor and collective bargaining in the postwar United States.

Nicole C. Raeburn is a Ph.D. candidate in the Department of Sociology at Ohio State University. Her areas of specialization include social movements, gender, and gay and lesbian studies. The reprinted selection (with Verta Taylor) is based on her master's thesis. She is currently working on her dissertation, entitled "The Rise of Lesbian, Gay, and Bisexual Rights in the Workplace."

E. Burke Rockford, Jr. is Professor of Sociology at Middlebury College. He has written extensively on the Hare Krishna movement and is author of *Hare Krishna in America* and coeditor of *Srila Prabhupada* (Bhaktivedanta Book Trust, forthcoming). A new book that addresses changing family structures and the development of the Hare Krishna movement during the 1980s and 1990s is in progress. He recently completed a worldwide survey of 2000 Hare Krishna devotees from over 50 countries.

Dr. Wolfgang Roehl is the director of the computer pool of the Faculty of Education at the University of Hamburg.

Suzanne Staggenborg is Associate Professor of Sociology at McGill University. She is the author of *The Pro-Choice Movement* and a number of articles on social movements and abortion politics. She is currently researching the development of the women's movement and conflicts between movements and countermovements.

Sidney Tarrow is Maxwell M. Upson Professor of Government at Cornell. He has worked for most of his career on the comparative study of social movements and political parties: first, in his published Ph.D. dissertation (*Peasant Communism in Southern Italy,* 1968); then in a reconstruction of the protest cycle on the 1960s in Italy (*Democracy and Disorder,* 1989); and most recently in his synthesis of social movement research in western democratic states (*Power In Movement,* 1994). He is currently working on an expansion of social movement theory into a general approach to contentious politics with Doug McAdam and Charles Tilly, and on a book called *Costumes of Revolt* on the presentation of self in contentious politics.

Verta Taylor is Associate Professor of Sociology at Ohio State University where she has won several teaching awards. Her research focuses on gender and social movements with an emphasis on women's movements and the lesbian and gay movement. She is coauthor (with Leila J. Rupp) on *Survival in the Doldrums: The American Women's Rights Movement, 1945 to the 1960s* and coeditor (with Laurel Richardson and Nancy Whittier) of *Feminist Frontiers IV.* Her most recent book, *Rock-a-by Baby: Feminine Self-Help and Postpartum Depression*, focuses on the transformation of feminism in the modern women's self-help movement and sets forth a framework for analyzing the intersection of gender and social movements.

Bert Useem is Professor of Sociology, University of New Mexico. He is the author of two books on prison riots. The most recent is the *Resolution of Prison Riots* (with Camille Camp and George Camp, Oxford University Press).

Edward J. Walsh and **Rex H. Warland** are Professors at Pennsylvania State University. They have recently completed a book (with D. Clayton Smith), *Recycle or Burn?* on the environmental justice movement. After concluding the Three Mile Island research, which is the topic of their article in this collection (see Walsh's *Democracy in the Shadows* [Greenwood, 1988] for a more comprehensive analysis of the TMI story), they focussed on the emergence and evolution of the national anti-incineration movement. Their research involving grassroots challenges to technological projects, such as nuclear reactors, nuclear waste facilities, and municipal incinerators, reveals both continuities and differences with more commonly studied equity struggles, such as the civil rights and women's movements, prompting them to suggest the theoretical usefulness of a distinction between equity and technology movements.

Nancy Whittier is Associate Professor of Sociology at Smith College. Her principal research focus has been on the women's movement in the Unites States, with emphasis on generational succession in the women's movement and, with David Meyer, on the influence of the women's movement on peace activism in the United States during the 1980s.

Steven K. Worden is Associate Professor at the University of Arkansas at Fayetteville. His interests include the study of prosaic symbolic interactionism, identity and transformation, and religious-occupational subcultures. His research projects currently entail a study of the multiple realities of the Salvation Army and a study of "Hoo-Hoo," an occupationally-based subcultural world in the timber industry.

Maurice Zeitlin is Professor of Sociology at the University of California, Los Angeles. His books include *Revolutionary Politics and the Cuban Working Class* (1967), *The Civil Wars in Chile* (1984), *Landlords & Capitalists* (1988), *The Large Corporation and Contemporary Classes* (1989), and, with J. Stephan-Norris, *Talking Union* (1996).

Lewis A. Zurcher, Jr. was Professor of Sociology and Social Work at the University of Texas at Austin. He passed away at relatively young age in the fall of 1987 following a distinguished career as a scholar, teacher, and administrator. Some of his more notable contributions were in the area of collective behavior and social movements.

Yvonne Zylan is Assistant Professor of Sociology at the University of Arizona. Her research interests include political sociology, the sociology of gender, and social movements. Her work focuses on the construction of gendered subjects and actors within state political institutions, through an examination of the development of welfare and regulatory policies for women in the post-World War II United States. She is also interested in the relationship between gender and social citizenship. ✦

Introduction

Social Movements: Conceptual and Theoretical Issues

Social movements and kindred collective action, such as protest crowds, riots, and revolutions, are conspicuous and significant social happenings. They are conspicuous in that they occur frequently and are striking features of the social landscape. Any daily newspaper or weekly news magazine is likely to refer to movement and protest activity in relation to one of the more hotly contested issues of our time: abortion, animal rights, civil rights, environmental protection, family values, gender equality, government intrusion, gun control, homosexuality, labor and management conflict, nuclear weapons, poverty, race and ethnic relations, religious freedom, and welfare reform. Indeed, it is difficult to think of a major social issue in which social movements are not involved on one or both sides.

The movements associated with such issues are important social phenomena, as well, capturing our attention because they bring into bold relief sizeable numbers of people attempting to promote or resist social change as they act on behalf of common interests or values about which they feel strongly. To understand the politics and conflicts associated with important contemporary and historical social issues, it is crucial to acquire an understanding of the character and dynamics of the social movements associated with these issues. The central objective of this book is to provide such an understanding by presenting readings that illuminate the dynamics of social movements—from their emergence, through the trials and tribulations of mobilization, to their tactical actions and consequences.

In this introduction, we provide a working conceptualization of social movements, explain the various components of that conception, iden-

tify the various sets of social actors relevant to social movements, discuss the relationship between social movements and other forms of collective action, and elaborate the logic for the substantive issues addressed and the way in which we have organized this book.

Conceptualizing Social Movements

Although there are many definitions of social movements, most conceptual efforts include the following elements: (1) collective or joint action; (2) change-oriented goals; (3) some degree of organization; (4) some degree of temporal continuity; and (5) some extrainstitutional collective action, or at least a mixture of extrainstitutuional (protesting in the streets) and institutional (political lobbying) activity. Blending these elements together, we can define a social movement as a collectivity acting with some degree of organization and continuity outside of institutional channels for the purpose of promoting or resisting change in the group, society, or world order of which it is a part.[1] To clarify this conceptualization of social movements, we turn to an elaboration of its various components.

Movements as Agents of Change

Since the promotion or resistance of change is the raison d'être for all social movements, we begin with this defining characteristic. Caution must be exercised, lest we generalize to all movements as if they are cut from the same cloth. Even though most social movements are carriers of change, they vary dramatically in the kinds and degree of change sought. Virtually all typologies of social movements acknowledge this point, at least with respect to the degree or amount of change pursued. Perhaps the most common distinction is between reform and revolutionary movements. Neil Smelser's approach (1962) is illustrative, as he divides social movements into two generic categories: norm-oriented and value-oriented. Norm-oriented movements are concerned with producing more limited but specific changes within a social system, particularly with respect to rules of access to and operation within the various institutional arenas of society. Thus, movements that have sought to introduce or change child labor laws, decriminalize or legalize drugs such as marijuana, and introduce measures to cut down on drunk driving might all be considered norm-oriented. Value-oriented movements, on the other hand, are said to be concerned with more fundamental change, and thus seek to alter basic values and the institutional bedrock on which they rest. The most obvious examples would be revolutionary movements, such as those that undergirded the French, American, and Russian revolutions, or broad-based struggles, such as the civil rights or women's movements, which have sought to transform race or gender relations in society.

A similar scheme is provided by Roy Wallis's distinction between world-rejecting and world-affirming movements (1984). Although this dichotomy was developed with religious movements in mind, its application parallels that of the value-oriented/norm-oriented distinction. Thus, world-rejecting movements, like Smelser's value-oriented movement, condemn the prevailing social order as a whole, both its underlying values and institutional arrangements. The world-affirming movement, like the norm-oriented movement, is less contemptuous of and hostile toward the social order in which it is embedded and thus can live within the world if certain modifications are made.

One of the problems with the above typologies is that they are based primarily on the single dimension of the amount of change sought. That change can have a different locus, or occur at different levels, is only implicitly considered.

The anthropologist David Aberle addresses this oversight in his book on the Peyote cult among America's Navajo Indians (1966). Aberle differentiates social movements based both on the amount or degree of change and the locus or level of change sought. The locus dimension directs attention to the target of change, which can vary from the individual to some aspect or level of social structure. The amount dimension, as we have seen, distinguishes among movements in terms of the degree of change sought, with some movements pursuing only partial change and other movements seeking total change. Although any set of movements can be situated along continua of both dimensions, the cross-classification of these two dimensions yields four generic types of movements, as diagrammed in the following table.

Table 1
***Types of Social Movements by
Change Orientation***

What Aberle calls *alterative* movements seek partial change in individuals (cell A). Presumed or actual character and psychological tendencies or habits are regarded as troublesome and in need of exorcism or repair. Examples of such individual tendencies or habits that have been targeted for change by social movements include the use of alcohol, sexual practices and contraceptive behavior, level of personal assertiveness, abusive interpersonal behavior, and low self-regard. In each case, the object of change is some individual shortcoming, deficit, or patterned tendency. The therapeutic and self-help movements that have flourished in the United States since the 1970s and 1980s are examples of movements that seek to do something about such shortcomings or tendencies. Some of the better known alternatives within this larger movement, often referred to as the human potential movement, include Silva Mind Control, Transcendental Meditation, and Erhard Seminar's Training, also known in terms of its italicized, lower-case acronym *est*.

It is reasonable to wonder whether such self-improvement efforts are really social movements inasmuch as the individual is the primary focus of change. Yet it is also difficult to argue with the contention that the alteration of thousands of individuals may be one avenue to social change. Insofar as self-help themes are mixed with the idea of social change through personal transformation, as is the case with the rhetoric of many such groups, they do constitute a type of social movement.

This linkage between individual change and social change is even more transparent in the case of what Aberle calls *redemptive* movements (cell B). These movements also focus on individuals as the object of change or control, but they seek total rather than partial change. From the vantage point of these movements, social ills and problems of all varieties are seen as rooted in individuals and their misguided behaviors or ill-informed ideas and beliefs. If individuals are transformed or redeemed, than the larger problem is resolved. Personal transformation is thus seen as the key to societal transformation. Religious movements and cults are among the best-known carriers of this highly individualistic approach to broader social issues. A large number of such movements surfaced and flowered in much of the Western world in the 1970s: few were as well known as the Hare Krishna movement, the Children of God, the "Moonies" or Unification Church, and the Nichiren Shoshu Buddhist movement. All are still active in varying degrees, and all still claim to be interested in transforming the world by affecting personal transformation of the masses.

The third category of movements in Aberle's typology is termed *reformative* (cell C). Movements of this ilk seek limited change in the social system in which they are embedded. There is no blanket rejection of the present order of things, but an attempt instead to rectify or neutralize specific perceived wrongs or threats. The objective may be to reduce or remove some actual or perceived threat to the interests of a specific human social group, such as neighborhood residents. Or it may be a category of threatened animals, as in the cases of the spotted owl of Oregon and the red squirrel on Mt. Graham in southern Arizona. The objective may also be to protect the environment, as with the movement to save the rain forests of the world. Perhaps even more

common are movements that seek to improve or preserve the lifestyle or treatment of a particular category of individuals, such as women, African Americans, Hispanic Americans, religious fundamentalists, and the physically disabled.

The final generic category of movements seek total change in the broader social structure and its associated ideational bedrock. Aberle termed such movements *transformative* (cell D), but these are more commonly referred to as revolutionary. Because the amount of change sought tends to be all-embracing and cataclysmic, these movements are typically the most dramatic and historically consequential. Some of the more notable examples include the classical revolutionary movements that raged in France from 1787 to 1800 and in Russia from 1917 to 1921, as well as the millenarian movements that seek to wipe the slate clean in preparation for the new millennial or new day on earth. One such millennial effort was the Anabaptist movement that arose in the first half of the 1500s in northern Europe in opposition to Roman Catholicism and the Lutheran Reformation. Its aim, as described by Norman Cohn in *The Pursuit of the Millennium* (1961), was to "sweep Christendom clean of ungodly rulers" and create a "New Israel" on earth.

The foregoing typology clearly helps to situate movements in terms of their dominant change orientation. Although movements seldom fit neatly into one of the four cells, they are typically skewed more in one direction than another along the two-change continua. Thus, a typology such as Aberle's is useful in helping to illuminate the diversity among movements, particularly in terms of their change-oriented objectives. But, as we will see, the course and character of social movements are influenced not only by their objectives, but also by the context in which they arise, external relations with the communities in which they exist, and their own internal dynamics.

However movements are categorized, the fact that there are different kinds raises questions about the sociohistorical conditions that account for their emergence and why some individuals rather than others participate in various movements. But these and other questions pertaining to the origins, operation, and dynamics of social movements will have to wait until we clarify the other elements of our conceptualization.

Movements as Collectivities Acting Outside of Institutional Channels

In thinking of movements as carriers of change, it is important to keep in mind that the unit of reference is a collectivity—that is, a group of interrelated persons engaged in joint action—rather than an aggregate of persons acting in a parallel but disconnected fashion. This understanding helps to distinguish social movements from other social phenomena that are sometimes related to but different from movements. *Social trends* are one such phenomenon. They refer to large-scale, far-reaching changes in patterns of social organization and behavior over an extended period of time. Prominent examples include industrialization, urbanization, and bureaucratization, as well as changes in patterns of employment, marital stability, and the like. Such trends affect the probability that specific events or life experiences will be altered, and may therefore provide the grievance or organizational base for social movements. But social trends are not in themselves social movements.

Nor are social movements coherent pockets of public opinion or what others have referred to as *sentiment pools*. McCarthy and Zald, for example, have defined social movements in this fashion by referring to them as "a set of opinions and beliefs in a population which represents preferences for changing some elements of the social structure or reward distribution of a society" (1977: 1217-1218). Sets of change-oriented opinions and beliefs do not constitute collective action, however. They are no doubt a necessary condition for such joint action, but in actuality they are only preference structures or unmobilized sentiment pools, not social movements.

Also sometimes confused with social movements are *mass migrations* of individuals, as in the case of a gold rush, a land rush, or the migration of large numbers of citizens from one region of a country to another or across national borders. Such mass movements share some characteristics of social movements, but not the most essential one, namely the pursuit or resistance of social change through engagement in noninstitutional tactical action. Additionally, the behaviors associated with mass migrations tend to be associated with individual rather than collective interests and objectives.

To argue that social trends, unmobilized sentiment pools, and mass migrations should not be equated directly with social movements is not to suggest that these phenomena may not have important implications for change in a particular society or across societies. Additionally, these phenomena may often be related to social movements in important ways, but they do not constitute social movements per se.

Interest groups comprise another set of collective phenomena that are often equated with social movements. Clearly interest groups, such as the American Medical Association and the National Rifle Association, and reform-oriented social movements, such as the pro-choice and anti-abortion movements, bear striking resemblances insofar as both seek to promote or resist change in some aspect of social life. Yet there are also striking differences. Probably the most important is that they stand in a different relationship to the mainstream political environment. Interest groups are embedded within that environment; they are typically regarded as legitimate actors within the political arena. Social movements, on the other hand, are typically outside of the polity, or overlap with it in a precarious fashion. Another important difference follows: interest groups pursue their collective objectives almost exclusively through institutionalized means, such as lobbying and soliciting campaign contributions, whereas social movements are more or less forced to resort to the use of noninstitutional means or tactics, such as conducting boycotts, blockades, encampments, and sit-ins, in pursuit of their collective ends. Social movements may sometimes engage in institutionalized action as well, but their action repertoires are almost always skewed in the direction of extrainstitutional lines of action. Thus, to paraphrase William Gamson (1990), interests groups and social movements are not so much different species as members of the same species positioned differently in relation to the polity. But that differential positioning is sufficiently important to produce different sets of strategic and tactical behaviors, and thus different kinds of collectivities.[2]

Movements as Organizations and Organized Activity

Dating back to the work of some of the early political sociologists, such as Lenin (1929) and

Michels (1949), the organizational dimension of social movements has been featured in most treatments of the topic. But it was not until McCarthy and Zald's (1973, 1977) articulation of the resource mobilization perspective that the organizational dimension took center stage and social movement organizations (SMOs) became the focal unit of analysis. Since then, there has been ongoing debate about the centrality of formal organization to the operation of social movements and about whether it impedes or facilitates a movement's goal-attainment efforts (Gamson 1990; Melucci 1989; Piven and Cloward 1977).

In attempting to clarify this debate, Tarrow (1994) has distinguished between social movements as formal organizations and the organization of collective action. We think this is an important distinction, but we also think it is difficult to understand the operation and dynamics of social movements, including most movement-related collective action, without reference to organization and organizational characteristics. When we think of the civil rights movement of the 1960s, for example, a number of organizational representatives spring to mind, such as the National Association for the Advancement of Colored People (NAACP), the Congress of Racial Equality (CORE), the Southern Christian Leadership Conference (SCLC), and the Student Non-Violent Coordinating Committee (SNCC). The same is also true of the women's movement, the pro-life and pro-choice movements, and the environmental movement.

In each of these movements, we see the interests of a particular constituency represented and promoted by a number of organizations that are routinely referred to in the literature as SMOs. Of course, some movements are associated with a single organization, as is more likely to be the case with locally-based movements. But whether movements are connected with one or more SMOs, those organizations function to carry and dramatize the concerns and grievances of their respective constituencies, thus making social movements and social movement organizations opposite sides of the same coin. It is for this reason that a semblance of organization needs to be included as a component of the conceptualization of social movements, but without specifying the character of the organization for any specific movement. We add this qualifica-

tion because the character of a movement's organization—whether it is formal or informal, tightly or loosely structured, for example—and its relevance to the movement's operation and goal-attainment efforts are variable phenomena that constitute important topics for investigation.

Movements Existing With Some Temporal Continuity

The final element of our conceptualization requiring brief elaboration is the observation that social movements exist or operate with some degree of temporal continuity. This characteristic helps to distinguish movements from more ephemeral kinds of collective behavior, such as unconventional crowds or gatherings. The point is that social movements are rarely, if ever, fly-by-night phenomena that are here today and gone tomorrow. The word movement itself implies some degree of development and continuity. Moreover, the kinds of changes movements pursue typically require sustained, organized activity. Indeed, it is difficult to imagine any movement making progress in pursuing its objectives without persistent, almost nagging, collective action. Continuity, like organization, is a matter of degree, of course. But some degree of sustained collective action is an essential characteristic of social movements, as we conceive of them.[3]

Categories of Actors Relevant to Social Movements

We have presented and elaborated our conceptualization of social movements as collectivities working with some degree of organization and continuity to promote or resist change through a mixture of extrainstitutional and institutionalized means. But what kind of collectivity is a social movement? What is the relationship between the various actors relevant to social movements? How do we conceptualize movement participants? How do they differ from other pertinent actors, and how is a movement bounded from other relevant collectivities and aggregations? Borrowing on the work of Hunt, Benford, and Snow (1994), we suggest that the various sets of actors relevant to the course and character of a social movement fall into three clusters or categories: protagonists, antagonists, and bystanders.

Protagonists

The protagonists include all groups and collectivities that are supportive of the movement or whose interests are represented by it. They include a movement's adherents, constituency, and beneficiaries. At the core of a movement's protagonists are its *adherents*. The adherents include those individuals who engage in movement activities that are conducted in pursuit of its objectives. At a minimum, such engagement typically involves participating in one or more movement activities, be it a protest rally, a sit-in, or a more formal organizational meeting. Presumably these individuals share certain key values and objectives and identify themselves with the movement. It is useful to keep in mind, however, that most adherents are not equally involved. Some may devote considerable time and energy to movement activities and campaigns, while others may do little other than pay dues or attend an occasional meeting or activity. It is therefore "useful to distinguish *activists* from the bulk of the adherents by the level of effort and sacrifice they give to the cause" (Turner and Killian 1987: 225).

Most movement adherents are drawn from its *constituency*, the second set of actors that comprise the movement's protagonist base. Although the term is borrowed from politics, it refers, in the context of social movements, to the aggregation of individuals the movement organization claims to represent and which typically is a major source of resources and support. In actuality, not all individuals who comprise a movement's constituency are wildly enthusiastic about it; some may be indifferent, others sympathetic but uninterested in or unable to provide direct support, while still others may constitute the movement's primary resource base. As suggested above, it is from this latter group of constituents that adherents are likely to be drawn.

Turning to the third category of protagonists, it is often assumed that a movement's constituents are also the direct *beneficiaries* of the changes it is trying to effect. Although this is typically the case, the relationship between a movement's constituency and its beneficiaries is not simple. If the good or change being pursued is a public one, such as clean air or clean water, then clearly it is not something that can be targeted or preserved for a specific group or aggregation.[4] Instead, the larger public benefits. In such cases, most of the beneficiaries can be thought of as *free riders* inasmuch as they have contributed neither sympathetic support nor more tangible resources to the movement.[5] In other cases, when the objective of a movement is to expand the rights and opportunities of a particular disadvantaged group, such as Native Americans, the disabled, and women, all of the direct beneficiaries may be constituents, but not all of the constituents will necessarily be beneficiaries. Consider, for example, straights marching in support of gay and lesbian rights, men linking arms with women in support of the Equal Rights Amendment, and over 1,000 northern college students, most of them white, volunteering to go to Mississippi in June 1964 to register black voters and staff "freedom schools" as part of the Freedom Summer campaign organized by the Student Non-Violent Coordinating Committee.[6] In each of these examples, individuals are supporting a movement without standing to benefit directly if movement objectives are obtained. Such individuals can be thought of as either *conscience adherents* or *conscience constituents*, depending on the nature of support they provide (McCarthy and Zald 1977).

Antagonists

Standing in opposition to a movement's adherents and constituents are the set of actors or groups we refer to as antagonists. Included among a movement's antagonists are the *targets* of its actions, such as a city, state, or national government, sometimes a corporation like Exxon, or perhaps a university where research or admissions practices are targeted. Any set of individuals, groups, or institutions can be the target of the change a movement is attempting to effect. Since many individuals and groupings within a movement's environment of operation may not only be unsympathetic to a movement's objectives and activities, but may also perceive the movement's interests as antithetical to their own, it is not uncommon for *countermovements* to emerge. The objective of these countermovements is straightforward: to halt or neutralize the goal attainment activities of the movement in question. Thus, the anti-abortion or pro-life movement emerged in response to the success of the pro-choice movement, as manifested most clearly in the 1973 Roe vs. Wade Supreme Court decision.

Bystanders

The third category of actors relevant to the operation of a social movement are bystanders, elements of a community which are initially uninterested in the issue at hand. Bystanders have no perceptible stake in the objectives and outcomes of a movement, and thus remain somewhat aloof and indifferent. But interest in a movement and its activities can be activated. In some instances, a change in orientation may result from the disruption of bystanders' taken-for-granted daily routines. When this occurs, bystanders are more likely to call for a cessation of protest activities than to choose a side. In other instances, bystander interest is piqued by movement activities and appeals, often through the media, and some bystander groups are transformed into constituents or even adherents. And in still other cases, the actions of movement antagonists, be they the police or countermovements, may engender opposition to the movement. Just as likely, however, is the possibility that police are perceived as overreacting and unwittingly generate sympathy for the movement. In light of these possibilities, it is clear that the relationship between a movement's protagonists, antagonists, and bystanders, including the media, is a dynamic and ongoing process that is central to a movement's career.

Social Movements as a Form of Collective Action

At several points throughout the course of this chapter we have suggested that social movements are a form of collective action as well as a sponsor of collective action. Since the term "collective action" is used broadly and sometimes interchangeably with the term "social movement" in the literature, it is useful to clarify the relationship between these concepts and such related constructs as collective behavior and crowds.

Although the term collective action is widely used, one is hard-pressed to find a clear, consensual definition of the term. Broadly and logically speaking, collective action encompasses any goal-directed activity jointly pursued by two or more individuals. The action is pursued jointly because an individual is unlikely to attain the objective. Thus, at a rudimentary level, collective action is joint action in pursuit of a common objective.

Since this basic conception encompasses a significant proportion of human behavior, it is useful to distinguish between those collective actions that are institutionalized or normatively sanctioned and those which fall outside of institutional channels. Since social movements are defined in part by their operation outside of institutional channels, introducing this distinction clearly reduces the number of joint actions that bear a resemblance to movements. As Sidney Tarrow notes: collective action not only "takes many forms," but "most of it occurs within institutions on the part of constituted groups who act in the name of goals that would hardly raise an eyebrow" (1994: 2).

Still, many collective actions fall into the non-institutional category. Traditionally, most of these non-institutional collective actions, including those associated with social movements, have been discussed and analyzed as varieties of collective behavior. Broadly conceived, collective behavior refers to "extrainstitutional, group-problem solving behavior that encompasses an array of collective actions, ranging from protest demonstrations, to behavior in disasters, to mass or diffuse phenomena, such as fads and crazes, to social movements and even revolution" (Snow and Oliver 1995: 571).

Thus, just as social movements are a form of collective action, so they also constitute a species of collective behavior. But they also differ from most of the other variants of collective behavior—such as crowds, panic, fads, and crazes—because of their change-oriented goals, semblance of organization, and temporal continuity.

To note the distinction between social movements and other species of collective behavior is not to assert that they do not overlap or commingle at times. The relationship between nonconventional crowd activity and social movements is illustrative. Although some crowds arise spontaneously and dissipate just as quickly, such as those that spring up around accidents and fires, others are the result of prior planning, organization, and negotiation. In such cases, they are typically orchestrated by a social movement and constitute part of its tactical repertoire for dramatizing its grievances and pressing its claims. When this occurs, which is probably the dominant pattern for most protest crowds or demonstrations, neither the crowd phenomena nor the movement can be thoroughly understood without understanding the relationship between them. Thus, while social movements can be distinguished conceptually from other varieties of collective action and collective behavior, social movements and some crowd phenomena are often intimately linked, especially when movements dramatize their concerns and press their claims in public settings.

Organization of the Book and Underlying Logic

We have chosen to organize this reader around three central issues: the emergence of social movements, the micromobilization process, and the dynamics of movements. We chose to use these issues as the book's "linchpins" because together they focus attention on the character and operation of social movements over their life course, from the conditions giving rise to them to their impact and consequences. Although we do not claim to have covered these focal issues exhaustively, we do believe that our coverage provides the basis for understanding the central issues in the life histories of social movements as well as the factors associated with movement participation.

The issue of emergence focuses attention on the various contextual conditions that nurture the soil for social movements and thus facilitate their development. The first section explores this issue, with Part 1 considering conditions of strain, such as conflict and breakdown, Part 2 taking up political opportunity as a condition of conduciveness, and Part 3 examining facilitative organizational contexts.

The second section explores the processes of micromobilization as they pertain to differential recruitment and participation—that is, why do some people participate rather than others? The role of social networks in relation to this issue is examined in Part 4. Part 5 turns attention to some of the barriers to and correlates of participation in movements. Part 6 examines the interpretive framing process in relation to micromobilization and participation. And Part 7 considers the relevance of conversion and commitment-building processes to movement participation.

The third section focuses on the dynamics or actual operation and functioning of social move-

ments. Part 8 considers movements in action by exploring strategic and tactical considerations. Part 9 examines the relationship between movements and various categories of actors in their environment of operation. Part 10 looks at internal movement processes and dynamics and their implications for the ongoing functioning of movements. And Part 11 addresses the question of whether movements make any difference by considering their outcomes and consequences.

It is our hope that the chapter introductions and corresponding selections will facilitate understanding of the factors that influence the course and character of social movements. We also hope that this book stimulates further interest in collective action and social movements.

Notes

1. This conceptualization of social movements borrows from and/or is almost identical to the ones provided by Benford (1992: 1880), Snow and Oliver (1995: 571), Turner and Killian (1987: 223), and Wilson (1973: 9).

2. For a more detailed discussion of the relationship between social movements and interest groups, see Bunis (1993).

3. See Turner and Killian (1987:224) for further discussion of this characteristic of movements.

4. Public goods are typically conceptualized as goods that are indivisible and nonexcludable. This means that public goods are shared by all within a community regardless of whether or not everyone contributed to their attainment or production. See Mancur Olson (1965).

5. "Free riders" are individuals who benefit from a public good without having contributed toward attaining it. For discussion of the concept of free rider, see Olson (1965).

6. For discussion and analysis of the freedom summer campaign, see McAdam (1988).

References

Aberle, David. 1966. *The Peyote Religion Among the Navaho*. Chicago: Aldine.

Benford, Robert D. 1992. "Social Movements." Pp. 1880-1887 in E. Borgatta and M. Borgatta (eds.), *Encyclopedia of Sociology*, Vol. 4. New York: Macmillan Publishing Company.

Bunis, William K. 1993. *Social Movement Activity and Institutionalized Politics: A Study of the Relationship Between Political Party Strength and Social Movement Activity in the United States*. Unpublished dissertation, University of Arizona.

Cohn, Norman. 1961. *The Pursuit of the Millennium*. New York: Harper and Row.

Gamson, William A. 1990. *The Strategy of Social Protest*. Second Edition. Belmont, CA: Wadsworth.

Hunt, Scott, Robert D. Benford, and David A. Snow. 1994. "Identity Fields: Framing Processes and the Social Construction of Movement Identities." Pp. 185-208 in E. Larana, H. Johnson, and J. R. Gusfield (eds.), *New Social Movements: From Ideology to Identity*. Philadelphia: Temple University Press.

Lenin, V. I. 1929. *What Is To Be Done? Burning Questions of Our Movement*. New York: International Publishers.

McAdam, Doug. 1988. *Freedom Summer*. Oxford University Press.

McCarthy, John and Mayer Zald. 1973. *The Trend of Social Movements in America*. Morristown, NJ: General Learning Press.

——. 1977. "Resource Mobilization and Social Movements: A Partial Theory." *American Journal of Sociology* 82: 1212-1241.

Melucci, Alberto. 1989. *Nomads of the Present: Social Movements and Individual Needs in Contemporary Society*. Edited by John Keane and Paul Mier. Philadelphia: Temple University Press.

Michels, Robert. 1949. *Political Parties: A Sociological Study of the Oligarchical Tendencies of Modern Democracy*. Glencoe, IL: Free Press.

Olson, Mancur. 1965. *The Logic of Collective Action: Public Goods and the Theory of Groups*. Cambridge: Harvard University Press.

Piven, Francis Fox and Richard Cloward. 1977. *Poor People's Movements*. New York: Vintage Books.

Smelser, Neil. 1962. *Theory of Collective Behavior*. New York: Free Press of Glencoe

Snow, David A. And Pamela Oliver. 1995. "Social Movements and Collective Behavior: Social Psychological Dimensions and Considerations." Pp. 571-599 in K. Cook, G. Fine, and J. House (eds.), *Sociological Perspectives on Social Psychology*. Boston: Allyn and Bacon.

Tarrow, Sidney. 1994. *Power in Movement: Social Movements, Collective Action and Politics*. New York: Cambridge University Press.

Turner, Ralph H. and Lewis Killian. 1987. Third Edition. *Collective Behavior*. Englewood Cliffs, NJ: Prentice-Hall,

Wallis, Roy. 1984. *The Elementary Forms of the New Religious Life*. London: Routledge & Kegan Paul.

Wilson, John. 1973. *Introduction to Social Movements*. New York: Basic Books. ✦

Unit One

Emergence: Facilitating Conditions

Social movements cannot be adequately understood by focusing solely on either their internal features and characteristics, such as their goals, organization, and adherents, or on the relevant external conditions that constitute their environment of operation. In this section, we focus on one aspect of the external context: the conditions within the ambient environment that facilitate movements' emergence. We begin with this set of external conditions not because they are more important than other external factors or internal dynamics to understanding the operation of social movements, but because all movements grow out of and are embedded in a particular sociohistorical context that requires elaboration if a movement's course and character is to be fully understood.

There are three broad sets of contextual conditions that are relevant to the emergence and operation of social movements. One set can be thought of as conditions of strain or breakdown; the second as conditions of opportunity; and the third as conditions of organization. None of these conditions is sufficient by itself to give rise to a social movement, but each is necessary inasmuch as social movements arise only in contexts that are generative of pressing grievances and yet sufficiently nurturant or facilitative of collective action aimed at repairing or removing the source of those grievances.

Part 1

Conditions of Strain: Conflict and Breakdown

Under what conditions do social movements emerge? What factors give rise to social movements? Questions such as these are among the most frequently asked in the study of social movements. Whatever the array of troublesome, unsettling social conditions that presumably stimulate the growth of social movements, they have generally been conceptualized as strains. The traditional argument is that social movements are by-products of rapid social change and disintegration triggered by wars, economic downturns, disasters, and the like, that, in turn, give rise to mounting tensions and frustrations that are vented through social movements. Because of its emphasis on social disintegration, this perspective has been aptly dubbed breakdown theory (Tilly, Tilly, and Tilly 1975).

Although the strain/breakdown perspective was once the dominant account of movement emergence, its popularity has waned considerably during the last thirty years based on a number of vexing observations and issues. First, the basic proposition that strain undergirds movement emergence is called into question by the observation that societies are rarely, if ever, in a state of stability and equilibrium. Rather, conflict, uncertainty, and other stresses are common features of society. Thus, strain or breakdown alone cannot account for the ebb and flow of social movement activity. Second, there is no determinant relationship between strain, however it is specified, and social movement activity. Not only is the relation-

ship between particular types of strain and specific kinds of movements indeterminant, but movements do not automatically follow a stressful event or trend. Sometimes there is apathy, indifference, and inaction; other times appeals may be made directly through existing political channels to dominant institutional actors; on other occasions citizens may take to the streets and demand that their grievances be resolved; and still other times they may engage in what James Scott has called everyday forms of resistance, such as "foot dragging, dissimulation, false compliance, pilfering, feigned ignorance, slander, arson, sabotage, and so forth" (1985: 29). Clearly, strain or tension alone can not account for such varied responses.

These concerns notwithstanding, we believe that some remnant of the strain idea should be retained for the simple reason that social movements do not arise in an issueless, trouble-free vacuum. Rather, they arise in response to issues and troublesome events or trends about which people have considerable concerns. No one who has ever studied or been involved in a movement would take exception with this statement. Indeed, the passion and depth of concern of movement actors can be readily seen on their faces and heard in their voices. It is partly for this reason that John Lofland (1985) has differentiated crowds or collective-action gatherings in terms of their dominant emotion: fear, hostility or joy. Not all crowd activity is associated with social movements, but those that are movement-sponsored are typically associated with strong feelings about an unsettling event or happening. We will defer discussion of the cognitive and interpretive factors that link such sentiments to participation in social movement activities until the second unit, and focus here on a select set of strains and conflicts found to have been associated with the emergence of social movements and related collective action.

Several cautionary considerations should be kept in mind, however. First, we do not assume that people respond automatically, in a stimulus/response-like fashion, to disrupting trends and events. Rather, as will be noted in Part 6, any response or action that evolves depends partly on interpretive/framing processes. At the same time, collective actors rarely, if ever, manufacture troublesome events entirely apart from the social context in which they find themselves. In other words, their framing of events is anchored in part to some set of empirical conditions. Here we want to highlight a number of the unsettling preconditions that have been linked with movement emergence.

One such precipitating strain or tension is population change. At least since the time of Thomas Malthus, the late eighteenth and early nineteenth century British economist who proposed a causal link between population growth and hunger and poverty, some observers of social movements have assumed that significant population increases will increase the scale of poverty to such a degree that social movement activity will escalate as well. Today it is generally agreed that there is little, if any, direct connection between human suffering and the propensity to engage in social movement activity. If there were, then, as Leon Trotsky, one of the architects of the Russian Revolution, once observed, "the masses would be always in revolt" (1959, p. 249)

However, the absence of a direct link between population growth and social movement activity does not rule out the possibility of a more indirect association. Jack Goldstone has recently taken this position (1991), arguing that state breakdown and revolution in early modern agrarian-bureaucratic states in both Europe and Asia were stimulated by dramatic population growth. In his examination of state breakdown in England between 1640-42, for example, he found that the English population grew from just over 2 million to more than 5 million between 1500 and 1650, and that London alone grew from 50,000 to 400,000 in-

habitants during the same period (1991: 83-84). Goldstone takes care to emphasize, however, that he does not advocate a simple demographic approach. Rather, he sees the associations between demographic change and state breakdown as more subtle and varied, as reflected in his linkage of population growth in England and elsewhere to declining state revenues and fiscal crisis, elite competition and turnover, and the mobilization potential of the masses. The passage included from his book, *Revolution and Rebellion in the Early Modern World*, clarifies his position, which he calls a structural/demographic model of state breakdown.

While Goldstone's model is clearly integrative and conjunctural in the sense that state breakdown results from the confluence of a number of interconnected factors, demographic change remains the starting point of the process and the unifying theme of his analysis. Moreover, he establishes population growth as the pivotal factor. However, it is important to keep in mind that the demographic change associated with social movement emergence may sometimes entail population decline rather than growth, as Russell Thornton (1981) found when he examined the relationship between population change of Native American and the Ghost Dance Movement of 1890.

The second precipitating strain or tension we consider is competition, particularly ethnic competition. The most fully developed model of the relationship between ethnic competition and movement emergence has been developed by Susan Olzak and her colleagues (Olzak 1992; Olzak and Nagel 1986). They propose that ethnic conflict and the prospect of movement mobilization increase when two or more ethnic groups within a nation-state find themselves competing for the same valued resources, such as jobs and housing. Sarah Bélanger and Maurice Pinard examine this thesis in the second selection included in this part. Specifically, they offer a partial reformulation of the model by proposing that ethnic competition leads to conflict and movement mobilization only when the competition is perceived as unfair and occurs in a context of low interdependence between the groups in question. Analysis of survey data on the independence movement in Quebec provides support for these proposed modifications to the model, suggesting that the causal connection between ethnic competition and mobilization is contingent on a number of intervening conditions.

The last selection in this part, by Bert Useem, focuses attention on the relationship between organizational disruption or breakdown and the emergence of collective action, in this case a brutal prison riot that occurred in New Mexico in 1980. Drawing on two different sets of interview data with prison guards and inmates, Useem reconstructs the structure of prison organization and relationships in the decade prior to the riot, and finds that the riot can be traced to a disorganizing process that began around five years earlier. Based on this and related findings, Useem concludes that students of collective action have been too quick to throw out the strain or breakdown model. Although this and his other conclusions are based on a single riot, we think the analysis raises new questions about the relationship between the disruption of organizational routines and expectations and the emergence of various forms of collective action, including social movements.

Taken together, the three selections in this part clearly underscore the importance of various unsettling trends, conflicts, and disruptions in relation to movement emergence. Additionally, they suggest that dismissing or ignoring this linkage because of the shortcomings of previous work associated with the strain/breakdown perspective undermines a thoroughgoing understanding of social movements.

References

Goldstone, Jack A. 1991. *Revolution and Rebellion in the Early Modern World.* Berkeley: University of California Press.

Lofland, John. 1985. *Protest: Studies of Collective Behavior and Social Movements.* New Brunswick: Transaction Books.

Olzak, Susan. 1992. *The Dynamics of Ethnic Competition and Conflict.* Stanford, CA: Stanford University Press.

Olzak, Susan and Joane Nagel (eds.). 1986. *Competitive Ethnic Relations.* Orlando: Academic Press.

Scott, James C. 1985. *Weapons of the Weak: Everyday Forms of Resistance.* New Haven: Yale University Press.

Thornton, Russell. 1981. "Demographic Antecedents of a Revitalization Movement: Population Change, Population Size, and the 1890 Ghost Dance." *American Sociological Review* 46: 88-96.

Tilly, Charles, Louise Tilly, and Richard Tilly. 1975. *The Rebellious Century, 1830-1930.* Cambridge: Harvard University Press.

Trotsky, Leon. 1959. *The History of the Russian Revolution,* edited by F. W. Dupee. New York: Doubleday. ◆

1

A Demographic/Structural Model of State Breakdown

Jack A. Goldstone

My primary conclusion is quite beautiful in its parsimony. It is that *the periodic state breakdowns in Europe, China, and the Middle East from 1500 to 1850 were the result of a single basic process.* This process unfolded like a fugue, with a major trend giving birth to four related critical trends that combined for a tumultuous conclusion. The main trend was that population growth, in the context of relatively inflexible economic and social structures, led to changes in prices, shifts in resources, and increasing social demands with which agrarian-bureaucratic states could not successfully cope.

The four related critical trends were as follows: (1) Pressures increased on state finances as inflation eroded state income and population growth raised real expenses. States attempted to maintain themselves by raising revenues in a variety of ways, but such attempts alienated elites, peasants, and urban consumers, while failing to prevent increasing debt and eventual bankruptcy. (2) Intra-elite conflicts became more prevalent as larger families and inflation made it more difficult for some families to maintain their status, while expanding population and rising prices lifted other families, creating new aspirants to elite positions. With the state's fiscal weakness limiting its ability to provide for all who sought elite positions, considerable turnover and displacement occurred throughout the elite hierarchy, giving rise to factionalization as different elite groups sought to defend or improve their position. When central authority collapsed, most often as a result of bankruptcy, elite divisions came to the fore in struggles for power. (3) Popular unrest grew, as competition for land, urban migration, flooded labor markets,

declining real wages, and increased youthfulness raised the mass mobilization potential of the populace. Unrest occurred in urban and rural areas and took the various forms of food riots, attacks on landlords and state agents, and land and grain seizures, depending on the autonomy of popular groups and the resources of elites. A heightened mobilization potential made it easy for contending elites to marshal popular action in their conflicts, although in many cases popular actions, having their own motivation and momentum, proved easier to encourage than to control. (4) The ideologies of rectification and transformation became increasingly salient. Spreading poverty and vagrancy, ever more severe and frequent harvest crises and food riots, and state ineffectiveness undermined the credibility of religious leaders associated with states and turned both elites and middling groups to heterodox religious movements in the search for reform, order, and discipline. The conjuncture of these four critical trends—state fiscal distress, intrastate conflicts, heightened mass mobilization potential, and, deriving in part from the other three, increased salience of the folk and elite ideologies of rectification and transformation—combined to undermine stability on *multiple* levels of social organization.

This basic process was triggered all across Eurasia by the periods of sustained population increase that occurred in the sixteenth and early seventeenth centuries and again in the late eighteenth and early nineteenth centuries, thus producing worldwide waves of state breakdown. In contrast, in the late seventeenth and early eighteenth centuries populations did not grow, and the basic process and its four subthemes were absent. Political and social stability resulted. In the early nineteenth century, one should note, several European states had greatly increased their financial resources; thus, even though population growth initiated a similar pattern, the first critical trend was muted, and the ensuing state crises in 1830 and 1848 were less severe. But their kinship with the earlier wave of state crises, and with contemporary state crises in the Ottoman and Chinese empires, remains clear. After 1850, most western European states had increased the flexibility of their economics through industrialization, and of their administrative and social structures through political revolution or reform; thus, population growth lost its ability to trigger the processes that earlier had led to state breakdown. Russia, China, and the Ottoman empire, however, with their still largely traditional economic, political, and social structures, remained vulnerable to population pressures, which continued through the nineteenth century and led to state breakdowns in the early years of the twentieth.

The power of this argument lies not merely in its ability to explain the timing, and the widespread coincidence, of such crises. It lies especially in displaying the linkages—between population growth and price inflation, and between both these factors and state fiscal crisis, elite mobility and competition, and mass mobilization potential—that shaped the development and key features of these crises. Thus for example, the fact that the English and French revolutions were both preceded by periods of unusual social mobility and triggered by fiscal crises can be understood as similar responses to similar historical situations, rather than as mere coincidence or superficial analogy.

Indeed, it is fascinating to find so many trends that English, or French, or Chinese, or Ottoman specialists have claimed to be the product of unique conditions appearing again and again across time and space. Moreover, this consistency lays to rest many old shibboleths and tortured debates. Thus, we clearly and repeatedly find that revolution and rebellion were *not* due to excessively high taxation by rulers, or to a simple lack of social mobility, or chiefly to class conflict, or to general impoverishment of society as a whole. Instead we find consistently that fiscal crises were due to *undertaxation* as elites systematically evaded taxes, so that state revenues barely kept pace with inflation, and hence never kept pace with the increasing *real* wealth of their societies. We find everywhere that *high* social mobility— *high* rates of turnover and displacement—preceded crises, while *low* social mobility characterized times of stability. Rapid turnover among high officials, strains on elite education and recruitment, and conflicts over patronage are seen in all states and empires approaching crisis. *Factional conflict within the elites*, over access to office, patronage, and state policy, rather than conflict across classes, led to state paralysis and state breakdown. We also find consistently that elites succeeded in shifting the burden of taxation to the middling classes, and that the conditions of the working classes and peasants declined while elites and commercial classes grew richer. Thus,

we consistently see a *polarization* of social wealth in the generations preceding crises. And the combination of declining state effectiveness, heightened conflicts over mobility, and increasing poverty at the bottom of the social scale raised the salience of reformist, disciplined, heterodox moral and philosophical schools, a salience that failed rapidly when these social trends ended. These trends are evident in the sixteenth and early seventeenth centuries, and in the eighteenth and early nineteenth centuries, across Eurasia. Certainly particular conditions in each society shaped the timing and magnitude of these trends. But in light of their near universal character, any claim that such trends were produced *solely* by unique local conditions is thoroughly undermined by the evidence.

Almost two decades ago, Lawrence Stone (1972, 26) wrote that "with both [the English and French] Revolutions, once historians have realized that their Marxist interpretation does not work very much better than the Whig, there has followed a period where there is nothing very secure to put in its place." I hope that the *demographic/structural* model can now take that place, as it explains the key features of both crises in better accord with the known facts than the Marxist or Whig views. It also deals far more effectively with the contemporary crises in China and the Middle East and avoids any of the objectionable teleology characteristic of other analyses.

There is no teleology because, although the basic processes and pressures that led to state breakdown occurred widely, the model allows that the precise responses to these pressures varied with the capacity of states to react, of elites to organize, and of popular groups to mobilize. Moreover, once state breakdown had begun, the struggle for power and the need for state reconstruction gave great scope to distinct ideologies, albeit constrained by existing cultural frameworks, to shape the future course of reaction or revolution. Thus, the same basic causal process gave rise to a range of outcomes, depending on the setting in which that process unfolded.

Historians have long debated whether the main causes of early modern revolutions and rebellions were social, economic, religious, or political cleavages. Such distinctions are illusory. Social and economic conflicts, religious heterodoxy, and political factionalization were not independent factors but related aspects of an underlying causal pattern. For a number of societies, this book demonstrates that the early modern crises were rooted in the simultaneous decline of traditional systems of taxation, elite training and recruitment, and popular living standards; hence, the increased salience and appeal of heterodox ideologies, under the pressure of ecological change.

This model offers several advantages over the Marxist interpretation, its "revisionist" adversaries, and the more recent theories of revolution such as Skocpol's. First, the state appears as an autonomous actor in *three* respects: (1) as an economic actor whose strength is affected by trends in the economy such as inflation and by changing real costs of governance brought by population growth; (2) as a political actor whose strength is affected by the demands of international competition and the demands of domestic elite and popular groups; and (3) as a cultural actor whose strength (and pace of future development) is affected by the tensions—or lack thereof—between state-supported orthodoxy and alternative ideological claims. Marxist interpretation tends to neglect the autonomy of political actions, the revisionists and Skocpol tend to neglect the impact of key shifts and cycles in economic history, and Skocpol and many Marxists tend to neglect the autonomy of cultural and ideological aspects of social change. The demographic/structural approach to state breakdown—combined with our analysis of the process of revolutionary struggles and their outcome—gives due attention to the economic, political, and cultural aspects of the state's relations with other states, elites, and popular groups.

Second, this analysis of elites identifies a variety of social conflicts, not just those between economically distinct classes. Instead, demographic and economic pressures are seen to create conflicts both *across* classes—between peasants and landlords and between urban artisans and urban oligarchies—and *within* classes—between factions of landed, merchant, professional, and religious groups. Recognition that social mobility can provide absorption or generate displacement and turnover, noting that the latter combination, in particular, generates intra-elite competition and conflict at a *multiplicity* of levels, allows a better understanding of the precise cleavages that broke across the Old Regimes when subjected to demographic pressure: reform versus conservative factions among ministerial, provincial, and town officials; bishops versus curés or preachers; international versus domestic merchants; older versus newer military officers; financiers versus professionals; and orthodox intellectuals versus heterodox reformers.

Understanding how demographic pressure gives rise to heightened elite competition also explains a particular, and heretofore puzzling, phenomenon: the simultaneous "boom" in University enrollments all across Europe and the overburdening of religious schools in the Ottoman Empire and of the imperial examination system in China in the late sixteenth and early seventeenth centuries, followed by the "bust" in those enrollments in Europe and an easing of educational strains in Asia in the late seventeenth and early eighteenth centuries. This sequence was followed by another "boom" in the late eighteenth and early nineteenth centuries. These boom and busts are too extreme to be explained by changes in population size per se. However, we need only recognize that the periods of growing population led to inflation, which created economic opportunities that, in turn, increased the number of people who considered themselves qualified to demand elite positions. At the same time, inflation and sharp resistance to increasing taxation limited each state's ability to increase the supply of elite positions. The result was heightened competition for such positions, which spurred a scramble for credentials. Conversely, periods of stable population give rise to little social mobility, and stable family size allowed much of the demand for elite positions to be satisfied by simple inheritance or family succession. Thus, the demand for formal credentials went "bust." Whether examining education or broad-based elite conflicts, consideration of the *interaction* of demographic, economic, and political relationships is far more fruitful than asserting the centrality of purely class, or purely political, factors.

Third, the demographic/structural approach to popular uprisings allows considerable scope for attention to *regional* differences in conflicts that occur within a crisis. Thus, an awareness of how demographic pressures produce land shortages, rising rents, falling real wages, and a more youthful population helps to explain why banditry, urban riots, and rural rebellions would all become more likely following periods of sustained population increase in agrarian-bureaucratic states.

However, the model dictates no particular form of popular unrest. Instead, the precise shape of popular action is determined by the way such pressures impinge on a particular region's distribution of resources and relationships between potential actors. Thus, one would expect different patterns of popular unrest in northern France, southwestern France, and rural England, for in each case the organization of peasants, and the resources of landlords, differed. Similarly, in China one would expect different patterns of popular unrest in the mountains of the west and in the waterways of the Yangzi delta. Regional differences, as well as international differences, are the logical outcome of a model in which similar *causal* forces, rooted in demographic change, act on a variety of *social structures* to produce various patterns of conflict.

Fourth, this analysis integrates material and cultural factors in a far richer way than do the Marxist or revisionist analyses, and in a way that rectifies Skocpol's underemphasis on ideologies. I argue that the material causes of state breakdown first give rise to evident decay in state effectiveness and increases in popular and elite discontent. This combination of decay and disaffection raises the salience of ideologies of rectification and transformation which may be longstanding but dormant elements of the political culture. Clear shifts in discourse and the spread of heterodoxy thus precede state breakdown, though these derive primarily from the collision of economic, political, and social structures with demographic change. If state crisis leads to state breakdown, however, the struggle for power polarizes and radicalizes discourse, further shaping and giving vent to ideological conflicts. When a victor emerges and sets a course for state reconstruction, these ideologies have a powerful molding effect on the postrevolutionary state. Moreover, ideologies of state reconstruction reflect not only the struggle for power but also the broader cultural framework of the society at large.

Ideologies reflect the available elements for conceptualizing change. Thus, European societies (as well as non-European societies later affected by European ideas), because of their linear and eschatological notions of time, their stock of apocalyptic imagery, were likely to respond to state breakdown through innovation; whereas Asian societies, with their primarily cyclic notions of time, were likely to respond to state breakdown with conservative state reconstruction. In this argument, both material and ideal factors play a leading role, although they do so in different phases of the process of state breakdown and reconstruction. This model also has the advantage, in regard to the Marxist view of history, of *not* interpreting the relative stagnation of Asia after the seventeenth century as the "absence" of change relative to Europe; instead it is seen as the result of a different *direction* of change, because of its different response to a similar crisis. In this respect, the model suggests parallels between the responses to the seventeenth-century crises in Hapsburg Spain, the Ottoman Empire, and China that merit further study. . . .

Population Growth: A Blessing or a Curse?

There is an old debate in demographic theory about whether there is an "ideal" level of population for a society, and whether increases in population are generally beneficial or detrimental to societal well-being. There have been famous pessimists, from Malthus to Keynes, and famous optimists, most recently Julian Simon and Ester Boserup, who have reiterated Dupréel's argument that "an increase in population is beneficial in itself, because it enhances competition and spurs individual initiative, and is thus a decisive factor in civilization and progress" (cited in Overbeek 1974, 118).

At first glance, the argument in this book appears pessimistic in tone, for population growth in early modern history was strongly associated with mass poverty, elite factionalism, and state crises. But this observation alone would be an excessively simple and misleading characterization of events. The actual matter of interest is not defined by movements of population alone, viewed as a single independent variable, but rather by a set of *balances:*

between population and agrarian output, between elite recruitment and eligible aspirants, and between state tax revenues and state expenditures. It was not population growth per se but rather growth beyond the absorptive capacity of early modern economic, social, and political institutions that undid these delicate balances and ruptured the social order. The lesson of early modern history is not that population growth is bad but rather that inflexible social structures are bad, at least in the sense that they become highly unstable in the event of sustained demographic change.

What, then, are the policy implications to be drawn from this book with respect to the pressing issue of population growth in the developing world? Will population growth lead to continued political instability?

The answer is that population increases *probably will* lead to political crises, but they need not. The argument of this book can be neatly divided into two parts. First, there is a theory of the conditions that create a likelihood of state breakdown, drawing on a conjunctural model of crises. This theory asserts that massive state breakdown is likely to occur only when there are *simultaneously* high levels of distress and conflict at *several levels* of society—in the state, among elites, and in the populace. We examined this conjuncture empirically through the *psi* equation, which combined attention to trends in state fiscal distress, elite mobility and competition (including both turnover and displacement), and mass mobilization potential. A sustained rise in all three elements is associated with state breakdown; a rise in two of these elements can produce a state crisis leading to major reforms or modest state breakdown; a rise in any one alone is unlikely to end a regime. This theory can be simply summarized: high *psi* implies a high probability of state crisis. Second, there is a more historically delimited theory that seeks to explain *why psi* rose to high levels in most Eurasian states in the two periods 1550-1660 and 1770-1850, an explanation that rests on the interaction of demography and institutions.

Since the two parts are logically independent, we can approach the problems of contemporary population growth and instability through two questions: Is population growth likely to raise *psi* in today's world? And are there other forces that could raise *psi*, and hence other, more worrisome, sources of state breakdown?

In the early modern world, population growth was a threat to societies that were fundamentally agrarian. As Gellner (1983, 110) has pointed out, "agrarian society .... unlike, it would seem, both its predecessor [hunter-gatherer society] and successor [industrial society] is Malthusian." Today, although many developing nations such as India, China, and most nations of Africa and northwest Latin America still have largely agrarian economies, they are no longer purely agrarian *societies*. That is to say, the wealth, political power, and military strength of each depend more on access to capital, technology, information, and often

electoral support and foreign assistance than on mere ownership of acreage. Without access to foreign and urban markets, without capital for machinery, fertilizer, fuel, and transportation, large landholdings today are nearly worthless. Without access to national party organizations, large landowners can be, at best, local *caudillos* or bosses; small farmers and tenants can be, at best, restive local forces. Technological improvements that are available in agriculture, production, communication, and transportation dwarf anything that was available in the early modern world. Thus, population growth need not overwhelm modern societies, provided they can harness modern resources to absorb their population increases.

In these circumstances, the question of whether population growth will undo crucial balances that sustain social stability has more to do with government policy, capital availability, and local organization than with the simple arithmetic of bodies and land. Policies of cronyism and corruption that drain or unproductively concentrate capital, and policies of urban investment and price-skewing at the expense of rural infrastructure and economies, are likely to create the same conditions of high mass mobilization potential among impoverished cultivators that simple population growth produced in the seventeenth and nineteenth centuries. Conversely, policies that create a well-capitalized, productive, domestic agriculture, and that can supply employment to the rural sector and food and raw materials to world markets and the urban sector, can cope with quite rapid population growth. Japan under the Meiji oligarchs experienced rapid population increase, but state policies of the latter type served to maintain political stability (Nishikawa 1986, 426; Macpherson 1987).

Development policies often focus on raising GNP per capita. Clearly, this approach need not succeed in reducing *psi*, which is not a simple matter of total social wealth. We have seen that the nations and empires that encountered crisis suffered from *polarization* in their income distribution, from high social mobility that unsettled and divided elites, and from failure of the state to gain resources to cope with rising real expenses. Eighteenth-century France, for example, raised its GNP per capita. But a lagging agricultural sector, and problems in the distribution of income and taxation, still produced a crisis. Thus development policies, if they wish to help counter political instability as well as create growth, need to do more than just raise GNP. Measures such as land reform and support for small farmers, which reduce income polarization and urban migration, and foreign aid aimed at avoiding excessive government debt while providing government resources for housing, education, and other population-linked infrastructural expenses, are more politically stabilizing than investments in concentrated industries. One must also consider the ability of the state, church, business, and social institutions to employ ambitious elites at levels that correspond to their self-perceived qualifications. It is politically risky to create new, professional, educated elites without also creating ample political and economic opportunities for them. It is in these areas that demographic change poses problems to contemporary governments.

In fact, rapid population growth in many Third World countries has had two extremely important political effects: rapid urbanization and the growth of new professional and managerial elites. The extreme urbanization reflects a common economic bias, wherein development policies, pricing policies, and foreign investment increase economic opportunities in cities rather than in the countryside (Bates 1981; Kelley and Williamson 1984; Bradshaw 1985). Unfortunately, such rapid urbanization places enormous strains on the capacity of governments to provide services, political organization and control, and employment for urban residents. Under such conditions, dissident elites may find ready recruits to mobilize in anti-state movements. Tehran and Managua in 1979 thus had the same potential—in terms of mass mobilization in politically crucial sites—as Paris in 1789 or Vienna and Berlin in 1848.

Dissident elites may arise when expanding urban markets offer opportunities to entrepreneurs in manufacturing and services and an expanding educational system produces professional degree holders, while traditional military and landowning elites, or a particular ruler or clique, seeks to monopolize power. Stable balances within a landed oligarchy, or between elite segments under the orchestration of an authoritarian ruler, may be undone by a relatively sudden expansion of urban population and markets.

The demands of traditional elites to preserve their privileged position often clash with the demands of new elites and popular urban and rural groups for broad economic expansion. Development plans must then meet many agendas, from satisfying current and emerging elites to keeping pace with overall population growth. A combination of agrarian reform, guided productive investment, and compensation to traditional elites has sometimes successfully overcome this dilemma, as in Japan during the Meiji era.

However, states with less political clout and fewer resources often seek to defer difficult choices by borrowing. In early modern times, such a course might have led straightforwardly to a state fiscal crisis. But contemporary states have a greater ability to externalize deficits by inviting foreign investment, printing money, and manipulating exchange rates. Thus, in analyzing the "fiscal crisis" component of *psi* for modern states, we may see rising inflation, loss of control of the economy to foreign interests, or wild swings or divergences from parity in the local currency, instead of simple state financial difficulties. Nonetheless, all of these disrupt the flow of resources to states, or to elite and popular groups who look to the state for control of these matters. Thus broadly defined, fiscal or economic crises are a common outcome of states' attempts to utilize borrowing and currency controls to meet foreign competition and the demands of changing elites and growing populations.

Again, we come face to face with the problem of population change and its effects on political and economic *structures*. Early modern states failed to cope with population growth because their economic, fiscal, and social structures—rooted in simple agrarian techniques and in aristocratic status and political systems—lacked sufficient flexibility to deflect or absorb the conflicts produced by that growth. Contemporary states rarely face such simple economic and traditional status institutions, and their attendant constraints. Thus, they often *can* absorb population growth; the question is whether, at a given time, they adopt the policies that will actually allow them to do so (cf. Johnson and Lee 1987).

The tenets that favor stability are simple: do not adopt fiscal policies that rely on debts in excess of what the economy and tax system can reasonably be expected to sustain; do not adopt economic policies that encourage urban growth at a faster rate than housing, services, employment, and civic organization can develop; do not adopt educational policies that produce graduates in excess of the state's and the economy's ability to give them meaningful responsibilities; and do not adopt political policies that exclude from power newly rising groups that are growing in numbers and wealth. States often fail to follow these tenets because it is in the short-term interests of rulers or particular elites to acquire debts, to favor rapid urban expansion, to implement educational expansion, or to seek monopolization of power. The problem is that these short-term, and thus short-sighted, policies undermine political stability in the long run. How a current regime weighs the short-run versus the long-run consequences of its choices is often the key to whether its prospects for stability are brief or extend far into the future.

These tenets are *not* merely matters of economic expansion or development. One can have economically stagnant states that follow these tenets and yet remain politically stable economic backwaters—for example, North Korea. And one can have economically dynamic states that fail to follow these tenets for stability and hence encounter state crisis—for example, Iran.

From 1956 to 1976, the population of Iran increased from just over twenty million inhabitants to nearly thirty-five million, an increase of 75 percent in two decades (B. Clark 1972). During these decades, the Pahlavi regime adopted a rural land reform program that left three-fourths of rural families with inadequate land to support commercial farming, and it adopted pricing and credit policies that starved the rural sector while subsidizing urban populations. The cities were also the focus of development efforts financed by massive borrowing. The state thus drew population to the cities more rapidly than adequate services or regular employment could be supplied, developing a large population of aggrieved urban families who looked to the mosque and bazaar, rather than to the state and modern economic sector, for material benefits, moral authority, and community leadership. The number of university students increased tenfold, many of them educated overseas for lack of domestic facilities (Abrahamian 1980). Witnessing the moral dissolution and poverty in the urban slums, along with the concentration of wealth among the shah's family and associates, many elites and students became dismayed at the moral failures and corruption of the regime.

Counting on future oil wealth, the shah borrowed heavily, and sought to complement his development effort with a military buildup. These expenditures stretched both the state budget and the economy to the limit. The resulting inflation undermined middle- and working-class incomes. Finally, seeking to monopolize power, the shah excluded from politics the professional and managerial groups and civil servants on which his modernization efforts depended, and attacked the bazaar merchants and the traditional religious elite (Keddie 1981; Green 1986).

The result of these policies was mounting state debt, roaring inflation, and political exclusion that made enemies among the salaried middle class and the traditional religious leaders and bazaar merchants. When these elite groups allied and began to mobilize the urban masses against the shah's government, given the questionable ability of the army to act against a broad popular movement (as in France in 1830 and 1848), the breakdown of the shah's regime became imminent (Abrahamian 1980). The shah's fall was thus a product of misguided policies, not an inevitable outcome of rapid development or Islamic fundamentalism. However, once state breakdown had begun, there followed the familiar sequence: an initially moderate, widely supported movement for rectification, then struggles for popular mobilization and power, with victory attained by extremist leaders. These leaders were a formerly marginal elite—the fundamentalist wing of the Shi'ite clergy—who drew on an eschatological ideology. The revolutionary process culminated in an aggressive Iranian nationalism that produced persecution of minorities and other internal "enemies," as well as foreign war.

In sum, population growth does pose problems for modern states. But they are not insoluble problems, as many examples from the newly industrialized countries show. Whether or not population growth will lead to instability depends on the policies adopted by particular regimes. Poor policy choices can create exactly the "high *psi*" conditions—state fiscal crises, elite factionalization and alienation, and rising mass (particularly urban) mobilization potential—that make state crises likely. In contrast, careful policy choices can maintain "low *psi*" conditions, and hence political stability despite rapid economic growth.

Given the explosive population growth that has occurred in the Third World during the twentieth century, often without the benefit of rapid industrialization or flexible political institutions, it is not surprising that this is a "century of revolution" in Third World states. Although a decline in per capita wealth has occasionally been a problem, this has not been the primary factor in modern revolutions. Instead, problems of wealth distribution among the population, weak state finances, and competition among elites, exacerbated by explosive population increases and inappropriate policy responses, have undermined political stability. Wherever rulers or elites have been tempted to put their own short-term interests ahead of long-term political stability for their respective societies, the resulting policy choices have created, over a span of few decades, the ingredients for state crises.

We should thus not be surprised if population growth and state crises, though not inevitably linked, remain companion phenomena in the contemporary Third World.[1]

Notes

1. For a more detailed consideration of contemporary revolutions, see Goldstone, Gurr, and Moshiri (forthcoming). ◆

2

Ethnic Movements and the Competition Model: Some Missing Links

Sarah Bélanger
Maurice Pinard

While many models of ethnic resurgence have been proposed, few have enjoyed as much popularity as the so-called competition model. Derived from a more sophisticated model first put forth by Barth (1969) and expanded by Hannan (1979), its recent formulation simply holds that "modernization increases levels of competition for jobs, housing, and other valued resources among ethnic groups," and that *"ethnic conflict and social movements based on ethnic (rather than some other) boundaries occur when ethnic competition increases"* (Olzak and Nagel 1986, p. 2, italics in original). Thus, the resurgence since 1960 of ethnic movements in many multicultural societies is alleged to have resulted from increased ethnic competition, especially job competition, and this increased competition is viewed as the result of modernization processes, especially urbanization, the expansion of the secondary and tertiary sectors of the economy, the expansion of the political sector and supranational organizations, and the increasing scale of organizations (Nagel and Olzak 1982; Olzak and Nagel 1986, pp. 3-4).

This elementary version of the competition model has been tested in studies of ethnic resurgence in Wales (Ragin 1979), Flanders (Nielsen 1980), Québec (Olzak 1982), in a comparison of Québec and Northern Ireland (See 1986), and in a large comparative study (Ragin 1987). It has also been tested in studies of urban racial and ethnic conflict in earlier eras (Olzak 1986, 1989b), in a study of ethnic awareness (Portes 1984), and in a study of the American women's movement (Ward and Rosenfeld 1987). However, the tests

"Ethnic Movements and the Competition Model: Some Missing Links." *American Sociological Review* 56: 446-457. Copyright © 1991 by the American Sociological Association. Reprinted with permission.

bearing on ethnic resurgence present inferential problems, and the evidence does not unequivocally support the competition model. Although the theory has merits, it is underspecified. Our critique leads to a reformulation that specifies the conditions under which ethnic competition leads to conflict and the types of competition likely to have been important in recent ethnic movements. Some of these ideas are then tested through an examination of the independence movement in Québec.

A Critical Assessment

Most earlier tests of the competition model that have focused on ethnic movements have been based on aggregate ecological data. In these studies, it was usually not possible to measure ethnic competition directly. Instead, the impact of ethnic competition was inferred from direct relationships between various measures of modernization and measures of support for ethnic parties or movements. Therefore, the key argument that ethnic competition, especially job competition, is the main mechanism linking modernization to ethnic movements could not be established empirically. Alternative mechanisms—the growth of financial or human resources, increased organizational strength, changes in beliefs, values, and culture, and/or changes in long-term political opportunities—could also account for these relationships (e.g., McCarthy and Zald 1973; Tilly 1978; McAdam 1982; Allardt 1981; Inglehart 1977).[1] The task remains of empirically assessing whether competition and/or these other mechanisms are involved in the resurgence of these movements.

Evidence for the presumed modernization/ethnic movement link is not strong. In the quantitative studies, most measures of modernization are indicators of industrial development, particularly employment in the secondary and tertiary sectors, although measures of urbanization, economic development (income), and state expansion have also been employed. For the Welsh movement, Ragin (1979) found that tertiary sector employment was positively related to support for the Welsh nationalist party, Plaid Cymru. But he also found that another common measure of modernization, employment in the secondary sector (peripheral industries), did not increase nationalist support. Support for the nationalist Liberal party also did not conform to his hypothesis—support was strongest in agricultural areas. Finally, support for Plaid Cymru was strongest in areas of strong cultural traditionalism. which tended to be the *least* developed areas. Indeed, only by holding traditionalism constant could Ragin obtain a positive association between tertiary sector employment and support for Plaid Cymru. (See also the comment by Lutz [1980] and rejoinder by Ragin [1980].)

Nielsen's (1980) results for Flanders are also mixed: Two indicators of modernization—tertiary sector employment and income—were positively related to support for the Flemish nationalist party, the Volksunie, but three other indicators (industrialization, agricultural employment, and rural residence) were either unrelated or not related as expected to nationalist support. Nielsen also reported (pp. 82-83) that support for the Flemish movement during the interwar years was concentrated in rural areas, contrary to predictions.

The model finds even less support in Olzak's (1982) analysis of Québec's independence movement. None of the many conventional measures of modernization were positively and significantly related to ethnic mobilization. In the case of state expansion, the relationships were negative. Only bilingualism, posited as an indicator of linguistic competition, was positively related to separatist support.

Finally, in a recent comparative test examining 36 linguistic minorities in Western Europe, Ragin (1987, pp. 133-49) found that the competition perspective could account only partially for some types of ethnic mobilization, and was inappropriate for others (for which the internal colonial model, although incomplete as well, was better suited). He suggested some preliminary amendments to the competition model (which differ from those we propose).[2] The inability of the ethnic competition model to account for so much of the evidence implies some theoretical difficulties.

The theory has merit: It is a dynamic model ultimately linking ethnic upsurges to changes in levels of modernization. While modernization is undoubtedly related to such ethnic upsurges, the specific dimensions of modernization and the intervening mechanisms have not been adequately identified; however, this question cannot be examined here. In addition, while the competition argument is certainly relevant, it requires some important specifications.

Hannan (1979, p. 268) explicitly stated that the phenomenon to be explained was "ethnic . . . collective action, either institutional or noninstitutional. . . ." Paradoxically, while the model may be more appropriate for institutionalized collective action, it has primarily been used to account for noninstitutionalized, contentious collective action involving open clashes and manifest conflicts. We claim that, in its present form, the model is unsuitable for that purpose.

First, we question the basic hypothesis of a direct link between competition and conflict. If conflict over the appropriation of scarce goods implies, by definition, competition, the reverse is obviously not true: Competition can occur—and often does occur—without conflict. Hence the important question that the theory ignores: Under what conditions does ethnic competition break into conflict, i.e., open, noninstitutionalized confrontation? We attempt to answer this question.

Second, if ethnic conflict—or conflict in general—often involves competitive striving for scarce goods (e.g., economic goods, status, or power resources), it can also result from disagreements over the desirability of certain goals, e.g., the maintenance of cultural differences. In the latter situation, groups do not compete for the same goods, but for different rewards (Kriesberg 1973, pp. 28-55). Although any conflict may involve both types of claims, the second type, which is central in some ethnic conflict theories (e.g., Smith 1969), is ignored in the competition model.

Finally, proponents of the competition model—Barth being a notable exception—have failed to take into account the fact that ethnic groups, even in developed societies, often reside in different geographical areas and/or participate in segmented institutions and organizations, particularly in the labor market. Such segmentation decreases the likelihood of *individual* competition across ethnic lines and hence, according to the model, decreases the likelihood of ethnic conflict. Indeed, Barth (1969, p.19) saw territorial separation as promoting "stability." Consider Flanders, the site of Nielsen's (1980) test: With a population that is approximately 95 percent Dutch-speaking (McRae 1986, pp. 280-81), there is little opportunity for contact with French speakers, let alone for job competition. This case is not exceptional: High levels of concentration and overall segmentation prevail in many multicultural societies and are certainly typical of the groups studied in Britain and Canada as well as in Belgium (see McRae 1974). Indeed, Horowitz (1985, pp. 105-35) rejected economic competition as a major source of ethnic conflict precisely because of the segmentation prevalent in various markets and the ensuing relative absence of such competition. Thus, it is not surprising that job competition did not appear to be an important factor in the research reviewed above.

A Partial Reformulation

Our reformulation addresses only the crucial competition/conflict relationship. We argue that for ethnic competition to lead to ethnic conflict, two previously ignored conditions must be present and a third factor is often relevant.

(1) *Ethnic competition leads to ethnic conflict and ethnic movements if, and only if, the competition is perceived to be unfair*. In principle, if competition proceeds according to accepted rules, it will tend to be perceived as fair and ethnic relations will tend to remain harmonious, as in the classic instances of competition between sports teams or between business entrepreneurs in a free market. In such instances, competition will at most lead to institutionalized collective action, as when competitors with a common ethnic background form an association to lobby for their interests through routine channels.

The notion of fairness is absent from the competition model, even in Barth's (1969) and Hannan's (1979) formulations. By assuming that "claims of injustice and inequality follow from ethnic mobilization rather than cause it," Nagel and Olzak (1982, p. 136n) can only consider the fairness or unfairness of competition as irrelevant. We assume first that collective action will not produce feelings of unfairness if there is no objective basis for them; second, if feelings of unfairness precede the action, which is not unusual, they will tend to lead to conflict. Most authors adopting a more general competition perspective also fail to specify unfairness as a condition of conflict, even if it is sometimes implicit in their discussions (e.g., Melson and Wolpe 1970; Wilson 1980; van den Berghe 1981; Brass 1985; Breton 1988).

Ethnic competition will tend to be perceived as unfair when it is seen as violating accepted norms (e.g., when discriminatory practices prevail), when it is seen as involving unjustified threats to claimed rights and possessions (e.g., infringing on one's turf), or when the rules of the game themselves are contested or the outcomes of competition are seen as unduly unbalanced (e.g., the same ethnic region wins government allocations more often than others).

But the main determinants of perceptions of unfairness are *structural*. Even if ethnic competition is "objectively" fair, it is likely to be perceived as unfair whenever it occurs within structures that generate grievances that spoil relations between competitors. This is likely to occur whenever the competition takes place within a larger context of ethnic inequality, subordination, or disadvantage of a class/economic nature (as in Hechter's [1975] internal colonial and Bonacich's [1972] split labor market models), a status nature (as in Horowitz's [1985] differential group worth model), a political nature (e.g, the Catholics in Northern Ireland), or a cultural nature. Empirically, these disparities often occur together, but not always (e.g., the Basques in Spain).

Our proposition is diametrically opposed to a central argument of the competition model that interethnic competition *and conflict* increase with interethnic (economic) *equality. We recognize that as ethnic disparities increase, the likelihood of competition and conflict decreases because of shortages in the disadvantaged group of resources, especially leadership, and of motivational factors like incentives and expectations of success. However, moderate* structural disadvantage, which is more common in ethnic relations than in class relations, does not entail serious shortages of these elements and thus does not prevent competition and conflict.[3]

We believe that including unfairness in the competition model and stating its structural determinants resolve its alleged incompatibility with both the internal colonial and split labor market models. Both a cultural division of labor and a split labor market are among the structural conditions of disparity most likely to lead to perceptions of unfair competition (see Laczko 1986). Our position is also consistent with the views of other competition theorists who, despite not stating explicitly that unfairness is a condition of conflict, nevertheless insist that the basic motives of conflict are found in competition occurring within a structural context of hierarchy, domination, coercion, or exploitation (see especially van den Berghe 1981, chaps. 3 and 4).

(2) For unfair ethnic competition to lead to conflict, *the competitors' relationships with each*

other must also be as purely competitive as possible or, to put it another way, as uncomplementary as possible. If high levels of complementarity or interdependence (or even dependence) are present, relationships are likely to be perceived as mutually beneficial and will therefore tend to be peaceful (although not necessarily friendly).

Barth (1969) attended to interdependence when he argued that stability may obtain when ethnic groups "provide important goods and services for each other, i.e., occupy reciprocal and therefore different niches but in close interdependence" (p. 19). For Barth, this was an ideal-type situation leading to stability, opposed to the ideal-type situation in which competition and instability prevailed. However, Barth also argued that, in reality, mixed situations are likely to obtain, so that "only quite gross simplifications can reduce them to simple types" (p. 20). Unfortunately, oversimplification has prevailed in the competition model. Neither the ideal type of interdependence nor the mixed empirical situations have been addressed in studies of ethnic movements. This neglect is particularly problematic because interdependence tends to increase with modernization (Barth and Noel 1972; van den Berghe 1981. p. 42). Indeed, one of Hannan's (1979, p. 267) central claims is that modernization increases "connectedness" between small ethnic groups, but he did not draw out the implications of this for the competitive relationships between such enlarged groups and others. The potential effect of interdependence has not, however, escaped notice from other theorists. Van den Berghe (1967, pp. 138-40; 1981, chap. 3), for instance, sees complementarity as a concomitant of competition in all stages of ethnic relations. (See also Lieberson 1970, pp. 12-15; Barth and Noel 1972, pp. 340-43; Brass 1985.) Therefore, competition cannot be considered independently of complementarity, and we hypothesize that *ethnic competition translates into nonroutine mobilization only among ethnic groups or individuals that perceive competition as unfair and are not highly interdependent.*

With these two conditions, our reformulation is consistent with the so-called contact hypothesis, which holds that interracial contacts breed tolerance and harmony only if they are equal status contacts and are contacts over common and interdependent goals (Allport 1958, chap. 16; Pettigrew 1971, pp. 274-78).

In line with previous work (Pinard and Hamilton 1986), we further hypothesize that perceptions of unfair competition and ethnic interdependence are likely to produce effects independently of competition. Perceptions of unfair competition produce a sense of ethnic grievance, whereas ethnic interdependence produces negative collective incentives. Specifically, we hypothesize an interaction effect between these two factors, although previous work has indicated additive effects as well (Pinard and Hamilton 1986).

(3) A third element is also relevant to ethnic conflict, although it is not a necessary condition. While individual experiences of unfair competition over some private goods may be a motivating factor for some, we believe they do not account for most current ethnic movements. *For conflict to be widespread and intense, it must be social rather than interpersonal, and the competition must be intergroup rather than interindividual. Above all, the objects of competition must involve collective goods rather than individual goods* (Rose 1971, pp. 300-301 and 445-46). Proponents of the competition model are ambiguous in this regard. While some insist that the competition be over political resources, which are clearly collective goods (e.g., Nagel 1984; see also Nagel and Olzak 1982, pp. 136-37), others stress job competition, with unspecified "other resources" sometimes mentioned (e.g., Nielsen 1980, pp. 79-80; Olzak 1985, p. 76; Ragin 1979, pp. 622, 627; Olzak and Nagel 1986, p. 2). But even in confrontations in which job competition has been the central issue, what was at stake was each group's share of the *labor market*, a collective good, not particular individuals' jobs. Hence, not only did the individuals actually competing for jobs become concerned and mobilize, others did too.

The recent resurgence of ethnic conflict has, however, generally involved competition over a much wider set of collective goods, e.g., political rights and regional-ethnic power, regional or group ethnic parity in the economy, group status including the status of the group's culture, and language. In addition, these conflicts have not been rooted only in competitive strivings, but also in disagreements over the promotion of cultural differences. (See, for example, Lorwin [1973] and McRae [1986] on Belgium; Rose [1971] and Urwin [1982] on Great Britain; Linz [1973] and Greenwood [1977] on Spain; Breton and Stasiulis [1980] and Pinard and Hamilton [1986] on Canada.) Wilson (1980, chaps. 5 and 6) explicitly rejects job competition as an important source of black/white conflict in the post-World War II period and claims instead that conflict was increasingly related to "competition for power and privilege . . . in the sociopolitical order" (p. 116). Breton (1988) makes a similar argument about French-English relations in Canada, examining a whole set of collective goods over which competition and conflict developed over the last two centuries.

Although grievances and demands are formulated in somewhat specific terms and packages in each country at each time, they are usually subsets of the general types of issues mentioned. Moreover, not only competing individuals, but competing groups or organizations, express such grievances and demand relevant collective goods. Therefore, competition arguments ought to be cast in the wider terms usually found in general competition theories (e.g., Park 1950; Melson and Wolpe 1970; van den Berghe 1967, 1981).[4]

The positive evidence reported in Olzak's (1986, 1989) recent work on early racial and ethnic conflicts in American cities is consistent with our reformulation. In that research, the previous modernization argument is largely ignored and direct measures of labor market competition are developed, e.g., racial and ethnic group internal migration and immigration. The historical evidence also suggests that, unlike contemporary ethnic movements, older, local ethnic confrontations were (1) more likely to involve labor market competition than competition over a broad set of collective goods, and (2) the competition tended to be perceived as unfair both by members of the indigenous population whose "acquired" rights were threatened and by migrants, who were exposed to discriminatory practices. Finally, there was little interdependence between these early groups. Hence the more positive results obtained in these studies, despite the missing links in the original model.

Data, Measures, and Methods

Our test relies on cross-sectional, individual-level data that are better-suited than ecological data to assess competition arguments. Unfortunately, these data lack a direct measure of our third factor—group competition over collective goods. Since we do not regard it as a necessary factor and since we posited that unfair competition over jobs or other private goods could be a motivating factor for some, we proceed with a partial test of our theory. While not ideal, this test is better than none.[5] Although we consider only job competition, we can evaluate our arguments concerning the impact of the two necessary factors—the fairness of competition and the degree of interdependence present. This is an important task in itself since these two factors are relevant for competition over any types of goods.

The data are from a study of the movement for the independence of Québec (S.M.I.Q.) carried out by the second author during the winter of 1970-1971. A stratified proportional sample of 1,982 Québec residents aged 18 and over were interviewed at home.[6] The analysis is restricted to full-time Francophone labor force participants. We seek to explain the ethnic mobilization of Francophones, who are the moving force behind the independence movement in Québec. Since job competition is an important variable, only Francophones in the labor force on a full-time basis, i.e., those in a position to compete with Anglophones for jobs, are included in the analysis.[7]

The ethnic mobilization of Francophones is measured by their support for the separation of Québec. Respondents were asked: "Personally, are you for or against the separation of Québec from the rest of Canada?" Respondents who were undecided were asked if they "would be more inclined to be for or against" it. Twenty percent of Francophone workers favored separation or were inclined to favor separation. This attitudinal measure is a good indicator of mobilization behind the independence movement because it identifies the movement's core supporters and eliminates those favoring milder options, such as a sovereign Québec remaining economically associated with Canada. Furthermore, it is a better indicator than support for the Parti Québécois (P.Q.), the political arm of the movement: Although most supporters of separation voted for the P.Q., many P.Q. voters were not in favor of separation, but preferred milder options or voted P.Q. for different reasons (Pinard and Hamilton 1977, 1978; for similar arguments, see also Nielsen 1986, pp. 173-74; Studler and McAllister 1988, pp. 53, 57).

Interethnic job competition is measured by the presence of English Canadians at the same and/or at higher levels in the Francophone respondent's workplace.[8] Francophones who work alone or in places where there are no English Canadians at similar or higher levels are considered to be not in job competition with them. We assume that Francophones with Anglophones at similar or higher levels in the workplace may have been and/or may still be competing for higher-level positions or job transfers.

The perceived fairness of this competition is measured by the respondent's evaluation of the relative chances of French and English Canadians obtaining job offers or promotions.[9] Competition is presumed to be unfair if Francophone respondents believe that an English Canadian has a better chance of obtaining a job offer or promotion than an equally competent French Canadian. Although some would argue that the perception of unfairness is a consequence and not a cause of mobilization, we believe that argument does not hold in this case. Repeated surveys since the early 1960s have shown that a high (over 50 percent) and relatively stable proportion of Francophones claim that Anglophones have better chances in the job market, while mobilization for separation has remained at lower levels over that period and, until recently, increased only gradually. Hence, for most the perceptions of unfairness could not have followed mobilization. (For a fuller discussion of this point and the evidence see Pinard and Hamilton 1986, pp. 235-41, 246.)

Finally, interdependence is measured indirectly as concern about the overall consequences of separation.[10] While we would prefer a stronger measure, this is the only one available. It is strengthened by data gathered through open-ended questions in which these concerns were often expressed in terms of interdependence, e.g., a belief that Québec and the rest of Canada need

one another or that at least the former needs the latter, particularly for economic reasons (Pinard 1975, pp. 87-90). Respondents who worry "somewhat" or "a lot" about the consequences of separation perceive this option as costly and we assume that they perceive a high degree of interdependence or complementarity between Québec and the rest of Canada.

Our analysis employs a logit model, with support for the separation of Québec as the dichotomous dependent variable. The independent variables included in this model are coded contrasts that reflect the predicted effects of job competition, perceived fairness of competition, and perceived interdependence on support for the separatist option.

Table 1 shows how the independent variables were introduced into the statistical model. Seven different contrasts were coded to correspond to our hypotheses. The first four contrasts are for the evaluation of the effect of job competition on the probability of supporting separatism within each possible combination of perceived fairness and perceived interdependence. Each contrast compares the "no competition" group to the "competition" group within one of the four possible combinations of fairness and interdependence. If job competition leads to separatism only under conditions of unfair competition and in the absence of perceived interdependence, only the first of these contrasts should be significant.

Our second hypothesis is that both perceived fairness and perceived interdependence have separate and direct effects on support for separation in Québec, regardless of the other variables. The fifth and sixth contrasts test these two "main"

Table 1
Coding Coefficients Assigned to Subgroups for Seven Orthogonal Contrasts Used as Independent Variables

	Subgroup			Orthogonal Contrast (Independent Variables)						
	Compet-ition	Fair-ness	Interde-pendence	(1)	(2)	(3)	(4)	(5)	(6)	(7)
(1)	No	No	No	−1	0	0	0	1/4	−1/4	−1/16
	Yes	No	No	0	0	0	0	1/4	−1/4	−1/16
(2)	No	Yes	No	0	−1	0	0	−1/4	−1/4	1/16
	Yes	Yes	No	0	1	0	0	−1/4	−1/4	1/16
(3)	No	Yes	Yes	0	0	−1	0	−1/4	1/4	−1/16
	Yes	Yes	Yes	0	0	1	0	−1/4	1/4	−1/16
(4)	No	No	Yes	0	0	0	−1	1/4	1/4	1/16
	Yes	No	Yes	0	0	0	1	1/4	1/4	1/16

Note: Fractions are used in contrasts 5 and 6 so that positive values add to 1 and negative values add to −1.

Table 2
Unstandardized Logit Coefficients Predicting Support for Québec Separation: Full-Time Francophone Workers, 1979-1971

Independent Variable	Unstandardized Logit Coefficients	χ^2
Intercept	1.490***	
Effect of job competition when		
(1) Competition unfair/	.350	5.38*
No interdependence	(.151)	
(2) Competition fair/	.267	1.00
No interdependence	(.267)	
(3) Competition fair/	−.033	.01
Interdependence	(.455)	
(4) Competition unfair/	−.023	.01
Interdependence	(.245)	
Main Effect		
(5) Fairness	1.907	10.01*
	(.602)	
(6) Interdependence	−3.955	45.56**
	(.606)	
(7) Interaction effect:	.339	.02
fairness x interdependence	(2.404)	
(8) Worker/farmer	−.851	13.86***
	(.229)	
Number of cases	659	

*$p<.05$ **$p<.01$ ***$p<.001$
Note: Numbers in parentheses are standard errors. Log-likelihood at convergence $(-2 \ln [L_0]) = 515.22$; χ^2 for full model $= 104.52$; degrees of freedom $= 8$; $p<.001$

effects, respectively. The seventh contrast tests the combined (interactive) effect of perceived fairness and perceived interdependence.

Other control variables were examined as possible sources of spuriousness (occupation, industrial sector, income, education, age, ethnicity of management, size of workplace, self-employment, region, and religious attendance). Occupation and region were significantly related to both job competition and support for separation at the zero-order level and were considered for the final logit model. However, statistical tests revealed an increment in explanatory power only for workers and farmers (coded as 1) compared to all other occupations (coded as 0), so that only this dummy variable was included in the final logit model (for more details, see Bélanger 1988).

Results

Table 2 presents the results of the logit model predicting support for separatism as a function of the seven contrasts and the worker/farmer dummy variable. The goodness-of-fit test for the overall model reveals that, as a group, the independent variables have a significant effect.

Of greater interest is the significance of the individual contrasts corresponding to the proposed hypotheses.[11] As predicted, job competition has a significant effect on support for separation only when the competition is perceived as unfair and the consequences of independence are not worrisome. Under the three remaining alternatives, job competition does not increase support for separation by a statistically significant amount.[12] Therefore, our central hypothesis is supported.

The main effect of perceived fairness is statistically significant, which supports our second hypothesis. The main effect of perceived interdependence is also statistically significant and the negative value of the logit coefficient indicates that those who worry about the consequences of separation are less likely to support it than those who are not worried. However, the effects of both perceived interdependence and perceived fairness on support for separation are independent of one another, since the interaction between these two exogenous variables is not statistically significant. This is mainly due to the fact that when competition is fair and interdependence is not perceived, support for separation is still relatively strong (see Table 3).[13]

Table 3
Predicted Probabilities of Support for Québec Separation: Full-Time Francophone Workers, 1970-1971

Subgroup	Workers/Farmers		Other Occupations	
	No Job Competition	Job Competition	No Job Competition	Job Competition
(1) Competition unfair/ no interdependence	.22	.37	.40	.58
(2) Competition unfair/ interdependence	.06	.05	.12	.12
(3) Competition fair/ no interdependence	.11	.18	.23	.33
(4) Competition fair/ interdependence	.02	.02	.05	.05

Note: Values are predicted probabilities calculated from the equation for the final logit model.

The dummy variable for workers and farmers is also statistically significant and negative, indicating that workers and farmers are less likely to support separatism than those in other occupations (e.g., see Pinard and Hamilton 1989, p. 91).[14] This is expected because the tests for its incremental contribution revealed the necessity of retaining this variable.

Table 3 translates the effects of the independent variables into the predicted probabilities of supporting independence for each category of respondents. The first row reveals that when there are *no worries* concerning the consequences of independence and a perception of *unfair* competition, job competition produces a significant increase in the probability of supporting separation. Among workers and farmers, the increase in probability is .15 (.37 −.22), whereas among those in other occupations, the difference is .18 (.58 −.40). For all other combinations of perceived fairness and perceived interdependence, the effects of job competition are weaker (and not statistically significant) or altogether absent. These results support our reformulation.

The statistically significant main effect of perceived unfairness can also be observed in Table 3 by comparing row (1) to row (3) and row (2) to row (4). In line with our argument stating that what is at stake is the group's share of the labor market, not only the jobs of those individuals actually in competition, we find that perception of unfairness in the job market has an effect on support for separatism whether or not one is actually involved in job competition.

In accordance with the results of the logit analysis, worries about the consequences of separation show the strongest independent effects, as revealed by the comparison between row (1) and row (2) and between row (3) and row (4). A lack of concern about the consequences of separation increases the probability of support for separation regardless of the presence of job competition, the fairness of competition, or occupation. In the absence of perceived interdependence, the probability of supporting separation depends on the joint presence of perceptions of unfairness and job competition itself, as well as on occupation. However, perceived interdependence greatly reduces the probability of supporting separation and virtually eliminates the effects of the other three explanatory factors.

Summary and Discussion

The theory of ethnic competition suggests a direct causal link between occupational competition and ethnic mobilization. Two conditions were posited as necessary for such a relationship to hold: Competition had to be perceived as unfair

and it had to take place within a context of low interdependence. These arguments were evaluated with survey data on the independence movement in Québec. The analysis confirmed our expectations. Job competition between Francophones and Anglophones in Québec leads Francophones to support separation only when competition is seen as unfair and there is no perception of interdependence with the Anglophone group. If these two conditions do not hold, job competition will not produce a significant increase in ethnic political mobilization.

Under the posited conditions, however, the significant positive effect of job competition on separatist support is not strong. This is not surprising given our argument that in recent ethnic movements, and in Québec in particular, the main objects of competition have not been individual jobs, but more general collective goods. Indeed, grievances regarding these more general issues exert stronger effects than those observed with job competition, even under specified conditions (Pinard and Hamilton 1986).

Our reformulation of competition theory can account for the otherwise puzzling case of Switzerland. Switzerland is a multicultural society that exhibits a high level of ethnic harmony at the national level, especially between its two largest groups, the French- and German-speaking Swiss. According to the original competition model, Swiss politics at the national level should be characterized by high levels of *conflict*, not harmony. Unlike corresponding groups in other countries that have been studied, the French- and German-speaking Swiss are virtually equal on various socioeconomic dimensions (McRae 1983, pp. 80-92; Schmid 1981, pp. 33-36), and the model predicts that "the more alike are the occupational distributions of two [ethnic] groups, the greater competition between them," and, hence, the greater the conflict (Hannan 1979, pp. 272-73). How can the ethnic harmony in Switzerland be explained? Competition theorists are silent on this issue.

Our hypothesis is that job competition between these groups—to the extent that it occurs under the prevailing high level of linguistic territorial concentration—is unlikely to be seen as unfair because of their basic socioeconomic equality and the unlikely presence of pervasive and one-sided linguistic job discrimination under such equality. Moreover, these groups are unlikely to perceive other forms of competition as unfair, especially competition over collective goods, because of the overall socioeconomic parity, status equality, and regional economic balance (McRae 1983, pp. 80-92), and because of the way political power is distributed and exercised. While political power is unequal, given that the number of German-speaking Swiss citizens is much larger than that of their French-speaking counterparts (74 percent vs. 20 percent), this is partly compensated for by the slightly higher prestige of the French language, which "effectively counterbalances [their] numerical weakness" (McRae 1983, p. 73; also pp. 59-68). Moreover, power is decentralized through federalism and the distribution of power goes beyond simple proportionality in the national government (McRae 1983, pp. 126-31). Above all, given the prevailing conditions of equality and balance, power can easily be exercised in a consociational manner, that is, through grand coalition governments and informal mutual veto powers that ensure that no group is a disproportionate loser. Switzerland is recognized as a prototype of consociational politics (Lijphart 1977, chap. 2) so that, despite divergent interests, there are few grievances over economic, status, political, or cultural issues. To the extent that linguistic competition occurs, it is likely to be harmoniously carried out through institutionalized channels in a consociational framework. Competition and harmony can go hand-in-hand.

Our reformulation is also consistent with another empirical generalization: the high propensity of intellectuals and the low propensity of managers and businessmen to support and lead current ethnic movements (Pinard and Hamilton 1989), despite the fact that intellectuals are less likely to be involved in individual interethnic competition compared to managers and businessmen. Intellectuals, in contrast with businessmen, are especially sensitive to unequal opportunities in the competition for collective economic position, status, and power, are particularly concerned with the preservation of cultural differences, and are less exposed or sensitive to material interdependence.

Notes

1. The argument that modernization leads to ethnic conflict through an increase in ethnic resources and organization sometimes appears with the more common competition argument. At other times, resources and organization are simply additional independent variables added to the modernization/competition link. (Cf. Olzak 1982, p. 254; Nagel and Olzak 1982, pp. 136-37; Olzak 1986, p. 77; Olzak and Nagel 1986, p. 3; see also Hannan 1979, pp. 270-72; Ragin 1987.) Notice, however, that a high level of organization within an ethnic group should increase segmentation and thus *reduce* interindividual competition.

2. Beer's (1980, chap. 3) ecological analysis of regionalist resurgence in France, cited as supporting the model, also presents contradictory results. Fitzsimmons-LeCavalier and LeCavalier (1989) found no support for the competition model in their study of Québec's non-Francophones' mobilization. See's (1986) comparative-historical evidence on Northern Ireland and Québec has been critically evaluated elsewhere (Pinard 1987). Olzak's (e.g., 1989) positive evidence concerning earlier ethnic confrontations in American cities is discussed below.

3. This implies a curvilinear relationship between ethnic inequality and nonroutine collective action: Groups must be disadvantaged enough to be dissatisfied (the deprivation theorists' argument), but also resource-rich enough to be able to challenge dominant groups (the resource mobilization argument). The latter argument is central in Hannan's (1979) formulation and was important in Jenkins and Kposowa's (1990) research (in which relative parity in resources is *the* measure of competition). Both, however, fail to fully appreciate the first argument.

4. Our reformulation deals mainly with problems of motivation; a more general model of nonroutine ethnic collective action should consider other determinants, such as ethnic segmentation or other conducive factors, ethnic beliefs and ideologies, material and human resources, opportunities, and social control or facilitation. (On political conduciveness, see Nielsen 1986).

5. The third factor has been examined indirectly in another study (Pinard and Hamilton 1986). Although not explicitly cast in terms of competition over collective goods, its examination of the strong impact of grievances regarding collective goods implies competition.

6. Details of the study are given in the S.M.I.Q. codebook (revised edition), April 15, 1976, which can be obtained from the authors.

7. Actually, the analysis includes all male labor force participants (the majority of whom work full-time) and full-time female participants because the measure of current job competition was available only for these groups. Unemployed, retired, and voluntarily inactive respondents were excluded because job competition was measured with respect to previous jobs. Other respondents (housewives, part-time female workers, students, and persons unable to work) were omitted because only husbands' or fathers' job competition was measured.

8. The questions asked were: "Among these people who work at the same place as you, how many are French-speaking Canadians: all, nearly all, about three quarters, about half, or less than half?" (For answers other than "all" or "works alone," ask: "What is the proportion of English-speaking Canadians among the people working at the same level as you: are there none, only a few, about a quarter, about half, or more than half?" and "What is the proportion of English-speaking Canadians among the people working at a higher level than you: are there none, only a few, about a quarter, about half, or more than half?")

9. The question asked was: "In the case of job offers or promotions, do you think that a French Canadian and an English Canadian who are equally competent have the same chances of getting them, that the French Canadian has a better chance, or that the English Canadian has a better chance?"

10. The question asked was: "When you think of all the consequences that independence could have, does it worry you or not?" (If yes) "Does it worry you a lot, somewhat, or just a little?"

11. Whereas the chi-square significance tests for these coefficients are revealing, the coefficients themselves are not easily interpretable as they represent the effect of each exogenous variable on the log of the odds of supporting separation. Of central interest are the predicted probabilities of supporting separatism, presented in Table 3. These probabilities, while slightly different from the actual percentages obtained by a crosstabulation, reveal the magnitude of the differences between the various subgroups.

12. The logit model was also run using a more restrictive measure of competition, i.e., the presence of Anglophones at the *same level* in the workplace. It was also run controlling for self-employment vs. being employed, to ensure that the effect of competition was not being enhanced by the absence of job competition among self-employed respondents. In both instances, the results were the same as those described except that in each case the fast contrast was significant at $p = .10$ instead of $p = .02$.

13. This is a special case whereby, in the absence of perceived costs, grievances can be replaced by aspirations as alternative internal motives (Pinard and Hamilton 1986, pp. 255-58).

14. Many factors may account for the low level of support among workers and farmers, e.g., a weaker concern for cultural, status, and political ethnic issues, stronger materialistic concerns, lesser exposure to nationalistic beliefs, weaker ethnic loyalties, a lower degree of political involvement, or dependence on fewer ethnic institutions (for data, see Pinard and Hamilton 1981). ◆

3

Disorganization and the New Mexico Prison Riot of 1980

Bert Useem

Few researchers now defend a "breakdown" or "disorganization" model of collective action, even though it dominated the field just two decades ago (Kornhauser, 1959; Smelser, 1962; Davies, 1962). According to the model, collective action arises from a breakdown in the structures of solidarity—church, family, work, and voluntary organizations—that normally channel people into conventional behavior.

The fact that the "breakdown" model is called what it is—rather than the "crisis" or "shock" model, say—reflects an underlying presumption that in normal times social structures exist which keep people from mobilizing for conflict. Two complementary facets of the breakdown model emphasize different sets of these controlling structures.

A Durkheimian (and Parsonian) facet emphasizes control over the individual's emotions, thoughts, and appetites. In normal times, the individual is integrated into the social whole; he feels a sense of commonality with other sectors of the society; his appetites are restrained to a manageable level. According to this view, then, disorganization produces collective action for two reasons. First, disorganization frees individuals from the regulatory mechanisms that inhere in social organization. Urbanization and migration, for example, uproot individuals from their social, political, and recreational activities, producing a mass of isolated, anomic individuals. These marginal individuals are then readily "available" for mobilization (Kornhauser, 1959; Smelser, 1962).

Second, disorganization increases "discontent" within a population. The isolated, anomic individual develops new, unpredictable, and poten-

tially unfulfillable desires; he develops irrational beliefs about how they can be fulfilled; he seeks to escape and overcome his isolation and discontent through collective action (Smelser, 1962; Davies, 1962, 1969).

The second, more economically-oriented facet of the breakdown model emphasizes society's ability in normal times to meet people's needs, needs that are considered as given and somewhat stable. Thus, the effect of unemployment on the individual is traded through his empty pockets rather than through his isolated condition. Without the rewards of work, discontent results, followed by protest (Piven and Cloward, 1977).

Of course, discontent need not be conceptualized as the result of "breakdown." Theorists of "pure" deprivation and relative deprivation emphasize the effect of discontent on protest without necessarily attributing it to the failure of pre-existing control mechanisms. Increased perceived deprivation, however, can be treated as the expression of "breakdown" if one adopts the assumption that a stable order normally has the mechanisms, cultural or economic, to ensure stable levels of contentment for all its constituents.

The breakdown model is consistent with the idea that protest occurs in periods of high rates of personal pathology and antisocial behavior, such as suicide, dissolution of families, alcoholism, vagrancy, and crime. Protest and high rates of pathology covary, according to breakdown theory, because both are products either of the dissolving of social controls or of increased deprivation.

The most ardent critics of breakdown approach are researchers working within the "resource-mobilization" tradition: "Breakdown theories of collective action and collective violence," the Tillys (1975:290) state, "suffer from irreparable logic and empirical difficulties." There are four major arguments against the breakdown model. First, resource-mobilization theorists claim that grievances are sufficiently widespread through all societies at all times that, as a constant, they explain little of the variation in collective action. Although resource-mobilization theorists would agree with the proposition that individuals who engage in collective action are dissatisfied with the existing order, they assert that this proposition has no predictive power (Jenkins and Perrow, 1977; Oberschall, 1978b:298; McCarthy and Zald, 1977:1214-15; Snyder and Tilly, 1972). Second, they maintain that the bar-

"Disorganization and the New Mexico Prison Riot of 1980." *American Sociological Review* 50: 667-688. Copyright © 1985 by the American Sociological Association. Reprinted with permission.

rier to insurgency is the access to resources, and that disorganized groups are least likely to have the requisite resources. Disorganized populations will tend to be powerless and unable to launch an insurgency. Third, the resource-mobilization theorists argue that collective action flows out of struggles among well-defined groups. They find implausible the idea that collective action occurs when groups becomes less organized, rather than more organized.

Finally, resource-mobilization theorists rest much of their charge against the breakdown model on the purportedly negative evidence they and others have collected. Collective action does *not* covary with indicators of personal pathology (e.g., crime, suicide, alcoholism) (Lodhi and Tilly, 1973:296; Tilly et al, 1975:76-81), non-membership in secondary and primary groups (Gerlach and Hime, 1970; Useem, 1980), and changes in the level of deprivation (Jenkins and Perrow, 1977; Snyder and Tilly, 1972; Skocpol, 1979:115).

One focus of this research has been the urban riots of the 1960s. The evidence indicates that the rioters compared to their nonrioting counterparts, were more likely to be politically sophisticated, racially conscious, socialized in the North, victims of racial discrimination, and similar to their counterparts on such variables as income, education and occupation (Bryan, 1979; Caplan and Paige, 1968; Feagin and Hahn, 1973; Sears and McConahay, 1973; Tomlinson, 1970). Further, rioting tended to occur in cities that had blocked political opportunities for blacks (Eisenger, 1973), whereas variation in the social conditions in the cities, such as percent of dilapidated housing as a measure of social disorganization, did not have an impact on riot propensity (once controls are introduced for region and percent of nonwhite population) (Spilerman, 1970; 1976). The Tillys sum up their interpretation of the evidence:

> As the dust settled and evidence accumulated, people began to see the discrepancies between what happened in Watts, Detroit, or elsewhere and theories which emphasized the explosion of accumulated discontent. . . . [The evidence] dispel[s] the idea that the participants came disproportionately from the ghetto's marginal, depressed, disorganized populations. (Tilly et al., 1975:293)

These arguments have convinced most researchers in the discipline. Even those researchers otherwise critical of the resource-mobilization approach have sided with its stand against the breakdown model (Pinard, 1983). Social movement/collective behavior textbooks now routinely report that breakdown model has, as Miller recently put it, "yielded few explanations of social movements that have withstood the probings of critics" (Miller, 1985:319; see also, Wood and Jackson, 1982:63-77; Washburn, 1982:201-203).

Despite the general opposition to the breakdown model, there is still research claiming support for it. One example is Piven and Cloward's (1977) work on the conditions that give rise to "poor" people's movements. They argue that "profound dislocations," such as massive unemployment or large scale migration, are needed "to virtually destroy the structures and routines of daily life" before protest can occur (1977: 10). A second exception has been Gurr and his collaborators, who found that "crime waves"—sharp increases in crimes of violence and theft—coincided with episodes of civil strife in London, Stockholm, New South Wales, and Calcutta during various periods in the 19th and 20th centuries (Gurr, 1976:82-90; Gurr et al., 1977:666-76).

Third, a number of researchers have found flaws in the standard research on the 1960s urban riots, and reported that properly assessed, the data support a breakdown model. Miller and associates (1976) show that many of the key tables supporting the resource-mobilization interpretation of the riots are percentaged in the wrong direction and conflate a critical distinction between nonviolent protesters and rioters. Once these errors are corrected, Miller and associates (1976:361) argue, the data reveal that the rioters were the "least socially integrated and lower elements of the community." Lieske (1978) found that cities with higher levels of social disorganization were more likely to experience a riot than cities with lower levels. Family disorganization (as measured by divorce and separation rates and illegitimacy rates), demographic dislocations (as measured by nonwhite population change and percent nonwhite change in residence), and high levels of criminal activity (as measured by police density) each contributed to the outbreak of the riots.

Finally, a greater number of researchers have been persuaded that deprivation and protest are causally associated (Useem, 1980; Walsh, 1981, 1983; Pinard, 1983). These researchers, however, still tend to reject the picture of collective action as the behavior of uprooted, disorganized people, and argue instead that organization and solidarity generate protest. They see the "breakdown" element as the failure of social mechanisms that were previously supposed to satisfy the needs of the discontented group, and not as the disruption of ties *within* that group.

This paper takes a new look at the breakdown model. We show that the breakdown model can more adequately account for a particular instance of collective action, the New Mexico prison riot of February 2, 1980, than the rival resource-mobilization model.[1]

Data and Riot

Before describing the data, we consider whether evidence on prison riots, in general, can be used to help adjudicate the debate between the breakdown and resource-mobilization approaches. Two considerations suggest it cannot. A mandated purpose of prisons is the deprivation of its clientele. Sykes (1958:63-83) describes five deprivations—liberty, goods and services, heterosexual relationships, autonomy, and security— that together lead all inmates to feel that "life in the maximum security prison is depriving or frustrating in the extreme" (1958:63). As a possible consequence, the effect of deprivation on protest may be different in prisons than it is elsewhere.

Further, inmates in maximum security prisons are (of course) convicted felons. The factors that cause this atypical subpopulation to rebel may differ from those that generate rebellion in the populations considered by resource-mobilization and breakdown proponents.

While these considerations serve as an important caveat—cautioning researchers not to overgeneralize the results from prisons to collective action elsewhere—it would be unwarranted to draw the stronger conclusion that the evidence on prison riots does not bear on the central controversies. Although all inmates experience a profound deprivation by virtue of their imprisonment, inmates do develop standards of just deprivation. It is the violation of these standards which, as in the non-prison world, is hypothesized to motivate protest.

The breakdown and resource-mobilization models, furthermore, have been applied to a heterogeneous assemblage of phenomena, including peasant involvement in revolutionary movements, strikes by workers in the early stages of industrialization, unionization of farmworkers in the United States, and participation in the U.S. civil rights and new Christian right movements, to name a few recent examples. These diverse foci make less troublesome the argument that prison populations are atypical of those usually studied. Additionally, both resource-mobilization theorists (e.g., Zald and Berger, 1978:843, 846, 847) and breakdown theorists (e.g., Smelser, 1962:236-37, 251-52, 254) *have* drawn on data on prison riots to support their respective models.

Finally, the resource-mobilization theorists emphasize protest by integrated, skilled, intelligent, organized sectors of a group, and oppose the image of rebellion as the work of the *canaille*. It is somewhat problematic for them, therefore, if the *canaille do* rebel. Because prison inmates often lack social skills and invariably lack organizational and material resources, pure resource-mobilization theory would predict their being a passive and easily-controlled group. Their high levels of deprivation ought not to alter this, because everyone has grievances. If they do rebel, a resource-mobilization theorist would be forced to posit some causative increase in resources or internal organization. It is therefore particularly problematic if prisoners rebel precisely when their deprivation is greatest, resources fewest, and social structure most atomized—as was the case in New Mexico.

The data on the New Mexico riot are drawn from two principal sources. As part of the official investigation of the riot, the New Mexico Attorney General's office interviewed, shortly after the riot, a random sample of 49 inmates and 28 guards. Of those selected to be interviewed, only three inmates and six guards refused to grant interviews (OAGSNM, 1980:A-2). The interviews lasted from two to four hours, and involved questioning the inmates and guards about prison conditions over a ten-year period. Verbatim transcripts of these interviews were obtained. The author and co-worker, in addition, interviewed 36 inmates in February, 1985. The sample consisted of all inmates in the penitentiary who had been there during the riot.[2]

The 1980 New Mexico prison riot is perhaps the most brutal (33 inmates killed, 400 injured [Lapham et al., 1984:218]) and costly ($200 million [Morris, 1983:225]) U.S. prison riot. It began when several inmates overpowered, stripped, and severely beat four guards who were conducting a routine inspection of a dormitory in the prison's south wing. Guards stationed at other south wing dormitories were quickly subdued. A number of security lapses allowed the inmates to take control over the entire institution: a security gate separating the south wing from the rest of the institution was left unlocked; a recently-installed, purportedly impenetrable window fronting the control center gave way when bashed by inmates; and renovation crews left behind acetylene torches that were used to burn open locked gates (OAGSNM, 1980; Serrill and Katel, 1980; Colvin, 1982).

No group of inmates attained clear leadership status. Control over hostages, walkie-talkies, and negotiations was fragmented, personalistic, and ephemeral. Some inmates, alone and in groups, took advantage of the situation to beat, rape, torture, and mutilate other inmates. One inmate had his head cut off with a shovel; another died from a screw-driver driven through his head; several others were immolated in their cells when inmates sprayed lighter fluid on them; and still others were tortured to death with acetylene torches. No inmate group made a serious attempt to prevent this. One inmate wrote:

> there were many such groups . . . ferociously slashing open stomachs, cutting of genitalia, beating on corpses that were strewn over the catwalks. The floors were covered with clotted pools of blood, the cells with bloody drag marks, the air with cries of men being tortured. (Stone, 1982:126)

The assaults and killing were selective. The primary targets were inmate informants ("snitches") and objects of personal grudges. An inmate stated,

> [M]ost of the people [attacked] were rats or they had jackets. . . . Some of them were killed over little petty beefs. . . . There was a reason behind every one of them. There wasn't, you know, helter skelter killing. (A.G. Interview)

Autopsy reports listed thirty of the thirty-three deaths as inmate-inflicted homicides (the cause of death could not be determined for the remaining three bodies, which were incinerated) (Lapham et al., 1984:222).

Twelve guards were taken as hostages, some of whom were repeatedly beaten, sodomized, and threatened with death. A hostage reported that an inmate approached a group of hostages with the severed head of a black inmate, saying, "This is what can happen to you. . . . We'll cut you in pieces and throw you out the window" (Quoted in

Hillman, 1981:1194). Another hostage reported that an inmate said to him: " 'First we're going to stab you fifteen times, then we're going to cut your hands off, then we're going to cut your head off.' " (Quoted in *New Mexican,* February 3, 1985, Sec. E, p. 3.)

Inmates killed no hostages for two reasons. First, they believed that a hostage killing would swiftly bring an armed assault. Second, as one inmate put it,

> a dead man does not suffer and they [the inmates] wanted to fuck them [the guards] up. . . . They succeeded in every case. Fucked them up bad. They didn't want to kill them. . . . [T]hey've been hurt for years by those fucking guards, and they wanted to get back at them, wanted to hurt them.[3] (A.G. Interview)

However, some guards received better treatment than others, and some were helped to escape by sympathetic inmates.

Not all inmates participated in the violence. This included the prison's 120 blacks (nine percent of the inmate population). They organized themselves for self-protection and eventually fled from the riot (OAGSNM, 1980:49).

Other inmates not participating in the brutality included a small group who had been active in prison reform and class-action suits. Led by respected jail-house lawyer Lonnie Duran, the group tried to transform the riot into a protest for prison reform (Colvin, 1982:459). Duran's group formulated a set of demands and established negotiations with the administration. Many inmates, however, simply paid no attention to or were unaware of these activities, and they had little impact on the course and outcome of the riot (Serrill and Katel, 1980; Colvin, 1982).

Findings

Both the inmate and guard interviews support a deprivation explanation of the riot. Most inmates reported that the conditions in the penitentiary before the riot were insufferably bad. One inmate, for example, stated:

> It was unlivable before the riot. . . . It's been too crowded, the food is bad, the goddamned guards talk to you like you're a dog. We're not dogs. (A.G. Interview)

Another inmate described the prison as a place of chronic violence:

There was one dormitory designed for 45 men, and they had 120 in there. It was a jungle after lights out. You couldn't go to the restroom at night without stepping on someone, and that was all it took for a fight to break out. The guards stayed down in the mess hall, drinking coffee. (*Albuquerque Journal*, 2/3/85, Sec. B, p. 4.)

A U.S. Justice Department study concluded that the Penitentiary was, before the riot, "one of the harshest, most punitive prison environments in the nation." (*Albuquerque Journal*, 9/24/80, quoted in Morris, 1983:111).

This evidence, though, does not persuade resource-mobilization theorists. Deprivation may have been a "constant" feature of the penitentiary, and thus cannot explain why the riot happened when it did. Indeed, Colvin (1982) rejects a deprivation explanation of the riot for just those reasons. He argues that inmate food and "services" had always been bad, and that while some services had deteriorated, others had improved. Further, guard brutality had been a permanent feature of the prison.

We found, however, that inmates perceived a dramatic worsening of conditions. The turning point, according to most inmates, occurred in 1975 when the deputy warden was fired and the warden (Felix Rodriguez) was transferred (under allegations of personal corruption) to a make-work job in the central administration. One inmate stated:

When we had Rodriguez everything was running good. . . . Ever since he left we got the rest of them wardens, they all change everything, from better to worse. (A.G. Interview)

Another inmate invidiously compared the Rodriguez period with the one that followed:

When Mr. Rodriguez was here you had programs here. . . . They had people going to college and everything. They had good programs. . . . They give them something to do and it improves their minds and their spirits and everything. We had a good year when they had those programs here. (A.G. Interview)

One inmate, himself, perceived a link between changes in the level of deprivation and an increased likelihood of a riot:

Inmate: [Before 1975] there was only about eight officers in the corridor at night, . . . and they'd call chow just about everybody at the same time, so there'd be 700 people out in the corridor.

Question: So it was easier to pull off a riot in those days?

Inmate: Oh, yeah, much easier. . . .

Question: But nobody wanted to?

Inmate: Yeah. Nobody cared about that thing because the conditions weren't that bad. I mean, the conditions were bad . . . we've always had rats and the water has always been cold in the showers and stuff like that. [B]ut people can live with that if they're treated like human beings. . . . It's really hard to live here. You just got that hatred in your mind all the time. (A.G. Interview)

Another inmate described the transition:

Inmate: It's just been getting worse ever since I got here. In '74 it was pretty mellow. It was alright. Shoot, by '79 it was smokin' hot. Just making you do things you didn't want to do . . . just to give you a hard time. Locking people up left and right. (A.G. Interview)

Another inmate stated:

Question: You've been here for the last five wardens. . . . Give me an idea as to how programs change when the wardens changed?

Inmate: They've all gone worse. Straight down hill.

Question: No bouncing around?

Inmate: No, no bouncing around, just boom, right from ten to zero. (A.G. Interview)

The guards also stated that the prison conditions for inmates had worsened, although some regarded this change as appropriate. One guard stated: "During [Rodriguez's] tenure, there was no escapes. There was no major stabbing, there was no killings, and that's because they [the inmates] had everything they wanted. It was ridiculous, but they did."

The evaluations made of different administrations in the 1980 inmate interviews also support the deprivation argument. Inmates compared the conditions under the various wardens 181 times. One-hundred-sixty of these comparisons indicated that conditions were better under Rodriguez. Table 1 classifies these comparisons by the area of prison life commented upon. In every area, inmates reported that the conditions under Rodriguez were better than under any of the other wardens.

According to breakdown theory, unemployment and absence of voluntary organizations make individuals more "available" for mobilization. When applied to the prison setting, the argu-

Table 1
Comparisons of Prison Conditions Under Various Wardens[a]

| | Prison Better Under: | | | | | | |
Condition Mentioned	Baker (1968-1969)	Rodriquez (1970-1975)	Aaron (1975-1976)	Malley (1976-1978)	Romero (1978-1979)	Griffin (1979-1980)	Same Under All
Officials/Warden Fair, Competent, or "Cares"	—	21	—	—	—	2	—
General Conditions	1	20	—	—	—	—	—
Food, Mail, TV, Case Workers, Recreation, Psych. Services, Canteen, Visitation	—	17	—	—	—	25	—
Inmate Programs	1	45	—	—	—	—	—
Inmate Informants	—	15	—	—	—	—	—
Treatment by Guards	—	18	—	—	—	—	2
Discipline, Restriction on Movement, Disciplinary Segregation	—	24	—	—	—	—	7

[a] This Table is based on the 1980 interviews only. The distribution of responses among the categories in part reflects the questions asked. For example, the inmates were asked to evaluate the programs under each of the wardens since 1970 but were not asked about changes in the quality of the food. Thus, we cannot infer from the table that inmates were more concerned about the inmate programs than, say, the food (although this is probably true). The table does demonstrate that inmates believed that the quality of prison life had declined in virtually every area.

ment implies that inmate programs and jobs make riot participation less likely. The data support this hypothesis. Under the Rodriguez regime, the majority of inmates participated in a wide range of programs and activities (OAGSNM, 1980:14). Programs included a college associate of arts program (213 inmates); a school release program for inmates nearing parole (20); an IBM key-punch work shop (184 inmates); counseling programs for drug, alcohol and sex-related offenders; and a number of clubs and community contact programs, such as the Outside Friends, Bible Study, Jay Cees Club, and Toastmasters. On their own initiative, inmates formed Toys for Tots, Concerned Convicts for Children, and other charitable activities (OAGSNM, 1980:14). According to the Attorney General's report, "programs and activities during the period (1970-1975) involved a majority of the inmates in some meaningful activity" (OAGSNM, 1980:24). The administration that replaced Rodriguez's sharply reduced the number of programs in the prison and stopped community-contact programs entirely (Colvin, 1982:454). The inmates were aware of these changes. One inmate commented:

Inmate: I joined one of those clubs.

Question: This was when Rodriguez was warden?

Inmate: Yes, and when the other wardens came in, they just stopped it.

Question: They closed down the other clubs too?

Inmate: Everything, everything. (A.G. Interview)

Another inmate stated:

I'll give Mr. Rodriguez credit for he knew how to run this goddam penitentiary for the things that were important to the inmates in here. He was a strong believer in programs. He knew when you have 'em in, you got to give 'em something to occupy their dead time. He was damn good at that, but it hasn't happened since then. (A.G. Interview)

The termination of the programs appears to have had many of the effects that breakdown theory would suggest. One decreased inmate incentives to comply with institutional rules.

Question: How has [the Penitentiary] changed over the years?

Inmate: I think it changed when Warden Rodriguez resigned. . . . That's when the big change came.

Question: What did they do?

Answer: They stopped all the programs. They just took everything away and nobody had anything to look forward to or no more incentive to try for. [Rodriguez] had programs . . . that a convict could shoot for. Now in this institution there's nothing to try for. (A.G. Interview)

The inmate added:

> We had outside entertainment at least once a month. It was something to look forward to, something to stay out of lock up. There wasn't near as much tension. . . . When Aaron came in [in 1975] he stopped all outside programs, everything. (A.G. Interview)

Another inmate offered this reflection:

> Every one of these wardens, I have begged 'em until I was blue in the face to get programs back in this institution. I've gotten other inmates together to get the lifers program here in this institution. The men that's here doing life and more you'd have to give them something for an incentive or you can't hold em. You're going to have to kill 'em or let 'em hit the fence. (A.G. Interview)

Breakdown theorists posit that there is an association between crime, interpersonal violence, and protest, since they stem from the same cause. Evidence on the ten-year period leading up to the riot supports that contention. Both inmates and guards report a dramatic rise in the level of inter-inmate assaults and assaults against guards. In an interview conducted in 1985, an inmate stated:

> Question: Did it make any difference when Malley and Aaron came in?
>
> Inmate: They introduced death here. In 1970 there was maybe one stabbing a year. I wasn't here in '71 and '72. I came back again in '73. There was maybe a few gang fights but no stabbings, not any real bad things. It didn't really start until '76 or '77. There was a guy killed in five, next month after that was another guy who got killed in cellblock 2. . . . Then it started increasing two or three (stabbings) every month. (U. and K. Interview)

Another inmate, in the same round of interviews, stated:

> [Malley] came in like a real maniac. People can say what they want about Rodriguez, and maybe he did have his finger in the pie, but all I know man, all I know empirically, when he was warden here, you didn't have guys stabbing each other in wholesale numbers, you didn't have guys breaking out and running up the fence 15 or 20 at a time because it was too heavy for them to do time here. . . . It was a mellow, laid-back place under Rodriguez. (U. and K. Interview)

The trend toward greater inmate crime and violence after 1975 is also reflected in the number of inmates housed in solitary confinement (punishment) and protective custody. During the early 1970s, one cellblock housed both the prison's disciplinary cases and its protection cases. It averaged around 50 inmates, representing less than 5 percent of the population, and held as few as 13 in 1971. By 1976, over 20 percent of the inmates were either in protective custody or in segregation units, forcing the administration to designate one block for segregation and another for protective custody. Each block had a rated capacity of 90 inmates, but held as many as 200 inmates. Two and sometimes three inmates lived in a cell designed for one (OAGSNM, 1980:18, 27).

Further, a "breakdown" in the prison community appears to have heightened the level of deprivation experienced by inmates. Inmates experienced deprivation in the late 1970s, not only because of the direct effect of the institutional conditions, but because inmates preyed upon each other. One inmate stated:

> Most trust was back in '69 and '70. It seemed like everybody trusted each other more. There wasn't too much ripping off the canteen and . . . a person didn't have to go to sleep with a shank in his pillow. (A.G. Interview)

Another inmate stated:

> Inmate: Inmates get up with there's nothing to do. . . . They're mad. They ask the case worker, "Why don't you get me a job, or work somewhere, or something." [They answer,] "Nah, you don't need no job."
>
> Question: Inmates sitting in a dormitory all huddled together, does that cause problems between [sic] the inmates?
>
> Inmate: Yeah, it's just like a snake pit. Inmates that don't do nothing, they build up and build up and they get tired of it. Maybe the inmate has borrowed something and they just going to jump him. But if they had something to do, this place [would] be better. (A.G. Interview)

Another inmate observed:

> Aaron came in, security tightened up, people started escaping, people started stabbing each other, people started killing each other. Sure, they got rid of the drugs, but the violence got worse. Your opportunity to go to school lessened, the educational services, the psychological services, everything was shrinking. (A.G. Interview)

Another factor causing inmates to distrust one another was the institution, by the administration, of a system of inmate informants. Prior to 1975, prison officials gathered information through several channels, including an inmate council consisting of inmates elected from each living unit. Inmates also passed information to the directors of the various inmate programs who, in turn, forwarded it to the warden. These avenues of communication were closed after 1975 with the abolishment of the inmate council and the curtailment of the inmate programs (OAGSNM, 1980:12, 23). In place of these programs, officials began a coercive "snitch" (informant) system. Officials threatened inmates with punishment unless they provided information on other inmates' misbehavior. The punishments included both direct disciplinary actions and the disclosure to other inmates that a noncooperative inmate was a "snitch" (OAGSNM, 1980:24). The snitch system increased the enmity among inmates.

> Question: During the six months before the riot, did inmates trust each other?
>
> Inmate: No. Hardly anybody trusted anybody else.
>
> Question: Why do you think that was?
>
> Inmate: It was because all that snitching was going on. (A.G. Interview)

There were fewer informants under Rodriguez's administration.

> Question: Is the snitch system pretty prevalent?
>
> Answer: Sure.
>
> Question: Under Rodriguez? Is that something that's changed?
>
> Answer: When Rodriguez was Warden there was no such thing as a protection unit [for snitches] and I think it was a whole lot better. (A.G. Interview)

Another inmate stated:

> Inmate: Just about three fourths of the inmates are snitching.
>
> Question: Really?
>
> Inmate: You can't hardly trust anybody.
>
> Question: Are there more [snitches] now than there used to be or are there less?
>
> Inmate: Seems like there are a lot more now than there was before. . . . Hell, you can't even trust your best friend anymore. . . . They'll snitch on you.
>
> Question: When did it start getting to be that bad?
>
> Inmate: In about seventy-six.

Finally, in a 1985 interview, an inmate reported that he believed that the increased use of snitches after 1975 contributed to the violence in the 1980 riot.

> It's [the snitch system] a real trashed out system. If that riot would have come down when Rodriguez was warden, I don't think 33 people would have died because I don't think there were 33 snitches in this whole penitentiary. When the riot [did] come down there was about a hundred and some odd down in Cell Block 4 (the protective custody unit), all of them stoned rats. (U. and K. Interview)

Outcome of Collective Action

Breakdown theorists and resource-mobilization theorists also disagree over the effectiveness of protest in solving the problems of an aggrieved constituency. Resource-mobilization theorists argue that protest can be an effective lever for change, but this depends upon the presence of a protest organization that can mobilize and channel unrest (e.g., Gamson and Schmeidler, 1984). In its absence, the resources and skills necessary for effective protest cannot be aggregated and used efficiently. Breakdown theorists are internally divided. Traditionally, they have tended to dismiss protest as an agent for change. Protest was presumed to be an irrational response to the breakdown of the social order, and one incapable of forcing constructive change (e.g., Smelser, 1963; Kornhauser, 1959).

Writing more recently, breakdown theorists Piven and Cloward (1977; see also, Cloward and Piven, 1984) share the resource-mobilization theorists' supposition that protest can effect change, but challenge the strategic value of building a protest organization. Piven and Cloward posit that "poor" constituencies do not have the skills, money and other resources needed to build and sustain an effective protest organization. The most effective option is to create pressure for reform through a strategy of mass defiance and disruption.

From our 1985 interviews, it was apparent that the 1980 riot was directly responsible for significant improvements in the living conditions, including the elimination of overcrowding, suppression of guard brutality, increased programming, less reliance on snitches for information, and fewer restrictions on personal property. One inmate stated:

> At that time [before the riot], they wasn't giving up anything. I mean it was a real fucked up place to be. You know it's still a real fucked up place to be. But at least a guy can live here with relatively safety, and you get fairly decent food and clean linen, showers and exercise. . . . I have been in bet-

ter joints than this, but the improvement now compared to before 1980 was—man—it's one-thousand percent better. Now they have pay jobs, and there is industrial jobs where you can work a day and get a day cut off your sentence. There's different pay jobs, but before the riot none of that. Shit, you know, probably seventy-five percent of the population was on idle. No one worked. (U. and K. Interview)

Speaking in 1985, a 1980 riot participant observed that he probably would not participate in another riot, because of the improved conditions.

Myself I wouldn't feel near as good about participating in another one because there have been some things that have gotten better. They've gotten off my case and they've gotten off a lot of people's cases, for the most part. . . . It's never going to be enjoyable but it's livable. . . . Now, that that [harassment] is not happening, well you feel a little better about yourself. You do your time. You know you got "x" number of years to do. You gonna do it the best way you can and hopefully get out in one piece. And I think you stand a better chance of that now then you did before. (U. and K. Interview)

Another inmate reported that the riot had caused groups outside of the prison to take an interest in the welfare of the inmates, which he and other inmates "appreciate a lot." Prior to the riot, he stated, "we had nothing coming from the public; nothing at all from the public." (U. and K. Interview).

As further evidence that riot contributed to the improvements in the penitentiary, the Department of Corrections Secretary, interviewed on the fifth anniversary of the riot, stated that the 1980 riot had motivated him to try to improve the prison (*Albuquerque Journal*, 2/3/85, Sec. E, p. 4). He said that, in his opinion, the riot was the product of inmate idleness, crowding, and understaffing, and that he was seeking to remedy these problems. Calling the snitch system "disgusting and immoral," he stated that it had been banned. He felt that these changes would decrease the likelihood of another riot. (*Albuquerque Journal*, 2/3/85, Sec. E, p. 4).

Discussion

During the 1970s, the State Penitentiary changed from a relatively benign and well-run institution, to one that was harsh, abusive, painfully boring, and without the "regulatory mechanisms" that had been in place in the early 1970s. With few programs or work assignments available, inmates remained confined to their living units with little to do or look forward to. Inmates became increasingly hostile not only toward prison officials and guards, but also toward one another.

The processes of disorganization within the prison not only increased the likelihood of a riot, but also determined its form. The fragmenting of bonds among inmates appears to have contributed to the weak and chaotic structures of leadership among the inmates during the riot, as well as to the brutal attacks of some inmates against other inmates.

This case study has a number of implications for the study of collective action. It demonstrates that researchers have been too quick to reject the breakdown model. The New Mexico riot appears to have been (in part) a response to the prison disorganization that began dramatically around 1975. The riot was a product of the termination of inmate programs, crowding, idleness, and a generally poorly-administered prison system. Furthermore, the alternative resource-mobilization model cannot account for the riot. There is no evidence whatsoever that the prison riot occurred in 1980 because of an increase in inmate resources or solidarity, which resource-mobilization theorists say must precede collective action.

At the heart of controversy between breakdown and resource-mobilization theorists is the issue of the relationship between crime/deviance and collective action. Resource-mobilization theorists hold that crime/deviance and collective action arise from different, if not opposite, processes. They argue that crime/deviance and collective action should not covary or, if they do, the links should be weak and negative. Breakdown theorists argue that crime/deviance and collective action covary because they arise from the same underlying condition. On this point, the New Mexico data support the breakdown position. The 1980 riot followed a period of dramatic increase in the level of personal violence in the prison, as described by the inmate interviews and as seen in the large increase in the number of inmates in protective custody and segregation.

Black (1984) has recently argued that much crime is an effort to seek justice by those who have a grievance but to whom law is relatively unavailable. Youths may vandalize property, for example, because they have grievances against adults but no legal recourse. Seen in this light, crime has much in common with protest (even as resource-mobilization theorists conceive the latter), in that both express a grievance by one person or group against another person or group. Resource-mobilization theorists have failed to see this link between protest and crime, not so much because of weaknesses in their model of protest, but because they underestimate the moral component of crime.[4]

The interviews and increasing punishment suggest, as well, a causal connection between crime and collective action. A secure, low-crime environment is a valued condition, and its absence may produce anger toward authorities or toward others in the community, or toward both. In New Mexico, inmates complained bitterly about the beatings and the absence of security in the prison before the riot. This dissatisfaction appears to have fueled the riot. When authorities respond regressively to increases in crime/deviance, but do not destroy all forms of resistance, the increased repression may add a further impetus to collective action. This proposition fits well with the evidence for the New Mexico riot. The prison administration responded to the increased level of crime/deviance with a coercive snitch system and a greater use of solitary confinement. Both of these policies appear to have angered inmates and to have helped motivate them to start the riot.

These findings, though, do not indicate the utility of accepting the full breakdown model as a general account of collective action. The case study provides no support for the presumption held by some breakdown theorists that collective action inevitably fails. The living conditions of the State Penitentiary were substantially better in 1985 than they were before the riot. The 1980 riot contributed to these improvements.

Furthermore, the evidence does not give much support to the Durkheimian strand of breakdown theory which emphasizes anomie, egoism, and the breakdown of a group's internal structure as causes of collective action. A similar model was applied to prisons by Sykes (1958), who argued that riots occurred when authorities suppressed the pre-existing social order and allowed unruly, violence-prone inmates to gain pre-eminence.

In examining both sets of interviews, we found no evidence that there was much of an inmate social order even under the Rodriguez administration, that any group of inmates lost or gained relative power after 1975, or that such

processes had anything to do with the outbreak of the riot.

Neither did we find the actions of most inmates during the riot to be irrational or characteristic of "magical beliefs." Most of the inmates we interviewed in 1985 described the riot as a more or less justified and successful attempt to relieve unjustly bad conditions of life. In fact, the quantity and quality of the violence, in its apparent savagery and irrationality, may have been the most effective possible strategy to motivate the state government to make sweeping improvements (Morris. 1983:225-26).

The evidence does, though, support Piven's and Cloward's thesis of the advantages of mass defiance, at least in the prison setting. The New Mexico riot forced substantial prison reforms in the absence of a protest organization. Although work comparing the relative "success" of prison riots is needed before we draw any firm conclusion, it would appear that fear of another high-cost prison riot provides a deeper impetus for prison reform than the concessions that inmate negotiators sometimes force officials to agree to during a riot. Once order is restored, inmates have no means to ensure compliance with these concessions, nor are state and prison officials likely to feel bound by them since officials agreed to them under duress.

Furthermore, collective action may have distinct subtypes, some promoted by the processes identified by the breakdown theorists, others by the processes specified by the resource-mobilization theorists. One possibility is that relatively spontaneous, short-lived actions, such as riots, arise primarily from breakdown processes, whereas the more enduring forms, such as social movements, flow from resource-mobilization processes. We find, however, no support for this proposition in the current theoretical literature. Breakdown theorists apply their model to social movements (Kornhauser, 1959; Piven and Cloward, 1977), and resource-mobilization theorists see their model as able to account for riots. More important, perhaps, are the prevailing historical and cultural conditions within which the collective action is embedded. For example, it could be argued that resource-mobilization processes—such as increased solidarity and heightened political struggles—were responsible for the urban riots of the late 1960s and the Attica riot of 1971. In contrast, both the black riots which occurred in Miami in 1980 (Porter and Dunn, 1984) and the New Mexico prison riot of 1980 may have been breakdown riots, in part because of the demise of a culture of opposition in the United States.[5]

The breakdown model, over the past decade, has fallen into disfavor among social movement researchers. This case study suggests that breakdown processes can contribute to at least certain instances of collective action. Furthermore, as noted at the outset, the evidence on the breakdown model in other contexts is equivocal, despite the claims of resource-mobilization theorists otherwise. The brief against the breakdown model rests on shaky empirical grounds.

Notes

1. Because the resource-mobilization model has been discussed extensively in the recent social movement literature, we do not further elaborate it here. See the useful overviews by Jenkins (1983), Wood and Jackson (1982:141-47), and Marx and Wood (1971), as well as the original formulations by Gamson (1975), McCarthy and Zald (1977), Oberschall (1973), and Tilly (1978).

2. Interviews conducted by the Attorney General's office and by the author and Peter Kimball are designated "A.G. Interview" and "U. and K. Interview," respectively. Wherever possible, we have relied on the Attorney General's interviews rather than our own. First, the Attorney General's researchers obtained a sample representative of the inmate population at the time of the riot, whereas our sample overrepresented inmates with long sentences and recidivists. Second, the Attorney General's interviews were conducted soon after the riots, whereas ours occurred almost five years later. At this point, inmates' memories may have faded. This is especially salient in regard to inmates' assessment of changes in the prison from 1975 to 1980, for which we rely almost exclusively on the 1980 interviews. Still, we noticed no major discrepancy between the two rounds of interviews.

3. A psychiatrist who treated 9 of the 12 guard hostages reports that the inmates did, indeed, "succeed" in terrorizing the hostages (Hillman, 1981). In addition to the physical brutality, most experienced extreme feelings of fear and helplessness. Many of them said "goodby" in their minds to their loved ones; they imagined the grisly ways that inmates would kill them; and they visualized their dead bodies being discovered after the riot. Most experienced acute and disabling aftereffects for at least one year following the riot.

4. Based, as it is, on Black's view of crime, this observation is tentative. Black and his associates (e.g., Baumgartner [1984] and Rieder [1984]) have opened a new perspective on crime and its relationship to other forms of "social control." The effort is still in its early stages, however, and lacks confirmatory evidence. It may turn out that Black and his associates are explaining the exceptional case rather than the modal one or even a frequent one.

5. Elsewhere, we have developed a theory to explain the variation in the form of prison riots. "Identification" is the key independent variable, which refers to a state in which individuals either model their behavior after other actors or choose their actions according to their effects on others (Useem and Kimball, 1985). ✦

Part 2

Conditions of Conduciveness: Political Opportunities

Writing in 1970, the political scientist Michael Lipsky (1970:14) urged scholars to be skeptical of

> system characterizations presumably true for all times and all places. . . . We are accustomed to describing communist political systems as "experiencing a thaw" or "going through a process of retrenchment." Should it not at be an open question as to whether the American political system experiences such stages and fluctuations? Similarly, is it not sensible to assume that the system will be more or less open to specific groups at different times and at different places?

Lipsky believed that the answer to both questions was yes. He assumed that the ebb and flow of protest activity was a function of changes that left the broader political system more vulnerable or receptive to the demands of particular groups. Three years later, another political scientist, Peter Eisinger (1973: 11), used the term *structure of political opportunities* to help account for variation in riot behavior in 43 American cities. Consistent with Lipsky's argument, Eisinger found that "the incidence of protest is . . . related to the nature of the city's political opportunity structure," which he defined as "the degree to which groups are likely to be able to gain access to power and to manipulate the political system" (Eisinger 1973: 25).

Within ten years the key premise underlying the work of Lipsky and Eisinger had been incorporated as the central tenet in a new *political process model* of social movements. Proponents of the model saw the timing and fate of movements

as largely dependent upon the opportunities afforded insurgents by the shifting institutional structure and ideological disposition of those in power.

Since then this central assumption and the concept of political opportunities has become a staple of social movement research. The emergence and development of instances of collective action as diverse as the American women's movement (Costain 1992), liberation theology (Smith 1991), peasant mobilization in Central America (Brockett 1991), the nuclear power movement (Meyer 1993c), and left-wing protest in Italy (Tarrow 1989b) have been attributed to processes that rendered the movements' opponents more vulnerable or receptive to movement demands.

The first selection, by Craig Jenkins and Charles Perrow, nicely illustrates this use of the political opportunity concept. Jenkins and Perrow compare two farm workers' movements that developed between 1946 and 1972. The first of these movements failed miserably; the second produced significant gains in the legal and material status of farm workers. Why did these two movements fare so differently? Jenkins and Perrow write:

> . . . [T]he difference between the two challenges was the societal response that insurgent demands received. During the first challenge, government policies strongly favored agribusiness; support from liberal organizations and organized labor was weak and vacillating. By the time the second challenge was mounted, the political environment

had changed dramatically. Government was now divided over policies pertaining to farm workers; liberals and labor had formed a reform coalition, attacking agribusiness privileges in public policy. The reform coalition then furnished the crucial resources to launch the challenge.

Most contemporary theories of revolution start from much the same premise, arguing that revolutions owe much less to the actions of revolutionaries in fomenting rebellion than to the effect of broad social, political, and economic crises which render existing regimes weak and vulnerable to challenge from various quarters (i.e., Arjomand 1988; Goldstone 1991b; Skocpol 1979). The revolutions of 1988-89 in Eastern Europe would seem to be good cases in point. As we now know, the entire Soviet system was beset with crushing economic problems. When then-Soviet Premier Mikhail Gorbachev stated publicly in 1986 his unwillingness to henceforth intervene militarily in defense of the Warsaw Pact countries, the die was seemingly cast. Weakened by popular discontent and economic woes, the removal of the Soviet military threat paved the way for the subsequent revolutions in East Germany, Hungary, Rumania, Poland, and Czechoslovakia.

In addition to the many studies that have sought to explain the rise of single social movements or revolutions on the basis of sudden changes in the vulnerability or receptivity of those in power, the stress on political opportunities has also spawned a comparative tradition in which researchers have attempted to explain the fate of the same movement in a number of countries on the basis of national-level differences in the structures of institutionalized power. Eisinger's aforementioned study of riot behavior exemplifies this tradition. So too does the second piece in this part, by Hanspeter Kriesi and his colleagues. In this selection, the authors attempt to show that the timing, extent, and ultimate fate of the various "new social movements" that arose in most West European countries in the 1970s and 80s can largely be explained by differences in the political opportunity structures of these countries.

The concept of political opportunities has thus proven to be a welcome and seemingly useful addition to the analytic arsenal of movement scholars. But the widespread adoption and general seductiveness of the concept carries with it its own set of dangers. The idea that successful collective action is necessarily preceded by objective structural changes that weaken the regime in question is an assumption shared by most movement researchers. But as important as this factor may be in many instances of collective action, we certainly do not regard it as a necessary feature of all successful social movements. The Iranian Revolution certainly stands out as a recent and dramatic instance of successful collective action. But, if we are to believe the argument made by Charles Kurzman in the final selection in this part, the Revolution occurred in the absence of any facilitative changes in the objective structure of political opportunities. In his conclusion, Kurzman underscores the significance of the Iranian case for general social movement theory. He writes:

> This finding suggests that social-movement theory should reconsider the relation between "objective" and "subjective" definitions of political opportunity. If opportunity is like a door, then social-movement theory generally examines cases in which people realize the door is open and walk on through. The Iranian Revolution may be a case in which people saw the door was closed, but felt that the opposition was powerful enough to open it.

For us, the bottom line is clear. Social movements and revolutions are complex social phenomena that probably do not conform to a single, universal model. Rather, there are a number of broad facilitative factors and general causal dynamics that recur with great frequency in the empirical study of collective action. A certain expansion in political opportunities is certainly among the most often noted features of successful social movements and revolutions. Not all of these factors and dynamics, however, will necessarily be present in any given instance of collective action.

References

Arjomand, Said. 1988. *The Turban for the Crown: The Islamic Revolution in Iran.* New York: Oxford University Press.

Brockett, Charles D. 1991. "The Structure of Political Opportunities and Peasant Mobilization in Central America." *Comparative Politics* 253-274.

Costain, Anne W. 1992. *Inviting Women's Rebellion: A Political Process Interpretation of the Women's Movement.* Baltimore: Johns Hopkins University Press.

Eisinger, Peter K. 1973. "The Conditions of Protest Behavior in American Cities." *American Political Science Review* 67: 11-28.

Goldstone, Jack. 1991. *Revolution and Rebellion in the Early Modern World.* Berkeley: University of California Press.

Lipsky, Michael. 1970. *Protest in City Politics.* Chicago: Rand McNally.

Meyer, David S. 1993. "Protest Cycles and Political Process: American Peace Movements in the Nuclear Age." *Political Research Quarterly* 47: 451-79.

Skocpol, Theda. 1979. *States and Social Revolutions*. Cambridge: Cambridge University Press.

Smith, Christian. 1991. *The Emergence of Liberation Theology*. Chicago: University of Chicago Press.

Tarrow, Sidney. 1989. *Democracy and Disorder: Protest and Politics in Italy, 1965-1975*. Oxford: Oxford University Press. ✦

4

Insurgency of the Powerless: Farm Worker Movements (1946-1972)

J. Craig Jenkins
Charles Perrow

From about 1964 until 1972, American society witnessed an unprecedented number of groups acting in insurgent fashion. By insurgency we mean organized attempts to bring about structural change by thrusting new interests into decisionmaking processes. Some of this insurgency, notably the civil rights and peace movements, had begun somewhat earlier, but after 1963 there were organized attempts to bring about structural changes from virtually all sides: ethnic minorities (Indians, Mexican-Americans, Puerto Ricans), welfare mothers, women, sexual liberation groups, teachers and even some blue-collar workers. The present study isolates and analyzes in detail one of these insurgent challenges—that of farm workers—in an effort to throw light on the dynamics that made the 1960s a period of dramatic and stormy politics.

Our thesis is that the rise and dramatic success of farm worker insurgents in the late 1960s best can be explained by changes in the political environment the movement confronted, rather than by the internal characteristics of the movement organization and the social base upon which it drew. The salient environment consisted of the government, especially the federal government, and a coalition of liberal support organizations. We shall contrast the unsuccessful attempt to organize farm workers by the National Farm Labor Union from 1946 to 1952 with the strikingly successful one of the United Farm Workers from 1965 to 1972.

The immediate goals of both movements were the same—to secure union contracts. They both used the same tactics, namely, mass agricul-

tural strikes, boycotts aided by organized labor, and political demands supported by the liberal community of the day. Both groups encountered identical and virtually insurmountable obstacles, namely, a weak bargaining position, farm worker poverty and a culture of resignation, high rates of migrancy and weak social cohesion, and a perpetual oversupply of farm labor, insuring that growers could break any strike.

The difference between the two challenges was the societal response that insurgent demands received. During the first challenge, government policies strongly favored agribusiness; support from liberal organizations and organized labor was weak and vacillating. By the time the second challenge was mounted, the political environment had changed dramatically. Government now was divided over policies pertaining to farm workers; liberals and organized labor had formed a reform coalition, attacking agribusiness privileges in public policy. The reform coalition then furnished the resources to launch the challenge. Once underway, the coalition continued to fend for the insurgents, providing additional resources and applying leverage to movement targets. The key changes, then, were in support organization and governmental actions. To demonstrate this, we will analyze macro-level changes in the activities of these groups as reported in the *New York Times Annual Index* between 1946 and 1972.

The Classical Model

In taking this position, we are arguing that the standard literature on social movements fails to deal adequately with either of two central issues—the formation of insurgent organizations and the outcome of insurgent challenges. Drawing on Gusfield's (1968) summary statement, the classical literature holds in common the following line of argument. See also Turner and Killian (1957; 1972), Smelser (1962), Lang and Lang (1961), Kornhauser (1959), Davies (1962; 1969) and Gurr (1970).

Social movements arise because of deep and widespread discontent. First, there is a social change which makes prevailing social relations inappropriate, producing a strain between the new and the old. Strain then generates discontent within some social grouping. When discontent increases rapidly and is widely shared, collective efforts to alleviate discontent will occur. Though there is disagreement about how to formulate the

"Insurgency of the Powerless: Farm Worker Movements (1946-1972)." *American Sociological Review* 42: 249-268. Copyright © 1977 by the American Sociological Association. Reprinted with permission.

link between strain and discontent, e.g., subjective gaps between expectations and satisfactions versus emotional anxiety induced by anomie, the central thrust is consistent. Fluctuations in the level of discontent account for the rise of movements and major changes in movement participation.

Recent research, though, has cast doubt on the classic "discontent" formulations. Disorders do not arise from disorganized anomic masses, but from groups organizationally able to defend and advance their interests (Oberschall, 1973; Tilly et al., 1975). As for relative deprivation, Snyder and Tilly (1972) and Hibbs (1973) have failed to find it useful in accounting for a wide variety of collective disruptions. Nor is it clear that we can use the concept without falling into post hoc interpretations (cf. Wilson, 1973:73-9).[1]

In this study, we do not propose to test each of the various "discontent" formulations currently available. *A priori*, it is rather hard to believe that farm workers' discontent was, for example, suddenly greater in 1965, when the Delano grape strike began, than throughout much of the 1950s when there was no movement or strike activity. Indeed, it seems more plausible to assume that farm worker discontent is relatively constant, a product of established economic relations rather than some social dislocation or dysfunction. We do not deny the existence of discontent but we question the usefulness of discontent formulations in accounting for either the emergence of insurgent organization or the level of participation by the social base. What increases, giving rise to insurgency, is the amount of social resources available to unorganized but aggrieved groups, making it possible to launch an organized demand for change.

As for the outcome of challenges, the importance of resources is obvious. Though the classical literature has rarely dealt with the issue directly, there has been an implicit position. The resources mobilized by movement organizations are assumed to derive from the aggrieved social base. The outcome of the challenge, then, whether or not one adopts a "natural history" model of movement development, should depend primarily upon internal considerations, e.g., leadership changes and communication dynamics among the membership.

However, are deprived groups like farm workers able to sustain challenges, especially ef-fective ones, on their own? We think not. Both of the movements studied were, from the outset, dependent upon external groups for critical organizational resources. Nor, as the history of agricultural strikes amply attests (McWilliams, 1939; London and Anderson, 1970; Taylor, 1975), have farm worker movements proven able to mobilize numbers sufficient to wring concessions from employers. For a successful outcome, movements by the "powerless" require strong and sustained outside support.

If this line of argument is correct, we need to contest a second thesis frequently found in the classical literature—the assertion that the American polity operates in a pluralistic fashion (cf. Kornhauser, 1959; Smelser, 1962). A pluralistic polity is structurally open to demands for change.[2] As Gamson (1968b; 1975) has put it, the political system should be structurally "permeable," readily incorporating new groups and their interests into the decision-making process. Once organized, groups redressing widely-shared grievances should be able to secure at least some part of their program through bargaining and compromise.[3] Yet our evidence shows that farm worker challenges have failed, in part, because of the opposition of public officials, and that a successful challenge depended upon the intervention of established liberal organizations and the neutrality of political elites.

We can then summarize the classical model as follows. (1) Discontent, traced to structural dislocations, accounts for collective attempts to bring about change. (2) The resources required to mount collective action and carry it through are broadly distributed—shared by all sizeable social groupings. (3) The political system is pluralistic and, therefore, responsive to all organized groups with grievances. (4) If insurgents succeed, it is due to efforts on the part of the social base; if they do not, presumably they lacked competent leaders, were unwilling to compromise, or behaved irrationally (e.g., used violence or broke laws).

In contrast, we will argue that (1) discontent is ever-present for deprived groups, but (2) collective action is rarely a viable option because of lack of resources and the threat of repression. (3) When deprived groups do mobilize, it is due to the interjection of external resources. (4) Challenges frequently fail because of the lack of resources. Success comes when there is a combination of sustained outside support and disunity and/or tolerance on the part of political elites. The important variables separating movement success from failure, then, pertain to the way the polity responds to insurgent demands.

Structural Powerlessness of Farm Workers

The major impediment to farm worker unionization has been the oversupply of farm labor, undercutting all attempted harvest strikes. There are few barriers of habit or skill that restrict the entry of any applicant to work in the fields. The result is an "unstructured" labor market, offering little job stability and open to all comers (Fisher, 1953). The fields of California and Texas are close enough to the poverty-stricken provinces of Mexico to insure a steady influx of workers, many of whom arrive by illegal routes (Frisbee 1975). Continuous immigration not only underwrites the oversupply of labor, but complicates mobilization by insuring the existence of cultural cleavages among workers.

Furthermore, there are reasons to believe that a significant number of workers have only a limited economic interest in the gains promised by unionization. The majority of farm workers, both domestic and alien, are short-term seasonal workers. During the early 1960s, farm employment in California averaged less than three months of the year (Fuller, 1967). This means that a majority of workers are interested primarily in the "quick dollar." Imposition of union restrictions on easy access to jobs would conflict with that interest. And for the vast majority of farm workers, regardless of job commitment or citizenship status, income is so low as to leave little economic reserve for risktaking. Since a major portion of the year's income comes during the brief harvest period, workers are reluctant to risk their livelihood on a strike at that time.

In addition to these structural restraints on collective action, there were the very direct restraints of the growers and their political allies. The California Department of Employment and the U.S. Department of Labor have long operated farm placement services that furnish workers for strike-bound employers. Insurgent actions that directly threaten growers, like picket lines and mass rallies, consistently have been the target of official harassment. Though never returning to the scale of the "local fascism" of the 1930s (McWilliams,

1942; Chambers, 1952), grower vigilante actions are not uncommon.

Bringing these considerations to bear on the comparison of farm worker challenges, there is reason to believe that circumstances were slightly more conducive to the mobilization efforts of the UFW. Between 1946 and 1965 farm wage rates rose slightly and a few public welfare benefits were extended, at least within California. Presumably, farm workers were slightly more secure economically by the mid-1960s. More significant, though, were changes in the social composition of the farm labor force. During the late 1940s farm workers in California were either "dustbowlers" or Mexican *braceros* (government-imported contract workers); by the mid-1960s the California farm labor force was predominantly Mexican-descent, short-term workers, most of whom only recently had migrated across the border. Not only were linguistic-cultural cleavages somewhat less pronounced, but these new immigrants were more likely to settle and develop stable community ties than their "Okie" predecessors.

Also, the United Farm Workers pursued a mobilization strategy better designed than that of the NFLU to sustain the participation of farm workers. From its inception, the UFW was an Alinsky-styled community organization. The primary advantage was that it offered a program of services and social activities that did not depend upon first securing a union contract. Members developed an attachment to the organization independent of the immediate gains that might derive from any strike. Though the National Farm Labor Union had taken limited steps in a similar direction, its program remained primarily that of the conventional "business" union, promising wage gains and better working conditions rather than social solidarity and community benefits.

But the critical issue is whether differences in either the structural position of farm workers or the mobilization strategy adopted by the movements affected either dependent variable. As we shall see, the impetus for both of the challenges came from the interjection, into an otherwise placid situation, of a professionally-trained cadre backed by outside sponsors. Farm worker discontent remained unexpressed in any organized way until outside organizers arrived on the scene.

As for the question of challenge outcome, despite the UFW's advantages, it experienced no more success in strike efforts than did the NFLU.

Where the NFLU had to contend with the semi-official use of *braceros* as strikebreakers, the UFW had to deal with vastly increased numbers of illegal aliens and short-term workers crossing the picket lines. The combination of structural constraints and direct controls insured that neither union was able to mobilize a sufficiently massive social base to be effective.

What separated the UFW success from the NFLU failure was the societal response to the challenges. The NFLU received weak and vacillating sponsorship; the UFW's backing was strong and sustained. Under the pressure of court injunctions and police harassment, the NFLU boycott collapsed when organized labor refused to cooperate. By contrast, the UFW boycotts became national "causes," receiving widespread support from organized labor and liberal organizations; though official harassment remained, the UFW did not deal with the same systematic repression confronted by the NFLU. The success of a "powerless" challenge depended upon sustained and widespread outside support coupled with the neutrality and/or tolerance from the national political elite.

Method

To test this argument we need two bodies of information, one bearing on events leading to the initiation of insurgency and the other dealing with the political environment shaping challenge outcomes. For the first, we have drawn on published accounts of the movements, filled in and corroborated by extensive interviews conducted with movement participants and informed observers. For the second, we have turned to newspaper sources to provide a picture of the societal response to the two challengers. By content coding the abstracts of news stories that dealt with farm labor issues printed in the *New York Times* over a twenty-seven-year period (1946-1972), we can determine the types of groups concerned with the question of farm labor, whether their actions favored the structural changes advocated by insurgents, the types of activities in which they were engaged and, finally, the pattern of interaction prevailing between these various groups during the course of the respective challenges. This way we have a systematic data base against which to test hypotheses bearing on movement-environment interaction.[4]

As with any data source, there are limits to the *Times* data. We cannot, for example, use it to test hypotheses on the internal dynamics of mobilization. For this, we leave gone to interviews and published sources. Nor, as Danzger's (1975) work has recently indicated, can we view the Times reportage as a complete picture of all insurgent activity and environmental responses to insurgency. Since it is a national newspaper, the *New York Times* will not provide us with day-to-day coverage, for example, of police repression in Delano, California. Nor can we count on the Times to reveal the hidden bargains and machinations that might underlie public positions and alliances.

We do not ask it to do so. What we are using the *Times* for is to construct a systematic, reliable index of the publicly visible political activities that formed the environment of each challenge. By comparing statistics drawn from this data base and relating these measures to differences in challenge outcome, we can see if our environmental thesis holds up.[5]

To see if the *New York Times* is a reliable source, we have compared the coverage given by the *Times* with that of two other newspapers, the *Chicago Tribune* for a more conservative picture and the *Los Angeles Times* for a more proximate source. After comparing the stories on farm labor carried by these three papers for one month (selected at the peak of activity for the three periods of analysis), we have concluded that the *New York Times* is basically a more complete version of the same "news." In the month selected from the first period (March, 1951), the *New York Times* covered seventeen events, only one of which was picked up by each of the other papers; no events in the "test" papers were missed by the *New York Times.* In the second period (April, 1958), the *New York Times* carried nine events, two of which the *Los Angeles Times* covered and none of which the *Tribune* covered; again the *New York Times* missed no events covered in the other papers. Only in the third period (October, 1968) did the *New York Times* miss an event, one involving a local organization that pressured the Los Angeles City Council to boycott grapes. This was reported in the *Los Angeles Times.* Of eight events covered by the *New York Times,* half appeared in the *Los Angeles Times* and none in the *Tribune.* In sum, if you want newspaper reportage on farm labor events, the *New York Times* is a more thorough source and reveals no clearly different bias than the other papers during one period of time, say, the NFLU challenge, than another, e.g., the UFW effort.

Finally, there is the question of whether news reportage, regardless of crossvalidation with other news sources, is valid. Danzger (1975) has argued that news coverage is affected by editorial policy, and that systematic error creeps in because the geographic location of national wire service offices produces uneven reportage of relevant events. It is important to note that we code events, not news stories. The prominence given to stories by the editors of the *New York Times* is irrelevant, as are the evaluations of the events by news personnel. Additionally, our data set should be relatively immune to the main source of error identified by Danzger. Both insurgencies centered in the same locale. Assuming that the corrective mechanisms within the news agencies identified by Danzger were operative, time-series data should be less vulnerable to error than cross-sectional data. Also, we should note the limitations to Danzger's conclusions given his own data base. As Snyder and Kelly (1976) have demonstrated, news-based conflict data dealing with violence appear quite valid; more error exists in nonviolent protest data (employed in Danzger's test). Extending that distinction to our own data set, we can place more confidence in our measures of "concrete" activities than those for "symbolic" ones.

Basic Variables

Our analysis centers on the comparison of three time periods. The first, 1946-1955, spans the challenge of the National Farm Labor Union. Chartered to organize farm workers at the 1946 American Federation of Labor convention, the NFLU launched a strike wave in the Central Valley of California that ended with the abortive Los Baños strike of 1952. The selection of 1955 as the end point of the period was somewhat arbitrary.

By comparison, the third period, 1965-1972, covers the sustained and successful challenge of the United Farm Workers. The 1965 Coachella and Delano strikes announced the UFW challenge; in 1970, after two years of nation-wide boycott efforts, the UFW brought table-grape growers to the bargaining table and began institutionalizing changes in the position of farm workers. (The Teamster entry in 1973 is not dealt with in this paper.)

During the period intervening between the two challenges, 1956-1964, important changes

took place in the political system that set the stage for a successful challenge. In the absence of a major "push" from insurgents,[6] issues pertaining to farm labor received a different treatment in the hands of established liberal organizations and government officials. We will argue that these years constituted a period of germination and elite reform that made possible the success of the late 1960s.

From the *New York Times Annual Index*, we have coded the types of groups involved, the direction and form of their activity and the issues involved. The groups are: (1) the farm worker associations and unions that represented farm worker insurgents; (2) federal, state and local governments; (3) the liberal organizations (religious, philanthropic, political action and "public interest" groups); (4) organized labor; (5) agribusiness associations, corporations and individual farmers, referred to collectively as the growers. Of these, the growers have the fewest events reported in the *Times*, probably because fewer of their activities are likely to constitute "notable" events in a journalistic sense—e.g., securing the services of local police, hiring strikebreakers, rounding up support among legislators. Their views are generally presented quite effectively by the Department of Agriculture so they need do little public relations on their own.

The first step is to break down group activity by direction—into actions favorable, unfavorable, ambiguous, or not relevant to the interests of farm workers. (Only government had significant numbers of both favorable and unfavorable actions. All other groups were either wholly favorable or unfavorable. Government was also the only type with a large number of "ambiguous" or "not relevant" actions. These are excluded from the analysis; they do not depart in terms of issue or type of action from "directed" actions.) We then can estimate the balance of favorable/unfavorable actions in the political system during the course of each challenge, and chart the fluctuations in favorable and unfavorable actions by different types of groups (see Figures 1 and 2).

In addition to group and direction, we are concerned with the form of action adopted. We will distinguish between "symbolic" and "concrete" actions. Purely rhetorical acts which attempt to shape public opinion, e.g., speeches or hearings, are "symbolic"; actions that attempt to directly allocate control over material resources, e.g., court rulings and mass protest, fall under the rubric of "concrete."

Issue is our final variable: (1) labor supply, which is largely centered around the importation of Mexican labor under the *bracero* and "green card" programs and which was the dominant issue during the NFLU challenge; (2) working and living conditions of farm workers, which dominated the remaining two periods; (3) unionization, i.e., the legality of collective bargaining in agriculture, a question which first appeared in significant measure only during the UFW challenge.

Two types of statistics drawn from this data set will be used. N's, percentages and percent differences set off the rough differences between the three periods of activity. To capture more precisely the divergent patterns of interaction taking place between insurgents and among various groups in the polity, Pearson product-moment correlations are reported. The scores entering the analysis are counts of actions taken by different groups, on different issues, for conventional calendar years. High *r*'s are taken to indicate that considerable concomitant activity took place over the time period between relevant pairs of groups, e.g., insurgents and liberals; low *r*'s, the absence of concomitant activity. Bringing this to bear on the environmental thesis, differences in descriptive statistics and *r*'s for relevant pairings of groups will reveal any differences that existed in the societal response to the challenges.[7]

Period I: The NFLU Conflict (1946-1955)

The first period illustrates in classical terms the obstacles to a sustained and successful farm worker challenge. In addition to the structural constraints restricting farm worker activity, the political environment confronting the insurgents was unfavorable. Government officials at all levels and branches came into the conflict predominantly on the side of the growers, despite the mandate of agencies such as the Department of Labor or the Education and Labor Committees in Congress to protect the interests of deprived groups like farm workers. Though external support was decisive in launching the challenge, it was weak and frequently ill-focused, dealing with the consequences rather than the causes of farm worker grievances. When support was withdrawn, the challenge soon collapsed.

Chartered at the 1946 convention of the American Federation of Labor, the National Farm Labor Union set out to accomplish what predecessors had been unable to do—successfully organize the farm workers of California's "industrialized" agriculture. The leadership cadre was experienced and resourceful. H. L. Mitchell, President of the NFLU, was former head of the Southern Tenant Farmers Union; the Director of Organizations, Henry Hasiwar, had been an effective organizer in several industrial union drives during the 1930s; Ernesto Galarza, who assumed prime responsibility for publicity efforts, had served as political liaison for Latin American unions and had a Ph.D. in economics from Columbia University.

Initially, the strategy was quite conventional: enlist as many workers as possible from a single employer, call a strike, demand wage increases and union recognition, and picket to keep "scabs" out of the fields. American Federation of Labor affiliates would then provide strike relief and political support to keep the picket line going. An occasional church or student group would furnish money and boost morale.

But the government-sponsored alien labor or *bracero* program provided growers with an effective strike-breaking weapon. According to provisions of the law, *braceros* were not to be employed except in instances of domestic labor shortage and *never* to be employed in fields where domestic workers had walked out on strike. Yet in the two major tests of union power, the DiGiorgio strike of 1948 and the Imperial Valley strike of 1951, the flood of *braceros* undermined the strike effort of domestic workers (London and Anderson, 1970; Galarza, 1970; Jenkins, 1975: ch. 3). In the Imperial strike, the NFLU used citizen's arrests to enforce statutes prohibiting employment of *braceros* in labor disputed areas. However, local courts ruled against the tactic and the Immigration Service refused to remove alien "scabs" from the fields (Galarza, 1970:78; Jenkins, 1975: ch. 4). Nor were affairs changed when the *bracero* administration was transferred to the U.S. Department of Labor in 1951. Domestic workers were pushed out of crops by *braceros*, and *braceros* reappeared in the Los Baños strike of 1952 to break the challenge (Galarza, 1970:79).

In response, the NFLU launched a two-pronged political challenge—a demand for termination of the *bracero* program and, to get around the problem of ineffective strikes, requests for organized labor's support of boycotts. Neither demand found a favorable audience. Lacking strong labor or liberal support, the demand for an end to the *bracero* traffic ended in minor reforms in the *bracero* administration (Galarza, 1970: ch. 4). As for the boycott, despite initial success, it collapsed when a court injunction was issued (improperly) on the grounds that the NFLU was covered by the "hot cargo" provisions of the Taft-Hartley Act. The National Labor Relations Board initially concurred and reversed its position over a year later. By then the Union's resources were exhausted and organized-labor support had long since collapsed (Galarza, 1970:73-92).

Figure 1 charts the level of favorable actions by selected groups, allowing us to gauge the societal response to insurgency. The curves delineating government, liberal, and farm worker activi-

Figure 1
Actions Favorable to Insurgents

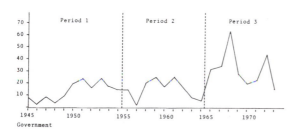

Government

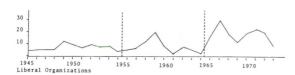

Liberal Organizations

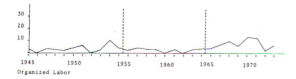

Organized Labor

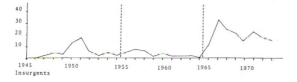

Insurgents

ties move roughly in concert. (Organized labor, though, played little public role in this or the next period.) Checking these impressions, Table 1 reports Pearson *r*'s on relevant pairs of groups. Largely a reflection of the pressure campaign waged by the NFLU, the strongest correlation is between insurgents and favorable government activity (.63), concrete activities seemingly being more efficacious (.70 versus .49 for symbolic acts). *R* for insurgent/government activity drops only slightly when controls are introduced for liberal activity (.57), indicating that liberal activity was not necessary for this measure of official re-

Table 1
Extent of Concomitant Activity—
Pro Farm Worker (r's)

	All Acts	Symbolic Acts[a]	Concrete Acts[a]
Period I (1946-1955)			
Insurgents and Government		.63	.49
Insurgents and Liberal Pressure Groups	.45	.56	−.02
Insurgents and Organized Labor	.08	−.08	—[b]
Liberal Pressure Groups and Government	.33	.37	−.17
Organized Labor and Government	.36	.35	—[b]
Period II (1956-1964)			
Insurgents and Government	−.26	−.26	−.42
Insurgents and Liberal Pressure Groups	−.10	.05	−.13
Insurgents and Organized Labor	.59	.67	−.33
Liberal Pressure Groups and Government	.50	.53	.25
Organized Labor and Government	.06	−.60	.58
Period III (1965-1972)			
Insurgents and Government	.26	.26	.04
Insurgents and Liberal Pressure Groups	.62	.06	.83
Insurgents and Organized Labor	.16	.43	−.01
Liberal Pressure Groups and Government	.04	.16	−.08
Organized Labor and Government	−.002	.46	−.54

[a] Symbolic or concrete for both types of groups.
[b] N for one group during this period was zero.

sponse.

The main issue for the period was labor supply. Looking at activities concerned with this issue, the correlation between insurgent and pro-farm worker government activities is high (.59); for the issue of living and working conditions, the relation disappears (-.08). The union attempted, through court actions, lobby efforts and public protest, to pressure government to end the *bracero* program since it was so central to the control of the labor supply. The official response, however, was largely symbolic. Though government tended to respond to concrete insurgency with favorable concrete actions, the majority of favorable governmental actions were actually symbolic (58%). Nor did many of these concrete moves decisively aid the farm worker cause. Key actions, such as pulling strikebreaking *braceros* out of the fields, did not occur.

What, then, are we to make of the fact that 50% of reported governmental actions were coded as favorable to the interest of farm workers? Was government responding to the conflict between insurgents and growers in some even-handed "pluralist" way? Here it is necessary to recall that we are using news media reportage on a social problem and efforts to redress that problem. The news media will be more sensitive to efforts attempting to define or solve that problem than to efforts to maintain the *status quo*. Consequently, unfavorable actions by government and growers are underrepresented in our data. If only 50% of news-reported government actions can be coded as favorable, then the full universe of governmental activities should, in the balance, be more favorable to growers.

The strength of this assertion is borne out by information on actions favorable to growers. Figure 2 charts these actions for government and growers. The correlation between pro-grower government activities and grower activities is quite high (.75), actually stronger than the respective *r* for insurgents. In quantitative terms, government was more responsive to agribusiness interests. Clearly, in critical instances, e.g., leaving *braceros* in struck fields, government policies favored growers over workers.

In addition to the predominantly unfavorable response of government, the NFLU failed to receive sustained, solid support from the liberal community. The major problem was the type of activities in which liberals engaged. When they acted, liberals consistently supported farm workers over growers but they rarely moved beyond symbolic proclamations. Only 24% of liberal actions during the period were concrete. By contrast, 38% during the UFW challenge were so. Even more indicative, though, is the modest level of the correlation between liberal and insurgent activity (.45). What concomitant activity did exist between these two groups involved only symbolic acts (.56 versus -.02 for concrete acts). Looking ahead, the respective *r*'s for the UFW challenge indicate a quite different liberal response. Overall, *r* was .62; for concrete actions, *r* was .83 and, for symbolic acts, .06. Where the UFW experienced consistent and concrete support, the NFLU found itself relatively isolated.

Though liberals did not rush to the side of the NFLU, they did play a role in the pressure campaign. When controls are introduced for government activity on the relation between insurgents and liberals, the modestly positive relation turns negative (-.10). Insofar as liberals did act alongside insurgents, apparently it was in the presence of public officials. But there were problems even with this limited-scale liberal support. Liberals focused almost exclusively on the working and living conditions of farm workers. Following the lead of Progressive Party candidate Henry Wallace in 1948, several religious and "public interest" associations sponsored conferences and issued study reports publicizing deplorable camp conditions and child labor. In what might be considered a typical pattern of liberalism of the time, they were concerned with the plight of the workers rather than the fact of their powerlessness or the role of the *bracero* program in underwriting that powerlessness. It was a humanitarian, nonpolitical posture, easily dissipated by "red baiting" in Congressional investigations and "red scare" charges by growers and their political allies throughout the late 1940s and early 1950s. The two issues, poverty and the question of labor supply, were not to be linked by the liberal organizations until well into Period II.

Period II: Elite Reform and Realignment (1956-1964)

In the late 1950s and the early 1960s, the second Eisenhower administration and the brief Kennedy period emerge from this and other studies in the larger project as a period of germination. Contrary to some interpretations, the remarkable insurgencies of the late 1960s did not originate with the Kennedy administration, but with developments that initially began to appear during Eisenhower's second term. Nor did the Kennedy years witness a dramatic escalation of insurgent activity. Indeed, in the case of farm workers, insurgency showed a decline (Figure 1). For our purposes, the two presidential administrations can be treated as a single period, one that witnessed important realignments and shifts in political resources in the national polity, culminating in a supportive environment for insurgent activity.

Farm worker insurgency during the reform period was at a low ebb. Actions by farm worker insurgents dropped from 16% to 11% of all proworker activity. In 1956-1957 the NFLU, now renamed the National Agricultural Workers Union (NAWU), secured a small grant from the United Auto Workers, enabling it to hang on as a paper organization. Galarza, by then the only full-time cadre member, launched a publicity campaign to reveal maladministration and corruption within the *bracero* administration. Aside from a brief and ineffective organizing drive launched in 1959 by the Agricultural Workers Organizing Committee (AWOC), generating only one reported strike (in

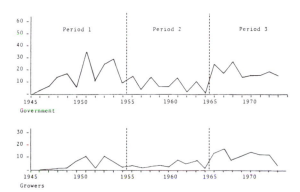

Figure 2
Actions Favorable to Growers

1961), this was the sum of insurgent activity for the nine-year Period II (Figure I). Growers remained publicly inactive and seemingly secure in their position, aroused only at renewal time for the *bracero* program to lobby bills through Congress. Until the insurgency of Period III began, growers retained a low profile in the *Times* (Figure 2).

With the direct adversaries largely retired from the public arena, affairs shifted into the hands of government and the liberals. Despite the absence of significant insurgency, the balance of forces in the national polity had begun to shift. Actions favorable to the interests of farm workers increased from 50% to 73%, remaining on the same plane (75%) throughout the following UFW period. Beginning during the last years of the Eisen-

hower administration, three interrelated developments brought about this new supportive environment: (1) policy conflicts within the political elite that resulted in a more "balanced," neutral stance towards farm workers; (2) the formation of a reform coalition composed of liberal pressure groups and organized labor that, in the midst of elite divisions, was able to exercise greater political influence; (3) the erosion of the Congressional power-base of conservative rural interests, stemming immediately from reapportionment.

The concern of liberal pressure groups initially was focused on the need to improve housing and educational conditions of migrant workers. In 1956, the Democratic National Convention included a plank for increased welfare aid to migrants. The next year, the National Council of Churches, already involved in the early civil rights movement in the South, began a study of migrant camp conditions and child labor. In early 1958, the Council brought public pressure to bear on Secretary of Labor James Mitchell to enforce existing laws regarding migrant camps throughout the nation. In late 1959, several liberal pressure groups were joined by the AFL-CIO in attacking the *bracero* program, scoring administrative laxity, and arguing that federal labor policies were the origin of social problems. The two as yet unrelated issues—poverty and labor policies—were now firmly in the public debate.

The fusion of these two issues was significant. Of course, economic conditions already had been linked with social deprivations in public parlance but the concern of liberal groups in the past had been with inspection of housing, assurances of educational opportunity, and public health measures. To argue now that a public program of importing foreign labor perpetuated the list of conditions deplored by liberals was a substantial change. As later happened more generally with the New Left (cf. Perrow, 1972), the advocates of reform had began to look at the source of problems in terms of a system.

About the same time, organized labor took a new interest in farm workers. In 1959, the AFL-CIO Executive Council abolished the NAWU and created the Agricultural Workers Organizing Committee (AWOC), headed by Norman Smith, a former UAW organizer. Despite strong financial backing, the AWOC produced little results. Concentrating on 4 A.M. "shake-ups" of day laborers, the AWOC managed to sponsor a number of "job actions" but only one major strike and little solid organization. Like the NFLU, the AWOC had to confront the problem of *braceros*. In the one reported strike, the Imperial Valley strike of February, 1961, the AWOC used violence to intimidate strikebreaking *braceros* and create an international incident over their presence. Officials quickly arrested the cadre, and the AWOC ceased to exist except on paper. Though the AWOC drive consumed over one million dollars of AFL-CIO funds, it produced neither contracts nor stable membership (London and Anderson, 1970:47-50, 77). Yet, and this indicates the shift, this type of financial support had never before been offered by organized labor.

The final element in the formation of a supportive environment was a shift in governmental actions. Actions favorable to farm workers increased from the unfavorable 50% prevailing during Period I to a more "balanced" 68% of all governmental actions. Of these, the portion coded "concrete," and therefore more likely to have impact, increased from 40% in Period I to 65%. Indicative of the change taking place in official views, the focus of governmental attentions shifted from the labor supply issue (56% of favorable actions during Period 1) to the question of

farm workers' living and working conditions (73% during Period II).

The change in official actions stemmed, in part, from internal conflicts within the political elite. Secretary of Labor James Mitchell was a surprise Eisenhower appointee from the Eastern wing of the Republican Party, a former labor consultant for New York department stores and a future protege of Nelson Rockefeller. Mitchell took the Department of Labor in a more pro-union direction than was thought possible, at the time becoming a "strong man" in the cabinet because of his success in mollifying unions.[8] In 1958, an open fight between the Taft and Eastern wings of the Republican Party developed, with the conservatives favoring a national "right-to-work" law. Mitchell, as an advocate of unionism and apparently jockeying for position for the Republican Vice-Presidential nomination, became a figure of elite reform within Republican circles.

A second factor contributing to the shift in official actions was the pressure campaign launched by the reform coalition. The effects of the campaign can be captured, in part, from the *Times* data. Though the correlation between liberal activity and government activity favorable to workers is modest (.50), it is considerably higher than during

Table 2
Extent of Concomitant Activity—Pro Grower (r's)

	All Issues	Work-Life Conditions[a]	Labor Shortage[a]	Unionization[a]
Period I (1946-1955)				
Insurgents and Government	.63	−.08	.59	—[b]
Insurgents and Liberal Pressure Groups	.45	.21	.76	—
Insurgents and Organized Labor	.08	.17	.08	—
Liberal Pressure Groups and Government	.33	.02	.40	—
Organized Labor and Government	.36	.18	.37	—
Period II (1956-1964)				
Insurgents and Government	−.26	−.28	−.04	—
Insurgents and Liberal Pressure Groups	−.10	−.13	−.04	—
Insurgents and Organized Labor	.59	.20	.58	—
Liberal Pressure Groups and Government	.50	.50	.23	—
Organized Labor and Government	.06	.21	−.05	—
Period III (1965-1972)				
Insurgents and Government	.26	.74	—[b]	−.21
Insurgents and Liberal Pressure Groups	.62	.84	—	−.21
Insurgents and Organized Labor	.16	.57	—	.09
Liberal Pressure Groups and Government	.04	.49	—	−.08
Organized Labor and Government	−.002	.13	—	.36

[a] Work-life for both types of groups; labor shortage for both, unionization for both.
[b] N for one group during this period was zero.

the other periods (.33 for the first and .04 for the third) and it is independent of insurgent activity.

Tangible effects of the pressure campaign appeared almost immediately. In 1957, under pressure from the liberal reform coalition, the Department of Labor under Mitchell's guidance carried out an internal review of farm labor policies. The upshot was a series of executive orders to tighten up enforcement of regulations covering migrant camps (Craig, 1971: 151-5). When the economic recession of 1958-1959 arrived, sensitivity within the Administration to rising unemployment levels increased. In response, Mitchell vowed to enforce more fully the 1951 statutes requiring farm employment to be offered to domestic workers prior to importation of *braceros*. Growers, long accustomed to having their *bracero* requests met automatically, rebelled when asked to provide more justification (Jacobs, 1963: 183-4). In February, 1959, Mitchell took an even stronger step, joining the liberal reformers in support of legislation to extend minimum-wage laws to agriculture and to impose new restrictions on the use of *braceros*.

The following year, the division within the Eisenhower Administration opened up into a full-scale, cabinet-level battle over renewal of the *bracero* program. The Farm Bureau and the state grower associations engaged that other administration "strong man," Secretary of Agriculture Ezra Taft Benson, to defend the program. In testimony before the House Committee on Agriculture, the White House took a neutral stance; Benson defended the program, while Mitchell argued that the program exerted demonstrable adverse effects upon domestic workers and should be abolished (Craig, 1971: 156-61). Into this breach in the political elite stepped the liberal-labor support coalition. At the same time, the House Committee on Public Welfare opened hearings on health and camp conditions, giving the Cotton Council and the Meatcutters Union a chance to air opposing views.

Initially, the reform effort failed. In March, 1960, Secretary Mitchell withdrew his program, resolving the dispute on the cabinet level. The next month, agribusiness pushed a two-year renewal of the *bracero* program through Congress. But, for the first time, the issue had been debated seriously and a loose coalition of liberal pressure groups (e.g., National Council of Churches, National Advisory Committee of Farm Labor, NAACP) and organized labor had formed.

Though the eventual termination of the *bracero* program did not undermine growers' ability to break strikes (there were other substitutes, e.g., "green card" commuters, illegal aliens), the fight against the program did refocus the concern of liberals and organized labor on the structural problem of farm worker powerlessness.

The reform coalition sustained the campaign over the next three years. In 1960, the Democratic platform condemned the *bracero* program. Once in office, the New Frontiersmen, though demanding no important statutory changes, did vow to enforce fully the laws restricting *bracero* use (Craig, 1971:174). By renewal time in 1963, the Kennedy Administration was in the pursuit of a public issue ("poverty") and courting minority-group votes. For the first time, the White House went formally on record against the program. Only at the last minute was a pressure campaign, mounted by Governor Pat Brown of California and the Department of State, responding to Mexican diplomatic pressure, able to save the program temporarily. Amid promises from Congressional farm bloc leaders that this was the last time the program would be renewed, a one-year extension was granted.

In addition to the efforts of the reform coalition, which played a critical role in other reforms of the same period, and the new elite-level neutrality, the fall of the *bracero* program stemmed from the narrowing power base of the Congressional farm bloc. Congressional reapportionment had visibly shaken the conservative farm bloc leaders. Searching for items in the farm program that could be scuttled without damaging the main planks, the farm bloc leaders fixed on the *bracero* program. The mechanization of the Texas cotton harvest had left California growers of specialty crops the main *bracero* users. When the test came, *bracero* users, as a narrow, special interest, could be sacrificed to keep the main planks of the farm program intact (Hawley, 1966).

Period II, then, emerges from this analysis as a period of reform and political realignment that dramatically altered the prospective fortunes of insurgents. Reforms, stemming from elite-level conflicts and a pressure campaign conducted by liberal public-interest organizations and organized labor, came about in the virtual absence of activity by farm worker insurgents. The activism of several key liberal organizations depended, in turn, upon broad economic trends, especially the growth of disposable income that might be invested in worthy causes (McCarthy and Zald, 1973). Insurgents did not stimulate these changes in the national polity. Rather, they were to prove the beneficiaries and, if anything, were stimulated by them.

Period III: The UFW Success (1965-1972)

During the NFLU period, the number of insurgent actions reported totalled 44. Most of these were symbolic in character, only 27% being concrete. Insurgency was brief, concentrated in a four-year period (1948-1951). However, in the third period, insurgency became sustained. Insurgent actions reached a new peak and remained at a high level throughout the period. A total of 143 actions conducted by farm worker insurgents were recorded. Significantly, 71% of these were concrete in character. By the end of the period, the success of the United Farm Workers was unmistakable. Over a hundred contracts had been signed; wages had been raised by almost a third; union hiring halls were in operation in every major agricultural area in California; farm workers, acting through ranch committees set up under each contract, were exercising a new set of powers.

The key to this dramatic success was the altered political environment within which the challenge operated. Though the potential for mobilizing a social base was slightly more favorable than before, the UFW never was able to launch effective strikes. Though the UFW cadre was experienced and talented, there is little reason to believe that they were markedly more so than the NFLU leadership; neither did the tactics of the challenge differ. The boycotts that secured success for the UFW also had been tried by the NFLU, but with quite different results. What had changed was the political environment—the liberal community now was willing to provide sustained, massive support for insurgency; the political elite had adopted a neutral stance toward farm workers.

As before, external support played a critical role in launching the challenge. The initial base for the United Farm Workers was Cesar Chavez's National Farm Workers Association (NFWA) and remnants of the AWOC still receiving some support from the AFL-CIO.[9] During the 1950s, Chavez had been director of the Community Service Organization, an Alinsky-styled urban community-organization with strong ties to civil rights groups, liberal churches and foundations. Frustrated by the refusal of the CSO Board of Directors to move beyond issues salient to upwardly-mobile urban Mexican-Americans, Chavez resigned his post in the winter of 1961 and set out to organize a community organization among farm workers in the Central Valley of California. Drawing on his liberal contacts, Chavez was able to secure the backing of several liberal organizations which had developed a new concern with poverty and the problems of minority groups. The main sponsor was the California Migrant Ministry, a domestic mission of the National Council of Churches servicing migrant farm workers. During the late 1950s, the Migrant Ministry followed the prevailing policy change within the National Council, substituting community organization and social action programs for traditional evangelical ones (Pratt, 1972). By 1964, the Migrant Ministry had teamed up with Chavez, merging its own community organization (the FWO) with the NFWA and sponsoring the Chavez-directed effort.[10]

By summer, 1965, NFWA had over 500 active members and began shifting directions, expanding beyond economic benefit programs (e.g., a credit union, cooperative buying, etc.) to unionization. Several small "job actions" were sponsored. Operating nearby, the remaining active group of the AWOC, several Filipino work-crews, hoped to take advantage of grower uncertainty generated by termination of the *bracero* program. The AWOC launched a series of wage strikes, first in the Coachella Valley and then in the Delano-Arvin area of the San Joaquin Valley. With the AWOC out on strike, Chavez pressed the NFWA for a strike vote. On Mexican Independence Day, September 16th, the NFWA joined the picket lines (Chavez, 1966; Dunne, 1967; London and Anderson, 1970).

Though dramatic, the strike soon collapsed. Growers refused to meet with union representatives; a sufficient number of workers crossed the picket lines to prevent a major harvest loss. Over the next six years, the same pattern recurred—a dramatic strike holding for a week, grower intransigence, police intimidation, gradual replacement of the work force by playing upon ethnic rivalries and recruiting illegal aliens (cf. Dunne, 1967; London and Anderson, 1970; Matthiessen, 1969; Kushner, 1975; Taylor, 1975).

What proved different from the NFLU experience was the ability of the insurgents, acting in the new political environment, to secure outside support.

Political protest was the mechanism through which much of this support was garnered. By dramatic actions designed to capture the attention of a sympathetic public and highlight the "justice" of their cause, insurgents were able to sustain the movement organization and exercise sufficient indirect leverage against growers to secure contracts. The UFW's use of protest tactics departed from that of rent strikers analyzed by Lipsky (1968; 1970). Though the basic mechanism was the same (namely, securing the sympathy of third parties to the conflict so that they would use their superior resources to intervene in support of the powerless), the commitments of supporting organizations and the uses to which outside support was put differed. Lipsky found that protest provided unreliable resources, that the news media and sympathetic public might ignore protestors' demands (cf. Goldenberg, 1975) and that, even when attentive, they often were easily satisfied with symbolic palliatives. Though the UFW experienced these problems, the presence of sustained sponsorship on the part of the Migrant Ministry and organized labor guaranteed a stable resource base.

Nor were the uses of protest-acquired resources the same. Lipsky's rent-strikers sought liberal pressure on public officials. For the UFW, protest actions were used to secure contributions and, in the form of a boycott, to exercise power against growers. Marches, symbolic arrests of clergy, and public speeches captured public attention; contributions from labor unions, theater showings and "radical chic" cocktail parties with proceeds to "*La Causa*" supplemented the budget provided by sponsors and membership dues.

Given the failure of strike actions, a successful outcome required indirect means of exercising power against growers. Sympathetic liberal organizations (e.g., churches, universities, etc.) refused to purchase "scab" grapes. More important, though, major grocery chains were pressured into refusing to handle "scab" products. To exercise that pressure, a combination of external resources had to be mobilized. Students had to contribute time to picketing grocery stores and shipping terminals; Catholic churches and labor unions had to donate office space for boycott houses; Railway Union members had to identify "scab" shipments for boycott pickets; Teamsters had to refuse to handle "hot cargo"; Butchers' union members had to call sympathy strikes when grocery managers continued to stock "scab" products; political candidates and elected officials had to endorse the boycott. The effectiveness of the boycott depended little upon the resources of mobilized farm workers; instead, they became a political symbol. It was the massive outpouring of support, especially from liberals and organized labor, that made the boycott effective and, thereby, forced growers to the bargaining table.

The strength of liberal-labor support for the UFW is indicated by the high level of concomitant activity between insurgents and their supporters. While the correlation of insurgent and liberal activities was modest in Period I (.45), it was strong during the third period (.62). More important, liberals were far more concrete in their support for insurgents. In the first period, concomitant activities were almost wholly symbolic (.56 versus .02 for concrete activities); during the UFW challenge, it was concrete activities (.81 versus .06 for symbolic activities). Nor do statistical controls for governmental actions favorable to farm workers reduce the correlation ($r = .64$). Given the fact that liberal activities rarely occurred jointly with pro-worker government activities ($r = .04$), it is clear that liberals directed their efforts toward supporting insurgents rather than pressuring government.[11]

The more "balanced," neutral posture of government that was the product of the reform period continued. Sixty-nine percent of all official actions were favorable to farm workers (as against 50% and 68% in Periods I and II). Concretely, this meant that court rulings no longer routinely went against insurgents; federal poverty programs helped to "loosen" small town politics; hearings by the U.S. Civil Rights Commission and Congressional committees publicized "injustices" against farm workers; welfare legislation gave farm workers more economic security and afforded insurgents a legal basis to contest grower employment practices. National politicians, such as Senators Kennedy and McGovern, lent their resources to the cause.

The most striking changes in official actions took place on the federal level. Actions favorable to firm workers rose from 46% of federal level activity in the first period, to 63% in the second and 74% in the third. State and local government, more under the control of growers (cf. McConnell, 1953:177; Berger, 1971), followed a different pattern. In Period I, when growers had opposition only from insurgents, only 26% of official actions were judged favorable to workers. In Period II, when farm workers were acquiescent but the liberal-labor coalition was experiencing growing influence in national politics, 67% were favorable, slightly more than on the federal level. But when insurgency reappeared in Period III, the percent favorable dropped to 45%, far lower than the federal level. Government divided on the question, federal actions tending to be neutral, if not supportive, of insurgents while state actions, still under grower dominance, continued to oppose insurgents.

Significantly little of the pro-worker trend in governmental actions during the UFW period is associated with either insurgent or liberal activities. For insurgent and favorable government actions, r is low (.26 versus .63 during the NFLU Period); the correlation between liberal organizations and favorable government actions drops to the lowest point in the study (.04 versus .33 and .50 for Periods I and II, respectively). Only organized labor appeared to be performing a pressure function. There is a modest correlation between symbolic activities by organized labor and government (.46), largely centering around the legitimacy of unionism in agriculture ($r = .35$). Official positions had already undergone important changes during the reform period. The termination of the *bracero* program had left government in a neutralized position. No longer a key player in the conflict, but still under the influence of the reform policies, government preserved its neutral stance despite less visible pressure from any of the partisans.[12]

There was, of course, opposition on the part of growers and allied governmental actors. There were numerous instances of police harassment, large-scale purchases of boycotted products by the Department of Defense, and outspoken opposition from Governor Reagan and President Nixon.

However, growers had lost their entrenched political position. Public officials no longer acted so consistently to enhance grower interests and to contain the challenge. An indication of the sharpness of the displacement of growers is given by the levels of concomitance between grower actions and pro-grower governmental actions. In Period I, r for grower-government activity was .75;

in Period II, .62. But, during the UFW challenge, the correlation dropped to a negligible .05. By the time the United Farm Workers struck in 1965, agricultural employers were no longer able to rely upon government, especially at the federal level, to be fully responsive to their interest in blocking unionization.

Conclusion

The critical factor separating the National Farm Labor Union failure from the United Farm Worker success was the societal response to insurgent demands. In most respects, the challenges were strikingly similar. In both instances, the leadership cadre came from outside the farm worker community; external sponsorship played a critical role in launching both insurgent organizations; both movements confronted similar obstacles to mobilizing a social base and mounting effective strikes; both resorted to political protest and boycotts. What produced the sharp difference in outcome was the difference in political environment encountered. The NFLU received token contributions, vacillating support for its boycott and confronted major acts of resistance by public authorities. In contrast, the UFW received massive contributions, sustained support for its boycotts and encountered a more "balanced," neutral official response.

The dramatic turnabout in the political environment originated in economic trends and political realignments that took place quite independent of any "push" from insurgents. During the reform period, conflicts erupted within the political elite over policies pertaining to farm workers. Elite divisions provided the opening for reform measures then being pressed by a newly active coalition of established liberal and labor organizations. Though the reforms did not directly effect success, the process entailed by reform did result in a new political environment, one which made a successful challenge possible.

If this analysis is correct, then several assumptions found in the classic literature are misleading. Rather than focusing on fluctuations in discontent to account for the emergence of insurgency, it seems more fruitful to assume that grievances are relatively constant and pervasive. Especially for deprived groups, lack of collective resources and controls exercised by superiors—not the absence of discontent—account for the relative infrequency of organized demands for change. For several of the movements of the 1960s, it was the interjection of resources from outside, not sharp increases in discontent, that led to insurgent efforts.

Nor does the political process centered around insurgency conform to the rules of a pluralist game. The American polity had not been uniformly permeable to all groups with significant grievances (cf. Gamson, 1975). Government does not act as a neutral agent, serving as umpire over the group contest. Public agencies and officials have interests of their own to protect, interests that often bring them into close alignment with well-organized private-interest groups. When insurgency arises threatening these private interests, public officials react by helping to contain insurgency and preserve the *status quo*. But if an opposing coalition of established organizations decides to sponsor an insurgent challenge, the normal bias in public policy can be checked. Sponsors then serve as protectors, insuring that the political elite remains neutral to the challenge.

The implications for other challenges are rather striking. If the support of the liberal community is necessary for the success of a challenge by a deprived group, then the liberal community is, in effect, able to determine the cutting edge for viable changes that conform to the interests of those groups still excluded from American politics. Moreover, there is the possibility of abandonment. Since liberal support can fade and political elites shift their stance, as has happened to the UFW since 1972, even the gains of the past may be endangered. The prospects for future insurgency, by this account, are dim. Until another major realignment takes place in American politics, we should not expect to see successful attempts to extend political citizenship to the excluded.

Notes

1. Shifts in perceptions, treated as central by relative deprivation theorists, in our view would be secondary to the main process—changes in social resources.

2. Note also the central role played in pluralistic interpretations by the "discontent" hypothesis. Assuming that all groups have ready access to the resources needed to mobilize, Rose (1967:249) argued: "As soon as a felt need for some social change arises, one or more voluntary associations immediately springs up to try to secure the change."

3. As the central tenet of pluralist theory, the "permeability" argument can be found in almost any presentation of the view. Dahl (1967:250) argues: "even minorities are provided with opportunities to veto solutions"; Truman's (1951) speculations about "poten-

tial groups" and Smelser's (1963:364-79) recommendations to elites for channeling "value-oriented" movements into "norm-oriented" ones both build on the assumption of a flexible political system based on a pluralistic social structure.

4. For a copy of the coding schedule used, contact the first author.

5. Inter-coder reliability was set at 90%; all items failing to meet this standard were excluded from the analysis.

6. The Agricultural Workers Organizing Committee (AFL-CIO) was chartered in 1959, but never posed a serious threat to growers (London and Anderson 1970: 46-78); the National Farm Worker Association was an independent community organization launched by Cesar Chavez in 1962 and entered the labor question in an offensive way only in 1965 (London and Anderson, 1970: 148-53).

7. Contrary to most time-series analyses, controls for auto-correlation are inappropriate. The correlation analysis does not causally relate a dependent variable (e.g., level of insurgent activity) to a set of independent variables (e.g., level of liberal activity). Instead, it is designed to reveal whether significant differences exist between time periods in movement-environment interaction. These differences are then held to account for the divergent outcomes. Instead of asking, "Does liberal activity cause insurgency?" we are asking, "Did insurgent and liberal activities co-occur to a different extent during one challenge than another? Did this difference relate to different challenge outcomes?"

8. *New York Times.* October 5, 1958, VI; 9: 2; October 20, 1964: 37: 1.

9. For a detailed discussion, see Jenkins (1975: chs. 7-8).

10. There was also a brief challenge launched in 1965 among black tenant farmers in the Mississippi Delta region (the Mississippi Freedom Labor Union). The dynamics of that challenge are virtually identical to the UFW-sponsorship by liberal churches, labor union, etc. (for a history, see Hilton, 1969). Given the low event-count for this challenge, though, the statistics reported pertain to the UFW.

11. Despite the fact that help from organized labor was critical to the boycott's success, our correlations hardly document the point. In the NFLU challenge, r was .08; in the UFW period, .16. This relation is weaker than that for liberal pressure groups, we would argue, because much of the supportive labor action was "local" in character and often went unreported in the *Times*.

12. Corroborating this interpretation, the correlation between insurgent/liberal actions and proworker government actions is considerably stronger (.74 and .59, respectively) once insurgent and liberal actions are lagged by one year. As a roughly neutral participant, government followed along a year behind the chief partisans, though not responding directly to pressure as before. Though not conclusive, the fact that this was the only instance in the study in which time-lags produced marked increases in r's lends the interpretation some plausibility. ✦

5

New Social Movements and Political Opportunities in Western Europe

Hanspeter Kriesi
Ruud Koopmans
Jan Willem Duyvendak
Marco G. Giugni

Introduction

The crucial contention of the so called "political process" approach to social movements is that social processes impinge indirectly on social protest, via a restructuring of existing power relations (McAdam, 1982). This contention has received considerable support from Skocpol's (1979) analysis of social revolutions. As she has shown, social revolutions are typically triggered by a political crisis that weakens the control on the population exercised by the political system. Similarly, the analysis of a century of collective violence in France, Germany and Italy by Tilly et al. (1975)[1] has indicated that the rhythm of collective violence did not so much depend on structural transformations of society, but was rather directly linked to shifts in the struggle for political power. More recently, the political context has also been shown to be of considerable importance for the mobilization and the impact of different types of new social movement. Thus, in what has probably been the first systematic study of the impact of the political context on the fate of a new social movement, Kitschelt (1986) has shown how the impact of the antinuclear movement varied according to specific characteristics of the political context of the countries he studied.

For the systematic analysis of the political context that mediates structural conflicts given as

latent political potentials, the notion of *political opportunities structure* (POS) has become fashionable. First introduced by Eisinger (1973), it has been elaborated by Tarrow (1983, 1989). We shall employ a modified version of this concept to show the importance of the political context for the mobilization of new social movements (NSMs) in Western Europe. Following the conceptualization of Kriesi (1991), we distinguish three broad sets of properties of a political system: its formal institutional structure, its informal procedures and prevailing strategies with regard to challengers, and the configuration of power relevant for the confrontation with the challengers. The first two sets of properties provide the general setting for the mobilization of collective action; they also constrain the relevant configurations of power. Together with the general setting, the relevant configuration of power specifies the strategies of the "authorities" or the "members of the system" with regard to the mobilization of the "challengers." These strategies, in turn, define (a) the extent to which challenging collective action will be facilitated or repressed by "members of the system," (b) the chances of success such actions may have, and (c) the chances of success if no such actions take place, which may be either positive if the government is reform-oriented, or negative if the government in power is hostile to the movement (Koopmans, 1990a).

In other words, the country-specific mix of facilitation/repression and chances of success and of reform is, in part at least, the result of strategic calculations of the authorities. However, it is not exclusively determined by such strategic calculations, since the general setting also restricts this country-specific mix in a way that is independent of the concrete strategies devised by the authorities. Finally, this country-specific mix determines the set of strategic options available for the mobilization of the "challengers." It provides the crucial link between the POS and the challengers' decision to mobilize or not, their choice of the form of mobilization, the sequence of events to be organized, and the target of their campaign. Figure 1 presents a graphical summary of this argument. As Koopmans (1990a) pointed out, the way the country-specific conditions enter into the challengers' strategic calculations will depend on the type of movement in question.[2]

After a brief discussion of each of these general concepts,[3] we shall test some hypotheses con-

"New Social Movements and Political Opportunities in Western Europe." *European Journal of Political Research* 22: 219- 244. Copyright © 1992 by the Kluwer Academic Publishers. Reprinted with permission.

Figure 1
Conceptual outline of the general argument.

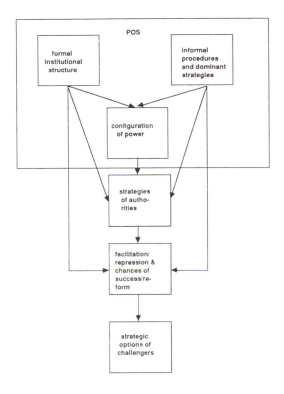

violent form which is reported in the newspapers we analyzed. Excluded from this definition are conventional legal actions (such as the filling of a legal suit), conventional political actions (such as participation in a consultation procedure), conventional media-oriented actions (such as press conferences or public resolutions), and strikes. The actions included range from petitions and demonstrations, through boycotts, disturbances and occupations to violent attacks against persons. In the Swiss case, they also include direct-democratic forms of action—initiatives and referenda. In other words, protest events have been defined irrespective of their goal.

For each event, a limited number of characteristics have been coded.[6] On the basis of the goal of the event, we have decided whether it was an event of a given NSM, or of some other movement. Among the NSMs we count the ecology movement (including its anti-nuclear energy branch), the peace movement, the solidarity movement (encompassing various branches mobilizing for humanitarian aid, political refugees, human rights, political regimes in the Third World, and against racism), the autonomous movement (including the squatters movement and the Swiss movement for youth centres), the women's movement, the gay movement, and the citizens' rights movement (mobilizing for democratic participation and against repression).

The General Political Context

For the conceptualization of the overall institutional setting, our approach follows the state-centered theories (Badie & Birnbaum, 1979; Zysman, 1983), which have usefully been applied to the field of new social movements by Kitschelt (1986). In this tradition, a distinction is often made between weak and strong states. Weak states are defined by their openness on the input side and by their lack of a capacity to impose themselves on the output side. Conversely, strong states are defined as closed and having a high capacity to impose themselves. The internal structure of the state institutions—the degree of their internal coherence or fragmentation—is thought to determine the overall strength or weakness of the state. Among our four countries, Switzerland clearly seems to have the weakest state, France the strongest one (see Badie & Birnbaum 1979), with the "semi-sovereign" Federal Republic of Germany (Katzenstein, 1987) coming closer to the

cerning the impact of the various aspects of the POS on the mobilization of NSMs in four Western European countries—France, the Federal Republic of Germany, the Netherlands, and Switzerland. These hypotheses will be tested using data on protest events, collected in a comparative project on the development of NSMs in these four countries in the period from 1975 to 1989. Following the lead of others (Kriesi et al., 1981; McAdam, 1983; Tarrow, 1989a; Tilly et al., 1975), we have collected systematic data on protest events on the basis of a contents analysis of newspapers.[4] In each one of the four countries, we have analyzed the Monday editions of one major newspaper for the period indicated.[5] Protest events constitute the basic units of an organized, sustained, self-conscious challenge to existing authorities or other political actors. This challenge, in turn, establishes a social movement according to the definition given by Tilly (1984).

We have defined as protest events any kind of public action of a demonstrative, confrontative or

Swiss case, and the rather centralized Netherlands more closely resembling the French one (Kriesi, 1990).

The informal procedures and prevailing strategies with respect to challengers are either *exclusive* (repressive, confrontative, polarizing) or *integrative* (facilitative, cooperative, assimilative). It is important to note that such procedures have a long tradition in a given country. According to Scharpf (1984: 260), they develop a powerful logic of their own. Efforts to change them are up against all the "sunk costs" of institutional commitments supporting them. Among our four countries, the French and the German legacy is typically one of exclusion and repression.[7] While the formal institutional structure of the Federal Republic has been completely rebuilt after World War II, the dominant strategy of its ruling elite with regard to challengers from below has continued to be marked by the experience of the past (Koopmans, 1991). In contrast to France, however, where the exclusive strategy is associated with a strong state, the exclusive strategy in the Federal Republic combines with a relatively weak state, which will result in a different overall setting for social movements in general, and for NSMs in particular. Integrative strategies are typical for the two small, consensual democracies—the Netherlands and Switzerland. Just as in the exclusive case, they are compatible with rather different formal institutional structures. A strong unitary Dutch state, with a system of cabinet government comparable to the "Westminster model," together with a relatively coherent bureaucracy, contrasts with a Swiss state weakened by its federalism, its fragmentation and its direct-democratic institutions.

Combining the distinction between strong and weak states with the distinction between exclusive and integrative dominant strategies, we arrive at four distinct general settings for dealing with challengers. As is indicated in Figure 2, each of these general settings corresponds to one of our four countries. The combination of a strong state with an exclusive dominant strategy we call a situation of *full exclusion*. In such a situation, the challenger can count on neither formal nor informal access to the political system. Because of its strength, the state can often choose merely to ignore challenges; if it does react, however, it will most likely confront the challenger with repression. Moreover, since the state is a strong one, the

Figure 2
The general settings fot the approach of members toward challengers.

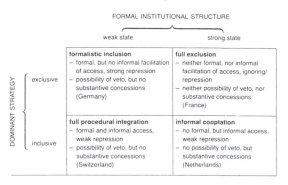

challenger is neither likely to have veto power, nor is he likely to obtain substantive concessions.[8] This case is represented by France.

In contrast to "full exclusion," we find the case of *full procedural integration*, which is characterized by the combination of a weak state with an inclusive dominant strategy. In such a situation, repression is comparatively weak and the challenger's access to the system is formally as well as informally facilitated. Given the weakness of the system, the challenger cannot count on important substantive concessions, but he may be able to block decisions by exercising a veto. This case is represented by Switzerland. The direct democratic institutions as well as the federalist structure of Switzerland provide for a large number of formal access points for challengers. The traditionally integrative strategy enhances the general effect of the formal structure.

Germany represents one of the two intermediate cases, that of *formalistic inclusion*. In this situation, the challenger can count on formal, but not on informal, facilitation of access. Moreover, he tends to be met with strong repression. There is a possibility of veto, but no concessions can be expected. The federal structure of the German Republic allows for a multiplication of points of access. Moreover, the strong position of the German judiciary provides the challengers with another set of independent access points. Compared to Switzerland, the number of formal regional and local access points is, however, more limited, because—apart from some exceptions[9]—the Federal Republic does not have direct democratic institutions. Moreover, the repressive legacy of the system implies that those who articulate themselves outside of the formally available channels will be confronted with strong repression.

The second intermediary case, of *informal cooptation*, is represented by the Netherlands. In such a general setting, challengers do not have a lot of formal access, but they can count on informal facilitation. Such informal measures may not go as far as the overt facilitation of action campaigns of social movements, but they may imply the facilitation of their organizational infrastructure. This includes public recognition, consultation, and even subsidization of SMOs. Since the Dutch state is also quite strong, it is able to make considerable substantive concessions, and it can prevent challengers from exerting a veto. Concessions have actually been forthcoming in the Dutch case, because of the prevailing inclusive strategies, which serve to preempt challengers.

These general settings can be expected to have a country-specific impact on all challenging mobilizations, not only on those of the NSMs, with respect to the general level of mobilization, the general form and strategy of the challenging mobilizations, and the system level at which mobilizations are typically oriented.

It is difficult to make predictions about *the general level of mobilization*. On the one hand, as we have just argued, inclusive strategies have a tendency to preempt protest. However, it also seems plausible to argue that inclusive strategies imply elaborate decision-making processes which increase the chances for challengers to intervene and to exercise a veto. A most telling example is provided by a series of non-decisions by the Dutch government with regard to the stationing of the cruise missiles in the early 1980s, which has given the Dutch peace movement ample opportunities to continue its anti-missiles campaign. On the other hand, one may argue that repressive strategies generally raise the costs of collective action, and thereby serve to limit its scope in a general way.

However, strong repression may also stimulate collective action. As is pointed out by Koopmans (1990a), there are at least three ways in which this may happen. First, repression reinforces the identity of countercultural movements, which may stimulate offensive reactions of a rather radical type on the part of these movements. Second, repression may itself become a crucial issue for the challengers. Finally and related to this

second point, repression may focus media attention on the challengers, which may result in the support of third parties that would otherwise not have supported the movement. Such supportive mobilization, in turn, may be expected to be of a rather moderate type.

Although it is thus very hard to say anything about the amount of unconventional mobilization, we can be more specific about two types of more conventional mass mobilization that require relatively little effort from the participants: petitions and direct-democratic actions. The latter, like petitions, amount to the collection and presentation of signatures, but they are different from petitions in that they formally compel the authorities to take a position and to submit the proposition to a vote by all the citizens. The possibility for this type of action is, as we have seen, restricted to the Swiss case, and offers an extra channel of mobilization to the citizens of that country. We may, therefore, expect that the existence of this possibility in Switzerland leads to a higher overall participation in protest events. Petitions, although of course equally possible in all countries, are not likely to be equally important in all of them. A petition is a very moderate form of action which entails only a small amount of direct pressure on the authorities. It is, therefore, a more likely form of mobilization in those countries where authorities can be expected to react favorably even to such a friendly show of public discontent. This means that petitions are expected to be most frequent in the two countries with inclusive informal strategies: Switzerland and the Netherlands.

To arrive at a comparable indicator of the general level of mobilization in each country, we have calculated the total number of persons mobilized in the events represented in our newspaper file per million inhabitants; that is, we have taken the sum of all participants[10] in the events we have recorded over the 15 years period, multiplied this by one million and divided by the total population of the country in question. For the events where we did not have any information about the number of participants, we calculated estimates on the basis of the median of the number of participants in comparable events in the same country.[11] In Table 1 the value of this rough indicator of the general level of mobilization is given for three types of mobilization: unconventional events mobilizing people in the streets (ranging from dem-

Table 1
General Level of Mobilization
(Participants/Millions)

Country	Unconventional Mobilisation	Petitions	Direct Democracy
The Netherlands	216,000	304,000	—
Germany	232,000	140,000	—
France	237,000	24,000	—
Switzerland	234,000	207,000	198,000

onstrations to violent events), petitions, and direct-democratic events.

If we look at the first column, we notice that the general level of unconventional mobilization is of the same order of magnitude in each of the four countries. This result reflects the difficulties we had in formulating hypotheses concerning this aspect of mobilization. We find the result quite puzzling. It suggests that there might be something like a "natural" level of unconventional mobilization which is attained—in different ways of course—in each country, irrespective of the POS or the level of structural problems. Of course, we have no way of knowing whether this finding is only accidental. It seems clear, however, that such a "natural level" can at the most extend to comparable, democratic countries. Dictatorial regimes, at least in the short and medium run, often succeed in limiting protest to a very low level.

However, turning to the more moderate forms of mass mobilization, significant differences emerge even between the countries under study. The more moderate forms are clearly more popular in the two inclusive, consensual democracies. Due to its additional direct-democratic possibilities, Switzerland now emerges with the highest level of overall mass mobilization. Strikingly, even outside of direct-democratic channels, quite a lot of petitioning is going on in this country, although the Netherlands rank even higher on this. In the two countries with exclusive dominant strategies, Germany and France, petitions are much less popular, especially in the fully exclusive French case, where people apparently do not have much faith in the effectiveness of such a moderate form of protest.

In line with the above considerations, we hypothesize that, with regard to *the general forms and strategies of action* typically used by challengers in the different countries, the French context of "full exclusion" invites disruptive strategies on the part of the challengers. As Wilson (1987: 283)

observed, the strength of the French state gives rise to its greatest weakness; unable to allow challengers to articulate their concerns through formal or informal channels of access, it is periodically confronted by large scale explosions of discontent. By contrast, the highly accessible Swiss system is expected to invite moderate, conventional strategies on the part of the challengers. Such a system functions much like a sponge; it absorbs all kinds of protest without granting much in the way of concessions to meet the demands of the challengers. In spite of a conspicuous lack of concessions, challengers may continue to mobilize in moderate ways, because procedural success is to some extent a functional equivalent of substantive success (Epple, 1988), and because occasionally the challenges may still exert a veto power. We may expect, however, that there will be considerable variation of this general theme within Switzerland, given that the informal procedures to deal with challengers vary quite substantially from one region to the other.

In the general setting of informal cooptation in the Netherlands, we may also expect collective action to be moderate. The Dutch tradition of pillarization will especially stimulate the growth of social movement organizations, working through conventional channels, that will be treated in much the same way as are the religious minorities for which the system was set up. This implies large scale subsidization, integration into advisory bodies, and even some relatively autonomous role in the implementation of government policies. On the other hand, the possibilities to influence policies will not be as large as in Switzerland, most importantly because of the lack of possibilities for direct-democratic intervention and because of the relative strength of the Dutch state. Therefore, the Dutch action repertoire may be expected to include a considerable amount of more radical, confrontative forms of action as well. The low level of repression enables social movements to use such forms but at the same time will ensure that the actions involved remain mainly of a non-violent nature.

Finally, in the case of Germany we may expect the relatively large number of formal access channels, and the possibility of blocking political decisions through such channels, to invite moderate mobilization. On the other hand, the level of state facilitation of social movements will be quite low, due to the repressive legacy of the German

Table 2
Form of Protest Events (in Percentages)

Level	Netherlands	Germany	France	Switzerland
New Social Movements				
1. Direct Democracy	—	—	—	4.8
2. Demonstrative	57.4	66.7	58.8	68.1
3. Confrontative	30.5	19.3	18.7	12.7
4. Light Violence	6.5	7.1	4.8	10.6
5. Heavy Violence	5.6	6.7	17.8	3.8
Total	100.0	100.0	100.0	100.0
n	(881)	(1795)	(811)	(811)
Other Movements				
1. Direct Democracy	—	—	—	13.3
2. Demonstrative	48.2	62.3	34.6	63.0
3. Confrontative	42.9	18.3	27.5	14.5
4. Light Violence	2.2	3.1	6.5	3.1
5. Heavy Violence	6.7	16.3	31.4	6.1
Total	100.0	100.0	100.0	100.0
n	(450)	(541)	(1430)	(511)

state. While this legacy may also be expected to push the bulk of the activists to more moderate, less risky forms of action, it will at the same time probably lead to the radicalization of another, smaller group that will turn to more radical, violent forms of action.

In our newspaper analysis, we have distinguished five broad forms of protest events of increasing radicalness: direct democratic events, demonstrative events (such as petitions and demonstrations), confrontative events (such as blockades and occupations), events of light violence (such as violent demonstrations and limited damage to objects) and of heavy violence (bombings, arson and violence against persons). For each of the four countries, Table 2 presents the distribution of events over these five forms of action. The distributions are given separately for NSMs and for other movements.

As the table indicates, collective protest in France is, indeed, more disruptive than elsewhere. Heavy violence clearly plays a larger role among French NSMs than among those in other countries. Such violence is not as prominent among the NSMs in France, however, (17.8% of their events belong to this category) as it is among the other French movements, for which it constitutes almost a third (31.4%) of the events. The other movements mainly associated with these violent actions are the French regional movements, especially those in Corsica and the Basque country.

Mobilization in Switzerland, on the other hand, is most moderate—given the possibility of mobilization in direct democratic channels. The direct-democratic possibilities turn out to be less frequently used by NSMs (4.8% of events) than by others (13.3%). In spite of the generally moderate character of the Swiss action repertoire, we also find a considerable amount of light violence (10.6% of events) among Swiss NSMs, and some heavy violence (6.1%) among the events produced by other movements. These violent events are largely caused by the urban autonomous movement of Zurich and by the regional movement of the Jura, and are thus explained by regionally specific factors.

In the case of the Netherlands, confrontative mobilization plays, indeed, the important role that we expected. A total of 30.5% of the events of NSMs and fully 42.9% of the events of other movements can be classified in this category. The Dutch action repertoire is thus clearly more radical than the Swiss, but it is still a moderate kind of radicalism that prevails.

In the German case, the overall repertoire of protest is quite moderate, and comparable to the Swiss. However, heavy violence plays a considerable role among the other movements (16.3% of the events). In fact, the same is true for the NSMs as well. Although the 6.7% of heavy violence is not that much higher than in the Netherlands (5.6%) and in Switzerland (3.8%), it includes very heavy acts of violence (among others committed by the Rote Armee Fraktion), in which several dozens of persons have been killed. The existence of such a violent minority in a generally moderate social movement sector is in line with our above expectations regarding the effect of repression;

moderating most and radicalizing a minority of protestors.

Highly conventional forms of action, such as lobbying and judicial action are not included in the above figures because such forms only rarely reach the newspaper columns. For the NSMs we have, however, an additional indicator that taps the extent to which such actions are undertaken. This is strength of formal, professionalized movement organizations (SMOs). In Table 3, the total

Table 3
Membership of New Social Movement Organisations (per Million Inhabitants)

Level	Netherlands	Germany	France	Switzerland
Ecological Movement	85,000	34,000	17,000	78,000
Solidarity Movement	18,000	2,000	2,000	18,000
Peace Movement	3,000	1,000	1,000	3,000
Total	106,000	37,000	19,000	100,000

SMO membership per million inhabitants is presented for the three most important NSMs.[12]

The international differences here are quite remarkable and fully in line with what we expected. In the two consensual democracies with integrative strategies, SMOs of NSMs turn out to be much larger than in the two exclusive countries. In both the Netherlands and Switzerland, SMOs receive considerable state subsidies and have a whole range of channels of access available to them. By contrast, in Germany and even more

so in France, SMOs have only limited access to the decision-making process, which makes them less attractive for possible members. Moreover, facilitation by the state is much less important in those countries. The differences among the four countries can also be seen when we consider the national branches of international SMOs only. Thus, for instance, the national chapters of Amnesty International and the World Wildlife Fund have, even in absolute terms, a larger membership in the Netherlands and in Switzerland than in Germany and France, although the number of inhabitants of the latter two countries is much higher. Equally remarkable are the differences between the three movements. The same pattern emerges in all four countries, with the ecology movement having by far the strongest organizational infrastructure, the solidarity movement being already a lot less organized and, finally, the peace movement being quite weak as far as its formalized organizations are concerned.

With regard to the system level at which mobilization is typically oriented, our hypothesis is simple. We maintain that mobilization is predominantly oriented at the national level in centralized states, while being above all oriented at the regional or local level in decentralized states. Table 4 largely confirms this hypothesis.

In the two federalist countries—Germany and Switzerland—mobilization is much more decentralized than in the two centralized ones—the Netherlands and France. The Swiss NSMs in particular are by far the most locally-oriented ones—43.5% of their events are locally oriented—whereas the German NSMs are about as locally

Table 4
System Level Towards Which Protest Events are Oriented (in Percentages)

Level	Netherlands	Germany	France	Switzerland
New Social Movements				
1. International	25.9	12.8	8.7	22.8
2. National	51.7	38.8	66.6	29.8
3. Regional	3.7	22.1	17.6	3.8
4. Local	18.7	25.3	7.2	43.5
Total	100.0	100.0	100.0	100.0
n	(870)	(1789)	(809)	(811)
Other Movements				
1. International	16.4	16.5	4.1	19.4
2. National	56.0	40.2	74.7	15.1
3. Regional	5.5	11.8	10.1	33.7
4. Local	21.9	31.4	11.1	31.8
Total	100.0	100.0	100.0	100.0
n	(439)	(532)	(1422)	(510)

oriented (25.3% of their events) as they are oriented toward the regional level (22.1%). The very limited regional orientation of the Swiss NSMs (3.8% of their events) is striking compared to the remarkably strong regional focus of the other Swiss movements (33.7%). Given the great weight of the regional, (cantonal) level in Swiss politics, the absence of a regional orientation of the Swiss NSMs is all the more astonishing. The concentration of the events of the French NSMs, as well as of the other French movements, on the national level corresponds to the far-reaching centralization of the French state. What also distinguishes the French movements from those in the other three countries is their lack of international orientation.

Summarizing, we conclude that the French pattern of mobilization is the most centralized, the least formally organized—and the most radical. As a result of their overall radicalism and lack of formal organization, the French movements also mobilize a comparatively small number of people in moderate forms. Thus, the French pattern of social movement mobilization mirrors the situation of "full exclusion" movements have to face in the same country. The Swiss pattern, by contrast, is the most decentralized and the most moderate one, mobilizing the comparatively largest number of people. Moreover, formalized SMOs operating through conventional channels are very strong in Switzerland, reflecting the characteristics of "full procedural integration" prevailing in this case. The Dutch and German patterns, finally, correspond to the contradictory situations the social movements are confronted with in these countries. Integrative strategies coupled with a strong state result in a centralized, but otherwise hybrid mobilization pattern in the Dutch case. This pattern combines strong formalized, fully integrated SMOs mobilizing comparatively large numbers of people in rather conventional forms with a moderate, non-violent radicalism of those protesting in the streets. "Formalistic inclusion" in the German case, finally, results in an equally hybrid, but nevertheless distinct pattern that combines a largely decentralized mobilization of the majority of protesters by relatively moderate, but little formally organized means with a far-reaching radicalization of a small violent minority.

The Configuration of Power in the Party System

We shall now turn to the third broad set of properties of the POS: the configuration of power. We shall here focus on the configuration of power in the party system. A more complete treatment should also take into account the corresponding configuration in the system of interest-intermediation, especially that in the union system. Moreover, the opportunities for a specific movement or set of movements (like the NSMs) will also depend on the composition of the social movement sector (SMS) at large. Compared to the configuration of power in the party system, these factors are in our opinion, however, of only secondary importance for the mobilization of NSMs, which is the main reason why we do not treat them systematically here.

The configuration of power in the party system refers to the distribution of power among the various parties as well as to the relations which exist between these parties. As is indicated in Figure 1, the configuration of power in a given political system can be thought of as an element of the POS that intervenes between the formal institutional structure and the system's general strategic legacy on one hand, and the country-specific mix of strategies applied to challengers on the other. Itself constrained by the general systemic context (such as the electoral system), the configuration of power in turn sets more specific limits to the strategies available to the authorities with regard to given challengers.[13] It modifies the openness of access channels and the system's capacity to act, and it modulates the general strategic legacy.

Not all the established parties have been of equal significance for the mobilization of NSMs in Western Europe. The supporters of NSMs typically belong to the electoral potential of the left (see Müller-Rommel, 1984, 1989; Kriesi & van Praag Jr., 1987). Therefore, we have to pay particular attention to the *configuration of power on the left*. As has been indicated in more detail elsewhere (Kriesi, 1991), two aspects of this configuration are of particular importance in the present context: whether or not the left is divided between a major Communist current and a Social Democratic/Socialist one, and whether or not the left participates in government.

Following Brand (1985: 322), we propose that under conditions of a *split left*, there will be relatively little action space for the NSMs in general, and that support for their mobilization by the Social Democrats will be strongly conditioned by their struggle for the hegemony on the left. By contrast, in a setting where the left has *not been divided* and where the class conflict has been pacified by the time of the emergence of the NSMs, there will be more action space for the NSMs and the Social Democrats can be expected to be much more likely to support the mobilization of these new challengers. To what extent they will be prepared to do so depends, however, on a second set of factors.[14]

With regard to this second set, we expect the Social Democrats to profit, if they are *in the opposition*, from the challenges that NSMs direct at the government. These challenges weaken their major opponents in the next elections. Moreover, since the supporters of NSMs also form part of the electoral potential of the left, the Social Democrats will appeal to them in the frame-work of a general strategy designed to build as broad an electoral coalition as possible. Being in the opposition, they will therefore tend to facilitate the mobilization of NSMs. On the other hand, being in the opposition, they have of course no possibility to make any material concessions to the NSMs. If *in government*, the Social Democrats will be much less amenable to the mobilization of NSMs, even if they may be willing to make limited concessions to some of them. The details of the strategy chosen by a Social Democratic governing party depend on its position in the government. If the Social Democrats govern alone, then they will be more able to make concessions than if they depend on a coalition partner. If they are only a minority partner in coalition governments, then they may not be able to make any concessions at all.

These considerations imply decisive changes in the POS of NSMs, when the left becomes part of the government, and when it resigns from government. If the left takes power, the necessity for mobilization decreases for NSMs, because of anticipated chances of reform in their favor. At the same time, their mobilization is no longer facilitated by their most powerful ally. The net result predicted is a clear cut decrease in the mobilization of NSMs, but not necessarily for other movements that are not dependent on the support of the left. Conversely, if the left resigns from government, the necessity for mobilization increases for NSMs, because the chances of reform in their fa-

vor become much more limited. Moreover, their mobilization is now facilitated by their most powerful ally. The net result to be expected in this case is a clear-cut increase in the mobilization of NSMs, but not necessarily of other movements that are not dependent on the support of the left.[15] The impact of these changes in the POS of NSMs may not exactly coincide with the change in government. We have to allow for some measure of anticipation or delay. For example, the deterioration of a government coalition where the left participates may already improve the POS of NSMs before the effective collapse of the coalition. Similarly, prolonged coalition formation and unstable prospects of a newly-formed center-right coalition may delay the mobilization of the left against the new government.

The general outline of the configuration of power on the left is given by the two crucial dimensions discussed so far—split/unified left, left in/out of government. It is also, finally, modified by the extent to which *new forces on the left* (the New Left, and Green parties in particular) have constituted themselves as new actors within the party system, and by the extent to which the traditional major parties on the left—Communists and Social Democrats—have been open with regard to these new forces.

We should briefly like to discuss the strategies chosen by the Social Democrats with regard to NSMs in the four selected countries in the light of these general theoretical expectations. Figure 3 indicates the situation of the Social Democrats in the four countries in the course of the last twenty years.

Let us first take a look at the French Social Democrats. Among the four countries selected, these are the only ones who have been faced by a major Communist party. In the early 1970s, the Communists were definitively the dominant force on the left. It was at that time that President Pom-

Figure 3
***Situation of the Social Democratic parties in the
countries under study.***

		Left divided into major Communist/Social Democratic parties	
		No	Yes
Social Democrats in government	Yes	Germany (1970s), Netherlands (until 1977, 1981/82), Switzerland	France (1980s)
	No	Germany (1980s), Netherlands (1980s)	France (1970s)

pidou predicted that, as a result of the bipolar dynamics of the presidential system, only two political forces would survive in French politics—the Gaullists and the Communists. He has, of course, been wrong. By the early 1980s, the Socialist Party (PS) has become the dominant force on the left.[16] To gain predominance on the left, the PS has opened itself to various leftist militants since the early 1970s. It has attracted important groups of militants from the CFDT, the PSU, left wing Catholics, and also from the NSMs. At that time, the PS appeared to be the best of all possible choices for NSM-supporters and activists (Ladrech, 1989). But, for the PS, the integration of the concerns of the NSMs remained superficial. It constituted a tactical choice rather than a fundamental reorientation.

As the renewed party rapidly gained success, it became increasingly less accessible to outside forces such as the NSMs (Lewis & Sferza, 1987). In the course of the late 1970s, the party's strategy has become less facilitative, although it has remained generally favorable to the NSMs. Not soon after the PS came to power in 1981, its strategy has changed again, in line with what we would have expected. The party abandoned the concerns of NSMs which would have imperiled its short-term management of the economy. Thus, it completely gave up its—admittedly always quite limited—anti-nuclear position (von Oppeln, 1989). Depending on the issues raised by NSMs, the PS in power has, at worst, followed a fully exclusive strategy, at best one of cooptation by material concessions and procedural integration. The only exception from this general pattern is the anti-racist movement, which received strong support from the socialists, even when they were in government.

The German Social Democratic party (SPD) has traversed a trajectory exactly opposite to that of the French PS. All through the 1970s and up to 1982, the SPD was the dominant partner in a coalition with the FDP. During this period, it followed a strategy which comes close to full exclusion—close to the one of the French socialists in power. To understand why, we should, first, note that the SPD had to govern in coalition with the FDP, which imposed a constraint on the amount of concessions they could have made to the NSMs. Second, the generally repressive legacy prevented the governing SPD from taking a more integrative stance toward the NSMs. Third, the terrorist at-

tacks during the 1970s, while being themselves in part a result of the generally repressive mood, reinforced the tendency of the governing SPD to resort to repression once again. Finally, although there was no Communist competition in Germany, the SPD nevertheless was under pressure from the strong union movement to stick to the traditional goals of the labor movement. However, contrary to the PS, the leadership of the SPD was not able to centralize debate on the new issues, or to keep internal discussions under control. This greater openness of the SPD can be attributed to a number of factors (von Oppeln, 1989): the federal structure of the German political system; the relatively strong position of the party's youth organization (Juso's); the challenge by a vigorous Green party since 1979; and the programmatic disorientation of the SPD in the final stages of the left-liberal coalition. When the coalition finally broke down in 1982 and the SPD had to join the ranks of the opposition, these factors resulted in a much more facilitative strategy with regard to the new challengers.

In line with the integrative strategy of the Dutch political system, the Dutch Social Democrats (PvdA) have been open to NSMs since the early 1970s. Under the impact of the depillarization of the Dutch political system and significant competition from New Left parties in the late 1960s and early 1970s, the PvdA had radicalized and attracted many New Left militants, who eventually gained control over the party (Kriesi, 1989b). Being the dominant government party from 1973 to 1977 tempered its support for NSM mobilization provisionally. But after its change into the opposition in 1977, the PvdA came even closer to the NSMs than it had already been. It joined the antinuclear power camp in 1979—after the Haltrisburg accident (Cramer, 1989: 66)—and, most importantly, it embraced the goals of the peace movement (Kriesi, 1989b). Except for its brief spell in government in 1981-82, one may describe the strategy of the PvdA with respect to NSMs during the first half of the 1980s as one of strong facilitation. This situation changed radically, however, after 1985. In this year, the PvdA's liaison with the peace movement finally proved to be a failure, when the government decided to deploy cruise missiles after all. When this decision did not lead to the hoped for electoral gains for the PvdA in the 1986 elections, the Social Democrats' close link to the NSMs was almost completely severed. This was the result of a new party strategy (finally successful in 1989) designed to make the PvdA acceptable to the Christian Democrats as a government partner once more. This example shows that there may be conditions under which even a Social Democratic party in opposition may refrain from supporting the NSMs.

The Swiss Social Democrats (SP/PS), finally, have had an ambiguous position with regard to NSMs. Having been part of the grand-coalition that has governed Switzerland since 1959, they shared the formal responsibility for the government's policies against which the NSMs mobilize. Having always been in a clear minority position within the governing coalition, they have at the same time been opposed to the government on specific issues, including several issues of concern to NSMs. The ambiguity of the party's position is reflected by its internal division into a party left and a party right. As a result of the most fragmented character of the Swiss party system, the specific configuration of power within the party has varied from one canton to the other.

Given the situations described, we first maintain that the NSMs have generally played a less important role in France than in the other three countries. The split in the left in France, as well as the absence of a pacification of class and other traditional conflicts,[17] are expected to have limited the action space of NSMs to a greater extent than elsewhere. The results presented in Table 5 confirm this hypothesis.

Table 5
The Relative Level Mobilisation of NSMs and Other Movements in the Four Countries

Country	Percentage of Events Caused by NSMs	Percentage of Participants Mobilised by NSMs
The Netherlands	66.1 (n = 1331)	72.9
Germany	76.9 (n = 2336)	81.4
France	36.1 (n = 2241)	81.4
Switzerland (without direct dem.)	63.7 (n = 1215)	47.7

The percentage of protest events caused by NSMs is considerably lower in France (36.1%) than elsewhere. Measured by the share of protest events, the preponderance of NSMs turns out to be particularly impressive in Germany (76.9%), but they dominate also in the two smaller countries where they cause around two-thirds of the events. Except for Switzerland, we get largely similar results if we measure the relative importance of the NSMs by the share of participants they have mobilized in each country. In the case of Switzerland, the share of participants (47.7%), turns out to be considerably smaller than the share of the number of events (63.7%). This means that, on the average, the events caused by Swiss NSMs are clearly less massive than those caused by other Swiss movements and that, in relative terms, they are also less massive than those generated by the NSMs in the other countries. Among the other Swiss movements, the regional movement of the Jura, in particular, has been able to mobilize large numbers of people over an extended period of time—much larger numbers than any of the NSMs of the country. Moreover, the fact that events associated with Swiss NSMs turn out to be less massive than those of other countries is clearly linked to their predominantly local orientation. Local events are typically smaller than events targeted at higher system levels in all the countries.

Second, following the above considerations about the effect of the Social Democrats' acceding to or resigning from government, we expect a clear decline in France in the level of mobilization of NSMs since 1981, the moment the left came to power. The mobilization of the labor movement is also likely to have declined, but not the mobilization of the other movements. Conversely, for Germany we expect an increase in the level of mobilization of NSMs, starting in the early 1980s. The left had lost power in 1982, but the coalition had already started to get into difficulties before that date, and competition from the Greens had set in since 1979. No corresponding increase is expected for the other movements—with the possible exception of the labor movement. In the Netherlands, the mobilization of NSMs, but not necessarily that of other movements, should have started to increase in 1978. For Switzerland, predictions are more difficult, since there has never been an explicit change in government as in the other countries. Alternatively, one might argue that the takeover of the Social Democratic party organization by its left wing in some cantons during the late 1970s may have had a clear mobilization effect on the NSMs in the regions concerned.

Figure 4 allows for a test of these expectations. It contains four diagrams, one for each country. In each diagram, the evolution of the number of events caused by NSMs and the one caused by all the other movements are shown.[18] Let us first look at the two large countries. The contrasting evolution of the number of NSM events in the two countries starting in the early 1980s is striking: whereas Germany experiences a surge of NSM activity after 1980, there is a decline of their mobilization in France. This contrast corresponds to our hypothesis about the impact of the loss of power of the left in Germany, and of its access to power in France. The level of mobilization of the other movements has hardly at all been affected by this change in the configuration of power, which also corresponds to our expectations. Here however, the aggregation of all other movements obscures important differences. Whereas left-wing mobilization follows the same declining pattern as the NSMs, mobilization from the right increases after the coming to power of the socialists.

Figure 4

Evolution of the number of events caused by NSMs and by other movements in the four countries between 1975 and 1989.

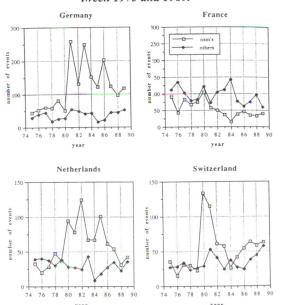

Turning to the two smaller countries, the case of the Netherlands confirms the general hypothesis once again. After the Social Democrats lost power, the level of mobilization of NSMs started to increase and reached impressive peaks in the early 1980s. The reaction to the change in power has not been as rapid as in France or Germany, but the general pattern conforms to what we have expected. Also as predicted, after 1985 the Dutch NSMs experience a relatively strong decline that coincides with the changes in the strategy of the Social Democrats. As in France and Germany, the other movements have once more not been affected by such changes in the configuration of power. In the Swiss case, we also find a substantial increase in the mobilization of NSMs at the beginning of the 1980s. This increase has, however, been almost exclusively a result of the mobilization of the urban autonomous movement at Zurich. This lends some support to our hypothesis that the change in power within the regional and local Social Democratic party may have been conducive to the enormous increase in the overall level of mobilization. Concerning the other Swiss movements, they have again hardly been affected by such changes in the configuration of power on the local level.

To conclude this section, we should draw the reader's attention to the fact that we have not offered any hypotheses about the course of the events once the mobilization of NSMs has reacted to a change in the configuration of power. The basic idea is that the initial change in the level of mobilization caused by a basic change in the configuration of power will establish a specific interaction context which will follow its own auto-dynamic course. Karstedt-Henke (1980), Tarrow (1989a, 1989b) and Koopmans (1990b) have presented some theoretical arguments about how such interaction contexts may develop. Finally, the argument presented has not taken into account differences between various NSMs with regard to their dependence on POS either. More detailed analyses show that not all NSMs react to the same extent to a change in the configuration of power (Duyvendak, 1990b; Giugni & Kriesi, 1990).

Conclusion

In this paper we have tried to elaborate the notion that "politics matter," even in the field of new social movements. In stressing the importance of conventional politics for movement politics, we have implicitly taken issue with the mainstream of NSM analyses in Western Europe, for which aspects of social and cultural change are central to the understanding of the evolution of NSM mobilization. In our view, social and cultural change only become relevant for the mobilization of social movements to the extent that they are mediated by politics. In focusing on politics we do not deny the relevance of other factors for the explanation of the origins and the development of social movements in general, and of NSMs in particular. However, we maintain that the overt collective action that constitutes the organized, sustained, self-conscious challenge to existing authorities is best understood if it is related to political institutions, and to what happens in arenas of conventional party and interest group politics. We interpret the general thrust of our results as a confirmation of this basic point.

The invisible side of social movements, the activity which does not become public and is not reported in the newspapers, is probably less related to the factors of POS. To stress the overt challenge of social movements is not to deny that movements have a less visible side as well. Since it does not treat the latent side of social movements at all, the theory presented here obviously is only a partial one. However, in our view, the crucial element of a social movement is its overt challenge to authorities—it is the series of action campaigns, constituted in interaction with the authorities, that defines a social movement in Tilly's (1984) terms.

As indicated, the argument presented in this paper presumes that the most relevant level of the POS is the national one. The other levels have entered into our argument only in a subsidiary way. This raises, finally, the question as to whether the theoretical argument is not only partial, but also one that is no longer pertinent for the explanation of the evolution of contemporary movements mobilizing in a world that increasingly becomes determined by international politics. The international POS certainly is becoming more relevant for movement politics as well. Today, changes in the international POS may have a structural impact on the level of the national POS. Thus, the breakdown of the formerly communist states in Eastern Europe and the end of the divide between East and West introduce fundamental changes in the POS of NSMs in the countries with a traditionally divided left. The end of the divide between East and West implies, in the not too long run, the end of the divided left in these countries. In this case, it is still the national POS which ultimately determines the mobilization of NSMs, although a national POS of an entirely different make-up. The relevance of the national POS may, however, decline in an even more fundamental way, if the

nation-state loses its prominence in conventional politics in a unified and/or regionalized Europe. There certainly are strong tendencies towards the decline of the nation-state, but we believe that they should not be exaggerated at this point. They do not yet challenge the crucial importance of the national-level POS for the mobilization of NSMs.

Notes

1. We adopt here the simple distinction between "members" and "challengers" as it has been made by Tilly (1978). While it is not always possible to separate members from challengers neatly, we stick to this distinction to simplify the exposition. We shall frequently refer to the "members" in terms of "authorities," that is, the two terms are used interchangeably.

2. We are aware of the fact that both types of strategy—those of the authorities and those of the challengers—are to some extent mutually independent. This interdependence does, however, not enter into the present discussion because the focus is on those aspects of the political context that have to be taken as given by the challenging actors. The mutually interdependent aspects of the political context belong to what we propose to call the "interaction context" of a specific challenge. The interaction context follows its own logic which will not be treated here.

3. For a more detailed account of these concepts and their implications, see Kriesi (1991).

4. For more details about this methodology and the problems it involves we refer the reader to the presentation of Tarrow (1989: 27-31, 349-66) and to the summary discussion of Olzak (1989a).

5. We used *Le Monde* for France, *Frankfurter Rundschau* for Germany, *NRC* for the Netherlands, and the *NZZ* for Switzerland. To limit the amount of work, we restricted ourselves to one issue per week. We chose the Monday edition, because a large number of protest events take place over the weekends, which means that we get at a larger number of events than if we had picked a day at random.

6. These characteristics include the location of the event in time and space, its form and thematic focus, the number of participants (if possible as reported by the organizers of the event), the organizations participating, the reactions of the authorities and the possible location of the event within larger action campaigns of the movements concerned.

7. As other Southern European countries, France has a long legacy of repression of the labor movement (Golden, 1986; Gallie, 1983).

8. We did not enter here into the discussion of the different forms of success. For a more detailed discussion of this point, see Gamson (1975: 28ff.), Kitschelt (1986: 66f.) and Kriesi (1991).

9. There are direct-democratic procedures *(Volksbege-hren)* in one member state of the Federal Republic—Bavaria—and on the community level in Baden-Württemberg.

10. In case the newspaper reports contained more than one estimate of the number of participants, we have chosen the highest figure reported, which is of course usually the version of the organizers.

11. The number of events with missing data about participants were not evenly distributed among our four countries: the percentage of missing data range from 4% for Germany, though 16% for the Netherlands and 20% for France to 28% for Switzerland. A comparable event was defined as an event of the same form (e.g., demonstration) in the same country (e.g., a demonstration in France).

12. The figures have been computed by adding the 1989 (or the year for which figures were available closest to that year) membership figures of all large formalized organizations for each movement, as reported by the organizations themselves. The figures have been rounded to whole thousands.

13. The configuration of power is, of course, also a function of the cleavage structure of a given society (see Lipset & Rokkan, 1967). We acknowledge this determinant factor, but we want to restrict our attention here to the interrelationships among the elements of the political system.

14. The structure of the union system also plays a role in this context. Thus, a strong union system may exert pressure on the Social Democrats to give priority to the traditional labor concerns, even if they do not face a serious trade-off in electoral terms.

15. The labor movement may be an exception, because it may also have a greater incentive to mobilize under these circumstances.

16. On the right, the Gaullists soon had to contend with a second major conservative force (UDF), not to talk about the rise of the Front National.

17. Apart from class conflict, other "traditional" conflicts still play an important role in French politics. In the whole period under study, regional conflicts played an important role in the social movement sector (responsible for 17.9% of all unconventional events), and in the 1980s conflicts around the position of religious education mobilized hundreds of thousands (responsible for 9.3% of all events and 17.5% of all participants).

18. Among the other movements, the labor movement is included. Since we have not taken strikes into account in our analysis, the number of events caused by the labor movement is relatively small in all the countries—it varies between 3.6% for Switzerland and 9.8% for France. In order to keep the presentation in Figure 5 as simple as possible, we have not shown the evolution of the labor movements separately. ✦

6

Structural Opportunity and Perceived Opportunity in Social-Movement Theory: The Iranian Revolution of 1979

Charles Kurzman

"*When a people which has put up with an oppressive rule over a long period without protest suddenly finds the government relaxing its pressure, it takes up arms against it.*"
Tocqueville 1955:176

Alexis de Tocqueville's famous dictum is based on two observations about the French Revolution. On one hand, the government undercut and alienated its bases of support through ill-conceived efforts at reform. On the other hand, the populace perceived a lessening of "pressure" and rose up to take advantage. The strength of Tocqueville's analysis lies in its combination of objective and subjective factors. It is not only the structural weakness of the state that precipitates revolution in Tocqueville's model, or the subjective sentiments of collective efficacy, but the combination of the two.[1]

Social-movement theory has recently revived this combined approach after years of veering between structuralist and subjectivist extremes (Foran 1993b; Klandermans, Kriesi, and Tarrow 1988; Morris and Mueller 1992). McAdam's (1982) oft-cited book, *Political Process and the Development of Black Insurgency,* may be the model for contemporary social-movement theorizing on structure and consciousness. McAdam argues that the "structure of political opportunities" is one of two major determinants of political

protest, the other being organizational strength: "The opportunities for a challenger to engage in successful collective action . . . vary greatly over time. And it is these variations that are held to be related to the ebb and flow of movement activity" (pp. 40-41). The "crucial point," he states, is that the political system can be more open or less open to challenge at different times (p. 41). But structural conditions, McAdam argues, do not automatically translate into protest: They are mediated by "cognitive liberation," an oppressed people's ability to break out of pessimistic and quiescent patterns of thought and begin to do something about their situation (pp. 48-51).

McAdam's (1982) analysis shows the tight fit between subjective perceptions and the structure of opportunities. The optimism of African Americans in the 1930s (pp. 108-10) and early 1960s (pp. 161-63) reflected structural shifts in Federal policies (pp. 83-86, 156-60). Conversely, in the late 1960s, perceptions of diminishing opportunities reflected the actual diminishing of opportunities (p. 202). State structure and subjective perceptions are treated as closely correlated.

Structural opportunities generally coincide with perceived opportunities in other recent studies in the Tocquevillean tradition. Tarrow (1994), for instance, recognizes the interplay between the macro- and micro-levels of analysis. He notes that "early risers"protest groups at the beginning stages of a cycle of widespread protest activitymay make opportunities visible that had not been evident, and their actions may change the structure of opportunities (pp. 96-97). However, over most of the protest cycle, perceptions closely follow the opening and closing of objective opportunities (pp. 85-96, 99). "The main argument of this study," Tarrow emphasizes, "is that people join in social movements in response to political opportunities" (p. 17).

Goldstone (1991a, 1991b) also combines aspects of the state's structure (state breakdown) and subjective factors (ideology and cultural frameworks) in his analysis of the early modern revolutions of the seventeenth and eighteenth centuries. State breakdown, the result of nonsubjective causes like "material and social change" (Goldstone 1991a: 408), is accompanied during revolutions by subjective perceptions of breakdown, namely "widespread loss of confidence in, or allegiance to, the state" (Goldstone 1991b:10).

"Structural Opportunity and Perceived Opportunity in Social-Movement Theory: The Iranian Revolution of 1979." *American Sociological Review* 61: 153-170. Copyright © 1996 by the American Sociological Association. Reprinted with permission.

Subjective perceptions do not play an independent role until after the state has broken down.

These Tocquevillean analyses recognize that structural opportunities and perceived opportunities may not always match. Cognitive liberation is a distinct variable that is not reducible to political opportunity structure, according to McAdam; "early risers" may protest despite unfavorable structural conditions in Tarrow's model; not all state crises lead to revolution, Goldstone notes. The Tocquevillean tradition, however, has focused on cases in which the opportunity structure and perceptions agree, and has not examined mismatches.

Protestors' Definitions of Opportunity

The correlation between subjective perceptions and structural conditions may not hold true for some cases. Two possible mismatches occur when (1) people fail to perceive opportunities, or (2) they perceive opportunities where none exists. The first possibility has been explored in many works, primarily in the Marxist tradition, which blame false consciousness and ideological hegemony for masking opportunities or deflecting attention from them.

The second mismatch has been raised in the critical-mass approach to collective action, which argues that protestors define opportunities primarily with reference to patterns of oppositional activity (Goldstone 1994; Granovetter 1978; Kuran 1989; Marwell and Oliver 1993; Oberschall 1994; Schelling 1978).[2] Individuals are more likely to participate in the protest movement when they expect large numbers of people to participate.[3] The critical-mass approach implies that individuals calculate opportunities, not simply in terms of changes in the structure of the state, as Tocqueville argued, but primarily in terms of the strength of the opposition. They may feel that widespread participation in protest changes the "balance of forces"what Gramsci (1971) calls the "relation of political forces"between the state, the opposition, and other interested parties. State crisis does not precipitate revolutionary mobilization, in this view, but "an evaluation of the degree of homogeneity, self-awareness, and organization attained by the various social classes" (Gramsci 1971:181).

The collective-behavior school of analysis, with its roots in symbolic interactionism, is a further precursor to critical-mass theory. Though collective-behavior analyses are often limited to the study of crowds, the approach is analogous: The fact that others are protesting, affects potential protestors and attracts them (Blumer 1969b). While critical-mass theory has relaxed the Gramscian assumption of class actors and the collective-behavior assumption of social disorganization, and has replaced the collective-behavior focus on irrational, emotive protest behavior with an assumption of rationality, these precursors provide an alternative to the Tocquevillean approach.

Empirical studies have confirmed elements of the critical-mass approach. Klandermans (1984a) and Opp (1988a) find a correlation between the expected numerical strength of a protest movement and the likelihood of participation. Other researchers find that expectations of repression are generally uncorrelated with protest participation (Muller, Dietz, and Finkel 1991; Muller and Opp 1986; Opp 1994; Opp and Gern 1993; Opp and Ruehl 1990a).

However, critical-mass studies do not emphasize the distinction between their findings and the state-centered Tocquevillean approach. For instance, Opp and his collaborators, whose work is increasingly influential in social-movement theory, write that their research program "is not in complete disagreement with a structural framework" (Opp and Gern 1993:661). Elsewhere, Opp (1994) notes that subjective-perception data "reflect the real situation" (p. 110) and that decreases in objective repression, "we assume" (p. 127), result in corresponding shifts in perceptions. Indeed, Opp's research on repression is intended to show that opportunity structure *does* have an effect, albeit a complex one, on protest activity. On one hand, he hypothesizes that repression increases the cost of protest and thereby chills it. On the other hand, repression may increase discontent and micromobilization processes, thereby inflaming protest (Opp and Ruehl 1990a). However, instead of the expected negative effect of repression, regressions consistently show a positive effect, or at best statistical nonsignificance, even after controlling for proxies for micromobilization. Although Opp and Ruehl (1990a:541) recognize that they were unable to control for all intermediary variables, their results show that expected repression does not deter people from protesting. If repression represents the structure of opportunities (as Opp, McAdam, and others argue), this finding suggests that protestors are either unconcerned about opportunities (and by extension about whether protest succeeds) or are defining opportunities in some different way.

I explore this latter possibility through an examination of the Iranian Revolution of 1979. Protestors *were* concerned with prospects for successthey did not participate in large numbers until they felt success was at hand. However, most Iranians did not feel that the state had weakened or that structural opportunities had opened up. Indeed, I argue that the state was *not*, by several objective measures, particularly vulnerable in 1978 when widespread protest emerged. Instead, Iranians seem to have based their assessment of the opportunities for protest on the perceived strength of the opposition. In other words, Iranians believed the balance of forces shifted, not because of a changing state structure, but because of a changing opposition movement.

Unlike the Tocquevillean cases, then, structural opportunities and perceived opportunities may have been at odds. Thus, the Iranian Revolution may constitute a "deviant" case for social-movement theory, one that allows a comparison between the relative effects of structural versus subjective factors. This is a historic issue in sociological theory, and far too weighty for the imperfectly documented Iranian case. However, the case at least raises the historic issue in a new guise for social-movement theory. In addition to researching the links between the structural and subjective levels of analysis, as social-movement theory has attempted to do in recent years (for instance, Klandermans et al. 1988), the case suggests that conflicts and disjunctures between these levels are also worth examining.

Methodology

As this paper is theory-driven, not case-driven, I will not discuss the many explanations for the Iranian Revolution. However, I take as measures of state structure four elements that are often cited in the literature on Iran: (1) the undermining of the monarchy's social support by reforms, (2) international pressure on the monarchy, (3) overcentralization and paralysis of the state, and (4) the state's vacillating responses to the protest movement. I argue that none of these factors represents a structural weakness of the state.

This is not the usual picture of the Iranian Revolution. Scholars who argue that the structure of the Iranian state was conducive to revolution usually presume that Iranians must have perceived it as such. Although some scholars have interviewed expatriate Iranian elites, no scholar has researched *popular* perceptions of the state. This is perhaps understandable, given the difficulties of studying a relatively closed society like post-revolutionary Iran. And, in a way, the past is also a closed society.

I draw on seven forms of eyewitness accounts of the Iranian revolutionary movement of 1977 to 1979, three of them contemporaneous and four of them after-the-fact: (1) journalists' accounts, both Iranian and foreign; (2) opposition publicists' *i'lâmîyih*'s, or pronouncements, some of them distributed clandestinely as a form of alternative journalism; (3) Government documents, especially U.S. diplomats' records, some of them seized and published by the militant students who occupied the U.S. embassy in Tehran (*Asnâd-i Lânih-yi Jâsûsî* 1980-1991), and some of them obtained through the Freedom of Information Act and published by a private nonprofit organization in Washington, D.C. (National Security Archive 1989); (4) memoirs by Iranians and foreigners resident in Iran during the revolution; (5) oral histories of prominent Iranians, mostly expatriates opposed to the post-revolutionary regime, conducted by projects at the Foundation for Iranian Studies (1991) and Harvard University (Harvard Iranian Oral History Collection 1987); (6) interviews with Iranians, again mostly prominent expatriates, that have been excerpted in academic and journalistic studies of the revolution; and (7) supplementary interviews with nonexpatriate and nonprominent Iranians I conducted in Istanbul, Turkey (see the Appendix). Taken together, these sources corroborate one another. The preponderance of evidence suggests that Iranians did not perceive the Pahlavî state to be weak; indeed, they feared a crackdown right through the regime's final days. However, in early September of 1978, they began to consider the revolutionary movement to be stronger than the state.

Because I do not proceed chronologically, a brief summary of the events leading to the fall of the Iranian monarchy in February 1979 is in order. The revolutionary movement is generally dated from mid-1977. when liberal oppositionists began to speak out publicly for reforms in the Iranian monarchy. Late in 1977, some of Iran's Islamic leaders called for the removal of Shâh Muhammad Rizâ Pahlavî, and their followers embarked on a series of small demonstrations that the regime suppressed with force. Casualties at each incident generated a cycle of mourning demonstrations throughout the first half of 1978. The bulk of Iran's population, however, did not participate in these events. The revolutionary movement attracted a large following, only in September 1978, following a suspicious theater fire and a massacre of peaceful demonstrators; both events persuaded many Iranians that the Pahlavî regime must fall. Beginning in September 1978, strikes began to shake the country and built up to a virtual general strike that lasted until the revolution's success in February 1979. By the end of 1978, the shah was actively seeking a reformist prime minister. When he finally found an oppositionist willing to take the position and left for a "vacation" in mid-January, the country had become ungovernable. Exiled religious leader Imâm Rûhullah Khumeinî returned to Iran to great acclaim at the end of January and named his own prime minister. Two weeks later, a mutiny in one of the air force barracks in Tehran sparked an unplanned citywide uprising. Within 40 hours, the military declared its "neutrality" and allowed the revolutionaries to take power.

The Structure of Political Opportunity

Scholars of the Iranian Revolution have generally characterized the Pahlavî regime as highly susceptible to collapse. Four structural weaknesses are often cited as constituting a structure of political opportunities conducive to revolution.

Monarchy's Social Support Undermined by Reforms

One alleged weakness of the state is the undermining of the state's social support, particularly by the elite, as a result of the monarchy's vigorous efforts at reform. This argument takes different forms depending on the affected group. For instance, the shah's land reforms of the 1960s threw the landed oligarchy into the opposition. The shah's industrialization policies and punitive price-control measures threw the traditional *bazaari* sector into the opposition. Harsh labor repression threw workers into the opposition. The overheated oil-boom economy led to the inflation of urban housing prices, throwing poor migrants into the opposition. Political repression threw intellectuals and the middle classes into the opposition. Secularizing reforms threw religious leaders into the opposition. In sum, the state "destroyed its traditional class base while failing to generate a new class base of support" (Moshiri 1991:121; also see Bashiriyeh 1984:94-95; Foran 1993a:391; McDaniel 1991:103-105).

There are three problems with this argument. First, the affected groups were not entirely oppositional. Second, even as reforms created enemies for the state, they also created new allies. Third, the shah needed relatively little internal support because of the state oil revenues and international support, and this internal autonomy may have strengthened rather than weakened the state.

The most affected elite group was the Islamic clerics. State reforms took away their longstanding judicial roles, limited their educational roles, and challenged their role in welfare distribution. Clerics had the clearest reason to resent the Pahlavî state. Yet prior to the revolution, relatively few clerics favored Khumeini's revolutionary proposals. During the revolutionary movement, senior clerics tried to dissuade protestors from confronting the state, and one cleric even met secretly with government representatives to seek a compromise (Kurzman 1994).

Similarly, leading oppositionist *bazaaris* and intellectuals opposed the revolutionary tide; they favored reforming the monarchy, not ousting it. Workers' demands centered on workplace gains and only switched to revolutionary demands in the fall of 1978, months after the revolutionary movement began (Bayat 1987:86-87). Urban migrants who suffered the most from the state's policies did not participate in large numbers in the revolutionary movement (Kazemi 1980:8895; Bauer 1983:157-60). Indeed, strikers at one factory blamed recent urban migrants for being too apolitical (Parsa 1989:5). In sum, the extent to which the shah's reform policies undermined his popular support should not be exaggerated.

Meanwhile, the state created new classes dependent on state patronage and therefore inclined to support the shah. The most important of these was the military, which expanded greatly during the shah's decades in power. The loyalty of the military remained largely unshaken to the end (see below). Another class created by state fiat was the industrial bourgeoisie, which emerged through credit subsidies (Salehi-Isfahani 1989) and royal patronage (Graham 1980:48). This class allegedly abandoned the shah by transferring its assets overseas and then emigrating at the first hint of trouble.

Certainly rumors to this effect were circulating during the fall of 1978 (Naraghi 1994:97). But evidence suggests that some of the bourgeoisie stayed and actively supported the shah to the end. Groups of industrialists met in November 1978 and January 1979 to determine common solutions to strikes and money shortages; representatives worked with the prime minister on these matters (Âhanchian 1982:370-85; National Security Archive 1989: Document 21-27). Thus, the shah was not totally abandoned by his allies.

In any case, the shah's access to oil revenues and foreign support made internal support less important than it was for most regimes. On theoretical grounds, it is difficult to say whether this is a sign of state weakness or strength. While reliance on foreign powers may create an image of a puppet regime, state autonomy is often identified as a strength, as the state can impose collective solutions on recalcitrant social groups (Migdal 1988). If the basis for autonomy breaks down, of course, the state is left without a reed to lean on. However, the shah retained international support during the revolutionary movement.

International Pressure on the Monarchy

The second alleged weakness of the state is the widespread impression that international constraints stayed the monarchy's hand and prevented the crackdown that would have crushed the protest movement. Many academic analyses have applied Skocpol's (1979) structural model to the Iranian Revolution, arguing that international pressures weakened the state and made it vulnerable to revolution (Ashraf and Banuazizi 1985:1920; Liu 1988:202-203; Milani 1988:30-31).[4] However, none of these analysts presents evidence of such pressure.

Jimmy Carter campaigned for President in 1976 on a platform that included the consideration of human rights in U.S. foreign policy, and he threatened to weaken U.S. support for the shah. But this threat never materialized. When the shah visited Washington in November 1977, Carter's meetings with him barely touched the subject of human rights (Carter 1978:2028-29, 2033). A month later, Carter made his famous New Year's toast to the shah in Tehran: "Iran, because of the great leadership of the Shah, is an island of stability in one of the more troubled areas of the world. This is a great tribute to you, Your Majesty, and to your leadership and to the respect and the ad-

miration and love which your people give to you" (*Weekly Compilation of Presidential Documents*, January 2, 1978, p. 1975).

As the revolutionary movement grew during 1978, the shah received no international complaints about his handling of Iranian protests, even when his troops shot hundreds, perhaps thousands, of unarmed demonstrators in Tehran on September 8. In fact, Carter telephoned the shah from Camp David two days later to express his continuing support (Carter 1979:1515).[5] When the shah installed a military government on November 6, U.S. officials voiced their full approval (*New York Times*, November 7, 1978, p. 14). National Security Advisor Zbigniew Brzezinski had telephoned the shah several days earlier to encourage him to be firm (Brzezinski 1983:364-65; Carter 1982:439; Pahlavi 1980:165). Riot-control equipment, blocked for months on human-rights grounds, was then shipped to Iran (*Newsweek*, November 20, 1978, p. 43). As late as December 28, 1978, the U.S. Secretary of State cabled to his ambassador in Tehran the firm statement "that U.S. support is steady and that it is essential, repeat essential, to terminate the continuing uncertainty" (National Security Archive 1989: Document 1972).

Throughout the fall of 1978, the shah met regularly with the U.S. ambassador, William Sullivan. The shah's final autobiography notes that "the only word I ever received from Mr. Sullivan was reiteration of Washington's complete support for my rule" (Pahlavi 1980: 161). In fact, according to Sullivan (1981), "the Shah himself in due course told me he was somewhat embarrassed by the constant reiteration of our public support, saying it made him look like a puppet" (p. 204).

The shah was apparently unaware of divisions within the U.S. administration (Pahlavi 1980:165; Sick 1985:345). Carter's cabinet was split into hostile camps over the extent of force the shah should use, the advisability of a coup d'état, and the desirability of a nonmonarchical government in Iran in short, how to respond to the Iranian revolutionary movement. This debate was never resolved. As a result, Washington never sent detailed recommendations to Iran. Ambassador Sullivan in Tehran repeatedly told the shah that he had "no instructions" from his superiors (Pahlavi 1980:161; Sullivan 1981: 191-92).

This lack of instructions may have deepened the shah's suspicions about the United States' true intentions. The head of the French secret service insisted to the shah that the United States was secretly planning his ouster (Marenches 1988:125-26), and the shah asked visitors on several occasions whether the United States had abandoned him (Naraghi 1994:124; Pahlavi 1980:155; Parsons 1984:74; Sick 1985:53, 88; Sullivan 1981:157). Offhand public remarks by U.S. officials suggesting that the United States was considering various contingencies in Iran reached the shah and worried him, despite official denials and reassurances (Sick 1985:88, 110).

In sum, the United States continued to pledge its support, although the shah did not entirely believe it. But there is no evidence of international pressure constraining the monarchy's response to protest.

Overcentralization and Paralysis of the State

A third alleged weakness focuses on the structure of the Iranian state. According to this argument, a concerted crackdown would have worked, but the state lacked the will to carry it out. At its basest, this explanation accuses individual officeholders of treason. At its most theoretical, this analysis argues that the Iranian state was structurally susceptible to paralysis because of its overcentralization around the person of the shah. Fatemi's (1982) analysis is perhaps the most succinct: "Since the *raison d'être* of this organizational structure was mostly to protect the shah and his throne from potential threats, such as military *coups d'état* and strong political rivals" (p. 49), the state demanded loyalty to the monarch, arranged overlapping responsibilities and rivalries, and forbade lateral communication. "To operate this system the shah had effectively made himself the sole decision-making authority in every significant phase of Iran's political affairs" (p. 49). Therefore, the system depended for its operation on a fully functioning shah. In 1978, however, the shah was ill with cancer. According to this thesis, the state was thereby paralyzed in its response to the protest movement (Arjomand 1988:114ff, 189ff; Zonis 1991).

There is abundant evidence of the centralization of the state around the person of the shah. There is also evidence of the shah's illness. He was under medication and appeared at times to be depressed or listless and not his usual decisive self (Kraft 1978:134; Sick 1985:52-53. 61; Sullivan 1981:156, 195, 196, 198). But evidence of paralysis is much less convincing. To be sure, the shah repeatedly stated his unwillingness to massacre his subjects in order to save his throne (Marenches 1988:130: Parsons 1984:147; Sullivan 1981:167). "The instructions I gave were always the same: 'Do the impossible to avoid bloodshed'" (Pahlavi 1980:168).[6] One general allegedly offered to kill a hundred thousand protestors to quell the disturbances. Another supposedly proposed to bomb the holy city of Qum. The head of a neighboring country suggested the execution of 700 mullahs. The shah vetoed all these plans (Mirfakhraei 1984:443: Reeves 1986:188; Stempel 1981:280).

However, the refusal to authorize slaughter does not necessarily indicate lack of will or structural paralysis. Less extreme measures were vigorously pursued. Throughout the fall of 1978, security forces routinely broke up protests at gunpoint. They arrested virtually every prominent oppositionist in the country at least once. At one time or another they occupied virtually all key economic and governmental institutions and forced striking personnel back to work in the oil fields, power stations, airlines, customs offices, and telecommunications centers (Kurzman 1992: 194-99). Plans began to be drawn up for a possible pro-shah military coup (Copeland 1989:252, Yazdî 1984:249-99).

Moreover, the Pahlavî regime—despite its pretensions—was a Third World state and not overly efficient in the best of times: Iran's intelligence service was hardly more than a glorified police force, according to the head of the French secret service (Marenches 1988:121); Tehran had no sewage system (Graham 1980:22); and industry suffered frequent power shortages (Graham 1980:120-21). The flurry of state actions in response to the revolutionary movement hardly represents paralysis.

State Vacillation

A fourth possible weakness concerns the state's "vacillating" (Abrahamian 1982:518; Keddie 1981:255) or "inconsistent" (Arjomand 1988:115; Cottam 1980:18) responses to the protest movement. The combination of concession and repression is said to have encouraged protestors while providing them with new reasons to protest. Because of this vacillation, according to these analyses, the Iranian revolution grew from a small and sporadic movement into a massive and continuous upheaval. The implication is that a more one-sided policy—either reform or crackdownwould have been more effective in stifling protest.

Such a conclusion goes against the advice of numerous royal advisors. In ancient India, Kautilîya (1972:414) instructed kings on how to deal with revolts: "Make use of conciliation, gifts, dissension and force." In eleventh-century Persia, Nizam al-Mulk (1960, chaps. 40. 44) urged caliphs to imitate the mercy and liberality of Harun ar-Rashid, but also the deviousness and repression of Nushirwan. In sixteenth-century Italy, Machiavelli (1980, chaps. 8, 17) advised princes to gain both the fear of the people and the love of the people, combining punishment and reward, cruelty and clemency. In the twentieth century, U.S. State Department analyst W. Howard Wriggins (1969:258-63) theorized on the strategic mix between rewarding the faithful and intimidating the oppositions. On theoretical grounds, then, it is not clear whether a combined state response constitutes vacillation and vulnerability, or carrot-and-stick and co-optation.

In any case, the shah had used a similar strategy for years. The two major pre-revolutionary studies of the Iranian political system make this point repeatedly. Zonis (1971) notes that co-optation of the opposition had become routine, to the extent that the shah told one foreign visitor not to worry about youthful subversives. "We know just who those young men are and will be offering them high-level jobs as appropriate" (pp. 331-32). Bill (1972:100) describes the state's "three-pronged strategy of intimidation, bribery, and selected concessions" toward student oppositionists. Both authors view the shah's repression and his co-optive concessions as complementary parts of a single coherent system of political opportunities.

This combined approach continued through 1978 (Kurzman 1992:81-91). At several crucial junctures, the shah cracked down on protestors, but at the same time offered minor concessions and promised future reforms. In mid-May, soldiers opened fire on a demonstration in Tehran, but troops were removed from the seminary city of Qum and a ban was announced on pornographic films, clearly gestures toward religious oppositionists. In early August, the shah announced that free elections were going to be held, but soon placed the city of Isfahan under martial law. In late August, the shah placed 11 cities under martial law, but also granted various concessions,

including freedom of the press, and appointed a new prime minister thought to be more acceptable to the religious opposition. In November, the shah installed a military government that flooded Tehran with armored vehicles and cracked down on the oilfield strikes. At the same time, the shah made an apologetic televised speech and promulgated limits on the royal family's business activities.

There was a definite logic to these state responses. The government sent protestors a mixed but consistent message: Continue protesting and you'll be killed; stop protesting and you'll get reforms. The combination of crackdowns with promises of future reforms was intended to defuse the short-term situation while reaffirming the long-term commitment to liberalization. The shah stuck to the structure of political opportunities he had maintained for decades, one that was conducive to co-optive political participation and inimical to revolutionary street protests.

The Perception of Political Opportunity

Perceptions of the State's Coercive Power

Casualties increased as the protest movement progressed.[7] Moreover, the Iranian people recognized that street protests were dangerous, including the large demonstrations that were legal, well-organized, and rarely repressed.[8] For instance, marches on the religious holidays of Tâsû'â and 'Âshûrâ in December 1978 were certain to attract millions of participants, but they still inspired fear. The leading cleric in Shiraz warned on the eve of the demonstrations: "Maybe we'll be killed tomorrow. We're facing guns, rifles and tanks. Whoever is afraid shouldn't come" (Hegland 1986:683). One man in Tehran wrote out his will before heading out to march (Pîshtâzân 1981:173).

Fear of state reprisal lasted through the final hours of the Pahlavî regime, as security forces continued to shoot and arrest protestors. In December 1978, Iranians feared that hundreds of CIA operatives were being smuggled into the country to squelch the revolutionary movement (Khalîlî 1981:128). In early February of 1979, just a few days before the shah's regime fell, one newspaper columnist noted: "In Tehran, conversations are limited to this: how will the revolution, which has gone half-way, deal with the fundamental power of the government? Will it resign? Will there be a fight? And how far would fighting go?" (Âyandigân, February 6, 1979, p. 12).

But recognition of the state's coercive power did not translate into obedience. Frequently, repression led to increased militancy. In late August, after the immolation of several hundred moviegoers in Abadana tragedy many Iranians blamed on the stateprotests increased from several thousand participants to hundreds of thousands. In early September, the day after hundreds and perhaps thousands of peaceful demonstrators were gunned down in Tehran's Zhâlih Square, wildcat strikes spread across the country. In early November, within weeks of the installation of a military government, the opposition denounced the government as illegal and began planning for huge confrontations during the Shi'i holy month of Muharram.

On an individual level, acts of repression that hit close to home were a major source of revolutionary zeal. An anthropologist who spent much of the revolutionary period in a village near Shiraz reports that this response was called "*az khud guzashtih*" or "*az jân guzashtih*" (literally, "abandoning oneself" or "abandoning life"):

> People felt this emotion and gained this attitude through hearing about or participating in events in which government forces treated people with violence and injustice. . . . Villagers reported to me their horror, fury, and frustration upon hearing about such events, as well as their resolve that they would never rest until the shah and the government that did such inhuman things to their fellow Iranians no longer existed. (Hegland 1983:233-34)

Repression was such a mobilizing force that the opposition circulated a hoax audio cassette, along with other opposition cassettes, on which an indistinct voice resembling the shah's was heard giving his generals formal orders to shoot demonstrators in the streets (Sreberny-Mohammadi 1990: 358). If scare tactics of this sort were revolutionary propaganda, and not counterrevolutionary propaganda, then something was clearly amiss with the shah's carrot-and-stick strategy.

Perceptions of the Opposition's Power

What was amiss, I propose, was the Iranian people's perception of political opportunities. Iranians continued to recognize and fear the state's coercive powers. However, they felt that these powers were insignificant compared with the strength of the revolutionary movement. Confirming critical-mass hypotheses, these percep-

tions caused Iranians to become more active, not to withdraw into freerider status. Popular perceptions are difficult to identify, particularly during a period of repression and unrest. But this is no excuse for leaving popular perceptions unexamined. The bits of evidence that exist show consistently that Iranians considered the strength of the protest movement to be a decisive factor in their decisions to participate.

At the first mass demonstration of the protest movement, on September 4 in Tehran, journalists reported a sense of euphoria among the protestors: "'The shah is finished,' they cry above all" (Brière and Blanchet 1979:46). This judgment was premature, but the sentiment seems genuine. Protestors felt that revolution was not only possible, but practically inevitable:

> A year before, I heard news about demonstrations, but I didn't feel that it was something very important. That is, I thought, well, something is happening, but I didn't think that it would bring about a basic change in my country. Later, in September 1978, at the start of school, when we began classes, everything had changed. All of a sudden, the feeling arose that things weren't that way anymore. (Maryam Shamlu, from an interview in May 1983)[9]

A lawyer from Tehran recalled a large demonstration:

> I had the sense that the bourgeois had come to see what was happening, without much conviction, to eventually, one day, be able to say, "I was there," and not to be looked upon badly by certain devout neighbors. The future was up in the air, better get on board. (Saint-James 1983: 191)

On a smaller scale, it appears that Iranians preferred to participate in a particular protest only if they had assurances that others would protest as well. U.S. diplomats in Tehran noted during the strike day of October 16, 1978:

> Most shops have closed during [the] morning, however, as shopkeepers evaluated [the] local situation: no one wants to have the only open shop on the block. . . . Everyone knew of Khomeini's appeal [to strike], yet [the] vast majority came to work, they decided to stay or return based on what neighbors were doing. (National Security Archive 1989: Document 1594)

At its margins, this desire to go with the flow shaded into fear of persecution for nonparticipation. "I could not go to [the] office against the will of my employees," said the managing director of a state agency that was on strike. "Besides, anything could happen to me" (Farazmand 1989:172). The owner of a tiny shop in central Tehran expressed a similar opinion:

> He explained candidly that he had put a photograph of the Ayatollah, whom he said he respected, in his store window because he feared it would be smashed otherwise. "Most of the people want an Islamic Republic," he said wearily. "And I want anything that most of the people want." (*New York Times*, February 2, 1979, p. A9)

The fear of violence should not be overestimated, however, despite the dark suspicions of several foreign observersnotably British Ambassador Anthony Parsons (1984:81), U.S. military envoy Robert Huyser (1986:22), and U.S. diplomats (*Asnâd-i Lânih-yi Jâsûsî* 1990-1991, vol. 25, p. 50; vol. 12, part 2, pp. 16, 79-80; vol. 13, part 1, p. 48; vol. 13, part 2, p. 71). The Iranian Revolution exhibited remarkably little retribution against backsliders, especially when compared with the revolutionary violence reported in South Africa, Palestine, and the Sikh independence movement in India.

Rather, the fear of violence should probably be considered part of the overall "bandwagon effect" (Hirsch 1986:382), whereby individuals' willingness to participate in a protest is correlated with their expectations of the size and success of the protest. Other critical-mass studies are better able to delve into the details of the social-psychological mechanisms at work here, given their more accessible research sites. In the Iranian case, in which random sampling is not possible, only the broad outlines of the process can be identified.

Perhaps the best evidence of the bandwagon effect comes from the reformist oppositionists who opposed outright revolution. These liberals are more fully represented than are other social groups in the Government, journalistic, and oral-history sources available for this research. Liberals were highly sensitive to the structure of opportunitiesthey had begun to speak out publicly for reform in 1977 when the shah allowed such opposition to be voiced. In late 1977, when the shah clamped down again after his cordial meetings with Carter, liberals muted their protests. In the summer of 1978, when the shah made a few concessions and promised to hold free elections, liberals were elated and rushed to take advantage of the new freedoms (Kurzman 1992:106-109). During the fall of 1978, liberals began to sense that the opposition movement was larger than they had imagined, and "out of our hands."[10] This sense

crystallized for some on September 4, when liberal *bazaar* oppositionists chased in vain after a massive revolutionary demonstration, trying to disperse the crowd and reminding people that they were not supposed to be demonstrating.[11]

In the following months, liberals joined the revolutionary movement, not because they now favored revolution, but because they felt the revolutionary movement was too strong to oppose. In a memorandum of November 5, 1978, the U.S. embassy reported that one leading liberal "privately accused Khomeini of irresponsibility and said he 'acts like a false god.' But we have no sign he or any other oppositionist dares to attack Khomeini publicly" (National Security Archive 1989: Document 1685). In a memorandum dated December 8, 1978, a U.S. diplomat reported asking a moderate Iranian religious leader if he and other clerics would approve a constitutional settlement to the crisis and go against Khomeini. The cleric, "perhaps not wanting his followers to understand, replied in broken English, 'That would be dangerous and very difficult'" (*Asnâd-i Lânih-yi Jâsûsî* 1980-1991, vol. 26, p. 61). By the end of 1978, when the shah was casting about for a prime minister, a series of liberal oppositionists turned down the position. Several months earlier they would have considered the appointment a dream come truenow they considered it futile.[12]

Perception Versus Structure

Confident of the revolution's ultimate victory, millions of Iranians participated in mass protests against the shah in the final months of 1978. Yet, at the end of the year, the shah's military remained largely intact. The two sides faced a potentially cataclysmic confrontation. But as protestors' perception of political opportunities clashed with the state's structural position, the structure of the state gave way.

As late as early December 1978, top generals still thought they could subdue the protest movement (Kamrava 1990:39). Thus, the collapse of the military followed, rather than preceded, mass mobilization of the protest movement. Like the broad state-breakdown argument, this suggests that military breakdown may be an outcome of mobilization rather than a necessary precondition (Chorley 1973; Russell 1974).

During demonstrations, protestors handed flowers to soldiers and chanted slogans such as: "Brother soldier, why do you kill your brothers?"

and "The army is part of the nation" (Kamalî 1979). On several occasions, large throngs of protestors persuaded soldiers to give up their arms, throw off their uniforms, and join the demonstration (Simpson 1988:33). On other occasions, protestors attacked security personnel and even military bases (Parsa 1989:231-37).

Nonetheless, the effectiveness of popular pressure on the military is unclear. Even in mid-January 1979, as the shah was about to leave Iran, desertions remained relatively low, only about a thousand a day out of several hundred thousand troops, according to the Iranian chief of staff (Gharabaghi 1985: 122). However, authorized leaves may have been increasing dramatically as soldiers requested furloughs to check on their families and property after riots and other disturbances (Zabih 1988:33). (In a Crisis Meeting on January 23, the chief of staff estimated that the armed forces were only at 55 percent of their strength, although the tone of his comments suggests that this figure was picked more for effect than for accuracy [*Misl-i Barf* 1987:175].[13]) Small mutinies increased (Parsa 1989:241-44). On December 21, 1978, the U.S. embassy reported:

> Base security has been tightened on more than one base or unit area, apparently because of indications of decreasing loyalty among junior personnel as well as concern that deserters may attempt to return in uniform to seize arms. (National Security Archive 1989: Document 1950)

Whether or not popular pressure was effective, however, military leaders were clearly worried about it. This concern prevented the military from being used to its full capacity because each military operation exposed the troops to fraternization and further appeals from protestors. On January 15, 1979, the head of the ground forces proposed keeping the soldiers away from this nefarious influence:

> We should round up the units and send them someplace where [the demonstrators] won't have any contact with the soldiers. Because yesterday they came and put a flower in the end of a rifle barrel, and another on the [military] vehicle. . . . The soldiers' morale just disappears. (*Misl-i Barf* 1987:50)

During the largest demonstrations, military commanders kept their troops well away from the march routes, guarding "key" sites and neighborhoods (National Security Archive 1989: Document 1900; *Âyandigan,* January 20, 1979, p. 2). On a few occasions they ordered the military back to barracks, twice as a direct result of defections (*Los Angeles Times,* December 19, 1979, pp. 1-22; *Hambastigî,* December 24, 1978, p. 2).

In early 1979, Iranian military commanders struggled to keep the military intact and gave up trying to use the military to govern the country. They had been trained to fear a Soviet incursion and saw the collapse of the Iranian military as an invitation to aggression (*Misl-i Barf* 1987:118-21). In Mashhad at the height of the unrest, one commander said that the military was unable to defend the nearby border with the Soviet Union. "The important border now is our own garrison" (*New York Times,* January 4, 1979, p. A10).

But several hundred thousand troops could not be held in their barracks for long.[14] A number of soldiers, even officers, slipped out and joined protests out of uniform, of course, because a uniform would attract dangerous attention from protestors and security forces that remained loyal (Balta and Rulleau 1979:59-60). In early February of 1979, when whole units of troops began to demonstrate in uniform against the shah, the military's disintegration was imminent. After only a day and a half of street fighting, the chiefs of staff declared the military's "neutrality" and allowed the revolutionaries to take power (Gharabaghi 1985:207-49).

Implications for Social-Movement Theory

I have argued that the Iranian state was not particularly vulnerable to revolution in 1978, according to several indicators. The Pahlavî regime's domestic support had not withered away, nor had its international support. State centralization and the shah's illness did not prevent the state from responding actively to the revolutionary movement, combining carrot and stick, cracking down on opposition activities while promising future reforms, as it had done for decades.

In terms of popular perceptions, the Iranian people considered the coercive power of the state to be intact right up to the end. At the same time, however, evidence suggests that the Iranian people considered political opportunities to have increased as a result of the growth of the opposition. The strength of the revolutionary movement induced even nonrevolutionary liberals to join in. Acting on this perception of opposition strength, Iranians altered the structure of opportunities by fraternizing with the military and making it partially unusable as a coercive force.

In more theoretical terms, there was a mismatch between the structure of political opportunities and popular perceptions of political opportunities. Rather than calculate opportunities solely on the basis of changes in the state, as Tocquevillean theory suggests, Iranians appear to have calculated opportunities on the basis of changes in the opposition. Ultimately, their perceptions proved self-fulfilling: The balance of forces had indeed tilted toward the opposition, and perceptions proved stronger than the state structure.

This finding suggests that social-movement theory should reconsider the relation between "objective" and "subjective" definitions of political opportunity. If opportunity is like a door, then social-movement theory generally examines cases in which people realize the door is open and walk on through. The Iranian Revolution may be a case in which people saw that the door was closed, but felt that the opposition was powerful enough to open it. These people were not millenarians, masochists, fanatics, or martyrsthe case is not dismissed so easily. It turns out that Iranians were able to open the door on their own.

Thus Iran is a "deviant" case for social-movement theory, a case suggesting that perceived opportunities may affect the outcome of revolutionary protest independent of structural opportunities. This conclusion is hardly novel. The critical-mass school, drawing on a long tradition in sociology, has often examined protestors' and potential protestors' perceptions. However, this school has avoided emphasizing its differences with the Tocquevillean tradition. The Iranian case makes these differences clear. However, a single "deviant" case cannot answer all the questions that it raises. Are perceptions always stronger than structures? Under what conditions do perceptions outweigh structures? Only through research on additional cases in which perceived opportunities and structural opportunities fail to coincide can the relative weight of each be understood.

Such research will encounter difficulties. First, the identification of appropriate cases will not be easy. Many theorists will assume that if protest occurs, structural conditions must have been conducive. Therefore, any case study proffered to the contrary may be dismissed out of hand. Furthermore, the Tocquevillean tradition

presents a moving target, as theories of political opportunity increase. Like any research program (Lakatos 1978), Tocquevillean theorists can develop new corollary analyses to bring seemingly deviant cases back into alignment. As a result, it may not be easy to convince these theorists that cases exist in which structural opportunities and perceived opportunities do not coincide.

Second, the measurement of popular perceptions will be difficult. The survey instruments developed by Opp, Muller, and their collaborators (Muller et al. 1991; Muller and Opp 1986; Opp 1994; Opp and Gern 1993; Opp and Ruehl 1990a) represent great strides in identifying the key perceptions involved in protest behavior. However, systematic surveys are not feasible in the midst of revolutionary turmoil, so the issue of recollected motivations enters the picture. In addition, the countries most amenable to survey research may be the least "deviant" cases from a Tocquevillean point of view. Countries like Iran, whose regimes are less open to the free flow of information and thus to independent survey analysis, may be precisely the countries in which information about the structure of opportunities is also not widely disseminated, so that perceptions of opportunities may be more out of synch.

Third, identifying a set of "deviant" cases in which perceived opportunities outweigh structural ones may be inherently self-defeating. Take, for instance, the hypothesis that regimes that block the free flow of information are more likely than other regimes to have mismatched structural opportunities and perceived opportunities. Haven't we, then, identified the structural conditions under which structural conditions are not important? In other words, haven't we simply redefined structure to include the free flow of information, thereby bringing structure back into alignment with perceptions?

Fourth, examining perceptions independently of structures places social scientists in an anomalous position because their privileged position as observers is called into question. In social-movement theory, structural opportunity means the social scientist's perception of opportunities. This scientific perception is more informed than contemporary popular perceptions because it is after-the-fact and arguably more objective. However, cases in which perceptions outweigh structures present the risk that scientific perceptions, for all their rigor and hindsight, may not be as important as the perceptions of the social-movement participants.

Fifth, if perceptions can outweigh structures, then protest may not be predictable, even in principle. The Tocquevillean tradition has embarked on one of the greatest quests in social science: To discover the regularities underlying irregular behaviorthe rules underlying behavior that flouts the rules. However, if protest results from perceptions and not structures, then there are no advance clues. Given social science's poor record of predicting major protest movements, including the Iranian Revolution, this conclusion may be comforting. But many social scientists may not want to abandon the quest for predictability.

The single case of the Iranian Revolution of 1979 cannot resolve any of these weighty issues. However, the mismatch between structural opportunities and perceived opportunities in this case has far-reaching implications for social-movement theory. The Tocquevillean tradition has avoided these disconcerting implications by failing to study such cases, and the critical-mass school has thus far not shown the desire to challenge the Tocquevilleans. My goal has been to show that the two approaches are at odds with each other and to stimulate further debate.

Appendix

Interview Evidence of Perceived Opportunities During the Iranian Revolution

To corroborate the fragmentary evidence concerning popular perceptions of the Iranian state and the revolutionary movement, I planned to interview a representative sample of Iranians in 1989 and 1990. When I was unable to obtain a visa to Iran, I pursued this research in Istanbul, Turkey, where many Iranians traveled at that time for tourism and business. In six months, I conducted semi-structured interviews in Persian with 83 temporary visitors who intended to return to Iran. This sample included Iranians from more diverse backgrounds than are found among expatriates. Nonetheless, this sample was not representative of the Iranian population at largeit was far more urban, somewhat more white-collar, and almost entirely male.

The study of closed societies through interviews abroad has been successful in several studies (Millar 1987; Whyte 1983). However, because of a lack of funds and a way to sample the fluid Iranian visitor population of Istanbul, my interviews could not be as systematic as in these other works. Although my interviews may give a "sense" of Iranian popular perceptions that is more representative than those of prominent expatriates who have been quoted in previous analyses of the Iranian Revolution, they cannot prove what those popular perceptions were.

The bulk of the interviews confirmed that respondents judged political opportunities not in terms of the power of the state, but in terms of the power of the opposition. Only a few of my respondentsgenerally the better educated onesmade any reference to the shah's liberalization reforms, and some of these references were derisive comments on the reforms' insincerity. One respondent attributed the shah's liberalization reforms to pressure from Carter. I asked if he had felt freer as a result. "No, things were getting worse. But we all had solidarity," he responded, clasping his hands together to demonstrate.[a] This impression of worsening political conditions was widespread.

Some of the more devout Muslim respondents said they worried that Islam was in danger, that the shah was systematically undermining the religious establishment.[b] Several respondents gave unsolicited accounts of being *"az khud guzashtih"* (see p. 73), although none used this term. One man attributed his revolutionary participation to the shooting of his brother. "It was this way for everyone," he said. "If my brother, or my friend, or my child was shot, I would get angry and pour out into the streets."[c]

However, the most common explanation for respondents' participation in the revolutionary movement referred to the strength of the opposition. Contrary to the stereotype of Shi'i Islam, most Iranians were not eager for martyrdom. When religious leaders urged Iranians to sacrifice themselves for Islam in late 1977 and early 1978, very few responded to the call. "I was prepared to be killed at that time, for our goals," one respondent recalled[d]but neither he nor most Iranians joined the protest movement until late in 1978, when they had safety in numbers:

The more people, the less fear. (Respondent 11, army conscript from Tehran, interviewed October 26, 1989)

I saw in the streets the crowds getting bigger and bigger. . . . I saw my friend in the street shouting, 'Death to the shah,' and my fear left me. (Respondent 46, unemployed former conscript from Tehran, interviewed November 22, 1989)

When everyone was in the streets, huge crowds, I'd go. I didn't go if there was going to be danger and shooting. (Respondent 48, telephone company official from Tehran, interviewed November 22, 1989)

It wasn't just one, two, or a thousand people. (Respondent 52, shopowner from Shiraz, interviewed November 27, 1989)

There were lots of people there. If it had been just one person. . . . (Respondent 58, government official from Gombad, interviewed December 1, 1989)

When everyone is shutting down [their shops], the rest shut down too. (Respondent 62, shopowner from Tehran, interviewed December 4, 1989)

When the people were of a piece (*yik-parchih*), I participated. (Respondent 67, high school student from Luristan, interviewed December 7, 1989)

Everyone was there. There were so many people. If it was just a small demonstration, I didn't go. But those huge demonstrations fear had no meaning then. (Respondent 72, high school student from Tehran, interviewed December 13, 1989)

It was not an individual decision. Everyone was of a piece. When everyone is of a piece, one person cannot stay separate. (Respondent 77, auto mechanic from Tehran, interviewed December 20, 1989)

Some of these voices were apologetic, as though admitting to a lack of heroism. Others distanced themselves, through their comments, from the tragic turns that the revolution later took. Others were proud of the country's unanimity in protest and of their participation. In any case, these voices constitute further evidence that Iranians' calculations about opportunities were focused on the strengthening of the opposition, not the weakening of the state.

Notes

1. Tocqueville discusses social-structural factors in addition to state structure. I do not address this aspect of Tocqueville's analysis here.
2. Another definition of opportunities comes from resource-mobilization theory: The perceived balance of forces may shift because of changes in the opposition's resource, organizational, or network base. Micromobilization theories offer another definition of opportunities; solidarity with one's peers is more important than the balance of forces and the expected success of protest.
3. Thus critical-mass models present a direct challenge to free-rider models, which argue that other people's participation provides disincentives for individual participation (Olson 1965; Tullock 1971; also see

Lichbach 1994 for a thorough review of the social-movement literature on this issue).
4. Skocpol (1982:267) denies that her theory applies directly to the Iranian Revolution, particularly with regard to international pressures.
5. Oddly, the shah denied that Carter called him (Pahlavi 1980:161).
6. The shah had given similar orders in previous crises, according to generals and politicians involved in episodes in the 1950s and 1960s (Afkhami 1985:941).
7. Tabulation of the "martyrs of the revolution" listed in *Lâlih'hâ* (circa 1980) finds increases of 30 to 150 percent each month through the fall and winter of 1978 and 1979. Bill (1988:487) has also used this source as a sampling of revolutionary fatalities. I appreciate Professor Bill's assistance in locating this book.
8. "Even if one assumes that the government had lost its will to repress people, it is not altogether clear that participants in the revolution were aware of this fact or would have believed it" (Moaddel 1993:156). However, Moaddel's explanation for revolutionary participation focuses on Islamic ideology, as opposed to popular perceptions of the opposition movement's strength and prospects.
9. Maryam Shamlu, former head of the Women's Organization of Iran, was interviewed in Washington, D.C. in May 1983 by Mahnaz Afkhami (Foundation for Iranian Studies 1991, transcript p. 24).
10. Eslam Kazemieh was interviewed in Paris on October 31, 1983 and May 8, 1984 by Shirin Sami'i (Foundation for Iranian Studies 1991, transcript p. 32).
11. Abol Ghassem Lebaschi was interviewed in Paris on February 28, 1983 by Habib Ladjevardi (Harvard Iranian Oral History Collection 1987, transcript of tape 3, p. 5).
12. Lebaschi (Harvard Iranian Oral History Collection 1987, transcript of tape 3, p. 10); Mohammad Shanehchi was interviewed in Paris on March 4, 1983 by Habib Ladjevardi (Harvard Iranian Oral History Collection 1987, transcript of tape 4, pp. 5-6).
13. *Misl-i Barf* (1987) purports to be a transcript of three meetings of military leaders in the last month of the Pahlavî regime; it cannot be verified, but seems highly realistic. The generals do not appear bloodthirsty or anti-Islamic, as might be expected of a fabricated transcript published in post-revolutionary Iran. According to comments in the transcript, the recordings were made on the orders of the chief of staff.
14. This point was raised by Respondent 98, a career soldier from Tehran interviewed in Istanbul on February 23, 1990.
a. Respondent 55, a Tehran bazaar worker, interviewed on November 29, 1989. (Occupations and place of residence are at the time of the revolution.)
b. Especially Respondent 16, an unemployed young religious activist in east Tehran, interviewed on November 1, 1989.
c. Respondent 59, a bank official from Tehran, interviewed on December 3, 1989.

d. Respondent 89, a company official from Khuzistan, interviewed on February 19, 1990. One of the stock comments I heard was, "Iranians know no fear." This comment was often, paradoxically, accompanied by accounts of how the respondent had run away when security forces opened fire. ✦

Part 3

Conditions of Organization: Facilitative Contexts

In Part 2 we focused on the role played by systems of institutionalized politics in the emergence, development, and ultimate fate of social movements. Such systems condition collective action by expanding or contracting the opportunities available for such action. Vulnerable and/or receptive systems encourage movement activity; strong and/or resistant systems tend to discourage it.

But opportunities alone do not make a movement. Even the most facilitative political environment only creates a certain structural potential for collective action. Among the most important factors determining whether this potential will be realized is the level of prior organization within the aggrieved group. In the absence of sufficient organization, a group is unlikely to act even when granted the opportunity to do so. To generate a social movement, then, insurgents must be able to take advantage of favorable political opportunities by fashioning an organized campaign of social protest. Many movement scholars believe that the established organizations and associational networks of the aggrieved group hold the key to this process.

The significance of these existing organizations or networks to the process of movement emergence would appear to be largely a function of the supportive infrastructure they afford insurgents. Three aspects of this infrastructure are especially critical: *a membership base*, *a communication network*, and *leaders*.

If there is anything approximating a consistent finding in the empirical literature, it is that movement recruitment normally depends on prior contact between prospective recruits and individuals already in the movement. The greater the social organization in the aggrieved community, the more likely that there will be a supportive membership base to facilitate contact and promote individual recruitment and the growth of the movement.

The established organizations and associational networks of a given community also constitute a communication network, the strength and breadth of which strongly influence the pattern, speed, and extent of movement expansion. Both the failure of a fledgling movement to take hold and the rapid spread of protest activity have been credited to the presence or absence of such a communication network. Jo Freeman (1973a) has argued that it was the recent development of such a network that enabled women in the 1960s to create a successful feminist movement. Conversely, Jackson et al. (1960: 38) document a case in which the absence of a readily cooptable communication network contributed to the collapse of an incipient California tax revolt. The movement failed, according to the authors, because "there was no . . . preestablished network of communication which would be quickly employed to link the suburban residential property owners who constituted the principal base of the movement."

All manner of movement analysts have asserted the importance of leaders and organizers in the generation of social movements. To do so requires not so much a particular theoretical orientation as common sense. In the context of favorable political opportunities and widespread discontent there still remains a need for the centralized direction and coordination of a recognized leadership. The existence of established groups within the movement's mass base often insures the presence of recognized leaders who can be called upon to lend their prestige and organizing skill to the burgeoning movement.

The three readings in this part underscore the importance of these infrastructural supports and established organization more generally in the emergence of collective action. In the first selection, James Petras and Maurice Zeitlin document the important role of communication networks in the spread of political rebellion in Chile. They show that agricultural areas surrounding mining towns steeped in Marxist or socialist thought were more apt to return large electoral majorities for Socialist-Communist candidates than were agricultural areas geographically removed from a mining town. The implication of the work is clear. Established Marxist or socialist organizations within the mining towns were instrumental in spreading their radical ideology to the surrounding "satellite" area.

Closer to home, the two remaining readings document the crucial role played by the established organizations of the African-American community in the resurgence of civil rights activity in the American South in the 1950s and early 1960s.

In his classic article, Aldon Morris documents the critical role played by black churches and colleges in the emergence and development of the 1960 student sit-in movement. Morris underscores the extraordinary extent to which the leadership of the sit-in campaign was drawn from these two institutions.

In an excerpt from his book, Doug McAdam shows the extraordinary growth experienced by urban black churches, black colleges, and local chapters of the National Association for the Advancement of Colored People (NAACP) between 1930 and 1955.

References

Freeman, Jo. 1973. "The Origins of the Women's Liberation Movement." *American Journal of Sociology* 78: 792-811.

Jackson, Maurice, Eleanora Peterson, James Bull, Sverre Monsen, and Patricia Richmond. 1960. "The Failure of an Incipient Social Movement." *Pacific Sociological Review* 3: 35-40. ✦

7

Miners and Agrarian Radicalism

James Petras
Maurice Zeitlin

Generally, empirical analyses of class and politics focus on the relative chances for given types of political behavior in different classes, but neglect *the interaction of these classes and the political consequences of such interaction*. Moreover, even when reference is made to the possible political relevance of such interaction, the emphasis has been on asymmetrical influence, i.e., on how the privileged classes may moderate the politics of the underprivileged.[1] For instance, the possibility that the working class might modify the political behavior of the middle classes has scarcely been entertained, nor has the possible impact of the workers on the development of political consciousness in other exploited classes been explored. The latter is precisely what we focus on in this article: the impact of organized workers in Chile on the development of political consciousness in the peasantry.

In Chile, agricultural relations have gradually become modernized, and traditional social controls have loosened considerably. In the central valley, where Chile's agricultural population is centered, the modernization favored by the Chilean propertied classes may be directly responsible for the growth of rural radicalism. As one writer has put it: "The principal impact of technological advance and farm rationalization has been to undermine the secure if impoverished position of the agricultural laborers which has been an important feature of the traditional system of employment. Wage rates are barely keeping up with consumer price increases and [these rates] may have fallen recently. Thus while the attempts to increase output and productivity have not been very successful, these attempts have led to changes which adversely affect the landless laborer. These changes in Chilean agriculture may lead to demands for a more radical transformation in the future."[2] This

breakdown of the traditional rural social structure, the growth of a "rural proletariat," and emergence of demands for radical reforms in the agrarian structure may allow other relatively oppressed groups who have similar demands and *are* highly organized to provide leadership for the peasantry as it enters the political struggle in Chile. The most highly organized and politically conscious working class centers in Chile are in the mining municipalities—centers from which the miners' political influence may be diffused into the surrounding countryside.

Organized Working Class Politics in Chile

In Chile, both the organized trade union movement and the emergence of insurgent political parties began in the northern areas of Tarapaca and Antofagasta, where 40 percent of the labor force was already employed in the mines by 1885. Soon after the middle of the last century, large-scale social conflict rivaling similar outbreaks in Europe were occurring with increasing frequency and intensity.[3] The northern nitrate city of Iquique and the southern coal mining area of Lota were frequently the scenes of struggles of civil war proportions in which hundreds if not thousands of workers were killed. The first general strike in 1890 originated in Iquique and spread throughout the country. Despite the violent reaction of the public authorities, the first labor organizations began to emerge—based predominantly in the nitrate mines of the north.[4] The Chilean Workers Federation was founded in 1908 by Conservatives as a mutual aid society. By 1917 it had become a militant industrial trade union; two years later it called for the abolition of capitalism. Between 1911 and 1920 there were 293 strikes involving 150,000 workers. In 1919 the Chilean Workers' Federation (FOCH) became affiliated with the Red Trade Union Federation. The FOCH, the largest national union, contained an estimated 136,000 members of which 10,000 were coal miners and 40,000 nitrate miners—miners accounting for almost 37 percent of all union members. Of all industries, it was only in mining that a majority of the workers were organized. In 1906, the first working-class Socialist leader, Emilio Recabarren, was elected from a mining area—although he was not allowed to take office.

The Socialist Party that grew out of the establishment of the so-called "Socialist Republic,"[5]

"Miners and Agricultural Radicalism." *American Sociological Review* 32: 578-586, 1967. Public Domain.

(June 4-16, 1932) had its most cohesive working-class political base among the copper miners. Although the Socialist Party condemned both the Second and Third Internationals, it claimed adherence to Marxism and the establishment of a government of organized workers as its goal. The Communists also secured their major base in the mining areas. In the municipal elections of 1947, the last relatively free election before the ten-year ban on the Community Party (1948-1958), the Communists received 71 percent of the coal miners' vote, 63 percent of the nitrate miners' vote and 55 percent of the vote of the copper workers: nationally, in contrast, they received only 1% percent of the vote.

The eleven major mining municipalities accounted for 20 percent of the total national Communist vote.[6] Their history of class conflict and organized political activity clearly established the miners as the most active revolutionary force in Chilean society. Their political radicalism is in line with the radicalism of miners all over the world,[7] in great part the result of the structure of the "occupational community" of the miners. The high degree of interaction among the miners results in very close-knit social organization. Since they are concentrated together, and in relative physical and social isolation from the influences of the dominant social classes in the society, it is highly likely that a shared class outlook based on the recognition of their common interests will develop. The question we deal with here is the impact, if any, that these highly organized, politically radical miners have on the traditionally conservative rural poor.

Rural Labor Force

Sharp divisions have existed between the urban and rural sectors of the Chilean labor force. A fundamental factor in the stability, continuity and power of the propertied classes was the social condition and attitudes of the rural labor force. The system of rural labor established in colonial times continued down through the twentieth century, little changed by the Revolution for Independence or by a century and a quarter of parliamentary and presidential democracy.

Formally free, the rural labor force was bound to the land by the fact that neighboring landowners would refuse to hire a tenant who had left a *hacienda* because he was discontented with his lot. The economic status of the *inquiline* (tenant worker) was the same throughout the nineteenth and most of the twentieth century: a few pennies a day in wages, a one- or two-room house, a ration of food for each day he worked, and a tiny plot of land. Usually he was required to supply labor for some 240 days a year.[8] Debt servitude was widespread and opportunity for the *inquiline* to advance from that status and become an economically independent farmer was nonexistent. The social and religious life of the *inquiline* was restricted by the landowners (*hacendados*) who preferred that their employees have minimal contact with outsiders. The landowners organized the fiesta, the amusements and the "civil jurisdiction" within the hacienda ("*fundo*"). In the middle 1930's these *fundos* approximated the "ideal type" of an authoritarian system of social control and rigid social stratification.

Within the larger society, where some voluntary associations defending working-class interests were able to establish themselves, the rural poor lived in conditions in which the apparatus of violence and force was regulated by a single owner or family, alternative sources of information were prohibited, and voluntary associations were forbidden. Middle-class parliamentary parties such as the *Radicales* did not advocate a program of socioeconomic reform of the traditional landed system. They were unable to mobilize the peasantry and lower-class rural populace against the landowners' rule. In turn, this forced the middle-class parties to forego a meaningful and dynamic program for industrial and democratic development, and allowed the Socialists and Communists, and then the Christian Democrats, to become spokesmen for the rural poor and agrarian reform.

In his control of the *inquilino*, the landowner held an effective counterweight to any political program of social and economic development that negatively affected his interests. The alliance of foreign investors, large landowners, and those urban entrepreneurs integrated with them, rested on the control the landowners had of the *inquilino*; this was the condition *sine qua non* for their continuing political hegemony.

Apart from the *inquilino,* there was a sector of the rural labor force which was not attached to the land, and consequently was less directly under the dominance of the landowners. These "free laborers" have constituted about one-third of the rural work force; three decades ago they were already said to "have the reputation of provoking many difficulties in the relation between the inquilino and the farm owner."[9] The free laborers were reputed to be frequently more independent in their outlook and more likely to object to any excesses committed by the landowners against the workers. With the gradual mechanization of agriculture and the increased payment in wages in recent years, the rural population has become like wage laborers.

Miners and Peasants: The Diffusion Process

Only with industrial development, and especially mining, did the agricultural labor force in Chile begin to have even a hint of political consciousness, impelled largely by their contact with industrial workers. The landowners' strategy had been to isolate the *inquilinos* from the urban working class, prohibiting their independent organization. By restricting their experience to the *fundo* itself, the *patron* had inhibited the development of their political awareness. With the rapid growth of the urban working class in the period after World War I, strikes spread to the rural districts for the first time in the history of the country. Uprisings took place on a number of *fundos*. The miners took the leadership in this early attempt at rural organization. In 1919, an abortive attempt was made to organize the *inquilinos* into a nationwide federation in the Cometa region in the Aconcagua Valley, "the intention being to federate the *inquilinos* with an organization of miners."[10] Again in the 1930's a broad militant movement of peasant unionization developed, supported by sectors of the urban working class; it was violently repressed by the state and politically defused by the electoral strategy that the leftist parties adopted during the Popular Front.[11]

In recent years the closed system of the large *fundos* has begun to change under the impact of the growth of commercial-capitalistic economic and social relations and, more important, as political organization, trade unions and outside communications networks have been able to undermine the information monopoly of the large landowners.

In the 1958 presidential election, significant sectors of the Chilean peasantry shifted their traditional allegiance away from the Right. The Socialist-Communist coalition, *Frente de Accion Popular* (FRAP) and the Christian Democratic Party are competing for the allegiance of this important and newly emerging social force; they have formed their own peasant "unions" and advocated programs for agrarian reform. In both the 1958 and the 1964 Presidential elections, FRAP campaigned actively throughout the countryside. With old political alignments shifting and the balance of social forces changing, the political direction which the Chilean peasantry will take is seen by all major political parties as a major factor in determining the future of Chilean society. The decisive role that the miners can play in determining the direction taken by the peasantry will become clear from our findings.

Our analysis is based on the electoral returns of the Presidential elections of 1958 and 1964, with primary emphasis on the 195 agricultural municipalities. An ecological analysis of these election results is meaningful: distortions of the results through vote-tampering and coercion are believed to have been minimal. In these elections, competing political programs that included the socialist alternative were presented to the Chilean peasantry at a moment when it is emerging as a national political force. Our focus here is on the political impact of the organized mining centers on the peasantry, and on the differential political response of different types of peasantry.

Findings

We define as agricultural municipalities those in which 50 percent or more of the economically active population are engaged in agriculture.[12] Mining municipalities are those in which at least 500 individuals or 50 percent or more of the economically active population are in the mining sector. Each of the 296 municipalities in the country was located on a map (in Mattelart, *Atlas Social de Las Comunas de Chile*) and each municipality that directly adjoined any mining municipality was defined as a "satellite."

The vote for Salvadore Allende, presidential candidate of the Socialist-Communist coalition (FRAP) is taken as an index of radical political behavior. We define a "high" vote for Allende in 1958 as 30 percent (the national average) or more in the municipality, and a "low" vote as 20 percent or less; in 1964, a "high" vote is 40 percent (the national average) or more in the municipality, and "low" is 25 percent or less.[13]

If our assumption is correct that the mining municipalities are not only centers of political radicalism but also centers from which political radicalism is diffused into surrounding non-mining areas, then we should find that the greater the number of mining municipalities a "satellite" adjoins, the more likely it is to have a "high" vote for Allende, the FRAP presidential candidate. (The number of mining municipalities adjoining a satellite ranges from one to four.) The municipalities that are neither mining municipalities nor adjoin any should be least likely to give a "high" vote to Allende.

As Table 1 shows, this is precisely what we find in both agricultural and non-agricultural municipalities in 1958 and in 1964. The same relationship holds when we look at the tail end of the vote—the "low" Allende vote (Table 2): The greater the number of mining municipalities adjoining it, the greater the likelihood in a municipality that Allende received a "high" vote (and the less the likelihood of a "low" vote). The greatest political differences are between the mining municipalities and the municipalities that are neither satellites nor have mines in them.

In addition to this demonstration of the political impact of the mining centers on surrounding non-mining areas, the following should be noted: (1) The agricultural municipalities, whatever their proximity to mining centers, have proportionately fewer "high" Allende municipalities among them than the non-agricultural ones. Despite FRAP's appreciable growth in strength in the agricultural areas, the non-agricultural, industrial and urban municipalities still provide the major electoral base of the Left. (2) Yet the strength of the Left grew throughout the agricultural municipalities from 1958 to 1964. This indicates that the *Frapistas* are penetrating and broadening their support in the peasantry as a whole, and not merely in particular peasant "segments" or strata, a point to which we shall return below. (3) It is beyond the scope of this article, but it should be pointed out that the miners' political influence apparently radiates out to other workers, perhaps even others in the "*clase popular*" made up of a variety of poor from pedlars to artisans and manual laborers. As a cohesive, organized, politically conscious community, the miners' political influence is critical not only in the peasantry but also among other lower strata. The existence of a major mining population whose political influence reaches other exploited strata may explain why class-based and class-conscious politics have emerged so much more clearly in Chile than in other countries in Latin America which, while having large strata of urban and rural poor, lack cohesive working-class centers.[14]

The Miners' Political Consciousness

The high degree of radical political consciousness in the mining areas of Chile was indicated by the results of Trade Union elections held shortly after Government troops killed 7 and wounded 38 miners during a military occupation of striking copper-mining areas in April, 1966. *El Mercurio,* the anti-Communist conservative daily, editorialized before the election: "The election of union officers that will take place in El Salvador,

---

Table 1
Percent "High" Vote for Allende Among Males in Municipalities Classified by Prevalence of Agriculture and Mining, 1958 and 1964

| | Prevalence of Agriculture | | | | | | | | |
| | Non-agricultural Municipalities | | | Agricultural Municipalities | | | Entire Country | | |
Prevalence of Mining	1958	1964	(N)	1958	1964	(N)	1958	1964	(N)
Neither "Satellites" nor Mining Municipalities	45	67	(58)	31	51	(162)	35	55	(220)
"Satellites"[a]	73	93	(15)	60	80	(30)	69	82	(45)
Mining Municipalities	93	93	(28)	..	..[b]	(3)	93	93	(31)

[a] A further breakdown of "satellites" according to the number of mining municipalities they adjoin also yields a direct relationship between proximity to mining centers and political radicalism. There are too few cases to examine the relationship among non-agricultural municipalities, however. Among agricultural municipalities, 58 percent of the "Satellites" of one mining municipality (N = 19) gave Allende a "high" vote in 1958, and 82 percent of the "satellites" of two to four mining municipalities (N = 11) gave him a "high" vote. In 1964, the respective figures are 74 percent and 91 percent. In the entire country, in 1958, of the first "satellite" group (N = 25), Allende got a "high" vote in 64 percent, and of the second group, 75 percent of the municipalities. The respective figures for 1964 in these groups are 76 percent and 90 percent.
[b] All three mining municipalities gave Allende a "high" vote in both elections, 1958 and 1964.

Table 2
Percent "Low" Vote for Allende Among Males in Municipalities Classified by
Prevalence of Agriculture and Mining, 1958 and 1964

| | Prevalence of Agriculture | | | | | | | | |
| | Non-agricultural Municipalities | | | Agricultural Municipalities | | | Entire Country | | |
Prevalence of Mining	1958	1964	(N)	1958	1964	(N)	1958	1964	(N)
Neither "Satellites" nor Mining Municipalities	21	10	(58)	49	20	(162)	41	17	(220)
"Satellites"	7	0	(15)	20	3	(30)	16	2	(45)
Mining Municipalities	4	0	(28)	..	..	(3)	3	0	(31)

Potrerillos and Barquito will be realized in an atmosphere of liberty adequate for the workers to express their preferences without the shadow of government pressure over the voters or candidates. These acts are of considerable importance because they will demonstrate what the spontaneous will of the workers really is when they do not feel menaced or intimidated by agitators. . . . Now the workers can take advantage of the new climate in the mines in order to form union committees that serve their interests rather than subordinating themselves to partisan politics."[15] The "spontaneous will" of the workers resulted in an overwhelming victory for the FRAP candidates, even when the elections were government supervised.[16] The point is that the way the miners voted in the presidential elections represents real support for the left—a high level of political consciousness that can be and is effectively transmitted to the peasantry.

In Chile, the organized mining workers' "isolated" communities have a high level of participation in activities, controversies, and organizations—features that are essential to a democratic society. The reason may be, as Lipset suggests, that the "frequent interaction of union members in all spheres of life . . . [makes] for a high level of interest in the affairs of their unions, which translates itself into high participation in local organization and a greater potential for democracy and membership influence."[17]

More important, these same miners consciously seek to influence the politics of others. *El Siglo,* the Communist daily, recently reported that "The two hundred delegates attending the Eighth National Congress of the Miners Federation . . . has adopted a resolution that, throughout the country, it will lend the most active class solidarity to the workers in the countryside in their struggles in defense of their rights and for the conquest

of a true Agrarian Reform. A few days ago the powerful unions [nitrate miners] of Maria Elena, Pedro de Valdivia and Mantos Blancos in the province of Antofagasta adopted a similar resolution."[18] The politicization of the peasantry by the miners is both a conscious effort and a "natural process."

The Left, conscious of the diffusion of radical ideas through informal communication between the working class and the peasantry, intervenes to maximize their advantages from this situation, accentuating and deepening the process of the diffusion of radical ideas. The importance that the Left attributes to this interaction between class conscious workers and the peasantry is shown by the remarks of Luis Corvalan, Communist Party General Secretary:

The political and cultural ties between the city and the country, between the proletariat and the campesinos, have developed in many ways. The children of campesinos who go to work in industry learn many things which they soon teach to their relatives and friends who have remained on the *fundo* or in the village and with whom they maintain contacts. Thousands of *inquilinos* . . . and small owners have become laborers in the construction of hydroelectric plants, roads, reservoirs and canals, or have been incorporated into the infant industries of sugar or lumber and live alongside numerous members of the proletariat who come from the cities. Furthermore, the crises and the repressive measures employed against the urban working class have caused many of the workers in the mines and factories to return to the country. *Throughout Chile, on the fundos and in the villages, we have seen many laborers, including some who were union leaders in the nitrate coal and copper* [industries]. It follows that the political work of the popular parties and especially of us Communists, should also figure among the principal elements that have influenced and are influencing the creation of a new social consciousness in the countryside.[19] (Our italics)

Table 3
Percent "High" Vote for Allende Among Males in Agricultural Municipalities Classified by Prevalence of Mining and Proprietors, 1964

	Percent Proprietors						
Prevalence of Mining	70 plus		50-69		30-49		under 30
Neither "Satellite" nor Mining Municipality	29	(35)	46	(24)	51	(37)	80	(54)
Mining "Satellites"	83	(6)	100	(3)	87	(8)	90	(10)

As urbanization and industrialization impinge on the peasantry and cause migrations of the labor force, so also is the political awareness of those individuals who have roots in both cultures heightened. These individuals bring the new ideas of struggle and of class solidarity to their friends and relatives still living in the rural areas and employed in agriculture. To the extent that the Left political parties are effective in organizing and politicizing these newly recruited industrial workers, they have an effective carrier of radicalism into the countryside.

The Diffusion of 'Political Culture' and the Structure of the Agricultural Labor Force

We discussed elsewhere the relationship between the structure of the agrarian labor force—the class composition of the countryside—and the FRAP presidential vote.[20] We find an inverse relationship between the proportion of proprietors in a municipality's agricultural labor force and the likelihood that it would give Allende a "high" vote. The higher the proportion of agricultural proprietors in a municipality the less likely it was to have a "high" Allende vote. This was consistent with our finding regarding the relationship between the proportion of wage laborers in a municipality's agricultural labor force and the vote—the higher the proportion of wage laborers, the greater the likelihood that the municipality gave Allende a "high" vote. From this evidence, we concluded that class position is a major determinant of peasant political behavior and that the rural proletariat, as distinguished from peasant proprietors, is apparently the major social base of the FRAP in the Chilean countryside.

The question now is what impact the organized political centers, the mining municipalities and their satellites, have on the class determination of voting in the countryside. We find that the political differences based on class position

among the peasants tend to disappear in the mining and satellite municipalities. In the non-mining, nonsatellite municipalities, however, class structure continues to determine voting patterns. The mining satellites are more likely, whatever the structure of the agricultural labor force (or class composition of the peasantry), to give Allende a "high" vote than the non-mining, non-satellite municipalities (Table 3). The theoretical point is clear: the mining and adjoining areas develop a distinct political culture, radical and socialist in content, that tends to eliminate the importance of class differences in the peasantry, and unite the peasants across class lines.

The fact is that the Chilean Left not only specifically directs its working class activists in the trade unions to unite with peasants in support of their demands but also emphasizes the role they can play in uniting different peasant strata: *El Siglo,* the Chilean Communist daily, writes: "All the workers in all the unions should unite with the peasants, wherever the unions are near agricultural properties in which the peasants are initiating struggles in defense of their interests. The miners' unions must be there to help the organization of the peasant unions. All our fellow miners must be there to bring all their moral and material support to the peasants who are struggling for possession of the land."[21] The Communist Party general secretary urges that "the forms of organization should be in accord with the wishes of the campesinos themselves; but we Communists believe that the best form of organization is that of the independent union, with headquarters in the village, in which are grouped the workers from various *fundos* and *all of the modest sectors of the rural population from the wage-hand to the small proprietor*, including the sharecropper, the poor campesino, etc."[22] Communist organizing strategy, the formation of independent organizations which include all of the rural "modest sectors . . . from wage hands to the small proprietor," adds a conscious element to further the general process of social interaction and diffusion of political conscious-ness that unites laborers and small proprietors in the areas adjoining mining centers.

Conclusions

The miners' organizational skills and political competence, the proximity of the mines to the countryside, the sharing of an exploited position, and conscious political choice, enable the miners to politicize and radicalize the Chilean country-side. The sense of citizenship and the necessity of having their own leaders that develops in the mining communities, where the miners themselves, rather than "other strata and agencies," run their affairs, also expresses itself in the political leadership and influence that their communities exert in adjoining rural areas. Further, the miners can supply legal, political, and economic resources to aid the peasants concretely, and thus demonstrate to them the power of organization and of struggle in defense of their common interests against land-owners. Where the miners have a strong political organization, peasant proprietors and agricultural wage laborers are equally susceptible to radical-ism. Political men, such as the Chilean miners, who make an effort to organize or influence peas-ant proprietors spread over the countryside, rela-tively isolated and atomized, can provide a link between them. The miners' leadership and ideol-ogy provide the peasants with a form of commu-nication and sharing of experience that is neces-sary for them to recognize and be able to act upon their common interests.

Notes

1. Cf. Seymour Martin Lipset, *Political Man*, New York: Doubleday &, Co., 1960, esp. pp. 231 and following.
2. Marvin Sternberg, "Chilean Land Tenure and Land Reforms" (unpublished doctoral dissertation), University of California, Berkeley, 1962, pp. 132-133.
3. Over one-third of all the strikes and popular dem-onstrations occurring in the period between 1851-1878 involved miners, according to Hernán Ramírez Necochea, *Historia de Movimiento Obrero en Chile: Antecedentes Siglo XIX*, Santiago: Editorial Austral, no date, pp. 133-134.
4. One of the worst massacres in labor history occurred in Chile at that time, when ten thousand nitrate miners marching in Iquique were machine-gunned, and two thousand died. Julio Cesar Jobet, *Ensayo Critico del desarrollo economico-social de Chile*, Santiago: Editorial Universitaria, 1955, p. 139.
5. Following the lbañez military regime, in the midst of a general economic crisis, the "Socialist Republic"

consisted of a series of four military juntas beginning on June 14, 1932, and ending on the 30th of that month. The officers had no social program and their only achievement was the establishment of the So-cialist Party under the leadership of one of them, Mar-maduke Grove.

6.

The Communist Vote in Mining Centers (1947)[a] (National Votes = 18 percent)	
Copper Mining Zone	%
Chuquicamata	68
Potrerillos	47
Sewell	50
Total	55
Nitrate Mining Zone	%
Iquique	34
Pozo Almonte	70
Lagunas	64
Toco	79
Pedro de Valdivia	72
Total	63
Coal Mining Zone	%
Coronel	68
Lota	83
Curanilahue	63
Total	71

[a] Ricardo Cruz Coke, *Geografía electoral de Chile,* Santiago: Editorial del Pacifico, 1952, pp. 81-82.

7. Lipset, *op cit.*, pp. 242-246. See also Clark Kerr and Abraham Siegel, "The interindustry Propensity to Strike—An International Comparison," in Arthur Kornhauser, Robert Dubin and Arthur Ross, (ed.) *Industrial Conflict,* New York: McGraw-Hill, 1954. pp, 200-201.
8. George McBride, *Chile: Land and Society*, New York: American Geographical Society, 1936, pp. 148-155.
9. *Ibid.*, p. 164.
10. *El Agricultor*, May, 1920, p. 113, cited in McBride, *op. cit.,* p. 166.
11. Luis Vitale, *Historia del movimiento obrero*, Santiago: Editorial POR, 1962, p. 88 *et passim*.
12. The data were compiled from several sources: *Censo Nacional Agricola—Ganadero,* Vols. I-VI, Santiago: Servicio nacionale de estadisticas y censos, Repub-lica de Chile, 1955; *Censo de Población*, Santiago: Dirección de Estadistica y Censos de la Republica de Chile, 1960; Armand Mattellart, *Atlas Social de las Comunas de Chila,* Santiago: Editorial del Pacifico, 1966.
13. We have used "high" and "low" ends of the voting spectrum as an *index* of radicalism because we are concerned with municipalities as social units, and relative radicalism as an *attribute* of the municipality. Thus, a municipality with a "high" FRAP vote is a "radical" municipality. This procedure differs from

simply taking the mean or median FRAP vote in the municipalities and therefore focusing on simple *quantitative* differences, whatever the actual vote. Neither procedure is intrinsically "correct." One or the other is more useful depending on the focus of the analysis; when looking for the determinants of political radicalism, in ecological analysis, we think our procedure is more useful.

14. We hope to deal extensively with this question in another article. The Agricultural Census makes it possible to gauge the impact of the miners on given agricultural strata but a comparable census for the non-agricultural areas of Chile does not exist. The regular census does not include occupational breakdowns on the municipal level. Such an analysis will require indirect indicators of class structure.

15. *El Mercurio*, April 15, 1966, p. 3.

16. The FRAP candidates obtained 16,227 votes, the Radical Party 3,287, and the Christian Democrats 3,263. The FRAP elected seven of the ten new union officers, replacing three Christian Democrats. *Ultima Hora* April 19, 1966, p. 2.

17. *Op. cit.,* p. 408.

18. *El Siglo,* February 20, 1966, p. 10.

19. Luis Corvalan. "The Communists' Tactics Relative to Agrarian Reform in Chile" in T. Lynn Smith (editor), *Agrarian Reform in Latin America,* New York: Knopf, 1965, p. 139. Our translation of the original differs slightly from the version in Smith's book.

20. James Petras and Maurice Zeitlin, "Agrarian Radicalism in Chile," *British Journal of Sociology,* forthcoming.

21. *El Siglo,* February 20, 1966, p. 10.

22. Corvalan, *op. cit.,* p. 141. ✦

8

Black Southern Student Sit-In Movement: An Analysis of Internal Organization

Aldon D. Morris

Scholars of the Civil Rights movement (Zinn, 1964; Oppenheimer, 1964; Matthews and Prothro, 1966; Meier and Rudwick, 1973; Oberschall, 1973; McAdam, 1979) and Civil Rights activists agree that the black Southern student sit-in movement of 1960 was a crucial development. The sit-ins pumped new life into the Civil Rights movement and enabled it to win unprecedented victories. Moreover, the sit-ins exercised a profound tactical and strategic influence over the entire course of social and political upheavals of the 1960s.

Apart from having a jarring impact on race relations, the sit-ins signaled the possibility of militant action at both Northern and Southern white campuses (Haber, 1966; Obear, 1970; Sale, 1973). A critical mass of the early leaders of the white student movement acquired much of their training, organizing skills, and tactics from the black activists of the student sit-in movement (Sale, 1973; Westby, 1976). Thus, the beginning of the white student movement as well as the quickened pace of Civil Rights activity can be traced to the black student sit-in movement.

The sit-ins were important because their rapid spread across the South crystallized the conflict of the period and pulled many people directly into the movement. How is such a "burst" of collective action to be explained? A standard account of the sit-ins has emerged which maintains that the sit-ins were the product of an independent black Student movement which represented a radical break from previous civil rights activities, organizations, and leadership of the Black community (e.g., Lomax, 1962; Zinn, 1964; Oppenheimer,

1964; Matthews and Prothro, 1966; Meier and Rudwick, 1973; Oberschall, 1973; Piven and Cloward, 1977).

In the standard account, various factors are argued to be the driving force behind the sit-ins, including impatience of the young, mass media coverage, outside resources made available by the liberal white community of the North, and support from the Federal Government. Although these writers differ over the proximate causes of the sit-ins, they nevertheless concur that the sit-ins broke from the organizational and institutional framework of the emerging Civil Rights movement. The data for the present study do not fit this standard account and suggest that a different account and interpretation of the sit-ins is warranted. The purpose of this paper is to present new data on the Southern student sit-in movement of 1960, and to provide a framework that will theoretically order the empirical findings.

Theoretical Context and Propositions

Classical collective behavior theory and the recently formulated resource mobilization theory are the major sociological frameworks that attempt to provide explanations of the origins, development, and outcomes of social movements. Classical collective behavior theory (e.g., Blumer, 1946; Turner and Killian, 1957; Lang and Lang, 1961; and Smesler, 1963) maintains that social movements differ substantially from institutionalized behavior. Social movements are theorized to be relatively spontaneous and unstructured. Movement participants are often portrayed as nonrational actors functioning outside of normative constraints and propelled by high levels of strain.

Classical collective behavior theorists do not deny that organizations and institutional processes play a role in collective behavior. Rather, organizations and institutional processes emerge in the course of movements and become important in their later stages. The standard account of the sit-ins fits the collective behavior imagery. Indeed, it can be argued that the diverse proponents of the "standard account" have been unduly influenced by classical collective behavior theory; their account largely ignores the organizational and institutional framework out of which the sit-ins emerged and spread.

The resource mobilization explanation (e.g., Oberschall, 1973; Gamson, 1975; Tilly, 1978;

McCarthy and Zald, 1973) of social movements differs markedly from classical collective behavior theory. In this view, social movements have no distinct inner logic and are not fundamentally different from institutionalized behavior. Organizations, institutions, pre-existing communication networks, and rational actors are all seen as important resources playing crucial roles in the emergence and outcome of collective action. In contrast to classical collective behavior theory, organizational and institutional structures are argued to be central throughout the entire process of collective action.

In its present formulation, resource mobilization theory is unclear about the type of organization and resources that are crucial for the initiation and spread of collective action. Some theorists (Oberschall, 1973; McCarthy and Zald, 1973; Jenkins and Perrow, 1977) argue that resources and organizations outside the protest group are crucial in determining the scope and outcomes of collective action. External groups and resources are argued to be especially critical for movements of the poor. In other formulations of this approach (e.g., Gamson, 1975; Tilly, 1978), emphasis is placed on the important role that internal organization plays in collective action. However, internal organization is but one of several variables (e.g., repression, bureaucracy, opportunity) that are investigated. In my view such an approach fails to capture the degree to which collective action is dependent on internal organization.

This paper focuses on the central function that internal organization played in the emergence and development of the sit-in movement. My analysis suggests that one-sided emphases on spontaneous processes or outside resources can lead to unwarranted neglect of internal structure. A case will be made that the diffusion of the 1960 sit-ins cannot be understood without treating internal organization as a central variable. The analysis will be guided by three propositions.

Proposition 1. Pre-existing social structures provide the resources and organizations that are crucial to the initiation and spread of collective action. Following Tilly (1978), collective action is defined here as joint action by protest groups in pursuit of common ends. This proposition maintains that collective action is rooted in organizational structure and carried out by rational actors attempting to realize their ends. This proposition is central to resource-mobilization theory and has

received considerable support from a number of empirical studies (Oberschall, 1973; Gamson, 1975; Tilly, 1975).

Proposition 2. The extent and distribution of internal social organization will determine the extent to which innovations in collective strategy and tactics are adopted, spread, and sustained. This proposition directs attention to a protest group's internal organization—its "local movement centers." A local movement center is that component of social structure within a local community that organizes and coordinates collective action. A local movement center has two major properties. First, it includes all protest organizations and leaders of a specific community that are actively engaged in organizing and producing collective action. During the sit-ins, the Southern Christian Leadership Conference (SCLC), Youth Councils of the National Association for the Advancement of Colored People (NAACP), Congress of Racial Equality (CORE), and "direct action" churches existed in numerous Southern black communities. A local center within the Civil Rights movement included all these organizations and leaders. Second, a local movement center contains a unit that coordinates protest activities within the local movement and between the local center and other institutions of the larger community. During the Civil Rights movement, a particular church usually served as the local coordinating unit. Through this unit the protest activities of the church community, college community, activist organizations, and their leaders were mobilized and coordinated. Thus, movement centers provide the organization and coordination capable of sustaining and spreading collective action.

Proposition 3. There is an interaction between the type of pre-existing internal organization and the type of innovations in strategy and tactics that can be rapidly adopted and spread by a protest group. This proposition addresses the issue of why a protest group adopts a particular tactical innovation rather than another.[1] Whereas Proposition 2 maintains that diffusion of an innovation in strategy is a function of the development and spread of internal social organization, Proposition 3 specifies that certain types of organization are more conducive than others to the diffusion and adoption of certain types of tactical innovation. In short, the framework for the analysis of the 1960 sit-ins consists of three interrelated propositions. One, collective action is initiated through pre-existing structures. Two, tactical innovation within a movement is a function of well-developed and widespread internal organization. Three, the type of innovation in strategy and tactics which can be rapidly disseminated and sustained is largely determined by the characteristic internal organization of a protest group.

Data

This study of the sit-ins is part of a larger study on the origins of the Civil Rights movement (Morris, forthcoming). A substantial part of the data were collected from primary sources—archives and interviews with Civil Rights participants. The archival research was conducted at various sites between May and September of 1978.[2] Thousands of original documents (i.e. memoranda, letters, field reports, organizational histories and directives, interorganizational correspondences, etc.) generated by movement participants were examined. These data contained a wealth of information pertaining to key variables—organization, mobilization, finance, rationality, spontaneity—relevant to the study of movements.

Interviews with participants of the movement constituted the second source of data. Detailed interviews with over 50 Civil Rights leaders were conducted. Interviews made it possible to follow-up on many issues raised by the archival data; and, since these interviews were semi-open-ended, they revealed unexpected insights into the movement. Whenever statements were heard that seemed novel or promising, interviewees were given freedom to speak their piece.

Methods

The strategy for the archival research was straightforward. The researcher examined every document possible within the time allocated for a particular site.[3] The main objective was to examine the roles played in the sit-ins by variables associated with Weberian theory and theories of collective behavior and resource mobilization. Following collective behavior theory, I was concerned with the extent to which the sit-ins were spontaneous and discontinuous with established social structure. From Weberian theory I was interested in whether a charismatic attraction between a leader and followers was sufficient to produce the heavy volume of collective action in the 1960 sit-ins. Finally, several issues addressed by

resource mobilization theory were of interest. I examined archival sources to ascertain the role of social organization and resources in the sit-ins. Also, I was concerned with whether the leadership, money, and skills behind the sit-ins were supplied by outsiders or by the indigenous Southern black community.

Three strategies were employed in the interview process. First, the researcher attempted to learn as much as possible about the movement from extensive library and archival sources before conducting interviews. This prior knowledge enabled the interviewer to ask specific questions and to assist interviewees in rooting their memories in the social, temporal, and geographical context of their actions twenty years earlier. Prior knowledge enabled the interviewer to gain the respect of interviewees and increased the likelihood that they would approach the interview in a serious manner.

Second, the interviews were semistructured, usually lasting two or three hours. An extended list of questions structured around the variables used in the archival research were formulated beforehand. The interviewees were instructed to feel free to deviate from the questions and to discuss what they thought to be important. Their "diversions" produced new information.

Third, the interview sample was assembled in two ways. While examining the archival material, the names of leaders associated with various activities turned up constantly. These were the initial individuals contacted for interviews. Once the interview process was underway, interviewees would invariably remark, often in response to queries, "you know, you really should speak to [so-and-so] regarding that matter." Subsequent interviews were arranged with many of these individuals. Thus, the snowball effect was central to the sampling process. Although the activists interviewed came from numerous organizations and represented different, if not conflicting, viewpoints, to our surprise they agreed on many basic issues.

Given that the sit-in movement occurred twenty years ago, it is reasonable to wonder whether interview accounts are reliable and valid. Moreover, there is the suspicion that participants might have vested interests in presenting the "facts" in such a way as to enhance their own status. Such problems of recall and vested interest have been minimized in this research because the analysis is not based on any one source. Rather, it is built on an array of published material, archival sources, and accounts of individuals who participated in and were eye-witnesses to the same events. Furthermore, cross references were made throughout the data collection process. Follow-up phone calls were made to clarify ambiguity and to obtain a comprehensive view of the sit-in movement. It appears that neither of these potential trouble spots produced fundamental defects in the data.

Early Sit-Ins: Forerunners

The first myth regarding the sit-in movement is that it started in Greensboro, North Carolina, on February 1, 1960. This research documents that Civil Rights activists conducted sit-ins between 1957 and 1960 in at least fifteen cities: St. Louis, Missouri; Wichita and Kansas City, Kansas; Oklahoma City, Enid, Tulsa, and Stillwater, Oklahoma; Lexington and Louisville, Kentucky; Miami, Florida; Charleston, West Virginia; Sumter, South Carolina; East St. Louis, Illinois; Nashville, Tennessee; and Durham, North Carolina.[4] The Greensboro sit-ins are important because they represent a unique link in a long chain of sit-ins. Although this paper concentrates on the uniqueness of the Greensboro link, there were important similarities in the entire chain. While other studies (Southern Regional Council, 1960; Oppenheimer, 1964; Matthews and Prothro, 1966; Meier and Rudwick, 1973) have not totally overlooked these earlier sit-ins, they fail to reveal their scope, connections, and extensive organizational base.

The early sit-ins were initiated by direct-action organizations. From interviews with participants in the early sit-ins (Moore, 1978; McCain, 1978; Lawson, 1978; Smith, 1978; McKissick, 1978, 1979; Luper, 1981; Randolph, 1981; Lewis, 1981) and published works (Southern Regional Council, 1960; Meier and Rudwick, 1973), I found that Civil Rights organizations initiated sit-ins in fourteen of the fifteen cities I have identified. The NAACP, primarily its Youth Councils, either initiated or co-initiated sit-ins in nine of the fifteen cities. CORE, usually working with the NAACP, played an important initiating role in seven of the fifteen cities. The SCLC initiated one case and was involved in another. Finally, the Durham Committee on Negro Affairs, working with the NAACP, initiated sit-ins in that city. From this data, we can conclude that these early sit-ins were a result of a multi-faceted organizational effort.

These sit-ins received substantial backing from their respective communities. The black church served as the major institutional force behind the sit-ins. Over two decades ago, E. Franklin Frazier argued that "for the Negro masses, in their social and moral isolation in American society, the Negro Church community has been a nation within a nation" (Frazier, 1963:49). He argued that the church functioned as the central political arena in black society. Nearly all of the direct-action organizations that initiated these early sit-ins were closely associated with the church. The church supplied these organizations not only with an established communication network, but also leaders and organized masses, finances, and a safe environment in which to hold political meetings. Direct-action organizations clung to the church because their survival depended on it.

Not all black churches supported the sit-ins. The many that did often supported sit-ins in a critical but "invisible" manner. Thus, Mrs. Clara Luper, the organizer of the 1958 Oklahoma City sit-ins, wrote that the black church did not want to get involved, but church leaders told organizers, "we could meet in their churches. They would take up a collection for us and make announcements concerning our worthwhile activities" (Luper, 1979:3). This "covert" role was central. Interviewed activists revealed that clusters of churches were usually directly involved with the sit-ins. In addition to community support generated through the churches, these activists also received support from parents whose children were participating in demonstrations.

These sit-ins were organized by established leaders of the black community. The leaders did not spontaneously emerge in response to a crisis, but were organizational actors in the full sense of the word. Some sit-in leaders were also church leaders, taught school, and headed up the local direct-action organization; their extensive organizational linkages provided blocks of individuals to serve as demonstrators. Clara Luper wrote, "The fact that I was teaching American History at Dungee High School in Spencer, Oklahoma and was a member of the First Street Baptist Church furnished me with an ample number of young people who would become the nucleus of the Youth Council" (Luper, 1979:1). Mrs. Luper's case is not isolated; leaders of the early sit-ins were enmeshed in organizational networks and were integral members of the black community.

Rational planning was evident in this early wave of sit-ins. During the late fifties, the Revs. James Lawson and Kelly Miller Smith, both leaders of a direct-action organization—Nashville Christian Leadership Council—formed what they called a "nonviolent workshop." In these workshops, Lawson meticulously taught local college students the philosophy and tactics of nonviolent protest (D. Bevel, 1978; Lewis, 1978).[5] In 1959, these students held "test" sit-ins in two department stores. Earlier, in 1957, members of the Oklahoma City NAACP Youth Council created what they called their "project," whose aim was to eliminate segregation in public accommodations (Luper, 1979:3). The project consisted of various committees and groups who planned sit-in strategies. After a year of planning, this group walked into the local Katz Drug Store and initiated their sit-in. In St. Louis in 1955, William Clay organized an NAACP Youth Council. Through careful planning and twelve months of demonstrations, members of this organization were able to desegregate dining facilities at department stores (Meier and Rudwick, 1973:93). In Durham, North Carolina in 1958, black activists of the Durham Committee on Negro Affairs conducted a survey of 5-and-10-cent stores in Durham (Southern Regional Council, 1960). The survey revealed that these stores were heavily dependent on black trade. Clearly, the sit-ins initiated by this group were based on rational planning. A similar picture emerges in Sumter, South Carolina and for all the early sit-ins.

Finally, these early sit-ins were sponsored by indigenous resources of the black community; the leadership was black, the bulk of the demonstrators were black, the strategies and tactics were formulated by blacks, and the finances came out of the pockets of blacks, while their serene spirituals echoed through the churches.[6]

Most of the organizers of the early sit-ins knew each other and were well aware of each other's strategies of confrontation. Many of these activists were part of the militant wing of the NAACP. Following the Montgomery bus boycott, this group began to reorganize NAACP Youth Councils with the explicit purpose of initiating direct-action projects. This group of activists (e.g., Floyd McKissick, Daisy Bates, Ronald Walters, Hosea Williams, Barbara Posey, Clara Luper,

etc.) viewed themselves as a distinct group, because the national NAACP usually did not approve of their direct-action approach or took a very ambivalent stance.

These militants of the NAACP built networks that detoured the conservative channels and organizational positions of their superiors. At NAACP meetings and conferences, they selected situations where they could present freely their plans and desires to engage in confrontational politics. At these gatherings, information regarding strategies was exchanged. Once acquainted, the activists remained in touch by phone and mail.

Thus, it is no accident that the early sit-ins occurred between 1957 and 1960. Other instances of "direct action" also occurred during this period. For example, Mrs. Daisy Bates led black students affiliated with her NAACP Youth Council into the all-white Little Rock Central High School and forced President Eisenhower to send in National Guards. CORE, beginning to gain a foothold in the South, had the explicit goal of initiating direct-action projects. We have already noted that CORE activists were in close contact with other activists of the period. Though these early sit-ins and related activities were not part of a grandiose scheme, their joint occurrences, timing, and approaches were connected via organizational and personal networks.

Sit-In Cluster

Organizational and personal networks produced the first cluster of sit-ins in Oklahoma in 1958. By tracing these networks, we can arrive at a basic understanding of this cluster and a clue to understanding the entire sit-in movement.

In August of 1958, the NAACP Youth Council of Wichita, Kansas, headed by Ronald Walters, initiated sit-ins at the lunch counters of a local drug Store (Lewis, 1981). At the same time, Clara Luper and the young people in her NAACP Youth Council were training to conduct sit-ins in Oklahoma City. The adult leaders of these two groups knew each other: in addition to working for the same organization, several members of the two groups were personal friends. Following the initial sit-ins in Wichita, members of the two groups made numerous phone calls, exchanged information, and discussed mutual support. This direct contact was important because the local press refused to cover the sit-ins. In less than a week,

Clara Luper's group in Oklahoma City initiated their planned sit-ins.

Shortly thereafter, sit-ins were conducted in Tulsa, Enid, and Stillwater, Oklahoma. Working through CORE and the local NAACP Youth Council, Clara Luper's personal friend, Mrs. Shirley Scaggins, organized the sit-ins in Tulsa (Luper, 1981). Mrs. Scaggins had recently lived in Oklahoma City and knew the details of Mrs. Luper's sit-in project. The two leaders worked in concert. At the same time, the NAACP Youth Council in Enid began to conduct sit-ins. A Mr. Mitchell who led that group (Luper, 1981) knew Mrs. Luper well. He had visited the Oklahoma Youth Council at the outset of their sit-in and discussed with them sit-in tactics and mutual support. The Stillwater sit-ins appear to have been conducted independently by black college students.

A process similar to that in Oklahoma occurred in East St. Louis, Illinois. Homer Randolph, who in late 1958 organized the East St. Louis sit-ins, had previously lived in Oklahoma City, knew Mrs. Luper well, and had young relatives who participated in the Oklahoma City sit-ins.

In short, the first sit-in cluster occurred in Oklahoma in 1959 and spread to cities within a hundred-mile radius via established organizational and personal networks. The majority of these early sit-ins were (1) connected rather than isolated, (2) initiated through organizations and personal ties, (3) rationally planned and led by established leaders, and (4) supported by indigenous resources. Thus, the Greensboro sit-ins did not mark the movement's beginning, but were links in the chain. But the Greensboro sit-ins were a unique link which triggered sit-ins across the South at an incredible pace. What happened in the black community between the late 1950s and early 1960s to produce such a movement?

Emergence of Internal Organization

During the mid-fifties the extensive internal organization of the Civil Rights movement began to crystalize in communities across the South. During this period "direct action" organizations were being built by local activists. Community institutions—especially the black church—were becoming political. The "mass meeting" with political oratory and protest music became institutionalized. During the same period, CORE entered the South with intentions of initiating protest, and NAACP Youth Councils were reorganized by young militant adults who desired to engage in confrontational politics.

However, neither CORE nor the NAACP Youth Councils were capable of mobilizing widescale protest such as the sit-ins of 1960, because neither had a mass base in the black community. CORE was small, Northern-based, and white-led, largely unknown to Southern blacks. Historically, the NAACP had been unable to persuade more than 2% of the black population to become members. Furthermore, the national NAACP was oriented to legal strategies, not sit-ins. Following the 1954 school desegregation decision, the NAACP was further weakened by a severe attack by local white power structures. Members of the Southern white power structures attempted to drive local branches of NAACP out of existence by labeling them subversive and demanding they make their membership public. NAACP officials usually refused to comply with this demand because their members might suffer physical and economic reprisals if identified. NAACP's opponents argued in the local courts that this noncompliance confirmed their suspicion that NAACP was subversive, and the courts responded by issuing injunctions which prevented NAACP from operating in a number of Southern states. For example the NAACP was outlawed in the state of Alabama from 1956 to 1965 (Morris, 1980). This repression forced the NAACP to become defensively-oriented and to commit its resources to court battles designed to save itself. Thus, neither CORE nor NAACP Youth Councils were able to provide the political base required to launch the massive sit-ins of 1960.

Nevertheless, between 1955 and 1960 new organizational and protest efforts were stirring in Southern black communities. The efforts attracted CORE southward and inspired the direct-action groups in the NAACP to reorganize its Youth Councils. The Montgomery bus boycott was the watershed. The importance of that boycott was that it revealed to the black community that mass protests could be successfully organized and initiated through indigenous resources and institutions.

The Montgomery bus boycott gave rise to both the Montgomery Improvement Association (MIA) and the Southern Christian Leadership Conference (SCLC). The MIA was organized in

December 1955 to coordinate the activities of the mass bus boycott against segregated buses and serve as the boycott's official decision making body. The MIA was a loose church-based Southern organization, whose leadership was dominated by local ministers of Montgomery, with the Rev. Martin Luther King serving as its first president. The dramatic Montgomery boycott triggered similar boycotts in a number of Southern cities. As in Montgomery, the boycotts were organized through the churches, with a local minister typically becoming the official leader. SCLC was organized in 1957 by activist clergymen from across the South to coordinate and consolidate the various local movements. SCLC's leadership was dominated by black ministers with King elected as first president, and the major organizational posts were filled by ministers who led local movements. Thus, SCLC was organized to accomplish across the South what the MIA had in Montgomery. The emergence of MIA and SCLC reflected the dominant role that churches began to play in confrontational politics by the late 1950s.

The Montgomery bus boycott demonstrated the political potential of the black church and church-related direct-action organizations. By 1955 the massive migration of blacks from rural to urban areas was well underway, and many Southern cities had substantial black populations. The black urban churches that emerged in these cities were quite different from their rural counterparts. The urban churches were larger, more numerous, and better financed, and were presided over by ministers who were better educated and whose sole occupation was the ministry (Mays and Nicholson, 1933; McAdam, 1979; Morris, 1980). Moreover, urban churches were owned, operated, and controlled by the black community.

These churches functioned as the institutional base of the Montgomery bus boycott. They supplied the movement with money, organized masses, leaders, highly developed communications, and relatively safe environments where mass meetings could be held to plan confrontations. This institutional base was in place prior to the boycott. Movement leaders transformed the churches into political resources and committed them to the ends of the movement. The new duty of the church finance committee was to collect money for the movement. The minister's new role was to use the pulpit to articulate the political responsibilities of the church community. The new

role of the choir was to weave political messages into the serene spirituals. Regular church meetings were transformed into the "mass meeting" where blacks joined committees to guide protests, offered up collections to the movement, and acquired reliable information of the movement, which local radio and television stations refused to broadcast. The resources necessary to initiate a black movement were present in Montgomery and other communities. They were transformed into political resources and used to launch the first highly visible mass protest of the modern Civil Rights movement.

The important role of the MIA in the emergence of the modern Civil Rights movement is seldom grasped. As a non-bureaucratic, church-based organization, MIA's organizational affairs were conducted like church services rather than by rigid bureaucratic rules, as in the case of the NAACP. Ministers presided over the MIA the way they presided over their congregations. Ultimate authority inhered in the president, Dr. King. Decisions pertaining to local matters could be reached immediately. Diverse organizational tasks were delegated to the rank-and-file on the spot. Rules and procedures emerged by trial and error and could be altered when they inhibited direct action. Oratory, music, and charismatic personalities energized MIA's organizational affairs. The structure of the organization was designed to allow masses to participate directly in protest activities. The MIA proved to be appropriate for confrontational politics because it was mass-based, nonbureaucratic, Southern-led, and able to transform pre-existing church resources into political power.

Southern blacks took notice of the Montgomery movement. Activists from across the South visited Montgomery to observe the political roles of the church and the MIA. For example, when Hosea Williams (at the time, an activist associated with the NAACP in Savannah, Georgia) visited the Montgomery movement, he marvelled at its dynamics:

> You had the NAACP lawsuits, you'd had NAACP chapters, who had much less than 5% participation anyplace. But here's a place [Montgomery] where they got masses of blacks—they couldn't get a church big enough where they could hold mass rallies. And then, none of them [masses] were riding the buses. I was interested in these strategies and their implementation and in learning how to

mobilize the masses to move in concert. [Williams, 1978]

Williams, like countless others, did more than marvel. In his words, "I went back to Savannah and organized the Youth Council and nonviolent movement." Thus, another direct-action organization emerged.

Black ministers were in the best position to organize church-related direct-action organizations in the South. Even while the Montgomery movement was in progress, ministers in other cities (e.g., Steele in Tallahassee, Shuttlesworth in Birmingham, and Davis in New Orleans) began to build mass-based movements patterned after the Montgomery movement. These ministers were not only in a position to organize and commit church resources to protest efforts, they were also linked to each other and the larger community via ministerial alliances. In short, between 1955 and 1960 a profound change in Southern black communities had begun. Confrontational politics were thrust to the foreground through new direct-action organizations closely allied with the church.

SCLC and Movement Centers

The creation of the Southern Christian Leadership Conference (SCLC) in 1957 marked a critical organizational shift for the Civil Rights movement. The ministers who organized SCLC clearly understood the historic and central institutional importance of the church in black society. They knew that the church nurtured and produced most of the indigenous leaders, raised finances, and organized masses, as well as being a major force in other aspects of black culture. By 1957 these ministers, many of whom were leading movements in their local communities, consciously and explicitly concluded that the church was capable of functioning as the institutional vanguard of a mass-based black movement. Hence, they organized SCLC to be a Southern-wide, church-based protest organization.

Prior to SCLC, the major black protest organization—NAACP—had been closely linked with the church. Yet, before SCLC was created, the NAACP, and not the church, functioned as the organization through which protest was initiated. With the emergence of SCLC, the critical shift occurred whereby the church itself, rather than groups closely linked to it, began to function as the institutional center of protest.

In 1957 the organizers of SCLC sent out a call to fellow clergymen of the South to organize their congregations and communities for collective protest. The remarks of Rev. Smith of Nashville typified the action of protest-oriented ministers:

> After the meeting [SCLC organizing meeting] and after the discussion that we had and all that, it became clear to me that we needed something in addition to NAACP. So I came back and I called some people together and formed what we named the Nashville Christian Leadership Council in order to address the same kind of issues that the SCLC would be addressing. [Smith, 1978]

Hundreds of ministers across the South took similar action.

From this collective effort resulted what can best be conceptualized as local movement centers of the Civil Rights Movement, which usually had the following seven characteristics:

1. A cadre of social-change-oriented ministers and their congregations. Often one minister would become the local leader of a given center and his church would serve as the coordinating unit.

2. Direct-action organizations of varied complexity. In many cities local churches served as quasi-direct-action organizations, while in others ministers built complex, church-related organizations (e.g., United Defense League of Baton Rouge, Montgomery Improvement Association, Alabama Christian Movement for Human Rights of Birmingham, Petersburg Improvement Association). NAACP Youth Councils and CORE affiliates also were components of the local centers.

3. Indigenous financing coordinated through the church.

4. Weekly mass meetings, which served as forums and where local residents were informed of relevant information and strategies regarding the movement. The meetings also built solidarity among the participants.

5. Dissemination of nonviolent tactics and strategies. The leaders articulated to the black community the message that social change would occur only through nonviolent direct action carried out by masses.

6. Adaptation of a rich church culture to political purposes. The black spiritual sermons, and prayers were used to deepen the participants' commitment to the struggle.

7. A mass-based orientation, rooted in the black community, through the church.

See Figure 1 for a schematic diagram of a typical local movement center.

Figure 1
Structure of a Typical Local Movement Center

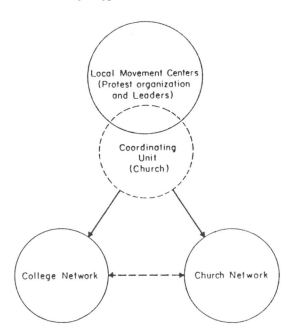

Most scholars of the movement are silent about the period between the Montgomery bus boycott and the 1960 sit-ins. My analysis emphasizes that the organizational foundation of the Civil Rights movement was built during this period and active local movement centers were created in numerous Southern black communities. For instance, between 1957 and 1960 many local centers emerged in Virginia. Ministers such as Reverends Milton Reid, L. C. Johnson, Virgil Wood, Curtis Harris, and Wyatt Walker operated out of centers in Hopewell, Lynchburg, Portsmouth, and Petersburg. The direct-action organizations of these cities were named Improvement Associations and were patterned after the original MIA. South Carolina also had its movement centers. For example, in 1955-1956, after whites began exerting economic pressure against blacks desiring school integration, the black community of Orangeburg initiated an economic boycott against twenty-three local firms. This extended boycott resulted in a vibrant movement center led by the Reverends Matthew McCollom, William Sample, and Alfred Issac and their congregations. Movement centers emerged in other South Carolina cities, such as Sumter, Columbia,

and Florence, organized by James McCain of CORE and activist clergymen.

In Durham, North Carolina, churches that made up the movement center were Union Baptist, pastored by Rev. Grady Davis; Ashbury Temple, pastored by Rev. Douglas Moore; Mount Zion, pastored by Rev. Fuller; St. Marks, pastored by Rev. Speaks; and St. Joseph's, pastored by Rev. Swann. Movement centers were also to be found in cities of the deep South such as Montgomery and Birmingham, Alabama; Baton Rouge, Louisiana; and Tallahassee, Florida.

So prevalent were these centers throughout the South that when Gordon Carey, a CORE field investigator, surveyed the situation in 1959, he reported:

> In some Southern cities such as Montgomery, Orangeburg, Tallahassee, and Birmingham nonviolent movements have been and are being carried on. But most of the South, with its near total segregation, has not been touched. Many places have *felt* the *spirit of* Martin Luther King, Jr. but too often this spirit has not been turned into positive action. [Carey, 1959, emphasis added]

The "spirit" to which Carey referred was in fact the church-based movement centers he found throughout the South, most of which were affiliated with or patterned after SCLC.

Elsewhere (Morris, 1980), I have analyzed how, in the late 1950s, these centers were perfecting confrontation strategies, building organizations, leading marches, organizing voter drives, and radicalizing members of the community. Scholars (e.g., Oberschall, 1973:223) persistently dismiss these centers as weak, limited, and unwilling to confront the white power structure. Yet the evidence suggests a different interpretation. For example, Rev. Fred Shuttlesworth and his mass-based movement center continually confronted Bull Connor and the white power structure of Birmingham throughout the late fifties. As a consequence, Shuttlesworth's home and church were repeatedly bombed.

In short, between 1955 and 1960 many local movement centers were formed and hardened. These centers, which included NAACP Youth Councils and CORE chapters, constituted the new political reality of Southern black communities on the eve of the 1960 sit-ins. It was these structures that were able to generate and sustain a heavy volume of collective action.

The Greensboro Connection

On February 1, 1960 Ezell Blair Jr., Franklin McCain, Joe McNeil, and David Richmond, all students at North Carolina Agricultural and Technical College, sat-in at the Woolworth's lunch counter in Greensboro, North Carolina. Though most commentators mark this as the first sit-in, the four protesters knew that they were not the first to sit-in in the state of North Carolina. Sit-in activity in the state had begun in the late fifties, when a young black attorney, Floyd McKissick, and a young Board member of SCLC, Rev. Douglas Moore, and a small group of other young people (including a few whites from Duke University) began conducting sit-ins in Durham.

These early Durham sit-ins were part of the network of sit-ins which occurred between 1957 and 1960. The activists involved in the early sit-ins belonged to the NAACP Youth Division, which McKissick headed, and their own direct-action organization called the Durham Committee on Negro Affairs. During the late fifties, McKissick and Moore's group conducted sit-ins at local bus stations, waiting rooms, parks, hotels, and other places (McKissick, 1978). In 1957, Rev. Moore and others were arrested for sitting-in at a local ice-cream parlor. The subsequent legal case became known as the "Royal Ice Cream Case." McKissick, who also headed the local Boy Scout organization, periodically would take the young "all-American" scouts into segregated restaurants and order food. In short, this Durham group persistently confronted the white power structure in the late fifties.

The four students who sat-in at Greensboro and sparked the widespread sit-in movement had been members of the NAACP Youth Council, headed by McKissick. According to McKissick, he knew them all well and they knew all about the Durham activities. Martin Oppenheimer (1964:398), an early historian of the sit-ins, confirms this: "All of the boys were, or at some time had been members of an NAACP Youth Council." Indeed, the four students had participated in numerous meetings in social-action oriented churches in Durham. Involvement with the NAACP Youth Council meant that they were not only informed about the Durham sit-ins, but also knew about many of the sit-ins conducted prior to 1960. Thus, the myth that four college students got up one day and sat-in Woolworth's—and sparked the movement—dries up like a "raisin in the sun" when confronted with the evidence.

The National office of the NAACP and many conservative ministers refused to back the Greensboro sit-ins. The NAACP's renowned team of lawyers did not defend the "Greensboro Four." Nevertheless, on the same day they sat-in the students contacted a lawyer who they considered to be their friend, and Floyd McKissick became the lawyer for the "Greensboro Four." The network of college students and adult activists had begun to operate in earnest.

Well-forged networks existed between and among black churches and colleges in North Carolina, facilitated by the large number of colleges concentrated in the state. Indeed, ten black colleges exist within a ten-mile radius of Greensboro (Wolff, 1970:590). Interactions between colleges and churches were both frequent and intense; many colleges were originally founded by the churches. A number of North Carolina churches were referred to as "college churches" because they had large student memberships. These two sets of social organizations were also linked through college seminaries where black ministers received their theological training.

These church-student networks enabled activist-oriented students to become familiar with the emerging Civil Rights movement via local movement centers and made it possible for adult activists to tap the organizational resources of the colleges. Leaders of student government and other campus groups facilitated student mobilization because they, like the ministers, had organizing skills and access to blocs of people. Moreover, the concentration of colleges in the state provided an extensive network of contacts. Fraternity and sorority chapters linked students within and between campuses, as did dating patterns and joint cultural and athletic events. Finally, intercollegiate kinship and friendship networks were widespread, and student leaders were squarely tied to these networks. Similarly, black communities across North Carolina could be rapidly mobilized through the churches, since churches were linked through ministerial alliances and other networks. By 1960 these diverse and interlocking networks were capable of being politicized and coordinated through existing movement centers, making North Carolina an ideal state for the rapid diffusion of collective action.

Within a week of the Greensboro protest, sit-ins rapidly spread across the South. In an extensive study, the Southern Regional Council (1960) reported that between February 1 and March 31 of 1960, major sit-in demonstrations and related activity had been conducted in at least sixty-nine Southern cities (see Table 1).[7]

Table 1
Number of Cities With Sit-ins and Related Protest Activities, February-March 1960, by State

State	Number
North Carolina	18
Florida	11
Virginia	9
South Carolina	7
Texas	5
Tennessee	4
Alabama	4
Georgia	2
West Virginia	2
Louisiana	2
Arkansas	2
Maryland	1
Ohio	1
Kentucky	1
Total	69

Compiled from: Southern Regional Council. "The student protest movement, winter 1960." SRC-13, April 1 1960 (revised).

Beyond Greensboro

As soon as the sit-ins started in Greensboro, the network of movement centers was activated. In the first week of February, 1960, students continued to sit-in daily at the local Woolworth's, and the protest population began to grow. The original four protesters were joined by hundreds of students from A & T College and several other local black colleges. Black high-school students and a few white college students also joined the protest. Influential local whites decided to close the Woolworth's in Greensboro, hoping to take the steam out of the developing mass-movement. It was too late.

Floyd McKissick, Rev. Douglas Moore, and others who had conducted previous sit-ins formulated plans to spread the movement across the state. They were joined by CORE's white field secretary, Gordon Carey, whose services had been requested by the local NAACP president. Carey arrived in Durham from New York on February the 7th and went directly to McKissick's home, where the sit-ins were being planned. Carey was a good choice because he had knowledge of nonviolent resistance and because of his earlier contact with movement centers in Southern black communities.

On February 8th—exactly one week after the Greensboro sit-ins—the demonstrations spread to nearby Durham and Winston-Salem. McKissick, Moore, Carey, and others helped organize these sit-ins, bringing students from the local colleges to churches where they were trained to conduct sit-ins. For example, the Durham students were trained at the same churches through which McKissick and Moore had planned direct action in the late 1950s. Following training and strategy sessions, the students went to the local lunch counters and sat-in.

The organizing effort was not limited to these two nearby cities. Within the first week of the Greensboro sit-in, McKissick, Carey, and Rev. Moore made contact with activists in movement centers throughout North Carolina, South Carolina, and Virginia, urging them to train students for sit-ins. They not only phoned these activists, but traveled to various cities to provide assistance. Upon arrival they often found sit-in planning sessions already underway. According to Carey (1978), "when we reached these cities we went directly to the movement oriented churches." When asked why, Carey replied, "Well, that's where the protest activities were being planned and organized." Thus, these sit-ins were largely organized at the movement churches rather than on the campuses. To understand the sit-in movement, one must abandon the assumption that it was a collegiate phenomenon. For different reasons, Rev. Moore attempted to convey this same idea in the early days of the sit-ins: "If Woolworth and other stores think this is just another panty raid, they haven't had their sociologists in the field recently" (Moore, 1960). The sit-ins grew out of a context of organized movement centers.

As anticipated above, the Southern Christian Leadership Conference was central to the rise of the 1960 sit-in movement. It is critical to remember that when Rev. Moore and other organizers visited churches in North and South Carolina and Virginia, they discovered that church leaders were already training students for sit-ins. Speaking of the ministers who headed these movement churches, Carey (1978) reported, "All of these ministers were active in the Southern Christian

Leadership Conference. At least 75% were getting inspiration from King." Additionally, these ministers had contacts with and often were leaders of both CORE and the activist wing of the NAACP.

Since the movement centers were already in place, they served as both receiving and transmitting "antennas" for the sit-ins. As receivers they gathered information of the sit-ins, and as transmitters they rebroadcast information throughout the networks. Because this internal network already existed, information was rapidly channeled to groups prepared to engage in nonviolent collective action.

During the second week of February 1960, plans were formulated to conduct sit-ins in a number of Southern cities. Communication and coordination between the cities was intensified. For example, early in the second week of February, the Rev. B. Elton Cox of High Point, North Carolina, and Rev. C. A. Ivory of Rock Hill, South Carolina, phoned McKissick and other leaders, informing them that their groups were "ready to go" (McKissick, 1978). Cox's group sat-in on February 11th and Ivory's on February 12th. Rev. Ivory organized and directed the Rock Hill sit-ins from his wheelchair. Within the week, sit-ins were being conducted in several cities in Virginia, most of them organized through the dense network of SCLC movement centers in that state (Southern Regional Council, 1960; Walker, 1978).

The movement hot lines reached far beyond the border states of North Carolina, South Carolina, and Virginia. Rev. Fred Shuttlesworth, an active leader of the Birmingham, Alabama, movement center, happened to be in North Carolina when the first wave of sit-ins occurred, fulfilling a speaking engagement for the leader of the High Point sit-ins—Rev. Cox. According to Shuttlesworth, "He [Rev. Cox] carried me by where these people were going to sit-in . . . I called back to Atlanta, and told Ella [Baker] what was going on. I said, 'this is the thing. You must tell Martin [King] that we must get with this, and really this can shake up the world'" (Shuttlesworth, 1978). Baker, the Executive Director of SCLC, immediately began calling her contacts at various colleges, asking them, "What are you all going to do? It is time to move" (Baker, 1978).

Carey and Rev. Moore phoned the movement center in Nashville, Tennessee, and asked Rev. Lawson if they were ready to move. The student

and church communities coordinated by the Nashville Christian Leadership Conference answered in the affirmative. According to Lawson,

> Of course there was organizing because after the sit-in, the first one in February, people like Doug Moore, Ella Baker, myself, did call around to places that we knew, said, 'Can you start? Are you ready? Can you go? And how can we help you?' So there was some of that too that went on. Even there the sit-in movement did not just spread spontaneously. I mean there was a readiness. And then there were, there were phone calls that went out to various communities where we knew people and where we knew student groups and where we knew minister groups, and said, you know, 'this is it, let's go.' [Lawson, 1978]

When asked, "Why did the student sit-in movement occur?" Lawson replied,

> Because King and the Montgomery boycott and the whole development of that leadership that clustered around King had emerged and was ready and was preaching and teaching direct action, nonviolent action, and was clearly ready to act, ready to seed any movement that needed sustenance and growth. So there was . . . in other words, the soil had been prepared. [Lawson, 1978]

These data provide insight into how a political movement can rapidly spread between geographically distant communities. The sit-ins spread across the South in a short period of time because activists, working through local movement centers, planned, coordinated, and sustained them. They spread despite the swinging billy clubs of policemen, despite Ku Klux Klansmen, white mobs, murderers, tear gas, and economic reprisals (Southern Regional Council, 1960; Matthews and Prothro, 1966; Oberschall, 1973). The pre-existing movement centers provided the resources and organization required to sustain the sit-ins in the face of opposition.

Sit-In Clusters of 1960

The organizational and personal networks that produced the first cluster of sit-ins in Oklahoma in 1958 have already been described. The cluster concept can be applied to the entire set of sit-ins of February and March 1960. Many of the cities where sit-ins occurred can be grouped by geographic and temporal proximity. A cluster is defined as two or more cities within 75 miles of each other where sit-in activity took place within a span of 14 days. In Table 2, forty-one of the sixty-nine cities having sit-ins during this two-month period have been grouped because they

Table 2
Clusters of Cities With Sit-ins and Related Activities, February-March 1960

Cluster	Number of Days Between First Sit-ins Within Cluster	Number of Miles Between Farthest Two Cities Within Cluster
Fayetteville, Raleigh, N. C. (2/9/60-2/10/60)	1	50
Tampa, St. Petersburg, Sarasota, Fla. (2/29/60-3/2/60)	2	50
Montgomery, Tuskegee, Ala. (2/25/60-2/27/60)	2	25
Columbia, Florence, Sumter, S. C. (3/2/60-3/4/60)	2	70
Austin, San Antonio, Tx. (3/11/60-3/13/60)	2	75
Salisbury, Shelby, N. C. (2/16/60-2/18/60)	2	60
Wilmington, New Bern, N. C. (3/17/60-3/19/60)	2	75
Charlotte, N. C., Concord, Rock Hill, S. C. (2/9/60-2/12/60)	3	50
Durham, Winston-Salem, High Point, N. C. (2/8/60-2/11/60)	3	75
Chapel Hill, Henderson, N. C. (2/25/60-2/29/60)	3	50
Jacksonville, St. Augustine, Fla. (3/12/60-3/15/60)	3	40
Charleston, Orangeburg, Denmark, S. C. (2/25/60-2/29/60)	4	70
Daytona Beach, Sanford, Orlando, Fla. (3/2/60-3/7/60)	5	54
Houston, Galveston, Tx. (3/5/60-3/11/60)	6	65
Richmond, Petersburg, Va. (2/20-60-2/27/60)	7	30
Hampton, Norfolk, Portsmouth, Newport News (2/11/60-2/22/60)	11	35

Compiled from: Southern Regional Council: "The student protest movement, winter 1960." SRC-13, April 1960

meet these criteria. Within this period 59% of the cities that had sit-ins and related activity were part of clusters. The percentage of these cities forming sit-in clusters is even more striking in the first month: during February, 76% of cities having sit-ins were part of clusters, while during March the percentage dropped to 44%.

The clustering differentials between the two months can be explained by taking region into account as shown in Table 3. In the first month (February) 85% of the cities having sit-ins were located in Southeastern and border states. This pattern had been established earlier, when most of the pre-1960 sit-ins occurred in border states. Most of the February sit-ins took place in cities of border states because repression against blacks was not as severe there as in the deep South. This made it possible for activists in border states to build dense networks of movement centers. We have already seen that North Carolina, South Carolina, and Virginia had numerous social-action churches and direct-action organizations. By the time the sit-ins occurred in Virginia, SCLC had affiliates throughout the state, and Rev. Wyatt Walker, who was the leader of Virginia's movement centers, was also the state Director of CORE and president of the local NAACP. Similar patterns existed in the other border states. Small wonder that in the month of February, 73% of cities having sit-ins were located in Virginia, North Carolina, and South Carolina. Similarly, these cities produced 88% of the February clusters. This clustering reflected both the great density of movement centers and a system of domination less stringent than that of the deep South.

Table 3
Cities With Sit-ins and Related Activities, February-March 1960, by Geographic Region

	Deep South	Southeastern and Border States	Non-South	All States
February-March 1960				
Number of Cities With Sit-ins, 2-Month Total	26	42	1	69
Region's % of 2-Month Total	38	61	1	100
February 1960				
Number of Cities With Sit-ins	5	28	0	33
Region's % of Feb. Total	15	85	0	100
% of 2-Month Total Occurring in Feb.	19	67	0	48
March 1960				
Number of Cities With Sit-ins	21	14	1	36
Region's % of March Total	58	39	3	100
% of 2-Month Total Occurring in March	81	33	100	52

Compiled from: Southern Regional Council. "The student protest movement, winter 1960." SRC-13, April 1 1960.
Note: Deep South states are Alabama, Florida, Georgia, Texas, Arkansas, and Louisiana. Southeastern and border states are South Carolina, North Carolina, Virginia, Tennessee, Maryland, Kentucky, and West Virginia. The non-South state is Ohio.

Table 3 reveals that in March a major change took place: the majority of the sit-ins occurred in cities of the deep South. With a few exceptions, the sit-ins in the deep South did not occur in clusters. They occurred almost exclusively in Southern cities where movement centers were already established: Montgomery and Birmingham, Alabama; Baton Rouge and New Orleans, Louisiana; Tallahassee, Florida; Nashville and Memphis, Tennessee; and Atlanta and Savannah, Georgia. Repression would have been too great on student protesters operating outside of the protection of such centers in the deep South. Thus, the decrease in clustering in the deep South reflected both the high level of repression and the absence of dense networks of movement centers. Focusing on the internal movement centers enables us to explain both the clustering phenomenon and its absence.

Given the large proportion of sit-ins occurring in clusters, we can say that they did not spread randomly. The clusters represented the social and temporal space in which sit-ins were organized, coordinated, spread, and financed by the black community.[8] Within these clusters, cars filled with organizers from SCLC, NAACP, and CORE raced between sit-in points relaying valuable information. Telephone lines and the community "grapevine" sent forth protest instructions and plans. These clusters were the sites of numerous midday and late night meetings where the black community assembled in the churches, filled the collection plates, and vowed to mortgage their homes to raise the necessary bail-bond money in case the protesting students were jailed. Black lawyers pledged their legal service to the movement and black physicians made their services available to injured demonstrators. Amidst these exciting scenes, black spirituals that had grown out of slavery calmed and deepened the participants' commitment. A detailed view of the Nashville sit-ins provides an example of these dynamics, because the Nashville movement epitomized the sit-ins whether they occurred singularly or in clusters.

The Nashville Sit-in Movement

A well-developed, church-based movement center headed by Rev. Kelly Miller Smith was organized in Nashville during the late 1950s. The center, an affiliate of SCLC, was called the Nashville Christian Leadership Council (NCLC). Rev. James Lawson, an expert tactician of nonviolent protest, was in charge of NCLC's direct-action committee. Lawson received a call from Rev. Douglas Moore about two days after the Greensboro sit-ins began. The Nashville group was ready to act because a cadre of students had already received training in nonviolent direct action. They had conducted "test sit-ins" in two large department stores in downtown Nashville prior to the 1959 Christmas holidays. Moreover, the group had already made plans in late 1959 to begin continuous sit-ins in 1960 with the explicit intention of desegregating Nashville (Smith, 1978; D. Bevel, 1978). Thus, Greensboro provided the impetus for the Nashville group to carry out its preexisting strategy.

Rev. Smith's First Baptist Church became the coordinating unit of the Nashville sit-in movement. A decision to sit-in at local lunch counters on Saturday, February 13 1960, was arrived at after much debate. The adults (mostly ministers) of the NCLC met with the students at movement headquarters and tried to convince them to postpone the demonstrations for a couple of days until money could be raised. According to Rev. Smith (1978), "NCLC had $87.50 in the treasury. We had no lawyers, and we felt kind of a parental responsibility for those college kids. And we knew they were gonna be put in jail, and we didn't know what else would happen. And so some of us said, "'we need to wait until we get a lawyer, until we raise some funds.'"

NCLC leaders told the students that they could collect the money through the churches within a week. Then, according to Rev. Smith:

> James Bevel, then a student at American Baptist Theological Seminary, said that, "I'm sick and tired of waiting," which was a strange thing to come from a kid who was only about nineteen years old. You see, the rest of us were older. . . . [Bevel said] "If you asked us to wait until next week, then next week something would come up and you'd say wait until the next week and maybe we never will get our freedom." He said this, "I believe that something will happen in the situation that will make for the solution to some of these problems we're talking about." So we decided to go on. [Smith, 1978]

The proximity of four black colleges in Nashville—Fisk University, Tennessee State College, American Baptist Theological Seminary, and Meharry Medical School—facilitated the mobilization of large numbers of students. In its extensive ties between students and churches, Nashville resembled the state of North Carolina. Indeed, John Lewis, James Bevel, and Bernard Lafayette, who became major sit-in leaders, were students at the American Baptist Theological Seminary and were taught there by Rev. Smith. Furthermore, they were student leaders:

> John Lewis, Bernard and myself were the major participants in the seminary. All of us were like the top student leaders in our schools. I think John at the time was the president of the Student Council. I was a member of the Student Council. I was one of the editors of the yearbook. Bernard was an editor of the yearbook. So all of us were like the top leaders in our school. [J. Bevel, 1978]

Thus the student leaders could rapidly mobilize other students because they already had access to organized groups. Other writers (Von Eschen et al., 1971; McAdam, 1979) have pointed out that these college networks played a key role in sit-in

mobilization. However, the sit-in movement cannot be explained without also noting the crucial interaction between black college students and local movement centers. Speaking of Rev. Smith and his church, Bevel recalled, "the First Baptist basically had the Baptist people who went to Fisk and Meharry and Tennessee State, and the Seminary were basically members of his church" (J. Bevel, 1978). These students had been introduced to the Civil Rights movement while they attended church.

On the first day of the sit-ins in Nashville, students gathered in front of their respective campuses. NCLC sent cars to each college to transport the students to Rev. Smith's church. Again, the major organizational tasks were performed in the church which served as the coordinating unit of the local movement center, rather than on the campuses. Coordination of sit-in activity between the college community and the churches was made less difficult because many of the students (especially student leaders) were immersed in the local movement centers prior to the sit-ins. The pattern of close connection between student demonstrators and adult leaders already existed in places such as Greensboro and even Oklahoma City in 1958; indeed, this pattern undergirded the entire movement. Rev. Jemison's (1978) remark that the Baton Rouge sit-in demonstrators "were schooled right over there at our church; they were sent out from here to go to the lunch counters" typifies the relationship between the students and the local movement centers.[9] Jemison continued, "The student leaders attended church here. We had close ties because they were worshipping with us while we were working together."

Once the Nashville students arrived at movement headquarters, they participated in workshops where they learned the strategies of nonviolent confrontation from experts like Rev. Lawson, Rev. Metz Rollins, Rev. C. T. Vivian, and the core group of students that Lawson had already trained. This pool of trained leaders was a pre-existing resource housed by NCLC. After the workshops, the students were organized into groups with specific protest responsibilities, each having a spokesperson who had been trained by Lawson during the late 1950s. They then marched off to confront Nashville's segregated lunch counters and agents of social control.

The adult black community immediately mobilized to support the students. Shortly after the demonstrations began, large numbers of students were arrested. According to Rev. Smith,

> We just launched out on something that looked perfectly crazy and scores of people were being arrested, and paddy wagons were full and the people out in downtown couldn't understand what was going on, people just welcoming being arrested, that ran against everything they had ever seen. . . . I've forgotten how much we needed that day, and we got everything we needed. [That particular day?] Yes, sir. About $40,000. We needed something like $40,000 in fives. And we had all the money. Not in fives, but in bail. Every bit of it came up. You know—property and this kind of thing . . . and there were fourteen black lawyers in this town. Every black lawyer made himself available to us. [Smith, 1978]

Thus, basic, pre-existing resources in the dominated community were used to accomplish political goals. It was suggested to Rev. Smith that a massive movement such as that in Nashville would need outside resources. He replied,

> Now let me quickly say to you that in early 1960, when we were really out there on the line, the community stood up. We stood together. This community had proven that this stereotyped notion of black folk can't work together is just false. We worked together a lot better than the white organizations. So those people fell in line. [Smith, 1978]

Rev. Smith's comments are applicable beyond Nashville. For example, in Orangeburg, after hundreds of students were arrested and brutalized, the adult black community came solidly to their aid. Bond was set at $200 per student, and 388 students were arrested. Over $75,000 was needed, and adults came forth to put up their homes and property in order to get students out of jail. Rev. McCollom, the leader of the Orangeburg movement center, remarked that, "there was no schism between the student community and the adult community in Orangeburg" (McCollom, 1978). Jim McCain (1978) of CORE, who played a central role in organizing sit-ins across South Carolina and in Florida, reported that community support was widespread. According to Julian Bond (1980), a student leader of Atlanta's sit-ins, "black property owners put up bond which probably amounted to $100,000" to get sit-in demonstrators released from jail.

These patterns were repeated across the South. This community support should not be surprising, considering the number of ministers and congregations involved before and during the movement. Yet, Zinn, an eyewitness to many of these events, wrote, "Spontaneity and self-sufficiency were the hallmarks of the sit-ins; without adult advice or consent, the students planned and carried them through" (1964:29). This myopia illustrates the inadequacies of analyses that neglect or ignore the internal structure of oppressed communities and protest movements. The continuing development of the Nashville sit-ins sheds further light on the interdependence of the movement and the black community. A formal structure called the Nashville Nonviolent Movement was developed to direct sit-in activities. Its two substructures, the Student Central Committee and the Nashville Christian Leadership Council, worked closely together and had overlapping membership (Reverends Lawson and Vivian were members of both groups). The Central Committee usually consisted of 25 to 30 students drawn from all the local colleges. NCLC represented adult ministers and the black community. The two groups established committees to accomplish specific tasks, including a finance committee, a telephone, publicity, and news committee, and a work committee. The work committee had subgroups responsible for painting protest signs and providing food and transportation. The city's black lawyers became the movement's defense team, students from Meharry Medical School were the medical team.

This intricate structure propelled and guided the sit-in movement of Nashville. A clear-cut division of labor developed between the Central Committee and the NCLC. The Central Committee's major responsibilities were to train, organize, and coordinate the demonstration. The NCLC developed the movement's financial structure and coordinated relations between the community and the student movement. Diane Nash Bevel, a major student leader of the Nashville sit-ins, was asked why the students did not take care of their own finances and build their own relationships with the larger community. She replied,

> We didn't want to be bothered keeping track of money that was collected at the rallies and stuff. We were just pleased that NCLC would do that, and would handle the book-keeping and all that trouble that went along with having money. . . . Besides, we were much too busy sitting-in and going to jail and that kind of thing. There wasn't really the stability of a bookkeeper, for instance. We didn't want to be bothered with developing that kind of stability. . . . We were very pleased to form this alliance with NCLC who would sponsor the rallies and coordinate the community support

among the adults and keep track of the money, while we sat-in and . . . well, it took all our time, and we were really totally immersed in it. My day would sometimes start . . . well we'd have meetings in the morning at six o'clock, before classes, and work steady to extremely late at night, organizing the sit-ins, getting publicity out to the students that we were having a sit-in, and where and what time we would meet. Convincing people, and talking to people, calming people's fears, going to class, at the same time. It was a really busy, busy time for all of the people on the Central Committee. We were trying to teach nonviolence, maintain order among a large, large number of people. That was about all we could handle. [D. Bevel, 1978]

Students are ideal participants in protest activities. Usually they do not have families to support, employer's rules and dictates to follow, and crystallized ideas as to what is "impossible" and "unrealistic." Students have free time and boundless energy to pursue causes they consider worthwhile and imperative (Lipset and Wolin, 1965:3; McCarthy and Zald, 1973:10). McPhail's (1971:1069) finding that young, single, unemployed males were ideal participants in civil disorders and McPhail and Miller's (1973:726) discussion of availability for participation in the assembly process parallels this notion that students are ideal participants in protest activities. Nevertheless, although black students were able to engage in protest activities continuously because of their student status, a one-sided focus on them diverts attention from the larger community, which had undergone considerable radicalization. Speaking of the adults, James Bevel (1978), a student organizer of the Nashville sit-ins, remarked, "But when you talk to each individual, they talked just like we talked—the students. They had jobs and they were adults. But basically, their position would be just like ours. They played different roles because they were in different—they had to relate based on where they were in the community" (J. Bevel, 1978).

The adults of the NCLC organized the black community to support the militant student sit-in movement. Once the movement began, NCLC instituted weekly and sometimes daily mass meetings in the churches. Rev. Smith (1978) recalled,

Sometimes we had them more than once a week if we needed to. When things were really hot we called a meeting at eight o'clock in the morning. We'd call one for twelve that day, twelve noon, and the place would be full. We had what we called our wire service. People got on telephones, that was our wire service, and they would fill that building. They'd fill that building in just a matter of relatively short time.

At these mass meetings, ministers from across the city turned over the money that their respective churches had donated to the movement. Thousands of dollars were collected at the mass meetings while black adults, ministers, and students sang such lyrics is "Before I'd be a slave, I'd rather be buried in my grave." Then too, bundles of leaflets were given to adults at mass meetings who then distributed them throughout the black community. This shows how the movement built communication channels through which vital information, strategies, and plans were disseminated.

During the Nashville sit-ins, word went out to the black community not to shop downtown.

We didn't organize the boycott. We did not organize the boycott. The boycott came about. We don't know how it happened. I tell you there are a lot of little mystical elements in there, little spots that defy rational explanation. . . . Now, we promoted it. We adopted it. But we did not sit down one day and organize a boycott . . . ninety-nine percent of the black people in this community stayed away from downtown during the boycott. It was a fantastic thing—successful. It was fantastically successful. [Smith, 1978]

Yet the boycott was largely organized by NCLC. According to Bevel, Dr. Vivian Henderson, who was head of Fisk University's economic department and a member of NCLC, played a key role in the boycott, because

Vivian Henderson was basically responsible for calling the boycott. He got up at a mass meeting and said, "at least what we could do to support students, if we've got any decency, we can just stop paying bills and just don't shop until this thing is resolved." A very indignant type of speech he made. It just caught on. All the bourgeois women would come to the meeting, and they just got on the phone and called up everybody, all the doctors' wives and things. They just got on the phone and called 300 or 400 people and told them don't shop downtown. Finally there was just a total boycott downtown. There would be no black people downtown at all. [J. Bevel, 1978]

Activists were stationed downtown to insure that blacks knew not to shop. According to Rev. Smith, shortly after the boycott was initiated, merchants began coming to his home wanting to talk. Diane Nash Bevel attributed the boycott's effectiveness to reduced profits during the Easter shopping season. It also changed the merchant's attitude toward the sit-ins.

> It was interesting the difference that [the boycott] made in terms of how the managers were willing to talk with us, because see we had talked with the managers of the stores. We had a meeting at the very beginning and they had kind of listened to us politely, and said, "well, we just can't do it. We can't desegregate the counters because we will lose money and that's the end of it." So, after the economic withdrawal, they were eager to talk with us, and try to work up some solution. [D. Bevel, 1978)

In early 1960 the white power structure of Nashville was forced to desegregate a number of private establishments and public transportation facilities. SNCC's *Student Voice* reported that in Nashville, "A long series of negotiations followed the demonstrations, and on May 10, 6 downtown stores integrated their lunch counters. Since this time others have followed suit, and some stores have hired Negroes in positions other than those of menial workers for the first time" (*Student Voice,* August, 1960). Daily demonstrations by hundreds of students refusing to accept bond so that they could be released from jail, coupled with the boycott, gave blacks the upper hand in the conflict situation. Careful organization and planning was the hallmark of the Nashville sit-in movement.

Discussion and Conclusions

Consistent with Proposition 1, I have presented evidence that pre-existing social structures played a central role in the 1960 sit-in movement. Pre-existing activist groups, formal movement organizations, colleges, and overlapping personal networks provided the framework through which the sit-ins emerged and spread. Previous writings on the sit-ins (e.g., Lomax, 1962; Zinn, 1964; Matthews and Prothro, 1966; Killian, 1968; Meier and Rudwick, 1973; Piven and Cloward, 1977) have persistently portrayed pre-existing organization as an after-the-fact accretion on student spontaneity. The dominant view is that SCLC, CORE, NAACP, and community leaders rushed into a dynamic campus movement after it was well underway, while my data provide evidence that those organizational and community forces were at the core of the sit-in movement from its beginning. Thus, preexisting organizations provided the sit-ins with the resources and communication networks needed for their emergence and development.

Prior to 1960 the sit-in was far from being the dominant tactic of the Civil Rights movement, yet in early 1960, sit-in demonstrations swept through thirteen states and hundreds of communities within two months. Almost instantly sit-ins became the major tactic and focus of the movement. A tactical innovation had occurred.

Consistent with Proposition 2, the data strongly suggest that the 1960 Greensboro sit-in occurred at the time when the necessary and sufficient condition for the rapid diffusion of sit-ins was present. That condition was the existence of well-developed and widespread internal organization. Because this internal organization was already firmly in place prior to 1960, activist groups across the South were in a position to quickly initiate sit-ins. The rapidity with which sit-ins were organized gave the appearance that they were spontaneous. This appearance was accentuated because most demonstrators were students rather than veteran Civil Rights activists.

Yet the data show that the student organizers of the sit-ins were closely tied to the internal organization of the emerging Civil Rights movement. Prior student/activist ties had been formed through church affiliations and youth wings of Civil Rights organizations. In short, students and seasoned activists were able to rapidly coordinate the sit-ins because both were anchored to the same organization.

Innovations in political movements arise in the context of an active opposition. The organization of the Civil Rights movement provided the resources that sustained diffusion of the sit-ins in the face of attack. This vast internal organization consisted of local movement centers, experienced activists who had amassed organizing skills, direct-action organizations, communication systems between centers, pre-existing strategies for dealing with the opposition, workshops and training procedures, fund-raising techniques, and community mobilization techniques.

The pre-existing internal organization enabled organizers to quickly disseminate the "sit-in" idea to groups already favorably disposed toward direct action. In the innovation/diffusion literature (e.g., Coleman et al., 1957; Lionberger, 1960; Rogers, 1962) a positive decision by numerous actors to adopt a new item is treated as a central problem. In the case of the sit-ins, the adoption problem was largely solved by the pre-existing organization. Since that organization housed groups that had already identified with "confrontational politics," little time was lost on debates as to whether sit-ins should be adopted. Thus, the diffusion process did not become bogged down at the adoption stage.

Repression might have prevented the diffusion process. The authorities and white extremist groups attempted to prevent the spread of the sit-ins by immediately arresting the demonstrators, employing brutal force, and refusing to report the sit-ins in the local press. The organizational efficiency of the movement centers prevailed against the opposition. Existing recruiting and training procedures made it possible for jailed demonstrators to be instantly replaced. When heavy fines were leveled against the movement, activists were able generally to raise large sums of money through their pre-existing community contacts. The pre-existing communication networks easily overcame the problems imposed by news blackouts. Moreover, skilled activists were able to weaken the stance of the opposition by rapidly organizing economic boycotts. Because the internal organization was widespread, these effective counter measures were employed in Black communities across the South. Thus, it was well-developed and widespread internal organization that enabled the 1960 sit-ins to rapidly diffuse into a major tactical innovation of the Civil Rights movement.

Proposition 3 maintains that pre-existing internal organization establishes the types of innovations that can occur within movements. The internal organization that gave rise to the sit-ins specialized in what was called nonviolent direct action. This approach consisted of a battery of tactics that were disruptive but peaceful. The nonviolent approach readily fitted into the ideological and organizational framework of the black church, and provided ministers, students, and ordinary working people with a method for entering directly into the political process.

The movement centers that emerged following the Montgomery bus boycott were developed around nonviolent approaches to social change. Indeed, the primary goal of these centers was to build nonviolent movements. Yet, nonviolent confrontations as a disciplined form of collective action was relatively new to the black masses of the South. The activists within the movement centers systematically introduced blacks to the nonviolent approach. They organized nonviolent workshops and conducted them on a routine basis in the churches and protest organizations. Literature from organizations (e.g., Fellowship of Reconciliation and CORE) that specialized in the nonviolent approach was made available through the centers. Skilled nonviolent strategists (e.g., Bayard Rustin, James Lawson, and Glenn Smiley) travelled between centers training leaders how to conduct nonviolent campaigns. The varied tactics—mass marches, negotiations, boycotts, sit-ins—associated with direct action became common knowledge to activists in the centers. Moreover, in the late fifties activists began experimenting with these tactics and urging the community to become involved with nonviolent confrontations. Meier and Rudwick (1976) have shown that sit-ins at segregated facilities were conducted by black activists in the nineteen forties and late fifties. But this tactic remained relatively isolated and sporadic and did not diffuse throughout the larger community. Meier and Rudwick (1976:384) conclude that diffusion did not occur before 1960 because the white mass-media failed to cover sit-ins. My analysis suggests another explanation: sit-ins prior to 1960 did not spread because the internal organization required for such a spread did not exist. In short, without visible internal social organization, innovations will remain sporadic and isolated. With organization, innovations can spread and be sustained. By 1960 the internal organization of the Civil Rights movement had amassed resources and organization specifically designed to execute nonviolent confrontations.

The sit-in tactic was well suited to the existing internal organization of the Civil Rights movement. It did not conflict with the procedures, ideology, or resources of the movement centers. Indeed, because the sit-in method was a legitimate tactic of the direct-action approach, it was quickly embraced by activists situated in the movement centers. Because these activists were already attempting to build nonviolent movements, they instantly realized that massive sit-ins could have a wide impact. Furthermore, they were well aware that they were in command of precisely the kinds of resources through which the sit-ins could be rapidly diffused. This is why they phoned activist groups and said, "This is it, let's go!" That is, the sit-ins became a tactical innovation within the movement because they fit into the framework of the existing internal organization.

In conclusion, this paper has attempted to demonstrate the important role that internal organization played in the sit-in movement. It is becoming commonplace for writers (e.g., Hubbard, 1968; Lipsky, 1968; Marx and Useem, 1971; McCarthy and Zald, 1973; Oberschall, 1973) to assert that the Civil Rights movement was dependent on outside resources: elites, courts, Northern white liberals, mass media, and the Federal Government. The present analysis suggests that this assertion may be premature, especially when the role of internal organization is ignored. Future research on collective action that treats internal organization as a topic in its own right will further increase our knowledge of the dynamics of social movements.

Notes

1. Why, for example, did the "teach-ins" spread rapidly between college campuses during the mid-sixties? This proposition suggests that the teach-in tactic was especially suited to the university-based internal organization of the white student movement. In its essentials the teach-in innovation was academically oriented and could be implemented by academic types who were entrenched in the "movement centers" of the various universities involved in the movement. Lecture halls, libraries, film clips, study groups, seminar notes, etc. were the preexisting indigenous resources used by agents of the movement via the teach-ins.

2. King papers at Boston University; SCLC papers at the Southern Christian Leadership Conference headquartered in Atlanta; Rev. Kelly Miller Smith's papers housed at First Baptist Church of Nashville.

3. All of the King papers at Boston University and all of SCLC's files in Atlanta were examined, as well as the portion of Rev. Smith's papers dealing with the sit-ins.

4. I suspect that further research will reveal that sit-ins occurred in more than these fifteen cities between 1957 and 1960.

5. Actual names of movement participants are used in this study rather than pseudonyms. I decided to use actual names because my study focuses on real places, movements, and activists. This approach will assist other researchers in evaluating the interview data, since they will know who said what and can conduct further interviews if the need arises. In addition, the respondents had data for this argument. Meier and Rudwick's account of early CORE suggests a similar conclusion.

7. To appreciate the volume of protest activity engendered by the sit-ins, it is necessary to note that the total number of cities (69) is not a count of actual day-to-day demonstrations, which during these first two months ran into the hundreds if not thousands.

8. Cities identified as part of a particular cluster may actually be part of another cluster(s). I assume that the probability of shared organization and coordination of sit-ins is high if two or more cities within a 75-mile radius had sit-ins within a two-week period. My data and analysis generally confirm this assumption.

9. For further evidence of the centrality of student church ties in other cities that had sit-ins see Morris, forthcoming. ✦

9

Institution Building in the African-American Community, 1931-1954

Doug McAdam

. . . At the close of the 1876-1930 period, the southern black population was only just beginning to develop the institutional strength so vital to the generation of social insurgency. However, so as long as blacks remained a predominantly agricultural labor force, the extent of institutional development was destined to be limited. The decisive break once again coincided with the demise of "King Cotton." Precipitated by the mix of factors reviewed earlier, the decline of cotton farming triggered a demographic revolution in the South that was to leave blacks in a much stronger position organizationally than ever before.

The Collapse of Cotton and the Demographic Transformation of the South

Despite developing contradictions, the South remained, on the eve of the Depression, essentially a semifeudal agricultural society. Nearly seven out of every ten southern blacks continued to live in rural areas as late as 1930. That same year, the number of black farm operators stood at 870,000, down only slightly from the record total reached in 1920. The apparent stability embodied in these numbers, however, was shattered by the Depression and the collapse of the world cotton market. Thereafter the combination of "push" factors reviewed earlier simply accelerated trends set in motion by the Depression. The extensiveness of this economic upheaval is captured in figure 3. From a total of 915,000 black farm operators in 1920 the number declined to only 267,000 in 1959 (U.S. Bureau of the Census, 1962a). Increasingly, "the traditional tenant labor force of the South . . .

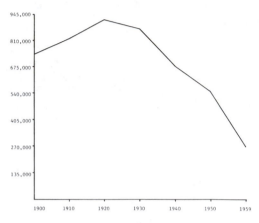

Figure 1
Number of Black Farm Operators in the South, 1900-1959

Source: U.S. Bureau of the Census (1962a): vol. 2, chap. 10.

found itself . . . obsolete, forced to search elsewhere for the means to subsist" (Piven and Cloward, 1979: 191).

Many of the displaced agricultural workers moved out of the South. However, many more stayed behind and were part of a massive rural to urban redistribution of blacks within the region. So thoroughgoing was this internal migration that by 1960 the proportion of southern blacks living in urban areas had increased to 58 percent, nearly double the figure for 1930 (Price, 1969: 11). Overall the increase in total southern black population was only 18 percent between 1930 and 1960. By contrast, the increase among urban blacks living in the South was 118 percent over the same period of time.

Like the parallel northward migration, this regional movement was fueled by a mix of "push" and "pull" factors. The push, of course, was supplied by the decline in cotton farming. The pull was the result of expanding economic opportunities in urban areas. Numerous studies have documented the significant upgrading of the southern occupational structure that occurred during this period (Simpson and Norsworthy, 1965: 198-224; Spengler, 1963: 26-63; Thompson, 1971: 38-53). Thompson has summarized the occupational advances that occurred in the 1930s and 1940s: "in the drastic readjustment of its economy from 1930 to 1950 the South made more economic progress than in any four previous decades. This is evident in the sizeable shifts from extractive to manufacturing and service economies as shown by the occupational shift of the working force" (1971: 52-53). Data reported by Simpson and Norsworthy indicate that the general occupational upgrading of the southern economy noted by Thompson continued apace during the 1950s (1965: 199). That blacks benefitted absolutely from these shifts in the southern occupational structure is also apparent from data presented by Simpson and Norsworthy. While continuing to lag well behind their white counterparts, southern blacks showed significant gains, between 1940 and 1960, in the proportion of their total work force employed in the higher-status occupations such as clerical and managerial positions, skilled craftsmen, and professionals (Simpson and Norsworthy, 1965: 209-10). As the authors note, "these shifts can be taken to mean improved occupational status for Negroes. Even their movement into operative, laboring, and service jobs was probably a step up from farming, in view of Negroes' low position within southern agriculture" (Simpson and Norsworthy, 1965: 207-8).

Through a combination, then, of decreased demand for agricultural labor and expanding occupational opportunities in urban areas, southern blacks were transformed, in the period from 1930 to 1960, from a predominantly rural to urban population segment. The dynamics of this transformation, however, concern us less than its effect on the pace of organizational development within the southern black community. In this regard, the demographic processes reviewed here acted to stimulate development in two principal ways.

First, the collapse of the cotton economy reduced the need for the oppressive system of social controls that had earlier been required to maintain it. Piven and Cloward comment: "with a massive agricultural and industrial transformation underway, a system of political domination based on terror and disenfranchisement was no longer essential to the southern ruling class in order to insure their labor needs on terms favorable to them" (1979: 192). The result was a gradual diminution after 1930 in the virulence of white control efforts. This trend is clearly visible in table 1. From an average of fifty-seven lynchings per year in the 1910-19 period, the number declined to twenty-eight during the 1920s, twelve in the 1930s, to only three a year between 1940 and 1949. This decline in supremacist violence encouraged organizing efforts in the black community both by diminishing the risks involved in such efforts and by signifying to insurgents that a certain "thaw" was underway in southern race relations.

The increased pace of urbanization after 1930 (and especially after 1940) served as a second stimulus to organizational development within

Table 1 Number of Lynchings by Year, 1882-1954					
1882	49	1906	62	1930	20
1883	53	1907	58	1931	12
1884	51	1908	89	1932	6
1885	74	1909	69	1933	24
1886	74	1910	67	1934	15
1887	70	1911	60	1935	18
1888	69	1912	61	1936	8
1889	94	1913	51	1937	8
1890	85	1914	51	1938	6
1891	113	1915	56	1939	2
1892	161	1916	50	1940	4
1893	118	1917	36	1941	4
1894	134	1918	60	1942	6
1895	113	1919	76	1943	3
1896	78	1920	53	1944	2
1897	123	1921	59	1945	1
1898	101	1922	51	1946	6
1899	85	1923	29	1947	1
1900	106	1924	16	1948	1
1901	105	1925	17	1949	3
1902	85	1926	23	1950	1
1903	84	1927	16	1951	1
1904	76	1928	10	1952	0
1905	57	1929	7	1953	0
				1954	0

Ploski and Marr (1976: 275-76).

the southern black community. Insofar as the incidence of supremacist violence was greater in rural than in urban areas, the move to the city granted an increasing number of blacks a measure of immunity from the more virulent forms of racism. More important, urbanization was accompanied by the occupational upgrading of the black population.

In turn, these occupational gains gave rise to an increase in personal income that afforded blacks more resources to support the growth of indigenous organizations. Burgess reports that median income for southern blacks, fourteen years of age or over, rose from $739 to $1,604 between 1949 and 1962, an increase the author links to the rapid urbanization of the southern black population over that same period of time (1965: 348-49). Though hardly staggering, this rise did represent an increase in financial resources available to support institutional development.

As important as the actual dollar increase was the greater financial independence that resulted from urbanization and the accompanying diversification of the southern occupational structure. As long as the majority of blacks were employed as agricultural workers, their vulnerability to various forms of debt bondage remained a serious obstacle to organizing efforts. The expansion of occupational opportunities in southern cities thus contributed to a marked decline in the financial vulnerability of the black population both by pulling people out of southern agriculture and by concentrating them in numbers sufficient to support a growing occupational structure independent of white control. As Higgs has observed: "with these . . . occupational shifts went a measure of upgrading in the black labor force. Also significant was the increasing independence from direct white supervision achieved . . . in the emergence of a 'group economy' in the larger cities. In this respect the incipient ghettos had obvious advantages, for they promoted a modicum of independence and physical security for growing numbers of blacks" (1977: 121).

The advances noted in regard to occupation and income were paralleled in education. Studies have consistently documented higher levels of educational attainment for urban blacks in the South than for their rural counterparts. Given these rural/urban differentials, it is hardly surprising that the 1930-60 period was witness to a higher rate of educational advance among southern blacks than had occurred in any previous thirty-year period.[1]

By the mid-1950s, the demographic transformation of the South set in motion by the collapse of the cotton economy had created a growing class of urban black residents possessed of the personal resources (education, occupation, income) traditionally associated with organizational activity. Writing in 1954, Burgess discussed these trends and linked them to organizational developments within the black community: "It is in the city that the greatest educational opportunities have become available to the Negro. It is here that expanding occupational opportunities have been possible, and that a rise in income and standard of living have gradually been realized. In the urban black belts, Negro institutions . . . have flourished. These social institutions provide the breeding ground for a new kind of leadership trained in the values and skills of the middle class" (1965: 344).

It was not only the personal resources of this emerging black urban middle class, however, that encouraged the institutional development noted by Burgess. The physical proximity and improved communications characteristic of urban life were crucial factors as well. So too was the sheer increase in the size of the black community in urban areas.

Between 1931 and 1954 this complex mix of factors combined to produce an era of institutional development in the black communities of the urban South that was to give rise to the organizational structure out of which black insurgency was to develop in the 1950s and 1960s.[2] In the forefront of this process was the burgeoning black middle class and the three institutions discussed earlier: black churches, black colleges, and local NAACP chapters.

The Southern Black Church, 1931-1954

Even while criticizing various aspects of the urban black church, numerous authors have acknowledged a greater propensity for social action among such churches than had been true for rural congregations (Bullock, 1967: 163; Johnston, 1954: 180; Mays and Nicholson, 1969). That the urban churches were much stronger organizationally than their rural counterparts has been amply documented as well. Conducted in 1930, the Mays-Nicholson study, *The Negro's Church*, provides relevant data on this point. Though not specifically designed as an organizational comparison of the urban and rural southern black churches, the study reports data that permit such a comparison. Table 2 summarizes a number of comparative measures of organizational strength reported by Mays and Nicholson.

As can be seen, the urban church ranks significantly higher than the rural church on all measures of organizational strength. The differentials range from an average membership size three times greater in urban than in rural churches to a 900 percent difference in the proportion of ministers holding advanced degrees. Moreover, what sketchy evidence is available strongly suggests that the southern urban church grew apace with the general expansion in black urban population during the 1931-54 period. For instance, Joseph Washington, in summarizing developments in the

Table 2
1930 Comparison Between the Southern and Urban Black Churches on a Variety of Measures of Organizational Strength

	Southern Rural Black Church	Southern Urban Black Church	Ratio of Southern Urban to Southern Rural Black Church
Mean Membership Size	145	442	3.0
% of ministers holding college or other degrees	2%	18%	9.0
Mean Ministerial Salary	$266	$1,268	4.8
Mean Expenditure Per Year	$436	$3,472	8.0

Mays and Nicholson (1969).

southern black church in the period following the publication of the Mays-Nicholson study, observes that, "during the decades since this study was made, there has been a general upgrading of ministerial standards, religious education, financial responsibility, and institutional outreach to meet the needs of the community" (1964: 293-94). Ruby Johnston (1956) in *The Religion of Negro Protestants* offers evidence consistent with Washington's statement. Finally, a simple comparison of the rates of growth in number of black churches and total black church membership affords an indirect measure of the growing organizational strength of the black church between 1926 and 1962. While the number of black churches increased by only 17 percent, total church membership was up 93 percent over this period of time.[3] Thus, as one measure of organizational growth, the average size of the black congregation increased significantly during the period of interest here.

Simultaneously with these advances, and perhaps because of them, the southern urban black church also evidenced increased involvement in social action after about 1940. On the eve of the Montgomery bus boycott, Johnston discussed this increased church involvement in secular affairs. After noting that "urban churches tend to emphasize some aspects of these programs more than rural churches," Johnston goes on to specify the types of programs she is referring to. The churches, she writes, "urge members to register and vote, offer instruction and information on voting procedures and candidates for office, and organize the political community; and they support the National Association for the Advancement of Colored People" (Johnston, 1954: 180). Similar observations have been made by others. In one particularly interesting study, Tucker documents the growing secular orientation of the southern urban black church through a series of historical portraits of the leading black churchmen in Memphis, Tennessee. The author shows that while the dominant church leadership in the 1900-1940 period was decidedly accommodationist and otherworldly in orientation, an important shift in emphasis was already discernible by the early 1940s. So rapid and thoroughgoing was the transformation of church leadership that, according to Tucker, by the early 1950s, "the majority of local ministers . . . had become outspoken civil rights advocates" (1975: 106-7).

The organizational strength of the southern black church increased enormously between 1930 and 1954. A measure of this increased strength is attributable to the rapid urbanization of the black population during this period. Whereas nearly seven in ten southern black congregants were members of small, weak, rural churches in 1930, by the mid-1950s better than half held memberships in the larger and organizationally stronger urban churches. Add to this significant population shift the organizational advances made by the church, the socioeconomic upgrading of urban congregants, and the increasingly secular orientation of black church leadership during this period, and one begins to comprehend the enormous institutional strength embodied in the black church on the eve of the outbreak of widespread black protest activity in the mid-1950s.[4]

The Black Colleges, 1931-1954

As impressive as the development of the black church was between 1931 and 1954, even more spectacular growth was registered by the black colleges over the same period of time. Perhaps the best evidence of this growth is that indicated in figure 2, which depicts the change in enrollment between 1900 and 1964. After experiencing little growth in the first decade and a half of this century, the enrollment for all black colleges increased sharply after 1915.

Figure 2
Total Enrollment in Black Colleges, 1900-1964

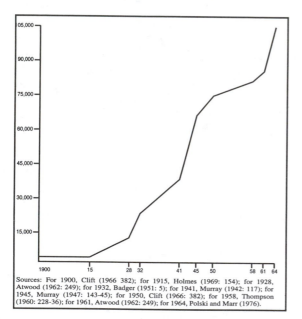

Sources: For 1900, Clift (1966 382); for 1915, Holmes (1969: 154); for 1928, Atwood (1962: 249); for 1932, Badger (1951: 5); for 1941, Murray (1942: 117); for 1945, Murray (1947: 143-45); for 1950, Clift (1966: 382); for 1958, Thompson (1960: 228-36); for 1961, Atwood (1962: 249); for 1964, Polski and Marr (1976).

Figure 2 also serves as a useful means of illustrating the effect of various factors shaping the growth of the black colleges over time. The 1915-16 Phelps-Stokes survey of black colleges served as an early impetus to expansion by dramatizing the inadequacies of the existing system of higher education for blacks. A decade later a similar study, conducted jointly by the Phelps-Stokes Fund and the federal Bureau of Education, had much the same effect. That the period roughly bounded by these two studies was one of significant growth for the black colleges is clear from an examination of figure 2. The growth stimulated by these two surveys was not simply in the area of enrollment, however. An especially beneficial result of the second study was the impetus it supplied for the

upgrading of the educational programs of the colleges as a condition of obtaining full accreditation. While only one school merited full accreditation in 1930, five others achieved the distinction three years later (Holmes, 1969: 198-99). During this period there were other encouraging signs of institutional growth as well. Total income for all black colleges doubled between 1915 and 1930 (Bullock, 1967: 184). The number of degrees awarded rose by approximately 200 percent over the same fifteen-year period (Guzman, 1952: 218). It is with considerable justification, then, that Stephen Wright has characterized the 1916-38 period as one in which "the Negro college began to come of age" (1960: 288).

Nonetheless, as figure 2 shows, the period of greatest growth in the black colleges came after 1940. The rate of increase was especially pronounced in the 1940s, with enrollment doubling from 37,203 in 1941 to 74,526 at mid-century. This represents a 54 percent rise in the proportion of southern blacks attending college. By comparison, the rate of increase for southern whites during the same decade was only 18 percent (Bullock, 1967: 175).

This phenomenal rate of growth was, in large measure, the product of an equally dramatic rise in financial support for the black colleges. Total income for all black colleges rose from slightly more than 8 million dollars in 1930 to more than 38 million seventeen years later (Bullock, 1967: 184). A measure of this increased financial support is attributable to a rise in philanthropic sponsorship of black higher education during the postwar era. Financial data on 23 black church-affiliated colleges for the 1944-59 period support this assertion. Support for these schools, in the form of church donations or other gifts and grants, rose from just under a million dollars in 1944 to approximately 2.5 million by 1959 (Trent, 1960: 360). Similarly, the founding of the United Negro College Fund in 1944 served as another important impetus to the expansion of educational opportunities for blacks. During its first year in existence, the fund raised more than three-quarters of a million dollars in support of black colleges. By 1959 that figure had increased to nearly 2 million dollars (Trent, 1960: 363).

Increased financial support was also forthcoming during this period from an unexpected source: the governments of the southern states. Indeed, the rate of increase in support from the southern states far exceeded that for any other source during this period. In 1914-15, only $422,356, or approximately 10 percent of the total expenditures of the black colleges, was provided by the southern states (Bullock, 1967: 184). By 1947-48, the total amount had risen to $10,881,932, or more than 30 percent of total expenditures (Guzman, 1952: 219).

The major reason for this increased generosity is clear. In 1938 the Supreme Court ruled, in the *Gaines* case, that the state of Missouri had either to admit Lloyd Gaines, a black applicant, to the University of Missouri Law School or establish a separate school within the state to accommodate him. In effect, the Court was instructing the southern states to honor the "separate but equal" doctrine or face compulsory desegregation of their educational facilities. As Trent notes, the effect of this ruling, though indirect, was powerful:

> The southern and border states began to take more seriously the need for more adequate financing of their public colleges and teacher training institutions. They not only appropriated more funds for the general educational program but also established new graduate and professional schools. It is clear that the purpose of this new concern was in the main to avoid admitting Negroes to the then white colleges and professional schools. But whatever the reason, the Negro public colleges began to grow and develop at a rapid rate (Trent, 1959: 267).

As a result, by mid-century the poorly supported, inadequately staffed black colleges of thirty years earlier had been transformed into some of the strongest and most influential institutions within the black community.

The Southern Wing of the NAACP, 1931-1954

Finally, the southern wing of the NAACP experienced a period of rapid expansion between 1931 and 1954. In fact, for the three institutions under discussion here, the NAACP's rate of growth during this period was greater than that for either the black churches or colleges. Total association membership rose from approximately 85,000 in 1934 to around 420,000 in 1946 (NAACP, 1948: 92; Wolters, 1970: 302). This represents a nearly fivefold increase in only thirteen years. Over this same period of time, there occurred a comparable rate of growth in the number of separate units officially incorporated by the

association.[5] The increase was from 404 units in 1934 to 1,613 in 1947 (NAACP, 1948: 3; Wolters, 1970: 302). In terms of the present argument, however, the NAACP's growth at the national level is not as significant as the rate of expansion in the association's southern wing. However, the figures on regional growth are, if anything, even more impressive than the national totals. Two separate observations are relevant here. First, growth in the association was disproportionately centered in the South throughout the period under examination here. St. James reports that, of the 310 units incorporated as of 1919, 131, or 42 percent, were located in the South (Hughes, 1962: 59; St. James, 1958: 53). By 1949 the proportion had increased to 63 percent, with 923 of 1,457 local units chartered in the South (NAACP, 1950: 63). This means that between 1919 and 1949 the number of nonsouthern units rose by some 200 percent while the rate of increase for southern units was approximately three times as great. In the context of the massive northward migration of southern blacks over the same period of time, these comparative figures are all the more significant.

Second, not only did NAACP growth between 1919 and 1950 take place disproportionately in the South, but the growth differential between the northern and southern wings of the association grew more pronounced as the period wore on. Evidence substantiating this observation is presented in figure 3. As the figure shows, the proportion of new southern branches increased steadily (with one decline between 1921 and 1925) throughout the association's history. By the 1946-50 period, nearly eight of ten newly incorporated units were being chartered in the South. In terms of this analysis, though, the more relevant comparison involves the respective proportion of new units that were located in the South pre- and post-1930. In this regard, only 28 percent (38 of 137) of the units chartered between 1911 and 1930 were located in the South as compared to 74 percent (956 of 1,288) in the succeeding twenty-year period. Thus, the dramatic growth in the association after 1935 was clearly centered in the South.

The causes of this rapid regional expansion in NAACP strength are both difficult to pinpoint and, no doubt, numerous. However, a number of probable factors can be identified. The decline in supremacist violence after 1935 would seem to have served as an important impetus to the growth of the association's southern wing. The outbreak

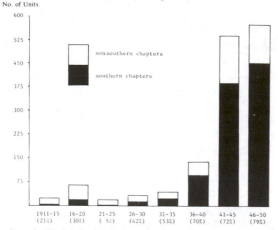

Figure 3
Proportion of Southern and Nonsouthern
NAACP Units Chartered in Successive
Five-Year Periods, 1911-50

Source: for 1911–45, Anglin (1949: 128); for 1946–50, NAACP Annual Reports (1947–50).

Percentages indicate southern proportion of new units chartered during each five-year period.

of World War II may also have facilitated NAACP organizing efforts in both substantive and symbolic ways. With regard to the latter, the glaring discrepancy between the thrust of American propaganda efforts during the war and the reality of Jim Crow racism at home no doubt served the association as an effective organizing device. As Dalfiume has observed:

> The hypocrisy and paradox involved in fighting a world war for the four freedoms and against aggression by an enemy preaching a master-race ideology, while at the same time upholding racial segregation and white supremacy, were too obvious. The war crisis provided American Negroes with a unique opportunity to point out, for all to see, the difference between the American creed and practice. The democratic ideology and rhetoric with which the war was fought stimulated a sense of hope and certainty in black Americans that the old race structure was destroyed forever (Dalfiume, 1970: 247).

Finally, it must be remembered that this rapid expansion in the association's southern wing occurred in the context of a dramatic rural to urban redistribution of the South's population. This transformation provided for larger concentrations of blacks in urban areas who possessed the characteristics associated with membership and were afforded a measure of protection from the more virulent forms of racism that probably inhibited organizing in rural areas. That southern NAACP chapters

were overwhelmingly located in urban areas is clear from an analysis of their geographic distribution throughout the South. Of those newly chartered southern NAACP units listed in the organization's annual reports for the years 1940 through 1950, fully 85 percent were located in urban areas.

Regardless of the precise mix and weight assigned to the various factors facilitating the NAACP's growth in the region, the fact remains that by mid-century the association was firmly established as one of the strongest institutions in the southern black community. In combination with the black churches and colleges of the South, the local NAACP chapters afforded that population a strong, integrated institutional network capable of concerted and sustained collective action. . . .

Notes

1. For figures confirming this statement see Johnson (1930:232); U.S. Bureau of the Census, *Census of the Population: 1950,* vol. 2 (1952); U.S. Bureau of the Census, *Census of the Population: 1960,* Characteristics of the Population, U.S. Summary (1962: table 239).

2. That the later protest campaigns were disproportionately centered in urban areas is obvious from an examination of available data. Of the 394 movement-initiated events reported by the *New York Times* that occurred in the South between 1955 and 1961, 386, or 98 percent, took place in urban areas. From "newspaper files and accounts published by the Southern Regional Council," Oppenheimer compiled a list of 102 sites that were witness to student-initiated protest activity during 1960. Of these, 98, or 96 percent, occurred in urban, as opposed to rural, locales, (Oppenheimer, 1963: 63-64). Since only 58 percent of the southern black population was residing in urban areas in 1960, the disproportionate urban locus of the demonstrations is indeed impressive. There may, of course, be a slight underestimation of rural protest activity built into these figures as a consequence of the decreased publicity that normally accompanies any event that occurs in an isolated locale (Danzger, 1975). But any such bias would probably be too small to reduce the significance of these figures. The fact remains that the migration to urban locales within the South facilitated insurgency by affording blacks the personal resources, physical proximity, and protection from the more virulent forms of white racism that they had lacked in rural areas.

3. The number of black churches rose from 42,585 in 1926 to 49,882 in 1962. The comparable increase in total church membership was from 5,203,487 in 1926 to 10,048,493 in 1962 (Murray, 1942: 94-95; Washington 1964:233).

4. One additional characteristic of the urban church strengthened its position as a potential vehicle for collective protest. Quite simply, in comparison to rural congregations, the urban church was, as a rule, far more independent of white control. This was true in two senses. First, the vast majority of urban churchgoers were themselves not as economically dependent on whites as their rural counterparts, a large percentage of whom remained tied to the tenant farm system. Second, as an institution, the urban church usually relied less on white support than the rural church did. As many observers have remarked, the black church, especially, in urban areas, represented the institution within the black community that was the least controlled or "penetrated" by whites (Matthews and Prothro, 1966: 185; Mays and Nicholson, 1969: 279-80; Washington, 1964: 229). Oberschall, in the following passage, touches on both these points: "In the middle-sized and large cities . . . the position of the large and relatively affluent black churches was much stronger. Its ministers and finances were truly independent of white control. Its middle-class, professional congregation enjoyed social leadership and prestige within the entire black community and possessed considerable financial resources independent of white control" (1973: 222).

5. The term "units" refers to all local NAACP-affiliated membership bodies. This includes all regular branches, youth councils, and college chapters. ✦

Unit Two

Processes of Micromobilization

In the first section we examined the external, social environmental factors that facilitate the rise of social movements and related collective action. Since the operation of these factors rarely applies to all aggregations within a society, they are likely to make some sets of individuals more inclined than others towards movement participation. Yet, these factors do not determine who will participate within an aggrieved or victimized constituency. Thus, there is an individual level analog to the emergence question: Why do only certain individuals come to be involved in social movement activity? Why does one individual sign a petition, join a protest march, or perhaps even engage in terrorist violence while the vast majority of similarly impacted citizens stay far removed from the social movement fray? What in other words, accounts for differential recruitment and participation? This question links the next four parts, and the readings address it in one fashion or another.

Part 4

Microstructural Factors: Social Networks

Until the mid-1970s, scholars tended to invoke explanations that parallelled the individualist, psychologistic orientation so prevalent in western culture when attempting to explain why only certain individuals participate in social movements and other forms of collective behavior. Differential recruitment and participation were explained by personality and/or psychological factors.

Lewis Feuer's account of the rise of the 1964 Free Speech Movement at Berkeley is an example of this kind of psychological theorizing. In his 1969 book, *The Conflict of the Generations,* Feuer argued that those who were drawn to the movement were apt to be those students—especially males—who saw in the movement a chance to play out unresolved emotional conflicts with their parents. Other observers, such as Eric Hoffer (1951) and Theodor Adorno (Adorno et al. 1950), argued that nondemocratic movements may disproportionately recruit those with "authoritarian personalities." Some proponents of the mass society approach (Kornhauser 1959) argue that movements provide "substitute communities" for those alienated, marginal members of society who are drawn to activism. And some psychological theories see activism as a form of aggression caused by various forms of frustration. These models are variations on the well established theme of frustration/aggression in psychology, which argues that much of human behavior, including activism, should be seen as a release of frustration through aggression. One specific application of this perspective to movement participation is the theory of relative deprivation. The theory rests on the underlying assumption that the perception that one is deprived relative to someone else creates "an underlying state of . . . psychological tension that is relieved by SM [social movement] participation" (Gurney and Tierney 1982: 36).

However intuitively and culturally appealing, these kinds of explanations have fared poorly in receiving empirical support. Summarizing his exhaustive survey of the literature on the relationship between activism and various psychological factors, Mueller (1980: 69) concluded that "psychological attributes of individuals . . . have minimal direct impact for explaining the occurrence of rebellion and revolution per se" (see also McPhail 1971).

Does this mean that psychological factors are irrelevant to the study of individual activism? Certainly not. In our view, various cognitive and motivational factors are very important in relation to differential recruitment and participation, but the nature of the relationship is more complicated than generally understood. The complexity of the relationship and the importance of motivational and cognitive factors will be taken up in the next several parts.

Here we wish to examine a structural line of argument that focuses on an individual's social-structural proximity to a movement. The argument, which has evolved over the past fifteen years, is that people participate in movements not simply because they are motivationally or cognitively inclined to but because their structural location makes them available for participation. Specifically, researchers have focused on the role of personal or organizational networks in facilitating movement recruitment. The articles in this part exemplify this line of research and the consistently supportive empirical findings it has yielded.

The first selection, by David Snow, Louis Zurcher, and Sheldon Ekland-Olson, was among the first to call researchers' attention to the network basis of movement recruitment. The authors' survey of nine studies of movement participation revealed that in eight of the nine cases, the vast majority of recruits were drawn into the movement by contact with a friend or relative previously involved with the group. The lone exception was Hare Krishna, which specifically targeted individuals lacking strong ties to friends and family.

The second selection, by Roger Gould, illustrates just how sophisticated the network approach to the study of movement recruitment has become. Using a variety of advanced statistical techniques, the author documents the role that overlapping networks played in shaping participation in the republican revolt that shook Paris in the spring of 1871. Gould shows that in contrast to the class-based revolt that took place in Paris 23 years earlier, the 1871 movement was rooted in overlapping patterns of neighborhood and National Guard solidarity.

In another interesting extension of the network perspective, Doug McAdam and Ronnelle Paulsen compare those who took part in the 1964 Mississippi Freedom Summer Project with those who applied and were accepted by project organizers, but did not participate. Using original project applications and follow-up surveys, the authors highlight a particular confluence of factors that greatly increased the likelihood of movement involvement. They show that applicants who framed participation in the project in terms of a salient prior identity (e.g., "Christian," "teacher," etc.), who were members of organizations supportive of this link between identity and action, and who encountered little opposition from parents or other significant others were overwhelmingly likely to make it to Mississippi.

Finally, in her interesting analysis of the rise of the women's liberation movement, Carol Mueller documents the crucial role that "submerged conflict networks" played, not only in drawing women into the burgeoning movement, but in facilitating the process by which pioneering activists fashioned the shared collective identity of feminism so crucial to the movement's growth. This is an important extension of the network perspective. Whereas most work on the topic has documented the role networks play in drawing recruits into a well established movement, Mueller shows that networks may also serve as the crucial social locations within which movements and the new conceptions of self and society they require are created in the first place.

References

Adorno, T.W., E. Frenkel-Brunswick, D.J. Levinson, and R.N. Sanford. 1950. *The Authoritarian Personality.* New York: Harper & Brothers.

Feuer, Lewis. 1969. *The Conflict of the Generations.* New York: Basic Books.

Gurney, J.N. and Kathleen Tierney. 1982. "Relative Deprivation and Social Movements: A Critical Look at Twenty Years of Theory and Research." *Sociological Quarterly* 23: 33-47.

Hoffer, Eric. 1951. *The True Believer: Thoughts on the Nature of Mass Movements.* New York: The New American Library.

Kornhauser, William. 1959. *The Politics of Mass Society.* Glencoe, IL: Free Press.

McPhail, Clark. 1971. "Civil Disorder Participation: A Critical Examination of Recent Research." *American Sociological Review* 36: 1058-1073.

Mueller, Edward N. 1980. "The Psychology of Political Protest and Violence." in Ted Robert Gurr (ed.) *Handbook of Political Conflict.* New York: Free Press. ✦

10

Social Networks and Social Movements: A Microstructural Approach to Differential Recruitment

David A. Snow
Louis A. Zurcher, Jr.
Sheldon Ekland-Olson

Among the various issues and questions relating to the study of social movements, few have generated as much discussion and research as those pertaining to differential recruitment. Why are some people rather than others recruited into a particular social movement organization?[1] Given the number of competing and functionally equivalent movement organizations frequently on the market at the same time, how is it that people come to participate in one rather than another? Why do some movement organizations attract a larger following and grow at a more rapid rate than others? Whether one scans the literature on religious cults and movements, political protest, the ghetto revolts of the 1960s, or student activism, the problem of differential recruitment surfaces as a dominant focal concern, both theoretically and empirically. Indeed, the study of movement recruitment has been "one of the most prominent characteristics of collective behavior research in recent years" (Marx and Wood, 1975:388).

Nonetheless, understanding of the process of differential recruitment, its underlying determinants, and implications for the spread and growth of social movements is still quite limited (Marx and Wood, 1975:393). As Zald and McCarthy (1979:240) concluded in their recent review of the resource mobilization approach, very little is known about the movement recruitment process

and the conditions under which various recruitment techniques are more or less successful.

The purpose of this article is to advance understanding of the movement recruitment process by assembling quantitative and qualitative data which bear on the relationship between movement recruitment and such microstructural factors as social networks, and by developing a set of corresponding propositions. Four focal questions structure the inquiry: (1) What are the microstructural avenues of movement recruitment? (2) What accounts for the differential availability of people for movement participation? (3) What are the structural characteristics of social movements which predict different recruitment strategies and patterns? (4) What implications do different recruitment strategies and patterns have for the spread and growth of a movement?

Data and Procedures

The article draws on three sets of data. The first is derived from an examination of social movement case studies through which we synthesize quantitative data pertaining to the recruitment process. References to the salience of such microstructural factors as social networks are not uncommon, but our review of the literature revealed that most of the references tend to be impressionistic. There is a dearth of hard data specifying the function of social networks in relation to differential recruitment to and the differential spread and growth of movements. However, we did find ten studies with quantitative data bearing directly on the recruitment process. The sample size of the ten studies varies from 31 to 310 participants, with the combined N totalling more than 1,200.

The second data set comes from an examination of recruitment to the Nichiren Shoshu Buddhist movement in America.[2] These data were derived from the senior author's observations and experiences as a participant-observer for a year and a half, his informal interviews with recruits and members, and his examination of a random sample of members' testimonies appearing in the movement's newspaper, *The World Tribune*.[3] Since most editions of the newspaper contain several members' testimonies, 504 were randomly selected from 1966 to 1974 (six per month), excluding a two-year period in which the newspaper was not readily available. Three hundred and thirty of the 504 testimonies provided information specifying mode of recruitment into the movement. These 330 cases, coupled with 15 other members from whom recruitment information was informally elicited, yielded a sample of 345. Informal interviews with 25 Hare Krishna devotees supplement the data pertaining to Nichiren Shoshu. Twenty of the interviews were with members of the Krishna commune in Los Angeles, and five were with members of the Dallas commune. The interviews were conducted during the course of six visits to the Los Angeles commune and two visits to the Dallas commune.[4]

The third data set is derived from a nonrandom sample of University of Texas students. A questionnaire designed to gather information pertaining to movement recruitment and participation was administered to 550 students enrolled in ten different university courses in the Spring semester of 1979. The first part of the questionnaire contained a list of twenty-five social movement organizations within the Austin, Texas, area. The respondents were initially asked to indicate for each movement whether they were (a) unfamiliar with it; (b) familiar but not sympathetic or supportive; (c) sympathetic but not a participant; or (d) associated with it as a participant at one time or another. Three hundred of the 550 respondents indicated that they either were movement participants or were sympathetic with the objectives of one or more of the movements.[5] Since we are concerned with differential recruitment, only the responses of the 135 participants and the 165 sympathizers are considered. The sympathetic nonparticipants constitute a kind of control group in that their responses shed light on the question of why it is that people who are in sympathy with and supportive of a movement's value orientation do not always participate in movement activities. A consideration of the responses of both participants and sympathizers should yield a better understanding of differential recruitment.

Findings and Discussion

The Microstructural Avenues of Recruitment

Movement recruitment has generally been approached from a social-psychological/motivational level of analysis, with various states-of-mind or psychological attributes posited as the major causal variables (see Cantril, 1941; Feuer, 1969; Glock, 1964; Hoffer, 1951; Klapp, 1969; Toch, 1965). However reasonable the underlying assumption that some people are more susceptible than others to movement participation, that view

deflects attention from the fact that recruitment cannot occur without prior contact with a recruitment agent. The potential participant has to be informed about and introduced into a particular movement. Thus, even if one accepts the popular contention that some individuals are predisposed social-psychologically to movement participation, the following question still remains: What determines which potential participants are most likely to come into contact with and be recruited into one movement rather than another, if into any movement at all?

It is a basic sociological tenet that social phenomena are not distributed randomly, but are structured according to aggregate or group membership, role incumbency, and the like. It thus seems reasonable to assume that movement recruitment, rather than being random or merely the function of social-psychological predispositions, will also be structured by certain sociospatial factors. Accordingly, we can begin to answer the above question by considering, first, the various sociospatial settings in which movements and potential participants can come into contact, and, second, the variety of generally available modes of communication through which information can be imparted.

Regarding the first concern, most spatial settings or domains of social life can be conceptualized in terms of a continuum ranging from public to private places.[6] Examples of the former include shopping malls, community sidewalks, airports, bus stations, and city parks. Country clubs, an office, a sorority or fraternity house, and an apartment or home are illustrative of the latter.

The means of information dissemination can be conceptualized generally in terms of whether they are face-to-face or mediated. By face-to-face communication, we refer to all information, whether it be verbal or nonverbal, that is imparted when two or more individuals or groups are physically present. In contrast, mediated communication refers to information dissemination through institutionalized mass communication mechanisms, such as radio and television, or through institutionalized, but individualized and privatized, communication mechanisms such as the mail and telephone.

The cross-classification of these two dimensions suggests four general and fairly distinct microstructural avenues for movement information dissemination and recruitment. Figure 1 sche-

Figure 1
Classification of General Outreach and Engagement
Possibilities for Movement Information Dissemina-
tion, Promotion, and Recruitment

FACE-TO-FACE

Face-to-face leafleting, petitioning, and proselytizing on sidewalks; participation in public events, such as parades; staging events for public consumption, such as sit-ins, protests, movement-sponsored conventions and festivals.	Door-to-door leafleting, petitioning, and proselytizing; information dissemination and recruitment among familiar others along the lines of promoter's extra-movement interpersonal networks.

PUBLIC CHANNELS ——————————————————— PRIVATE CHANNELS

Promotion and recruitment via radio, television, and newspapers.	Promotion and recruitment via mail and telephone.

MEDIATED

matically summarizes these alternative avenues, each of which is distinguished by the spatial domain of social life in which contact can be established and the means through which information can be imparted.

Given the alternative microstructural avenues, the question arises as to the relative yield of each in terms of actual recruits. In other words, is recruitment among strangers in public places more productive than recruitment along the other avenues, or are movement recruits typically drawn from existing members' extramovement friends, acquaintances, and kin?

Examination of the movement literature strongly suggests that the network channel is the richest source of movement recruits. Numerous studies allude to the importance of social networks as a conduit for the spread of social movements. While some of these works are theoretical or critical in orientation (Oberschall, 1973; Tilly, 1978; Useem, 1975; Wilson, 1973; Wilson and Orum, 1976), most are empirical studies of religious movements (Bibby and Brinkerhoff, 1974;

Table 1. Studies with Data Specifying Mode of Recruitment to Various Movements (Percentage)

			Mode of Recruitment			
			Recruited through Social Networks			% Recruited Outside Networks[b]
Investigator	Movement	N	% By Relatives	% By Friends, Acquaintances[a]	Tot. % Rec. thr. Ntwks.	
Sills (1957)	March of Dimes	234	[c]	90	90	10
Murata (1969)	Sokagakkai	100	16	76	92	9
Dator (1969)	Sokagakkai	120	65	35	100	[d]
White (1970)	Sokagakkai	[e]	24	86	96	4
Gerlach and Hine (1970)	Pentecostal	77[f]	47	32	79	21
Harrison (1974)	Catholic Pentecostal	169	[g]	59	59	[g]
Bibby & Brinkerhoff (1974)	Evangelistic Protestantism	132	45	29	74	26
Leahy (1975)	Anti-Abortion	31	26	65	91	9
Judah (1974)	Hare Krishna	63	0	3	3	97

[a] Includes all individuals recruited through networks other than familial or kinship (e.g., occupational, neighborhood).

[b] Includes all individuals recruited by strangers in the street or at mass meetings, or who sought out the movement after learning about it through the public media, or who joined on their own initiative.

[c] Percent recruited by relatives, if any, not reported. Of the 90% recruited through networks, 52% were recruited by friends, 20% through community network, and 18% through organizational and occupational networks.

[d] Data derived from 200 testimonials of American members in a Sokagakkai newspaper. Of the 60% (120) indicating mode of recruitment, none was recruited by strangers or through the media. The reason for the large percentage recruited by relatives is that the majority of the individuals in the sample were American GI's stationed in Japan who were married to Japanese members.

[e] Sample size not given. Percent figures based on the average of three to five different surveys. Percent figure for friends and acquaintances based on the average of three surveys; percent figure for relatives and the last two columns based on the average of five surveys.

[f] Figures based on the compilation of Gerlach and Hine's (1970:79–80) reported findings regarding two separate Pentecostal churches.

[g] Percent recruited by relatives or strangers, if any, not reported. Therefore the actual percentage recruited through networks may have been greater than the 59% reported.

Dator, 1969; Gerlach and Hine, 1970; Harrison, 1974; Heirich, 1977; Judah, 1974; Lee, 1967; Lofland, 1966; Murata, 1969; White, 1970) or political protest or reform-oriented movements (Freeman, 1973a; Jackson et al., 1960; Leahy, 1975; Marx, 1969; Orum, 1972; Petras and Zeitlin, 1967; Pinard, 1971; Tygart and Holt, 1972; Von Eschen et al., 1971; Woelfel et al., 1974; Zurcher and Kirkpatrick, 1976). Although suggestive, few of the investigations provide hard data specifying the relation between social networks and differential recruitment. However, ten studies were found with quantitative data bearing on the recruitment process. Table 1 summarizes the findings of all but one of the studies,[7] clearly demonstrating the salience of social networks as a recruitment avenue. For each of the movements studied, with the exception of Hare Krishna, extramovement social networks constitute the primary source of recruits.

Our findings regarding recruitment to Nichiren Shoshu are consistent with those just presented. As indicated in Table 2, Nichiren Shoshu members are typically recruited into the movement by one or more members with whom they have a preexisting, extramovement, interpersonal tie. Although Nichiren Shoshu members devote a considerable amount of time and energy to proselytizing in public places, these information dissemination and recruiting forays are not very productive. The senior author accompanied members on over forty such expeditions, and only twice were recruits attracted. In contrast, all but one of the twenty-five Krishna devotees we interviewed were recruited "off the street" by other members who were strangers at the time of contact. (Factors which account for the different recruitment patterns of Hare Krishna and the other movements will be discussed later.)

Table 3. Recruitment Avenues of a Sample of University Students Participating in Various Movements (Percentage)

| Recruitment Avenues | Movements | | |
	Political (N:81) Percent	Religious (N:54) Percent	Totals (N:135) Percent
Public Places	7	0	4
Social Networks	63	80	70
Mass Media	30	20	26
Mail/Telephone	0	0	0

The important bridging function of social networks in relation to movement recruitment is further demonstrated by our findings regarding the sample of university students participating in various social movements. Additionally, these findings suggest that network linkages are not only important in accounting for religious movements, but also for political movements. As indicated in Table 3, 63% of the students participating in political movements were drawn into their respective movement's orbit of influence through a preexisting, extramovement personal tie.

The findings associated with the three data sets not only corroborate each other, but they also clearly demonstrate the importance of preexisting social networks in structuring movement recruitment. It is thus reasonable to suggest the following summary position:

Proposition 1: Those outsiders who are linked to one or more movement members through preexisting extramovement networks will have a greater probability of being contacted and recruited into that particular movement than will those individuals who are outside of members' extramovement networks.

The Importance of Social Networks in Accounting for Differential Availability

Proposition 1 and the data in which it is grounded suggest that recruitment among social networks is likely to be more productive than recruitment via the other microstructural avenues. However, the fact remains that not all relatives, friends or acquaintances of movement members participate in movement activities when invited. The findings reported in the preceding section report that, for all the movements studied, at least some members were recruited "off the street" or through the public media. The findings pertaining to Hare Krishna in particular suggest that some movements recruit most of their members through

Table 2. Recruitment Patterns for Nichiren Shoshu and Hare Krishna (Percentage)

Recruitment Avenues	Nichiren Shoshu (N:345) Percent	Hare Krishna (N:25) Percent
Public Places	17	96
Social Networks	82	4
Mass Media	1	0
Mail/Telephone	0	0

channels other than social networks. The question thus arises as to who out of the pool of individuals contacted either through existing ties or through other recruitment avenues is most likely to become a movement participant?

One plausible answer is suggested by the many works that posit a psychofunctional linkage between social-psychological attributes (conceptualized as susceptibilities) and the goals and ideologies of movements (construed as appeals). According to this view, participation in movement activities is largely a function of certain fertile dispositions, such as alienation (Bolton, 1972; Oppenheimer, 1968; Ransford, 1968), relative deprivation (Aberle, 1966; Davies, 1971; Glock, 1964; Gurr, 1970), and authoritarianism (Hoffer, 1951; Lipset, 1960; Lipset and Raab, 1973). Although of longstanding popularity, the social-psychological dispositional approach has in recent years been called into question on both theoretical and empirical grounds.[8] Moreover, our research suggests that the reason why some rather than other individuals join a movement once they have been introduced to it can be explained in large part by their structural availability. Specifically, the findings pertaining to Nichiren Shoshu and the sample of movement sympathizers suggest that the reason for participating in movement activities once invited is largely contingent on the extent to which extramovement networks function as countervailing influences. Since sets of social relationships can be more or less demanding in regard to time, energy, and emotional attachment (Etzioni, 1975; Kanter, 1972), it follows that they can also vary in the extent to which they constitute countervailing influences or extraneous commitments (Becker, 1960) with respect to alternative networks and lines of action. Hence, some individuals will be more available for movement exploration and participation because of the possession of unscheduled or discretionary time and because of minimal countervailing risks or sanctions.

In the case of Nichiren Shoshu, these observations seem to hold for both those members recruited from the street and those recruited through social networks. Most were under 30, single, in a transitional role (such as that of student), employed in a line rather than in a managerial position, or in a state of occupational marginality. As a consequence, they tended to possess a greater amount of unscheduled time and generally lacked the kinds of extraneous commitments that are

likely to inhibit movement participation. Aside from the absence of a social tie to one or more members prior to initial contact, those recruited from the street differed from those recruited through networks only in that they were structurally more available for participation. This observation is illustrated by the following account of how and why one street-recruit, a twenty-five-year-old male, came to join Nichiren Shoshu:

> I found myself here in L.A. with nothing but the clothes I was wearing. I didn't know anybody. I didn't have a lot of money. It was a really strange situation.
>
> I had just flown into L.A. airport, and all my baggage came up missing. This was on a Saturday night. Since I didn't know anybody and didn't have any place to go, I went to the airport police station and was told to go to Travelers' Aid. But I learned that they wouldn't be open until Tuesday, since this was a Labor Day weekend. So I waited around the airport until Tuesday and then went down to Travelers' Aid. They sent me to the Welfare Department. After spending four days waiting and filling out forms, I was told that I couldn't qualify for welfare because I wasn't a California resident.
>
> At this point I didn't know what to do. So I spent a few nights at the Midnight Mission, and then decided to go to the Santa Monica Beach. That evening while I was walking around downtown Santa Monica, this guy came up to me and started talking about Nam-Myoho-Renge-Kyo (the Nichiren Shoshu chant), and asked if I would like to go to a meeting. Since I didn't have anything else to do, I went along.
>
> All of a sudden I find myself at this meeting where everybody was chanting. I didn't have the faintest idea about what was going on. I had never heard of the chant before, and didn't even know there was such a group as NSA. But since everybody was telling me to give chanting a try, I figured why not. I literally didn't have anything to lose. So I joined, and I've been chanting ever since—which is about four months.

Although this account differs somewhat from the stories of other street-recruits in its particulars, it underscores what was common to the life-situation of the 85 street-recruits about whom we were able to gather information.[9] They were either recent arrivals to or passing through the area in which they were recruited, or they were minimally involved in proximal and demanding social relationships.[10] Although one might argue that these street-recruits were "susceptible" to the "appeals" of the movements they joined because they were "social isolates," "loners," or "outcasts," we do not subscribe to such an interpretation. Rather, we think it is sociologically more compelling to argue that individuals who join social movements share the kinds of demographic and social characteristics that allow them to follow their interests and/or engage in exploratory behavior to a greater extent than individuals who are bound to existing lines of action by such extraneous commitments as spouse, children, debts, job, and occupational reputation.[11]

This microstructural interpretation is also suggested by our findings regarding the movement sympathizers in our sample of university students. By movement sympathizers, we refer to those individuals who indicate verbal support of or agreement with the goals of a movement, but who do not devote any time, energy, or other resources to advancing the movement's objectives. The major reasons given by the sympathizers for

Table 4. Reasons for Not Participating Given by Movement Sympathizers (Percentage)

| Reasons | Movements | | |
	Political (N:115) Percent	Religious (N:50) Percent	Totals (N:165) Percent
1. Didn't know anyone actively involved	73	66	71
2. Not enough time	64	61	63
3. Wasn't asked	57	47	54
4. Just didn't want to get involved	18	16	18
5. Fear of negative reaction by nonmovement significant others	7	12	9
6. Don't know/other	4	4	4

remaining on the sidelines and not getting involved are indicated in Table 4. Most relevant to the present discussion is the finding that nearly two-thirds indicated that they did not have enough time to participate. Had their lines of action not been constrained by competing, extramovement commitments and demands, and had they been asked to participate by a member with whom they were acquainted, then presumably they would have become a participant or "constituent" rather than just a sympathizer or "adherent."

In light of these corroborating findings and observations, it seems reasonable to suggest that, given the existence of a social tie to one or more movement members, differential recruitment is largely a function of differential availability,

which is best conceptualized as a microstructural phenomenon. That is, it is a function of how tightly individuals are tied to alternative networks and thus have commitments that hinder the recruitment efforts of social movement organizations. The following propositions summarize the argument. The first pertains to the relation between social networks and availability for movement participation. The second concerns the connection between structural availability and the probability of actual participation.

Proposition 2A: The fewer and the weaker the social ties to alternative networks, the greater the structural availability for movement participation.

Proposition 2B: The greater the structural availability for participation, the greater the probability of accepting the recruitment "invitation."

Here it might be argued that even though a social bond with one or more movement members and structural availability increase the probability of movement participation, they are not sufficient conditions. We would agree, especially since social action on behalf of noncoercive organizations is unlikely in the absence of instrumental, affective, or ideological alignment (Etzioni, 1975; Kanter, 1972; Parsons and Shils, 1962). However, it is important to emphasize that people seldom initially join movements per se. Rather they typically are asked to participate in movement activities.[12] Furthermore, it is during the course of initial participation that they are provided with the "reasons" or "justifications" for what they have already done and for continuing participation. As C. Wright Mills emphasized some time ago (1940), vocabularies of motives are frequently supplied "after the act" to explain the "underlying causes of the act," even though they have little to say about how the act came about. We would thus argue that the "motives" for joining or continued participation are generally emergent and interactional rather than prestructured. That is, they arise out of a process of ongoing interaction with a movement organization and its recruitment agents. Although this alignment process has not received much empirical attention, its salience in relation to movement recruitment has been illustrated by Lofland's (1977a; 1977b) reexamination of the process by which one becomes a "Moonie" and by Snow's (1976) description of how Nichiren Shoshu strategically goes about the business of "luring" and "securing" recruits. In both cases the recruitment process is organized so as gradually to "sell" prospects on the "benefits" of participation and to provide them with "reasons" for remaining a member. This is not to suggest that prestructured cognitive states and tensions are irrelevant for understanding movement joining. Rather, it is to emphasize that they must be aligned with the movement's value orientation, given specific forms and means for expression and amelioration, and put into the service of the movement (Zygmunt, 1972).[13] In light of these observations, we argue that initial and sustained participation is largely contingent on the countervailing influence of alternative networks and intensive interaction with movement members. Whereas the first factor determines whether one is structurally available for participation, the second factor gives rise to the rationale for participation.

Structural Influences on Movement Recruitment Strategies and Patterns

In analyzing the recruitment process from the point of view of the movement itself, the relationship between movement structure (as determined by its network attributes) and recruitment opportunities and patterns requires attention. As indicated earlier, there are four general outreach and engagement channels that movements can exploit for information dissemination and recruitment: (1) They can channel their promotion and recruitment efforts among strangers in public places by face-to-face means; (2) They can promote via the institutionalized, mass communication mechanisms; (3) They can recruit among strangers in private places by such means as door-to-door canvassing; (4) They can promote and recruit through members' extramovement social networks. The question thus arises as to what determines the patterning and channelling of a movement's recruitment efforts.

Depending on their resource base and strategy, all nonsecretive movement organizations interested in expanding their ranks can exploit the first three recruitment possibilities. However, not all such movements are structurally able to use the network channel to the same extent since they do not all constitute open networks. Some movements are more restrictive and exclusive than others in that membership eligibility is contingent on the possession of certain ascribed or achieved attributes. In other movements, such as Hare Krishna, core membership may even be contingent upon the severance of extramovement inter-

personal ties. Since movement organizations can vary in the extent to which they are linked to or isolated from other networks of social relations, it follows that their recruitment opportunities can vary considerably. Accordingly, it seems reasonable to suggest the following propositions regarding the relation between a movement's network attributes and the channelling and patterning of its recruitment efforts:

> *Proposition 3A:* Movements requiring exclusive participation by their members in movement activities will attract members primarily from public places rather than from among extramovement interpersonal associations and networks.

> *Proposition 3B:* Movements which do not require exclusive participation by their members in movement activities will attract members primarily from among extramovement interpersonal associations and networks, rather than from public places.

These two propositions are suggested when we compare our findings regarding recruitment into Nichiren Shoshu with those pertaining to Hare Krishna. As mentioned earlier, more than three-quarters of our sample of NSA members reported that they were recruited into the movement by relatives, friends, or acquaintances. In contrast, only one of the twenty-five Krishna devotees we interviewed was recruited by a former acquaintance. Judah (1974:162) similarly found that only 3.32% of the Krishna devotees he interviewed "learned about it through a friend who was a devotee." The majority (66%) came into contact with the movement by encountering a public chanting session or a devotee in the street. Judah (1974:162-3) concludes that

> . . . the results seem to indicate rather clearly the importance of the Movement's method of proselytizing. It has attracted the attention of many by its practice of chanting the Hare Krishna mantra in public. During these public ceremonies, other devotees sell the literature and engage the curious in conversation about Krishna.

Anyone with firsthand knowledge of the Krishna movement will find little reason to quibble with Judah's (1974) observations. However, he fails to note that the movement in general and devotees in particular have little choice other than to turn to the streets in search of recruits. Since core membership in Hare Krishna requires an austere communal lifestyle and the severance of extramovement interpersonal ties, the movement is structurally compelled to concentrate its recruitment efforts in public places. Consequently, most of its members are recruited "off the streets."

In contrast, the Nichiren Shoshu movement does not involve communal life or require its members to sever their extramovement interpersonal ties. It is, therefore, structurally able to recruit both in public places and through members' extramovement networks. Consequently, it draws the bulk of its membership from those networks.

Implications of Recruitment Strategies for Movement Spread and Growth

The differential spread and growth of social movements has generally been analyzed in terms of the appeal of movement goals and value orientations to various target populations in the ambient society. That a movement's organizational structure, and particularly its network attributes, might function as an important determinant of its spread and growth has received only brief attention in the literature (Curtis and Zurcher, 1973; 1974; Messinger, 1955; Zald and Ash, 1966; Zurcher and Kirkpatrick, 1976). We now address this issue. Specifically, do differences in network attributes and recruitment opportunities have a significant impact on the success of a movement's recruitment efforts, as measured by the number of outsiders actually recruited? The answer hypothetically depends not only on a movement's value orientation, but also on whether recruitment among social networks typically yields a greater return than does recruitment "off the street" or through the media. If the latter is generally more productive, then a movement's network attributes would be of little relevance to its overall growth. However, if recruitment among strangers is not as effective as recruitment among movement members' acquaintances, friends, and relatives, then a movement's network attributes would constitute a significant and important variable in relation to its growth and spread.

Our findings indicate that for those movements which recruit both in public places and through networks, recruitment among acquaintances, friends, and kin is generally more successful than recruitment among strangers. We thus conclude that a movement's network attributes and corresponding recruitment patterns do indeed make a significant difference in a movement's recruitment efforts and growth. Hence, the following propositions:

Proposition 4A: The success of movement recruitment efforts, measured by the numbers of outsiders actually recruited, will vary with the extent to which movements are linked to other groups and networks via members' extramovement interpersonal ties, such that:

Proposition 4B: Movements which are linked to other groups and networks will normally grow at a more rapid rate and normally attain a larger membership than will movements which are structurally more isolated and closed.

Aside from a few exceptions (Craven and Wellman, 1974a; Curtis and Zurcher, 1973; Turk, 1970), most social network analyses have focused on the individual and his or her interpersonal ties, with a paucity of social ties taken as evidence of objective or structural social isolation. That focus may be useful for understanding the structural determinants of individual behavioral patterns and propensities. However, it obscures the fact that social isolation can also occur at the group or movement level, as when a movement has few, if any, direct links with other groups and therefore constitutes a closed network or insulated system of social relations. When this occurs, Propositions 4A and 4B suggest that such movements will differ markedly from structurally less isolated movements in recruitment opportunities and patterns, and overall growth.

Empirical support is provided for the propositions by a comparison of the membership claims of the Nichiren Shoshu and Hare Krishna movement organizations in the United States. Since 1970 Nichiren Shoshu's membership claims have consistently hovered between 200,000 and 250,000. In contrast, members of the Los Angeles and Dallas Krishna communes have reported that the number of communal Krishna devotees throughout the country totals no more than 4,000. While efforts to reach an objective estimate of Nichiren Shoshu's membership suggest that it is about half of what the movement claims (see Snow, 1976:137-44), the point still remains that Nichiren Shoshu's membership far exceeds that of Hare Krishna. Given the fact that both are active, proselytizing movements, the question arises as to why the spread and growth of Nichiren Shoshu have far outdistanced those of Hare Krishna. Differences in the value orientation, promises, and membership demands of the two movements certainly constitute important variables in accounting for the difference in their spread and growth.[14] However, Propositions 4A and 4B point to a perhaps more significant determinant of the differential spread and growth not only of these two movement organizations, but also of social movement organizations in general: the extent to which a movement organization is linked to or structurally isolated from other groups and networks within its environment of operation.

Summary and Conclusions

In recent years the study of differential recruitment to and the differential spread and growth of social movements has been characterized by concern with the process through which movement organizations strategically expand their ranks and mobilize support for their cause. Yet, as both Useem (1975:43) and Zald and McCarthy (1979:240) have noted, there has been relatively little systematic research conducted on the details of the influence process. In order to shed greater empirical and theoretical light on the recruitment process, we have presented data derived from three sources. Our findings indicate that the probability of being recruited into a particular movement is largely a function of two conditions: (1) links to one or more movement members through a preexisting or emergent interpersonal tie; and (2) the absence of countervailing networks. The first condition suggests who is most likely to be brought directly into a movement organization's orbit of influence and thereby subjected to its recruitment and reality-construction efforts. The second indicates who is structurally most available for participation and therefore most likely to accept the recruitment invitation. Our findings also indicate that a movement's recruitment strategies and its resultant growth will vary considerably in the degree to which it constitutes a closed or open network of social relations. Taken together, these findings indicate that both the network attributes of movement organizations and members function as important structural determinants of differential recruitment to and the differential growth of movement organizations.[15]

Several theoretical and empirical implications are suggested by our findings and correspondent propositions. First, in contrast to the traditional assumption that movement recruitment efforts are largely a function of goals and ideology, our findings indicate that the mobilization process in general and the recruitment process in particular are likely to vary significantly with changes in organizational structure. Indeed, our findings indicate that movement goals and organizational structure may occasionally contradict each other. When this occurs, as in the case of Hare Krishna, the organizational structure will function as the more important determinant of recruitment patterns.

Second, since social networks constitute microstructures, the findings suggest that microstructural variables are of equal, and perhaps greater, importance than dispositional susceptibilities in the determination of differential recruitment. We do not urge that dispositions be wholly ignored in attempts to understand the recruitment process. The notion "disposition" perhaps usefully could be integrated with the network perspective by conceptualizing it in terms of the normative, instrumental and affective ties among current and potential participants. People can become encapsulated (Lofland, 1977a; 1977b) by a movement when they are "dispositionally" linked to the proselytizing network, and when that connection becomes expanded by exposure to increasingly broadened socialization messages.

Third, our analysis suggests that the question of "why" people join social movements cannot be adequately understood apart from an examination of the process of "how" individuals come to align themselves with a particular movement. Indeed, it is our contention that the "whys" or "reasons" for joining arise out of the recruitment process itself. We would thus argue that further examination of movement joining and participation should give more attention to how movements solicit, coax, and secure participants, and more attention to the factors that account for variations in recruitment strategies and their efficacy. An examination of such factors should move us beyond our current knowledge about the recruitment process, which has, according to Marx and Wood (1975:393), reached "a point of diminishing returns."

Notes

1. Here we are following McCarthy and Zald's (1977:1217-9) distinction between a social movement and a movement organization. They define a social movement as "a set of opinions and beliefs in a population which represents preferences" in support of or opposition to social change. A social movement organization is defined as "a complex, or formal, organization which identifies its goals with the preferences of a social movement or a countermovement and attempts to implement those goals." We think this

is a conceptually useful distinction since individuals are recruited into and devote time and energy to movement organizations.

2. Nichiren Shoshu of America (NSA) is a Japanese-based, culturally transplanted, proselytizing Buddhist movement that seeks to change the world by changing individuals. It was formally introduced into America in 1960 and claims to have since attracted more than 200,000 members, the vast majority of whom are Occidental. For a detailed examination of the movement's ideology, goals, and operation in America, see Snow (1976; 1979).

3. *The World Tribune* is published five times weekly in Santa Monica, California. It was first issued in August 1964 and now has over 55,000 monthly subscriptions. It constitutes a useful record of the growth and history of the Nichiren Shoshu movement in America.

4. For a discussion of the origins, goals and ideology, and operation of Hare Krishna, see Daner (1976) and Judah (1974).

5. Classification of Respondents by Relationship to and Type of Movement

Movement Type	Participants[a]	Sympathizers[b]	Totals
Religious or Psychiatric[c]	54	50	104
Political[d]	81	115	196
Totals	135	165	300

[a] "Participants" refers to those individuals who devote time, energy, and other resources to the movement organization with which they are affiliated. They are what McCarthy and Zald (1977:1221) refer to as the "constituents" of a social movement organization.

[b] "Synpathizers" refers to those individuals who believe in or agree with the goals of a movement or movement organization, but do not devote any personal resources to it. They are what McCarthy and Zald (1977:1221) refer to as "adherents."

[c] Movements classified as "Religious or Psychiatric" include Transcendental Meditation, Church of Scientology, Baha'i, Jehovah's Witnesses, Campus Crusade for Christ, etc.

[d] Movements classified as "Political" include: National Organization for Reform of Marijuana Laws, NOW, Right to Life, Young Socialist Alliance, Lesbian-Gay Alliance, John Birch Society, Common Cause, University Mobilization for Survival (Anti-Nuke), etc.

6. Following Goffman (1963) and Lyman and Scott (1967), "public places" refer to those regions or areas in a community or society that are freely and officially accessible to most members of that community or society. "Private places," on the other hand, refer to those spatial domains that are off-limits to all but acknowledged members and guests, and in which outsiders are considered as actual or potential intruders.

7. Heirich's (1977) findings regarding conversion to Catholic Pentecostalism do not neatly fit into Table 1. However, the findings are consistent with those reported in Table 1. Among the 118 respondents "introduced to the movement by trusted associates," 75% were converts. In contrast, among the 187 respondents who were not introduced to the movement by trusted associates, only 31% were converts. Based on similar findings for other social influence variables, Heirich (1977:667) concluded that "it is clear that members of the movement, when recruiting, turn to previous friends and to persons they meet daily."

8. Much of the literature touching on the hypothetical association between preexisting social psychological strains and participation in movements suggests a relatively indeterminate relationship (see Aberle, 1965; Bolton, 1972; Marx and Wood, 1975; Petras and Zeitlin, 1967; Portes, 1971a; Useem, 1975). Also the magnitude of statistical association between measures of social psychological variables and participation in movements and protest has generally been quite small and unconvincing (see Lewis and Kraut, 1972; McPhail, 1971; Moinat et al., 1972; Portes, 1971a; Snyder and Tilly, 1972). For varied criticisms of the social psychological-dispositional approach to movement joining, see McCarthy and Zald (1977: 1214-5), Snow and Phillips (1980), Turner and Killian (1972: 365), Useem (1975:11-18), and Zygmunt (1972).

9. The information pertaining to street-recruits is based on the testimonies of 61 Nichiren Shoshu members recruited off the street and on in-depth interviews with two street recruits to NSA and with 24 Hare Krishna devotees.

10. It thus follows that relatively few people are recruited directly off the streets for two basic reasons: First, most people walking the street are engaged in the business of completing a particular line of action—such as shopping, going to a movie, and the like—and, therefore, have little if any unscheduled or free time when confronted by movement recruiters. Second, most individuals walking the street in most urban areas have a number of fairly strong, proximal social relationships that function as countervailing influences, at least when confronted by a proselytizing stranger.

11. This interpretation is suggested by McCarthy and Zald (1973) in their initial discussion of resource mobilization, and by McPhail and Miller's (1973) treatment of the assembling process. Although one must be cautious about assuming that the dynamics underlying participation in civil disorders and social movements are the same, it is worth noting that this interpretation is consistent with McPhail's (1971) reinterpretation of the riot participation literature, Lachman and Singer's (1968) findings regarding participation in the 1967 Detroit riot, and Snyder and Kelly's (1979) discussion of the development of urban disorders. (Also see National Advisory Commission on Civil Disorders, 1968:123.) Darley and

Batson's (1973) work on helping behavior also suggests that unscheduled or discretionary time is perhaps the most important determinant of Good Samaritanism.

12. This has been amply illustrated by a number of studies. In his examination of recruitment and conversion to the Unification Church, Lofland (1977a:306) found that initial contact "commonly involved an invitation to dinner, a lecture, or both" (see also Bromley and Shupe, 1979:171-4). Snow's (1976) findings regarding the recruitment practices of the Nichiren Shoshu movement reveal similar patterns. When recruiting in public places, Nichiren Shoshu members coaxed prospects to attend discussion meetings, chanting sessions, and other movement activities. Our observations of the recruitment efforts of Krishna devotees also indicate that the first step was to get prospects to the local temple. They were invited to attend a devotional session, to listen to discussion of the philosophy, or to attend a Sunday "love feast" (see also Judah, 1974).

13. In arguing that the "motives" for movement participation are largely emergent and interactional in character, we are at least implicitly questioning the rational calculus assumptions accepted by resource mobilization theorists. That perspective is most clearly represented in the work of McCarthy and Zald (1973; 1977) and Oberschall (1973). For an extensive critique of this "utilitarian" strand of resource mobilization theory, see Fireman and Gamson (1979) and Zurcher and Snow (forthcoming).

14. Regarding the differences in the value orientations and promises of the two movements, Nichiren Shoshu is more practical and this-worldly in orientation. Rather than calling for a renunciation of worldly attachments and promising a transcendence of the material world, as is the case with Hare Krishna, Nichiren Shoshu promises the realization of personal enlightenment and happiness in the immediate here-and-now. It is thus reasonable to assume that Nichiren Shoshu would appeal to a greater number of people than would Hare Krishna. Relatedly, membership in Nichiren Shoshu is much less demanding. Not only are Krishna devotees required to surrender to the movement their personal possessions and desiderata, but they are also required to sever their preexisting, extramovement interpersonal associations and ties. In contrast, Nichiren Shoshu members are merely required to surrender some time and energy, and perhaps be willing to risk a negative reaction by nonmovement significant others. In short, not only is it easier to be a Nichiren Shoshu member than a Krishna devotee, but Nichiren Shoshu adherents also live in and are "into" the here-and-now material world to a much greater extent than are the saffron-robed chanters and promoters of the Krishna mantra.

15. Our concentration upon microstructural factors in movement recruitment is not intended to detract scholars from equally necessary macrostructural probings of movement emergence, growth and decline. Blumer's (1951) identification of general social movements as seedbeds for specific movements remains heuristically important. The shifts in societal trends, especially in values and their interpretations, can influence the relevance of networks (and rhetoric in networks) for potential movement recruits. ◆

11

Multiple Networks and Mobilization in the Paris Commune, 1871

Roger V. Gould

A decade ago, Snow, Zurcher, and Ekland-Olson (1980) pointed to the importance of social networks for understanding the mobilization of social movements, but the state of research in this area is still best described as inchoate. Despite widespread acceptance of the idea that "network" or "structural" factors play a role in mobilization or recruitment, only a handful of studies have made genuine progress toward understanding the significance of these factors.

A principal reason for this state of affairs is that often because of data considerations researchers have typically used purely scalar variables to measure networks of social relations. "Network effects" are examined by simply counting social ties and using these counts as interval variables in regression equations, so that the process by which social ties influence mobilization is analyzed as though it operates exclusively on the individual level. This in turn means that two key issues—network structure and multiplexity—have received insufficient consideration in theory and research.

My goal is to demonstrate that the effect of social relations on the mobilization of collective action depends on the way in which these relations are structured and, more precisely, on the correspondence between *organizational and informal* networks. I use data on patterns of insurgency during the Paris Commune of 1871 to show that successful mobilization depended not on the sheer number of ties, but on the interplay between social ties created by insurgent organizations and pre-existing social networks rooted in Parisian neighborhoods. Organizational networks maintained solidarity because they were structured along neighborhood lines. Paradoxically, neighborhood ties even determined the importance of organizational links that cut *across* neighborhoods.

Previous studies have rarely demonstrated that structural properties of relational systems are important for social movements, and there is no discussion in the literature of the ways in which formal and informal networks interact in the mobilization process. In the conclusion, I argue that these issues are best addressed through data collection procedures and analytic strategies that respect the structure of networks rather than reducing networks to individual-level counts of social ties.

Network Factors in Mobilization

The notion of social structure, in various guises, has played a role in theories of collective action for a long time (Smelser 1963; Oberschall 1973). However, it was only with the publication of Snow, Zurcher, and Ekland-Olson's (1980) seminal article that a specifically network-based conceptualization of structure gained currency in social movement research. Reacting to the undersocialized view of human behavior characteristic of early versions of the resource mobilization perspective (McCarthy and Zald 1973, 1977; Gamson 1975), Snow and his colleagues demonstrated that social ties to members of Nichiren Shoshu of America were instrumental in drawing new members into the organization. This was a significant finding because it focused attention on the "microstructural" bases of social movement recruitment.

Subsequent research has yielded similar results, most notably in McAdam's (1986, 1988b) study of recruitment to the 1964 Mississippi Freedom Summer project. But in each case, supposedly "structural" factors in recruitment are measured as individual-level variables: Ties between participants and movement activists that predate recruitment are counted and the resulting number used as an independent variable in a regression equation. In some cases, organizational affiliations or respondents' subjective evaluations about how integrated they are have been substituted for network data (see, e.g., Cable, Walsh, and Warland 1988).

While the difficulty of collecting and analyzing true network data make this a practical approach, it masks the complexity inherent in social networks and does not permit inquiry into the pos-

"Multiple Networks and Mobilization in the Paris Commune, 1871." *American Sociological Review* 56: 716-729. Copyright © 1991 by the American Sociological Association. Reprinted with permission.

sibility that network influences on mobilization operate on a supra-individual level. The effect on A of a social tie to B may depend on whether A is also tied to C, but this kind of interlock disappears when networks are reduced to numerical counts of ties.

Recently, researchers have begun to address this issue by exploring the effects of specifically structural aspects of social networks. In a later study of the Freedom Summer project, Fernandez and McAdam (1988b) analyzed the effect on participation of an individual's network prominence—a measure of centrality that uses the first eigenvector of the network matrix to weight each person's ties by the centrality of the people to whom he or she is tied. This specification of network effects permits an individual's *position* in a social structure to play a role in movement recruitment. A simulation study by Marwell, Oliver, and Prahl (1988) explored the effect of group-level variables—network centralization and resource heterogeneity—on aggregate contributions to a collective good.

While these research efforts represent an important advance, inasmuch as they refuse to treat social ties in piecemeal fashion and place an emphasis on networks as such, they focus on single networks and thus neglect the second key issue, network multiplexity.[1] Yet one of the key reasons network structure is significant is that mobilization typically creates organizational networks that overlay and interact with pre-existing informal networks. Thus, a focus on network structure entails a simultaneous examination of formal and informal networks.

There are three principal reasons why the Paris Commune of 1871 is an especially useful setting for an investigation into the problem of social networks and social movements. First, insurgent mobilization was effected through a highly visible formal organization, the Paris National Guard, so that it is possible to make precise statements about how participants were recruited to the uprising. Second, National Guard units were generally organized along neighborhood lines, with the important exception of 35 volunteer battalions. This means that mobilization outcomes across units can be compared with respect to a critical variable: the availability of neighborhood social ties as a source of solidarity. Finally, the connection between the *organizational* structure of the insurgent effort and the *social* structure of

neighborhoods permits an examination of the extent to which social networks and organizational networks interact in affecting social movement mobilization.

The Communal Revolution of 1871

The late 1860s were a period of social and political ferment in Paris as well as the rest of urban France.[2] In part because of an 1864 law legalizing strikes and an 1868 law liberalizing controls on the press and public meetings, but also because of growing discontent with the regime of Emperor Louis Napoleon, strikes became more frequent throughout France's industrial regions and calls for social and political reforms became more vociferous. Although France's economy had grown and industrialized since the declaration of the Second Empire in Bonaparte's "Eighteenth Brumaire" of 1851, the growing prosperity had chiefly benefitted propertied classes and finance capitalists at the expense of the working population, which included proletarianized industrial workers as well as artisans (Edwards 1971).

Unlike the revolutions of 1789 and 1848, the events of 1871 were not preceded by a nationwide agricultural crisis. The combination of an economic recession and a misguided war with Prussia over the succession of a Hohenzollern prince to the Spanish throne were sufficient to sweep away the Empire without a shot being fired. A series of embarrassing defeats of France's armies, including the encirclement of one force at Metz and the capture of a second—along with the Emperor himself—at Sedan, led to the proclamation of a Republic in Paris on September 4, 1870.

The defeats continued, however, and Paris was subjected to a four-month winter siege by the Prussian army. In January 1871, the rural population of France elected a National Assembly determined to sign a peace treaty with Bismarck, the Prussian Chancellor. The radical deputies from Paris, who wanted to continue the war rather than surrender, were outvoted, and the capital was ceded to the Prussian army (although the victorious forces were permitted only to march through, not occupy, the city). A struggle ensued between the conservative government of Adolphe Thiers and the people of Paris over the disposition of the artillery of the Paris National Guard, the popular militia force of 300,000 men that had been armed during the Prussian siege. A poorly planned attempt by the French army to seize the cannon on

March 18 became a complete fiasco when the troops refused to fire on the crowds protecting the artillery parks. Thiers ordered the army to retreat to Versailles, leaving Paris by default in the hands of the Central Committee of the National Guard, a largely radical group elected by the working-class battalions of the Guard in February 1871. The next day, the Committee announced elections to the Commune, simultaneously invoking the revolutionary Commune of 1789 and the tradition of municipal independence favored by nine-teenth-century socialists like Proudhon (Greenberg 1973).

The proclamation of the Commune on March 26 initiated a two-month experiment in democratic socialism. The Commune established workers' cooperative enterprises throughout the city, instituted universal free education, declared the separation of church and state, and passed resolutions on specific economic issues such as the abolition of night work for bakers. But as Marx (1940), noted, "The greatest social measure of the Commune was its own working existence. Its special measures could but betoken the tendency of a government of the people by the people" (p. 65).

Although the Commune was not a class war in the sense of a proletarian revolt against capitalism, its suppression was every bit as brutal as if it had been motivated by the class hatred Marx attributed to the French bourgeoisie. From the first hostilities between the Paris National Guard and the movement on March 30, the Versailles forces chose to execute rather than detain many of the insurgents they captured. The fighting increasingly absorbed the Commune's attention, until the Versailles army re-entered Paris on May 21. In a re-enactment of the June Days of 1848, the people of Paris tore up cobblestones, gratings, and anything else that was available to build barricades and defend the city against the government troops. Officers and soldiers of the French army continued to execute those they captured at each barricade, prompting the massacre by Parisians of dozens of hostages taken by the Commune. At the end of the *semaine sanglante* (or "bloody week") of May 21 to 28 when the city had finally been subdued, about 25,000 Parisians were dead, most of them shot after surrendering to the army. In contrast, of the 15,000 Communards actually tried for their role in the insurrection (about 40,000 were arrested, but most of these were dismissed after a preliminary interrogation), only 23 were executed by the military courts (Appert 1875). About one-fifth of those tried were acquitted; the rest were either deported to the French penal colonies in New Caledonia or imprisoned in France for periods ranging from one to 20 years.

In the short term, the upheaval of 1871 imperiled the infant French republic by reinforcing Bourbon and Bonapartist calls for the maintenance of social order through a strong monarchy. But in 1879, after nearly a decade of right-wing reaction under the presidency of Marshal MacMahon, the monarchist general who had engineered the crushing of the Commune, Republicans finally gained a majority in both houses of the legislature. Less than a year later, a general amnesty was approved for all those still imprisoned for participating in the 1871 uprising. In the ensuing months, thousands of convicted insurgents returned to France—leaving behind hundreds who had died serving their sentences.

Social Networks and Social Movement Mobilization

Mobilization does not just depend on social ties; it also creates them. Although members of a protest organization may have joined because of a pre-existing social tie to an activist, they also form new social relations while participating in collective protest (for a discussion of some of the long-term effects of such ties, see McAdam 1988b). Without addressing the matter directly, the current view of how social networks influence mobilization implies that pre-existing ties do not matter once someone has been recruited. For example, Marwell, Oliver, and Prahl's (1988) simulation treated an actor's contribution to a collective good as unproblematic once he or she had been contacted by a movement organizer. Fernandez and McAdam (1988b) argued that their focus on the organizational affiliations of applicants to the Freedom Summer project was "ideally suited for studying the network or other factors that maintain commitment to the project among the set of applicants" (p. 360). These approaches implicitly presuppose that the ties established during the process of mobilization tell us everything we need to know about continued participation; pre-existing ties may have helped create these new ties by facilitating initial recruitment, but they have no further influence.

Evidence from the final week of the Paris Commune strongly suggests that this view is incorrect. The residential recruitment system of the National Guard, which assigned people to battalions on the basis of the neighborhood in which they lived, provided more than an organizational framework for the insurgent effort.[3] Rather, the policy of recruitment along residential lines was crucial for mobilization until the last moments of fighting because it linked the informal social networks defined by neighborhoods to the formal network generated among insurgents by joint membership in the National Guard. Members of each battalion were tied to each other not only through their shared organizational affiliation, but also by the fact that they were neighbors.

The importance of neighborhood solidarity in maintaining the cohesiveness of residentially organized units was clearly evident in the persistence with which rank-and-file National Guardsmen associated their participation in the insurgent effort with a neighborhood-based identity. One group of Guardsmen in the second battalion, which was recruited primarily in the eighth Paris *arrondissement*, protested their inclusion in a Guard unit from another neighborhood:

> The undersigned National Guards, inhabitants of the chaussée d'Antin in the ninth *arrondissement*, forming part of the 2nd battalion of which four companies reside in the eighth *arrondissement*;
> Request that the companies residing in the ninth be turned over to one of the battalions of the ninth *arrondissement*, or any other assignment deemed useful for the communal defense. (Archives Historiques de l'Armée de Terre, Series Ly, carton 35)[4]

Similarly, a group of officers of the 148th battalion expressed their desire "to perform no service but that of their own *arrondissement*," arguing that this was the only way to ensure the protection of their neighborhood from reactionary forces. Moreover, they viewed the deployment of an outside battalion in their arrondissement as "a sign of mistrust, and consequently as an insult to their republican patriotism" (Archives Historiques de l'Armée de Terre, Series Ly, carton 44).

Petitions and letters were not the only means by which insurgents expressed their neighborhood loyalty. The localism of National Guard battalions is a recurrent theme in historical treatments of barricade fighting during the *semaine sanglante*. According to numerous accounts, the central obstacle to a concerted defense of the city against the Versailles army was the obstinate refusal of Guardsmen to fight outside their residential areas.

Rougerie (1971) argued that the final call to the barricades issued by the Commune's War Delegate, Charles Delescluze, served to "dismantle what was left of the organized Communard troops, each one running to the defense of its *quartier* [neighborhood] rather than forming a front" (p. 252). Edwards (1971) reported that Jean Allemane, a battalion commander in the fifth *arrondissement* who rose to prominence as a labor leader in the 1880s, was unable to prevent two units from the eleventh and twelfth *arrondissements* from going home to fight during the final week. Clifford (1975) reported a similar incident in which Guardsmen from the Right Bank abandoned a large barricade they were defending on the Left Bank saying they were going to protect their own areas from the army. Clearly, neighborhood social structure left its imprint on the behavior of insurgents long after the initial stages of recruitment.

Historical accounts of the Commune have consistently pointed to the damaging effects of neighborhood loyalty on efforts to mount a coordinated military struggle against the Versailles army. But this emphasis on *strategy* misses the crucial sociological point that the mapping of National Guard units onto residential areas had unmistakably positive effects on *mobilization*. In fact, neighborhood social structure was the principal source of commitment to the insurgent effort. This is evident when the arrest patterns of residentially recruited battalions are compared with the patterns for the 35 volunteer units. Aside from the fact that Guards in volunteer units were recruited without regard to residence, differences between these two types of battalions were minimal. While volunteer battalions remained independent of the administrative apparatus of the National Guard Federation, even this distinction became irrelevant as all traces of central control vanished in the last week of fighting.

Figure 1 reveals critical differences between the two groups with respect to the cumulative distribution of arrests across the eight days of the *semaine sanglante*. Raw data for this figure are drawn from the army's official report to the National Assembly (Appert 1875). For the volunteer battalions, nearly half (45.2 percent) of all those arrested during the fighting had already been detained by the second day. In contrast, the proportion for residentially based units at this point was a little over one-fourth (26.4 percent). The insurgents' typical approach to resistance during the "bloody week" was to defend each barricade until it was overcome and then either to surrender or, if they were not trapped, to retreat to another barricade (Edwards 1971; Tombs 1981). Thus this difference in the timing of arrests appears to reflect a higher level of solidarity in residential battalions than in volunteer units. The pattern for the first two days is particularly striking in light of the fact that there was very little serious fighting during this period; most arrests at this point were the result of surrender rather than capture. For example, on the morning of May 22, the second day of the *semaine sanglante*, 1,500 National Guards from several battalions surrendered when an army regiment entered the city gates at the Porte Maillot and overran the battery of cannon in the Parc Monceau (Clifford 1975; Edwards 1971). Given that this incident accounted for half of the 3,000 arrests reported for that day (Appert 1875), it is clear that at this stage the army had not yet encountered much resistance.

Figure 1
Cumulative Distribution of Arrests of National Guardsmen by Day, for Volunteer Battalions and Residential Battalions: Paris Commune, May 21-28, 1871

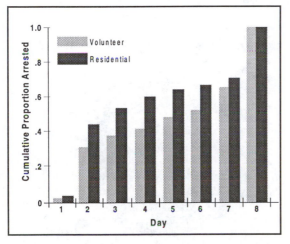

For battalions recruited along neighborhood lines, 42.7 percent of the total arrests for the week were made in the last two days, compared with 31.9 percent for Guardsmen in volunteer battalions. In general, insurgents in neighborhood-based units were arrested at considerably later stages in the fighting, indicating that these battalions were more cohesive than those that were not organized residentially.

It is apparent from these data that informal social networks are implicated in social movement mobilization well past the initial stages of recruitment. Pre-existing social ties helped to maintain solidarity in the 1871 insurrection even after participants were firmly embedded in organizational networks because National Guard battalions tied people together in ways that mirrored the division of the Parisian social world into well-defined neighborhoods. Thus, neighborhood social structure contributed not only to the *formation* of insurgent organizations, but also to their *effectiveness* as tools for mounting collective protest.

Solidarity and Structure

These findings could be interpreted as showing only that social ties need to be counted more accurately, i.e., network multiplexity might only imply that different kinds of ties contribute additively to mobilization and the maintenance of solidarity. If this were true, sociologists would still not need to consider structure: they would simply need to remember that pairs of people can be tied in more than one way and that multiple ties (friendship, shared organizational membership, and so on) can exert simultaneous but independent effects on mobilization.

But this is not the whole story. Neighborhood ties and organizational ties created by the National Guard acted jointly to maintain solidarity in the ranks of Parisian insurgents; and it is because of this interaction between the two networks that their structure must be taken into account.

Despite the general policy of residential recruitment, a substantial number of Guardsmen were enlisted in battalions outside their own neighborhoods. Thus, they were linked by the insurgent *organization* to people who were not tied to them as neighbors; conversely, they were linked as *neighbors* to other insurgents with whom they did not have organizational ties. In other words, these insurgents constituted organizational links across neighborhoods and neighborhood links across organizations.

The analysis presented below shows that the network of social ties created by overlapping enlistments had important consequences for the insurgent effort. These overlaps made levels of commitment to the insurrection interdependent across residential areas: the degree to which each neighborhood was successful in mounting resistance to the Versailles army depended on levels of resistance in the other neighborhoods to which it was linked.

Data and Methods

The most effective test of the claim that resistance levels are interdependent is a regression model that explicitly takes enlistment overlaps into account by means of a term for network autocorrelation. The model takes the following form:

$$y = \rho \, Wy + X\beta + e,$$

where **W** is a matrix of weights representing network links among the 20 *arrondissements* of Paris, ρ is a coefficient representing the degree of interdependence among the observations, **y** is a vector of outcomes on the dependent variable, and the remainder of the equation is the standard linear regression model. This model posits an influence process in which a district's resistance level is a function of a set of exogenous variables *and of the resistance levels of all the other districts,* weighted by the strength of its links with them. This specification implies that each district simultaneously influences and is influenced by each other district in the network, resulting in "endogenous feedback" (Erbring and Young 1979) that operates through network ties. Moreover, because the entire network is taken into account, neighborhoods are hypothesized to influence each other directly, through their ties to each other, and indirectly, through their ties to other neighborhoods. My arguments imply that we should observe positive values of p resulting from the network of overlapping enlistments. Estimation of the model is accomplished through maximum-likelihood techniques (Doreian 1981; Odland 1988).

Data are drawn from both archival and published sources. Because variation in levels of resistance is difficult to capture with a single variable, two dependent measures are used. The first is the average battalion size for each *arrondissement.* The number of battalions formed in each *arrondissement* was based on the number of adult males living there, and in principle each battalion should have consisted of 1,500 men. Despite a series of decrees issued by the Commune's War Delegates to the effect that men who failed to perform their Guard service would be disarmed and imprisoned, the exigencies of the war effort and the inefficiency of the organization made enforcement impracticable. Consequently, the number of Guardsmen actually reporting for duty varied considerably and usually fell well below the target. Since these shortfalls presumably resulted from apathy or a lack of resolve on the part of recruits, the average battalion size measures each district's success in mobilizing its male population during the insurrection.

Battalion commanders filed daily dispatches to the Commune's War Ministry reporting on the discipline and morale of their units and on the number of men actually serving. These dispatches were seized by the army during the final week of fighting and are preserved in the Archives Historiques de l'Armée de Terre at Vincennes (Series Ly, cartons 37 through 123). Although these records are incomplete, reports are available for 176 of the 215 battalions acting under the Commune. For this study, battalion size was recorded at two time points: The first week in May, after enlistment lists were closed and disloyal or "recalcitrant" battalions had been dissolved or reorganized; and the end of the third week in May, on the eve of the Versailles army's final assault on the capital. This makes it possible to determine if the extent of interdependence among neighborhoods changed in the course of the uprising. Figure 2 depicts average battalion size in late May. Not surprisingly, there are no reports dated after May 21, the day the army entered the city's western gates.

Figure 2
Average Battalion Size in Late May, by **Arrondissement:** *Paris Commune, 1871*

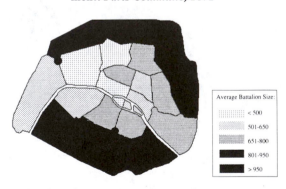

Note: Although battalion sizes vary from early to late May, the differences are not noticeable in this form of presentation.

The second dependent variable is the number of deaths per 1,000 inhabitants for each *arrondissement* during the month of May. Ideally, deaths from natural causes should be subtracted *from arrondissement* totals, but this information is unavailable. Given the large increase in the number of deaths during the insurrection, however, it is likely that most of the variation in this variable is attributable to differential rates of participation in the fighting rather than to variation in the death rates from other causes. There is one other source of measurement error: the dozens of wounded insurgents who died in military hospitals during the *semaine sanglante* tend to inflate the totals for *arrondissements* containing large hospitals.[5] Consequently, the analyses of death rates include a term for the number of deaths from military injuries that occurred in each district in February 1871. Since fighting with the Prussians ceased in January, any military deaths in February presumably occurred in hospitals; this variable should therefore correct for distortions in the death rates for May 1871 that result from the presence of large hospitals. Data for these measures come from the city's monthly bulletin of vital statistics (Ville de Paris 1872). Figure 3 shows death rates by *arrondissement*.

Figure 3
Standardized Deaths per 1,000 Inhabitants, by Arrondissement: Paris Commune, May 1871

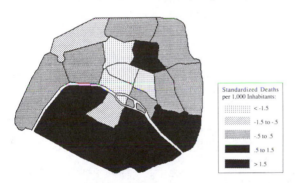

Note: Since death rates are confounded by the presence of military hospitals in some neighborhoods, these data represent deaths net of this confounding factor. These rates are standardized residuals from an OLS regression of raw death rates on deaths from military injuries in February 1817 (see text).

W is a 20 x 20 matrix in which each element, w_{ij}, is the number of Guards living in the *i*th *arrondissement* who served in the *j*th legion, divided by the total number of that district's Guards who served in other legions (each legion corresponds to a particular *arrondissement*). Thus **W** is a nonsymmetric, row-normalized matrix of weights in which the diagonal elements are set to zero.[6] Raw data for this matrix are drawn from the official military report on the insurrection and its repres-

sion (Appert 1875). Figure 4 shows these enlistment overlaps for each *arrondissement*.

Figure 4
Numbers of National Guardsmen Serving in Legions Outside Their Arrondissement of Residence, by Arrondissement: Paris Commune, 1817

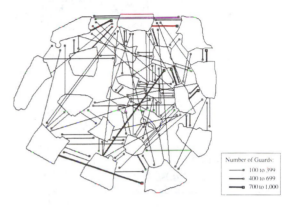

Note: Enlistment overlaps of fewer than 100 National Guardsmen are not shown; inclusion of such links would connect each arrondissement with nearly every other. Directionality is indicated by a hollow square, i.e., if 150 inhabitants of District A serve in a National Guard battalion from District B, this would appear as a thin line from A ending in a square near B.

The exogenous variables measure aspects of each *arrondissement's* social composition that may have influenced resistance levels: the number of poor people per 1,000 inhabitants; the percentage of the population classified in the 1872 census as skilled salaried workers; the percentage classified as unskilled (day-laborers); and the percentage who were white-collar employees (Loua 1873). The contrast category consists of people with bourgeois or professional occupations.

Poverty is hypothesized to have contributed positively to resistance levels for two reasons. First, the poor people of Paris had suffered the greatest hardship during the four-month Prussian siege and were therefore most likely to be hostile toward the French government for having surrendered. Second, National Guardsmen were paid a small daily indemnity (1 franc 50 centimes) under the Commune. This incentive to participate in the insurrection probably had the greatest effect among the poorest segments of the population.

Following similar reasoning, the percentage of each district's population with a working-class occupation is expected to exert a positive effect on resistance levels because the openly pro-labor policies of the Commune's elected government presumably generated greater support in working-class sections of the city and greater hostility in bourgeois areas. Voting records for the March 26 elections to the Communal Council demonstrated a clear relationship between class composition and support for radical and socialist candidates (for election data, see Rougerie 1971). At the same time, however, it is important to distinguish white-collar workers, who often came from middle-class families, from salaried artisanal workers with a tradition of activism (Moss 1976; Sewell 1980). Likewise, unskilled day-laborers were more marginal and geographically mobile than skilled artisanal workers and consequently less likely to participate in an insurrection that depended on the social integration of urban neighborhoods. For this reason, my analyses separate the working population of each district into skilled, unskilled, and white-collar workers.

Since my hypotheses are directional, all of the statistical tests are one-tailed. Thus, estimates of ρ and of coefficients for the exogenous variables are treated as statistically significant only if they deviate from chance levels in the predicted direction.

Results

The first four columns of Table 1 present estimates for the models predicting battalion size in both early May and late May; columns 5 and 6 report results for the models predicting death rates during the month of May. To test whether autocorrelation is a result of cross-district enlistments rather than simple geographical diffusion, two versions of the model are estimated. The "spatial model" substitutes a spatial adjacency matrix for the enlistment network used in the "network model." The hypothesis is that autocorrelation through the enlistment network is larger (more positive) than autocorrelation through spatial contiguity. In the spatial model, w_{ij} is coded as 1 if district i borders on district j, and 0 otherwise; the **W** matrix is then row-normalized as with the network model. Because sampling logic is inappropriate for these data, standard significance tests are not used. The significance levels reported are based on a null model of "randomization" of the observed values of **y** with respect to the **W** and **X** matrices (Odland 1988). The estimates of ρ and β are compared with the distribution of the estimates that would result from a random assignment of the observed values of **y** to the 20 cases.[7] Coefficient estimates are statistically significant at the .05 level if fewer than 5 percent of random assignments produce estimates of equal or greater value.

As predicted, all of the exogenous variables contribute positively to battalion size and death rates in all models, although the only statistically significant effect is that for percentage salaried workers. Since the reference category for the oc-

Table 1
Coefficient Estimates for Average Battalion Size and Death Rate on Selected Independent Variables:
Paris Commune, 1871

	Battalion Size				Death Rate, May 1871	
	Early May		Late May			
	Network Model	Spatial Model	Network Model	Spatial Model	Network Model	Spatial Model
Independent Variable	(1)	(2)	(3)	(4)	(5)	(6)
Autocorrelation ρ	.289*	−.118	.477**	.038	.487*	.030
February Military Deaths	—	—	—	—	.076**	.068**
Poverty Rate	2.217	2.419	2.217	2.320	16.818	18.103
Percent Skilled Workers	9.163*	9.311**	8.040*	8.164**	.064	.054
Percent Unskilled Workers	7.671	7.743	8.523	7.765	.081	.068
Percent White-Collar Employees	8.434	6.667	12.074	10.869	.066	.036
Constant	−148.918	180.656	−347.618	8.597	−4.650	−1.715
Fit[a]	.728	.722	.703	.674	.471	.441
Number of *arrondissements*	20	20	20	20	20	20

*$p<.05$ (one tailed) **$p<.01$ (one tailed)
[a] "Fit" is the square of the correlation between the observed and predicted values of the dependent variable. While it roughly corresponds to R^2 in standard regression analysis, it is not strictly comparable and should not be interpreted as the percentage of variance explained.

cupational composition variables is bour-geois/professional, the coefficients confirm the hypothesis that resistance was stronger in areas that were poor and working-class. The expectation that white-collar and unskilled workers would play less prominent roles in the insurrection is not supported.

The most important finding is that the auto-correlation term, ρ, is positive and significant in the network models for battalion size in early May and late May. A significant autocorrelation effect is observed only when **W** represents cross-district enlistments; there is no evidence of autocorrelation through spatial adjacency in either early or late May. In addition, the estimate of ρ in the network model for late May is significantly larger (p .05) than the estimate in the spatial model.[8] Similar results obtain for the number of deaths per 1,000 inhabitants (columns 5 and 6). The network of militia enrollments made levels of insurgency significantly interdependent across districts, whereas spatial proximity did not.[9] The fit of the models predicting late May battalion size and death rates improves when the enlistment network rather than spatial adjacency is used.

These findings show that insurgents in different neighborhoods influenced each other's degree of commitment to the insurrection through the network of links created by overlapping enlistments. High levels of commitment in one area enhanced commitment elsewhere when enlistment patterns provided a conduit for communication and interaction. This effect cannot be explained in terms of purely spatial diffusion, demonstrating that resistance levels were rendered interdependent across districts through a fundamentally social network.

Even more intriguing is the fact that this influence process worked in one direction only: Neighborhoods responded to events in other areas where their residents served in National Guard units. For instance, resistance in the fifth *arrondissement* was positively affected by the fact that many of its residents served in the thirteenth legion, whose members demonstrated a strong commitment to the insurgent effort. However, this does not imply that resistance in the thirteenth *arrondissement* was affected by the presence of Guardsmen from the fifth.[10]

Indeed, Table 2 shows that this was not the case by estimating the network models using the transpose of the enlistment matrix **W** (written **W'**).

Here, each element (w'_{ij}) represents the number of Guards serving in the ith legion who live in the jth district, divided by the total number of Guards in the ith legion who live outside the ith district. Under this model, each district is influenced by other districts through the Guardsmen who lived in these other areas, not by its own residents serving as Guardsmen in other areas.[11]

Using **W'** instead of **W**, the coefficient estimate for autocorrelation through the enlistment network is not significant for any of the dependent variables. Furthermore, the model for battalion size in early May yields an estimate of ρ that is significantly lower (p .05) than the estimate using **W**. The fit for the equation predicting battalion size in late May drops from .703 in the model using **W** to .673 in the model using **W'**: the fit for the model predicting death rates drops from .471 to .441.

Table 2
Coefficient Estimates for the Network Model Using the Transpose of the Enlistment Network: Paris Commune, 1871

Independe Variable	Battalion Size		Death Rate
	Early May	Late May	May 1871
Autocorrelation (ρ)	−.271	−.017	.268
February Military Deaths	—	—	.072[*]
Poverty Rate	2.617	2.371	16.177
Percent Skilled Workers	9.063[*]	8.162[**]	.058
Percent Unskilled Workers	7.446	7.868	.079
Percent White-Collar Employees	6.827	10.576	.044
Constant	302.492	47.489	−3.070
Fit	.724	.673	.441
Number of *arrondissements*	20	20	20

[*] $p < .05$ (one tailed) [**] $p < .01$ (one tailed)

This analysis indicates that levels of resistance in each *arrondissement* were affected by the experiences of its own residents serving in the National Guard in other districts, but not by the experiences of Guardsmen who lived in other districts. On an individual level, then, the influence process occurred because insurgents serving away from home had an impact on the behavior of their neighbors serving at home; but these insurgents did not affect the behavior of the Guardsmen with whom they served.

This finding provides strong evidence that formal and informal networks do not affect mobilization independently. The organizational links the National Guard generated through overlapping enlistments established a kind of cross-neighborhood solidarity in the form of interdependent levels of resistance, but this interdependence only emerged because the insurgents whose battalion memberships constituted these organizational ties also had informal ties to people in their own neighborhoods. Thus, the influence of formal and informal networks on mobilization cannot be described in additive terms; rather, neighborhood and organizational ties interacted to forge and maintain solidarity among insurgents.

Discussion

The reductionist treatment of network factors in social movement research has obscured important aspects of their effects on mobilization. Sociologists have typically treated network data as they would any other variable: Information on social ties among movement participants has been collected and analyzed at the individual level. A few scholars (Fernandez and McAdam 1988b; Marwell, Oliver, and Prahl 1988) have pointed to the advantages of an approach that is more sensitive to structural properties of networks, but the issue of network multiplexity has not been studied until now.

This study demonstrates not only that multiplexity and structure are both central to an understanding of network effects on mobilization, but that the impact of structure cannot even be appreciated without taking multiplexity into account. The importance of neighborhood identity and the pattern of arrests showed that pre-existing social ties among neighbors and organizational ties formed by the National Guard worked together to maintain solidarity in the insurgent ranks. Formal ties alone cannot explain the localistic behavior of residentially recruited battalions or the fact that they were more cohesive during the final week of fighting than volunteer battalions. Thus, it is inappropriate to focus exclusively on networks created by formal movement organizations, even when discussing the latest phases of mobilization.[12]

But it is precisely because mobilization is simultaneously affected by more than one network that network structure cannot be ignored.[13] The cross-district influence process uncovered in the Paris Commune resulted from the *interaction of* informal neighborhood networks with the organizational network of the Paris National Guard.

Cross-neighborhood solidarity could not have emerged in the absence of enlistment overlaps that linked each residential area with Guard units in other areas; but these overlaps only made resistance levels interdependent across areas because mobilization was rooted in social ties among neighbors.

The interaction of multiple networks demonstrates the importance of structure in two ways. First, the notion of a network of overlapping enlistments presupposes that informal ties grouped people into neighborhoods and organizational ties grouped people into residentially based National Guard units. That is, it is not even possible to *discuss* enlistment overlaps without first recognizing that residential areas linked people informally as neighbors, and that National Guard battalions linked people formally as members of an insurgent organization. To recognize that formal and informal ties clustered people into neighborhoods and organizational units is to recognize that these ties exhibit a structure.

Second, the process by which neighborhoods influenced each other through these overlapping enlistments can only be analyzed by considering the entire network of overlaps. Each neighborhood simultaneously affected and was affected by the levels of resistance in other neighborhoods, both directly (to the extent that it was directly linked to each of these neighborhoods) and indirectly (to the extent that each of these other neighborhoods was itself influenced by still other neighborhoods, and so on). In other words, the influence process occurred not just between isolated pairs of neighborhoods, but through chains of neighborhoods linked directly and at various removes. The interdependence of resistance levels across residential areas was thus intimately tied not only to the quantity, but also to the structure of overlapping enlistments. This intricate pattern would be obscured in an analysis that disaggregated networks into scalar counts of ties.

I have concentrated on the interplay between two specific social networks: one consisting of neighborhood ties, and the other defined by membership in a military organization. This focus derives from the nature of the event because mobilization in the 1871 uprising revolved around the construction and defense of barricades—a distinctly neighborhood-oriented revolutionary tactic—by a militia recruited along residential lines.

But this study's findings have implications for social movement research that go beyond the roles of neighborhoods and militias. Mobilization itself creates new social ties, even as it relies on pre-existing ties as a source of solidarity. In general, then, it should be possible to characterize any mobilization in terms of a mapping of formal organizational ties onto an indigenous network of informal ties—a mapping that can be quantified using techniques for comparing adjacency matrices. Where social movement organizations are isomorphic to preexisting social structure (e.g., if National Guard enlistments had mirrored neighborhood boundaries perfectly, with no cross-district enrollments), formal networks should have minimal effects on solidarity. In such a situation, formal organization might make social protest more effective by rationalizing participation, but not by inducing greater commitment. On the other hand, formal organizations that mobilize people in ways that completely cut across pre-existing networks, as in the volunteer Guard units, should experience considerable difficulty in sustaining commitment unless they manage to supplant such networks by creating total institutions (see, e.g., Walzer's [1980] discussion of revolutionary vanguards and Kuhn's [1971] treatment of the role of Triad societies in the Taiping Rebellion).[14]

The intermediate case, in which mobilization groups people in ways that largely follow the contours of indigenous social structure but also generates some interaction across pre-existing boundaries, provides the greatest potential for formal and informal networks to jointly influence solidarity and commitment to social movements. Most instances of social movement mobilization, like the present one, fall into this middle category. Consequently, future research should focus on informal and organizational ties concurrently rather than individually. This shift in focus will make discussion of the structure rather than the number of network ties indispensable.

Notes

1. In Marwell, Oliver, and Prahl's (1988) simulation study, only one kind of relation is assumed to exist: Individuals are either tied to each other or not, and there is no provision for multiple social ties. Similarly, Fernandez and McAdam (1988b) restricted their attention to the network of social ties generated by joint membership in activist organizations, thus neglecting the effects of any social ties not specifically connected with the mobilization of activism.

2. This historical account is necessarily brief. Detailed histories in English may be found in Home (1965) and Edwards (1971); Tombs (1981) focused on the military aspects of the uprising. The classic account in French is Lissagaray [1876] (1969); Serman (1986) provided a recent synthesis.

3. The Paris National Guard was divided into 20 legions, each corresponding to one of the city's 20 *arrondissements,* or administrative districts. Each legion was subdivided into battalions drawn from particular neighborhoods within the *arrondissement.* The statement that insurgents belonged to the same unit as their neighbors should therefore be taken literally: Participants in the insurrection routinely fought beside people who lived on the same street, even in the same building.

4. As this example makes clear, the continual reshuffling of National Guard companies in the early weeks of the Commune resulted in numerous organizational anomalies, so that most battalions included some Guardsmen who lived outside the appropriate neighborhood. The implication of these enlistment overlaps is dealt with in detail below.

5. For example, the Hôpital des Invalides in the upper-class, politically conservative seventh *arrondissement* probably explains many more of the deaths that occurred there in May 1871 than insurgency could.

6. Row-normalization of **W** is required for the estimation procedure used here. The likelihood function for the estimates of ρ and the other coefficients is in general undefined when any of the eigenvalues of **W** exceeds 1; consequently, the rows of **W** must sum to unity to ensure that the largest eigenvalue of **W** equals 1.

Although row-normalization is a technical necessity, it also has substantive implications. Forcing all the rows of **W** to sum to 1.0 means that the effect on A of a network tie to B can only be modeled *relative to* the total number of ties A has to other nodes. Thus, the model is insensitive to variation in degree (number of ties) across nodes in the network: A node with 1,000 ties is assumed to be subject to the same amount of network influence as a node with 2,000 ties. This situation could be rectified if the model permitted the value of ρ to vary across nodes, but techniques to estimate such a model have not been developed.

If the absolute number of ties were the key determinant of the magnitude of network influence, it would be undesirable to make this assumption. In the present case, however, this limitation of the model does not pose a problem. Indeed, row-normalization provides a necessary control for variation in population size across *arrondissements.* For each *arrondissement,* the total number of Guardsmen enlisted in outside legions is roughly proportional to the size of the adult male population (r = .78). Row-normalization permits the model to reflect the theoretical supposition that 1,000 cross-enlisted insurgents from a district with 40,000 men would have about the same effect as 2,000 insurgents from a district with 80,000 men.

7. Doreian (1981) provides formulae for computing standard errors based on the assumption of sampling observations from a normally distributed population. Because the 20 *arrondissements* analyzed here constitute the population in question, the randomization model is more appropriate. The distributions of ρ and β are generated through simulation in which the model is repeatedly estimated with randomly generated permutations of the values of **y** with respect to the 20 *arrondissements*.

8. Tests for differences in ρ between the two equations are performed in a manner analogous to those for the point estimates within each equation. Estimates are iteratively calculated for random assignments of the values of **y** to the observations, and for each iteration the estimate of ρ is computed once for each specification of the **W** matrix. This procedure generates a distribution of differences between estimates of ρ for a given set of data and two networks.

9. This result could reflect a causal relationship in which battalion size influenced the pattern of enlistment overlaps rather than the reverse. For instance, if neighborhoods with extremely high enlistment rates sent their overflows to other neighborhoods, but not to neighborhoods with very low rates, a positive autocorrelation effect would be observed. Three considerations militate against this interpretation, however. First, it seems unlikely that cross-district enlistments were the result of oversubscription in some areas because battalion sizes nowhere reached the target level of 1,500 men: The largest average battalion size was 1,155 for the fifteenth *arrondissement* (1,287 in early May). Second, enlistment rolls were closed at the end of April, so if autocorrelation were the result of the restructuring of battalions in response to disparities in enlistment rates, a stronger effect would have been observed in early May rather than in late May. Finally,

the fact that the analysis of death rates produces the same result suggests that the autocorrelation in Table 1 is not an artifact of the way resistance levels are measured.

10. Table 1 does indicate, however, that commitment to the insurrection in the thirteenth *arrondissement* was influenced by the enlistment of some of *its* residents in the fifth legion.

11. The spatial adjacency matrix is by definition symmetric, so that for spatial data, **W** = **W'**. Consequently, it would be redundant to re-estimate the spatial models for Table 2.

12. Fernandez and McAdam (1988b) noted that their data permit a discussion only of the later stages of mobilization, and acknowledge that other (unobserved) networks may have played significant roles earlier in the recruitment process. But they do not consider the possibility that informal relationships may continue to affect recruitment late in the mobilization process. Effects of prior networks are thus implicitly assumed to be mediated by, rather than interacting with, the network of organizational affiliations.

13. There is nothing particularly original in the claim that structure is closely related to network multiplexity. White, Boorman and Breiger (1976) made multiple networks a pivotal component of the blockmodelling approach to social structure. Still, this issue has not come up in social movement research despite increasing interest in network factors.

14. On the other side of the barricades, history has repeatedly shown how difficult it is for elites to make effective use of military organizations whose members interact regularly with the population they are supposed to control. This is the central theme of Traugott's (1985) study of the Parisian insurrection of 1848, and is echoed in most work on the February Revolution in Russia (Chorley 1943: Fitzpatrick 1982). Indeed, fraternization between the French army and the people of Paris was a key factor in the government's embarrassing defeat on March 18, 1871. ◆

12

Specifying the Relationship Between Social Ties and Activism

Doug McAdam
Ronnelle Paulsen

In recent years much attention in the social-movements literature has been focused on the role of social or organizational ties in movement recruitment. The result has been a growing body of studies that appear to attest to the causal importance of organizational ties (Barnes and Kaase 1979; Curtis and Zurcher 1973; Fernandez and McAdam 1988a; Gould 1991; McAdam 1986; Rosenthal et al. 1985; Orum 1972; Walsh and Warland 1983) or prior contact with a movement participant (Bolton 1972; Briët, Klandermans, and Kroon 1987; Gerlach and Hine 1970; McAdam 1986; Snow, Zurcher, and Ekland-Olson 1980; Zurcher and Kirkpatrick 1976) as strong predictors of individual activism. But while they remain important, these studies are nonetheless plagued by a troubling theoretical and empirical imprecision that raises important questions about their ultimate utility. This imprecision stems from three sources.

First these studies are generally silent on the basic sociological dynamics that account for the reported findings. That is, in most cases, no theory is offered to explain the observed effects of social ties on activism (for exceptions, see Opp 1989a; Fernandez and McAdam 1988a; and Gould 1993, 1991). So there remains a fundamental question about what the findings mean.

A second source of imprecision stems from the failure of movement scholars to specify and test the precise dimensions of social ties that seem to account for their role as facilitators of activism. As Marwell, Oliver, and Prahl (1988, p. 502) note, "it is widely agreed that participants in social movement organizations are usually recruited through preexisting social ties. . . . But exactly

how and why social ties are important is less well established."[1] This second problem is very much related to the first. Having failed to advance a theory that specifies the precise link between social ties and activism, empirical researchers have been content to assess the basic strength of the relationship instead of testing the causal power of the various dimensions of social ties. Accordingly, we do not really know whether it is the presence of a tie, the number of ties, or the salience, centrality, or strength of a tie that determines its effectiveness as a recruitment agent.

Finally, and perhaps most important, the existing studies fail to acknowledge conceptually or treat empirically the fact that individuals are invariably embedded in many organizational or associational networks or individual relationships that may expose the individual to conflicting behavioral pressures. This weakness is due to all the well-known dangers of sampling on the dependent variable. Almost invariably, the studies of movement recruitment start by surveying activists after their entrance into the movement. But showing that these activists were linked to the movement by some preexisting network tie does not *prove* the causal potency of that tie. No doubt there are many others who also had ties to the movement but did not participate in its activities. We suspect one of the principal reasons for the failure of the tie to impel participation in these cases is the existence of other, perhaps more salient, ties that are constraining involvement. But, to date, our lack of conceptual models of the recruitment process and the tendency to study activists after the fact of their participation has left the effects of these "multiple embeddings" unexamined.

In this article we hope to address these shortcomings in the network literature on recruitment. We will begin by briefly reviewing the existing literature on recruitment to activism and placing the recent emphasis on structural or network factors in the context of a broader discussion of other possible causal influences. We will then sketch a very rudimentary model of recruitment as mediated by social ties. In doing so we will take conceptual account of the multiple embeddings typical of social life. We will then use this model as a basis for examining the role of social ties in mediating individual recruitment to the 1964 Mississippi Freedom Summer Project. Specifically, we will seek to determine (a) which dimensions of social ties (e.g., salience, strong vs. weak, etc.) have the most causal potency and (b) how competing ties affect the decision of whether or not to participate in the project.

Review of the Literature

Among the topics that have most concerned researchers in the field of social movements is that of "differential recruitment" (Jenkins 1983, p. 528; Zurcher and Snow 1981, p. 449). What accounts for individual variation in movement participation? Why does one individual get involved while another remains inactive? Until recently, researchers have sought to answer these questions on the basis of individual characteristics of movement activists.

Psychological or Attitudinal Accounts of Activism

The basic assumption underlying such accounts is that it is some psychological or attitudinal "fit" with the movement that either compels participation or, at the very least, renders the individual susceptible to recruiting appeals.

For all their apparent theoretical sophistication, empirical support for all of these individually based psychological or attitudinal accounts of participation has proved elusive. Summarizing this exhaustive survey of the literature on the relationship between activism and various psychological factors, Mueller (1980, p. 69) concludes that "psychological attributes of individuals, such as frustration and alienation, have minimal direct impact for explaining the occurrence of rebellion and revolution per se." Much the same conclusion has been reached as regards the link between attitudes and activism. On the basis of his analysis of 215 studies of the relationship between individual attitudes and riot participation, McPhail (1971) concludes that "individual predispositions are, at best, insufficient to account" for participation in collective action.[2]

Does this mean that psychological characteristics or attitudes are irrelevant to the study of individual activism? Certainly not. In our view, both remain important insofar as they demarcate a "latitude of rejection" (Petty and Cacioppo 1981) within which individuals are highly unlikely to get involved in a given movement. However, in the case of most movements the size of the pool of recruits—the "latitude of acceptance"—is still many times larger than the actual number of persons who take part in any given in-stance of activism. Klandermans and Oegema (1987) provide an interesting illustration of the size of these respective groups in the Netherlands. On the basis of before-and-after interviews with a sample of 114 persons, the authors conclude that 26% of those interviewed were unavailable for recruitment because of their basic disagreement with the goals of the demonstration. That left nearly three-quarters of the sample as potentially available for recruitment. Yet only 4% actually attended the rally. It is precisely this disparity between attitudinal affinity and actual participation that, of course, requires explanation. One thing seems clear, however; given the size of this disparity, the role of individual attitudes (or the psychological factors from which they derive) in shaping activism must be regarded as fairly limited. If 96% of all those who are attitudinally or psychologically disposed to activism choose, as they did in this case, not to participate, then clearly some other factor or set of factors is mediating the recruitment process.

Microstructural Accounts of Activism

Since psychological and attitudinal explanations of individual participation have been weak, there has been increased usage of alternative microstructural explanations. The microstructural account posits that it is relatively unimportant if a person is ideologically or psychologically predisposed to participation when they lack the structural location that facilitates participation. Without structural factors that expose the individual to participation opportunities or pull them into activity, the individual will remain inactive. A number of recent studies appear to demonstrate the strength of structural or network factors in accounting for activism (Fernandez and McAdam 1989; Gould 1990, 1991; Marwell et al. 1988; McAdam 1986; McCarthy 1987; Orum 1972; Paulsen 1990; Rosenthal et al. 1985; Snow et al. 1980)

Interpersonal Ties. Knowing someone who is already involved in social movement activity is one of the strongest predictors of recruitment into the membership (Briët et al. 1987; Gerlach and Hine 1970; Heirich 1977; McAdam 1986; Orum 1972; Snow 1976; Snow et al. 1980; Von Eschen, Kirk, and Pinard 1971; Zurcher and Kirkpatrick 1976; Bolton 1972). Strong or dense interpersonal networks encourage the extension of an invitation to participate and they ease the uncertainty of mobilization. Oliver (1984), for example, finds that one of the best predictors of participation in neighborhood organizations is residence in the same area as one's closest friends or relatives. Oliver also states that "social ties may be thought of as indicators of subjective interest in the neighborhood, as factors influencing the availability of solidarity incentives for participation in collective action or as factors reducing the cost of action by making communication easier" (1984, p. 604). These notions elaborate on why social ties are an important measure in the prediction of participation.

Membership in Organizations. Organizational membership is another microstructural factor that has been linked to individual activism. There are two possible explanations for the relationship, the first of which has already been mentioned. Membership in organizations is an extension of the interpersonal social tie. Acquaintances made in the formal setting of the organization form elaborate structures of interpersonal ties. In other words, belonging to an organization is a good way to meet people and the likelihood of being pulled into social-movement activity increases through this contact with others. Movement organizers have long appreciated how difficult it is to recruit single isolated individuals and therefore expend most of their energies on mobilizing support among existing organizations.

The alternative explanation draws on the relationship between organizational membership and feelings of personal efficacy. It appears that individuals who hold membership in several organizations have a stronger sense of efficacy than those who have few or no memberships (Finkel 1985; Neal and Seeman 1964; Sayre 1980). A strong sense of efficacy is also a good predictor of participation in collective action (Craig 1979; Paulsen 1990, 1991; Sutherland 1981; Travers 1982).

Whether the positive relationship between membership in organizations and activism is explained using networks of interpersonal ties or the development of a sense of efficacy, its existence is well established. Empirical evidence supporting the relationship is clear in a wide variety of social-movement contexts including the civil rights movement (McAdam 1986), student sit-ins (Orum 1972), and the antinuclear movement (Walsh and Warland 1983).

Toward an Elaborated Microstructural Model of Recruitment

In our view, the recent emphasis on structural or network factors in movement recruitment represents a welcome corrective to the earlier individualistic accounts of activism. And certainly the empirical evidence linking individual or organizational ties to movement participation appears to be stronger than the simple association between either psychological attributes or attitudes and individual activism.

Not discounting this progress, serious conceptual and methodological lacunae continue to plague the structural network approaches to the study of movement recruitment. Three such problems were noted above. First, we still lack a general sociological explanation of the empirical effects reported in these studies. In short, we have demonstrated a strong association between social ties and activism, but have largely failed to account for the relationship theoretically. Second, perhaps owing to the absence of any real social structural theory of recruitment, with a few notable exceptions (Fernandez and McAdam 1988a; Gould 1991, 1993; Marwell et al. 1988) researchers have failed to distinguish empirically between various dimensions of social ties. So it remains unclear which aspects of a social tie (e.g., strength, salience, centrality) accounts for its effectiveness as a recruitment agent. Finally, as both Roger Gould (1991, 1993) and Andrew Marchant-Shapiro (1990) have perceptively noted, our efforts to assess the link between social ties and activism have thus far been seriously hampered by a highly truncated view of this relationship. As Gould (1990, p. 14) notes, these studies rest on "the presupposition that existing social relations exert an unconditionally positive influence on a group's capacity to mobilize for collective action." In point of fact, social ties may constrain as well as encourage activism. Our failure to acknowledge the variable impact of social ties is due, in turn, to our failure to take account of the "multiple embeddings" that characterize people's lives. The effect of these two limiting presumptions has been to structure empirical analysis in ways that virtually assure positive effects. First, we have tended only to study activists, thereby inflating the positive influence of existing social ties. And second, instead of examining a range of social ties, we have restricted our attention to a single class of ties: those linking the subject to others in the movement. This leaves unexamined (a) all those nonactivists who also had ties to the movement and (b) the effect of other social ties—parents, peers, and so forth—on the recruitment process. To truly test the utility of a structural/network account of activism we must take account of both phenomena. To do so, however, first requires a fuller conceptualization of the role of social ties in the recruitment process. In sketching such a conceptualization, we will begin by stressing the importance of two concepts: *multiple ties* and Sheldon Stryker's notion of *identity salience* (1968).

All of us, except perhaps for the occasional hermit, are embedded in many relationships. Some of these are mediated by formal organizational processes; the rest by informal interpersonal dynamics involving one or more persons. The presence of these multiple ties points up the fundamental flaw in most existing studies of movement recruitment, which focus solely on the presence or absence of a prior tie between the subject and someone in the movement. The question is, Why should this tie be granted causal primacy? Why should it be examined in the absence of all others? The fact that we are embedded in many relationships means that any major decision we are contemplating will likely be mediated by a significant subset of those relationships. This, of course, would apply to participation in any significant forms of activism, especially those of the "high-risk" variety (McAdam 1986; Wiltfang and McAdam 1991). The fact that the recruitment decision is likely to be influenced by a number of people, in turn, raises the critical question of how the individual goes about aggregating the advice she or he receives. It is unlikely that all the advice will be consistent. It is more likely that the contemplated action will invite a range of responses from those party to the decision-making process. We thus need a model of how these responses are aggregated to yield a final decision.

Here is where Stryker's (1968) notion of *identity salience* may prove useful.[3] For Stryker (1981, pp. 23-24), "identities are conceptualized as being organized into a hierarchy of salience defined by the probability of the various identities being invoked in a given situation or over many situations." In turn, the salience of any particular identity is a function of the individual's "commitment" to it, defined "as the degree to which the

individual's relationships to specified sets of other persons depends on his or her being a particular kind of person" (1981, p. 24). So, for Stryker, it is the centrality and importance of our relationships with others that serve to establish and sustain the salience of various identities.

When applied to the recruitment process, the perspective above suggests that the decision to join or not join a movement will be mediated by the salience of the identity invoked by the movement and by the support or lack thereof that the prospective recruit receives from those persons who normally serve to sustain or reinforce the identity in question. This suggests a three-step recruitment process by which a prospective recruit brings the intended behavior—in this case, movement participation—into alignment with their existing hierarchy of identities. First, the individual must be the object of a recruiting appeal (whether direct or, in the case of the media, indirect) that succeeds in creating a positive association between the movement and a highly salient identity. This linkage creates the initial disposition to participate in the movement. Second, the recruit discusses this disposition with those persons who normally sustain the identity in question. In effect, the recruit is seeking to confirm the linkage between movement and identity and thus the ultimate "correctness" of the intention to participate. Should the recruit receive this confirmation, she or he would still need to reconcile the intended action with the demands of any countervailing identities that may be even more salient. This would again open the individual up to influence attempts by those persons on whose support these more salient identities rest. The ultimate decision to participate, then, would depend on the confluence of four limiting conditions: (1) the occurrence of a specific recruiting attempt, (2) the conceptualization of a tentative linkage between movement participation and identity, (3) support for that linkage from persons who normally serve to sustain the identity in question, and (4) the absence of strong opposition from others on whom other salient identities depend. The prohibitive nature of these conditions may help explain why so few of those whose attitudes place them in the "latitude of acceptance" (Petty and Cacioppo 1981) actually engage in activism.

This perspective would also help to account for the oft-noted role of established organizations (Curtis and Zurcher 1973; McAdam 1982; Morris

1984; Oberschall 1973; Rosenthal et at. 1985) in the recruitment process. Provided that the identity invoked by the organization (e.g., "Christian," "feminist," etc.) is highly salient to its members, it would be hard to imagine a more efficient way to recruit movement adherents.[4] In effect, when organizations serve as recruiting agents, the three-step process outlined above is reduced to a two-step process. The initial recruiting appeal is immediately merged with efforts to confirm the "correctness" of the link between member status and movement participation. Moreover, the organization may well retain a virtual monopoly on those significant others who have long sustained the identity in question. To the extent that these referent others have affiliated with the movement, it will be difficult for the individual in question not to do so as well.

But the ultimate utility of this perspective will not derive from the plausible interpretation it affords past findings, but rather from how well it accords with data designed to test its merits. This is what we hope to do in the remainder of the article.

The Study

In seeking to assess the role of social ties in movement recruitment, we will focus on a single instance of high-risk activism: participation in the 1964 Mississippi Freedom Summer Project. That campaign brought hundreds of primarily white, northern college students to Mississippi for all, or part of, the summer of 1964 to help staff "Freedom Schools," register black voters, and dramatize the continued denial of civil rights throughout the South. As instances of activism go, the summer project was time-consuming, physically demanding, and highly newsworthy.

The project itself began in early June with the first contingent of volunteers arriving in Mississippi fresh from a week of training at Oxford, Ohio. Within ten days, three project members, Mickey Schwerner, James Chaney, and Andrew Goodman, had been kidnapped and killed by a group of segregationists led by Mississippi law-enforcement officers. That event set the tone for the summer as the remaining volunteers endured beatings, bombings, and arrests. Moreover, most did so while sharing the grinding poverty and unrelieved tension that was the daily lot of the black families that housed them.

Preliminary to their participation in the campaign, all prospective volunteers filled out detailed applications providing information on, among other topics, their organizational affiliations, previous civil rights activities, and reasons for volunteering. On the basis of these applications (and, on occasion, subsequent interviews), the prospective volunteer was either accepted or rejected. Acceptance did not necessarily mean participation in the campaign, however. In advance of the summer, many of the accepted applicants informed campaign staffers that they would not be taking part in the summer effort after all. Completed applications for all three groups—rejects, participants, and "no-shows"—were copied from the originals which are now housed in the archives of the Martin Luther King, Jr., Center for the Study of Non-violence in Atlanta, and the New Mississippi Foundation in Jackson, Mississippi.[5] A total of 1,068 applications were coded in connection with this study. The breakdown of these applications by group is as follows: 720 participants, 239 no-shows, 55 rejections, and 54 whose status as regards the summer project is unclear.

Besides the five pages of information included on these forms, the applications also served as the methodological starting point for a followup survey of those who applied to the project. Specifically, several items of information from the original applications—alma mater, parents' address, major in school—functioned as crucial leads in efforts to obtain current addresses for as many of the applicants as possible.

The result of these efforts were verified current addresses for 556 of the 959 participants and withdrawals for whom there were applications. Of these, 382 (of a total of 720) had been participants in the project, while another 174 (of 239) had withdrawn in advance of the summer. Separate questionnaires were then prepared and sent to the participants and to the no-shows. Participants were questioned about the influences that led them to apply, their activities immediately preceding the summer, as well as their personal and political experiences during and since the project. The questionnaire sent to the no-shows dealt with these topics as well as the reasons why they withdrew from the project. In all, 212 (or 56%) of the participants and 118 (or 68%) of the no-shows returned completed questionnaires. In addition, in-depth interviews were conducted with 40 volunteers and another 40 no-shows to flesh out the information gleaned from the questionnaires. Together, the applications, questionnaires, and interviews provide a rich source of data for an analysis of the ways in which social ties mediated the decision of whether or not to take part in the project.

Results

In seeking to learn more about the relationship between social ties and movement recruitment, we will address two principal topics. First, we will take up the issue of multiple ties by examining for each applicant the breadth of support they received for participation across five categories of possible ties (parents, friends, civil rights organizations, other volunteers, and religious groups or figures). Second, we will seek to determine which dimensions of social ties appear to account for their important role in recruitment. Specifically, we will look at three such dimensions: (1) the strength of the tie (weak vs. strong), (2) the locus of the tie (face-to-face or geographically removed), and (3) the salience of the tie.

Multiple Ties

As Gould (1991) and Marchant-Shapiro (1990) have argued, prior network studies of recruitment have failed to take account of the multiple ties that comprise a person's social world. Instead, researchers have focused on the presence or absence of a particular type of tie—prior contact between the recruit and another activist—as the crucial relationship mediating entrance into the movement.[6] An earlier analysis of recruitment to the Freedom Summer project shares this deficiency (see McAdam 1986). To illustrate the point as well as to provide a statistical baseline for what is to follow, we have rerun, using updated data, the final logit regression from the earlier paper.[7] Table 1 reports the results of this analysis.

The dependent variable in the analysis is participation/nonparticipation in the summer project. The independent variables include a variety of measures, among which are the applicant's gender, race, age, college major, highest grade completed, and home and college regions. But the single best predictor of participation is the existence of a prior strong tie linking the applicant to another volunteer. However, this is the lone network or social-tie item included in the analysis. No effort has been made to assess the impact of other kinds of ties on the recruitment process. The result is precisely the kind of truncated analysis of the relationship between social ties and activism

Table 1
Logit Regression Predicting Freedom Summer Participation by Various Independent Variables

Independent Variables	Dependent Variable (b)	Summer Status SE(b)[a]
Level of Prior Activism	.020	.039
N of Organizational Affiliations	.118*	.059
Strong Tie to a Volunteer	.491**	.191
Weak Tie to a Volunteer	.141	.098
Strong Tie to a No-Show	−.169	.325
Major:		
Social Science	.167	.324
Other	−.137	.182
Home Region:		
West North Central	−.204	.324
New England	−.372	.387
Mid-Atlantic	.294	.583
East North Central	−.517	.486
West	.694	.468
South	−.411	.484
College Region:		
West North Central	−.144	.297
New England	−.447	.327
Mid-Atlantic	−.251	.555
East North Central	.439	.486
West	−.444	.358
South	.748*	.333
Race = white	−.135	.218
Gender = female	−.446**	.178
Age	.022+	.013
Highest Grade Completed	−.014	.022
Distance From Home to Mississippi	−.0003	.0002
Constant	1.039	.636

Note: N = 766.
[a]No-shows = 0; volunteers = 1.
+*P*<.10.
**P*<.05.
***P*<.01.

about which critics such as Gould and Marchant-Shapiro have rightly complained.

To remedy this deficiency we have sought in the present analysis to assess the effect of various types of ties on the decision to take part in the Freedom Summer project. Specifically, we have differentiated the applicants on the basis of whether or not they report having received support for participation from each of five categories of others: parents, friends, religious groups or figures, civil rights organizations, or another volunteer. The data on the first three support categories were taken from a single item on the follow-up survey distributed to the applicants. The item asked respondents to rank order, from a fixed list, all those groups or individuals who "*positively* influenced your decision to apply to the Freedom Summer Project." The first three support categories listed above were included in the responses provided to subjects.[8] The subject's responses to these three support categories were coded separately to yield three dichotomous variables. For example, subject's responses to the category "parents" were coded "0" and "1" to create the variable "parental support." Listing parents as a positive influence resulted in a code of "1"; failure to list was coded as "0." The same coding procedures were used in regard to the other two categories of ties as well.

The fourth support category, civil rights organizations, was generated using the list of organizational affiliations provided on the original applications. Those subjects reporting membership in a civil rights organization were coded as "1" on this variable; those lacking such an affiliation were coded as "0." The final support category, "other volunteers," makes use of the variable, "strong tie to another volunteer," included in the earlier logit regression (see table 1). This variable was created using information provided on the original project applications. One item on the application asked the subjects to list at least 10 persons whom they wished to be kept informed of their summer activities. The most common categories of names supplied by the applicants were those of parents, parents' friends, professors, ministers, and any other noteworthy or influential adults they had contact with. Quite often, however, applicants would list another applicant. This enabled us to construct a measure of the interpersonal ties connecting the applicant to (a) other Freedom Summer volunteers and (b) no-shows. In doing so, we were careful to distinguish between "strong" and "weak" ties (Granovetter 1973). Persons listed directly on the subject's application were designated as strong ties. Weak ties were defined as persons who, although not listed on the subject's application, were nonetheless linked to them by way of an intervening strong tie.

The applicant's responses to this application then were coded to produce a fifth dichotomous variable, termed "volunteer support." Only those applicants who reported a strong tie to a volunteer were coded as "1" on this variable. All other responses, including weak ties, were coded as "0."

Table 2 reports the percentage of volunteers and no-shows who received support from each of these five support categories. The percentage dif-

ference between volunteers and no-shows was significant in regard to the following forms of support: that from parents, civil rights organizations, and other volunteers. Moreover the differences are in the expected direction. The differences are especially great in regard to the first and last of these categories. The percentage of volunteers reporting support from parents was nearly double the figure for the no-shows. And the proportion of volunteers reporting support—in the form of strong ties—from other volunteers was 75% greater than the comparable figure for no-shows. But these simple bivariate comparisons tell us little about the impact of these various forms of support, either in relation to each other or to the other significant variables shown in table 1. For that we turn to table 3, which reports the results of a sec-

Table 2
Percentage of Volunteers and No-Shows Reporting Support From Various Sources

	Volunteers		No-Shows	
	%	N	%	N
Parents	26**	55	14	17
Friends	46	98	52	61
Religious Groups or Figures	14	30	19	22
Civil Rights Groups	43+	313	37	89
Other Volunteers	41**	210	24	36

+$P<.10$.
*$P<.05$.
**$P<.01$.

ond logit regression predicting participation.

Included in the analysis shown in table 3 is a pared-down version of the model reported in table 1 (including all the significant relationships from the earlier analysis), plus the five support variables. The results generally mirror the findings reported for table 1, while simultaneously confirming the suggestion contained in table 2.[9] That is, in the aggregate, those who made it to Mississippi did have the benefit of greater support from parents and project peers. Or, if one prefers the negative interpretation, the no-shows were handicapped by relatively low levels of support from these two important groups. Whichever interpretation one prefers—and both are probably operative—the results support a complex, differentiated view of the role of social ties in movement recruitment. Ties to persons not in the movement—in this case, to parents—may also influence recruitment decisions. And, those ties may, as in the case of the no-shows and their parents, constrain as well as encourage participation.

Table 3
Logit Regression Predicting Freedom Summer Participation by Various Independent Variables, Including Tie Categories

Independent Variables	Dependent Variable (b)	Summer Status SE(b)[a]
Level of Prior Activism	.085*	.041
N of Organizational Affiliations	.217+	.129
Weak Tie to a Volunteer	−.524	.403
Strong Tie to a No-Show	−.504	.546
Race = white	−.026	.522
Gender = female	−.555+	.338
Age	.192*	.069
Highest Grade Completed	−.016	.056
Distance From Home to Mississippi	.0004	.0003
Support Categories:		
Parent	1.223*	.497
Friends	−.491	.368
Religious Groups	−.548	.526
Civil Rights Groups	.149	.433
Other Volunteers	1.360**	.455
Constant	−4.810**	1.850

Note: $N = 206$.
[a]No-shows = 0; volunteers = 1.
+$P<.10$.
*$P<.05$.
**$P<.01$.

Prior Contact with Another Volunteer: Interpreting the Relationship

While our efforts to broaden the study of the relationship between social ties and activism have produced results suggesting the importance of various types of ties (e.g., to parents), they have done nothing to undermine the special significance previously ascribed to contact with another activist, in this case, another Freedom Summer volunteer. On the contrary, regardless of what other ties or additional variables are introduced into the analysis, a strong tie to another volunteer remains, to this point, the best predictor of participation in the summer project. The robustness of this finding suggests a conclusion that is both interesting and perhaps broadly relevant in seeking to make a behavioral decision in the face of conflicting advice from multiple others: *behavioral,* as opposed to rhetorical or attitudinal, support is likely to prove decisive. That is, in supporting with their own actions the applicant's original behavioral intention, other volunteers provided a

more dramatic and, perhaps, more meaningful form of support than the other ties whose influence we have sought to measure.

But apart from this generalization, we do not really know what it is about these ties to other volunteers that accounts for their predictive significance. What dimensions of these ties are especially facilitative of activism? In the remainder of this article, we will explore this question in some detail. Specifically, we will take up two dimensions of these ties: "strength" and salience.

1. *Strength of ties.*—Much has been made in the movement literature of the "strength of weak ties" (Granovetter 1973) as a force for the diffusion of collective action. Numerous studies have shown that movements often spread by means of diffuse networks of weak bridging ties (Freeman 1973a; McAdam 1982; Oppenheimer 1989) or die for lack of such ties (Jackson et al. 1960). These findings suggest that, at the meso level, the critical function performed by social ties for a movement is one of communication. However, the findings reported earlier in tables 1 and 3 suggest a very different role for social ties at the individual level. The significant positive relationship between strong ties and participation and the absence of any relationship between weak ties and involvement suggests that, at the microlevel, ties are less important as conduits of information than as sources of social influence. And the stronger the tie, the stronger the influence exerted on the potential recruit. This implies that the ultimate network structure for a movement would be one in which dense networks of weak bridging ties linked numerous local groups bound together by means of strong interpersonal bonds. But for our purposes, the mesolevel structure of a movement is irrelevant. Our concern is solely with the microlevel function of social ties. And in this regard, our results support a strong conclusion: as dimensions go, the strength of a social tie appears to account for much of its power as a predictor of activism. But before we pronounce certainty on this issue, let us turn our attention to one other dimension of social ties.

2. *Salience of ties.*—Given the theoretical importance ascribed to the salience of a tie at the outset of the paper, it is especially important that we try to assess the significance of this dimension in shaping the applicant's decision regarding the summer project. To do so we will make use of several items from the original project applications.

The principal item is an open-ended question asking the individual to explain why they "would like to work in Mississippi this summer." These answers were content-coded along a number of dimensions. But the important dimension for our purposes concerns the extent to which, in their statements, the applicants explicitly aligned themselves with a specific community or reference group. Some examples of these types of "aligning" statements follow:[10]

If I'm to continue *calling myself a Christian,* I must act NOW to put my abstract conception of brotherhood into practice.

All of us in the movement must join forces if the Summer Project is to succeed.

In my group of future teachers I make it a point to ask each of them, "Why do you want to go into education?"

When combined with the organizational affiliations listed on the application, these statements allowed us to create the variable, "recruitment context," to capture the principal communities/identities that served to draw people into the project. Five such communities emerged from our reading of the open-ended question. These were teachers, religious community, socialists/leftists, liberal Democrats, and the civil rights movement. Along with the category, "no discernible group," these five communities or reference groups comprised the coding scheme for the variable, "recruitment context." But to be coded as belonging to any of these communities, it was not enough that the applicants express identification with the group in their statements. They also had to include among the organizational affiliations listed on their applications at least one organization tied to the community in question. So, for example, to be coded as belonging to the "liberal Democratic community," the applicants would have had to assert this identity in their statements and report membership in either their campus chapter of Young Democrats or in a similar group (see Appendix). The variable, then, has both a subjective identification and objective organizational dimension.

The significant, but hardly surprising, finding from our perspective concerns the much higher rates of participation among those in all five of the aforementioned recruitment contexts. Table 4 reports the percentages of no-shows and volunteers in each of the five contexts with the comparable figures for those not identified with any discernible context.

Only 65% of those lacking an identifiable recruitment "community" made it to Mississippi, as compared to from 83% to 87% of those so embedded.[11] The apparent causal influence of these recruitment contexts would appear to be due to two factors. First, the subject's expressed identification with these communities suggests a high degree of salience for the identities embodied in each. And second, their membership in organizations associated with these communities no doubt afforded these subjects strong support for their expressed identity as well as for the link between that identity and participation in the Freedom Summer project. This is exactly the combination of a highly salient identity and strong social support for activism based on that identity that we stressed at the outset as crucial to the process of movement recruitment. But one might complain that organizational membership alone could well predict activism and that combining it with subjective identification makes it impossible to tease out the effects of each. We will turn to this issue in our final analysis.

Table 4
Recruitment Context by Status on the Summer Project[*]

	Church/ Religious		Civil Rights		Liberal Democrats		Socialist/ Leftist		Teachers		No Context		Total	
	%	N	%	N	%	N	%	N	%	N	%	N	%	N
Volunteers	83	94	87	82	85	51	83	93	87	87	65	320	75	727
No-Shows	17	19	13	12	15	9	17	19	13	13	35	169	25	241
Total	100	113	100	94	100	60	100	112	100	100	100	489	100	968

[*]Only two applicants were coded as affiliated with more than one recruitment context. Rather than lose data by excluding these subjects, we coded them as being affiliated with whatever context they first aligned themselves in their response to the open-ended item.

Assessing the combined effects of these dimensions.—So far we have sought to assess the independent effects of various factors or dimensions on the relationship between social ties and activism. But what of the combined effects? When taken together, which of these factors or dimensions appear to account for the role of social ties in constraining or facilitating activism? To answer this question, we report the results of four logistic models incorporating all but one of the significant variables touched on previously.[12]

The results reported in table 5 serve to underscore the importance of the combination of a highly salient identity and structural support for same in encouraging activism. Three specific results from the table bear comment. First, membership in any of the five recruitment contexts is shown in the full model (model 4) to bear a strong, positive relationship to participation in Freedom Summer.[13] Second, none of the simple organiza-

tional variables—including number of organizational affiliations, as well as the specific categories of organizational membership—are predictive of participation when included in the same model as the recruitment contexts. Finally, even the heretofore significant effect of a strong tie to another volunteer washes out in the face of the predictive power of the context variables.

The conclusion is unmistakable: neither organizational embeddedness nor strong ties to another volunteer are themselves predictive of high-risk activism. Instead it is a strong subjective identification with a particular identity, *reinforced by organizational or individual ties,* that is especially likely to encourage participation. Does this mean that organizational or individual ties are irrelevant to the recruitment process? Hardly; it does, however, suggest that if the identity sustained by the tie is neither linked to participation nor particularly salient to the person in question, it is not

Table 5
The Effects of Various Independent Variables on Participation in Freedom Summer Project

Independent Variables	Model 1 (b)	Model 1 SE(b)	Model 2 (b)	Model 2 SE(b)	Model 3 (b)	Model 3 SE(b)	Model 4 (b)	Model 4 SE(b)
Level of Prior Activism	.037*	.015	.024	.171	.030+	.018	.001	.020
Race = White	-.144	.189	-.097	.192	-.051	.196	-.006	.200
Gender = Female	-.291+	.157	-.311*	.158	-.338*	.161	-.311+	.165
Age	.064**	.016	.066**	.017	.061**	.017	.048**	.018
Highest Grade Completed	-.042*	.019	-.036+	.019	-.037+	.019	-.032+	.019
Distance From Home to Mississippi	.00008	.0001	.00009	.0001	.0001	.0001	.00009	.0001
N of Organizational Affiliations	.110*	.051	.102*	.052	.089	.056	.050	.057
Weak Tie to a Volunteer	.504**	.190	.119	.261	.145	.264	.090	.269
Strong Tie to a No-Show	-.260	.340	-.290	.353	-.239	.353	-.352	.361
Support Categories:								
Civil Rights Group			-.277	.189				
Other Volunteers			.570+	.336	.561+	.339	.524	.349
Proximity of Tie:								
Proximal			-.013	.176	-.028	.177	-.017	.181
Distal			.238	.189	.237	.190	.241	.194
Membership:								
Religious Organization					-.429+	.242	-.271	.296
Civil Rights Organization					-.241	.197	-.354+	.202
Democratic Party Organization					.198	.253	.362	.282
Socialist or New Left Organization					.074	.228	.143	.277
Teachers Organization					-.434	.372	-.270	.431
Recruitment Context:								
Religious							.723*	.341
Civil Rights							1.057**	.390
Liberal Democrat							1.210**	.414
New Left							.798*	.344
Teaching							.867*	.382
Constant	-.177	.481	.104	.603	1.258	1.129	.426	1.000

Note: $N = 766$.
+$P<.10$. *$P<.05$. **$P<.01$.

likely to encourage activism. What about the opposite question? Is strong identification with a particular identity enough to promote involvement in the absence of structural support for same? It is significant that we cannot directly answer this question with our data. None of our subjects expressed strong identification with any of these five identities without also being structurally embedded in the relevant organizational community supportive of that identity. That is, identity salience would itself seem to be a social product.

We are left, then, with the kind of necessary but not sufficient relationship sociologists are so fond of. Prior ties—either through organizations or particular others—would seem to be necessary, but not sufficient, for recruitment to high-risk activism. In the absence of (a) a strong identification with the identity sustained by the tie and (b) a link between that identity and the movement in question, prior ties are no more productive of participation than the absence of ties. Such prior ties provide the crucial social context in which identities may achieve salience and the linkage between identity and activism can be forged, but the existence of such ties does not ensure that these crucial processes will, in fact, take place.

Before concluding with a discussion of the significance of these findings, a few words are in order regarding the strength of the relationship linking integration into the "teaching context" with participation. Of the five contexts it would appear to be the one with the least relevance for an explicitly political project such as Freedom Summer. In point of fact, however, the relationship is entirely consistent with the contemporary "framing" (Snow and Benford 1988) of the project and, as such, represents a nice nonintuitive example of the broader social psychological dynamic sketched earlier.

As noted earlier, one of the two principal components of the project was the campaign to establish a network of "freedom schools" throughout the state. These schools were to expose students to a broader range of subjects and more information on African-American history than they typically got in the historically impoverished "separate but equal" institutions they normally attended. The prominence accorded the freedom school effort in planning for the summer (see Holt 1965a; McAdam 1988a), made the recruitment of qualified teachers a major goal of project organizers. Toward this end they sought and received

official endorsement for the project from the major national teacher's associations, including the American Federation of Teachers and the National Educational Association.

These endorsements, coupled with the specific steps taken by organizers to recruit upper-division education majors on campus, represent exactly the kinds of efforts to link a particular identity with participation that we expect to be especially effective in encouraging participation. Though historically not as disposed to political action as those integrated into the other four recruitment contexts, prospective teachers were, in this case, the object of specific recruiting appeals that sought to link their future occupational identity to involvement in the Freedom Summer project.

Discussion and Conclusion

All of this calls to mind the model of movement recruitment outlined at the outset of this article. We suggested that the ultimate decision to participate in a movement would depend on four limiting *conditions:* (1) the occurrence of a specific recruiting attempt, (2) the successful linkage of movement and identity, (3) support for that linkage from persons who normally serve to sustain the identity in question, and (4) the absence of strong opposition from others on whom other salient identities depend.

The results reported in table 5 can certainly be interpreted as consistent with the above account of recruitment. All of our subjects—no-shows and volunteers alike—shared the first two limiting conditions noted above. Clearly they were aware of the project (condition 1) and, given their willingness to apply, appear to have viewed the project as consistent with some salient identity (condition 2). In our view, what differentiates the volunteers from the no-shows is the extent of support they received for this linkage (condition 3) and the relative absence of opposition from salient others (condition 4). Not only were the volunteers embedded in more organizations, but also in ones—civil rights organizations, teacher associations, and so forth—ideally suited to reinforcing the linkage between identity and action. Moreover, as the greater support from parents suggests, the volunteers also appear to have received less opposition (or more support) from other salient relationships in which they were involved.

All of this may help to explain the surprising lack of statistical significance of the relationship linking a strong tie to another volunteer with participation. While this relationship had been significant in all previous analyses, it appears that it was merely a proxy for the recruitment contexts included in table 5. That is, the volunteers' ties to other volunteers were themselves a function of the participants' greater integration into specific recruitment contexts that served as the microstructural basis for their decisions to take part in the project.

If this is the case, then, the analyses presented here do more than simply support the general model of recruitment outlined earlier. Our findings also argue for a much stronger effect of organizational (or otherwise collective) as opposed to individual ties in mediating entrance into collective action. Clearly much work remains to confirm this conclusion, but it is an intriguing one and one that accords with "bloc recruitment" accounts of the emergence and rapid spread of collective action (Oberschall 1973). Ties to individuals may well mediate the recruitment process, but they appear to do so with special force and significance when the tie is embedded in a broader organizational or collective context linking both parties to the movement in question.

We would be remiss, however, if we closed the article on the structural note above. Clearly, the most important implication of this research is as much sociopsychological as structural. Network analysts of movement recruitment have been overly concerned with assessing the structure of the subject's relationship to the movement without paying sufficient attention to the social psychological processes that mediate the link between network structure and activism. As Gould has recently argued, "It is risky to make generalizations about the impact of network structure in the absence of detailed information about collective action settings" and the "influence process" by which people come to participate in a social movement (1993, p. 195).

More specifically, prior ties would appear to encourage activism only when they (a) reinforce the potential recruit's identification with a particular identity and (b) help to establish a strong linkage between that identity and the movement in question. When these processes of identity amplification and identity/movement linkage take place, activism is likely to follow. In the absence of these processes, prior ties do not appear to be predictive of participation. Movement analysts,

then, need to be as attuned to the *content* of network processes as to the structures themselves.

Appendix

Organizational Fields

Space constraints do not allow for a complete listing of all the organizations that were coded as constituting the "organizational field" for the five recruitment contexts. We can, however, provide the following broad description of these five "fields."

1. *Religious organizations.*—Any reported affiliation with a specific church or temple was coded as a "religious organization." So too were any campus- or community-based religious groups (e.g., Episcopal Society for Cultural or Racial Unity, Young People's Fellowship). In all, 106 organizations were coded as constituting this category.

2. *Civil rights organizations.*—Forty-one groups were coded under this category. Besides the so-called "big five" civil rights organizations—SNCC (including Friends of SNCC), CORE, SCLC, NAACP, and the Urban League, another 36 campus- or community-based civil rights organizations were included under this category (e.g., the Orangeburg Freedom Movement, Georgia Students for Human Rights, Vassar Civil Rights Organization).

3. *Liberal Democratic party organizations.*—This category comprised the smallest number of specific organizations, but even so, 16 groups were included under the heading. Far and away the most frequently listed organization in this category was the Young Democrats. In addition, however, 15 other reform Democratic groups were counted as part of this category (e.g., Heights Reform Democrats, Riverside Democratic Club).

4. *Socialist/leftist organizations.*—This category comprised 19 organizations. Some of these were campus-based New Left organizations such as Students for a Democratic Society (SDS), but most were more traditional socialist or "old" left groups such as the Student Peace Union, War Resisters League, or the Industrial Workers of the World (IWW or "wobblies").

5. *Teachers or other educational organizations.*—Any professional association of teachers (e.g., American Federation of Teachers, Glen Rock Teachers Organization) was coded under this category as were any campus-based groups of

future teachers or education majors (e.g., Future Teachers of America, Indiana University Association of Student Teachers). Thirty-one groups were coded under this category.

Notes

1. The paper by Marwell et al. (1988) is perhaps the only empirical work to date that takes seriously the need to distinguish and test the causal significance of various dimensions of social ties.

2. In general, the discrepancy between attitudes and behavior has been borne out by countless studies conducted over the years. In summarizing the results of these studies, Wicker (1969) offered what remains the definitive word on the subject. Said Wicker, there exists "little evidence to support the postulated existence of stable, underlying attitudes within the individual which influence both his verbal expressions and his actions" (p. 75).

3. Stryker is hardly alone in stressing the idea that the self is made up of a hierarchy of identities. McCall and Simmons's (1978) notion of "role salience" and Rosenberg's (1979) concept of "psychological centrality" also rest on this fundamental premise.

4. For a slightly different but highly compatible argument, see Taylor and Whittier (1992a).

5. Our deep appreciation goes to Louise Cook, the former head librarian and archivist at the King Center, and to Jan Hillegas—herself a Freedom Summer volunteer—of the New Mississippi Foundation, for all their help in locating and copying the application materials used in this project.

6. The work of David Snow and several of his colleagues provide an important exception to this general assessment. In their pioneering theoretical work on the role of social ties and social networks in recruitment, Snow et al. (1980) acknowledge the importance of "multiple embeddings" in structuring a person's "differential availability" for movement participation. Later, Snow and Rochford (1983), in their study of recruitment into the Hare Krishna movement, sought to analyze the effect of various social ties on the recruit. They conclude that "a substantial majority of . . . recruits had few countervailing ties which might have served to constrain their participation in the movement." In his later book on the movement,

Rochford (1985) provided additional data consistent with this conclusion.

7. Since the publication of this analysis in 1986, the first author has acquired additional data that has allowed for a recording of the network items (strong tie to a volunteer, weak tie to a volunteer, and strong tie to a no-show). Table 1 is included, then, not only to provide a baseline model for the results to follow in this paper but to update the key analysis from the earlier paper.

8. The other responses included in the list given respondents were "spokespersons for movement groups," "movement literature," and "other."

9. The reader should note that the N for the analysis reported in table 3 is only 206, as compared to 630 for table 1. The reason for the reduced N has to do with a shift in the sources of data used in computing tables 1 and 3. All the variables in table 1 were generated using data taken from the original project applications. Excluding those whose applications were rejected and those whose project status could not be determined, the number of such applications was 959. However, the data from which the support variables shown in table 3 were constructed were taken from the 330 follow-up surveys returned by project applicants. In order to test to see what effect, if any, reducing the N would have on the magnitude of all variables other than the support categories, a separate logit regression was run. It is reassuring to note that a comparison of these two logits (the original with an N of 206 and the one described above with an N of 630) revealed no significant differences in the direction or magnitude of the other coefficients.

10. These quotes were taken from the summer project applications. In each case the emphasis is my addition.

11. When we use an overall chi-square test, these differences are significant at the .01 level.

12. The one exception is the measure of parental support used in table 3. Given that the measure was based on information taken from the follow-up survey, including it here would have reduced the overall N for the analysis from some 600 to 200.

13. "Recruitment context" is a single categorical variable in the logit regression. The coefficient for each context reflects the effect that is in addition to the base category, "no discernible group." ✦

13

Conflict Networks and the Origins of Women's Liberation

Carol M. Mueller

Increasing cross-fertilization of social movement theory has occurred from both sides of the Atlantic over the last five years. The European "new social movements theory" and the North American theory of "resource mobilization," developed since the tumultuous 1960s, have been the major contributors.[1] Resource mobilization theory is based in a strategic approach to the study of social movements; it emphasizes the mobilization and allocation of resources by movement actors in the context of opportunities and constraints imposed by the social and political environment. Particular attention focuses on the role of formal social movement organizations as the key social actors planning strategies and mobilizing resources. Grievances are treated as a given preference structure in some of the most powerful statements of the theory.

New social movement theory has, strangely, emphasized issues that are largely ignored by resource mobilization. Instead of being taken as given, grievances are at the center a theory that locates their source in both social structure and the social psychological processes underlying their identification and development as part of movement culture. For many North American scholars, the strength of new social movement theory lies at the intermediate and the macro levels of analysis. New social movement theory has pointed to the need for a social psychology based in the social interaction of movement actors as well as the need to identify the source of grievances and collective actors for particular social movements in their historically variable structural context, particularly the changing class structure and symbolic environment of postindustrial, capitalist so-

cieties. While the latter contribution has been largely ignored,[2] interest in the intermediate level of analysis where social conditions are defined as grievances and personal misfortunes are translated into a collective sense of injustice has coincided with a developing focus on the creation of meaning by social movement actors among those who seek to expand the resource mobilization paradigm.[3]

As contributions to social movement theory increasingly merge into a more comprehensive whole it is important to explore the components of each theory more carefully and to "test" it against empirical studies on both sides of the Atlantic. Particularly important to scholars interested in developing the new emphasis on social construction processes has been the work of the Italian new social movement theorist Alberto Melucci. Melucci's (1989) theory develops the role of "submerged networks" in the process of creating collective identities, interpreting grievances, and evaluating the potential effectiveness of collective action. Despite this interest (see works by Gamson 1992; by Klandermans 1986, 1990b, 1992; and by Taylor and Whittier 1992a) and the publication of Melucci's book *Nomads of the Present,* Melucci's theory of "collective identity" and "submerged networks" has not been systematically evaluated in the context of North American social movements. This chapter rectifies this omission through a critical examination of Melucci's theory as applied to the origins of women's mobilization in the United States during the period from 1960 to 1970. It will then be possible to assess its role in a broader theory of the social construction of social movements. Of primary interest is Melucci's contribution to the intermediate level of analysis where social movement culture is generated and dominant cultural codes are challenged.

Melucci's Theory of Socially Constructed Collective Identities

Melucci's point of departure is what he characterizes as the false unity attributed by observers to collective action. He argues:

> The collective phenomenon—whether a panic, a social movement, or a revolutionary process—is treated as a *unified empirical datum,* which, supposedly, can be perceived and interpreted by observers. It is supposed that, first, individuals' behavior forms *a unitary character* or *gestalt.* Sec-

ond, this assumption is then transferred from the phenomenological to the conceptual level and acquires ontological consistency: the collective reality is seen to exist as a thing. (1989, 18)[4]

Melucci attributes the error of false unity to a model of analysis that grew out of the class struggles of the nineteenth century and the actions of the supposedly unitary working class as it [*sic*] demanded the expansion of citizenship rights to encompass suffrage, political association, free speech, and so forth (1989, 19). The working-class movement, in this historic context, was tied to the idea of social movements "as historical agents marching toward a destiny of liberation" (1988, 330).

It is this perception of a social movement as ossified in a unitary "collective identity" that Melucci seeks to correct with his own theoretical model. He attempts to explain social movements at an intermediate level of social processes that occur in face-to-face interactions. These processes connect the sense of personal misfortune that people experience in their everyday lives with a collective interpretation of these conditions as injustice or grievances that justify collective action. He seeks to identify those groups processes "by which individuals evaluate and recognize what they have in common and decide to act together" (1988, 339). Thus, he seeks to create a theory that links the structured practices of social life with the collective action of a social movement through the intermediate steps of face-to-face interaction and meaning construction.

There are three key features of his theory: (1) the content or outcome of the process of social construction, the "collective identity" of the movement that comes to exist as a part of the movement culture; (2) the social processes by which the collective identity is created in "submerged networks" of small groups concerned with the ongoing routines of everyday life; and (3) the emotional investments that enable individuals to recognize themselves as the "we" in a collective identity.

The first feature of Melucci's theory is his conception of the collective identity, which he defines as "nothing else than a shared definition of the field of opportunities and constraints offered to collective action: 'shared' means constructed and negotiated through a repeated process of 'activation' of social relationships connecting the actors" (1985, 793). For Melucci, the content of the

collective identity or sense of "we" consists of a social resolution of three orders of orientation: "the *ends* of actions (i.e., the sense the action has for the actor); those relating to the *means* (i.e., the possibilities and the limits of action); and finally those relating to relationships with the *environment* (i.e., the field in which the action takes)" (1988, 33). In other words, people will interact in "submerged networks" where they will arrive at a new definition of their situation. This definition is different from the ordinary outcomes of daily social interaction in that it is action oriented, and it includes a goal, tactics, and a strategy for collective action on behalf of shared grievances.

The incubation period during which new collective identities are formed occurs in submerged social networks out of view of the public eye. Melucci argues that by the 1980s when he conducted his research on three different movement groups in Milan, collective actions were created within networks composed of many groups that were dispersed throughout the urban landscape. They are fragmented in terms of their relationships with each other and they were invisible because of their immersion in everyday life. Not only are the networks submerged in the sense that their cultural experimentation is not readily visible to the wider public but they are transitory in that individuals have multiple memberships with temporary and limited involvement (1989, 60). The submerged network is a system of small, separate groups engaging in cultural experimentation, and it is also a system of exchange in which persons and information circulate freely within the network. These networks act as "cultural laboratories" submerged within civil society (1980, 60). Some agencies, such as local free radios, bookshops, and magazines provide sources of unity (1985, 800).

In these cultural laboratories, new collective identities are constructed from the expressive interactions of individuals experimenting with new cultural codes, forms of relationships, and alternative perceptions of the world. The creation of the collective identity occurs in the midst of tensions created by the inadequacy of the means currently available for reaching personal and collective goals. From these tensions, as well as the close face-to-face interaction, develops a heavy emotional investment that encourages the individual to share in the collective identity. As the collective identity is created to address these tensions, both leadership and organization attempt to give permanence through their tentative resolution. This process involves the negotiation of the three orientations given the constraints of resources and political opportunities within emotionally enriched relationships.

For Melucci, the hidden networks become visible only when collective actors "confront or come into conflict with a public policy," that is, when they confront the state (1989, 90). This confrontation adds to a state of tension and enhanced emotional investment. Melucci argues, for instance, that the massive peace mobilizations of the 1980s were based in the submerged networks of women, young people, ecologists, and alternative cultures. Thus, Melucci's submerged networks point to what he calls the relationship between the latency and visibility poles of collective action. [5]

While Melucci associates the submerged networks in which collective identities are formed with the relatively quiescent period of the 1980s in both Europe and the United States, other scholars have identified similar incubation networks in periods prior to mass mobilization. Aldon Morris (1984), for instance, describes the "halfway houses" throughout the southern United States that served as laboratories for working out a collective identity of ends (civil rights and racial integration), means (nonviolence), and environmental relations (the development of a network of alliance systems linking North and South) prior to the public phase of the civil rights movement that began in the mid 1950s. Doug McAdam's (1982) political process theory also posits a stage of "cognitive liberation" that precedes mass mobilization. Similarly, Verta Taylor (1989a) describes the "abeyance processes" that link the periods of feminist activism in the United States from the suffrage movement of the early twentieth century to the contemporary movement.

Although Melucci argues that this process of constructing collective identities is a unique characteristic of highly complex societies, he may also underestimate how universal the process of cultural transformation has been as a prelude to previous periods of mass mobilization. The development of a collective identity centered on class consciousness among the working class in England (1780-1830), France (1830-1833), and Russia (1900-1914) point to a similar combination of social analysis contained within a new collective identity and institution building within sub-

merged networks as prelude to collective action (see this analysis and a comparison with political consciousness of African Americans by Morris in Morris and Mueller 1992).

The basic thrust of Melucci's conception of submerged networks is the proposition that the initial challenge to the prevailing order takes principally on symbolic grounds. That is, the status quo must be challenged at the cultural level in terms of its claims to legitimacy before mass collective action is feasible. Thus, Melucci argues that submerged networks "challenge and overturn the dominant codes upon which social relationships are founded. These symbolic challenges are a method of unmasking the dominant codes, a different way of perceiving and naming the world" (1989, 75). By concentrating only on the visible, public signs of a social movement's challenge to the existing order, previous theories of social movements have failed to appreciate the contribution of these cultural transformations. Melucci argues, for instance, that our concept of success should be expanded to encompass these cultural changes. This is the investment of the nascent movement in what he calls a "latency phase" as dominant cultural codes are unmasked and overturned.

Melucci contributes to a growing interest among students of social movements in the way that cultural codes are challenged; in the connection of social structure to culture through a social psychology that identities face-to-face patterns of interaction and their location in submerged networks where cultural experimentation actually occurs; and in the new cultural codes that can serve as the basis of collective action. These are important contributions that have been too little appreciated. In addition, it has been too little realized that the tensions and emotional investments associated with the process of generating collective identities and initiating collective actions are often accompanied by internal dissension and organizational segmentation.

Nevertheless, there are unresolved issues in Melucci's theory that must also be identified before it can be successfully applied to a case study. While Melucci is unique in pointing to the role of externally derived tension in the development of new cultural configurations within social movements, his focus on resource and environmental constraints as the major source of tension fails to consider the important role of internal conflict and competition as an additional dynamic contributing to the generation of new collective identities (see, as examples, Mueller 1987; Tarrow 1989b; Taylor and Whittier 1992a). There are other unresolved issues in Melucci's theory as well, but the most important for present purposes is his disavowal of the role of the collective identity as historic actor. In his focus on an intermediate level of analysis, the face-to-face interactions where collective identities are forged, he unnecessarily abandons the cultural level of analysis at which the product of the submerged networks enters political culture. It is at this point that the social movement emerges as historic actor and agent of political change. These two concerns—the role of internal conflict in shaping the collective identity and the level of analysis—are brought together here in the course of applying his theory to a specific case, the origins of the contemporary women's movement in the United States. This application may also suggest the utility of Melucci's theory for readers who do not have access to his Italian case materials (see an evaluation of these materials in Johnston 1991).

Collective Identity and the Mass Mobilization of Women

To demonstrate the importance of submerged networks in challenging dominant codes and creating new collective identities that facilitate mass mobilizations, it is necessary to document that this configuration of the new identity was not already widely available. This seemingly simple condition is often ignored in empirical demonstrations of cultural innovations but is essential for the current case study of the creation of a new collective identity for women.

In the United States, the decade after World War II was characterized by later feminists as the "decade of domesticity" because of its high birthrates and its emphasis on home, family, and women's traditional roles. So pervasive was the dominant cultural code prescribing a narrow set of roles for women that few social scientists recognized its existence. To characterize women's condition as one of inequality much less as oppression would have been regarded as heresy. Yet, in 1951, an article appeared in an American sociological journal strangely titled, "Women as a Minority Group" (Hacker [1951] 1979). The author, Helen Hacker, took the lonely position that women's characteristic behavior and position of

social inferiority paralleled that of Jews and Negroes, groups well recognized as "minorities" in U.S. culture. Hacker's article can be taken as a benchmark for its characterization of women according to the dominant cultural code of the United States in the 1950s. Despite its poor reception at the time, it brought to consciousness a set of cultural assumptions that were largely taken for granted.

After itemizing discriminatory patterns against women in economic, political, and social life, Hacker noted that, although women showed no conscious self-awareness of their inferior status, other aspects of their behavior supported the analogy. She cited data from the World War II period indicating high levels of self-hatred associated with the status of being a woman. In surveys, women showed high levels of dislike for other women, women expressed a preference for working under the direction of men, women had misgivings concerning the value of participation in public life, and high proportions of women, compared to men, wished they had been born in the opposite sex. Hacker showed parallels in the castelike behavior and treatment of women and Negroes. She noted, for instance, high social visibility and frequent attributions of an inferior intelligence, a smaller brain, irresponsibility, emotional instability, and moral weakness (514). Like the Negro, the woman accommodated to her inferior status with smiles, laughter, rising inflection in conversation, and downward glances. She cultivated an appearance of helplessness and pursued her goals with a flattering manner and "feminine wiles." Yet, after Hacker identified a deeply repressed sense of inferiority, she issued no call for women to overcome their condition and seemed to see little possibility for change. Instead, she pointed out that there were a few women, like those in nontraditional, professional occupations, who broke the dominant cultural code and recommended that these should be studied (520). Although there were other women who had long challenged the assumptions of the dominant code among minority women (Hooks 1981) and among a small group of feminists who had pursued the Equal Rights Amendment since 1922 (Rupp and Taylor 1987), both groups were largely invisible because the challenge they represented had been marginalized and assimilated.

Hacker was not the only one who saw little potential for a change in women's collective identity. More than ten years later, at a conference called by the prestigious American Academy of Arts and Sciences, a dozen of America's leading intellectuals contemplated women's condition (Lifton 1967). Many of the leading male scholars celebrated women's traditional virtues. Erik Erikson noted that women inhabit a special "inner space," while Robert J. Lifton praised women's possession of insight and wisdom. David Riesman noted that the greater resourcefulness of the contemporary generation of young women was possible "without storming the barricades at home or abroad" (Riesman 1964, 97). Carl Degler, a historian, pointed to the revolutionary changes taking place in women's growing paid employment, but he noted that women would probably remain in segregated and low-paying jobs because there was no strong feminist push to improve their condition. He was pessimistic about any such change because, "The whole truth is that American society in general, which includes women, shuns like a disease any feminist ideology" (Degler 1967, 203). That is, in Melucci's terms, the male scholars either saw no need for a collective identity for women or, like Degler, found it impossible to imagine the conditions under which such a profound cultural transformation might be brought about.

There was one member of this august gathering, however, who was soon to achieve a certain notoriety for her paper, "Equality between the Sexes: An Immodest Proposal." The author, Alice Rossi, drew on Helen Hacker's paper from the 1950s to call for uncompromising equality in the socialization, schooling, and adult responsibilities of men and women (Rossi 1967, 98-143). Her paper was received with little enthusiasm by either male or female participants at the conference. Degler (1967) responded to Rossi's "immodest proposal" by asserting that, "in America the soil is thin and the climate uncongenial for the growth of any seedlings of ideology" (210).

Although this conference indicated the increasing concern with women's status in society, at this level of discourse where scholars and intellectuals bring issues to public awareness, only Rossi's paper suggests a potential for cultural reconstruction and a new collective identity. Clearly, some of the best informed leaders of American intellectual life were unaware that they were sitting on the brink of a massive shift of consciousness in the culturally prescribed roles for women and an unprecedented mass mobilization. How did it happen? Did scholarly discourse on the plight of women escalate from papers like that given by Rossi at the Academy of Arts and Sciences conference? Did women's organizations disseminate persuasive communications on what should be done? Did young women defy the advice of their elders and take to the barricades? Did small groups of women get together in submerged networks removed from the public eye and renegotiate their identities as women and consider tactics and strategies that would challenge the dominant cultural code? Clearly, all of these things happened, but paramount place must go to the submerged networks where a transformed collective identity developed in the tense atmosphere of disagreement and conflict over the nature of the collective identity that would become the basis of a new set of goals and programs for change. Once this collective identity had been created, however, it would take on a life of its own as historic actor and source of political influence. The process by which the collective identity is created demonstrates the basic value of Melucci s theory.

The Origins of the Women's Movement

While the origins of women's mobilization in the United States are well documented,[6] two different explanations have been proposed to account for the beginning of the movement. The first explanation corresponds to the structural theories of the European new social movements literature that attempt to link changes in the objective condition of the mobilized group with changes in consciousness. Survey research is the tool usually employed with the goal of correlating clusters of attitudes reflecting a new collective consciousness with the subgroup defined by the objective condition. The key proponents of this approach for the U.S. women's movement have been Joan Huber (1976) and Ethel Klein (1984).[7] The second explanation corresponds in many ways to Melucci's emphasis on the generative role of submerged networks. Major contributors to this approach are Jo Freeman (1973a) and Sara Evans (1980). A review of these theories suggests both the strengths and the weaknesses of Melucci's conceptions of submerged networks and collective identities in an understanding of the origins of the U.S. women's movement. To make these theories accessible to a European audience, I characterize them as the structural and the submerged network theories.

Structural Theories

Explanations based on changes in technology and the division of labor argue that "the decline in fertility and the shift of productive work from home to factory in the past two centuries has upset the equilibrium of sex stratification in industrial societies," thus paving the way for a shift of consciousness and the mobilization of women (Huber 1976, 372). Based on a historic analysis of women's work and child-care responsibilities, Huber documents that, after 1940, the female work force was increasingly composed of married women with children. She argues that the double burden of paid work and domestic work was so onerous that women were compelled to see that they were treated unjustly by society (1976, 372). From Huber's perspective, the contemporary women's movement is the "unplanned result" of the technological changes that transformed women's work and child-care responsibilities. She predicts that the movement will continue as long as women bear this double burden.

Although Huber describes objective conditions that might logically lead women to develop an "injustice frame," she does not demonstrate empirically that the women experiencing these changes were, in fact, developing a new consciousness (or collective identity). For this kind of data, it is necessary to turn to Klein (1984) who has made this connection between structural position and changed consciousness. Looking at three different dimensions of women's traditional roles—domestic employment, motherhood, and marriage—she, like Huber, describes changes brought about through mature industrialization. She links these objective, structural changes to shifts over time in public opinion toward greater tolerance for women's work outside the home, for reduced fertility and family size, and for the social acceptability of either single status or divorce. Despite the momentous changes occurring in women's lives throughout the century, she notes, it was not until the 1960s that public opinion polls indicated large numbers of women were endorsing a nontraditional role.

Klein's (1984) analysis is based on the over-time data from the National Election Studies, which have been gathered since the 1950s by the Survey Research Center at the University of Michigan. They indicate that, by the end of the 1960s, the majority of women were in favor of nontraditional, roles for women based on social equality, and an increasing number felt that women faced discrimination (91). Klein characterizes this cluster of attitudes as a "feminist consciousness." Her data indicated that, by 1972, women who were psychologically more likely to support nontraditional roles for women were themselves found in structural positions where they were more likely to work outside the home, to have a job with high occupational status, to achieve more than a high school education, to be single, divorced, or separated, to live in a large metropolitan area, to have a mother who had worked, to be politically liberal, and to be little involved in organized religion (106-19). The more of these characteristics a woman possessed, the more likely she was to have a highly developed feminist consciousness.

Klein's data reveal a paradoxical finding, however. Despite the sharp increase in feminist consciousness among women, it was even higher among men. By 1972, men were even more likely than women to believe that society rather than nature or biology was responsible for women's roles; to support an equal role for women in business and industry; and to endorse equal employment treatment (100). Yet, needless to say, men did not create the women's movement nor did they encourage women's mass mobilization. This anomalous finding points to the limitations of the structural explanation of the origins of the women's movement. Despite Klein's careful connection of structural changes in women's roles to changes in public consciousness, to some extent, changes in social structure affected the consciousness of men and women similarly.

The structural theories and Klein's careful documentation of the rise of a feminist consciousness help to account for the large public support for the women's movement during the 1970s and, also, its considerable political influence after the period of mass mobilization beginning in 1970, but it cannot explain the origins of the movement for two simple reasons: (1) a new consciousness that is shared equally by men and women cannot explain why women rather than men formed a movement; and (2) widespread support among women for greater equality does not explain why some few specific individuals of the millions of American women affected by structural changes did, in fact, create a movement. To try to explain the origins of the movement with a structural analysis alone faces the same limitations that Melucci has identified in some of the European literature on new social movements: "Approaches based on the *structure/motivation* dualism . . . view collective action either as a product of the logic of the system or as a result of personal beliefs" (1989, 21). The basic problem is that "both the macrostructural factors and the individual variables imply an unbridgeable gap between the level of explanation proposed and the concrete process that allows a certain number of individuals to act together" (1988, 332).

Melucci's proposed solution is an intermediate level of analysis in which submerged networks are studied as the source of new collective identities that encompass the definition of specific possibilities and limits of action. At the same time, relationships are activated within localized, submerged networks and particular individuals make commitments to act together in pursuit of specific goals (1988, 332). Applied to the origins of women's liberation, a generally diffuse feminist consciousness, while perhaps necessary, is not enough. To explain origins, specific individuals must be identified who have formed emotional bonds from their interaction, negotiated a sense of group membership, and made a plan for change (or series of plans), however tentative, with goals, means, and a consideration of environmental constraints: a collective identity.

The Submerged Networks

Previous scholarship on the women's movement has provided many of the pieces necessary for the kind of analysis that Melucci proposes. Freeman's (1973a) and Evans's (1980) work on the origins of the U.S. women's movement are best known in this tradition. As Freeman indicates, the movement originated simultaneously in two different social locations in the mid to late 1960s from their respective sources among, first, the "older branch" of women active in national politics who were involved in the new State Commissions on the Status of Women, and, a second, "younger branch" of women who had been participants in the civil rights movement and the New Left. Freeman (1973a) argues that the origins of the movement in these two branches can be explained by the availability of compatible communications networks, a series of "crises" that fo-

cused each branch of women on feminist issues, and experienced organizers in the younger branch who could weld together local groups into a national movement. It was the older branch that created the National Organization for Women (NOW), which eventually became the major social movement organization for the movement. The younger branch developed the small groups, consciousness-raising, and the less conventional tactics of the movement. Evans (1980) provides an in-depth study of how the younger women were radicalized by the humiliations they experienced from their male colleagues in the social movements of the 1960s. In the course of describing what Melucci would characterize as "submerged networks," Evans also indicates the degree to which conflict and struggle played a role in developing collective identities in the submerged networks of both branches of the movement. It was in part the struggle over the notion of the emerging collective identity that led to cultural innovation, organizational segmentation, and the spread of movement groups in the five years preceding the Women's Strike. This event, in August 1970, marked the symbolic beginning, the public "coming out," of the movement.

The processes of negotiation and identity construction in the two branches reflected the very different political cultures of electoral and movement politics in the mid 1960s. The older branch, or what came to be called "equal rights feminism," was based in the policy debates, organized interests, and campaign obligations of political actors in state and federal governments. The conflicts that led to changes in women's consciousness arose from policy debates regarding women's rights. In this context, the collective identity that developed followed the model of the civil rights movement in emphasizing the source of women's problems in systematic patterns of discrimination that could be eliminated or mitigated primarily through appropriate legislation, regulations, litigation, and enforcements but not excluding marches and demonstrations. Through conflict with Commission members, congressional representatives, officials, and the media over the Equal Rights Amendment, the interpretation of Title VII of the Civil Rights Act, employment policy, the enforcement practices of the Equal Employment Opportunities Commission, and a host of other policies, a relatively small network of politically well-connected women developed a conception of gender equality or collective identity that was thoroughly radical in its implications[8] (see Hole and Levine 1971, 15-107; Carden 1974, 103-47; Freeman 1975, 44-102).

The conflict that occurred over the formulation of this identity among equal rights women led to a proliferation of organizations devoted to efforts on behalf of specific constituencies, issues, or policies. In 1967, for instance, women from the United Auto Workers were forced to withdraw from NOW because their union opposed inclusion of the Equal Rights Amendment in the NOW Bill of Rights (they formed the Congress of Labor Union Women). Further segmentation occurred with inclusion of abortion in the NOW Bill of Rights, which led women more concerned with issues of economic discrimination to leave and form the Women's Equity Action League (WEAL). Further division occurred when younger women from the New York NOW chapter charged the national organization with an elitist decision making structure and formed the October 17 Movement (later known as The Feminists). In 1968, two of NOW's lawyers walked out in disgust over the inefficiency of the organization, taking two of its most important cases. They then formed other social movement organizations—first, Human Rights for Women and, later, the Legal Defense Fund—to support sex discrimination cases (Freeman 1975, 80-81). The proliferation of equal rights organizations reflected not only important differences of emphasis among women searching for political solutions to multiple sources of discrimination but also the pursuit of an area of action where individual women could create a highly personal interpretation of their collective identity. Unfortunately, for present purposes, accounts of these conflicts are devoted almost exclusively to the policy provisions involved in the debates and tell us little about the face-to-face process of collective identity construction as it occurred.

In contrast, there is a rich literature on the evolution of collective identity in the submerged networks of younger women who came to constitute the women's liberation branch of the movement. Whereas the older branch identified what they came to understand as the "overt" discrimination against women that appeared in employment, politics, credit, and educational opportunities, the younger branch turned to the personal politics that Helen Hacker ([1951] 1979) had associated with women's status as a minority. The collective identity that emerged had no precursor in the liberal politics of the early civil rights movement. It came to be identified as "women's liberation."

Prior to 1970, women's liberation had been a "movement of friends" in the submerged networks of civil rights and the New Left. Several detailed historical accounts indicate the intensity of the social interactions and the high level of emotional investment of the young people who were experimenting with the creation of new social forms of living as well as the means of achieving political goals. From 1964 to 1967, isolated pairs or small groups of activist women began to voice a sense of uneasiness to each other about what they perceived as a different and unequal role for women in the actual day-to-day activities of these movements. As Evans (1980) points out, attempts to articulate this uneasiness about women's assignment to the mundane and routine activities of kitchen work, mimeographing, typing, and cleaning evoked reactions of scorn and fury from the male radicals—first in the Student Nonviolent Coordinating Committee (SNCC), the major youth organization of the civil rights movement, and soon after in Students for a Democratic Society (SDS), the leading student organization of the New Left in the United States throughout the 1960s. The younger women were rebuffed time after time as they tried to discuss their concerns regarding gender differences within the limits of debate prescribed by the leaders of the civil rights and New Left movements. Conflict, ridicule, and exclusion greeted their attempts to extend the emotional bonds forged during the early 1960s to the sense of injustice and grievances arising from women's personal experiences within the movements.

As they continued to receive rebukes and scorn from the male radicals—at a SNCC staff meeting in the summer of 1964; at the SNCC Waveland Retreat in November 1964; at an SDS conference in December 1965; at a 1966 SDS convention; and, finally and most dramatically, at the first nationwide gathering of New Left groups in Chicago, the National Conference for a New Politics (NCNP), in September 1967—women's confusion and search for a new identity turned to rage and alienation (Evans 1980; Hole and Levine 1971, 109-16). The submerged networks of women that had developed within the New Left organizations moved outside to begin an autonomous existence in major cities in the East Coast and the Midwest.

The transitory processes that Melucci describes of conflict, segmentation, and dissolution of organizations is illustrated in Figure 1, which represents one year in the life of the New York women's liberation groups after they separated from the New Left in 1968. The collective identity that came to be associated with "women's liberation" in the early 1970s developed out of this process of conflict and negotiation. Figure 1 illustrates schematically how this process occurred in one location. The upper left-hand column indicates the processes of repeated conflict and segmentation of the New York radical feminists which, at the same time, gave rise to a series of collective actions that symbolically depicted the common understandings developing within the network. In contrast to the older branch of equal rights feminists, the radicals challenged the personal characteristics and patterns of social interaction assigned to women by the dominant cultural code through public actions and confrontations that increasingly gained national media coverage and public attention. By fall 1968, the Atlantic City demonstrations against the image of women portrayed in the Miss America bathing suit contests brought front page coverage throughout the country. A live sheep was crowned Miss America and bras, girdles, and other "instru-

ments of torture" were dumped into a Freedom Trashcan. Young women, with their open disrespect for "Miss America" and the image of women it celebrates, were soon dubbed "bra burners" by the mass media. Despite this distortion of their collective actions (or because of it), their numbers continued to grow. By November, a national meeting gave a sense of common purpose while contributing to the formation of additional radical groups that continued the process of conflict, segmentation, and dissolution throughout 1969. At the same time the rudiments of a new collective identity were taking shape.

Although New York drew on an unusually large constituency of radical women, their experiences reflected a microcosm of centers of mobilization around the country. Throughout the year, an understanding of women's oppression (in contrast to discrimination) developed among the New York women that emphasized a politics of interpersonal relations; the bonding of women as an oppressed class; the use of rapping (later, "consciousness raising") to bring out the emotional pain of women's lives; a fear of leadership and hierarchy; and the creation of novel and innovative tactics to voice women's anger against the symbols of conventional femininity. These common understandings grew in an emotional atmosphere of tension and conflict over major points of disagreement within the emerging identity of radical

Figure 1
Conflict and Segmentation among New York 'Women's Liberation' Groups, 1968

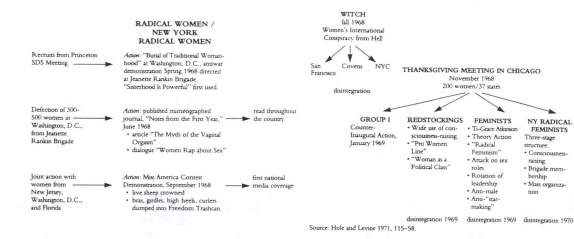

Source: Hole and Levine 1971, 115–58.

feminists. Every action and every organizational split reflected both a conflict over identity and the emergence of a new basis of understanding.

Through the processes associated with identity construction, the movement experienced extraordinary growth between 1969 and 1970. By mid 1970, *Notes from the Second Year,* a feminist journal of 126 pages, sold over forty thousand copies (Hole and Levine 1971, 158). The number of movement periodicals increased from two in 1968 to sixty-one in 1972. Small groups proliferated throughout the country, and regional conferences to coordinate their activities had become commonplace by 1970 (Carden 1974). By August 1970, the highly diverse submerged networks of equal rights feminists and women's liberation were ready to emerge as womanhood united, the historic actor.

The Women's Movement as 'Historic Actor'

Melucci has rightfully pointed to the origins of social movements at an intermediate level of analysis: the submerged networks of face-to-face interactions like those of the New York radical feminists who created the basis of a new collective identity during a short period of cultural experimentation. In the process of testing new representations through collective actions, experiences of conflict, internal dissension, and organizational segmentation and dissolution, new understandings were developed that became the basis for challenging the dominant cultural code at its roots. As this identity developed, however, it gathered increasing support from the structural changes that had altered the lives of U.S. women throughout the twentieth century and led to a massive shift in consciousness among both men and women. As the two branches of the movement increasingly engaged in common actions during the summer of 1970, they found that the collective identity they represented has massive appeal.

Like other new movements, the women's movement in the United States first achieved widespread national recognition and political influence at its point of initial mass mobilization. Women's Strike for Equality Day, August 26, 1970, marked the symbolic starting point for the contemporary women's movement in the United States. Sponsored by a broad coalition of women's movement organizations coordinated by the National Organization for Women (NOW)

to commemorate the fiftieth anniversary of the Suffrage Amendment, tens of thousands of women went "on strike" for equality. It was the largest protest on behalf of women in U.S. history (Hole and Levine 1971, 420). Women across the country marched and picketed, held rallies and attended teach-ins. In New York, women set up a child-care center in City Hall Park; in Chicago, sit-ins were held at restaurants barring women (Deckard 1975, 343); in New York, feminists went to the editor of the *New York Times* to protest an editorial titled "Henpecked House," against the Equal Rights Amendment (ERA); and in Minneapolis, a guerrilla theater group portrayed the parts of key figures in the universal abortion drama for downtown audiences (Hole and Levine 1971, 263, 299). The most memorable event in media coverage, however, was the unprecedented outpouring of tens of thousands of women who marched down Fifth Avenue in New York carrying signs that read, "Don't Cook Dinner—Starve a Rat Today!" "Eve Was Framed," and "End Human Sacrifice! Don't Get Married!!" (Hole and Levine 1971, 78; Deckard 1975, 343). Despite its label as "Equality Day," the protests, demonstrations, guerrilla theater, chants, and banners that marked the day represented not only the discrimination issues of equal rights feminists but also the personal politics of women's liberation.

Equality Day marked a turning point in terms of women's political influence and the nature of the women's movement. The size of the mobilization made it clear that the movement would now have to be taken seriously (Freeman 1973a, 84). Only after Equality Day did Congress act on behalf of women. During the 1960s, Congress had considered 844 bills concerned with women's issues and passed only 10 (Klein 1984, 22). The Ninety-second Congress passed more women's right legislation than the total of all previous legislation combined (see Freeman 1975, 202-5). By 1980, 71 bills had been passed on behalf of women (Costain 1988, 161). In addition to political influence in Congress, media interest in women began a sharp upward trend after Equality Day as well (Cancian and Ross 1981). Public awareness of the new movement almost immediately reached 80 percent of adult Americans (Hole and Levine 1971, 269), and public opinion polls began to show a marked increase in support for improvements in the status of women. Women began to win elections to local, state, and federal office in unprecedented numbers (Mueller 1987).

The movement itself was transformed by the publicity associated with the Strike. New members had been recruited primarily through personal networks of activists in the period from 1965 to 1970, but after the Strike, contact with the movement through the media played an increasing role (Carden 1974, 32-33). Because of its greater visibility and respectability, the new recruits flooded the modest NOW offices in major cities. Chapters often expanded by as much as 50 to 70 percent in a few months (Freeman 1975, 85). The National Organization for Women mushroomed from a membership of several thousand in 1969 to fifteen thousand by 1972 (Carden 1974, 194). By the end of the decade, it had become a mass membership organization of several hundred thousand (Costain and Costain 1987).

For three years after the Equality Day Strike, the Women's Movement acquired the character of that mythical, historical actor that Melucci has typified as a "unified empirical datum" or collective reality that is seen to exist as a "thing" (Melucci 1988, 330; 1989, 18). This "thingness" of the movement's collective identity in the eyes of the national media, Congress, the state legislators, and, probably the general public is anathema to Melucci because it denies the diversity and the tentativeness of the "real" social movement that he has observed in submerged networks. Yet, there is considerable evidence to suggest that The Movement as historical actor was thought to represent an aroused and angry womanhood. Congress yielded to its demand for equality in their passage of legislation on behalf of women.[9] For a brief moment, a very brief moment, women emerged as historic actor with a seemingly homogeneous identity centered on a wide-ranging quest for equality.

Despite the impressive evidence that a homogeneous and unitary movement was demonstrated by the Equality Day marches, both feminist activists at the core of the movement then and scholars who have studied the movement since have realized that The Movement was a highly diverse aggregation of women with many different grievances, programs of action, and visions of the future. As Melucci has claimed for the European "new social movements, " at the level of interpersonal, face-to-face relationships, the movement was not then, nor has it ever been, a unified whole.[10] Yet, a more comprehensive analysis would encompass not only the interactions and meanings of the core actors who created the movement or even those who were recruited to it but also its contributions to public discourse and political culture. To understand the political influence of the movement would require consideration of the impression of unity created by the Equality Strike and its media coverage as a major datum to be explained. Such an analysis would draw from much of the new work on social construction that seeks to explain the consequences as well as the origins of social movements. To address this level of public discourse and political influence is not to deny that origins of movements lie in submerged networks and must be analyzed with a different set of conceptual and empirical tools. Nevertheless, it requires an analysis that includes but extends beyond Melucci's important contributions.

Conclusion

This case study focuses on two moments in the life of the contemporary women's movement—first mass mobilization of U.S. women in the Women's Equality Day Strike of August 1970, and the five-year period preceding the Strike—when the two branches of contemporary U.S. feminism were constructing a new identity through a process of internal conflict and organizational segmentation. These two stages in the development of the movement point to both the strengths and the weaknesses of Melucci's intermediate level of analysis for a comprehensive theory of social construction.

Melucci's theory is most telling when it calls attention to that level of face-to-face interaction where collective identities are developed in submerged networks through a process of social negotiation. It is at this point that structural sources of personal injury—such as the contradiction that younger branch women felt between their high levels of education and the low status they experienced in the personal politics of the 1960s movements—are translated into a shared sense of injustice focused on grievances that are articulated as part of a program for change. The case study also demonstrates, however, that the creative tensions that fuel these negotiations spring as much from internal competition and conflict within movement networks as from the inadequacy of means for realizing goals. Although the new collective identity of women continued to change in the submerged networks of the movement and to be challenged by counter movements such as those that arose in the mid 1970s to oppose early feminist victories in abortion rights and the Equal Rights Amendment, the collective identity soon took on a life of its own.

The independent existence or "thingness" of the identity of women" that existed in the early 1970s suggests that a comprehensive theory of social movement construction cannot restrict its attention to the intermediate level of submerged networks if it is concerned with the political influence and cultural changes achieved by the movement. The collective identities created within submerged networks achieve an independent existence once they become public through the movement's explanatory apparatus of manifestos, programs, press conferences, banners, slogans, insignia, costumes, and guerrilla theater that attempt to account for the movement and its collective actions. Through these devices, a collective identity becomes public that has a potential for political influence. It is then subject to attempts at distortion and marginalization of state, media, and countermovements. (See Gitlin's [1980] description in his excellent study of media treatment of Students for a Democratic Society [SDS] during the 1960s.) At this public stage of movement development, when the collective identity becomes a historic actor, it would be an empirical as well as a theoretical mistake to equate the public persona of this collective identity (an object of political culture and public discourse) with the collective identity of Melucci's submerged networks (an object of continuing negotiation and renegotiation amid fluid but intense face-to-face interactions).

The distinction between these two levels of analysis is important not only for our appreciation of Melucci's strengths and weaknesses but also for locating his contribution within the developing work on the social movement of social movements. As this work has proliferated, it has become increasingly important to identify theoretical contributions in terms of appropriate levels of analysis.

The most comprehensive attempt to specify these levels is Klandermans's (1992) essay in which he distinguishes three levels of social construction: (1) public discourse and the formation and transformation of collective identities; (2) persuasive communication during mobilization

campaigns by movement organizations, their opponents, and countermovement organizations; and (3) what he terms "consciousness raising" during episodes of collective behavior. At the first level, he combines the two construction processes that have been distinguished here: public discourse such as William Gamson's (1988) work on "issue packaging" by the media and Melucci's (1989) conception of the construction of collective identities in submerged networks. The second level of persuasive communication by social movement organizations and their opponents encompasses Klandermans's (1984a) own work on consensus mobilization and the work of David Snow and his associates (1986) on frame alignment. At the third level, Klandermans includes the changes of meanings and perception that occur during the course of experiencing collective action as described, for instance, in the work of Rick Fantasia (1988) on industrial strikes.

Klandermans distinguishes these three levels in terms of two implicit criteria: the number of people involved and the degree to which social construction is purposive or spontaneous. Public discourse is a diffuse process encompassing major media of communication for a society or sector of society. Social constructions created by social movement organizations are purposive and reach a more limited audience than public discourse. Finally, construction processes involving the participants and spectators at a collective action event are even more limited by the situational opportunities for direct participation or observation.

While Klandermans's typological distinctions are extremely useful in ordering this growing field of research, our lengthy consideration of Melucci's theory of collective identity suggests several modifications. After Melucci has so carefully indicated that the submerged networks are part of the latency phase of social movements, an "invisible process" out of the public eye, it is inappropriate that this process should be considered a part of public discourse. In fact, as Melucci argues, it is partly the freedom from public scrutiny that permits people to interact in small groups where experimentation and negotiation of identities can result in the development of new social codes and goals for action. Thus, when selecting groups for study in Milan, Melucci deliberately chose the most grass-roots level of participation because, he noted, leaders were more likely to present, what was to him, a falsely unified version of the collective identity if they had to interact frequently with public actors such as media representatives or officials (1989, 242). It was only it the grass-roots level, he felt, that such false presentations (which should properly be considered part of public discourse) could be avoided and maximum heterogeneity in experimentation and negotiation be observed.

On the other hand, our case study of the public phase, or "coming out" of the women's movement at the Women's Strike for Equality Day indicates that collective identities do become a part of public discourse and, potentially, historic actors if the movement attempts to bring about social or political change. At this public level of analysis, a different set of social and political actors, particularly the representatives of formal organizations, will attempt to influence the nature of the collective identity and fit it to their own interests and systems of meaning.

These observations suggest the utility of four rather than three levels of analysis: public discourse, persuasive communication initiated by movement organizations, "consciousness raising" from participation in episodes of collective action, and the creation of collective identities in submerged networks. To the extent that the four levels of analysis have a natural sequencing in a cycle of protest, it seems likely that social movements based on a major reconstruction of collective identities will require either a lengthy or an intensive period for the gestation of the new identity. An ideal typical sequence would progress from least to most public awareness (and, undoubtedly, back again). Groups of individuals in submerged networks would experiment with new collective identities and action proposals, increasingly taking their new social constructions into conflict with targets of change or potential converts outside their own small circle just as the New York radical feminists crowned a sheep "Miss America." As a collective identity takes shape, potential activists may come together and create a social movement organization with a public declaration announcing their new collective identity like the women from the State Commissions on the Status of Women who formed the National Organization for Women and drew up a Bill of Rights for women in the mid 1960s. Collective actions such as those associated with women's Strike for Equality Day offer opportunities for direct experience of action and perceptual change

based on the newly revealed collective identity. Finally, the national media may be attracted by the newsworthiness of the confrontation or the importance of the values at stake, and the social reconstruction represented by the new collective identity may become a part of public discourse. (See Freeman on the "grand press blitz" of the women's movement, January through March 1970 [1975, 148-51].) Over the course of any social movement, these processes of social construction will cycle back and forth between levels in increasingly complex patterns depending on the degree to which all sectors of society become involved and how quickly the movement is controlled.

Yet, the search for stages is somewhat premature in a field that is only now beginning to distinguish one level of analysis from another. In this chapter, I have attempted to distinguish two of these levels and to suggest that Melucci's contribution lies in highlighting an intermediate level of analysis in a latency phase that may precede the creation of formal organizations. His work suggests the importance of the opening skirmishes between members of submerged networks and symbolic representations of the dominant cultural code through collective actions that begin a more public phase of the movement.

Although the political fortunes of any subordinate group, such as women, demand that it enter a public phase to challenge the cultural order directly and to influence public affairs, such an analysis would not explain how women came to develop and identify with an analysis of women as a minority group and to share what Gamson and his colleagues (1982) call an "injustice frame" and McAdam (1982) terms "cognitive liberation." To understand how several hundred women throughout the United States constructed the new identity of women as historic actor that became an influential political force for change in the status of women, it is necessary to understand the origins of the women's movement in the preceding decade. It is here that Melucci's theory is most convincing.

Notes

1. Increased awareness began with the New School Volume, edited by Jean Cohen (1985a), which was followed by a series of papers by Bert Klandermans and Sidney Tarrow (see Klandermans 1986; Klandermans and Tarrow 1988; Klandermans 1990b).

2. But see *From Structure to Action,* in which Klandermans, Kriesi, and Tarrow attempt to connect social structure to collective action. In the introduction, Klandermans and Tarrow (1988) indicate that the volume seeks to "bridge that gap between structure and participation" (10).

3. Important representations of this developing interest in social movement culture and processes of social construction as applied to social movements are found in contributions to *Frontiers in Social Movement Theory,* edited by Aldon Morris and Carol Mueller (1992).

4. Later, I argue that the "unified empirical datum" is not necessarily a false reification but is instead a cultural artifact that serves to enhance or detract from the movement's political influence. A similar perception of unity in crowd behavior by observers is also a starting point for recent theories of collective behavior (see the first edition of *Collective Behavior* [Turner and Killian 1957]).

5. The latent/manifest distinction refers to the difference between the private, "submerged" life of the movement in groups and communities that experiment and negotiate challenges to the dominant cultural code and the visible, public challenges to that code that usually begin in collective action events or in symbolic insignia of dress or behavior (see also Taylor and Whittier 1992a).

6. The most authoritative accounts are those by Hole and Levine (1971); Carden (1974); Freeman (1973a, 1975); Deckard (1975); Cassell (1977); Evans (1980); and Ferree and Hess (1985).

7. Corresponding examples for the new social movement approach in Europe are Inglehart 1977 and Barnes, Kaase, and Allerbeck 1979.

8. Just how radically different their collective identity had become from women outside the movement could not be appreciated until it was incorporated into the Congressional hearings that became the basis for interpreting the implications of the Equal Rights Amendment (see Brown et al. 1971). These implications, including the obligation of women to perform military service and to surrender their (largely inoperative) support prerogatives in divorce proceedings, became the target of attack in a ferocious campaign in the mid 1970s by conservative women that undermined the impression of the women's movement as united womanhood, a historic actor (see Mansbridge 1986).

9. Margaret Heckler was Republican leader of the Congressional Women's Caucus throughout much of the 1970s. She was one of two women first appointed to the Cabinet by President Ronald Reagan in an attempt to woo the women's vote.

10. Nevertheless, the power of the unitary image is revealed in comments by Freeman (1975), who notes, "The pluralistic nature of the women's liberation movement is a characteristic that has not been adequately appreciated either by the movement's participants or by its critics" (150). ✦

Part 5

Motivational Factors I: Barriers to and Correlates of Participation

The previous readings demonstrated the importance of various kinds of networks and interpersonal ties in linking prospective adherents to social movement organizations and their activities. However, social networks are only information conduits and bridges that channel the diffusion of movement activity. As such, they facilitate rather than determine individual recruitment and participation. Equally important is the variable of individual motivation. Are those individuals introduced to a movement activity or event sufficiently motivated to devote some portion of their time and energy to the activity in question? Moreover, can they be counted on to participate consistently when called upon? Of course, the character of participation varies across social movements, with some movements demanding relatively little time, energy, and personal resources, while others are comparatively greedy, demanding a great deal from their members (Coser 1974; Turner and Killian 1987). Wherever a movement falls on this continuum of participant demands or expectations, however, their relative success in securing adherents depends in part on the prospective adherents' motivation.

Recruiting individuals who are sufficiently motivated to devote time and energy to movement activity is not a simple, routine task. A movement's constituency—that pool of individuals whose material and/or lifestyle interests are consistent with those that the movement claims to be promoting—is typically much larger than the number of individuals a movement can count on to participate in a fashion consistent with its objectives and activities. Thus, neither being linked to a movement through social networks nor being a probable beneficiary of a movement's objectives is sufficient to guarantee participation.

The problem of motivation is illustrated and elaborated by the four selections in this part. The first, by Dirk Oegema and Bert Klandermans, shows that sympathy with the cause a movement represents does not guarantee action in support of the movement. In their terms, "action preparedness" does not automatically lead to "action participation." They identify two factors or paths that account for nonparticipation among those who expressed sympathy with the cause in question (the People's Petition against cruise missiles in the Netherlands): one is erosion, which involves the dissipation of sympathy; the other is nonconversion, the failure to transform sympathizers into active participants.

The second selection, by Karl-Dieter Opp and Wolfgang Roehl, explores the relationship between the motivation or incentive to participate in protest actions and the repressive acts of state officials. Although it is often assumed that repression, or its threat, constrains individual participation in social movement activities, Opp and Roehl show that this is not always the case. They attempt to elaborate the conditions under which repression either facilitates or impedes participation in social movement activities. Among other things, this article demonstrates that the relationship between conditions thought of as disincentives to participation, such as repression, and actual participation varies depending on a number of contextual factors.

The third selection, by Pamela Oliver, reveals a paradox in participation in neighborhood improvement associations in Detroit: those community residents with a strong sense of collective identity and positive regard for their neighbors were less likely to absorb the costs of participation than those individuals who had less respect for their neighbors and who were pessimistic about the prospect of their engaging in collective action. This paradoxical finding points to three complexities of the motivational issue: at least in some cases, positive identification with a group, including shared interests, does not guarantee acting on its behalf; people may not be more likely to participate when they believe others will; and the free-rider dilemma may be more pronounced in contexts where there are clear-cut activists.

Ed Walsh and Rex Warland examine this relationship between activists and free-riders even more thoroughly in the final selection, a study of movement involvement in the wake of the 1979 nuclear accident in the Three Mile Island area of Pennsylvania. Based on the questionnaire responses of a random sample of citizens in four threatened communities, they found that free-riding was both more pervasive and more complex

than generally thought. Not only did a small percentage of the thousands of threatened citizens get involved, but free-riding was not based solely on self-interested calculations, such as the belief that others would act on their behalf. Rather, more complicated ideological, communicative, psychological, and structural factors separated free-riders from activists.

Taken together, the following selections sensitize us in different ways to the complexity of the motivational issue. In particular, they remind us, first, that sympathy for a cause or group does not readily translate into supportive action or engagement; second, that there can be important differences among activists, token participants, and constituents more generally, and that it is therefore important to be clear about which members or participants are our points of reference when considering the factors accounting for participation; third, that the costs and risks associated with movement participation are not purely objective factors, but are subject to change; and, fourth, that the motivation for free-riding is based on much more than merely rational or self-interested calculation.

References

Coser, Lewis. 1974. *Greedy Institutions*. New York: Free Press.

Turner, Ralph H. and Lewis M. Killian. 1987. *Collective Behavior*. Third Edition. Englewood Cliffs, NJ: Prentice-Hall. ✦

14

Why Social Movement Sympathizers Don't Participate: Erosion and Nonconversion of Support

Dirk Oegema
Bert Klandermans

Activating individuals who are already sympathetic to a movement—or, in Klandermans's (1994) words, action mobilization—is more difficult than one might imagine. Movement participation, we have previously argued, evolves in four steps: (1) one becomes a sympathizer of the movement, then (2) a target of mobilization attempts; next (3) one becomes motivated to participate, and finally, (4) one overcomes the barriers to participation (Klandermans and Oegema 1987). Action mobilization involves the last three steps of this sequence. Our analysis of a large peace demonstration in the Netherlands reveals what every organizer knows from experience: There is a big difference between being a sympathizer and becoming an active participant, and many a sympathizer fails to become active.

There is every reason to assume that the proportion of sympathizers that potentially can be activated varies over time, by the situation, and by the activity. For instance, Klandermans (1984a) observed that, within a single union, union members varied considerably in their willingness to participate in union action depending on the specific action proposed. Moreover, in different companies the proportion of the union membership willing to participate in industrial action also varied considerably. Studies of many social movements record a similar variability in participation. To cite only a few examples: Walsh (1988) observed different levels of participation in the various communities surrounding Three Mile Island; Henig (1982a) found variation among different

neighborhoods in Boston during the anti-busing protests; and Briët, Klandermans and Kroon (1987), in a study of the women's movement, found substantial differences in levels of participation, depending on the particular activity, among a population of women in a Dutch town. Such differences in levels of participation (or between subsets of) the same population can originate at each transition point in the four-step model of movement participation, and the relative contribution of each step to the final number of participants points to the strengths and weaknesses of a mobilization campaign.

In this paper we depart from the usual approach to studying movement campaigns and focus on a campaign's *failure* to activate sympathizers. The literature on social movements offers little information on nonparticipation in response to action mobilization campaigns. Mass mobilizations have generally been studied in terms of what they achieve rather than what they fail to achieve. Consequently, we know more about participants than about nonparticipants (see McAdam 1986 for a similar criticism). There might be a methodological reason for this neglect of the dynamics of nonparticipation—a lack of proper quantitative longitudinal data. Without such data, which help us map preexisting levels of sympathy, it is difficult to make valid estimates of the proportion of movement sympathizers who actually end up being inactive.

We propose two terms to identify two different forms that nonparticipation can take. First, a campaign can fail to transform sympathizers into active participants, an outcome we call *nonconversion.* Second, people who initially support the movement may change their minds and become unwilling to become active. In this case, the problem isn't that sympathy is not converted into action, but rather that sympathy disappears—hence our use of the term *erosion.* Nonconversion and erosion of support are two measures of a mobilization campaign's effectiveness or ineffectiveness. From the standpoint of movement organizers, of course, neither is desirable: Organizers must convert support into action.

We assume that rates of nonconversion and erosion vary over time and across movements, movement organizations, campaigns, actions, communities, and subsets of populations. We elaborate here on these assumptions and offer explanations for this variation. We test these expla-

"Why Social Movement Sympathizers Don't Participate: Erosion and Nonconversion of Support." *American Sociological Review* 59: 703-722. Copyright © 1994 by the American Sociological Association. Reprinted with permission.

nations on data we collected from a study of participation in the Dutch peace movement.

Theory

Generalized Action Preparedness, Specific Action Preparedness, and Action Participation

To further define and explain nonconversion and erosion, we distinguish and describe three stages in the mobilization process: generalized action preparedness, specific action preparedness, and action participation. *Generalized action preparedness* describes an individual's expressed willingness to support a movement, to take part in different types of collective action the movement might stage. Adherents of the movement possess this disposition to a greater or lesser degree. A movement's mobilization potential in a society can be thought of as the proportion of individuals within that society that is inclined to support the movement (Klandermans and Oegema 1987). This proportion is relatively stable over time and defines the participation limits of mobilization campaigns. The mobilization potential of a movement, then, theoretically encompasses those individuals with a generalized action preparedness greater than zero.

Generalized action preparedness *for a particular movement* can be seen as a function of the existence and magnitude of grievances and the existence and appeal of a movement addressing these grievances (Oegema and Klandermans 1992). The more individuals who believe that a specific movement can effectively mobilize to redress shared grievances, and the more serious these grievances are, the higher the generalized action preparedness for this movement (Schwartz and Paul 1992).

But ideological commitment alone does not guarantee participation in concrete action: Action mobilization campaigns must transform generalized action preparedness into actual participation. In successful mobilization campaigns, generalized action preparedness is successfully converted into the preparedness to participate in specific actions, and this *specific action preparedness* materializes as actual action participation.[1] If individuals are not being targeted by mobilization attempts, however, it is unlikely that they will participate (Klandermans and Oegema 1987). Incentives contingent on the particular action and the circumstances of the individual further influence

an individual's motivation to participate. For any individual, the lower the perceived costs of participation and the higher the benefits, the more motivated he or she will be to participate (Klandermans 1984a; Opp 1989a). Whether motivation—that is, specific action preparedness—is converted into actual participation depends on the presence of barriers, for example sickness or lack of transportation (Klandermans and Oegema 1987). The more barriers that exist, the less likely it is that an individual will participate. The process

Figure 1
Process of Action Mobilization

of action mobilization is represented by the simple schema shown in Figure 1.

We can now define nonconversion and erosion in terms of these concepts. *Nonconversion* is the nonparticipation of individuals who are prepared to participate but somehow fail to convert their preparedness into actual participation. *Erosion* is the nonparticipation of individuals who, though once prepared to participate, have changed their minds and lost their preparedness to take action.

We hypothesize that nonconversion occurs when individuals have not been targeted by mobilization attempts, and/or they find that the ratio of costs to benefits is unfavorable, and/or barriers prevent them from participating. Erosion, we hypothesize, occurs when individuals perceive the ratio of costs to benefits as *becoming* less favorable over time, and/or their grievances are no longer pressing, and/or their sympathy for the movement wanes.

The Antecedents of Nonconversion and Erosion

Nonconversion, then, seems to be related to circumstantial factors that make the conversion of action preparedness (general or specific) into actual participation less likely. Mobilization attempts, incentives, and barriers do not occur randomly throughout a population, but coincide with characteristics of political opportunity structures, characteristics of movement organizations, campaign characteristics, specific actions, characteristics of individual communities, and social categories. The more favorable the political opportunity structures, the more likely it is that action preparedness will be converted into participation (Duyvendak forthcoming; Koopmans 1995). The more extensive a movement's networks, the more likely it is that individuals will be targeted (Snow, Zurcher, and Ekland-Olson 1990). Sophisticated mobilization techniques increase the likelihood of conversion (Oliver and Marwell 1992). Strategic choices of specific actions influence the balance of costs and benefits (Oberschall 1973; McAdam 1986). Characteristics of communities, such as their social and political composition, help determine incentives for participation (Opp 1988a, 1989b). And persons from different social categories—such as male versus female or young versus old—traditionally differ in their action participation (Barnes and Kaase 1979).

Erosion depends on changing circumstances that undermine existing action preparedness, be it general or specific. Although erosion of support occurs not only in the context of action mobilization—other contexts might be movement decline, changes in public opinion, and issue attention cycles—we limit our inquiry to the erosion of support during action mobilization campaigns. We hypothesize that action mobilization can backfire and produce a reverse effect because it generally polarizes a population—cognitively and socially. *Cognitive* polarization takes place because, in the context of action mobilization, the mobilizing organization's features become especially distinct: Goals and means become pronounced, rhetoric changes, and interactions with opponents become confrontational. Opposing parties argue, previously mild debates sharpen, and latitudes of indifference become smaller and smaller. Opponents and countermovement organizations are often extremely skilled in creating caricatures of the movement and sowing doubt in the hearts of halfhearted sympathizers (Conover and Gray 1983; Mansbridge 1986). Often a movement organization bears within itself the ammunition for a countercampaign (Chafetz and Dworkin 1987).

In other words, action mobilization forces a shift in public discourse: In the media and in informal conversations among citizens, public discourse becomes increasingly focused on campaign issues. As a result, individual citizens and societal actors are forced to take sides.

Action mobilization thus implies *social* polarization, for it splits multi-organizational fields (Klandermans 1989; Rucht and Della Porta forthcoming) into the movement organization's alliance and conflict systems. An individual's social environment becomes rearranged into proponents and opponents of the movement. Most individuals live in a fairly homogeneous social environment and will find themselves unambiguously in one camp or the other, but some may discover that groups, organizations, or parties with which they identify are suddenly in their enemy's camp or that groups and people with whom they feel little affinity have become allies. If they don't like the social identity implied by these new arrangements, they may choose to detach themselves from the movement. In the context of election campaigns, Lazarsfeld, Berelson, and Gaudet (1948:56-64) referred to this process of conflicting identifications as "cross pressure" (see also Lane 1964:197-203).

Data and Methods

The data come from a longitudinal study of the mobilization campaign for the People's Petition against cruise missiles, organized in 1985 by the Dutch peace movement. The People's Petition was the final act of a campaign that had lasted almost 10 years and was able to orchestrate the two largest demonstrations the Netherlands had ever experienced (Oegema 1991; Rochon 1988). The Petition was an attempt to demonstrate once again the movement's maximum strength. In the months preceding November 1, 1985—the day the Dutch government had committed itself to decide on deployment—the movement tried to have a petition against deployment signed by as large a proportion of its constituency as possible. Its organizers estimated—and the polls indicated—that they would be able to win the support of close to 50 percent of the Dutch population 15 years old and older. If they could achieve this goal, the government would be in trouble because a large proportion of its own constituency would be among the signers.

To realize a maximum response, organizers chose an action that made it easy for even marginal sympathizers to support the movement: signing a petition directed at the parliament. Assuming that merely signing a petition required little or no effort, the organizers supposed that all they had to do was to reach everybody who was prepared to support the peace movement. Accordingly, they invested a great deal of effort in a campaign designed to guarantee that no potential supporter would be overlooked. They mailed signature cards to every postal address in the country and made sure that as many homes as possible were visited by activists collecting the cards. A single card could carry up to five signatures. Signed cards could be mailed in or handed to the collectors going from door to door. Five-and-one-half million signature cards were distributed, and an estimated 50,000 volunteers were involved in door-to-door card collection (this number, by the way, was 30,000 short of what the movement had calculated would be necessary [Kriesi and Van Praag 1988]). The campaign proper started on August 31, but from May onward local peace groups were involved in organizing. In many communities these groups made use of the canvassing experience of local political party activists.

In the course of the campaign, the cruise missile issue was hotly debated within and between political parties. The government—composed of the Conservatives and the Christian Democrats—feverishly attempted to formulate a compromise. During the campaign it became clear that, over the preceding two to three years, the peace movement had become an antigovernment coalition, welcoming everyone opposed to the government and the parties in office. As we will see, this development had a significant impact on sympathizers who identified with one of those parties. Meanwhile the movement became more controversial and, occasionally, countermobilization occurred.

Eventually, 3.75 million people signed signature cards. This number constituted 30 percent of the Dutch population 15 years old and older. Although this was an impressive percentage that was possible only because of sophisticated organizing, it was a disappointment to the movement. Thirty percent was too far below their initial goal and also was too low a turnout to unsettle the government. On November 1, 1985 the government did indeed decide to deploy cruise missiles in the Netherlands.

Samples

Between May 23 and June 13, 1995 (at the start of the campaign) we conducted telephone surveys among random samples of the population in four communities from different parts of the Netherlands (sample 1).[2] Those people who in May and June stated that they would sign the petition were interviewed for a second time between November 9 and November 28 (after the campaign was over) so we could ascertain whether they did in fact sign. Unless otherwise specified, all analyses are based on sample 1. However, we also selected a second sample that consisted of individuals who were interviewed only in November (sample 2). We use this second sample occasionally to control for the effect of repeated measurement.

For both samples 1 and 2, 100 addresses were randomly drawn from the most recent telephone directories for each of the four selected communities. A letter was mailed to each address explaining that the residents would be contacted by telephone for an interview regarding peace, disarmament, and the peace movement. As it turned out, 16 cases in sample 1 (May/November) and 9 in sample 2 (November only) no longer belonged to the population (they had moved to another town or their phone had been disconnected); thus our net sample sizes were 384 and 391 respectively. We achieved response rates of 58 percent (224 cases) and 61 percent (231 cases) respectively for the two samples; for both samples we could not arrange interviews for 160 addresses. Of these, 11 percent in the first sample (8 percent in the second) proved impossible to contact. We were able to reach the remaining 89 percent (92 percent), but for various reasons they were not able or willing to interviewed: 17 percent (15 percent) were not in good health or were too old; 12 percent (12 percent) had no time; 11 percent (11 percent) were opposed to interviews in general; 4 percent (15 percent) disliked the topic; 30 percent (20 percent) mentioned some other reason; and 15 percent (19 percent) refused without giving any clear reason. The resulting samples are, of course, not random samples of the entire Dutch population. But we were interested, not in assessing the extent of popular support of the peace movement in the Netherlands (see Oegema 1991; and Rochon 1988 for such estimates), but in the rate of petition-signing among supporters of the movement and in opinion changes that occurred over time among supporters. A comparison of the two resulting samples revealed that they did not differ significantly in terms of such variables as age, level of education, and party identification. There was, however, a significant difference in gender composition (49 percent male in May, 59 percent in

November, $F = 4.84$, $p = .03$). We adjusted our repeated measurement tests for this sample bias.

The interviews took place between 6:30 p.m. and 10:00 p.m. At each address the interviewer asked to speak to the person whose birthday was closest to the interview date and who was older than 17 years. If necessary, the interviewer made an appointment to call again later. If no contact was established after four attempts, the address was given up. Interviews lasted 20 minutes on average, and we followed a structured questionnaire format.

The 154 respondents from sample 1 who in May/June announced that they planned to sign the petition were approached again in November for a follow-up interview. Eighty-six percent (132) responded. In 22 cases a second interview could not be arranged: 12 of the subjects could not be reached; 10 refused. The nonrespondents did not differ from the respondents on any of the key variables.

Variables

The following sets of variables were included in our analyses:

Participation. (1) *May/June preparedness* to sign a petition against the deployment of cruise missiles. Two groups were distinguished: (a) individuals who were not prepared to sign, and (b) individuals who said they were prepared to sign. (2) *Signing behavior* in November. Here we distinguished three groups: (a) individuals who did not sign and had indicated that they had not wanted to sign, (b) individuals who did not sign but emphasized that they had wanted to sign, (c) individuals who did sign.

Generalized Action Preparedness. (1) Adapting Barnes and Kaase's (1979) action potential scale, we constructed a measure of generalized preparedness to participate in peace movement activities. Unlike Barnes and Kaase, however, we employed partial credit modeling (Masters 1982) rather than Gutman-scaling to construct a *generalized action preparedness scale* (GAP-scale) for the peace movement (Prins 1990). The GAP-scale indicates an individual's willingness to participate in peace movement activities on a continuum from modest action (signing a petition) to violent action (sabotage). (2) As noted earlier, theoretically, generalized action preparedness is a function of grievances and the individual's evaluation of the movement. In the case of the peace movement, concern about the nuclear arms race rather than firsthand experiences or instances of personal harm generated the grievances the movement wanted to redress. Therefore we included a scale to measure concerns about the nuclear arms race constructed from three statements about nuclear armament: "Nuclear arms are needed to guarantee peace"; "I am really concerned about the arms race"; "Would you favor a decision to deploy cruise missiles?" (Cronbach's alpha = .71). (3) The individual's *evaluation of the peace movement* was measured by a scale consisting of four questions, (a) about the movement ("I have a very positive attitude toward the peace movement"); (b) the movement's goals ("I have a very positive attitude toward the goals of the peace movement"); (c) the movement's activities ("I am fully endorsing the activities of the peace movement"); and (d) the people in the movement ("I feel strongly akin to the people in the peace movement") (Cronbach's alpha = .86).

Specific Action Preparedness. From Klandermans's (1984a) participation model we inferred the following variables related to preparedness to sign the People's Petition: (1) *agreement with the petition's goal* (preventing deployment of cruise missiles); the reaction of significant others—(2) in May/June, the *expected reactions* if one were to sign ("How would people who are important to you, such as members of your family and friends, respond if you signed the petition?" [positive, negative, indifferent]), and (3) in November, the *experienced reactions* to one's signing or not signing ("How did people who are important to you, such as members of your family and friends, respond to your signing of the petition?" [positive, negative, indifferent]).

The Presence of Barriers. In each community, organizers offered the population a number of opportunities to sign the petition. Signature cards were distributed by mail, cards were available at stands in shopping areas, a card collector could call at the door, and so on. If by chance none of these opportunities were available (the person was not a target of the mobilization attempt), a person had no choice but to try to find his or her own way to sign. In a campaign that required as modest an effort as signing a petition, this was the only barrier we could think of.

Perceived Social Environment. Although the characteristics of one's social environment are reflected in the expected and experienced reactions of significant others, we included three additional perceived characteristics in our analyses, as it was our assumption that characteristics of the environment and changes in the environment are important factors in nonconversion and erosion. These three characteristics are: (1) the *perceived opinion of the peace movement* among people in one's environment, (2) the *expected number of one's acquaintances who would sign* (in May/June), and the *perceived number of acquaintances who did sign* (in November),[3] and (3) the extent to which *cruise missiles were discussed within one's environment by others and by oneself.*

Left Party Identification. In the Netherlands the political parties can be placed on a left-right continuum. For our analyses we have combined the small rightist and leftist parties in two clusters. The result is the following continuum (from the political right to the political left): radical rightist parties, Conservatives (VVD), Christian Democrats (CDA), Centre Democrats (D'66), Social Democrats (PVDA), and radical leftist parties. In some analyses the first two parties are combined into "right-wing parties" and the last three are combined into "left-wing parties." All political parties had clear opinions on the cruise issue (right-wing and Christian Democrats favored deployment, the left wing opposed it).

Demographic Variables. Demographic measures included *age,* level of *education,* and *sex.*

Controlling for Repeated Measurement

Because our research question concerned changes over time it was crucial that we eliminate repeated measurement as an alternative explanation for observed difference: between May and November (Campbell and Stanley 1963). We did this by comparing samples 1 and 2. None of our tests suggested any effect of repeated measurement: Levels of signing were virtually the same in the two samples, and those individuals in the May sample who signed did not differ from the signers in the November-only sample with respect to any of the key variables; similar proportions of the two samples indicated their intention to sign, and those from the May sample who had wanted to sign did not differ from those who had wanted to sign in the November sample with respect to any of the key variables. Moreover, logistic regression analyses of the November correlates to

signing and nonsigning revealed identical determinants in the May sample and November sample. We thus concluded that repeated measurement could be ruled out as an alternative explanation for any of our findings. Accordingly, we could safely conduct our study of nonconversion and erosion using the interviews in May/June and November using sample 1 alone.

Results

We present our results from two different angles. First, we describe the respondents' preparedness to sign in May/June and their subsequent reports of signing in November and try to distinguish erosion from nonconversion. Next we explain why some of those individuals who in May/June said they would sign ultimately failed to do so.

Figure 2
Preparedness to Sign a Petition Against the Deployment of Cruise Missiles and Actual Petition Signing: Respondents to Telephone Interviews, the Netherlands, 1985

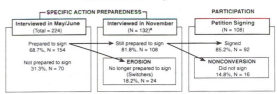

[a] Of the 154 respondents in May/June, 22 were not available for interviews in November.

Preparedness to Sign and Actual Signing

Figure 2 presents the basic parameters of our results. In May/June, at the start of the campaign, over 68.7 percent of our respondents ($N = 224$) were prepared to sign; among the respondents from this group that were interviewed in November ($N = 132$), 19.2 percent had changed their minds and indicated that they no longer wanted to sign (we refer to these respondents as "switchers"). The other 91.9 percent remained prepared to sign ("nonswitchers"). Of those who maintained their preparedness ($N = 108$), 14.9 percent failed to sign ("nonsigners"); the remaining 85.2 percent did indeed sign ("signers"). In other words, 69.6 percent of those who were prepared to sign in May/June and were later interviewed in November ($N = 132$) did in fact sign the petition. The remaining 30.3 percent, who despite their initial preparedness to sign did not do so, consists

Table 1
Not Prepared, Erosion, and Nonconversion: Three Forms of Nonparticipation in Signing Among Respondents to
Telephone Interviews, the Netherlands, 1985

Independent Variable	N	Percent							
		Not Prepared	+	Erosion	+	Nonconverison	=	Nonsigning
Total	224	31.2	+	12.5	+	8.3	=	52.0
Sex								
Male	109	30.3	+	10.9	+	13.1	=	54.3
Female	113	31.8	+	14.3	+	4.0	=	50.1
Age								
<31	51	21.6	+	16.5	+	12.4	=	50.5
31-39	66	18.2	+	12.8	+	7.2	=	38.2
40-56	58	37.9	+	10.4	+	10.3	=	58.6
>56	48	50.0	+	10.6	+	2.6	=	63.2
Communities								
Zuiderstad	62	24.8	+	12.1	+	2.8	=	39.7
Randstad	63	27.0	+	10.4	+	8.4	=	45.8
Kleinoord	50	30.0	+	16.5	+	12.3	=	58.8
Grootland	49	46.9	+	11.2	+	11.2	=	69.3
Party Identification								
Conservatives	38	69.7	+	12.1	+	9.1	=	90.9
Christian Democrats	49	47.1	+	20.7	+	10.7	=	78.5
Left-wing	93	5.4	+	5.0	+	8.1	=	18.5

Note: For these computations, the 22 respondents who could not be interviewed again are presumed to have the same distributions as those interviewed twice.

of individuals representing the two processes: nonconversion (those who said they wanted to sign but failed to do so—12.1 percent of those prepared to sign and who were re-interviewed in November) and erosion (switchers who deliberately did not sign—18.2 percent).

When we introduced the concepts of erosion and nonconversion we hypothesized that different subpopulations would manifest different rates of erosion and of nonconversion. In Table 1 we compare several subpopulations. As expected, nonsigning in these subpopulations could be attributed to strikingly different factors.

Sex. In May/June the number of male and female respondents who were not prepared to sign was virtually the same, but in the course of the campaign the proportions changed. Had the change been caused only by erosion, more females than males would have refrained from signing—an outcome that would have been in line with the literature on action participation (Barnes and Kaase 1979). But due to a low level of nonconversion—very few women who wanted to sign failed to do so—the reverse happened: More males than females failed to sign.

Age. Consistent with the general finding that young people are more likely to take part in col-

lective action than are old people (Barnes and Kaase 1979), we found a highly significant correlation between age and preparedness to sign. But because each of the four age cohorts in Table 1 manifested a different pattern of erosion and nonconversion, this correlation did not remain when it came to actual signing. Although among the second group (ages 31 to 39) we found the expected low percentage of nonsigning, the high levels of erosion and nonconversion in the youngest age group, and the very low level of nonconversion in the oldest age group compensated for the differences in preparedness to sign reported in May/June.

Community. The four selected communities followed strikingly different routes to nonsigning. This pattern coincides remarkably well with our knowledge of the local campaigns. The most successful campaign was that in Zuiderstad. An average degree of erosion combined with an extremely low level of nonconversion produced the lowest proportion of nonsigning respondents in any of the four communities. Indeed, Zuiderstad had the highest number of card collectors relative to its population size, a fact that accounts for the very low level of nonconversion there. Comparing Zuiderstad with Kleinoord is illuminating. In

May/June the proportions of the samples in the two communities which were not prepared to sign were similar. In November, however, almost 60 percent of the original sample in Kleinoord did not sign, as compared to 40 percent in Zuiderstad. The low support in Kleinoord was the result of a high level of erosion combined with a relatively high level of nonconversion. The high degree of erosion in Kleinoord is undoubtedly related to the intense countercampaign conducted in that community. In Grootland, the community with the highest proportion of Conservatives and Christian Democrats of the four communities, the number of people not prepared to sign was initially high. In addition, the anticruise missile campaign conducted there was relatively weak. Grootland, in fact, had the lowest number of card collectors relative to population size of the four communities. Thus, Grootland had the lowest turnout of the four communities: Two-thirds of the respondents ended up not signing the petition.

From a theoretical standpoint, these four communities illustrate the separate processes of erosion and nonconversion. First, the proportion of respondents prepared to sign in May/June differed significantly from one community to another, largely because the political composition of the population of the four communities differed. Second, the one community in which a vigorous countercampaign emerged had the highest degree of erosion. Third, the community with the most sophisticated and elaborate campaign had the lowest level of nonconversion. In other words, different characteristics of the four communities accounted for different effects of the process of action mobilization.

Party Identification. As expected, we found widely divergent patterns among the constituencies of the main political currents in the country—the right, the Christian Democrats, and the left. Not surprisingly, the turnout among the three constituencies varied dramatically: 90 percent of the respondents from the right and more than 75 percent of the Christian Democrats did not sign the petition. Among the respondents on the left, however, fewer than 20 percent failed to sign. Clearly, these results have their origins in the beginning of the campaign: In May, two-thirds of the right, almost one-half of the Christian Democrats, but only one-twentieth of those on the left were not prepared to sign. Then, during the campaign, erosion and nonconversion combined to produce the divergent patterns reflected in the November results. Most striking are the differences in erosion among the constituencies of the three political groups. Twenty-one percent of the Christian Democrats who initially supported the petition withdrew their support, compared to only 5 percent of the left. Proportionally, loss of support due to nonconversion was about equal for all three political groups.

Determinants of Preparedness, Erosion, and Nonconversion

The remainder of our analysis concentrates on three questions: (1) Why were some people prepared to sign the petition while others were not? (2) Why did some of the respondents who, in May, were willing to sign, eventually change their minds? (3) Why did some of those respondents who in November maintained their willingness to sign the petition ultimately fail to sign it? Thus framed, our research questions are akin to the multiple kinds of events Allison (1985) has dis-

Table 2
Logit Coefficients for Regression of Preparedness to Sign a Petition in May/June on Selected Independent Variables: Responses to Telephone Interviews, the Netherlands, 1985

Independent Variables	Model 1	Model 2
Constant	−5.24***	1.94
Demographic Variables		
Female	.02	−.18
	(.19)	(.26)
Age	−.04***	−.02
	(.01)	(.02)
Education	.07	−.08
	(.08)	(.11)
Left Party Identification	1.20***	.31
	(.23)	(.28)
Generalized Action Preparedness Scale	—	2.07***
		(.45)
Agreement With Goal	—	1.24***
		(.30)
Likelihood Ratio	180.73	106.24
Degrees of Freedom	214	212
Change in Likelihood Ratio	90.61	74.49
Degrees of Freedom	4	2
P-Value of Likelihood Test	.000	.000
Number of Observations	219	219

***p<.001 (two-tailed tests)
Note: Numbers in parentheses are standard errors. Preparedness is coded so that positive coefficients indicate that a higher level of the independent variable is associated with increased odds of being prepared to sign.

cussed as being appropriate for modeling with a sequence of binomial logit analyses.

Prepared to Sign Versus Not Prepared. Table 2 presents the results of two logistic regressions of preparedness versus nonpreparedness to sign the petition on two categories of independent variables. Model 1 confirms our previous results.

The respondents who were not prepared to sign were older than those who were prepared to sign. With respect to political affiliation, the further to the right the respondents were, the less inclined they were to want to sign. The fit of the model indicates that on the basis of age and political affiliation alone, we can predict fairly accurately the odds of preparedness and nonprepared-

ness to sign. Model 2, which includes the attitudinal determinants, not only improves the fit considerably but renders both age and party identification insignificant. In other words, age and party identification are related to signing *because* people who were generally prepared to take action on behalf of the peace movement and who were against deployment of cruise missiles were younger and more often identified with the political left. Altogether, the results of the final model are fairly straightforward: People were not willing to sign the petition because they were in general not prepared to take action on behalf of the peace movement and because they were not against the deployment of cruise missiles. Note that attitude

Table 3
Logit Coefficients for Regression of Nonswitching and Signing on Selected Independent Variables:
Respondents to Telephone Interviews, the Netherlands, 1985

Independent Variables	Nonswitching			Signing (Among Nonswitchers)		
	Model 1	Model 2	Model 3	Model 1	Model 2	Model 3
Constant	−3.71*	.75	2.04	−4.97*	−3.33	−8.37*
	(1.71)	(2.23)	(2.82)	(2.44)	(2.96)	(4.22)
Demographic Variables						
Female	.01	−.43	−.05	.65	.44	1.51*
	(.26)	(.30)	(.41)	(.35)	(.37)	(.67)
Age	.01	.02	.02	.03	.04	.05
	(.02)	(.02)	(.02)	(.03)	(.03)	(.04)
Education	.11	−.03	.04	.16	.10	.25
	(.11)	(.15)	(.19)	(.13)	(.16)	(.22)
Party Identification (Left)	.76***	−.14	.17	.83**	.49	.97
	(.24)	(.32)	(.41)	(.32)	(.37)	(.52)
May/June						
Generalized Action Preparedness Scale	—	2.32***	—	—	.89	—
		(.72)			(.72)	
Expected Positive Reactions of Others	—	.80**	—	—	.89	—
		(.32)			(.35)	
Agreement With Goals	—	.56	—	—	.65	—
		(.43)			(.50)	
November						
Generalized Action Preparedness Scale	—	—	2.15*	—	—	.89
			(.90)			(.72)
Expected Positive Reactions of Others	—	—	1.52**	—	—	.77
			(.52)			(.60)
Agreement With Goals	—	—	.91	—	—	.29
			(.55)			(.84)
Presence of Barriers	—	—	−.45	—	—	−2.75**
			(.82)			(.88)
Likelihood Ratio	95.64	66.69	46.84	65.57	60.22	37.19
Degrees of Freedom	116	113	112	96	93	92
Change in Likelihood Ratio	12.86	28.95	19.79	11.97	5.37	22.06
Degrees of Freedom	4	3	1	4	3	1
P-Value of Likelihood Test	.01	.000	.000	.02	.15	.000
Number of Observations	121	121	121	101	101	101

*$p<.05$ **$p<.01$ ***$p<.001$ (two-tailed tests)
Note: Numbers in parentheses are standard errors. Switching and signing are coded so that positive coefficients indicate that a higher level of the independent variable is associated with increased odds of nonswitching or signing.

toward deployment contributes to the explanation of preparedness independent of generalized action preparedness. This finding is important because it indicates that it was not just general commitment to a movement that made people willing to sign the petition, but also dedication to a specific cause.

As the campaign was designed to activate sympathizers rather than persuade opponents, the canvassers made no attempt to change peoples' minds. Indeed, only two individuals who were not prepared to sign in May/June changed their minds and ended up signing.

Switching Versus Nonswitching. Our next set of logistic analyses explores the determinants of erosion. The first three columns in Table 3 displays the logit coefficients for regression of switching versus nonswitching on the independent variables as measured in May/June and November. Model 1 indicates that erosion was more likely among people who identified with parties on the right. If we refer to our observations in Table 1, we find that the respondents primarily responsible for this outcome are those who identify with the Christian Democratic Party. Model 2, however, indicates that the differences in generalized action preparedness and the expected reactions of significant others related to party identification account for most of the observed impact of party identification. Model 2 improves on the first model, implying that individuals who indicated a lower level of generalized action preparedness in May/June and also expected less supportive reactions from significant others in May/June were more likely to switch.

In Model 3 the May/June parameters are replaced by the November parameters. This model represents a considerable improvement over Model 2. The basic pattern yielded by the November data is similar to that produced by the data collected in May/June: In terms of generalized action preparedness, switchers and nonswitchers are dispersed, whereas in terms of the reaction of significant others, their experiences fit their May/June expectations. Note that switching is not related to the presence of barriers.

Signing Versus Nonsigning. Not everyone who was prepared to sign the petition did eventually sign. Nonconversion occurred among 15 percent of those who remained willing to sign. The last three columns in Table 3 examine the determinants of such nonconversion. Model 1 reveals

the significance of party identification. The odds of nonconversion were higher among people who identified with parties on the right. Model 2 does not improve the fit; that is, in May/June nonsigners and signers did not differ in terms of generalized action preparedness, expected reactions of significant others, or attitudes toward deployment. Model 3, however, implies a substantial improvement over Model 2. It is theoretically important that neither generalized action preparedness nor attitude toward deployment nor the expected or experienced reactions of significant others affected petition signing. Hence, it is not changing attitudes or environments that produce nonconversion. The most important determinant is whether an individual has been the target of mobilization attempts, or, by implication, has encountered barriers to participation. Interestingly, when controlling for the other parameters, respondent's sex makes a difference: The degree of nonconversion was lower among women than among men—not, as one might hypothesize, because women were targeted more often than men. Our results indicate that, regardless of whether they were targeted, women who were prepared to sign did so more often than men who said they were prepared to sign. Among male respondents, however, those who were not targeted failed to sign more often than those who were. The effect of gender that we already encountered in Table 1, then, appears to hold in multivariate analysis.

Finally, a comparison of nonswitchers and signing nonswitchers in Table 3 reveals theoretically meaningful differences between the two configurations of determinants. The first three columns display an expanding attitudinal gap between switchers and nonswitchers together with their increasingly divergent perceptions of the social environment. Nothing of the kind is apparent in the second two columns. To be sure, nonconversion was more likely among respondents who identified with right-wing parties, but it was predominantly the lack of mobilization attempts among these groups that determined their nonsigning. This conclusion is supported by two analyses not reported in Table 3. A model (not shown) that included both the May/June and November parameters revealed a fit significantly better than that produced by Model 3 in the case of switching versus nonswitching (change in likelihood ratio = 15.76, d.f. = 3, p .001). The fit, however, does not change in the case of nonsigning versus signing. In other words, the odds of switching—unlike the odds of signing—were affected by changing circumstances between May/June and November.[4]

In sum, for respondents who, at the start of the campaign, intended to sign the petition we registered reports of actual signing among those who still intended to sign at the end of the campaign. Our objective was, of course, to determine the extent to which intentions expressed in May/June could predict actual signing. In the absence of erosion and nonconversion, intentions expressed in May would be perfect predictors of actual signing and other variables measured at later times would fail to improve our models. In fact, our assessment that almost one-third of those who intended to

sign in May/June and who were also interviewed in November; $N = 132$) failed to do so because of erosion or nonconversion (see Figure 2), already implies less than perfect prediction. Indeed, the results demonstrate that determinants measured in May/June *did* predict signing and nonsigning. But, the results reveal also that determinants as measured in May/June are not sufficient predictors of the eventual outcomes—not in the case of erosion and definitely not in the case of nonconversion. Interestingly, erosion and nonconversion each has its own configuration of predictors: for erosion, generalized action preparedness as measured in May/June and November, and expected and experienced reactions of significant others: for nonconversion, respondent's sex, and the ab-

Table 4

Logit Coefficients for Regression of Nonswitching and Signing on Concerns Over Nuclear Arms Race and Four Measures of Appreciation of the Peace Movement: Respondents to Telephone Interviews, the Netherlands, 1985

Independent Variable	Nonswitching		Signing (Among Nonswitchers)	
	Model 1	Model 2	Model 1	Model 2
Constant	−2.01*	1.34	−.69	.99
	(.82)	(.65)	(1.17)	(.65)
May/June				
Concerns About Nuclear Arms	1.42**	—	1.75**	—
	(.46)		(.55)	
Evaluation of Peace Movement				
Appreciation of Peace Movement	1.47	—	.77	—
	(.50)		(.54)	
of goals	.76	—	.07	—
	(.42)		(.60)	
of activities	.33	—	.47	—
	(.33)		(.36)	
of people	−1.08**	—	−.49	—
	(.41)		(.40)	
November				
Concerns About Nuclear Arms	—	1.13*	—	1.34*
		(.48)		(.58)
Evaluation of the Peace Movement				
Appreciation of the Peace Movement	—	.35	—	−.38
		(.36)		(.49)
of goals	—	−.20	—	−.02
		(.36)		(.43)
of activities	—	−.23	—	.66
		(.34)		(.40)
of people	—	1.38**	—	.02
		(.47)		(.40)
Likelihood Ratio	81.67	66.43	62.96	64.69
Degrees of Freedom	114	114	92	92
Change in Likelihood Ratio	32.67	47.91	17.42	−15.42
Degrees of Freedom	5	5	5	5
P-Value of Likelihood Test	.000	.000	.004	.01
Number of Observations	120	120	98	98

*$p<.05$ **$p<.01$ (two-tailed tests)

Note: Numbers in parentheses are standard errors. Switching and signing are coded so that positive coefficients inidicate that a higher level of the independent variable is associated with increased odds of nonswitching or signing.

sence of mobilization. In other words, changes in the determinants of signing during the campaign produced a rate of signing different from what one would have expected given the values of these determinants in May/June.

For switchers the results confirm an interpretation that nonsigning occurred because of erosion of support. A generalized action preparedness that was no more than moderate at the start of the campaign eroded; moreover, these respondents changed their minds in the context of a social environment they perceived as becoming less supportive of signing the petition.

Nonconversion is the most plausible interpretation of nonsigning for those who maintained their willingness to sign. Unlike the switchers, the nonswitchers failed to sign because of an absence

of mobilization attempts rather than a change of mind.

Declining Generalized Action Preparedness and Unsupportive Social Environments

A decline in generalized action preparedness and an unsupportive social environment appear to correlate with erosion; for nonconversion, however, the correlate was an absence of mobilization attempts.

Declining Generalized Action Preparedness. The decline in generalized action preparedness is elaborated further in Table 4. Theoretically, generalized action preparedness for a movement is a function of the population's appreciation of the movement and the intensity of the grievances the movement seeks to redress. We trans-

Table 5
Logit Coefficients for Regression of Nonswitching and Signing on Five Measures of Perceived Social Environment

Independent Variable	Nonswitching		Signing (Among Nonswitchers)	
	Model 1	Model 2	Model 1	Model 2
Constant	−23	.83	3.92	−4.35
	(1.30)	(1.56)	(1.69)	(1.56)
May/June				
Expected Positive Reactions of Others	.76*	—	.72a	—
	(.32)		(.37)	
Perceived Positive Opinion of Peace Movement	.36	—	−.45	—
	(.35)		(.42)	
Expected Number of Acquaintances Who Would Sign	.62	—	−.61	—
	(.48)		(.56)	
Cruise Missiles Discussed in Environment	−.22	—	.05	—
	(.54)		(.67)	
Did Discuss Cruise Missiles Recently	.82	—	.07	—
	(.59)		(.59)	
November				
Expected Positive Reactions of Others	—	1.34*	—	.11
		(.50)		(.52)
Perceived Positive Opinion of Peace Movement	—	.14	—	−1.15
		(.42)		(.74)
Number of Acquaintances Who Signed	—	1.03	—	2.80**
		(.66)		(.93)
Number of Acquaintances Who Signed Unknown	—	−1.05	—	−2.32
		(.80)		(1.03)
Cruise Missiles Discussed in Environment	—	−.59	—	−1.28
		(.84)		(.96)
Did Discuss Cruise Missiles Recently	—	1.29	—	2.09*
		(.84)		(1.10)
Likelihood Ratio	92.03	70.05	71.63	49.56
Degrees of Freedom	110	109	98	88
Change in Likelihood Ratio	17.70	38.92	4.22	26.28
Degrees of Freedom	5	6	5	6
P-Value of Likelihood Test	.003	.000	.519	.000
Number of Observations	116	116	95	95

*$p<.05$ **$p<.01$ a$.10>p>.05$ (two-tailed tests)
Note: Numbers in parentheses are standard errors. Switching and signing are coded so that positive coefficients indicate that a higher level of the independent variable is associated with increased odds of nonswitching or signing.

lated "grievances" into concern over the nuclear arms race and divided "appreciation for the peace movement" into three elements: appreciation of goals, of activities, and of people. In Table 4, switchers and nonswitchers and signers and non-signers are once again compared, here in terms of these antecedents of general action preparedness.

These logistic regression analyses confirm our argument and provide some important supplementary details. Even in May/June, switchers were less concerned about the nuclear arms race and less positive about the peace movement than were nonswitchers (Model 1). Interestingly, the sign of the logit for the respondents' appreciation of the people in the movement is negative. Indeed, in May/June switchers and nonswitchers were more alike in their attitudes toward the people in the movement than in their appreciation of any other aspects of the movement. In Model 2 the measures for November are entered in the equation, and they produce a considerable improvement of fit, which can be attributed to concerns over the nuclear arms race and the appreciation of the people in the movement, but this time with a *positive* sign. Apparently, during the campaign the initially relatively positive feelings among switchers toward the people in the movement changed into strongly negative ones: In November they no longer felt any sympathy for the people in the movement. This factor, together with their already less than positive feelings toward other aspects of the peace movement, contributed to their change of mind.

The second two columns of Table 4 reveal a completely different picture, which underscores our argument regarding nonconversion. In May/June signers were more concerned about the nuclear arms race than nonsigners, and in November that was still the case. Except for this one difference the two group are similar in all respects in May/ June as well as in November. This finding underlines the distinction between erosion and nonconversion as two theoretically separate forms of nonparticipation.

Unsupportive Social Environments. As indicated, unlike nonswitchers, switchers perceived their social environment as increasingly unsupportive. Table 5 refines this observation by specifying particular characteristics of the respondents' social environment: perceived opinions in their environment, expected and reported signing by

acquaintances, and discussions on cruise missiles with individuals in their environment.

In May/June nonswitchers expected more supportive reactions for signing than did switchers. Similarly, at that time signers expected more supportive reactions than nonsigners. As for the other characteristics, the two groups experienced similar social environments in May/June. Five months later the situation changed. The social environment of switchers and nonswitchers and of nonsigners and signers became increasingly disparate. For switchers and nonswitchers a difference materialized in changes in experienced reactions of significant others—they became even less supportive of signing than had been expected a few months before (means for switchers in May/June was −.73 and in November it was −1.05, as compared to .12 and .24 for nonswitchers).

Among the nonswitchers, signers and non-signers experienced different changes in their social environments. In November perceived reactions of significant others no longer influenced the individual's actions. The actual signing by acquaintances and awareness of actual signing became more important, as did the extent to which cruise missiles were discussed in one's environment. As for actual signing, signers knew the rate of signing among their acquaintances and reported that most of their acquaintances signed. Nonsigners, however, were either not aware of the rate of signing by their acquaintances or reported low rates of signing. As for discussions on cruise missiles, signers more often discussed cruise missiles with people in their environment than did nonsigners. Indeed, if we compare the means, nonsigners were in the only groups that did *not* report an increase in discussions (means for switchers: .83 [May/June] and 1.17 [November] for discussions in their environments and .79 [May/June] and .92 [November] for discussing themselves; means for signers: 1.15 [May/June] and 1.65 [November] and 1.24 [May/June] and 1.65 [November]; means for nonsigners: 1.06 [May/June] and 1.06 [November] and 1.06 [May/June] and .88 [November]).

Not included in Table 5 are two additional findings. Among the respondents who signed, two-thirds could cite at least one active member of the peace movement among his or her acquaintances, whereas among those who switched positions the proportion was a little less than and among those who planned to sign but didn't, the proportions was one-third.

Party identification is the last element in the social environment we consider. Three-quarters of those who turned away from the peace movement identified with the Conservatives or Christian Democrats, the two parties that were in office at the time and which constituted a government determined to deploy cruise missiles. It was among supporters of these two parties in particular that initial sympathy for the peace movement eventually evaporated (difference between May/June and November was −.49 as compared to .13 for the remaining respondents; $F = 3.52, p < .01$).

In summary, erosion occurred predominantly among sympathizers who identified with one of the two political parties in power in the government. These individuals reported that their social environments became less supportive during the antimissile campaign, and because their support was only lukewarm to begin with, the increasingly negative environment undermined their motivation to sign (as shown by lower values on such variables as positive evaluation of the peace movement and rejection of cruise missiles). Interestingly, these individuals reported an increase in the number of their personal conversations about cruise missiles. This increase and the fact that their decision *not* to sign evoked supportive reactions from significant others are evidence of social pressure. We emphasize, however, that it is the *combined* impact of these factors that accounts for erosion. Identification with one of the two parties in government was not in itself sufficient to produce erosion—after all, three-fifths of those who identified with one of the parties had wanted to sign or did indeed sign. Rather, the turnabout from sympathizer to switcher was the result of a combination of factors: identification with one of the two parties; the perception that one's environment did not support the movement; plus, initially, the expectation, and later, the experience, of negative reactions from significant others, which weakened an already halfhearted motivation.

Nonconversion, too, can be linked to characteristics of the individual's social environment, but in a different way. It was not social pressure but the lack of it that was responsible for the failure to sign of "nonconverts." These individuals were only moderately supportive throughout the campaign, thus the minor barrier of not having been offered the opportunity to sign sufficed to

discourage them from signing. Their social environment was conducive to such an outcome: For instance, only one-third of these individuals could identify one or more movement activists among their acquaintances, and contrary to the general trend they reported a decline in the number of conversations about cruise missiles. They were not affected by the campaign and did little to put themselves in situations where they would be.

Discussion

Social movement organizations repeatedly face the challenge of converting action preparedness into active participation. But willingness to participate, as we found, is no guarantee of actual involvement: The absence of mobilization attempts, the presence of barriers, and/or an unsupportive social environment may ultimately prevent a person from participating (for similar findings, see Ajzen and Fishbein [1980] and Granberg and Holmberg [1988]).

Patterns of nonconversion and erosion appear to vary across subpopulations. Counter to the general finding that women participate in collective action less often than men (Barnes and Kaase 1979, but see Wallace and Jenkins forthcoming), we found that women signed the peace petition more frequently than men. As the campaign proceeded women seemed to become more sensitive to the controversial tone that gradually marked public discourse, as witnessed by a higher degree of erosion. But, this trend was more than offset by a high degree of conversion among women. In addition, men who were not targeted by the campaign failed more often than women to overcome this barrier. Similarly, the combined impact of erosion and conversion nullified the traditionally negative correlation between age and active participation. And with respect to political party identification, cross pressure (Lazarsfeld et al. 1948) produced high degrees of erosion among adherents of the Christian Democratic Party. Finally, our comparison of four communities emphasizes the differential impact of the intensity of campaigns and countercampaigns: An intense mobilization campaign in one community produced high levels of conversion; an intense countercampaign in another community produced high levels of erosion.

Our results reveal mobilization to be a complicated process in which preexisting levels of action preparedness, characteristics of mobilization campaigns and countercampaigns, and characteristics of the individual's social environment interact to determine movement participation. When preexisting levels of preparedness are high, even poor campaigns can be effective. Low levels of action preparedness, however, require elaborate campaigns, because prospective supporters need more incentives to join and are more susceptible to countercampaigns. Effective mobilization campaigns have low rates of nonconversion especially in the context of a supportive social environment; effective countercampaigns produce high degrees of erosion, and are especially successful in a context of a nonsupportive social environment.

Paradoxically, these conditions make campaigns designed to mobilize low-risk support (Ennis and Schreuer 1987) more vulnerable to erosion than campaigns for high-risk activities. Because the strength of low-risk campaigns is in the potentially high numbers of participants, they must appeal to as large a proportion of the population as possible, and include marginal sympathizers. The fact that only a low-risk, undemanding act of support is requested does not necessarily make erosion less likely, because the public debate can still be intense, as this petition campaign demonstrated.

Generalized action preparedness could account for a considerable proportion of the differences in the probability of nonsigning versus signing even four months later. But by incorporating specific factors we improved our models substantially. This finding may help resolve the classic question of whether movement participation is a function of relatively stable ideological commitment to a movement or the relatively fluctuating incentives associated with a specific activity (Opp 1989a).

Our findings question once again the importance of the free-rider problem. Recent social movement theory argues that the free-rider problem is not, in fact, a major obstacle for movements that mobilize through community networks and rely on purposive commitment and solidarity (Fireman and Gamson 1979; Klandermans 1988; Oliver and Marwell 1992; Ferree 1992). Even in the case of low-risk forms of action, such as signing a peace petition, levels of action preparedness, friendship networks, weak mobilization attempts, and the presence of barriers seem to be more important than free-rider logic. Indeed, shortfalls occur not so much because sympathizers take a free ride, but because people with moderate levels of action preparedness either lose sympathy for the movement or are embedded in social networks that fail to put their principles into practice (that is, their networks do not impel them to act).

To what extent can we generalize from these findings? Signing a petition is a very minimal act. Although we can expect nonconversion and erosion to occur in most mobilization campaigns, we can assume that different types of action will balance the various factors that lead to nonconversion or erosion in different ways. There was every reason to expect that the petition campaign as a whole would produce extremely low levels of nonconversion. First, it involved a low-risk activity, and one would expect low levels of nonconversion in this case. However, our finding that high expected and experienced rates of signing in an individual's personal environment increased the odds that he or she too would sign is similar to what McAdam (1986) discovered in his study of applicants for the Mississippi Freedom Summer. McAdam explicitly placed his observation in the context of high-risk participation. Our study demonstrates that the same mechanisms work at the opposite end of the scale, in the context of low-risk participation. Second, the petition campaign was extremely well organized and was designed to reach as high a level of conversion as possible. Less well organized campaigns will not reach such high levels, as illustrated by the divergent results of the campaigns in our four communities. Third, the petition campaign was one phase in an extended campaign that had been going on for several years. Consequently, social networks that in other circumstances might have remained indifferent had already been co-opted by the movement. The activity of these networks helped to lower the level of nonconversion.

Note, however, that factors that decrease nonconversion do not necessarily produce lower levels of *erosion*. We assumed that erosion results from the sharpening of loosely defined goals, countercampaigns, and polarization. Because these conditions may accompany even highly effective campaigns, some of the factors that reduce nonconversion may well foster erosion.

Notes

1. Although our tripartite distinction is related to McCarthy and Zald's (1976) distinction between

movement adherents and movement constituents, the two distinctions are not identical: The latter concerns attitudinal support, whereas generalized action preparedness, specific action preparedness, and actual participation all concern action *participation,* be it preparedness to act or actual participation, and the three stages combined can be conceived of as a funneling process in which sympathizers face increasingly intense demands.

2. We applied the same interview strategy we had used in previous studies (Klandermans and Oegema 1987). In the regions where we conducted our field work, telephone density was above 95 percent, so we did not risk much bias by restricting ourselves to addresses that could be reached by phone. To increase response rates, we adopted a strategy suggested by Frey (1983): We sent an introductory letter informing respondents that they would be contacted for an interview. Because we needed the combination of telephone numbers and addresses for this strategy, we used telephone books to determine our samples. This approach had the disadvantage of missing people with unlisted numbers, but the advantage that private numbers could be distinguished from business numbers.

3. The question about the number of acquaintances who signed produced a high proportion of "don't knows" (28.6 percent). Because SPSS logistic regression analysis works with listwise deletion of missing values, we were forced to relate the "don't knows" to our scale from 0 = nobody through 4 = almost everybody, rather than eliminate these respondents. Assigning them to 0 = nobody seriously influenced the outcomes of the analyses. Therefore we chose a more conservative strategy by giving them the mean of those who did know how many in their environment signed.

4. Further confirmation is provided by univariate analyses of the changes in these parameters. Whereas the GAP-scale declined for categories, it dropped most strongly among switchers, and only switchers experienced more reactions from significant others supportive of nonsigning than they had expected. All others experienced more supportive reactions to signing than they had expected. ✦

15

Repression, Micromobilization, and Political Protest

Karl-Dieter Opp
Wolfgang Roehl

It is generally known that repressive acts of state officials (such as those associated with the police, courts, and governments) constraining political protest are important factors in shaping the rise and decline of social movements and individual participation in social movement activities. Also well documented by empirical studies is that the effects of repression vary: increasing repression may promote or impede mobilization processes. There has been little effort, however, to develop propositions that explain *under what conditions* repression advances or inhibits the growth of social movements and participation in protest actions. This article suggests such propositions that focus on individual participation in social movement activities and tests these propositions with data from a panel study of opponents of nuclear power in West Germany. Our concern is not the complex interplay of social movement tactics and more or less repressive reactions by governing regimes. Yet a theory about the effects of repression on individual decisions about whether to take part in social movement activities is a significant element of such a broader issue. "Movements may occur in broad macro context, but their actual development clearly depends on a series of more specific dynamics operating at the micro level" (McAdam 1988b:127). This article focuses on some of these "more specific dynamics," which in turn specify the processes on the microlevel that explain relationships between repression and protest on the macrolevel.

Theory

The major theories explaining political protest make different predictions about the effects of repression on protest. *Deprivation and relative deprivation theory* proposes that "imposed sanctions are deprivations, the threat of sanctions is equivalent to the concept of anticipated deprivation, the innate emotional response to both is anger" (Gurr 1970:238). Its general prediction is that repression of political action raises political protest and thus has a radicalizing effect.

The *resource mobilization perspective* seems to predict that tightening social control impedes the mobilization of protest groups (Oberschall 1973:138,163; see also Barkan 1980a:282; Barkan 1980c:953; Jenkins & Perrow 1977:251; Tilly 1978:114). Yet litigation and civil disobedience may be used by social movements to increase both the commitment of their members and public support, thereby strengthening the movement (Barkan 1980c:948; Gerlach & Hine 1970; Zald & McCarthy 1980). The resource mobilization perspective leaves open what exactly the circumstances are under which repression hinders or promotes the growth of social movements and individual participation in movement activities.

According to the *theory of collective action* (Olson 1965; Hardin 1982; Oliver 1980a) repression is a negative selective incentive. Thus, if adherents of a social movement expect repression for participation, they will be less inclined to participate in social movement activities. This is also the general prediction of rational choice theory upon which the theory of collective action is based (see, e.g., McKenzie & Tullock 1978:189). Yet this prediction rests on the *ceteris paribus* clause, which states that an increase in punishment has a deterrent effect only if no other costs and benefits of the punished behavior change. If this assumption is rejected, different predictions about the effects of repression or punishment can be derived (see, e.g., Cameron 1988; DeNardo 1985).[1]

The results of empirical research about the effects of repression are also inconclusive. In analyses of aggregate data on social unrest and political violence, for example, the relationship between repression (x-axis) and the extent of political violence (y-axis) corresponds to a reversed U-curve (Gurr 1969; Muller 1985; Muller & Seligson 1987; Weede 1987). Other studies, however, do not agree with this result (Hibbs 1973:180-95; see also Weede 1977).

Disparate effects of repression are also reported in case studies. For example, in Barkan's (1984) analysis of the effects of legal control on

"Repression, Micromobilization, and Political Protest." *Social Forces* 69: 521-547. Copyright © 1990 by the University of North Carolina Press. Reprinted with permission.

the Southern civil rights movements, he observed that such repressive acts as arrests or state court injunctions alternately hindered and helped organizing efforts of protest groups (see also Marx 1979:119-23; McAdam 1982,1983; White 1989.) If repression sometimes deters and sometimes radicalizes the participants of political protest, a change in the definition of the problem is necessary. The question should no longer be whether repression has a deterring or a radicalizing effect, but which effect is to be expected under what conditions.

The following hypotheses that address this question proceed from an idea that is most clearly stated in the labeling approach in the sociology of deviant behavior, which is that official negative sanctions promote rather than prevent deviant behavior because sanctions initiate processes of stigmatization that push the norm violator into a deviant career. Legal punishment thus gives rise to social reactions that increase delinquency (see, e.g., Becker 1963; Lemert 1931). In other words, repression frequently has an *indirect* effect on criminal activity by influencing the values of intervening variables that promote behavior. These variables are reactions of the social environment to legal sanctions.

When this hypothesis is applied to protest, labeling theory predicts that official sanctions will result in social processes that raise protest. For example, members of social movements who have been exposed to official sanctions may experience special attention or other positive reactions from protest-promoting groups, yet they may be stigmatized by a large number of others in their social environment. This would push protesters into a "protest career": protest groups would become their reference groups and existing ties would weaken. In extreme cases, "bridge burning" would occur (see Gerlach & Hine 1970; Kornhauser 1962), i.e., previous social ties would be completely cut.

Similar processes have been observed for social movements. DeNardo (1985:191) notes: "When demonstrators become the victims of brutal repression, their movement often gains sympathy and even material support from people who have not suffered directly from the government's excesses." Repression sets in motion *micromobilization processes* that raise the rewards and diminish the costs of participation. These processes are "a structural bridge mediating the relationship between macro political conditions and the individual decision to act on those conditions" (McAdam 1988b:134). Our hypotheses focus on one of these "macro political conditions," namely repression.

In contrast to the labeling perspective, it is also possible that repression sometimes brings about social reactions that endorse the effects intended by repressive agencies. For example, persons convicted for political acts of violence may be sanctioned negatively by their friends.

Aside from the indirect effects of repression, scholars agree that repression is inherently disagreeable for the persons concerned. Repression always has a direct effect on protest: repression is a cost and therefore a negative incentive for protest. This effect is relatively strong if the subjective probability of repression in case of protest is high and if repression is evaluated highly negatively. Whether a deterring or radicalizing effect occurs depends on the strength of the direct and indirect effects of repression.

To arrive at testable propositions about the indirect effects of repression, the kinds of micromobilization processes that could be set off by repressive acts of legal authorities have to be specified. Our hypotheses are summarized in Figure 1. Proceeding from the social movements literature (Fireman & Gamson 1979; Klandermans 1984b; Mitchell 1979; Muller & Opp 1986; Opp 1986, 1989; Tillock & Morrison 1979; Walsh & Warland 1983), we distinguish the following kinds of incentives that may change because of exposure to legal sanctions. First, repression may generate or raise expectations of important others not to abstain from protest but to increase it. Moreover, informal positive sanctions (prestige, approval, or attention granted to persons who have been exposed to repressive acts) may be generated. Expectations of reference persons and positive sanctions are rewards and raise protest.

Yet repression may also generate informal negative sanctions for protest: persons who have been exposed to official sanctions may be shunned by friends or confronted with disadvantages on the job. Such reactions are costs and reduce protest.

Repressive acts may also prompt psychological reactions. DeNardo (1985:192) observed that "the moral distress or disutility created by the regime's repression" increases the likelihood of participation (see also Barkan 1980c:948). Repression may thus be regarded as immoral, and individuals who are exposed to repression or who know about it may feel a moral obligation to support a movement's cause and even to regard violence as justified (White 1989).

Figure 1
A Model Explaining the Effects of Repression

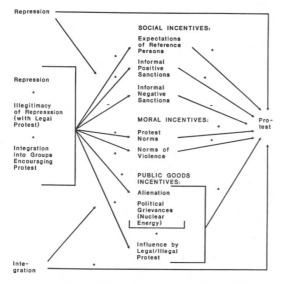

Note: + and - denote proposed positive and negative causal effects;
* denotes a multiplicative relationship.

We differentiate between two types of felt moral obligation to protest. "Protest norms" refers to the extent to which persons think they should participate in protest generally, and "norms of violence" denotes the extent to which persons consider violent protest justified. Acting in accordance with norms or justifications of protest is associated with a good conscience, whereas inaction leads to a bad conscience.

Another psychological reaction to repression may be that citizens "become disillusioned with the established order and can be more easily recruited" (Gerlach & Hine 1970:192; see also Marx 1979:118). Repression may cause system alienation, i.e., discontent with a society's political institutions, which will in turn lead to more protest if persons believe they can change these conditions by means of protest. We thus expect an interaction between alienation and perceived political influence in their effect on protest.

White (1989:1293) found evidence that repression may increase the perceived efficacy of violence in achieving political aims. Later in this

article, we suggest that under certain other conditions repression will also bring about an increase in the perceived efficacy of legal political action.

In sum, repression may affect three types of incentives to protest: *social incentives* (expectations of reference persons and informal positive and negative sanctions), *moral incentives* (protest norms and norms of violence), and *public goods incentives* (system alienation and perceived influence by legal and illegal political action). Because system alienation means that the political order is regarded as a public evil, we can say that repression raises the preference for an alternative political order that is regarded as a public good.[2]

Participation in social movements is also affected by specific grievances or, in terms of the theory of collective action, by specific public goods incentives. For the respondents in the study used to test our model, discontent with nuclear energy is an important grievance conducive to participation in political protest (Opp 1988). Although repression does not change their discontent, because our model includes protest as a dependent variable (see Figure 1), we have to include "discontent with nuclear energy" as a variable that directly affects protest. As for alienation, the strength of the effect of discontent with nuclear energy depends on the perceived influence in reducing the use of nuclear energy by means of legal or illegal protest (see Opp 1988).

Under what conditions will the psychological and social incentives mentioned above be created? The nature of reactions to encounters with authorities depends on the extent to which the activities of authorities are regarded as *legitimate* (Gamson, Fireman & Rytina 1982:26). With regard to repression, Barkan (1980c:948) notes that in the civil rights movement, "legalistic"—as opposed to "violent"—actions of authorities acquired legitimacy and made mobilization less successful (Barkan 1984:562; see also Gurr 1970:238; Marx 1979:118). Thus the micromobilization processes outlined above may be more likely to occur the more repression is considered *illegitimate,* i.e., as unjust or unjustified. We further assume that repression is judged as highly illegitimate if it is directed against *legal* protest actions,[3] which implies that the social and psychological reactions mentioned above will occur more often (or, for informal negative sanctions discussed below, less often) if persons are involved in legal actions before experiencing repression.

Numerous empirical studies have shown that integration into groups supporting the goals of a movement is positively related to group members' protest activities (see, e.g., Oberschall 1973; Opp 1989a; Snow et al. 1980; Useem 1980). These groups are important micromobilization contexts (McAdam 1988b). Accordingly, we assume that micromobilization processes are set off in particular for persons who have been exposed to repression that they and their social environment regard as illegitimate *and* who are integrated into protest-encouraging groups. More specifically, expectations of reference persons to continue or even intensify protest will increase sharply if persons are integrated into protest-encouraging networks because most reference persons will be members of those networks and will empathize with fellow members who have been exposed to repression.

Persons integrated into protest-encouraging networks who are exposed to repression will also be faced with strong positive sanctions from their fellow members. Because highly integrated persons are more involved in protest than those less integrated, however, they frequently interact with persons of other political persuasions. For some of these other persons, official sanctions may indicate that the sanctioned behavior and/or the cause of the group are morally wrong, and they may therefore withhold positive sanctions. But if the general population shares the political aims of a group and if the sanctioned behavior is generally accepted, those exposed to repression will receive more positive reactions outside their group.

As noted, the respondents in the studies we use to test our hypotheses are opponents of nuclear power in West Germany. Opinion polls indicate that the majority of the West German population was skeptical about the use of nuclear energy when the data were collected (see Opp & Roehl 1990b). Since the respondents exposed to repression usually did not perpetrate violence, we predict that for integrated persons exposed to repression, positive sanctions will increase more than they will for less integrated persons, although the differences may be slight.

A similar argument holds for informal negative sanctions: we expect them to change little for integrated persons because although they will receive some negative sanctions outside their group, they will receive few from fellow group members.

Persons not integrated into protest-encouraging groups will usually receive more negative sanctions if they protest. If they are exposed to repression that is generally regarded as illegitimate, however, informal negative sanctions will decline strongly since their actions are legal and their political aims widely shared. Furthermore, norms stating that legal protest is desirable despite the dangers of repression will be strongly advanced by members of protest-promoting groups, and justifications of violence will often be accepted as a reaction to repressive acts.

The extent of system alienation will strongly increase for members of protest-encouraging groups. They will be the first to become skeptical about the functioning of a political system that will not accept what they see as just political aims and that uses illegitimate means to oppress them.

Repression will raise perceived influence by illegal means only for those having employed legal means for a long time without success. They may see repression as an outgrowth of a political system that cannot be changed legally. But in a democratic society in which the public goods that a movement advocates are on the political agenda, repression will usually increase perceived influence by legal means. In particular, persons integrated into protest-encouraging networks will notice that for legal kinds of political actions their mobilization base in the general population expands as a result of increased repression and that opportunities to achieve their political aims through legal forms of protest therefore increase. Because the respondents and groups we are concerned with in our studies primarily participate in and encourage legal forms of protest only,[4] we assume that most of our respondents regard official sanctions as illegitimate.

In sum, whether repression raises protest depends first on the extent to which repression is considered illegitimate. We assume that repressive acts against legal protest are viewed as illegitimate. Second, the effect of repression on protest depends on the extent to which actors are integrated into networks encouraging legal protest. There is thus an interaction effect of the three variables "repression," "illegitimacy of repression," and "integration in protest-promoting groups."

We further assume that repression and integration into protest-encouraging groups have additive effects on the incentive variables. For example, those exposed to repression will usually experience some positive incentives: because they have tried to contribute to the provision of a public good that they believe benefits many others, they should therefore be viewed with respect.

In protest-encouraging networks extensive interpersonal rewards are exchanged which we could not measure with our social incentive variables. We assume that our measure of integration into groups encouraging protest captures some of these kinds of social incentives, and integration is therefore expected to have a direct effect on protest.

Because of the results of dimensional analyses of the data we use to test our model (see the next section), we distinguish between legal and illegal forms of protest. Our measures are composite scales of statements referring to action as well as intention (see the Appendix). To simplify our language, however, we will use the terms legal and illegal protest to cover both actions and intentions.

Research Design and Measurement of Variables

A two-wave panel of opponents of nuclear power, administered in 1982 and 1987, was used to test our model. When the first survey was administered, the antinuclear movement in West Germany was at a low ebb. There were no large-scale activities, just a few isolated actions. This changed dramatically after the nuclear accident at Chernobyl on April 26, 1986.

The second data wave was collected between January and March 1987 after the peak of protest activities, when action was again focused on particular nuclear power stations and a nuclear waste recycling plant under construction in Wackersdorf, a small village in Bavaria.

The first wave consisted of 398 opponents of nuclear power in two locations: a district of Hamburg, where many counterculture people and opponents of nuclear power live (229 interviews), and a small town near Hamburg (Geesthacht), which has an atomic power station nearby (169 interviews). These locations were chosen to get variation in the variables. We interviewed 211 from a snowball sample beginning with a random sample of 187.[5]

Of the first wave, 227 respondents agreed to be reinterviewed, and 121 interviews were completed in 1987. Our panel thus consists of 121 respondents interviewed in both 1982 and 1987. Of the 106 respondents who were not reinterviewed, only 26 refused the second interview. The others could not be located (unknown addresses, $N = 28$; moved, $N = 25$; other reasons, $N = 27$).

Respondents and nonrespondents of the two waves were compared in terms of age, gender, family status, type of school attended, occupational education and position, income, and religious affiliation. Statistically significant differences at the .05 level were obtained for age and income, indicating that low-income and young people were slightly overrepresented among the nonrespondents. This finding can probably be accounted for by the students in the 1982 sample who were relatively mobile.

It is important to keep in mind that this study is not concerned with the representativeness of the opponents of nuclear power in the sample, but with a test of theoretical propositions. For this purpose no representative sample is necessary (see Zetterberg 1965:128-30).

We measured the variables of our model with response scores to various interview statements and questions. A detailed account is given in the Appendix.

Results

Indirect Effects of Repression

After the reactor accident at Chernobyl, several demonstrations against nuclear power plants in West Germany took place in which "hard" police actions occurred, some against peaceful demonstrators. In a public place in Hamburg, for example, more than 800 participants in a demonstration were surrounded by police and kept there for more than 13 hours, until they were arrested. In a later lawsuit this action was declared illegal. In Wackersdorf and other places with nuclear plants, legal demonstrations took place in which many demonstrators were hurt by police.

Respondents were asked to assess these police actions (see Table 1). Their responses provide a direct measure of the impact of repression from their perspective. Since the police actions were directed against persons who had engaged in legal protest, we assume that most of the respondents considered these actions illegitimate. Consequently, we expect the police actions to have had more of a radicalizing than a deterring effect, which is confirmed by the responses to statements 1, 2 and 7 in Table 1, although a slight deterring effect is seen in the responses to statement 3.

Table 1
Reactions of Respondents to Recent Police Actions (1987)

Items	% Agree	% Disagree
Questions Referring to a Deterring Effect		
(1) The police actions deterred me from taking part in demonstrations.	33.1	52.1
(2) I'm downright afraid now to take part in a demonstration.	28.1	50.4
(3) I would advise him[a] to take part in less dangerous actions.	47.9	24.8
Questions Referring to a Radicalizing Effect		
(4) Now I feel more obliged than ever to take action against nuclear power.	57.9	20.7
(5) After these police actions, I have supported others to become active now more than ever.	47.1	36.4
(6) I will participate in demonstrations now more than ever to demonstrate that I won't just accept such police actions.	43.0	31.4
(7) I would go with him[a] to the next demonstration.	40.5	17.4
(8) I would encourage him[a] to keep up his involvement.	75.2	0.0

Note: The difference to 100% corresponds to a response of "undecided."
[a]The question read: "Let's assume one of your friends is arrested in the course of such a police action. How would you react?"

The responses to statement 8 indicate that repression stimulates positive sanctions: 75% of the respondents said that they would encourage a friend who had been arrested by the police to continue protesting. The responses to statement 5 support this result: 47.1% of the respondents replied that they had especially encouraged others to participate in demonstrations following the police actions, while 36.4% replied that they had not. The responses to statements 4 and 6 show that repression activates norms held by the respondents.[6] We also asked our respondents whether they had personally experienced some of the police actions referred to in Table 1, i.e., whether they had been exposed to repression, and ascertained whether the respondents were members in protest-encouraging groups.

Our model assumes an interaction effect of repression and integration into protest-encouraging groups on the incentive variables. To derive the implications of this effect using our dichotomous repression and integration variables, we first address the effects of repression and integration on the *positive* incentive variables. In Figure 2A the x-axis represents the two values of the dichotomous variable "exposure to recent police actions" (no = 0, yes = 1), and the y-axis represents the values of the positive incentive variables (expectations of reference persons, positive sanctions, protest norms, norms of violence, system alienation, influence by legal and illegal protest). According to our model, we predict that the values of the positive incentives *increase* more for integrated than for nonintegrated persons (i.e., the slope of the line representing integrated persons is positive and larger than the slope for noninte-

grated persons). We further expect the incentives to be, on average, larger for integrated than nonintegrated persons (i.e., the intercept of the line for integrated persons should be higher than that for nonintegrated persons).

Responses to statements in Table 1 measuring the effect of repression directly should be similar: respondents who had experienced police actions *and* were integrated into protest-encouraging groups should have felt especially "practicalized." To examine this prediction we constructed a composite measure termed "personal radicalization" by adding each respondent's scores based on their replies to items 4 through 8.

Figure 2A
Exposure to Repression and Positive Incentives: Expected Relationships

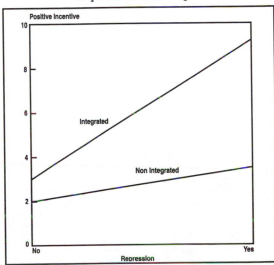

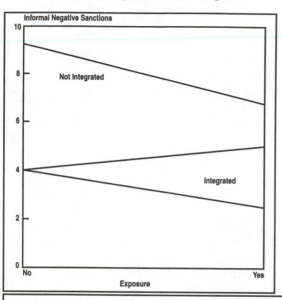

Figure 2B
Exposure to Repression and Informal Negative Sanctions: Expected Relationships

With regard to the interaction effects of repression and integration on informal *negative* sanctions (see Figure 2B), we expect negative sanctions to *decrease* more for persons who are not integrated than for persons who are. For integrated persons the informal negative sanctions should change little (as illustrated by the two lower lines in Figure 2B). Further, nonintegrated persons will usually experience more informal negative sanctions than will those who are integrated (i.e., the intercept of the curve for nonintegrated persons is expected to be higher than for integrated persons).

To test these predictions, we regressed, for nonintegrated and integrated persons separately, each incentive variable (including personal radicalization) on "exposure to repression." To facilitate comparison of the unstandardized coefficients, the quantitative variables were assigned a value from 0 to 10.

With regard to the *positive* incentives, both predictions (i.e., the expected interaction effects)

Table 2
Interaction Effects of Repression and Integration: Incentives to Protest (Dependent Variables) Regressed Against Repression (Independent Variable) for Nonintegrated and Integrated Respondents (1987)[a]

| | Independent Variable: Exposure to Repression | | | |
| | Nonintegrated | | Integrated | |
Dependent Variables	Intercept	B/Beta	Intercept	B/Beta
Social Incentives				
Expectations of Reference Persons	.41**	.16	.56**	.27**
		(.12)		(.30)
Informal Positive Sanctions	3.60**	−.38	4.86**	.01
		(−.08)		(.00)
	4.91**	−.43	4.53**	.15
		(1.10)		(.05)
Moral Incentives				
Protest Norms	7.22**	.31	7.67**	1.15**
		(.04)		(.30)
Norms of Violence	2.05**	1.22	2.27**	1.32**
		(.24)		(.31)
Public Goods Incentive				
Political Alienation	6.47**	.46	6.54**	.71
		(.11)		(.20)
General Influence	5.43**	.95	6.49**	1.51**
		(.13)		(.32)
Influence by Legal/Illegal Protest	.46**	−.03	.32**	.14
		(−.02)		(.14)
Direct Measure of the Effects of Repression				
Personal Radicalization	4.51**	−.22	4.63**	1.79**
		(−.04)		(.38)
N	44		77	

*p<.05 **p<.01
[a]Unstandardized regression coefficients, standardized regression coefficients (or Pearson correlation coefficients) are in parentheses.

are confirmed (see Table 2): the unstandardized B-coefficients are positive for the integrated persons and the slopes are larger for integrated than for nonintegrated persons.[7] For three incentive variables the B-coefficient for nonintegrated persons is even negative ("informal positive sanctions," "influence by illegal protest," and "personal radicalization"), which means that exposure to repression does not raise but rather reduces the effect of these variables for those not integrated into protest-encouraging groups.

Table 2 also shows that the constants of the curves referring to nonintegrated persons are smaller than those referring to integrated persons—with the exception of "influence by illegal protest": integrated persons consider illegal protest less successful than legal protest, which contradicts a finding in White's (1989) study.

The informal *negative* sanctions of nonintegrated persons decrease when these persons are exposed to repression (B = −.43), and the intercept for nonintegrated persons is higher than for those who are integrated (4.91 vs. 4.53). The informal negative sanctions for integrated persons increase slightly when they experience repression (B =

.15). These results are also in line with our predictions.

To examine the asserted additive effects of repression and integration on the incentive variables, we computed the bivariate correlations of "exposure to repression" and "integration into protest-encouraging groups" on one hand and the incentive variables (including "personal radicalization") on the other. As Table 3 indicates, all correlations of the positive incentives are, as expected, positive, and most are statistically significant. With the exception of "informal positive sanctions," the coefficients for "exposure" are larger than for "integration." The correlation coefficients for "informal negative sanctions" are negative, as expected, but they are only slightly so. The latter holds also for "influence by illegal protest."[8]

If "exposure" and "integration" are included as independent additive variables in a multivariate regression equation (see the last two columns of Table 3) and if we compare the resulting standardized regression coefficients with the bivariate correlation coefficients, we see that the latter are

Table 3
Additive Effects of Exposure to Repression and Integration on Incentives to Protest (1987)[a]

Dependent Variables	Bivariate Correlations		Regression Analyses (B and Beta)		
	Exposure	Integration	Exposure	Integration	Adj. R^2
Social Incentives					
Expectations of Reference Persons			.25**	.17	
	(.29)**	(.24)**	(.24)	(.17)	.10
Informal Positive Sanctions			−.09	1.35**	
	(.06)	(.30)**	(−.02)	(.31)	.08
Informal Negative Sanctions			.01	−.25	
	(−.02)	(−.08)	(−.00)	(−.08)	−.01
Moral Incentives					
Protest Norms			.95*	.63	
	(.24)**	(.19)*	(.20)	(.14)	.06
Norms of Violence			1.30**	.25	
	(.32)**	(.14)	(.30)	(.06)	.09
Public Goods Incentives					
System Alienation			.65	.12	
	(.19)*	(.08)	(.18)	(.03)	.02
General Influence			1.38**	1.19**	
	(.32)**	(.29)**	(.25)	(.22)	.13
Influence by Legal/Illegal Protest			.10	−.10	
	(.06)	(−.08)	(.09)	(−.10)	−.00
Direct Measure of the Effects of Repression					
Personal Radicalization			1.31**	.57	
	(.31)**	(.20)*	(.27)	(.12)	.09

*p<.05 **p<.01

slightly reduced in size as a result of their inter-correlation of .28.

The question arises whether the additive and interaction effects are preserved if they are tested simultaneously. Since the two independent variables "exposure" and "integration" are dichotomous, we computed for each dependent incentive variable an analysis of variance. The interaction effects turned out to be weak and not statistically significant, with the exception of "personal radicalization" for which the interaction effect was significant at the .05 level. This finding and the consistency of the interaction effects across all incentives suggest that these effects are real and not due to chance.

In sum, the predictions concerning the additive and interaction effects of exposure to repression and integration into protest-encouraging groups were generally confirmed, with the interaction effects being weaker than additive effects.

Direct Effects of Repression

Our hypotheses about the indirect effects of repression presuppose that individual participants experience repression in protest actions. With regard to the direct effects, our theoretical argument implies that expected repression usually has direct effects on protest. To test this prediction we have included a composite measure termed "expected official sanctions" (see the Appendix), which refers to the extent to which a respondent expects to receive official sanctions if he or she engages in protest.

Since "expected official sanctions" was measured in both waves of the panel—in contrast to "exposure to repression" which was measured only in the second wave—we are now able to use both waves to test the hypotheses about the direct effects of the incentive variables on legal and illegal protest. The bivariate correlations of both repression variables are shown in Table 4 (first wave) and Table 5 (second wave), columns 1 and 3. The results for both waves are similar: we find consistent positive correlations (which are identical to the bivariate standardized regression coefficients) ranging from .19 to .45. Repression thus has a clear radicalizing effect for legal as well as illegal protest.

Our model does not include any prediction about bivariate correlations of repression and protest, only about a negative *direct* effect on protest if the other incentive variables are controlled for

Table 4
Direct Effects of Expected Official Sanctions and Other Incentives on Protest (1982)[a]

Independent Variables	Legal Protest		Illegal Protest	
	1	2	3	4
Repression				
Expected Official Sanctions	.41**	.28**	.34**	.17
	(.45)	(.31)	(.29)	(.15)
Adj. R²	.20		.07	
Social Incentives				
Expectations of Reference Persons	.62*	.64*	.62	.63
	(.14)	(.15)	(.11)	(.11)
Informal Positive Sanctions	.17*	.14*	.05	.03
	(.17)	(.14)	(.04)	(.02)
Informal Negative Sanctions	−.19*	−.30**	−.18	−.25*
	(−.13)	(−.21)	(−.10)	(−.14)
Integration into Protest-Enc. Groups	.59*	.41	.01	−.10
	(.14)	(.09)	(.00)	(−.02)
Moral Incentives				
Protest Norms	.22*	.21*	.10	.09
	(.19)	(.18)	(.07)	(.06)
Norms of Violence	.13	.09	.51**	.48**
	(.11)	(.08)	(.34)	(.33)
Public Goods Incentives				
Composite Public Goods Term (With General Infl.)[b]	.42**	.37**	.50**	.47**
	(.40)	(.35)	(.37)	(.34)
Adj. R^s	.52	.59	.41	.42

*p<.05 **p<.01
[a]Unstandardized regression coefficients, standardized coefficients are in parentheses.
[b]Additive scale of "system alienation" and "discontent with nuclear energy" multiplied by "general influence." "Influence by illegal means" was only measured for 1987.

(see Figure 1). The positive correlational effect of repression and protest should become negative in a multivariate regression analysis in which repression and the other incentive variables are included. We expect this to hold, however, only if all incentive variables that are influenced by repressive acts of legal authorities and have a direct effect on protest are included in the model and measured without error. Since this can hardly be assumed in any survey—the explained variances are far from 100%—the bivariate unstandardized and standardized regression coefficients for our repression variables can be expected to be higher than the corresponding coefficients in multivariate analyses in which the incentive variables are also included.

We first tested this prediction with the data of the first wave. In column 1 of Table 4 we present—after the model including only "expected official sanctions"—the results of a regression

Table 5
Direct Effects of Exposure to Repression, Expected Offical Sanctions, and Other Incentives on Protest (1987)[a]

Independent Variables	Legal Protest		Illegal Protest	
	1	2	3	4
Repression				
Exposure to Repression	1.54**	.23	2.01	.77
	(.33)	(.05)	(.32)	(.12)
Adj. R^2	.10		.10	
Expected Official	.16*	.03	.25*	.04
Sanctions	(.19)	(.03)	(.23)	(.04)
Adj. R^2	.03		.04	
Exposure to Repression	1.41**		1.75**	
	(.30)		(.28)	
Expected Official	.09		.17	
Sanctions	(.11)		(.15)	
Adj. R^2	.11		.11	
Social Incentives				
Expectations of	.31	.26	−.06	−.23
Reference Persons	(.07)	(.06)	(−.01)	(.04)
Informal Positive	.04	.05	−.01	.02
Sanctions	(.04)	(.05)	(−.01)	(.02)
Informal Negative	−.11	−.12	−.12	−.14
Sanctions	(−.07)	(−.08)	(−.06)	(−.07)
Integration into				
Protest-Encouraging	.61	.57	.64	.48
Groups	(.14)	(.13)	(.10)	(.08)
Moral Incentives				
Protest Norms	.14	.14	.05	.03
	(.14)	(.14)	(.04)	(.03)
Norms of Violence	−.07	−.08	.26	.21
	(−.07)	(−.08)	(.18)	(.15)
Public Goods Incentives				
Composite Public	.32**	.31**	.17**	.17**
Goods Term	(.30)	(.28)	(.26)	(.25)
Direct Measure of the Effects of Repression				
Personal Radicalization	.35**	.34**	.35**	.31*
	(.36)	(.35)	(.27)	(.24)
Adj. R^2	.48	.47	.31	.32

*$p<.05$ **$p<.01$

[a]The additive public goods term with general influence is included in the equation for legal protest, and the additive public goods term with influence by legal/illegal protest is included in the equation for illegal protest. See also the note in Table 4.

carried out for illegal protest (Table 4, columns 3 and 4).

A comparison of the coefficients of the models shows that the bivariate coefficients of "expected official sanctions" are substantially reduced in the full model (columns 2 and 4), e.g., for legal protest the beta coefficients decrease from .45 to .31, and for illegal protest from .29 to .15. If we compare the standardized coefficients of the "pure" incentives model with the full model, we see that they remain largely stable.[9]

A second test of the predicted direct effects of repression is provided by data from the second wave of the panel (see Table 5). This time we include two measures of repression, "exposure to repression" and "expected official sanctions." Table 5 shows the results of regression analyses of (1) a model including only exposure to repression," (2) a model including only "expected official sanctions," (3) a model including both repression variables, (4) a "pure" incentives model, and (5) a full model including the incentive variables (together with our direct measure of the effects of repression, personal radicalization") and both repression variables. These models are computed for both legal and illegal protest.

Table 5 shows that because of the intercorrelation of the two repression variables of .26, their unstandardized and standardized coefficients decrease slightly if they are included together in a regression analysis. In the full model (columns 2 and 4) the coefficients of the repression variables are greatly reduced and become statistically insignificant. All other standardized coefficients remain remarkably stable. The explained variances of incentive models with and without repression variables are usually similar, so repression explains only a very small percentage of the variance of the dependent variables.

If we compare the relative impact of the incentives on legal and illegal protest, we see that incentives specifically measured for legal and illegal protest show expected high correlations. This holds for norms of violence and the composite public goods terms. The other incentives were measured without explicit reference to legal and illegal protest. Most of these incentives have a stronger effect on legal than illegal protest. We suppose that respondents usually think of legal kinds of political action when answering questions that refer to protest in general, possibly be-

analysis including only the incentive variables (second block of column 1) as independent variables and legal protest as a dependent variable. The full model is estimated with "expected official sanctions" as well as the incentive variables (column 2 of Table 4). We can thus see to what extent the coefficients of the repression variable and the incentive variables change if both sets of variables are combined. The same analyses are cause most respondents have engaged in legal action or intend to in the future.

Our data allow a third test of the direct effects of repression and the other incentives on protest using both waves of the panel together[10]: we examine the effects of repression and the other incentives measured in the first wave (1982) on legal and illegal protest measured in the second wave (1987).[11] In such models the lagged variable is usually included as an independent variable in the regression equations. We thus have to include "legal protest 1982" and "illegal protest 1982" in the equation(s) if we regress "legal protest 1987" and "illegal protest 1987" on the incentives. This procedure causes two problems.

First, if a cross-sectional model with "protest" as a dependent variable has a relatively high explained variance, the multicollinearity in the panel model (consisting of the independent variables measured for 1982 and the dependent variable measured for 1987) is high. For example, if the incentives measured 1982 explain "legal protest 1982" very well, there are large correlations between "legal protest 1982" and these corresponding incentives, which results in high multicollinearity in a model with "legal protest 1987" as a dependent variable. Second, if the lagged variable correlates strongly with the corresponding dependent variable, little is left for the other independent variables to explain. The correlation of "legal protest 1982" and "legal protest 1987," for example, is .69 (the corresponding correlation for illegal protest is .49). If we regress "legal protest 1987" on the incentives measured for 1982 and include "legal protest 1982" as the lagged variable, there is relatively little variance left for the incentives to explain. Because of these problems we present the results of the regression

Table 6
Lagged Effects of Repression and Other Incentives (1982) on Legal and Illegal Protest (1987)[a]

Independent Variables (1982)	Legal Protest 1987				Illegal Protest (1987)			
	1	2	3	4	5	6	7	8
Repression								
Expected Official Sanctions '82	.28**		.16*	−.02	.12		−.05	−.13
	(.31)		(.17)	(−.02)	(.10)		(−.04)	(−.10)
Adj. R²	.09				.00			
Protest 1982								
Legal Protest '82	—	.62**	—	.64**	—	—	—	—
		(.62)		(.63)				
Illegal Protest '82	—	—	—	—	—	.40**		.42**
						(.38)		(.40)
Social Incentives								
Expectations of Reference Persons	.03	−.35	.04	−.36	.30	.03	.29	.01
	(.01)	(−.08)	(.01)	(−.08)	(.05)	(.01)	(.05)	(.00)
Informal Positive Sanctions	.29**	.18*	.27**	.18*	.11	.07	.11	.09
	(.29)	(.18)	(.27)	(.18)	(.08)	(.05)	(.08)	(.06)
Informal Negative Sanctions	−.13	−.03	−.19	−.02	−.13	−.05	−.11	.0
	(−.10)	(−.02)	(−.15)	(−.01)	(−.07)	(−.03)	(−.06)	(.00)
Integration into Prot.-Enc. Groups	.79*	.42	.69*	.43	.52	.55	.55	.62
	(.18)	(.10)	(.16)	(.10)	(.09)	(.09)	(.09)	(.11)
Moral Incentives								
Protest Norms	.18	.04	.18	.04	.03	−.03	.03	−.03
	(.15)	(.04)	(.15)	(.04)	(.02)	(−.02)	(.02)	(−.02)
Norms of Violence	−.00	−.08	−.02	−.07	.37*	.13	.38*	.13
	(−.00)	(−.08)	(−.02)	(−.07)	(.23)	(.08)	(.24)	(.08)
Public Goods Incentives								
Composite Public Goods Term	.24*	−.02	.21*	−.02	.31*	.16	.32*	.17
	(.23)	(−.02)	(.20)	(−.02)	(.21)	(.11)	(.22)	(.12)
Adj. R²	.32	.50	.34	.50	.14	.22	.13	.22

*p<.05 **p<.01
[a]The additive public goods term with general influence is included in the equation for legal protest, and the additive public goods term with influence by legal/illegal protest is included in the equation for illegal protest. Unstandardized regression coefficients, standardized coefficients in parentheses.

analyses both with and without the corresponding lagged variables.

We regress "legal protest 1987"on (1) "expected official sanctions 1982" alone, (2) the other incentives for 1982 with the lagged variable "legal protest 1982," (3) these incentives without the lagged variable "legal protest 1982," and (4) both "expected official sanctions 1982" and the other incentives for 1982 together. The same analyses are carried out for illegal protest. Table 6 shows a radicalizing effect of "expected official sanctions 1982" on "legal protest 1987" (B = .28, beta .31), which is consistent with our previous results.

If we compare the incentive models with and without the lagged legal protest variable (columns 1 and 2), all of the coefficients in the model with the lagged variable are, as expected, smaller than those in the model without it. In the full model (including "expected official sanctions 1982") without the lagged variable (column 3) the coefficients for the repression variable are reduced (from .28/.31 to .16/.17). If the lagged legal protest variable is included, the corresponding coefficients are near zero and negative (−.02/−.02, column 4). The other incentives remain largely stable.

The results of the analyses for illegal protest are similar. There is also a positive correlation of expected official sanctions, but the size of the coefficient is smaller than for legal protest. In the full models (with and without the lagged protest variable) the coefficients of the sanctions variable are also negative.

These analyses confirm the results obtained when we analyze each wave of the panel separately. In contrast to the separate analyses, however, we find that in some analyses the direct effect of repression becomes negative, as suggested by our model (see Figure 1).

Is There a Feedback Effect of Repression and Protest?

Throughout this article we assume that repression has an effect on protest, which our data confirms. This finding, however, does not imply anything about a possible feedback effect: although repression affects protest, the probability of being exposed to repression may increase how frequently people protest.

We did not measure exposure to repression in both waves, only the extent to which official reactions are expected and valued negatively. If protest leads to repression, respondents heavily engaged in protest activities will presumably expect more official sanctions.

We test this proposition first by regressing "expected official sanctions 1987" on (1) the corresponding lagged variable ("expected official sanctions 1982"), (2) "legal protest 1982," and (3) "illegal protest 1982." As Table 7 indicates, only the lagged variable has a statistically significant positive effect (column 1). The coefficients for "illegal protest 1982" are only little short of the .05 level of significance (p = .06), and "legal protest 1982" has a small negative effect on "expected official sanctions 1982." In other words, illegal protest increases expectations of repression whereas legal protest reduces them.

The correlation of the sanctions variables, measured for 1982 and 1987, is only .43, which does not cause a problem of multicollinearity, but the legal and illegal protest scales correlate at .63. It is thus useful to estimate several partial models including only legal and illegal protest (see columns 2 and 3 of Table 7). In the model with legal protest the coefficients are positive but near zero;

Table 7
Legal and Illegal Protest as Causes of Expected Official Sanction

Independent Variables	Dependent Variable: Expected Official Sanctions 1987					
	1	2	3	4	5	6
Expected Official Sanctions '82	.47**	.47**	.44**	—	—	—
	(.41)	(.41)	(.38)	(—)	(—)	(—)
Legal Protest '82	-.11	.04	—	.12	.27*	—
	(-.09)	(.03)	(—)	(.09)	(.22)	(—)
Illegal Protest '82	.19	—	.15	.20	—	.25**
	(.20)	(—)	(.15)	(.20)	(—)	(.26)
Adj. R²	.19	.17	.19	.06	.04	.07

*p<.05 **p<.01

in the model with illegal protest the coefficients are almost equal to those in the full model (column 1) and again just short of the .05 level of significance (p = .08).

In the next three models (columns 4 to 6 of Table 7) the lagged sanctions variable is omitted. One model includes both protest scales, and the two others include only one protest scale. We find that the coefficients of the protest variables are higher than in the models including the lagged sanctions scale. These results suggest that there are small effects of legal and illegal protest on the expectation of official sanctions.

Discussion

This article presents a model that addresses how repression, in conjunction with other incentives and disincentives, affects political protest. Repression is initially assumed to be a cost and thus to have a direct deterring effect on protest. If repression is considered unjustified and persons are integrated into networks encouraging protest, however, micromobilization processes are set in motion that promote protest. Depending on the strength of repression and the extent to which micromobilization processes provide positive incentives to protest, the direct deterring effect of repression is endorsed, overcompensated (i.e., a radicalizing effect is generated), or neutralized (i.e., there is no effect). On the basis of a two-wave panel survey of opponents to nuclear energy in West Germany, this model was tested and generally confirmed. Our model and findings, together with existing theory and research on the effects of repression, suggest several directions for future research.

We argue that in the multivariate regression analyses the direct effects of repression do not become negative in most of the analyses because the incentives explain only part of the variance of the dependent variables. This raises the question of how our model could be expanded. White (1989:1296) mentions identification with persons suffering from repression as a factor for the transition from legal to illegal protest. In our model this variable might have the same status as repression and thus may affect the other incentives and protest directly.

Another exogenous variable that should be added to our model is the visibility of repression. Repression may especially trigger micromobilization processes if a person's social environment

knows about her or his exposure. Tests also should be conducted to determine whether there is a threshold that the severity of repression must reach before it sets in motion micromobilization processes. To test this proposition a research design is required in which expected repression has a relatively large variance. Future studies should also include measures of legitimacy attributed to repressive acts of authorities.

A second direction of research should involve the expansion of our model by regarding some of our exogenous variables as dependent. For example, one of our independent variables is "expected official sanctions." To predict the effects of actual official sanctions on protest, hypotheses are needed that link real sanctions with expected sanctions: the question to be answered is how expectations are formed on the basis of actual sanctions. There is, of course, a positive relationship between actual and expected sanctions, but this relationship may differ for actors in different social positions. The expectations of social movement activists, for example, may differ from those of citizens not engaged in political action. Frequent exposure to repression and prior contact with government officials might also influence the perception of sanctions. A model is therefore needed that specifies the relationships between actual and expected official sanctions. Another question to be considered is under which conditions are certain forms of official sanctions regarded as more or less legitimate: does legitimacy depend on the evaluation of government performance or on the extent of alienation from the political system?

Also on the agenda for future research is the linkage of micro- and macroresearch on the effects of repression. A first step could be to spell out the implications of our model for the explanation of macrofindings. The reversed U-curve between protest (y-axis) and repression (x-axis) mentioned earlier, for example, could be explained with our model as follows: In countries where repression is perceived as illegitimate, where a relatively strong infrastructure encouraging legal forms of protest exists, and where discontent and perceived influence by legal protest are high, increased repression should launch large-scale micromobilization processes that raise protest. Beyond a certain degree of repression, however, the costs of protest become so large that the benefits derived from the positive incentives evoked by micromobilization processes can no longer compensate for the costs. Thus the direct deterring effect of repression protest becomes strong.

In Western democracies repression is relatively weak, so a radicalizing effect is more likely to occur in them (rising part of the curve). This is particularly true in societies with a large counterculture network such as West Germany. For these countries the maximum of the U-curve is far right, whereas in other societies the costs of legal and especially illegal protest are so large that a deterring effect occurs (falling part of the curve). This example suggests that different patterns of relationships between repression and (legal or illegal) protest on the macrolevel can be explained by our model. Testing theoretical accounts that specify such implications requires a research design in which data on both the macro- and the micro-levels exist for different countries. Such data would also allow a test of hypotheses addressing such issues as the effects of "objective" repression and perceived official sanctions.

Appendix: Measurement of Variables

Legal and Illegal Protest. In each wave, we presented respondents with a list of 14 legal and illegal actions that people may undertake to protest construction of nuclear power plants, e.g., petitioning, participating in legal demonstrations, working in citizen initiatives, seizing construction sites, and resisting police who attack demonstrators. We first asked whether respondents had engaged in any such actions and then asked whether they intended to do so in the future. Using five response categories ranging from "in no case" to "quite certain," each response to the first question (scored 1 for "have not done," "2 for "have done") was multiplied by the corresponding intention score for the second question (scored from 1 to 5), with a high score indicating that the action was most likely to occur. The resulting product terms were subjected to a principal component analysis for each wave. Three factors were extracted, the first explaining 45% (1982) and 41% (1987) of the variance; the second, 14% (1982) and 17% (1987); and the third, 8% (1982 and 1987). The four illegal actions loaded on one factor. One of the two other factors showed high loadings on more costly legal activities such as working in a citizen initiative, and the last factor

on less costly legal actions such as wearing buttons.

Covariance structure analysis was used to ascertain whether the construction of two separate scales for legal and illegal protest was justified. For each wave we estimated measurement models with two and three latent variables according to the results of the principal component analyses. A model with two latent variables (referring to legal and illegal protest) could explain the data as well as a model with three latent variables. We decided therefore to use four composite measures: two *legal protest scales* were constructed by adding the product terms for legal protest measured in 1982 and 1987, respectively, and two *illegal protest scales* were constructed by adding the product terms for illegal protest measured in these two years. Because of the skewed distribution of the illegal protest scales, they were log transformed (to base 10).

Informal Positive, Informal Negative, and Expected Official Sanctions. A list of 14 positive and negative consequences of protest—mostly reactions of other persons or institutions to the respondent's protest activity or inactivity—was presented, including statements such as "I am labelled as 'leftist,' 'crazy,' etc." and "I get social approval by opponents of nuclear power." We asked respondents to evaluate each reaction (the five response categories ranged from "very good" to "very bad" and were coded 1, .5, 0, −.5, −1) and to what degree they expected a reaction to occur (the response categories ranged from "quite certain" to "not at all" and were coded 1, .75, .50, .25, 0). The utilities and probabilities of each reaction were multiplied.

Principal component analyses of the 14 products resulted in three factors for each wave. The first factor explained 32.5% (1982) and 28.7% (1987) of the variance; the second, 18% (1982) and 20.2% (1987); and the third, 9.5% (1982) and 10.5% (1987). On the first factor the positive sanctions showed high loadings, as did the negative sanctions on the two other factors. In general, the "expected official reactions" and "informal negative sanctions" loaded on different factors. We therefore constructed three sanction scales for each wave by adding the product terms that corresponded to each scale. These scales—"informal positive sanctions," "informal negative sanctions," and "repression (formal negative sanctions)"— were transformed so that values under each one had a possible range of –10 to +10. Initial values under informal negative sanctions and repression were multiplied by –1, so high values denote high costs.

Exposure to Repression. Respondents were first asked whether they remembered any police actions, examples of which were enumerated in the questionnaire, and all answered that they did. They then were asked whether they had personally experienced such police actions—66.9% had. The variable was coded 0 for "not experienced" and 1 for "experienced."

Integration in Protest-Promoting Groups. In each wave the respondents were presented with a list of 29 groups and organizations and asked to indicate whether they were a member. Only in the 1987 survey was each member also asked whether he or she thought that most other group members opposed nuclear energy and encouraged protest against it. If more than 50% of the 1987 respondents replied affirmatively to this question a group was defined as protest promoting for both 1987 and 1982 since the group's political aims presumably had not changed. From these group classifications we constructed the scale "number of memberships in protest-promoting groups" for 1982 and 1987 by counting the number of protest-promoting groups in which each respondent was a member.

Norms of Protest and Violence. The respondents were first presented with four statements concerning "norms of protest" (an obligation to take part in protest against the use of nuclear energy), e.g., "If I were not active against atomic power stations, I would have a bad conscience." Their responses fell into one of five categories based on whether they more or less agreed. Two other statements were used that referred to justifications of violence: "I think that violence against property is morally justified" and "I think that violence against persons is morally justified." The respondent could reply "never," "sometimes," "mostly," and "always." High values denote a strong acceptance of protest norms and a strong approval of violence.

The first four statements refer to protest in general. Since most respondents had engaged in legal protest, we assume that these statements express a felt obligation to use legal forms of protest in particular. Accepting "norms of protest" is thus an incentive for legal protest, whereas accepting justifications for violence is more conducive to illegal forms of protest.

The six statements were subjected to a principal component analysis for each wave, for which two factors were extracted. On the first factor, which explained 31.7% (1982) and 39.9% (1987) of the variance, the first four statements exhibited high loadings, and on the second factor, which explained 20.8% (1982) and 18.3% (1987) of the variance, the other two statements showed similarly high loadings. So, two scales—"protest norms" and "norms of violence"—were constructed for each wave by adding response values for the corresponding items.

System Alienation. The statements in the alienation scale were originally used in a study in West Germany (Muller 1979). The scale consists of six statements with which a respondent can agree to a greater or lesser degree. Responses fall into one of five categories, scored from 0 to 4, with a high score denoting extreme alienation. Examples of statements include, "At present, I feel very critical of our political system" and "In general, one can rely on the federal government to do the right things." The items from 1982 and 1987 were subjected to separate principal component analyses, and in each wave, one factor was extracted, explaining 43.7% (1982) and 41.6% (1987) of the variance, respectively. The response scores were added yielding the scale "political alienation."

Discontent With Nuclear Energy. This scale is measured by scores based on yes/no responses to five statements, with 1 expressing high discontent and 0 low discontent. Examples of statements are, "I am really afraid of atomic power stations" and "I sometimes think about atomic power stations, but they do not play an important role in my life." Each statement was subjected to a principal component analysis for both waves. The analysis for 1982 yielded two factors explaining 45% and 20% of the variance. Since the eigenvalue of the second factor was only 1.01 and could not be interpreted meaningfully we decided to include all statements in an additive scale. The analysis of the statements for 1987 yielded only one factor, and an additive scale was constructed from them as well.

General Influence and Influence by Legal and Illegal Protest. The perceived efficacy of protest was measured by response scores to six statements, with five response categories ranging from "strongly agree" to "strongly disagree." Examples of statements include, "The activity of a single person against the erection of atomic power stations cannot prevent the use of nuclear energy" and "Everyone who is active against atomic power stations makes a small contribution." The statements were subjected to a principal component analysis for both waves, with analyses yielding two factors: the first explained 35% (1982) and 42% (1987) of the variance, and the second 23% (1982) and 17% (1987). In the analyses for both 1982 and 1987, the four statements measuring the influence of the individual loaded on the first factor, and the two other statements measuring individual influence via the antinuclear movement showed a high loading on the second factor. The first four items were used to construct the additive scales "general influence 1982" and "general influence 1987," with high values denoting high perceived influence. The scales were transformed to a possible range from 0 to 1, then multiplied by the additive public goods variable. In all other analyses these scales and all other quantitative variables were transformed to a range from 0 to 10.

One question, asked only in the second wave, measured the extent to which respondents believed they could influence the use of nuclear energy by legal or illegal means. Almost 60% of the respondents said that only legal actions could help the cause of the antinuclear movement, and 36% said that it depended on the situation whether legal or illegal actions would be successful. No respondent said illegal actions would be effective, and only 6 thought their participation would be ineffective. We dichotomized this variable, assigning 1 to the responses of those who thought only legal actions would help and 2 to the responses of those who believed illegal actions might help.

Personal Radicalization. Only in the 1987 survey were respondents first asked whether they recalled some recent police actions (which everyone did). Then several statements were presented concerning, among other things, the extent to which they felt these police actions deterred them personally from taking part in further protest. The statements are presented in Table 1. A principal component analysis showed that statements 4 through 8 had high loadings on the first component (explaining 38.1% of the variance) and that statements 1 through 3 loaded on the second component (explaining 22.4% of the variance). From the statements of the first component the additive

scale "personal radicalization" was constructed. High values indicate that the respondents felt motivated by the police actions to continue or even to increase protest in the future.

Missing Values. Missing values for individual items were replaced by the mean value for that item. This did not present a major problem since there were few missing values. Otherwise, correlations with the dependent variables were computed with and without mean substitution. This procedure is justified since the results were almost identical in every case.

Value Range of Variables. To facilitate the interpretation of the results, particularly of the unstandardized regression coefficients, all variables—except the dichotomies that were coded 0/1—were transformed to a value from 0 to 10.

Notes

1. An extensive body of theory and research on the effects of punishment can be found in the social psychology of learning literature (for reviews see Axelrod & Apsche 1983; Bandura 1986:262-82). There is, however, no coherent and generally accepted theory that can predict the effects of repression on the emergence of social movements and social movement participation under various conditions.

2. A public good is defined as "any good such that, if any person X_i in a group $X_1, , X_i, , X_n$ consumes it, it cannot feasibly be withheld from the others in that group" (Olson 1965:14). A public evil is something that cannot feasibly be withheld from the members of a group but that is valued negatively.

3. Some indirect evidence for this assumption is provided by the results of the studies we employ to test our hypotheses. The social environment of our respondents favors legal political action. Respondents in the second wave who were presented with the statement, "Some people whose opinion I value criticize my activities against nuclear power," were asked whether such criticism was most likely to be evoked if they were to engage in legal or illegal protest, or both. Of the respondents, 76% said that criticism would be evoked only in the case of illegal political action. If legal action is therefore regarded as legitimate, it is plausible to assume that repression of those actions is regarded as unjustified.

4. For evidence of this, see note 3.

5. The random sample for Hamburg was drawn by the Bureau of Statistics (Statistisches Landesamt). For Geesthacht we selected a random sample from an address book. We sent letters explaining our interest, and in a preliminary interview we identified opponents of nuclear energy who we then asked for a full personal interview. We succeeded with 80% of the cases in Hamburg and 87% in Geesthacht. Demo-

graphic differences between the samples were not large enough to require separate analyses (for details of the sample, see Opp et al. 1984).

6. It might be argued that the responses to the statements in Table 1 are partly attributable to a social desirability effect: respondents, particularly those involved in protest actions, may not admit that they are intimidated by repression or potential repression. The following facts do not support such an objection.

   First, in the full sample of the first wave, we correlated a social desirability scale and various properties of the interviewers (age, gender, attitude towards nuclear energy) with our scales. The correlations were approximately 0 (Opp 1986). Further, the interviewers' general ratings of the reliability of the respondents' answers were mostly positive. Finally, the results reported in Table 1 are consistent with those described later in this article.

7. Purely additive effects would exist if the B-coefficients for a given incentive were equal for nonintegrated and integrated persons and if only the intercepts differed.

8. It may be argued that the correlation of exposure to repression and protest is necessary since only those who protest can be exposed to repression. The latter assertion, however, is not true, since spectators at demonstrations are often the object of repressive acts. Furthermore, our protest scales are quantitative and are composite measures of action and intention, not only of action. As is seen elsewhere in this article, it is by no means logically necessary (and no truism) that increasing values of the protest scales signify exposure to repressive acts or are a result of such acts. If the correlations were necessary, they would be very high, but they are only .32 (repression and legal protest) and .33 (repression and illegal protest).

9. The change of the unstandardized dichotomous variables "expectations" and "integration" is relatively strong since they are coded 0/1 and the values of the other variables range from 0 to 10. A narrow value range yields relatively large unstandardized coefficients (steeper slopes) because the values of the independent variables are compressed.

10. The reason for carrying out only cross-sectional analyses in testing our hypotheses about the *indirect* effects of repression is, it may be recalled, that we did not measure "exposure to repression" and "personal radicalization" in the first wave. However, we can test our hypotheses about the *direct* effects of the incentives without these variables.

11. In estimating this and other models we did not use covariance-structure analyses (with programs like LISREL and EQS), but Ordinary Least Squares regression analyses. In a panel, the main argument for using covariance-structure analysis is that for lagged variables measurement errors may be correlated, which violates OLS assumptions. Since the time period between our two waves is about five years, correlated measurement errors are unlikely. We tested this by estimating measurement models for each lagged variable separately, with the models specified on the basis of the results of principal-component analyses. For each lagged variable, we estimated models with and without the introduction of correlated errors of the same indicators at two points in time. Because the quality of these models was almost identical, with the correlations of the error terms averaging about .25, the use of OLS is justified. ◆

16

'If You Don't Do It, Nobody Else Will': Active and Token Contributors to Local Collective Action

Pamela E. Oliver

When many people share an interest in some collective good, there are often wide discrepancies in the extent to which they contribute to obtaining it. Some people do nothing at all, others make only small token contributions such as signing a petition or paying dues, while a third group contributes substantial amounts of time and effort. What explains these differences in the willingness to absorb costs in the provision of local collective goods? Why are some people willing to make some real commitment of their time to a cause, while others give only token support or lip service? Are those who make the larger commitments simply those who are more interested in the collective goal and have more at stake in its provision? Do they have an unusually great faith in the willingness of their fellow citizens to back them in their efforts? Are they people with a lot of spare time on their hands, looking for a way to avoid boredom? Are they power-hungry moguls exploiting community needs as an avenue to their own advancement?

There is much less research on the question of explaining active versus token contributions than one might expect. Much of this is because it is assumed that the motivation to leadership is relatively unproblematic, that of course people want to be leaders so that they can have access to power in an organization. But scholars of voluntary associations (as opposed to large bureaucratic organizations) know better. Pearce (1980) compared cooperatives which employed paid staff with those relying solely on volunteers. She ob-

served that in employing organizations, leadership positions were hard to get and were sought after by the participants, while in all-volunteer organizations, leadership positions were easy to get but avoided by the participants. In all-volunteer cooperatives, the leaders absorbed high costs with low compensating rewards. Rich (1980b) studied a variety of neighborhood organizations; the leaders of organizations relying solely on volunteers and voluntary contributions absorbed the high cost of their participation while personally realizing relatively little of the collective goals. In short, the active members of all-volunteer local organizations are frequently underrewarded workhorses who provide collective benefits for their often unappreciative constituencies. Why do they do it?

This paper reports the differences among residents of Detroit who were nonmembers, token members, or active members of their neighborhood associations. Consistent with previous research, active members are more highly educated than token members. But an additional predictor has not been recognized in previous research: active members are more *pessimistic* than token members about the prospects for collective action in their neighborhoods. This perhaps surprising finding is, in fact, quite consistent with what activists often say and with recent theoretical work on collective action.

Theory and Predictions

The concept of collective action provides a framework for understanding the common dilemmas in a wide variety of situations, and many scholars have treated participation in community organizations as a form of collective action (for example, Rich, 1980a,b; O'Brien, 1974; Henig, 1982b; Wandersman, 1981; Smith, 1981; Sharp, 1978; Stinson and Stam, 1976). The term "collective action" refers to activities which produce collective or public goods, that is, goods with the nonexcludability property that their provision to some members of a group means that they cannot be withheld from others in the group (Olston, 1965:14). People who live in the same local area share common interests which lead to the existence of collective goods, both environmental, such as floods, wind storms, noxious fumes, or commuter traffic, and social, such as garbage collection, street repair, police patrols, and public schools.

Neighborhood organizations are explicitly formed to address these collective goods. Surveys

" 'If You Don't Do It, Nobody Else Will': Active and Token Contributors to Local Collective Action." *American Sociological Review* 49: 601-610. Copyright © 1984 by the American Sociological Association. Reprinted with permission.

of neighborhood organizations find that they address a wide variety of collective goods, such as housing, general city services, various types of crimes, street safety and traffic problems, recreation, senior citizen needs, education, unemployment, health services, commercial revitalization, redlining, highway construction, drug abuse, planning, tenant issues, and pollution (Green, 1979; National Commission on Neighborhoods, 1979; Oliver, 1980b).

From our theoretical understanding of collective action, four general factors can be expected to determine varying levels of involvement in neighborhood organizations. The first two are the basic economic factors of interests and costs. Very simply, we expect that larger contributions will come from people who value neighborhood collective goods more or who experience lower costs from their contributions. A third factor, social ties among group members, is stressed by sociologists such as Fireman and Gamson (1979), Tilly (1978), and Granovetter (1973).

The fourth general factor concerns predictions about others' behavior, specifically pessimism about the prospects for collective action by others. In some situations, notably in "large groups" (Olson, 1965), any individual's contribution is too small to make a noticeable difference in the level of the collective good, so everyone's contribution is irrational no matter what anyone else does. But in "small groups," such as the active members of a community organization, individual contributions do make a noticeable difference (Rich, 1980b) and predictions about others' behavior *are* relevant. People who believe others will provide the collective good are motivated to ride free; people who do not believe others will provide the collective good are motivated to provide the good themselves or do without.

More specific predictions can be developed for each of these four factors in turn, beginning with pessimism about others' behavior.

Pessimism About Others' Collective Action

It is commonly assumed that people are more willing to participate in collective action if they believe that others will. But if you ask someone why he or she agreed to chair a fundraising drive or be recording secretary of a local organization, a common answer is: "If I don't do it, nobody else will." That is, activists are often quite pessimistic,

believing it unlikely that they will be able to rely on the efforts of their neighbors.

Recent work on collective action by Oliver et al. (1984) argues that there is an interaction between beliefs about others' willingness to contribute to collective action and the character of the collective good. Optimism about collective action by others makes a person more willing to contribute when contributions have an accelerating impact on the collective good. But when there are diminishing marginal returns to contributions, pessimism about others' actions, not optimism, makes a person more willing to contribute. Contributions have diminishing marginal return when jobs are relatively finite, or when the earliest contributions have the biggest impact. Keeping an organization's checkbook, arranging to rent games for a school fair, or preparing a newsletter have this property: once the job is being done at all, additional contributions produce smaller (although not zero) increments in the collective good. If the job is being done, there is little marginal payoff for helping out, and free riding is likely.

Local activism often exhibits this property of diminishing marginal returns. Thursz (1972) stresses that successful community organizations do not require mass participation, citing Alinsky's claim that participation by 3 percent of a community would ensure success of a community organization. Bolduc (1980) provides a typical case study of a neighborhood in which only a dozen residents participated actively in the neighborhood organization although it was viewed as a legitimate representative body by the majority of residents. Since active members and leaders of local voluntary organizations absorb high costs for low rewards, it stands to reason that they are more likely to make this sacrifice when they believe no one else will.

Private incentives (Olson, 1965; Oliver, 1980a) could minimize the impact of this factor, but it is unusual in voluntary community action for the incentives for participation to be large enough to make a person want to absorb the costs of involvement. The incentives for active participation in community organizations are usually found to be psychological, including social contacts, deference or respect, self-actualization, learning new skills, or feeling a sense of accomplishment (Smith, 1981; Salem, 1978; Rich, 1980b; Sharp, 1978).

Interest in the Collective Good

A person's level of interest in the collective good should always have a positive effect on participating in collective action, but the strength of this impact may vary. We may distinguish subjective interest, as indicated by statements of concern about neighborhood problems, from objective interest, as indicated by demographic characteristics.

Concerning subjective interests, several studies and literature reviews indicate that various attitudinal measures which tap what can be thought of as the person's concern about the collective good are important predictors of participation in community organizations (McKenzie, 1981; Uzzell, 1980; Nanetti, 1980; Parkum and Parkum, 1980). However, these studies do not distinguish among levels of participation. One study which concerns leaders specifically (Rich, 1980b) argues that psychological incentives, not concern about the collective good, are the best predictors of the willingness to be a leader in an all-volunteer neighborhood organization.

The relevant "objective" interest for neighborhood organizations is being a homeowner. Home-ownership is likely to distinguish members from nonmembers, but is less likely to distinguish active from token members. The correlation with membership is high because renters are quite unlikely to belong to neighborhood organizations, but too little variance is left to distinguish active from token members. In theoretical terms, gross-category membership is relevant for defining the population at risk, but not for determining the level of contribution a person is willing to make.

Costs

It seems obvious that active members of local organizations absorb higher costs of action than do token members (Pearce, 1980; Rich, 1980a,b). Token members presumably absorb higher costs than nonmembers, although the difference may not be great. It is difficult to make comparisons across people of the costs of action, but it is possible to draw inferences about such costs by making assumptions about the nature of various actions and the effects of people's life circumstances.

Education and Income. One of the most well-documented correlations in social science is the positive correlation between socioeconomic status and all forms of political or organizational participation (see, e.g., Verba and Nie, 1972; Smith and Freedman, 1972), including participation in community organizations (see Parkum and Parkum, 1980; Vedlitz and Veblen, 1980; Verba and Nie, 1972; Smith and Freedman, 1972). This finding has been explained in cost-benefit terms by many authors, perhaps most forcefully by O'Brien (1974, 1975). The explanation is grounded in the high costs of participation for the poor. O'Brien argues that poor people are too concerned about survival to have time for leisure activities, that their failure to participate in community organizations is not due to "apathy" but to an acute case of the free-rider problem in which the costs of participation far outweigh the individual's share of the collective good.

Psychological costs are also relevant in this context. Organizational activity usually requires skills that are more common among educated people, such as public speaking, Roberts Rules of Order, understanding technical explanations, or knowing how to call City Hall. This means that the cost of such activities is much higher for less-educated people.

These cost considerations should hold true both for distinguishing members from nonmembers, and for distinguishing active members from token members of community organizations.

Free Time. Free or discretionary time is often posited as an important factor in collective action (McCarthy and Zald, 1973). The stereotype of the community volunteer as a bored housewife or retiree is common. Certainly this is a plausible account in cost-benefit terms, since the opportunity cost of an investment of time is lower for a person with more free time.

Since we lack direct measures of free time, we may make plausible inferences about free time from certain demographic characteristics. Other things being equal, people who are employed full time should have less free time than those who are not. Free time is also doubtlessly negatively related to the number of children one has.

As plausible as the free-time account is, especially for women's behavior, and especially considering recent publicity about the decline in volunteerism as women have entered paid employment, there is some contrary evidence. Several studies have found positive correlations between employment and voluntary community participation among women, especially less-educated women (Flynn and Webb, 1975; Schoenberg, 1980; and several unpublished studies cited by Schoenberg, including Schoenberg and Rosenbaum, 1979; Dabrowski, 1979; and Holmes, 1979). These studies argue that the skills and self-confidence obtained from paid employment are necessary for a woman to feel willing to engage in community participation. Having children was a positive predictor of participation in at least one older study (Wright and Hyman, 1958), although Ahlbrandt and Cunningham (1979) report that it did not predict participation in neighborhood organizations in six Pittsburgh neighborhoods.

Social Ties

In the substantive literature on neighborhoods, a major theme is the social solidarity or social integration within a neighborhood (see, e.g., Warren and Warren, 1977). It is usually assumed that this factor is an important element in a neighborhood's ability to act collectively in response to some threat, although this assumption is rarely subject to test. Sociologists such as Tilly (1978), Fireman and Gamson (1977), Granovetter (1973, 1982), and Snow et al. (1980) stress the importance of social ties for collective action. Tilly (1978) distinguishes feelings of identity or solidarity from network ties. Granovetter (1973, 1982) and Duff and Liu (1972) distinguish weak ties of acquaintance from strong ties of friendship, arguing that weak ties are important for collective action.

Social ties may be thought of as indicators of subjective interest in the neighborhood, as factors influencing the availability of solidary incentives for participation in collective action, or as factors reducing the cost of action by making communication easier. All these theoretical interpretations yield the same empirical prediction, that social ties will generally have a positive effect on collective action. None distinguishes theoretically between active and token contributions. In this paper, the effects of social ties are assessed without attempting to determine the best theoretical interpretation of these effects.

Methods and Procedures

Sample

The analysis in this paper is based upon data originally collected in Detroit neighborhoods in 1969 under the direction of Donald Warren; more details on data collection and sampling procedures may be found in Warren (1975). Twenty-eight elementary school attendance areas within the central city of Detroit were sampled purposively; sixteen of these were over 90 percent black and twelve were over 90 percent white. Individuals were randomly sampled within neighborhoods. The 1456 respondents included in the analysis were of the majority race in their neighborhood and were missing information on less than six of the original variables in the analysis. Cases missing information on a variable were assigned the mean for interval variables and the median for ordinal variables, a procedure which is conservative since it tends to attenuate correlations.

Measures of Dependent Variables

The three dependent dummy variables are types of participation in neighborhood improvement organizations: membership, activism, and leadership. Each reported organizational membership was classified by type of organization, "neighborhood improvement association" was an original response category. The handful of people who were members of more than one neighborhood organization were simply coded as members, as there were too few of them to analyze. For each organizational membership, the respondent was asked "How active have you been in the past three years?" The codes *active* and *not active* were entered for each of the years 1966, 1967, 1968, and 1969. The variable employed in the present analysis contrasts those who were active in any of the four years with all others. Leadership was indicated by the answer to the question: "Have you ever held an office or position of leadership in any of these groups? If yes, which ones?"

Measures of Predictions About Others' Collective Action

Respondents were asked to indicate on a five-point scale from "certainly will" to "certainly won't" their assessment of "how ready you think your neighbors would be to help each other in various situations." Two were collective: "If the principal of the local school was doing a very poor job, how much could you count on your neighbors for help in doing something about it'?" and "If the city were to announce a project that would hurt this neighborhood, and some of the neighbors tried to organize a protest, how would the others feel about joining?" The analyzed variable is an index created by summing these two items.

Measures of Interest in the Collective Good

Membership in the appropriate objective interest groups is indicated by whether the person owns or is buying (as opposed to rents) his or her home.

Subjective interest in neighborhood improvement is measured with a composite index based on six variables. The first variable is the number of "problems" the respondent said existed in his or her neighborhood.[2] The other five variables are the level of dissatisfaction with five city services (parks and playgrounds, sports and recreation centers, police protection, garbage collection, schools), each having four levels of response from generally satisfied to very dissatisfied. Principal-axis factor analysis with varimax rotation identified only one significant dimension; all other factors were of roughly equal weight and unique to a variable. The analyzed variable is the weighted regression factor score.

Costs

Education and Income. Education is coded as years of formal education. Income was assessed with the 1960 Census groupings; each category was assigned its midpoint, and the variable was treated as interval.

Free Time. Respondents employed full time were contrasted with those who have no paid employment or only part-time employment. Respondents were coded for the presence or absence of children under age 18 in the household.

Measures of Social Ties

The analyzed variables are three indices tapping important dimensions of social ties: positive affect or liking for the neighborhood; the number of acquaintances one has in the neighborhood; and the extent of one's close ties of friendship or kinship in the neighborhood.

To create these indices, eight variables were subjected to factor analysis:

(1) The person's liking for the neighborhood, measured with a composite index created by summing four questions. The first asked, "At your present time in life, how close are your neighbors to what you think neighbors should be like?" and was recorded on a four-point scale from "very close" to "not close at all." The second asked, "In general, how do you feel about this neighborhood?" with four responses ranging from good to very poor. The third and fourth used four responses from "like very much" to "dislike very much" for "your own block" and "the people living right nearby."

(2) Another measure of positive affect, how close the person's neighbors were to their ideal.

(3) An index created by summing the responses to questions on the perceived likelihood that one's neighbors would engage in five kinds of "personal" helping: keeping an eye on children; caring for a child while away for a week; helping you when sick; keeping an eye on the house for a month; lending you a few dollars.

(4) A measure of the person's perception of being like other people in the local area. Respondents were asked, "In general, would you say you and your neighbors share the same or different views on the following matters: best way to raise children, religious beliefs, attitudes about race problems, political attitudes, goals for children, way to enjoy leisure time, kind of person to have as a friend, how to furnish a house in good taste, how to get ahead in the world." An index was constructed by subtracting the number of "different" answers form the number of "same" answers.

(5) The number of "weak" ties: the number of neighbors the person knows "well enough so that you might spend half an hour or so with them now and then." Responses for separate questions for "on this block" and "in this area but not on this block" were summed.

(6) A measure of somewhat stronger ties: how often the person gets together with neighbors "at their home or yours," ranging from never to daily.

(7) A measure of the strong ties of friendship: whether at least one of the person's three closest friends is in the neighborhood.

(8) A measure of the strong ties of kinship: the proportion of the person's relatives in the Detroit area who live in the immediate neighborhood: all, most, about half, only a few, or none.

The factor analysis reveals only one "significant" dimension for these variables, a generalized satisfaction with the neighborhood. However, the three-factor solution produced theoretically meaningful dimensions, so the three weighted-regression factor scores were used in the analysis to allow specification of the relationship between social ties and local collective action. The variables which loaded high on the first factor were the liking index, whether the neighbors are ideal, the personal helping index, and the attitude-similarity index: this factor score is called the Liking for Neighborhood Scale. The most important variable in the second factor is the number of people known, with visiting with neighbors and believing the neighbors would give personal help also loading on this factor, this factor score is called the Acquaintances Scale. Having one's closest friends in the neighborhood is the only variable which loads highly on the third factor, with having relatives in the neighborhood having a moderate loading; this factor score is called the Close Ties Scale.

Control Variables

Race and gender were controlled in the analysis. There is substantial evidence that blacks participate more in community organizations than whites (Warren, 1975, 1974; Ahlbrandt and Cunningham, 1979; London and Hearn, 1977; Phillips, 1975). In addition, men have been found to be more active in some areas of community participation and women in others (Parkum and Parkum, 1980).

Preliminary analyses found no significant effects for age, length of residence in the neighborhood, and marital status, so they are excluded from the reported analyses. People in the broadly defined "middle ages" of 35-60 have often been found to be more active (Parkum and Parkum, 1980), although Edwards (1977) reports finding no age effect on general social involvement, and McPherson and Lockwood (1980) use time-series data to demonstrate that the age difference arises because memberships accumulate over time, with younger people having higher rates of membership. There is usually a positive correlation between the length of time a person has lived in a local area and involvement in community activities (Bell and Force, 1956: Ross, 1972; McKenzie, 1981; Parkum and Parkum, 1980). There is no reported finding that marital status has any significant effect on community participation.

Preliminary analysis also controlled for the number of other organizational memberships to determine whether active members of neighborhood organizations were simply "joiners." Other memberships is highly correlated with membership in neighborhood organizations but, among members, not with being active. The only effect of including this variable on the other parameters in any equation reported below is to make income nonsignificant as a predictor of membership.

Mode of Analysis

Since the dependent variables are dichotomies, probit analysis is an appropriate statistical tool. The contrast between members and nonmembers is assessed with the total sample. The contrast between token members and active members is assessed with the subsample who are members of the appropriate organization. This mode of analysis plausibly assumes that people are first selected to membership in an organization and, once members, face further selection for becoming active.

Results

Table 1 shows the distributions of the dependent variables and their interrelations. Nineteen percent of the respondents were members of neighborhood improvement associations at the time of the survey. Of the members, 22 percent said they had been a leader or officer of such a group, and 27 percent said they had been active in the group in at least one of the past four years. Thirty percent of the past leaders were currently active in their organizations, and 25 percent of those currently active had been leaders.

Table 1
Frequencies and Correlations Among Types of Participation in Neighborhood Organizations

| | | Percent of Row Group in Column Group | | |
	Number	Current Member	Past Leader	Currently Active
Total Sample	1456	19%	4%	5%
Members	278		22%	27%
Leaders	64	97%		30%

Table 2
Descriptive Statistics for Independent Variables[a]

Variable	Mean	Standard Deviation
Race (white = 1, black = 0)	.427	.495
Education (in years)	10.535	3.369
Income (in $1000s)	9.121	4.493
Has Children	.593	.491
Employed Full TIme	.544	.498
Sex (female = 1, male = 0)	.466	.499
Homeowner	.736	.441
Subjective Interest Scale	.002	.883
Liking for Neighborhood Scale	−.001	.751
Acquaintances Scale	−.001	.651
Close Ties Scale	.000	.708
Neighbors' Likelihood of Collective Action Scale (range 2 to 10)	8.069	1.608

[a]Number of Observations = 1456.

The means and standard deviations for all the independent variables are given in Table 2.

Table 3 shows the coefficients for a probit analysis of membership and, among members, of the two kinds of active participation. The findings for membership are reasonably consistent with previous research. Members are significantly more likely than nonmembers to be black, to have higher incomes, to own their homes, to score high on the subjective interest scale, to know many of their neighbors, and to believe their neighbors would respond collectively to a collective problem. The fact that those with relatively few friends or relatives in the neighborhood are more likely to be members is perhaps inconsistent with the theoretical literature but somewhat consistent with McCourt's (1977) findings.[3] The negative coefficient for having children is counter to Wright and Hyman's (1958) work, but somewhat consistent with free time as an explanation for involvement.

Turning to the contrast between active and token members, only two variables predict both indicators of active contributions: education and beliefs about the neighbors' willingness to act collectively. First, former leaders and current activists are more highly educated than other members. This result is in line with past research, and is probably due to the kinds of skills educated people acquire which make such activities easier (and therefore less costly) for them. Secondly, both for-

mer leaders and current activists are *less* optimistic than other members about the prospects for collective action on the part of their neighbors. Presumably they do not believe they can free ride on their neighbors' efforts.

Several factors are different for former leaders than for current activists. Former leaders are more likely than other members to be black, to score high on the subjective interest scale, and to know many of their neighbors. By contrast, current activists are less likely to be homeowners, less likely to like their neighborhood, and more likely to have close social ties with the neighbors they know (although they know nonsignificantly fewer of them). The negative coefficient on homeownership is difficult to explain theoretically and may be nothing more than a random quirk of these data, but it remains when controls for age and length of residence in the neighborhood are included.

Let us review the results for each set of predictors. The various measures of social ties in these data have no consistent effects on active participation, although they do have some meaningful patterns. First, members know more people than nonmembers, and leaders know more people than other members, consistent with the "weak ties" arguments. Secondly, members have fewer close ties in the neighborhood than nonmembers, but currently active members have *more* close ties while generally liking the neighborhood less than

Table 3
Probit Analysis of Membership and Active Participation in Neighborhood Organizations

| | Whole Sample Membership | | Members of Neighborhood Groups Only | | | |
| | | | Has Been Leader | | Currently Active | |
	Estimate	Standard Error	Estimate	Standard Error	Estimate	Standard Error
Race (white)	−0.842*	0.100	−0.563*	0.304	−0.017	0.249
Education	0.020	0.014	0.099*	0.034	0.067*	0.031
Income	0.021*	0.011	−0.025	0.024	−0.021	0.023
Has Children	−0.218*	0.087	−0.213	0.197	0.141	0.188
Full-time Employment	0.008	0.100	−0.020	0.220	-0.262	0.206
Gender (female)	0.070	0.094	−0.027	0.207	−0.173	0.199
Homeowner	0.564*	0.108	0.205	0.283	−0.996*	0.244
Subjective Interest	0.177*	0.049	0.277*	0.108	−0.006	0.104
Liking Scale	0.095	0.068	0.093	0.147	−0.246*	0.144
Acquaintances Scale	0.236*	0.073	0.575*	0.170	−0.152	0.162
Close Ties Scale	−0.153*	0.061	0.223	0.145	0.251*	0.136
Neigh Act Coll	0.108*	0.030	−0.122*	0.069	−0.139*	0.063
Constant	−2.261*	0.293	−0.837	0.682	1.091*	0.626
G-Square	1205.0		244.1		276.1	
D.F.	1443		265		265	

*p<.05, one-tailed

inactive members. This suggests that current activism arises not from a generalized collective neighborhood spirit, but rather from particularistic ties and, perhaps, even a sense of distance from one's neighbors. Wilson (1973) argues that personalized exchanges are an important mechanism for producing local collective goods, although his description may apply more to acquaintances than close friends.

Interests also have mixed effects on active participation. As expected, members are much more likely than nonmembers to be homeowners and to score high on the subjective interest scale. However, among members, the only significant positive effect is that of subjective interest on having been a leader. As discussed above, homeowners are surprisingly less likely than others to be currently active as members. We may say that interest in the collective good seems to move people from doing nothing to doing something, but interests do not seem to be critical for moving people from doing less to doing more. There is, however, some indication that people who take on leadership roles are especially interested in local issues.

Costs of participation were not measured directly, but we assumed that people with more resources would experience lower opportunity costs than those with fewer resources. Time is the central resource for active participation in neighborhood groups, but indicators of free time—not being employed full time and not having children—failed to predict such participation. Members are less likely to have children than nonmembers, but neither of these variables is a significant predictor of leadership or current activism. Although these factors are often thought to be more salient for women, tests for interactions with gender found no significant coefficients. Furthermore, there was a nonsignificant tendency for men's activism to be lower when they were employed or had children, but for women's to be higher. Thus, such trends as there are run counter to the conventional wisdom that community activists are women who do not have the demands of jobs or children.

Higher-income people have more financial resources, and more highly educated people have cultural resources and skills for organizational participation. Income is a weak predictor of membership, while education strongly distinguishes active from token members. This suggests that the salient resource limiting active participation is the skills involved, rather than money or time.

Finally, although members are more optimistic than nonmembers about the prospects for neighborhood collective action, both former leaders and currently active members are more pessimistic than token members about such prospects. As a bit of a check on the generality of this finding, the same analysis was performed for parent-teacher associations; the coefficients for former leadership and current activism in PTAs are not significant, but they are negative. Active participants in community organizations seem definitely to be more skeptical of their neighbors' cooperativeness than token members.

Conclusions

To summarize, two factors consistently distinguish active from token contributors to neighborhood organizations: active members are more highly educated and they are more pessimistic about their neighbors' willingness to make active contributions. Distinguishing among the types of active contributors, leaders are interested in local issues and know many people, while those currently active have negative feelings about their neighbors in general but have their closest friends or relatives in the area.

The positive effect of education is well known, but the significance of activists' pessimism about their neighbors has not been previously recognized and merits further discussion.

Some of the pessimism effect may be consequence rather than cause. People who get involved in community activities often experience frustration when they try to get others involved. Although the numbers involved are very small, the people in these data who had been leaders in past years but were not active in the current year had more pessimistic beliefs about the prospects for action than other active members. Optimism about collective action may be due to simple naivete: many people do not understand the collective-goods dilemma and are shocked when they try to organize collective action.

Experience may teach people about the collective dilemma. But whether they are pessimistic from the start, or become so through experience, people who make active contributions have less faith in the collective spirit of their neighbors than people who are only token members. This pattern is easily understood within a general collective-action model. Active contributors make a noticeable difference in the provision of the public good.

Furthermore, many local collective goods have the property of diminishing marginal returns, in that early contributions have much greater impact than later contributions of the same size. Under these conditions, rational individuals take account of the likelihood that the collective good will be provided through the efforts of others, and are less likely to contribute the more they believe others will.

There is a kind of paradox of community life. People with the greatest sense of collective identity and positive regard for their neighbors may not absorb the costs of community activism because they assume that someone else will take care of the problems. The people who are willing to absorb these costs are often precisely those who have less respect and liking for their neighbors and more of a belief that if they want something done they will have to do it themselves. There is often a real tension between community activists and their communities.

Of course, in some neighborhoods community activists are able to mobilize widespread activism whenever it is necessary and there are close ties between leaders and residents. But just as Olson's (1965) work made us realize that collective action is problematic, so we need to recognize that this is an exception to be explained rather than a natural or likely turn of events.

Notes

1. The two former neighborhood organization leaders who were not currently members of neighborhood organizations (Table 1) were dropped from the analysis of leadership.

2. These were: racial strife; people not keeping their houses up; unemployment; wild teenagers; nationality or religious conflict; people not knowing how to get along in the big city; pressure to keep up with the Joneses; young children not supervised properly; "it's no use trying" attitude toward solving local neighborhood problems; conflicts between older and younger children; people with strange behavior; fear of street crime; militant pressure groups; police harassment; traffic and noise; lack of police services. Several analytic approaches failed to reveal any interesting sub-dimensions, factors or clusters within these items, so the count of all yes answers is treated as a single variable.

3. McCourt's (1977) study of about 30 women in a white working-class Chicago neighborhood found that having one's own parents in the neighborhood had no effect on level of participation in the neighborhood organization, while having one's husband's parents in the neighborhood had a strongly negative effect. ✦

17

Social Movement Involvement in the Wake of a Nuclear Accident: Activists and Free Riders in the TMI Area

Edward J. Walsh
Rex H. Warland

The logic as well as the predictors of social movement participation are problematic. In his seminal work which has figured prominently in the transformation of the sociological subfield of social movements and collective behavior during the past 15 years, Mancur Olson insists that ". . . rational, self-interested individuals will not act to achieve their common or group interests" (1965:2). Although developed within his own field of economics, Olson's argument has also had a significant influence in psychology (e.g., Kerr and Bruun, 1983), political science (e.g., Moe, 1980), and sociology (e.g., Oberschall, 1973; McCarthy and Zald, 1977). This paper reports on the first empirical test of central hypotheses from Olson involving social movement phenomena within a natural setting.

Depending heavily on the concepts "public good"[1] and "selective incentive,"[2] Olson challenges interest group as well as Marxist theories of mobilization as he insists that "the logic of collective action" inclines individuals to resist appeals to unite with others in pursuit of public goods. It is not sufficient, according to him, that large numbers of persons recognize their common interest in creating a public good. He (1965:2) writes:

> The notion that groups of individuals will act to achieve their common or group interests, far from being a logical implication of the assumption that the individuals in a group will rationally further

their individual interests, is in fact inconsistent with that assumption.

Considering those who join public interest groups for altruistic motives to be "wildly unrepresentative," Olson (1979:149) ironically argues that the only way large numbers of people can be induced to become involved in a collective pursuit of the public good is to offer them something different from—perhaps even unrelated to—the group's goals. In the absence of such selective incentives, he predicts that the large majority of individuals will choose to ride free on the efforts of the few.[3] The strong version of the free-rider hypothesis predicts that nobody will contribute to the provision of the public good (Brubaker, 1975), while a weaker version suggests that the provision of the public good will be suboptimal because of the many free riders (Samuelson, 1954; Marwell and Ames, 1979). When the pursuit of a public good includes the initial formation of a social movement organization (SMO), the higher cost for the organizers makes the entire venture even more problematic (Olson, 1965:129).

Olson's model has not been without its critics. Marwell and Ames (1979, 1980), for example, argue that the magnitude of the free-rider problem is exaggerated by Olson's theory. After finding surprisingly large numbers of subjects contributing unexpectedly high percentages of tokens in their clever but contrived experiments with high school students confronted with investment opportunities, they speculate that the utilitarian assumptions underlying the free-rider hypothesis are less powerful than Olson and other economic theorists would have us believe (1979:1359).

More theoretical critics of Olson emphasize the importance of group solidarity, "collective bads," and the role of imperfect information. Fireman and Gamson (1979:22), for example, suggest various solidary relationships which make it likely that a person will "contribute his or her share even if the impact of that share is not noticeable," when collective action is urgent. Mitchell (1979) argues that the "no exit" (Hirschman, 1970) quality or public bads such as polluted air and water makes it quite reasonable, even in the absence of selective incentives, to contribute to their elimination. Moe (1980) challenges Olson's assumption of perfect information on the part of potential activists, suggesting that imperfect information may prompt some people to join organizations in which they miscalculate their own contributions and costs. By implication, imperfect information may also explain free riding.

Olson's model figures prominently in the writings of social movement analysts using what have come to be called "resource mobilization" (RM) perspectives (Oberschall, 1973; Gamson, 1975; McCarthy and Zald, 1973, 1977; Tilly, 1978). In contrast to earlier frameworks emphasizing such mental factors as common grievances and shared ideologies in the emergence of social movements (e.g., Smelser, 1963: Gurr, 1970), the RM perspectives emphasize networks and other structural variables which support and constrain such phenomena (see Walsh, 1978).[4]

Some RM writers, viewing SMO organizers as political entrepreneurs motivated by enlightened self-interest, assume that supporters are sustained in their involvement by a variety of selective incentives (Oberschall, 1973; McCarthy ind Zald, 1977). Others emphasize the importance of purposive incentives (Wilson, 1973) or principle (Fireman and Gamson, 1979), but RM perspectives "[have] not been particularly strong on the role of ideas and political consciousness in shaping collective action" (Gamson et al., 1982:8). Most RM writers emphasize the latent group solidary links—operating via organizational or friendship networks, for example—which are considered more important than ideological or attitudinal factors such as discontent or altruistic concern for the public good (Snow et al., 1980; McCarthy and Zald, 1977) in promoting activist involvement.

Without ignoring the genuine advances provided by RM perspectives, we argue that logic as well as empirical evidence suggest a more comprehensive model of social movement involvement (see Zurcher and Snow, 1981).[5] Although the role of ideology in recruitment has been given little systematic attention by empirical researchers (see Marx and Wood, 1975; Ferree and Miller, n.d.), individuals' ideas and attitudes prior to the impact of suddenly imposed grievances such as court-ordered busing (Useem, 1980), a massive oil spill (Molotch, 1970), or a nuclear accident (Walsh, 1981) are likely to facilitate or impede protest mobilization. Socioeconomic status is another important variable which has generally been found to relate positively to political participation (Verba and Nie, 1972), but negative correlations have also been reported (Useem, 1990). Researchers should also consider specific griev-

ances which may become important contributing factors in prompting people to participate in social movements (Walsh, 1981; Law and Walsh, 1983).

In summary, Olson predicts a high percentage of free riders in any collective effort to achieve a public good or, by implication, challenge a public bad. He suggests that the main reason for the free riding will be individualistic calculations of personal costs associated with activism. Olson's critics, on the other hand, argue that his model ignores the role of solidarity (Fireman and Gamson, 1979) as well as the threat of public bads (Mitchell, 1979) in prompting people to overcome the free-rider problem. Marwell and Ames (1979, 1980) insist that Olson's model greatly exaggerates the levels of free riding which occur in everyday mobilization attempts. Building on the valuable insights of RM theorists who have responded to Olson, we suggest an additive model including a variety of indicators from an actual mobilization process in our attempt to distinguish activists from free riders in the communities around Three Mile Island (TMI).

Research Setting

In late March 1979, more than 150,000 residents of communities in the vicinity of the TMI nuclear power station evacuated as news of this nation's most serious nuclear accident leaked out along with the radiation from the Unit 2 (TMI-2) reactor (Flynn, 1979). Some residents who did not evacuate later acknowledged that they felt constrained to stay behind because of occupational, familial, or other obligations. After a few weeks, when most evacuees had returned to their homes, public meetings were hosted by federal, state, and local officials in the various communities. A major anti-nuclear rally in Washington, D.C., was organized in response to the accident, and an estimated 200,000 people from around the nation gathered on May 6, 1979, with special places of honor given the TMI community organizations. Throughout the spring, and into early summer, the print and electronic media in the TMI communities carried regular announcements of meetings, rallies and other events intended to help educate and/or mobilize citizens vis-à-vis TMI issues. The President's Commission on the TMI accident, for example, under the direction of John Kemeny, conducted public hearings in the area; federal and state officials also chaired public meetings where information was shared and citizen input encouraged. In addition, most local communities had their own public meetings during these first few months after the accident to address TMI-related issues.

Community protest organizations emerged in Middletown, Newberry Township, York, Lancaster, and a number of small towns around TMI. An existing anti-TMI SMO from Harrisburg coordinated the mobilization processes for ten additional communities. Confronted with a proposed restart of Unit 1 (TMI-1), which just happened to be down for routine refueling at the time of the accident, as well as the extensive and threatening TMI-2 cleanup operations,[6] the twin goals of these community groups were to shut down TMI-1 and monitor the cleanup of TMI-2 (see Walsh, 1981, 1983). In addition to public meetings, these SMOs conducted door-to-door campaigns in an attempt to obtain petition signatures, contributions, and more active members. Stories about legal cases and lobbying activities in which these groups were involved appeared regularly in the local media, and newsletters were widely distributed, gratis, during the first few months after the accident.

Some TMI-area residents became active politically in the wake of the accident while others, who essentially agreed with the general goals of the citizen protest groups, never contributed any time or money to these SMOs. Between these extremes were those who contributed some time or money but did not become very active or else decreased their level of involvement after a relatively short time. We compare the most politically active citizens in four key communities around TMI with random samples of free riders. We distinguish the free riders from the broader population not expressing attitudinal opposition to the TMI nuclear facility.

Focal Hypotheses

The widespread mobilization processes occurring in the wake of the TMI accident provided an opportunity to operationalize and evaluate a number of generalizations distilled from Olson's model and related social movement literature. These focal hypotheses are used to organize the following analysis.

First, we estimated the percentage of free riders in an important and well-publicized mobilization attempt. The TMI issues were ones which tended to polarize surrounding communities into opponents and supporters of the nuclear industry. Relatively few persons remained undecided. Although Olson never specifies any expected percentage of free riders, the experimental data of Marwell and Ames (1979, 1980) has been used to argue that free riding is less of a problem than Olson's logic suggests. Our first hypothesis summarizes Olson's (1965) argument:

Hypothesis 1: The majority of TMI opponents will ride free on the efforts of citizen activists.

The second orienting hypothesis focuses on the reasons for whatever free riding did occur in the TMI mobilization effort. Olson (1965) suggests that the perceived irrationality of incurring the costs of participation in a struggle for public goods should explain most free riding. The second hypothesis again summarizes Olson (1965):

Hypothesis 2: Self-interested rationality will be the primary reason for whatever free riding does occur in the TMI area.

With the third hypothesis, we turn to comparisons between the most active citizens and the free riders. Although various RM analysts emphasize the importance of solidary relationships deriving from organizational and interpersonal networks as SMO recruitment mechanisms (Oberschall, 1973; Zald and McCarthy, 1979; Snow et al., 1980), there is vagueness in the RM literature over the solidarity concept. Some RM writers distinguish solidarity and interests (Oberschall, 1973; Zald and McCarthy, 1979), thus allowing for the possibility that social solidarity might serve as either a facilitator or inhibitor of protest mobilization. The distinction is not emphasized by other RM analysts, however, and an important recent empirical test of the RM model ignores the solidarity/interest distinction (Useem, 1980).[7] Solidarity comes in a variety of forms, and the empirical researcher should examine the possibility that these are not correlated. Our data permit us to address that issue. The general thrust of these perspectives provides what we will call the RM hypothesis:

Hypothesis 3: Activists in the TMI area will report more solidary relationships than will the free riders.

Although earlier social movement theorists were more inclined than are contemporary RM writers to emphasize the importance of beliefs in accounting for involvement, the systematic consideration of ideology has been generally neglected by sociologists. This variable, however, figures prominently in our research design. First of all, we distinguish free riders from the rest of the population in terms of their attitudinal opposition to TMI. Secondly, we examine political, religious, and issue-specific ideological differences between the activists and free riders in attempting to account for SMO involvement. At this point, however, we will simply list a fourth orienting hypothesis which directs attention to the role of attitudes and ideas in activist recruitment:

Hypothesis 4: Activists will be more ideologically inclined toward political involvement prior to actual affiliation than will the free riders.

The final hypothesis focuses on the role of specific grievances in fostering protest activism. Olson's model does not suggest that they will be important independent predictors of mobilization, and some RM analysts seem to deny any role to discontent (e.g., McCarthy and Zald, 1977).[8] In the TMI case, citizens' evaluations of the seriousness of the accident as well as their evacuation behavior appeared to be important enough influences to deserve special consideration. Our fifth orienting hypothesis asserts that attitudinal and behavioral indicators of discontent will be stronger for activists:

Hypothesis 5: Activists will report higher levels of specific grievances associated with the emergency period than the free riders.

The time dimension is frequently ignored in social movement analysis. This can lead to conceptual confusion, especially where pre- and postinvolvement variables are mixed together. When researchers do not *attempt* to distinguish between pre- and postinvolvement solidarity, ideology, or discontent, for example, they may use SMO affiliation as an indicator of solidarity, and/or they may explain discontent levels and ideological similarities as causes rather than effects of SMO affiliations. In the absence of longitudinal data, we attempt to avoid difficulties such as these by asking respondents to distinguish pre- and postinvolvement indicators. Despite the imperfections of this method, we cannot imagine any realistic alternatives when studying an actual mobilization process. Our analysis will focus primarily on the preinvolvemnt indicators because they are the most theoretically interesting.

Operational Definitions

The theoretical vagueness of central concepts such as *activist* and *free rider* presents a challenge for empirical research. When an SMO emerges in pursuit of a public good, what criteria should researchers use to distinguish the *activists*? Whether the *activists* are called *members* (Turner and Killian, 1972:334 ff.), *constituents* (McCarthy and Zald, 1977:1221), or *participants* (Snow et al., 1980:789), various levels of involvement are acknowledged by most writers. Should those who do not join an SMO designed to pursue a particular public good (or avoid a public bad), but who sign petitions, write letters to public officials, vote for appropriate candidates, or simply express support for the SMO goals, for example, be considered activists? Such behavior could, conceivably, be said to contribute to the attainment of the public good. We exclude such from our *activist* category because we are interested in structured involvement. In line with the RM emphasis on the problems and perspectives of organizers (Zald and McCarthy, 1979: 1), our *activists* are those so defined by the SMO leaders themselves (as will be explained in more detail below).

The operational meaning of *free rider* is even less agreed upon by researchers than is that of *activist*. Our *free-rider* category includes citizens other writers would label *adherents* (McCarthy and Zald, 1977:1221), *sympathizers* (Snow et al., 1980:789), or *supporters* (Useem, 1980:360), but it also includes people who agree with the goals of the SMO, but say they have never heard of the protest organization itself. Although the inclusion of those who have never heard of the SMO may seem, at first, too broad a definition of "free rider," we consider it preferable to other alternatives. Those who have not heard of the SMO present just as much of a challenge to SMO leaders as those who fail to contribute because they disagree with the way a particular SMO is pursuing its goals, because they are too uneducated or preoccupied with personal issues, or because the SMO's efforts are futile. It seems reasonable, both from a theoretical and from an operational viewpoint, to employ an *objective free-rider* category to refer to all people expressing a preference for a public good being sought by some SMO, regardless of whether they have heard of the SMO or agree with its mode of operating. When the *objective free-rider* category is decomposed, as we will do in this paper, it results in useful information for both organizers and practical theorists.[9]

After our discussion of the samples, models, and measures, we will address each of the focal hypotheses.

Methodological Issues

Samples

Before the survey was carried out, the first author spent 18 months of intense observation in the TMI area (Walsh, 1981). Insights gained were instrumental in the subsequent construction of questionnaires for activists and free riders in Middletown, Newberry Township, Harrisburg and Lancaster. As a result of the fieldwork, enough trust had been established with the SMO leaders in these communities to obtain their cooperation in providing lists of their most involved members and securing these activists' support. Leaders in the four SMOs were not given any target numbers when asked to name people they considered active in their organizations. These lists (N=165) included people who performed a wide variety of tasks for the SMOs, including "cadre," "staff," "workers" and even a few members of "transitory teams" (McCarthy and Zald, 1977:1227). The activist list did not include those whose only action was to sign a petition to close TMI, to purchase tickets at raffles sponsored by the SMO, to attend a few public meetings, or who were merely nominal supporters according to the leaders.[10] The fieldwork prior to questionnaire construction not only helped build the trust essential for such a project, but also provided important insights into the dynamics and most salient issues of the protest processes. Questionnaires, usually delivered and picked up from the respondents on the same day, were received from 149 activists. The response rate was 90 percent (149 of 165).

A pro-TMI citizens' group, sponsored by the utility and composed primarily of TMI workers and their families, emerged approximately one year after the accident. Thus area residents who favored the restart of TMI-1 had an organization representing their preferences, and those who had not contributed any time or money to the pro-TMI group could be called "free riders." We estimated the percentages of free riders on both sides of the TMI issue. Because our primary interest was on the anti-TMI free riders serving as a comparison group for the activists, the pro-TMI free riders were dropped after an initial screening.[11]

Random samples of adults were drawn from the same four communities as the activists and interviewed by a professional telephone survey firm. Respondents were selected by a process of random digit dialing to assume that those with unlisted numbers had an equal probability of being included. A filter questionnaire was used to determine free-rider status. After first being asked their position on the TMI issues, respondents were then asked whether they knew of any group of like-minded persons in the area. Those who did were also asked whether they had contributed any time or money to the group. The free riders on each side were those who either did not know or the group of like-minded persons in their area or had not contributed any time or money to it.[12]

Extended telephone interviews, including many of the same questions asked of the activists, were administered to the anti-TMI free riders. At the outset of the study, it was decided to attempt to interview twice as many free riders as activists in order to have enough observations to perform certain statistical analyses. In all, 673 persons answered the filter questionnaire, representing 80 percent of those contacted. Of these, 288 were anti-TMI free riders who answered the larger questionnaire, making the free-rider sample nearly twice the size of the activists' (288 to 149).

The data gathering for both the activists and free riders in the four communities occurred between December 1980 and September 1981. TMI issues continued to be salient throughout this period, but no significant events occurred which were likely to introduce bias deriving from the delay between the initial and final interviews. Although systematic checks were not made, we had no reason to think that the use of questionnaires with the activists and telephone interviews with the free riders introduced any systematic bias into our data.

This is the first sampling design we are aware of in the social movement literature to focus comparisons exclusively on those indicating support for the goals of the SMO under consideration. Unless such general ideological controls are introduced, however, it is difficult to interpret the significance of whatever similarities and differences do reveal themselves between SMO participants and the comparison groups selected.

Model Specifications and Measurement

Insights from both the fieldwork and the literature prompted us to focus on background, solidary networks, ideology, and accident-specific discontent in our comparisons between activists and free riders. Because the large majority of activists became involved within weeks of the accident itself, we distinguished pre- and postaccident time periods for our solidarity and ideology items in the following analysis. After having joined the protest movement in their community, it is to be expected that activists' attitudinal and behavioral differences from the free riders would increase. Our data support that presumption, but our primary focus is upon the differences between the two groups prior to the activists' involvement with their community SMOs.

A summary of the measures used in this paper is included in Figure 1. Among the background variables, the occupation of the principal wage earner was requested, and respondents were asked to give the title, kind of work, and the business, industry, or agency involved. We subsequently coded this information into the six general categories listed in the figure. The income categories were intentionally made quite wide lest the activists, especially, resent our prying. In addition to the general sensitivity of the income topic, activists also knew that citizens opposing nuclear power elsewhere had been sued by the industry.

Percent Solidarity. Although we estimated the effects of several other solidarity variables not included in Figure 1, those retained were the primary ones accounting for differences between the activists and free riders.[13] Our preliminary analyses prompted us to distinguish *general*, *political*, and *issue-specific* preaccident solidarity. Items on neighborhood solidarity and club/organizational affiliation were used as *general* indicators (Figure 1.B.1), and *political* solidarity was measured by asking respondents whether they voted in the 1976 presidential election (see Boor, 1981). The *issue-specific* items included estimates of the respondent's solidarity with both veteran and newly emergent activists (Figure 1.B.3).

A factor-analysis of the nine solidarity measures (the five presented in the paper plus the four not included) was conducted to determine whether a solidarity index could be created. One factor, containing only two items (neighborhood and community solidarity), emerged from the analysis. An inspection of the correlation matrix revealed that 57 percent of the intercorrelations were under 10, whereas only 9 percent were over .20. This evidence suggested that solidarity was a diffuse and multidimensional concept.

Preaccident Ideology. We distinguished three types of beliefs relevant to the analysis. During the early fieldwork stage, some activists themselves suggested that religious faith seemed to prompt numerous people to remain uninvolved because they believed that such things were "in God's hands." We included an item asking respondents how important faith in God was in their lives (Figure 1.C.1). In light of the fact that opposition to nuclear power is commonly seen as a liberal viewpoint, we also included an item asking respondent's "usual stand on political issues" (Figure 1.C.2). In addition to these *religious* and *political* ideology items, we also included three *issue-specific* ones involving attitudes toward nuclear power plants in general, TMI in particular, and the continuing development of nuclear weapons before the TMI accident (Figure 1.C.3).

Emergency Period Discontent. Because the initial fieldwork suggested that the experience of the accident, regardless of solidary networks or ideological factors, contributed independently to the protest mobilization processes in the area (Walsh, 1981), we used two measures of respondents' discontent during that period. One was attitudinal, asking how serious the accident was perceived to be, and the other focused on behavior, asking whether the person had actually evacuated from the area during the initial emergency period (Figure 1.D).

Postaccident Attitudes and Behavior. The accident itself changed many persons' attitudes and behaviors. Some of the activists said that they would never have imagined themselves becoming involved in a political protest organization prior to their accident experiences. Once they did become involved, however, we would expect their attitudes and behavior to become increasingly distinct from that of the free riders because of group interaction processes.

Federal, state, and local officials held numerous public meetings and hearings in the weeks and months after the accident, and the emerging protest groups also hosted a few rallies during the same period.[14] We asked both the activists and free riders whether they attended any of these public meetings. Other items involving behavior included evacuation during the krypton venting in

Figure 1
Concepts, Variables and Specific Measures

Concepts and Variables	Descriptions and Measurement
A. Background	
1. Education	Categories ranged from (1) none . . . (4) completed high school, (5) some college/vocational, (6) completed college, (7) graduate or professional school.
2. Occupational Status	Specific occupational data subsequently coded into six general categories: (1) laborer and semi-skilled; (2) service and protective workers, (3) skilled blue collar, foremen; (4) sales or clerical; (5) small owner/small manager; (6) professional, semi-professional, managerial (relatively large).
3. Household Income	Categories ranged from (1) under $5,000 . . . (4) $13,000 to $18,000, (5) $18,000 to $25,000, (6) $25,000 to $50,000, (7) over $50,000.
B. Preaccident Solidarity	
1. General Neighborhood	"Please try to think back *before the accident,* and tell me how much you felt in common with . . . most of your neighbors," with categories ranging from (1) nothing . . . (3) don't know, (4) pretty much, (5) very much.
Clubs and Organizations	Total number of clubs and organizations with which respondents were affiliated *before the TMI accident.* List included labor unions, religious groups, fraternal organizations, veterans' organizations, business, civic groups, PTAs, neighborhood clubs, sports teams, political clubs, card clubs and social clubs, charitable organizations.
2. Political	Voted in 1976 presidential election. Coded "yes" or "no."
3. Issue-Specific Anti-Nuclear	"Please try to think back *before the accident,* and say how much you felt in common with the anti-nuclear activists." Same options as in B.1 (neighborhood) above.
SMO ties	Number of persons who subsequently became involved in their local community protest group whom R knew *before the accident.*
C. Preaccident Ideology	
1. Religious	"Whether or not you attend religious services, how important is faith in God to your life?" Four response categories were collapsed into two, "important" and "unimportant."
2. Political	"Which of the following best describes your usual stand on political issues?" (1) conservative, (2) middle of the road, (3) liberal, (4) other (please specify).
3. Issue Specific Nuclear Power TMI-1 Restart Nuclear Weapons	Respondents were asked, in separate items, how they felt about TMI, commercial nuclear power in general, and the continuing development of nuclear weapons, *before the accident.* The five response options ranged from (1) strongly favor . . . (3) neutral . . . (5) strongly oppose.
D. Emergency Period Discontent	
1. Seriousness of Threat	"How serious a threat did you feel the TMI nuclear power plant was for your own and your family's safety during the two-week emergency period right after the accident?" (1) no threat; (2) somewhat of a threat; (3) serious threat; (4) very serious threat.
2. Initial Evacuation	"Did you evacuate during the first week or so of the accident?" Coded "yes" or "no."
E. Postaccident Attitudes/Behavior	
1. Public Meetings	"Did you attend any public meetings concerning the TMI accident?" Coded "yes" or "no."
2. Nuclear Attitudes Nuclear Power TMI-1 Restart Nuclear Weapons	Respondents were asked, in separate items, how they felt about TMI, commercial nuclear power in general, and the continuing development of nuclear weapons, at the same time of the survey (approximately 2 years after the accident). Same options as in C.3 above.
3. Krypton Opposition	R's attitude toward venting of radioactive krypton into atmosphere in June 1980. Five options from (1) strongly in favor . . . (3) no opinion or d. k. . . . (5) strongly opposed.
4. Krypton Evacuation	"Did you evacuate during the actual venting of the Krypton in June, 1980?" Coded "yes" or "no."
5. Political Solidarity	Voted in the 1980 presidential election. Coded "yes" or "no."
6. Political Ideology	R's candidate in 1980 presidential election. Coded "liberal" if Carter, Anderson or some more radical write-in candidate.
7. TMI in 1981	"And how about today, how serious a threat do you feel the Three Mile Island nuclear plant is for you and your family's safety?" (1) no threat; (2) somewhat of a threat; (3) serious threat; (4) very serious threat.
8. Civil Disobedience Attitude	"Some people support the use of nonviolent civil disobedience as a means of making viewpoints known or bringing about change, while others disapprove of such tactics under any circumstances. How about yourself? How do you feel about such tactics as refusing to pay part of a utility bill, or blocking traffic with a peaceful demonstration? Do you . . . (1) strongly disapprove; (2) mildly disapprove; (3) feel undecided; (4) mildly approve; (5) strongly approve."
9. Move Residence	"If TMI-1, the undamaged reactor, is allowed to be returned to service as a nuclear power plant, which of the following probably comes closest to how you will feel about such a decision?" (1) Favor the decision; (2) Oppose it, but remain living in area; (3) Oppose it, and think of moving; (4) Definitely move away from the area.

June 1980, voting in the 1980 election, and the probability that the respondent would move from the area if Unit 1 restarted (Figure 1.F).

Attitudinal indicators for this postaccident period included items on the same nuclear issues (commercial nuclear power, TMI, and nuclear weapons) that were asked for the preaccident period, opposition to the krypton venting in June 1980 cleanup, liberal vote in the 1980 election, and the respondent's evaluation of the seriousness of the TMI situation during the time of the survey in 1981. We also asked about the respondent's attitude toward nonviolent civil disobedience (Figure 1.E).

Although all of our preaccident measures are subject to the pitfalls of retrospective indicators, we are reasonably confident of their accuracy in reflecting respondents' actual attitudes prior to the accident. It is very common, for example, to hear postaccident local activists admitting their preaccident lethargy or even a tendency to favor TMI and nuclear power because of its presumed economic benefits. Many activists, especially in the two communities closest to TMI (Middletown and Newberry Township), acknowledge a basic sympathy with the free riders and other less-active citizens because they themselves were never politically active prior to the accident. The modest correlations (ranging from .25 to .45) between the pre- and postaccident measures of attitudes toward TMI and commercial nuclear power for both groups suggest the importance of the accident experience in modifying ideology.[15]

Findings

We turn, first, to the question of free riding in the TMI area. Our data enable us to estimate both the extent of, and reasons for, the phenomenon in this actual mobilization process. We will then turn to comparisons between the anti-TMI free riders and the most active citizens in the four focal communities.

Free Riding and Reasons for It

The results in Table 1 speak to our first focal hypothesis, and show 87 percent (288 of 330) of the TMI opponents and 98 percent of the TMI supporters as selective free riders. The fact that only 5 percent of the total random sample were undecided shows how salient the TMI issues were among residents of the four communities. Marwell and Ames (1979:1358-59) generalized from their own unique research design to raise questions about the power of the free-rider problem in other collective action situations. The data in Table 1 show, however, that free riders are indeed a major problem for organizers. Even when imperfect information is partially controlled for, by dropping those who never heard of the SMO, the magnitude of the free-rider problem is still much greater than Marwell and Ames (1979, 1980) suggest.

Although tens of thousands of people had their lives seriously disrupted by the accident and evacuation, only a very small percentage became actively involved in the protest movement. The data in Table 1 show that relative deprivation is a poor predictor of protest activism. This is not to argue, however, that the suddenly imposed griev-

Table 1
Telephone Survey Results in TMI Area Communities

	Subgroup Free Riders	Total %	(N)
A. Opposed to TMI-1 Restart and/or Water Dumping[a]			
1. Objective Free Riders[b]	87%	43%	(288)
2. Contributors		6%	(42)
B. In Favor of TMI-1 Restart			
1. Objective Free Riders[b]	98%	45%	(303)
2. Contributors		1%	(7)
C. Undecided		5%	(33)
		100%	(673)

[a]The primary focus of the Lancaster citizens' group was the prevention of the dumping of radioactive water from the TMI-1 into the Susquehanna River.
[b]When those who say they never heard of their local SMOs are dropped from the totals, this reduces the percentages of anti-TMI free riders to 84% (213 of 253), and the pro-TMI percentage of free riders to 86% (42 of 49).

fluence in promoting the protest mobilization. To the contrary, there were anti-nuclear citizen organizations in the TMI area which languished for lack of citizen support prior to the accident (see Walsh, 1981). Even though only a small proportion of the relatively deprived became actively involved, however, the widespread discontent was certainly a favorable condition for the emergence and growth of protest organizations. As Tillock and Morrison (1979:153) observe, a large number of persons valuing a public good "may increase the incentive to contribute on the part of those who value it more highly."

For the remainder of this paper, we will only be using the anti-TMI free-riders from Table 1 (A.1) to compare with the most active citizens in the four focal communities. A few of these activists were also identified as "contributors" (Table 1.A.2) in the course of the random telephone survey,[16] but the activists used for the following comparisons were much more involved in protest processes than the majority of "contributors," who merely reported giving some time and money to their local group. As noted in an earlier section, our activists were named by SMO leaders as the most involved citizens in their respective communities.

The second focal hypothesis, summarizing the utilitarian approach to free riding, suggests that self-interested rationality is the primary reason for this phenomenon. Using open-ended items, we asked both activists and free riders about this. Activists were asked to guess why persons who were essentially in agreement with their local SMO's goals did not become actively involved with the group,[17] and the free riders were asked why they themselves did not become involved. Table 2 summarizes those responses.

Both the activists and the free riders suggested a more heterogeneous list of reasons for

---

Table 2
Imagined (by Activists) and Reported (by Free Riders) Reasons for Free Riding in the TMI Area

	Activists' Opinions[a]	Free Riders' Reasons[b]
1. Political Powerlessness[c]	65%	5%
2. Familial and Personal Preoccupations[d]	37%	18%
3. Denial of Problem's Seriousness[e]	36%	4%
4. Social Pressures[f]	33%	2%
5. Economic Pressures[g]	24%	7%
6. Technical Complexity of the Issue[h]	14%	2%
7. Overt Free Riding on Others' Efforts[i]	4%	5%
8. Opposed to Joining Any Groups[j]	2%	9%
9. Critical of Local SMO's Method of Operating[k]	2%	6%
10. Never Invited to Join Local SMO	0	8%
11. Never Heard of Local SMO	0	26%
12. Other (e.g., "no reason," "don't know," or "don't care")	0	8%
		100%

[a]More than one possible reason for free riding was given by many activists, and thus column percentage exceeds 100%. Reasons are listed in order of frequency of mention by the activists.
[b]With very few exceptions, only one reason for noninvolvement was given by free riders. For these few exceptions, the first or most dominant was selected here, making the total 100%.
[c]These and following sample comments are from free riders: "You are fighting a hopeless battle." "Any small group can't buck a big industry." "Can't win against city hall."
[d]Examples: "I'm afraid to leave the kids at home to go to meetings." "I just didn't have the time." "I'm too old to get involved."
[e]Examples: "If I'd evacuated and thought it was that serious, I probably would have become involved." "I got tired hearing about the nuclear power crap."
[f]Examples: "Because of certain social activities, I couldn't get involved whether pro or con." "Because of religious matters I could not get involved in the controversy."
[g]Examples: "I work 14 to 16 hours a day and don't have the time." "I can't get involved because I'm a police officer." "I work nights and can't go to meetings."
[h]Examples: "I'm not too educated, and if I don't understand it, it doesn't hold my interest." "I don't believe in getting involved in something I don't understand."
[i]Examples: "Enough people are involved, but I suppose I really should help out." "I'm just lazy, I guess." "I just never took the time to find out when and where they were meeting."
[j]Examples: "I'm not one to get into organizations." "I don't want to be in any group." "I'm an individual and can do my own thinking."
[k]Examples: "In the beginning, they were not clear as to what they wanted to do." "I thought they were radical." "A lot of them are looking for front page publicity." "I think a lot of this stuff is communist inspired."

noninvolvement than the merely calculating and self-interested ones emphasized by the utilitarians. Many activists gave more than one possible reason for the free riders' behavior, but only 4 percent gave ones that could be classified as "overt free riding" (see Table 2.7). Because of the multiple possible reasons given by the activists, their column in Table 2 does not sum to 100 percent. The activists mentioned political powerlessness most frequently, but also included a variety of other possible inhibitors to collective action. Some of the activists' imagined reasons for noninvolvement centered on personal costs in the familial, social, and economic spheres (Table 2:2,4,5), but others focused on the specific issue itself (Table 2:3,6). Only 2 percent of the activists mentioned the possibility that their SMO's operating procedures might explain noninvolvement, and none of them suggested communication or recruitment shortcomings as a possible explanation (Table 2:10, 11).

In contrast to the activists, very few free riders gave more than one reason for their lack of involvement, and we coded the first one for the few exceptions so that their column in Table 2 sums to 100 percent. The largest number (26%) of free riders said they had never heard of their local protest group (Table 2:11). Familial preoccupations were the second most frequently mentioned reason (18%). The other categories as well as samples of actual comments are included in Table 2 and its footnotes.

The activists' and free riders' explanations for the same phenomenon are not necessarily mutually exclusive. Many free riders never heard of their local SMO only because they were poorly informed about the TMI issue. The widespread coverage received by the various protest groups, in fact, prompted some free riders to accuse them of wanting too much publicity (Table 2, footnote k). Many of the free riders who said they never heard of their local protest groups probably avoided newspaper, radio, and TV coverage of the TMI topic—perhaps due to feelings of powerlessness, or to personal problems, job pressures, or various other reasons. Criticism of the SMO's method of operating, given the open meetings and democratic decision-making processes used in each group, could also be interpreted to mean that the respondent just did not want to become involved.

Any adequate explanation for the lack of involvement by the free riders, according to these data, includes some combination of self-interested calculations, SMO communication failures, and a variety of additional psychological, demographic, and structural factors. These data warn against assumptions of perfect information and an overemphasis on self-interested rationality in accounting for free riding. Even among the free riders who knew of the SMOs, many seem never to have made a considered decision not to become involved.[18]

We turn now to comparisons of the most involved activists in the four communities with the anti-TMI free riders (Table 1.A.1) in those same communities.

Activists and Free Riders Compared

The time dimension is a critical factor in analyses of social movement involvement. Because it was impossible to predict such an event, we could only ask respondents in each group about their preaccident affiliations, networks, and attitudes when the data were collected—i.e., after the event. The data in Table 3 are organized into preaccident (A, B, and C), emergency period (D), and postaccident (E) time periods.

Background Characteristics. The top panel of Table 3 shows the activists were in higher educational, occupational, and income categories than the free riders. This is what we would expect on the basis of most previous research (Verba and Nie, 1972).

Preaccident Solidarity. The data in Table 3.B show that different types of solidarity had differential implications for mobilization in the TMI area. Activists reported higher levels of general organizational affiliation, political solidarity, and specific anti-nuclear or anti-TMI ties, but the free riders indicated higher levels of neighborhood solidarity.

A possible explanation for the finding that activists exhibited lower levels of neighborhood solidarity than the free riders may be found in the adoption-diffusion literature. It has been found that innovators (activists, in this case) are usually less integrated into the local community or neighborhood than those who prefer to wait and see how a new idea/action works out (Rogers and Shoemaker, 1971). Innovators with background characteristics similar to those of the TMI activists have been found to have more social ties outside their own neighborhoods and communities.

Table 3
Comparisons Between Activists and Free Riders[a]

	Activists (N = 149)	Free Riders (N = 288)
A. Background		
1. Education	5.5	4.3
2. Occupational Status	4.7	3.8
3. Income	5.0	4.2
B. Pre-Accident Solidarity		
1. General		
Neighborhood Solidarity	3.0	3.6
Number of Clubs/Organizations	1.6	1.0
2. Political		
Voted in 1976 Election	90%	70%
3. Issue-Specific		
Anti-Nuclear Solidarity	2.8	2.1
SMO ties	2.0	.4
C. Preaccident Ideology		
1. Religious		
Faith in God Important	72%	94%
2. Political		
Liberal Sympathies	51%	13%
3. Issue-Specific		
Opposition to Nuclear Power Plants	3.6	3.0
Opposition to TMI	3.7	3.1
Opposition to Nuclear Weapons	3.9	3.3
D. Emergency Period Discontent		
1. Initial Seriousness of Accident	3.8	3.3
2. Evacuated During Initial Emergency	87%	56%
E. Postaccident Attitudes and Behavior		
1. Attended Public Meetings on TMI	95%	8%
2. Opposition to Nuclear Power Plants	4.9	3.8
3. Opposition to Unit 1 Restart	5.0	4.4
4. Opposition to Nuclear Weapons	4.5	3.5
5. Opposition to Krypton Venting	4.7	4.0
6. Evacuated During June, 1980, Krypton Venting	39%	10%
7. Voted in 1980 Election	94%	71%
8. Liberal Vote in 1980 Election	76%	23%
9. Seriousness of TMI Situation in 1980	3.6	2.8
10. Approval of Nonviolent Civil Disobedience	4.5	2.8
11. Consider Moving if Unit 1 is Restarted	52%	26%

[a]All differences in Table 3 are significant at the .01 level or beyond, using χ^2 or two-tailed t-tests.

Preaccident Ideology. The results in Table 3.C show the activists much more likely than the free riders to report liberal political sympathies (51% vs. 13%) prior to the accident and mobilization processes. The activists were also more opposed, even before the accident, to commercial nuclear power in general, TMI in particular, and the increased production of nuclear weapons—although the reader will note that the means for each group are only between the "neutral" (3) and "mildly oppose" (4) response categories for each of the three.

The data in Table 3.C also support the impressions of those activists who suggested the religious faith seemed to immobilize some people. The free riders attributed more importance to faith than the activists.

Emergency Period Discontent. The terror and near chaos associated with the evacuation prompted many white residents to refer to March 30, 1979 as "Black Friday." Although the accident started on Wednesday, March 28, it was not until Friday that its full seriousness became public and widespread evacuation occurred. The decision to evacuate, and the actual experience of leaving home and neighborhood (perhaps for the last time), was a "bridge-burning act" (Gerlach and Hine, 1970) for many activists. Some vividly recall promising themselves, their families, and/or their neighbors that if they ever did return they would work to close the TMI nuclear facilities. The activists were higher than the free riders on the two discontent measures. As seen in Table 3.D, the means for both the activists and the free riders are between "serious" and very serious" in their evaluations of the accident during the emergency period. The actual evacuation rate was over 50 percent for both groups, with the activists more likely to have fled the area than the free riders (87% vs. 56%).

Postaccident Attitudes and Behavior. The TMI area became a beehive of political activity during the months following the accident. Local, state, and federal officials chaired public meetings which typically included presentations by medical, health, and/or technical personnel followed by an open period for comments and questions from the audience, which usually numbered in the hundreds.

Three of the four protest organizations also emerged during the months following the accident (the Harrisburg SMO already existed) and all four advertised regular public meetings to which all area residents were invited. In addition, there were a few protest rallies in each community during this time (see Walsh, 1981).

Approximately a year after the original accident, authorities began publicizing their intention to vent the trapped radioactive krypton gases from TMI-2 into the surrounding atmosphere. Again, public meetings were held and many area residents made strong public statements against it. Despite widespread local opposition, however, the NRC gave the TMI owners permission to go ahead with the venting. Many people evacuated for a second time in June 1980.

By the time of our survey, in 1981, the various community-based SMOs had become the carriers of the citizen protest against the TMI. Their newsletters and regular public meetings were sources of information for the media for their respective communities. The interaction among the activists helped strengthen their own opposition to TMI and influence the attitudes and behavior of group members. The frequent discussion of nuclear issues, the krypton venting, political candidates po-

sitions on nuclear power, civil disobedience as a protest tactic, and residence relocation in the event of a restart doubtlessly help explain the increasingly marked differences between the activists and free riders in the bottom panel of Table 3.

Table 3.E displays a dramatic difference between the two groups as far as public meeting, hearing, or rally attendance was concerned (95% vs. 8%). We also see that the differences between the two groups regarding nuclear power plants and nuclear weapons had increased (compare Table 3.C.3 to 3.E.2 and 4).[19] The same panel of the table shows the activists significantly more opposed to the krypton venting, more likely to have evacuated because of this venting, more likely to have voted in the 1980 presidential election, much more likely to have voted for a liberal candidate in that election, and possessing grimmer views of the seriousness of the TMI situation two years after the initial emergency period. The final two items in this section show the activists' general approval of civil disobedience (in contrast to the free riders' disapproval) and indicate that they were twice as likely to say they would probably move from the area in the event of a Unit 1 restart.

Summarizing Table 3, the bivariate analysis shows the activists with higher socioeconomic status and more solidary links at the organizational, political, and issue-specific levels. The activists were also more politically liberal prior to the accident, and more inclined to be somewhat suspicious of both commercial nuclear power and the weapons industry. During the actual emergency period, the activists were more likely to consider the TMI accident a very serious threat and to have evacuated. The free riders, on the other hand, reported stronger neighborhood solidarity and were more inclined to trust in God to protect them in their daily lives. After the protest groups had evolved, the differences between the activists and free riders became even more marked.

To determine whether the bivariate relationships would remain when control variables were introduced, several multivariate analyses of the data were performed. The next step in our inquiry is the examination of the relative importance of background, preaccident ideology, and discontent and discontent variables in predicting activist involvement.[20]

Table 4
Logistic Regression Analysis

Variables	Model 1 B	Model 2 B	Model 3 B	Model 4 B	Model 5 B
A. Background					
Education	.82***	.73***	.74***	.67***	.71***
B. Preaccident Solidarity					
Neighborhood		−.31**		−.08	−.10
Voted in 1976		.91*		1.10*	1.23**
Anti-Nuclear Solidarity		.31**		.17	.17
Activist Acquaintances		.33***		.32***	.35***
C. Preaccident Ideology					
Importance of Faith in God			−.13	−.30	−.16
Liberal Sympathies			.66***	.62**	.87***
Issue-Specific Nuclear Index (cf. Table 3.C:3)			.26***	.20**	.15*
D. Emergency Period Discontent					
Initial Seriousness of Accident					1.50***
Evacuated During Initial Emergency					.68**
Intercept	−4.66	−5.13	−8.53	−9.18	−16.55
R²	.17	.30	.28	.36	.46
D	.18	.28	.26	.32	.37
PAC	.24	.36	.35	.43	.51
−2LogL	411.44	318.84	309.70	250.73	213.66

*p<.05. **p<.01. ***p<.001.

Logistic Regression Analysis

Logistic regression analysis was used instead of standard regression techniques to avoid the estimation problems occasioned by dichotomous dependent variables (Nerlove and Press, 1973). Because of missing data, we dropped three variables from Table 3 in the logit analysis. Preliminary analyses indicated that income as well as occupational status contributed little additional explanatory power. The relatively large number of missing cases on these variables discouraged us from forming an SES index. The same missing data problem, as well as its unimportance as an explanatory variable in the final equations, prompted us to drop the organizational affiliation variable from the solidarity items.[21]

The three issue-specific ideology items (Table 3.C:3) were combined into a single index for the logit analysis. The alpha coefficient for this index was .75.

The results of five separate logit analyses are displayed in Table 4.[22] As one moves from Model 1 to Model 5 in the table, additional variables are included and their explanatory power is assessed by means of several measures of fit included at the bottom of each column.[23]

Turning first to Model 1, in which only education, our sole background variable, was included, we find it making an important contribution to explained variation between the activists and free riders. When the preaccident solidarity factors are added in Model 2, all four of them are statistically significant. The measures of fit also increase substantially. As noted above, solidarity factors are commonly emphasized by the RM theorists as important predictors of social movement involvement.

Model 3 omits solidarity and includes only the background and ideology measures. The measures of fit are similar to those of Model 2, and two of the three variables are statistically significant. The data in Model 3 suggest that ideology is comparable to solidarity in importance, although RM theorists may argue that one's solidary relationships determine ideology. The contrary argument, of course, could also be made—that ideology determines solidary relationships—but we see in Model 4 that when solidarity and ideology variables are both included in the model the measures of fit are better than when either factor is included separately.[24] Furthermore, both preaccident solidarity and ideology indicators are statistically significant.

Finally, Model 5 shows that the emergency period discontent variables make a substantial independent contribution to the explanation of the difference between activists and free riders in the TMI area.[25]

In sum, this logistic multiple regression analysis suggests that *both* the structural variables advocated by RM theorists *and* more social psychological ones such as ideology and discontent should be considered by analysts seeking a better understanding of the factors inclining people toward activism.[26]

Summary and Discussion

The data from this actual mobilization process provide qualified support for Olson over his critics and also suggest an additive model of social movement involvement which incorporates insights front both traditional and RM perspectives.

Remarkably high levels of free riding on both sides of the TMI issue support Olson (1965) vis-à-vis critics who question the magnitude of the free-rider problem (Marwell and Ames, 1979, 1990). When only 12 percent of a sub-group defining itself as discontented contributes *any* time or money to an organized political response by fellow citizens, free riding has to be considered a major problem. Although Olson's more theoretical critics do not specify the percentage of potential free riders they expect to be persuaded to collective action by solidary relationships (Fireman and Gamson, 1979) or the "no exit" nature of collective bads (Mitchell, 1979), the implications of their logic suggest higher percentages of activists than emerged in the TMI area. More than one of the five solidary factors listed by Fireman and Gamson (1979) are applicable to the majority of persons in the communities, and the widespread concern over the possibility of another nuclear accident in the event of a TMI-1 restart makes it logical, according to Mitchell's (1979) line of argument, to contribute to the elimination of that threat.

Although a significant percentage of the free riders' reasons for their own lack of involvement included considerations of calculating self-interest, as Olson (1965) predicted, SMO communication failures and other explanations (see Table 2) accounted for the largest number of free riders. More conceptual clarification of the various categories of free riding and empirical research documenting their prevalence are obviously suggested by these data.

Regardless of the percent of those becoming politically active from those at risk to mobilization in the wake of the TMI accident, activists' numbers were large enough to mount a serious challenge to the nuclear industry. The data suggest an additive model of social movement involvement incorporating structural, ideological, and grievance variables. RM perspectives emphasizing the importance of solidary networks were generally supported, but the data also suggested that some patterns of solidarity may have negative impacts on SMO recruitment. We suspect that the patterns of correlation between the various forms of solidarity and SMO involvement depend, to a significant extent, on the specific issues around which the mobilization process forms and also upon the networks activated by the initial organizers.

Social psychological variables, frequently ignored by RM writers, were shown to be additional independent predictors of activism. Even after ideology was used to filter the comparison group so that only opponents of TMI were interviewed, other ideological factors were as important as solidary networks in explaining protest involvement. Our data also showed that people's perceptions of, and reactions to, the same focal grievances contributed to political activism.

In sum, protest activism is a relatively rare phenomenon with a variety of contributing factors. Depending on the nature of the grievances, various structural and psychological factors will become significant predictors of involvement. The relative importance of structural and ideological variables probably varies from one instance of collective action to another, and this should be considered an empirical question inviting additional research. In the case of the TMI mobilization processes, background variables, preaccident solidary networks, preaccident ideology, and issue-specific discontent each made its own significant independent contribution toward explaining who did, and who did not, become actively involved. Our additive model assumes that these mobilization processes were not atypical, and that any attempt to explain SMO involvement without including both structural and social psychological variables is unrealistic and misleading.

Notes

1. A "public good" is one that, once supplied for any individuals in a collectivity, is automatically available for consumption by all individuals in that collectivity. Olson (1965:14) defines it thus: "A common, collective, or public good is here defined as any good such that, if any person X_1 in a group $X_1, \ldots, X_i, \ldots,$

X_n consumes it, it cannot feasibly be withheld from the others in that group."

2. A "selective incentive," in contrast to the public good, works to the advantage of those individuals who join the organization working for the collectivity's interests (Olson, 1965:51). The author discusses both positive (inducements) and negative (constraints) selective incentives.

3. Olson (1965:49ff.) makes exceptions for what he calls "privileged" and "intermediate" groups, but because we will be focusing on latent groups (communities) with thousands of citizens in them, such exceptions are not relevant to our discussion.

4. There is more variation in traditional collective behavior perspectives than some RM literature reviews lead one to imagine (see Turner, 1981, for an excellent summary), and there is also considerable variation in the RM camp (Perrow, 1979: Turner, 1981; Walsh, 1981). For a thoughtful summary, synthesis and critique of both perspectives, see Zurcher and Snow (1981).

5. Bert Useem (1980) makes a similar observation about the need for more integration of insights from different models. In his own paper, however, he combines activists and free riders to compare them with the rest of the population. In doing this, he ignores the most interesting and important comparison, in our opinion—i.e., between those who in his words "support" (ride free?) and those who "participate" (become actively involved?).

6. Lancaster residents, especially, were concerned that the utility might attempt to dispose of more than 1 million gallons of radioactive water by dumping it into the Susquehanna River only a few miles upstream from that city's drinking water intake.

7. Useem's first focal research question (1980:359) is: "Did social solidarity promote or inhibit participation in the anti-busing movement?"

8. In a personal letter commenting on an earlier draft of this paper, Mayer Zald wrote: "Although John [McCarthy] and I made a lot of provocative statements in our 1977 paper, we both believe in the strength of 'hard grievances' in mobilization. Grievance definition by movement cadre is a long-term process dealing with soft and disaggregated grievances" (December 10, 1992).

9. The objective free-rider concept seems especially appropriate in this TMI research because each community had its own SMO which received widespread publicity in the print and electronic media, and also because of the relatively open nature of the decision-making processes within each group. Notices of SMO meetings were carried regularly in the community newspapers, and particularly important meetings/rallies were also announced over radio and TV.

10. Activists' work included organizing public meetings, contacting political and business officials, directing and conducting petition drives, editing and circulating newsletters, seeking funding for legal cases involving the utility, speaking to the public, and a variety of related activities. People who became involved immediately after the accident but then had dropped away by the time of the survey were not included on the activist list by leaders, nor were those who only made token contributions to the SMO. As will be noted below, however, our survey instrument did include items designed to eliminate such nonactivist "contributors" from the free-rider category.

11. Early contacts were made with the pro-TMI citizens' group in the spring of 1980 by the first author. The charged emotional atmosphere surrounding TMI issues made it impossible to move from side to side without arousing suspicion and becoming involved in ethical dilemmas with implications for the research project. Such considerations led to the decision to concentrate on the anti-TMI SMOs.

12. The anti-TMI SMOs received much more coverage in the mass media than the pro-TMI group. The latter was generally viewed as less of a genuine citizens' SMO than a utility-sponsored interest group of TMI workers' relatives and friends.

13. The items not included are marital status, time lived in neighborhood, and solidarity measures at the household and community levels. The first three failed to differentiate activists and free riders. Community solidarity was highly correlated with neighborhood, and only the latter was included.

14. There were various meetings at which federal, state and local officials invited attendees to comment on their accident-related experiences, thoughts, feelings, etc. The Kemeny Commission, for example, held a few of its sessions in the TMI area. In early 1980, federal officials again held public meetings to discuss the atmospheric venting of the radioactive krypton gases trapped since the accident.

15. Regardless of the persuasiveness of such post hoc justifications, of course, the primary reason we relied on memory was that we wanted to introduce the time factor into our analysis and really had no alternative except recall.

16. Because those who said they had contributed some time or money to their community SMO were not asked any further questions, we have no systematic data on the number of those classified as activists who were also identified as "contributors" in the random surveys. Three activists mentioned having been contacted in the telephone survey during later conversations with the first author. The reader should note, however, that "burnt out" former activists (survey was approximately 2 years after the incident) as well as persons sending donations, purchasing t-shirts or rally tickets. etc., might all identify themselves as "contributors."

17. Many of the activists' reasons seemed to be summaries of their own problems deriving from, or threatening, continued involvement.

18. Sherry Cable, a graduate student at Pennsylvania State University, is analyzing the related question re-

garding activists' reasons for involvement, in her doctoral dissertation. Olson's (1965:60) model emphasizes the importance of selective economic incentives, but these were irrelevant in the TMI mobilization processes because the various SMOs were unable to offer such incentives. Very briefly, solidarity and principle in a collective endeavor (Fireman and Gamson, 1979) to avoid a public "bad" (Mitchell, 1979) were the main reasons for activists' involvement.

19. Fieldwork helped us realize the important distinction between being anti-nuclear and being anti-TMI. It is obvious that the only reason the difference between the two groups had not increased on the TMI issue was because of the ceiling effect on the activists' mean.

20. We omit the postaccident variables for both theoretical and statistical reasons. Theoretically, social scientists need not be reminded of the importance of a cohesive group for influencing attitudes and behavior.

21. Once income, occupation, and organizational affiliation were eliminated, fewer than five percent of the cases were missing from any of the remaining variables. The logistic regression analysis program required casewise deletion, but even so, none of the logit analyses had more than fifteen percent of the cases missing.

22. Because we were primarily interested in preaccident correlates of SMO involvement, we dropped activists who were residing outside the TMI area at the time of the accident from our logit analysis. The deletion of these activists and missing data reduced the total number of cases from 437 to 390 in Table 4. An analysis of the items listed in Table 3 based upon 390 cases resulted in exactly the same pattern of results as did the analysis based upon the 437 cases.

23. Three measures of fit are reported in Table 4: R^2 (see Knoke and Burke, 1980), D (see Harrell, 1980), and a predictive accuracy coefficient (PAC) which is based on the equations' ability to predict activism (Harrell, 1980). We are not here concerned with the relative merits and demerits of the R^2, D, and PAC coefficients, but only in the relative changes of each across the various models.

24. An inspection of the twelve intercorrelations between the four solidarity measures and the three ideology measures displayed in Model 4 indicated that these two sets of measures were weakly correlated. Of the possible twelve intercorrelations, only one (anti-nuclear solidarity and the issue-specific nuclear index, r = .45) was greater than .30. Most (9 of 12) were less than .20.

25. As explained in the first section of this paper, we think the most useful definition of the free-rider category is that which includes all those expressing a preference for the goal(s) of the SMO in question—even though some may not have heard of the SMO. One *ASR* reviewer challenged our inclusion of those who had not heard of the SMO in our free-rider category. When we reanalyzed our data, after dropping the 26 percent who had they have never heard of their local SMO (see Table 2:11), the same variables which were statistically significant in Table 4 were also significant (all but three at the same level of statistical significance). The measures of fit as well as the pattern of fit over the five models were also similar to those reported in Table 4. Thus this reanalysis, using a more restrictive definition of free riders, made no substantive differences in the results.

26. We note, in passing, that when we included the postaccident variables from Table 3 in our logit analysis, the percentage of variance explained increased dramatically (R^2, for example, went from .46 to .70). It is important, we insist, to distinguish pre- and post-SMO involvement when examining issues such is those discussed here. While we agree, theoretically, that longitudinal data on social movement involvement would be better than relying on respondents' own recall of pre-SMO phenomena, we cannot conceive of many instances where researchers would be in a position to obtain such data. ✦

Part 6

Interpretive Factors: Framing Processes

The motivational issue explored in Part 5 is problematic because identifying the motives for people's action is seldom a simple task. Not only are individuals typically ensnared in webs of cross-cutting commitments and interests, but those commitments and interests cannot be inferred automatically from their social positions or their enveloping contexts. The same situation or social object can be defined or perceived differently depending on the meanings attached to it. In other words, the objects that constitute our social world can be subject to differential interpretation. In order to understand the motives or reasons associated with particular lines of action, it is important to understand the meanings attached to those action possibilities by the individuals and groups involved.

This observation is consistent with one of the central premises of the symbolic interactionist perspective in sociology: that humans seldom respond to things directly or solely in terms of their utility, but also, and often primarily, in terms of the arbitrary meanings attached to those things or objects by our social environment. Human behavior, in other words, is partly contingent on what the object of orientation symbolizes or means. Furthermore, the meanings objects or events hold for us are not intrinsic—they do not, in other words, attach to them automatically—but are assigned or imputed through interpretive processes. Additionally, it is assumed that these meanings are not fixed or static but subject to change as the social context changes. Shifting patterns of interaction and identification are especially likely to alter the meanings we attach to persons, events, or things. The upshot of these assumptions is that the key to understanding the motivations for participation resides in the interpretive processes through which meanings are generated, debated, and diffused.

Within the past decade, a perspective has surfaced within the study of social movements that takes this interpretive process seriously. Referred to as the *framing perspective,* it views movements not merely as carriers of existing ideas and meanings, but as signifying agents actively engaged in producing and maintaining meaning for their constituents, antagonists, and bystanders. Drawing on the work of Erving Goffman (1974), the verb *framing* is used to conceptualize this signifying work, which is one of the activities that social movement organizations and their adherents do on a regular basis. That is, as Snow and Benford put it: "they frame, or assign meaning to and interpret, relevant events and conditions in ways that are intended to mobilize potential adherents and constituents, to garner bystander support, and to demobilize antagonists" (1988: 198). The three selections in this part illustrate, elaborate, and refine this argument as it pertains to participant mobilization.

The first selection, by David Snow, Burke Rochford, Steven Worden, and Robert Benford, constitutes one of the initial contributions to the framing perspective. It introduces the idea of frame alignment, which is presented as a major mechanism through which grievances are interpreted as social movement organizations attempt to link their interests and interpretations with those of prospective adherents. The authors then elaborate four ways in which such alignment occurs. These frame alignment processes include: the *bridging* of movement interpretive frames to ideologically similar perspectives of unmobilized sentiment pools or public opinion clusters; the *amplification* of the beliefs and values of prospective adherents; the *extension* of a movement's interpretive framework to encompass interests and perspectives that are not directly relevant to its primary objectives but are of considerable importance to potential adherents; and the *transformation* of old meanings and understandings and the generation of new ones.

Since this initial work on frame alignment processes, the framing perspective has been broadened and refined in a number of ways (see, for example, Gamson 1992; Jenness 1995; Snow and Benford 1988, 1992; Tarrow 1992; and Snow and Oliver 1995: 586-589, for a brief summary). One such development concerns the extent to which a collective action frame sometimes comes to function as a *master frame* in relation to movement activity by coloring and constraining the orientations and activities of other movements. Rita Noonan explores this and related issues in the second selection in this part through a historical case study of the mobilization of women against the state in Chile. In particular, she finds that while the leftist master frame of the 1950s and 1960s focused only on working class issues and did not accommodate feminism, its subsequent repression and the emergence of a more elaborated democracy frame in the 1980s created space for a variety of movement-specific frames, including the reemergence of feminism. She also reports that, during the era of authoritarian military rule, women mobilized under the rubric of a maternal frame that provided them with a measure of immunity and safety because of its resonance with both Catholicism's and the state's traditions and discourse regarding women. These findings show that master frames do indeed vary in terms of how restrictive or exclusive they are, and that this variation can significantly affect the mobilization of some aggregations or potential constituencies in comparison to others.

The third selection, by Steven Ellingson, further extends and refines understanding of the relationship between framing processes and participant mobilization by examining the connection between collective action frames and actual collective action events. Based on an in-depth, historical analysis of public debate and rioting over abolitionism in Cincinnati in the 1830s, Ellingson finds evidence of a dialectical relationship between movement framings and discourse and collective action events. More concretely, his findings demonstrate how collective action events (in this case riots) can be incorporated into existing frames and even force movement actors to create new framings that enhance the mobilization of both resources and adherents. Thus, the mutual influence of collective action frames and collective action events exemplifies the dynamic fashion in which the two are linked.

Together, the readings in this part clearly remind us that the recruitment and mobilization of adherents for engagement in movement activities cannot be adequately understood apart from the various meanings those activities have for the adherents; that social movement organizations play an important role in the generation and diffusion of these meanings for adherents, antagonists, and bystanders through various framing processes; that the resulting collective action frames sometimes function as master frames inasmuch as they restrict or broaden the prospect of alternative but related framings and movements; and that movement interpretive framing processes are linked in a dialectical fashion to movement events.

References

Gamson, William A. 1992. *Talking Politics*. New York: Cambridge University Press.

Goffman, Erving. 1974. *Frame Analysis*. New York: Harper Colphon.

Jenness, Valerie. 1995. "Social Movement Growth, Domain Expansion, and Framing Processes: The Gay/Lesbian Movement and Violence Against Gays and Lesbians as a Social Problem." *Social Problems* 42: 145-170.

Snow, David A. and Robert D. Benford. 1988. "Ideology, Frame Resonance, and Participant Mobilization." Pp. 197-217 in *International Social Movement Research*, Vol. 1. Greenwich, CT: JAI Press.

Snow, David A. and Robert D. Benford. 1992. "Master Frames and Cycles of Protest." Pp. 133-155 in *Frontiers of Social Movement Theory*, ed. by Aldon D. Morris and Carol M. Mueller. New Haven: Yale University Press.

Snow, David A. and Pamela E. Oliver. 1995. "Social Movements and Collective Behavior: Social Psychological Considerations and Dimensions." Pp. 571-599 in *Sociological Perspectives on Social Psychology*, edited by Karen S. Cook, Gary Alan Fine, and James S. House. Boston: Allyn and Bacon.

Tarrow, Sidney. 1992. "Mentalities, Political Cultures, and Collective Action Frames: Constructing Meanings Through Action." Pp. 174-202 in *Frontiers in Social Movement Theory,* ed. by Aldon D. Morris and Carol M. Mueller. New Haven: Yale University Press. ◆

18

Frame Alignment Processes, Micromobilization, and Movement Participation

David A. Snow
E. Burke Rochford, Jr.
Steven K. Worden
Robert D. Benford

A long-standing and still central problem in the field of social movements concerns the issue of support for and participation in social movement organizations (SMOs) and their activities and campaigns. There is growing recognition that a thoroughgoing understanding of this issue requires consideration of both social psychological and structural/organizational factors. This realization is reflected in recent literature reviews and critiques (Ferree and Miller, 1985; Gamson et al., 1982:7-12; Jenkins, 1983:527, 549; Zurcher and Snow, 1981) as well as in research on the correlates of support for or involvement in a variety of contemporary social movements (Isaac et al., 1980; Klandermans, 1984a; McAdam, 1984; Useem, 1980; Walsh and Warland, 1983; Wood and Hughes, 1984). To date, however, little headway has been made in linking together social psychological and structural/organizational factors and perspectives in a theoretically informed and empirically grounded fashion.

Our aim in this paper is to move forward along this line, both conceptually and empirically, by elaborating what we refer to as frame alignment processes and by enumerating correspondent micromobilization tasks and processes. By *frame alignment,* we refer to the linkage of individual and SMO interpretive orientations, such that some set of individual interests, values, and beliefs and SMO activities, goals, and ideology

are congruent and complementary. The term "*frame*" (and framework) is borrowed from Goffman (1974:21) to denote "schemata of interpretation" that enable individuals "to locate, perceive, identify, and label" occurrences within their life space and the world at large. By rendering events or occurrences meaningful, frames function to organize experience and guide action, whether individual or collective. So conceptualized, it follows that frame alignment is a necessary condition for movement participation, whatever its nature or intensity. Since we have identified more than one such alignment process, we use the phrase *frame alignment process* as the cover term for these linkages.[1] By *micromobilization,* we refer simply to the various interactive and communicative processes that affect frame alignment.[2]

We illustrate these processes with data derived primarily from our studies of the Nichiren Shoshu Buddhist movement (Snow, 1979, 1986), of Hare Krishna (Rochford, 1985), of the peace movement (Benford, 1984), and of urban neighborhood movements.[3] Drawing upon these empirical materials, on Goffman's frame analytic perspective (1974), which we extend and refine for our purposes, and on a range of literature pertinent to the issue of movement participation, we discuss and illustrate the frame alignment processes we have identified, and elaborate related micro-mobilization tasks and processes. Before attending to this agenda, however, we consider several major problems that plague most extant analyses of participation in SMOs and movement-related activities and campaigns. This excursion will provide a more solid grounding for our utilization of Goffman's frame analytic scheme and our elaboration of the various frame alignment processes.

Theoretical and Empirical Blind Spots and Shortcomings

Most analyses of movement participation can be conceptualized as variants of two generic perspectives on social movements: the psychofunctional perspective, variously referred to as convergence theory (Turner and Killian, 1972), the hearts and minds approach (Leites and Wolf, 1970), and breakdown theory (Tilly et al., 1975); and the resource mobilization perspective associated with the work of McCarthy and Zald (1973, 1977), Oberschall (1973), and Tilly (1978), among others. Although these approaches are routinely juxtaposed as countervailing perspectives on social movements, both share three fundamental shortcomings with respect to the participation issue. They neglect the process of grievance interpretation; they suggest a static view of participation; and they tend to over-generalize participation-related processes.

Neglect of Grievance Interpretation and Other Ideational Elements

The most striking shortcoming is the tendency to gloss questions concerning the interpretation of events and experiences relevant to participation in social movement activities and campaigns. This tendency is particularly evident in the treatment of grievances. Too much attention is focused on grievances per se and on their social psychological manifestations (e.g., relative deprivation, alienation), to the neglect of the fact that grievances or discontents are subject to differential interpretation, and the fact that variations in their interpretation across individuals, social movement organizations, and time can affect whether and how they are acted upon. Both the psychofunctional and resource mobilization perspectives ignore this interpretive or framing issue. The psychofunctional approaches do so by assuming an almost automatic, magnetic-like linkage between intensely felt grievances and susceptibility to movement participation.[4] Lip service is given to subjective/interpretive considerations, but they are rarely dealt with thoughtfully or systematically.

Resource mobilization perspectives also skirt this interpretive issue by assuming the ubiquity and constancy of mobilizing grievances. This assumption is stated most strongly by Jenkins and Perrow (1977:250-51, 266), McCarthy and Zald (1977:1214-15), and Oberschall (1973:133-34, 194-95). Tilly (1978:8) can be read as having reservations about the assumption, but deferring it to others for analysis. However, it is not so much this ubiquity/constancy assumption that we find troublesome,[5] but rather the meta-assumption that this exhausts the important social psychological issues and that analysis can therefore concentrate on organizational and macromobilization considerations. This leap skirts, among other things, "the enormous variability in the subjective meanings people attach to their objective situations" (McAdam, 1982:34). Questions concerning the interpretation of grievances and their alignment

with social movement organizations' goals and ideologies are thus ignored or taken for granted.

There are, however, a handful of students of social movements who have alluded to this oversight, thereby implicitly suggesting the importance of this line of inquiry. Turner (1969b), for one, has argued that the emergence of a significant social movement requires a revision in the manner in which people look at some problematic condition or feature of their life, seeing it no longer as misfortune, but as an injustice. In a similar vein, Piven and Cloward (1977:12) emphasize that "the social arrangements that are ordinarily perceived as just and immutable must come to seem both unjust and mutable" before collective action is likely, a process that McAdam (1982) calls "cognitive liberation." And Gamson et al. (1982), drawing on Moore (1978) and Goffman (1974), suggest that rebellion against authorities is partly contingent on the generation and adoption of an injustice frame, a mode of interpretation that defines the actions of an authority system as unjust and simultaneously legitimates noncompliance.

Taken together, these observations buttress the contention that what is at issue is not merely the presence or absence of grievances, but the manner in which grievances are interpreted and the generation and diffusion of those interpretations. But such interpretive issues have seldom been the object of empirical investigation or conceptual development. Recent social psychological work, taking a rational calculus perspective, appears at first glance to have attempted to remedy this neglect by focusing attention on the process by which prospective participants weigh the anticipated costs of action or inaction vis-à-vis the benefits (Granovetter, 1978; Klandermans, 1983, 1984a; Oberschall, 1980; Oliver, 1980a). But that decision-making process has tended to be treated rather mechanistically and non-processually. Aside from considering a limited number of variables, such as expectations regarding group support, little attention is given to the actual process by which certain lines of action come to be defined as more or less risky, morally imperative in spite of associated risks, or instrumentally pointless. Klandermans' (1984a) distinction between consensus and action mobilization alludes to the importance of these definitional concerns,[6] but his empirical research addresses only the matter of action mobilization. Consequently, the interpretive issues implied by the notion of consensus mobilization remain undeveloped.

The neglect of grievance interpretation not only side-steps the previously noted observations, but also flies in the face of long-standing concern in the social sciences with experience and its interpretation (Bateson, 1972; Berger and Luckmann, 1966; James, 1950; McHugh, 1968; Mead, 1932; Schutz, 1962), the most recent notable contribution being Goffman's *Frame Analysis* (1974). For Goffman, as well as for those on whom he builds, concern with interpretive issues in the everyday world is grounded in the readily documentable observation that both individual and corporate actors often misunderstand or experience considerable doubt and confusion about what it is that is going on and why.[7] Such common interpretive problems are particularly relevant to understanding the operation of SMOs and the generation of support for and participation in social movement activity. SMOs and their activists not only act upon the world, or segments of it, by attempting to exact concessions from target groups or by obstructing daily routines, but they also frame the world in which they are acting. Moreover, the strategic action pursued by SMOs, their resource acquisition efforts, and their temporal viability are all strongly influenced by their interpretive work. Accordingly, a thoroughgoing understanding of the participation process requires that closer attention be given to the interpretation of grievances and other ideational elements, such as values and supportive beliefs. The concept of frame alignment and its various processes are developed with these considerations in mind.

Static View of Participation

A second shortcoming that pervades the literature is the tendency to treat participation (or willingness to participate) as a rather static dependent variable based in large measure on a single, time-bound, rational decision. This tendency, which is especially prominent among work informed by both psychofunctional and rational calculus perspectives, is misguided in several ways. First, it overlooks the situation/activity-based nature of much movement participation. Seldom do individuals join a movement organization per se, at least initially. Rather, it is far more common for individuals to agree to participate in some activity or campaign by devoting some measure of time,

energy, or money (Lofland and Jamison, 1984; McAdam, 1984; Snow et al., 1980).

Just as movement activities and campaigns change with developments in a movement's career and environment of operation, similarly there is variation in the individual's stake in participating in new or emergent activities. Decisions to participate over time are thus subject to frequent reassessment and renegotiation. Indeed, we have been repeatedly struck by the fact that the various movement participants we have observed spend a good deal of time together accounting and recounting for their participation; they jointly develop rationales for what they are or are not doing.

While this sense-making or account-construction might be subsumed under the rubric of rational calculus, it is clear to us that it is neither an individual nor time-bound entity. Rather, rationales for participation are both collective and ongoing phenomena. This dynamic aspect of the social psychology of participation is not easily grasped, however, by procedures that tend to abstract the participant/respondent from the context and networks in which the rationales are developed and embellished. Because of this tendency participation is rarely conceptualized or studied as a processual, even stage-like or step-wise, phenomenon. The concept of frame alignment and its variant forms are elaborated in part with this more processual and activity-oriented understanding of participation in mind.

Overgeneralization of Participation-Related Processes

A third shortcoming with much of the work on movement participation involves the failure to specify the extent to which various participation-related processes, such as bloc recruitment (Oberschall, 1973:125), network recruitment (Rochford, 1982; Snow et al., 1980; Stark and Bainbridge, 1980), mobilization of pre-existing preference structures or sentiment pools (McCarthy and Zald, 1977; McCarthy, 1986) and conversion (Snow and Machalek, 1983, 1984), vary across social movements. The tendency is to write and speak in terms that are too general, as if there are one or two overarching microstructural or social psychological processes that explain participation in all movements, regardless of variation in objectives, organizational structure, and opposition.

This tendency, which is due in large measure to the practice of studying and then using as a basis for generalization a single SMO, a segment of its membership or a particular activity, such as a strike or freedom ride, is even reflected in the previously cited works that emphasize the importance of injustice frames or interpretations. But are shifts in interpretive frames a necessary condition for participation in all kinds of social movements and across all forms of collective action, regardless of variability in the costs or risks of participation? Is the mobilization of sentiment pools the major process that accounts for participation in most contemporary movements, or is it more pertinent to some kinds of movements and activities than it is to others? Similarly, is conversion a general process that obtains across all movements, or is it relevant to participation in only some movements? The notion of frame alignment processes also addresses these questions and concerns.

Types of Frame Alignment Processes

Earlier we defined frame alignment as the linkage or conjunction of individual and SMO interpretive frameworks. We now propose and elaborate four types of frame alignment processes that are suggested by our research observations, and which attend to the blind spots and questions discussed above. The four processes include: (a) frame bridging, (b) frame amplification, (c) frame extension, and (d) frame transformation. For each variant of alignment we indicate correspondent micromobilization tasks and processes. The underlying premise is that frame alignment, of one variety or another, is a necessary condition for movement participation, whatever its nature or intensity, and that it is typically an interactional accomplishment.

Frame Bridging

By frame bridging we refer to the linkage of two or more ideologically congruent but structurally unconnected frames regarding a particular issue or problem. Such bridging can occur at the organizational level, as between two SMOs within the same movement industry, or at the individual level, which is the focal concern of this paper. At this level of analysis, frame bridging involves the linkage of an SMO with what McCarthy (1986) has referred to as unmobilized sentiment pools or public opinion preference clusters. These sentiment pools refer to aggregates of individuals who share common grievances and attributional orien-

tations, but who lack the organizational base for expressing their discontents and for acting in pursuit of their interests. For these sentiment pools, collective action is not preceded by consciousness or frame transformation, but by being structurally connected with an ideologically isomorphic SMO.

This bridging is effected primarily by organizational outreach and information diffusion through interpersonal or intergroup networks, the mass media, the telephone, and direct mail. In recent years, opportunities and prospects for frame bridging have been facilitated by the advent of "new technologies," namely the computerization of lists of contributors or subscribers to various causes and literature (McCarthy, 1986). The micromobilization task is first to cull lists of names in order to produce a probable adherent pool, and second to bring these individuals within the SMO's infrastructure by working one or more of the previously mentioned information channels.

Evidence of frame bridging abounds in contemporary social movements. Indeed, for many SMOs today, frame bridging appears to be the primary form of alignment. Well-known examples include Common Cause, the National Rifle Association, the prolife and prochoice movements, and the Christian Right. In the case of the latter, for example, frame bridging was crucial to its rapid growth. Liebman (1983) reports that in its initial year, the Moral Majority infrastructure raised in excess of 2.2 million dollars via mass mailing campaigns, which in turn, supplied the funds to appeal to religious conservatives in general and tie them into the organization's network through extensive media campaigns. Richard A. Viguerie, a new Christian Right organizer and strategist, further underscores the role of direct mail as an important bridging mechanism in the outreach and mobilization activities of the Christian Right:

> We alert our supporters to upcoming battles through the mail. We find new recruits for the conservative movement through the mail. Without the mail, most conservative activity would wither and die. . . . (Viguerie, 1980:123-27)

For Viguerie and other new right leaders, the utility of direct mail as a key bridging mechanism rests on the presumption of the existence of ideologically congruent but untapped and unorganized sentiment pools. Computer scanning and name culling provide the lists of prospective constituents; direct mail provides the key to frame bridging.

The use of such bridging techniques and avenues is not peculiar to the Christian Right. Research on the peace movement in Texas revealed, for example, that peace groups also utilize the direct mail and similarly develop their mailing lists from a variety of sources, including lists of individuals who attend events sponsored by other liberal organizations and who subscribe to left-oriented periodicals such as *Mother Jones, The Texas Observer*, and *The Progressive* (Benford, 1984). As with other SMOs that rely on frame bridging techniques for diffusion and mobilization, the peace movement subscribes in part to the assumption of ideologically consistent or frame-compatible sentiment pools. In the words of a local peace activist, "we assume that most anyone whose name appears on one of these lists would share our views on the nuclear arms race, apartheid, and U.S. interventionism in Central America." This assumption is also shared at the national movement level, as reflected in a recent SANE (Committee for a Sane Nuclear Policy) fundraising letter:

> I'm sure you're well aware that most people in this country oppose the nuclear arms buildup by the two superpowers. . . . An overwhelming majority of Americans are deeply concerned that the arms race poses an awesome danger to our lives and to the future of the world.
> In sending this letter, I make one assumption. I assume you are one of those millions of Americans.

The foregoing illustrations point to the widespread existence of frame bridging as an alignment process and suggest its salience for mobilizing participants and other resources. But frame bridging does not sufficiently explain all varieties of participation in all forms of movements or movement activities. Yet, most work within the resource mobilization tradition concerned with participation has approached it primarily in terms of frame bridging. The orienting assumption that grievances are sufficiently generalized and salient to provide support for SMOs turns subjective orientations into a constant, and thus focuses attention on the mechanistic process of outreach and bridging.

The appropriateness of viewing micromobilization as largely a bridging problem has been suggested by a number of recent studies demonstrating the salience of both interpersonal and group networks in relation to the emergence and diffusion of social movements and their SMOs

(Morris, 1981; Oberschall, 1973; Rochford, 1982; Snow et al., 1980; Stark and Bainbridge, 1980). Yet, to focus solely on networks as the key to understanding participation patterns can easily yield a misguided and overly mechanistic analysis (Wallis and Bruce, 1982). Networks frequently function to structure movement recruitment and growth, but they do not tell us what transpires when constituents and bystanders or adherents get together. Since a good portion of the time devoted to many SMO activities is spent in small encounters, an examination of the nature of those encounters and the interactional processes involved would tell us much about how SMOs and their constituents go about the business of persuading others, effecting switches in frame, and so on. McCarthy and Zald alluded to such concerns when they suggested that sometimes "grievances and discontent may be defined, created, and manipulated by issue entrepreneurs and organizations" (1977:1215), but this provocative proposition has neither been examined empirically nor integrated into a more general understanding of constituent mobilization. Our elaboration of the other variants of frame alignment addresses these considerations, thus moving us beyond the frame bridging process.

Frame Amplification

By frame amplification, we refer to the clarification and invigoration of an interpretive frame that bears on a particular issue, problem or set of events. Because the meaning of events and their connection to one's immediate life situation are often shrouded by indifference, deception or fabrication by others, and by ambiguity or uncertainty (Goffman, 1974), support for and participation in movement activities is frequently contingent on the clarification and reinvigoration of an interpretive frame. Our research experiences and inspection of the literature suggest two varieties of frame amplification: value amplification and belief amplification.

Value Amplification. Values can be construed as modes of conduct or states of existence that are thought to be worthy of protection and promotion (Rokeach, 1973; Turner and Killian, 1972). Because individuals subscribe to a range of values that vary in the degree to which they are compatible and attainable, values are normally arrayed in a hierarchy such that some have greater salience than others (Rokeach, 1973; Williams,

1970). Value amplification refers to the identification, idealization, and elevation of one or more values presumed basic to prospective constituents but which have not inspired collective action for any number of reasons. They may have atrophied, fallen into disuse, or have been suppressed because of the lack of an opportunity for expression due to a repressive authority structure (Tilly, 1978) or the absence of an organizational outlet (McCarthy, 1986); they may have become taken for granted or cliched (Zijderveld, 1979); they may not have been sufficiently challenged or threatened (Turner and Killian, 1972); or their relevance to a particular event or issue may be ambiguous (Goffman, 1974). If one or more of these impediments to value articulation and expression is operative, then the recruitment and mobilization of prospective constituents will require the focusing, elevation, and reinvigoration of values relevant to the issue or event being promoted or resisted.

Examples of value amplification were readily apparent among several of the SMOs we studied. Particularly striking was the ongoing value amplification in which local neighborhood activists and SMOs engaged in order to generate mobilizable sentiment pools. In following the careers of five local SMOs associated with three different campaigns through 1985, values associated with family, ethnicity, property, and neighborhood integrity were continuously highlighted and idealized. In the case of generating neighborhood opposition to the proposed relocation of the local Salvation Army shelter for the homeless, for example, SMO activists appealed to prospective constituents on the basis of familistic values. Proximate relocation of the shelter was repeatedly portrayed as a threat to women and children in particular. Once such sentiments were validated, amplified, and diffused, periodic mobilization of neighborhood constituents to engage in other organizational activities, such as signing petitions, carrying placards, and participating in media displays of neighborhood solidarity, became considerably less problematic.

The use of value amplification as a springboard for mobilizing support was also evident in the peace movement. Fundamental values such as justice, cooperation, perseverance, and the sanctity of human life were repeatedly embellished. The movement's most frequently idealized values, however, were those associated with democ-racy, particularly the values of equality and liberty. Peace activists amplified such values by asserting their "constitutional right" to speak out on the nuclear arms race, national security, and foreign policy. A popular movement speaker, for example, often bracketed his speeches with the Preamble to the U.S. Constitution and excerpts from the Declaration of Independence. Similarly, the Texas Coordinator of the Nuclear Weapons Freeze Campaign, when asked in an interview what he thought needed to be done in order to achieve a nuclear freeze and move toward disarmament, responded succinctly, "just make the democratic system work."

By framing their mobilization appeals in the language of cherished democratic principles, peace activists not only attempt to build "idiosyncracy credit" (Hollander, 1958; Snow, 1979), but they also seek to redefine their public image as a movement serving the best interests of their country, in part through revitalization of what they see as atrophied values such as the right to redress grievances and express dissent.

Belief Amplification. Broadly conceived, beliefs refer to presumed relationships "between two things or between some thing and a characteristic of it" (Bem, 1970:4), as exemplified by such presumptions as God is dead, the Second Coming is imminent, capitalists are exploiters, and black is beautiful. Whereas values refer to the goals or end-states that movements seek to attain or promote, beliefs can be construed as ideational elements that cognitively support or impede action in pursuit of desired values.[8]

There are five kinds of such beliefs discernible in the movement literature that are especially relevant to mobilization and participation processes: (1) the previously discussed beliefs about the seriousness of the problem, issue, or grievance in question (Gamson et al., 1982; McAdam, 1982; Piven and Cloward, 1977; Turner, 1969b); (2) beliefs about the locus of causality or blame (Ferree and Miller, 1985; Piven and Cloward, 1977; Zurcher and Snow, 1981); (3) stereotypic beliefs about antagonists or targets of influence (Shibutani, 1970; Turner and Killian, 1972); (4) beliefs about the probability of change or the efficacy of collective action (Klandermans, 1983, 1984a; Oberschall, 1980; Olson, 1965; and Piven and Cloward, 1977); and (5) beliefs about the necessity and propriety of "standing up" (Fireman and

Gamson, 1979; Oliver, 1984; Piven and Cloward, 1977).

Since it is sociologically axiomatic that the nature of action toward any object is contingent in part on beliefs about that object, it follows that participation in movement activities to eliminate, control, or change a category of individuals, a lifestyle, or an institutional practice is more likely given a positive articulation between beliefs about the object of action and the nature of that action. The reality of everyday life in the modern world, however, is such that the relationship between beliefs and objects is not always transparent or uniformly unambiguous and stereotypic, and often times the relationship between beliefs and lines of action is antithetical or contradictory as well (Berger and Luckmann, 1966; Borhek and Curtis, 1975; Goffman, 1974). Consequently, participation in movement activity is frequently contingent on the amplification or transformation of one or more of the foregoing sets of beliefs. Since the first two sets will be discussed in relation to frame transformation, we illustrate the relevance of belief amplification to participant mobilization here by considering the latter three varieties of belief.

Examples of the amplification of stereotypic beliefs about antagonists or targets of influence are not difficult to find in the social movement arena, especially since such beliefs frequently function as unambiguous coordinating symbols that galvanize and focus sentiment. The efforts of neighborhood organizers to mobilize citizens to oppose the relocation of the Salvation Army shelter provides a graphic illustration. As previously noted, proximate relocation of the shelter was portrayed as a significant threat to the neighborhood ideal and to familistic values. The problem confronting organizers was to substantiate unambiguously the claim that the shelter would indeed "destroy our neighborhoods." Since the Salvation Army has long been identified with the values of Christian charity, it did not readily lend itself to rhetorical broadsides by neighborhood activists. Effective mobilization thus required a more negatively evaluated target of opposition. The growing number of homeless, transient males who had migrated to Austin and were served by the Salvation Army provided such a target. As one neighborhood activist candidly explained:

Everybody believed we couldn't fight the Salvation Army because it is good. But you can make anything look bad. So we focused on the transients, and emphasized how they threatened neighborhood residents, particularly women and children.

And indeed the activists did. Public hearing after public hearing in city council chambers were little more than rituals of vilification. Personified as slothful, alcoholic, mentally deranged, criminalistic, and sex-crazed, the homeless population came to be seen not only as an unambiguous threat to neighborhoods, but as being outside of the normative order and thus beyond what Coser (1969) has labelled the "span of sympathy." Neighborhood activists did not invent these negative typifications, though. Rather, they focused attention on and amplified selected beliefs and characterizations that have been associated historically with transient men so as to unify neighborhood residents, on the one hand, while neutralizing countervailing themes and interpretations, on the other. As one observer of the micromobilization process noted, "everybody can agree to spit at sort of half-alcoholic, twenty- to twenty-eight-year-old, unshaven men."

Moving from beliefs about antagonists to beliefs about the efficacy of collective action, we turn to what has been the primary concern of recent efforts to integrate social psychological considerations with the resource mobilization perspective. The basic proposition, rooted in value-expectancy theory, is that social action is contingent on anticipated outcomes (Klandermans, 1984a). If people are to act collectively, it is argued, then they "must believe that such action would be efficacious, i.e., that change is possible but that it will not happen automatically, without collective action" (Oliver, 1985:21). Optimism about the outcome of a collective challenge will thus enhance the probability of participation; pessimism will diminish it. We do not quibble with this proposition, especially since it has received considerable empirical support from different quarters (Forward and Williams, 1970; Gamson, 1968a; Klandermans, 1984a; Paige, 1971; Seeman, 1975). But we do find troublesome the tendency to take for granted the process by which optimism or a sense of efficacy is developed and sustained. Our research observations suggest that such beliefs or expectancies are temporally variable and can be modified during the course of actual participation and by the micromobilization efforts of SMOs as well. As one formerly pessimistic neighborhood activist recounted:

Much to my surprise, I came to the Austin neighborhood movement with more conservative expectations than other neighborhood representatives on matters such as development politics, environmental concerns, and the real possibilities of influencing change. . . . But after three months with the movement, I had more hope for grass-roots influence. . . .

The problematic nature and processual development of efficacy were also evident in our peace movement research. Nuclear disarmament activists were often heard to lament about finding themselves confronted by audiences who, on the one hand, agreed with the movement's assessment of the dangers of the nuclear arms race, but, on the other hand, did not seem to share the activists' beliefs that ordinary people can have any effect on the course of defense policy. Consequently, much of the micromobiliztion activity engaged in by peace activists involves the amplification of beliefs regarding the efficacy of their campaigns. Toward that end, disarmament leaders frequently cite and embellish the apparent successes of past movements. A favorite analogy is drawn between present attempts to rid the world of nuclear weapons and the nineteenth-century abolitionist movement. Parallels are drawn between those who believed that slavery would never be abolished and those who believe that nuclear weapons cannot be eliminated. Likewise, peace activists cite the presumed achievements of the anti-Vietnam War movement, as illustrated by the following excerpt from a campus rally speech:

> Some people think decisions are made in Washington and Moscow, but this is not necessarily the case. Decisions are made by the people. The decision that brought an end to the war in Vietnam was not made by politicians in Washington. The decision to stop it was made right here by people like you and me.

Such observations suffice to illustrate that beliefs about the efficacy of collective action are temporally and contextually variable and subject to micromobilization efforts to amplify them. Such is also the case with beliefs about the necessity and propriety of "standing up" and "being counted." Beliefs about necessity refer to beliefs about the instrumentality of one's own efforts in pursuit of some movement objective. Such beliefs are often of the "if-I-don't-do-it-no-one-will" genre, and are thus rooted in part in pessimism about the prospects of other potential participants "taking up the sword." As Oliver (1984:608-609) found in her research that compared active and token contributors to local collective action, activists were "more pessimistic about their neighbors' willingness to make active contributions" and therefore believed "that if they want(ed) something done they (would) have to do it themselves."

Our research on neighborhood movements and the peace movement similarly revealed pessimism on the part of activists about stimulating and sustaining constituent participation. But such pessimism was typically privatized. Moreover, it was frequently seen as something that might be neutralized in part through micromobilization activities to generate "a sense of necessity" on behalf of potential participants. Thus, organizers of a movement in opposition to expansion of the city airport exhorted proximate neighborhood residents to "speak up, emphasizing not only that their "voices count," but that it is a matter of necessity "because no one else will stand up for your home." In a similar vein, local peace activists emphasized repeatedly how critical it is to communicate to individuals that their contribution to the peace movement is of utmost necessity if nuclear war is to be prevented. As one leader related:

> Personally, I'm more pessimistic, but I think to be involved is the only alternative. If you're not involved the nuclear holocaust will happen, for sure. To be involved is the only slight chance that maybe it won't. That's what we have to emphasize.

Implied in such comments is a connection between beliefs about the necessity and instrumentality of standing up, on the one hand, and the propriety of doing so, on the other. Indeed, beliefs about the former are often associated with and buttressed by beliefs about the moral propriety of standing up. Propriety can be conceptualized in terms of what Fireman and Gamson (1979:31-32) call loyalty and responsibility, both of which are properties of cultural codes or belief systems and not merely individual attributes. As Fireman and Gamson (1979:32) correctly note, "individuals exist in a climate of cultural beliefs about their obligations to those groups with which they identify." But since there is considerable variability in the salience of these beliefs both individually and culturally, it is often necessary to amplify them so as to increase the prospect that some potential participants will see their involvement as a moral obligation. The leadership of the Nichiren Shoshu movement seemed to understand this well. Members were constantly reminded of their obligation to carry out "a divine mission that was set in motion thousands of years ago." In the words of the movement's Master, "members were born into this world as Bodhisattvas of the Earth whose noble mission is to propagate true Buddhism throughout the world." Similarly, peace movement leaders often invoked notions of moral obligation and duty as mobilizing prods in their efforts to activate adherents, as illustrated by the comments of a media personality, before a crowd of demonstrators gathered at the gates of the Pantex nuclear weapons facility on the 40th anniversary of the Hiroshima bombing: "I've learned that we not only have a right, but a responsibility to tell our government . . . when they have gone against our wishes."

Frame Extension

We have noted how SMOs frequently promote programs or causes in terms of values and beliefs that may not be especially salient or readily apparent to potential constituents and supporters, thus necessitating the amplification of these ideational elements in order to clarify the linkage between personal or group interests and support for the SMO. On other occasions more may be involved in securing and activating participants than overcoming ambiguity and uncertainty or indifference and lethargy. The programs and values that some SMOs promote may not be rooted in existing sentiment or adherent pools, or may appear to have little if any bearing on the life situations and interests of potential adherents. When such is the case, an SMO may have to extend the boundaries of its primary framework so as to encompass interests or points of view that are incidental to its primary objectives but of considerable salience to potential adherents. In effect, the movement is attempting to enlarge its adherent pool by portraying its objectives or activities as attending to or being congruent with the values or interests of potential adherents. The micromobilization task in such cases is the identification of individual or aggregate level values and interests and the alignment of them with participation in movement activities.

Evidence of this variety of frame alignment was readily discernible in the movements we studied. In the case of the peace movement, frame extension is commonplace. Movement leaders frequently elaborate goals and activities so as to encompass auxiliary interests not obviously associated with the movement in hopes of enlarging its adherent base. The employment of rock-and-roll

and punk bands to attract otherwise uninterested individuals to disarmament rallies, and the dissemination of literature explicating the services sacrificed by a community as a result of an escalating defense budget are illustrative of this practice. A recent decision by the Austin Peace and Justice Coalition (APJC) illustrates this alignment process even more concretely. Since its inception four years ago, this city-wide coalition of some 35 peace groups had organized most of its activities around the movement's goals of "nuclear disarmament, stopping military intervention, and redirecting military spending to the needy." During this period, the movement appealed primarily to "white middle-class baby-boomers." Efforts were made to mobilize racial and ethnic minorities under the banner of "peace and justice," but with little success. A recent APJC memo attributes the failure of this outreach campaign to two factors, and urges an expansion of the movement's framework:

> Two important reasons for this lack of interracial coalition are: (1) APJC's failure to actively work on issues important to minority groups such as hunger, better public housing, and police brutality; and (2) APJC's stated goals and purposes do not clearly define its intention to oppose racism and unjust discrimination.
>
> . . . With the recent rapid growth of the anti-apartheid movement in Austin, it is time for APJC to definitively affirm its intentions and sympathies, which were previously only implied.

As a solution, APJC decided to add a fourth goal to its statement of purpose and promotional literature: "To promote social justice by nonviolently confronting racism, sexism, and all forms of discrimination and oppression." Whether this frame extension will broaden the movement's constituency remains to be seen, but it clearly illustrates the way in which the peace movement has attempted to enlarge its adherent pool.

Frame extension also surfaced on occasion during research on local neighborhood movements. The most vivid example occurred when the proprietors of bars and restaurants within a popular downtown nightlife strip were confronted with the prospect of the Salvation Army shelter being built in their area. In order to protect their interests, they quickly attempted to win the support of neighborhood residents throughout the city by invoking the already successful neighborhood frame and identifying their interests with those of

Austinites in general. Thus, the rallying slogan became: "Let's Save 6th Street—Austin's Neighborhood." Once the frame was extended, organizers played upon and amplified the pieties of neighborhood in hopes of mobilizing support, as illustrated by the following appeal extracted from a flyer and newspaper advertisement:

> WE NEED YOUR HELP!! We feel about our neighborhood just as you do about yours—and we ask the same consideration. If Austin is to keep the Sixth Street Neighborhood as we know it, and it is to be utilized by all of the people of Austin as it is now, then you must help!! Please take a few minutes to call the Mayor and the City Council Offices. Tell them how you feel about YOUR NEIGHBORHOOD—Sixth Street. Ask them to seek an alternative to this problem. Please do it now!!

Frame extension was also operative in both the Nichiren Shoshu and Hare Krishna movements, but at a more interpersonal level. In the case of Nichiren Shoshu, the operation of this process was particularly evident at the point of initial contact between prospective recruits and movement members. The primary aim of these initial recruitment encounters was not to sell the movement or to get individuals to join, but simply to persuade the prospect to attend a movement meeting or activity. Toward that end, members attempted to align the prospect's interests with movement activities, practices, or goals. They did this by first trying to discover something of interest to the prospect, and then emphasized that this interest could be realized by attending an activity or chanting. In a similar manner, Hare Krishna devotees strategically attempted to assess the interests of persons contacted in various public places in an effort to relate the movement's religious philosophy to individual interests and concerns. As one ISKCON leader explained:

> The principle, basically, is just trying to relate the book to where a person is at. . . . So devotees are really just trying to scope the person out as they are coming up to them. Trying to be more sensitive to them, asking them what their job is and even going so far as X (a devotee known within ISKCON as the king of book distribution) who would approach somebody and say: "What are you into, man?" Y: "I'm into guns." X: "Well, here take this because in this book there are a lot of things about all kinds of ancient weapons from 5000 years ago."

Since the purpose of such encounters is to encourage the prospect to attend or contribute to a movement function, members' appeals can vary widely, ranging from playing a musical instrument to meeting members of the opposite sex. Consequently, the reasons or interests prompting initial investigation of movement activity may not be relevant, if related at all, to the decision to join and become, at the very least, a nominal member. As one Nichiren Shoshu member related when discussing how he got involved in the movement and why he joined:

> I didn't want to go to a meeting when first asked. But then the person who recruited me started telling me about the many pretty girls that would be there. So I said, "Well, it can't be that bad if they have all those pretty girls in this religion." So I agreed to go to a meeting that night and take a look at all those girls. . . . But that isn't why I joined Nichiren Shoshu. It was the happiness and friendliness of the members, and the fact that I kind of liked chanting, that made me decide to become a member and receive my Gohonzon (sacred scroll). But that decision didn't occur until, gee, several weeks after attending my first meeting.

And just as the interests that prompted investigation of movement activity were not always the same as those that motivated joining, so the latter were not always the same as the interests that sustained participation. This was clearly illustrated by comparison of the accounts of the same members over an extended period of time. What was found was that the interests associated with participation were frequently redefined or elaborated. The longer the member's tenure, the more likely he or she would articulate interest in world conditions and peace rather than in material or physiological matters, which was typically the case with novitiates. As one member noted when reflecting on her four and a half years in the movement:

> When I first joined I was concerned most with my looks and with getting a nice car and a nice apartment. But I eventually came to realize that those material things don't really count that much. What really matters to me now is whether people are happy.

Inspection of the accounts of Krishna devotees similarly revealed temporal variation in and elaboration of motives for participation. As one Krishna devotee recounts:

> When I first joined in 1973, 1 didn't know much about the philosophy, but I was suffering greatly at the time. When I met the devotees the second time I knew that I would join them. . . . Now I realize that this life and body are temporary and miserable, and that ISKCON is divine.

These findings indicate that sustained participation in movements such as Nichiren Shoshu and Hare Krishna is frequently contingent on a change in interpretive frame, thus suggesting that for some individuals in some movements, frame extension is but a "hooking" (Lofland, 1977) process that functions as an initial step along the path to the more thoroughgoing type of alignment we refer to as frame transformation.

Frame Transformation

Thus far we have noted how the alignment of individuals and SMOs may be effected through the bridging, amplification, and grafting or incorporation of existing interpretive frames and their attendant values and beliefs. The programs, causes, and values that some SMOs promote, however, may not resonate with, and on occasion may even appear antithetical to, conventional lifestyles or rituals and extant interpretive frames. When such is the case, new values may have to be planted and nurtured, old meanings or understandings jettisoned, and erroneous beliefs or "misframings" reframed (Goffman, 1974:308) in order to garner support and secure participants. What may be required, in short, is a transformation of frame.

According to Goffman (1974: 43-44), such a transformation, which he refers to as a "keying," redefines activities, events, and biographies that are already meaningful from the standpoint of some primary framework, in terms of another framework, such that they are now "seen by the participants to be something quite else." What is involved is "a systematic alteration" that radically reconstitutes what it is for participants that is going on (Goffman, 1974:45).

We have identified two such transformation processes that are pertinent to movement recruitment and participation: transformations of domain-specific and global interpretive frames. We shall first consider the similarities between these two alignment processes, and then turn to their differences.

The obvious similarity is that both involve a reframing of some set of conditions, be they biographic or social, past, present, or future. The objective contours of the situation do not change so much as the way the situation is defined and thus experienced. Two analytically distinct aspects comprise this interpretive change. First, as noted earlier, there is a change in the perceived seriousness of the condition such that what was previously seen as an unfortunate but tolerable situation is now defined as inexcusable, unjust, or immoral, thus connoting the adoption of an injustice frame or variation thereof (Gamson et al., 1982).

But the development and adoption of an injustice frame is not sufficient to account for the direction of action. A life of impoverishment may be defined as an injustice, but its relationship to action is partly dependent, as attribution theorists would argue, on whether blame or responsibility is internalized or externalized. Thus, the emergence of an injustice frame must be accompanied by a corresponding shift in attributional orientations.

Evidence of such a shift manifested itself repeatedly in research on conversion to the Nichiren Shoshu Buddhist movement, as illustrated by the words of a 20-year-old convert:

> Before joining Nichiren Shoshu I blamed any problems I had on other people or on the environment. It was always my parents, or school, or society. But through chanting I discovered the real source of my difficulties: myself. Chanting has helped me to realize that rather than running around blaming others, I am the one who needs to change.

Since Nichiren Shoshu is a religious movement that emphasizes personal transformation as the key to social change, it might be argued that this feature of alignment is pertinent only to participation in religious, personal growth, and self-help movements. But this clearly is not the case; for a shift in attributional orientation is also frequently a constituent element of mobilization for and participation in movements that seek change by directly altering sociopolitical structures. In the case of participation in such movements, however, the shift involves a change from fatalism or self-blaming to structural-blaming, from victim-blaming to system-blaming, as documented by research on leftist radicalism in Chile (Portes, 1971a, 1971b), unemployed workers' movements in the U.S. (Piven and Cloward, 1977) and Cuba (Zeitlin, 1966), protest orientations among American blacks (Forward and Williams, 1970; Gurin et al., 1969; Isaac et al., 1980) and on the development of feminist consciousness (Bird, 1969; Deckard, 1975). Moreover, this literature suggests that this shift can not be assumed.

We have thus far suggested that transformations of both domain-specific and global interpretive frames are contingent on the development and adoption of injustice frames and correspondent shifts in attributional orientation, but we have yet to distinguish between the two types of transformations. We now turn to that consideration by examining how they differ in terms of scope.

Transformation of Domain-specific Interpretive Frames. By transformation of domain-specific interpretive frames, we refer to fairly self-contained but substantial changes in the way a particular domain of life is framed, such that a domain previously taken for granted is reframed as problematic and in need of repair, or a domain seen as normative or acceptable is reframed as an injustice that warrants change. We construe "domain" broadly to include an almost infinite variety of aspects of life, such as dietary habits, consumption patterns, leisure activities, social relationships, social statuses, and self-perception. While each of these as well as other domains of life can be and frequently are interconnected, they can also be bracketed or perceptually bounded (Goffman, 1974:247-300), as often occurs in the case of single-issue movements. The interpretive transformation that occurs with respect to one domain may affect behavior in other domains, but the change of frame is not automatically generalized to them.[10]

Domain-specific transformations frequently appear to be a necessary condition for participation in movements that seek dramatic changes in the status, treatment, or activity of a category of people. Concrete examples include movements that seek to alter the status of a category of people such as women, children, the aged, handicapped, and prisoners, or that seek to change the relationship between two or more categories, as in the case of many ethnic and racial movements. In each case, a status, pattern of relationships, or a social practice is reframed as inexcusable, immoral, or unjust. In the case of Mothers Against Drunk Driving, for instance, the misfortune of the tragic loss of a loved one has been redefined as an injustice that demands an increase in the severity and certainty of penalties for drunk driving. However, as Turner (1983) has suggested, participation involves not only coming to see as an inexcusable tragedy what was formerly seen as an unfortunate accident, but also redefining the status of drunk driver in more negative terms than was previously the case.

While movements for the liberation or integration of negatively privileged status groups have considerably broader and more far-reaching goals, the success of their mobilization efforts also rests in part on effecting changes in the way their potential constituents view not only their life situation, but also themselves. As Carmichael and Hamilton argued in *Black Power* (1967:34-35):

> . . . we must first redefine ourselves. Our basic need is to reclaim our history and our identity. . . . We shall have to struggle for the right to create our own terms through which to define ourselves and our relationship to society, and to have those terms recognized. This is the first right of a free people. . . .

Domain-specific transformations have also been central to the participation process in the many self-help and personal growth movements that have flowered during the last 15 years or so, such as est and TM (Katz, 1981). A less obvious but important linkage between domain-specific transformation and the participation process is also frequently found among movements whose mobilization efforts involve in part a reframing of heretofore taken-for-granted aspects of everyday life. A case in point is provided by one of the neighborhood movements we studied that has sought to curtail encroaching development in the name of "historical preservation." The mobilizing potency of that ideology, however, was contingent on the prior and ongoing transformation of stylistically outdated residential structures into architecturally unique repositories of historically sacred values and sentiments. As one neighborhood resident explained:

> We are shaped by these houses, their architecture, their floorplans, what the spaces between the houses, the absence of driveways and garages, and the sidewalks all say about the conduct of human life. We are close to our grandparents' values here. When we preserve houses, we keep with us the people whose lives were expressed here.

Support for and participation in some SMOs is thus partly contingent in the reframing of some domain-specific status, relationship, practice, or environmental feature or condition. Yet there are still other movements for which a far more sweeping transformation is frequently required in order to secure more than nominal participation.

Transformations of Global Interpretive Frames. In this final frame alignment process, the scope of change is broadened considerably as a new primary framework gains ascendance over others and comes to function as a kind of master frame that interprets events and experiences in a new key. What is involved, in essence, is a kind of thoroughgoing conversion that has been depicted as a change in one's "sense of ultimate grounding" (Heirich, 1977) that is rooted in the "displacement of one universe of discourse by another and its attendant rules and grammar for putting things together" (Snow and Machalek, 1983:265-66). Domain-specific experiences, both past and present, that were formerly bracketed and interpreted in one or more ways are now given new meaning and rearranged, frequently in ways that previously were inconceivable, in accordance with the new master frame. As a female convert to Nichiren Shoshu recounts:

> I am an entirely different person now. I never thought I would have much of a future or grow up to enjoy the world. I was against everything. I hated myself most of all, but I didn't know it until chanting and the Gohonzon (the sacred scroll) showed that there was a different kind of world. Now I see things totally different.

One of the major consequences of this more sweeping variety of frame transformation is that it reduces ambiguity and uncertainty and decreases the prospect of "misframings" or interpretive "errors" and "frame disputes" (Goffman, 1974:301-38). In short, everything is seen with greater clarity and certainty.

This pattern also manifested itself in discussions and interviews with some peace activists. One veteran activist noted, for example, that during the course of her involvement the perceptual boundaries between war and peace issues and other aspects of the world gradually dissolved until there were no longer any distinctive, mutually exclusive domains. Nearly every domain of life, from her interpersonal relations to global issues, came to be reframed in terms congruent with the peace movement.

> . . . The planet is all one system. And therefore it follows logically that we're all one people living on it. And, if people see that, how in the world could they get into a thing, you know, that's going to hurt each other? You've got to try to figure out how to make it all work. I mean, to me, it's a political, spiritual thing that's totally tied together. And I feel that it's the way it is whether or not people realize it. I'm sure of it. And the only real hope is for more people to realize it and to do whatever it takes to make them realize it.

What it takes, in those cases where there is little if any transparent overlap between the perspectives of potential adherents and SMOs, is frame transfor-mation or conversion. In those cases, the micromobilization task is to affect conversion by "keying" the experiences of prospective participants, including events that they observe, so that what is going on for them is radically reconstituted (Goffman, 1974:45), as reflected in the above activist's account of her transformation from a "right wing racist" into a peace movement activist:

> My senior year was the time when I changed from the extreme right to . . . left of liberal. . . . Everything I learned about it (the peace movement) convinced me how wrong and racist it was to be, you know, right wing. . . . I was in Oklahoma City then, and the peace movement was really late getting there.

While this radical transformative process may be a necessary condition for the participation of some individuals in an array of movements, it is undoubtedly more central to the participation process of some movements than others. Hare Krishna provides a case in point, as graphically illustrated by the following remarks routinely made to recruits at the New York ISKCON temple in 1980:

> As Krishna explains in the *Bhagavad-Gita*, our lives thus far have been in darkness, in the mode of ignorance. *All our learning up to now has been illusion, garbage.* This is because this past learning we have received does not allow us to know the Absolute, Krishna Consciousness [leader's emphasis].

Summary and Implications

We have attempted to clarify understanding of adherent and constituent mobilization by proposing and analyzing frame alignment as a conceptual bridge that links social psychological and structural/organizational considerations on movement participation. We have pursued this task by addressing three deficiencies in research on movement participation—neglect of grievance interpretation, neglect of the processual and dynamic nature of participation, and overgeneralization of participation-related processes, and by identifying and elaborating six concrete points. First, participation in SMO activities is contingent in part on alignment of individual and SMO interpretive frames. Second, this process can be decomposed into four related but not identical processes: frame bridging, frame amplification, frame extension, and frame transformation. Third, initial frame alignment cannot be assumed, given the existence of either grievances or SMOs. Fourth, frame alignment, once achieved, cannot be taken for granted because it is temporally variable and subject to reassessment and renegotiation. As we have noted, the reasons that prompt participation in one set of activities at one point in time may be irrelevant or insufficient to prompt subsequent participation. Fifth, frame alignment, in one form or another, is therefore a crucial aspect of adherent and constituent mobilization. And sixth, each frame alignment process requires somewhat different micromobilization tasks.

Taken together, these observations suggest several sets of questions and propositions that subsequent research ought to address. A first set of questions concerns the relationship between types of frame alignment and types of movements. Is each of the frame alignment processes identified more likely to be associated with some kinds of movements rather than others? Frame bridging, for example, appears to be the modal type of alignment associated with low demand, professional social movements that often are difficult to distinguish from conventional interest groups. Similarly, value amplification might be hypothesized as the modal type of alignment associated with two sets of movements: those that are reactive in the sense that they defend the status quo, such as many conservative movements; and those that arise among people who are segmentally organized in relation to dominant power structures (in the sense discussed by Oberschall, 1973:118-24) and who have constituted, as a result, long-standing subcultures of resistance and contention, such as Catholics in Northern Ireland, Palestinians in the Middle East, Rastafarians in Jamaica, the Basque in Spain, and Blacks in South Africa. In a similar vein, we suspect that frame transformation of the global variety, given its extensive scope and radical nature, is most likely to be associated with participation in movements that share two characteristics: they have "world-transforming" goals or aspirations in the sense that they seek total change of society across all institutions (Bromley and Shupe, 1979a); and they are comparatively "greedy" in terms of time, energy, and orientation (Coser, 1974). Examples of movements that can be defined in these terms include Hare Krishna, the Unification Church, Nichiren Shoshu, most millenarian movements, and early communism.

While each of the frame alignment processes may be operative in varying degrees at some point in the life history of most movements, what we are

hypothesizing is that there is a kind of elective affinity between forms of alignment and movement goals and perspectives, such that we can speak of modal types of alignment for particular types of movements. Investigation of this hypothesized relationship becomes especially important when we consider that the differential success of participant mobilization efforts may be due in part to variation in the capacity of SMOs to skillfully effect and then sustain a particular type of alignment.

A second issue concerns the relationship between types of frame alignment and what Tarrow (1983a, 1983b) has referred to as "cycles of protest." Cycles of protest are characterized by, among other things, "the appearance of new technologies of protest" that "spread from their point of origin to other areas and to other sectors of social protest" (Tarrow, 1983a:39), thus adding to what Tilly (1978) refers to as the "repertoire" of protest activity. But cycles of protest do not function only as crucibles out of which new technologies of social protest are fashioned; they also generate interpretive frames that not only inspire and justify collective action, but also give meaning to and legitimate the tactics that evolve. Just as some forms of innovative collective action become part of the evolving repertoire for subsequent SMOs and protesters within the cycle, so it seems reasonable to hypothesize that some movements function early in the cycle as progenitors of master frames that provide the ideational and interpretive anchoring for subsequent movements later on in the cycle. If so, then the corollary proposition follows that there ought to be cyclical variation in the predominance of particular types of frame alignment, such that transformation is more likely to be predominant in the early stages, followed by amplification and bridging.

Perhaps the occurrence, intensity, and duration of protest cycles are not just a function of opportunity structures, regime responses, and the like, but are also due to the presence or absence of a potent innovative master frame and/or the differential ability of SMOs to successfully exploit and elaborate the anchoring frame to its fullest. Hypothetically, the absence of innovative master frames may account in part for the failure of mass mobilization when the structural conditions seem otherwise ripe; or a decline in movement protest activity when the structural conditions remain fertile may be partly due to the failure of SMOs to exploit and amplify the anchoring frame in imaginative and inspiring ways. In either case, latent structural potential fails to manifest itself fully.

A third set of issues implied by the foregoing considerations concerns the factors that account for variation in the relative success or failure of framing processes in mobilizing potential constituents. In arguing that one or more varieties of frame alignment is a necessary condition for movement participation, we have proceeded as if all framing efforts are successful. But clearly that is not the case. Potential constituents are sometimes galvanized and mobilized; on other occasions framing efforts fall on deaf ears and may even be counter-productive. This obdurate fact thus begs the question of why framing processes succeed in some cases but not in others. There are at least two sets of factors at work here.

One involves the content or substance of preferred framings and their degree of resonance with the current life situation and experience of the potential constituents. Does the framing suggest answers and solutions to troublesome situations and dilemmas that resonate with the way in which they are experienced? Does the framing build on and elaborate existing dilemmas and grievances in ways that are believable and compelling? Or is the framing too abstract and even contradictory? In short, is there some degree of what might be conceptualized as frame resonance? We propose that one of the key determinants of the differential success of framing efforts is variation in the degree of frame resonance, such that the higher the degree of frame resonance, the greater the probability that the framing effort will be relatively successful, all else being equal. Many framings may be plausible, but we suspect that relatively few strike a responsive chord and are thus characterized by a high degree of frame resonance. Consideration of this issue calls for closer inspection than heretofore of not only the nature of the interpretive work and resources of SMOS, but also of the degree of fit between the resultant framings or products of that work and the life situation and ideology of potential constituents.

The second set of factors that we think bears directly on the relative success or failure of framing efforts concerns the configuration of framing hazards or "vulnerabilities" (Goffman, 1974:439-95) that confront SMOs as they go about the business of constructing and sustaining particular frame alignments. The excessive use of frame bridging techniques by SMOS, for example, may lead to an oversaturated market. Consequently, a movement may find itself vulnerable to discounting, particularly when potential adherents and conscience constituents are inundated by a barrage of similar impersonal appeals from a variety of competing SMOS.

Frame amplification, too, has its own vulnerabilities, as when a movement fails to consistently protect or uphold those core values or beliefs being highlighted. If, on the other hand, a value becomes discredited or loses its saliency, or a belief is popularly refuted, it may drag associated frames down along with it.

Similar hazards may be associated with the frame extension process. If, for instance, an SMO fails to deliver the promised auxiliary and incidental benefits, suspicion of the construction of an exploitative fabrication may arise. Moreover, the very use of such inducements that are not central to the movement's stated goals may result in the trivialization of the sincerity of its claims and objectives, and perhaps of even the movement itself. Social movement organizations and coalitions further run the risk of clouding a frame when they extend their primary frame to encompass goals and issues beyond the scope of their original platform. Adherents and conscience constituents may not embrace the extended frame as enthusiastically as they would a relatively clear, domain-specific frame. Indeed, popular support may be withdrawn following a frame extension strategy, as was the case when some nuclear freeze proponents attempted to link nuclear disarmament goals with a defense of social welfare programs.

Frame transformation is not immune to its own vulnerabilities. Domain specific conversion, for example, though resistant to small changes in opinion climate, is often so narrowly based that either a sudden failure or an unexpected success may test the organization's adaptive abilities. Another risk associated with this form of frame alignment is the occasional fostering of an excessive and unbridled enthusiasm that threatens to spill over into domains extraneous to the movement's frame, thereby undermining its integrity and the movement's mode of operation. Movements involved in global transformation, on the other hand, are less likely to find such generalized enthusiasm problematic, but may find themselves devoting a greater proportion of their resources to internal frame maintenance or "ideological work"

(Berger, 1981) to ward off external symbolic threats in the form of ridicule or the downkeyings of "deprogrammers" and other opponents.

The foregoing observations suffice to illustrate that the frame alignment process is an uneasy one that is fraught with hazards or vulnerabilities throughout a movement's life history, and particularly at certain critical junctures, as when SMOs seek to establish coalitions or when they are attacked by countermovements. The ways in which SMOs manage and control these frame vulnerabilities, as well as interpretative resources in general, thus seem as crucial to the temporal viability and success of an SMO as the acquisition and deployment of more tangible resources, which to date have received the lion's share of attention by research informed by the resource mobilization frame.

By focusing on the role SMOs play in the frame alignment process, we have not intended to suggest that there are not other micromobilization agencies or contexts. Clearly, there is evidence that everyday social circles and local, non-movement communal organizations can function as important micromobilization agencies. The organizing role of the black churches in the early stages of the civil rights movement has been well documented (McAdam, 1982; Morris, 1984), as has the similar role performed by Islamic Mosques throughout the Middle East (Snow and Marshall, 1984). Mass protests that exist apart from SMOs have also been suggested as important mobilizing vehicles by European scholars (Melucci, 1980; Pizzomo, 1978; Touraine, 1981), and single protest events have been hypothesized to function in a similar manner as well (Tarrow, 1983a, 1983b). Precisely how these latent mobilizing structures and incidents of collective behavior affect frame alignment, and thereby facilitate consensus or action mobilization, is not clear, however. Thus, a fourth issue subsequent research ought to address concerns the relationship between extra-movement, micromobilization agencies and the various types of frame alignment, focusing in particular on the processes and mechanisms through which frame alignment is effected in different contexts.

One might ask, of course, what difference it makes whether we can specify empirically how and in what contexts frame alignment of one variety or another is effected. Is it not enough to know that frame alignment is produced and constituents are mobilized? The answer is *no* for several reasons. As Tilly (1978) and his associates have shown, collective actors come and go. Some show up when not anticipated. Others fail to mobilize and press their claims, even when they appear to have a kind of natural constituency. And those that do show up vary considerably in terms of how successful they are. The argument here is that the reasons why some show up and others do not, why some stay in contention longer than others, and why some achieve greater and more enduring success, have to do not only with changes in opportunities and the expansion and appropriation of societal resources, but also with whether frame alignment has been successful effected and sustained.

Notes

1. The concept of alignment as used here should not be confused with what Stokes and Hewitt (1976) have termed "aligning actions." These refer to "largely verbal efforts to restore or assure meaningful interaction in the face of problematic situations."

2. The term micromobilization has been used only sparingly in the literature to refer to a set of interactive processes that are relevant to the operation of SMOs and that are analytically distinguishable from macro-mobilization processes such as changes in power relationships and opportunity structures (Gamson et al., 1982:1-12; Walsh, 1981:3). Our use of the concept is consistent with this previous usage; however we would broaden the conceptualization to refer to the range of interactive processes devised and employed by SMOs and their representative actors to mobilize or influence various target groups with respect to the pursuit of collective or common interests. Although the specific targets of these mobilization or influence attempts can vary considerably from one movement to another, the literature suggests that there are at least seven distinct target groups relevant to the life histories of most SMOs: adherents, constituents, bystander publics, media, potential allies, antagonists or counter-movements, and elite decision-makers or arbiters. Although there are specific micromobilization tasks pertinent to each of these groupings, we are concerned in this paper only with those micromobilization tasks and processes that pertain to participation in general and to what we have called frame alignment in particular.

3. Since the first three studies are described in the works cited, it will suffice to note here that each was based on ethnographic fieldwork lasting over a year and involving first-hand participation in SMO activities, campaigns, and rituals, informal and in-depth interviews with other participants, and systematic inspection of movement-related documents. The study of urban neighborhood movements in Austin, Texas, has traced to date the careers and micromobilization ac-

tivities of five different SMOs associated with three different campaigns, one to curtail development, another in opposition to expansion of the city's airport, and a third in opposition to the relocation of the local Salvation Army Shelter in or near residential neighborhoods. This research is also based on ethnographic fieldwork procedures, which we have found particularly well-suited for studying and capturing the interactive, dynamic, and multifaceted nature of micromobilization and participation related processes.

4. For varied and pointed criticism of this psychofunctional breakdown approach, see Turner and Killian (1972:365), Useem (1975:11-18), Zurcher and Snow (1981), and Zygmunt (1972).

5. Observations regarding the prevalence of grievances are rather commonplace, ranging from Trotsky's (1959:249) observation that if privations were enough to cause an insurrection the masses would be always in revolt, to public surveys (ISR, 1979:4) revealing that Americans readily avow numerous anxieties and problems.

6. Action mobilization involves the activation of individuals who already support movement goals and activities; consensus mobilization refers to an SMO's efforts to drum up support for its views and aims. In the language of McCarthy and Zald (1977:1221), action mobilization refers to the process of turning adherents into constituents, whereas consensus mobilization involves the generation of adherents.

7. This is not to demean the interpretive capacity of everyday actors. Rather, it underscores the obdurate reality that interpretation is a problematic enterprise that can be encumbered by intentional deception, incomplete information, stereotypic beliefs, disputes between allegedly "authoritative" interpreters, and so on. Indeed, much of Goffman's *Frame Analysis* is devoted to the analysis of such encumbrances.

8. For a more thoroughgoing discussion of the distinction and relationship between beliefs and values, see Bem (1970) and Rokeach (1968, 1973).

9. For overviews and discussion of attribution theory, see Crittenden (1983), Jones and Nisbet (1971), Kelley and Michela (1980), and Stryker and Gottlieb (1981).

10. That such self-contained reframings can occur is not only suggested by Goffman (1974), but is also consistent with Mills' vocabularies of motive thesis (1940) and Kelley's work on causal schemata (1972). ✦

19

Women Against the State: Political Opportunities and Collective Action Frames in Chile's Transition to Democracy

Rita K. Noonan

Introduction

Queremos democracia en el país y en la casa. (Adriana Santa Cruz, 1985)

"We want democracy in the nation and in the home." This slogan of the contemporary Chilean women's movement has come to symbolize the new direction of women and politics in Latin America. Since the bloody reign of the Augusto Pinochet regime ended, and the democratically elected Christian Democratic government of Patricio Alywin peacefully took power in March 1990, the old question of women and democracy has become increasingly urgent. How are women using this new political opening? Will they have a voice in the new postauthoritarian politics of Chile? It is still somewhat premature to predict how women will fare under more democratic conditions, but the shape of the future is clearer if we understand the past.

In September 1973, one of Latin America's longest standing democracies was overthrown. The democratically elected government of Salvador Allende was forcibly dismantled by a military coup d'etat. Although most Chileans thought the military regime of Pinochet was temporary, it ruled Chile for over 15 years using some of the most repressive tactics in the history of Latin America. State-sponsored terrorism, concentration camps, "disappearances," and executions comprised what many Chileans have termed a "reign of terror."

Although Pinochet's campaign to eviscerate unions, extinguish the left, and push women back into traditional roles earned him a good number of enemies, his most visible adversaries were women. The mothers, sisters, and daughters of the detained and/or "disappeared" were the first to protest against the human rights offenses of the Pinochet regime, and they had an instrumental role in undermining its legitimacy. It is quite ironic that the conservative ideology of traditional womanhood, typically espoused by Pinochet himself, was used by women to subvert the state.[1] This ironic source of feminine power has only recently been explored in the literature on women in Latin America (e.g., Alvarez, 1990; Jaquette, 1991).

While transitions to democracy have been hailed as the most important phenomena of this century, few scholars understand the role that women have played in these metamorphoses. Specifically, two questions are poorly understood. First, why do women mobilize and have political "voice" at seemingly inopportune times (i.e., under authoritarianism)? Traditional explanations usually focus on structural elements of protest: the political opportunity structure (see Tarrow, 1988, for a review) and the availability of resources (e.g., McCarthy and Zald, 1977). Yet these theoretical approaches tend to overlook how cultural and ideational factors (e.g., gender ideology) shape opportunities for protest, and they do not operate well in an authoritarian context. Second, given that structural analyses fall short, how do broad cultural themes and movement ideologies affect women's collective action? Similarly, social movement approaches that highlight ideational elements such as ideology and beliefs (e.g., Snow and Benford's 1988 and 1992 work on collective action frames) do not adequately explain social movements under conditions of authoritarianism because they assume democratic conditions (e.g., public discussion and freedom of the press).

In this paper I take a new look at the concepts of political opportunities and collective action frames. First, I examine the limitations of current political opportunity models, which fail to assess the "informal," nontraditional power that women in Third World countries often wield. Next, I broaden previous analyses of collective action frames to include the dynamics of social movement activities under conditions of authoritarianism. Furthermore, in this section I extend a "frame analysis" approach to social movements by suggesting that collective action frames create opportunities for protest even when structural conditions do not seem otherwise ripe, and by exploring the relationship between master frames and movement-specific frames, proposing that some frames create space for specific ideas (e.g., feminism) while others do not. Third, after modifying these two theoretical approaches to accommodate women and the authoritarian context, I provide an in-depth case study of women's collective action against the state in Chile. Although some work has been done on collective action frames (e.g., Snow and Benford, 1988, 1992; Snow et al., 1986), very few in-depth case studies have been done, and none to my knowledge has addressed the military authoritarian context. I close by making recommendations for new hypotheses regarding the use of collective action frames in a nondemocratic setting.

Extending Political Opportunity Structure and Frame Analysis

Political Opportunity Structure

Many scholars working within popular American schools of social movement research (e.g., resource mobilization) have made use of the concept of political opportunities (e.g., Jenkins and Perrow, 1977; McAdam, 1982; Tarrow, 1989a; Tilly, 1978). Until recently, researchers did not have an adequate understanding of how political structures and processes shaped, encouraged, or discouraged collective action. For example, what are the conditions under which states become vulnerable to political protest? Tarrow (1988) summarizes the main variables in models of political opportunity: (1) degree of openness in the polity, (2) stability or instability of political alignments, (3) presence or absence of allies and support groups, (4) divisions within the elite or its tolerance for protest, and (5) and the policymaking capacity of the government. Undoubtedly, these variables have increased our ability to "understand variations in the strategies, structures, and outcomes of similar movements that arise in different places" (Tarrow, 1988:430). However, because the models have been used almost exclusively in Western democracies (for exceptions, see O'Donnell et al., 1988; Stepan,

1985), they sometimes obscure rather than elucidate the political processes associated with Third World states, especially authoritarian regimes.

More specifically, I have three reservations about traditional political opportunity models. First, because these models have been based primarily on Western democracies, they are biased in favor of explaining opportunities for the kinds of mobilizations normally found in these same countries (e.g., protection or extension of legal rights). In contrast, social movements in Latin America are more often based on crises of "consumption," such as lack of food, health, and other basic resources (Escobar and Alvarez, 1992). Prime examples are the mass riots against International Monetary Fund austerity measures that have dotted the map of Latin America over the last decade (see, e.g., Nash, 1990; Walton and Ragin, 1990).

Second, women's political power is not well captured by a traditional examination of political opportunities. Jaquette's (1991) research on Latin American women demonstrates that their sources of power are often more informal and nontraditional (i.e., not based on electoral politics). Power resides in different places for various segments of the population (see also Bookman and Morgen, 1988). In fact, many of the key hypotheses of these models are dramatically overturned when we consider women under authoritarian conditions. The case of Chile demonstrates that women's political power came out of a "closed" polity, during a time of intolerance for protest, and where the policymaking capability of the government was at an all-time high in terms of extinguishing popular mobilizations. Thus, less political "space" (in the generic sense) led to a greater "voice" for women. Examples are offered in this case study.

Third, political opportunities, as Tarrow (1988:430) notes, can be a subjective issue, meaning many opportunities must first be

perceived to exist before actors can take advantage of them. Without this subjective component the issue of human agency is strangely absent. How do we account for how people make sense of a "ripe" situation? Is it just dumb luck that they take advantage of opportunities from time to time? Below I shall argue that most theories of social movements do not attend adequately to ideational elements such as beliefs, perceptions, and values. To this end, I argue for greater analytic attention to collective action frames.

It seems clear that Third World and authoritarian states do not fit neatly into existing frameworks of political opportunity structure, nor do political opportunity models explain why women were actively protesting at a time when their male counterparts were silenced. Part of the problem with this literature is a lack of attention to cultural factors; that is, we do not have a concept of "cultural opportunity structure," but perhaps we should (see Rucht, 1992, for a similar point). By examining changes in collective action frames, cultural themes, and master frames available to different groups in the population, we are one step closer to a culturally sensitive understanding of social protest.

Collective Action Frames

The idea of "collective action frames" is relatively new in the social movements literature. The term *frame*, made popular by Snow and his associates (1986), was first introduced by Goffman (1974:21) to denote "schemata of interpretation" that enable individuals "to locate, perceive, identify, and label occurrences within their life space and the world at large." In Snow and Benford's (1992:137) words,

> it refers to an interpretive schemata that simplifies and condenses the "world out there" by selectively punctuating and encoding objects, situations, events, experiences, and sequences of actions within one's present or past environment. . . . Collective action frames not only perform this focusing and punctuating role; they also function simultaneously as modes of attribution and articulation.

Thus, a frame is a mechanism through which individuals may understand what happens around them, identify sources of their problems, and devise methods for addressing their grievances. For example, the civil rights movement framed its activity in terms of deeply entrenched and firmly held American cultural beliefs such as inalienable rights, "liberty and justice for all," and other liberal political concepts. The movement understood the problem as a lack of basic rights and privileges that are normally guaranteed on the basis of citizenship. The culpable parties were those who denied them those rights (e.g., shopkeepers, lawmakers). The tactics of addressing these deprivations were channeled into on-site, nonviolent demands for these basic rights (e.g., to sit at a lunch counter). Clearly, an important reason for the success of the civil rights movement was the extent to which the collective action frame struck a chord in dominant cultural beliefs. In this sense, the frame had cultural *resonance* (Snow and Benford, 1988).

However, a frame is not simply a constant or a static "worldview." It is actively created by participants in a movement as part of a struggle over symbols and meanings (Snow and Benford 1988, 1992; Snow et al., 1986). In Snow and Benford's words, "movement organizations and actors [are] actively engaged in the production and maintenance of meaning for constituents, antagonists, and bystanders or observers" (1992:136). Hence, Snow and other proponents of this approach use the verb framing to denote an active process of constructing meaning for themselves, the movement participants, potential adherents, and opponents.

It is important to underscore the importance of human agency in this approach, as framing activities are not simply reflections of a passive internalization of ideology. In this sense, collective action frames, or the results of framing activities, make a theoretical break from previous treatments of ideology in social movement research. Ideology, rather than being overlooked, is put squarely into the realm of mobilizational strategies. Previous social movement theories, such as "resource mobilization," have paid scant attention to the importance of mobilizing beliefs, values, and other meanings (for critiques of previous theories, see Snow and Benford, 1988, 1992; Snow *et al.,* 1986).

Collective action frame analysis represents an attempt to bring social psychological factors back into analyses of social movements, while maintaining the notion that participants are rational actors engaged in the construction of their own mobilizing beliefs and strategies. In the past, few scholars argued for the need to examine *both* social psychological and structural/organizational factors (for exceptions, see Ferree and Miller, 1985; Snow and Benford, 1988; Snow et al., 1986; Zurcher and Snow, 1981). It was not until quite recently that social movement researchers, many from the resource mobilization tradition, have made a concerted effort to move in this direction (see Morris and Mueller, 1992). Accordingly, it is important to stress that social movement participants do not frame their campaigns in a cultural or social vacuum. The larger political and social context matters.

Attention to broader cultural themes and larger mobilizational frames is at the heart of Snow and Benford's most recent work (1992). They make a strong argument for the importance of *master frames,* or larger cultural frames that "provide the interpretive medium through which collective actors associated with different movements . . . assign blame for the problem they are attempting to ameliorate" (1992:139). Furthermore, they state that "Master frames are to movement-specific collective action frames as paradigms are to finely tuned theories. Master frames are generic; specific collective action frames are derivative" (1992:138). Snow and Benford distinguish between "restricted" and "elaborated" master frames. Elaborated master frames are more flexible and inclusive than restricted ones, allowing "numerous aggrieved groups to tap it and elaborate their grievances in terms of its basic problem-solving schema" (1992:140). In other words, master frames shape and constrain movement-specific frames.

Similarly, Gamson (1988) introduces the idea of ideological "packages," or sets of related ideas about an issue. Gamson uses the notion of a "package" to refer to a kind of discourse, and says that packages have an internal structure—a frame. In his words, "At [a package's] core is a central organizing idea or frame for making sense of relevant events . . . [t]he frame suggests what the issue is about" (1988:222). He goes on to argue that there are broad cultural themes (akin to worldview, ideology, and *Weltanschauung),* each of which has a countertheme; more specifically there are issue cultures, or a "particular issue arena," in which there is a relevant discourse used "in the process of constructing meanings relevant to the struggle" (1988:221).[2]

Snow and his colleagues, as well as Gamson, have added a great deal to our knowledge of ideology, ideational elements, and social movements more generally. However, their approaches too must be extended to fit the Third World and authoritarian context. Both Snow and Gamson posit the importance of mass media, counterthemes, and oppositional frames in the making of a social movement. After all, participants are supposed to be opposed to something, and presumably need to get their message out in order to effect change. While these assumptions generally hold, specific

questions arise in the case of mobilization under military authoritarianism. First, how do participants use an oppositional frame *and* make their claims public? The obvious problem is becoming targeted for repression (e.g., death or "disappearance") for such subversive activity. The case study below demonstrates that, in fact, using the *same* discourse and frame as the state may be the most effective, and certainly the safest, mobilization strategy.

Second, what happens to master frames during periods of crisis or under conditions of repression? Specifically, the use of the leftist master frame, generated by the very active labor movement and the Communist and Socialist parties, was made a crime against the state in Chile. Again, torture, death, or disappearance was not unusual for those who espoused leftist ideas. The examples below suggest that the lack of availability of the once very dominant leftist master frame opened up ideological and political space for women to organize. In Snow and Benford's (1992) words, it allowed for the creation of a new "innovative master frame." This innovation, it seems, opened the door for movements—like feminism—that historically were edged out or excluded by leftist party politics (see Chuchryk, 1984, ch. 4, for a similar point).

The relationship between master frames and movement-specific frames offers an interesting extension of previous work. The notion of master frames is very new to the literature (Snow and Benford, 1992). In fact, the incipient theorizing consists of relatively untested hypotheses about how bigger frames give meaning to many movement-specific frames in the same wave or "cycle" of protest. There is a sense of complementarity among the smaller frames. In contrast, I argue below, collective action frames within a "cycle" can compete with each other, with competition being more likely under conditions of a restricted master frame. The rise and fall of master frames may shape how movement-specific frames compete, decay, and transform, as some master frames create space for certain ideas while others do not.

To explore these issues, I shall take an historical look at women's mobilization in Chile. I begin by providing a brief history of women's activism in Chile, necessary for grasping the contemporary issues concerning women and social mobilization. As traditional social movement theory predicts, economic and political upheavals created many opportunities for mobilization in Chile. As Snow and Benford suggest (1992), the availability of resonant frames also creates or denies opportunities. Regarding the creation of what I shall term the "maternal" frame, two issues are important until 1978: the tension between feminism and the left in Chile, which resulted in the decay of a "feminist" frame and a peculiar insertion of women's interests into traditional (electoral) politics in the 1950s; and the role of early (mid-1960s) mothers' organizations.[3] After 1978 three issues are important: the transformation of women's consciousness as they enter the "public" realm; the expansion of women's survival organizations (especially after the collapse of Chile's "economic miracle" in 1982); and the cooperation among various aggrieved groups, which resulted in the introduction of a "return to democracy" master frame, and a movement-specific "feminist" frame.

History of Women's Activism

Women have always been active in protest movements in Latin America. Their participation ranges from the independence struggles against Spain in the early 19th century to the guerrilla wars of the 1960s and 1970s (Jaquette, 1991; Miller, 1981). Even before women won the right to vote, they participated in various street demonstrations and strikes, and they joined political parties (Gaviola et al., 1986; Jaquette, 1991). Over time, poor women have been especially active in urban organizations demanding better access to schools, health facilities, and housing (Lechner and Levy, 1984; Magendzo et al., 1985; Valenzuela, 1987). Rural women waged battles over land titles, potable water, and development plans, to name a few (Deere, 1986; Nash and Safi, 1986).

Chilean women are no exception. Beginning with the early 20th century struggle for suffrage, I will outline key theoretical turning points in the relationship between women's mobilizations and collective action frames.

The Rise and Fall of a Feminist Frame (1913-1953)

The first half of the 20th century was marked by a flowering of women's organizations, many of which devoted themselves to the struggle for women's suffrage. Women's reading circles, a political party *(Partido Cívico Femenino)*, a proemancipation organization, and a confedera-

tion of over 200 women's organizations are just a few examples of the activist organizations that marked the political landscape in Chile before 1953 (see Chuchryk, 1984; Gaviola et al., 1986; Kirkwood, 1983a, 1986). According to Kirkwood (1983a), this was a time during which women concentrated on female oppression and feminist critiques of social systems that subordinate women. In other words, a "feminist" frame was developed to make sense out of women's disadvantaged status in society. Within four years after the vote was won in 1949, nearly all feminist organizations disappeared, beginning a 25-year period of "feminist silence" (Kirkwood, 1983a:634). This section highlights how the early feminist frame was edged out by the Chilean left's focus on class as a source of social oppression.

Most women's organizations in the early 20th century demanded civil and political rights (Gaviola et al., 1986; Miller, 1991). Like its counterpart in the United States, the feminist strand of the Chilean suffrage movement was closely associated with the rise of liberalism; women wanted a share of what was constitutionally guaranteed to men on the basis of citizenship, inalienable rights, and so on (see Jaggar, 1983, for an excellent discussion of feminism and liberalism). Women had great faith that access to the voting booth would solve most of their problems (Change International Reports, 1981). Also like the North American experience, the single issue of suffrage created a tenuous alliance among various organizations, a coalition that disbanded soon after the vote was won.

Despite the feminist victory in the battle for suffrage, or perhaps because of it, 1949 marked the "beginning of the end" of the feminist agenda. Kirkwood states that "priority attention began to be given to class, which eventually prevailed" (1983a:634). The final decline of the feminist movement, she claims, is due to the fact that great numbers of both men and women viewed oppression based on class, not gender, as the most pressing problems of the day. The "absolute supremacy attributed to the class struggle by large groups of women eventually impeded further denunciation of patriarchal attitudes. *Feminism was dismissed as a bourgeois issue*" (1983a:634, emphasis mine). Miller (1991:142) also describes this same emphasis on class during the 1950s and 1960s:

Since the late nineteenth century the main strand of feminism in Latin America had been closely associated with the rise of secular liberalism, and this impulse remained the predominant influence until the late 1950s, when the prescriptions of democratic liberalism seemed increasingly inadequate to address the glaring social, political, and economic problems of the region.

In other words, as the legitimacy of liberalism eroded, so did feminism. The left in Chile turned to a typical class analysis that viewed feminism as a divisive, bourgeois issue. Although very little is written about women during this time period, it seems that the master frame of the left (one that criticized social systems, not individuals, for their problems) probably was compatible with feminist ideas at the time. More troublesome, it seems, was the movement-specific frame used by the labor movement—that of "working-class radicalism"— a frame that competed with a much weaker feminist frame.[4]

The Chilean left was not unusual in its hostility toward feminism. Countless examples from the former Soviet Union (e.g., Mamonova, 1984), Mexico (Miller, 1981), Cuba, and Nicaragua (Molyneux, 1985) demonstrate that "progressive" and even "revolutionary" politics on the left rarely include a feminist critique of social power relationships. Women in these countries found that the insistence on articulating programs solely in terms of class or "the people" served to perpetuate traditional patterns of male dominance. As Vilma Espín, Cuban revolutionary and wife of Raúl Castro, states: "Unfortunately, many feminist groups take away forces that could strengthen the *genuinely* revolutionary movement" (Hahner, 1980, cited in Miller, 1991:189, emphasis mine). The message is clear: women's strategic concerns should come after the "real" revolution succeeds.

Another important and related trend was occurring in Chilean politics during the late 1930s and 1940s. Although this time period signaled the first recognition of women as a potentially significant political force, the left was slower to support equal rights for women. Part of the explanation lies in the left's rejection of gender inequality as a valid frame for progressive or revolutionary politics; the other cause is the persistent perceptions of women's "inherent" conservatism (Chancy, 1979; Miller, 1991).[5] It was widely believed that women's vote would be heavily influenced by the Catholic Church, and thus a conservative impediment to change. Interestingly, women in Chile, Brazil, and Peru were enfranchised by conservative governments, with the "explicit intention of using the women's vote to counter the growing political radicalism of an increasingly mobilized male electorate" (Jaquette, 1991:3).

The theoretical importance of this time period (1913-1953) in relationship to collective action frames is clear. The early "feminist" frame in Chile was edged out by the left's "working-class radicalism" frame.

Inception and Creative Use of the 'Maternal' Frame (1953-1978)

After the deterioration of the feminist frame, women adopted dominant cultural and political themes to frame their activities around maternal and family issues. This outcome was not necessarily a foregone conclusion in the wake of the feminist frame's demise. A body of ideological and material resources that reinforced traditional (i.e., maternal) roles for women were not only available, but promoted, by state agencies and political parties. This section documents the creation of a "maternal" collective action frame, a justificatory frame for mobilizations on both the right (e.g., *El Poder Femenino*) and the left (e.g., groups opposed to Pinochet). Interestingly, the discourse produced in the creation of the maternal collective action frame mirrored the dominant discourse espoused by the authoritarian regime of Pinochet.

Peculiar Insertion of Women's Issues in Politics. Although this 25-year period was characterized by an absence of feminism, women's day-to-day interests, which revolve around their socially assigned duties, became no less important.[6] Women who were politicized after the franchise turned to political parties, expressing their social concerns in terms of health care and social welfare (Chancy, 1979; Miller, 1991). In *Supermadre* (supermother), Chaney demonstrates that women's involvement in Chilean politics during this time was an extension of their role in the family. As civil servants, female politicians acted like "big" mothers for the country, concerning themselves with family welfare, child health, and balanced budgets. Important decisions, these women argued, should be left up to the men (Chaney, 1979). Therefore, Chaney (1979:21) argues,

women overwhelmingly agree to a division of labor in the polity that parallels the traditional, unequal roles of men and women in the family. Both men and women believe that women should participate in politics, but in a style that is a reflection of the political institution of the division of tasks in the family.

Hence, larger cultural themes of mothering and appropriate activities for women made their way into both family and political life in Chile. Kirkwood (1983a) argues that during this period women's feminist demands toward greater liberation were no longer voiced, and all of women's interests soon became confused with the mother-child relationship. Mother-child relationships extended into the area of social welfare and came to be seen as women's *only* concerns. It seems that women's practical interests came to the fore at a time when their strategic or feminist interests were not accepted by any party. In other words, the concept of women's issues got inserted into politics by parties that refused to view women or their social concerns as anything other than "maternal."

Notwithstanding the importance of practical interests, the dismissal of feminist goals at this time seems to have dealt a crushing blow to the future relationship between women and electoral politics in Chile. The sole incorporation of women's practical or maternal interests carved out a very narrow place for women's issues in party politics. As Chaney (1979) argues, women agreed to this division of labor in the polity, further perpetuating the understanding of women's concerns through what I term a "maternal collective action frame." Hence, Kirkwood's analysis seems to be quite accurate: over time the variety of women's political affairs became collapsed into and confused with a very specific, though important, aspect of women's lives—their reproductive function. The way women's concerns were framed at this time is important because it gave shape and form to women's subsequent political mobilizations.

Mothers' Centers. Political parties further created and reinforced the maternal frame by developing mothers' and housewives' centers for poor women. The first mothers' centers were organized around sewing workshops in an effort to integrate women into the labor force. In 1954, a private organization started the "*Ropero del Pueblo*" (the Poor People's Closet). In 1962, the women's section of the Christian Democratic Party multiplied mothers' centers "in an effort to root the party and its social reforms among the poor" (Bunster, 1988:490). At this time the Christian Democratic Party of Eduardo Frei was not yet in power, but it seems likely that this political

move was geared toward giving the party extra appeal among women in the upcoming elections of 1964. Women were probably targeted since they were largely responsible for voting the conservative party of Alessandri into power in the 1958 election.

In 1964 Eduardo Frei won the presidential election, beating his opponent Salvador Allende by nearly 20 percentage points (Wynia, 1990). In his second "State of the Union Address" (1966) he outlined a plan for increased community action programs. His plan was called "popular promotion" *(promoción popular),* a program designed to integrate marginal sectors of the society into the national life, and to provide them with organizations that "represent their aspirations" (Frei, 1966:26). This flowering of grass-roots organizations under *promoción popular* culminated in more than 15,000 cooperatives, neighborhood councils, mothers' centers, art groups, and the like. Some of the most prominent groups were housewives' centers (over 400,000 people); community training centers (over 450,000 people); Neighborhood Councils; Rural Social Movements (grew from 24 to 500 agricultural trade unions); and trade unions (from 1900 in 1964 to 3600 in 1967; *Ministerio de Relaciones Exteriores*, 1968).

Regarding housewives' centers, a Chilean government report (*Ministerio de Relaciones Exteriores,* 1968: no page number provided) describes the following:

> Mothers' centers to the number of 8,500 have been opened, and more than 400,000 women have taken advantage of their workshops or educational courses, and, above all, of the opportunity for social gatherings, which in many cases has metamorphosed their formerly downtrodden, drab and empty lives.

Similarly, Bunster (1988) states that women initially joined these centers to buy their own sewing machines, but they continued to thrive because they allowed women to become involved in neighborhood activities.

Under the Allende government in the early 1970s, mothers' centers were regenerated through COCEMA *(Confederación Nacional de Centros de Madres)* and eventually became meeting places for women to discuss community affairs. Later these mothers' centers became integrated into government agencies dealing with price regulations and fair distribution of commodities among the Chilean population (Bunster, 1988:490). According to Bunster, these organizations played an important role "because they were active at a time when those women opposing the Allende regime were producing a 'black market fright.'" Moreover, "price wars became regime"anti-regime wars, and women were on the 'front lines' of both sides" (1988:490).

The theoretical importance of these centers is that they gave women a core of resources, both material and ideological, that strengthened the maternal frame.[7] As Tilly (1986b) suggests, in subsequent mobilizations, people will use familiar frames and "repertoires of mobilization." Similarly, Snow and Benford (1992) argue that the existence of a collective action frame creates opportunities for subsequent mobilizations. In this case, I argue, the available and culturally resonant maternal frame was used fruitfully by women on both the right and the left when a change in state form threatened the integrity and safety of their families. Below I outline two examples of women's mobilizations explicitly framed around women's maternal duties to care for family and country.

On the Front Lines: El Poder Femenino (Feminine Power). In light of the aforementioned events surrounding the development of the maternal frame, it should not be surprising to find that conservative women (primarily middle and upper class) mobilized themselves in defense of the status quo. President Salvador Allende took office in 1970 with the goal of leading Chile down the "democratic road to Socialism" (Skidmore and Smith, 1989). International boycotts, a reduction in copper prices on the world market, national strikes, inflation, and drastically reduced purchasing power plagued the Allende economy and led to an economic collapse in 1972 (Arriagada, 1991; Remmer, 1991). In response to these economic and political events, women organized the famous march of the "pots and pans" in December 1971, the first large-scale mobilization against the new government. In this protest, middle and upper class conservative women banged pots and pans together to symbolize their opposition to deteriorating economic conditions and the threat of communism. Out of this mobilization El Poder Femenino (EPF) was formed.

EPF engaged in its share of subversive activities designed to undermine the legitimacy of the Allende government. Examples include making stink bombs to drive customers away from busi-

nesses that refused to strike against the government, supposedly operating a plant that manufactured "*miguelitos*" or nail-like spikes to scatter over highways in an effort to sabotage nonstriking truck drivers, and helping mobilize the armed forces into action (Crummett, 1977; Mattelart, 1975). One particularly humorous example of EPF's actions is that some women went to the military academy and threw chicken feed at the soldiers, attacking their manhood and accusing them of cowardice (Crummett, 1977).

By framing their activities as maternal duties, EPF was able to justify very nontraditional behavior. Leaders of this group suggested that their "womanly intuition" and "maternal instincts" allowed them to truly understand the dangers of communism (Crummett, 1977:110). Another leader says, "women felt their fundamental values of family and motherhood threatened at the onset of Marxism; it touched the inside of women's being . . ." (Crummett, 1977:137). The threat of communism, they cried, was beginning to destroy families and social order (Chuchryk, 1984, 1989, 1991; Crummett, 1977; Jaquette, 1991).

After the 1973 Military Coup: Women Against Authoritarianism. Pinochet's military regime ushered in a new era of what is sometimes called Catholic traditionalism, extolling the values of religion, patriotism, motherhood, and the free market. Paradoxically, the introduction of these values and military authoritarianism resulted in greater political opportunities or "space" for women. By framing their activities in congruence with the state's discourse concerning women, the maternal collective action frame was both safer and more effective than an oppositional frame.

Similar to EPF, women found it necessary to repudiate the state in the defense of family integrity. After all, they were only being "good" wives and mothers searching for the thousands of beloved family members who disappeared. A report from the Inter Church Committee on Human Rights estimated that as many as 30,000 people were killed in the first few months after the military coup (Chuchryk, 1991). Moreover, the creation of Pinochet's private secret police force in 1974 (Dirección de Inteligencia Nacional) facilitated the systematic extermination of political figures on the left.[8] As a result, many women who had never been political before—the wives, sisters, mothers, daughters of the victims—were the first to mobilize against the repression (Bunster, 1988; Chuchryk, 1984, 1989, 1991). Women became the primary voice against the regime because, as Chuchryk (1991:156) states,

> Men were the victims of repression more often than women, in part because women had tended to play what were considered marginal or secondary roles in the targeted organizations, principally political parties and trade unions. In this sense, it was precisely women's traditional public invisibility which allowed them to become political actors during a time when it was extremely dangerous for anyone to do so. Furthermore, this political involvement has been legitimated by their traditional roles as wives and mothers.

Less than three weeks after the coup, the *Association of Democratic Women* (*Agrupación de Mujeres Democráticas*) was formed to do solidarity work with political prisoners and their families. Much of this work had to be done clandestinely, and because the military often ignored women, they were suited better than men (Chuchryk, 1991). Other organizations, such as The Chilean Association of the Relatives of the Detained and Disappeared, were formed in 1974 after the same women, seeking information about missing family members, kept bumping into each other outside of prisons, hospitals, and government offices. After being met with silence and denial from the government, these groups resorted to more extreme forms of protest. In 1975 these women were the first to "take to the streets" to demonstrate against the regime, resulting in numerous arrests (Agosín, 1987; see Chuchryk, 1984, 1989, and 1991, for a longer discussion of these groups).[9]

Discourse and Framing: Women and the State Speaking the Same Language. Obviously the cultural theme of traditional family values and gender roles was available for many groups to use in their framing strategy. The most interesting part of this whole picture is that Pinochet and the angry women, both using the same discourse, framed their campaigns around the defense of this cultural theme. Women were defending the integrity of the family and the lives of their loved ones; Pinochet was defending the future of the Fatherland against communism. In particular, both the state and women agreed that motherhood and family constitute the cornerstone of Chilean life. Below I will briefly outline the dominant discourse concerning women.[10]

Since its takeover in 1973, the military has made quite deliberate use of the traditional gender ideology, especially the "proper" role for women in the family and society. An explicit part of Pinochet's social and economic programs addressed the role of the family in society. For example, his socioeconomic program for 1981-1989 declares that "the political constitution of the state defines the family as the fundamental core of the society" (*Oficina de Planificación Nacional*, 1981:26). Women, as mothers, were assigned the duty of defending the integrity of the Chilean family, and raising the next generation of patriotic (meaning apolitical) citizens (Bonder, 1983; Chuchryk, 1989, 1991; Kirkwood, 1983a, 1986). In Pinochet's words:

> Chile needs and thanks the technical contribution of the female professionals, and appreciates their brilliant capacities, but it should not underestimate the anonymous work in the laboratory that is home, where women silently work looking after what is most precious to the Nation, the care of children, the future hope of the Fatherland. On the contrary, we believe that it is necessary to deepen the consciousness of woman in herself and of society in the task that is hers. (cited in Change International Reports, 1981)

"Deepening" the Female Consciousness. In order to "deepen the consciousness" of women as mothers, Pinochet used two specific institutions: mothers' centers and the National Secretariat for women. Government-sponsored mothers' centers, first created by the reformist government of Eduardo Frei in the mid-1960s, were reorganized and transformed into an ideological tool to disseminate images of the "good" woman: self-sacrificing, patriotic, and apolitical (Bonder, 1983; Change International Reports, 1981; Kirkwood, 1983a). The mothers' centers (CEMA) were designed ostensibly to empower women and their families by offering courses, workshops, and producing goods for commercial sale (e.g., arts; Lechner and Levy, 1984).

To some extent Pinochet's use of these centers did earn him the respect and admiration of poor women. But more importantly, according to both Bunster (1988) and Lechner and Levy (1984), the centers manipulated women into performing their "proper" roles, thus rendering them apolitical. In the words of CEMA's leader and Pinochet's wife, Lucía Hiriart de Pinochet, "CEMA-CHILE is no longer a political entity" (Lechner and Levy, 1984:38). This process was facilitated by garnering volunteer participation among conservative, pro-Pinochet, upper class women who wanted to "earn their uniforms" by helping at the centers. Many of these volunteers were wives of military personnel (Agosín, 1987).

The National Secretariat for women, founded by Salvador Allende in the early 1970s, was taken over and put to further ideological use. Headed by Pinochet's wife, the self-professed mission of the Secretariat was to "propagate national and family values to form a consciousness and a correct comprehension of the dignity of women and their mission within the family" (UN INSTRAW Review, cited in Change International Reports, 1981).

The idea of self-sacrificing, dutiful motherhood was a long-standing cultural theme, often invoked by Allende, as well as by Pinochet:

> The fact that Allende and Pinochet, despite their cavernous political gulf between them, could share similar views about women's proper role and sphere amply dramatizes the vitality of the tradition which relegates men and women to very different economic and political "space" in Latin America. (Wasserspring, cited in Chuchryk, 1989:139)

Scholars note that Latin America's long history of idealizing "true" womanhood has been supported by the Church. For example, historically the Church has been partially responsible for "marianismo," the female equivalent of "machismo," where women are idealized for their moral superiority, self-abnegation, "semi-divine" devotion to others, and general commitment to domesticity (Ehlers, 1991). This broad theme was a readily available "policy tool" that Pinochet was able to manipulate for his own purposes.

Despite "marianismo" and Pinochet's two ideological institutions, which reached thousands of women in Chile (over 230,000 in mothers' centers alone), his mission to put women "in their place" and render them apolitical did not work. In fact, women became politicized in order to perform their duties properly (i.e., defending life). It is important to note that even a conservative or repressive state ideology may provide political opportunities and sometimes liberation. Similarly, in the Marxist sense, an oppressive system may contain the seeds of its own destruction. From 1978 onward, many Chilean women continued framing their protest in terms of women's relationship to the family; however, the maternal frame gave life to a new "feminist frame," and the broader issue of democracy dominated the political landscape.

Development of the 'Return to Democracy' Master Frame and the Movement-Specific 'Feminist' Frame (1978 onward)

This period is marked by an explosion of women's political activism.

Not only did feminism reemerge, but human rights organizations and *pobladora* (poor women's) community survival organizations joined feminists in the repudiation of military authoritarianism. Three important processes are underscored in this section. First, increasing financial hardship caused by the collapse of Chile's economic miracle and the onset of the debt crisis organized poor women around basic needs, which included human rights. Women came to recognize the government as the source of their grievances. Second, the outcome of women's protests against Pinochet was contradictory: as "traditional," nonpolitical women went into the realm of public protest and community action, they became politicized. In fact, many survival organizations transformed into feminist organizations. Third, the "days of protest" against the government in 1983 started a new wave of protest based on a fundamental call for democracy. A "return to democracy" master frame emerged in this cycle of protest, and many groups used it fruitfully to guide and shape their own movement-specific efforts.

Responses to Economic Crisis: Pobladoras and Other Urban Groups. In addition to torture and murder, Pinochet seemed to add hunger to his list of repressive techniques (Change International Reports, 1981; Chuchryk, 1989). In the early part of the Pinochet era (1973-1975), several urban-based groups sprung out of the postcoup chaos. With close affiliations to the Church, groups formed to deal with issues related to political asylum, detentions, and disappearances (Agosín, 1987; Magendzo et al., 1985; Molina, 1990).[11] Poor economic conditions and the frequent loss of a breadwinner added even more strain to many families' survival. Although Pinochet's neoliberal economic campaign enjoyed some success during the late 1970s (i.e., the "economic miracle" from 1977-1980), it is generally regarded as a source of additional hardship for the poor (see Arriagada, 1991; Chuchryk, 1984, 1989, 1991; Muñoz Dálbora, 1987; Remmer, 1991).[12] After the collapse of Chile's so-called economic miracle and the onset of the debt crisis in 1982, more urban groups formed to combat hunger, declining health, and unemployment.

In 1981 the economic miracle burst, leaving 25% of the labor force unemployed and driving the gross national product down 15% (Arriagada, 1991:51). By the second quarter of 1983, the unemployment rate rose to 34%, with estimated rates up to 50% in poor neighborhoods, and 60% or more among the youth in poor areas (Arriagada, 1991:54; see also Remmer, 1991; Sigmund, 1984). As a result, the urban landscape became dotted with community survival groups, such as popular economic organizations (*organizaciones económicas populares,* or OEPs). For example, *comedores infantiles* (soup kitchen for children), and hundreds of *ollas comunes* (community kitchens) were developed to provide the poor with hot meals. Poor women (*pobladoras*) created and ran most of the OEPs, which numbered over 1125 in Santiago by 1985 (Chuchryk, 1991). Workshops and unemployment bureaus were additional responses by the poor who suffered tremendous hardships with the onset of economic crisis (Magendzo et al., 1985; Valenzuela, 1987).

Women in the "popular sector" not only took it upon themselves to find solutions to community problems of feeding the hungry; they were often responsible for providing economic sustenance for the family since many men "disappeared" or lost their jobs. Women knit together, made tapestries (the famous *arpilleras,* see Agosín, 1987),[13] and found other creative ways of earning income.[14] In this sense, women assumed a triple role: caretaker of the home and children, economic provider for the family, and caretaker of the community.

In response to this problem, some urban groups have addressed many of the specific difficulties facing women in their communities (see Chuchryk, 1991; Magendzo et al., 1985). It is likely that the multiple burdens placed on women eventually led to an awareness of specific social processes that assign more work to women than men. In fact, below I will describe some of these *pobladora* groups that transformed into feminist organizations.

The surge in organizations among the poor provided another source of protest against Pinochet as the agenda of many survival organizations expanded to include human rights. In a sense, these organizations demanded a broader definition of the necessities of life. Human rights were added to the basic rights of food, housing, and standard of living. Magendzo et al. (1985:5) state that

> an effort arises [among the poor] to reclaim their survival organizations. The primary objective is to improve permanent problems: health, housing, culture, and human rights. This reclamation is based on the right to acknowledge the basic necessities of the poor, orienting the struggle against the representative of the system that has taken those rights: the government.[15]

This passage demonstrates that not only did the agenda expand, but the target of popular hostility became identified—the government. Apparently, those "permanent problems" such as health, quality of life issues, and now human rights turned poor women's attention toward the "representative of the system that has taken those rights away: the government" (Magendzo et al., 1985:5). It seems that identifying a target of hostility may facilitate frame expansion and transformation.

'Days of Protest.' In this atmosphere of economic and social crisis, a series of protests that began on May 11, 1983, shook the nation. The "days of protest" consisted of five demonstrations against the dictatorship, roughly one per month from May to September. The first protest, called by the Copper Workers Union, was supposed to be a general strike, but with severe government repression and a reserve labor army available to replace participating workers, the strike was replaced by a call for a "national day of protest." On the evening of May 11, the capital city of Santiago, especially the middle and upper middle class neighborhoods, "reverberated with the deafening noise of Chileans beating on pots and pans and honking car horns to express their profound dissatisfaction with the military regime" (Arriagada, 1991:55).

Pinochet's response was brutal. Curfews were declared for the subsequent protests, and arrests jumped from 1213 in 1982 to 4537 in 1983 (Arriagada, 1991:63). As Pinochet stepped up his repression and the results of protest seemed to bear little fruit, support for the demonstrations among the middle and upper middle class began to decline. Arriagada notes that after the first two days of protest, demonstrations "were rapidly becoming an expression of predominantly lower-class discontent, with the greatest support coming from young Chileans in poor neighborhoods"

(1991:57). In other words, those with little to lose were the voices for democracy.

By the third day of protest it was clear that neither the Copper Workers Union nor any other organized body of workers could take a leading role in the demonstrations. Strikes were simply not effective under conditions of high unemployment, as evidenced by the dismissal of 1800 strikers after the second day of protest (Arriagada, 1991). Moreover, workers' organizations were too often crushed by Pinochet. Thus, the containment of the traditional left in Chile opened up "space" for other social actors to carry forward the demand for democracy. For example, when the government intimidated the Copper Workers Union into canceling a strike, women's human rights, survival organizations, and feminists continued demonstrating. Despite their very different agendas, these three groups came together to demand democracy. In the course of this wave of protest, a new master frame became apparent—the "return to democracy." This master frame accommodated the various movement-specific frames such as feminist and maternal since all groups had a vested interest in a new state form.

It seems that the return to democracy anchoring master frame did not shut out feminism as the "working-class radicalism" frame had done in the 1950s because feminists found meaningful, creative ways to use the frame of democracy. For example, feminists made innovative use of the "democracy" frame by drawing links between the state and the family. Democracy became an issue in the home as well as the nation, and authoritarian tendencies were identified in the institution of the family (Alvarez, 1990; Chuchryk, 1989, 1991; Feijoó, 1991; Jaquette, 1991; Kirkwood, 1983b).

Similarly, the sexual abuse meted out by Pinochet's henchmen raised the issue of violence against women in the home and in the streets. The military's "divide-and-conquer" scheme in which family members were forced to report on one another, and the exploitation of family ties to increase the effectiveness of torture, illuminated the regime's hypocritical glorification of the family (Bunster Burotto, 1986). The exalted status of mothers was the most glaring inconsistency because the regime, in the name of "national security," routinely robbed mothers of their children via murder, torture, or "disappearances" (Bunster Burotto, 1986; Feijoó, 1991; Jaquette, 1991). In the broadest sense, the underlying distinction between public and private began to erode as feminists drew analogies between the state and the home.

Feminists' ability to use creatively the frame of democracy does not entirely explain the reemergence of feminism, however. Ironically, the preexisting maternal frame, which encouraged women to become active in the "public" sphere in increasing numbers, had an unexpected outcome: women became politicized in the process, often leading to important frame transformations from maternal to feminist.

Frame Transformation. One major reason for the partial transformation of the maternal frame to the feminist frame is the duality of collective action based on women's conventional roles. On the one hand it is an acceptance of their traditional roles and responsibilities in the family; on the other it is a means for expressing rather radical politics, an untraditional occurrence in Latin America. In all of these cases, political "voice," even if an extension of women's traditional responsibilities, gave women a sense of self-transformation that was highly empowering (Chaney, 1979; Chuchryk, 1989, 1991). Many women publicly stood by their convictions for the first time, entered positions of leadership in the community, and learned how to manage organizations. For example, some of the community survival organizations did not allow men to help them do anything. They wanted to show that they could fix their own roofs, manage their own organizations, and learn how to empower themselves (Chuchryk, 1991).

Below, I illustrate just a few of these frame transformations using Chuchryk's research on women's groups in Chile during the mid-1980s. In the early 1980s, three prominent women's groups were formed: the committee for the Defense of Women's Rights (CODEM), Women of Chile (MUDECHI), and the Movement of Shanty-town Women (MOMUPO). Chuchryk notes that "CODEM and MUDECHI both emerged as a response to the political and economic crises, focusing their activities around survival issues and defining as their central priority the struggle against the dictatorship" (1991:164). Over time, the first two of these three organizations slowly began to incorporate women's strategic interests into their agenda. After a long internal political battle, CODEM now identifies itself as a feminist organization.

MOMUPO's activities center on the pobladoras from the northern section of Santiago. As previously mentioned, the general pobladora movement began as a response to economic crisis as women found creative survival strategies. Later, consciousness-raising, sexuality, women's rights, and self-education were added to their list of priorities. By 1985, according to Chuchryk, MOMUPO began to identify itself as a feminist organization.

In 1983, the Feminist Movement (MF) was organized. According to Chuchryk (1991:166),

> Women wanted to participate, as *feminists,* in the Days of Protest, which were initiated by the Copper Workers Union in May 1983 when the regime successfully intimidated them to cancel a strike they had called. On August 11, 1983, the fourth day of protest, approximately 60 women staged a 5-minute sit-in on the steps of Santiago's National Library under a banner which read "Democracy Now! The Feminist Movement of Chile."

This event marked the first feminist, as opposed to women-led, demonstration in Chile during the Pinochet era.

Another important group that emerged in 1983, Women For Life (*Mujeres Por la Vida*), began as a group of 16 women, many of whom were well-known political figures from a diversity of political perspectives. To demonstrate that women across political lines could band together in the name of peace, they organized a demonstration in December of 1983 where over 10,000 women turned out at the Caupolicán Theater. Chuchryk notes that "men were not permitted to attend, not even journalists, for the simple reason that these women wanted to demonstrate to the men of the opposition how unity could be achieved" (1991:167).

Rethinking Opportunities and Frames

Opportunities

Economic and political upheavals provided the context and many of the opportunities for mobilization in Chile's history. Surely the economic crises during Allende's administration, Pinochet's violation of human rights, the collapse of the economic miracle, and the global debt crisis have created the dislocation, grievances, and necessity of organizing around survival issues. As caretakers of families and communities, women were the ones who created and ran these survival organizations. Similarly, when state control changed hands it was women who took to the streets in protest. From what we know about political opportunity structures, it is not unusual for mobilized groups to find success at moments of "instability" or when elites are "divided." But why women? Even if one were to argue that a "closed" polity and violent repression of political protest often creates rather than destroys opportunities, why was it *women,* and not men, who found these moments opportune? Why were they effective?

I have tried to demonstrate that women's power, especially in Latin America, often resides in "informal," nonelectoral arenas. Ironically, women's traditional responsibilities in the family and community have translated into political power, especially in protests against Pinochet in the 1980s. How did they do it? The answer, I have argued, lies in collective action frames. When the state forms changed, women mobilized the preexisting maternal frame, thus manipulating dominant cultural themes in a safe manner, to identify the culpable parties, guide their action, and justify their "nontraditional" behavior. Women's use of the available maternal frame not only shows an historical continuity, but serves to explain why women were able to protest at a time when their male counterparts were silenced. Women had a mobilizational opportunity men did not have. Ostensibly Pinochet respected motherhood and family, and these women were only performing their duties as "good" women. Moreover, due to the historical longevity and cultural resonance of the maternal frame, women most likely perceived an opportunity to mobilize on this basis.

Political opportunity models cannot account for this phenomenon for two reasons: they tend to neglect cultural opportunities (e.g., the availability of a resonant frame) and they are gender blind. Until we have culturally sensitive, gendered analyses of state and political processes, nontraditional sources of power will be overlooked (see, e.g., Orloff, 1992).

To be sure, resources and organizational bases were important in this process as well. The mothers' and housewives' centers of the 1960s gave women a place to meet, a way to get involved in their neighborhoods, and a core of experiences *based on their traditional role in the family.* Motherhood and housewifery were organizing principles. I am not claiming that each participant in the protests against Pinochet was necessarily a "veteran" or a member of a mothers' center. Rather, the organizational forms associated with such centers reinforced a cultural ideal that gave strength to the "maternal frame." In subsequent protests women could draw on this frame's tactics (e.g., organize women at the local level, protest in streets), analysis (e.g., the government is hurting our families), and the justification for action (e.g., only being a "good" mother/wife/daughter).

The *pobladora* organizations provide another example of an important resource base, one linked directly to protests against Pinochet. Women worked together to provide basic needs for their families and communities. Again, because they were responsible for this kind of care, women were increasingly drawn into the "public" realm of community action where they formed networks and raised their consciousness about basic needs (including human rights), women's rights, and authoritarianism. Women of these organizations were a visible part of the protests against Pinochet.

Collective Action Frames

Gamson says that "[S]ocial psychology bashing among students of social movements is over" (1992a:53). In the past, social movement researchers shied away from models that included discontent, ideology, beliefs, and other "psychological" elements. Resources, most claimed, explained the emergence of a movement. Recently, however, scholars are beginning to realize that we need more cross-fertilization between the "rational" and "psychological" models. Collective action frames can begin to bridge this divide.

The case of women in Chile suggests that women had a powerful, resonant maternal frame to use during periods of economic and political upheaval. Since both labor unions and leftist political parties effectively edged out feminist ways of understanding social problems in the 1950s, the working-class radicalism frame became dominant. As in other times and places in the world, the left was hostile toward feminism. Consequently, labor unions and political parties helped push women's issues into political practice and cultural/political discourse as reproductive issues only. Subsequent movements on both the right and left have made use of the available frame and attendant discourse.

The story of women in Chile hints at the ways in which the theoretical concept of master frames

can be developed further. The nature of the master frame may shape the competition between movement-specific frames, as a more "elaborated" frame (such as the "return to democracy") allows room for a variety of interests to be expressed. The "restricted" master frame, however, may cause more intense competition among movement frames since there is not sufficient "space" for all groups to participate. For example, I hypothesize that the leftist master frame of the 1950s and 1960s *could* have accommodated feminism, but did not. The narrow way in which the overarching theme of "systems of oppression" got played out solely in terms of working-class issues, is what signed feminism's death warrant. The narrow or "restricted" expression of the leftist frame provided little room for feminism. However, after 1973 the leftist master frame was pushed underground. Chuchryk (1984) explains that the absence of the left created "space" for other kinds of organizations, especially church groups and community/shantytown organizations. I contend that because the leftist frame was crushed, in public practice at least, there was also room for a feminist frame again. The horror of Pinochet's Chile turned the left's 1971 chants for "Socialism Now" into cries for "Democracy Now" in the 1980s (Winn, 1986:256). The new master frame of democracy was broad enough to accommodate feminist, maternal, and labor concerns. In sum, it is likely that collective action frames within a "cycle" not only compete for dominance, but do so in a manner that is shaped by the master frame. More research needs to be done in this newly developing area of social movement theory.

Moreover, little is understood about how frames operate in a nondemocratic context. Although much more research needs to be done in this area, this case study suggests a few areas of inquiry.

First, we should not assume that opposition movements are using an oppositional frame. Under conditions of authoritarianism, actors may be able to legitimate their actions by using the dominant discourse, or the same language as the repressive state. By using the maternal frame women were afforded some safety and legitimacy.

Second, we ought to examine the importance of master frames in relation to political upheaval. What happens when master frames are crushed by a police state? Examining periods of political change (e.g., democracy to authoritarianism and vice versa) offers a window into the processes involved in the creation of new frames, and the transformation of old ones.

Third, important international research has pointed out that women are key to our understanding of activism under conditions of state repression (e.g., Alvarez, 1990; Chuchryk, 1984, 1989, 1991; Fisher, 1989; Jaquette, 1991; Molina, 1990). Not only are they typically considered nonpolitical (and therefore nonthreatening), they are responsible for family and community care. This combination can radicalize women. It seems that they are key actors in the mobilization against repressive states because of the way in which their activities are framed. More comparisons across states are needed.

Fourth, in terms of transitions to democracy, we should look at the ways in which frames were used during previous democratic periods in the country. These insights may not have predictive power about how different groups will fare in the new context, but they help us understand how framing activities worked or failed beforehand.

Conclusion

Now that Chile is making the difficult transition to democracy, what will happen to women's political power? It is still unclear whether women's mobilization in the 1980s was just another example of short-term "crisis" politics. As Jaquette notes, "in the past, women have usually withdrawn from politics after a surge of activism" (1991:206). Will women quietly go back into their position as mere party appendages (i.e., part of women's branches of political parties)?

Many scholars are skeptical of democracy. Phillips (1991) argues that democracy in fact does not provide the same freedom and liberties to women as it does to men. Historians have reminded us that periods of greater democratization (e.g., after the French Revolution) often result in the codification and reinforcement of gender hierarchies (e.g., Faure, 1991; Hunt, 1992). Latin American feminists have speculated that the introduction of democracy may close off political participation for the vast majority of women (see Jaquette, 1991). Ironically, some argue, under authoritarianism women had the most input in state affairs that they may ever have.

I am not as pessimistic. Undoubtedly, as formal political channels are reinstated, women's informal political power will wane. Men will continue to dominate formal, electoral politics for some time to come. However, two particular historical shifts are working in women's favor. First, the historically difficult relationship between women and the left has changed. I predict that a somewhat younger, fragmented, and realistic left in Chile will not shun feminism the way it once did. After all, their history shows them that a "democratic road to Socialism" is not coming anytime soon. We have already seen some cooperation between progressive parties and women.

Second, the thousands of women who learned leadership skills, coordinated neighborhood programs, and protested in the streets have become politicized, perhaps against their will. The advent of democracy cannot turn back the clock to a time when women were assumed to be mere objects or recipients of political actions. They have proven their power to change the way politics operate, and they may decide to use their collective force. To be sure, the future of women's political "voice" in Chile rests with the brave women who were not afraid to oppose state tyranny.

Notes

1. In one of his many references to motherhood, Pinochet stated, "When a woman becomes a mother she does not expect anything more on a material plane; she searches and finds in her own [child] the purpose of her life, her only treasure and the finishing line where her dreams come true" (Munizaga and Letelier, 1987, cited in Bunster, 1988:488).

2. I refer to discourse as a "social dialogue which takes place through and across societal institutions, among individuals as well as groups, organizations and . . . political institutions themselves" (Donati, 1992:138). Therefore, in accordance with Donati, (1992), Gamson (1988), and Taylor and Wittier (1992b), I assume that discourse is used to help create a collective action frame.

3. The term "maternal collective action frame" will be used to capture the notion of collective action based on traditional gender and family roles for women. It is not meant to assume that all female participants in these social movements were mothers—just that the ethic of care is better characterized as maternal than "individual," "working class," or any other label.

4. By framing issues in terms of "class," particularly "working-class" radicalism, women were generally excluded. Leftist (especially Marxist) arguments that conceptualize the point of production as the primary locus of "human" oppression overlook the manifold sites in which women are oppressed (e.g., the family). Furthermore, a radical agenda based on workers' problems tends to exclude the many women who are

not involved in the paid labor force. Due to cultural standards, many Chilean women leave the work force when they marry.

5. This is a summary of a complex historical phenomenon. Scholars have debated whether and why women are indeed more conservative than men. See Chaney (1979) and Chuchryk (1984).

6. As a shorthand way of expressing different kinds of interests, I will borrow Molyneux's (1985:240) distinction between "practical" and "strategic" gender interests. Practical interests relate to women's responsibilities due to the division of labor in society: interests in maintaining the family, ensuring that children are fed, etc. Strategic interests are those that grow out of a critique of the unequal division of social power: interests in fighting violence against women, working for suffrage, and eliminating women's oppression more generally. These are often termed feminist interests. Sometimes these divisions are not very clear, as when practical interests turn into strategic interests.

7. Thus, mothers' centers provided an unintended infrastructure for subsequent political action. While not identical, this process is analogous to the social movement "half-way houses" of the U.S. civil rights movement that Morris (1984) describes, or the consciousness-raising groups of the U.S. women's movement (see Freeman, 1973a; Ferree and Hess, 1985).

8. Dirección de Inteligencia Nacional was disbanded in 1977 and replaced with the Centro Nacional de Inteligencia.

9. Ximena Bunster Burotto's (1986) "Surviving Beyond Fear" is a vivid and horrifying account of the sexual violence and torture women often experienced when they were arrested or "picked up" by the military.

10. Space considerations prevent me from discussing some "concrete" outcomes of Pinochet's campaign to reinforce women's "proper" roles. For example, changing laws prohibited women from wearing slacks (Andreas, 1976); employment discrimination against women was permitted (women could be tested for pregnancy and then fired; see Chuchryk, 1984, for discussion).

11. The Catholic Church provided protection to various women's human rights organizations. Pinochet monitored the Church closely, so women were better able to work under its aegis as the regime tended to view women as apolitical.

12. His neoliberal economic plan formally began in 1975, closely guided by Chicago economists (termed "Chicago Boys"). A variety of pressures forced Pinochet to modify his approach over the years. See Sigmund (1984), Remmer (1991), and Arriagada (1991) for more detailed discussions of his economic policies.

13. Agosín demonstrates how women's knitting groups were also used as clandestine forms of protest. Her book *Scraps of Life* is a study of how the famous *arpilleras* were used to portray scenes of political repression.

14. Space prohibits me from providing more examples of poor women's collective strategies to fight poverty during the debt crisis of the 1980s. Structural adjustment policies had profound effects on women and their communities. For a good discussion of this point, see Centro de Comunicación y Participación de la Mujer (1989), *Mujer, Participación Social Y Politica.*

15. Author's translation. ✦

20

Understanding the Dialectic of Discourse and Collective Action: Public Debate and Rioting in Antebellum Cincinnati

Stephen Ellingson

Throughout the 1830s many communities in the United States were embroiled in conflict over slavery and the new antislavery or abolition movement. Abolitionist agitation triggered public outcry, resolutions for antiabolition legislation, and riots to silence the reformers. Situated in a border state and as the most important western center for the North-South trade, Cincinnati became a battleground to test the resolve of the fledgling abolition movement and the strength of Northern racism. Initially the battle was waged with words, but on July 30, 1836, city residents, frustrated by the inefficacy of words, took to the streets with bricks and clubs to destroy the abolitionist press in a night of rioting.

From August 1835 through the months following the riot of July 30, Cincinnati citizens argued over the propriety and right of antislavery advocates to publish and distribute their newspaper in the city. Yet the debate did not hinge on the question of slavery or abolition but rather on the antinomies of individual and communal rights, freedom and despotism, order and chaos. Three groups of citizens participated in the debate, creating discourses from which to contest the meaning of the debate and to mobilize action. Antiabolitionists claimed that abolitionism threatened the city's trade with the South, as well as the security of the city and the nation. They demanded an absolute cessation of abolition activity and sanctioned collective violence to secure that end. The abolitionists defended their right to publish

on the subject of slavery and charged the antiabolitionists with trading Northern civil liberties for Southern dollars. A third group, "The Friends of Law, Order and the Constitution," created a discourse that rejected the positions of the other two as dangerous to the law, civil liberties, economy, and good order of the city. They advocated tolerance and upholding the law as the means to resolve the conflict, but their message was largely ignored until after the riot.

Before the riot, the struggle appeared to have been won by the antiabolitionists. Their discourse received widespread public support. They used this discourse to drive law and order supporters from the field and mobilize residents to silence the hated abolitionists through collective violence. However, their victory was short-lived. In a dramatic turnaround of public sentiment, the antiabolitionists and their discourse were repudiated after the riot, while the law and order position won public approval and abolitionism was granted legitimacy. What might account for the antiabolitionists' pyrrhic victory and the revitalization of law and order claims?

I argue that this turnaround—the delegitimization and repudiation of antiabolitionism—was made possible by the successful reframing of the debate by law and order and abolitionist speakers.[1] More generally my explanation rests on understanding the dialectical relationship between discourse and events. In the following analysis I demonstrate how the discursive struggle over abolitionism shaped the two episodes of collective action that interrupted the ongoing debate and, conversely, how these events changed the content, form, and legitimacy of competing discourses and altered the configuration of the discursive field. Before turning to this analysis, I will situate my study within the literature on culture and collective action, outline my theoretical position that links events to the production and reception of discourse, and describe the data and historical background of the case.

Theory and Method

In recent years many social scientists have made the "linguistic turn" and have accorded great explanatory power to language.[2] Yet too often how and why language influences events (e.g., collective action) or processes of social and cultural change remains unspecified, hidden behind the jargon of discourse analysis or obscured when all social phenomena (e.g., institutions, relations of authority, collective actions) are defined as "texts" (e.g., Barthes 1972, 1986; Foucault 1980; Stedman-Jones 1983; see Palmer [1990] for a critique). However, this problem is being addressed by analysts who have identified how cultural objects (such as discourses or ideologies) may be used by actors to form lines of action (e.g., Swidler 1986) or how they enable actors to define certain issues, beliefs, and forms of action as legitimate and others as illegitimate—thus reproducing or challenging social structures and relations of power (Bourdieu 1991; Best 1990; Wagner-Pacifici 1986; Lears 1985; Gusfield 1981a).³ Yet many studies that examine the relationship between culture and action concentrate too narrowly on the shaping power of cultural objects and thus fail to take seriously how the nature and course of events (i.e., sequences of actions occurring through time) influence the meanings and forms of the cultural objects involved, and how the construction and reconstruction of meaning occurs at the nexus of event and cultural object (see Archer [1988] and Kane [1991] regarding the interdependent influence of culture and action on social change). At best, events are treated as arenas where the effective manipulation of cultural objects produces specific actions or results in some form of social change (e.g., see Wagner-Pacifici 1986; Condit 1990; Beisel 1993).

Sahlins (1981, 1985, 1991) and Sewell (in press) note that although events are shaped by some set of ideas, beliefs, or rules embodied in ritual, symbol, or speech (e.g., the killing of Captain Cook was predicated on the religious myths and ritual cycle of the Hawaiian islanders), they also transform these same cultural objects and social structures. Events disrupt the operative systems of ideas, beliefs, values, roles, and institutional practices of a given society (Sahlins 1991, p. 44). In so doing, events change the way in which social actors think about the meaning and importance they assign to modes of action and the rules that govern interaction, groups and their discourses, symbols, and rituals. In the event, the meanings carried by cultural objects are embodied in historic actors and actions and then reinterpreted and reconfigured based on the consequences (real or perceived) the event has for particular actors (Sahlins 1985, pp. xiv, 138, 144-49; Sewell 1992, p. 18).⁴

Recent work on social movements and collective action also stresses the definitional power of culture. In the shift from more structurally oriented theories of collective action (i.e., resource mobilization) to more culturally oriented approaches, scholars have focused attention on explaining how social movement organizations and actors interpret grievances and generate consensus on belief and action (Klandermans 1984a, 1988a), create collective identities (Melucci 1989), and produce the frames of meaning (Snow et at. 1986; Snow and Benford 1988, 1992; Gamson, Fireman, and Rytina 1982), vocabularies of motives, and social dramas necessary to mobilize constituents (Benford 1993b; Benford and Hunt 1992). Although this new approach adds a needed corrective in the literature, it tends to focus on the ideological and discursive work of movements without explaining how this work is related to collective action events that are primarily oriented toward demonstrating (rather than producing) a movement's or group's ideology (e.g., strikes, riots, marches; for exceptions see Tarrow [1994, pp. 129-33], Benford [1993a, pp. 689-94], and Gamson and Modigliani [1989, pp. 17-21]). In other words, we do not fully understand how episodes of collective action influence the processes of meaning construction and the content of movement frames or discourses.

Klandermans (1992) acknowledges this theoretical and empirical gap in the literature, noting that little attention has been given to the "social construction of meaning in action situations" or to the "processes of interpreting, defining, and consciousness raising that occur among participants who interact during episodes of collective action" (p. 81; see also Gamson 1992a, p. 70; Tarrow 1992, p. 175). The relationship between collective action events and the success or failure of movement discourses remains undertheorized and ungrounded in detailed empirical studies. Too often the events that scholars identify as having a powerful influence on movement discourses or frames are not collective actions engaged in or engendered by social movements but dramatic, nonmovement events such as humanmade disasters, major court decisions, or wars (McAdam 1994, p. 40; Snow and Benford 1992, pp. 149-50). These events are conceptualized as external forces that may generate attention on a particular problem, win credibility for a movement's frame, encourage new organizations to join a movement, or serve as a model of success that foments expectations among constituents of future movement victories (see Klandermans 1988a, p. 185; 1992, pp.

92-93; Gamson 1988, pp. 233-37; McAdam 1982, pp. 48-51). This research points to the importance of events for understanding changes in consciousness or collective beliefs, and I build upon it by demonstrating *how* events are incorporated into existing sets of meaning and force movement actors to create new sets of meaning that will garner resources, attract constituents, or realize movement goals (see Tarrow 1989; Hirsch 1990; McAdam 1983; Gamson and Modigliani 1989).

To a certain degree the shift to culture in the social movement field has also been a shift inward. This inward shift is especially prominent in work that focuses on discourse (e.g., Gamson 1988; Gamson and Modigliani 1989; Johnston 1991b; Benford and Hunt 1992; Hunt 1992; Benford 1993b). The strength of these studies lies in their detailed analyses of the rhetorical strategies, media practices, or linguistic devices movement actors employ to construct injustice frames and rationales for action, link them to the interests and beliefs of specific audiences, or challenge the ideologies or frames of authorities, countermovements, or movement factions. Because many authors are primarily concerned with identifying and describing the various strategies movement actors use to construct meaning (e.g., the frame alignment process of Snow et al. [1986] or the dramaturgical techniques identified by Benford [1993a]), they tend to give little theoretical and empirical attention to how collective action events might influence the process of meaning construction.[5] Why do discourses change in the wake of collective action events? Do such events discredit frames of meaning or undermine rationales for action? Do they break the link between the interests and expectations of movements and their audiences and thus cause both sets of actors to evaluate, rework, or jettison all or part of a movement's discourse?

I address these questions by explicating the dialectical relationship between meaning construction (through discourse) and collective action. That is, I demonstrate how the two episodes of collective action in Cincinnati (events that are analytically separable from the discourses and seen as such by speakers) were shaped and made meaningful by the competing discourses and how they also brought about changes in the specific discourses and the configuration of the discursive field.

A second area of my study concerns the relationship between how meaning is produced and how movement actors and their audiences interact. In the extant literature, the discursive field is often conceived in narrow terms, thus simplifying the complex discursive and action-oriented relationships among various speakers and audiences.[6] A number of scholars are attending to this problem by examining the competitive relationships that exist among movements, government agencies, nonmovement organizations (e.g., churches), and the media. However, they tend to treat these relationships in a theoretical manner and do not test their ideas in extended empirical analyses (e.g., see Tarrow 1994, pp. 122-34; Klandermans 1988a, pp. 185-86; Gamson 1988). In a recent work, Klandermans (1992, pp. 94-99) highlights the importance of conceptualizing movement fields as being populated by multiple organizations in systems of alliances and rivalries, but he only begins to discuss how patterns of interaction, discursive production, and collective action are related. Similarly, Hunt, Benford, and Snow (1994) explain how social movements construct the identities of protagonists, antagonists, and audiences within a movement field and frame outsiders' claims about the movement, but they do not discuss how outsiders or nonmovement groups construct counterframes or demonstrate how identities and claims change as a result of the interaction among competing groups. We have studies that ably discuss discursive work within a single movement (e.g., Snow et al. 1986; Snow and Benford 1988; Benford 1993b), between movement factions (e.g., Benford 1993a), or between challengers and authorities (e.g., Gamson et al. 1982), but these studies generally do not analyze patterns of creation and reception among all the parties within a movement field during a specific event or period of time.[7] These studies do not address the ways in which groups within the field alter their discourses in response to one another or identify how the field expands or contracts based on the course of discursive struggle amidst episodes of protest (e.g., see Gamson and Modigliani 1989). In this article, I show how events and discursive production serve as catalysts for new (and outside) voices to become involved, for some audiences to organize, and for others to become quiescent.

A final issue that has not been fully addressed by studies that focus on movement discourse and framing is identifying which audiences are targeted by which movements and other groups within a field and for what reasons (on this critique, see Klandermans 1988a, p. 192).[8] Although several recent studies illustrate how movements engage in different framing tasks or tailor their claims to appeal to targeted audiences, they are not concerned with understanding how these audiences interpret competing claims or how reception influences the continued use or alteration of specific arguments (e.g., Snow et al. 1986, pp. 468, 472; Benford 1993a, pp. 687-91; Gerhards and Rucht 1992). Yet if successful mobilization depends on linking movement frames with those held by targeted audiences (Snow et al. 1986; Snow and Benford 1988; Klandermans 1988a), tapping into collective beliefs (e.g., Tarrow 1992), or constructing collective identities that are congruent with those held by specific audiences, then identifying the operative interests, expectations, and beliefs of a movement's targeted audiences is vital. Do movement and nonmovement speakers adopt different mobilization strategies (e.g., sets of arguments that identify problems or rationales for action) depending on the audiences they address? Are some audiences more important and thus more likely to influence the content and form of discourses within a field? How do speakers incorporate the responses of particular audiences to episodes of collective action into their frames of meaning?

In sum, my study extends the extant work on framing, movement discourse, and the role of meaning by scholars within the constructivist approach to collective action by focusing on the dialectical relationship between collective action events and the production of discourses. I contend that we need to examine how episodes of collective action influence the strategies of meaning construction, the nature of discursive competition, and the content of the discourses within a particular field to more fully understand how speakers construct and reconstruct their diagnoses and solutions and how and why mobilization efforts succeed or fail. . . .

Discourse and Collective Action

I define a discourse as a relatively bounded set of arguments organized around a specific diagnosis of and solution to some social problem.[9] This definition narrows attention to those discourses oriented toward advocating or preventing some form of social change and thus toward the discursive work in social movement, political, or civic arenas. This definition also suggests that discourses are situated within a field of debate wherein speakers struggle with one another to establish meaning, earn legitimacy, and mobilize consensus on belief and action (see Bourdieu 1991, Volosinov 1986; Lears 1985; Hall 1982; Foucault 1965, 1980). Because discourses are created in reference and opposition to one another, an imperative of differentiation characterizes the process of creation and contestation. One of the common modes of differentiation is for speakers to structure their discourses (and the field) around various sets of poles (i.e., pairs of fundamental oppositions) that condense what the debate is about, what can be discussed, and what problems can be addressed (Bourdieu 1991, pp. 185-91; Wuthnow 1989, p. 13).[10] Fields then become primary sites of contention, where competing speakers battle over which poles will govern debate because control over them endows some speakers with the power to set agendas and guide the direction and content of debate.

Speakers rely on a variety of strategies to establish or contend more effectively over the meaning and organization of the debate. These strategies include (1) shifting the definition of the situation from a specific or practical level (e.g., abolitionism injures the city's businesses) to a more general or conceptual level (e.g., the issue is not about abolitionism but about whether civil liberties will be preserved), (2) changing the focus of a discourse to render it more salient and resonant with a targeted audience or to gain entry into a debate (e.g., the abolitionists dropped their moral and economic arguments and concentrated on political arguments when only the latter generated support and attracted the attention of the other participants in the debate) and (3) reordering the institutional locus of the debate or bringing a specific discourse into closer articulation with institutional values, symbols, or practices (e.g., the law and order and abolition factions shifted the institutional locus from economics to politics and defined their positions as preserving the civil liberties and laws necessary to ensure orderly economic and social activity).

Discursive struggles often take place at the level of arguments, which are the building blocks of discourse. Arguments are both the means by which speakers create and justify their diagnoses and solutions and the carriers of economic, political, or moral goals and interests that motivate public debate. Speakers craft new arguments or adopt preexisting ones (in Cincinnati, speakers drew upon extant arguments about mobs, social order, commerce, and republican ideals . . .), then arrange these arguments in different combinations in order to accomplish their goals. These goals might include advancing alternative conceptions of what the debate is about and what the potential consequences are, contesting ideologies or the meaning of categories that undergird different discourses (e.g., order or civil liberties), challenging or reinforcing collective beliefs, and discrediting rival speakers' arguments by aligning them with illegitimate ideologies or social groups (e.g., antiabolitionists tried to discredit the law and order position by linking it to abolitionists' arguments) or by constructing rivals as public enemies (see Edelman 1988, pp. 66-89; Rogin 1987; on strategies of discursive creation and contestation see Thompson [1990, pp. 60-67]; Edelman [1971, 1988]; Terdiman [1985]). As suggested by the social constructivist perspective in the social movements and social problems literature, the effectiveness of a particular discourse (or claims-making endeavor) may hinge on the fit between diagnosis and solution or between arguments and the interests of audiences (see Snow and Benford 1988; Benford 1993a, pp. 691-94; Best 1990, pp. 24-42- Edelman 1988, pp. 12-36). Speakers will reject solutions, change goals, or rework arguments when they contradict or fail to resonate with their audiences. Failure to do so may undermine the legitimacy of their position or impair their capacity to mobilize audiences. In the Cincinnati case, the antiabolition solution of collective violence undermined both the economic goal of prosperity and the political goal of ensuring a secure environment from which to conduct business. Instead of refitting the economic and political goals of Cincinnatians to the new context of vigilantism and collective violence, residents and the previous supporters of antiabolitionism alike rejected the discourse and solution of antiabolitionism during the third phase of the conflict.

Meaning is thus constructed through the ongoing process of contestation within a discursive field as speakers jockey to gain legitimacy for their positions, the support of targeted audiences, and the opportunity to implement their solutions. During this struggle, "issues are redefined, and means of action and outcomes are reevaluated; movement organizations, opponents, and coun-

termovement organizations may be discredited; beliefs and ideologies are challenged or refuted; and competing organizations are deemed unreliable" (Klandermans 1992, p. 90).

Yet meaning is not constructed solely on the basis of the interaction among speakers; meaning is also produced as speakers modify their discourses in response to the episodes of collective action constituted by the debate and to the reception of discourse and event by audiences. During the course of discursive struggles over social change, actors implement actions designed to resolve specific problems; these actions disrupt the struggle and open the way for speakers to resignify what the debate means (Gamson 1988, p. 237; Archer 1988, pp. 154-82). Episodes of collective action provide new information actors use to evaluate the practical consequences of specific solutions, to confirm or refute arguments, and to assess how well competing arguments and poles articulate with the interests, beliefs, and experiential bases of particular audiences (i.e., their horizons of expectations).[11] This new information also may be defined as proof or evidence by competing groups to justify their particular claims. Both speakers and their audiences engage in this work of interpreting the event and assigning meaning to the potential consequences or implications of it for themselves, their social world, and the course of debate. Speakers' goals and interests (e.g., winning support for a particular diagnosis and solution) also may be subject to reevaluation and adjustment when collective action is seen as an inadequate means for realizing or protecting them, especially when audiences no longer view arguments favorably.

When the fit between collective action and horizons is loose (e.g., when rioting subverted the common interest of preserving social order), when collective action undermines diagnoses or solutions, or when it fails to achieve the intended results, audiences may alter their interests and beliefs, change the meaning of these interests and beliefs, or look for new means to realize them. As horizons change, some solutions may be rejected and some diagnoses judged incorrect, while others are accorded greater authority. Speakers respond to the event and altered horizons by reworking their discourses—jettisoning arguments that are untenable, adopting those of their rivals, or crafting new ones that incorporate the event (i.e., the episode of collective action) as the ground from which to assess the viability and legitimacy of old and new arguments—to make them more resonant with their audiences' new horizons of expectations and to help speakers compete more effectively within the field of debate. In short, collective action challenges or discredits some arguments and their underlying ideas, lends support for others, and in effect alters the social and cultural context of meaning production. This process compels speakers to reconstruct their discourses around the experience and consequences of collective actions.

Speakers, Audiences, and Data

Identifying the interests of speakers and the expectations of audiences helps the analyst to understand why a discourse is created and how it is received, as well as to assess the fit between the discourse and the interests and expectations (Griswold 1987). There were three groups of speakers involved in the Cincinnati debate over abolitionism: antiabolitionists, abolitionists, and the law and order faction. Each group organized its discourse around a set of arguments that were appropriated from a preexisting stock of arguments about mobs and disorder, race and abolitionism, and civil liberties and community rights. The members of all three groups were largely from the commercial and professional classes, although they differed in terms of occupational and social status.[12]

Table 1 divides the three groups according to the occupations of their members.[13] Although the professional class was equally represented among the three groups, members of the commercial class were more likely to belong to the antiabolition faction. Moreover, the city's social, economic, and political elite (i.e., wholesale merchants, owners of foundries or mills, bankers,

lawyers and doctors with large practices, and ministers of the largest churches in the city) were disproportionately represented among antiabolitionists. Nearly 90% of the commercial antiabolitionists were from the upper tier of the city's elite, and over 40% (11 of the 27) of the professional men were prominent attorneys who often represented these commercial elites or were engaged themselves in real estate speculation or commercial investment (Glazer 1968, pp. 107-9).[14]

Abolitionists and the law and order group represented the middle level of the commercial and professional classes (e.g., small retailers, teachers, and clerks). Only one member of the law and order faction belonged to the commercial elite, and only six (or 15%) were high-status professionals. Similarly, abolitionists lacked the wealth, status, and social authority of the antiabolitionists. Only six abolitionists (about 21%) were from the elite, and over half of its professionals were low-status, low-paid schoolteachers (three men taught free blacks and three were women).

Although each group represented a specific population of the professional and commercial classes, all three directed their discourse toward the city's elite, who, as political officials and the primary employers in the city, held the authority to sanction or prevent a riot. Members of the three groups, especially the abolitionists, were probably aware that elites had condoned, sanctioned, and in some cases participated in previous antiabolition and antiblack riots (e.g., in New York City in 1833 and 1834, in Boston in 1835, and in Utica, N.Y., in 1835) and understood that most episodes of collective violence would not be allowed unless elites considered them unlikely to seriously threaten the law or their property (see Gilje 1987, pp. 17-25, 32-44, 83; Feldberg 1980,

Table 1
Occupational Classification of the Three Discursive Groups

Group	Commercial[a]	Professional[b]	Artisan[c]	Unknown[d]	N
Antiabolition	44 (52)	27 (32)	4 (5)	10 (12)	85
Law and Order	7 (18)	12 (30)	10 (25)	11 (28)	40
Abolition	9 (31)	11 (38)	4 (14)	5 (17)	29

Note: Nos. in parentheses are % of sample engaged in that class.
[a]Members of the commercial class include wholesale merchants, bankers, and owners of stores, real estate, foundries, mills, breweries, life insurance companies, or utility companies.
[b]Members of the professional class include attorneys, judges, ministers, editors, medical doctors, civil servants, clerks or managers of businesses, and school teachers.
[c]Members of the artisanal class include saddlers, hatters, machinists, carpenters, wire workers, bricklayers, and river pilots.
[d]Participants in this category either were not listed in the city directory or no occupation was given.

pp. 26, 42-44; Hammett 1976; Richards 1970, pp. 131-33; Weinbaum 1979, pp. 35, 41-42, 62). Thus all three groups hoped to persuade this powerful audience to support their claims and to legitimate their positions. The three groups also appealed to members from middle-class occupations, who were likely participants in any riot.[15] Many in both audiences were opposed to abolitionism, held racist opinions, and tended to value economic growth more than moral reform (see Aaron 1992, pp. 82-83, 29599; Folk 1978, chap. 3 [on the 1829 Cincinnati race riot], pp. 58-62, 83; Pih 1969; Wade 1954; Woodson 1916). Antiabolitionists possessed a distinct advantage over abolition and law and order speakers because they were speaking to two sets of listeners generally committed to their ideas and plan of action. In order to effectively counter antiabolitionism, the other two groups would be forced to overcome Cincinnatians' racism, hostility to abolitionism, and fears of losing the Southern trade.

At the same time, abolitionists and antiabolitionists targeted specific audiences who were likely to be receptive to their respective messages and possessed important resources (e.g., money or willingness to engage in action) each group hoped to tap. Abolitionists directed their message to an audience of state and national abolitionists because they hoped to secure the support, financial resources, and pressure of public opinion of a larger audience than was available to them in Cincinnati.[16] Antiabolitionists directed their message to Cincinnati's Southern neighbors, especially those in Kentucky and in South Carolina, in order to maintain amicable trade relations and avert a potential economic boycott. They also hoped to win the support and participation of those laborers engaged in work dependent on the Southern trade (e.g., steam engine manufacturing) and therefore scheduled their public meetings when workers in the manufacturing shops and mills were on their way home.

I drew the data for the textual analysis—editorials, letters to the editor, proceedings of public meetings, and narratives of the riot—primarily from six of Cincinnati's daily (*Whig, Republican, Gazette, and Post*) and weekly (*Philanthropist*, and *Cincinnati Journal and Western Luminary*) newspapers.[17] These papers represented the two political parties (Whig and Democrat), the abolition movement, and the Presbyterian community. The four dailies carried economic and political news

and catered to a mercantile and professional audience. They had circulations that ranged from about 1,200 to 4,000 and were financed through subscriptions and local advertising.[18] Fear of losing the financial support of this audience certainly contributed to the strong antiabolitionist position taken by three of the four, although the editor of the *Gazette* was willing to risk the loss of subscription and advertising dollars to defend the abolitionists' civil liberties (see Aaron 1992, p. 238).[19] *The Philanthropist* was owned by the Ohio Anti-Slavery Society (OASS), and though it was financed primarily by subscriptions (it relied on some advertising revenue, but only a small part was from local businesses; see Nerone [1989, pp. 265, 2731) the society covered shortfalls (see OASS 1837, 1841, 1842, 1843). Thus James Birney, editor of the *Philanthropist,* did not face the same financial pressures to avoid positions contrary to the interests of Cincinnati's businessmen and could advance controversial causes, such as abolitionism, more easily than other editors could.[20] Although the majority of the articles in the *Philanthropist* were directed at abolitionists and thus dealt with slavery, abolitionism, or moral reform, it also published articles on local and national politics, economic news, and short stories. Birney was not, however, just preaching to the converted. He used the newspaper to attract new supporters and to engage the editors of Cincinnati's other papers in a discussion of slavery and the city's economic and political interests. Moreover, Birney could expect that many city residents would read the paper, given the common practice among readers from all classes of sharing newspapers and the easy access to newspapers in the city's reading rooms and taverns.[21] Table 2 links

Table 2
Discursive and Organizational Position of Cincinnati Newspapers

Newspaper	Editor	Party/Organization	Position
Gazette	C. Hammond	Whig	Law and Order
Whig	J. Conover	Whig	Antiabolition
Post	E. S. Thomas	Whig	Antiabolition
Republican	C. Ramsay	Democrat	Antiabolition
Philanthropist.	J. Birney	OASS	Abolition
Cincinnati Journal & Western Luminary	T. Brainerd	Presbyterian	Law and Order

each paper with its party or organization and with its discursive position during the debate.

The *Whig*, *Gazette*, and *Philanthropist* were the primary voices of the antiabolition, law and order, and abolition positions, respectively. These three newspapers were the main producers of editorials and publishers of letters to the editor and of commentaries on the riot and debate from non-Cincinnatians. Editorials, letters, and outside commentaries accounted for 85% of the texts produced (192 of 225 texts; 43% [97] were editorials, while letters and commentaries each accounted for roughly 21% [47 and 48, respectively]). The discursive struggle was divided into three discrete stages, punctuated by two episodes of collective action. During the first stage of the debate, speakers relied on editorials to establish their positions, especially the editor of the *Philanthropist*, who penned nearly half (14 of 30) of them. In the second stage, textual production was evenly split between editorials (23 of 54) and letters (21 of 54). The *Whig* was the most active editorial voice in this stage, and its pages were opened to both antiabolition and law and order speakers who struggled to define and defend different conceptions of social order and the means to preserve it. The final stage was dominated by the fight between the editors of the *Whig* and the *Gazette,* and a much stronger law and order voice was heard. The Whig published few letters in this stage and instead returned to editorials (two-thirds of its published texts). On the other hand, the Gazette produced 10 editorials and published 13 letters from new law and order supporters. The other law and order paper, the *Cincinnati Journal and Western Luminary* (hereafter referred to as CJWL) doubled its editorial production from the previous stage (from three to seven) and reprinted six outside commentaries that condemned the July 30 riot. The *Philanthropist* also followed this strategy by publishing extracts from 24 different newspapers across the North. . . .

Establishing the Abolition Press: The Dialectic of Discourse and Action

As noted previously, the conflict over abolitionism in Cincinnati was divided into three discrete periods of public debate and separated by two episodes of collective violence. In the following analysis I demonstrate how these episodes provided new information that the three groups and their audiences used to evaluate the claims

and solutions articulated in the preceding period of debate. After each episode, speakers altered their discourses by framing new diagnoses and solutions according to the real and perceived outcomes of collective violence and formed new discursive alliances in order to gain legitimacy and support for their positions.

The Historical Context of Antebellum Collective Violence

The 1836 riot occurred in an environment marked by heightened concerns about order, sectionalism, and race and ethnicity; increasingly these concerns were translated into collective violence.[22] National identity and institutions remained unsettled, and groups that challenged the political basis for the Union or threatened white labor or Protestantism were often made the object of ideological and physical attack (e.g., Masons, Catholics, Irish immigrants, free blacks). Rioting was considered a quasilegitimate means of voicing popular opinion about or disapproval of political events, labor relations, and public morality, as well as a means for "the people" to correct "social abuses in instances where the legal system was unable or unwilling to act" (Grimstead 1972, p. 365).[23]

One of the primary focuses of social conflict and rioting during the 1830s was the abolition movement. It challenged commonly held beliefs about race relations, citizenship rights, and the nature of republican government. Thus it generated heated opposition. This opposition was based on the perception that the movement questioned the legitimacy of the Constitution and the compromises necessary to create the nation, promised to destroy the Southern economic system and thus the networks of trade between Northern merchants and manufacturers and Southern cotton growers, promoted black citizenship rights and racial amalgamation, and denounced all institutions that would not promote emancipation. Although Democrats were especially opposed to abolition, the perceived dangers of the movement engendered bipartisan and widespread popular opposition (see Hammett 1979, pp. 859-63; Henig 1969, pp. 48-51; Silbey 1985, pp. 89-90).

The year 1835 witnessed a dramatic upsurge of abolitionist activity that was met in the South with economic threats against the North and demands for legal action against abolitionists. The American Anti-Slavery Society (AASS) initiated a campaign to flood the South with its propaganda, and Southerners interpreted this campaign as an attempt by abolitionists to encourage slave insurrection and destroy the legalized system of slavery. Throughout the summer of 1835 and into the early months of 1836, Southern communities (especially in South Carolina) intercepted the mail, demanded an immediate end to the campaign, and urged the North to prove their commitment to the South and the Constitution by suppressing abolitionism. Mass meetings were held in both the South and the North at which abolitionists and their propaganda campaign were condemned and Northern communities pledged not to interfere with or discuss the slavery question (see Dumond 1961, pp. 204-10; Wyatt-Brown 1965; Savage 1938; Richards 1970, pp. 14-43). The crowds did more than listen; they acted collectively to destroy abolitionist presses and property, disrupt meetings, or tar and feather antislavery lecturers. The leading abolition newspapers reported 209 incidents during the 1830s and 1840s, while a less biased source, the *Niles' Weekly Register*, reported 48 (see Richards 1970, p. 14; Feldberg 1980, p. 5). New York City, Utica, New York, Boston, Philadelphia, and Alton, Illinois, were scenes of major antiabolition and antiblack riots between 1833 and 1838. The majority of antiabolition protests and riots (about three-quarters) were planned by the local professional and commercial elites and were intended to force abolitionist leaders to abandon movement activities (see Richards 1970, p. 111; Feldberg 1980, pp. 45-46).

It was not surprising that Cincinnati should be the scene of a riot against abolitionists. In 1834, city residents protested when the students at Lane Seminary formed an antislavery society, and the board of trustees avoided a riot by outlawing the new society. To protest the AASS's propaganda campaign, Cincinnatians held a mass meeting in the summer of 1835 at which they pledged to defend the constitutional right of Southern citizens to hold slaves and urged Northern citizens to stop the abolitionists (Savage 1938, p. 50). In addition, the city's economy depended on Southern trade and Southern visitors.[24] Cincinnati's merchants began planning to build a rail line to Charleston in 1835 and 1836 that would expand their markets and minimize trade losses to other Western river cities (see Aaron 1992, p. 296).[25] Abolitionism represented a threat to the new transportation link

and the Southern trade in general. Merchants, manufacturers, and workers (especially those from shipyards and engine foundries) responded as they had to previous threats to the city's businesses by acting collectively to preserve their businesses and jobs as well as the city's long-term economic vitality (see Aaron 1992, pp. 82-83; Marcus 1991, p. 56). . . .

In short, the 1836 antiabolition riots in Cincinnati occasioned changes in the discourses and organization of the field of debate. Speakers from all three groups responded by reframing the debate around the question of how best to preserve social order while addressing the presence of abolitionism in the city. In turn, some speakers switched allegiances and new actors joined the debate in support of preserving the law and social order. After the second mob, abolitionists and law and order speakers renewed their arguments that antiabolitionism threatened the political and economic security of the city. These arguments were more compelling to city residents who had witnessed the destruction the angry mob wreaked and who lived in fear of continued rioting for nearly a week. Mob action was rejected as a legitimate solution by many of its earlier advocates—the business and political elite—as well as by many of the city's other residents. The law and order position won widespread support, the discourse of antiabolitionism was reworked to closely resemble the law and order position, and abolitionism gained publicity, new constituents, and tacit permission to continue its activities in the city.

Conclusion

In a recent article, Gamson (1992a, p. 70) claims that "there is an important and complicated relationship between the characteristics of events and the success of certain frames," and then argues that the key to understanding this relationship lies in examining how speakers and audiences interpret the event and why a particular interpretation is adopted. Unfortunately, most constructivist studies of collective action leave the nature of this relationship—how it is organized and how it changes—unspecified. We do not know how episodes of collective action affect the success or failure of different frames, nor whether and how speakers change arguments, extend frames, or tap into alternative collective beliefs following these episodes.

In this study of the Cincinnati antiabolition riot of 1836 I offer some answers to these question. First, I argue that the relationship between collective action and discourse is dialectical. Speakers shuttle between creating diagnoses and solutions to some social problem, implementing a solution through collective action, and then incorporating the action into their particular discourses as the grounds for evaluating and reworking arguments or redefining the subject of the debate. Competition among speakers defines and narrows the problem at hand and the possibilities for collective action. Episodes of collective action may lead speakers to reopen the discursive struggle by providing evidence for speakers and audiences who witnessed the event to assess the accuracy of competing diagnoses, measure the efficacy of the solution, or articulating arguments. Events, then, may change the underlying ideas or beliefs that make up the discourses and frames used by movement actors, resignify which set of collective beliefs are salient, and alter the meaning of actors' interests—all of which affect the power of a particular discourse or frame.

Law and order and abolition speakers reorganized the discursive struggle around the relationship of collective violence to order rather than the relationship of abolitionism to economic interests. In so doing, they changed the grounds by which to understand and judge the antiabolitionists' solution. Once this solution (i.e., mob action) was implemented, they had the evidence necessary to discredit antiabolitionism and demonstrate that their position was more congruent with the goal of preserving the political order that made economic activity possible and profitable. The power of this discursive position was evident not only by the support it received from previously unmobilized audiences but also by the support it received from antiabolitionists during the third stage. By focusing on this dialectic, we can enrich studies of movement tactics and protests that do not explicitly address how the arguments, frames, or beliefs that mobilized constituents are created and recreated following collective action (e.g., Tarrow 1989; Hirsch 1990).

Second, by conceptualizing the relationship in a dialectical manner, I also illustrate how actors within a discursive field use episodes of collective action to change alliances and reconfigure relations within a discursive field, which in turn may alter a group's legitimacy, base of support, and

power to sanction or prevent further collective action. After the first mob, the law and order voices became more active in the debate as old and new speakers came to see that mob violence threatened their economic or civic interests. Meanwhile, abolitionists strategically adopted the arguments of the law and order group in a bid to define the movement as the champion of constitutional liberties instead of as the champion of the more unpopular ideas of emancipation and racial equality. They changed their argument to gain legitimacy, win new supporters, and forestall additional mob violence directed at them.

In addition, examining the dialectic between events and discursive production may help us understand more completely how and why frames of meaning are extended or transformed. Snow and his collaborators (Snow et al. 1986; Snow and Benford 1988; Benford 1993a, 1993b) suggest that movement frames, vocabularies of motives, or arguments are changed or fail because speakers tap into the wrong set of collective beliefs, advance goals that are incongruent with those of their audience, fail to create ideological or organizational alliances with other movements, or do not develop robust and interconnected diagnoses, solutions, and rationales. Yet as I argue, these processes of frame alignment are influenced as well by the course and interpretation of collective action events. Such events intervene in the process of creating frames or discourses, change the value actors assign to collective beliefs, and motivate some groups to abandon a set of arguments and adopt those of a rival or create new ones. They also provide some speakers with new information that they can use to substantiate their claims and discredit the claims. In the case at hand, I argue that abolition and law and order speakers drew upon a preexisting discourse and set of collective beliefs about the sanctity of constitutional rights and the threat mobs posed to them to counter the antiabolitionists' political and commercial threat arguments. Their antimob and civil liberties arguments provided an alternative definition of what was at stake in the debate and how to preserve social order and the Southern trade. Although these arguments did not prevent the riot, they became the lens through which the riot and antiabolitionism were interpreted, discredited, and rendered indefensible during the third stage of the debate. Future research in the constructivist paradigm would not only benefit by attending more carefully to how and under what conditions collective action episodes shape meaning-making processes but will further our understanding of the dialectic between discourse and action by specifying how different forms of collective action (e.g., consciousness-raising campaigns, strikes, sit-ins, and riots) influence different framing tasks or discursive strategies.

Third, this study indicates that speakers occupying different positions within a field of debate may respond to episodes of collective action and construct their arguments in very different ways. Those speakers who occupy the challenger role (e.g., abolitionists and law and order speakers) may be more willing to extend and transform their discourses in order to win a place in the debate, influence the agenda, and even "force the sponsors of a legitimating frame to defend its underlying assumptions" (Gamson 1992a, p. 68). The strategies challenger groups adopt to accomplish these goals and, in the Cincinnati case, to defeat the antiabolitionists' discourse and favored course of collective action may include: taking a morally or politically unassailable position (e.g., defending constitutional liberties); changing the stakes of the debate so that short-term solutions cannot resolve problems defined as deep-seated and requiring radical social-structural change; offering alternative diagnoses and solutions that reinforce and more closely fit the new horizon of expectations; and depicting the actions of opponents as imminent threats to the overall security of the social system, while redefining one's own group as the victim of the unjust actions.

Finally, this study demonstrates that we will be able to develop more comprehensive accounts of how and why arguments are constructed and reconstructed and discursive fields are reconfigured by attending more carefully to which audiences speakers target, how well their diagnoses and solutions serve the interests and goals of those audiences, and how adept speakers are at responding to the changes in their audiences' beliefs, interests, or goals occasioned by collective action. In the Cincinnati case, the critical audience for all three groups was the economic and political elite, who possessed the power to sanction or prevent collective violence. Law and order and abolition speakers reframed the debate to change the meaning of order and to discredit collective violence as the best means to preserve order. This reframing allowed them to build a compelling case after the

riot that violence and the antiabolition economic justifications for it were illegitimate and harmful to the interests of the elite. In the end, elites withdrew their support for antiabolitionism or became vocal supporters of the law and order position. The key to explaining these changes lies in understanding the ways in which speakers incorporate episodes of collective action into their preexisting discourses in order to make those discourses resonate more closely with an audience's new horizon of expectations or to win the support of new audiences. In sum, attending to the dialectic of culture and event helps us understand how and why social action is organized and its effect on discursive creation.

Notes

1. Discursive success refers to situations in which the arguments of one group determine the issues of debate, speakers abandon their own arguments and adopt those of others, or speakers are forced to alter their discourse in response to the claims or alternative definitions of rival speakers. It may also be identified by the degree to which audiences demonstrate their approval or support of one discourse over another.

2. See Palmer (1990) for a detailed account of the linguistic turn in the social sciences; Thompson (1990) and Bourdieu (1991) for more theoretical treatments of discourse; and Wuthnow (1992), Wagner-Pacifici (1986), Hunt (1984), and Sewell (1980) for empirical studies of discourse.

3. Griswold (1987, p. 4) uses the term "cultural objects" to "refer to shared significance embodied in form, i.e., to an expression of social meanings that is tangible or can be put into words." This definition allows the analyst to specify more concretely the nature and content of culture under study, which minimizes problems regarding operationalization and facilitates an analysis that concentrates on how individuals (both speakers and audiences) interact with a cultural object to create meaning.

4. Sahlins (1991, pp. 80-82) conceptualizes the event as unfolding in three moments: *instantiation,* when social and cultural categories are represented by persons, objects, and acts; *denouement,* when the actual incidents occur; and *totalization,* when the consequences of the event are incorporated into and change the cultural categories that shaped the event.

5. Although some scholars acknowledge that new frames, identities, or collective beliefs are constructed according to the experiences of movement actors and audiences in specific structural, historical, and event-driven contexts, the literature fails, both theoretically and empirically, to address how collective action and discourse, event and meaning are interrelated (e.g., Benford 1993b, p. 210; Gamson 1988, p. 242). Gamson (1988, pp. 235-36) notes that "events take their

meaning from the discourse in which they are embedded and collective action helps to shape these meanings for both movement constituents and a larger audience," but he fails to specify how this dialectic actually operates. He identifies the occupation of the Seabrook, New Hampshire, nuclear reactor site as an important event that opened up the nuclear power discourse, but he does not discuss how this event changed the discourse of the antinuclear movement. In a later article Gamson and Modigliani (1989, pp. 17-21) discuss how different "media packages" about nuclear energy incorporated the Seabrook demonstration and how a new package emerged after the event, but again they do not explicitly discuss how the competition between different actors over the meaning of the event changed the discourse about nuclear power.

6. In this study I define speakers as those agents who both create discourses and articulate them in written and oral form. Speakers may refer to individuals or to the group that they represent.

7. Tarrow's (1989) work on the cycle of protest in Italy during the 1960s and 1970s provides a detailed map of the tactics and ideological positions of political parties, social movements, unions, and student organizations, but it is not explicitly concerned with explaining the relationship between meaning construction, discursive struggle, and collective action.

8. For example, some studies treat audiences as an undifferentiated public (see Benford 1993b; Benford and Hunt 1992; Gamson and Modigliani 1989).

9. An argument is a series of claims, images, or tropes combined in a coherent manner and intended to persuade an audience through an appeal to logic, fact, belief, emotion, or external authority (Thompson 1990, p. 289).

10. I am not making a strong structuralist argument that all discourses and fields are organized around binary oppositions. I recognize that fields often are populated by multiple voices, each of which may address the issues or problems in complex and nonreductionistic ways. At the same time, speakers may construct the field and their discourses around poles as a way of simplifying the issues, setting the limits of what can be discussed, and more clearly distinguishing one discourse from another. Polarizing the field may also allow speakers to create clearly defined moral or political positions that will discredit other discourses and win legitimacy for some, thus forcing or encouraging audiences to support one position over another. In short, I see the polarization of discourses and discursive fields as an event-driven phenomenon rather than a necessary result of the internal logic of discourse (see Alexander 1992; Rogin 1987; Edelman 1988, pp. 66-89; Gusfield 1981, pp. 167-68).

11. I am borrowing the term "horizon of expectations" from Griswold (1987, p. 10), who uses it to designate the bundle of experiences, interests, or beliefs an audience brings with it when it receives a cultural object.

12. I obtained the names and occupations of the active creators and participants of the three groups from the proceedings of public meetings, organizational statements, published letters from participants, the city directory for 1836 (*Cincinnati Directory for the Years 1836/37* 1836), the OASS annual reports for 1835 and 1836 (OASS 1836, 1837), and app. A in Richards (1970, p. 174). There were not significant differences in political party affiliation among the three groups, because Whigs were dominant in each (Richards estimates roughly 60%-70% of each group were Whigs), although abolition and law and order discourses more strongly reflected Whig concerns about the pernicious effects of mobs on society.

13. Table 1 represents the leaders of the three groups. The low number of artisans included in the table is not indicative of the actual number who participated in the riot nor who were members of an abolition society (Richards [1970, p. 140] notes that artisans were underrepresented because they were not among the leadership or active core of the society). Folk (1978, p. 108) suggests that many of the rioters were employed in the foundries and shipyards owned by antiabolitionist leaders or were employed in jobs dependent on the Southern trade.

14. My classification agrees with Richards's (1970) assessment of the elite nature of the antiabolition coalition. Glazer (1968, pp. 109-10) divides the commercial class into a core of wealthy elites and a large class of small retailers of more modest wealth. He notes that of the 2,044 men involved in commercial occupations (excluding manufacturers) in 1840, only about 100 were involved in large-scale, wholesale activities and were extensively involved with the Southern trade, where the vast majority were small retailers who owned small amounts of property and were engaged in local trade. Only 5 of 43 or just over 10% of antiabolitionists in the commercial class were shop owners.

15. Several historians suggest that participants in antebellum riots were generally from the middle classes and owned some property (see Gilje 1987, pp. 162-70; Feldberg 1983, pp. 43-53; Hammett 1976, p. 863; Grimstead 1972, p. 386).

16. Although there were only about 100 abolitionists in Cincinnati, the surrounding rural communities in southwest Ohio constituted one of the movement's strongholds (see Volpe 1990, p. 12). Nerone (1989, p. 44) suggests that many subscribers to Cincinnati's papers resided in these communities. As the official newspaper of the OASS, the Philanthropist had a statewide readership and many of its articles were reprinted in antislavery papers in New England, New York, and Pennsylvania.

17. These newspapers, along with the *Baptist Cross and Journal*, *Western Christian Advocate*, and *Workingman's Friend* are available at the Cincinnati Historical Society or the Ohio State Historical Society.

18. The *Gazette* published daily, weekly, and triweekly editions with a circulation of about 4,100. The circulation levels of the *Post* and *Whig* ranged between 1,200 and 1,800 for daily, triweekly, and weekly editions (see Hooper 1933, p. 90; Cist 1841, pp. 93-94). The *Republican* (a leading Democratic paper) had a combined daily and weekly circulation of 1,800 (Hooper 1933, p. 90; Nerone 1989, p. 293). The number of weekly subscribers to the *Philanthropist* grew from about 1,000 to over 1,700 during 1836 (Aaron 1992, p. 307). The circulation figures for Cincinnati's newspapers are similar to those for the average New York City daily (Folk 1978, p. 87).

19. Throughout its history the *Gazette* risked alienating subscribers and the business community by opposing slavery, championing the civil liberties of minority groups (including blacks and abolitionists), and defending freedom of the press and editorial independence (see Hooper 1933, pp. 74-77; Weisenburger 1934, pp. 413-27; Folk 1978, pp. 49-54; Nerone 1989, pp. 152-53; Aaron 1992, pp. 301-13).

20. Ohio abolitionists were not nearly as radical, however, as their New England counterparts, and Birney ran the risk of alienating some of his subscribers if his message were to approach the extremism published by William Lloyd Garrison in the Liberator, the newspaper of the New England abolitionists (see Gamble 1977).

21. Readership data for pre-Civil War America is scarce, and historians are reluctant to make conclusive statements regarding readership. However, they contend that readership was much larger than circulation figures (see Nerone [1989, pp. 41-46] for an overview; see also Aaron 1992, p. 235).

22. There was a significant increase in the frequency and intensity of urban collective violence during the 1830s. Richards (1970, p. 12) notes that there were 21 mobs during the 1820s, 115 during the 1830s (77% between 1834 and 1836), and 64 in the 1840s. Richards defines mobs as, "those situations where dozens, hundreds, or even thousands of persons tem-porarily assisted one another and in a violent or turbulent manner broke up meetings, assaulted abolitionists, damaged or destroyed property" (p. 5).

23. Riots or mob violence were considered quasi-legitimate in part because they posed no real threat to existing structures of society and in part because the upper classes believed that the lower classes would not act independently and that they could control the lower classes (see Grimstead 1972, p. 365; Weinbaum 1979, p. 62). Thus many riots received the explicit or tacit approval of civic authorities and the local elite. Although both parties tolerated rioting, Whigs were far more likely to voice disapproval and alarm than Democrats, because mobs subverted the foundations of society: established authority and law (Hammett 1976, p. 858; Ashworth 1987, pp. 52-61, 11 1-25; Howe 1979, pp. 23-42). The Democratic ideology of popular sovereignty was used to justify extralegal collective violence (see Feldberg 1980, pp. 90-91, 96-97; Grimstead 1972, pp. 368-74).

24. The importance of the Southern trade is evident in the following statistics regarding Cincinnati exports: In 1830 the value of steam engines and sugar mills sent to New Orleans was estimated at $300,000 (with a value of total manufactures at $1,000,000). By 1835 local production of steam engines, cotton gins, sugar mills, and steamboats was valued at $4 million to $5 million (Beery 1943, p. 235). During the 1830s, manufactured goods accounted for approximately one-fourth to one-third of the city's total exports, while pork accounted for 30%-40% of total exports (see Pred 1973, p. 133; Glazer 1968, p. 56; Beery 1943, p. 253). Folk (1978, p. 90) notes the importance of Southern visitors to the city's service industry during the summer months.

25. This early plan for a Southern rail link was put on hold by an inability to raise $500,000 in start-up money, resistance by canal and steamboat interests, and technological infeasibility of bridging the Ohio River (see Stover 1961, pp. 19-42; Reed 1966). ◆

Part 7

Motivational Factors II: Conversion and Commitment

The demonstrated importance of social networks and framing processes in relation to differential recruitment does not necessarily account for sustained participation and such kindred phenomenon as group solidarity and mutual identification. In order for a movement to maintain its viability as a collective enterprise, it must not only secure potential adherents, but also transform some of these participants into committed members or devotees.

Commitment, Kanter (1972) tells us in her study of the differential viability of nineteenth century utopian communes, requires a willingness:

> to do what will help maintain the group because it provides what [people] need . . . commitment means the attachment of self to the requirements of social relations that are seen as self-expressive. Commitment links self-interest to social requirements. (1972: 66-67)

To be committed in this sense is to follow a line of action consistent with the expectations and goals of the movement, not because one is compelled to do so, but because one's interests and identity are tied to the movement.

The generation of such commitment is not an easy task, however, as it appears that the proportion of participants in most movements who end up as committed adherents is relatively small. To illustrate, McCarthy and Zald (1973, 1977) have argued that many contemporary movements consist of little more than a small cadre of professionals who periodically mobilize a team of transitory constituents for engagement in some movement activity. While it might be argued that these so-called professional movements—like Common Cause and the National Rifle Association—are more interest groups than movements, it is interesting to note that even in movements that appear to have an ideological mandate for a much larger core of committed adherents, as in the case of many religious movements, most participants are ephemerally involved. In their study of participation rates in religious and para-religious movements in Montreal, Canada in the late 1970s, for example, Bird and Reimer (1982) found that 75.5 % of those who participated became involved for only a short while and then dropped out, and that the typical participant was essentially a "transitory affiliate" (1982: 1). Still, a core of participants were found to have become committed members of the religious movements in question. Without such a core of highly committed adherents the religious movements examined would have ceased to function. This is true of all other movements as well, however much they vary in terms of their membership requirements and demands. But how is commitment to a movement and its activities developed and maintained? What are its sources? And to what extent do movements vary in their capacity to affect or produce commitment?

One necessary condition for commitment to some movements for some individuals is that they undergo or experience conversion. Conversion can be thought of as a radical transformation of consciousness in which a new or formerly peripheral universe of discourse comes to function as a person's primary frame of reference (Machalek and Snow 1993; Snow and Machalek 1983). It is akin to frame transformation and involves corresponding change in identity or self-concept as well. But how does it occur? What are the underlying mechanisms that affect conversion from one primary framework or interpretive scheme to another?

The first two selections address these questions. The initial article, by John Lofland, reassesses the now classic conversion model that he and Rodney Stark propounded—based on Lofland's field study of a small idiosyncratic movement that became known as the Unification Church or the "Moonies"—in order to explain how some individuals become converts to strange and deviant groups (Lofland and Stark 1965). In this selection, Lofland reexamines some components of his and Stark's theory, and offers some additional observations based on the movement's conversion efforts a decade later. These new observations are particularly interesting because they focus attention on the "how" of conversion—that is, on what committed members actually do (e.g., picking-up, hooking, encapsulating) as they go about the business of attempting to effect conversion. The substance of these conversion practices, which appear to be pursued in a strategic and sequential fashion, may vary across movements in which conversion is a necessary condition for participation. But whatever the substance of conversion practices from one movement to another, by focusing on them Lofland illuminates the group-based and highly interactive character of the conversion process.

The next selection, by David Snow and Cynthia Phillips, further underscores the importance of group-based interactive processes in relation to conversion. Drawing on data derived from an ethnographic study of recruitment and conversion to the Nichiren Shoshu Buddhist movement in America between the mid-1960s and mid-1970s, Snow and Phillips critically examine all seven conditions proposed by Lofland and Stark as necessary for conversion to occur. Their findings call into question all but two of the postulated conditions: formation of affective bonds with one or more members, and involvement in intensive interaction with other members. Based on these findings, they argue that affective and intensive interaction between prospects and converts were not only essential for conversion to the movement they studied, but that conversion in general is highly improbable in the absence of these two factors. Additionally, the findings highlight the importance of framing processes in relation to conversion; biographical reconstruction or reinterpretation was found to be both a salient feature and product of the conversion process.

The next two selections turn from conversion to commitment. In the first of these two pieces, Eric Hirsch examines what prompts participants to sacrifice their personal welfare for a movement cause. In other words, he asks what commits people to pursue high-risk collective action? He explores this and related questions with data derived from a study of a student protest movement at Columbia University that demanded that the school divest itself of stock in companies with business interests in South Africa. His findings identify four processes that generate the commitment necessary to sustain action in support of the cause: consciousness-raising, collective empowerment, polarization, and group decision making, all group-level, interactive processes. Thus, we find the suggestion that the key to understanding sustained involvement in movement protest activity, and thus commitment, resides in ongoing group dynamics rather than in individual-level characteristics.

In the final selection, John Hall explores the question of whether all communal groups have the same capacity to generate commitment by employing similar commitment-building mechanisms. He examines this question through a reassessment of Kanter's analysis of 30 nineteenth century utopian communes (1972), in which she found that the most successful communes were those that were able to activate various kinds of commitment through various commitment-building mechanisms. Hall's reanalysis does not so much refute Kanter's findings as refine and extend her thesis. Specifically, he found, upon constructing a typology of communal groups, that only two of the five alternative types possessed the capacity to generate and sustain commitment, and that this differential capacity was rooted in different cultural and structural characteristics of the communal groups.

The four selections suggest a number of important summary observations regarding conversion and commitment. First, neither commitment nor such related phenomena as solidarity and collective identity are merely by-products of pre-participation bonds, grievances and the like, but often evolve and are typically strengthened during the course of participation in protest and social movement activities. Second, the key to understanding both conversion and commitment resides in group-based, interactive processes rather than in the psychological characteristics of prospective converts or adherents. Some individuals may be more psychologically inclined toward movement activity, but such inclinations can best be understood as dispositions toward rather than determinants of engagement in a particular line of activity. The selections in this part suggest that the mechanisms for activating or aligning such dispositions reside in movement activities and interactive practices. And third, just as "movements vary greatly in the commitments they require" (Turner and Killian 1987: 337), so they vary in their capacity to generate and sustain commitment.

References

Bird, Frederick and Bill Reimer. 1982. "Participation Rates in New Religious and Para-Religious Movements." *Journal for the Scientific Study of Religion* 21: 1-14.

Kanter, Rosabeth M. 1972. *Commitment and Community: Communes and Utopias in Sociological Perspective.* Cambridge, MA: Harvard University Press.

Lofland, John and Rodney Stark. 1965. "Becoming a World Saver: A Theory of Religious Conversion." *American Sociological Review* 30: 862-874.

Machalek, Richard and David A. Snow. 1993. "Conversion to New Religious Movements." Pp. 53-74 in *Religion and The Social Order: The Handbook on Cults and Sects in America,* Volume 3B. Greenwich, CT: JAI Press.

McCarthy, John and Mayer and Zald. 1973. *The Trend of Social Movements in America.* Morristown, NJ: General Learning Press.

——. 1977 "Resource Mobilization and Social Movements: A Partial Theory." *American Journal of Sociology* 82: 1212-1242.

Snow, David A. and Richard Machalek. 1983. "The Convert as a Social Type." *Sociological Theory* 1:259-289.

Turner, Ralph H. and Lewis Killian. 1987. *Collective Behavior,* 3rd Edition. Englewood Cliffs, NJ: Prentice Hall. ✦

21

Becoming a World-Saver Revisited

John Lofland

More than a decade ago, Rodney Stark and I observed a small number of then obscure millenarians go about what was to them the desperate and enormously difficult task of making converts. We witnessed techniques employed to foster conversion and observed the evolution of several people into converts. We strove to make some summarizing generalizations about those conversions in our report "Becoming a World-Saver" (Lofland and Stark 1965), a report that has received a gratifying amount of attention over the years. I want here to offer some new data on the conversion efforts of the same millenarian movement as it operates a decade later, to assess the new data's implications for the initial world-saver model, and to share some broader reflections on the model itself.

DP Conversion Organization Revisited

The conversion efforts witnessed by Rodney Stark and myself in the early sixties were in many respects weak, haphazard, and bumbling. The gaining of a convert seemed often even to be an accident, a lucky conjunction of some rather random dom flailing (Lofland 1966, pt. 2). Starting about 1972, however, all that was radically changed and transformed. The DPs [Deployable Personnel], as I continue to call them,[1] initiated what might eventually prove to be one of the most ingenious, sophisticated, and effective conversion organizations ever devised. I will describe its main phases and elements as it operated at and out of "State U City" and "Bay City," the same two West Coast places where the action centered in *Doomsday Cult* (Lofland 1966).

DPs of the early sixties and seventies alike believed that their ideology was so "mind blowing" to unprepared citizens that they could not expect simply to announce its principal assertions and make converts at the same time. As documented

throughout *Doomsday Cult,* effort was made to hold back the conclusions and only reveal them in a progressive and logical manner to prospective converts. They were dogged by a dilemma: They had to tell their beliefs to make converts, but the more they told the less likely was conversion.

They dealt with this dilemma by using a carefully progressive set of revelations of their beliefs and aims, starting from complete muting or denial of the religious and millenarian aspects and ending with rather more disclosure. This process may be conceived as consisting of five quasi-temporal phases: picking up, hooking, encapsulating, loving, and committing.

Picking Up

Reports of people closely involved with the movement suggest that the multi-million-dollar media blitzes and evangelical campaigns that made DPs famous and virtual household words in the seventies were not significant ways in which people began DP conversion involvement. Perhaps most commonly, it began with a casual contact in a public place, a "pickup." DPs spent time almost daily giving hitchhikers rides and approaching young men and women in public places. Display card tables for front organizations[2] were regularly staffed in the public areas of many campuses as a way to pick up people.

The contact commonly involved an invitation to a dinner, a lecture, or both. Religious aspects would be muted or denied. As described in *Doomsday Cult* (Lofland 1966, ch. 6), this strategy of covert presentations was employed in the early sixties with but small success. It became enormously more successful in the early seventies due to several larger-scale shifts in American society. First, the residue of the late sixties' rebellion of youth still provided a point of instant solidarity and trust among youth, especially in places like State U City, in a major locale of public place pickups. Second, even though the number of drifting and alienated youth was declining from the late sixties, there were still plenty of them. They tended to be drawn to certain West Coast college towns and urban districts. DPs concentrated their pickups in such areas, with success.

While of major importance, pickups were not the sole strategy. Some minor and rudimentary infiltrations of religious gatherings continued (cf. Lofland 1966:90-106), and one center specialized in sending "voluptuous and attractive" women to visit "professors at area colleges and persuade them to come to meetings under the guise of Unified Science" (Bookin 1973).

This shift in the strategy of first contact and shifts in the large trends of American society (see Lofland 1977c) resulted in a decisive shift in the recruitment pool of the movement. Converts I studied in the early sixties were decidedly marginal and rather "crippled" people, drawn from the less than advantaged and more religiously inclined sectors of the social order. Hence, I quoted the apostle Paul on the choosing of "mere nothings to overthrow the existing order" (Lofland 1966:29). As it became fashionable in the late sixties and early seventies for privileged and secular youth of the higher social classes to be alienated from their society and its political and economic institutions, a portion of such youth encountered the DPs. Some converted. Some of them were offspring of the American upper class, a fact that has caused the organization considerable trouble. What is signaled here is that the major pattern of prior religious seeking I reported seemed to fade in significance. People with strong prior political perspectives and involvements (e.g., Eugene McCarthy workers) started converting. (Such changes must also be considered in conjunction with a growing political element within the DP itself.)

Hooking

By whatever device, a prospect was brought into DP territory. Treatment varied at this point. In mid-1974 Chang himself was still experimenting in the New York City Center with Elmer's ancient notion of playing tape-recorded lectures to people (Lofland 1966:125-29). Fortunately for recruitment to the movement, other centers went in different directions. The most successful hooked into their dinner and lecture guests with more intensive and elaborate versions of the promotion tactics I originally described in *Doomsday Cult* (Lofland 1966, ch. 9). As practiced at the West Coast State U City Center—the most convert-productive center in the country—these went as follows.

The prospect arrived for dinner to find fifty or more smiling, talkative young people going about various chores. The place exuded friendliness and solicitude. He/she was assigned a "buddy" who was always by one's side. During the meal, as phrased in one report, "various people

stopped by my table, introduced themselves and chatted. They seemed to be circulating like sorority members during rush." Members were instructed to learn all they could about the prospect's background and opinions and to show personal interest. In one training document, members were told to ask: " 'What do you feel most excited about . . .'. *Write down* their hooks so that the whole center knows in follow up." The prospect's "buddy" and others continually complimented him: "You have a happy or intelligent face"; "I knew I would meet someone great like you today"; "your shoes are nice"; "your sweater is beautiful"; and so forth (cf. Lofland 1966:175-77). The feeling, as one ex-member put it, was likely to be: "it certainly felt wonderful to be served, given such attention, and made to feel important." DPs had learned to start conversion at the emotional rather than the cognitive level, an aspect they did not thoroughly appreciate in the early sixties (Lofland 1966:189).

It is on this foundation of positive affect that they slowly began to lay out their cognitive structure. That same first evening this took the form of a general, uncontroversial, and entertaining lecture on the principles that bound their family group. Key concepts include sharing, loving one another, working for the good of humankind, and community activity (Taylor 1975). Chang and his movement were never mentioned. At State U City (and several other places with the facilities), prospects were invited to a weekend workshop. This was conducted at The Farm in the State U City case I am following here, a several-hundred-acre country retreat some fifty miles north of Bay City. A slide show presented the attractions of The Farm. During the three years of most aggressive growth (1972–74), probably several thousand people did a weekend at The Farm. Hundreds of others had kindred experiences elsewhere.

Encapsulating

The weekend workshop (and longer subsequent periods) provided a solution to two former and major problems. First, by effectively encapsulating[3] prospects, the ideology could be progressively unfolded in a controlled setting where doubts and hesitations could be surfaced and rebutted. Second, affective bonds could be elaborated without interference from outsiders. Focusing specifically on The Farm, the encapsulation of prospects moved along five fundamentally facilitating lines.

Absorption of Attention. All waking moments were preplanned to absorb the participant's attention. The schedule was filled from 7:30 a.m. to 11:00 p.m. Even trips to the bathroom were escorted by one's assigned DP "buddy," the shadow who watched over his/her "spiritual child."

Collective Focus. A maximum of collective activities crowded the waking hours: group eating, exercises, garden work, lectures, games, chantings, cheers, dancing, prayer, singing, and so forth. In such ways attention was focused outward and toward the group as an entity.

Exclusive Input. Prospects were not physically restrained, but leaving was strongly discouraged, and there were no newspapers, radios, televisions, or an easily accessible telephone. The Farm itself was miles from any settlement. Half of the fifty or so workshop participants were always DPs and they dominated selection of topics for talk and what was said about them.

Fatigue. There were lectures a few hours each day, but the physical and social pace was otherwise quite intense. Gardening might be speeded up by staging contests, and games such as dodgeball were run at a frantic pitch. Saturday evening was likely to end with exhaustion, as in this report of interminable square dancing.

> It went on for a very long time—I remember the beat of the music and the night air and thinking I would collapse and finding out I could go on and on. The feeling of doing that was really good—thinking I'd reached my limit and then pushing past it. [At the end, the leader] sang "Climb Every Mountain" in a beautiful, heartbreaking voice. Then we had hot chocolate and went to bed.

A mild level of sexual excitement was maintained by frequent patting and hugging across the sexes. Food was spartan and sleep periods were controlled.

Logical, Comprehensive Cognitions. In this context, the DP ideology was systematically and carefully unfolded, from the basic and relatively bland principles (e.g., "give and take"; Lofland 1966:15-16) to the numerologically complex, from the Garden of Eden to the present day, following the pattern I reported in Chapter 2 of Doomsday Cult. If one accepted the premises from which it began, and were not bothered by several ad hoc devices, the system could seem exquisitely logical. The comprehensiveness combined with simplicity were apparently quite impressive to reasonable numbers of people who viewed it in The Farm context. The "inescapable" and "utterly logical" conclusion that the Messiah was at hand could hit hard: "It's so amazing, its so *scientific* and explains everything." The encapsulating and engrossing quality of these weekends was summed up well by one almost-convert:

> The whole weekend had the quality of a cheer—like one long rousing camp song. What guests were expected (and subtly persuaded) to do was participate . . . completely. That was stressed over and over: "give your whole self and you'll get a lot back," "the only way for this to be the most wonderful experience of your life is if you really put everything you have into it," etc.

Loving

The core element of this process was deeper and more profound than any of the foregoing. Everything mentioned so far only in part moved a person toward a position in which they were open to what was the crux: the feeling of being loved and the desire to "melt together" (a movement concept) into the loving, enveloping embrace of the collective. (We learn again from looking at the DPs that love can be the most coercive and cruel power of all.)

The psychodynamic of it is so familiar as to be hackneyed: "People need to belong, to feel loved," as it is often put. People who want to "belong" and do not, or who harbor guilt over their reservations about giving themselves over to collectivities, are perhaps the most vulnerable to loving overtures toward belonging. The pattern has been stated with freshness and insight by a young, recently-Christian woman who did a Farm weekend, not then knowing she was involved with the DPs:

> When I did hold back in some small way, and received a look of sorrowful, benevolent concern, I felt guilt and the desire to please as though it were God Himself whom I had offended. What may really have been wisdom on my part (trying to preserve my own boundaries in a dangerous and potentially overwhelming situation) was treated as symptomic of alienation and fear and a withholding of God's light. Those things are sometimes true of me, and I am unsure enough of my own openness in groups that I tended to believe they were right. Once, when [the workshop leader] spoke to us after a lecture, I began to cry. She'd said something about giving, and it had touched on a deep longing in me to do that, and the pain of that wall around my heart when I feel closed off in a group of people. I wanted to break through that badly enough that right then it almost didn't matter

what they believed—if only I could really share myself with them. I think that moment may be exactly the point at which many people decide to join [the DPs].

The conscious strategy of these encapsulating weekend camps was to drench prospects in approval and love—to "love bomb" them, as DPs termed it. The cognitive hesitations and emotional reservations of prospects could then be drowned in calls to loving solidarity:

> Whenever I would raise a theological question, the leaders of my group would look very impressed and pleased, seem to agree with me, and then give me a large dose of love—and perhaps say something about unity and God's love being most important. I would have an odd, disjointed sort of feeling—not knowing if I'd really been heard or not, yet aware of the attentive look and the smiling approval. My intellectual objection had been undercut by means of emotional seduction.

Sometimes the group would burst into song: "We love you, Julie; oh, yes we do; we don't love anyone as much as you. I read it this way: we *could* love you if you weren't so naughty." And, of course, they *would* love her. This incredibly intense encapsulating and loving did not simply "happen." DPs trained specifically for it and held morale and strategy sessions among themselves during the workshops:

> On Sunday morning, when I woke really early, I walked by the building where some of the Family members had slept. They were up and apparently having a meeting. I heard a cheer: "Gonna meet all their needs." And that did seem to be what they tried to do. Whatever I wanted—except privacy or any deviation from the schedule—would be gotten for me immediately and with great concern. I was continually smiled at, hugged, patted. And I was made to feel very special and very much wanted.

As characterized by investigative reporter Andrew Ross (1975), people were "picked up from an emotional floor and taken care of." "The appeal is love—blissed out harmony and unity." Ross and his coworkers discovered some converts who had been in the movement four to six months who truly seemed to have attended to little or nothing regarding Chang and his larger movement. They were simply part of a loving commune. Some, on being pressed explicitly with Chang's beliefs and aims, declared they did not care: their loyalty was to the family commune. Such, as Stark and I discussed with regard to "affective bonds," is an important meaning of love (Lofland and Stark 1965:871-72).

Committing

It is one thing to get "blissed out" on a group over a weekend, but it is quite another to give one's life over to it. And the DPs did not seem immediately to ask that one give over one's life. Instead, the blissed-out prospect was invited to stay on at The Farm for a week-long workshop. And if that worked out, one stayed for an even longer period. The prospect was drawn gradually—but in an encapsulated setting—into full working, street peddling, and believing participation.

Doubts expressed as time went on were defined as "acts of Satan" (Lofland 1966:193-98), and the dire consequence of then leaving the movement would be pointed out (Lofland 1966:185-88). A large portion of new converts seemed not to have had extramovement ties to worry about, but those who did—such as having concerned parents—seemed mostly to be encouraged to minimize the impact of their DP involvement to such outsiders and thereby minimize the threat it might pose to them.

A part of the process of commitment seemed to involve a felt cognitive dislocation arising from the intense encapsulating and loving. One prospect, an almost-convert who broke off from his "buddy" after a weekend, reported: "As soon as I left Suzie, I had a chance to think, to analyze what had happened and how everything was controlled. I felt free and alive again—it was like a spell was broken."

Another, on being sent out to sell flowers after three weeks at The Farm, had this experience:

> Being out in the world again was a shock; a cultural shock in which I was unable to deal with reality. My isolation by the church had been so successful that everyday sights such as hamburger stands and TVs, even the people, looked foreign, of another world. I had been reduced to a dependent being! The church had seen to it that my three weeks with them made me so vulnerable and so unable to cope with the real world, that I was compelled to stay with them.

This "spell," "trance," or "shock" experience is not as foreign, strange, or unique as it might, at first viewing, appear. People exiting any highly charged involvement—be it a more ordinary love affair, raft trip, two-week military camp, jail term, or whatever—are likely to experience what students of these matters have called "the reentry problem" (Irwin 1970, ch. 5). Reentry to any world after absence is in many circumstances painful, and a desire to escape from that pain increases the attractiveness of returning to the just-prior world. Especially because the DP situation involved a supercharged love and support experience, we ought to expect people to have reentry unreality, to experience enormous discontinuity and a desire to flee back. DPs created their own attractive kind of "high"—of transcending experience—to which people could perhaps be drawn back in much the same way Lindesmith (1968) has argued people employ certain drugs to avoid withdrawal (reentry pains?) as well as exploiting them for their own inherently positive effects (Lofland and Lofland 1969:104-16).

The World-Saver Model Revisited

A first and prime question is: What are the implications of the above for the world-saver model that Stark and I evolved from an earlier era of DP conversion organization? As summarized in the report's abstract, the model propounds:

> For conversion a person must experience, within a religious problem-solving perspective, enduring, acutely-felt tensions that lead to defining her/himself as a religious seeker; the person must encounter the cult at a turning point in life; within the cult an affective bond must be formed (or preexist) and any extra-cult attachments, neutralized; and there he/she must be exposed to intensive interaction to become a "deployable agent" [Lofland and Stark 1965:862].

My impression is that the situational elements of the model, at least, are so general and abstract that they can, with no difficulty, also accurately (but grossly) characterize the newer DP efforts. They are general and abstract to the point of not being especially telling, perhaps reflecting the rather pallid data with which Stark and I had to work. The play of movement and external "affective bonds" and "intensive interaction" continues, certainly, but the new DP efforts now permit much more refined and sophisticated analysis, a level of refinement and sophistication at which I have only been able to hint in my descriptions of "encapsulating" and "loving." Close study of the two major DP conversion camps could result in a quantum step in our understanding of conversion, for the DPs have elaborated some incredible nuances.

Relative to the more "background" elements, the concept of the turning point is troublesome because everyone can be seen as in one or more important ways at a turning point at every moment of their lives. Like concepts of tension, it is true and interesting but not very cutting. There seems

to have been a definite broadening of the range of people who get into the DP. The pattern of prior and universal religious seeking, at least in its narrow form, became far less than universal. People not previously religious at all have joined in noticeable numbers. Only further study can sort out the contexts and meanings underlying the diverse new patterns. Further study ought to address the possibility that an entire generation of youth became, broadly speaking, religious seekers in the early seventies and frenzied themselves with a fashion of "seeker chic," a sibling of Wolfe's (1976) aptly identified "funky chic." Last, there seems no reason to modify our polymorphic characterization of tension, which remains a virtually universal feature in the human population.

Be all that as it may, let me now step back and view the world-saver model as an instance of *qualitative process theorizing*. I have been impressed that, although there have been efforts to give the model a quantitative testing, to employ it in organizing materials on conversion to other groups, and to state the correlates of conversion, almost no one has tried their own hand at qualitative process models of conversion. The world-saver model was intended as much as an analytic description of a sequence of experiences as it was a causal theory, and it was very much informed by Turner's (1953:609-11) too-neglected formulation of the distinction between "closed systems" and "intrusive factors." That kind of logic has not caught on, despite the oddity that much lip service is given to it, and the world-saver model provides an example of it, as do the widely known and generically identical models of Becker (1953) on marihuana use, Cressey (1972) on trust violation, and Smelser (1963) on collective behavior. Indeed, and I think now in error, my own effort to generalize the world-saver model to all deviant identities lapsed into the mere causal-factorial approach in providing eleven social-organizational variations that affect the likelihood of assuming a deviant identity and reversing it (Lofland with Lofland 1969:pts. 2, 3). Such an approach is fine and necessary, but it is a retreat from the study of process, signaled in my all too abstract, brief, and shakily founded depiction of "escalating interaction" (Lofland with Lofland, 1969:146-54).

I would have hoped that by now we might have at least half a dozen qualitative process models of conversion, each valid for the range and kind of event it addressed, and each offering insights, even if not the most sophisticated account that might be given. We then could be well on our way to talking about types of conversion and types of qualitative conversion processes. Instead, some investigators get "hung up" in trying to determine whether the world-saver model is right as regards the group they have studied. Such investigators would advance us better by looking at the conversion process directly and reporting what they saw. Stark and I did not feel it necessary to wear anyone's specific model when we went to look at conversion. People ought not to compulsively wear the tinted spectacles wrought by Lofland and Stark when they go to look at conversion. I would urge a knowledge of the logic of a qualitative process point of view, but an eschewing of harassing oneself to look at the world through a specific application of that logic (Lofland 1976, pt. 1).

Stepping back yet further, I have since come to appreciate that the world-saver model embodies a thoroughly passive actor—a conception of humans as a "neutral medium through which social forces operate," as Herbert Blumer (1969a) has so often put it. The world-saver model is anti-interactionist, or at least against the interactionism frequently identified with people such as Blumer.

It is with such a realization that I have lately encouraged students of conversion to turn the process on its head and scrutinize how people go about converting themselves. Assume that the person is active rather than merely passive (Lofland 1976, ch. 5). Straus' (1976) "Changing Oneself: Seekers and the Creative Transformation of Life Experience" is an important initial effort to lay down new pathways of analysis within such an activist-interactionist perspective. I hope there will soon be many efforts of its kind.

Looking back from the perspective of a decade, students of conversion have ample reason for celebration and optimism. Stark and I had very few models and theoretical and substantive material to guide us. Limitations aside, there is now a solid and rich body of reasonably specific ideas and data bits that can guide investigators. We now know more about conversion than we did a decade ago, and I have every confidence that we will know enormously more in a decade.

Notes

1. Because of DP fame, my pseudonyms are now somewhat labored, but I must continue to protect the anonymity of the movement for the reasons indicated in Lofland 1977, n. 1. The main phases of the development of the DP movement from 1959 through 1976 are chronicled in my epilogue to the Irvington edition of *Doomsday Cult* (Lofland 1977). Transformations in membership size and composition, modes of operation, funding, and other aspects are as startling as the changes in conversion organization I reported here. My account is drawn from the diverse sources described in Lofland (1977, n. 2.), save here again for to acknowledge the indispensable help of Andrew Ross, Michael Greany, David Taylor, and Hedy Bookin.

2. DPs evolved dozens of front organizations from behind which they carried on an amazing variety of movement-promoting activities (see Lofland 1977, phase two, sec. 4, "Missionizing").

3. I use the concept of encapsulation here in a related but not identical manner to that introduced in analysis of the deviant act (Lofland with Lofland 1969:39-60).◆

22

The Lofland-Stark Conversion Model: A Critical Assessment

David A. Snow
Cynthia L. Phillips

The proliferation of religious movements and mass therapies during the past decade has prompted some observers to suggest that America is currently "gripped by an epidemic of sudden personality change" (Conway and Siegelman, 1978:11; Zurcher, 1977) and that we are living in an "age of conversion" (Richardson and Stewart, 1978:24). Although one can quibble over the accuracy of such characterizations, there is little question that the phenomenon of conversion has indeed captured the attention of a growing number of laymen and of social scientists (Colson, 1976; Conway and Siegelman, 1978; Enroth, 1977; Patrick, 1976; Richardson, 1978).

Within sociology, conversion has traditionally been explained as a sequential "funneling" process, including psychological, situational and interactional factors (see Gerlach and Hine, 1970; Richardson et al., 1978; Seggar and Kunz, 1972; Shibutani, 1961; Toch, 1965; Zablocki, 1971). Of the various works representative of this approach to conversion, the most prominent is the model propounded well over a decade ago by Lofland and Stark (1965; see also Lofland, 1966). Based on a field study of the early American devotees of Sun Myung Moon (hereafter referred to as the Unification Church), the model suggests that "total" conversion, involving behavioral as well as verbal commitment, is a function of the accumulation of seven "necessary and constellationally-sufficient conditions" (Lofland and Stark, 1965:874). Specifically, a person must (1) experience enduring and acutely-felt "tensions," (2) within a "religious problem-solving perspective," (3) which results in self-designation as a "relig-

ious seeker." Additionally, the prospective convert must (4) encounter the movement or cult at a "turning point" in life, (5) form an "affective bond" with one or more believers, (6) "neutralize" or sever "extracult attachments," and (7) be exposed to "intensive interaction" with other converts in order to become an active and dependable adherent. The first three factors are classified as "predisposing." They hypothetically exist prior to contact with the group and function to render the individual susceptible to conversion once contact is established. The remaining four factors are regarded as "situational" contingencies. They hypothetically lead to recruitment to one group rather than another, if any other, and to the adoption of the group's world view. In the absence of these situational factors, total conversion will not occur, no matter how predisposed or susceptible the prospective convert may be. Accordingly, the conversion process is conceptualized as a value-added process in which the addition of each new condition increases the probability that conversion will occur.

The purpose of this paper is to contribute to our understanding of conversion by critically examining the Lofland-Stark model and the extent to which it applies to our findings on conversion to the *Nichiren Shoshu* Buddhist movement in America. Two issues guide the inquiry. The first has to do with the model's empirical generalizability. Lofland initially suggested that the application of the model was "universal" (1966:61). Whether this is in fact the case remains an empirical question. Although the Lofland-Stark model is the most widely cited conversion scheme in the sociological literature (see Richardson, 1978; Richardson and Stewart, 1978; Richardson et al., 1978; Robbins and Anthony, 1979; Wilson, 1978), it has rarely been subjected to rigorous empirical examination.[1] Instead, most studies have uncritically used the model as a *post factum* ordering scheme for classifying data pertaining to the group under investigation (e.g., Judah, 1974; McGee, 1976). Moreover, neither Lofland and Stark nor those scholars drawing on the model have fully considered the extent to which the conversion process may vary across movements—according to differences in value orientations, organizational structure, and the way a movement is publicly defined. Given that communal groups tend to be more demanding than noncommunal groups (Kanter, 1972; 1973), it seems reasonable

"The Lofland-Stark Conversion Model: A Critical Assessment."
Social Problems 27: 430-447. Copyright © 1980 by the Society for the Study of Social Problems. Reprinted with permission.

to assume that such differences in organizational structure might lead to differences in the conversion process. Similarly, we might expect the conversion process to vary according to whether a group is publicly defined as "respectable," "idiosyncratic" or "revolutionary" (see Snow, 1979; Turner and Killian, 1972:257-59). Consideration of such factors seems especially important given the fact that *Nichiren Shoshu* is a noncommunal group in contrast to the Unification Church.

Aside from the issue of empirical generalizability, several components of the model strike us as theoretically questionable when viewed from the complementary perspectives of Mead (1932, 1936, 1938), Burke (1965, 1969a,b) and Berger and Luckmann (1967) and the related work on "accounts" or "motive talk" (see Blum and McHugh, 1971; Mius, 1940; Scott and Lyman, 1968). In particular, two aspects of this work inform our approach to conversion and therefore our theoretical critique of the Lofland-Stark model. The first suggests that social conditions and the various elements of one's life situation, including the self, constitute social objects whose meanings are not intrinsic to them but flow from one's "universe of discourse" (Mead, 1934:89) or "informing point of view" (Burke, 1965:99) or "meaning system" (Berger, 1963:61). The second and corollary principle emphasizes that meaning itself is constantly in the process of emergence or evolution; that personal biographies as well as history in general are continuously redefined in the light of new experiences.[2] Since conversion involves the adoption and use of a new or formerly peripheral universe of discourse and its attendant vocabulary of motives, it follows, as Burke (1965) and Berger and Luckmann (1967) have emphasized, that this ongoing process of retrospective interpretation would be heightened and more extensive in conversion than is customary in the course of everyday life.

Drawing on these concepts and on data pertaining to conversion to the *Nichiren Shoshu* Buddhist movement, we will critically examine the extent to which the Lofland-Stark model is conceptually useful and empirically on target.

The data on which this examination is based were collected by the senior author during a year and a half ethnographic study of the *Nichiren Shoshu* Buddhist movement in America (hereafter referred to as NSA). The movement was formally introduced in the U.S. in 1960 as a foreign extension of *Sokagakkai*—a Japanese Buddhist movement that emerged as a significant religious and political force in post-World War II Japan.[3] At the time of its establishment in 1960, NSA claimed fewer than 500 followers, nearly all of whom were Japanese brides of American G.I.'s. Today the movement claims over 200,000 variously committed adherents, over 90 per cent of whom are Occidental and most of whom have joined since 1966.

The movement's primary goals are similar to those of the Unification Church. Although NSA promises the attainment of personal regeneration and happiness in the immediate present through the realization of an endless stream of material, physical and spiritual "benefits," its ultimate objective is the construction of a new civilization. Like the Unification Church, it seeks to change the world by incorporating an ever-increasing number of people within its ranks and changing them in accordance with its doctrine.[4] Personal transformation is thus seen as the key to social transformation. However, unlike the Unification Church, NSA does not accept Christ or some variant thereof as the "one way." Instead, the answer for NSA resides in the repetitive chanting of *Nam-Myoho-Renge-Kyo* to the *Gohonzon* (a small sacred scroll inscribed in Japanese and regarded as the most powerful object in the world) and in the practice of *Shakubuku*, the act of bringing others into contact with the *Gohonzon* and the key to unlocking its power—*Nam-Myoho-Renge-Kyo*.[5]

Organizationally the movement is composed of numerous units and cells linked together not only through a clear-cut leadership hierarchy but also through intersecting movement associations and interpersonal ties between members of different cells.[6] Members are typically recruited into one of these cells; and it was at this organizational level that the senior author initially gained entrée into the movement and began a year and a half association with it as a nominal convert and active participant observer. Since core members would spend all their leisure time engaged in NSA activities, the role of participant observer called for the devotion of considerable time and energy to the movement. This intensive involvement included daily phone calls (at all hours) from members, attending meetings on the average of three nights per week, accompanying members on recruiting missions into public places, visiting other members in their homes, and even giving "an experience" (testimony) when called upon during

Shakubuku (conversion) meetings. Although an attempt was made to be as open and honest as possible about the researcher's sociological identity, neither this identity nor the purposes of the research were announced in each movement-related situation. As a consequence, not all members who functioned as informants were aware of the research interests to which they were contributing. The nature of the senior author's association with the movement was thus participatory and intense, and overt and covert at one and the same time.[7]

In addition to observational and experiential data, we also draw on information obtained from in-depth, conversational interviews with fifteen core members and an examination of a random sample of members' testimonies (experiences) appearing in the movement's newspaper, *The World Tribune*.[8] Since most editions of *The World Tribune* contain several members' testimonies, we randomly selected 504 experiences from 1966 to 1974 (six per month), excluding the years 1972 and 1973 which were not accessible during this phase of the research. The testimonies were examined for demographic data and information pertaining to manner of recruitment, accounts of past life situations, motivational accounts for joining, benefits received, length of membership and nature of participation. These data pertain more to the highly committed and active members than to the entire membership. This is suggested by the

fact that the mean length of membership at the time of each testimony was twenty months, with the mode being one year and the median around fourteen months. Also, because the *World Tribune* is, in part, a promotion vehicle and recruitment aid, the less active and more peripheral members are less likely to be called upon or to volunteer to give testimony in the newspaper. We thus assume that the population from which the sample was drawn consists primarily of "core converts" or "true believers." While this sample would undoubtedly be too limited for some purposes, it is well-suited to our interests. It not only complements and provides a "validity check" for the observational and experiential data, but also makes it possible to assess the Lofland-Stark model with quantitative data.

Findings and Discussion

Predisposing Conditions

Tension. Lofland and Stark suggest that a state of acutely-felt tension or frustration is a necessary predisposing condition for conversion. This tension, as well as the other predisposing conditions, are viewed as "attributes of persons" that exist "prior to their contact with the cult" or group in question (1965:864; their emphasis). We would thus expect our data to demonstrate that

TABLE 1

Personal Problems Retrospectively Referred to as Characterizing Life Situation Prior to Conversion

Problems*	Number of Members Referring to Category (N: 504)		Number of Problems Referred to within Category (N: 1,580)		Average Number of Problems Per Member**
Spiritual[a]	(346)	69%	(526)	33%	1.52
Interpersonal[b]	(244)	48%	(309)	20%	1.26
Character[c]	(262)	52%	(284)	18%	1.08
Material[d]	(214)	43%	(255)	16%	1.19
Physical[e]	(151)	30%	(206)	13%	1.36

* The following problem categories are those used by members when recruiting and giving testimony.

[a] Problems coded as "spiritual" include meaninglessness, lack of direction and purpose, a sense of powerlessness, poor self-image.

[b] Problems coded as "interpersonal" include marital problems, child rearing problems, parental problems, and other relational problems.

[c] Problems coded as "character" include drugs, alcohol, self-centeredness, and various personality problems such as uncontrollable temper.

[d] Problems coded as "material" include unemployment, job dissatisfaction, finances, and school-related problems.

[e] Problems coded as "physical" include headaches, nervousness, chronic illness, obesity, lack of energy, and so on.

** This column is equal to column two divided by column one. On the average, members reported 3.13 problems.

NSA members experienced severe tension and acutely-felt needs prior to joining the movement.

At first glance, it would appear as if our data corroborate this expectation. As indicated in Table 1, like Lofland and Stark's informants, NSA members characterize their preparticipation life situations in terms of various problems and tensions. Sixty-nine percent of the sample, for example, indicated that prior to or at the time of encountering NSA they were experiencing one or more "spiritual" problems, such as meaninglessness, a lack of direction or purpose, or a sense of powerlessness. Perhaps even more revealing than the specific problems alluded to is the finding that, on the average, core members reported at least three problems per person just prior to conversion (see column three, Table 1).

Looked at uncritically, these findings, and the fact that they are consistent with those of Lofland and Stark (1965) and Richardson et al. (1978), suggest that a state of acutely-felt tension is indeed an important precipitant of conversion. Yet, in the absence of a control group that is representative of the larger population, such a conclusion is methodologically untenable. Until we know whether the problems experienced by preconverts are greater in number or qualitatively different from those experienced by the larger population, it is unreasonable to assume a causal linkage between prestructured tension and susceptibility to conversion.

Acknowledging this issue, Lofland and Stark (1965:867) suggest that while the problems experienced by preconverts and the larger population "are not qualitatively different," the former experience their problems "rather more acutely and over longer periods of time than most people do." Although they offer no evidence in support of this assertion, a number of studies and polls regarding the worries and problems of American adults suggest that Lofland and Stark are probably right on the first account. A 1957 University of Michigan survey of how American adults viewed their mental health revealed that roughly 41 percent experienced marital problems, 75 percent encountered problems in raising their children, 29 percent had job-related problems, 35 percent avowed various personality shortcomings, and 19 percent felt they were on the verge of a nervous breakdown at one time or another.[9] These and findings of similar surveys (Cantril, 1965; Chase, 1962; Gallup, 1978; Stouffer, 1955) suggest that Americans not only have an overriding concern with themselves and "their immediate environment," but also often "admit" to having "weaknesses and problems" (Gurin et al., 1960:xxiv-xxv).[10] Since the kinds of worries and tensions noted in public opinion polls and surveys are of the same genre as those alluded to by NSA converts and summarized in Table 1, Lofland and Stark appear to be correct in arguing that the worries and problems that plague most Americans are not qualitatively different from those of the preconverts.

However, what about the corollary contention that it is the magnitude and duration of stress, rather than stress *per se,* that render people differentially susceptible to conversion? This is a difficult question, especially since studies such as those cited above shed little direct light on the matter. However, our data do not indicate a state of acutely-felt and prolonged tension to be a necessary precipitating condition. Although many NSA converts typically characterize their respective preconversion life situations as being laden with several personal problems (Table 1), many others report that they were not aware of having had any severe problems prior to conversion to NSA. Consider the following statements extracted from members' testimonies during movement meetings or presented in the movement's newspaper:

> Male, Caucasian, single, under 30: When I joined I didn't think I was burdened by any problems. But as I discovered, I just wasn't aware of them until I joined and they were solved.

> Female, Caucasian, single, under 30: After I attended these meetings and began chanting, I really began to see that my personal life was a mess.

> Male, Caucasian, single, under 30: Now as I look back I feel that I was a total loser. At that time, however, I thought I was pretty cool. But after chanting for a while, I found out that my life was just a dead thing. The more I chanted, the more clearly I came to see myself and the more I realized just how many problems I had had.

> Male, Caucasian, married, over 30: After you chant for a while you'll look back and say, "Gee, I was sure a rotten, unhappy person." I know I thought I was a saint before I chanted, but shortly after I discovered what a rotten person I was and how many problems I had.

These statements indicate that, for many individuals, conversion to NSA involves either the redefinition of life before conversion as being fraught with problems or the discovery of personal problems not previously discernible or regarded as troublesome enough to warrant remedial action. In either case, these findings suggest not only that conversion can occur in the absence of preexisting strains, but also that the strains or problems alluded to by converts may indeed be a product of conversion itself—that is, of the internalization of a new interpretive schema and its attendant vocabulary of motive. Although this interpretation runs counter to what Lofland and Stark lead us to expect, it is quite consistent with the Meadian thesis that the past is not a static entity but is subject to change with new experiences and alterations in one's universe of discourse. It is also consonant with the corollary observation that one of the more significant consequences of conversion, religious or secular, is that it entails a total or partial reinterpretation of one's biography (Berger, 1963; Berger and Luckmann, 1967; Burke, 1965; Shibutani, 1961; Travisano, 1970). We would thus argue on both empirical and theoretical grounds that while a state of acutely-felt and prolonged tension may be associated with conversion, it is not necessarily a predisposing condition.[11]

Parallel Problem-Solving Perspectives. Personal problems can be defined and dealt with in terms of a number of functional alternatives (Emerson and Messinger, 1977). Lofland and Stark suggest that the remedy chosen is partly dependent on the correspondence between the individual's problem-solving perspective and the remedial alternative in question. If the alternative is political, but the individual views the world primarily from a religious or psychiatric standpoint, then conversion to that alternative is not likely. If, on the other hand, the two are congruent, then the prospect of conversion is heightened. Accordingly, Lofland and Stark initially hypothesized that conversion to a religious movement is contingent on the possession of a religious problem-solving perspective.

While concurring with this hypothetical linkage between problem-solving orientation and susceptibility to conversion, Richardson and Stewart (1978) have sought to extend and refine the linkage by proposing several modifications. First, they suggest, in addition to the religious, political and psychiatric perspectives, a "physiological" perspective (e.g., drugs, alcohol, dieting, exercise). Second, they contend that Lofland and Stark have neglected the role of prior socialization in furnishing individuals with perspectives for de-

fining problems and their solutions and thereby facilitating susceptibility to conversion. Drawing on the hypothesis that some religious traditions make people prone to frustration (Fromm, 1950; Pattison, 1974; Toch, 1965) and on the observation that some converts to the Unification Church and the Jesus movement came from a background of Christian fundamentalism, Richardson and Stewart hypothesize that prior socialization as a fundamentalist not only increases the probability of having a religious problem-solving perspective, but also renders those individuals more susceptible to participation in religious cults and movements.

Although this hypothesis with its emphasis on prior socialization is sociologically appealing, our observations suggest that it may be overstated.[12] In particular, we find no compelling evidence suggesting that converts to NSA were raised in a fundamentalist environment. Moreover, our data provide little support for the corollary proposition that the possession of a religious problem-solving perspective is a necessary precondition for conversion to a religious cult or movement. This is illustrated in the first section of Table 2, which indicates that less than 25 percent of the converts clearly fell into the religious problem-solving category prior to encountering NSA. In other words, more than three-quarters of the sample saw both the source and solution to problems, whether personal or social, as residing in forces or structures other than mystical, supernatural or occult. As one such member, a twenty-three year old female convert who viewed herself as a "political revolutionary" prior to joining NSA, relates:

> I've come from the revolution, but I've since learned that the real revolution is through NSA and its human revolution. It's not the superficial revolution of a culture or a government or an economic system. It's finally gotten down to the revolution of myself and others through chanting to the *Gohonzon.*

Similarly, a male convert in his early twenties describes his view of things prior to encountering NSA:

> Right up until I joined NSA I harbored hostility toward my parents, and had a cynical attitude toward society in general. I blamed my parents for my hang-ups and criticized the U.S.'s foreign policy, the President, and so on. I realize now that because I was miserable inside, I perceived the environment as miserable. And I also came to realize

that if I wanted things to improve, I had to change myself first.

These statements, which are not exceptional, cast further doubt on the hypothesis that preparticipation ideological congruence is a necessary condition for conversion. They also suggest that conversion to NSA frequently effects a significant change in problem-solving perspective. Not only do converts to NSA reinterpret their past by redefining some aspects of it as more problematic than before, but also they frequently come to redefine or discover the source of blame for their more acutely defined or recently acquired problems.

Some might argue that these observations and findings do not necessarily preclude a causal linkage between prior religious socialization and conversion; the former may still influence which of the many groups, both conventional and offbeat, the potential convert will select or find appealing. With this we have no quarrel, since it seems quite reasonable to expect that those raised in a fundamentalist tradition might find the Unification Church or the Children of God more appealing than NSA or some other Buddhist- or Hindu-inspired movement. In either case, we still maintain that preparticipation ideological congruence is not a necessary condition for conversion in general. To argue otherwise is inconsistent with the logic of the constant comparative method (Glaser and Strauss, 1967). It also ignores the fact that movements function as important agitational, problem-defining, need-arousal and motive-producing agencies. Social movements have traditionally been viewed as vehicles for the expression of prestructured beliefs and dispositions (see Cantril, 1941; Glock, 1964; Hoffer, 1951; Klapp, 1969; Toch, 1965). However, attendance at an NSA meeting demonstrates that movements also function to construct social reality.[13] When this is the case, then ideological congruence, if and when it exists, constitutes a facilitative rather than a necessary precondition for conversion.

Religious Seekership. The final background factor that Lofland and Stark posited as a necessary precipitant of conversion is religious seekership. The prospect must come "to define himself as a religious seeker," as "a person searching for some satisfactory system of religious meaning to interpret and resolve his discontent" (1965:868). Recently, Lofland (1978:12,20) has suggested that perhaps this dimension of the model is not as important as originally assumed, since "people

not previously religious at all have joined" movements such as the Unification Church "in noticeable numbers" since the late sixties.

Although Lofland offers no substantial evidence in support of his recent observation, our data suggest that it is well-grounded. Specifically, if we take experimentation with other religious alternatives as an indicator of religious seekership, then, as indicated in the first section of Table 2, the vast majority of our sample were not seekers in the sense of "searching for some satisfactory system of religious meaning" (Lofland and Stark, 1965:868). We do not suggest, however, that religious seekership was not operative in the case of many preconverts. As one married female convert in her mid-twenties recounts:

> I have been a member of several religions, and try as I did to live by them I somehow fell away. I didn't realize then, but my reason for leaving was always the same. They all lacked something I was searching for. I read many books about different religions. But every way I tried I failed to reach the guidance and fulfillment I was seeking.

Seekership is also suggested by the fact that 22 percent of the sample could be classified as "seekers." Yet, the fact that 78 percent or more were not self-designated religious "experimenters" or "searchers" suggests that the linkage between seekership and conversion is not a necessary one.[14] Moreover, even when people do define themselves as religious seekers, we are again confronted with the problem of interpreting retrospective accounts. Did the avowed state of religious seekership actually exist prior to joining the group in question, or did conversion lead to a reconstruction of personal biographies such that converts came to reevaluate their lives prior to joining as ones seeking some ultimate authority?

Situational Factors

Turning Point. Situational factors refer to those conditions that lead to the successful recruitment and conversion of those individuals who are so inclined on the basis of the foregoing predispositions. One such factor is that prospects encounter the movement shortly after or at the same time as the occurrence of what is perceived as a "turning point" in life. That is, preconverts must come into contact with the movement at or about the same time as being confronted with the necessity or opportunity of doing something different with their lives because of the completion or disruption of old obligations and lines of action. The kinds

TABLE 2
Percentage and Frequency Distribution for Orientation,
Turning Points and Mode of Recruitment

I. Preconversion Problem-Solving Orientation	No.	%
Physiological[a]	117	35
Religious[b]	72	22
Psychiatric[c]	39	12
Political[d]	32	10
Mixed[e]	70	21
Totals*	330	100

II. Possible Preconversion Turning Points	No.	%
Unemployed/Lost Job	52	16
Divorced/Separated	46	14
Military/Draft	38	12
School Dropout	36	11
Institutionalized	34	10
Close Encounter with Death	15	4
Attempted/Contemplated Suicide	17	5
None Mentioned	92	28
Totals*	330	100

III. Mode of Recruitment	No.	%
Recruited through Social Networks	270	82
By Friends	(190)	(58)
By Relatives	(80)	(24)
Recruited Outside of Social Networks	60	18
Totals*	330	100

* Although there were 504 cases in our sample of testimonies, 174 of them did not include information pertaining to orientation, possible turning point or mode of recruitment. Therefore, this table is based on 330 rather than 504 cases.

[a] Physiological orientation includes references to being "into" or resolving personal difficulties through drugs, alcohol, dieting, exercise, sex and the like.

[b] Religious orientation includes self-designation as a religious searcher and/or identification of the supernatural or occult (God, unseen forces) as the key to resolving problems.

[c] Psychiatric orientation includes references to being "into" psychoanalysis, psychotherapy, and groups such as est. Includes statements indicating that manipulation of the self or psyche is seen as key to resolving personal difficulties.

[d] Political orientation includes references to belief that life situation is determined primarily by political and social arrangements. Being "into" peace movement, political activism and civil rights movement.

[e] Mixed orientation includes self-designation as hippie, street person, wanderer or drifter.

of personal incidents and situations that Lofland and Stark (1965:870) allude to as turning points include objective changes such as loss of job; completion, failure or withdrawal from school; divorce; and residential change.

Insofar as such specific events are taken as reliable indicators of turning points, then our data seemingly provide some support for the hypothetical linkage between turning points and conversion. As indicated in the second section of Table 2, 72 percent of the usable cases in our sample report personal experiences that might be construed as turning points. Additionally, if we include as being at a turning point the 21 percent who referred to themselves as "hippies" or "wanderers" at the time of encountering NSA, then roughly 93 percent of the converts in our sample were at a turning point in their lives sometime before or concurrently with their encounter with

NSA. While these findings do not unqualifiedly indicate that a turning point is a necessary condition for conversion, they do suggest that it may be an important facilitative condition in that it appears to increase one's susceptibility to conversion.

Yet, looked at more critically, the concept of the turning point and its relation to conversion are, as Lofland (1978:20) has recently commented, quite "troublesome." The reasons are several. First, the turning point concept is ambiguous. Whether a particular situation or point in one's life constitutes a turning point is not a given, but is largely a matter of definition and attitude. There are few, if any, consistently reliable benchmarks for ascertaining when or whether one is at a turning point in one's life. As a consequence, just about any moment could be defined as a turning point. Relatedly, when seeking to establish the occurrence of turning points in the past, we again face the problem of retrospective reporting. Events once seen as routine or inconsequential may emerge as highly significant after one has adopted the world view of NSA. In addition, when NSA converts discuss turning points in their lives, they seldom refer to the kinds of objective major life changes emphasized by Lofland and Stark. As indicated in Table 2, such changes as divorce, unemployment, and completion of school are frequently mentioned, but not as turning points. Instead, this designation seems to be reserved for that point at which members come to align themselves with the movement emotionally, cognitively, and morally—seeing themselves at one with the group. Furthermore, this realization typically occurs during the course of their practice as a member, rather than prior to or at the time of encountering the movement. As one middle-aged convert, employed as a nurse and who was the mother of a seventeen-year-old, relates:

> Although I had been a member for some time, things weren't going well. I was beginning to lose my patience and motivation at work, and my son was going through some troublesome phases. I continued to chant, but it wasn't until the *Nichiren Shoshu* San Diego Convention that I began to develop a real faith in the practice and a sense of mission. . . . When I got home, things started happening. My whole attitude seemed changed. When I went to work I felt a real sense of confidence that was never there before. . . . As I look back now, the convention was the turning point in my life.

Similarly, an unmarried female convert in her early twenties, employed as a retailer in a clothing store, recounts how the turning point in her life came upon seeing President Ikeda, the movement's principal leader, during the movement's 1974 San Diego Convention:

> Prior to the Convention I felt a gap in my life. I loved NSA activities and devoted every spare moment to them, but something was missing in the world outside of NSA. In the month before the convention I came to realize I needed to capture the spirit of President Ikeda. The opportunity came when the Convention Cultural Festival began and I found myself sitting five seats away from him. As I watched he turned and waved in my direction. Astonished, I waved back. And then he gave me the "V" sign. It was beyond my greatest dreams. Now I feel that I could follow him anywhere. At that moment I felt a real connection with President Ikeda that has opened up a whole new aspect in my life. You stay in your nest until you're ready to fly. This is the first time I've been out of the nest. I feel like I've been born again.

Such accounts, in conjunction with the earlier observations, suggest that the turning point concept may be related to conversion, but not necessarily in the way initially hypothesized by Lofland and Stark. We see two differences. First, rather than assuming that major objective life changes are necessarily perceived by converts as turning points (see Lofland and Stark, 1965:870), we contend that what is defined as a turning point is largely contingent on the interpretive schema of the group in question. Thus, a turning point may be indicated by extramovement status passages or role changes, as Lofland and Stark assume, or it may be constituted by some illuminating insight or by heightened or renewed faith. In either case, it is subjectively determined rather than objectively given. The second difference follows from the first. Rather than occurring prior to or around the time in which the movement is encountered, the turning point is more likely to come after contact with the movement and exposure to its world view. Inasmuch as conversion involves the acquisition of a new or more clearly articulated universe of discourse and its attendant vocabulary of motive, then these observations are neither surprising nor unreasonable. Accordingly, the turning point might be conceptualized as an artifact of the conversion process, rather than as a precipitating condition. Indeed, the turning point may symbolize conversion itself, for converts are gripped by the realization that they are not the same as they were moments ago and that their life situation and view of the world have changed, and for the better.

Cult Affective Bonds. None of the hypothetical precipitants of conversion are regarded as more important than the development of a positive, interpersonal tie between the prospect and one or more movement members. However amenable an individual is to the appeals of a cult or movement, Lofland and Stark (1965:871) argue that for conversion to occur "an affective bond must develop, if it does not already exist." Such a bond may emerge during the course of movement-specific interaction between two former strangers, or it may be the result of a preexisting, extramovement, interpersonal association. Lofland and Stark found that once the initial bond between the founder and the first convert developed, nearly all subsequent conversions "moved through preexisting friendship pairs or nets."

Our findings tend to agree with those of Lofland and Stark. Examination of the conversion careers of the fifteen most active members of the chanting cell with which the senior author was associated revealed that an affective bond was not only discernible in each case, but that the bond was typically preexisting rather than emergent and movement-specific. Two of the fifteen members were recruited by a spouse, one by another relative, ten by friends or acquaintances, and only two by strangers. All but two of the most active members in the chanting cell were thus drawn into sustained contact with the movement by being linked to a member through a preexisting, extramovement interpersonal tie. Further investigation revealed that the same pattern was evident for the vast majority of NSA members brought into the movement's orbit of influence. As indicated in the third section of Table 2, 82 percent of our sample were recruited by members with whom they had preexisting, extramovement ties. Although the remaining 18 percent were recruited directly from the street by members who were strangers, first-hand association with such recruits suggests that their subsequent conversion was contingent on the development of an affective bond with one or more members of the cell into which they were recruited.

That an affective interpersonal tie between the prospect and one or more members might constitute a necessary condition for conversion is not surprising. Such a bond can function to bridge the information gap between prospect and movement, increase the credibility of the message and cause, and intensify the pressure to consider the message and the corresponding practice. We would thus argue that while conversion involves more than "coming to accept the opinions of one's friends" (Lofland and Stark, 1965:871), it is rather unlikely in the absence of such an affective bond to one or more members.[15]

Weak Extracult Affective Bonds. The third situational factor Lofland and Stark deem necessary for conversion is the absence or neutralization of extracult attachments. Given the fact that converts to the group they studied had few (if any) strong, proximal, interpersonal ties, and given the corollary finding that "conversion was not consummated" when extracult bonds were not weakened or neutralized (Lofland and Stark, 1965:873), such a proposition seems well-grounded. Moreover, it is consistent with the argument that extraneous ties and commitments can function as countervailing influences with respect

to the interests, demands and ideology of a cult or movement (see Becker, 1960; Kanter, 1972).

However plausible the above hypothesis, both the work of Richardson and his associates and our own findings cast considerable doubt on its generalizability. In their work on conversion to a fundamentalist sect, Richardson et al. (1978:51) found that while "many members did not have especially rewarding" preexisting "ties" and while "most such ties were generally weakened or broken at least for a time after a person became a member of the group," the "sect members were not isolated from their society to the extent that Lofland and Stark found in their study." Even more significantly, they report finding a number of extragroup significant others, particularly parents, who felt positively toward the group and were even supportive of the convert's participation (Richardson et al., 1978:51; Richardson and Stewart, 1978:37).

Our findings similarly provide little support for the hypothesis that either neutralized extramovement ties or social isolation constitutes a necessary condition for conversion. As noted earlier, 82 percent were recruited into the movement via preexisting, extramovement social networks. Moreover, our data suggest that conversion to NSA generally may lead to a strengthening of extramovement bonds, particularly among family, co-workers and classmates. There are two reasons for this. First, because NSA's interpretive beliefs include the karmic principle that one's present life condition is largely contingent on one's own actions, both past and present, converts come to blame themselves for their misfortunes. Consequently, they seek to change themselves rather than others, thereby improving rather than worsening extramovement relations. The account of an unmarried twenty-three year old female convert illustrates our assertion:

> I now realize that the reason I didn't get along with my roommate wasn't her fault, but my fault. Chanting and the *Gohonzon* made me realize that the things I criticized about her were the very faults I possessed. By chanting and changing my character we are now able to get along.

Or, as an unmarried male convert in his early twenties similarly recounts:

> I discovered that I was running from myself. I came to realize that everything I hated was part of me. This realization made me a better person, because I am now correcting what was wrong with

me instead of blaming it on my parents, the school, and the country.

In addition, since NSA is a noncommunal, proselytizing movement that seeks to change the world by expanding its ranks, all nonmembers, and particularly extramovement familiar others, are defined as potential converts: as one informant put it, "like freshly sown seeds, [they] will eventually blossom if only they are tended to." Accordingly, members are constantly reminded to build and nurture extramovement ties in order to facilitate the movement's spread.

These observations suggest that affective ties to both movement members and nonmembers are not necessarily contradictory, and that extramovement affective ties may function to facilitate rather than to counteract conversion. There are at least two reasons why these findings are inconsistent with those by Lofland and Stark. One is that the Unification Church they studied had a communal structure and NSA's is noncommunal. Because communally organized groups are generally more demanding (Kanter, 1972, 1973) or "greedy" (Coser, 1967b), the neutralization or severance of extragroup ties and other countervailing influences may well be necessary in order to effect conversion. In contrast, such a break with the outside world hardly seems necessary for conversion to noncommunal movements such as NSA. The other reason is that the relationship between extramovement affective ties and conversion may also be influenced by the public reaction a movement engenders (see Turner and Killian, 1972:257-59; Snow, 1979). Conversion to movements that are publicly defined as "revolutionary" or "peculiar" or "idiosyncratic" may be contingent on the weakening of extramovement ties—in order to neutralize the stigma frequently associated with participation in such movements. In contrast, participation in movements defined as "respectable" may not be encumbered by resistance from nonmovement significant others. Hence, the maintenance of extramovement ties may not impede conversion to more "respectable" movements. Given the fact that NSA has made a longstanding and concerted effort to render itself respectable and legitimate in the public eye, such an hypothesis seems quite plausible (see Snow, 1979).

Intensive Interaction. While they regard the confluence of the six previous items (three predisposing conditions and three situational factors) as sufficient for the production of verbal conversion,

Lofland and Stark contend that commitment remains only verbal, and that conversion remains incomplete, in the absence of intensive interaction with group members. Such interaction hypothetically transforms the avowed convert into a "deployable agent" by securing behavioral as well as verbal commitment, and they regard it as the final condition that rounds out the conversion process.

Our observations are not only in line with those of Lofland and Stark but suggest that intensive interaction is perhaps the most important factor in the conversion process once the prospect has been informed about and brought into contact with the movement. In the case of NSA, the interaction begins in earnest once the prospect has been persuaded to attend a cellular (district) discussion meeting.[16] Conducted four evenings per week, these meetings are highly organized affairs staged for the expressed purpose of giving "newcomers the best possible reasons for receiving their own *Gohonzon* (scroll) and to begin chanting."[17] If the prospect agrees to give chanting a try, he or she is formally initiated into NSA in a conversion ceremony (*Gojukai*) held at one of its regional temples and conducted by NSA priests. Following this and the enshrinement of the *Gohonzon* in the newcomer's place of residence, the new member typically becomes the primary responsibility of the member who was the recruiter. Referred to as a Junior Group Leader, this member constitutes the initial primary link between the novitiate and the movement. More than anyone else in the movement, the group leader is expected "to know the situation of the new member, what sort of hopes [he/she] has, and what [his/her] desire is to practice." Moreover, the group leader is to "strive to establish a warm and close relationship with the member [he/she] is taking care of."

The ultimate aim is to get the new member to "stand alone," to be a "self-motivated member," to be, in Lofland and Stark's terms, a "deployable agent." But a new member is only "at level one toward becoming an active, vigorous member of NSA," and has to be "brought along." It is here that the Junior Group Leader comes into play. Alternating between the roles of instructor, informer and confidant, the Junior Leader is charged with maintaining constant contact with the new member—answering questions, advising about movement activities, and nurturing faith. This leader is also responsible for taking new members on recruiting expeditions into public places; coaxing them to attend meetings; introducing them to other group members and movement leaders; and visiting them at home to "help them chant correctly." By performing such duties the Junior Leader is a role-model of what it means to be a member, of how members think, talk and act—not only in relation to NSA but with respect to the world in general. It is thus through the Junior Group Leader and through attendance at and participation in movement activities that the new member begins to learn what NSA is all about and begins to become oriented cognitively, emotionally and morally. Members are constantly reminded that "if the link between the new member and the Junior Group Leader is cut off," then "the new member is virtually left out of the rhythm of NSA and is likely to fall away."

In the absence of such constant and intense interaction, conversion to NSA seems unlikely. Since this observation is not only consistent with Lofland and Stark's work, but also is suggested by studies of Hare Krishna (Daner, 1976; Judah, 1974) and Pentecostalism (Gerlach and Hine, 1970; Heirich, 1977), it would appear that the salience of intensive interaction to conversion cannot be overemphasized.

Summary and Conclusions

We have sought to extend our understanding of the conversion process by critically examining the Lofland-Stark conversion model. Our data, derived from a study of recruitment and conversion to the *Nichiren Shoshu* Buddhist movement in America, have not supported the model in its entirety. Our analysis has suggested that several components of the model are theoretically questionable, while others seem more defensible.

Our findings are especially at odds with the contention that personal tension, ideological congruence, and religious seekership are necessary predisposing conditions for conversion. These factors were present in some individual cases, but missing in many others. Moreover, even if they had been uniformly operative, such factors might be best interpreted as consequences rather than precipitants of conversion. Our argument is admittedly inconsistent with the longstanding tendency to approach recruitment and conversion to movements primarily from a social psychological-motivational standpoint which focuses on various prestructured tensions and cognitive orientations as the major explanatory variables (see

Cantril, 1941; Glock, 1964; Hoffer, 1951; Klapp, 1969; Peterson and Mauss, 1973). But we believe that this traditional approach is itself empirically questionable and theoretically unfounded. It ignores the fact that motives for behavior are generally emergent and interactional. It also assumes that the explanations given by converts for their conversion were necessarily those that motivated or precipitated it in the first place. We question such an assumption because conversion involves the reconstruction of one's past, frequently including the discovery of personal needs and problems not previously discernible or troublesome enough to warrant remedial action. Hence, the old past and the new past bear slight resemblance to each other.

The findings and analysis here also call into question the necessity of two of the situational factors that were components of the Lofland-Stark model: that of the turning point and that of weak or severed extracult attachments. Their original conceptualization of the connection between the turning point and conversion is at best problematic. Because the identification of something as a turning point is largely a function of the interpretive schema in use, the turning point really cannot be known *a priori* or without familiarity with the world view in question. Therefore, instead of conceptualizing the turning point as a precipitant of conversion, it might best be thought of as a consequence that can function to *symbolize* conversion itself.

We found that recruitment and conversion to NSA were typically contingent on the *maintenance* of extracult affective ties, rather than being associated with weakened or neutralized extramovement affective ties. Data were also reported suggesting that conversion to NSA may even function to strengthen some extramovement ties. These findings ran counter to what the Lofland-Stark model led us to expect, and we suggested that the difference was probably related to: 1) whether the groups involved were organized communally (as was the Unification Church) or noncommunally (true of NSA); and 2) whether the movements involved were considered "respectable" or not by the general public.

Although we have questioned many features of the Lofland-Stark model, our findings indicate that two remaining factors in their model—cult affective bonds and intensive interaction—are essential for conversion to NSA. We would even argue that conversion in general is highly improbable in the absence of affective and intensive interaction. Some critics (Lofland, 1978; Straus, 1976) might object to such a conclusion on the grounds that it views the human actor as a relatively passive agent whose outlook and behavior is unwittingly molded and controlled by various social factors. However, we are not arguing that prospective converts are empty and disinterested vessels into which new ideas and beliefs are poured. To the contrary, we take it for granted that most converts were initially interested in exploring the perspective or group with which they are currently associated. After all, aside from the deprogramming "business" (cf. Patrick, 1976; Shupe et al., 1978), there is little, if any, evidence to suggest that the bulk of contemporary conversions are involuntary or coerced. But to suggest that an individual once had an interest in or taste for something is not to explain how that something—whether a philosophy, a life style or a form of music—became a burning preoccupation, in James' (1958:162) words, "the habitual centre of [one's] personal energy." The key to such a transformation, we contend, is in the process of intensive interaction between prospect and converts. Of course people may facilitate their own conversion, but before they can "go about converting themselves" (Lofland, 1978:22) they must be privy to a universe of discourse that renders such transformations desirable and possible. Moreover, when a virtual smorgasbord of transformative world views exists, the question arises as to how and why one alternative is selected over another: the answer again seems to lie within the process of affective and intensive interaction.

In summary, our findings and analysis not only question the generalizability of some key elements of the Lofland-Stark model, they also raise questions about related models of conversion that place considerable emphasis on prestructured tensions and cognitive states, and on prior socialization. The analysis also suggests that instead of being the same in all groups, the conversion process may vary, depending, for example, on whether the group in question is communal or noncommunal, and "respectable" or "idiosyncratic." Our analysis, finally, suggests that the interactive process holds the key to understanding conversion. Future research should emphasize understanding this process more fully and pay special attention to the extent to which it varies across groups differing in ideology, organization and public reaction.

Notes

1. Aside from the work of Richardson et al. (1978), we know of only two studies which might be considered "tests" of the Lofland-Stark model. The first, Seggar and Kunz's (1972) examination of conversion to Mormonism, not only had mixed results, but we question (for reasons that will become clear later in the paper) the extent to which conversion can be adequately studied solely by means of *post factum*, structured interviews. We also question whether an examination of conversion to an institutionalized religious denomination constitutes a fair test of a conversion model pertaining to "deviant" cults or belief systems. The second study examines the relation between psychological stress, prior socialization and direct social influence (Heirich, 1977). Because its findings bear upon some related components of the Lofland-Stark model but neglect others, it cannot be regarded as a test of the Lofland-Stark model in its entirety.

2. In *The Philosophy of the Present* (1932:31), Mead notes, for example: "If we had every possible document and every possible monument from the period of J. Caesar, we would unquestionably have a truer picture of the man and of what occurred in his lifetime, but it would be a truth which belongs to the present, and a later present would reconstruct it from the standpoint of its own emergent nature." Similarly, Mead writes in *The Philosophy of the Act* (1936:616): ". . . that which arrives that is novel gives a continually new past. A past never was in the form in which it appears as a past. Its reality is in its interpretation of the present."

3. For a discussion of the *Sokagakkai* movement, see Babbie, 1965; Dator, 1969; Murata, 1969; White, 1970. Since NSA is a foreign extension of *Sokagakkai*, it is important to note that for strategic reasons NSA has attempted to deemphasize its relationship to the *Sokagakkai* and to establish its own separate identity. In 1966, for example, the name of the movement was changed from *Sokagakkai* of America to *Nichiren Shoshu* of America. Unlike the *Sokagakkai*, NSA has refrained from mixing politics and religion. For an analysis of these differences and of NSA's highly accommodative behavior, see Snow (1979).

4. In their recent examination of the Unification Church, Bromley and Shupe (1979a:22) refer to it as a "world transforming movement, i.e., one which seeks total, permanent structural change of society across all institutions." This orientation was also evident in the early years of the movement. Its major goal then, as now, was "a complete restoration of the world to the condition of the Garden of Eden" (Lofland and Stark, 1965:826). Since NSA's "unchangeable mission," according to its major leader, is the "building of a new culture," it might also be classified as a world-transforming movement.

5. Nam-Myoho-Renge-Kyo is variously translated as "Adoration to the Scripture of the Lotus of the Perfect Truth," I devote myself to the inexpressibly profound and wonderful truth embodied in the *Lotus Sutra*," or, as most core members prefer, "Devotion to the mystical, universal law of cause and effect through sound."

6. NSA shares with Pentecostalism, the Black Power movement, and the Women's movement a segmented and reticulated organizational structure, but has more centralized leadership and decision making. For a discussion of these dimensions of movement organization, see Gerlach and Hine (1970).

7. Although it was not the senior author's intent to engage in secretive research, the nature of participant observation often militates against total candidness. On some occasions it is easy to forget that one is not merely a participant, and on the other occasions to announce one's identity as a researcher is to disrupt and contaminate a flow of interaction deemed natural both by the members and the researcher. Much research is both secretive and nonsecretive: "All research is secret in some ways and to some degree—we never tell the subjects everything" (Roth, 1962:283). For a more detailed account of the ethnographic stage of the research, see Snow (1976:1-38).

8. *The World Tribune* is published five times a week in Santa Monica, California. It was first issued in August 1964, and has been published ever since. It now has over 55,000 monthly subscribers and constitutes a useful record of the growth and history of the *Nichiren Shoshu* movement in America.

9. Although the sample consisted of 2,460 American adults over 21, the base for the above figures ranges from 922 for work problems to 2,455 for feelings of impending nervous breakdown. The figures were extrapolated from Gurin et al., 1960: Tables 2.6, 3.4, 4.8, 5.8 and 6.1.

10. A 1976 survey of over 2000 American men and women about their feelings of well-being and distress suggests that Americans still readily avow numerous anxieties and problems. The study reveals that today people tend to be somewhat more anxiety-ridden and "unhappy about their communities and country, their jobs, and their interpersonal lives" than in 1957 (Institute of Social Research, 1979:4).

11. That prestructured tension or stress may not be a necessary precondition for conversion is also suggested by Heirich's (1977:666) finding "that stress, at least as measured here, is insufficient to account" for conversion to Catholic Pentecostalism. Here it is also interesting to note that Heirich's findings suggest that perhaps converts to Catholic Pentecostalism are not as inclined as are converts to *Nichiren Shoshu* to define their past as problematic and stressful. If this is true, it suggests either that converts to NSA are more "troubled" than converts to Catholic Pentecostalism or that whether converts see their past as stress-ridden is largely dependent on the newly acquired interpretive schema. As argued above, we prefer the latter explanation. This explanation is also consistent with Emerson and Messinger's more general observations (1977:23) about the natural history of personal difficulties or "troubles." Among other things, they note that troubles initially "appear vague to those concerned. But as steps are taken to remedy or manage that trouble, the trouble itself becomes progressively clarified and specified."

12. Our observations here are also consistent with Heirich's finding (1977:66) that conversion to Catholic Pentecostalism, as indicated by attending Mass, "does not result from previous conditioning."

13. This is also amply demonstrated by attendance at an Erhard Training Seminar (est) or an evangelistic revival, or by spending an evening at a Krishna Commune or with the Moonies, each of which we have done on one or more occasions.

14. Even though Balch and Taylor (1978) and Straus (1976) argue convincingly that many people who participate in contemporary religious groups and mass therapies are "seekers," we find no reason to modify our contention that seekership is not essential for conversion. Based on our observations, we think it is more reasonable to argue that while "there are undoubtedly personality types who are attracted to any movement," only rarely do they ever constitute "more than a small fraction of its members" (Turner and Killian, 1972:365).

15. In their study of participation in the Bo and Peep UFO cult, Balch and Taylor (1978) report findings apparently questioning the importance of group affective bonds to conversion. They note that "new recruits almost never established close affective ties with members of the cult before they joined," and that "even after a seeker decided to join, he got very little social support from members of the cult." *Yet,* they also note that "members of the UFO cult were not converts in the true sense of the word." Instead, they were "metaphysical seekers" who defined "their decision to follow the Two" as "a reaffirmation of their seekership . . . as a logical extension of their spiritual quest." If the members of the cult had undergone conversion, then it was not to the UFO cult but to the metaphysical world view which came to function for them as a primary authority prior to encountering the Two and their followers. Because the conversion process was not involved in affiliation with the cult, it seems unreasonable to argue that Balch and Taylor's findings contradict either the Lofland-Stark model or our own conclusions about the importance of group affective bonds in relation to conversion.

16. We do not intend to provide in this paper a detailed account of the interactive process leading to conversion to *Nichiren Shoshu;* only a brief overview of the process is included below. For a detailed analytic description of the process, see Snow (1976:219-57).

17. This and the following quoted material are derived from the *World Tribune,* from members' comments during movement meetings, and from informal discussions with the senior author. ✦

23

Sacrifice for the Cause: Group Processes, Recruitment, and Commitment in a Student Social Movement

Eric L. Hirsch

Early analyses of protest movement mobilization emphasized the irrationality of movement participation and argued that marginal, insecure people join movements because of a need for social direction. This approach has lost popularity because many movement participants are socially integrated and quite rational. A popular current approach, rational choice theory, counters by suggesting that movement participation is the result of individual cost-benefit calculations. But even the most elaborate individual incentive models cannot fully account for the manner in which group political processes influence movement participants to sacrifice individual interests in favor of a collective cause.

This article develops an alternative perspective on recruitment and commitment to protest movements; it emphasizes the importance of the development of *political solidarity,* that is, support for a group cause and its tactics. Mobilization can then be explained by analyzing how group-based political processes, such as *consciousness-raising, collective empowerment, polarization,* and *group decision-making*, induce movement participants to sacrifice their personal welfare for the group cause. Empirical support for this perspective comes from a detailed analysis of a Columbia University student movement that demanded that the university divest itself of stock in companies doing business in South Africa. . . .

Impact of Group Process

The best way to explain recruitment and commitment in protest movements is to reject both rational choice and social disorganization views and focus instead on explaining how groups create commitment to their goals and tactics. The following discussion builds on the work of movement theorists (Gamson 1975; Schwartz 1976; Tilly 1978; Gamson, Fireman, Rytina 1982; McAdam 1982, 1986, 1988b; Ferree and Miller 1985; Hirsch 1986, 1989; Rosenthal and Schwartz 1989)[1] and conflict theorists (Simmel 1955; Coser 1956, 1967a; Edelman 1971; Kriesberg 1971; Sherif, Harvey, White, Hood, Sherif 1988) to provide an explanation of recruitment and commitment to protest movements that emphasizes how four group processes—*consciousness-raising, collective empowerment, polarization*, and *group decision-making*—create a willingness to sacrifice personal welfare for a collective cause.

Consciousness-Raising

Potential recruits are not likely to join a protest movement unless they develop an ideological commitment to the group cause and believe that only non-institutional means can further that cause. Consciousness-raising involves a group discussion where such beliefs are created or reinforced. It may occur among members of an emerging movement who realize they face a problem of common concern that cannot be solved through routine political processes. Or it may happen in an ongoing movement, when movement activists try to convince potential recruits that their cause is just, that institutional means of influence have been unsuccessful, and that morally committed individuals must fight for the cause. Effective consciousness-raising is a difficult task because protest tactics usually challenge acknowledged authority relationships. Predisposing factors, such as prior political socialization, may make certain individuals susceptible to some appeals and unsympathetic to others.

Consciousness-raising is not likely to take place among socially marginal individuals because such isolation implies difficulty in communicating ideas to others. And it is not likely to happen among a group of rational calculators because the evaluation of society and of the chances for change is often influenced more by commitment to political or moral values than by self-interest calculations (Fireman and Gamson 1979; Ferree and Miller 1985). Consciousness-raising is facilitated in non-hierarchical, loosely structured, face-to-face settings that are isolated from persons in power; in such *havens* (Hirsch 1989), people can easily express concerns, become aware of common problems, and begin to question the legitimacy of institutions that deny them the means for resolving those problems (Gerlach and Hine 1970; Rosenthal and Schwartz 1989).

Collective Empowerment

The recruitment and commitment of participants in a protest movement may also be affected by a group process called collective empowerment. While recruits may gain a sense of the potential power of a movement in consciousness-raising sessions, the real test for the movement comes at the actual protest site where all involved see how many are willing to take the risks associated with challenging authority. If large numbers are willing to sacrifice themselves for the movement, the chances for success seem greater; a "bandwagon effect" (Hirsch 1986) convinces people to participate in this particular protest because of its presumed ability to accomplish the movement goal. Tactics are more easily viewed as powerful if they are highly visible, dramatic, and disrupt normal institutional routines.

Polarization

A third important group process is polarization. Protest challenges authority in a way that institutional tactics do not because it automatically questions the rules of the decision-making game. The use of non-routine methods of influence also means that there is always uncertainty about the target's response. For these reasons, one common result of a protest is unpredictable escalating conflict. Each side sees the battle in black and white terms, uses increasingly coercive tactics, and develops high levels of distrust and anger toward the opponent (Kriesberg 1973: 170-3).

Polarization is often seen as a problem since it convinces each side that their position is right and the opponent's is wrong; this makes compromise and negotiation less likely (Coleman 1957). Since it leads each side to develop the independent goal of harming the opponent, movement participants may lose sight of their original goal. Finally, escalation of coercive tactics by those in power can result in demobilization of the movement as individual participants assess the potential negative consequences of continued participation.

But if other group processes, such as consciousness-raising and collective empowerment, have created sufficient group identification, the protesters will respond to threats as a powerful, angry group rather than as isolated, frightened individuals. Under these circumstances, polarization can have a strong positive impact on participation (Coser 1956, 1967a; Edelman 1971). The sense of crisis that develops in such conflicts strengthens participants' belief that their fate is tied to that of the group. They develop a willingness to continue to participate despite the personal risks because they believe the costs of protest should be collectively shared. Greater consensus on group goals develops because the importance of social factors in perception increases in an ambiguous conflict (Sherif et al. 1988); protesters become more likely to accept the arguments of their loved fellow activists and less likely to accept those of their hated enemy. Because of the need to act quickly in a crisis, participants also become willing to submerge their differences with respect to the group's tactical choices (Coleman 1957).

Collective Decision-Making

Finally, collective decision-making often plays an important role in motivating the continuing commitment of movement participants. Movements often have group discussions about whether to initiate, continue, or end a given protest. Committed protesters may feel bound by group decisions made during such discussions, even when those decisions are contrary to their personal preferences (Rosenthal and Schwartz 1989). Participation in a protest movement is often the result of a complex group decision-making process, and not the consequence of many isolated, rational individual decisions.

The Columbia Divestment Campaign: A Case Study

The importance of these four group processes—consciousness-raising, collective empowerment, polarization, and group decision-making—in recruitment and commitment in a protest movement is illustrated by the Columbia University divestment protest. In April of 1985, several hundred Columbia University and Barnard College students sat down in front of the chained doors of the main Columbia College classroom and administrative building, Hamilton Hall, and stated that they would not leave until the university divested itself of stock in companies doing business in South Africa. Many students remained on this "blockade" for three weeks. This was a particularly good case for the analysis of movement recruitment and commitment because the majority of the participants in the protest had not been active previously in the divestment or other campus protest movements.

Protest actions of this kind can create problems for researchers because the organizers' need for secrecy often prevents the researcher from knowing of the event in advance. The best solution is to use as many diverse research methods as possible to study the movement after it has begun. I spent many hours at the protest site each day observing the activities of the protesters and their opponent, the Columbia administration. I also discussed the demonstration with participants and non-participants at the protest site, in classrooms, and other campus settings; and examined the many leaflets, position papers, and press reports on the demonstration.

During the summer of 1985, I completed 19 extended interviews, averaging one and one-half hours each, with blockaders and members of the steering committee of the Coalition for a Free South Africa (CFSA), the group that organized and led the protest. The interviews covered the protester's political background, previous experience in politics and protest movements, her/his experiences during the three weeks of the protest, and feelings about the personal consequences of participation. All quotes are taken from transcripts of these interviews.

I also analyzed responses to a survey distributed to the dormitory mailboxes of a random sample of 300 Barnard and Columbia resident undergraduates during the third week of the protest. The 28-question survey assessed attitudes toward those on both sides of the conflict, the extent of the respondent's participation in the protest and in campus politics and social organizations, the respondent's general political values, and demographic information.

Of the 300 surveys, 181, or 60.3 percent, were returned. Given the situation on campus at the time and the fact that the semester was drawing to a close, it was difficult to increase the return rate through followup letters and questionnaires. If those who returned the questionnaires differed in a significant way from those who did not, survey results would be biased. However, it wasn't only

divestment activists who returned the survey; a wide variety of opinions was expressed by respondents. Nine-tenths of respondents had not been active in the divestment movement prior to the blockade, and only about half favored divestment or felt that the blockade was justified when they first heard about it. A copy of the questionnaire and a summary of the results are available from the author upon request.

Consciousness-Raising

The Coalition for a Free South Africa (CFSA) was founded in 1981 to promote Columbia University's divestment of stock in companies doing business in South Africa. It was a loosely structured group with a predominantly black steering committee of about a dozen individuals who made decisions by consensus, and a less active circle of about 50 students who attended meetings and the group's protests and educational events. The group was non-hierarchical, non-bureaucratic, and had few resources other than its members' labor. The CFSA tried to convince Columbia and Barnard students that blacks faced injustice under apartheid, that U.S. corporations with investments in South Africa profited from the low wages paid to blacks, that Columbia was an accomplice in apartheid because it invested in the stock of these companies, and that divestment would advance the anti-apartheid movement by putting economic and political pressure on the white regime of South Africa.

This consciousness-raising was done in a variety of small group settings, including dormitory rap sessions, forums, and teach-ins. Coverage of the CFSA's activities in the Columbia student newspaper and television reports on the violent repression of the anti-apartheid movement in South Africa increased student consciousness of apartheid and encouraged many students to support divestment.

Even in this early period, conflict between the CFSA and the Columbia administration affected the views of potential movement recruits. At first, the CFSA tried to achieve divestment by using traditional avenues of influence. In 1983, the organization was able to gain a unanimous vote for divestment by administration, faculty, and student representatives in the University Senate, but Columbia's Board of Trustees rejected the resolution. As one protester pointed out, that action was interpreted by many students as an indication that traditional means of influence could not achieve divestment:

> I remember in '83 when the Senate voted to divest. I was convinced that students had voiced their opinion and had been able to convince the minority of administrators that what they wanted was a moral thing. It hadn't been a bunch of radical youths taking buildings and burning things down, to destroy. But rather, going through the system, and it seemed to me that for the first time in a really long time the system was going to work. And then I found out that it hadn't worked, and that just re-affirmed my feelings about how the system at Columbia really did work.

The result of CFSA's extensive organizing work was that many students were aware of the oppressed state of blacks in South Africa, the call for divestment by anti-apartheid activists, and the intransigence of the university president and trustees in the face of a unanimous vote for divestment by the representative democratic body at the university.

Collective Empowerment: The Initiation of the Blockade

In the next phase of the movement, the CFSA sponsored rallies and vigils to call attention to the intransigence of the trustees. Few students attended these demonstrations, probably because few supporters believed they would result in divestment. Deciding that more militant tactics were necessary, the CFSA steering committee began to plan a fast by steering committee members and a takeover of a campus building. The plan called for chaining shut the doors of the building and blocking the entrance with protesters; this, it was assumed, would lead to a symbolic arrest of a few dozen steering committee members and other hard-core supporters of divestment. The intent was to draw media coverage to dramatize the continuing fight for divestment.

Because they had worked hard on publicity, the steering committee of CFSA expected a large turnout for their initial rally, but fewer than 200 students gathered at the Sundial in the center of campus on the morning of April 4. Speeches were made by a local political official, a representative of the African National Congress, several black South African students, and members of the CFSA steering committee. Many of those interviewed had been at the rally, but none felt that the speeches were any more or less inspiring than speeches they had heard at previous CFSA events.

At the conclusion of the speeches, nearly all of those present agreed to follow one of the CFSA steering committee members on a march around campus. Most expected to chant a few anti-apartheid and pro-divestment slogans and return to the Sundial for a short wrap-up speech. Instead, they were led to the steps in front of the already-chained doors at Hamilton Hall. The protesters did not understand at first why they had been led to this spot, and few noticed the chained doors.

The steering committee member then revealed the day's plan, stating that this group of protesters would not leave the steps until the university divested itself of stock in companies doing business in South Africa. At least 150 students remained where they were; no one recalls a significant number of defections. Within two hours, the group on the steps grew to over 250.

Why did so many students agree to participate in this militant protest? The CFSA steering committee did not have an answer. Student participation in their relatively safe rallies and vigils had been minimal, so they certainly did not expect hundreds to join a much riskier act of civil disobedience. According to one steering committee member:

> Needless to say, I was quite startled by the events of April 4. By noon, there must have been hundreds more people than I expected there would be. I was hoping for 50 people, including the hard core. We would all get carted off, and whatever obstacles were blockading the door would be cut, removed, or thrown up. That's what everyone was expecting. We would have a story written and the press would report that we had done this. Jesus Christ, what happened that day was absolutely mind boggling! I still haven't gotten over it.

It was hard for anyone to predict the high level of mobilization based on the prior actions and attitudes of the participants because so few had been active in the divestment movement prior to April 4. Only 9 percent of the random sample of students reported that they had been at least somewhat active in the divestment movement, yet 37 percent participated in blockade rallies and/or slept overnight on the steps of Hamilton Hall. In fact, these students did not know that they would join this militant protest until it was actually initiated.

It is unlikely that the decision to participate was due to a narrow individual cost/benefit analysis including such costs as the time involved and the definite possibilities of arrest and/or disciplinary action by the university. Regarding personal benefits, it is hard to see how any Columbia student could gain from the divestment of South Africa-related stock.

Rather, participation was due to a belief in the cause and the conviction that this protest might work where previous CFSA actions had failed. Consciousness-raising had convinced these students of the importance of divestment, but they had not participated in the movement because they did not believe its tactics would work. Once several hundred were in front of the doors, many demonstrators felt that such a large group using a dramatic tactic would have the power to call attention to the evils of apartheid and cause the university to seriously consider divestment:

> Often when I would see a rally, I'd think that here was a bunch of people huffing and puffing about an issue who are going to be ignored and things are going to go on just as they were before this rally. The fact that there were a couple of hundred people out there with the purpose of altering the way the University does business gave me the feeling that this would be noticed, that people would pay attention.

The belief in the potential power of the tactic was reinforced by the willingness of several leaders of the movement to sacrifice their individual interests to achieve divestment. Two black South African students who spoke at the rally faced the possibility of exile or arrest and imprisonment upon their return home. About half a dozen CFSA steering committee members had fasted for nearly two weeks simply to get a meeting with the university president and trustees; two of these students were eventually hospitalized. As one blockader testified:

> The fasters were doing something that personally took a lot of willpower for them, and that gave you a little extra willpower. To have to go into the hospital because you were off food for 15 days, and the trustees won't even speak to you. It really made me angry at the trustees, so I was determined that this was not something that was just going to whimper off. At least I was going to be there, and I know others felt the same way.

The leaders of the protest recruited participants by taking personal risks that demonstrated their own commitment to the cause and to this particular tactic; other students in the blockade ignored individual interests in favor of the cause as well.

> I do think it has something to do with the support of peers, just seeing that there were people who were willing to extend themselves and put their own asses on the line. I guess it's the self-sacrifice

aspect of it that appealed to me, that really drew my attention. These people were willing to sacrifice their own personal interests in a big way, or a larger way than usual. That's something that hit a chord with me. It was the degree to which people were willing to give up self-interest.

Another factor influencing participation may have been the fact that the protesters were not forced to decide to join the protest at all. Instead, they were led as a group to a position in front of the doors, unaware that this was an act of civil disobedience; the only decision to be made was whether or not to leave the protest. Although this was done because CFSA did not want to reveal its plans to campus security prematurely, the unintended consequence was to maximize participation; it was difficult for demonstrators to leave the steps because of the public example of self-sacrificing black South Africans and the fasters.

Of course, each protester had many less public opportunities to leave the protest during the three weeks after April 4th. Most stayed, partly because of growing evidence of the power of this tactic. The protest soon gained the public support of a variety of groups locally and nationally, including Harlem community groups and churches, the Columbia faculty, unions on and off the campus, the African National Congress, and the United Nations. Students on other campuses engaged in similar protests. This support made the blockaders believe that their challenge to the authority of the Columbia administration was moral, necessary, and powerful. One blockader described this as being "part of something that was much larger than myself." Another suggested:

> One thing I believe now is that people in a grass-roots movement can actually have an impact, that we're not all completely helpless. I guess it was that sense of power that I didn't have before.

Polarization and Increased Commitment

Because the blockade was an unconventional attempt to gain political influence, the steering committee of CFSA was unable to predict how many would participate. For the same reason, they were unable to predict their opponent's reaction to their tactic. Based on the information they had on recent South African consulate and embassy protests, they assumed they would be arrested soon after the doors of Hamilton Hall were chained. As these expectations of a mostly symbolic arrest were communicated to the less politically experienced blockaders, a consensus developed that the blockade would be shortlived.

However, the administration did not order the arrest of the protesters. Instead, Columbia's president sent a letter to everyone at the university arguing that the students were "disruptive" and "coercive," and that they were trying to impose their will on the rest of the university. He suggested that "countless avenues of free speech" in the university community were open to them and that what they were doing was illegal, that divestment would probably hurt rather than help blacks in South Africa, and that the university was doing all it could to fight apartheid.

University officials began to videotape the protesters in order to prosecute them under university regulations on obstructing university buildings and disrupting university functions. They sent letters threatening suspension or expulsion to the members of the CFSA steering committee and a few others. Guarantees were given that those who reported for individual disciplinary hearings would be treated more leniently than those who did not. They also obtained a court order calling on participants in the blockade to cease and desist.

By threatening suspensions and expulsions, the administration had raised the stakes; the protesters felt much more threatened by these academic penalties than by symbolic arrests. There were other costs associated with participating in this protest, including dealing with the cold and freezing rain; missing classes, exams, and study time; and losing close relationships with non-blockaders. Ignoring these costs, the steering committee members who received letters refused to go to the disciplinary hearings, suggested that the administration was engaging in unfair selective prosecution, and reiterated their determination to remain in front of Hamilton Hall until the university divested.

Such actions were to be expected from the strongly committed CFSA steering committee. The surprise was that the less experienced majority of protesters also refused to be intimidated and remained on the blockade. They did so in part because of an example of self-sacrifice by one of their own. One of the politically inexperienced students, a senior with three weeks to go before graduation, received a letter threatening him with expulsion. Initially, he was scared:

> I was petrified, especially since Columbia has not been fun for me but rather painful. I really wanted to get out of here, and I was horrified by the thought that I would either have to come back to Columbia or go somewhere else and lose credits by transferring. My reaction was, "Why do they have to pick me? Why do I have to be the focal point of this whole thing?"

But he decided not to report for disciplinary action. He felt that he could not give in to his fears in the face of the sacrifices being made by the fasters and South African students.

> Listening to the commitment on the part of the steering committee people who had received letters made me feel bad that I even considered leaving the blockade. One other factor was the fasters, the fact that there were South Africans involved in it, and that these people had more on the line than I did. I felt like I could not let these people down. I also felt that I was a sort of representative of a lot of people on the blockade and I felt I could not set a precedent by leaving and backing down.

His example was extremely important for the maintenance of commitment by the other inexperienced blockaders:

> They threatened (the blockader) with expulsion. It was sobering in a way. But it helped bond us together. It was stupid to do that because it just made people more furious, and it made people more resolved to stay. We just said we're not going to let him be expelled. We're all going to stick together in this.

The protesters responded as a group to administration threats, not as isolated individuals. Individual concerns about disciplinary actions were now secondary; each blockader saw her or his welfare as tied to the group fate. Paradoxically, the potential for high personal costs became a reason for participation; protesters wanted to be part of an important and powerful movement and they did not want fellow activists to face the wrath of the authorities alone. The night the threat of arrest was assumed to be greatest, Easter Sunday, was also the one night out of 21 with the greatest number sleeping out on the blockade. Soon after this, 500 students signed a statement accepting personal responsibility for the blockade.

Collective Decision-Making and the End of the Blockade

Another group process which influenced participation in this protest was collective decision-making. Open-ended rap sessions among the blockaders, lasting up to four or five hours, were begun after administration representatives delivered the first disciplinary letters to the protesters. In all cases, a serious attempt was made to reach consensus among all those on the steps; votes were held on only a few occasions. One of the main questions was whether to continue the protest. This discussion was initiated by members of the CFSA steering committee because of their commitment to democratic decision-making, and because they understood that the blockaders would be more likely to continue the protest if they participated in a collective decision to do so. During the first two weeks of the protest, the consensus was to continue the blockade.

By the third week, though, some of the protesters began to feel that the protest should be ended. The sense of crisis had been dulled by the lack of action by the administration to back up their threats. It was now clear that there were no plans to call in the police to make arrests. As one blockader put it, the "university's policy of waiting it out was becoming effective." Also, an event can be news for only so long, and the image of Columbia students sitting on some steps became commonplace. Diminishing television and print coverage reduced the collective belief in the power of this particular tactic. As one protester suggested:

> It was during the third week that I started spending nights at home and coming up in the morning. During the last week I probably spent three nights out [on the steps] and four nights at home. During that third week a kind of mood of lethargy hit, and it became a chorelike atmosphere. There was a lot of feeling that it was kind of futile to stay out there.

In the face of declining participation, long and heated discussions were held about ending the protest. Proponents of continuing the action argued that protesters ought to honor their commitment to stay in front of the doors until Columbia divested. Those who advocated ending the protest argued that divestment was not imminent and that the blockade was no longer effective. As one protester put it:

> The blockade ended because a very thoughtful and carefully planned decision was made. It was a question of what we could do that would be most effective for divestment. We decided that the blockade had done a lot, but at this point other things would be better, seeing how the administration was willing to sit us out.

On the 25th of April, the blockade officially ended with a march into Harlem to a rally at a Baptist Church. Five months later, the Columbia trustees divested.

Survey Results

Participant observation of the protest as well as extended interviews with the protesters revealed that certain group processes—consciousness-raising, collective empowerment, polarization, and group decision-making—influenced recruitment to and motivated continuing participation in the blockade. Findings from the survey support this conclusion.[2]

One question on the survey asked the respondent to report on his or her level of involvement in the protest. Responses indicated that 18 percent completely avoided the demonstration, 44 percent stopped by out of curiosity, 20 percent participated in the rallies supporting the blockade or frequently joined the demonstration during the daytime, and 17 percent spent at least one night sleeping on the steps.

Table 1 shows a multiple regression analysis with responses to the participation question as the dependent variable and a variety of possible correlates of participation as independent variables. The resulting equation explains 59 percent of the

Table 1
Regression Between Level of Participation in the Blockade and Selected Independent Variables: Columbia University, 1985

Independent Variables	b	Beta
Conservative-Liberal Scale	.25	.32**
Support for Divestment X Effectiveness of Blockade	.09	.24**
Personal Expense Caused by Blockade Justified?	.10	.15*
Opinion of University President Declined	.18	.13*
Divestment Will Influence South African Government?	.17	.14*
Extent of Prior Participation in Divestment Movement	.32	.09
Membership in Campus Political Action Organization	.09	.04
Number of Campus Organization Memberships	–.01	–.01
First-Year Student	.05	.02
No Religious Affiliation	–.08	–.03
Constant	–.17	—

*$p<.05$ **$p<.01$
Note: $R^2 = .59$; N = 176.

variance in participation. The single most important predictor is being politically liberal or radical, indicating that general ideological predisposition, not just commitment to the specific cause, has an important impact on protest participation. This is consistent with the findings of Walsh and Warland (1983) and Mueller and Opp (1986).

Another important factor associated with participation is the interaction effect between support for Columbia's divestment of all stock in companies doing business in South Africa, and a belief that Columbia would divest as a result of the blockade.[3] This result indicates the importance of both consciousness-raising and collective empowerment processes in recruitment and commitment to protest; it shows that those who support the specific cause and believe in the power of the tactic to further that cause are likely to participate in a protest.

That participation is associated with a belief in the power of the collective tactic to further movement goals is given further support by the fact that those who felt that divestment would influence the policies of the South African government were more likely to join the movement. Finally, the equation shows an independent association of a declining opinion of the university president with participation, supporting the notion that a polarization process had an important effect on participation in the blockade.

A variety of other factors were entered in the equation to assess the propositions of rational choice and collective behavior theories. Those who felt that any personal expense or inconvenience suffered as a result of the blockade was justified were more likely to participate in the protest. In other words, participants were committed to the group cause and felt that personal costs suffered as a result of participation were justified. Other factors emphasized by resource mobilization theories of participation, such as prior participation in the divestment movement or in a political action group on campus, were not highly associated with joining the blockade. Propositions about the association between social marginality or a lack of values and recruitment to movements are not supported; being a first-year student, lacking a religious affiliation, and being a member of a small number of campus groups were not highly correlated with participation in the blockade.

Conclusion

Rational choice theories cannot explain why students joined and became committed to this protest action because group processes are not just the sum of individual preferences or predispositions. Such frameworks cannot easily account for why participants felt willing to accept the personal costs associated with this protest; it is contradictory to argue that students stayed on the blockade to enjoy the selective incentive of self-sacrifice. Recruitment and commitment to the blockade can only be understood through the analysis of how group discussions, empowerment, conflict, and decision-making led participants to a willingness to sacrifice self-interest in pursuit of a valued collective goal using a noninstitutional tactic.

Collective behavior theory is right about the importance of group-level processes in the mobilization of noninstitutional movements. But its proposition that protest originates in disorganized unrest certainly does not apply here. Years of well-organized activities by the CFSA were crucial in raising consciousness about the apartheid issue and on the need for noninstitutional means of influence to achieve divestment. The blockade itself was initiated only after two months of careful planning by the CFSA steering committee.

The blockaders were not just isolated individuals with preferences for divestment nor a set of confused, insecure people; rather, they were people who had been convinced by CFSA meetings that apartheid was evil, that divestment would help South African blacks, and that divestment could be achieved through protest. They joined the blockade on April 4th because it appeared to offer a powerful alternative to previously impotent demonstrations and because of the example of self-sacrificing CFSA leaders. The solidarity of the group increased after the administration's escalation of the conflict because group identification among the protesters was already strong enough so that they responded to the threat as a powerful group rather than as powerless individuals. Protesters remained at this long and risky protest partly because of the democratic decision-making processes used by the group.

This analysis of the 1985 Columbia University divestment protest indicates that useful theories of movement mobilization must include insights about how individual protesters are convinced by group-level processes to sacrifice themselves for the cause. This means asking new kinds of questions in movement research: What kinds of arguments in what kinds of settings convince people to support a political cause? Why do potential recruits decide that noninstitutional means of influence are justified and necessary? Under what circumstances is the example of leaders sacrificing for the cause likely to induce people to join a risky protest? Why do some tactics appear to offer a greater chance of success than others? Under what conditions do threats or actual repression by authorities create greater internal solidarity in a protest group? Under what conditions do threats or repression result in the demobilization of protest? What kinds of group decision-making processes are likely to convince people to continue to participate in a protest movement?

Generalizing from case studies is always difficult. Some aspects of student movements make them unusual, especially the ability of organizers to take advantage of the physical concentration of students on campuses. But the important impact of group processes on movement recruitment and commitment is not unique to the 1985 Columbia anti-apartheid movement. The development of solidarity based on a sense of collective power and polarization was also found in a Chicago community organization (Hirsch 1986). And these same group processes were crucial in the mobilization and development of the Southern civil rights movement of the 1950s and 1960s. Consciousness-raising occurred in black churches and colleges. The collective power of protest was evident to those who participated in bus boycotts, sit-ins, freedom rides, and in Freedom Summer. The movement relied heavily on the creation of polarized conflict between the white Southern segregationist elite and black protesters to recruit participants, to gain national media attention, and ultimately to force federal intervention to redress the social and political grievances of Southern blacks (McAdam 1982; Morris 1984). Finally, two of the major mobilizations in the 1960s student movement—the Berkeley Free Speech movement in

1964 and the Columbia conflict in 1968—developed in a manner similar to the 1985 divestment movement (Heirich 1970; Avorn 1968).

Notes

1. I have elsewhere (1989) labelled this theoretical tradition "solidarity theory." Perrow (1979) calls those who emphasize the development of movement solidarity "resource mobilization I" theorists, but this term is better reserved for theories that emphasize the similarities between institutional and noninstitutional politics and are sympathetic to rational choice perspectives. Others working in this tradition have described it as "political process theory" (McAdam 1982), but until recently (McAdam 1986; 1988b) this theory has generally emphasized macro movement processes and ignored micromobilization. The best approach to further theoretical development in the field of social movements is to elaborate the connections between a macro political process theory and a theory of micromobilization like the one described here.

2. A single cross-sectional survey cannot assess the importance of group processes. If one finds a political attitude to be highly correlated with participation in the blockade, how does one know whether the attitude caused participation or participation caused the attitude? This demonstrates the need for the qualitative methods of participant observation and extended interviews. Analysts should do baseline surveys to assess attitudes before a movement begins, as some analysts have done (Klandermans 1984a; Klandermans and Oegema 1987; McAdam 1986; 1988b). But as Walsh and Warland (1983) have pointed out, it is often difficult to predict the need for such baseline surveys before the outbreak of protest.

3. Klandermans' work (1984a) inspired the use of an interaction term. Running the equation with the "support for divestment" question substituted for the interaction term results in an equation that explains 57 percent of the variance in participation. A similar result is obtained if only the question about whether Columbia would divest as a result of the blockade is included. If both questions are included and the interaction term omitted, the percentage of variance explained is 58 percent. In other words, the percent of variance explained is higher in the equation with only the interaction effect than with the main effects entered separately or together. ✦

24

Social Organization and Pathways to Commitment: Types of Communal Groups, Rational Choice Theory, and the Kanter Thesis

John R. Hall

Functionalist theory holds that, for a social system to persist, institutional arrangements have to draw individuals into social roles. Rosabeth Kanter (1968, 1972) elaborated this theory by proposing commitment as the link by which individual biographies and group objectives become aligned. For a sample of 30 19th-century American communal groups, Kanter showed that various mechanisms promoting commitment tended to be employed more often by successful groups than by unsuccessful ones. This finding does not imply that all commitment mechanisms are equally viable in all types of groups. Questions remain about whether (and how) overarching cultural patterns of social organization affect groups' capacities to resolve problems of commitment. The present study uses quantitative ideal-type analysis, factor analysis, and a path model to test a theory about relationships between type of social organization, commitment, and success in communal groups. The results, discussed in terms of rational choice theory, indicate two things. First, not all types of groups have the same capacities to employ commitment mechanisms. Second, successful groups may achieve commitment through cultural structures that shape the relationship between individual and group in fundamentally different ways.

The Commitment Thesis and Social Groups

The connection between individuals' actions and the maintenance of a social order has been an enduring issue of social theory (Alexander 1982; Coleman 1986; Collins 1986). Kanter's theory of commitment elaborates Talcott Parsons' (1951; Parsons and Shils 1951) functionalist approach to the problem by positing commitment as the central process by which the personality system and the social system become articulated. For Kanter, there are three basic problems of commitment: (1) *continuance,* involving perceptions that individual interests are sustained by participation; (2) *cohesion,* or individuals' affective solidarity with a group; and (3) *control,* the exercise of group authority with moral force, without untoward domination. For each of these commitment problems, social organization affects individuals by both *dissociative processes,* which "free the personality system from other commitments," and *associative processes,* which "attach the personality to the current object of commitment" (Kanter 1968, p. 504). The central hypothesis is that "(s)ystems with all three kinds of commitment, with total commitment, should be more successful in their maintenance than those without" (Kanter 1968, p. 501).

Kanter (1968, p. 500) noted that different types of social systems (e.g., a corporation, a family) may vary in the centrality of one or another commitment problem, but her empirical research on communal groups does not pursue this line of analysis. Instead, it shows that an array of *commitment mechanisms* (specific practices held to build commitment, e.g., eating meals communally) are found more frequently among groups that succeeded, i.e., survived for 25 years. Left unanswered is the question of whether different communal groups face distinctive commitment problems. Nor is it evident whether various commitment mechanisms are mutually independent, either in the pattern of mechanisms adopted in a group or in the distribution of patterns from group to group. Previous studies (Olson 1968; Stephan and Stephan 1973; Hechter 1978, 1983, 1987; Hougland and Wood 1980; Morris and Steers 1980; Knoke 1981) suggested that basic aspects of group structure constrain the possibilities of solidarity. But it is still necessary to systematically theorize the relationships between types of groups, processes of commitment, and group viability. Such an agenda should be pursued on a wide range of organizations, but to permit comparison, I reanalyze Kanter's data on 19th-century communal groups. First I describe five types of communal groups. This typology in turn suggests formal propositions about communal groups' potentialities for resolving problems of commitment. These propositions are tested on Kanter's sample by factor analysis and path analysis.

Ideal Types of Communal Groups and Commitment

Utopian communal groups may be defined as groups of three or more individuals, some of whom are unrelated by blood or marriage, who live in a single household or interrelated set of households and engage in attempts at value achievement not available in society-at-large. This definition does not yet delineate a sociologically coherent pattern of action (cf. Weber [1922] 1977, p. 20). In fact, communal groups differ radically from one another, and understanding their sociological dynamics requires a way of distinguishing their meaningful differences. For this purpose, I draw on a systematic typology based on Karl Mannheim's theory of utopias, which I have used previously to study modern American communal social-movement organizations (Hall 1978, 1987). The typology identifies ideal types in terms of two phenomenological dimensions: (1) orientations toward time; and (2) modes of social enactment in relation to the symbolic construction of reality (see Table 1). Research on contemporary communal groups (Hall 1978, pp. 200-208) showed that the types could be further specified along social and political dimensions. These specified types represent alternative ideal, but objectively possible, overall patterns of communal life. The question of whether these patterns are associated with alternative processes of commitment that affect group viability will be the standard for judging whether the typology is a useful one in the present context (cf. Weber [1922] 1977, p. 213).

There are five ideal types. In the frame of the "natural attitude" in which the world as experienced is taken for granted as real (Schutz [1933] 1967), *communes* are relatively individualistic, pluralistic, and egalitarian associations of family-like solidarity that lack goals of utopian perfection, or even institutional longevity. Second, among types involving a "produced" or socially legitimated symbolic construction of reality, *otherworldly sects* prophesy the apocalyptic end of time in a society at large and gather together true believers to create post-apocalyptic "timeless" heavens on earth separated from the "evils" of this world. The rationalistic type, the *intentional association*, promotes principles of pluralism, individual freedom, equality, and justice—all based on the diachronic treatment of time as a commodity, such that the clock coordinates social action. On the other hand, the *community* embraces an egalitarian solidarity and shared ideology of the "many who act as one," temporally mediated through communion in the "here and now." Third, in the "transcendental" mode of social enactment, a natural or produced enactment is suspended in favor of the *ecstatic association*—a group dedicated not to reformation through doctrine, philosophy or rational scheme, but to "breaking out" of ordinary reality by orgiastic celebration or meditation. (On the typology, see also Appendix, section 1.)

How do the different types of communal groups resolve problems of commitment? This question can be addressed for each of Kanter's three commitment problems—continuance, cohesion, and control—in relation to both "dissociative" processes (which free individuals from nongroup commitments) and "associative" processes (which bind individuals to the group). Empirical cases will vary, but the consequences of each type can be explored in strictly theoretical terms (cf. Roth 1971, p. 126). As Table 2 indicates, we may expect certain types of groups to have much greater capacity than others for resolving commitment problems. On theoretical grounds, the commune lacks any substantial capacity to resolve

Table 1
Typology of Communal Groups

Mode of Social Enactment	Mode of Organizing Time:		
	Diachronic	Synchronic	Apocalyptic
Natural		Commune	
Produced	Intentional Association	Community	Other-Worldly Sect
Transcendental		Ecstatic Association	

Note: Table available from Hall 1978, p. 202.

Table 2
Theorized Capacities of Types of Communal Groups to Resolve Commitment Problems

Type of Group	Continuance		Cohesion		Control		Total
	Sacrifice	Investment	Renunciation	Communion	Mortification	Surrender	
	(D)	(A)	(D)	(A)	(D)	(A)	
Commune	–	–	–	+/–	–	–	7
Intentional Association	–	+/–	–	–	–	+/–	8
Ecstatic Association	+/–	+/–	+/–	+/–	–	+/–	11
Community	+/–	+	+/–	+	+/–	+/–	14
Other-Worldly Sect	+	+	+	+	+	+	18

Note: D: dissociative process of commitment; A: associative process of commitment (Kanter 1968, p. 504). – = 1 = low, +/– = 2 = moderate or indeterminate, + = 3 = high capacity to resolve commitment problem.

mune lacks any substantial capacity to resolve commitment problems. In a pluralistic "natural enactment" of putatively equal, "multiple realities," no instituted basis exists for establishing mechanisms of continuance or control, and the problem of cohesion is resolved, at best, if group participants can sustain family-like communion. This is not an easy trick for individuals who have not nurtured family ties over a long period of time (cf. Abrams and McCulloch 1976, p. 188).

The intentional association has little better chance of success, but for different reasons. Definitionally, the commune involves what Weber termed a "communal" relationship, in which "the orientation of social action is based on a subjective feeling of the parties, whether affectual or traditional, that they belong together." On the other hand, Weber ([1922] 1977, pp. 40–41) viewed "associative" relationships as "based on a rationally motivated adjustment of interests or a similarly motivated agreement, whether the basis be absolute values or reasons of expediency." In the intentional association, commitment is bound up in associative processes tied to rationally calculative investment and individuals' limited "surrender" to social control within the framework of agreed-upon goals. This "organic solidarity" (Durkheim [1893] 1933) does not lend itself to resolving broader problems of group cohesion, and it can offer its participants no compelling justification for undergoing mortification in submission to social control.

Like the intentional association, the ecstatic association is based on associative rather than communal relationships. But there is a crucial difference: in the ecstatic association, associative relationships involve an absolute value—the pursuit of transcendence—which requires significant face-to-face interaction. Thus, the ecstatic association may be postulated to engender more communion than the intentional association, where the clock coordinates individuals often disjoined in time and space. In addition, pursuit of transcendence requires a somewhat greater renunciation of extra-group ties. Still, because the value-rational purpose of transcendence, not the group itself, is paramount, cohesion derives only from a shared goal, and its resolution is incomplete. Similarly, because association is the basis of group life, surrender to "mystagogic" authority does not necessarily require surrender in other matters, and submission to social control does not inherently extend to mortification. Finally, in the quest for transcendence, the problem of continuance may well be resolved, not through emergence of a relatively stable set of participants, but through the capacity of an inner circle to recruit a succession of other persons who pass through the group (cf. Troeltsch 1932, p. 378).

Both the community and the other-worldly sect have substantially greater capacities than other groups to resolve problems of commitment. As types, the two are similar: the community is established on a totally communal basis, which nevertheless does not require renunciation of the historical world or individuals' previous connections to it. For the other-worldly sect, an apocalyptic time does not necessarily increase the communion founded in the here and now of the community, nor can it command greater than the total investment required of the community's participants. But an apocalyptic time legitimates prophets who call on their followers to make special sacrifices, to renounce the "evils" of this world and submit to the total social control of the group, which acts to fulfill God's will on Earth. In this light, the imposition of sexual mores, ascetic practices, mutual criticism, and other commitment mechanisms seems especially tenable in the otherworldly sect. Compared to the intentional association or the commune, the community has a substantial basis for resolving all three problems of commitment, but the other-worldly sect resolves the problem of total commitment.

Some types of groups face especially formidable problems of commitment, whereas others seem advantageously positioned organizationally to solve commitment problems. If the commitment mechanisms described by Kanter are aspects of social organization, comparative ideal type and case analysis offers a frame for Kanter's variable analysis. What is the significance of such a seemingly technical shift in method? A null hypothesis would suggest that problems of commitment are basically the same for all communal groups, that tendencies to resolve commitment problems by employing the diverse commitment mechanisms are independently variable (cf. Kanter 1968, p. 500), and that comparative analysis across types of groups will add no new information. My hypothesis, in contrast, is this: since alternative types of communal groups have unequal capacities to resolve problems of commitment, some groups—notably ones approximating the other-worldly sect and to a lesser degree the community—are more likely to be successful than others. If communal groups cluster according to ideal type with respect to their "mixes" of commitment mechanisms, it will tend to substantiate my theoretical analysis, which suggests that commitment-building processes represent broad alternative pathways structured by overarching patterns of social organization.

Methodology

What are the empirical relationships between communal groups, their commitment processes, and their success? I addressed this question by reanalyzing Kanter's sample of groups with the following overall strategy. First, I specified the ideal types of communal groups in terms of dummy variables that reflect key theoretical dimensions of variation among them. I then used the same dummy variables to measure the degree to which each of the groups in the sample approximated each of the ideal types. Second, I treated Kanter's nominal level measurements of commitment mechanisms in communal groups as interval level

dummy variables. I subjected a matrix of commitment-mechanism variables to R-type factor analysis to reduce the matrix to a set of empirical "commitment factors," for which I could calculate factor scores for each communal group. Then I used the two sets of measures—group approximations to ideal types and group commitment-factor scores—along with a measure of group success in multiple regression and path analysis.

The Sample

Included in the analysis are the 30 19th-century American communal groups that Kanter studied. Kanter (1968, p. 503) identified groups for which at least two independent sources of information were available and constructed the sample on a purposive, non-random basis. Practically all groups that survived for more than 25 years were included; the sample's more short-lived groups represent all major social movements and 19th-century time periods. Since Kanter's sample is not random, I use statistical procedures only for descriptive, rather than inferential, purposes. Nevertheless, because a wide range of groups is included, descriptive statistical analysis can reveal something generally about processes of commitment, their empirical bases, and effects. This is the assumption on which Kanter's original study is based, and much quantitative research depends on the same assumption (Haas 1982).

Measurement

I measured communal group success by the same dummy variable used by Kanter (1972, p. 245): "survival for at least twenty-five years, the sociological definition of a generation." By this criterion, 21 groups, lasting from 6 months to 15 years, failed, while 9 groups, surviving from 33 to 184 years, succeeded (Kanter 1972, pp. 246-48).[1] Measuring group approximations to ideal types and group commitment-factor scores involved more elaborate procedures.

Communal Group Approximations to Ideal Types. The five ideal types of communal groups were theoretically specified with six dichotomous variables. These included four variables reflecting the two dimensions (orientation to time and mode of social enactment) by which the typology of communal groups was generated and two variables describing basic aspects of social relationships (egalitarianism and pluralism) that further specified the original typology (Hall 1978, pp. 200-208) (see Appendix, section 2). The ap-

Table 3
Specification of Ideal Types of Communal Groups

		Ideal Type			
Dichotomous Variable	Commune	Intentional Association	Community	Other-Worldly Sect	Ecstatic Association
Temporal Mode					
1. Diachronic		Yes			
Synchronic[a]	Yes		Yes		Yes
2. Apocalyptic		Yes		Yes	
Enactment Mode					
Natural[a]	Yes				
3. Produced		Yes	Yes	Yes	
4. Transcendental					Yes
Social Relations					
5. Egalitarianism	Yes	Yes	Yes		
6. Pluralism	Yes	Yes			

[a]Redundant variable omitted in analysis.

empirical communal group to each ideal type of group was specified in terms of the same six vari-ables (see Appendix, section 3). In other words, I compared the observed characteristics of each

Table 4
Dichotomous Variable Values and G Indices of Agreement of Communal Groups With Ideal Types

Nineteenth Century Group	Dichotomous Variables	G Index With Ideal Types				
		Commune	Intentional Association	Community	Other-Worldly Sect	Ecstatic Association
1. Zoar	--+-+-	.333	.333	1.000	.333	.333
2. Amana	--+---	.000	.000	.667	.667	.667
3. North American Phalanx	+-+-++	.333	1.000	.333	-.333	-.333
4. New Harmony	+-+-++	.333	1.000	.333	-.333	-.333
5. Saint Nazianz	--+-+-	.333	.333	1.000	.333	.333
6. Yellow Springs	----++	1.000	.333	.333	-.333	-.333
7. Kendal	+-+-++	.333	1.000	.333	-.333	-.333
8. Bishop Hill	-++-+-	.000	.000	.667	.667	.000
9. Harmony Society	-++-+-	.000	.000	.667	.667	.000
10. Oneida	-++-+-	.000	.000	.667	.667	.000
11. Hopedale	+-+-+-	.000	.000	.667	.667	.000
12. Northampton	+---++	.667	.667	.000	.000	-.667
13. Wisconsin Phalanx	+-+-++	.333	1.000	.333	-.333	-.333
14. Shakers	-++---	-.333	-.333	.333	1.000	.333
15. Fruitlands	--+++-	.000	.000	.667	.000	.667
16. Brook Farm	+-+-++	.333	1.000	.333	-.333	-.333
17. Preparation	------	.333	-.333	.333	.333	.333
18. Jasper Colony	--+-+-	.333	.333	1.000	.333	.333
19. Blue Spring	--+-++	.667	.667	.667	.000	.000
20. Iowa Pioneer Phalanx	--+-++	.667	.667	.667	.000	.000
21. Order of Enoch	-++-+-	.000	.000	.667	.667	.000
22. Modern Times	+-+-++	.333	1.000	.333	-.333	-.333
23. Oberlin	--+-+-	.333	.333	1.000	-.333	-.333
24. Communia	+-+-++	.333	1.000	.333	-.333	-.333
25. Snowhill	-++-+-	.000	.000	.667	.667	.000
26. Bethel and Aurora	--+-+-	.333	.333	1.000	.333	.333
27. Skaneateles	----++	1.000	.333	.333	-.333	-.333
28. Nashoba	+-+---	-.333	.333	.333	.333	.333
29. Jerusalem	--+---	.000	.000	.667	.667	.667
30. Utopia	+-+-++	.333	1.000	.333	-.333	-.333

Note: Dichotomous variable values for each group are listed in order corresponding to Table 3.

group to the theoretical characteristics of each ideal type (see Table 4). This was done on an additive linear scale using the G Index of Agreement (Holley and Guilford 1964), a coefficient that has the properties of, and may be treated as, an interval-level correlation coefficient.[2] With the G Index, a greater number of shared characteristics between a group and an ideal type is reflected in a higher positive coefficient of correlation. Note that ideal types and groups as cases, not variables, are correlated with each other.

Commitment Factors. Forty-seven of Kanter's original commitment-mechanism variables that had substantial amounts of missing data were eliminated from the analysis. I then applied an R-type oblique-factor analytic procedure to the remaining matrix of 46 commitment-mechanism variables. There was considerably less than random variance among these variables, or, to put it differently, certain variables were practically redundant with one another. Indeed, the factor space spanned by these variables was only 13; that is, the factor analysis essentially involved a reduction of the data matrix that produced 13 empirically derived, but theoretically interpretable commitment factors, which together reflect 100 percent of the variance in the matrix of 46 commitment variables. In this solution, none of the factors is correlated with another at a level of greater than +/".27. Table 5 lists the factors, names them, and indicates commitment-mechanism variables that were highly loaded on the factors in the factor-pattern matrix (cf. Rummel 1976, p. 399-401). Though the empirical-commitment factors sometimes combine more than one dimension of commitment theorized by Kanter, the important point is that each process of commitment continues to be represented after reduction of the 46-variable commitment-mechanism matrix to a smaller matrix of commitment factors reflecting its total variance. For each of the factors, commitment-factor scores of each communal group were calculated by the complete estimation method and used in subsequent analysis to reflect the groups' commitment processes (see Appendix, section 4).

Method of Analysis

Measurement procedures yielded three kinds of variables, with values for each communal group: (1) the G Index degree of approximation to each ideal type; (2) commitment-factor scores on each of 13 factors; and (3) a dichotomous measure of success (Hall 1988). Given these variables, evaluation of the study's hypotheses was

Table 5
Commitment Factors and Commitment–Mechanism Variables With Factor Pattern Loadings

Factor Name	Commitment Mechanisms With Highest Loadings
1. Privileged Leader	leadership immunities [.803]; special address for leaders [.788]; leadership prerogatives [.724]; clothing owned by the community [.600]
2. Ethnicity	common ethnic background [–.948]; foreign language spoken [–.936]
3. Social Communalism	communal dining halls [.762]; land owned by community [.636]
4. Financial Contribution	financial contribution for admission [.719]
5. Religious Colony	community derived from prior organization or group [.824]; outside perceived as evil and wicked [.692]; common religious background [.609]
6. Oligarchy	top leaders were founders or named by predecessors [–.699]
7. Spiritual Hierarchy	formally structured deference to those of higher moral status [.874]; members distinguished on moral grounds [.838]
8. Ideological Order	furniture, tools, equipment owned by community [.513]; personal conduct rules [.512]; commitment to ideology required [.466]; clothing and personal effects owned by community [.433]; ideology a complete, elaborated philosophical system [.403]
9. Religious Communalism	demands legitimated by reference to a higher principle [.859]; no charge for community services [.755]
10. Non–Monogamy	free love or complex marriage [.652]
11. Acquaintance	prior acquaintance of members [.733]
12. Confession	regular confession [.713]; confession on joining [.684]; slang, jargon, other special terms [.675]
13. Homogeneity	uniform style of dress [–.700]

Note: All commitment variables with loadings of +/–.600 or greater are listed in order of decreasing magnitude, with all loadings of +/–.400 or greater listed for factors otherwise uninterpretable. To avoid the confusion of double-negatives, factors 2, 6 and 13 were named in relation to the highly loaded negative variables, and the signs associated with these factors were reversed in subsequent tables. This consistent labeling convention was introduced after the fact and had no effect on statistical analyses.

relatively straightforward. For Kanter's hypothesis that commitment-building mechanisms have a positive effect on group success, the commitment factors were included in a multiple-regression analysis with success as a criterion variable.

My hypothesis holds that alternative types of groups have different propensities to employ commitment mechanisms, and thereby succeed or fail. Since this hypothesis argues that overarching types of social organization are causally prior to commitment factors, I evaluated the hypothesis in a two-stage path-analytic model, with success as the dependent variable regressed on all other variables and commitment factors regressed on group approximations to ideal types. I then evaluated a series of stepwise regression equations. A commitment factor was retained for the path model if it contributed greater than 5 percent additional variance explained when included in a stepwise multiple regression of all commitment factors, with success as the dependent variable. On this basis, four commitment factors—ethnicity, spiritual hierarchy, confession, and homogeneity—were retained. The same 5 percent criterion was applied in stepwise multiple regressions including all ideal-type approximation variables, with each of the four selected commitment factors as dependent variables. Two ideal types—the community and the other-worldly sect—met the criterion for inclusion in subsequent analysis. Multiple-regression equations and standardized beta weights were calculated for a just-identified two-stage path model with the retained variables (Land 1969, p. 34) to determine the relative significance and causal interrelations among approximations to ideal types of communal groups, commitment factors, and success.

Social Structure, Commitment and Group Persistence

My analysis supports Kanter's theory that resolution of commitment problems contributes to group success, and it establishes the relative importance of the commitment factors. Beyond Kanter's thesis, my hypothesis gains strong support: the prevalence of particular commitment-producing strategies seems to derive in part from basic differences in social organization. Certain types of communal groups—the community and, especially, the other-worldly sect—are relatively successful.

Commitment and Success

Four commitment factors—ethnicity, spiritual hierarchy, confession, and homogeneity—explain 67.1 percent of the variance in group success (see Table 6). Addition of any of the nine other commitment factors to the equation adds less than 5 percent to the variance explained. Possibly, some of the nine less significant factors reflect processes that resolve commitment problems in one group or another, while failing to differentiate the sample as a whole. But in terms of the entire sample, only the four major commitment factors are consistently decisive. Each relates to the theory of commitment that Kanter (1968, p. 501) described. Two—ethnicity and homogeneity—are tied to the commitment problem of cohesion, and two—confession and spiritual hierarchy—to that of social control.

For social cohesion, ethnicity is a historically given attribute of group composition that promotes an associative commitment process of communion, grounding the collective feeling, as Weber put it, of belonging together. An "ethnic

Table 6 Multiple Regression of Commitment Factors With Success		
Commitment Factor	Partial Correlation	Standardized Beta With Success
Ethnicity	.601	.447
Spiritual Hierarchy	.515	.358
Confession	.425	.295
Homogeneity	.460	.320
Multiple R	.819	
R^2	.671	

boundary" (Barth 1969) differentiates group members from other individuals, establishing the grounds for deriving identity, status, and rewards from participation. The second important factor tied to social cohesion—homogeneity—reflects a dissociative commitment process, renunciation of individualism, marked by the factor's highly loaded variable, a uniform style of dress.

The other two commitment factors strongly correlated with group success—confession and spiritual hierarchy—relate to the problem of social control. Confession, tied to the *dissociative* process of mortification, inhibits individuals from covertly maintaining attitudes and practices that would be considered alien. It subjects the thoughts and actions of individuals to public scrutiny. The mortification of individuals by this process is considerable: the self is sacrificed to a public cognitive reality through organized ritual action. The second social-control commitment factor—spiritual hierarchy—seems more closely linked to the *associative* commitment process of surrender (or transcendence [Kanter 1972]): members are distinguished on moral grounds, and those of higher moral status receive deference.

If a spiritual hierarchy represents surrender (Kanter originally classified it as mortification), the four commitment factors that best predict group success represent dissociative and associative processes of cohesion and social control, the commitment problems that Kanter (1968, p. 501) suggested are of a higher order than the problem of continuance. Continuance commitment processes—individual sacrifice and investment—may be necessary, but they do not seem sufficient to establish a group on a successful basis.

Considering all commitment factors in one regression equation consolidates Kanter's separate measurements of commitment mechanisms in a way that more directly tests her original theoretical formulation concerning the total problem of commitment. Commitment does seem to involve analytically distinct processes that are functionally necessary for group success. Among

19th-century communal groups, these processes are parsimoniously summarized by four commitment factors: homogeneity and ethnicity as social cohesion, and confession and spiritual hierarchy as social control.

Types of Communal Groups, Commitment, and Success

The question remains: do alternative types of communal groups possess differential capacities for resolving commitment problems measured by the four major commitment factors associated with success? This question can be addressed by examining a path model constructed from (1) beta weights of the two ideal-type approximation variables when each of the four major commitment factors is used as a dependent variable; and (2) beta weights of group ideal-type approximation variables and commitment factors as independent variables when success is used as a dependent variable. The model (see Table 7) lends support to the hypothesis of Table 2 that the other-worldly sect and, to a lesser degree, the community have stronger capacities than other types of groups for resolving commitment problems.

The community and the other-worldly sect as types of communal groups account for a little more than 15 percent of the variance in commitment processes of homogeneity, ethnicity, and

Table 7
Multiple Regressions for Path Model of Communal Group Success

	Independent Variable	Partial Correlation	Standardized Beta With Dependent Variable	Multiple R	R^2
Dependent Variable					
Homogeneity	Community	−.257	−.278		
[Renunciation]	Other-Worldly Sect	.410	.471		
				.412	.170
Ethnicity	Community	.277	.298		
[Communion]	Other-Worldly Sect	.192	.202		
				.435	.189
Confession	Community	−.065	−.069		
[Mortification]	Other-Worldly Sect	.377	.428		
				.399	.159
Spiritual Hierarchy	Community	−.412	−.344		
[Surrender]	Other-Worldly Sect	.748	.857		
				.750	.562
Success	Community	.418	.316		
	Other-Worldly Sect	−.106	−.116		
	Homogeneity	.495	.356		
	Ethnicity	.510	.368		
	Confession	.445	.284		
	Spiritual Hierarchy	.444	.413		
				.858	.737

confession, and a little more than half of the variance in spiritual hierarchy, but the pattern is not the same for the two types. Approximation of a group to the other-worldly sect as a type strongly promotes homogeneity, whereas approximation to the community tends a bit more toward encouraging heterogeneity. Similarly, the otherworldly sect tends to employ confession as a vehicle of mortification, whereas whether a group approximates the community as a type says very little about its tendency to employ confession mechanisms. Further, the other-worldly sect very strongly favors spiritual hierarchy, whereas the community has a rather strong tendency in the opposite direction. Only with respect to the commitment process of communion is the community notably associated with a factor, ethnicity, that is decisive in contributing to the persistence of communal groups. The other-worldly sect is associated with all four commitment factors and with one of them, the existence of a spiritual hierarchy, quite strongly.

In turn, when both the approximations of groups to the two ideal types and the commitment factor scores are included as independent variables in a multiple regression with success as the dependent variable, the existence of spiritual hierarchy is the best single predictor, followed in order of beta-weight magnitude by ethnicity and homogeneity. Combining multiple-regression analyses using the two kinds of dependent variables, commitment factors and success, yields a comprehensive just-identified path model (i.e., including all beta weights given in Table 7). The total causal path of each ideal type to success may be calculated as its direct path (i.e., standardized beta weight) to success plus the sum of all indirect paths to success (namely, the path from a type to a commitment factor times the commitment factor's path to success). The total causal path to success of the community as an ideal type is .165, while that of the other-worldly sect is .434. Moreover, the strongest single basis to predict the success of the community is by the direct path, that is, by aspects of the community unrelated to the commitment factors in the model. As a type, the community is negatively associated with all of the commitment factors aside from ethnicity, and ethnicity represents a preexisting fact of group composition that grounds commitment, rather than an adopted strategy. By contrast, communal groups that approximate the other-worldly sect are more likely than communities to be successful, and this tendency results from the other-worldly sect's capacity to involve all four commitment factors that, taken together, are strongly associated with group success.

Two Pathways to Commitment

Kanter (1968, p. 504) suggested that, in theory, there might be functionally equivalent ways in which commitment problems are resolved. My analysis shows distinctive causal pathways of commitment at work in the two successful types of communal groups—the community and the other-worldly sect. Insofar as the community's success depends on processes measured by the four major commitment factors, commitment of members is basically grounded in the process of communion, through ethnicity. Apparently, ethnicity grounds formation of a boundaried status group, the social and economic benefits of which are restricted to members (Weber [1922] 1977, p. 387; Barth 1979). But ethnicity also seems to limit the capacity of a group to invoke other commitment-building processes associated with success. As Weber ([1922] 1977, p. 391) observed, "The sense of ethnic honor is a specific honor of the masses, for it is accessible to anybody who belongs to the subjectively believed community of descent." As a form of solidarity based on the "lowest common denominator" (Simmel [1912] 1950) of a cultural marker, ethnicity would tend to rule out requirements that compel conformity of participants on bases narrower than the group boundary badges of membership. In other words, communion is sustained by the "leveling" sentiment of ethnicity, which in turn delimits the extent to which social control can be established in a spiritual hierarchy and confession. The community thus resolves or fails to resolve commitment problems largely on the basis of the communion flowing from ethnic solidarity.

How then does the community deal with the problem of social control? More specifically, how does the community resolve the "free-rider" problem (Olson 1968) of individuals deriving benefits from a public good without contributing to its maintenance? We have seen that the egalitarian ethos of the community does not lend itself to emphasis on hierarchy. Given this limit on a potent basis of social control, free-riders would seem to pose a significant threat to a collective economy and shared work ethic (as indeed happened in groups like Robert Owen's New Harmony). In the absence of a spiritual hierarchy, monitoring of compliance to group requirements cannot so easily follow the typical route (Hechter 1987), in which "principals" with the highest stakes in a group enforce the relevant conformity of others in work, consumption, and social life. But, employing Hechter's framework, it can be argued that an alternative regimen of monitoring can be instituted in the community, such that the need for hierarchical social control is lessened. Given the "mass" or egalitarian basis of the community, each participant can in principle claim equal material and social benefits. On this basis, all members have at least some interest in monitoring others to protect their own benefits. These diffuse interests in monitoring are probably not so pronounced as those of a narrower set of presumably more privileged principals in a less egalitarian group. But diffuse monitoring interests among the mass of participants may make monitoring, and thus social control, more pervasive group processes that effectively permeate all social strata of the group.

The circumstances of the other-worldly sect are quite different. They derive from the call away from this world, to establish a "heaven-on-earth" of the "elect." Independently of any putatively ethnic basis of communion, the capacity to promote social cohesion by enforcing the renunciation of significant extra-group ties may be derived from effective social control. Here, the other-worldly sect is better positioned than the community. If the members of an other-worldly sect recognize the legitimacy of their group's prophecy, the principle of a spiritual hierarchy is not difficult to establish. Experimental laboratory research (Marwell and Ames 1979) suggests that investment in a public good most likely occurs in small, unequal groups. In a parallel way, a spiritual hierarchy in the other-worldly sect is based on the principals' moral standards, which negatively assess individuals who act in ways perceived to threaten the material and social enterprise and reward individuals who comply with group expectations. This distribution and denial of religious benefits represents what Weber ([1922] 1977, p. 54) called the "psychic coercion" of "hierocratic domination." For it to succeed, the individual must abandon personal value standards and embrace the socially legitimated standards that define grounds of spiritual deference. In this light, confession and a spiritual hierarchy are two sides

of group social control. A spiritual hierarchy identifies principals charged with monitoring relevant conduct and legitimates group standards they use to confer rewards and punishments. Ritualized confession in turn offers one basis on which the relatively privileged principals enact social control, i.e., by monitoring individual commitment to group values and behavioral requirements.

Yet if social control is the strong suit of the other-worldly sect, cohesion remains an awkward problem. The very principle of spiritual hierarchy contravenes ethnicity as a basis of communion, for the group is formed from the elect. The other-worldly sect is thus antagonistic to the leveling involved in mass participation. Under such conditions, social cohesion must be promoted on another basis than ethnicity. One possible avenue invokes the asceticism involved in the self-sacrifice to a transcendent religious cause as a basis of homogeneity, for example, through the wearing of uniforms. Thus, homogeneity in the other-worldly sect is a *dissociative* process of social cohesion that can substitute for a less than complete *associative* process of cohesion. Over the long run, enforcement of homogeneity through such "outer" cultural markers can promote the cohesion of surrogate ethnicity.

Conclusion

Each of the 19th-century communal groups studied by Kanter has a distinctive cultural structure of social organization that forms a more or less consistent basis of meaningful group life. The differences between their social organization seem substantial enough that alternative types of communal groups cannot be considered equivalent social systems having, in principle, equal chances of resolving the various functional problems of commitment. To the contrary, groups that approximate one or another ideal type had different historical trajectories that constrained or enhanced their ability to resolve problems of commitment. Groups that approximate the commune and the intentional association—the Owenist groups, the Fourierist phalanxes, groups founded on personal friendship, and a smattering of anarchist and socialist endeavors—do not seem to have been capable, on average, of resolving such problems, and they were short-lived. Given that few groups in the sample approximate the ecstatic association as a type, we can say nothing empirically about commitment in such groups. The question might more fruitfully be posed for recent countercultural groups, studied most comprehensively by Zablocki (1980).

Unlike the unsuccessful American communal groups of the 19th-century, the ones that persisted at least 25 years were religious social-movement organizations. Some were religious communities of colonization fleeing persecution in Europe, often interpreting their migrations in apocalyptic terms. Others were native American religious movements, sometimes, like the Mormons, as apocalyptic as the European ones. Whether immigrant or native, the groups mirrored the classic ideal types of church and sect formulated by Troeltsch (1932) and typologically delineated by Weber (1977, p. 1164). In groups approximating the community, on the one hand, ethnicity, community, and religion were but different facets of a "leveling" church-like organization where the blessings of salvation were in principle available to all. Though such groups were always religious, religion did not always dominate group life; sturdy faith, rather than explicit theology or extensive religious organization, was the order of the day. On the other hand, in the other-worldly sects among the 19th-century groups (and, as Troeltsch and Weber suggested, in sects in general), a regimen based on a clearly delineated spiritual revelation was strictly maintained. Participants' commitment was enhanced through procedures of confession that discerned their qualification to live and work in a community of the elect set apart from an alien and evil world.

This study suggests two distinctive pathways of commitment deriving from alternative cultural structures of social organization, that of the community, keyed to social cohesion via ethnicity, and that of the other-worldly sect, directed to social control through hierocratic domination. Ethnicity and religion long have been recognized as the important sources of communal group persistence. I argue that we can explain these patterns by identifying a pathway of commitment attached to each source of persistence. In future research, it remains to be seen whether the diffuse and hierarchical monitoring explanations attached to the two pathways have wider application. In general, the study of the two pathways in other contexts and the construction of similar models may offer a useful basis for tying rational choice explanations to patterns of social structure. In the study of organizational commitment, the identification of

pathways offers a foundation for further research. The two pathways are distinctive and even logically incompatible, but they are not necessarily mutually exclusive. To the contrary, it may be that when organizations combine ethnicity and sectarian hierarchy, they enhance commitment beyond that sustained by either logic in itself. Such a possibility seems both theoretically significant and relevant to modern social movements, but its investigation lies beyond the focus of this study.

Appendix

Section 1. The typology of communal groups has empty cells that result from the synchronic temporal mode's subsumption of other temporal possibilities in the natural and transcendental modes of social enactment. The commune involves an episodic pluralism of times, while the ecstatic association transcends all cognitive elaborations of time (Hall 1978, p. 16). In the construction of typologies, dimensions are not necessarily independent of one another; as Parsons (1951, pp. 152ff.: cf. Stinchcombe 1968, p. 47) recognized in a similar context, some combinations of elements seem more sociologically coherent than others. An additional type from the original typology, the preapocalyptic warring sect, is not treated in the present analysis because the sample does not include any groups that approximated it.

Section 2. The five ideal types and the 30 communal groups were specified on the basis of the following questions. *Diachronic time:* "Did the group calculate members' labor contributions in terms of objective temporal measurements and either pay them wages or credit them with having fulfilled their labor obligations on the basis of accumulated credits?" *Apocalyptic time:* "Did the group have a well developed theory of the end of history, in which members considered themselves as existing or paving the way for existence beyond 'this' world, in an exclusive heaven-on-earth of the chosen or saved?" *Produced enactment:* "Did the group share some basic philosophy from which the form of communalism derived (rather than simply holding out a value ideal of communalism, or living together principally as friends, family, or for convenience)?" *Transcendental enactment:* "As a central group activity, did group participants try to attain a mystical, symbolically transcendent form of consciousness and act in terms of that 'vision'?" *Egalitarianism:* "In principle, aside from a brief novitiate, did the members of the group deemphasize status distinctions and deference, even when people differed in skills or spiritual development, by trying to treat people equally?" *Pluralism*: "Even if the group shared an overall philosophy as a basis for collective life, in general did the group and its members tolerate individual differences in viewpoints and beliefs and seek to accommodate a variety of members?" The specification of ideal types with these variables follows the logic of Max Weber's methodology, applied to quantitative analysis (Murphy and Mueller 1967, p. 14; Bailey 1973; Hall, 1984a, 1984b). Types may be more or less similar, and actual communal groups may approximate one or more types to a greater or lesser degree (cf. Weber [1922] 1977, p. 20). It would be possible to specify the typology by any number of variables reflecting clear theoretical characteristics of the types, ranging upward from the minimum number necessary to define the conceptual space of the typology (in the present study, four variables). Using six variables is a compromise between refining the typology and limiting type specifications to variables that do not reflect specific commitment mechanisms measured by Kanter.

Section 3. For the approximations of groups to ideal types, characteristics of cases were specified in terms of the above questions, based on examination of the historical sources cited by Kanter (1972, p. 270ff.). Values derived in this manner were crosschecked with selected variables Kanter had measured but had not defined in the original study as commitment mechanisms. To provide a stringent test of the present hypothesis, cases were identified as involving apocalyptic time only if this temporal orientation was *central to* group life. Thus, there were some groups which shared a sense of apocalypse as a basic tenet of Protestantism, but no group action became predicated on it in any substantial way. While the question of type-approximation validity ultimately turns on complex issues of historical interpretation that remain open by definition, the present specification of case approximations to types can, at a minimum, be regarded as reliable, both with respect to Kanter's original study and in terms of the consistency of categorization decisions across groups. One specification question, diachronic time, substantially recreated a variable, "communistic labor, no compensation for labor," used by Kanter to reflect a commitment mechanism, and the commitment-

mechanism variable was not included in the matrix subjected to factor analysis.

Section 4. Kanter's original analyses are based on subsamples of communal groups that vary from nine to the full sample of 30 cases, depending on the amount of missing data about a given commitment mechanism. The difference of means tests apparently (Kanter 1972, p. 505) were calculated for indices that combined individual commitment-mechanism variables based on different subsets of the overall sample. Kanter's quantitative analysis thus is based on the assumption that the tendency for a group to employ or fail to employ different commitment mechanisms within a subset is uncorrelated with its propensity for missing data. Because there were substantial missing commitment-mechanism data in Kanter's original study, if all cases and all variables had been used in the present study, the resulting correlation coefficients for the factor analysis, like Kanter's difference of means tests, would be based on substantially different subsets of the sample. To resolve this problem, a commitment-mechanism variable was eliminated from the analysis if data for over four of the thirty groups (13.3 percent) was missing. On this basis, 46 variables, still representing all dissociative and associative processes of commitment, remained for analysis. Of the 46 variables, 12 had no missing values, 16 had one missing, seven had two, seven had three, and four variables had four missing values, for an average percentage of missing data of 4.86 percent. In the calculation of zero-order correlation coefficients for factor analysis, a case was eliminated from the computation of a given coefficient if its value for either variable was missing. This procedure maximizes the use of data in calculating coefficients without estimating values for missing data.

The 46 variables were subjected to R-type factor analysis using an oblique rotation procedure. The requirement of orthogonality was relaxed because there was no reason to assume that different empirical factors of commitment were uncorrelated with one another, and since the purpose of factor analysis in this study was to produce factors that reflected empirical variance (rather than to maximize the variance explained with each successive factor) (Rummel 1976, p. 386ff.). A series of factor analyses, using different delta values (specifying the degree of obliqueness among factors) was performed, and, by inspection, I determined that a delta $= -.5$ provided a solution under which the strength of loadings of commitment-mechanism variables on factors was maximized. With the exception of Factor 8, Ideological Order, all the factors from the solution described are easily interpretable, because only a few commitment-mechanism variables are highly loaded on them, and the highly loaded variables are theoretically related. Because Factor 8 includes variables that are theoretically unrelated, the interpretation is more tenuous. But, in any event, the factor does not figure prominently in subsequent analysis. Factor scores were calculated for each case on each factor by using the complete estimation method, in which a factor-score coefficient for each variable in the analysis is included in the equation. In case of a missing observation for a variable (i.e., on average, for 4.86 percent of the observations), the observation was replaced by the standardized mean of the variable, i.e., zero, so that the resulting factor score is really the sum of nonmissing terms in the equation (Nie, Hull, Jenkins, Steinbrenner, and Brent 1975, p. 489). This is a conservative procedure that reduces a case's factor score and its contribution to variance, in proportion to the case's number of variables with missing observations.

Notes

1. Statistical analyses were also carried out using an interval-level measure of success—years of existence. The results were slightly different than those reported here, yet would not have required any different interpretation. Because distribution of groups' years of existence was skewed, the interval measure gave undue statistical weight to certain cases (e.g., the Shaker colonies, which endured for 184 years) and to variables (e.g., the homogeneity commitment factor) on which outlying cases were differentially loaded. Kanter chose the 25-year break point for the success variable to focus on processes promoting initial generational survival of a communal group. Using this approach in my study both maintains continuities with Kanter's study and, by avoiding excessive statistical influence of exceptionally long-lasting groups, yields a more stringent test of hypotheses about success than would an interval measure.

2. The G Index of Agreement is calculated by the subtraction of the proportion of *noncorresponding* characteristics for any two cases (one "yes," the other "no") from the proportion of *corresponding* characteristics of the two cases (both "yes" or both "no"). ◆

Unit Three

Movement Dynamics

In the previous two units we examined the broad societal conditions associated with the emergence of social movements and the actual micro-level processes that account for differential recruitment and participation. But what happens once mobilization has occurred at the macro- and micro-levels? What do we know about social movements once they are up and running? How do they go about the business of strategically and tactically pressing their claims? What is the character of their external relations with various relevant groupings in society? How does their internal organization affect their operation? And what difference do they make in the end? What are their consequences? We address these and related questions in this final section as we attempt to understand the factors and processes that influence the operation, impact, and life course of social movements.

Part 8

Movements in Action: Strategies and Tactics

In this part we examine one of the most inter-esting and dynamic aspects of collective ac-tion: the use of various tactics and strategies to advance movement aims. Besides its intrinsic scholarly appeal, the topic is critically important to movements and those who would seek to direct them. Consider the unique dilemma that confronts movements. They generally develop among less powerful segments of the population. Moreover, by organizing outside conventional political insti-tutions—such as parties and formal interest groups—movements eschew politics through "proper channels." They typically do this for two reasons. First, they tend not to have access to these institutions and the conventional forms of action (e.g., lobbying, electoral politics, etc.) associated with them. Second, as relatively powerless groups, they may fear that their aims will be com-promised by pursuing them through "proper chan-nels," those institutionalized channels of decision making that tend to be controlled or dominated by conventional political/economic elites.

This rejection of conventional political means may make sense for movement groups, but it nonetheless poses a dilemma. By opting for politics by other means, movements must answer a difficult question: what should these other means be? How will the movement seek to over-come its relative powerlessness and press effec-tively for the realization of its interests?

What do we know about this crucial topic? Perhaps not as much as we know about the dy-namics of movement emergence or differential re-cruitment; but, as the following articles show, we are slowly beginning to understand some of the processes that shape the tactical decisions and out-comes of collective action. In this introduction we will focus on three such processes, each of which is illustrated by one of the articles in the part. We start with the reading by Sidney Tarrow. How do movement activists select the tactics they em-ploy? No doubt there are a number of factors that influence the selection process, but among the most important is the cultural availability of any given tactic. The fact is, for all the seeming spon-taneity and unpredictability of social movements, their selection of tactics tends to be patterned and predictable. At any given historical moment, ac-tivists—especially those sharing a general ideo-logical orientation—have available to them a fairly narrow "tool kit" of protest tactics. Move-ment scholars have coined the term *repertoires of contention* (Tarrow 1994; Tilly 1977) to refer to those established means of popular protest that are known and regarded as legitimate within a given social milieu. It is difficult for movements—espe-cially at the outset—to choose forms of action that are unknown or otherwise unavailable to them.

In the first selection, Tarrow adds to our understanding of repertoires of contention by linking it to another concept—that of the protest cycle—also current in the movement literature. *Cycles of protest* refer to those periods of intense and more or less continuous mobilization that pe-riodically arise in most modern societies. The tur-bulence of the 1960s and early 1970s in the U.S. is a case in point. Tarrow uses the Italian protest cycle of the same period to document the important role that such cycles play in expanding and refining the repertoire of contention available to insurgents in any given society.

But surely movements are not entirely bound by the conventional forms of protest characteristic of the historical period in which they develop. If movements were truly restricted in their selection of protest forms, we would never be able to account for change in these repertoires of convention. And change does, indeed, occur. Movements are themselves sources of innovation in protest behavior, expanding, through their actions, the forms of contention which will be available to succeeding generations of activists.

How does this innovation occur? What are the dynamics that give rise to new protest tactics? In the second selection, Doug McAdam takes up this interesting question. Part of the answer to the question, McAdam asserts, lies in the ongoing tactical interaction between movement groups and their opponents, both within and outside of the state. The portrait that emerges from McAdam's study of the civil rights movement is that of an elaborate tactical chess match that, by fits and starts, gradually expands the available repertoire of contention. But what is the dynamic that drives the search for new tactical forms? According to McAdam, it is the movement's ongoing efforts to offset the enormous power disparity that exists between itself and its opponents. To do this it must keep its foes off guard by finding new ways to disrupt "business as usual" which, in turn, force the opposition to bargain in good faith with the movement. In the case of the civil rights movement, McAdam shows that the ebb and flow of protest activity and major movement victories was closely related to the introduction of a series of major tactical innovations that temporarily afforded the movement the leverage needed to wrest concessions from the federal government. But each innovation eventually produced a tactical response from southern segregationists, which effectively neutralized the original tactic and sent movement activists back to the drawing board. It is through such interactive chess moves that new protest forms arise.

Finally, there is the all important question of tactical effectiveness. What do we know about the impact of various kinds of tactics? Which forms of protest seem to be related to movement success? McAdam's piece contains a provocative and perhaps counterintuitive suggestion: movement success depends on the disruptive force of movement tactics. In a political system that has long stressed the utility of compromise and bargaining, what are we to make of this suggestion? In the final selection, William Gamson seeks to systematically answer this question. To do so, Gamson studied 53 challenging groups and sought to relate various dimensions of these groups to their success in gaining new advantages and gaining acceptance by established political elites. Gamson reports the results of his analysis of the relationship between both dimensions of success and the tactics employed by his 53 groups. The results may surprise you. On average, those groups who used disruptive forms of protest were more successful, both in gaining acceptance and new advantages, than were those groups who eschewed such tactics. On the issue of violence, Gamson is more equivocal. While groups who used violence had slightly higher rates of success than those who did not, Gamson is cautious in interpreting this finding. It may be that only those groups which are strong enough in other dimensions use violence in the first place, thus making it hard to know whether it is their general strength or their use of violence which accounts for their higher rates of success. However you interpret this latter finding, the overall thrust of Gamson's results is clear: like it or not, a degree of disruption may be functional for movement success. In movement politics, as often in life, the squeaky wheel may, indeed, get the grease.

References

Tarrow, Sidney. 1994. *Power and Movement: Social Movements, Collective Action and Politics.* New York: Cambridge University Press.

Tilly, Charles. 1977. "Getting It Together in Burgundy." *Theory and Society* 4: 479-504. ✦

25

Cycles of Collective Action: Between Moments of Madness and the Repertoire of Contention

Sidney Tarrow

Moments of madness—when "all is possible"—recur persistently in the history of social movements. In such turbulent points of history, writes Aristide Zolberg, "the wall between the instrumental and the expressive collapses." "Politics bursts its bounds to invade all of life" and "political animals somehow transcend their fate" (1972: 183). Such moments are unsettling and often leave even participants disillusioned—not to mention elites and political authorities. But they may be "necessary for the political transformation of societies," writes Zolberg, for they are the source of the new actors, the audiences, and the force to break through the crust of convention (1972: 206). In Kafka's parable: "Leopards break into the temple and drink to the dregs what is in the sacrificial pitchers; this is repeated over and over again; finally it can be calculated in advance, and it becomes a part of the ceremony."[1]

With de Tocqueville, look at the 1848 Revolution, when "a thousand strange systems issued impetuously from the minds of innovators and spread through the troubled mind of the crowd. Everything was still standing except the monarchy and parliament, and yet it appeared as if society itself had crumbled into dust under the shock of revolution" (1942; quoted in Zolberg 1972: 195). Or look with Edgar Morin at May 1968 in France. It "was carried away by 'the great festival of youthful solidarity,' the 'permanent game' which was also a serious strategy, in which revolutionary incantations achieved a 'genuine socialization' " (1969; in Zolberg 1972: 184). In

such moments, the impossible becomes real—at least in the minds of participants.

But an important question about such moments is often overlooked: their relation to the historical development of the repertoire of contention. Some observers think that such moments create totally new forms of collective life.[2] But when we confront the creative aspects of moments of madness with the historical development of the repertoire of collective action, we find a puzzle. For as Tilly has shown, the repertoire developed slowly and haltingly and no faster than the development of states and capitalism. If moments of madness produce as rich a tapestry of collective action as we think, why has the repertoire developed as slowly as it has? Is it because the forms of contention that explode during such exceptional moments are not as exceptional as they seem at the time? Or is it because—precisely because they are so exceptional—they are rejected and repressed when order returns? Or rather, is the incremental pace of the repertoire's change due to the fact that the absorption of new forms of contention is mediated by institutional processes?

The Repertoire of Contention

The question can be posed in more analytical terms if we return to the concept of the repertoire as it was developed by Charles Tilly in the 1970s and 1980s.[3] Tilly sees the repertoire as the whole set of means that a group has for making claims of different kinds on different individuals or groups (1986a: 4). Because different groups in similar circumstances have similar repertoires, he speaks more loosely of a general repertoire that is available to the population as a whole. At any point in time, he writes, the repertoire available to a given population is limited, despite the possibility of using virtually any form of contention against any opponent. The repertoire is therefore not only what people do when they make a claim; it is what they know how to do and what society has come to expect them to choose to do from within a culturally sanctioned and empirically limited set of options (Tilly 1978: 151).

It follows from this definition that the repertoire of contention changes very slowly, constrained by overarching configurations of economics and state-building and by the slow pace of cultural change. As Arthur L. Stinchcombe writes in a perceptive review of Tilly's The Contentious French:

"Cycles of Collective Action: Between Moments of Madness and the Repertoire of Contention." *Social Science History* 17: 2 (Summer), pp. 281-308. Copyright © by the Social Science History Association, 1993. Reprinted with permission.

The elements of the repertoire are . . . simultaneously the skills of population members and the cultural forms of the population. . . . Only rarely is a new type of collective action invented in the heat of the moment. Repertoires instead change by long run evolutionary processes. The viability of one of the elements of a repertoire depends on what sorts of things work in a given social or political structure, on what forms of protest have been invented and disseminated in a population and on what grievances a given form is appropriate to express. (1987: 1248, 1249)

But if Stinchcombe is right, what then is the effect of Zolberg's "moments of madness," in which men and women not only "choose their parts from the available repertoire" but "forge new ones in an act of creation" (1972: 196)? Are the newly forged acts no more than chimeric explosions against the slowly evolving drama of the history of contention, doomed to disappear as participants tire, supporters melt away, and the forces of order regroup and repress their challenges? Or are they related in some way to longer-term changes in collective action? How do history's moments of madness relate to the long, slow progress of the repertoire of contention?

This essay proposes a solution to that problem through the concept of systemic cycles of protest. I will argue that moments of madness do not transform the repertoire of contention all at once and out of whole cloth, but contribute to its evolution through the dynamic evolution of larger cycles of mobilization in which the innovations in collective action that they produce are diffused, tested, and refined in adumbrated form and eventually become part of the accepted repertoire. It is within these larger cycles that new forms of contention combine with old ones, the expressive encounters the instrumental, traditional social actors adopt tactics from new arrivals, and newly invented forms of collective action become what I call "modular." Cycles of protest are the crucibles in which moments of madness are tempered into the permanent tools of a society's repertoire of contention. Let us begin with the concept of the protest cycle.

Cycles of Protest

That there are regular variations in political or social phenomena is scarcely a new or surprising idea. Wilhelm Buerklin, for example, writes that "virtually all time series describing and explaining social and political change display deviations or fluctuations of one sort or another" (1987: 1). Students of history recognize cycles in various forms: reform cycles, electoral cycles, generational cycles, economic cycles.[4] Yet empirical studies of political cycles rarely go beyond these generic classifications and seldom escape their putative dependence on economic fluctuations.

Elements of Cyclicity

Although protest waves do not have a regular frequency or extend uniformly to entire populations, a number of features have characterized such waves in recent history. These features include heightened conflict, broad sectoral and geographic extension, the appearance of new social movement organizations and the empowerment of old ones, the creation of new "master frames" of meaning, and the invention of new forms of collective action. Since these elements provide the skeleton for the rest of this analysis, I will briefly outline them here.

1. Heightened Conflict: Protest cycles are characterized by heightened conflict across the social system: not only in industrial relations, but in the streets; not only in the streets, but in the villages or in the schools. For example, in their time-series data on France, Shorter and Tilly correlated the rate of violence per year with other forms of collective action. They reported that "since the 1890s, the times of extensive collective violence in France have also been the times of hostile demonstrations, mass meetings, explicitly political strikes and calls for revolution" (1974: 81). Similar findings emerged from my study on the Italian wave of protest in the late 1960s and early 1970s. It is this co-occurrence of turbulence across the social sector that brings it to the attention of elites and sets in motion a process of institutional adaptation or collapse (Tarrow 1989: chap. 3).

2. Geographic and Sector Diffusion: Cycles of protest also have traceable paths of diffusion from center to periphery, as was discovered by Rudé in the grain seizures he studied in France from the 1770s; by Shorter and Tilly in the nineteenth- and twentieth-century French strikes that they analyzed; and by Beccalli in her study of Italian strikes. Such cycles also spread from heavy industrial areas to adjacent areas of light industry and farming, as Beccalli found in Italy in the 1970s. Particular groups recur with regularity in the vanguard of waves of social protest (e.g., miners, students), but they are frequently joined during the peak of the wave by groups that are not generally known for their insurgent tendencies (e.g., peasants, workers in small industry, white-collar workers).[5]

3. *Social Movement Organizations:* Protest cycles are often touched off by unpredictable events, and they almost never are under the control of a single movement organization. The high point of the wave is often marked by the appearance of supposedly spontaneous collective action, but in fact both previous traditions of organization and new forms of organization structure their strategies and outcomes. Nor do existing organizations necessarily give way to new movements in the course of the wave. From the wave of industrial unrest in Western Europe in the 1968-72 period we have evidence that—while organized groups were taken by surprise—many of them quickly recouped their positions and adapted to the new forms of collective action created at the peak of the strike wave (Dubois 1978: 5; Klandermans 1990a).

The importance of movement organizations in cycles of protest is that they have a vested interest in contentious collective action because protest is their major—and often their only—resource. To the extent that these organizations become the major carriers of a protest wave, contention will not cease just because a particular group has been satisfied, repressed, or becomes tired of life in the streets. A major reason for the acceleration in the appearance of protest cycles in the past 150 years is the invention of these organized actors with their stake in contentious collective action.

4. *New Frames of Meaning:* Protest cycles characteristically produce new or transformed symbols, frames of meaning and ideologies that justify and dignify collective action and around which a following can be mobilized.[6] These frames typically arise among insurgent groups and spread outward, which is how the traditional concept of "rights" expanded in the United States in the 1960s. The rights frame eventually spread to women, gays, Native Americans, and advocates of the rights of children and animals (Snow and Benford 1988). These new cultural constructs are born, tested, and refined within the cycle and may then enter the political culture in more diffuse and less militant form, serving as a source of the symbols mobilized by future movement entrepreneurs.

5. *Expanding Repertoires of Contention:* A final characteristic of protest cycles is perhaps their most distinctive trait: they are crucibles within which new weapons of social protest are fashioned. The barricades in the French revolutions of the nineteenth century; the factory occupations of 1919-20; the sitdown strikes of the French Popular Front period; the direct actions of the 1968-72 period in Italy—new forms of collective action develop within the experimental context of cycles of protest. The most successful—and the most transferable—become part of the future repertoire of collective action even during quieter times.

In a number of cases, forms of collective action are not merely the instrumental means that people use to demand new rights and privileges; rather, they themselves express the rights and privileges that protesters are demanding and are diffused as general expressions of their claims and similar ones. For example, the 1960 lunch counter sit-ins in the American South were not simply a way of gaining attention or opposing racism; by sitting-in at lunch counters, African American college students were actually practicing the objective they sought. Honed, tested, and refined into known and adaptable forms, this new form of collective action was then applied in bus stations, movie theaters, and welfare agencies. Surviving beyond the end of the cycle as a permanent form of popular politics, it contributed to the evolution of the entire repertoire of contention.

To summarize: A cycle of protest will be operationalized in this essay as an increasing and then decreasing wave of interrelated collective actions and reactions to them whose aggregate frequency, intensity, and forms increase and then decline in rough chronological proximity. This leads to three related questions:

First, what is the balance within a cycle of protest between the institutionalized forms of collective action from the inherited repertoire and the less institutionalized ones that reflect something like Zolberg's moments of madness?

Second, what kinds of activities does the moment of madness contain? Is it predominantly made up of violence? Of conventional forms of action used in greater magnitude? Or of a combination of violent, confrontational, and conventional forms of participation?

Third, how are these forms of collective action translated into permanent changes in the repertoire of contention?

These questions will be examined in the case of a ten-year period of mass mobilization and protest in Italy from 1965 through 1974.

Assumptions and Data

A few simplifying assumptions will have to be accepted in order to fit Zolberg's intuitive concept of moments of madness into an empirical and historical framework. We will identify moments of madness with the sudden onset of collective action near the beginning of a protest cycle. We will operationalize new social and ideological actors with the presence and frequency of unorganized protest. And we will reduce Zolberg's complex question of "lasting political accomplishments" to the character of collective action observable at the close of the cycle.

The data that will be used to illustrate the incidence and impact of moments of madness come from both machine-readable and qualitative newspaper data collected in Italy for the 1965-74 period from a daily reading and coding of Corriere della Sera that have been presented in greater detail elsewhere (della Porta and Tarrow 1986; Tarrow 1989). For each protest event identified, information was recorded on the forms of action used, the participants, the groups targeted, the claims made, and the outcomes that could be observed. The newspaper data were supplemented by archival research, interviews with former participants, and documentary sources.[7] Secondary data from other studies supplemented the primary Italian data.

The Italian Protest Cycle

Historical memory always foreshortens histories of collective action into long, shallow valleys and short, pointed peaks that punctuate them. But when we reconstruct cycles of protest from both public records and private memories, the peaks that leave indelible impressions in public consciousness are really only the high ground of broader swells of mobilization that rise and fall from the doldrums of compliance to waves of mobilization more gradually than popular memory recognizes.[8]

For example, although the year 1789 had world-historical importance beyond most others, it could probably not have occurred if not for the "pre-revolution" of 1787-88 and the campaign of public assemblies that preceded the taking of the Bastille. Similarly, the 1848 revolution was presaged by food riots, land seizures, and public demonstrations in the guise of public banquets. As for the explosive year 1968, the subtitle of Todd Gitlin's book says it all: Years of Hope, Days of Rage (1987).

In Italy the public record shows a rise and fall in contentious collective actions beginning in the mid-1960s and continuing in large numbers into the early 1970s. Figure 1 presents the number of codable events recorded from our reading of the Corriere data for each half year from the beginning of 1965 through the end of 1974. The curve is based on the total number of conflictual events found in the daily newspaper record, from routine petitions, delegations, and strikes to public marches and demonstrations, occupations, and traffic obstructions to violent clashes and organized attacks on others.[9] It shows that Italy in the mid-1960s was entering a period of extensive social and political conflict.

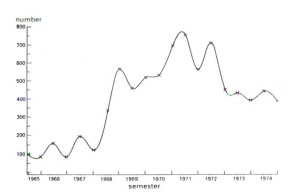

Figure 1   Number of conflictual events, Italy, 1965–74.

There is a puzzle in Figure 1 that can help us understand the relationship between the cycle's most memorable moment and its long-term dynamic: 1968 has been remembered as the peak of the cycle, yet the evidence in Figure 1 shows that collective action continued to rise in quantity until after the turn of the decade.[10] Was 1968 a false spring, a mere reflection of what was happening across the French Alps during the same time? Or did it have special characteristics that distinguish it from the larger, quantitative peak of collective action later on? Unraveling the puzzle will require us to turn from the quantitative data to their changing character in the course of the cycle. We can do so first by distinguishing the institutional from the noninstitutional aspects of collective action and then by looking at the appearance of new social actors.

Convention and Contention

The most important contribution of Tilly's concept of the repertoire is to help us disaggregate the popular notion of protest into its conventional and less conventional components. In each period of history some forms of collective action are sanctioned by habit, expectations, and even legality, while others are unfamiliar, unexpected, and are rejected as illegitimate by elites and the mass public alike. Consider the strike. As late as the 1870s it was barely known, poorly understood, and widely rejected as a legitimate form of collective action. By the 1960s, however, the strike can be considered as an accepted part of collective bargaining practice.

Looking again at the Italian data from the 1960s and 1970s, we find routine and conventional forms alongside confrontational and violent ones. As "confrontation," we shall operationalize forms such as occupations, obstructions, forced entries, and radical strikes, and as "violence" attacks on property, on antagonists and on authorities, and clashes with police. "Conventional" forms contain petitions, audiences, and legal actions,[11] marches and public meetings, and strikes and assemblies. We consider the inherited repertoire as the presence and relative frequency of the conventional forms of collective action as opposed to the use of both confrontation and violence. The question here is, within a generalized period of contentious collective action, do the conventional forms give way to disorder and violence, or do they rise in magnitude along with more unruly and contentious actions?

Figure 2 shows that the answer to the question is unambiguous: just as confrontational and violent forms of collective action rose during the period, so did routine and conventional ones. Italians at the peak of their protest cycle were fighting, raiding, obstructing, and occupying premises far more often than they had in the recent past. But they were also—and predominantly, in quantitative terms—engaging in well-known routines of collective action inherited from the conventional repertoire. The most common forms of collective action enumerated from the newspaper data in It-

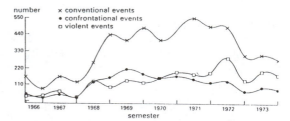

Figure 2 Incidence of conventional, confrontational, and violent events, Italy, 1966–73.

aly between 1966 and 1973 were strikes, marches, and public meetings (see Table 1). Just behind these were the confrontational forms of occupations and obstructions, with the conventional forms of assemblies and petitions close behind them. Only then do we find the four main forms of violent conflict.[12]

The numerical predominance of the conventional repertoire is not surprising when we take into account the fact that the late 1960s were a period of mass collective action. When we consider

Table 1
Incidence of All Forms of Collective Action as Percentages of Total Forms of Action, Italian Newspaper Data, 1966-73

Action Form	% of All Forms	Incidence
Strike	20.3	1,974
March	12.4	1,206
Public Meeting	9.8	955
Occupation	8.3	812
Obstruction	8.2	797
Assembly	7.3	709
Petition	6.6	639
Violent Attack	6.0	589
Attack on Property	6.0	584
Violent Clash	5.1	497
Clash With Police	3.9	382
Forced Entry	1.0	100
Hunger Strike	.7	70
Rampage	.6	58
Direct Action	.4	48
Leafleting	.3	33
Symbolic Protest	.3	33
Legal Action	.2	18
Random Violence	.1	15
Theft	.1	11
Campout in Public Place	.1	7
Miscellaneous Other	1.6	154
Unclassified	.4	48
Total	99.7	9,739

Source: Tarrow (1989): 68.

the difficulties in mobilizing large numbers of people into any form of collective action, it becomes clear that it must be particularly hard to get them to participate in high-risk confrontational and violent protest. When movement organizers think of how best to mobilize large numbers of people against superior forces, they therefore most naturally turn to the inherited repertoire. What is most interesting is that moments of madness and institutional forms of collective action co-occurred all through the cycle.[13]

But note the differences in the employment of the different types of collective action over time. In Figure 2 the numerous types of collective action from Table 1 have been aggregated into three main curves (conventional events, confrontational events, and violent events) and their numerical appearance traced over the eight-year period for which we have detailed data. As the figure shows, while all three major types increased during the upward slope of the cycle, their respective curves differed. While violent forms of attack increased mainly toward the end of the cycle,[14] the much larger conventional curve peaked in 1971. As for confrontational forms of collective action, these reached their height in 1968-69—the years celebrated in popular memory as the peak of contestation. This contrast between the peaks of conventional and confrontational collective action will help us to understand the internal dynamic of the cycle and the role of the moment of madness of 1968-69 within it.

New Social Actors and Identities

Something else occurred during the 1968-69 period: the appearance of new social actors and collective identities, operationalized here as the relative absence in the protests of known movement organizations and parties. Throughout the Italian cycle, both organized and nonorganized protests were found in great numbers. At times, however, organized actors were more prominent than at others.[15]

The years 1968-69 produced the largest percentage of protest events with no known organizations. Two thirds of the protests in the mid-1960s had involved known organizations, and half of these were organized by the trade unions. Even the 1966 bombings in Alto Adige were carried out by known nationalist organizations and—as for protests against the war in Vietnam—the majority were mounted by the institutional left-wing parties or their youth affiliates (Tarrow 1989: chap. 9). But by 1969 the proportion of protests in which known organizations could be identified fell to less than half of the total, and only one-quarter involved the unions.[16]

The 'Hot Autumn'

The trend continued in 1969 and expanded from the university to the factory. In the autumn of that year a wave of factory-level strikes, often sparked by grass-roots committees outside the unions, began. This "hot autumn," which stretched through the winter of 1970, was largely propelled by younger, unskilled "mass workers," many of them of southern parentage, who lacked the discipline and respect for work of their northern elders. Many workers adopted the forms of collective action experimented with by the student movement in 1968 and added new twists to conventional strikes (see below). This tactical flexibility was a major challenge to industrialists, but it also was a challenge for the trade unions, which were forced to respond by absorbing the new forms of organization that had been invented at the base (Regalia 1979).

Organizing Disruption

By 1971 the trend had begun to reverse itself in both factories and universities. Two major organizational developments changed the nature and extent of collective action during this period. First, the trade unions integrated many of the younger workers into their base-level structures; and second, the student movement was increasingly absorbed by the Leninist-type organizations that had emerged from the mass movement of 1968 (Lumley 1983). By 1973 more than half of the events studied were led by either the unions or by these new extraparliamentary groups. Although the two trends were different in many ways—for example, in the degree of violence they produced—they were united in helping to bring collective action back within an organizational framework after the moment of madness of 1968-69.[17] Disruption was being increasingly organized.

The Moment of Madness

Thus, the years 1968-69 brought a wave of confrontational collective action to Italy that placed workers and students in unprecedented confrontation with authority in the absence of the traditional mediating leadership of unions and parties. Yet the capacity of these social actors for organizing protest did not seem to be impaired. This can be seen first in their level of tactical flexibility. It also can be seen, for the workers, in the radicalization of the strike, and, for the students, in the form of collective action that most dramatically marked their protests—the occupation of university premises.

Tactical Flexibility

To some, in order to be effective, social protests must be well-organized (Hobsbawm 1978), but to others, disruptiveness is actually dependent on the emergent quality of the movement, which implies a lack of stable leadership and organization (Piven and Cloward 1977). As protest intensified, did the decline in the presence of known organizations imply a loss in tactical ability? Quite the contrary. During this period the degree of tactical flexibility increased, as evidenced by the increase in the average number of forms of action used in each protest event.

Figure 3 presents the average number of tactical forms observed per event in the protest events. It shows a rapid increase in organizational capacity in 1967-69, just as the confrontational forms of collective action we saw earlier were peaking and as the presence of known organizations declined. If the ability to array a variety of forms of collective action in the absence of known organizations and of confrontations with authorities is a sign of a moment of madness, then the academic year 1967-68 was just such a moment.

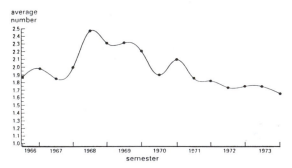

Figure 3 Action forms per event, Italy, 1966–73.

Radicalizing the Strike

Strike behavior—especially during periods of contract negotiation—follows a national and sectoral logic in Italy that is both regular and predictable (Frinzosi 1981), and strikes were the

most common and most conventional form of collective action we found during the period studied.[18] As we saw in Table 1, strikes appeared in 40 percent of the events and made up more than 20 percent of the forms of action that were recorded. Strikers almost always put forward instrumental demands, although some of these—like the demand for equal pay increases for all classes of workers—had strongly expressive elements (Pizzorno 1978).

The largely conventional role of striking can be seen in the rhythm of the strike rate during periods of national and sectoral contract renewal.[19] These conflicts often followed an almost ritualistic sequence. First, the unions would hold conferences at which platforms were elaborated and voted on; then brief strikes would be called in key firms or industries—usually those in which the unions were strongest; then, building on the momentum that had been demonstrated in these strongholds, national strikes would be called; finally, contract negotiations would begin (Golden 1988).

But toward the end of the 1960s a new phase was added to the sequence; plant committees began to regard contract agreements reached at the national level, not as a ceiling, but as a floor on which to construct more ambitious plant-level agreements. This meant that industrial conflict extended beyond contract renewal periods into the trough between them and that the center of gravity of the strike fell from the national level to the plant or local level.

The dramatic rise of plant-level disputes that this change signified can be seen in Figure 4, which breaks down the strike data into those that were observed only at the local level and those that were organized nationally. The curves show a sharp proportional increase in local strikes from the middle of 1968, when the first plant-level wildcat strikes broke out. The number of national strikes—although they included many more workers—expanded much more slowly throughout the period.

The extension of the strike to the plant level was more than quantitative; it reflected a flowering of new strike forms, some inherited from past cycles of industrial conflict, but others invented on the spot (Dubois 1978). A whole new vocabulary of strike forms rapidly developed, from the sciopero bianco (go-slow) to the sciopero a singhiozzo (literally, hiccup strikes) to the sciop-

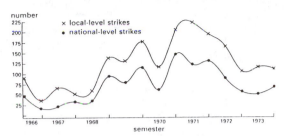

Figure 4   Incidence of national and local-level strikes, Italy, 1966–73.

ero a scacchiera (chessboard strikes) to the corteo interno (marches around the factory grounds to carry along undecided workers) to the presidio al cancello (blocking factory gates to prevent goods from entering or leaving the plant). The logic of these innovations in the strike repertoire was to attempt to produce the maximum amount of disruption with the minimum expenditure of resources.

In addition to these permutations within the strike, workers learned to combine distinctly different forms of collective action with striking. In the factory, occupations, obstructions, and forced entries challenged assembly-line rhythms and the authority of foremen. Collective action extended outside the factory as workers adopted public forms of display, expressive forms of action, and traffic blockages to publicize their demands. These public demonstrations often contained symbolic military elements (e.g., mechanics would frequently bang on milk cans with pipes as they marched), but they also contained important elements of play and theater and bore a resemblance to the traditional carnival.[20]

Both the expansion in the forms of conflict within the workplace and its extension into the public sphere can be seen in Table 2, which analyzes the strikes in our newspaper data for their combination with other forms of collective action. As the table shows, the ratio of other forms of action to strikes was much higher in 1968 and 1969 than either earlier or later in the period. During their moment of madness, workers were simultaneously going public and intensifying disruption in the workplace.

The Occupation as Collective Life

As in the United States during the 1960s, occupying institutional premises was the form of collective action most frequently used by Italian students, and it owed much to the American example. At first, such occupations were enthusiastic and joyful activities, especially in the takeovers of university faculties carried out during the 1967-68 academic year (Ortoleva 1988). Lumley writes of one of the first important university sit-ins— that of the architecture faculty in Milan—that "an environment was created which was functional to collective living, debate and shared work; all major decisions were taken by the general meetings" (1983: 164).

But although some faculties were almost continuously occupied from early in the 1967-68 academic year until the spring of 1969, the magic of shared participation and achievement could not endure. Not only did vacations and ever more frequent roustings by the police prevent the occupations from achieving their goal of creating "free spaces" in the universities, but such actions became institutionalized, as "commissions were set

Table 2
Strike Events: Use of Nonstrike forms by Strikers; Aggregated Protest Forms by Year (Number of Events)

Forms of Action	1966	1967	1968	1969	1970	1971	1972	1973
Public Display	31	28	78	107	97	110	78	74
Assembly	10	15	40	69	84	59	43	33
Routine Action	13	15	37	59	88	77	87	14
Confrontation	32	15	52	118	72	70	31	33
Violent Encounter	20	5	33	18	23	34	16	15
Attack on Property	12	4	13	28	19	12	3	8
Attack on Persons	2	3	4	19	9	10	4	6
Total Other Forms	120	85	257	418	392	372	262	183
Total Strike Events[a]	127	117	196	306	319	416	269	224
Ratio Other/Total	.94	.73	1.31	1.37	1.23	.89	.97	.82

[a]Strike events are defined nominally as all events in which a strike took place.
Source: Tarrow (1989): 189.

up to examine political and educational issues with the participation of some lecturers" (ibid.), and factional groupings formed their own organizations that attempted to gain control of the various assemblies and commissions.

By 1969-70 the university occupations had taken on a ritualistic character, with standard banners and posters that reflected the ideological line of this or that movement organization, a servizio d'ordine of security guards—some of whom would later appear as the military cadres of the extraparliamentary groups—and almost as ritualistic police roustings and counterdemonstrations. By the early 1970s the main force of the occupations had moved to the secondary schools, where far less sophisticated leaders turned them into staging grounds for battles over turf.

The Diffusion and Modularization of Protest

Thus, the most innovative and confrontational forms of collective action that arose in the Italian moment of madness declined after 1969. Unions—never absent from the factory—had regained control of the strike movement by 1970. In the universities, extraparliamentary groups turned student protests into set piece productions that soon took on a routine character. When participation lagged, the extraparliamentary groups moved into the secondary schools. In those instances where the police moved in, clashes ensued, providing an opportunity for the groups' armed servizi d'ordine to gain prominence and inducing much of the mass base to vanish.[21]

What was the impact of the moment of madness on Italian society and on its continuing repertoire of protest? To answer that question, we will have to ask what parts of the new repertoire survived the collapse of the movements of 1968-69. As we saw in Figure 2, while the sharpest decline in institutionalization and the greatest increases in confrontation and tactical innovation occurred in 1968 and 1969, conventional collective action continued to grow in magnitude until 1971. That such mobilization increased after tactical creativity declined suggests that the period legitimated protest in sectors of Italian society that otherwise would not have engaged in it.

Most of the effects were less than creative—and some were often violent. But this does not negate the significance of the diffusion and legitimation of protest throughout Italian society. Social

groups and regions that had not participated in the first wave of mobilization began to strike, demonstrate, and—in a few cases—loot and burn in the early 1970s.[22] Collective action frames that the students developed in the context of university occupations—such as the theme of autonomia—spread to the workers and other groups and became a key slogan (albeit with different implications) during the conflicts of the early 1970s. And forms of protest that were first experimented with in university faculties and the large factories of the north became general models for collective action in other settings and in other regions—for example, the practice of self-reduction, which can serve as an archetypical example of the modularization of protest.

Autoriduzione

Production and institutional routines do not have to be attacked by straightforward striking; they can be disrupted by simple noncooperation, as was the case for the prison revolts that broke out in 1969, or by setting one's own schedule, as was the case for the autoriduzione campaigns that began in the Pirelli factory near Milan in the same year. The skilled Pirelli workers sensed that the increase in factory orders in the context of a labor shortage gave them an unusual degree of leverage vis-à-vis management. As the practice spread, workers would simply decide on their production rate, ignoring piecework schedules in coordinated passive resistance. According to Lumley, autoriduzione "captured the imagination of a wide section of activists on the shopfloor, in the Left, within the trade unions, and in the social movements more generally" (1983: 329-39).

Observers of the period thought they saw spontaneity here; but it took enormous coordination for a technically advanced productive process to be deliberately slowed down in a self-reduction campaign. By the early 1970s the technique had been extended to urban movements by well-organized national extraparliamentary organizations like Lotta Continua—for example in the self-reduction of rents in public housing projects and in the mass refusal to pay gas and electricity bills and transit fares (Perlmutter 1987; 1988). Between 1968, when it was invented in the Pirelli factory, and the mid-1970s, when it was turned into a weapon of urban struggle, autoriduzione became modular—that is, a model of collective action that was diffused across a wide range of social and territorial space and adapted to a variety of social and political conflicts.

As it was diffused, the practice became more routinized, with professional movement organizers teaching their supporters how it was done. As this occurred, autoriduzione became stylized and modular, permitting it to be employed with a minimum of organizational effort in a variety of social and economic settings—much as the sit-in had been diffused to a variety of protest groups in the United States. But repetition and modularization had another effect; unlike its first employment at Pirelli, where it caught management off-guard, elites and authorities soon learned how to respond.

If workers could self-reduce their assembly lines, piecework rates could be adjusted to penalize them for it; if rate-payers refused to pay their utility bills, their gas or electricity could be cut off; and if commuters failed to pay their bus or tram fares, the fare itself could be canceled, as occurred in one Italian city, with the cost transferred to general revenue collection. Modularization of the new forms of collective action made them easier to diffuse to new sectors and social actors, but it also facilitated social control.[23]

The Assembly in the Place of Work

Not all of the innovations in collective action that first appeared in the moment of madness were as easily defeated as Autoriduzione was. Before 1969, union organizers had been unable to gain access to factories to meet with workers. They were forced to waylay them at the factory gates after a hard day's work or organize meetings after hours. Some of the most dramatic moments in the Hot Autumn of 1969 occurred when insurgent workers triumphantly carried their leaders onto factory grounds, where tumultuous assemblies were organized and strike votes taken.

As the cycle wound down and the unions reasserted their control, workers returned to more conventional and institutionalized forms of collective action. Of course, the factory councils that organized factory assemblies soon lost their tumultuous character, and their elected delegates often felt "elected and abandoned" by their unions (Regalia 1985). But the assembly in the place of work remained a permanent conquest for the workers and an institutionalized accretion to the repertoire of collective action.

Moments, Cycles, Ages of Contention

In his intuitive and perceptive article Zolberg concludes of moments of madness that they bring about significant transformations in three distinct ways:

> First of all, the "torrent of words" involves a sort of intensive learning experience whereby new ideas, formulated initially in coteries, sects, etc., emerge as widely shared beliefs among much larger publics. . . .
> Secondly, these new beliefs expressed in new language are anchored in new networks of relationships which are rapidly constituted during such periods of intense activity. . . .
> Thirdly, from the point of view of policy . . . the instant formulations become irreversible goals which are often institutionalized in the not-very-distant future. (206)

Each of Zolberg's themes implies an indirect and a mediated—rather than a direct and unmediated—effect on political culture, which is why we need to look beyond great events and crises to the cycles of protest they trigger in order to observe their effects. Let us turn from the discourse of the movements that preoccupied Zolberg to their effects on the repertoire of collective action to ask if there is a similar logic.

In the first case, just as new ideas filter down from their originators to those who vulgarize and domesticate them, the new forms of collective action invented in the enthusiasm of the moment of madness become modular. One thinks of the practice of autoriduzione as it spread from Pirelli to other factories, then to urban protests for rent and rate reductions, and finally (and in its most farcical version) as a teenager's justification for breaking into rock concerts without a ticket. Not the new invention itself, but its distilled, refined, and often routinized products become part of a more lasting practice of collective action.

In the second case, just as networks of people that form in the heat of a moment of madness diffuse new ideas, they also spread out across society—to the cities, the factories, the schools—and induce others to take up tactics that they have found successful. College students who go home for the weekend teach younger brothers and sisters how to organize an occupation; arrested militants who are shifted from troublesome urban prisons to more remote ones teach common criminals how to politicize their discontent; radicalized workers who become union organizers bring their militant practice to smaller and less politicized factories.

In the third case, through changes in public policy (in which Zolberg includes the creation of new political institutions as well as new programs), society absorbs a portion of the message of moments of madness. This can be as true for the practice of collective action as it is for ideas and substantive policies. For example, one thinks of the factory councils that became the grass-roots institutions of the Italian trade unions after being created in shop floor conflicts or of the practice of decisions made through assemblies that affected life in Italian universities for years to come.

Each of these hypothetical effects requires separate—and much more qualitative—investigation than we have been able to give them here. (And, needless to say, they should be examined in countries other than Italy as well.) If true, these effects imply an intervening and dynamic process connecting the utopian dreams, the intoxicating solidarity and the violent rhetoric of the moment of madness, and the glacially changing, culturally constrained, and socially resisted pace of change. I have proposed such a mediation in the concept of cycles of protest.

Few people dare to break the crust of convention. When they do so during moments of madness, they create the opportunities and provide the models for others. Moments of madness—seldom widely shared, usually rapidly suppressed, and soon condemned even by their participants—appear as sharp peaks on the long curve of history. New forms of contention flare up briefly within them and disappear, and their rate of absorption into the ongoing repertoire is slow and partial. But the cycles they trigger last much longer and have broader influence than the moments of madness themselves; they are, in Zolberg's words, "like a flood tide which loosens up much of the soil but leaves alluvial deposits in its wake" (206).

Notes

1. From Franz Kafka, Parables and Paradoxes (1937): 92-93.

2. Listen to Henri Lefebvre as he speaks of the Paris Commune: "in this movement prompted by the negative, and therefore creative, elements of existing society—the proletariat—social action wills itself and makes itself free, disengaged of constraints" (1965; quoted in Zolberg: 190).

3. The discussion here is based on Tilly (1978, 1986a). For a more detailed examination of Tilly's concept in a historical context, see Tarrow (1993).

4. The discussion below is a summary from two more developed versions of my argument about the structure and dynamics of protest cycles in Tarrow (1991a and 1991b). For a formal model of revolutionary violence that emphasizes the importance of the dynamics of conflict, see Tsebelis and Sprague (1993).

5. The best evidence on how grain seizures spread comes from Rudé (1964: chap. 1). On the spread of strikes from areas of large to small industry in France, see Shorter and Tilly (1974: 106); in Italy, see Beccalli (1971).

6. My argument here owes much to the work of David Snow and Robert Benford. See, in particular, Snow and Benford (1988). Also see Gamson (1988) and Klandermans (1988a) for related discussions of the importance of framing discourses in the social construction of collective action.

7. The data collection strategy owes much to Tilly's monumental work on British contentious events. For a brief discussion of the British project, see Horn and Tilly (1986a). A similar discussion of the Italian project can be found in Project on Social Protest and Policy Innovation, Project Manual, Cornell University, Ithaca, New York (1985), available from the author on request. Many of these data summarized below were presented in different form in my final report (Tarrow 1980).

8. For example, see the excellent example of the development of the themes and networks of the future women's movement in the doldrums of the 1940s and 1950s in the United States in Rupp and Taylor (1987).

9. Two points: first, the figure includes both coded events and those for which a defining grievance, a starting date, or a disruptive form of collective action could not be identified; therefore, they were not coded further. The analysis in the remainder of this essay is based on only the first type, for which these basic data could be gathered. Second, for the years 1965 and 1974 a one-month-in-four sampling procedure has been used, while for the remaining eight years in the series, the entire population of codable events was used. For further details on sampling and enumeration of the protest events, see Tarrow (1989: Appendixes A and B), and Project Manual (1985).

10. The puzzle was reinforced by the memories of participants, many of whom remembered 1968 as the cathartic moment of the cycle, even in the face of the quantitative record of increasing collective action in later years. For the interview evidence, see Tarrow (1989: chap. 9).

11. Strictly speaking, the Italian study focused only on contentious collective action, which was operationalized as actions that disrupted the lives of someone else and did not enumerate "audiences, petitions and legal actions." These appear in the data only when they accompanied at least one disruptive form of collective

action in the same protest event. Thus, the overall use of these conventional forms is probably grossly underestimated in the data, which makes their magnitude here even more striking.

12. Notice that the table calculates the forms that were used as a proportion of the total forms of collective action, since several forms of action were often employed in the same event. Calculating the presence of each form as a proportion of events (N = 4,980) changes the weight of each only slightly.

13. I am grateful to Arthur Stinchcombe for putting clearly, in his comments on an earlier version of this essay, what had been only implicit in an earlier discussion. For a fascinating historical parallel from the Russian Revolution, see his "Milieu and Structure Updated" in Theory and Society (1986: 909-11) on the relationship between elite and mass parts of the movement.

14. On this point, see della Porta and Tarrow (1986) and Tarrow (1989: chap. 12). For the most careful analysis of the left-wing terrorism that followed, see della Porta (1991).

15. There is a risk here of mistaking journalistic ignorance for spontaneity. But it is interesting that detailed inspection of some portions of the data showed that the absence of known organizations in a protest correlates closely with expressive modes and the formation of new collective identities, as suggested by Pizzorno (1978).

16. For evidence that the replacement of party or interest group leadership by new actors and groups using confrontational forms of collective action occurs elsewhere than Italy, see Diarmuid Maguire's Ph.D. thesis, "Parties into Movements," Cornell University, Department of Government, 1990.

17. In a personal correspondence to the author, J. Craig Jenkins points out that something similar happened in the United States, where "unnamed groups launched the protest, then national social movement organizations and coalitions of SMOs (social movement organizations) took over by the late 1960s." I am grateful to Jenkins, whose excellent work on this question has been published in a joint article with Craig Eckert (1986).

18. Strikes are defined as the withdrawal of labor or (in the case of nonproducing institutions like schools) noncooperation in the institution's functioning. We shall see that strikes were frequently accompanied by more public and more confrontational forms of action.

19. A large technical literature exists on the fluctuation in the strike rate during this period (see Franzosi 1981; Bordogna and Provasi 1984; and the sources cited in those works).

20. The finest evocation of this aspect of the movement will be found in Lumley (1983). Some, but not all, of his rich and evocative analysis is carried forward in his book, States of Emergency: Cultures of Revolt in Italy from 1968 to 1978 (1990).

21. The appearance of violence—even in its early, disorganized stages—seems to have been an important motive in the defection of many young women from the movement, as could be seen from a number of interviews carried out in the study. For a particularly significant case of violence and the resulting defection of women from an important extraparliamentary group, see Tarrow (1989: 327-28).

22. The notorious case of the "Revolt of Reggio Calabria," in which a city was paralyzed by right-wing mobs, and thousands of police ringed the city for months, is a prime example. (See Tarrow 1989: chap. 9, for a brief discussion.)

23. In a similar way, Diarmuid Maguire recounts how CND (Committee for Nuclear Disarmament) activists tried to encourage the use of nonviolent direct action among British printmakers and miners, both of whom went on strike in the mid-1960s. But there were legal and cultural obstacles to diffusion in both cases, and the attempt to apply this successful peace movement tactic to another sector failed miserably. In contrast, CND was able to use NVDA (non-violent direct action) successfully in protesting local antinuclear waste dumping, even in conservative constituencies. (Personal communication to the author. See Maguire (1990) for the relationship between conventional and unconventional protest in the British peace movement.) ◆

26

Tactical Innovation and the Pace of Insurgency

Doug McAdam

Sociological analysis and theory regarding social movements has tended to focus on the causes of insurgency. By comparison, relatively little attention has been devoted to the dynamics of movement development and decline.1 This article represents a modest attempt to address this "hole" in the movement literature by analyzing the effect of one factor on the ongoing development of a single movement. It studies the relationship between *tactical interaction* and the pace of black insurgency between 1955 and 1970.

The Significance of Tactics and the Process of Tactical Interaction

The significance of tactics to social movements derives from the unenviable position in which excluded or challenging groups find themselves. According to Gamson (1975:140): "the central difference among political actors is captured by the idea of being inside or outside of the polity. . . . Those who are outside are challengers. They lack the basic prerogative of members— routine access to decisions that affect them." The key challenge confronting insurgents, then, is to devise some way to overcome the basic powerlessness that has confined them to a position of institutionalized political impotence. The solution to this problem is preeminently tactical. Ordinarily insurgents must bypass routine decision-making channels and seek, through use of noninstitutionalized tactics, to force their opponents to deal with them outside the established arenas within which the latter derive so much of their power. In a phrase, they must create "negative inducements" to bargaining (Wilson, 1961).

Negative inducements involve the creation of a situation that disrupts the normal functioning of society and is antithetical to the interests of the

group's opponents. In essence, insurgents seek to disrupt their opponent's realization of interests to such an extent that the cessation of the offending tactic becomes a sufficient inducement to grant concessions.

Findings reported by Gamson (1975:72-88) support the efficacy of negative inducements or disruptive tactics for many challenging groups. In summarizing his findings, he concludes that "unruly groups, those that use violence, strikes, and other constraints, have better than average success" (Gamson, 1975:87). Piven and Cloward's (1979) analysis of several "poor people's movements" supports Gamson's conclusion. As they note, ". . . it is usually when unrest among the lower classes breaks out of the confines of electoral procedures that the poor may have some influence, for the instability and polarization they then threaten to create by their actions in the factories or in the streets may force some response from electoral leaders" (Piven and Cloward, 1979:15).

In most cases, then, the emergence of a social movement attests to at least limited success in the use of disruptive tactics. To survive, however, a movement must be able to sustain the leverage it has achieved through the use of such tactics. To do so it must either parlay its initial successes into positions of institutionalized power (as, for instance, the labor movement did) or continue to experiment with noninstitutional forms of protest. Regarding the latter course of action, even the most successful tactic is likely to be effectively countered by movement opponents if relied upon too long. Barring the attainment of significant institutionalized power, then, the pace of insurgency comes to be crucially influenced by (a) the creativity of insurgents in devising new tactical forms, and (b) the ability of opponents to neutralize these moves through effective tactical counters. These processes may be referred to as *tactical innovation* and *tactical adaptation,* respectively. Together they define an ongoing process of *tactical interaction* in which insurgents and opponents seek, in chess-like fashion, to offset the moves of the other. How well each succeeds at this task crucially affects the pace and outcome of insurgency.

As crucial as this interactive dynamic is, it has received scant empirical attention in the social movement literature.[2] Instead research has tended to focus on the characteristics or resources of either opponents or insurgents rather than the dynamic relationship between the two.

Political Process as a Context for Tactical Innovation

As important as the process of tactical innovation is, it derives much of its significance from the larger political/organizational context in which it occurs. That is, the process only takes on significance in the context of the more general factors that make for a viable social movement in the first place.

Elsewhere (McAdam, 1982) is outlined a *political process* model of social movements that stresses the importance of two structural factors in the emergence of widespread insurgency. The first is the level of indigenous organization within the aggrieved population; the second the alignment of groups within the larger political environment. The first can be conceived of as the degree of organizational "readiness" within the minority community and the second, following Eisinger (1973:11), as the "structure of political opportunities" available to insurgent groups. As necessary, but not sufficient, conditions for social insurgency, both factors are crucial prerequisites for the process of tactical innovation. Indigenous organizations furnish the context in which tactical innovations are devised and subsequently carried out. Such organizations serve to mobilize community resources in support of new tactical forms and to supply leaders to direct their use, participants to carry them out, and communication networks to facilitate their use and dissemination to other insurgent groups.[3] This latter point is especially significant. The simple introduction of a new protest technique in a single locale is not likely to have a measurable effect on the pace of movement activity unless its use can be diffused to other insurgent groups operating in other areas. It is the established communication network's characteristic of existing organizations that ordinarily make this crucial process of diffusion possible.[4]

The Pace of Insurgency

But the effectiveness of such organizations and the tactical innovations they employ also depend, to a considerable degree, on characteristics of the larger political environment which insurgents confront. Under ordinary circumstances, excluded groups or challengers face enormous obstacles in their efforts to advance group inter-

ests. They oftentimes face a political establishment united in its opposition to insurgent goals and therefore largely immune to pressure from movement groups. Under such circumstances tactical innovations are apt to be repressed or ignored rather than triggering expanded insurgency. More to the point, it is unlikely even that such innovations will be attempted in the face of the widely shared feelings of pessimism and impotence that are likely to prevail under such conditions. Tactical innovations only become potent in the context of a political system vulnerable to insurgency. Expanding political opportunities then create a potential for the exercise of political leverage which indigenous organizations seek to exploit. It is the confluence of these two factors that often seems to presage widespread insurgency.

Certainly this was true in the case of the black movement (McAdam, 1982: see especially Chapters 5-7). By mid-century the growing electoral importance of blacks nationwide, the collapse of the southern cotton economy, and the increased salience of third world countries in United States foreign policy had combined to grant blacks a measure of political leverage they had not enjoyed since Reconstruction. Equally significant was the extraordinary pace of institutional expansion within the southern black community in the period of 1930-1960. Triggered in large measure by the decline in cotton farming and the massive rural to urban migration it set in motion, this process left blacks in a stronger position organizationally than they had ever been in before. In particular, three institutions—the black church, black colleges, and the southern wing of the NAACP— grew apace of this general developmental process. Not surprisingly, these three institutions were to dominate the protest infrastructure out of which the movement was to emerge in the period 1955-1960. It is against this backdrop of expanding political opportunities and growing organizational strength, then, that the emergence of the civil rights movement must be seen.

The confluence of indigenous organization and expanding political opportunities, however, only renders widespread insurgency likely, not inevitable. Insurgents must still define the "time as ripe" for such activity and commit indigenous organizational resources to the struggle. Then, too, they must devise methodologies for pressing their demands. It is only at this point that the process of tactical innovation becomes crucial. For if expanding opportunities and established organizations presage movement emergence, it is the skill of insurgents in devising effective protest tactics *and* their opponents' ability to counter such tactics that largely determine the pace and outcome of insurgency. In the remainder of this article attention will center on this dynamic and its effects on the unfolding of black protest activity in this country between 1955 and 1970.

Institutionalized Powerlessness and the Politics of Protest

By any measure of institutionalized political power blacks were almost totally powerless in the middle decades of this century. Of the nearly eight and three-quarter million voting age blacks in the country in 1950 only an estimated three million were registered to vote (Berger, 1950:26), in contrast to the estimated 81 percent registration rate for whites in 1952 (Danigelis, 1978:762). While no contemporaneous count of black elected officials nationwide is available, the number was certainly very small. At the national level, only two Congressman—Dawson (R-IL) and Powell (D-NY)—held elective office. Institutionalized political impotence was most extreme for southern blacks. Some ten and a quarter million blacks still resided in the South in 1950, with barely 900,000 of them registered to vote (Bullock, 1971:227; Hamilton, 1964:275). No blacks held major elective office in the region and none had served in Congress since 1901 (Ploski and Marr, 1976). Moreover, with blatantly discriminatory electoral practices still commonplace throughout the region—especially in the Deep South—the prospects for changing this state of affairs were bleak. Yet a scant 20 years later significant change had come to the South. An entire system of Jim Crow caste restrictions had been dismantled. Black voter registration rates had risen from less than 20 percent in 1950 to 65 percent in 1970 (Lawson, 1976:331). The number of black elected officials in the region climbed to nearly 1,900 after the 1970 elections (Brooks, 1974:293). And with the election of Andrew Young and Barbara Jordan, black southerners were represented in Congress for the first time since 1901.

The pressure for these changes came from an indigenous movement organized and led primarily by southern blacks. In the face of the institutional political powerlessness of this population it is important to ask how this pressure was generated and sustained. The answer to this question is, of course, complex. However, any complete account of how blacks were able to mount such a successful insurgent campaign must focus squarely on their willingness to bypass "proper channels" in favor of noninstitutionalized forms of protest. Having "humbly petitioned" the South's white power structure for decades with little results, insurgents logically turned to the only option left open to them: the "politics of protest." It was the potential for disruption inherent in their use of noninstitutionalized forms of political action that was to prove decisive.

Methods

To measure the pace of black insurgency over this period all relevant story synopses contained in the annual *New York Times Index* (for the years, 1955-70) under the two headings, "Negroes—U.S.—General" and "Education—U.S—Social Integration," were read and content-coded along a variety of dimensions. The decision to restrict coding to these headings was based on a careful examination of the classification system employed in the *Index,* which indicated that the overwhelming majority of events relevant to the topic were listed under these two headings.

To be coded, a story had to satisfy four criteria. It first had to be relevant to the general topic of black civil rights. As a result, a good many other topics were excluded from the analysis, for example, stories reporting the achievements of black athletes or entertainers. Besides this general criterion of relevance, to be coded, synopses also had to be judged unambiguous as to (1) the nature of the event being reported (e.g., riot, sit-in, court decision); (2) the individual(s) or group(s) responsible for its initiation; and (3) geographic location of the event. The former two variables, "type of action" and "initiating unit," figure prominently in the analysis to be reported later.

In all, better than 12,000 synopses were coded from a total of about 29,000 read. Coding was carried out by the author and a single research assistant. By way of conventional assurances, intercoder reliability coefficients exceeded .90 for all but one variable. For all variables employed in this article, however, reliability ratings exceeded .95.[5]

Black Insurgency and the Process of Tactical Innovation

To assess the effect of tactical innovation on the pace of black insurgency between 1955 and 1970 requires that we be able to measure both insurgent pace and innovation. Two code categories noted in the previous section enable us to do so. The variable, "initiating unit," provides us with frequency counts of all civil rights-related actions for all parties to the conflict (e.g., federal government, Martin Luther King, Jr., etc.). One major category of initiating unit employed in the study was that of "movement group or actor." The com-

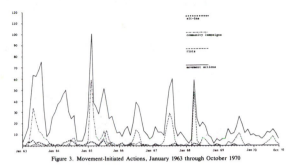

Figure 3. Movement-Initiated Actions, January 1963 through October 1970

Source: *Annual Index* of the *New York Times*, 1963–1970.

THE PACE OF INSURGENCY

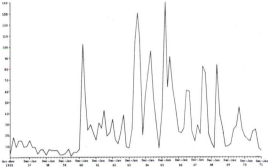

Figure 1. Movement-Initiated Actions, Oct–Nov 1955 through Dec–Jan 1971

Source: *Annual Index* of the *New York Times*, 1955–1971

bined total of all actions attributed to movement groups or actors provides a rough measure of the pace of movement-initiated activity over time. Figure 1 shows the frequency of such activity between October 1955 and January 1971.

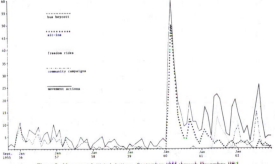

Figure 2. Movement-Initiated Actions, September 1955 through December 1962

Source: *Annual Index* of the *New York Times*, 1955–1962.

What relationship, if any, is there between tactical innovation and the ebb and flow of movement activity? By coding the "type of action" involved in each reported event, we can compare the frequency with which various tactics were used to the overall pace of insurgency shown in Figure 1. Figures 2 and 3 show the specific activity frequencies for five novel tactical forms utilized by insurgents during the course of the movement.

As these figures show, peaks in movement activity tend to correspond to the introduction and spread of new protest techniques.[6] The pattern is a consistent one. The pace of insurgency jumps sharply following the introduction of a new tactical form, remains high for a period of time, and then begins to decline until another tactical innovation sets the pattern in motion again. A more systematic view of this dynamic is provided in Table 1.

Table 1 reports the use of five specific tactics as a proportion of all movement-initiated actions during each of the first 12 months following the introduction of each technique.

As the "Total" column makes clear, the sheer number of actions is highest immediately following the introduction of a new protest form, as is the proportion of all actions attributed to the new technique. Thus, tactical innovation appears to trigger a period of heightened protest activity dominated by the recently introduced protest technique. This is not to suggest that the older tactical forms are rendered obsolete by the introduction of the new technique. Table 1 shows clearly that this is not the case. In only 22 of the 60 months represented in the table did the new tactical form account for better than 50 percent of all move-

Table 1
Tactical Innovations as a Proportion of a Month's Activity by Months Since First Use of Tactical Form

Month Since First Use[a]	Bus Boycott	Sit-In	Freedom Ride	Community Campaign	Riot	Total
0	.86 (6/7)	.57 (24/42)	.19 (4/21)	.06 (1/17)	.14 (7/51)	.30 (42/138)
1	.82 (9/11)	.83 (50/60)	.59 (13/22)	.35 (7/20)	.38 (14/37)	.62 (93/150)
2	.67 (4/6)	.91 (30/33)	.45 (9/20)	.64 (9/14)	.21 (5/24)	.59 (57/97)
3	1.00 (5/5)	.74 (14/19)	.54 (7/13)	.20 (2/10)	.04 (1/26)	.40 (29/73)
4	.50 (4/8)	.53 (8/15)	.83 (5/6)	.50 (3/6)	.00 (0/18)	.38 (20/53)
5	.29 (2/7)	.44 (4/9)	.60 (3/5)	.11 (1/9)	.00 (0/11)	.24 (10/41)
6	.83 (5/6)	.40 (4/10)	.00 (0/17)	***	.00 (0/12)	.23 (11/48)
7	.67 (6/9)	.63 (12/19)	.05 (1/20)	***	.00 (0/8)	.37 (22/60)
8	***	.73 (8/11)	.00 (0/14)	.79 (15/19)	.00 (0/14)	.39 (24/61)
9	.67 (4/6)	.36 (4/11)	.00 (0/10)	.23 (6/26)	.00 (0/17)	.20 (14/70)
10	.29 (2/7)	.29 (2/7)	.00 (0/6)	.08 (1/12)	.11 (1/9)	.15 (6/41)
11	***	.62 (5/8)	.00 (0/9)	***	.29 (6/21)	.33 (15/45)

[a]Listed below are the months of first use for the five tactical forms shown in the table:

Bus Boycott:	December, 1955
Sit-In:	February, 1960
Freedom Ride:	May, 1961
Community Campaign:	December, 1961
Riot:	August, 1965

***Fewer than five movement-initiated actions.

ment-initiated actions. On the contrary, tactical innovation seems to stimulate the renewed usage of *all* tactical forms. Thus, for example, the economic boycott, largely abandoned after the bus boycotts, was often revived in the wake of sit-in demonstrations as a means of intensifying the pressure generated by the latter technique (Southern Regional Council, 1961). Then, too, during the community-wide campaign all manner of protest techniques—sit-ins, boycotts, etc.—were employed as part of a varied tactical assault on Jim Crow. This resurgence of the older tactical forms seems to underscore the importance of the process of tactical innovation. The presumption is that in the absence of the heightened movement activity triggered by tactical innovation the older protest forms would not have reappeared. Their use, then, is dependent on the altered protest context created by the introduction of the new technique.

What of the "valleys" in movement activity shown in Figures 2 and 3? A closer analysis suggests that the lulls in insurgency reflect the successful efforts of movement opponents to devise effective tactical counters to the new protest forms. For a fuller understanding of this interactive dynamic, we now turn to a more detailed qualitative examination of the processes of tactical innovation and adaptation surrounding the protest techniques listed in Table 1.

Bus Boycott

The first such technique was the bus boycott. Certainly the most famous and successful of these boycotts was the one organized in Montgomery, Alabama, (1955-56) by the church-based Montgomery Improvement Association (MIA) led by Martin Luther King, Jr. The technique, however, was not original to Montgomery. In 1953 a similar boycott had been organized by the Rev. Theodore Jemison in Baton Rouge, Louisiana.

If not the first, the Montgomery campaign was unique in the measure of success it achieved and the encouragement it afforded others to organize similar efforts elsewhere. In a very real sense the introduction of this technique marks the beginning of what is popularly called the "civil rights movement." From extremely low levels of activism in the early 1950s, the pace of black protest rose sharply in 1956 and 1957.

Consistent with the theme of this article, it is appropriate that we date the beginnings of the movement with a particular tactical, rather than substantive, innovation. After all, the specific issue of discriminatory bus seating had been a source of discontent in the black community for years. Repeated efforts to change such practices had always met with failure until the Montgomery boycott was launched. Why did this tactic succeed where all others had failed? The answer to this question lies in the contrast between the institutional powerlessness of southern blacks at this time and the leverage they were able to mobilize outside "proper channels" by means of the boycott. Outside those channels blacks were able to take advantage of their sizeable numbers to create a significant "negative inducement" to bargaining. That inducement was nothing less than the economic solvency of the bus lines, which depended heavily—70-75 percent in Montgomery—on their black ridership (Brooks, 1974:110). Such leverage was telling in Montgomery and elsewhere.

The U.S. Supreme Court, on November 13, 1956, declared Montgomery's bus segregation laws unconstitutional. Five weeks later, on December 21, the city's buses were formally desegregated, thereby ending the black community's year-long boycott of the buses. During the boycott an estimated 90-95 percent of the city's black passengers refrained from riding the buses (Walton, 1956).

A similar boycott begun on May 28, 1956, in Tallahassee, Florida, did not result in as clearcut a victory for insurgents as did the Montgomery campaign. Nonetheless, the boycott once again demonstrated the power of widespread insurgent action by blacks. With blacks comprising 60-70 percent of its total ridership, the city bus company quickly felt the effect of the boycott. Barely five weeks after the start of the campaign, the bus company was forced to suspend service. With revenues cut by an estimated 60 percent, it simply was no longer feasible to maintain bus service (Smith and Killian, 1958). Several months later bus service was resumed, thanks to several forms of public subsidy devised by city officials. Still the boycott held. Finally, following the Supreme Court's ruling in the Montgomery case, organized efforts to desegregate Tallahassee's buses were instituted. Despite continued harassment, legal desegregation had come to Tallahassee. Finally, the impact of the Tallahassee and Montgomery boycotts (as well as those organized elsewhere) was felt in other locales. Apparently fearing similar disruptive boycotts in their communities, at least a dozen other southern cities quietly desegregated their bus lines during the course of the Tallahassee and Montgomery campaigns.

As effective as the boycott proved to be, it was in time effectively countered by southern segregationists. The adaptation to this tactic took two forms: legal obstruction and extralegal harassment. The latter consisted of violence or various forms of physical and economic intimidation aimed at members of the black community, especially those prominent in the boycott campaigns. In Montgomery,

> buses were fired upon by white snipers, a teenage girl was beaten by four or five white rowdies as she got off the bus. Four Negro churches were bombed at an estimated damage of $70,000, the homes of Ralph Abernathy and Robert Graetz were dynamited . . . and someone fired a shotgun blast into the front door of . . . Martin Luther King's home. (Brooks, 1974:119)

Similar responses were forthcoming in Tallahassee and in other boycott cities (Smith and Killian, 1958:13). These incidents had the effect of increasing the risks of participation in insurgent activity to a level that may well have reduced the likelihood of generating such campaigns elsewhere.

These extra-legal responses were supplemented by various "legal" maneuvers on the part of local officials which were designed to neutralize the effectiveness of the bus boycott as an insurgent tactic. Several examples drawn from the Tallahassee conflict illustrate the type of counter moves that were instituted in many southern communities at this time.[7]

— City police initiated a concerted campaign of harassment and intimidation against car pool participants that included arrests for minor violations and the detention of drivers for questioning in lieu of formal charges.

— The executive committee of the I.C.C., the organization coordinating the boycott, was arrested, tried, and found guilty of operating a transportation system without a license. Each member of the committee received a 60-day jail term and a $500 fine, a sentence that was suspended on condition the defendants engaged in no further illegal activity.

— Following the Supreme Court's desegregation ruling in the Montgomery case, the Tallahassee City Commission met and rescinded the city's bus segregation ordinance replacing it with one directing bus drivers to assign seats on the basis of the "maximum safety" of their passengers. Segregation, of course, was deemed necessary to insure the "maximum safety" of passengers.

Though unable to stem desegregation in the long run, these countermeasures (in combination with the extra-legal techniques reviewed earlier) were initially effective as tactical responses to the bus boycotts.

It wasn't just the short-run effectiveness of these tactical responses, however, that led to the declining pace of black insurgency in the late 1950s (see Figure 2). In point of fact, the bus boycott was a tactic of limited applicability. Its effectiveness was restricted to urban areas with a black population large enough to jeopardize the financial well-being of a municipal bus system. It was also a tactic dependent upon a *well-organized* black community *willing* to break with the unspoken rule against noninstitutionalized forms of political action. This point serves once again to underscore the importance of organization and opportunity in the generation and sustenance of protest activity. Given the necessity for coordinating the actions of large numbers of people over a relatively long period of time, the bus boycott tactic made extensive organization and strong community consensus a prerequisite for successful implementation. Tactical innovation may have triggered the boycott, but once again it was the confluence of existing organization and system vulnerability—in the form of municipal bus lines dependent on black patrons—that provided the context for successful insurgency. Not surprisingly, these conditions were fairly rare in the South of the mid '50s. Therefore, truly mass protest activity had to await the introduction of a protest tactic available to smaller groups of people. That tactic was the sit-in.

The Sit-In

According to Morris (1981), blacks had initiated sit-ins in at least 15 cities between 1957 and February 1, 1960. The logical question is why did these sit-ins not set in motion the dramatic expansion in protest activity triggered by the February 1 episode in Greensboro, North Carolina? The answer helps once again to illustrate the importance of organization and opportunity as necessary prerequisites for the dynamic under study here. First, as Morris's analysis reveals, the earlier sit-ins occurred at a time when the diffusion network linking various insurgent groups had not yet developed sufficiently for the tactic to spread beyond its localized origins. Indeed, within a narrow geographical area the expected escalation in protest activity *did* occur. For example, in August, 1958, the local NAACP Youth Council used sit-ins to desegregate a lunch counter in Oklahoma City, Oklahoma. Following this success, the tactic quickly spread, by means of organizational and

personal contacts, to groups in the neighboring towns of Enid, Tulsa, and Stillwater, Oklahoma, and Kansas City, Kansas, where it was used with varying degrees of success (McAdam, 1982:269; Morris, 1981:750; Oppenheimer, 1963:52).

Secondly, the "structure of political opportunities" confronting southern blacks was hardly as favorable in 1957-58 as it was in 1960. Every one of the pre-Greensboro sit-ins occurred in "progressive" border states (e.g., Missouri, Oklahoma, Kansas). This is hardly surprising in light of the strong supremacist counter-movement that was then sweeping the South (Bartley, 1969; McAdam, 1982). Between 1954 and 1958 southern segregationists mobilized and grew increasingly more active in resisting school desegregation and the organized beginnings of the civil rights movement. White Citizen Councils sprang up throughout the region and came to exercise a powerful influence in both state and local politics (McMillen, 1971). As part of a general regional "flood" of segregationist legislation, several states outlawed the NAACP, forcing the state organization underground and seriously hampering its operation. But the resistance movement was to peak in 1957-58. Total Citizen Council membership rose steadily until 1958, then fell off sharply thereafter. The volume of state segregation legislation followed a similar pattern, peaking in 1956-57 and declining rapidly during the remainder of the decade. By 1960 a noticeable "thaw" was evident in all regions except the "deep South."

Faced, then, with a more conducive political environment and the dense network of organizational ties that make for rapid and extensive diffusion, it is not surprising that the tactic spread as rapidly as it did in the spring of 1960. The events surrounding the Greensboro sit-in are, by now, well known. There on February 1, 1960, four students from North Carolina A & T occupied seats at the local Woolworth's lunch counter. In response, the store's management closed the counter and the students returned to campus without incident. After that, events progressed rapidly. Within a week similar demonstrations had taken place in two other towns in the state. By February 15, the movement had spread to a total of nine cities in North Carolina as well as the neighboring states of Tennessee, Virginia, and South Carolina (McAdam, 1982). By the end of May, 78 southern communities had experienced sit-in demonstrations in which at least 2,000 had been arrested (Meier and Rudwick, 1973:102).

The effect of this tactical innovation on the overall pace of black insurgency is apparent in Figure 2. From low levels of movement activity in the late 1950s, the pace of insurgency increased sharply following the first sit-in in February and remained at fairly high levels throughout the spring of that year. This dramatic rise in movement activity was almost exclusively a function of the introduction and spread of the sit-in as a new tactical form. Not only did local movement groups rush to apply the tactic throughout the South, but these various campaigns soon stimulated supportive forms of movement activity elsewhere. Sympathy demonstrations and the picketing of national chain stores began in the North. At the same time, the existing civil rights organizations rushed to capitalize on the momentum generated by the students by initiating actions of their own (Meier and Rudwick, 1973: 101-104; Zinn, 1965:1-9).

Why did the introduction of this tactic have the effect it did? Two factors seem to be crucial here. The first is the "accessibility" of the tactic. Even a small group of persons could employ it, as indeed was the case in the initial Greensboro sit-in. Nor was the tactic reserved only for use in large urban areas, as was the case with the bus boycott. In the South nearly all towns of any size had segregated lunch counters, thereby broadening the geographic base of insurgency.

The second factor accounting for the popularity of the tactic was simply that it worked. By late 1961, facilities in 93 cities in ten southern states had been desegregated as a *direct* result of sit-in demonstrations (Bullock, 1970:274). In at least 45 other locales the desire to avoid disruptive sit-ins was enough to occasion the integration of some facilities (Oppenheimer, 1963:273). These figures raise another important question: *why* was the tactic so successful? At first blush the underlying logic of the sit-ins is not immediately apparent. Certainly the logic of the boycott does not apply in the case of segregated facilities. Given that blacks were barred from patronizing such facilities in the first place, they could not very well withdraw their patronage as a means of pressing for change. Instead they sought to create a very different inducement to bargaining. By occupying seats at segregated lunch counters, insurgents sought to disrupt the ordinary operation of business to such an extent that the effected stores would feel compelled to change their racial policies.

The hoped-for disruption of business was only partly a function of the routine closing of the lunch counter that normally accompanied sit-in demonstrations. Obviously, the revenues generated by the lunch counter were only a small fraction of the store's total income and insufficient in themselves to induce the store to negotiate with insurgents. For the tactic to work, there had to occur a more generalized store-wide disruption of business. This, in turn, depended upon the emergence, within the community, of a general "crisis definition of the situation." When this occurred, the store became the focal point for racial tensions and violence of sufficient intensity to deter would-be shoppers from patronizing the store. An example will help to illustrate this point. It is drawn from an eye-witness account of the violence that accompanied a 1960 sit-in in Jacksonville, Florida. The account reads:

> Near noon the demonstrators arrived at Grant's store. . . . Grant's then closed its counters after demonstrators sat-in for about five minutes. The sitters then left. As they proceeded toward other stores, a group of about 350 armed white men and boys began running down the street toward the store. Some Negroes broke and ran. The majority, however, proceeded in good order, until four or five members of the Youth Council also panicked and ran. At this point the mob caught up to the demonstrators. A girl was hit with an axe handle. Fighting then began as the demonstrators retreated toward the Negro section of town. . . . A boy was pushed and hit by an automobile. . . . By 12:50, only an hour after the first sit-in that day, Police Inspector Bates reported the downtown situation completely out of hand. A series of individual incidents of mobs catching Negroes and beating them took place at this time. (Oppenheimer, 1963:216)

Clearly, under conditions such as these, shoppers are not likely to patronize the target store let alone venture downtown. The result is a marked slowdown in retail activity amidst a generalized crisis atmosphere. This state of affairs represents a twofold tactical advance over that evident during a bus boycott. First, the crisis engendered by a boycott affected fewer people directly and took longer to develop than did a sit-in crisis. Second, as Oberschall (1973:268) notes, "the cost of the boycott fell heavily upon the boycott participants, many of whom walked to work over long distances.

Only after months had passed did the loss of income from bus fares create a financial situation worrisome to the municipal administration." By contrast, the financial cost of the sit-in campaign was felt immediately by the segregationists themselves, making it a much more direct and successful tactic than the boycott.[8]

As is the case with all tactics, however, the impact of the sit-in was relatively short lived. As Figure 2 shows, following the peak in movement activity during the spring of 1960, the pace of insurgency declined sharply in the summer and fall of the year. Part of this decline can, of course, be attributed to the effectiveness of the tactic. Having desegregated facilities in so many cities, there were simply fewer targets left to attack. However, far more important than this in accounting for the diminished use of the tactic was the process of tactical adaptation discussed earlier. Having never encountered the tactic before, segregationists were initially caught off guard and reacted tentatively toward it. Over time, however, they devised tactical counters that proved reasonably effective.

In his thorough analysis of the sit-in movement, Oppenheimer (1963) makes reference to this two-stage phenomenon. He distinguishes between several phases in the development of the typical sit-in. The initial or "incipient state" of the conflict is characterized by "the relatively unplanned reaction to the movement of the police in terms of arrests, by the managers of the stores in terms of unstructured and varying counter-tactics which may vary from day to day (Oppenheimer, 1963:168). However, through this process of trial and error, movement opponents were able to devise consistently effective responses to the sit-in tactic (and share them with one another) during what Oppenheimer calls the "reactive phase" of the conflict. These responses included mass arrests by the police, the passage of state or local anti-trespassing ordinances, the permanent closure of the lunch counters, and the establishment of various biracial negotiating bodies to contain or routinize the conflict. The latter adaptation proved especially effective. By defusing the crisis definition of the situation, the disruptive potential of the sit-in was greatly reduced, resulting in a significant decline in the leverage exercised by the insurgents. Indeed, this must be seen as a general aspect of the process of tactical adaptation regardless of the protest technique involved. All protest tactics depend for their effectiveness on the generation of a crisis situation. Yet prolonged use of the tactic necessarily undercuts any definition of crisis that may have obtained initially. James Laue (1971) has termed this process the "neutralization of crisis." He explains: "crisis tolerances change as communities learn to combat direct action and other forms of challenges. In most cities in the early 1960s, sit-ins were enough to stimulate a crisis-definition, but today they are dealt with as a matter of course and are generally ineffective as a change technique" (Laue, 1971:259). And so it was in the South after the initial wave of sit-ins. As a result, the pace of insurgency dropped sharply and civil rights activists resumed their search for potent new tactical forms.

The Freedom Rides

The tactic that revived the movement was the freedom ride. First used by the Fellowship of Reconciliation in 1947 to test compliance with a Supreme Court decision (*Morgan v. Virginia*, 1946) outlawing segregated seating on vehicles engaged in interstate transportation, the tactic was reintroduced by CORE in May 1961. Prompting its reintroduction was another Supreme Court decision—*Boynton v. Virginia*—extending the ban against segregation in interstate travel to terminal facilities as well as the means of transportation themselves. To test compliance with the ruling two CORE-organized interracial groups left Washington, D.C., on May 4, bound by bus for New Orleans. The buses never reached their destination. Following the burning of one bus near Anniston, Alabama, and a savage mob attack in Birmingham, the riders had to fly to New Orleans to complete their journey. Nevertheless, the ride had more than accomplished its original purpose. Not only had it dramatized continued southern defiance of the Supreme Court's ruling, but it also served, in the words of a contemporary analyst, "as a shot in the arm to civil rights groups just when interest on the part of Southern Negro students seemed to be flagging . . ." (Oppenheimer, 1963:277).

Figure 2 supports Oppenheimer's assessment. Following the initial wave of sit-ins during the spring of 1960, the pace of movement activity foundered badly. Except for a brief flurry of activity in February-March 1961 (stimulated, once again, by the introduction of a minor protest technique, the jail-in) the pace of insurgency had dropped to pre–sit-in levels. The initial CORE-sponsored ride changed all this. Inspired by that effort, *and* anxious to capitalize on the momentum it had generated, SNCC activists initiated a second Freedom Ride, which departed from Nashville on May 17. After surviving a mob attack three days later in Montgomery, the second group of riders pressed on to Jackson, Mississippi, where they were arrested and jailed on May 24, on charges of trespassing. Thereafter, the tactic was picked up by groups all over the country. From May to August, separate groups of riders poured into Jackson at the rate of nearly one group a day. By summer's end better than 360 persons had been arrested in connection with the rides (Meier and Rudwick, 1973:140).

In accounting for the impact of the freedom rides one must again point to the ability of insurgents to create a crisis situation of formidable proportions. In this they were helped immeasurably by local segregationists, who responded to the "threat" posed by the rides with a series of highly publicized, violent disruptions of public order. These responses, in turn, prompted a reluctant federal government to intervene in support of the riders. The Justice Department asked a federal district court in Montgomery to enjoin various segregationist groups from interfering with interstate travel; Robert Kennedy ordered 600 marshals to Montgomery to protect the riders; and under administration pressure on September 22, 1961, the Interstate Commerce Commission issued an order barring segregation in interstate travel. Indeed, it seems as if federal intervention had been the goal of insurgents all along. James Farmer, CORE director and chief architect of the rides, described the strategy underlying the campaign: "our intention was to provoke the Southern authorities into arresting us and thereby prod the Justice Department into enforcing the law of the land" (Farmer, 1965:69).

Thus, like the earlier tactics, the rides were used to create a crisis situation. The nature of this crisis, however, was very different from those generated by either the bus boycotts or the sit-ins. It marked the movement's initial use of a protest dynamic whose recognition and conscious exploitation would fuel the heightened pace of insurgency during the period widely regarded as the heyday of the movement. That period begins with the inauguration of John Kennedy as president in January of 1961 and ends with the close of the Selma campaign in May 1965 and the movement's consequent shift to the urban north as a locus of protest activity.

The dynamic in question can be described simply. Impatient with the slow pace of social change achieved through confrontation at the local level, insurgents sought to broaden the conflict by inducing segregationists to disrupt public order to the point where supportive federal intervention was required. This dynamic again emphasizes the crucial importance of political opportunities in setting the context within which the process of tactical innovation operates. With Kennedy's election, the vulnerability of the federal government to this type of pressure increased enormously. Whereas Eisenhower had owed little political debt to black voters or the Democratic South, Kennedy owed much to both groups. The "black vote," in particular, had been widely credited with playing the decisive role in Kennedy's narrow electoral victory over Richard Nixon the previous fall (c.f. Lawson, 1976:256). Kennedy thus came to office with a need to hold his fractious political coalition together and to retain the support of an increasingly important black constituency. This rendered his administration vulnerable to the "politics of protest" in a way Eisenhower's had never been. Recognition of this vulnerability is reflected in the evolution of the movement's tactics. Whereas the earlier tactics had sought to mobilize leverage at the local level through the disruption of commercial activities, the tactics of the next four years aimed instead to provoke segregationist violence as a stimulus to favorable government action. During this period it was the insurgent's skillful manipulation of this dynamic that shaped the unfolding conflict process and keyed the extent and timing of federal involvement and white opposition. Data presented in Figure 4 supports this contention.

The figure clearly reflects the determinant role of movement forces in shaping the unfolding conflict during the early '60s. In their respective patterns of activity, both segregationist forces and the federal government betray a consistent reactive relationship vis-à-vis the movement. With regard to the first of these groups, the pattern of movement stimulus/segregationist response noted earlier is quite evident. In Figure 4 peaks in segregationist activity are clearly shown to follow similar peaks in black insurgency.

The relationship between the federal government and the movement is a bit more complex.

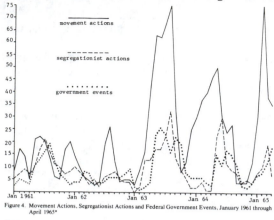

Figure 4. Movement Actions, Segregationist Actions and Federal Government Events, January 1961 through April 1965*

Source: *Annual Index* of the *New York Times*, 1961–1965

*The final eight months of 1965 have been excluded from this figure because they mark the termination of the dynamic under analysis here. In large measure this is due to the shifting northern locus of movement activity.

Government activity is still responsive to the pace of black insurgency, but as expected, much of this responsiveness derives from the ability of the movement to provoke disruptive segregationist activity. This can be seen more clearly through a logit regression analysis intended to assess the effect of a variety of independent variables on the odds of a federal civil-rights–related action.[9] The odds were computed separately for each of six tactical forms—bus boycotts, sit-ins, freedom rides, and three community-wide protest campaigns in Albany, Birmingham, and Selma. For each of the first seven weeks following the initial use of the tactic (or beginning of the campaign), the number of movement *actions* that were followed the very next week by federal *events* in the same state was recorded.[10] Likewise the number of movement actions that were *not* followed the next week by government events was also noted. The log odds of a movement action being followed by a federal event constitutes the dependent variable in the analysis.

Nine independent variables were utilized in the analysis. Each of the six tactics listed above were treated as independent variables. Five dummy variables were created, with "sit-in" employed as the left-out category. Use of sit-in as the omitted category reflects the fact that it had the least effect of any of the tactics on the dependent variable. In addition to these six tactics, three other independent variables were also entered into the analysis. The first was the number of weeks, ranging from 0-6, since the initial use of the tactic. The second was the total number of movement actions during any given week. The final independent variable was the presence or absence of a segregationist action during the week following

and in the same state as the initial movement action.

As reported in Table 2, the results of the logit regression analysis show clearly that not all of the six tactical forms were equally productive of federal action. Indeed, only three of the tactics showed a significant positive relationship with the dependent variable. Not surprisingly, all of these tactics were employed during the Kennedy presidency rather than the "Eisenhower years." As noted earlier, the tactical forms of the "Kennedy years" were designed to prompt favorable federal action by inducing disruptive segregationist violence. Table 2 reflects the operation of this characteristic dynamic.

Both the pace of movement action and the

Table 2
Summary of Logit Regression Analysis of Odds of Federal Action in Relation to Various Independent Variables

Tactic	b	\bet	F
Bus Boycott	−.344	.132	.681
Freedom Rides	.838**	.155	29.084
Community Campaigns			
Albany	.225	.151	2.206
Birmingham	.806**	.113	50.604
Selma	.854**	.102	69.994
Number of Weeks			
Since First Use	−.744**	.187	15.789
Number of Movement			
Actions	.416*	.150	7.654
Segregationist Response	.593**	.752	62.226
Constant	−1.308	.111	138.401
R² 67			

*Significant at the .10 level.
**Significant at the .01 level.

presence or absence of a segregationist response to movement action are significantly related to the odds of federal action. It is the relationship between segregationist action and the odds of a federal response, however, that is the stronger of the two. Federal activity, then, is still responsive to the overall pace of black insurgency, but as expected, much of this responsiveness appears to derive from the ability of the movement to provoke disruptive segregationist activity. More accurately, then, much of the strength of the relationship between federal and movement activity is indirect, with the stimulus to government involvement supplied by the intervening pattern of segregationist activity.

Returning to Figure 4, we can identify four periods that, in varying degrees, reflect this characteristic three-way dynamic linking black protest activity to federal intervention by way of an intermediate pattern of white resistance. The first of these periods, as noted earlier, occurred between May-August 1961, during the peak of activity associated with the freedom rides.

However, even this tactic was not able to sustain high levels of insurgency indefinitely. By August the pace of the rides, and movement activity in general, had declined dramatically. In this decline we can once again see the process of tactical adaptation at work. Following the two violence-marred rides through Alabama, and the federal intervention they precipitated, law enforcement officials in Mississippi worked hard to prevent any reoccurrence of violence in their state. In effect, they had learned to short-circuit the dynamic discussed above by failing to respond violently to the demonstrators' tactics. Over time the arrival and arrest of a new group of riders in Jackson took on a fairly routine character. The "crisis atmosphere" that had pervaded the initial rides had again been "neutralized." Fortunately for insurgents, the effectiveness of these counter-maneuvers was negated by the ICC's desegregation order on September 22. The issue of segregation in interstate transportation was dead. Then too, so was the freedom ride tactic and the momentum it had afforded the movement.

Community-wide Protest Campaigns

With the cessation of the freedom rides there again followed a period of diminished movement activity as insurgents groped to develop new protest tactics. The next breakthrough occurred in December 1961 in Albany, Georgia, with the initiation of the first of what might be called the "community-wide protest campaigns." Such campaigns represented a significant tactical escalation over all previous forms of protest. Instead of focusing on a particular lunch counter, bus terminal, etc., insurgents sought to mobilize the local community for a concerted attack on all manifestations of segregation in the target locale. This escalation was a logical response to the routinization of the other protest methodologies discussed previously. Quite simply, the "crisis tolerance" of local segregationists had increased to the point where bus boycotts, sit-ins, or freedom rides were no longer sufficient in themselves to generate the

leverage required by insurgents. Nothing short of a community-wide crisis would suffice to precipitate the sort of disruption that would grant insurgents increased leverage to press their demands. Indeed, in Albany not even this escalation in tactics was able to achieve significant progress. Yet, over the next three years this tactic was to be refined through a process of trial and error to the point where it was responsible for the most dramatic campaigns of the entire movement.

The Albany campaign took place during the final two months of 1961 and the summer of the following year. Figure 2 again mirrors a rise in movement activity during these two periods. What was absent during the campaign was the pattern of reactive segregationist violence and subsequent federal intervention evident in the freedom rides. Consistent with this view, Table 2 shows only a weak positive relationship between that campaign and subsequent government action. Accounts of the Albany campaign stress the firm control exercised by Police Chief Laurie Pritchett over events there (Watters, 1971:141-229; Zinn, 1962). While systematically denying demonstrators their rights, Pritchett nonetheless did so in such a way as to prevent the type of major disruption that would have prompted federal intervention. To quote Howard Hubbard (1968:5), "the reason . . . [the movement] faded in Albany was that Chief Pritchett used force rather than violence in controlling the situation, that is, he effectively reciprocated the demonstrator's tactics." Even in "defeat," then, the dynamic is evident. Failing to provoke the public violence necessary to prompt federal intervention, insurgents lacked sufficient leverage themselves to achieve anything more than an inconclusive stand-off with the local segregationist forces in Albany.

The experience of Albany was not without value, however, as the following remarkable passage by Martin Luther King, Jr., attests:

> There were weaknesses in Albany, and a share of the responsibility belongs to each of us who participated. However, none of us was so immodest as to feel himself master of the new theory. Each of us expected that setbacks would be a part of the ongoing effort. There is no tactical theory so neat that a revolutionary struggle for a share of power can be won merely by pressing a row of buttons. Human beings with all their faults and strengths constitute the mechanism of a social movement. They must make mistakes and learn from them, make more mistakes and learn anew. They must

taste defeat as well as success, and discover how to live with each. Time and action are the teachers.

When we planned our strategy for Birmingham months later, we spent many hours assessing Albany and trying to learn from its errors. (King, 1963:34-35)

The implication of King's statement is that a fuller understanding of the dynamic under discussion here was born of events in Albany. No doubt a part of this fuller understanding was a growing awareness of the importance of white violence as a stimulus to federal action. As Hubbard (1968) argues, this awareness appears to have influenced the choice of Birmingham as the next major protest site. "King's Birmingham innovation was preeminently strategic. Its essence was not merely more refined tactics, but the selection of a target city which had as its Commissioner of Public Safety, 'Bull' Connor, a notorious racist and hothead who could be depended on not to respond nonviolently" (Hubbard, 1968:5).

The view that King's choice of Birmingham was a conscious strategic one is supported by the fact that Connor was a lame-duck official, having been defeated by a moderate in a run-off election in early April 1963. Had SCLC waited to launch the protest campaign until after the moderate took office, there likely would have been considerably less violence *and* less leverage with which to press for federal involvement. "The supposition has to be that . . . SCLC, in a shrewd . . . stratagem, knew a good enemy when they saw him . . . one that could be counted on in stupidity and natural viciousness to play into their hands, for full exploitation in the press as archfiend and villain" (Watters, 1971:266).

The results of this choice of protest site are well known and clearly visible in Figure 4 and Table 2. The Birmingham campaign of April-May 1963 triggered considerable white resistance in the form of extreme police brutality and numerous instances of segregationist violence. In turn, the federal government was again forced to assume a more supportive stance vis-à-vis the movement. The ultimate result of this shifting posture was administration sponsorship of a civil rights bill that, even in much weaker form, it had earlier described as politically inopportune (Brooks, 1974). Under pressure by insurgents, the bill was ultimately signed into law a year later as the Civil Rights Act of 1964.

Finally there was Selma, the last of the massive community-wide campaigns. It was in this campaign that the characteristic protest dynamic under discussion was most fully realized. To quote Garrow (1978:227):

> . . . it is clear that by January 1965 King and the SCLC consciously had decided to attempt to elicit violent behavior from their immediate opponents. Such an intent governed the choice of Selma and Jim Clark [Selma's notoriously racist sheriff], and such an intent governed all of the tactical choices that the SCLC leadership made throughout the campaign. . . .

These choices achieved the desired result. Initiated in January 1965, the campaign reached its peak in February and March, triggering the typical reactive patterns of white resistance and federal involvement (see Figure 4 and Table 2). As regards segregationist violence, the campaign provoked no shortage of celebrated atrocities. On March 9, state troopers attacked and brutally beat some 525 marchers attempting to begin a protest march to Montgomery. Later that same day, the Reverend James Reeb, a march participant, was beaten to death by a group of whites. Finally, on March 25, following the triumphal completion of the twice interrupted Selma-to-Montgomery march, a white volunteer, Mrs. Viola Liuzzo, was shot and killed while transporting marchers back to Selma from the state capital. In response to this consistent breakdown of public order, the federal government was once again pressured to intervene in support of black interests. On March 15, President Johnson addressed a joint session of Congress to deliver his famous "We Shall Overcome" speech. Two days later he submitted to Congress a tough Voting Rights Bill containing several provisions that movement leaders had earlier been told were politically too unpopular to be incorporated into legislative proposals. The bill passed by overwhelming margins in both the Senate and House and was signed into law August 6 of the same year.

However, for all the drama associated with Selma it was to represent the last time insurgents were able successfully to orchestrate a coordinated community-wide protest campaign. Part of the reason for this failure was the growing dissension within the movement. As the earlier consensus regarding goals and tactics gradually collapsed around mid-decade, so too did the ability of insurgents to mount broad-based community campaigns. "The movement—in the special sense of organizations and leaders working together toward agreed goals . . . fell apart after Selma" (Watters, 1971:330).

But growing internal problems were only part of the reason for the movement's diminished use of this tactic. As was the case with earlier innovations, movement opponents learned to counter the specific tactic and in so doing short-circuit the more general protest dynamic under discussion here. The key to both outcomes lay in the opponents' ability to control the violent excesses of the most rabid segregationists. Through the process of tactical interaction they learned to do exactly that. Von Eschen et al. (1969:229-30) explain:

> The response of the movement's opponents was bound to become less extreme. For one thing, a movement is a school in which both the movement and its opponents learn by trial and error the most appropriate moves. Thus, much of the success of the movement had depended on the untutored, emotional responses of the Southern police. In time, however, authorities learned that such responses were counter-productive. In some areas, authorities learned responses sufficiently appropriate to deny the movement its instrument of disorder and to totally disorganize its leadership. In Maryland, for instance, Mayor McKeldin responded to CORE's announcement that Baltimore was to become CORE's target city with a warm welcome and an offer of aid, and the temporary chief of police, Gelston, used highly sophisticated tactics to defuse CORE's strategies.

Finally, the increasing northern locus of movement activity made use of the tactic and the characteristic three-way dynamic on which it depended virtually impossible to sustain. The reason centers on the very different form that white resistance took in the North as opposed to the South.

> One of the functional characteristics of the Southern segregationists was that they could be counted on, when sufficiently provoked, to create the violent disruptions of public order needed to produce federal intervention. No such convenient foil was available to the movement outside the South. . . . Without the dramatic instances of overt white oppression, the movement was deprived of both the visible manifestations of racism so valuable as organizing devices and the leverage needed to force supportive government involvement. Having developed an effective mode of tactical interaction vis-à-vis one opponent, insurgents were unable to devise a similarly suitable response to the changed pattern of northern resistance. (McAdam, 1982:214-15)

Urban Rioting

The last of the major tactical innovations of the period was the urban riot of the mid to late 1960s. Though by no means the first use of the tactic, the Watts riot of 1965 seemed to inaugurate an era of unprecedented urban unrest (see Downes, 1970:352). In the three years following the Watts riot "urban disorders" increased steadily. The peaks in riot activity shown in Figure 3 for the summers of 1966-68 reflect the spread of rioting during this period.

That there were differences between the riots and the tactical forms discussed earlier should be obvious. Most importantly, no evidence has ever been produced to indicate that the riots were deliberately planned or carried out by specific insurgent groups, as were the other tactics. There is little question, however, that the riots came to be *used* rhetorically by black leaders as a tactic and widely interpreted as a form of political protest within the black community (Fogelson, 1971:17). Then, too, the often noted selectivity of riot targets suggests that at the very least the rioters were animated, in part, by a limited political definition of their own actions.

In addition to their political use and interpretation, the riots share two other similarities with the other protest techniques discussed above. First, all occasioned a significant breakdown in public order. And, except for the bus boycotts and sit-ins, all served to stimulate directly supportive federal action.[11] Evidence to support this latter contention is drawn from a number of sources. For example, Button (1978) documents a strong (though by no means consistent) pattern of increased federal expenditure for programs benefiting blacks (and poor whites) in 40 American cities following urban riots in those locales. Consistent with the general thrust of Button's work are the data on school desegregation (U.S. Commission of Civil Rights, 1977:18). They suggest a close connection between disruptive insurgency and the pace of federally sponsored school desegregation efforts. Finally, the work of Isaac and Kelly (1981), and Schram and Turbett (1983), among others, argues for a close connection between the riots and the expansion in welfare benefits in the late 1960s.

With use, however, all new tactical forms become less effective, and so it was with the urban riot. After 1965—and especially after 1967—the ameliorative federal response to the riots was increasingly supplanted by a massive control response at all levels of government which was designed to counter the continued threat posed by the disorders. That these efforts had a measurable effect on the actual handling of the riots is suggested by a comparison of data on the 1967 and April 1968 disorders, the latter occurring in the wake of Martin Luther King's assassination.

The first finding of note involves a comparison of the number of law enforcement personnel used in quelling these two sets of disturbances. As shown in Table 3, the force levels used in the 1968 disorders were on the average 50 percent greater than those used the previous year. As Skolnick (1969:173) notes:

> . . . 1968 represented a new level in the massiveness of the official response to racial disorder. In April alone . . . more National Guard troops were called than in all of 1967 . . . and more federal troops as well. . . . *Never* before in this country has such a massive military response been mounted against racial disorder.

The presence of increased numbers of enforcement personnel facilitated the more thoroughgoing containment efforts desired by those charged with controlling the disorders. As the data in Table 3 indicate, all major indices of official repression, save one, showed increases between 1967 and April 1968. The average number of injuries per disorder

in 1968 was nearly 40 percent higher than in 1967. Even more dramatic was the nearly two-fold increase in the average number of arrests between the two years.

In the face of this massive control response, it is hardly surprising that the intensity and pace of movement activity dropped sharply in the final two years of the period under study (Feagin and Hahn, 1973:193-94; Skolnick, 1969:173). Confronted by government forces increasingly willing and able to suppress ghetto disorders with force, and painfully aware of the costs incurred in the earlier rioting, insurgents gradually abandoned the tactic. In effect, the government's massive control efforts had proven an effective tactical adaptation to the riots. Though no doubt sensible, the abandonment of rioting as a form of protest deprived insurgents of the last major tactical innovation of the era. And with the abandonment of the tactic, insurgency once again declined sharply (see Figure 1).

The failure of the insurgents to devise new tactical forms must ultimately be seen as a response to the shifting political and organizational realities of the late 1960s and early 1970s. Just as the earlier innovations had depended upon the confluence of internal organization and external opportunity, the cessation of innovation can be seen, in part, as a function of a certain deteriora-

Table 3
Comparative Statistics on Racial Disorders During 1967 and April, 1968[a]

	Year 1967	April 1968	Totals
Number of Disorders	217	167	384
Cities	160	138	298
States	34 (+ Wash., D.C.)	36 (+ Wash., D.C.)	70 (+ Wash., D.C.)
Arrests	18,800	27,000	45,800
Avg. No. of Arrests Per Disorder	87	162	119
Injured	3,400	3,500	6,900
Avg. No. Injured Per Disorder	16	22	18
Killed	82	43	125
Property Damage[b]	$69,000,000	$58,000,000	$127,000,000
National Guard			
Times Used	18	22	40
Number Used	27,700	34,900	62,600
Federal Troops			
Times Used	1	3	4
Number Used	4,800	23,700	28,500

Source: Adapted from Lemberg Center for the Study of Violence, "April Aftermath of the King Assassination," Riot Data Review, Number 2 (August 1968), Brandeis University, p. 60. (mimeographed).

[a]Excluded from the totals reported in this chart are "equivocal" disorders, so termed by the authors of the study because of sketchy information on the racial aspects of the event.

[b]Property damage refers to physical damage to property or loss of stock (usually through looting), estimated in dollars.

tion in these two factors. Organizationally the movement grew progressively weaker as the '60s wore on. In the face of the collapse of the strong consensus on issues and tactics that had prevailed within the movement during its heyday, insurgents found it increasingly difficult to organize the strong, focused campaigns characteristic of the early 1960s. Instead, by 1970, insurgent activity had taken on a more diffuse quality with a veritable profusion of small groups addressing a wide range of issues by means of an equally wide range of tactics. Unfortunately, the diversity inherent in this approach was all too often offset by a political impotence born of the absence of the strong protest vehicles that had earlier dominated the movement.

Second, reversing a trend begun during the 1930s, the "structure of political opportunities" available to blacks contracted in the late 1960s in response to a variety of emergent pressures. Chief among these was the mobilization of a strong conservative "backlash" in this country fueled both by the turbulence of the era and the conscious exploitation of "law and order" rhetoric by public officials. When combined with the emergence of other competing issues and the declining salience of the black vote, this "backlash" served to diminish the overall political leverage exercised by insurgents and therefore the prospects for successful insurgency.

Summary

The pace of black insurgency between 1955 and 1970 has been analyzed as a function of an ongoing process of *tactical interaction be*tween insurgents and their opponents. Even in the face of a conducive political environment and the presence of strong movement organizations, insurgents face a stern tactical challenge. Lacking institutional power, challengers must devise protest techniques that offset their powerlessness. This has been referred to as a process of *tactical innovation*. Such innovations, however, only temporarily afford challengers increased bargaining leverage. In chesslike fashion, movement opponents can be expected, through effective *tactical adaptation,* to neutralize the new tactic, thereby reinstituting the original power disparity between themselves and the challenger. To succeed over time, then, a challenger must continue its search for new and effective tactical forms.

In the specific case of the black movement, insurgents succeeded in doing just that. Between 1955 and 1965 they developed and applied a series of highly effective new tactical forms that, in succession, breathed new life into the movement. For each new innovation, however, movement opponents were eventually able to devise the effective tactical counters that temporarily slowed the momentum generated by the introduction of the technique. With the abandonment of the riots in the late 1960s, insurgents were left without the tactical vehicles needed to sustain the movement. Reflecting the collapse of the movement's centralized organizational core and the general decline in the political system's vulnerability to black insurgency, by decade's end the movement had not so much died as been rendered tactically impotent.

Notes

1. I am not alone in noting the relative lack of attention paid to the dynamics of movement development and decline in the sociological literature. Gamson (1975), Piven and Cloward (1979), and Snyder and Kelly (1979) have made similar comments in other contexts. The introduction of resource mobilization and other "rationalistic" theories of social movements, however, has helped focus more attention on the ongoing dynamics of movement development. In the work of such theorists as Tilly (1978), McCarthy and Zald (1973, 1977), and others, one begins to discern the outlines of a systematic framework for analyzing not just the emergence but subsequent development/decline of social movements.

2. Though hardly a major focus of theoretical attention, the dynamic has at least been acknowledged and discussed by a number of movement theorists. Zald and Useem (1982), for example, apply a similar interactive perspective to the study of the ongoing relationship between movements and the countermovements they give rise to. Such a perspective also informs Tilly's (1978) model of social movements. Finally, elements of an interactive conception of movement development are implied in McPhail and Miller's work (1973) on the "assembling process."

3. In his analysis of the emergence and spread of the sit-in tactic, Morris (1981) offers a richly drawn example of the organizational roots of tactical innovation. In this case it was the indigenous network of southern black churches, colleges, and local movement affiliates that supplied the organizational context essential to the successful application and diffusion of the sit-in tactic.

4. A possible exception to the rule involves the urban riots of the mid to late 1960s. In the case of these loosely organized, more diffuse forms of protest, it is likely that the media—particularly television—served as the principal vehicle of diffusion linking rioters in different cities. Within the same city, how-

ever, several authors have noted the importance of indigenous associational networks in the spread of the riot (cf. Feagin and Hann, 1973:48-49; Wilson and Orum, 1976:198).

5. For a more complete discussion of the coding procedures employed in this analysis the reader is referred to McAdam, 1982:235-50.

6. In most cases the protest techniques were not really new. Indeed, most had been employed by insurgents previously. What distinguished their use from previous applications was the adoption of the tactic by other insurgent groups. The extensiveness of the adoption is largely attributable to the dense network of communication ties that had developed between insurgents by 1960. Morris (1981) provides a detailed illustration of the crucial importance of formal and informal ties in the process of tactical diffusion in his analysis of the spread of the sit-in tactic. His analysis merely underscores a fundamental point made earlier: the significance of the process of tactical innovation depends heavily on the organizational resources available to insurgent groups. A well-developed communication network linking insurgents together is perhaps the most critical of these resources.

7. All of the examples are taken from Smith and Killian's (1958) account of the bus boycott in Tallahassee, Florida, and the conflict that stemmed from it.

8. Nor was the cost of the sit-ins for the segregationists merely financial. The symbolic consequences were enormous as well. For southern blacks and whites alike the sit-ins served to shatter certain myths that had served for decades to sustain the racial status quo. Southern blacks who had long felt powerless to effect basic changes in "their" way of life were galvanized by the realization that they were in fact doing just that. For their part many segregationists found it increasingly difficult to maintain their long-held invidious moral distinction between blacks and whites as a result of the glaring symbolic contrast evident in the sit-ins. The dilemma is nicely captured by an editorial that appeared in the prosegregationist *Richmond News Leader* on February 22, 1960, in the wake of sit-ins in that city. In part the editorial read:

> Many a Virginian must have felt a tinge of wry regret at the state of things as they are, in reading of Saturday's "sit-downs" by Negro students in Richmond stores. Here were the colored students, in coats, white shirts, ties, and one of them was reading Goethe and one was taking notes from a biology text. And here on the sidewalk outside, was a gang of white boys come to heckle, a ragtail rabble, slack-jawed, black-jacketed, grinning fit to kill, and some of them, God save the mark, were waving the proud and honored flag of the Southern States in the last war fought by gentlemen. Ehew! It gives one pause. (quoted in Zinn, 1965:27)

In accounting for the sit-ins, then, one must consider the symbolic consequences of the demonstrations, no less than the financial cost to the segregationists.

9. My use of logit regression was motivated primarily by a concern for the likely heteroskedasticity of my data. For an excellent introduction to the technique and its possible uses see Swafford (1980). The unit of analysis in the logit regression was the first seven weeks following the introduction of each protest tactic. The analysis was based on a total of 84 observations.

10. In coding story synopses a distinction was made between two general types of movement-related activity. *Statements* referred to any written or oral pronouncements related to the topic of civil rights that were issued by a party to the conflict. *Actions* represented a broad category consisting of all other types of activity *except* for statements. The term *event* was used to designate the total of all statements and actions attributed to a particular initiating unit.

11. This is not to suggest that the bus boycott and sit-ins were unsuccessful. It must be remembered that, unlike the later tactics, the goal of the boycott and sit-ins was not so much to stimulate federal intervention as to mobilize leverage *at the local level* through the creation of negative financial inducements. In this they were largely successful.

This analysis is based on all *events* initiated by the federal government but only the *actions* attributed to movement and segregationist forces. This convention reflects my conception of the dominant conflict dynamic operative during the early 1960s. Movement and segregationist forces tended to engage in a chesslike exchange of strategic *actions* (e.g., marches, court orders, arrests, sit-ins, beatings) within a localized conflict arena. Much of this local maneuvering, however, was played out for the benefit of federal officials, whose *actions* and *statements* came, in turn, to exert a crucial influence over the course of local events.

A second methodological convention should also be clarified at this point. The decision to lag movement actions one month behind both segregationist actions and government events was made *before* the completion of data collection and was based on my reading of many impressionistic accounts of specific movement campaigns. Those accounts invariably stressed the *delayed reaction* of segregationists to movement activity in their community. Thus, for example, we are told that "Birmingham residents of both races were surprised at the restraint of [Bull] Connor's [Birmingham's notorious chief of police] men at the beginning of the campaign" (King, 1963:69). Once mobilized, however, local segregationists could generally be counted on to respond with the flagrant examples of public violence that made a virtually *instantaneous* federal response necessary. ✦

27

The Success of the Unruly

William A. Gamson

It is a happy fact that we continue to be shocked by the appearance of violence in social protest. Apparently, frequency is no great cushion against shock for, at least in America, social protest has been liberally speckled with violent episodes. One can exaggerate the frequency—a majority of challenges run their course without any history of violence or arrests. But a very substantial minority—more than 25 percent—have violence in their history. The fact that violence is a common consort of social protest in the United States is not a matter of serious contention.

The consequences of violence are at issue. It is commonly believed to be self-defeating. Evaluating the validity of this belief is made elusive by a tendency that we all have, social scientists and laymen alike, to allow our moral judgments to influence our strategic judgments and vice versa. Kaplowitz has suggested the following general hypothesis. If strategic rationality does not clearly specify a course of action as desirable but normative criteria do, people will tend to believe that the normatively desirable course of action is also strategically rational.[1]

Violence is relatively unambiguous morally. At most, it is regarded as a necessary evil which may be justified in preventing or overcoming some even greater evil. And for many, the situations in which it is justified are scant to nonexistent. The issue depends on one's image of the society in which violence takes place. In a closed and oppressive political system that offers no nonviolent means for accomplishing change, the morality of violence is not as clear. But when it is believed that effective nonviolent alternatives exist, almost everybody would consider these morally preferable.

In the pluralist image of American society, the political system is relatively open, offering access at many points for effective nonviolent protest and efforts at change. With this premise, the

use of violence by groups engaged in efforts at social change seems particularly reprehensible. The above reasoning should apply not only to violence as a means of influence but as a means of social control as well. The use of violence and other extralegal methods for dealing with protestors is also morally reprehensible.

While the moral issues may be clear, the strategic ones are ambiguous. There is no consensus on the set of conditions under which violence is a more or less effective strategy, and the issue has been seriously analyzed only in the international sphere. The Kaplowitz hypothesis, if correct, explains the strong tendency for people to believe that something so immoral as domestic violence is not a very effective strategy in domestic social protest. It also helps us to recognize that the fact that many people regard violence as self-defeating is no evidence that it is actually futile.

The pluralist view, then, acknowledges that collective violence has taken place in the United States with considerable frequency but argues that it is effective neither as a strategy of social influence when used by challenging groups nor as a strategy of repression when it is used by the enemies of such groups. We treat this view here as an hypothesis. It would be comforting to find that moral and strategic imperatives coincide, but the evidence discussed below suggests that they do not.

Violence Users and Recipients

I mean by the term "violence" deliberate physical injury to property or persons. This does not embrace such things as forceful constraint—for example, arrest—unless it is accompanied by beatings or other physical injury. It also excludes bribery, brainwashing, and other nasty techniques. To use the term violence as a catch-all for unpleasant means of influence or social control confuses the issue; other unpopular means need to stand forth on their own for evaluation, and we will explore some of these as well.

Among the 53 groups, there were 15 that engaged in violent interactions with antagonists, agents of social control, or hostile third parties. Eight of these groups were active participants; they themselves used violence. It is important to emphasize that these "violence users" were not necessarily initiators; in some cases they were attacked and fought back, and in still others the sequence of events is unclear. No assumption is made that the violence users were necessarily the aggressors in the violent interaction that transpired.

Whether they initiate violence or not, all of the violence users accept it, some with reluctance and some with apparent glee. Wallace Stegner (1949, pp. 255-56) describes some of the actions of Father Coughlin's Christian Front against Communism. "In Boston, a *Social Justice* truck went out to distribute the paper without benefit of the mails. When a *Boston Traveler* photographer tried for a picture, the truck driver kicked his camera apart while a friendly cop held the photographer's arms." In another incident in the Boston area, a printer named Levin was approached by Christian Fronters who handed him *Social Justice* and told him, "'Here, you're a Jew, Levin. You ought to read about what your pals have been doing lately. Take a look how your investments in Russia are coming.' . . . One morning, . . . Levin came down to his shop to find it broken open and its contents wrecked." In New York, as Stegner describes it (p. 252), Christian Fronters would start fights with passing Jews, would beat up one or two opponents, and then vanish. Another source, Charles Tull (1965, p. 207) writes, that "it was common for the Coughlinite pickets . . . to be involved in violence with their more vocal critics. . . . Street brawls involving Christian Fronters and Jews became frequent in New York City. . . ." Now these accounts are at best unsympathetic to the Christian Front. Some of the clashes may well have been initiated by opponents of the group. For example, Tull points out that the "most notable incident from the standpoint of sheer numbers occurred on April 8, 1939, when a crowd of several thousand people mobbed ten newsboys selling *Social Justice*." Although the Christian Fronters may have been passive recipients of violence in this particular case, on many other occasions they clearly played the role of active participant or more.

The active role is even clearer in the case of the Tobacco Night Riders. . . . [There was some] violence directed against their constituency, but much of their violence was directed at the tobacco trust as well. "The Tobacco Night Riders were organized in 1906 as a secret, fraternal order, officially called 'The Silent Brigade' or 'The Inner Circle.' Their purpose was to force all growers to join the [Planters Protective] Association . . . and to force the [tobacco] trust companies to buy tobacco only from the association" (Nall, 1942).

The violence of the Night Riders was the most organized of any group studied. They "made their first show of armed force at Princeton [Kentucky], on the morning of Saturday, December 1, 1906, when shortly after midnight approximately 250 armed and masked men took possession of the city and dynamited and burned two large tobacco factories. . . . Citizens in the business district opened windows and looked out on bodies of masked men hurrying along with guns on their shoulders. They saw other masked and armed men patrolling the sidewalks and street corners and they heard commands: 'Get back!' And if they did not obey, bullets splattered against the brick walls near by or crashed through the window panes above their heads. . . . Several squads of men had marched in along the Cadiz road and captured the police station, the waterworks plants, the courthouse, and the telephone and telegraph offices. They had disarmed the policemen and put them under guard, shut off the city water supply, and taken the places of the telephone and telegraph operators. . . . Within a few minutes the city was in control of the Riders and all communication with the outside was cut off." With their mission accomplished and the tobacco factories in flames, the men "mounted their horses and rode away singing 'The fire shines bright in my old Kentucky home'" (Nall, 1942, p. 69).

About a year later, the Night Riders struck again at the town of Hopkinsville, Kentucky. It is worth noting, since the argument here views violence as instrumental rather than expressive, that the Hopkinsville raid was twice postponed when it appeared that the town was prepared to resist. "The Night Riders were not cowards," Nall writes, "but their cause and methods of operation did not demand that they face a resistant line of shot and shell to accomplish their purposes." The Night Riders made heavy use of fifth columnists in the town to assure that their raid could be successful without bloodshed. As in the Princeton raid, they carried out the operation with precision, occupying all strategic points. During this raid, they "shot into the . . . residence of W. Lindsay Mitchell, a buyer for the Imperial Tobacco Company, shattering electric lights and windowpanes. A group entered the house and disarmed him just in time to keep him from shooting into their comrades. He was brought into the street and struck over the head several times with a gun barrel, sustaining painful wounds. The captain of the squad looked on until he considered that Mr. Mitchell had 'had enough' then rescued him and escorted him back to his door" (Nall, p. 78). After the raid, they reassembled out of town for a roll call and marched away singing. The sheriff and local military officer organized a small posse to pursue the raiders and attacked their rear, killing one man and wounding another before the posse was forced to retreat back to Hopkinsville. One might have thought that the Night Riders would have retaliated for the attack made on them by the posse, and, indeed, Nall reports that "some of the Riders considered a second raid to retaliate . . . but such was not considered by the leaders. They had accomplished their purpose" (p. 82).

The Native American, or American Republican Party, a nativist group of the 1840s, was heavily implicated in less organized violence directed against Catholics. "Traversing the Irish section [of Philadelphia], the [nativist] mob was soon locked in armed conflict with equally riotous foreigners. The Hibernia Hose Company house was stormed and demolished; before midnight, more than thirty houses belonging to Irishmen had been burned to the ground. . . ." A few nights later, "roaming the streets, the rioters finally came to Saint Michael's Catholic Church. A rumor that arms were concealed within the building proved sufficient grounds for attack, and while the presiding priest fled in disguise, the torch was applied. . . ." The mob also burned St. Augustine's Church and "throughout the city, priests and nuns trembled for their lives" (Billington, 1963, pp. 225-26). Party leadership repudiated much of this mob action but especially deplored and emphasized the counterattacks: "the killing of natives by foreign mobs." The central involvement of American Republicans was, however, substantial and well-documented.

The other violence users were all labor unions involved in clashes with strikebreakers or police and militia called out to assist and defend the strikebreakers. Among the violence users, then, the challenging group is sometimes the initiator but not always; sometimes the leadership openly defends and advocates the practice but not always. To be classified as a violence user, it is only necessary that the group be an active participant in the violent interactions in which it is involved.

The recipients of violence were passive recipients—they were attacked and either did not or, because they had insufficient means, could not

fight back. The International Workingmen's Association, the First International, is one example. In September, 1873, a major financial panic occurred in the United States, resulting in subsequent unemployment and economic dislocation. A mass demonstration was called for January 13, 1874, in the form of a march of the unemployed in New York City. To quote John Commons (1966, p. 220), " It was the original plan of the Committee that the parade should disband after a mass meeting in front of the city hall but this was prohibited by the authorities and Tompkins Square was chosen as the next best place for the purpose. The parade was formed at the appointed hour and by the time it reached Tompkins Square it had swelled to an immense procession. Here they were met by a force of policemen and, immediately after the order to disperse had been given, the police charged with drawn clubs. During the ensuing panic, hundreds of workmen were injured."

Abolitionists were frequent recipients of violence in the form of antiabolitionist riots. The object of the violence was primarily the property and meeting places of abolitionists rather than their persons, although there were frequent threats and some physical abuse as well. The National Female Anti-Slavery Society was victimized on various occasions, although the women themselves were never attacked. Once, when the hall in which they were scheduled to hold a meeting was set on fire by an antiabolitionist mob, the women sought refuge in the home of Lucretia Mott. "As the rioters swarmed through nearby streets, it seemed as if an attack on the Mott house were imminent but a friend of the Motts joined the mob, and crying, 'On to the Motts' led them in the wrong direction" (Lutz, 1968, p. 139). William Lloyd Garrison was attacked at one of the meetings and dragged through the streets. The American Anti-Slavery Society was similarly abused. Eggs and stones were thrown at the audience of several of their meetings. In Cincinnati, rioters attacked the shops and homes of abolitionists, particularly Englishmen. An abolitionist printer in Illinois, Elijah Lovejoy, was killed when he attempted to resist an antiabolitionist mob destroying his shop. Lovejoy's resistance was isolated and provoked a controversy in the fervently nonviolent society. Lovejoy had had his printing presses destroyed three times, "his house was invaded, and his wife was brought to the verge of hysterical collapse. When a fourth new press arrived, Lovejoy determined that he would protect it. . . . When his press was attacked he raised his pistol but was quickly gunned down by one of the mob." Even under such circumstances, "abolitionists in the American Anti-Slavery Society and elsewhere were divided on whether or not to censure Lovejoy's action" (Sorin, 1972, p. 91). They did not censure Lovejoy but reasserted their commitment to nonviolent means of achieving the end of slavery.

Members of the National Student League were attacked in the familiar manner of northern civil rights workers going south in the 1960s. In one instance, the cause was the bitter struggle of coal miners in Harlan County, Kentucky. "At Cumberland Gap, the mountain pass into Kentucky, the full impact of Kentucky law and order descended. The road was almost dark when the bus turned the corner over the boundary; out of the approaching night the scowling faces of a mob of more than 200 people greeted the visitors. Cars drove up and surrounded the bus; most of the throng were armed, wearing the badges of deputy sheriffs. . . . There were derisive cat-calls, then the ominous lynch-cry: 'String 'em up' " (Wechsler, 1935). Students were shoved and some knocked down, but none seriously injured on this occasion.

The recipients of violence, then, unlike the users, played essentially passive roles in the violent episodes in which they were involved. The success or failure of the violence users will enable us to say something about the effectiveness of violence as a means of influence; the success or failure of the violence recipients will help us to evaluate the effectiveness of violence as a means of social control.

The Results

What is the fate of these groups? Are the users of violence crushed by adverse public reaction and the coercive power of the state? Do the recipients of violence rouse the public sympathy with their martyrdom, rallying to their cause important bystanders who are appalled at their victimization and join them in their struggle?

Figure 1 gives the basic results. The violence users, it turns out, have a higher-than-average success rate. Six of the eight won new advantages, and five of these six established a minimal acceptance relationship as well. Of

course, some paid their dues in blood in the process as we have seen in the descriptions above. The seven recipients of violence also paid such dues but with little or nothing to show for it in the end. One, The Dairymen's League, established a minimal acceptance relationship with its antagonist, but none of them were able to gain new advantages for their beneficiary. With respect to violence and success, it appears better to give than receive.

Figure 1
Arrests and Outcome

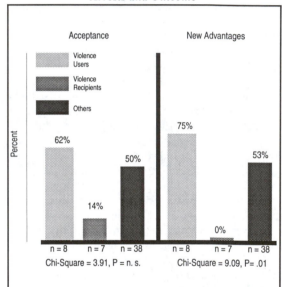

* This excludes 12 groups that were involved in violent interactions and experienced arrests.

† This excludes 3 groups that were involved in violent interactions but did not experience arrests

It is worth asking whether the different goals of these groups might account for the difference. The most relevant variable . . . is whether the displacement of the antagonist is part of the goals. Two of the eight violence users have displacement goals, and two of the seven violence recipients do also. Figure 2 makes the same comparison as Figure 1 but only for those groups that are not attempting to replace their targets. It reveals that every violence user with more limited goals is successful, although the Night Riders were not accepted; every violence recipient was unsuccessful, although the Dairymen's League won minimal acceptance. The earlier result is, if anything, sharpened.

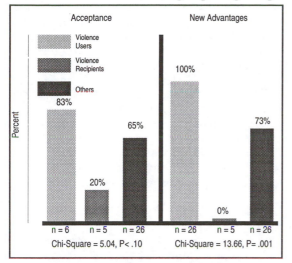

Figure 2
Violence and Outcome Excluding Displacing Groups

Does Violence Pay?

Am I ready to conclude then that violence basically works? Not quite, or at least not in any simple fashion, and my caution is not due simply to the small number of cases involved and the real possibility of sampling error. It is easier to say what these data refute than what they prove.

Specifically, the data undermine the following line of thinking: violence is the product of frustration, desperation, and weakness. It is an act of last resort by those who see no other means of achieving their goals. In this view, the challenging group, frustrated by its inability to attract a significant following and gain some response from its targets of influence, turns to violence in desperation. However, this merely hastens and insures its failure because its actions increase the hostility around it and invite the legitimate action of authorities against it.

When authorities use violence against challenging groups, there are similar dynamics in this argument. Frightened by the growing strength of the challenging group and unable to halt its rising power by legitimate means, tottering on their throne and unwilling to make concessions, the threatened authorities turn to repression. But this attempted repression simply adds fuel to the fire, bringing new allies to the cause of the challenging group and increasing its chances of ultimate success.

However compelling these images may be, they clearly do not fit the data presented here. The interpretation I would suggest is almost the opposite. As Eisinger (1973) puts it in discussing protest behavior in American cities, one hypothesis is that protest is as much a "signal of impatience as frustration." Violence should be viewed as an instrumental act, aimed at furthering the purposes of the group that uses it when they have some reason to think it will help their cause. This is especially likely to be true when the normal condemnation which attends to its use is muted or neutralized in the surrounding community, when it is tacitly condoned by large parts of the audience. In this sense, it grows from an impatience born of confidence and rising efficacy rather than the opposite. It occurs when hostility toward the victim renders it a relatively safe and costless strategy. The users of violence sense that they will be exonerated because they will be seen as more the midwives than the initiators of punishment. The victims are implicitly told, "See how your sins have provoked the wrath of the fanatics and have brought this punishment upon yourselves."

The size of the violence users and recipients supports this interpretation. The violence users tend to be large groups, the recipients small ones. Only one of the eight violence users is under 10,000 (the Night Riders) while five of the seven violence recipients are this small. Such growth seems more likely to breed confidence and impatience, not desperation.

I am arguing, then, that it is not the weakness of the user but the weakness of the target that accounts for violence. This is not to say that the weakness of a target is sufficient to produce violence but that, in making it more likely to be profitable, it makes it more likely to occur. As Figure 2 showed, many challenging groups are able to gain a positive response without resorting to violence, and many collapse without the added push of repression. But groups that are failing for other reasons and authorities that are being forced to respond by rising pressures generally do not turn to violence. This is why, in my interpretation, violence is associated with successful change or successful repression: it grows out of confidence and strength and their attendant impatience with the pace of change. It is, in this sense, as much a symptom of success as a cause.

It is worth noting that, with the exception of the Night Riders, none of the groups that used violence made it a primary tactic. Typically it was incidental to the primary means of influence—strikes, bargaining, propaganda, or other nonviolent means. It is the spice, not the meat and potatoes. And, if one considers the Night Riders as merely the striking arm of the respectable Planters Protective Association, even this exception is no exception.

The groups that receive violence, with one exception, are attacked in an atmosphere of countermobilization of which the physical attacks are the cutting edge. They are attacked not merely because they are regarded as threatening—all challenging groups are threatening to some vested interests. They are threatening *and* vulnerable, and most fail to survive the physical attacks to which they are subjected.

Other Constraints

This argument can be further evaluated by extending it to other constraints in addition to violence. "Constraints are the addition of new disadvantages to the situation or the threat to do so, regardless of the particular resources used" (Gamson, 1968a). Violence is a special case of constraints but there are many others.

Twenty-one groups (40 percent) made use of constraints as a means of influence in pursuing their challenge. We have already considered eight of them, those that used violence, and we turn now to the other 13. The most common constraints used by these groups were strikes and boycotts, but they also included such things as efforts to discredit and humiliate individual enemies by personal vituperation. Discrediting efforts directed against "the system" or other more abstract targets are not included, but only individualized, ad hominem attacks attempting to injure personal reputation.

Included here, for example, is A. Philip Randolph's March on Washington Committee, designed to push President Roosevelt into a more active role in ending discrimination in employment. A mass march in the spring of 1941 to protest racial discrimination in America would have been a considerable embarrassment to the Roosevelt administration. America was mobilizing for war behind appeals that contrasted democracy with the racism of the Nazi regime. Walter White of the NAACP described "the President's skillful attempts to dissuade us" (quoted in Garfinkel, 1969). The march was, from the standpoint of the administration, something to be avoided, a new disadvantage which the committee was threatening.

William Randolph Hearst's Independence League made liberal use of personal vituperation against opponents. "Most of Hearst's energy was devoted to pointing out the personal inequities of boss Charles F. Murphy. He found himself obliged to go back to the time of Tweed to discover any parallel in political corruption. . . . 'Murphy is as evil a specimen of a criminal boss as we have had since the days of Tweed'" (Carlson and Bates, 1936, pp. 146-47).

The League of Deliverance made primary use of the boycott weapon, employing it against businesses that hired Chinese labor. They threatened worse. The League's executive committee proposed to notify offenders of their desires and if not complied with, "after the expiration of six days it will be the duty of the Executive Committee to declare the district dangerous. . . . Should the Chinese remain within the proclaimed district after the expiration of . . . 30 days, the general Executive Committee will be required to abate the danger in whatever manner seems best to them" (Cross, 1935). The League, however, never had call to go beyond the boycott tactic.

Among the 13 nonviolent constraint users are three groups that were considered earlier as vio-

Figure 3

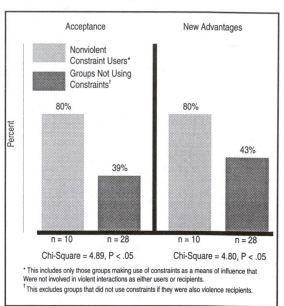

* This includes only those groups making use of constraints as a means of influence that Were not involved in violent interactions as either users or recipients.
† This excludes groups that did not use constraints if they were also violence recipients.

lence recipients. Including them makes it more difficult to interpret the relationship of success to the use of constraints since this is compounded by physical attacks on the group. Therefore, in Figure 3, we include only those ten groups that employed constraints but were not involved in violent interactions as either user or recipient. The advantage again goes to the unruly. Four-fifths of the constraint users and only two-fifths of the others are successful.

Constraints other than violence can also be used as a means of social control. In particular, many groups experience arrest and imprisonment or deportation of members which can be equally as devastating as physical attack, if not more so. Almost two-fifths of the sample (20 groups) had members arrested at some time or another during the period of challenge. These 20 included all eight of the violence users and four of the seven recipients, leaving only eight groups that were not involved in violent interactions but were subjected to arrests.

The Young People's Socialist League had people arrested during both its periods of challenge. "'You're under arrest,'" began an article in *The Challenge,* the YPSL paper. "This was not the first time members of the Young People's Socialist League had heard this pronouncement by officers while they were peacefully demonstrating against injustice." During its period of challenge in the World War I era, the national secretary of the group, William Kruse, was arrested, tried, convicted, and sentenced to 20 years imprisonment but ultimately won on appeal.

The German-American Bund was subject to arrests on a number of occasions. Fritz Kuhn, the group's major leader, was convicted of embezzling Bund funds, income tax evasion, and forgery. Other members were indicted on more political charges such as espionage. Some were tried in New York State under a rarely invoked statute passed in 1923 as a measure against the Ku Klux Klan, but Bundists won on appeal (Rowan, 1939, p. 178).

The American Birth Control League also experienced its share of official harassment. Soon after its organization, Margaret Sanger arrived at Town Hall in New York with her featured speaker, Harold Cox, editor of the *Edinburgh Review.*

> She found a crowd gathered outside. One hundred policemen, obviously intending to prevent the meeting, ringed the locked doors of the hall. When

the police opened the doors to let people already inside exit, those outside rushed in, carrying Mrs. Sanger and Cox before them. Once inside, Mrs. Sanger tried several times to speak, but policemen forcibly removed her from the platform. . . . Cox managed only to blurt, "I have come across the Atlantic to address you," before two policemen hauled him from the stage. The police arrested Mrs. Sanger and led her out of the hall while the audience sang, "My Country, 'Tis of Thee."

A few weeks later, with evidence of complicity of the Catholic Church in the raid emerging, Mrs. Juliet Barrett Rublee, a friend of Mrs. Sanger, was arrested "while she was in the act of testifying at an investigation into the charge of church influence behind the [earlier] raid" (Kennedy, 1970, pp. 95-96).

Figure 4 considers the eight groups subjected to arrest, again excluding all groups involved in violent interactions.[2] Only two of the eight groups were successful while nearly 60 percent of the remainder were. The results seem even clearer when we examine the two exceptions. Only two of the eight groups made use of nonviolent constraints—the League of Deliverance used the boycott and the United Brotherhood of Carpenters and Joiners of America used strikes and boycotts. These two groups were the only successes among the eight groups considered in Figure 4. In other words, groups that used neither violence nor any other form of constraint and yet experienced arrest were uniformly unsuccessful. In the absence of offsetting tactics by challenging groups, arrest seems to have the same connection with outcome as receiving violence, both are associated with failure for the receiving group.

There is another interesting fact about the six groups in Figure 4 that experience both arrests and failure. Five out of the six were attempting to displace antagonists as part of their goals, and three of the six advocated violence in principle even though they never actually employed it. Eisinger points out that "as long as protestors do not manipulate the threat of violence explicitly, they enjoy a slim legality, even, occasionally, legitimacy. Once they employ the threat openly, however, they open the way for authorities to suppress their movement or action" (1973, p. 14).

Groups like the Communist Labor Party, the Revolutionary Workers League, and the German-American Bund put themselves in the position of advocating or accepting violence as a tactic without actually using it. One might call this the strat-

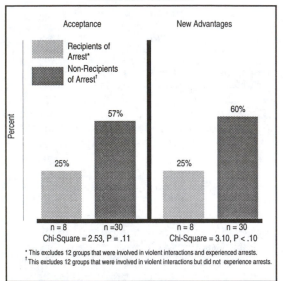

Figure 4
Arrests and Outcome

egy of speaking loudly and carrying a small stick. These groups seem to pay the cost of violence without gaining the benefits of employing it. They are both threatening and weak, and their repression becomes a low-cost strategy for those whom they attempt to displace.

Summary

The results on arrests and other constraints seem to parallel those on violence very closely. Unruly groups, those that use violence, strikes, and other constraints, have better than average success. Of the 21 groups that use some form of constraint, fully two-thirds win new advantages and 71 percent win acceptance. Among the ten groups that use no constraints but receive either violence or arrests, none is successful on either criterion. The 22 groups that neither experience

nor use constraints fall in the middle, 54 percent (12) win new advantages and half win acceptance.

Virtue, of course, has its own, intrinsic rewards. And a lucky thing it does too, since its instrumental value appears to be dubious. If we cannot say with certainty that violence and other constraints are successful tactics of social influence or social control, we must at least have greater doubt about the proposition that they lead to failure. When used by challenging groups, there is no evidence that they close doors that are open to those who use only inducements and persuasion. When used against challenging groups, there is no evidence that such tactics bring allies and sympathetic third parties to the effective aid of the beleaguered groups, allowing them to gain what would have been impossible acting alone.

Perhaps it is disconcerting to discover that restraint is not rewarded with success. But those who use more unruly tactics escape misfortune because they are clever enough to use these tactics primarily in situations where public sentiment neutralizes the normal deviance of the action, thus reducing the likelihood and effectiveness of counterattack.

Notes

1. Kaplowitz has explored the interaction between normative and strategic criteria experimentally (1973). He also argues for the complementary hypothesis to the one stated above: If normative criteria do not clearly specify a course of action while strategic criteria do, people will tend to believe that the strategically rational choice is the more normative one.

2. Only three of the 15 groups involved in violent interactions escaped arrests, all violence recipients. The violence in these cases came from hostile third parties—for example, antiabolitionist mobs—and the perpetrators of violence also escaped arrest. ◆

Part 9

Movement Careers: Extra-Movement Dynamics

In Part 8, we focused almost exclusively, on the internal tactical dynamics of social movements. That is, we sought to explore the factors that shape a movement's choice of tactics, the dynamics of tactical innovation within movements, and the relationship between tactics and movement success. Only occasionally did we reference the broader interactive dynamics that link movements to other groups in society. But movements do not operate in isolation. Normally, they confront a broad environment populated by a wide array of groups, each of which has considerable power to shape the ongoing development and ultimate impact of the movement. In this part, then, we wish to take better account of these groups and the ways in which they seek to constrain, control, or occasionally aid a given movement.

The sheer variety of such groups complicates our task. It is impossible to touch on all the main parties to the ongoing conflict in a single chapter, let alone devote readings to each of them. In the following selections we focus exclusively on the two groups that have received the most scholarly attention by movement researchers. These are the *state* and those *countermovements* that often arise to directly challenge the original movement. In some cases, agents of the state may act as allies or even active partisans in the countermovement, as southern elected officials did at the height of the American civil rights movement. More often, the three groups—movement, countermovement, and state—are enmeshed in a complex set of re-

lationships reflecting the often contradictory sets of interests which each brings to the conflict. The way these relationships evolve over the life of the conflict is perhaps the single most important factor shaping the ongoing development and ultimate impact of the movement. You will no doubt get a sense of this when we review the following three selections. Before we do, however, it is worth at least mentioning three other major groups whose actions may also prove consequential to the life of a movement: the media, non-governmental elites, and the general public.

The media's impact on social movements, though clearly important, is not well understood. Most academic observers, such as the sociologist Todd Gitlin (1980), have tended to be critical of the media's "sensationalist" coverage of social movements; coverage, they charge, that more often focuses on violence and charismatic leaders rather than the movement's substantive message. No doubt there is merit to this critical view. But the doggedness with which most movement groups seek media attention should caution us against a wholly negative view of the media. Movement organizers know that, for all their limitations, the various media are crucial to their aims. Having rejected proper political channels, movements must be able to get their message to the general public and the powers that be in some other way. The media are frequently the central conduit through which the movement seeks to influence public opinion and policy in their efforts to promote or resist change in society. While the general public does not set policy or implement political decisions, it can, when mobilized, affect both. It does so principally in two ways. First, supportive public opinion increases the pressure on state officials to react in ways favorable to the movement. Second, by mobilizing public support for a set of issues, a movement also increases the pool of people who might be drawn into more active roles in the struggle. So the number of people willing to give money, join a demonstration, or even go to jail for a cause invariably grows in the face of increased public awareness and support for a movement.

Finally, we should not underestimate the role of non-state elites in the emergence and development of social movements. Numerous examples exist. In the case of the American civil rights movement, various non-state elites played important roles. Numerous national foundations were active in funneling money to civil rights organizations to aid in voter registration campaigns. A variety of national religious organizations, such as the National Council of Churches came out four-square for the movement, at least during its non-violent civil rights phase. Even some generally conservative national corporations, fearing loss of revenues from their southern holdings, worked behind the scenes to restore public order, if not to directly press for civil rights goals. In a more contemporary vein, it would be hard to tell the story of the pro-life movement without mentioning the crucial support the movement has received throughout its history from the Catholic Church.

For all their importance, however, the aforementioned three groups generally pale in significance when compared to the two others mentioned above. To illustrate the importance of state officials and countermovement groups to a general understanding of social movement dynamics, we turn to the readings included in this part. In summarizing the three articles, we hope to provide a feel for the kinds of interactive dynamics involving movements, the state, and countermovements that very often determine the fate of a given struggle.

In the first selection, Ruud Koopmans analyzes the distribution and dynamics of protest activity in Germany between 1965 and 1989. He finds that novel, confrontational actions predominated in the early years of the "protest wave." Later, in response to complex patterns of state repression and facilitation, the new social movements which contributed most to the protest cycle increasingly split into two distinct wings. Benefiting from various kinds of state sponsorship, the moderates turned primarily to large, peaceful demonstrations to press their claims. The radicals, meanwhile, grew ever more violent and extreme in their actions, inviting state repression in the process. For Koopmans, then, the development of "a protest wave is the outcome of the interplay between the external constraints of facilitation . . . [and] repression . . . and activists choices among the different strategic options."

In the second selection, Steve Barkan also analyzes the interaction between movement forces and state authorities. His emphasis is on the differential impact of various forms of state repression on the southern civil rights movement. When state officials responded violently to civil rights demonstrators, it was the movement that generally benefited as a result of increased media attention, public outrage, and the supportive intervention of federal authorities. In contrast, when southern authorities resisted the urge to violence and used various legal weapons—mass arrests, high bail, court proceedings lacking due process—to tie up the movement, the result was a stalemate which left the status quo unchanged.

In the final selection, James Jasper and Jane Poulsen shift the focus from the interaction of state and movement to the dynamic interplay between movement and countermovement. Their empirical referent is three separate campaigns in the contemporary animal rights movement. By highlighting the different responses of the three targets to the protest campaigns mounted by the movement, the authors underscore the powerful effect that countermovements have on the ultimate outcome of social movement activity. It is not simply the state that mediates the conflict process, but a range of other parties including countermovement groups.

References

Gitlin, Todd. 1980. *The Whole World Is Watching.* Berkeley: University of California Press. ◆

28

The Dynamics of Protest Waves: West Germany, 1965 to 1989

Ruud Koopmans

The fluctuation between periods of contention and periods of acquiescence has long been a source of fascination and scientific interest. Protests usually occur in waves that wash over a country, but in many cases they have an international character. "What needs to be explained is not why people periodically petition, strike, demonstrate, riot, loot, and burn, but rather why so many of them do so at particular times in their history, and if there is a logical sequence to their actions" (Tarrow 1989b, p. 13). Tarrow (1988) called this "the largest current problem in collective action research" (1988, p. 435), and McAdam, McCarthy, and Zald (1988) cited "our relatively underdeveloped knowledge about the dynamics of collective action past the emergence of a movement" among "the most glaring deficiencies in the literature" (p. 728; see also Rucht 1990, p. 168; McAdam 1983, p. 735). One reason for this lack of attention for movement development may be that dynamic processes of interaction are difficult to grasp theoretically and analyze empirically. This is already the case for relatively simple interactions, involving a few, clearly circumscribed actors, which suggests that analyses of the dynamics of protest face formidable difficulties. Social movements are characterized by a low degree of institutionalization, high heterogeneity, a lack of clearly defined boundaries and decision-making structures, and a volatility matched by few other social phenomena. Moreover, the dynamics of protest are shaped by many actors. Social movements usually consist of informal, shifting, and often temporary coalitions of organizations, informal networks, subcultures, and individuals. In many cases, several such coalitions exist, each representing a usually vaguely bounded "current." In addition, social movements engage in cooperative or conflictive interactions with other actors, e.g., other social movements (including countermovements), allies within established politics, the police, and governments.

Given this complexity, a search for patterns in protest waves may appear doomed to failure. The sheer number of possible combinations of strategies and developmental trajectories make it unlikely that regularities will emerge among different protest waves. Any regularities that do exist may be buried under idiosyncrasies and be as easy to identify as a needle in a haystack.

However, recent studies of protest waves— the American civil rights movement (McAdam 1982), the Italian protest wave of the 1960s and 1970s (Tarrow 1989b), and new social movements in Western Europe (Duyvendak, van der Heijden, Koopmans, and Wijmans 1992; Koopmans 1992b, 1992c)—indicate that such skepticism may be premature. These studies reveal striking similarities among protest waves of different movements in different political contexts, which suggest that, at least for stable, Western democracies in the postwar period, recurrent patterns can be traced.

Identifying such patterns is one thing, explaining them is more difficult. The shortage of theories of protest development, let alone the lack of clearly specified hypotheses, implies that the explanations presented here must be tentative and based primarily on inductive and exploratory analyses rather than rigorous tests of hypotheses. My aims are to sketch the broad contours of the *terra incognita* of protest dynamics and to point at some main roads for exploring it.

Data

The analysis focuses on protest events produced by "new social movements" (NSMs) in West Germany between 1965 and 1989. New social movements include the peace, ecology, Third World solidarity, squatters', women's, gay, and student movements (including the radical Communist and terrorist groups that sprang from the student movement). These movements became the major form of social protest in Western Europe after the mid-1960s. This is especially true for West Germany, where they account for more than two-thirds of all protest events in the period studied (see Koopmans 1992c, p. 63).

"The Dynamics of Protest Waves: West Germany, 1965 to 1989." *American Sociological Review* 58: 637-658. Copyright © 1993 by the American Sociological Association. Reprinted with permission.

The validity of the concept of "new social movements" is hotly debated and can only be touched upon here (Dalton and Kuechler 1990; D'Anieri, Ernst, and Kier 1990; Tucker 1991). I do not necessarily subscribe to the idea advanced by Touraine (1978) and Offe (1985) that these movements represent a new political paradigm whose form and content differ radically from those of "old" social movements, like the labor movement. What matters for my present purpose is that empirical research has shown that these movements share a common social base in sections of the new middle class and that levels of support for the various NSMs are strongly correlated at the individual level (Kriesi 1989c, 1993). Moreover, the peaks and valleys in the levels of mobilization achieved by the different NSMs tend to be strongly clustered in time (see Duyvendak et al. 1992 for the Netherlands; Duyvendak 1992 for France; Giugni 1992 for Switzerland; and Koopmans 1992c for West Germany). Together, this evidence indicates that NSMs form a "social movement family" (Della Porta and Rucht 1991) that is distinct, though perhaps not dramatically different from other movement families (e.g., movements of the traditional left or the extreme right).

Figure 1 shows that NSM protests in Germany were concentrated in two periods—one in the late 1960s and one in the 1980s. Protests by other movements, in contrast, were infrequent throughout the period and were hardly affected by the ups and downs in the level of NSM protest. For this reason, I exclude protest events produced by other movements from the analyses.

Both waves of NSM protest originated in changes in the political opportunity structures confronting these movements, particularly changes in the position of the West German Social Democrats (Koopmans 1992c; Kriesi, Koopmans, Duyvendak, and Giugni 1992a).[1] My interest here, however, is in how the two protest waves developed after their emergence and the factors that contributed to their ultimate decline.

Data on protest events were obtained by content coding the Monday issues of the *Frankfurter Rundschau*, one of West Germany's leading daily newspapers. The concentration on Monday issues of the newspaper differs from other newspaper-based studies of protests, which generally have included all issues of a newspaper or are based on newspaper indexes. Whereas sampling is the dominant form of data gathering in many fields, protest event analysis is haunted by what Tarrow called "the fetish of thoroughness" (1989b, p. 363). However, sampling protest events substantially reduces the amount of time and resources needed for data gathering and thus may permit more studies and the inclusion of more movements, longer time periods, or several countries. For the analysis of many forms of protest (labor strikes are the main exception) the use of Monday issues is a particularly efficient way of sampling. In modern Western democracies, protests are heavily concentrated on weekends.[2] This is especially true for important protests like mass rallies and demonstrations. Because some important protests take place on weekdays, I have also coded all weekday protests referred to in the Monday paper.[3] Important events that had taken place during the week were often referred to in announcements or follow-up articles in the Monday papers (for details of the sampling and coding procedures and the methodological issues involved, see Koopmans 1992c, pp. 247-69).

For 1975 through 1989, the period of the second protest wave, the sample included all Monday issues of *Frankfurter Rundschau*. For the period 1965 to 1974, the sample was limited to issues on the first Monday of each month. Thus, for the time series reported below, data for the period 1965 to 1974 were weighted by a factor 4.33. The burden of proof, therefore, mainly rests on the data for 1975 to 1989; the data for the earlier period were included to test the generality of trends found in the second wave.

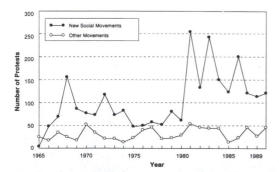

Figure 1. Number of Protests by Year for Types of Social Movements: West Germany, 1965–1989

I also systematically compare the West German findings to similar data on protest waves in the Netherlands, Italy, and the United States. These data on protest waves of different movements in different countries provide a broad basis for generalizations on the dynamics of protest waves.

Variables

The analysis concentrates on the dynamic interplay of four variables: two characteristics of social movement mobilization (the action forms employed and the degree and type of organizational support) and two types of external interference in protest (repression and facilitation).

Action Forms. I distinguish four main action strategies on the basis of increasing radicalness.[4] *Demonstrative* actions are legal actions that usually aim at mobilizing large numbers of people. Examples of such actions are demonstrations (legal and nonviolent), rallies, and petitions. *Confrontational* actions are also nonviolent, but they aim to disrupt official policies or institutions, and for that reason are usually illegal. Confrontational actions are associated with the strategy of "civil disobedience" (e.g., blockades, occupations, illegal [but nonviolent] demonstrations, and disturbances of meetings of political adversaries). Actions involving *light violence* include limited forms of movement-initiated violence (e.g., breaking windows or throwing stones at the police during a demonstration). A demonstration was coded as violent only if it was clear from the report that demonstrators initiated the violence. Peaceful demonstrations that turned violent because of violent intervention by the police were coded as peaceful demonstrations. If the report contained conflicting versions of who initiated violence or if the evidence was inconclusive, the coders were instructed to give the demonstrators the benefit of the doubt and to code the action as a peaceful demonstration. Finally, actions involving *heavy violence* include severe and usually conspiratorial violence, directed against property (arson, bombings, sabotage) or people (political murders, kidnappings).

Organizational Support. This variable indicates types of organizations mentioned in the newspaper report as organizers of a protest event. Protests for which no organizer was mentioned were coded as *no organization*. Of course, some of these protests may have been organized by a social movement organization (SMO) or by an external ally the newspaper failed to mention. Nevertheless, I assume that such events had a significantly lower level of organization than did protests for which an explicit organizer was reported. For protests for which an organizer was mentioned, four types of organization were distinguished. Among social movement organizations, *terrorist organizations* and *Communist vanguard groups* were distinguished from the much larger category of *other SMOs*. The fourth category consists of protests organized by or organized jointly with *external allies,* e.g., established political parties, labor unions, or churches.

Repression. Repression was measured using a simple dichotomous variable indicating the presence or absence of repressive intervention by the authorities. The most frequent types of repression reported were police interventions, such as arrests and violence. In other cases, repression was indicated if authorities depicted activists or organizers as criminals. In the case of conspiratorial forms of heavy violence (e.g., bombings or arson), the reports usually did not report a repressive reaction because the authorities' responses took place outside the public's view (police investigations), or only became known some time after the event (arrests, convictions). Therefore, I excluded these conspiratorial action forms when computing levels of repression.

Facilitation. This variable indicates the presence or absence of support from established political actors for an action. In the case of the NSMs, such support came primarily from left-wing political parties, labor unions, or churches. A protest event was coded as facilitated if an established organization was mentioned as an organizer or co-organizer, or if the protest was organized by a peak SMO that included one or more established organizations among its members.

Two Theories

Two theories provide a promising starting point for a search for patterns in waves of protest.[5]

Karstedt-Henke: The Counterstrategies of Authorities

In her analysis of the emergence of terrorism in West Germany, Karstedt-Henke (1980) argued that protest waves typically pass through four phases. In the initial phase of mobilization, authorities overreact to the emergence of protest.

In an attempt to quell unrest, they follow a strategy of repression, but because they are caught off guard they do so in an inconsistent and undifferentiated way that provokes public outrage and leads to further protests (1980, pp. 200-209). Their initial strategy of repression having failed, authorities, in the second phase, combine continued repression of some actions and organizations with efforts to appease other parts of the protest movement with concessions or facilitation. However, this double strategy cannot yet be implemented effectively because the authorities still have difficulty differentiating between "good" and "bad" protesters, and sometimes apply the wrong measures to the wrong group (1980, pp. 209-13). Thus, the radical and moderate wings of the movement continue to grow, but become increasingly distinguishable. In the third phase, this differentiation among activists, which often provokes internal conflicts, offers the authorities opportunities to exploit the double strategy. Moderate wings are integrated into the political system and will gradually abandon protest activities, while radical wings are not satisfied with the gains that have been made, and decisions about further protest activities increasingly become their exclusive domain. This radicalization of a movement's actions is reinforced by the authorities' reactions. Robbed of their moderate allies within and outside the movement, radicals are now confronted with full-scale repression. The result is spiraling violence and counterviolence, which produces terrorist organizations (1980, pp. 213-17). Ultimately, integration and radicalization lead to a decline in protests—moderates are no longer interested in protest activity as their attention shifts to conventional channels of political participation, while the extreme actions of radicals become too costly for most social movement participants. Moreover, radical groups become closed to new participants because they are forced underground and because they develop an exclusive ideology and organizational structure. The combined result of these tendencies is the fourth phase: latency of the potential for protest (1980, pp. 217-20).

Tarrow: Competition Among Organizations

Tarrow's (1989a, 1989b) theory of protest dynamics is more complex than Karstedt-Henke's model. According to Tarrow (1989a), social movements emerge "when new opportunities are at hand—such as a less repressive climate, splits within the elite, or the presence of influential allies or supporters" (p. 51). Subsequently, protests spread through the diffusion of tactical innovations developed by early protesters to other themes, groups, and locations. Such diffusion is not a spontaneous process, however, but:

> follows an organized logic through competition and tactical innovation within the social movement sector. . . . Competition intensifies the evolution of the repertoire toward more radical forms, as movements try to show they are more daring than their opponents. . . . At the peak of mobilization the increased propensity to engage in disruptive collective action leads to the formation of new movement organizations and draws old organizations into the social movement sector. The competition between these SMOs for mass support leads to a radicalization of tactics and themes. The resulting intensification of conflict reduces the audience for social movement activity and triggers a spiral of sectarian involution, on the one hand, and of goal displacement, on the other. . . . [As a result,] the cycle declines through a symbiotic combination of violence and institutionalization. (1989a, pp. 8, 54; 1989b, pp. 14, 16)

Tarrow thus shares Karstedt-Henke's belief that violence and institutionalization are linked products of protest waves and that the combination of these processes is the main cause of their decline. However, the explanations for these developments differ. In Karstedt-Henke's model, factors external to the social movement, particularly the shifting counterstrategies of the authorities, determine the development of protest. Tarrow, on the contrary, emphasizes internal factors and sees competition among social movement organizations and between SMOs and established political organizations as the crucial mechanism.

The Development of the Action Repertoire

From the available studies of protest development, a surprisingly regular pattern emerges that conforms to Karstedt-Henke's and Tarrow's hypotheses about the shifts in action repertoires that occur over the course of protest waves.

In his study of the Italian protest wave between 1965 and 1975, Tarrow found that nonviolent, confrontational actions like blockades and occupations peaked early in the wave. More moderate, demonstrative actions peaked a few years later, and they increasingly involved established allies like unions. Violence, finally, was most common in the late stages of the wave, after other forms of action had begun to decline (1989b, p. 70). Moreover, mass violence was increasingly replaced by more extreme forms of violence by small groups (Della Porta and Tarrow 1986, pp. 618-19; Tarrow 1989b, p. 306).

McAdam's (1982) study of the American civil rights movement provides additional evidence for these basic trends. Here as well, the wave started with confrontational actions like bus boycotts and sit-ins, gradually took on a mass character, and subsequently began to disintegrate as radicalization (e.g., ghetto rioting) and institutionalization (e.g., increased external support for the more moderate NAACP) set in (McAdam 1982, pp. 209, 222, 253).

Analyses of Dutch protests for the period 1975-1989 also confirm this pattern (Koopmans 1992a, 1992b). The initial protests around 1980 were disruptive (e.g., squatting and blockading nuclear power stations and ammunition transports). This was followed by a series of mass demonstrations by the peace movement that were strongly supported by political parties, churches, and labor unions. In the second half of the 1980s, protests declined, and violent action forms became more common and increased in intensity to include arson and bomb attacks. At the same time, institutionalization set in, which led to spectacular gains in memberships for professional social movement organizations.

Similar developments can be traced in the two German protest waves. Figure 2 shows the occurrences of the four main strategies used by NSMs between 1965 and 1989. As in the Italian, American, and Dutch cases, confrontational actions were heavily concentrated in the initial stages of the two waves, around 1968 and 1981, respectively. As McAdam (1983) and Tarrow (1989a, 1989b) noted, these strategies often included important tactical innovations that enabled movements to transcend the constraints attached to traditional repertoires of contention (Tilly 1986a, p. 4). In the 1960s, a whole range of new action forms were introduced in West Germany. Many of these actions crossed the Atlantic, having been developed first by the civil rights and anti-Vietnam-War movements in the United States: teach-ins, sit-ins and go-ins, occupations of universities and an overarching strategy of nonviolent civil disobedience. The tactical innovations that helped launch the second wave partly consisted of the extension of these forms of protest outside the stu-

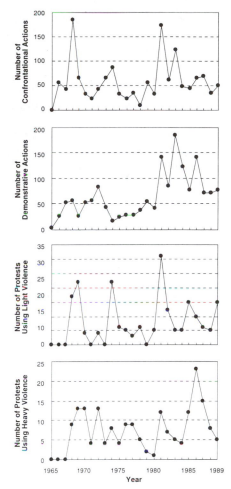

Figure 2. Types of Actions Used by New Social Movements, by Year: West Germany, 1965–1989

dent milieu and their adaptation to new goals. In addition, new tactics were introduced, of which site occupation[6] and squatting were the most important (see Koopmans 1992c, pp. 132-36). The authorities were generally unprepared for such strategies, whose novelty and spectacular nature ensured wide coverage in the media. Thus, these innovations partly offset the unequal balance of power between challengers and authorities, and their initial success contributed to the rapid diffusion of protests in the early stages of the two waves.

However, as their novelty waned and authorities learned to respond more effectively, confrontational actions declined, although they made a modest comeback in the late stages of the two waves. In the periods immediately following the

1968 and 1981 outbreaks of protests, more moderate, demonstrative actions that often mobilized large numbers of people, increasingly dominated the stage. As I will show below, this tendency reflects the increasing involvement of professional SMOs and external allies.

Protests involving light violence followed a trajectory similar to confrontational protests, with a somewhat stronger resurgence in the waves' final stages. Activists often turned to light violence as a response to increasing repression of confrontational tactics. Thus, 1969 was the peak year for occurrences of light violence in the first wave, i.e., one year after the peak year for confrontational protests. In the second wave, confrontational protests and protests involving light violence both peaked in 1991. Confrontational actions, however, declined sharply during the second half of the year while the number of protests involving light violence reached a maximum intensity in late 1981 and early 1982, after the authorities started an offensive against squatters (resulting in the death of one activist) and violently cleared an occupied runway construction site near Frankfurt (Mulhak 1983; Rucht 1984; Koopmans 1992c, pp. 178-94).

Thus, the seeds of institutionalization and radicalization were planted by the growing involvement of professional SMOs and external allies on the one hand, and the increasing repression of confrontational actions, on the other. In the late stages of the waves, these trends became increasingly prominent—heavy violence peaked late in the two waves, after the aggregate number of protests had already declined substantially. This trend is not immediately clear for the first wave because most actions involving heavy violence occurred relatively early, between 1969 and 1972. However, these figures obscure the radicalization that occurred within this category: Of the protests involving heavy violence between 1968 and 1973, only 8 percent involved violence against people, whereas between 1974 and 1977, 50 percent were directed against people. This trend culminated in a series of terrorist attacks by the *Rote Armee Fraktion* (Red Army Faction, RAF) and other groups between 1975 and 1977, in which several dozen people were killed, many of them high-ranking politicians, judges, and businessmen. In the second wave, the increase in heavy violence was also particularly pronounced for violence against people. Of the protests involving heavy violence between 1980 and 1984, only 4 percent involved violence against people, whereas from 1985 onward 25 percent involved violence against people. Thus Della Porta and Tarrow's (1986) findings on the development of different forms of violence are confirmed by the German data.

Whether this tendency toward radicalization in the late stages of the two protest waves was accompanied by a trend toward institutionalization can be answered only to a limited extent by the protest event data. The increasing dominance of demonstrative actions in the years around 1972 and 1983 and the increasing involvement of established allies in these actions are the first signs of institutionalization. After these years, however, the relative importance of demonstrative actions and the involvement of allies in protests declined again. However, the movements did not de-institutionalize. At first, institutionalization may lead to a shift toward more moderate goals and actions and increased involvement of established allies and professional SMOs in unconventional protest. As institutionalization proceeds, however, the movement increasingly turns toward conventional strategies and exits from the protest scene. This may take several forms. SMOs may institutionalize themselves by substituting a reliance on access to the media and the conventional policy process for mobilization of their constituency, and by replacing the active involvement of adherents with that of a few professionals, who are paid with the membership contributions of an otherwise passive constituency.

Institutionalization may also find expression within the party system, either in the emergence of new parties, or in increased support for established parties. In the first wave, institutionalization was primarily reflected in increased support for the Social Democratic Party (SPD) and its reform program. After 1968, the SPD made large electoral gains and it even became the largest party in the elections of 1972. Moreover, hundreds of thousands of new members swelled the ranks of the party, particularly its youth organization, the *Jusos*.[7] The most important form of institutionalization in the second wave was the success of the Green Party. Federal election results for the Green Party increased from 1.5 percent in 1980 to 5.6 percent in 1983 and 8.3 percent in 1987.[8] Moreover, since 1985—when the first coalition between the SPD and the Green Party was formed in Hesse—the Green Party has increasingly participated in government on the state level. Further signs of the institutionalization of protest were the inclusion of NSMs' themes in the SPD's program and the co-optation of several movement leaders among its personnel. This time, however, institutionalization was not limited to party politics. The late 1980s also saw strong membership increases for several national, professional SMOs, primarily within the ecology movement. The total membership of such SMOs increased from about 100,000 in 1975 to well over one million in 1989. Membership gains were strongest after 1985, when mass participation in unconventional protests had begun to decline.

Thus the two German protest waves reveal striking parallels in the development of their action repertoire. In turn, the two German waves parallel the development of NSM protests in the Netherlands, the Italian protest wave of the 1960s and early 1970s, and the American civil rights movement. Each of these protest waves started with confrontational actions, subsequently entered a phase dominated by more moderate mass mobilization, and ended in a twin process of institutionalization and radicalization.

Repression and Facilitation

Although Karstedt-Henke's model may hinge too much on a single explanatory factor—the reactions of political elites—and is somewhat deterministic in that it sees terrorism as an inevitable outcome of protest waves, it nonetheless offers valuable insights. Her explanation for the seemingly contradictory development of protest waves toward institutionalization and radicalization, although perhaps incomplete, is quite convincing. Political elites can choose between two basic reactions to protest: confrontation or integration. Both repression and facilitation typically are selective: Activists with radical goals and strategies are more likely to be subjected to repression, whereas moderate wings are more likely to receive facilitation. Thus, different wings of social movements receive different strategic cues.

Radical wings, which disproportionally confront repression, are likely to be further radicalized and develop anti-systemic identities that may escalate violence on both sides. Moderates, on the other hand, receive cues that work toward further moderation (see also Koopmans 1990a, 1992c). Political parties may support the moderate sections of a movement conditional upon de-radical-

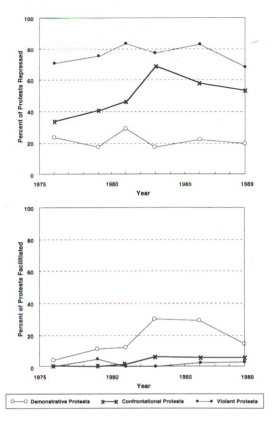

Figure 3. Percent of Protests Repressed and Facilitated by Year for Three Types of Protests: West Germany, 1975–1989

izing demands and the strategies used to advance them. State facilitation or co-optation of social movement organizations may occur as well, but again, it is unlikely to be granted unconditionally. Thus, the reactions of established political actors typically reinforce divisions among the activists, which leads to a twin process of moderation and radicalization. This development need not be the result of a conscious "divide and rule" strategy by the authorities, as is suggested by Karstedt-Henke. Members of the polity may themselves be internally divided (e.g., among government parties, between government and opposition or between political authorities who prefer integrative strategies and law enforcement authorities who prefer more repressive strategies).

Nevertheless, the data suggest that repression and facilitation are also employed strategically in attempts to create or reinforce divisions among protesters. Figure 3 shows, for the period 1975 to 1989, the percent of protests using each of three main social movement strategies that were repressed or facilitated (actions involving light violence or heavy violence are combined).[9]

Clearly, repression increases with increasingly radical strategies used by protesters. More interesting, here, however, is the development of repression over time. Karstedt-Henke's hypothesis that authorities overreact to initial protests receives only limited support: For all three strategies, repression is somewhat higher in 1981 than it is in the preceding years, but the differences are rather small. However, the changes in the use of repression after 1981 are more significant. The percent of violent protests and demonstrative protests that encounter repression remains relatively stable throughout the period—about 75 percent of violent protests and 20 percent of demonstrative protests. However, repression against confrontational protests changes considerably over the course of the protest wave. Initially, repression against such actions resembles that for demonstrative actions, but then increases substantially and ends up at a level close to that for violent protests. Interestingly, a similar pattern can be traced for the 1980s protest wave in the Netherlands (Koopmans 1992b).

Thus, instead of a general rise or decline in repression over the course of the wave, only repression against confrontational but nonviolent protests increases. This strategic increase in repression is perfectly suited to the creation of divisions within movements.[10] As nonviolent disruption becomes more costly and its practitioners are depicted and treated as criminals, protesters who use such strategies are increasingly forced to choose sides. The increased costs of nonviolent disruptions favor a turn to more moderate actions, a trend that is often reinforced by the involvement of established actors in the protests. Figure 3 shows that the increase in facilitation by established political actors in the course of the 1980s wave was heavily concentrated on the more moderate demonstrative protests. The percentage of demonstrative protests that were supported by established political parties,[11] labor unions, or churches rose from 4 percent in the 1975 to 1977 period to a maximum of 30 percent in the 1982 to 1987 period. By contrast, external support for confrontational protests increased slightly from 3 percent in the 1975 to 1977 period to 7 percent between 1982 and 1989. Facilitation of violent protests was negligible throughout the wave. Thus, intensified repression increased the relative costs of nonviolent disruptions over the course of the wave, while facilitation by established actors decreased the relative costs of moderate protests.[12]

On the other hand, increased repression may have provoked some activists to turn to violence. Repression against nonviolent protest de-legitimizes the state's monopoly on violence and strengthens the position of those activists who see reactive violence as legitimate. Moreover, the shift to violence is facilitated because the cost of violence compared to the cost of nonviolent disruption decreases. The final result of these countervailing pressures is an erosion of the middle ground of the action repertoire—nonviolent confrontations—and the simultaneous development of moderation and radicalization as hypothesized by Karstedt-Henke.

Organization and Spontaneity

Two Views on the Role of Organizations

Tarrow's explanation for the changing repertoire of protest emphasized the role of organizations and the competition among them. In the early phase of a protest wave, competition among SMOs, which try to outbid each other in radicalness and determination, still plays a positive role and accounts for the diffusion of disruptive tactics: "The expanding phase of the cycle is the result, not of pure spontaneity, but of the competition between movement organizations and their old competitors for mass support" (Tarrow 1989b, p. 10; see also pp. 186, 193). However, as new organizations are attracted by the successes of pioneer SMOs, the social movement sector becomes increasingly crowded, and organizers are forced to adopt more radical strategies in order to maintain their organization's positions or to create a niche for themselves. "In a competitive social movement sector, when the most extreme groups adopt violent stands, it is difficult for any group to come out against violence" (Tarrow 1989b, p. 284). This violence turns people off and ultimately draws the protest wave to a close.[13]

Tarrow's view of SMOs as sources of disruption and violence differs sharply from the view of Piven and Cloward (1977), who argued, "Whatever influence lower-class groups occasionally exert in American politics does not result from organization, but from mass protest and the disruptive consequences of protest. . . . Protest wells up in response to momentous changes in the institutional order. It is not created by organizers and leaders" (p. 36). Thus, organizations are not the driving force behind protest expansion and disruption, but on the contrary, take the disruptive sting out of protests, by diverting resources into more conventional—and in the view of Piven and Cloward less effective—channels.[14]

These two diametrically opposed views of the role of organizations cannot both be true. Tarrow's interpretation implies two hypotheses: (1) disruption should be highest when organizational competition is strongest; (2) protests in which organizations are involved should be more disruptive than "unorganized" protests. The first hypothesis is proven wrong by Tarrow's own data: Nonviolent disruptions peaked early in the Italian protest wave, in 1968 and 1969 (Tarrow 1989b, p. 81). However, in those same years, unorganized protests peaked as well (Tarrow 1989b, pp. 65-66). In other words, organizations declined in importance at a time when protests spread spectacularly and their disruptiveness peaked. It is hard to see how competition can be strongest at a time when the "market" expands dramatically and the number of competitors is at its lowest point relative to the size of the market.

With regard to the second hypothesis, however, the Italian evidence seems to confirm Tarrow's expectation: Protests that involved no organizations were the least disruptive; protests in which a union was involved were slightly more disruptive; protests in which an "external group" was involved were much more disruptive; and protests involving a union and an "external group" were even more disruptive. Therefore, Tarrow concluded that "competition for worker support was a direct cause of disruption and thus of the high point of social movement mobilization" (Tarrow 1989b, p. 186). However, apart from the fact that this conclusion contradicts Tarrow's other findings, other reasons cast doubt on this conclusion. Tarrow's claim would have been strong if his data referred only to attempts to mobilize a worker constituency. However, Tarrow combined all protests, including the many protests in which "extreme left- and extreme right-wing groups attacked one another's headquarters or engaged in physical confrontations in the streets" (Tarrow 1989b, p. 232). In other words, not all protests between 1966 and 1973 were designed to mobilize workers. In fact, a sizable proportion of the "external groups" were mobilizing against that constituency. Violent conflicts between left-

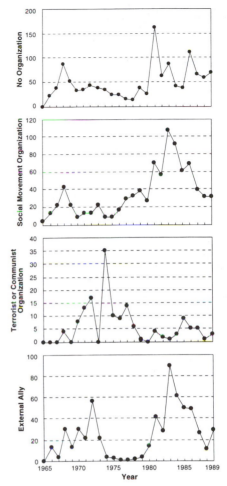

Figure 4. Number of Protests by Year Involving Different Organizations: West Germany, 1965–1989

wing and right-wing groups can hardly be interpreted as competition for a single "market."[15]

Organization and Spontaneity in the West German Protest Waves

What is the relation between the spread of protests, organization, and the radicalness of the action repertoire in Germany? Is the diffusion of protests the work of SMOs, or is it spontaneous? Are disruption and violence a result of competition among organizations, or does organization lead to a moderation of the action repertoire? Figure 4 shows the development of the number of protests that involved particular organizations. Consistent with Tarrow's data, for each wave the year with the greatest increase in the number of protests (1968 and 1981) was also the year in which the proportion of protests that were unorganized[16] was highest (56 percent in 1968; 64 percent in 1981). These years were also characterized by a particularly high level of confrontational events (see Figure 2). In other words, as in Italy, the involvement of organizations and the competition among them cannot account for the rapid spread of protests or their disruptive characters.[17]

However, organizations were more important before and after these peak years. Thus, organizations were heavily involved in the early stages of the 1960s' protest wave. Until 1966, most protests were organized by two national SMOs, the Socialist German Student League (SDS), and the peace movement's Campaign For Disarmament. However, after 1967, the roles of these organizations declined sharply. After the SDS and the Campaign For Disarmament had cleared the ground, protests began to diffuse much more spontaneously, often as a direct reaction to repression (e.g., the shooting of a demonstrator in June 1967 and the assault on student leader Rudi Dutschke in April 1968). By 1970, both the SDS and the Campaign For Disarmament dissolved because they had lost control of events and were torn apart by factional strife (Fichter and Lönnendonker 1977, pp. 140ff.; Otto 1977, pp. 172ff.).

As Figure 4 indicates, their place in the protest scene was taken over by other, rather different, organizations. The increase in protests brought more moderate external allies into the social movement sector. Most prominent among these were the youth organizations of the SPD, the liberal Free Democratic Party (FDP) and the unions. Although the goals supported by these allies were generally much more moderate than the goals of the period around 1968, facilitation was an important vehicle for extending protests to a mass public: On average, facilitated protests mobilized over four times as many people as unfacilitated protests. These tendencies toward institutionalization were accompanied by radicalization of sections of the movements. Like their comrades in Italy, these radical sections saw the creation of tightly structured vanguard organizations as a prerequisite for the continuation and radicalization of protests. Thus, from 1969 on, the number of protests produced by radical Communist groups or terrorist organizations increased.

Figure 4 illustrates the transitional character of the mid-1970s, which bore the imprint of the decline of the first wave and signaled the rise of the second wave. Protests that were supported by

an external ally declined sharply after 1972 as a result of the SPD's turn toward conservatism following the resignation of Chancellor Willy Brandt. The involvement of Communist groups reached its zenith around the middle of the decade, but subsequently these groups were quickly marginalized. The actions of terrorist groups increased until the fall of 1977, but declined rapidly after the suicides of the RAF's leaders in Stammheim prison. Meanwhile, however, protests organized by other SMOs began to increase, dominated in this period by a new type of organization, the so-called *Bürgerinitiativen* (civic initiatives), which were locally-based, nonideological, loosely organized groups that mobilized heretofore acquiescent sections of the population. Thus, as in the 1960s, organizations played an important role in the initial phase of the second protest wave. Again, the role of organizations was more modest in the period during which protests spread most spectacularly: Between 1978 and 1981, the increase in unorganized protests was over five times greater than the increase in protests organized by SMOs.

The Bürgerinitiativen had experimented with new forms of action and organization, and their successes had raised the public's belief in the efficacy of protest. Nevertheless, in doing so, they had opened up space for protests that to a large extent was filled by others—initially by relatively spontaneous actions (e.g., the squatters' movement), and later by the Green Party, the SPD, the churches, and the unions, as well as professional SMOs.

Radicalization in the second wave differed from that in the first wave. The confrontational and violent protests after 1968 were dominated by Communist vanguard organizations and terrorist groups, but the radicals of the 1980s tended to reject organization, not least because of the failure of their radical predecessors' organizational models. Thus, although Figure 4 shows a modest increase in the actions by terrorist organizations in the second half of the 1980s, the majority of the violence in this period was produced by small and nameless circles of activists, as reflected in the revival of unorganized protests.

Summarizing, the role of organizations varies over the course of a protest wave. Informal, loosely-structured organizations that rely more on the commitment and imagination of activists than on other resources (e.g., the SDS and the civic in-

Table 1
Percentage Distribution of Protests by Involvement of Organization, for Types of Protest: West Germany, 1965-1989

Type of Organization	Demonstrative Protests	Confrontational Protests	Protests Using Light Violence	Protests Using Heavy Violence	Total Protests
No Organization	37.3	63.8	79.7	63.6	47.7
Communist	1.2	2.4	2.0	0.0	1.5
Terrorist	0.0	2.7	2.7	30.7	2.9
Other SMO	27.4	20.1	11.5	4.3	23.1
External Ally	15.6	5.8	1.4	0.7	11.5
Other SMO + External Ally	18.5	5.1	2.7	0.7	13.3
Total percent	100.0	99.9	100.0	100.0	99.9
Number	1,296	412	148	140	1,996

itiatives) are important at the start of a protest wave. In this initial phase, protests require strategic planning and patience. However, once early protests have shown the way, the costs and difficulties of staging subsequent protests decrease. Actions that might require months or even years of preparation in less conducive circumstances may be accomplished almost instantaneously at these times of general arousal. Leaflets, rumors, intensified media coverage, or brutal police repression may then do the job of movement organizers, who often are unable to control the energies their pioneer actions have unleashed. In that sense, the diffusion of protests is neither spontaneous nor organized, but rather an often uneasy combination of the two.

After disruptive protests have peaked, the importance of organizations increases again. However, the organizations that dominate in this period often differ from the organizations that started the wave. Basically, these later organizations reflect the twin tendencies toward radicalization and institutionalization. External allies try to profit from the mobilization by entering the social movement sector, which extends protests to a wider public and exerts a moderating influence on goals and actions. In addition, pre-existing or newly founded professional SMOs may try to get a slice of the protest pie. Radicalization may be accompanied by the formation of new organizations, too, although the high degree of organization characteristic of the radicalism of the 1970s seems to be a result of the Marxist theories and Leninist models of organization that predominated at the time.

Table 1 shows the relationship between the involvement of organizations and the action rep-

ertoire. Contrary to Tarrow, moderate protests more often involved SMOs or external allies than did the more radical protests. Two-thirds of demonstrative protests were supported by established allies, "other SMOs," or a combination of the two. The large majority of the more radical protests did not involve an organization: Only one-third of confrontational events and one-fifth of the protests involving light violence were supported by an SMO or an established ally.[18]

The patterns of involvement of organizations that appear in the two German protest waves are confirmed by studies of other protest waves. Dutch protests in the period 1975 to 1989 reveal a remarkably similar pattern: Loosely-structured organizations and ad hoc initiatives dominated in the initial phase of the wave, but few organizations were involved in the rapid spread of protests between 1980 and 1982. Subsequently, professional SMOs and external allies dominated, while protests—organized and unorganized—involving violence also increased. As in Germany, unorganized protests were the most radical in the Netherlands, while protests involving SMOs or external allies were more moderate (Koopmans 1992b).

Killian's (1984) analysis of two campaigns of the civil rights movement in Tallahassee, Florida, also found that the initial phase of a protest wave is characterized by a "mixture of planning and spontaneity. . . . Spontaneity is especially likely to be important in the early stages of a social movement and during periods of transition from one type of action to another" (pp. 777-80). Oberschall (1978), studying the role of SMOs in the American protest wave of the 1960s, concluded:

Created hastily and expanding rapidly, SMOs controlled but a small part of their total social interaction field. Only a small fraction of the total resources expended upon movement activity by transitory teams and the wider circles of sympathizers actually passed directly through a central leadership group with a resource allocation capacity. The communications network between the leadership and rank and file was rudimentary and relied heavily on the mass media over which SMOs had little direct control. (p. 267)

McAdam's (1982, pp. 147-48) study of the civil rights movement found that the grassroots organizations that dominated the movement's early phase gradually became less prominent, while the involvement of formal movement organizations and external support increased.

These findings support Piven and Cloward's argument that the involvement of organizations has a moderating influence rather than a disruptive influence as Tarrow suggests. The blockades and violent demonstrations after the assault on Dutschke in April 1968 were not orchestrated by organizations. Similarly, the 1981 squatters' protests were more a result of spontaneous imitation and the mobilization of pre-existing networks of activists than of careful planning and organization. Nevertheless, the role of spontaneity in the spread of disruptive protests should not be overemphasized. These episodes would never have occurred without the groundwork laid by organizations like the SDS and civic initiatives, which successfully experimented with new strategies and introduced new issues into the political agenda. Only after the peak of disruption do organizations become a moderating force, as professional SMOs and established allies join the movements to exploit the pool of members, adherents, and voters revealed by the eruption of protests. Thus, Piven and Cloward's stress on the spontaneity of disruptions and the moderating influence of organizations, and their critics' emphasis on the importance of organizations in preparing the ground for disruption, both contain an element of truth. The main difference between these interpretations is their focus on different types of organizations and different periods in the mobilization process.

Discussion: Determinants of the Rise and Fall of Protest Waves

The findings presented point to striking regularities in the development of protest waves that are independent of the particular themes addressed and movements involved and that can be found in countries as divergent as Germany, the Netherlands, Italy, and the United States. Karstedt-Henke's explanation for these regularities, which emphasizes the effects of repression and facilitation by established political actors, finds more support in the data than does Tarrow's focus on competition among organizations.

Nevertheless, Karstedt-Henke's explanation is not wholly satisfactory: It assumes that the fragmentation of social movements into moderate and radical components and the ensuing decline in protests are the result of cunning counterstrategies devised by the authorities, and that social movements are powerless victims in their hands. Although repression and facilitation can have powerful effects on the relative costs and benefits of different strategies open to social movements, Karstedt-Henke's explanation ignores the fact that authorities cannot *force* activists to institutionalize or build terrorist organizations. The theory must consider why, within the constraints set by their environments, social movement activists consciously choose one strategy and not another.

What are the basic strategic options available to social movements in their efforts to change existing policies? Different answers have been proposed to this question. Some authors, especially those working in the classical tradition, have stressed violence as the basic resource available to social movements (Gurr 1970). De Nardo (1985), on the other hand, emphasized the "power of numbers," although he acknowledged that "violence can be used to compensate for inadequate support" (p. 200). Tarrow (1989a) argued that "the power of protest lies neither in its numbers . . . nor in its level of violence. . . . but in its threat to burst through the boundaries of the accepted limits of social behavior" (p. 7; Piven and Cloward [1977] argued in a similar vein). Rochon's (1990, p. 108) view that all three elements of movement power—which he labels *militancy, size,* and *novelty*—are important seems more realistic than a reductionist emphasis on one of these elements. These three elements are particularly relevant here because they can be easily linked to the three main action strategies: Demonstrative protests aim primarily to mobilize the power of numbers; confrontational protests are most suited to capitalize on the advantages of novelty; and violence clearly aims to change policies through a display of militant force and determination.

Social movements derive power from large *size* because the more people who are mobilized, the more the legitimacy of the authorities and their policies is called into question. Moreover, in democracies, participants in social movements and their sympathizers are also voters, so that size can become a considerable electoral factor.

The power of *novelty* lies, apart from the media attention it attracts, in its unpredictability and the insecurity it provokes among established actors about the limits and consequences of protests (Tarrow 1989b, p. 59). Moreover, novelty gives protesters a strategic advantage—authorities are unprepared for new strategies, political actors, and themes. Given the inertia of institutional politics, effective responses develop slowly, whereas in the early phase of rapid diffusion, social movements are highly flexible—they appear and disappear in ever-changing guises at unpredictable times and places.

Militancy is the most direct power available to social movements. Radical protests, especially when they involve violence, almost invariably attract media coverage. Moreover, the authorities are forced to react to serious disturbances of law and order that challenge their monopoly on the use of violence. However, violence employed by social movements is a risky tool. The individual costs are likely to be high for those arrested, and the probability of backlash is high. Nevertheless, if the violence is sufficiently enduring and massive, it may succeed. Repression can backfire, especially when it is excessive and badly directed. Moreover, repression is costly, and in some situations these costs may induce authorities to give in to the movement's demands.

These three sources of power for social movements are also associated with specific phases in the development of protest waves. Clearly, in the initial phase of a wave, novelty is the most important basis of power. Because the public at large is not yet mobilized, pioneer movements attract few participants, which rules out strategies that depend on large size. Violence is also not an attractive option because the public and the media have serious moral objections and will consider violence only as a last resort. Moreover, in the initial phase, protesters can attract attention with less militant and less risky actions. Thus, pioneer activists are likely to opt for actions that are novel and unconventional enough to attract media attention and militant enough to concern authorities but

that do not depend for effectiveness on large numbers of participants. Confrontational protests, like occupations, sit-ins, and blockades, satisfy these criteria and thus are important in the expansive phase of a protest wave. [19]

Similar considerations affect the organizational support for protests. Formal, professional movement organizations do not play dominant roles in the initial phase of a protest wave. Such organizations, if they exist when protests start, tend to suffer from the same structural inertia as do established political actors. Therefore, they are unlikely to spawn tactical and thematic innovations. Also, in the face of insecurity about the outcomes of such "experiments," they are reluctant to risk their resources (e.g., access to decision makers or to the media, mass membership, subsidies, salaried staff, etc.). Nor are the pioneers of protest waves likely to opt for formal organizations because such organizations require an already mobilized mass constituency that offers members and funding. Oberschall (1979) argued that in a group that is not yet represented by an existing SMO or political organization, "the first individuals to attempt organization run high personal risks as a result of innovator-loss dynamics; there are free rider tendencies; and the sheer length of time that would pass before SMO efforts might bring relief, even if they could get under way . . . make an organized challenge unlikely" (p. 63). Moreover, formal organization would not be fruitful strategically. Unpredictability, novelty, and fluidity are an emergent movement's main resources, whereas the involvement of formal organizations makes a movement's boundaries clearer, its leaders identifiable and accountable, and its strategies more predictable.

However, this initial strategic model is inherently unstable, and alternative strategic options gradually become more attractive. Tactical innovations, like site occupation and squatting, lose their ability to surprise and are no longer attractive to the media—and authorities learn to deal with such actions more effectively (Freeman 1979b, p. 186; Hilgartner and Bosk 1988, pp. 62-63; Rochon 1988, p. 186).

Similarly, the initial model of loosely structured organizations is difficult to sustain (Oberschall 1979, p. 67). In the initial phase of a protest wave, such organizations often have the field to themselves. However, as the wave progresses, they are increasingly faced with competition from professional SMOs and external allies on the one hand and from radical groups on the other. Because they lack the resources and internal coordination to compete effectively with professional SMOs and established allies for media access and mass support, and because they lack the strong identity that underlies the mobilization capacity of radical groups, these organizations become increasingly marginal. As Oberschall (1978) argued, this marginalization will be reinforced by the reactions of the media and the authorities, who are interested in "structuring" protests by focusing on a few identifiable leaders and organizations—"the media contributed in making leaders out of some who otherwise might not have been, and created more structure in the movements than they actually possessed" (p. 272). When protests begin to decline, the positions of the loosely structured parts of social movements become even more precarious. To survive declining participation, social movements must have either an enduring organizational structure with resources that do not depend on mass participation (McAdam et al. 1988, pp. 716ff.) or a strong identity that allows them to continue to mobilize even under unfavorable circumstances. The organizations and spontaneous collectives that dominate the initial phase of protests possess neither of these traits and are therefore likely to be the first victims of decline (Jenkins and Eckert 1986, p. 816).

Social movements must compensate the loss of novelty by increased numbers or increased militancy. A strategy to increase numbers is favored if established political actors, pre-existing SMOs, and social movement entrepreneurs are interested in allying themselves to movements. However, support from these groups is often accompanied by a moderation of strategies and goals, which may lead to friction with the more radical activists who do not wish to compromise on the original strategies and demands. Since these radicals are unable to outstrip the moderates and their allies in numbers, they resort to increased militancy, and some of them ultimately to violence, to make themselves heard. The presence of a radical minority may in turn strengthen the moderate faction's tendency toward moderation and institutionalization. "The presence of 'extremist' SMOs can actually help to legitimate and strengthen the bargaining position of more moderate SMOs [and may encourage] funding support for the 'moderates' as a way of undercutting the

influence of the radicals" (McAdam et al. 1988, pp. 718-19).

Thus, over the course of a protest wave social movements split over strategy, and the moderate and radical wings are increasingly separated. This division need not have immediate negative consequences on the protests. Initially, the involvement of allies may broaden public support for the movement's activities and enhance the media presence of the movement. Nevertheless, if institutionalization and radicalization continue, protests will ultimately decline. When established allies incorporate a movement's demands into their programs, when "movement parties," like the Green Party, enter parliaments or governments, and when professional SMOs gain acceptance as representatives of a movement's demands in the media and in policy making, many movement sympathizers find protests less urgent. Because participation in social movements is relatively costly and time-consuming compared to voting, for a sympathetic party or joining an SMO, institutionalization leads many to shift to such alternatives.

Increased radicalism may also lead to a decline in protests. Few activists are prepared to endure the repression that radical actions entail. Moreover, the increasingly hostile reactions of the authorities and the increased efficiency of repressive measures push radical groups toward covert actions involving a small activist core. The repression and marginalization of these groups also stimulates sectarian conflicts and distrust among activists, which diverts energy from external activities and discourages outsiders from participating (De Nardo 1985). Finally, if radicalization escalates to extreme violence or terrorism, it may provoke a backlash that undercuts the general legitimacy of protests.

A decline in protests may be reinforced by a decline in the chance of success of protests, which makes participation less attractive. I hypothesize that the chance of success erodes over the course of a protest wave. Social movements tend to succeed first when opportunities are most favorable (e.g., by focusing on issues with large public support and on which elites are divided). Being rational actors, activists focus on such "ripe apples" first. As a printed guide for movement organizers stated, "It is desirable to make the first organized project of the group a short term one that has a high probability of success. Your first issue should be an attainable goal which will provide you with your first victory" (as quoted in Fireman and Gamson 1979, p. 30). Once success has been attained or a compromise has been reached on these initial demands, the movement must continue mobilization on issues for which opportunities and public support are less favorable. Thus, subsequent successes are increasingly difficult, which gradually erodes the motivation to participate.

The increasing lack of success may reinforce tensions between moderates and radicals. While the prospects for success are favorable, different factions may find a common ground, or at least agree to a "peaceful co-existence." Once things go wrong, however, strategic debates often erupt in full force, and these internal conflicts can substantially weaken a movement. This happened to the German peace movement after the government decided to deploy Cruise and Pershing missiles in 1983 (Koopmans 1992c, pp. 201-206).

Summarizing, my explanation for the dynamics of protest waves combines external and internal factors. The progress of a protest wave is the outcome of the interplay between the external constraints of facilitation, repression, and success chances, and activists' choices among the different strategic options. These factors provide a plausible explanation for the trajectories of action repertoires and involvement of organizations discernible in the protest waves discussed in this article.

Because theory and empirical research on the development of social movements after their emergence are still in their infancy, my explanation provides only a rough map of the territory of protest dynamics. Besides action repertoires and organizational forms, other aspects of protests to explore in a dynamic perspective include patterns of territorial diffusion and thematic shifts (Tarrow 1989b; Snow and Benford 1992). Further, the empirical base for generalizations is still rather narrow. Additional studies of protest waves of different movements and in different political and cultural contexts can show whether the trends found in the four cases examined here reflect general patterns. Protest waves may differ in nondemocratic countries in which the constraints on social movement activity are much stronger. Further, the dynamics of social movements that address economic issues (e.g., the labor movement) rather than political authorities may differ from the dynamics of the movements discussed here.

Another question to investigate is whether the model developed here is limited to left-wing, progressive movements, or whether it extends to right-wing movements, like the recent anti-foreigner actions in Germany.[20]

Notes

1. This political opportunity perspective also suggests why the developmental trajectories of other movements are unrelated to those of the NSMs. The labor movement, the extreme right, and farmers' movements have their own unique opportunity structures, so that political situations that stimulate the mobilization of NSMs may be totally irrelevant, or even detrimental, to the mobilization of these other movements.

2. In Germany and most Western European countries, Monday newspapers report the news of both weekend days. If a Sunday newspaper were published, the appropriate method would be to code Sunday and Monday issues.

3. In such cases, the original report of the event was consulted to code the necessary information. Non-weekend events constitute about one-fifth of the sample (Koopmans 1992c, p. 258).

4. This categorization is similar to that employed by Tarrow (1989b), except that Tarrow's "conventional" category is here termed "demonstrative." I reserve the label "conventional" for those political actions that are usually associated with conventional or established politics, e.g., lobbying, litigation, and press conferences. For a full list of the action forms included in each category, see Koopmans 1992c, p. 264.

5. Three other bodies of theory also address aspects of the dynamics of protest: "natural history" models of revolutions (Edwards 1965; Brinton 1959); theories within the resource mobilization perspective on the development of social movement organizations (Zald and Ash 1966); and the population ecology model of organizational development (Hannan and Freeman 1987; Carroll 1988). However, these theories are not very helpful here. Revolutions are a unique type of protest, and, in addition, natural history models are descriptive and deterministic at the same time (for a devastating critique, see Rule and Tilly 1972). Theories of SMO development, like resource mobilization theory in general, address only organizational aspects of social movements. Moreover, the development of SMOs is not representative of the development of protest waves at large. As I show below, the growth of SMOs is more a product than a cause of protest waves. This problem is shared by the population ecology model. Moreover, the population ecology model's basic assumption of a relatively stable "carrying capacity" (Hannan and Freeman 1987, p. 912; Hilgartner and Bosk 1988, p. 59; for a critique, see Young 1988) of the social systems it analyzes seems to be untenable for the social movement sector,

which, as Figure 1 indicates, is characterized by sharp fluctuations over relatively short periods of time.

6. The strategy consists of occupying the site of a future nuclear power plant, runway, or road. This strategy had the advantage that, in most cases, the protesters were not immediately evicted because the authorities lacked a legal basis to intervene. Subsequently, the occupiers often constructed makeshift "hut villages" on the site, which developed into small, self-sustaining worlds serving as organizational centers and as places where solidarities could be forged, bridges between moderates and radicals could be built, and the continuity of mobilization could be assured (Ehmke 1987, pp. 67-76; Himmelheber and Philipp 1982).

7. Similarly, in Italy the Communist Party enlisted several hundred thousand new members (Tarrow 1990, p. 269). In the Netherlands, the New Left parties and the Communist Party were the main beneficiaries of the institutionalization of protest (Koopmans 1992a).

8. The Green Party was less successful in the elections of 1990, in which they received (in former West Germany) only 4.8 percent of the vote. However, these elections were unusual because they were heavily dominated by the issue of unification. In state elections, support for the Green Party has been relatively stable since 1987.

9. Because the numbers of violent protests and confrontational protests were low in some years, I combined data for the periods 1975-1977, 1978-1980, 1981, 1982-1984, 1985-1987 and 1988-1989. (Figures for 1965-1974 are not shown for the same reason). The figure for 1981 refers to that year only, to permit a test of Karstedt-Henke's idea of initial overreaction.

10. That such a strategy was at least partly deliberate is indicated by a "New Internal Security Strategy for the 1980s," that was unfolded by a leading police theorist in an article in the journal of the German police and in a book published in early 1982. Although this strategy envisaged a more tolerant approach to moderate sections of the NSMs, a tougher line was recommended against militant minorities to isolate them from the rest of the movements (Brand 1988, p. 212).

11. The Green Party is not included within this category. Including the Green Party does not significantly alter the results. The main difference is that the increase in facilitation for confrontational protests is somewhat larger, from 3 percent in 1975 to 1977 to a maximum of 15 percent between 1982 and 1984.

12. McAdam (1982) found similar patterns in the reactions of authorities and external supporters to the civil rights movement. Repression focused on the more radical organizations like SNCC and CORE, whereas the NAACP received more benevolent treatment. The sharp increase in external support after 1964 benefited the NAACP, while support for the other groups declined (McAdam 1982, pp.209-17).

13. Della Porta and Tarrow (1986) explained the particularly high level of violence in the Italian protest wave in a similar manner: "To the extent that violence is a tactical differentiation within an overcrowded social movement sector, it is the size of the 'market' for social protest that determines the extent of violence that will result from it. And Italy's was surely a highly developed social movement sector" (p. 629). This is not confirmed in the German data. Although the protest wave of the 1980s was more "developed" in every respect than the wave of the 1960s, and thus more "overcrowded," violence played a much larger role in the action repertoire of NSMs in the first wave (Koopmans 1992c, pp. 89, 100).

14. Adherents of the resource mobilization approach have challenged this position and have demonstrated the important role of organizations in the diffusion of disruptive protests, even in the cases studied by Piven and Cloward (Gamson and Schmeidler 1984; Morris 1984; Valocchi 1990).

15. Tarrow remarked that almost all violent conflicts in his sample were of this type (Tarrow 1989b, p. 304). In other words, violence within the Italian protest wave can only to a limited extent be seen as the result of competition for a single constituency. This violence can more aptly be described as a "war" between the extreme left and the extreme right. Of course, wars can be interpreted in terms of competition, but competition that aims to destroy competitors differs sharply from the competition among parties for the support of the electorate or the competition among SMOs for the support of a constituency. In the case of war, the most violent competitor is indeed likely to win. In a competition for a constituency, violence is only one option and probably not the most effective choice, since competition for a constituency often hinges on winning the support of the moderate center.

16. "Unorganized" protests are not purely spontaneous outbursts of collective action by isolated individuals, as suggested by "classical" models of collective behavior. In many cases, such protests originate in informal networks and subcultural and countercultural infrastructures, i.e., in the social organization of a movement's constituency. The term "unorganized" conveys only that such protests are not the result of mobilization by formal SMOs, although they may be an unintended by-product of such efforts.

17. The analyses of strike waves in Haimson and Tilly (1989) confirm this conclusion. In their introduction to the volume, Haimson and Brian concluded: "This process of 'deinstitutionalization' [wildcat strikes] was to a degree characteristic of all the major strike waves scrutinized in this volume" (Haimson and Brian 1989, p. 39). Cronin summarized the conclusion of his contribution as follows: "Strike movements built unions, but unions did not overall do a great deal to increase strike propensity" (Cronin 1989, p. 98).

18. The relation between organizations and type of protest seems to change at the far radical end of the action repertoire. Protests involving heavy violence were more organized than protests involving light violence. Moreover, among protests involving heavy

violence, those directed against people involved an organization in two-thirds of the cases, a level similar to that for demonstrative protests. This is, of course, related to the conspiratorial nature of such protests, which require careful planning: Kidnappings or political murders do not happen spontaneously.

19. Of course, what is novel and unconventional may vary over time and among countries. Thus, civic initiatives in West Germany initially attracted attention by their mere existence, although their action repertoire initially mainly consisted of moderate actions like petitions and small demonstrations. In West Germany, the average citizen has long been politically passive. Thus, the fact that citizens who did not belong to the small radical fringe were challenging decisions of the authorities was novel enough to be of interest to the media and to concern the authorities.

20. Social movement mobilization in East Germany during and after the revolution of 1989 has some interesting parallels with the model presented here. The revolution started with small actions organized by loosely structured civic initiatives like *Neues Forum*. These were followed by a series of illegal demonstrations that were largely spontaneous initially, but quickly drew the attention of (primarily West German) political parties. The elections of March 1990 provided further evidence of this trend toward institutionalization. The dissident groups that started the revolution fared poorly, while the established West German parties received the support of the large majority of the electorate. In this view, subsequent anti-foreigner protests can be interpreted as the revolution's radical offshoot, which carried the theme of nationalism and the slogan "We Are One People" to xenophobic and violent extremes. ✦

29

Legal Control of the Southern Civil Rights Movement

Steven E. Barkan

Following Durkheim ([1895] 1966), macrosociological theories traditionally tend to see major social events as consequences of underlying social structures and forces. As a result, they tend to overlook the impact of strategic and tactical decisions by leaders who exploit, or fail to exploit, the potential for change provided by the underlying structures.

Much contemporary work in political sociology, social change, and social movements now attempts to integrate structural and tactical explanations of social events (e.g., Linz, 1978; Oberschall, 1973; Tilly, 1978). In the field of social movements, the emerging "resource mobilization" (RM) and "political process" (PP) perspectives both emphasize tactical choices and consequences, though they differ in other respects (see McAdam, 1982). This emphasis represents a departure from traditional perspectives on social movements that focused on social psychological explanations of individual participation in collective action (Davies, 1962; Gurr, 1970; Smelser, 1963).

While the RM and PP models stress tactics, their focus tends to be limited in that they devote more attention to the tactics of movements than to those of their opponents (but see Marx, 1979; McAdam, 1983). This limits understanding of the development and outcome of insurgent challenges, since the social control tactics of movement opponents can have a major impact. The limitations of this focus in allowing us to understand the Southern civil rights movement will be discussed below.

One major difference between the RM and PP perspectives concerns their views on the potential power of social movements. Several proponents

of the RM perspective[1] have argued, for example, that a movement's mass base commonly lacks the indigenous resources that are important for success and has little, if any, disruptive potential. As a result, most movements are potentially weak and can succeed only if they receive external support from groups such as liberal organizations, labor unions, churches, and foundations (Jenkins and Perrow, 1971; Lipsky, 1968; McCarthy and Zald, 1973, 1977).

In contrast, proponents of the PP model have argued that the mass base of movements typically has many more resources, especially pre-existing organizational networks, and much more disruptive potential than assumed by the RM perspective. As a result, most movements are potentially powerful and need not depend so much, if at all, on external support for success (McAdam, 1982; Morris, 1981; Piven and Cloward, 1979; Schwartz, 1976). As McAdam (1982:30-31), the clearest exponent of this model, puts it,

> Except for the most deprived segments of society, aggrieved groups possess the ability to exert significant leverage on their own behalf and certain indigenous resources facilitative of organized social protest. . . . In characterizing the majority of such groups as politically impotent, resource mobilization theorists are to be faulted for their failure to acknowledge the power inherent in disruptive tactics.[2]

Scholars of the Southern civil rights movement have similarly disagreed over the movement's potential indigenous power. Expressing the RM perspective, several (e.g., Marx and Useem, 1971; Lipsky, 1968; McCarthy and Zald, 1973) argue that the origins and successes of the movement depended heavily on the outside support of Northern liberals, church groups, mass media, and the federal government. In marked contrast, those using the PP model (McAdam, 1982; Morris, 1981; Piven and Cloward, 1979) trace the origins of the movement to its indigenous organizational network and resources, and emphasize the role played in its successes by its own capacity for disruption. While PP theorists such as McAdam (1982, 1983) and Piven and Cloward (1979) concede the importance of federal action for the movement's major success, they imply that the movement was able to *compel* such action by engaging in mass protest that typically provoked a violent white response, prompting federal intervention on behalf of the movement.[3] Thus McAdam (1983:749), calling this triad of black protest\riawhite

"Legal Control of the Southern Civil Rights Movement." *American Sociological Review* 49: 552-565. Copyright ©1984 by the American Sociological Association. Reprinted with permission.

violence\riafederal intervention a "characteristic protest dynamic" in the South, argues (1982:174) that "southern supremacists . . . could be counted on, when sufficiently provoked, to create the violent disruptions of public order needed to produce federal intervention."

The RM-PP debate over the black movement's power has, however, overlooked the use of the Southern legal system to frustrate civil rights protest and goals, despite earlier treatments (e.g., Friedman, 1965; Killian, 1968; Lusky, 1964; Peltason, 1961; Vander Zanden, 1965) of the use of legal machinations to resist school desegregation in the 1950s. This neglect of Southern legal control also impoverishes a more general understanding of the dynamics of protest in the South.

This paper examines the white response to major protest campaigns in several Southern cities, and suggests that local Southern leadership could, by the choice of appropriate legal tactics, both effectively resist black demands and forestall extensive white violence and federal intervention. It will argue that the black protest\riawhite violence\riafederal intervention dynamic empirically established by McAdam (1983) was not an inevitable sequence, and that the sequence could have been broken with appropriate tactical choices by the white leadership.

Thus the paper has three purposes:

(1) to introduce protest and control tactics even more explicitly into social movement theory by indicating the importance of studying the tactical choices available to movement opponents.

(2) to refine our understanding of the dynamics of civil rights protest by showing that Southern elites could by the proper choice of tactics avoid the white violence that was an important stimulus for federal intervention;[4] and

(3) to contribute to the RM-PP debate outlined above by suggesting that civil rights forces did not have the power to win major successes by themselves, or to compel federal intervention, when confronted by intransigent white resistance relying on the legal process.

By examining situations in which black protest was met by legal control instead of the white violence that so often occurred, this study constitutes a deviant-case analysis. As Kendall and Wolf (1941) and Horst (1955) point out, deviant-case analysis allows the researcher to demonstrate the relevance and consequences of factors that had not been considered previously. Horst (1955:173) argues that the case study method may be "par-

ticularly useful" in the analysis of deviant cases. The attempt here is to show how law could be used to prevent the creation of a situation in which extreme white violence emerged, and to show how the consequences of different tactical choices are worked out within conflict situations. Several cases in which the conditions were such that white violence was quite possible were selected for analysis, in order to show how different elite decisions led to very different consequences for the emergence of white violence, and, as a result, for the prospects of federal intervention.

The protest campaigns examined here took place in Montgomery, Alabama, 1955-56; Albany, Georgia, 1961-63; Danville, Virginia, 1963; Birmingham, Alabama, 1963; and Selma, Alabama, 1965. Two models of white response to civil rights protest can be distinguished in these cities. The first, used in Montgomery, Albany, and Danville, involved the frequent use of arrest, prosecution, and other forms of legal harassment to suppress dissent.[5] Although the use of legal procedure instead of other, more brutal means of social control theoretically gave civil rights groups various procedural guarantees under the law, in Albany and Danville its use eventually proved overwhelming, while the Montgomery campaign would have failed had not the U.S. Supreme Court handed down a favorable ruling at the last moment. Moreover, the legitimacy conferred by the legal setting used in each city helped minimize the criticism that would have arisen had other, extralegal methods of control been employed (compare Balbus, 1973).[6]

The second model, characterizing Birmingham and Selma, is distinguished from the first by the use of police and civilian violence which undermined attempts by officials to use legal means to control dissent. Publicized across the nation, such violence negated the legitimacy surrounding the official use of legal procedure and helped pressure the federal government into taking action. Without white violence, moreover, the legal control of black protest in Birmingham and Selma might very well have defeated the civil rights forces.[7]

Legal Problems of Civil Rights Protesters: An Overview

Before proceeding to the analysis, it will be helpful to discuss briefly the various legal difficulties confronting civil rights groups in the South (a more detailed treatment is available in Barkan, 1980a, 1980b).

For the Southern civil rights movement the legal system proved a mixed blessing. At the federal level, the Supreme Court, the Fifth Circuit Court of Appeals, and a few District Judges rendered many decisions favorable to the movement's aims. At the state and local levels, however, the law served as an effective instrument of social control. "Legal repression" (Balbus, 1973) is not too strong a term to use here, for many Southern communities experienced "a wholesale perversion of justice, from bottom to top, from police force to [state] supreme court" (Lewis et al., 1966:289). The legal difficulties facing the movement were in many ways similar to those confronting other movements. In the South these problems were especially severe because of the particular historical and social context in which the civil rights effort found itself. The entire legal machinery of the South became a tool for social control of civil rights protest. For example, soon after lunch-counter sit-ins started sweeping the South in February 1960, several state legislatures passed new laws designed for application to the special characteristics of sit-ins. State and federal judges in the South also aided the social control effort when they granted injunctions that limited or banned civil rights activity (Bell, 1973).

Criminal courts also presented the movement with serious obstacles. The fate of civil rights activists was no different from that of Southern blacks caught in "conventional" criminal proceedings (Myrdal, 1944; Sitton, 1962; Galphin, 1963), but the civil rights movement and the passions it aroused intensified the difficulties encountered by activists and their attorneys (see Barkan, 1980a, 1980b). Most judges, prosecutors, and jurors were hostile to civil rights goals, making it almost impossible for civil rights defendants to win acquittals. The movement also suffered from a lack of defense attorneys, as most Southern attorneys were not willing to defend civil rights activists. Those that did represent such clients faced threats of contempt and disbarment in court, and possibilities of physical attack, loss of business, and social ostracism outside of court.

The two other branches of the criminal justice system, the police and the prisons, also posed serious difficulties for the movement; arrest was a daily threat, and the Southern jail an ugly institution. Southern police made arrests in virtually any

kind of sit-in, march, or demonstration, and also arrested known activists in the absence of actual protest activity. Most of these arrests were for actions that would have been legal outside the South. Southern jails also sapped the strength of the movement. Jailhouse living conditions were substandard for civil rights and conventional inmates alike, and prison guards and white inmates were especially hostile to civil rights defendants. Thus the rigor of Southern jails prevented the consistent use of the "jail, no bail" tactic advocated by CORE and SNCC members (Meier and Rudwick, 1973), forcing local and national movement groups to spend large sums of money on bail bonds before trial, appeal bonds after conviction, fines, and costs of legal defense.

All these problems were exacerbated by the nature of civil rights protest in many cities. The protests were not discontinuous, but rather parts of ongoing campaigns intended to dramatize civil rights goals, to achieve Northern support, and to force concessions from local officials by causing economic and social disruption. They would last days, weeks, or months at a time, lead to intimidating arrests of many dozens or hundreds of activists within a relatively short period, and, because of the mass nature of the arrests, prove financially and legally burdensome. These burdens helped defeat civil rights forces in Albany and Danville, and might very well have frustrated protest efforts in Birmingham and Selma had not law enforcement officials overreacted, prompting federal intervention. Legal harassment would also have defeated the Montgomery campaign, had the U.S. Supreme Court not intervened at a critical moment.

The Protest Campaigns

Montgomery, 1955-1956

The celebrated Montgomery bus boycott that propelled Martin Luther King, Jr., into national prominence has been recounted often, but the part played by law and the criminal justice system remains less understood. The boycott began, of course, with the December 1955 arrest of Rosa Parks for violating a segregation ordinance by refusing to move to the back of a city bus (Parks, 1977). Her arrest galvanized Montgomery's black community. Black leaders in the city had been waiting for an arrest of a "respectable" person to help start a bus boycott and decided that this would be the one.

Two negotiating sessions later in December between black and white leaders led nowhere. In January 1956, the mayor announced what he called a "get tough" policy. Two days later Martin Luther King was arrested for driving five miles an hour faster than the speed limit. At the end of January, police began ticketing and arresting the drivers of vehicles that were part of the car pool that enabled the bus boycotters to get to work. These arrests tied up the funds of the Montgomery movement (Martin, 1977). People waiting for rides had to stand away from bus stops, so that drivers could not be arrested for operating illegal taxi services. Many blacks waiting for rides were threatened with arrest for vagrancy or hitchhiking. The police tactics made many blacks afraid to continue driving for the car pool, forcing several boycotters to walk (Lewis, 1970). As a result, the bus boycott almost ended three months after it began.

The legal effort of the city escalated on February 21, when a county grand jury charged some 100 boycott leaders, including almost all of Montgomery's black ministers, with violating a 1921 state law that made it a misdemeanor to interfere with lawful business (the law had been enacted to impede unionization in Birmingham [Raines, 1977]). The arrests of the boycott leaders, however, unified the black community instead of intimidating it. By March, white merchants had lost more than $1 million in sales because blacks were not riding the buses to their stores.

Finally, in November 1956, city officials asked a state court to enjoin the Montgomery Improvement Association, the group sponsoring the boycott, from operating an illegal transit system—the car pool. The city's request for an injunction "noticeably diluted the ardor of the black community" (Lewis, 1970:79). Had the injunction been granted, the movement would have suffered a serious, perhaps fatal blow. As King and other boycott leaders waited in court November 13 for the judge's decision on the injunction, they feared the worst (Miller, 1968). But word came that the U.S. Supreme Court had affirmed a lower court's decision that the bus segregation statutes in Montgomery were unconstitutional; the original suit had been filed nine months earlier by Montgomery blacks. The Supreme Court's ruling not only desegregated Montgomery buses, it also saved the boycott effort. As one black resident said upon hearing of the Court's decision, "Praise the Lord. God has spoken from Washington, D.C." (in Lomax, 1962:94).

The Montgomery movement, it is true, was able to capitalize on the arrests of Parks and King and the later ones of the boycott leaders. Despite the arrests and police harassment of car-pool drivers and riders, the boycott lasted a year and proved costly to white merchants. Nevertheless, the arrests and other police tactics seriously weakened the boycott effort, and the injunction might have destroyed it had not the Supreme Court handed down a favorable ruling.[8] As the Albany and Danville campaigns will make clear, perhaps the mistake of Montgomery officials lay in not arresting more often, for while early arrests and prosecutions may galvanize a social movement, continued arrests and trials may frustrate spirits and pose increasing legal and financial burdens. The protest tactic chosen by the Montgomery movement made it difficult for the city to arrest more often. In seeking only to desegregate the buses, Montgomery blacks had a limited goal, albeit one difficult to achieve. Their main tactic was the boycott, and not marches and demonstrations, thereby reducing the possibility of arrest inherent in these more active forms of protest. Movement groups in other cities had wider goals; of necessity they initiated marches, rallies, and the like, at the same time subjecting themselves to greater possibilities of legal harassment and control.[9] The Albany campaign illustrates the dilemma they faced.

Albany, 1961-1963

In Albany, Georgia, one of the first concerted efforts in the South to desegregate bus and train terminals, lunch counters and restaurants, and other public facilities and accommodations began in November of 1961 and lasted through the summer of 1963. In this period, more than 1,000 people were arrested during sit-ins, marches, and rallies. Despite the mass protest and arrests, little desegregation occurred, as civil rights forces encountered an intransigent local government willing to use a legal system that provided an effective means of control. Partly because of the involvement of Martin Luther King and his Southern Christian Leadership Conference (SCLC), national attention was focused on the city during much of this period, and the failure of civil rights groups to desegregate Albany was thus emphasized as a telling blow for the movement. It still remains an important example of the use of the entire legal system of a city to thwart civil rights goals.

The city's most effective legal tactic involved a policy of continuous arrests by local police. Albany's police chief, Laurie Pritchett, was cited and, in many places, praised for his method of dealing with civil rights demonstrators. His police force arrested protesters in almost every demonstration, and, most important, did so without violence: in the months before the Albany protests, the city police had been trained to make arrests without violence and had seen films of demonstrations in other areas. Pritchett's tactics burdened the local movement with huge legal costs and other difficulties and effectively depicted a police force that quickly, efficiently, and impartially dealt with protesters breaking the law, especially in contrast with the beatings of "Freedom Riders" the previous spring in several Southern cities. As a result, U.S. Attorney General Robert Kennedy sent Pritchett a telegram congratulating him for the peaceful arrests (Raines, 1977). Reflecting the praise of Pritchett, an Atlanta newspaper reported that he was "widely known—not only in the South, but throughout the world—as a stalwart exponent of the nonviolent method of quelling integrationist uprisings" (McLendon, 1963:14).

The Albany Movement, a coalition of SNCC, the NAACP, and local black ministers, was formed November 17, 1961. Five days later, five local college students sat down in the Trailways bus terminal and were arrested. Arrests again occurred December 10th, when black and white SNCC members rode a train from Atlanta to Albany. After they entered the white waiting room of the train terminal, Pritchett ordered them to leave. As they were entering cars to depart, they were arrested for obstructing traffic, disorderly conduct, and failure to obey an officer (Zinn, 1962).

During the next week, the Albany Movement held large meetings in black churches and sponsored several downtown marches that ended in many arrests. One of the demonstrators said later, "I didn't expect to go to jail for kneeling and praying at city hall" (Zinn, 1962:4). On the day of the city court trial of the December 10th train riders, 400 students were arrested as they marched downtown to demonstrate against the trial. On December 16, Martin Luther King and Ralph Abernathy spoke at a black church and led another march downtown, with 200 more arrested, including King. By now 737 had been taken to jail. Negotiations began between city officials and Movement leaders. The latter agreed to call off the demonstrations in return for desegregation of the terminals, release of those still in jail on property bonds, except for the December 10th protesters, and the agreement of the city commission to discuss Movement demands in January.

The city commission refused, however, to take any action after meeting with Movement leaders on January 23. A month later city officials began trying the 737 protesters arrested in the December marches. In March the county court appeal trial of those arrested December 10th in the train terminal began. In April four Movement leaders were convicted of disorderly conduct for picketing a downtown store that refused to hire black workers. Thirty people were arrested in lunch-counter sit-ins. In June, nine more were arrested for picketing downtown stores (see Zinn, 1962; Walters, 1971).

The Albany Movement then scheduled a large prayer vigil for July 21, but the city obtained a temporary injunction at midnight on the 20th from Federal District Judge J. R. Elliott, prohibiting all marching, picketing, and congregating. As a result, the planned vigil did not take place, as King, the featured speaker, refused to violate the order of a federal judge (Lewis, 1970). That night, however, 160 blacks were arrested in a protest march for defying the injunction. Two days later 47 more were arrested for marching.

On July 24 a federal Fifth Circuit judge set aside the temporary injunction. A few days later, King and Abernathy were again arrested when they and a few Albany Movement leaders went to city hall to ask to talk with the city commissioners. By August more than 1,200 had been arrested since the previous November. In the early part of the month, federal Judge Elliott heard arguments by the city for a permanent injunction on demonstrations. On August 10, King, Abernathy, and the other defendants from the recent city hall arrests were convicted. A Northern minister who attended the brief trial said, "The trial was a farce. The judge had his opinion and judgement written out when he came into the court" (in Miller, 1968:133).

The mass protests and arrests of these ten months of the Albany Movement did not desegregate public facilities and accommodations. This was not to occur until after the Congress passed the 1964 Civil Rights Act (Bleiweiss, 1969). An NAACP official put it well: "Albany was successful only if the goal was to go to jail" (in Miller, 1968:139), an assessment shared by much of the press and many civil rights activists (Cleghorn, 1963; *Southern Patriot,* 1963). Others have taken a more positive view, asserting that, at the very least, the Albany campaign focused attention on Southern racism (Walker, 1963) and showed that an entire black community could be mobilized to attack segregation (Miller, 1968; Piven and Cloward, 1979).[10]

In the years since the Albany Movement, at least two explanations of its failure to desegregate have been advanced (Piven and Cloward, 1979). One argues that leaders of the Movement should have concentrated on one or two examples of racial discrimination in the city instead of launching a general attack, which spread the Movement too thinly (Lewis, 1970; Zinn, 1962). The second attributes the Movement's failure to factionalism among its various member groups. The two explanations are not mutually exclusive, and some observers agree with both.

If the organizational problems of the Albany Movement proved fatal, however, the intransigence of city officials provided a decisive blow. And here the criminal justice system of Albany played a crucial role, a point overlooked by Piven and Cloward (1979). Most of the more than 1,200 arrests that took place through the summer of 1962 were without legal merit. As Zinn (1962:21) points out, "There was no consideration of imminent disturbance, or impending violence, no concern with what is the prevailing judicial rule for the limits of free speech—the existence of a 'clear and present danger.'" Similarly, the head of the Southern Regional Council asserted, "There are legitimate grounds for saying that in Albany sophisticated police work has done the traditional—almost legendary—job of the mob, i.e., the suppression of Negro dissent" (in Zinn, 1962:vi).

The many arrests presented the Albany Movement with serious legal problems. With cash bonds of $200 required for most of those arrested, the Movement had to obtain some $200,000 in bail money. Although in many communities property bonds are allowed as collateral, Pritchett purposely refused them in order to create financial problems for the Movement (Pritchett, 1977). The Movement was also never able to overflow the local jails and force the city to spend large sums on incarceration. Long before King and the SCLC had come to Albany, Pritchett had read of King's admiration of Gandhi's method of filling the jails, and determined that this would not happen in Albany. Arrangements were made to send anyone arrested to jails up to 100 miles from the city. Protesters were booked, fingerprinted, photographed and taken immediately on buses to these jails, where several were beaten. Pritchett (1977:399) said later of his tactics, "I think this is one thing that Dr. King was surprised at. This did away with his method of overextending the facilities." As Cleghorn (1963:16) notes, the Albany city jail "proved a bottomless pit." The arrests also overwhelmed C. B. King, the only lawyer in the area willing to represent the more than 1,200 civil rights defendants, as the demands on his time hampered effective legal representation. Guilty verdicts were a foregone conclusion, and his normal practice suffered because of the time required by his civil rights clients.

Just as important, arrests and prosecutions in the long run proved intimidating. In the late spring and summer of 1963, the Albany Movement showed signs of rebirth, but it never achieved the number of participants of the previous year (Sitton, 1963). By that time the prospect of arrest for any protest action aimed at the elusive goal of desegregation was uninviting. As a Northern law student working for C. B. King that summer observed, "The young people are not interested in peaceful demonstrations in the street. That only means arrest with no bail money. The people here have been going to jail for over two years now. They are tired of going to jail" (Roberts, 1965:n.p.).

For those still willing to protest, jail was a certain fate. In June 1963, for example, about 100 people picketing and leafletting white businesses in support of a boycott were arrested for disturbing the peace, effectively "crippling the Negroes' efforts to boycott department stores" (Cleghorn, 1963:16). In late June, 20 out of 26 SNCC workers in Albany were arrested, usually for vagrancy. Thus by the middle of the summer a certain amount of despair had settled over Albany's black community. C. B. King remained busy. As his law student said,

> There is no way to explain how overworked we are, how impossibly far behind, how many things

have to be skipped, how much "private" practice is lost. Because we just don't have the time. We don't practice law here: we run around complying with all the irrelevancies. (Roberts, 1965:n.p.)

Noting the low attendance at protest meetings, he also commented, "People are just physically exhausted and feel forgotten and hopeless" (Roberts, 1965:n.p.).

The final legal blow to the Albany Movement came in August 1963, and, ironically, derived from a federal prosecution of Movement activists which SNCC workers charged was designed to appease Southern communities (Carson, 1981). Nine members of the Movement and of SNCC were indicted by a federal grand jury for perjury and obstructing justice. The defendants had been involved in the June picketing and leafletting of white-owned businesses. One of the store owners had been a juror in a federal suit filed by a black resident against a local sheriff for alleged brutality; an all-white jury ruled against the resident. On August 9 the grand jury indicted three of the nine activists for interfering with a federal juror by boycotting the juror's store, and the rest for perjury in their testimony before the grand jury (Bay Area Friends of SNCC, 1963; Zinn, 1965). All nine were later convicted.

Having regarded the federal government as an ally, Albany blacks were "stunned" and demoralized by the indictments (*Southern Patriot,* 1963: 1). As one resident said, "Even the federal government's a white man" (in Roberts, 1965:n.p.). The indictments also led to other problems. Some Albany blacks were now afraid to associate with members of the Movement; one black businessman refused to allow activists to enter his restaurant, pool hall, or liquor store, and several other black-owned restaurants followed suit (Forman, 1973). Moreover, police harassment of SNCC workers in Albany increased after the indictments. On August 16 one SNCC member who was taken from a porch to the police station for questioning was told by an officer, "Now that the federal government is going to put the Movement's ass in jail, we will put your ass in, too, if you don't stay off the street" (in Roberts, 1965:n.p.).

Thus we see how legal procedure affected the Albany Movement at every turn. Indeed, it is impossible to understand the Movement's development and demise without considering the part played by the police, courts, and prisons.

Pritchett's "nonviolent method" of arrests masked the fact that they were without legal merit and limited criticism of the police response. The city's request for injunctions was another nonviolent, legal method of control that proved effective without arousing national outrage.

Birmingham, 1963

From his defeat in Albany, Martin Luther King went on to victory in Birmingham, thanks in large part to the violence of the white response. After the Albany failure, King debated whether even to continue with his civil rights efforts (Young, 1977), but finally decided to stay in the movement. Thus when Birmingham civil rights leader Fred Shuttlesworth asked King and SCLC for help in May 1962, King quickly accepted. A boycott of downtown white merchants had already weakened the white position, increasing the chances of success if additional pressure were applied. The city's Police Commissioner, Bull Connor, was known for his hostility to civil rights efforts (Hubbard, 1968; Watters, 1971). The stage was thus set for a dramatic confrontation, as SCLC realized and even hoped that demonstrations would prompt police violence (Cleghorn, 1970; Garrow, 1978). Shuttlesworth (1977:168) said many years later, "I think the idea of facing 'Bull' Connor was the thing. We knew that we would have at least the spotlight."[11]

The Birmingham campaign has been recounted elsewhere (Garrow, 1978; Lewis, 1970; Miller, 1968), and space considerations allow only a brief summary here. In the middle of January 1963 King began a speaking tour in which he announced the planned Birmingham campaign and obtained pledges of bail money for arrests in the city. Sit-ins finally began April 3, 1963, with 20 arrested at a local department store. Three days later a protest march led by Shuttlesworth ended in 42 arrests, and by the end of the first week more than 150 had been arrested. Of these, 24 had already been convicted of various offenses, fined $100 each, and sentenced to six months in jail. The city also obtained a local court injunction prohibiting demonstrations.

On Good Friday, April 12, King, Abernathy, and Shuttlesworth led some 50 marchers to city hall, thus defying the injunction. All were arrested. On Easter Sunday, about 2000 blacks gathered at the city jail to protest the arrests, and some people in the crowd threw rocks at the police. In return the police swung clubs and used police dogs.

The use of the clubs and dogs marked a significant departure from the nonviolent tactics of the Albany police. While the latter had trained for mass arrests, Birmingham's had not. One of Birmingham's police captains later revealed that the city's police were "quite taken by surprise that this thing would happen, and they were not—well, they were not really prepared fully from a tactical point of view" (Evans, 1977:189).

In early May the local movement group, the Alabama Christian Movement for Human Rights (ACMHR), decided to use school children in protest marches. In the previous week, demonstrations had "reached rock bottom" (Kunstler, 1966:189). On Thursday, May 2, the police arrested 959 children and nine adults during several marches; more arrests would have taken place if the police had not run out of wagons. Five hundred more marched the next day, but were repelled by police using fire hoses and dogs. News photographs of the hoses and dogs "shocked the world" (Lewis et al., 1966:220). On Monday, May 6, about 1000 more children were arrested for marching to city hall. The number of arrests now exceeded 2000.

With no room left in the local jails, 500 children who marched May 7 were not arrested, prompting SCLC leaders to send 3000 more children downtown the same day. Police used fire hoses, and members of the crowd threw rocks in return; about 50 were arrested. That night, 575 state troopers came to Birmingham at the request of Bull Connor. National attention had now centered on the city. Serious negotiations had begun between civil rights leaders, black and white clergy, and white merchants, and a three-day halt in the demonstrations began May 7. By this time the local movement had run up about $257,000 in bail costs, which were paid by Northern contributors, the bulk coming from the United Auto Workers and the National Maritime Union.

Fearing further violence, the federal government had threatened to send in troops if a compromise were not reached. On Friday, May 10, the 790 protesters still in jail were released on bail, and that afternoon an agreement between the city and civil rights forces was announced. The agreement called for the desegregation of lunch counters, rest-rooms, and the like in all downtown stores, the hiring of blacks in various jobs in the stores, and release of those already convicted. In the next few weeks, white businessmen voted to support the settlement, while on May 20 the U.S. Supreme Court ruled that Birmingham's segregation ordinances were unconstitutional and overturned the convictions of all those arrested under the laws. The events in Birmingham "changed the thinking" of the Kennedy Administration, which had previously opposed new federal civil rights legislation (Lewis et al., 1966:121), and on June 19 Kennedy introduced in Congress the legislation that was to become the 1964 Civil Rights Act.

The protest campaign in Birmingham was generally similar to that in Albany. Protest strategy in each city involved the use of sit-ins and especially mass marches. In each city large numbers of arrests occurred as a result, although Birmingham had twice the number of Albany. Yet the campaign in Birmingham succeeded where, in many ways, it had failed in Albany. In addition to the better organization of the Birmingham effort, several factors seem to account for these different outcomes. First, in Albany the police sent demonstrators to jails outside the city, thus preventing the jails from overflowing, while in Birmingham, a much larger city, the jails did become full. Second, in Albany the Movement had trouble raising bail money, while in Birmingham it was provided by external supporters such as labor unions and Northern liberals. Third, and perhaps most important, the police in Albany arrested without violence, while those in Birmingham were violent. Fourth, in Albany the business community refused to negotiate a compromise, while in Birmingham it agreed to a settlement, partly because of the boycott in downtown stores, partly at the urging of the Justice Department, and partly because of the police violence. The violence of black protesters may also have raised fears of an even greater conflagration. For all these reasons, the Birmingham campaign achieved its goals in only six weeks, while Albany's encompassed some 18 months with little success, allowing time for frustration to set in and spirits to lag.

As a model of official control of civil rights dissent, then, Birmingham is distinguished from Albany and Montgomery by the violence of its police response. To succeed, Birmingham's campaign had to succeed quickly, lest it encounter the legal and financial problems that beset the Albany Movement. But this probably would not have been possible without the response of the Birmingham police, whose violence was exactly what SCLC and ACMHR had desired, and who had made no plans to send arrested demonstrators out of the city. Ironically, a Birmingham police official had consulted with Laurie Pritchett before the demonstrations, but the former's pleas for a nonviolent police response were vetoed by Bull Connor (Evans, 1977; Pritchett, 1977). Thus the Birmingham campaign might very well have failed if the city had followed the Albany and Montgomery pattern of legalistic control. The contrast between the two models is made clear once more in the Danville and Selma campaigns.

Danville, 1963

The success at Birmingham inspired demonstrations in many other areas (Franklin, 1969). One of the most prolonged protest efforts occurred in Danville, Virginia. There the local civil rights movement followed the Birmingham strategy. The city, however, patterned its strategy on that used in Albany, and the Danville protests largely failed to achieve their goals.

The Danville Christian Progressive Association (DCPA) began marches May 31, 1963. A few days later, negotiations began between black and white leaders. On June 5, however, two DCPA leaders were arrested for inciting to riot when they refused to leave city hall, where they had gone to try to talk to the mayor; their bail was set at $5000 each. The arrests ended the biracial negotiations. The DCPA then asked SNCC, SCLC, and CORE for help, and SNCC soon sent 18 field secretaries. On June 6, city Judge Thomas Aiken issued a temporary injunction forbidding further civil rights demonstrations, but in the next few days 105 were arrested for violating the injunction (Belfrage, 1963; Holt, 1965b).

Trials of the 105 began June 17. When the handful of civil rights attorneys walked into court, police took their pictures and searched the black attorneys in the group. Judge Aiken initially refused to tell the attorneys which defendant would be tried first. When he then told attorney Len Holt that the first defendant would be one of his clients, Holt asked for a continuance so that he would have time to prepare the case. Aiken denied the request and then refused Holt's client a jury trial. When Holt challenged the segregated seating in the courtroom, Aiken banned all spectators from the room, saying, "Sure, my courtroom is segregated, but not today, because nobody's allowed

in" (in Belfrage, 1963:11). Aiken then refused to tell Holt which section of the injunction his client had allegedly violated. Holt said he couldn't proceed with the case. The judge replied, "That's your problem," and sentenced the defendant to 90 days in jail and a $25 fine, reading an opinion on the defendant's guilt that had been written before the trial began. He then refused to allow the defendant to stay out of jail while his conviction was being appealed, meaning that the defendant would have served his jail term long before his appeal had been decided. The next day Aiken sentenced a second defendant to 60 days in jail, and later ordered the remaining defendants to be in court every day until all the individual trials had been completed (Belfrage, 1963; Holt, 1965b).

On June 22, a local grand jury indicted 14 Danville civil rights leaders for inciting blacks to riot. Thirteen of the 14 were arrested and released on $5000 bail each, which was raised by local blacks who pledged their homes as security, while the fourteenth, SNCC leader James Forman, left the city in secret. The remaining 13 were forced by the indictments to restrict their civil rights activities (Holt, 1965b).

In July, the Danville police chief, wishing to avoid the error of Bull Connor, asked Laurie Pritchett for advice in dealing with mass protests (Holt, 1965b). Martin Luther King arrived July 11, and 60 blacks who marched to city hall to mark his arrival were arrested. The next day, however, King flew to New York to help plan the March on Washington scheduled for August. About the same time, Chief Judge Simon Sobeloff of the federal Fourth Circuit Court heard the Danville movement's request to dissolve city Judge Aiken's temporary injunction. A week later Sobeloff said the full Circuit Court would hear the matter in late September, but that in the meantime the injunction would stay in effect (Holt, 1965b). His decision to delay a ruling dismayed Danville activists: "To say that we were profoundly distressed by the court's action would be the understatement of the summer" (Kunstler, 1966:228). City officials, on the other hand, greeted the news happily, one of them saying, "I couldn't believe the good news at first" (in Kunstler, 1966:229). The Danville police chief announced that anyone violating Aiken's injunction would be arrested, and that black tobacco workers who took part in demonstrations would not be able to find work later.

During the next two weeks the Danville movement was quiet, thanks to the injunction. Then, on July 28, 80 people were arrested for marching to city hall. The next day, Aiken made his injunction permanent, which "completely paralyzed the protest movement" in Danville (Kunstler, 1966:230). In yet another legal stratagem, Aiken transferred 41 of the injunction contempt cases from Danville to counties 80 to 250 miles away. His action intensified the legal intimidation of the city: "The prospect of having to travel hundreds of miles to be tried would keep most of Danville's Negro citizens from daring to violate the injunction" (Kunstler, 1966:321). However, a three-judge panel of the federal Fourth Circuit Court stopped all the cases until its late September hearing. Sobeloff also suggested that the opposing parties in Danville try to reach a compromise.

But on the day after this suggestion, six of the nine members of Danville's city council said they would not take part in the negotiations requested by three black clergy. The Danville movement had hoped and expected that King and the SCLC would return to the city, but obligations elsewhere prevented them from returning (Lewis, 1970). Despite the roughly two months of protest, "no dramatic gains resulted from Danville's hectic activities" (Miller, 1968:185).

The Danville movement's failure to desegregate can be traced to several factors. In contrast to Birmingham, King and the SCLC came to the city for only a few days. Danville activists were never able to mobilize the numbers that had marched and been arrested in Birmingham, or even in Albany. However, as in Albany, perhaps the primary reason for the movement's defeat was the use of legal means by Danville officials. Thus in August 1963 a *New York Times* reporter wrote that the "Danville method," one that followed the legalistic model of Albany and Montgomery, was being studied by other communities: "Officials of other Virginia cities have traveled here to observe and learn in an unspoken compliment to a strategy that is the most unyielding, ingenious, and effective of any city in the South" (Franklin, 1963:71).

Selma, 1965

Garrow (1978) has discussed the Selma campaign in great detail, and thus only a brief summary is needed here. Before 1965, arrests by Selma police and state court injunctions had "greatly hindered" (Miller, 1968:216) organizing efforts by SNCC in the city. On July 6, 1964, for example, 50 blacks attempting to register to vote were arrested. Three days later, a local judge issued an injunction prohibiting public gatherings of more than three people; the injunction "halted" (Garrow, 1978:34) weekly mass meetings that had been taking place.

Hoping for a violent white response, SCLC decided to focus on Selma to dramatize the call for Congressional passage of voting rights legislation, and it soon became clear the Selma law enforcement personnel had not learned the lessons of earlier protest campaigns (Garrow, 1978). As Laurie Pritchett (1977:404) later observed, "The people that were most responsible" for civil rights successes were Bull Connor and Jim Clark, sheriff of Selma. "Dr. King, when he left Albany, was a defeated man. In my opinion, right or wrong, if Birmingham had reacted as Albany, Georgia, did they'd never got to Selma."

In late January 1965, the SCLC campaign began, and by February 5 some 3000 had been arrested in a series of marches. The climactic events of Selma began Sunday, March 7, when SCLC had scheduled a march from Selma to Montgomery. Governor George Wallace signed an order prohibiting the march, and announced that state troopers with tear gas would stop the march if it took place. As 525 people marched across a bridge on the way to Montgomery, they were ordered to turn back by a state trooper official. When they did not retreat, troopers and Selma police used tear gas and beat the marchers with nightsticks as they tried to run away. Then Jim Clark ordered his police on horses to "get those niggers—and get those goddam white niggers" (in Miller, 1968:221); the horses plunged into the crowd. The press conveyed the police violence to the entire country, and several members of Congress came to Selma to investigate complaints of civil rights forces. As one SCLC member said, "Jim Clark is another Bull Connor. We should put them on the staff" (in Piven and Cloward, 1979:249). In response to a call by Martin Luther King for clergy and laity to come to Selma, hundreds began to arrive in the city Monday, March 8. Two days later, four members of the Ku Klux Klan beat to death a white minister.

The violence at Selma led to protests across the country that demanded federal intervention in Alabama and passage of federal voting rights legislation (Garrow, 1978). Then, on March 15, President Johnson announced that he would submit such legislation to Congress. A few days later, 380 persons, most of them white ministers, were arrested in Selma for picketing and praying in front of the mayor's house. Finally, on Sunday, March 21, more than 10,000 people marched from Selma to Montgomery. At the latter city they were joined by 25,000 others from many other states.

In Selma we see the impact of the two methods of white control that have been identified. The legalistic method used in Montgomery, Albany, and Danville had worked for Selma officials before the SCLC began its campaign, when SNCC activists were in the city. Legal means were also used in the early phases of the SCLC campaign. Finally, however, control actions followed the Birmingham pattern of violence by law enforcement personnel, leading once more to federal intervention. If the Selma police and Alabama state troopers had followed the legalistic path, however, they might very well have defeated the SCLC's campaign.

Conclusion

This paper has identified two models of control of civil rights protest in the South. In the first, characterizing Montgomery, Albany, and Danville, the pattern of white resistance was "legalistic," eschewing violence in favor of frequent questionable arrests, high bail, court proceedings lacking due process, and injunctions without legal foundation. Because of the legal means that were used, this approach acquired a measure of legitimacy, when compared to earlier episodes of violence, and muted criticism. Thus mass protests in Albany and Danville were not enough and in the long run created legal problems that helped defeat civil rights forces. This method of legal control would also have succeeded in Montgomery had not the U.S. Supreme Court intervened at the eleventh hour.

In the second model, characterizing Birmingham and Selma, police violence accompanied legalistic means of control and, because of the Northern sympathy and federal action that resulted, enabled civil rights forces to succeed in spite of the legal and financial problems inherent in mass protest.

Killian (1968:32) observed some time ago that the slow pace of Southern school desegregation in the 1950s was "created primarily by legal-

ists who did not crudely defy the law but cleverly used it to limit change to a minimum." This paper has argued that Southern whites could also have used legal tactics to thwart civil rights goals in the protest phase of the movement. Protest may be very effective at times, and it resulted in unprecedented, if often limited, gains in the South in many areas. But this paper has suggested that the major successes of the movement would not have been possible without inappropriate tactical choices by Southern officials. If this is true, then the movement's major successes derived not from its own ability to compel white violence and hence federal intervention by the use of mass protest, but from the crude and unlearned responses of certain Southern officials to such protest. Put more directly, movement groups were able to win major successes only when they were fortunate enough to find opponents who "could be counted on in stupidity and natural viciousness to play into their hands" (Watters, 1971:266).[12] In thus emphasizing the movement's weaknesses in the face of stubborn white resistance that resorted to legal repression, the paper provides support for the resource mobilization argument in the debate discussed earlier.

More generally, this paper has presented a detailed analysis of the variety of legal tactics available to social movement opponents. Arrests, prosecutions, and injunctions have long been effective weapons in controlling dissent, and were used in earlier eras against antebellum abolitionists (Campbell, 1970), striking workers (Frankfurter and Greene, 1930), and critics of U. S. involvement in World War I (Peterson and Fite, 1957). Such tactics helped destroy the Industrial Workers of the World early in this century (Chafee, 1941) and posed serious burdens for Communist Party leaders after World War II (Belknap, 1978). Despite this history of the legal control of dissent, however, sociologists have paid little attention to the impact of legal procedure on movement challenges.

The study of "political justice" (Kirchheimer, 1961), then, is essential for a full understanding of the dynamics of protest and control in times of social movement unrest. Future research will contribute further to the debate addressed by this paper and increase our knowledge of the interplay between the legal process and social and political dissent.

Notes

1. The term "resource mobilization" actually refers to many different viewpoints that have been grouped under this one rubric. The variant discussed here, as noted by McAdam (1982:262), is that which Perrow (1979) calls "RM II."

2. Scholars identified with the older collective behavior tradition are of two minds on the issue of external support. While some scholars (e.g., Smelser, 1963) assume that resources derive from a movement's mass base, Turner and Killian (1957:329, 1972:247-65; Turner, 1969a:825, 1970:151-52; Killian, 1964:432-35) clearly emphasize the importance of support by the general public and specific third-party groups with established power for the success of social movement challenges.

3. McAdam (1982, 1983) and Piven and Cloward (1979) do not explicitly say that the movement was able to *compel* federal action in this manner. Without this element of compulsion, however, their argument merely emphasizes the importance of federal intervention (and not the movement's disruptive capacity) and thus does not differ from that of RM theorists.

4. White violence did not always lead to federal intervention, as shown by the lack of federal response to extensive white violence in cities such as McComb, Mississippi (Carson, 1981), and St. Augustine, Florida (Goodwyn, 1965). An analysis of the conditions under which white violence did lead to federal intervention is important, for an understanding of the civil rights movement, though it is not the purpose of this paper. It is generally true, however, as McAdam (1983) has empirically demonstrated, that federal intervention was a response to white violence, which in turn was a consequence of black protest.

5. While white violence did occur in Montgomery (Brooks, 1974), the primary effort of white officials to control the movement was "legalistic" in nature.

6. In looking at the effective white resistance to school desegregation in the 1950s, Killian (1968:70) similarly notes the tendency of legalistic means of control to keep criticism to a minimum:

   > It is ironic that the white South was extremely successful in minimizing the impact of the desegregation decisions of the federal courts without arousing the indignation of the rest of the nation. As much as the White Citizens Councils and the Ku Klux Klan are invoked as symbols of the southern resistance, they and their extralegal tactics did not make this possible. Far more effective were the legal stratagems, evasions, and delays that led Negroes to realize that although they had won a new statement of principle they had not won the power to cause this principle to be implemented.

7. As Gamson (1980:1043) notes. "There is no more ticklish issue in studying social protest than deciding what constitutes success." Elsewhere he (1975:28-29, 1980:1045-50) and Jenkins (1981) discuss the many conceptual issues that arise in defining success. In this paper a local protest effort is defined as successful if it achieved most or all of the *immediate* goals of desegregation and the like that were sought by the protesters themselves. If it was essential for the larger movement's success that it have at least some local successes, then it is proper, and important, to study the factors affecting local successes. In determining the degree of success, I follow Gamson (1975:29) in taking "the group's own perspective and aspirations as the starting points" and in drawing on the perceptions of the group itself (and of its allies in the larger movement), its antagonists, and the view of historians and contemporary observers. Admittedly, this definition and analysis of success leave aside several conceptual questions, e.g., the achievement of goals that are "empty of real meaning" (Gamson, 1975:28).

8. This is a point that McAdam (1983) misses when he attributes the success of the Montgomery boycott to the fact that Montgomery blacks were able to deal a severe financial blow to the bus lines they boycotted. While I do not wish to minimize the impact of the boycott, my analysis suggests that it would have failed had it not been for the Supreme Court. McAdam (1983) notes the use of a similar pattern of legal harassment by Tallahassee officials in response to the 1956 bus boycott in that city. I take no issue with his (1983:741) observation that other cities desegregated their bus lines in the wake of Montgomery and Tallahassee, though I would argue that they could have defeated the boycotts through legal intimidation.

9. This point illustrates McAdam's (1982:264) observation that the choice of protest tactics greatly influences the form of control adopted by officials. The more "passive" form of protest used in Montgomery made it less likely that officials would, or could, resort to violence. Although "active" forms of protest like marches and demonstrations may increase the chances of official violence, as in Birmingham and Selma, they do not guarantee it, as Albany and Danville will illustrate.

10. Carson (1981:65) shares both views on the Albany outcome.

11. In discussing how the personalities and desires of law enforcement officials like Pritchett (in Albany), Connor (in Birmingham), and, later, Clark (in Selma) influenced outcomes, the analysis emphasizes personalities rather than structural forces. Characteristic of other works as well (e.g., Garrow, 1978; McAdam, 1982, 1983; Piven and Cloward, 1979), this view is unavoidable, precisely because the personalities and attitudes of each law enforcement official did play such a large role, as SCLC officials realized at the time and as later accounts have confirmed. Although sociology has, at least since the time of Durkheim, emphasized the influence of structural forces over that of individual personalities, we cannot escape the fact that in the protest campaigns described here the identity and attitudes of the primary law en-

forcement officials involved played a key, and even crucial, role. Just as sociology should avoid an "over-socialized" view of the individual (Wrong, 1961), so should the discipline avoid an "over-structuralized" view when studying social movements.

12. McAdam's (1983) analysis suggests the weaknesses of civil rights forces in the absence of white violence. First, he notes the effectiveness of decisions by law enforcement officials in Mississippi in 1961 to avoid the use of violence against Freedom Riders, neutralizing the "crisis atmosphere" that had occurred in earlier violent episodes. Second, in commenting on Albany he (1983:748-49) observes, "Failing to pro-voke the public violence necessary to prompt federal intervention, insurgents *lacked sufficient leverage themselves* to achieve anything more than an inconclusive stand-off with the local segregationist forces in Albany" (emphasis added), thus contradicting his earlier (1982:30) statement, quoted at the beginning of this paper, that "aggrieved groups possess the ability to exert significant leverage on their own behalf." Third, he (1983:750) notes that after Birmingham and Selma, whites finally learned to react moderately, "and in so doing short-circuit the more general protest dynamic under discussion here," as was the case in Baltimore (Von Eschen et al., 1969). ◆

30

Fighting Back: Vulnerabilities, Blunders, and Countermobilization by the Targets in Three Animal Rights Campaigns

James M. Jasper
Jane D. Poulsen

Introduction

In 1977 a small group of animal protectionists stopped a long-running research program on cat sexuality at the American Museum of Natural History in Manhattan. Ten years later (1987-1988), in response to pressure from an animal rights group named Trans-Species Unlimited, a researcher at the Cornell Medical School returned her federal funding for a long-running cat experiment on drug addiction. In 1988-1990—at the height of the animal rights movement—the same group, using the same tactics, failed in its efforts to stop drug addiction experiments on monkeys at New York University (NYU). Since then, there have been almost no victories in similar antivivisection efforts. Three battles in a growing war on animal experimentation, these campaigns raise obvious questions. Why do some social movement campaigns succeed while others fail? And why, in this case, does there seem to be an inverse relationship between the size of a movement and its ability to win campaigns?

Most explanations of social movement success concentrate on the tactics and traits of protest groups and on the responses of the state, largely ignoring the characteristics and responses of other targeted organizations. Yet the outcomes of protest campaigns are often influenced by the actions of the organizations under attack: their preexisting vulnerabilities (Walsh, 1986), their strategic responses to the protest, especially damaging "blunders," and their ability to mobilize a countermovement. Examination of these factors helps us see the relationship between different forms of success, which might include membership growth and accumulation of resources, institutional acceptance and longevity, and the attainment of stated goals. In particular, we shall see the possibility that the larger a movement becomes, the more countermobilizing it may inspire, and the less it may be able to attain specific stated goals.

Our evidence comes from participant observation at the NYU demonstrations and the meetings that planned them, from interviews with protestors and officials of the targeted institutions, and from exhaustive review of all the available published accounts of the three campaigns. (For interview data on the NYU protestors, see Jasper and Poulsen, 1989; for a broader interpretation of the animal rights movements, see Jasper and Nelkin, 1992.)

Theoretical Background

In the 1970s, "resource mobilization" explanations of social movement success typically concentrated on the characteristics, resources, and strategies of social movement organizations (SMOs) and their supporters (Ash, 1972; Gamson, 1975; Piven and Cloward, 1977). With the rise of "political process" approaches (Tilly, 1978; McAdam, 1982; Kitschelt, 1986) attention shifted to state institutions, with their power to tax and spend and to use violence to repress protest. Because protestors were viewed as insurgents demanding access to the polity, the state was naturally their preeminent opponent. McAdam (1982:25) even defined social movements as "those organized efforts, on the part of excluded groups, to promote or resist changes in the structure of society that involve recourse to noninstitutional forms of political participation." Others simply assumed that movement goals involved changes in state policies (Gamson, 1975).

Much of the "political opportunity structure" literature had two generic blind spots, overlooking additional strategic actors besides protestors and the state as well as missing the dynamic interaction between protestors and their environment. Because of its focus on the state, such research tended to ignore movement goals such as changes in public awareness, changes in the practices and beliefs of protestors themselves, or changes in the attitudes and practices of other targeted, but nonstate, institutions (Troyer and Markle, 1983, are an exception). Because many social movements try to change the practices of nonstate actors—such as corporations, universities, or professional associations—the responses of these targets often affect movements' success or failure. What is more, both state agencies and these other actors respond energetically with their own strategies. Doug McAdam (1983:736) explains the pace and outcome of protest in terms of "(a) the creativity of insurgents in devising new tactical forms, and (b) the ability of opponents to neutralize these moves through effective tactical counters." Protest campaigns are elaborate strategic games (see Staggenborg, 1986, and Hirsch, 1990, for examples), often with more than two players.

We hope to suggest ways of filling these lacunae by examining the role of targeted organizations in the outcomes of protest campaigns. Three factors prove especially important: preexisting vulnerabilities on the part of these targets, their strategic responses to attack, and broader countermobilization that they and similar organizations mount.

Vulnerabilities

Certain characteristics or practices of targeted organizations make them vulnerable to attacks by protestors. Edward Walsh (1986) analyzed the "target vulnerabilities" of General Public Utilities (GPU)—the owner of the Three Mile Island nuclear reactor—during the battle over cleanup and restart of the twin, undamaged reactor. Following the 1979 accident, GPU's credibility was further undermined when the utility filed a lawsuit against the reactor makers, as the suit inadvertently revealed GPU's own improper management and falsification of operating data, cheating by reactor operators in examinations for promotions, and leaking steam tubes at the undamaged Unit 1 reactor. Several engineers also charged that the cleanup was not proceeding in a safe manner. These vulnerabilities influenced public opinion, regulators, and elected officials. Walsh does not distinguish between types of vulnerability, some of which were ongoing conditions at the company, while others were blunders the company made in responding to the attacks by protestors. We reserve the term "vulnerability" for preexisting conditions (even if they are only brought to light during the controversy), and use the term "blunder" for actions taken in response

to criticism. Both vulnerabilities and blunders can occur at the level of the entire organization, for example in its official response to controversy, or at the sublevel of the project under attack, for example a particular research experiment or laboratory.

SMOs understandably look for targets with project vulnerabilities. National antinuclear organizations cultivated the Diablo Canyon reactor as a symbol of nuclear energy, because it was near an earthquake fault and had extreme cost overruns. Animal activists focused on experiments using cats because, given public tastes in animals, they are more evocative than research using rats. Protestors also look for weaknesses in targeted institutions such as internal cleavages, financial instability, or failure to perform according to publicly stated standards (cf. Freudenburg, 1993). Once an institution is spotlighted by protest, its activities are closely watched, and organizational problems unconnected with the controversy can be uncovered. Its general reputation for competence and credibility can be undermined, indirectly providing fuel for its critics. Disagreements between elites may yield an institutional vulnerability, by isolating the target from potential supporters.

Blunders

In addition to preexisting (and relatively passive) vulnerabilities, targeted organizations actively deploy, in response to public criticism, a range of strategies that may be either wise or mistaken. Protestors attempt to goad their opponents into mistakes, while targets try to reduce their preexisting vulnerabilities and avoid blunders. Many vulnerabilities are revealed during this interaction;[1] they can be seen as "accidents" revealing intentions and power structures that institutions often try to hide (Molotch, 1970). A strategic blunder can weaken an organization's reputation for competence, honesty, or benevolence. A classic case is Eugene "Bull" Connor's ferocious attacks on peaceful civil rights demonstrators in Birmingham, Alabama; transmitted through the news media, they created national sympathy for the demonstrators (Garrow, 1978:133-160; McAdam, 1982). Similarly, Steven Barkan (1984) found that southern communities which responded to civil rights protest with violence were less successful at defeating it than those using legal means. In other words, blunders become

Table I. Examples of Vulnerabilities and Blunders

	Vulnerabilities	Blunders
Project level	Experimental use of popular species; lack of obvious public benefits; potential environmental impact; criticism by external experts.	Deception or arrogance on the part of individual researcher; inability to communicate with the public or media.
Institutional level	Reputation for sloppy management, unsafe practices, or previous controversies; weak financial position; internal cleavages or frictions; failure to perform according to organization's own stated standards or goals.	Deception or denial; infiltration of the movement, or unsuccessful efforts to belittle it; brutal repression of peaceful protest.

new issues to be added to the original causes for protest (Oberschall, 1979:47).

Countermobilization

Whether an organization attacked by protestors reacts effectively or poorly often depends on the experiences of similar organizations that have been attacked or that perceive themselves at risk of attack. When a critical mass of organizations feel threatened, they may organize a counter-movement. Professional or trade associations, for example, can serve as countermovement organizations, giving aid to targeted individuals and institutions, coordinating their responses, providing resources, and sharing information about effective strategies. Counterorganizations thus help targeted institutions hide preexisting vulnerabilities and avoid blunders. (Their ability to do this shows that it is partly possible to predict what strategies will be blunders, rather than seeing this only in retrospect; otherwise blunders could only be recognized by their effects.)

As McAdam suggests, social movement success depends on whether the movement or its countermovement mobilizes more rapidly and effectively. Gamson (1975) argues that counterorganization is more immediate if a social movement explicitly names its target. Zald and Useem (1987:254) and Mottl (1980:624) claim that social movement successes spur countermobilization, unless they are "crushing victories." For example, the early successes of the pro Equal Rights Amendment movement aroused a broad backlash, because the issue "provided a link with the fundamentalist churches" and "mobilized a group, traditional homemakers, that had lost status over the two previous decades and was feeling the psychological effects of the loss" (Mansbridge, 1986:5-6). Most research on countermovements views

them as efforts to undo the social changes brought about by social movements, rather than as active opponents of the social movements (often directly attacking movement organizations, as in lawsuits).

The interaction between mobilization and countermobilization can be summarized by tracing the life cycle of protest movements. Charles Tilly (1978:122) plotted movement success ("collective goods produced") as a function of mobilization and protest activity ("resources expended"). Although his picture is static, the relationship can be seen as the life cycle of a growing movement: no action yields negative results (as the group's interests are not protected); a little action, because repressed, yields worse losses; extensive action yields significant results, but at some point there are diminishing returns (Fig. 1, "Early Losses"). Yet the two segments of Tilly's curve with negative slopes actually seem driven by two distinct factors: early repression by the state, and later countermobilization by other groups. This pattern fits the labor movement, which historically faced swift state responses. But how general is this pattern? Does it fit movements that avoid state repression?[2]

The target and opponent of many protest movements is not the state, but other actors in civil society. For these movements, which are not automatically repressed by the state, a small amount of action can yield substantial results. An incipient movement, still a collection of scattered groups, can be very successful. Jasper (1990:109) sug-

Figure 1
Effect of Mobilization on Outcomes Differs in Absence of State Repression

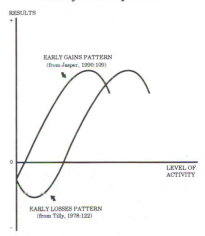

RESULTS

EARLY GAINS PATTERN
(from Jasper, 1990:109)

LEVEL OF ACTIVITY

EARLY LOSSES PATTERN
(from Tilly, 1978:122)

gested that antinuclear groups stopped several planned nuclear reactors in the 1960s—places like Bodega Head, Cayuga Lake, Malibu, Lloyd Harbor, Nippomo Dunes—before the national antinuclear movement emerged. These groups succeeded because electric utilities felt that if one site was controversial, they could find another. Once the national movement gelled in the early 1970s, however, antinuclear groups were unable to stop the construction of reactors, as utilities universally mobilized to fight back (plants were, however, canceled for reasons other than public protest). Antinuclear groups did not face early state repression—hence they achieved early gains rather than early losses—but they did ultimately face countermobilization.

If a movement is recognized in the media and perceived as a threat by its targets, every battle has wider—symbolic, if not material—implications. If it appears likely that a controversy will persist, targeted institutions counterorganize, bringing powerful national pressures to bear on local antagonists; witness the federal government's interference to stop New York State's arrangements to retire the Shoreham nuclear plant. In both curves in Fig. 1, the increasing size of a social movement ultimately spurs countermobilization; they differ in that the "early gains" pattern assumes little state repression in the early stages of mobilization. There may also be vulnerabilities and blunders that protestors can exploit in the early stages of a movement but which decrease over time. The conditions for the early success may simply disappear; more surprisingly, the early success may itself undermine its own conditions (by inspiring countermobilization).

The success or failure of social movements has often been analyzed as a consequence of resource distributions rather than as an open-ended game depending on clever moves. When this structuralist perspective is relaxed, SMOs can be seen as strategic agents; with political process models the state is also seen as a key strategic agent (Tilly, 1978; McAdam, 1983). But there has been little effort to theorize the active role of nonstate organizations under attack by protestors. Not only their preexisting vulnerabilities, but their individual blunders and collective countermobilization have a crucial effect on movement success.

Three Campaigns Against Animal Experiments

We now try to explain the outcomes of two successful and one failed campaign against particular animal experiments. The cases are similar in many ways. All three campaigns attacked institutions located in Manhattan. All involved higher-order mammals—cats and monkeys—for which there is widespread public sympathy. The same animal rights group, Trans-Species Unlimited, conducted two of the campaigns. While all three cases attracted national media attention, they were organized by local animal groups or chapters. At the same time certain differences between these cases highlight our theoretical concerns. The level of countermobilization by the research community increased over time across the three cases, and the pattern of vulnerabilities and blunders also differed in the three cases.

While these three campaigns are tactically similar to many others around the country, we do not claim they are representative. Protests have stopped relatively few animal experiments. Mainly they have caused delays and inspired costly protective measures. But it is useful to examine those campaigns that do succeed in their specific goals if we are to explain the determinants of success and failure. Why could activists stop these two experiments, when most of their efforts have failed?

The American Museum of Natural History

In 1976, several years before a discernible animal rights movement emerged, several activists who had taken a course on animal liberation taught by philosopher Peter Singer learned of an experiment on the sexual behavior of cats at the American Museum of Natural History. Underway since 1959, this research involved mutilating cats—castrating them, removing parts of the brain, destroying the sense of smell—to observe the effects on their sexual preferences and abilities. The activists had been searching for a target in New York (for better access and media attention) that involved dubious and easily parodied research. Experiments on feline sexual practices seemed ideal.

The campaign was organized by a new coalition, although several proanimal organizations were involved. Henry Spira, former union and civil rights activist, emerged as the key figure. As a newcomer to animal protection, he could avoid jealousies between existing animal groups. The campaign went public in June 1976. The museum received 8000 letters of protest in 1976, but its directors refused to talk with the campaign organizers. Picket lines formed outside the museum every weekend for 18 months, and because the museum has one main entrance, the activists could distribute informational leaflets to all visitors. One large rally drew 1000 people. Protestors claimed the experiments were not just cruel, but bad science and a waste of public funds. This last issue provided an opportunity for Congressman Ed Koch to visit the lab and report his skepticism: "I said to this professor, 'Now, tell me, after you have taken a deranged male cat with brain lesions and you place it in a room and you find that it is going to mount a rabbit instead of a female cat, what have you got?' There was no response. I said 'How much has this cost the government?' She said '$435,000' " (Spira, 1985:199). Protestors provided a grandstand for a politician fond of posturing and sarcasm.

Like Ed Koch, the news media had fun with the weaker aspects of the experiment. Gleefully reporting the protestors' slogans ("Curiosity Kills Cats," and "Castrate the Scientists"), they also questioned the research itself ("Cutting up Cats to Study Sex—What Fun!" *Chicago Sun Times*, July 25, 1976). Given broad public ambivalence about science, basic research, which appears driven by sheer curiosity, may be more vulnerable than applied research. The nature of the experiments— basic research, use of a popular species, sexual behavior—provided project vulnerabilities for protestors to exploit. Even *Science* magazine wryly commented that the research "sounds like no picnic" (Wade, 1976).

The federal agency funding the research, the National Institutes of Health (NIH), was inundated with letters from the public and inquiries from Congress. Upon investigation it found that the internal museum committee that had reviewed the experiments had been composed of two of the project's principal investigators and an outside veterinarian. An NIH official reported, "This violates the spirit of the animal welfare committee's function." This was a strong preexisting vulnerability (of both the project and the institution) that helped to alienate an important financial player.

By the fall of 1977, NIH and the museum agreed to capitulate. NIH stopped funding the experiment, and the museum dismantled the labs. In 1980 the museum abolished the entire Department of Animal Behavior in which the experiments had taken place. Unknown to the animal activists, this department had occupied a weak position within the museum—an institutional vulnerability that prevented a united position to protect the research. Research in museums usually focuses on the assembly and study of collections; behavioral research had been marginal at the museum. Tension between the two kinds of research had recently surfaced in the process of filling new staff positions. The animal rights campaign aggravated this conflict, providing an excuse for museum directors to abandon a unit they already regarded as peripheral.

Cornell Medical College

In the decade following the museum case, animal rights groups proliferated, their activities accelerated, and the movement came to be widely recognized as a threat to animal experimentation. New groups were formed especially from 1981 to 1985, partly inspired by several notorious challenges to animal experiments, including a 1981 case in Silver Spring that resulted in the indictment of the principal investigator and a 1984 case in which grisly videotapes were taken from a trauma research lab at the University of Pennsylvania (Jasper and Nelkin, 1992). Trans-Species Unlimited (TSU) was founded in 1981 in eastern Pennsylvania, and its largely autonomous New York City chapter grew to be its largest. While TSU solicited funds through mailings, its forte was public protest and civil disobedience. The New York chapter had monthly meetings typically attended by over 100 people. It held a "Fur-Free Friday" each November as well as other protests, letter-writing campaigns, and outreach activities. Each spring it targeted a local scientific research project, and in 1987 it selected one at the Cornell Medical College in Manhattan.

The Cornell experiments, funded by the National Institute on Drug Abuse (NIDA), examined the effects of barbiturates on cats by means of electrodes implanted in the animals' skulls. A pharmacology professor had been conducting this work since 1973 on around 200 cats. Animal activists target drug addiction research, on the grounds that the money should go to help real human addicts instead. As in the museum case, the use of cats made the project vulnerable to public opinion. But unlike the museum case, TSU claimed to have chosen the Cornell experiments because they were typical, not because they were especially vulnerable. In a fund-raising brochure, TSU President George Cave (no date) boasted that "We met the Cornell experiments head-on . . . the public learned that the cat addiction studies were not simply an isolated instance of 'bad' research but an all-too-typical example of useless drug addiction experiments." Furthermore, unlike the situation at the museum, the experiments had the full support of the funding agency and the medical school administration—there were no obvious institutional vulnerabilities.

The campaign began with a protest outside the school on April 24, 1987—World Day for Laboratory Animals. Roughly 350 people demonstrated, and 56 were arrested for civil disobedience. TSU benefited from the growing animal rights movement not only through the publicity surrounding World Day for Laboratory Animals, but also by networking with 65 other organizations to generate phone calls and letters of protest. NIDA received over 10,000 written protests, and 80 congressional offices made inquiries. Several scientists—involved in the national animal rights movement as counterexperts—drafted a critique of the experiments, arguing that, because the cat was a poor model for human barbiturate dependence, the research had no relevance for treating addicts.

Medical School officials made several surprising moves that added up to a fatal blunder. In August they met with TSU President George Cave and science advisor Murray Cohen (who advises many animal rights groups around the country). According to Cave, the officials said that the "experiments were over," and that the renewal grant, approved in May, would not be used. He cited a letter, drafted by a Cornell committee, and sent to legislators and the media over the signature of the associate dean for sponsored programs at the medical school. While defending the pharmacologist's research, the letter ambiguously said, "The research . . . that required the use of the cat model has essentially been completed." TSU claimed victory.

Two months later the researcher applied to NIDA for a renewal grant to continue the cat studies and develop an experimental model using rats. The proposal, consigned by the dean who had sent out the earlier letter, was funded. When TSU learned of this, it renewed its letter-writing campaign, insisting that Cornell had lied or reversed its stated intentions. Cornell's reaction placed it in an increasingly awkward position. Personally harassed, with little support from Cornell, the researcher returned the grant money in September 1988. Cornell officials said that this was done to preserve "institutional credibility" and also that it was the investigator's own personal decision. The university itself temporarily funded her research, which turned to rats as experimental models.

TSU's Steve Siegel called the case "the first time a major experiment has ever been stopped simply because of the lack of value of the research itself." It is one of the few large experiments stopped by the animal rights movement, though for political rather than scientific reasons. However, it may also be the last. Angry scientists around the country wrote to Cornell, arguing that the university's responsibility was to protect researchers from "extremists," and that Cornell's decision was a "disastrous precedent." Even NIDA attacked the university's "ostrich-like stance" and hinted the decision might affect future funding. The fact that a major private university had stopped an ongoing research project galvanized the biomedical community. New organizations have been founded to defend the use of animals in research. Professional associations discuss tactics for countering the animal rights movement, and counsel research institutions to take unyielding positions. This activity was accelerated by the Cornell case.

New York University

Believing it had already won the Cornell campaign, TSU targeted the New York University medical school in the spring of 1988. The experiments in this case involved Macaque monkeys (like cats, a popular species), which were taught to self-administer toluene, a common industrial solvent used in glues and paints. The purpose was to understand the effects of toluene in early stages of use, for children and teens occasionally sniff toluene for pleasure. Supported by NIDA, a professor of environmental medicine was conducting the experiments 40 miles north of NYU's Manhattan campus, in a research facility at Sterling Forest.

TSU's campaign against NYU resembled the Cornell protest. It involved pickets in front of the NYU library and administration building and extensive letter writing to legislators and NYU officials. In April 1988 and again in April 1989 nearly 1000 demonstrators participated, compared to 350 in the 1987 Cornell protest. TSU did not try to talk with NYU administrators, as demonstrators had in the museum and Cornell campaigns.

TSU had little practical effect on NYU's research. Although leaders claimed some success because the campaign mobilized new supporters and attracted media coverage, the experiments were not changed in any significant way (beyond tighter security measures). TSU put little effort into organizing the second (1989) rally. After their failure to influence NYU in 1988, many TSU members turned their attention to other animal issues, and the TSU meeting just before the 1989 NYU protest gave more time to furs than to the NYU action. In April 1990 there was no protest against NYU. The campaign was effectively over. (TSU underwent internal splits at this time, and it eventually collapsed. Other animal rights groups demonstrated at NYU in April 1991, attracting almost 300 protestors, but their focus was not these experiments.)

From the start, NYU's response to the campaign was aggressively "proactive" rather than defensive and "reactive." The day before each protest, NYU held a press conference to praise both the targeted experiments and scientific research in general. In 1988 this meeting centered on a sick 8-year-old and his mother, both with down-home Kentucky accents. The boy was a victim of a blood vessel tumor that trapped white cells and prevented blood coagulation, and scientists claimed he would not be alive except for procedures developed through animal experimentation. He and his mother proclaimed their love for animals, but also their gratitude that some animals were sacrificed to save people. Most of the news coverage of the next day's protest included clips from this conference. In the battle over public opinion NYU had found an emotional appeal to equal that of furry animals caged and victimized, and its reaction reduced the vulnerability of the project. It could contest protestors' "framing" of NYU as a heartless bureaucracy (Snow et al., 1986; Snow and Benford, 1988). The university unintentionally won another symbolic battle: the protests were held in front of the building housing university administrators, which is also the main library. The disturbing image was of protestors shouting at a place symbolic of learning, while the experiments took place miles away.

TSU faced practical disadvantages as well. Held on Saturdays, the protests did not disrupt university activity, and demonstrators could not speak to university officials. Unlike the museum, there were no clear places where they could contact people entering the university. That NIDA, the funding agency for both the Cornell and the NYU experiments, had disapproved of Cornell's capitulation was not lost on NYU. Moreover, the scientific response and the counterorganization following the Cornell case had strengthened the resistance of other universities to animal rights protests. The message was clear to NYU, which ignored the demonstrators and courted public sympathy.

Cornell and NYU may be seen as end points in a continuum from defensive and reactive to positive and proactive responses, and research institutions are drawing lessons from these and similar experiences. As state and national organizations of scientists spread information about tactics, targeted institutions are increasingly likely to adopt the proactive response that worked for NYU. Analysis of our three cases suggests the result may be even fewer victories for future animal rights campaigns.

Analysis

Why did the Cornell and museum campaigns succeed in stopping the experiments, while the NYU campaign, like most attacks on scientific experiments, failed? One set of explanatory factors are the choices and activities of the SMOs: their

Figure 2
Factors in the Three Cases

Variable	American Museum	Cornell University	New York University
Scope of SMO goal	Limited	Limited	Limited
Defense of research by funding agency	Weak	Strong	Strong
Project vulnerabilities	Sympathetic mammal; basic research poor internal review	Sympathetic mammal	Sympathetic mammal
Institutional vulnerabilities	Department lacked institutional support	None	None
Blunders	None	Misled public	None
Level of counterorganization	Low	Medium–high	High
Outcome	Experiment stopped	External funding stopped	Continued unchanged

goals, tactics, recruitment, organizational structure, and mobilization of resources. Second are the preexisting vulnerabilities of the targeted institutions: project vulnerabilities such as the nature of the research, and institutional ones such as internal conflict. Third are the active responses of targeted organizations, including the presence or absence of blunders and the effect of counterorganization. The differences between the cases are summarized in Table 2.

Table II. Factors in the Three Cases			
Variable	American Museum	Cornell University	New York University
Scope of SMO Goal	Limited	Limited	Limited
Defense of Research by Funding agency	Weak	Strong	Strong
Project Vulnerabilities	Sympathetic mammal; basic research poor internal review	Sympathetic mammal	Sympathetic mammal
Institutional Vulnerabilities	Department Lacked Institutional support	None	None
Blunders	None	Misled Public	None
Level of Counterorganization	Low	Medium–High	High
Outcome	Experiment stopped	External funding stopped	Continued unchanged

In each campaign, the SMOs made similar choices. They targeted experiments that might be offensive to a broad segment of the population because they used furry mammals and could be attacked as apparently pointless. These were significant choices, given the whole range of experiments (most of them using rodents) underway in New York laboratories. All three SMOs relied on a standard repertory of tactics: tabling to provide public information, letter writing, and a combination of occasional large rallies with more frequent picketing. All three employed mild civil disobedience, blocking traffic in order to be arrested or blocking the entrance to the museum. The rhetoric, both verbal and visual, was similar in the three campaigns (Jasper and Nelkin, 1992, discuss this rhetoric).

The three campaigns mobilized similar numbers of demonstrators, and NIDA and the American Museum received comparable numbers of letters. The museum campaign encouraged people to send letters of protest, and those more dedicated to join picket lines. The other two campaigns encouraged people to join TSU and participate through this organization. While TSU is inevitably concerned with its own survival, it emphasizes public action rather than fundraising. It probably has more bureaucracy than an *ad hoc* coalition focused on one experiment, but organizational interests did not seem to interfere with TSU's efforts. And these organizational interests obviously do not explain the different outcomes of the NYU and Cornell campaigns.

More important in these cases than the actions of the SMOs were the vulnerabilities and responses of the targeted institutions. The museum research was vulnerable in several ways. The experiments lacked obvious practical implications, and their intellectual implications were easy to lampoon. While the experiments were bringing in outside funds, the museum depended much more heavily on public contributions. If one unit, already in a precarious position within that organization, threatened public goodwill, it could be sacrificed. Finally, the centralized physical plant, with limited access, facilitated contact between picketers and museum-goers. The museum made no egregious blunders in handling the protest, but it did not need to. The preexisting project and institutional vulnerabilities were sufficient for protestors to stop the experiment.

In contrast, Cornell made blunders in its reaction to the controversy. When the campaign began, it seemed to be in a strong position, and TSU viewed it that way. The targeted research had practical applications, even though it involved a popular species. Cornell is a private research university more dependent on government funding and alumni support than on the general public. The funding agency had no desire to stop the experiments; in fact, it strongly favored their continuation. But the medical school made strategic mistakes in dealing with the protestors. Its public relations representatives were relatively inactive. Perhaps they thought that the protestors would go away if palliated with vague promises; or that they were too weak to force Cornell to stick to its apparent promise; or that they simply would not know if the experiment continued. Having made verbal and written assurances implying the research would end, Cornell could be shamed into keeping them. Behavior that SMOs can effectively portray as lies are devastating blunders.

Although its project used appealing animals, NYU managed to minimize both its vulnerabilities and its blunders. Learning from prior experience, the university worked to maintain its strong position by trying to defuse media attention through its own emotional appeals. A large (nine-person) public relations office at the NYU medical school, with long experience in animal controversies (NYU had been attacked by other animal rights groups in 1979 and 1986), made a difference. Beyond that, the university tried to avoid misleading public statements. It sent the targeted researcher to a media training school in order to avoid embarrassments in the form of misstatements at press conferences. TSU found few preexisting vulnerabilities and triggered no blunders.

Federal funding agencies were involved in all three cases, but their influence was not strong. In the museum case, the funder actually became a source of weakness since it was the object of congressional scrutiny and seemed willing to let the research disappear. In contrast, NIDA pressured both NYU and Cornell to stand firm. In the Cornell case, the university capitulated despite NIDA's firm support of the project, while NYU resisted the animal rights campaign. So the actions of funding agencies were not decisive to the outcomes of these cases. Nonetheless, indirectly, federal agencies funding biomedical research have become enthusiastic players in the countermovement against animal rights.

The responses of the targeted institutions reflected the life cycle of the animal rights movement, for the strategies of both SMOs and their targets change as controversies mature. In the early stages of a conflict, public awareness and media coverage are limited (Jasper, 1988). Then, as awareness grows, both sides tend to seek favorable public opinion. By 1988 neither the protestors nor NYU representatives were willing to talk to each other, although NYU had negotiated with other demonstrators as recently as 1986. Instead, both sides believed themselves engaged in a battle for the uncommitted public.

For the animal rights movement, the growth of a national controversy encouraged this expansive strategy. The national movement and the spread of organizational know-how and tactical innovation helped animal rights organizations mobilize members and accumulate funds. Photographs and videotapes taken from laboratories were widely distributed and proved to be effective recruiting devices. However, expansion of the controversy also spurred countermobilization by scientists. Targeted groups began to mobilize resources, share tactical information and expertise, and develop strategic sophistication to counterattack. In the 1970s, the museum case was seen as

an isolated, fluke incident at an institution not primarily devoted to research. But victories like that against Cornell demanded attention. The subsequent counterorganization will probably be successful in showing future targets how to avoid blunders in resisting animal rights campaigns. No fewer than 19 state-level groups have been established since 1983 to defend biomedical research. The head of the Alcohol, Drug Abuse, and Mental Health Administration, Frederick Goodwin, decided to attend NYU's 1989 press conference himself, and said,

> They succeeded at Cornell. They got the higher levels of the university to worry about contributions from alumni. They got bad publicity. So the researcher gave up the grant; taxpayers' money was wasted. And this really got the attention of the scientific community. I don't think they're going to pull that off again. I don't think NYU is going to do that. I don't think Cornell would do that again. I think we all learned a very tough lesson.

We can see how success in specific campaigns can hurt longer term success for a protest movement as a whole. In the absence of state repression, a movement may attain early gains. But these may in turn inspire even more rapid and energetic countermobilization. Then, as the controversy matures, SMOs may attend more to convincing the broader public about their cause than to attaining specific short-term goals. Future success for the animal rights movement may come through federal regulations and policies, not by stopping individual experiments.

One straightforward way that scientific institutions have reduced their vulnerabilities is by improving the conditions of laboratory animals. These movement successes (tighter federal regulations, institutional animal care and use committees) may prevent it from attaining more sweeping goals such as the abolition of certain categories of experiments or (sought by some) of all live-animal experiments. In this case, the movement simply has partly contradictory goals (reform vs. abolition). Yet it remains an open question as to whether mild success dampens a movement's fervor or encourages even more radical demands.

Additional research is necessary to uncover more complex relationships between different forms of social movement success. Perhaps some kinds of early victories do not lead to countermobilization—for example, decisive ones or imperceptible ones (Zald and Useem, 1987). Some kinds of blunders may be more difficult for a countermovement to suppress than others—for example, when institutional responses are multiple and decentralized, or when elites themselves are divided over the proper response.

Conclusions

The importance of target vulnerabilities, blunders, and countermobilization suggests that larger social movements are not necessarily more successful than smaller ones in attaining their stated goals. In the absence of state repression, movements can succeed in specific campaigns when they are still small, before they have inspired countermobilization. In the three animal rights campaigns discussed in this paper, the size of the movement and the choices of the SMOs were less important than the vulnerabilities and responses of the targeted institutions. The SMOs had to choose vulnerable targets, and to take advantage of blunders made during the disputes. But most critical were the responses of targeted groups, shaped in part by the timing of the campaign in the life of the entire animal rights movement.

One implication of this argument is that radical tactics may not always help movements succeed. Most research has found violent and other radical tactics to aid a group in attaining its demands, largely because the state is threatened in its role as keeper of order. But when movement success depends primarily on affecting nonstate actors (including the public), dialogue and compromise may be more effective. Jasper and Nelkin (1992) argued that this is true for the animal rights movement.

To set these findings in theoretical context, we propose that more attention be paid to strategic choices made on *both* sides of a social conflict. Recent work on social movements has recognized the importance of conscious actions and decisions made by social movement organizers and strategists, but the surrounding environment has been seen as a set of inflexible structures, a stage for social movement actors. In Tilly's model, state repression is almost automatic, not a choice, whereas we have shown one set of cases where early state repression is absent—a pattern we believe common for many contemporary protest movements. Especially in the absence of automatic state intervention, targeted institutions other than the state, become important strategic actors whose decisions and actions heavily influence the outcomes of social movement campaigns.

Notes

1. We say "revealed" because we assume that the vulnerabilities are already there, and are exploited by rather than created by movement leaders. Otherwise the concept becomes tautological, in that anything the activists can use to their advantage becomes a vulnerability.

2. The abscissa reflects both the level of collective action and the size of the challenger. We assume that these typically vary together, although further research is needed to separate their effects. See Oberschall (1979:61). ◆

Part 10

Movement Careers: Intra-Movement Dynamics

In Part 9, we looked at the relationship between social movements and various groups and institutions within the broader society, concentrating on the dynamic interaction among movements, countermovements, and the state. But the course and character of social movements are not determined solely by external constraints and pressures. Equally important in understanding the trajectories or life courses of movements are the structure and character of their own internal operations. Now, we focus on internal or intra-movement dynamics and processes.

The importance of internal factors in understanding the dynamics of social movements has been noted for some time. In their now classic essay on social movement organizations, Zald and Ash (1965-66) highlighted the importance of internal movement processes in examining factionalization, leadership, and movement transformation. In the various editions of their collective behavior text, spanning three decades, Turner and Killian (1957, 1972, 1987) stressed how patterns of social control and organizational and leadership characteristics were critical to understanding the dynamics of social movements. The relevance of different organizational characteristics and forms to understanding various movement processes—such as organizational maintenance and transformation, tactical action, and goal attainment—have been explored and debated by others as well (see, for example, Curtis and Zurcher

1974; Gamson 1990; McCarthy and Zald 1977; Piven and Cloward 1977).

The four selections in this part reflect the on-going interest in how various intra-movement factors and processes affect the course and character of social movements. The first selection, by Verta Taylor, furthers understanding of the persistence or continuity of social movement organizations. Drawing on data on women's activism between 1945 and the 1960s, Taylor shows that the movement did not die after its suffrage victory in 1920, only to rematerialize in the 1960s. Rather, it was alive but in abeyance during a portion of that period. The term *abeyance* is used to refer to a holding pattern in which movements sustain themselves in a political environment that is non-receptive or antagonistic. Taylor illuminates how the movement was able to persist by identifying and elaborating five characteristics of what is termed *movement abeyance structures*. In addition to helping us understand how movements persist when in the doldrums, Taylor's analysis suggests at least one mechanism that links together organizationally and ideologically the different periods of peak activity in a movement's career or history.

The second selection, by Suzanne Staggenborg, examines the consequences of McCarthy and Zald's (1973, 1977) professionalization thesis in relation to social movements by analyzing the impact of three types of leadership (professional, nonprofessional volunteers, and nonprofessional staff) and two types of organizational structure (formal and informal) in the pro-choice movement. Using data drawn from 13 organizational case histories of pro-choice (abortion rights) movement organizations, Staggenborg finds that while professional leaders are not entrepreneurial in the sense of initiating movements and creating new tactics, they do tend to formalize the movement organizations they lead. Additionally, formalized social movement organizations are found to be more adept than informal ones at maintaining themselves, especially during difficult times. These and other findings suggest refinements in the professionalization thesis and also advance our understanding of the effects of different types of leadership and organizational structures.

The third and fourth selections explore issues relevant to factionalism in social movements. The third selection, by Herbert Haines, investigates the effect of factionalism in the civil rights movement by examining how black radicalization during the 1960s influenced the ability of moderate civil rights organizations to attract funding from external supporters. Using trend data on donations to seven black movement organizations, Haines finds that the more moderate organizations received increased financial support from white groups, especially during the late 1960s, while the funding received by the more militant groups declined. Haines attributes this finding to the operation of a positive *radical flank effect* which occurs when the actions of radical groups generates support for more moderate elements within a movement. The findings indicate that factionalism does not automatically have negative implications for social movements and raise questions about the generality of radical flank effects across different types of movements.

In the final selection, Burke Rochford describes and analyzes the events that gave rise to factionalism, group defection, and schism within the Los Angeles Hare Krishna commune following the death of the movement's (International Society for Krishna Consciousness) charismatic leader. Rochford notes that a succession crisis did not materialize uniformly through all of the movement's communes in the aftermath of the founder's death, but was concentrated in those experiencing ongoing social conflict, particularly in relation to power. The factionalism that surfaced in the Los Angeles commune was found to be rooted in intense and longstanding cleavages. Rochford traces how this conflict unfolded in the Los Angeles commune and the fate of the dissident factions. The analysis forces us to think more carefully about the trajectory of movements in the wake of charismatic leadership succession, about the sources of factionalism and group defection, and about the impact of such events for the broader movement.

Taken together, the four selections in this part underscore the importance of taking internal organizational characteristics and dynamics into consideration when attempting to understand the character and careers of social movements. In general, these articles caution against overgeneralizing about intra-movement processes, such as abeyance, professionalization, radical flank effects, and factionalism. Rather, the way in which these processes unfold, and their implications for movements, depends on different constellations of internal and external conditions.

References

Curtis, Russell L., Jr. and Louis A. Zurcher, Jr. 1974. "Social Movements: An Analytical Exploration of Organizational Forms." *Social Problems* 21: 356-370.

Gamson, William A. 1990. *The Strategy of Social Protest.* Second Edition. Belmont, CA: Wadsworth.

McCarthy, John D. and Mayer Zald. 1977. "Resource Mobilization and Social Movements: A Partial Theory." *American Journal of Sociology* 82: 1212-1241.

Piven, Francis Fox and Richard Cloward. 1977. *Poor People's Movements.* New York: Vintage Books.

Turner, Ralph H. and Lewis M. Killian. 1957, 1972, 1987. *Collective Behavior.* Englewood Cliffs, NJ: Prentice-Hall.

Zald, Mayer and Roberta Ash. 1966. "Social Movement Organizations: Growth, Decay and Change." *Social Forces* 44: 327-341. ✦

31

Social Movement Continuity: The Women's Movement in Abeyance

Verta Taylor

Introduction

Scholars of the social movements of the 1960s have by and large held an "immaculate conception" view of their origins. These "new social movements" (Klandermans 1986) seemingly emerged out of nowhere and represented a sudden shift from the quiescent 1940s and 1950s (Flacks 1971; Touraine 1971; McCarthy and Zald 1973; Jenkins 1987). Recent empirical work, however, challenges this view, suggesting that the break between the sixties movements and earlier waves of political activism was not as sharp as previously assumed (e.g., Isserman 1987; McAdam 1988a). The overemphasis on movement origins and on new elements in the sixties movements has blinded students of social movements to the "carry-overs and carry-ons" between movements (Gusfield 1981b, p. 324). What scholars have taken for "births" were in fact breakthroughs or turning points in movement mobilization.

This paper develops a framework that specifies the processes of movement continuity. The framework is grounded in research on the American women's rights movement from 1945 to the mid-1960s. Most accounts trace its origins to the civil rights movement (Freeman 1975; Evans 1979). Yet the women's movement, like the other movements that blossomed in the 1960s, can also be viewed as a resurgent challenge with roots in an earlier cycle of feminist activism that presumably ended when suffrage was won. My approach relies heavily on the central premises of resource mobilization theory: political opportunities and an indigenous organizational base are major factors in the rise and decline of movements (e.g.,

Oberschall 1973; McCarthy and Zald 1977, McAdam 1982; Jenkins 1983). The paper makes a new contribution by elaborating certain abeyance processes in social movements and by specifying features of social movement abeyance organizations. The term "abeyance" depicts a holding process by which movements sustain themselves in nonreceptive political environments and provide continuity from one stage of mobilization to another.

After discussing data sources, the analysis briefly describes the history of the American women's movement and the persistence of a small band of feminists who, in the 1940s and 1950s, continued to remain faithful to the political vision that had originally drawn them into the suffrage movement nearly a half century earlier. Because the cultural and political climate had changed, these women found that their ideals and commitment to feminism marginalized and isolated them from the mainstream of American women. I argue that their form of activism is best understood as a social movement abeyance structure. Finally, I delineate the features of abeyance structures that were a source of movement continuity by tracing the consequences of postwar activism for the contemporary women's movement. I conclude by exploring the implications of the abeyance hypothesis for understanding the organizational and ideological bridges between earlier activism and the development of other movements of the 1960s.

Abeyance Processes in Social Movements

The term "abeyance" is borrowed from Mizruchi (1983) and is central to a theory of social control. Abeyance structures emerge when society lacks sufficient status vacancies to integrate surpluses of marginal and dissident people. The structures that absorb marginal groups are abeyance organizations. They temporarily retain potential challengers to the status quo, thereby reducing threats to the larger social systems. Abeyance organizations have certain properties that allow them to absorb, control, and expel personnel according to the number of status positions available in the larger society (Mizruchi 1983, p. 17).

Although Mizruchi recognizes the social change potential of abeyance organizations, he does not address this aspect systematically (Kimmel 1984). I both challenge and extend Mizruchi's thesis to hypothesize that social movement abey-

"Social Movement Continuity: The Women's Movement in Abeyance." *American Sociological Review* 54: 761-775. Copyright © 1989 by the American Sociological Association. Reprinted with permission.

ance organizations, by providing a measure of continuity for challenging groups, also contribute to social change. I hold that the abeyance process characterizes mass movements that succeed in building a support base and achieving a measure of influence, but are confronted with a nonreceptive political and social environment. A central tenet of resource mobilization theory concerns the role that changing opportunity structures play in the emergence and the attenuation of collective action (McCarthy and Zald 1973; Barkan 1984: Jenkins 1983). As a movement loses support, activists who had been most intensely committed to its aims become increasingly marginal and socially isolated. If insufficient opportunities exist to channel their commitment into routine statuses, then alternative structures emerge to absorb the surplus of people. These structures both restrain them from potentially more disruptive activities and channel them into certain forms of activism. In short, a movement in abeyance becomes a cadre of activists who create or find a niche for themselves. Such groups may have little impact in their own time and may contribute, however unwillingly, to maintenance of the status quo. But, by providing a legitimating base to challenge the status quo, such groups can be sources of protest and change.

The following factors are relevant to the abeyance process. First, certain factors external to a movement create a pool of marginal potential activists. These include *changes in opportunity structures* that support and constrain the movement and an *absence of status vacancies* to absorb dissident and excluded groups. Second, there are internal factors or organizational *dimensions of social movement abeyance structures: temporality, commitment, exclusiveness, centralization,*and *culture.* Since these dimensions were inductively derived, I elaborate them with the case at hand. The significance of abeyance lies in its linkages between one upsurge in activism and another. I delineate three ways that social movement abeyance structures perform this linkage function: through promoting the survival of *activist networks,* sustaining a repertoire of *goals and tactics,* and promoting *a collective identity* that offers participants a sense of mission and moral purpose.

Data

Most accounts describe the American women's movement as peaking in two periods (Chafe 1972; Freeman 1975; Klein 1984). The first wave, generally referred to as the suffrage movement, grew out of the abolitionist struggle of the 1830s, reached a stage of mass mobilization between 1900 and 1920, and declined after the passage of the suffrage amendment. The second wave emerged in the mid-1960s, reached a stage of mass mobilization around 1970, and continued into the 1980s (Carden 1974; Evans 1979; Ferree and Hess 1985).

Curiosity about what happened to the organizations and networks of women who participated in the suffrage campaign led to the research described here. There are two reasons for focusing on the period from 1945 to the mid-1960s. First, other researchers have explored the period from 1920 to 1940 (Lemons 1973; Becker 1981; Cott 1987). Second, most researchers see the civil rights movement as the major predecessor to the contemporary women's movement (e.g., Freeman 1975; Evans 1979; McAdam 1988a). By examining feminist activity in the decades just prior to the resurgence of feminism as a mass movement, I hoped to shed light on the accuracy of this view.

The data for this study come from documentary material in public and private archival collections and interviews with women who were activists from 1945 to the 1960s. Fuller description of the movement in this period and complete documentation are available in Rupp and Taylor (1987).

(1) Archival data included the papers of the National Woman's Party and the League of Women Voters, the two major factions of the suffrage movement, and the papers of the President's Commission on the Status of Women (1961-63), whose activities facilitated the resurgence of the contemporary women's movement. Other material examined were unofficial and official organizational documents, publications, personal letters, and memos in public and private collections, most of which are housed at the Schlesinger Library at Radcliff College or the Library of Congress. The papers of individual women provided an important source of information, not only about their organizational careers, but also about the activities of diverse women's organizations.

(2) The second source of data was 57 open-ended, semistructured, tape-recorded interviews, conducted between 1979 and 1983, with leaders and core members of the most central groups in-

volved in women's rights activities. Twelve of the women were active at the national level and 33 at the local level. Twelve other transcribed interviews conducted by other researchers and available in archival collections were used.

The Women's Movement in the Postsuffrage Decades: The Transformation of Feminist Activism

Feminist activism continued in the years after the suffrage victory but was transformed as a result of organizational success, internal conflict, and social changes that altered women's common interests (Lemons 1973; Becker 1981; Buechler 1986; Cott 1987). Deradicalization and decline of the women's movement left militant feminists limited avenues through which to pursue their political philosophy.

In 1920, with the vote won, the women's movement was left with no unifying goal. Moreover, tactical and ideological differences divided militant from moderate suffragists and those who saw winning the vote as a means from those who viewed it as an end. As a result, the major social movement organizations of the suffrage movement evolved in two opposing directions.

The militant branch of the movement, the National Woman's Party (NWP), launched a relentless campaign to pass an Equal Rights Amendment (ERA) to the constitution. The NWP was never a mass organization but saw itself as a feminist vanguard or elite (Lunardini 1986). Hoping to enlist the support of former suffragists, NWP leader Alice Paul instead alienated both socialists and moderate feminists by her dictatorial style and the decision to focus on the ERA. The vast majority of suffragists feared that the ERA would eliminate the protective labor legislation that women reformers had earlier struggled to achieve (Balser 1987).

The mainstream branch of the movement, the National American Woman Suffrage Association, formed the nonpartisan League of Women Voters. It spearheaded the opposition to the ERA, educated women for their new citizenship responsibilities, and advocated a broad range of reforms. Other activists in the suffrage campaign channeled their efforts into new or growing organizations that did not have an explicitly feminist agenda but promoted a vast range of specific causes that, in part, grew out of the expanded role

options available to women (Cott 1987). Thus, even though the women's movement was rapidly fragmenting, feminist activism continued throughout the 1920s and 1930s. But in the face of increasing hostility between the two camps of the suffrage movement, cooperation developed on only a few issues.

In addition to goal attainment and internal conflict, a third factor contributed to the dissipation of the mass base of the women's movement. Ironically, the role expansion for which the movement had fought fractured the bonds on which the solidarity of the movement had been built. As women's lives grew increasingly diverse, the definition of what would benefit women grew less clear.

As a result, the NWP—which alone continued to claim the title "feminist"—had become increasingly isolated from the mainstream of American women and even from women's organizations. With the demise of the large mass-based organizations that propelled the suffrage movement, the more radical feminists sought out the NWP. When the NWP captured the feminist agenda, however, the broad program of emancipation narrowed to limited goals and tactics pursued by an elite group of women (Cott 1987). This spelled the final demise of feminism as a mass movement.

Feminist Activism from 1945 to the 1960s: The Women's Movement in Abeyance

From 1945 to the 1960s, women's rights activists confronted an inhospitable political and social environment. Women who advocated equality found few outlets for their activism and became increasingly marginal and isolated from the mainstream of American women. Two social processes had this effect: first, advocates of women's rights lacked access to and support from the established political system; and, second, the cultural ideal of "the feminine mystique" that emerged after World War II affirmed the restoration of "normal family life" and discredited women who protested gender inequality.

Changing Opportunity Structure: Nonreceptive Political Elites

Despite an increase in the female labor force and the female student body in institutions of higher education, support for women's rights and opportunities declined sharply following the Second World War. By 1945, the women's movement had further fragmented into three overlapping interest groups, each with a different political agenda (Harrison 1988, p. 7). Because women's issues were not generally salient, the three groups lacked political access and influence. Just as important, when they did gain access to political elites, they often canceled out each other's influence.

One interest group consisted of a coalition of women's organizations associated with the Women's Bureau of the Department of Labor. Throughout the 1940s and 1950s, this coalition sought to improve women's working conditions and defeat the ERA. Despite its governmental status, the Women's Bureau had little political clout, and the coalition used much of its influence to fight supporters of the ERA.

A second group consisted of a network of women in politics, including women active in the women's divisions of both the Democratic and Republican parties. They advocated the election and appointment of women to policy-making positions despite a dramatic decline in women's political opportunities after the Second World War. For the most part, the selection of women for policymaking positions was done by party women without regard for their position on women's issues (Harrison 1988, p. 6-4). Since women officials generally had no policy role and little influence on women's issues, advocating token appointments of women diverted attention from major policy questions such as the ERA.

A third group, the National Woman's Party, remained furthest outside the established political order. By 1944, the NWP had begun a major campaign to get Congress to pass the ERA and had managed to garner support from a few women's organizations. Confronted with the establishment of the National Committee to Defeat the Unequal Rights Amendment, spearheaded by the Women's Bureau, the NWP sought the support of both political parties. Presidents Truman and Eisenhower endorsed the ERA, both party platforms advocated it, and Congress considered it in 1946, 1950, and 1953. Yet such support was more a nod to women than a serious political consideration (Freeman 1987).

None of these three groups made much progress in attaining their goals in the 1940s and 1950s. Although women's organizations succeeded in having 236 bills pertaining to women's rights introduced into Congress in the 1950s, only 14 passed (Klein 1984, p. 18). This reflected not only organized women's lack of political access and their conflicts, but also the exaggerated emphasis on sex roles that emerged on the heels of the Second World War.

Status Vacancy and Marginality

Following the war, a variety of social forces helped to reinstitutionalize traditional family life supported by rigid sex role distinctions (Friedan 1963; Breines 1985; May 1988). Women whose roles did not center on the home and family were considered deviant. In 1957, 80 percent of the respondents to a national poll believed that people who chose not to marry were sick, immoral, and neurotic (Klein 1984, p. 71). As a result of the pressure, fewer married women remained childless in the 1950s than in the 1900s—only 6.8 percent compared to 14 percent (Rupp and Taylor 1987, p. 15). Indicative of the tide, in 1945 only 18 percent of a Gallup Poll sample approved of a married woman's working if she had a husband capable of supporting her (Erskine 1971).

In addition to criticizing women who did not conform to the cultural ideal, the media denounced feminism, discredited women who continued to advocate equality, and thus thwarted the mobilization of discontented women (Rupp 1982). The most influential attack came from Ferdinand Lundberg and Marynia Farnham's popular and widely quoted book, *Modern Woman: The Lost Sex* (1947), which denounced feminists as severe neurotics responsible for the problems of American society. In the face of such criticism, only the NWP continued to claim the term "feminist." In fact, the core group of women in the NWP differed in major respects from the cultural ideal. An analysis of the 55 leaders and most active members of the NWP indicates that, by 1950, the majority were white, middle- or upper-class, well educated, employed in professional or semiprofessional occupations (especially law, government, and higher education), unmarried or widowed, and older (in their fifties, sixties, or seventies).[1] Specifically, 71 percent of the women were employed; 97 percent were over the age of 50; and 60 percent were unmarried or widowed. In short, the lifestyles of the women, while relatively advantaged, were not normative. Feminists were largely unattached women with time, money, and other resources that facilitated their activism. Yet the retreat of a broad-based women's movement left few outlets to express their views either inside or outside the established political arena.

In summary, as the political and cultural wave that had once carried feminism forward receded, members of the NWP paid for their lifelong commitment with a degree of alienation, marginality, and isolation. Nevertheless, the NWP provided a structure and status capable of absorbing these intensely committed feminists and thus functioned as an abeyance organization.

Dimensions of Social Movement Abeyance Structures

The abeyance process functions through organizations capable of sustaining collective challenges under circumstances unfavorable to mass mobilization. Properties of abeyance organizations help an organizational pattern to retain potentially dissident populations. My analysis of the women's rights movement in the postwar period suggests that the most relevant variables with respect to the abeyance process are: temporality, purposive commitment, exclusiveness, centralization, and culture. Since these variables are derived from a single case, each dimension is treated as a hypothetical continuum with respect to other cases.

Temporality. By definition, of course, an abeyance structure persists throughout time, but temporality refers to the length of time that a movement organization is able to hold personnel. Activism provides a community that is an alternative source of integration and, thus, can have an enduring effect beyond a particular period in an individual's life (Coser 1974; White 1988).

During the 70-odd years of the first wave of the women's movement, a number of women's rights groups emerged and provided alternative status vacancies for large numbers of mainly white and middle-class women (Flexner 1959; Buechler 1986; Chafetz and Dworkin 1986). Among the 55 leaders and core activists of the NWP, 53 percent had been recruited at least four decades earlier during the suffrage campaign.

For NWP members, early participation in high-risk activism (McAdam 1986), including picketing the White House, engaging in hunger strikes while imprisoned, and burning President Wilson's speeches, kept them involved long after the suffrage victory. Lamenting the passage of

that period, Florence Kitchelt asked a fellow suffragist in 1959 whether she ever felt "as I do that the modern woman is missing something very thrilling, uplifting, as well as unifying in not being able to take part in a suffrage campaign? Those were the days!"[2] Katharine Hepburn, mother of the actress, in a speech to women's rights activists, described her experiences in the suffrage struggle. "That whole period in my life I remember with the greatest delight," she said. "We had no doubts. Life was a great thrill from morning until night."[3] Involvement in the suffrage movement had a powerful and enduring effect on participants, so much so that they continued even into the 1950s to promote women's rights in a society antagonistic to the idea. The strong and lasting effects of participation in high-risk activism is supported by McAdam's (1988a) study of participants in the 1964 Freedom Summer project.

By the 1940s and 1950s, a core of women in the NWP had devoted a major portion of their lives to feminist activity. Typical participation patterns are reflected in the comments of two members. In 1952, one woman wrote, "Since 1917 I have devoted all my spare time to feminism."[4] Another woman asked in 1950 for a "cure for giving too much of one's time to one thing," although she still continued to devote herself to passage of the ERA.[5] Not surprisingly, the most striking characteristic of the NWP membership was advanced age. Isserman (1987, p. 24) found a similar age structure in another organization that provided continuity between two stages of mass mobilization, the American Communist Party in the 1940s and 1950s. Constant numbers—even if small—are better for morale than steady turnover, so temporality enhances the likelihood that an organization will continue to endure.

Purposive Commitment. Commitment refers to the willingness of people to do what must be done, regardless of personal rewards and sacrifices, to maintain a collective challenge and is essential for holding an organizational pattern alive between stages of mass mobilization. Research on social movement involvement has focused primarily on the types of incentives that induce activists to make an initial commitment to a movement (e.g., Pinard 1971; Fireman and Gamson 1979; Oliver 1983; McAdam 1986). In exploring movement continuity, we must pose a different question: why do individuals maintain radical or unpopular convictions over time?

The few studies that have explored this question suggest that the nature of and incentives for commitment depend on a movement's stage in the mobilization process. Kanter's (1972) research on American communes concludes that groups characterized by high commitment are more likely to retain participants and to endure. Other research suggests that, although individuals may become activists through solidary or material incentives, continued participation depends upon high levels of commitment to group beliefs, goals, and tactics (Hirsch 1986; White 1988).

From its inception, the NWP appealed to women with strong feminist sympathies. By the 1950s, continued participation depended largely on the singleness of members' devotion to the principle of sexual equality embodied in the Equal Rights Amendment. Rejecting all other proposals for a feminist program, NWP leaders insisted that ideological integrity and the dogged pursuit of legal equality, not membership gain, would guarantee triumph.

A dedicated core of NWP members worked for the ERA by lobbying Congress and the president, seeking endorsements from candidates for political office and from other organizations, establishing coalitions to support the amendment, and educating the public through newspaper and magazine articles, letters to the editor, and radio and television appearances. Commenting on the persistence of feminists' lobbying efforts, one Representative from Connecticut wondered in 1945 "whether or not the Congress meets for any other purpose but to consider the Equal Rights Amendment."[6] Since the NWP depended entirely on the volunteer work of members, commitment was built on sacrifices of time, energy, and financial resources. Recognizing the impact of such high levels of commitment, one new recruit commented that "the secret of the ability of the group to do so much in the face of such odds is that it can attract just such devotion and loyalty."[7]

Commitment, then, contributes to the abeyance process by ensuring that individuals continue to do what is necessary to maintain the group and its purpose even when the odds are against immediate success. Moreover, such intense commitment functions as an obstacle to participation in alternative roles and organizations.

Exclusiveness. Organizations vary according to their openness to members, some having more stringent criteria than others. Mizruchi

(1983, p. 44) hypothesizes that the expansion-contraction of an abeyance organization's personnel occurs in response to changes in the larger social system's requirements for absorption, mobility, or expulsion of marginal populations. To absorb large numbers of people who are unattached to other structures requires organizations to be inclusive, as happens during the peak mobilization of social movement organizations. In cycles of decline, however, when challenging groups lack widespread attitudinal support, organizations become exclusive and attempt to expel or hold constant their membership. Zald and Ash (1966) contend that exclusive movement organizations are more likely to endure than inclusive ones.

At the peak of the suffrage struggle, the NWP was inclusive across the class and political spectrum (Cott 1987, pp. 53-55). It attracted wage-earning women from a variety of occupations as well as elite women social activists. Its members had ties to political parties, government, and industry, as well as to the socialist, peace, labor, and antilynching movements. But when the NWP launched its ERA campaign, many bodies organized on occupational, religious, and racial grounds and devoted to other policy issues began to absorb women from mainstream suffrage groups and siphon off NWP members. This left the NWP with a small and relatively homogeneous permanent core of feminists.

By the end of World War II, the NWP had lost most of its members and was not attracting new ones. Compared to its 60,000 members in the last years of the suffrage campaign, the NWP had about 4000 "general" members by 1945 and only 1400 by 1952. More revealing, it listed 627 "active" members in 1947 and 200 by 1952. Although the NWP also lost members as a result of an internal conflict over whether to expand membership in 1947 and again in 1953, the leadership preferred to keep the organization a small elite vanguard. As one member put it, "no mass appeal will ever bring into the Party that type of woman who can best carry forward our particular aims. We are an 'elect body' with a single point of agreement."[8]

Just as important, the membership of the NWP also grew increasingly homogeneous and socially advantaged over the decades. Of 55 core activists, 90 percent of the employed held professional, managerial, or technical positions. Several researchers have noted that intellectuals and other privileged groups are likely to be overrepresented among the leadership and supporters of neo-liberal and communal movements. Some have attributed this to the risks and resources that participation entails (Lenin 1970; McCarthy and Zald 1973; Oberschall 1973, p. 161), while others look to the unique political culture of intellectuals and professionals (Pinard and Hamilton 1988).

Despite the fact that the NWP leaders preferred a small homogeneous membership, they recognized the significance of size and diversity for public impact. In order to give the appearance of a mass constituency, the NWP devised certain strategies. Members maintained multiple memberships in women's organizations in order to win endorsements for the ERA; they established coalitions to give the impression of a large membership; they financed a "front" organization to give the appearance of cooperation between feminists and labor women; and they recruited leaders of the National Association of Colored Women in order to obtain its endorsement of the ERA. Yet, despite attempts to appear inclusive, the NWP did not seriously try to build an indigenous base of support.

Organizational exclusivity is closely related to the commitment variable. Organizations that insist upon high levels of purposive commitment and make stringent demands of time and financial resources cannot absorb large numbers of people. They are, however, good at holding constant those members that they have. Thus, exclusiveness is an important characteristic of abeyance organizations because it ensures a relatively homogeneous cadre of activists suited to the limited activism undertaken.

Centralization. Organizations vary in their centralization of power. Some operate through a "single center of power," whereas decentralized groups distribute power among subunits (Gamson 1975, p. 93). Although centralization contributes to a decline in direct-action tactics (Piven and Cloward 1977; Jenkins and Eckert 1986), it has the advantage of producing the organizational stability, coordination, and technical expertise necessary for movement survival (Gamson 1975; Wehr 1986; Staggenborg 1989).

By the end of World War II, the NWP functioned almost entirely on the national level with a federated structure in which local and state chapters had little control. State branches, which had been active in the 1920s, consisted in most cases of little more than a chairman and served the or-

ganization primarily as letterheads to use in lobbying senators and representatives.[9]

A national chairman headed the NWP. The Party's founder and leading light, Alice Paul, however, directed and kept a tight reign on its activities, even though she formally occupied the chair for only a brief period from 1942 to 1945. As one member described it, Paul "gave the chairman all deference. But if you were a wise chairman, you did what Alice Paul wanted, because she knew what was needed."[10] The chairman headed a national council that met periodically at the Washington headquarters. There was also a national advisory council composed of prominent women who lent their names to the group's work.

Paul, reputedly a charismatic leader committed to the point of fanaticism, maintained tight control over the ERA campaign. She decided when it was time to press Congress and when to maintain a low profile and, according to members' reports, worked from six in the morning until midnight. On at least two occasions serious conflict erupted over the lack of democratic procedures in the Party. It focused specifically on Alice Paul's autocratic leadership style and on the refusal of the national leadership to allow state branches to expand membership. A letter, circulated in 1947, contained charges typical of those directed against Paul: "You have made it clear that you consider yourself and the small group around you an elite with superabundant intellect and talents, and consider us, in contrast, the commonfolk."[11] Thus centralization of leadership, like exclusiveness, had the potential to provoke conflict among members. But it also had advantages in a nonreceptive political environment.

Paul used her influence to direct a small group of activists with highly specialized skills—lobbying and researching, testifying, and writing about policy issues—who viewed themselves as an embattled feminist minority . The NWP was able to finance its activities with some invested funds, dues, contributions from members, and revenue from the rental of rooms in its Washington property. As a result, activists did not have to expend energy generating resources to maintain the organization.

This kind of central direction allowed the NWP to sustain the feminist challenge through the years by concentrating on a single strategy that could be carried out by a dedicated band of activists with highly specialized skills. Thus, centralization contributes to the abeyance process by ensuring the maintenance of organization and at least minimal activity during periods when conditions do not favor mass mobilization.

Culture. The culture of a social movement organization is embodied in its collective emotions, beliefs, and actions. Although all social movements create and bear culture, movement organizations vary in the character and complexity of their cultures (Lofland 1985b).

The effectiveness of an organization with respect to its abeyance function depends, in part, on its capacity to motivate persons to assume certain positions. As the larger political and cultural atmosphere becomes less hospitable to the social movement, recruitment of personnel becomes difficult. In order to make participation more attractive, organizations must elaborate alternative cultural frameworks to provide security and meaning for those who reject the established order and remain in the group. Previous research suggests that the more highly developed an organization's culture, the more it offers members the satisfaction and other resources necessary for its survival (Kanter 1972, Lofland 1985b).

The NWP developed an elaborate and expressive culture through activities at the Alva Belmont House, its national headquarters in Washington, D.C. Belmont House served not only as an office for national council meetings, but also as a center where lobbying efforts were coordinated and where the monthly newsletter was published. It also created the kind of female world essential to the maintenance of feminism (Freedman 1979; Rupp 1985). A few women lived at Belmont House and in two other Party-owned houses, while lobbyists stayed there from a few days to several months. In addition, Belmont House was the site of feminist events and celebrations: teas to honor women politicians or sponsors of the ERA, victory celebrations, and parties on Susan B. Anthony's birthday or on the anniversary of the suffrage victory. The activities and relationships women formed at Belmont House provided both ideological and affective support for participation in women's rights work.

Although NWP members believed in the pervasiveness of discrimination against women, the Party did not develop and advance a well-articulated ideological and theoretical position. Rather, feminism was defined principally through a culture that promoted a feminist worldview. One

member expressed her world view, complaining of "Masculinity running rampant *all over the earth!*"'and rebelling at the "utter manmindedness" she saw all around her.[12] Alice Paul characterized women's rights advocates as sharing a "feeling of loyalty to our own sex and an enthusiasm to have every degradation that was put upon our sex removed."[13] Despite occasional conflict over whether men should be brought into the movement, the NWP retained a separatist strategy. To ensure that the Party remain committed to its original vision—collective action by women for women—wealthy benefactor Alva Belmont included a clause in her bequest revoking her legacy if men ever joined or participated in the organization.

In addition to reinforcing feminist beliefs, the culture harbored at Belmont House fulfilled expressive and symbolic functions that contributed to the survival of feminism. Women who lived and worked at the house became, for some, the "Woman's Party family." Many who could not live at the house, because of family, work, and financial constraints, made regular pilgrimages in order to remain a part of the women's community. One member wrote that she was "looking forward with joy to my return home, and *Home* to me now, means the dear Alva Belmont House. "[14] In fact, bringing friends to Belmont House was the primary way that women recruited new members.

Personal ties of love and friendship among members were an important cultural ideal. A willingness to shape personal relationships around the cause was, in large measure, what made possible the intense commitment of members. NWP members described their ties as mother-daughter or sororal relationships, and members' letters to one another were filled with expressions of intimacy and friendship. Ties among members took the form of close friendships, intense devotion to Alice Paul, and couple relationships. Having another woman as life partner seemed to facilitate feminist work because these women's personal lives meshed well with their political commitments.

Movement organizations that cultivate and sustain rich symbolic lives, then, enhance the abeyance function by helping to hold members. This finding is consistent with other research that demonstrates that commitment to peers and to a shared political community promotes sustained involvement in social movements (Rosenthal and

Schwartz forthcoming; McAdam 1988a; White 1988).

In summary, I have described the NWP in the post-1945 period as an organizational pattern characterized by high longevity of attachment; intense levels of individual commitment to movement goals and tactics; high exclusiveness in terms of membership; high centralization that ensures a relatively advanced level of specialized skills among core activists; and a rich political culture that promotes continued involvement in the movement. This appears to be the ideal combination of factors necessary to hold a movement in abeyance until the external forces make it possible to resume a more mass-based challenge.

Consequences for the Resurgent Women's Movement

However movement success is measured, the women's rights movement from 1945 to the mid-1960s was not successful in its own time. But a more important question is: what consequences, if any, did the actions of feminists in this period have for the revitalized movement for gender equality in the late 1960s? The founding of the National Organization for Women (NOW) in 1966 serves as a useful signpost marking the rise of the contemporary women's movement. NOW brought together labor union activists, government employees, and longtime feminist activists and took leadership of the liberal branch of the movement (Freeman 1975). At about the same time, younger women involved in the civil rights and New Left movement formed the more locally organized radical branch.

Studies have not generally recognized connections between the existing women's rights movement and the resurgent one. My analysis suggests three ways in which the activism of the NWP shaped the feminist challenge that followed. It provided preexisting *activist networks,* an existing repertoire of *goals and tactics,* and a *collective identity* that justified feminist opposition. These elements constitute the most important consequences of abeyance structures for future mobilization around persistent discontents.

Activist Networks

A substantial body of research documents the significance of preexisting links and organizational ties among individuals for the rise of collective action (e.g., Snow, Zurcher, and Ekland-

Olson 1980; Freeman 1979b, 1983; Rosenthal et al. 1985). The feminist network of the 1940s and 1950s affected the resurgent movement of the 1960s in two ways. First, activism by NWP members played a crucial role in two key events: the establishment of the President's Commission on the Status of Women, convened by President Kennedy in 1961, and the inclusion of sex in Title VII of the Civil Rights Act of 1964, which forbade discrimination in employment. Second, many women who participated in the struggle for women's rights in the 1940s and 1950s became active in the resurgent women's movement, especially the liberal branch. NWP members were among the founders and charter members of NOW. Of the 10 individuals who signed NOW's original Statement of Purpose, 4 were members of the NWP (Friedan 1976). In her account of the early years of NOW, founder Betty Friedan (1976, pp. 110-17) describes an "underground network" of longtime committed feminists who provided crucial resources necessary for the formation of NOW. Even Alice Paul joined NOW, although she criticized NOW members for acting "as if they've discovered the whole idea."[15]

Although less common, a few NWP members established ties to the radical branch. One member met with the women's caucus of the National Conference on New Politics in Chicago in 1967, a conference that helped spark the formation of the radical branch. Another member attended a speech by Kate Millett at Purdue University in the early 1970s and handed out ERA literature to the crowd. Contrasting vividly the feminists of her generation with those of the 1970s, she noted that she was the only one there in a hat and that everyone else, including Millett, had long hair.[16] Thus a committed core of activists helped to provide resources for a resurgent more mass-based movement.

Goals and Tactical Choices

Tilly's (1979) concept of repertoires of collective action provides the greatest insight into the ways that actions of a challenging group at a given point in time can affect actions of a subsequent group. Thus, the forms of action available to a group are not unlimited but are restricted by time, place, and group characteristics. Movement goals and strategies are learned, and they change slowly. Extending Tilly's hypothesis, the array of collective actions that a movement develops to sustain itself should influence the goals and tactics adopted by the same movement in subsequent mass mobilizations.

This is indeed the case with respect to the American women's rights movement. Although the NWP abandoned disruptive and militant strategies after the suffrage victory, it retained the same goal—a constitutional amendment. Largely as a result of NWP pressure, NOW voted at its second conference in 1967 to endorse the ERA, which became the most unifying goal of the movement by the 1970s (Ferree and Hess 1985; Taylor 1989). Further, NOW adopted many of the NWP's institutionalized tactics, such as lobbying, letter writing, and pressuring the political parties. NOW even made use of the NWP's political connections and its list of ERA sponsors.

The ERA example illustrates the ways that existing repertoires of action can both facilitate and constrain a movement. The final campaign for the ERA in the late 1970s and early 1980s mobilized massive numbers of participants, swelling the ranks of NOW to almost 200,000 and its budget to nearly 3 million dollars (Gelb and Palley 1982; Mueller unpublished). During its early years, with its equal rights emphasis which appealed mainly to white and middle-class women, NOW alienated black and union women (Giddings 1984). Thus, the liberal branch of the contemporary women's movement, by adopting the goals and strategies of earlier feminists, found it difficult to shake the class and race limitations of its predecessors.

For a movement to survive periods of relative hiatus, it must develop a battery of specialized tactics that can be carried out by an activist cadre without the support of a mass base (Oliver and Marwell 1988). These become a part of a group's repertoire of collective action and influence the subsequent range of actions available to future challenges.

Collective Identity

Collective identity is the shared definition of a group that derives from its members common interests and solidarity. Although resource mobilization theorists minimize the importance of group identity and consciousness in the rise of social movements (McCarthy and Zald 1973, 1977; Jenkins and Perrow 1977), these factors are central to theorists of the "new social movements" (e.g., Pizzorno 1978; Cohen 1985b; Melucci

1985; Klandermans 1986). They suggest that, by definition, social movements create a collective oppositional consciousness. Mueller's (1987, p. 90) research on the women's movement suggests that changes in consciousness can have long-term significance because they can serve as a resource for future mobilization.

The creation of a shared collective identity requires the group to revise its history and develop symbols to reinforce movement goals and strategies (Gusfield 1970, p. 309-13). For the 1960s women's movement, the NWP, because of its ties to suffrage, became an important symbol of the long history of women's oppression and resistance. As a result of its historical significance and prime location, Belmont House was used throughout the 1970s for celebrations of women's movement history, as a temporary residence for scholars and students engaged in feminist research, and as a place for ERA lobbyists to meet. Moreover, Alice Paul, who earlier had sparked so many conflicts, became the quintessential symbol of feminist commitment. In 1977, NOW sponsored a birthday benefit for her at Belmont House that was attended by members of a wide range of feminist organizations. Even after Paul's death in 1977, the NWP continued to list her as founder on its letterhead and to advertise "Alice Paul Jail Jewelry," a replica of the famous jailhouse door pin proudly worn by imprisoned suffragists.

The significance of the NWP grew as younger and more radical women discovered the legacy of militant feminism. Even in 1981, the NWP's symbolic importance remained great enough to inspire an attempted takeover by a group of younger feminists, led by Sonia Johnson, who claimed the militants who first formed the NWP as their foremothers and even adopted the original name of the Party. Ironically, as the contemporary women's movement grew stronger and more militant, the actual heirs of the early militants grew increasingly isolated and less central in the struggle for women's rights.

In an abeyance phase, a social movement organization uses internally oriented activities to build a structure through which it can maintain its identity, ideals, and political vision. The collective identity that it constructs and maintains within a shared political community can become an important symbolic resource for subsequent mobilizations.

Conclusion

This paper presents new data that challenge the traditional view that no organized feminist challenge survived in the 1940s and 1950s. I have used the NWP case to highlight the processes by which social movements maintain continuity between different cycles of peak activity. I analyze the factors associated with adaptations of Mizruchi's (1983) abeyance process. Abeyance is essentially a holding pattern of a group which continues to mount some type of challenge even in a nonreceptive political environment. Factors that contribute to abeyance are both external and internal to the movement. Externally, a discrepancy between a surplus of activists and a lack of status opportunities for integrating them into the mainstream creates conditions for abeyance. Internally, structures arise that permit organizations to absorb and hold a committed cadre of activists. These abeyance structures, in turn, promote movement continuity and are employed in later rounds of mass mobilization.

Although any theory based on a single case is open to challenge, recent research points to the utility of the abeyance model for understanding other movements of the 1960s, particularly the civil rights (McAdam 1988a), New Left (Gittlin 1987; Isserman 1987; Hayden 1988), and gay rights (D'Emilio 1983) movements. But this work has not yet had major impact on revising theory about the sixties movements or on social movement theory in general.

Why have scholars of social movements neglected sources of continuity between cycles of movement activity and, instead, preferred an "immaculate conception" interpretation of social movements? First, scholars generally are more interested in movements undergoing cycles of mass mobilization and have done little research on movements in decline and equilibrium. Second, the limited conceptualization of movement organization in the literature has perpetuated classical conceptions of social movements as numerically large and mass-based. Research on a variety of organizational forms, including becalmed movements (Zald and Ash 1966), professional movements (McCarthy and Zald 1973), movement halfway houses (Morris 1984), elite-sustained movements (Rupp and Taylor 1987), and consensus movements (McCarthy and Wolfson unpublished), is now challenging the classical

view by suggesting that these types of movements are capable of sustained activism in nonreceptive political climates (Staggenborg 1988). Third, existing approaches overlook social movement continuity by neglecting to think about outcomes (Gamson 1975). Focusing on short-term gains ignores the possibility that social reform proceeds in a ratchetlike fashion, where the gains of one struggle become the resources for later challenges by the same aggrieved group (Tarrow 1983a).

The research presented above specifies the ways that organizational and ideological bridges span different stages of mobilization. Most movements have thresholds or turning points in mobilization which scholars have taken for "births" and "deaths." This research suggests that movements do not die, but scale down and retrench to adapt to changes in the political climate. Perhaps movements are never really born anew. Rather, they contract and hibernate, sustaining the totally dedicated and devising strategies appropriate to the external environment. If this is the case, our task as sociologists shifts from refining theories of movement emergence to accounting for fluctuations in the nature and scope of omnipresent challenges.

Notes

1. This analysis of the leadership and core membership is based on a careful reading of archival material, particularly correspondence, as well as research in biographical sources. For 55 women identified as leaders and core members, information was recorded about race, class, education, occupation, age, place of residence, political affiliation, political views, marital status, presence and number of children, living situation, and time of first involvement in the women's movement. In addition, any comments made by participants about the social characteristics of the membership were noted.

2. Florence Kitchelt to Katharine Ludington, August 14, 1950, Florence Kitchelt papers, box 6 (175), Schlesinger Library (SL), Radcliffe College, Cambridge, Massachusetts.

3. Katharine Hepburn, speech to the Connecticut Committee, n.d.[1946]. Kitchelt papers, box 6 (153), SL.

4. Betty Gram Swing to Ethel Ernest Murrell, October 3, 1952, National Woman's Party (NWP) papers, reel 99.

5. Mary Kennedy to Agnes Wells, July 12, 1950, NWP papers, reel 97.

6. Joseph E. Talbot to Florence Kitchelt, February 12, 1945, Kitchelt papers, box 8 (234), SL.

7. Mamie Sydney Mizen to Florence Armstrong, October 25, 1948, NWP papers, reel 94.

8. Open letter from Ernestine Bellamy to Ethel Ernest Murrell, May 24, 1953, NWP papers, reel 99.

9. I use the term "chairman" because that was the term used at the time. It seems historically inaccurate to change this usage.

10. Interview no. 2.

11. Laura Berrien and Doris Stevens, "An Open Letter to Miss Alice Paul," Committee on Information, Bulletin No. 4, July 30, 1947, Katharine A. Norris papers, box 2 (7), SL.

12. Rose Arnold Powell, diary entry, Nov. 2. 1960, Powell papers, box 1, v. 8, SL; Rose Arnold Powell to Mary Beard, June 1-3, 1948, Powell papers, box 2 (27), SL.

13. Alice Paul, "Conversations With Alice Paul: Woman Suffrage and the Equal Rights Amendment," an oral history conducted in 1972 and 1973 by Amelia R. Fry, Regional Oral History Office, University of California, 1976, p. 197.

14. Mary Alice Matthews to Alice Paul, March 24, 1945, NWP papers, reel 85.

15. Interview no. 12.

16. Mary Kennedy to Alice Paul, February 11, 1971, NWP papers, reel 112. ◆

32

The Consequences of Professionalization and Formalization in the Pro-Choice Movement

Suzanne Staggenborg

As a result of the conceptual work of McCarthy and Zald (1973, 1977), the notion of the "professionalized" social movement is now firmly associated with the "resource mobilization" approach to collective action (cf. Jenkins 1983). They argue that professionalized movements are increasingly common as a result of increases in sources of funding for activists who make careers out of being movement leaders. In contrast to what they term "classical" movement organizations, which rely on the mass mobilization of "beneficiary" constituents as active participants, "professional" social movement organizations (SMOs) rely primarily on paid leaders and "conscience" constituents who contribute money and are paper members rather than active participants. Importantly, this analysis suggests that social movements can be launched with adequate funding. "Entrepreneurs" can mobilize sentiments into movement organizations without the benefit of precipitating events or "suddenly imposed major grievances" (Walsh 1981) and without established constituencies.

McCarthy and Zald's analysis of professional movement organizations recognizes that there are different types of movement participants and different kinds of SMOs, which require different levels and types of participation. Although few theorists have expanded on the McCarthy-Zald analysis of professional movement organizations (exceptions are Cable 1984; Jenkins and Eckert 1986; Kleidman 1986; and Oliver 1983), such conceptual development is important because different types of organizational structures and participants have consequences for movement goals and ac-

tivities. Examination of the effect of organizational leadership and structure is relevant to debates over movement outcomes, such as those generated by Piven and Cloward's (1977) thesis that large formal movement organizations diffuse protest.

This paper explores the consequences of professionalization in social movements by analyzing the impact of leadership and organizational structure in the pro-choice movement. My analysis is based on documentary and interview data gathered on the pro-choice movement (Staggenborg 1985) and focuses on a sample of 13 pro-choice movement organizations, including 6 national organizations and 7 state and local organizations from Illinois and Chicago (see Table 1). Documentary data cover the histories of the organizations from their beginnings to 1983.[1]

Fifty individuals were interviewed, including leaders and rank-and-file activists, who were active in the organizations during different periods. I analyze the changes in leadership and internal structures of the SMOs and the impact of these changes on the movement. In particular, I focus on changes in three major periods of the abortion conflict: the years prior to legalization of abortion in 1973; 1973 to 1976, when Congress first passed the Hyde Amendment cutoff of federal funding of abortion; and 1977-1983 following the antiabortion victory on the Hyde Amendment.

I begin by making some conceptual distinctions among three types of movement leaders and two major types of SMOs and then use these distinctions to classify the organizations by structure (see Table 2). Next, I examine the impact of leadership on the formation of movement organizations and the formalization of SMOs. Then I examine the impact of formalization on the maintenance of SMOs, their strategies and tactics, and coalition work. Tables 3 through 6 summarize data for each SMO on the pattern of leadership and structural influence. More detailed case material illuminates processes under certain circumstances that may be more generalizable. Finally, I argue that the professionalization of social movements and activists does not necessarily help expand the social movement sector by initiating activities and organizations, but that professionalization and formalization importantly affect the structure and maintenance of social movement organizations, their strategies and tactics, and their participation in coalition work.

Table 1
Sample of National and State/Local Pro-Choice SMOs

	Dates
National Organizations	
National Abortion Rights Action League (NARAL), formerly National Association for the Repeal of Abortion Laws (NARAL) until 1973	1969-
Religion Coalition for Abortion Rights (RCAR)	1973-
Zero Population Growth (ZPG)	1968-
National Organization for Women (NOW)	1966-
National Women's Health Network (NWHN)	1975-
Reproductive Rights National Network (R2N2)	1978-1984
State/Local Organizations	
National Abortion Rights Action League of Illinois (NARAL of Illinois), formerly Illinois Citizens for the Medical Control of Abortion (ICMCA) until 1975 and Abortion Rights Association of Illinois (ARA) until 1978	1966-
Illinois Religious Coalition for Abortion Rights (IRCAR)	1975-
Chicago-area Zero Population Growth (Chicago-area ZPG)	1970-1977
Chicago Women's Liberation Union (CWLU)	1969-1977
Chicago National Organization for Women (Chicago NOW)	1969-
Chicago Women's Health Task Force (CWHTF)	1977-1979
Women Organized for Reproductive Choice (WORC)	1979-

Conceptual Distinctions

Types of Leadership in SMOs

With the professionalization of social movements and the availability of funding for staff positions, several types of leaders are found in SMOs (cf. McCarthy and Zald 1977, p. 1227; Oliver 1983, pp. 163-64). *Professional managers* are paid staff who make careers out of movement work. Professional managers are likely to move from one SMO to another and from movement to movement over their careers (see McCarthy and Zald 1973, p. 15). Two types of *nonprofessional leaders* are *volunteer leaders* and *nonprofessional staff leaders*. Volunteer leaders are not paid.[2] Nonprofessional staff leaders are compensated, for some or all of their time, but are not career activists. Rather, they serve as SMO staff for a short term and do not regard movement work as a career. As I argue below, there may be significant differences in orientation of leaders within this category based on whether the nonprofessional staff leader is temporarily dependent on the movement income for a living. Those who are dependent on the income may behave like professional managers in some respects, whereas those with other sources of income (or those willing to live at subsistence level) may behave more like volun-

Table 2
Organizational Structures of Sample SMOs Over Time

SMO	Pre-1973	1973-1976	1977-83
National			
NARAL	informal	transition to formalized	formalized
RCAR		formalized	formalized
ZPG	informal	informal	transition to formalized
NOW	informal	transition to formalized	formalized
NWHN		informal	transition to formalized
R2N2			informal
State/Local			
ICMCA/ARA/NARAL	informal	informal	formalized
IRCAR		informal	transition to formalized
Chicago-area ZPG	informal	(inactive)	(inactive)
Chicago NOW	informal	transition to formalized	formalized
CWLU	informal	informal	
CWHTF			informal
WORC			informal

Note: Details on organizational structures of sample SMOs are provided in Tables 3 and 4.

Table 3
Organizational Characteristics of Sample SMOs: Informal SMOs

SMO	Decision-making Structure and Division of Labor	Membership Criteria/Records	Connections to Subunits	Leadership
Pre-1973 NARAL	informal control by a small group of leaders on executive committee; board of directors representative of state organizations had no power; little division of labor	list of supporters rather than formal members, not formally maintained	loose connections to completely autonomous organizational members	volunteers and one nonprofessional staff director
Pre-1977 ZPG	control by self-appointed board of directors; no participation by rank-and-file membership in national decision making; division of labor between Washington lobbying office and California office	dues-paying membership, lack of reliable membership records	very poor communication with chapters, lack of national-level coordination	volunteers
Pre-1973 NOW	elected board and officers; major decisions made by membership at annual conference; division of labor between administrative office, public information office, and legislative office	dues-paying membership, lack of reliable membership records	very poor communication with chapters, lack of national-local coordination	volunteers
Pre-1977 NWHN	decision making by informally recruited board of directors and five founders; informal division of labor	local organizations signed up by founders, no criteria for active involvement	loose connections to completely autonomous organizational members	volunteers
R2N2	decision making initially done by membership at two annual membership conferences; later, regionally elected steering committee and annual membership conference; informal division of labor	membership open to any organization sharing principles; no criteria for active involvement	difficulty integrating many organizational members into organization	volunteers and one staff coordinator
ICMCA/ARA	informal decision making by board and executive director; informal division of labor created by director as needed	list of supporters rather than formal members	informal connection to autonomous "chapters" in other parts of state	volunteers and nonprofessional staff director
Pre-1977 IRCAR	Policy Council of informally selected individuals active in member denominations; informal division of labor among small group of activists	religious organizations in agreement with principles; no criteria for active participation	difficulty in involving subunits in organization	volunteer leaders and coordinator
Chicago-area ZPG	informal decision making and division of labor among small number of activists and coordinator	no formal membership or records	loose connections to area chapters until they declined	volunteers
Pre-1973 Chicago NOW	informal decision making by board consisting of most active members; informal creation of committees by interested members	dues-paying membership	committees form and act independently	volunteers
CWLU	decision making by steering committee and in citywide meetings of membership; many experiments with structure, attempts to involve all members.	List of supporters, dues initially voluntary, later required but not always collected; anyone active in workgroup or chapter was a "member	Loosely connected workgroups and chapters that were completely autonomous	Volunteers and nonprofessional, part-time staff
CWHTF	informal decision making and division of labor by small group of activists	exclusive "membership" of small group of friends	no subunits	volunteers
WORC	changing structure consisting of steering committee and various issues and work committees; attempts to rotate tasks and include all members	list of supporters; members include anyone who participates	typically not large enough for subunits; committees form and dissolve as needed	volunteers and one part-time nonprofessional staff

Table 4
Organizational Characteristics of Sample SMOs: Formalized SMOs
(Including SMOs in Transition to Formalized Structure)

SMO	Decision-making Structure and Division of Labor	Membership Criteria/Records	Connections to Subunits	Leadership
Post-1973 NARAL	decision making by elected board of directors, executive committee; division of labor by function with paid staff as lobbyists, media experts, fundraisers, etc.	dues-paying membership, professional direct-mail techniques	formalized connections to affiliates; training and funds provided	professional leaders along with volunteer board
RCAR	decision making by board of directors consisting of formal representatives of denominational members; division of labor by function using paid staff	denominations that agree with principles; expectation of active involvement	financial support to affiliates that report activities annually to national organization	professional leaders along with volunteer board
Post-1977 ZPG	decision making by board of directors and staff; division of labor by function using paid staff	dues-paying membership, professional direct mail; list of active members who participate in letter writing	some financial aid for chapter projects; formal guidelines for chapters developed	professional staff along with volunteer board
Post-1973 NOW	decision making by elected board and officers and delegates at national convention; division of labor by function using paid staff	dues-paying individuals, professional direct mail; chapters	communication with chapters established as national organization expanded staff and increased finances; state and regional organizations created to further coordination	professional leaders
Post-1977 NWHN	decision making by formally elected board of directors; division of labor using paid staff	dues-paying membership, professional direct mail; attempts to actively involve organizational members	organization of first official chapters	professional staff together with volunteer board
NARAL of Illinois	decision making by board of directors elected on rotating basis; division of labor among committees using paid staff	dues-paying membership plus activists	committees created to perform needed tasks	professional director together with volunteer board
Post-1976 IRCAR	formally elected Policy Council consisting of representatives from member denominations; creation of area units of activists	denominations agreeing with principles; attempts to encourage more active participation	more formalized ties to members and creation of formal area units	paid part-time director and volunteers
Post-1973 Chicago NOW	elected officers and board of directors; committees based on priorities screened by board and voted by membership; division of labor increasingly based on function using paid staff	dues-paying members plus activists	committees tightly integrated into organization, no longer autonomous	professional staff and paid officers

teers. All three types of leaders are, by definition, involved in organizational decision making. All three are also included in the category of activists, as are other nonleader members who are actively involved in the SMO as opposed to being paper members.

Paid leaders, then, may or may not be "professionals" in the sense of making careers out of movement work and, as Oliver (1983, p. 158) shows, may come from the "same pool" as volunteers. Of course, leaders who do not begin as movement professionals may become career ac-

Table 5
Consequences of SMOs: Informal Organizations

SMO	Maintenance/Expansion/Decline	Major Strategies and Tactics	Coalition Work
Pre-1973 NARAL	23 organizational members in states, 500-2,000 individual members, 1-2 staff, budgets of $30-70,000	demonstrations, support for abortion referral services, coordination of state lobbying campaigns, encouragement of litigation	minor participation in short-lived coalitions
Pre-1977 ZPG	high of 400 affiliates, 35,000 members in early 1970s; drop to about 60 affiliates, 8,500 members with budget of $350,000 in mid-70s	demonstrations, abortion referral work, state legislative lobbying, educational activities prior to 1973; Congressional lobbying, educational work after 1973	staff support for Congressional lobbying coalition after 1973
Pre-1973 NOW	initial membership of 1,200 individuals, 14 chapters; budget of $7,000 in 1967	participation in demonstrations on abortion	minor participation in short-lived coalitions
Pre-1977 NWHN	initial participation of about 50 activists	support for local demonstrations	no active participation
R2N2	50-90 affiliates, high budget of $50,000; dissolution in 1984 due to lack of resources	demonstrations; grassroots organizing; petition campaign against Hyde amendment; educational work	experienced great difficulty in attempts to participate in lobbying coalition, lack of communication with other SMOs in coalition
ICMCA/ARA	active core of 30-35, part-time director, mailing list of about 700 contributors up until about 1976, when organization declined to about 60 paying members	demonstrations, state legislative lobbying, encouragement of litigation, educational activities prior to 1973; continued state legislative lobbying, Congressional letter-writing campaigns, educational work until decline in 1976	minor participation in largely unsuccessful pre-1973 coalition and short-lived 1977 coalition
Pre-1977 IR-CAR	small core of activists; initial budget of $2,500, 8 denominational members, volunteer director through 1976	participation in demonstrations, lobbying in state legislature, letter-writing campaigns to Congress, educational activities	no major coalition work
Chicago-area ZPG	high of about 11 area chapters, low of 3 and small core of activists in early 1970s; largely inactive after 1973 with exception of failed attempt to revive the organization in 1977	participation in ICMCA demonstrations, lobbying activities prior to 1973; inactive after early 1970s	minor participation in largely unsuccessful pre-1973 coalition; endorsement of coalition activities in 1977 prior to dissolving
Pre-1973 Chicago NOW	about 20 active members, a few hundred paying members in early 1970s	participation in demonstrations, support for abortion referral work and support for ICMCA lobbying work by head of abortion committee	participation in short-lived coalitions

tivists. Both professional and nonprofessional leaders learn skills (e.g., public relations skills) that they can easily transfer from one organization to another and from one cause to another. Both professionals and nonprofessionals can serve as entrepreneurs—leaders who initiate movements, organizations, and tactics (cf. Kleidman 1986, pp. 191-92). However, as I argue below, nonprofessional leaders are more likely to initiate movements (as opposed to SMOs) and tactics than are professionals.

Types of Movement Organizations

Changes in the structures of SMOs have occurred along with the professionalization of social movement leadership. In contrast to "classical" SMOs, which have mass memberships of beneficiary constituents, McCarthy and Zald (1973, 1977) argue that movement organizations with professional leadership have nonexistent or "pa-

per" memberships and rely heavily on resources from constituents outside of the group(s) that benefit from movement achievements. Professional movement activists are thought to act as entrepreneurs who form such organizations by appealing to conscience constituents. The difficulty with this characterization of the structural changes in SMOs led by professionals is, as Oliver (1983) notes, that many such SMOs have both active and paper memberships. Similarly, organizations may rely on a mix of conscience and beneficiary constituents for resources.

An alternative characterization of structural differences in SMOs is based on differences in operating procedures. Formalized SMOs[3] have established procedures or structures that enable them to perform certain tasks routinely and to continue to function with changes in leadership. Formalized SMOs have bureaucratic procedures for

Table 6
Consequences of SMO Structure: Formalized Organizations (Including SMOs in Transition to Formalized Structure)

SMO	Maintenance/Expansion/Decline	Major Strategies and Tactics	Coalition Work
Post-1973 NARAL	10,000 members, 4-8 staff, budget reaches $200,000 by 1976; 40 state affiliates, 140,000 members, 25 staff, budget reaches $3 million by 1983	Congressional lobbying, litigation from 1973 on; campaign work, PAC contributions, grassroots organizing beginning in late 1970s	began working in Congressional lobbying coalition in 1973; leadership role in lobbying coalition by mid- to late 1970s
RCAR	began with 24 organizational members, 13 affiliates, several staff, budget of $100,00; 31 organizational members and 28 affiliates, 8-10 staff and budget of $700,000 by 1983	educational work, Congressional lobbying since 1973; increased local organizing in late 1970s	began working in Congressional lobbying coalition in 1973; leadership role in lobbying coalition by mid- to late 1970s
Post-1977 ZPG	about 20 affiliates, 12,000 members, budget of $65,000	Congressional lobbying	cooperation in letter-writing campaigns in response to alerts from coalition leaders
Post-1973 NOW	40,000 members, 700 chapters by 1974; budget of $500,000 by 1976; membership reaches 250,000, budget reaches $6,500,000 by 1983	Congressional lobbying work, educational work after 1973; political campaign work and PAC contributions by late 1970s	participation in Congressional lobbying coalition
Post-1977 NWHN	membership of 300 organizations, 13,000 individuals, budget of $300,000 by 1983	educational work; Congressional testimony	participation in Congressional lobbying coalition
NARAL of Illinois	high of 200 active members, 4,000 paying members, budget of $80,000, full-time director and 3-4 part-time staff in early 1980s	legislative lobbying in late 1970s combined with political campaign work in early 1980s	participation in coalitions in late 1970s; leadership role in Illinois Pro-Choice Alliance
Post-1976 IRCAR	mailing list of 600-15,000, 13 denominational members, part-time paid director, budget high of $10,000	legislative lobbying, educational work; expansion of state organizing efforts in 1980s	participation in coalitions in late 1970s; increased role in 1980s

decision making, a developed division of labor with positions for various functions, explicit criteria for membership, and rules governing subunits (chapters or committees). For example, the formalized SMO may have a board of directors that meets a set number of times per year to make organizational policy; an executive committee of the board that meets more frequently to make administrative decisions; staff members who are responsible for contacts with the mass media, direct mail campaigns, and so forth; chapters that report to the national organization; and an individual rank-and-file membership. As I argue below, this type of SMO structure is associated with the professionalization of leadership. In contrast, *informal* SMOs[4] have few established procedures, loose membership requirements, and minimal division of labor. Decisions in informal organizations tend to be made in an ad hoc rather than routine manner (cf. Rothschild-Whitt 1979, p. 513). The organizational structure of an informal SMO is frequently adjusted; assignments among personnel and procedures are developed to meet immediate needs. Because informal SMOs

lack established procedures, individual leaders can exert an important influence on the organization; major changes in SMO structure and activities are likely to occur with changes in leadership. Any subunits of informal SMOs, such as work groups or chapters, tend to be autonomous and loosely connected to one another. Informal organizations are dominated by nonprofessional, largely volunteer, leaders.

The SMOs in my sample are classified by structure in Table 2 based on the above criteria; details explaining the classifications are provided in Table 3.[5] The major categories of formalized and informal SMOs are, of course, ideal types. In reality, some SMOs share elements of each type, often because they are in the process of changing structures. When SMOs formalize, they typically do so very gradually. Some SMOs look formalized on paper, but are informal in practice. Important differences also appear among SMOs within each of the two major categories (e.g., some are centralized and others decentralized; cf. Gamson 1975). Nevertheless, the two major types of

SMOs do differ from one another in important ways discussed below.

The Impact of Professional Leadership

The Initiation Of Social Movements

Because professional movement activists can easily transfer their skills from one movement to another, McCarthy and Zald suggest that professional activists are likely to become entrepreneurs who start new organizations in which to work. If this is the case, an increase in movement careers should help to expand the social movement sector. Grievances can be manufactured by professional activists and SMOs, making the formation of social movements at least partially independent of overt grievances and environmental conditions (cf. Oberschall 1973, p. 158).

The McCarthy-Zald argument has been challenged on grounds of lack of evidence that professional managers and their SMOs originate insurgent challenges, although they may play a role in representing unorganized groups in more established interest group politics (Jenkins and Eckert 1986, p. 812). In the case of the civil rights movement, researchers have shown that informal indigenous SMOs initiated and led the movement (Morris 1984; Jenkins and Eckert 1986). In the case of the pro-choice movement, all of the SMOs in my sample that were active in the early movement were informal SMOs (see Table 2). The leaders who initiated SMOs that formed in the period prior to legalization were all nonprofessional leaders, mostly volunteers (see Table 3).

Professional managers may act as entrepreneurs in creating SMOs (as opposed to movements and collective action), but my data, together with cases from the literature, suggest that professionals are less likely than nonprofessionals to act as entrepreneurs. When professionals do initiate movement organizations, they are likely to be formalized rather than informal SMOs. Common Cause, for example, was initiated by a professional manager who created a formalized organization (see McFarland 1984). Many community organizations, which are often created by professional leaders, are also formally organized (see Delgado 1986). In my sample only the national Religious Coalition for Abortion Rights (RCAR) was initiated by individuals who might be called professional leaders; they included a staff member of the United Methodist Board of Church and Society. All of the other SMOs in my sample were initially organized by nonprofessional activists as informal SMOs (see Tables 2. 3, and 4). Significantly, RCAR is also distinctive in that it originated as a formalized organization to mobilize existing organizations for institutionalized tactics (e.g., lobbying Congress) in a period when the movement as a whole was becoming more established.[6]

Given the lack of evidence that movement professionals initiate movements and informal SMOS, it is necessary to reconsider the relationship between the roles of movement "professional" and movement "entrepreneur." McCarthy and Zald suggest that, in response to the availability of resources, movement professionals become movement entrepreneurs, initiating movement activities and organizations because they are career activists looking for preferences to mobilize. Although no systematic evidence on the entrepreneurial activities of professional and nonprofessional leaders has been collected, my data indicate that the roles of "entrepreneur" and "professional" are, in some cases, distinct (cf. Roche and Sachs 1965).

An example of a nonprofessional entrepreneur in the abortion movement is Lawrence Lader, a writer and family planning advocate who published a book (Lader 1966) reporting on the large number of abortions being performed by licensed physicians in the U.S. and advocating legal abortion. After his research was published, Lader was inundated with requests for the names of doctors from women seeking abortions. He began to make referrals to women and then announced his referral service publicly as a strategy intended "to stir as much controversy and debate as possible while bringing the facts to the public" (Lader 1973, p. xi). Lader played a role in getting others to employ this strategy, including the clergy who founded the Clergy Consultation Services on Abortion (see Carmen and Moody 1973). He later helped to found NARAL in 1969 and, more recently, founded another organization, the Abortion Rights Mobilization. Although remaining intensely interested in abortion and related family planning issues, Lader has not made a professional career out of his movement work; he continued to pursue his career as a writer while playing an entrepreneurial role in the movement.

Examples of nonentrepreneurial professionals in the pro-choice movement who have moved among established movement and political positions include Karen Mulhauser, an executive director of NARAL who became the executive director of Citizens Against Nuclear War after leaving NARAL in 1981. The NARAL director who succeeded her, Nanette Falkenberg, had previously been involved in union organizing work. In Illinois, the first professional leader of NARAL of Illinois was involved in community organizing work before taking the position of NARAL executive director and became a staff member of a political campaign after leaving NARAL.

These examples suggest that different factors may be responsible for the creation of two distinct roles. Movement entrepreneurs, the initiators of movement organizations and activities, may become paid activists who benefit from the existence of the same resources that support professional managers, but they typically do not make careers out of moving from one cause to another and they may never find paid positions that suit them. Rather, they found movement organizations and initiate tactics for the same reasons that other constituents join them. That is, they have personal experiences and ideological commitments which make them interested in the particular issue(s) of the movement. They are also tied into the social networks and preexisting organizational structures that allow the movement to mobilize and are influenced by environmental developments (e.g., legalization of abortion in 1973) that make movement issues salient and provide opportunities for action (cf. Oliver 1983).

Professional managers, on the other hand, are not likely to be the initiators of social movements. They make careers out of service to SMOs and are often hired to come into SMOs that already have formal structures or are in the process of becoming formalized. Professional leaders are likely to care very much about the cause of the SMO—even if they aren't initially motivated out of particular concern for the issue(s) of the SMO. However, professionals' concerns with the particular causes of SMOs are part of their more general concern for a range of issues—the orientation toward social activism that made them choose a professional reform career.

Professionalization and the Formalization of SMOs

Not only are movement entrepreneur and professional distinct roles, but movement entrepreneurs and other nonprofessionals are likely to dif-

fer from professional managers in their organizational structure preferences. While McCarthy and Zald (1977) suggest that movement entrepreneurs create "professional" SMOs, my data support the argument that movement entrepreneurs prefer informal structures and may resist creation of formalized SMOs run by professional leaders. The professionalization of social movements (i.e., the rise of career leadership) is associated with the formalization of SMOs for two reasons: (1) professional managers tend to formalize the organizations that they lead; and (2) the SMOs that have the resources to hire professional managers are those with formalized structures.

Movement entrepreneurs prefer informal structures that enable them to maintain personal control. As the analogy to business entrepreneurs suggests, movement entrepreneurs are risk-takers (cf. Oliver 1983) who initiate movement organizations without certainty of success, just as capitalist entrepreneurs risk investment in new products. Like capitalist entrepreneurs, movement entrepreneurs are likely to be personally involved in the enterprise, desiring personal control over decision making because they have taken the risks to establish an organization or movement. In contrast to the professional manager who brings skills to an organization and expects to operate within an established structure, movement entrepreneurs may try to prevent the creation of an organizational structure in which decision making is routinized and, therefore, less subject to personal control.

The history of leadership in NARAL, which was founded in 1969 as the National Association for the Repeal of Abortion Laws, reveals that conflict between entrepreneurial leadership and formalization occurs in some circumstances. NARAL founders were not professional movement organizers in the sense of being career movement activists; rather, they were persons who had become dedicated to the cause of legal abortion as a result of their prior experiences, primarily in the family planning and population movements that provided the most important organizational bases for the rise of the single-issue abortion movement (see Staggenborg, 1985). Because the decision-making structure was informal (see Table 3), a movement entrepreneur who became chairman of the executive committee exerted a large amount of control over the organization; as he commented in a 1984 interview about his own style of leadership:

Let's face it. . . . I don't believe in endless meetings, I like to make quick decisions. Maybe I acted unilaterally sometimes, although I was always careful to check with the executive committee. Some people objected to my calling [other members of the executive committee] and getting their approval on the phone. [But] we couldn't meet, we had to move fast, so I polled the exec committee around the country by phone. (Personal interview)

Although there were some disagreements among NARAL executive committee members in the pre-1973 years, the informal decision-making structure seems to have worked fairly well at a time when the movement was very young, abortion was illegal in most states, and it was necessary to act quickly to take advantage of opportunities for action and to meet crises (e.g., the arrests of leaders involved in abortion referral activities).

After legalization, however, conflict over the decision-making structure occurred as NARAL attempted to establish itself as a lobbying force in Washington and to expand by organizing state affiliates. At this point, there was a power struggle within the organization between long-time leaders and entrepreneurs of NARAL and newer activists who objected to "power being concentrated in the hands of a few men in New York City" and who supported having persons "who are doing the work of the field—the State Coordinators" on the board (documents in NARAL of Illinois papers; University of Illinois at Chicago). The latter faction won a critical election in 1974 resulting in a turnover of leadership on the NARAL executive committee. Although the executive committee remained the decision-making body of the organization, practices such as the use of proxy votes and phone calls to make important decisions were discontinued (personal interview with 1974 NARAL executive director), resulting in more formalized decision-making procedures that involved more activists at different levels. Another major change that occurred at this point was that for the first time the executive director and other paid staff became more important than the nonprofessional entrepreneurs as NARAL leaders. It was only with the defeat of movement entrepreneurs as organizational leaders that NARAL began to formalize and eventually grew into a large organization capable of acting in institutionalized arenas.[7]

If movement entrepreneurs interfere with the formalization of SMOs, as this case suggests, professional managers encourage formalization.

While informal structures are associated with nonprofessional leadership, all of the organizations in my sample that have moved toward a more formal structure have done so under the leadership of professional managers (see Tables 3 and 4). Although further study of the leadership styles of professional managers compared to nonprofessional SMO leaders is necessary, my data suggest some reasons why professional managers tend to formalize the SMOs that they lead. Insofar as a bureaucratic or formalized structure is associated with organizational maintenance (Gamson 1975), professional leaders have a strong motivation to promote formalization: ongoing resources are needed to pay the salary of the professional manager. However, the motivation to promote financial stability is also shared by nonprofessional staff who are dependent on their income from the SMO position; moreover, it is possible to secure stable funding by means other than formalization. It is also important that professional managers are interested in using and developing organizing skills and expanding the SMOs they lead because this is what they do for a career. A formalized structure, with its developed division of labor, enables the professional manager to achieve a degree of organizational development not possible in informal SMOs.

The case of the Abortion Rights Association of Illinois (formerly Illinois Citizens for the Medical Control of Abortion and later NARAL of Illinois) reveals the role of professional leadership in the creation of organizational stability and bureaucracy. From 1970 to 1976, ICMCA/ARA was led by a nonprofessional director who was paid a small salary, but who volunteered much of her time and was often not paid on time due to financial problems of the organization. She was extremely effective, but did not create a structure such that others could easily carry on her work. Rather, organizational activities were carried out by force of her personality.[8] Moreover, volunteer efforts were channeled into instrumental tactics like lobbying, and little emphasis was placed on organizational maintenance activities such as fundraising. When she resigned in early 1976, ARA entered a period of severe decline due to inept leadership and neglect of organizational maintenance.

A new director hired in 1978 was the first to develop a stable source of financial resources for the SMO. Although not a professional manager, the new director was highly motivated to secure funding because, unlike the previous directors, she was a graduate student who did not have a husband who made enough money to support her while she volunteered her time. She needed the money from the job and did not intend to work as a volunteer when there was not enough money to pay her salary (about $11,000 a year for part-time work) as had previous directors. Consequently, she set about trying to figure out how to bring a stable income to the organization. She eventually was able to do so by personally convincing the owners of a number of abortion clinics in the city to make monthly financial contributions to NARAL (personal interview with 1978-80 NARAL of Illinois director). Thus, it was important that the leader of Illinois NARAL was someone who, while not a career activist, did need to be paid and was therefore motivated to provide the organization with financial stability. However, the financial stability was based on the personal appeal of the organization's director: the contributions from clinics were received as a result of personal relationships with clinic owners established by the NARAL director. After she left NARAL and a new director replaced her in the fall of 1980, the organization lost these contributions and went through a period of budget tightening.

It was not until the first career professional took over leadership of NARAL of Illinois that the organization became more formalized and less dependent on the personal characteristics of its leaders. The director hired in 1980, who stayed with NARAL until 1983, was a young woman who had previously done community organizing work and who, unlike her predecessor, wanted a career in "organizing." She did not have any experience working on the abortion issue prior to being hired as the director of Illinois NARAL, but saw the job as a good experience for her, a way to develop her own skills and enhance her career objectives. Like other leaders, the professional manager was highly committed to the goals of the movement, both because of pro-choice views formed prior to directing NARAL and because of her experiences in working with NARAL. But the professional director's orientation to her job led her to make important changes in the structure of the organization.

Until Illinois NARAL's first professional manager took over, the board of directors was selected from the same pool of long-time activists, many of whom were highly involved in other organizations like Planned Parenthood and not very active in ARA/NARAL. Consequently, there was little division of labor in the organization and it was heavily reliant on the abilities of its executive director. When she was hired in 1980, the new director insisted that the board selection procedures be revised so that active new volunteer recruits could serve on the board and so that the terms of service on the board were systematically rotated. This procedure was implemented in 1980, resulting in a board composed of active volunteers along with some old board members who continued to serve on a rotating basis to provide experience to NARAL. The result was that a formal procedure for bringing new and active members into the decision-making structure of the organization was established for the first time. This change was important in making the organization less exclusively dependent on its executive director for leadership. It also made volunteers more available to the executive director for use in organizational maintenance activities, such as the NARAL "house meeting" program,[9] which provided an important source of funds to the SMO in the early 1980s. In Illinois NARAL and in other SMOs (see Table 4), formalization occurred as professional managers took over leadership. Once a formalized structure is in place, SMOs are better able to mobilize resources and continue to hire professional staff (see below).

The Consequences of Formalization

The Maintenance of Social Movement Organizations

While informal movement organizations may be necessary to initiate movements, formalized SMOs do not necessarily defuse protest as Piven and Cloward (1977) argue; rather, they often perform important functions (e.g., lobbying) following victories won by informal SMOs (Jenkins and Eckert 1986, p. 827). And, while informal SMOs may be necessary to create the pressure for elite patronage, formalized SMOs are the usual beneficiaries of foundation funding and other elite contributions (Haines 1984b; Jenkins 1985b; Jenkins and Eckert 1986). Consequently, formalized SMOs are able to maintain themselves—and the movement—over a longer period of time than are informal SMOs. This is particularly important in periods such as the one following legalization of abortion, when movement issues are less pressing and mobilization of constituents is more difficult.

Jenkins (1985b, p. 10) argues that one of the reasons that formalized SMOs are able to sustain themselves is that foundations prefer dealing with organizations that have professional leaders and "the fiscal and management devices that foundations have often expected of their clients." In the case of the civil rights movement, foundations "selected the new organizations that became permanent features of the political landscape" through their funding choices (Jenkins 1985b, p. 15). It is important to recognize, however, that this selection process is a two-way street. Formalized SMOs do not just passively receive support from foundations and other elite constituents; they actively solicit these resources. They are able to do so because they have organizational structures and professional staff that facilitate the mobilization of elite resources. Most importantly, professional staff are likely to have the know-how necessary to secure funding (e.g., grant-writing skills and familiarity with procedures for securing tax-exempt status).

The ability of formalized SMOs to obtain foundation funding is part of a broader capacity for organizational maintenance superior to that of informal SMOs. Paid staff and leaders are critical to the maintenance of formalized SMOs because they can be relied on to be present to carry out tasks such as ongoing contact with the press and fundraising in a routine manner. A formalized structure ensures that there will be continuity in the performance of maintenance tasks and that the SMO will be prepared to take advantage of elite preferences and environmental opportunities (cf. Gamson 1975). Of course, volunteers might well have the skills to perform such tasks, and some informal SMOs do maintain themselves for a number of years, even in adverse environmental conditions (cf. Rupp and Taylor 1987). However, it is much more difficult to command the necessary time from volunteer activists on an ongoing basis. When informal SMOs do survive for many years, they are likely to remain small and exclusive, as was the case for the National Women's Party studied by Rupp and Taylor (1987) and Women Organized for Reproductive Choice in my sample (see Table 5).

The superior ability of formalized SMOs to maintain themselves is documented by the experiences of organizations in my sample (see Tables 5 and 6). On the national level, all of the surviving pro-choice organizations have at least moved in the direction of formalization (see Table 2). The one organization that did not do so, the Reproductive Rights National Network, was formed in a period of intense constituent interest in the abortion issue created by events such as passage of the Hyde Amendment cutoff of Medicaid funding of abortion in late 1976 and the election of anti-abortion president Ronald Reagan in 1980, but was unable to maintain itself after this period. On the local level, the movement industry declined in the period after legalization due to the lack of formalized SMOs (see Tables 2 and 5). The exception was Chicago NOW, which was moving toward formalization but was concentrating its energies on the Equal Rights Amendment rather than on the abortion issue. In the period after the environmental stimulus of the Hyde Amendment, the local pro-choice SMOs that became stable were those that began to formalize. Among informal SMOs, only Women Organized for Reproductive Choice (WORC) has survived and it has remained a small organization. Thus, on both the national and local levels, formalized SMOs have been stable organizations that helped to sustain the movement during lulls in visible movement activity brought about by environmental developments.

Not only do formalized SMOs help keep a movement alive in periods when constituents become complacent, such as that following legalization of abortion, but they are prepared to take advantage of opportunities for mobilization when the environment changes. In the late 1970s, when the anti-abortion movement scored its first major victories, including the cutoff of Medicaid funding for abortions, adherents and constituents were alerted by visible threats to legal abortion, and the ability of the pro-choice movement to mobilize was greatly enhanced. However, it was important not only that the environment was conducive to mobilization but also that the pro-choice movement had formalized organizations that were stable and ready for combat (cf. Gamson 1975). In NARAL, professional leaders were available with the skills and know-how necessary to form a political action committee, launch a highly successful direct-mail drive, create an educational arm, obtain foundation grants, and organize state affiliates.

In contrast to the success of NARAL and other formalized SMOs in mobilizing resources (see Table 6), informal movement organizations were not as prepared to take advantage of constituent concerns in the late 1970s. The Reproductive Rights National Network (known as R2N2), an informal SMO formed in the late 1970s, received a donation of money to undertake a direct-mail campaign during this period, but the attempt to raise money and recruit activists in this manner was unsuccessful because activists in the organization's national office did not have the experience to carry out the program properly (personal interviews with 1980-83 R2N2 coordinator and steering committee member). There might have been local activists in the organization with direct-mail skills who could have directed this campaign, but in this instance, and in others, the informal structure of the organization made access to such skills difficult to obtain. As one steering committee member commented in an interview, R2N2 suffered from "the classic leadership problem"—the difficulty of trying to get people "to do what they are supposed to do" and the problem of "no one being around" to coordinate work—that has long affected the "younger branch" of the women's movement (see Freeman 1975) of which R2N2 was a descendent. Ultimately, this structural problem led to the demise of R2N2 after the period of heightened constituent interest in abortion ended.[10]

Formalized SMOs, then, are able to maintain themselves during periods when it is difficult to mobilize support and are consequently ready to expand when the environment becomes more conducive. An important reason for this is that they have paid leaders who create stability because they can be relied on to perform ongoing tasks necessary to organizational maintenance. However, stability is not simply a matter of having paid activists; it is also important that formalized SMOs have structures that ensure that tasks are performed despite a turnover in personnel. It is the combination of formalized structure and professional leadership that facilitates organizational maintenance in SMOs.

Strategies and Tactics

While Piven and Cloward (1977) appear to be mistaken in their claim that formalized SMOs necessarily hasten the end of mass movements, their argument that formalization leads to a decline in militant direct-action tactics remains important. Formalization does affect the strategic and tactical choices of SMOs. First, formalized SMOs tend to engage in institutionalized tactics and typically do not initiate disruptive direct-action tactics. Second, formalized SMOs are more likely than informal SMOs to engage in activities that help to achieve organizational maintenance and expansion as well as influence on external targets.

Formalization and Institutionalized Tactics. The association between formalization and institutionalization of strategies and tactics occurs for two reasons: (1) As environmental developments push a movement into institutionalized arenas, SMOs often begin to formalize so they can engage in tactics such as legislative lobbying (cf. Cable 1984). Formalization allows SMOs to maintain the routines necessary for such tactics (e.g., ongoing contacts with legislators through paid staff and an established division of labor. (2) Once SMOs are formalized, institutionalized tactics are preferred because they are more compatible with a formalized structure and with the schedules of professional activists. For example, institutionalized activities can be approved in advance: the amount and type of resources expended for such efforts can be controlled; and activities can be planned for the normal hours of the professional's working day.

The history of the pro-choice movement clearly reveals that formalization accelerated as environmental events forced the movement into institutionalized arenas. Prior to 1973, the movement to legalize abortion was an outsider to established politics. Although institutionalized tactics were employed in this period, no SMO confined its activities to institutionalized arenas; demonstrations and quasi-legal or illegal abortion-referral activities were common tactics (see Table 5).[11] After legalization in 1973, the arena for the abortion conflict switched to Congress and SMOs like NARAL began to formalize in order to act in that arena. After the Hyde amendment was passed in 1976, the political arena became the primary battlefield for the abortion conflict, and formalization of SMOs within the movement accelerated. Although informal SMOs in my sample did engage in some institutionalized tactics, the organizations that sustained a heavy use of tactics such as legislative lobbying and political campaign work were most commonly formalized SMOs (see Tables 5 and 6). It is possible for informal SMOs to engage in such tactics, but only as long as the leaders of the organization have the necessary know-how and other organizational resources. Formalized organizations are able to maintain such activities, despite changes in leadership, due to their structural division of labor.

Environmental forces and events, including countermovement activities, do place strong constraints on the tactics of SMOs. When environmental events call for nonroutine direct-action tactics, informal movement organizations typically play a critical role in initiating these tactics (Jenkins and Eckert 1986). In the case of the civil rights movement, for example, Morris (1984) shows that the formalized NAACP preferred to focus on legal and educational tactics, while informal SMOs were engaging in direct-action tactics. However, even the NAACP engaged in some direct-action tactics through its youth divisions at a time when it was clear that progress could only be made through tactics such as the sit-ins initiated by informal SMOs.

When formalized SMOs do engage in direct-action tactics, however, they are likely to be nondisruptive, planned versions of the tactics. NARAL's use of the "speak-out" tactic in the period following 1983 provides some evidence on this point. This was a period when the pro-choice movement was beginning to take the offensive in the legislative and political arenas, particularly after anti-abortion forces failed in their attempt to pass a Human Life Bill through Congress in 1982 and the Supreme Court delivered a ruling in 1983 that struck down most of the restrictions on abortion that had been passed by state and local legislatures. The anti-abortion movement responded to these developments by forcing a switch away from the institutionalized arenas, in which pro-choice forces were beginning to gain the upper hand, to public relations tactics such as the film *The Silent Scream.*12 As a result of media coverage that began to focus on the issue of fetal rights (cf. Kalter 1985), pro-choice organizations such as NARAL were forced to respond. NARAL chose to employ a version of the speak-out tactic originated by women's liberation groups in the late 1960s. Originally, the speak-out was a spontaneous type of public forum at which women spoke out about their experiences as women, relating their own stories about illegal abortions and so forth. NARAL's version of this tactic was a planned one; to focus media and public attention on women rather than on the fetus, NARAL asked women around the country to write letters about

their experiences with abortion addressed to President Reagan and other elected officials and send the letters to NARAL and its affiliates. The letters were then read at public forums on a scheduled day. This case suggests that formalized organizations can switch from tactics in institutionalized arenas to other tactics when necessary, but the tactics they choose are likely to be orderly versions of direct-action tactics originated by informal SMOs.

Formalization and Organizational Maintenance Tactics. Not only are the tactics of formalized SMOs typically institutionalized, but they are also frequently geared toward organizational maintenance and expansion, in addition to more instrumental goals. This was certainly the case for NARAL and its affiliates, which embarked on a "grassroots organizing" strategy known as "Impact '80," intended to expand NARAL, and its political influence, in the late 1970s (see, for example, *NARAL News,* November 1978). It was also the case for NOW, which engaged in a number of high-profile tactics around abortion that were used in membership appeals in the 1980s (see, for example, *National NOW Times*, September/October 1979). In Chicago NOW, there was explicit discussion of the membership-expanding potential of the abortion issue in the late 1970s and early 1980s (personal interview with Chicago NOW executive director).

The experiences of organizations in my sample suggest that professional leaders play an important role in influencing organizations to adopt tactics that aid organizational maintenance. In several organizations, professional staff were responsible for undertaking direct-mail campaigns that helped to expand the organization. In NARAL, an experienced director who took over in 1974 began a direct-mail campaign that was later expanded by other professional leaders (personal interviews with 1974-75 and 1975-81 NARAL executive directors). In the NWHN, an executive director succeeded in expanding organizational membership in the late 1970s through direct mail despite the concerns of nonprofessional leaders that direct mail would bring uncommitted members into the organization (personal interviews with NWHN board members). In ZPG, a professional manager was responsible for reversing the decline in individual membership in the organization through direct mail after he finally convinced the nonprofessional leaders on the ZPG board to undertake the campaign (personal interview with 1976-80 ZPG executive director).

The case of Illinois NARAL is particularly valuable in revealing the role of professional leaders in advancing strategies that aid organizational expansion. In the early 1980s, the NARAL affiliate made important changes in its strategies and tactics, switching from an emphasis on legislative lobbying to heavy involvement in political campaign work. This switch was part of the national NARAL Impact '80 program, which began to be implemented by Illinois NARAL in 1979. However, it was not until the early 1980s, after a professional manager took over, that Illinois NARAL really became committed to the new tactics, which included political campaign work and workshops to train volunteers, house meetings to recruit new members, and an "I'm Pro-Choice and I Vote" postcard campaign.

One reason why the switch in mobilization tactics occurred after 1980 was that the national NARAL organization had by this time become much better organized in implementing the grassroots organizing program through training and grants to local affiliates (see Table 4). As the national organization became more formalized, it was able to extend more aid through its bureaucratic structure to affiliates and to exert more influence over their tactics. In fact, NARAL affiliates signed formal contracts in exchange for national funds to carry out programs in the early 1980s. The other reason was that there were important differences in the state of the organization and in the orientations of the Illinois NARAL directors who served from 1978-1980 and from 1980-1983, which resulted in different strategies and tactics.

Because ARA was in a state of decline when she was hired in 1978 (see Table 5), the new director spent much of her time in administrative tasks; securing funding, renewing contacts with members, and organizing the office. Due to her organizational skills and attractive personal style, she was highly successful at reviving the organization. In doing so, she used the skills of constituents but did not create a formalized organization. NARAL's strategies and tactics were determined solely by the pragmatic and instrumental approach of the 1978-80 executive director. Rather than concentrating on bringing large numbers of activists into the organization, she recruited volunteers with particular skills, including her

friends, for specific tasks. Tactics were aimed less at gaining exposure for NARAL than at accomplishing specific objectives. For example, when a Chicago alderman moved to introduce an ordinance in the city council restricting the availability of abortions, the NARAL director worked to have the measure killed through quiet, behind-the-scenes maneuvers. In this instance and in lobbying work in the state legislature, she made use of the skills and influence of seasoned activists.

Due to her success with such tactics and her lack of concern with organizational expansion, the 1978-80 director was not sold on the national NARAL "Impact '80" program, which was intended to expand NARAL and make the organization a visible political force. In accordance with the national organization's wishes, she tried to implement the program, conducting a limited number of house meetings. But she remained unconvinced of their effectiveness, preferring more efficient methods of fundraising and recruitment. She had similar objections to other parts of the national NARAL grassroots organizing program. When I asked her about the political skills workshops, she replied:

> I refused to do those political skills workshops. I didn't have time, I said [to national NARAL], I'm doing the house meetings program—that's enough. I really just didn't think they were necessary—there are enough organizations like the League of Women Voters which do political skills training. From an organizational point of view, I guess it's good to do your own skills training to show that the organization is really involved. (Personal interview)

Although she recognized the organizational value of such tactics, this director was not primarily concerned with organizational expansion, but with more specific goals, such as defeating particular pieces of anti-abortion legislation. She was accustomed to using individual skills for this work rather than mobilizing large numbers of activists. When asked about campaign work, she replied:

> I do think the "I'm Pro-Choice and I Vote" [postcard campaign] was important in getting the message across to legislators and candidates in a public way. I put a lot of emphasis on [abortion] clinics for postcards because there was a ready-made setting for getting people to sign them. . . . As far as the campaign work, it was clear to me at the time that Reagan was going to be elected. It was too late in 1980 to make a difference. And, on the local level, there are already liberal groups . . . that almost always support pro-choice candidates any-

way. . . . I'm just not that much on duplicating efforts which I think NARAL is doing with the campaign work. (Personal interview)

As these comments indicate, the 1978-80 Illinois NARAL director preferred instrumental tactics rather than organizing tactics as a result of her background and experiences. She saw the house meetings as an inefficient way to raise money, and, while she recognized that political-skills workshops and campaign work were good for organizational visibility, she was not convinced of their effectiveness for achieving movement goals—her primary concern. She used the "I'm Pro-Choice and I Vote" postcards as a signal to legislators rather than as an organizing tool. Due to her influence, most of Illinois NARAL's activities during her tenure were instrumentally targeted at state legislators.

It was not until an executive director with experience in community organizing work and with ambitions for a movement career was hired in 1980 that the Illinois NARAL affiliate enthusiastically implemented the national NARAL grassroots organizing program. In contrast to her predecessor, who had no interest in organizing *per se,* the new director was anxious to engage in "organizing" work to expand the local affiliate and eagerly began to develop the house meeting program that was part of the national NARAL organizing strategy. One of the reasons that she was successful in doing so was that, as described above, she created a more formalized organization. Whereas her predecessor had been reluctant to delegate certain tasks, including speaking at house meetings, the new director made heavy use of a division of labor that had not existed in the previously informal SMO. Aided by her past experience with community organizing, she was highly successful at training volunteers to conduct house meetings and, with funds raised from the meetings and some financial aid from national NARAL, was able to hire an organizer to run the house meeting program, thereby increasing the division of labor in the SMO.

The new director's strategic approach was clearly influenced by her professional interest in organizing tactics. She used the NARAL house meeting program to raise money, but also as a means of bringing new activists into the NARAL organization. And just as the house meetings were used as an organizing tool, so were the NARAL postcards. As the NARAL director explained:

The best thing about the postcards was that they gave us new contacts. We would set up tables in different places and people would come up and sign and say things like "I'm really glad someone is doing something about this issue." And then we'd say, "Would you like to get more involved?" and we got a number of activists that way. We also got names for a mailing list. So the postcards were good as a way of making contacts, a means of exposure for the organization. The actual effect of the postcards on legislators was, I think, minimal. I know some of the legislators never even opened the envelope; when we delivered an envelope-full to Springfield, they'd just throw them away. (Personal interview)

Thus, Illinois NARAL employed tactics oriented toward organizational goals after moving toward formalization. This local case history suggests that professional leaders may be more likely than nonprofessional staff and volunteers to influence SMOs to engage in tactics that have organizational maintenance functions rather than strictly instrumental goals because they have organizational skills that they want to use and develop.

Coalition Work

The formalization of social movement organizations also has implications for coalition work within movements. In my sample, formalized SMOs have played the dominant roles in lasting coalitions (see Tables 5 and 6). Coalitions among formalized SMOs are easier to maintain than are coalitions among informal SMOs or between formalized and informal SMOs because formalized SMOs typically have staff persons who are available to act as organizational representatives to the coalition and routinely coordinate the coalition work. Just as paid staff can be relied on to carry out maintenance tasks for SMOS, they can also be relied on to maintain contact with the representatives of other SMOs in a coalition. When all of the SMO representatives are paid staff, coordination is easiest. While volunteers can represent SMOs in coalitions, it is more difficult to keep volunteers in contact with one another and to coordinate their work, particularly in the absence of a formalized coalition organization with paid staff of its own. Thus, paid staff help to maintain coalitions, thereby lessening the organizational problems of coalition work (see Staggenborg 1986, p. 387).

The experiences of the Illinois Pro-Choice Alliance (IPCA), a Chicago-based coalition organization, reveal the impact of organizational structure on coalition work. Formalized movement organizations, including NARAL of Illinois and Chicago NOW, have played a major role in this coalition, while informal organizations, such as Women Organized for Reproductive Choice (WORC), have had a difficult time participating in the coalition. One past director of the Illinois Pro-Choice Alliance recognized this problem, commenting in an interview:

> . . . there is a real difference between groups which have paid staff and the grassroots groups which are all volunteers. The groups with paid staff have a lot more opportunity to participate [in the coalition]—even trivial things like meeting times create problems. The groups with paid staff can meet in the Loop at lunch time—it makes it easier. Also . . . people from the grassroots groups tend to be intimidated by the paid staff, because as volunteers the grassroots people are less informed about the issue. Whereas for the staff, it's their job to be informed, and they have the resources behind them. . . . I think too that the grassroots people have higher expectations about what can be done. They're volunteers who may have worked all day, then they do this in the evenings; they're cause-oriented and they expect more out of people and projects. Paid staff are the opposite in that they work on the issue during the day and then want to go home to their families or whatever at night and leave it behind. They want to do projects with defined goals and time limits, projections as to the feasibility and all that. Not that paid staff are not committed people. I think it's good to have a balance between the grassroots and staffed groups. Without the grassroots people, I think things would be overstructured; with just the grassroots people, well, there's too much burnout among them. The staffers tend to last a lot longer. (Personal interview)

These perceptions are borne out by the difficulties of Women Organized for Reproductive Choice in trying to participate in the IPCA. WORC members interviewed also spoke of the problems they had attending IPCA meetings at lunchtime in downtown Chicago, a time and place convenient for the staff of formalized SMO members of the coalition but difficult for WORC members, who tended to be women with full-time jobs in various parts of the city.

Another reason for the difficulty is that the coalition has focused on institutionalized lobbying activities, tactics for which WORC members have neither the skills nor the ideological inclination. Efforts by WORC to get the coalition to engage in a broader range of tactics, including direct-action tactics, have been unsuccessful. On the national level, the Reproductive Rights National Network had nearly identical problems participating in the Abortion Information Exchange coalition (see Staggenborg 1986). Formalized SMOs play an important role in maintaining coalitions, but they also influence coalitions toward narrower, institutionalized strategies and tactics and make the participation of informal SMOs difficult.

Conclusion

While professionalization of leadership and formalization of SMOs are not inevitable outcomes of social movements, they are important trends in many movements (cf. McCarthy and Zald 1973, 1977; Gamson 1975, p. 91). There is little evidence, however, that professional leaders and formalized SMOs will replace informal SMOs and nonprofessionals as the initiators of social movements and collective action. While systematic research on the influence of different types of movement leaders is needed, my data show that the roles of entrepreneur and professional manager are in some cases distinct. This is because environmental opportunities and preexisting organizational bases are critical determinants of movement mobilization; movement entrepreneurs do not manufacture grievances at will, but are influenced by the same environmental and organizational forces that mobilize other constituents. Contrary to the arguments of McCarthy and Zald (1973, 1977), nonprofessional leaders and informal SMOs remain important in initiating movements and tactics that are critical to the growth of insurgency (cf. McAdam 1983).

Professionalization of leadership has important implications for the maintenance and direction of social movement organizations. My data suggest that professional managers, as career activists, tend to formalize the organizations they lead in order to provide financial stability and the kind of division of labor that allows them to use and develop their organizational skills. Once formalized, SMOs continue to hire professional managers because they have the necessary resources. Contrary to the arguments of Piven and Cloward (1977), formalized SMOs do not diffuse protest but play an important role in maintaining themselves and the movement, particularly in unfavorable environmental conditions when it is difficult to mobilize constituents. Formalized SMOs are better able to maintain themselves than are informal ones, not only because they have paid staff who can be relied on to carry out organizational tasks, but also because a formalized structure ensures continuity despite changes in leadership and environmental conditions. Thus, a movement entrepreneur who prevents formalization by maintaining personal control over an SMO may ultimately cause the organization's demise. A movement that consists solely of informal SMOs is likely to have a shorter lifetime than a movement that includes formalized SMOs. Similarly, a coalition of informal SMOs has less chance of survival than a coalition of formalized SMOs.

While formalization helps to maintain social movements, it is also associated with the institutionalization of collective action. Formalized SMOs engage in fewer disruptive tactics of the sort that pressure government authorities and other elites to make concessions or provide support than do informal SMOs. Formalized SMOs also tend to select strategies and tactics that enhance organizational maintenance. Given the prominent role of professional managers in formalized SMOs, these findings raise the Michels ([1915] 1962) question of whether formalized organizations with professional leaders inevitably become oligarchical and conservative, as Piven and Cloward (1977) argue. Based on my data, I dispute the conclusion that formalized SMOs necessarily become oligarchical. In fact, many seem more democratic than informal SMOs because they follow routinized procedures that make it more difficult for individual leaders to attain disproportionate power. As Freeman (1973) argues, "structureless" SMOs are most subject to domination by individuals.

The tendency of formalized SMOs to engage in more institutionalized strategies and tactics than informal SMOs might be interpreted as a conservative development, given findings that militant direct-action tactics force elite concessions (cf. Jenkins and Eckert 1986). Informal SMOs, with their more flexible structures, are more likely to innovate direct-action tactics. However, the institutionalization of movement tactics by formalized SMOs does not necessarily mean that movement goals become less radical; an alternative interpretation is that movement demands and representatives become incorporated into mainstream politics. For example, the National Organization for Women is now an important representative of women's interests in the political arena. While the long-term implications of

this phenomenon for the social movement sector and the political system require further investigation, it is certainly possible for formalized SMOs to exert a progressive influence on the political system.

Finally, my research raises the question of whether movements inevitably become formalized or institutionalized, as suggested by classical theories of social movements, which argue that movements progress through stages toward institutionalization (see Lang and Lang 1961; Turner and Killian 1957 for discussions of such stage theories). In the case of the pro-choice movement, there has clearly been a trend toward formalization. As Gamson (1975, p. 91) notes, there does seem to be a kernel of truth to theories that posit an inevitable trend toward bureaucratization or formalization. However, as Gamson also notes, "the reality is considerably more complex" in that some SMOs begin with bureaucratic or formalized structures and others never develop formalized structures. Although neither Gamson nor I found cases of SMOs that developed informal structures after formalization,[13] such a change is conceivable under certain circumstances (e.g., if nonprofessional staff are hired to replace professional managers, a development most likely at the local level). Classical theories of the "natural history" of a movement focus on the institutionalization of a movement as a whole and ignore variations in the experiences of different SMOs within the movement. My research shows that SMOs vary in the ways in which they deal with internal organizational problems and changes in the environment. Formalization is one important means of solving organizational problems, particularly as SMOs grow larger; however, SMOs can also develop alternative structures. Important variations exist within the two broad categories of SMO structure that I have identified; further empirical research on leadership roles and SMO structures and their impact on organizational goals and activities is necessary.

Notes

1. Manuscript collections used include the Women's Collection at Northwestern University, which contains newsletters and documents from NARAL, RCAR, ZPG, CWLU, ICMCA/ARA/ NARAL of Illinois, and several coalitions; the papers of ICMA/ARA/NARAL and Chicago NOW at the University of Illinois, Chicago; the CWLU papers at the Chicago Historical Society; the Lawrence Lader pa-

pers at the New York Public Library; the public portions of the NARAL and NOW papers at the Schlesinger Library of Radcliffe College; and private papers provided by informants.

2. Volunteers may be "professionals" in the sense that they spend many years, perhaps a lifetime, doing movement work. However, they differ from professional managers in that they do not earn a living through movement work.

3. The term bureaucratic might be substituted for "formalized" (cf. Gamson 1975). However, I have used the latter because SMOs are never as bureaucratic as more established organizations such as corporations and government agencies (cf. Zald and Ash 1966, p. 329).

4. I have used the term *informal* to describe this type of SMO structure for want of a more positive label. The terminology of the existing literature on organizations and social movements is inadequate. The term *classical* used by McCarthy and Zald (1973, 1977) does not describe the structure of the SMO. The more descriptive term *grass roots* implies a mass membership base that may or may not be present in either "formalized" or "informal" SMOs. The term *collectivist* used by Rothschild-Whitt (1979) refers to a specific type of decision-making structure which is distinguished from "bureaucratic" organization; not all informal SMOs are collectivist. Freeman's (1979, p. 169) term *communal* for "small, local, and functionally undifferentiated" organizations is inappropriate because not all informal SMOs are local organizations.

5. An appendix with further details on sample SMOs is available on request from the author.

6. The distinction between such formalized SMOs and interest groups or lobbies is not a sharp one (cf. Useem and Zald 1982). There is clearly a need for greater conceptual clarification of the differences between formalized SMOs and interest groups based on empirical research.

7. The conflict between entrepreneurial and professional roles also became apparent to me when I interviewed the anti-abortion leader Joseph Scheidler as part of another study. Scheidler helped to form several anti-abortion groups and was fired as executive director from two organizations for engaging in militant direct-action tactics without going through the proper organizational channels (see Roeser 1983). He finally founded his own organization in 1980, the Pro-Life Action League, in which he is unencumbered by bureaucratic decision-making procedures. As he told me in a 1981 interview:

> I don't like boards of directors—you always have to check with them when you want to do something—and I was always getting in trouble with the board. So I resigned, or they fired me, however you want to put it, because they didn't like my tactics. . . . The Pro-Life Action League is my organization. I'm the

chairman of the board and the other two board members are my wife and my best friend. If I want to do something, I call up my wife and ask her if she thinks it's a good idea. Then I have two-thirds approval of the board! (Personal interview)

Additional examples of such conflict between the entrepreneurial and professional roles in the social movements literature can be cited. In the farm worker movement, there has been conflict over the leadership of Cesar Chavez, who attempted to maintain personal control over the United Farm Workers at a time when others wanted to create a more bureaucratic union structure (see Barr 1985; Jenkins 1985a, pp. 204-6). In the gay rights movement, the "brash" activist Randy Wicker left the New York Mattachine Society to found "the Homosexual League of New York, a one-man organization designed to give him a free hand to pursue his own plans" (D'Emilio 1983. pp. 158-59). In the environmental movement, Friends of the Earth founder David Brower was ousted from the organization after he failed in his attempts to maintain control over the SMO and prevent it from becoming formalized (Rauber 1986). And in Mothers Against Drunk Driving (MADD), there has been conflict over the role of MADD's entrepreneur, Candy Lightner, who has attempted to maintain personal control over a bureaucratizing organization (Reinarman 1985).

8. By all accounts this leader had an extraordinary ability to recruit volunteers for various tasks. As one of my informants explained, "She was really effective at getting people to do things. She would keep after you so that it was easier to do what she wanted rather than have her continue to bug you." Another activist concurred. "There was nothing like having her call you at 7 a.m. and tell you what you were going to do that day!" The problem of reliance on the personal characteristics of this director was later recognized by a board member who commented that the problem with the long-time director was that she kept knowledge about the organization "in HER head" (document in private papers), making it difficult for her successor to assume control.

9. The "house meeting" tactic, which involved holding meetings in the homes of NARAL members or other interested persons, was a recruitment tool developed as part of a national NARAL grassroots organizing program.

10. The delay experienced by Women Organized for Reproductive Choice in obtaining the 501(c)3 tax status that allows a nonprofit organization to obtain tax-deductible contributions also reveals the difficulties that informal SMOs have with organizational maintenance. Although there were several local Chicago foundations willing to fund organizations such as WORC, the SMO was unable to take advantage of

these opportunities for some time because it had not obtained the necessary tax status. When I asked WORC's sole part-time, nonprofessional staff leader why the tax status had not been obtained, she replied that the delay occurred because she was the only one who knew how to apply for the status, but that she simply had not had the time to do it yet.

11. Abortion-referral activities were regarded by many activists as a militant means of challenging the system (see Lader 1973). In the case of women's movement projects such as the CWLU Abortion Counseling Service, there was an attempt to create an alternative type of organization as well as to serve the needs of women.

12. *The Silent Scream* attempted to use sonography to make its case that the fetus suffers pain in an abortion. The film was distributed to members of Congress and received a great deal of media attention, helping to shift the debate on abortion to "scientific" issues.

13. Although it never developed a structure that could be called formalized, one SMO in my sample, Women Organized for Reproductive Choice, did become even more informal as it became smaller. ✦

33

Black Radicalization and the Funding of Civil Rights: 1957-1970

Herbert H. Haines

Nearly all social movements divide into "moderate" and "radical" factions at some point in their development, although the meaning of these labels is continually changing. Bifurcation has occurred, for example, in the U.S. labor movement (Rayback, 1966), the women's movement (Freeman, 1975), the anti-nuclear movement (Barkan, 1979), and the black revolt in the United States (Allen, 1969; Killian, 1972). Analysts of social movements have largely neglected how radical groups alter the context in which moderate groups operate. In other words, what happens to moderates when radicals appear? Does a backlash ensue? Or do policymakers and other important audiences become more receptive to moderate claims? In the face of militant challenges, do moderates find it easier or more difficult to pursue their goals?

These questions are complex, and they touch upon an issue which is crucial to understanding social movements and social issues: the relationships between factionalism and responses to competing varieties of collective action. Though theoretically important, this issue has received little attention from sociologists and political scientists. This paper addresses these topics by examining changes in the funding of civil rights organizations in the United States during the late 1950s and the 1960s—a period when portions of the black movement were becoming increasingly militant in both their goals and their tactics. The paper begins with a discussion of the sparse literature dealing with the effects of radical factions on moderate groups. Following this brief review, I will describe the escalation of the goals and tactics of organized black activists during the twentieth century. I will then present and discuss data on the funding of civil rights organizations during the period from 1957 through 1970. Although white reactions to black collective action during those turbulent times were diverse, these data will show that radicalization of segments of the black community had the net effect of improving the resource bases of more moderate civil rights organizations by stimulating previously uninvolved parties to contribute ever increasing amounts of financial support.

Theoretical Background

Activists and scholars alike have suggested that the activities of radicals in a social movement can undermine the position of moderates by discrediting movement activities and goals, and by threatening the ability of moderates to take advantage of the resources available from supportive third parties. I refer to this general backlash as the *negative radical flank effect.* The history of social movements in the United States provides several examples of the fear of such negative effects among movement participants. Moderate abolitionists of the early 19th century worried that antislavery extremists would discredit their cause and delay the emancipation of black slaves (Nye, 1963). Groups opposed to nuclear power plants have expressed the fear that violent or obstructionist tactics and efforts to expand the movement to embrace nuclear disarmament and anti-corporatism will hurt the immediate goal of stopping nuclear power development (Barkan, 1979). Some scholars have suggested that black radicalization and rioting during the 1960s weakened the position of such mainstream civil rights groups as the National Association for the Advancement of Colored People (Masotti *et al.,* 1969; Muse, 1968; Powledge, 1967). Others have blamed the failure of the Equal Rights Amendment on the statements and actions of militant feminists (Felsenthal, 1982).

Conversely, a *positive radical flank effect* can occur when the bargaining position of moderates is strengthened by the presence of more radical groups. This happens in either (or both) of two ways. The radicals can provide a militant foil against which moderate strategies and demands are redefined and normalized—in other words, treated as "reasonable." Or, the radicals can create crises which are resolved to the moderates' advantage. Freeman (1975) has argued that mainstream reformist women's organizations would have been dismissed as "too far out" during the late

"Black Radicalization and the Funding of Civil Rights: 1957-1970." *Social Problems* 32:31-43. Copyright © 1984 by the Society for the Study of Social Problems. Reprinted with permission.

1960s and the early 1970s had it not been for more radical groups: lesbian feminists and socialist feminists appear to have improved the bargaining position of such moderate groups as the National Organization for Women. Ewen (1976) and Ramirez (1978) have suggested that demands by the labor movement for an eight-hour day and collective bargaining became negotiable only after the emergence of serious socialist threats in the early 20th century. Others have argued that the emergence of black militants in the 1960s helped to increase white acceptance of nonviolent tactics and integrationist goals (Elinson, 1966; Killian, 1972).

An understanding of radical flank effects would greatly enhance current social movement theory.[1] The literature on social and political movements abounds with more or less casual references to these effects, and they have been frequently debated by movement activists; but they have received almost no systematic attention. Gamson's (1975) research represents the most direct investigation of the effects of factionalism on protest outcomes. He examined the conditions under which groups came to represent a set of constituents and managed to gain "new advantages" for those constituents. Among the many conditions Gamson examined was the existence of moderate and radical groups championing the same broad issues. He tested—and rejected—the hypothesis that the existence of more militant organizations enhanced the success of less militant organizations. Gamson's test is less than conclusive for several reasons. There were measurement and coding problems (Goldstone, 1980). He examined only 30 groups. Labor unions were over-represented in the sample. And, most important, he focused upon only two dimensions of reactions to moderate organizations: (1) the designation of a group as a legitimate representative for a group of constituents; and (2) the group's success in winning significant benefits for its constituents. While these dimensions are important, a number of others remain to be examined. Radical groups might, for example, increase or decrease the level of public *awareness* of moderate groups. They might alter public *definitions* of moderates as more or less "extreme," "reasonable," or "dangerous." Radicals might increase or decrease moderates' *access to decisionmakers*. And, finally, radical flank effects might influence the capacity of moderate groups to *attract resources* from supporters who are not members of the moderate groups

themselves. This paper focuses upon the last of these dimensions.

The Black Revolt in the United States

The black revolt in the United States after the Second World War is well-suited for studying radical flank effects because it involved a variety of organizations, ideologies, and strategies, and has experienced rapid tactical and rhetorical escalation, especially during the 1960s. This section briefly traces the escalation of black insurgency, highlighting those movement transformations upon which radical flank effects were based.

The National Association for the Advancement of Colored People (NAACP) was the preeminent organizational representative of black interests in the United States from its incorporation in 1910 to the Supreme Court's landmark school desegregation decision in 1954. Other organizations existed, such as the National Urban League, the Commission on Interracial Cooperation (renamed the Southern Regional Council in 1944), and Marcus Garvey's Universal Negro Improvement Association. But none of these matched the NAACP in long-term influence. The NAACP functioned mainly as a legal group; its primary tactic was litigation. Initially, the NAACP did not challenge legalized racial segregation and discrimination. Well into the 1930s it aimed to ensure equality of rights and facilities under the "separate but equal" doctrine established in *Plessy v. Ferguson* (1896), rather than to attack the doctrine outright. During the 1930s, however, this goal changed. The NAACP launched a protracted campaign of litigation, culminating in *Brown v. Board of Education of Topeka* (1954), in which the Supreme Court invalidated segregation in public schools. Thereafter, the nature of the black revolt was fundamentally transformed.

Prior to 1954, many groups in the United States periodically defined and attacked the NAACP as a radical organization. This was especially true in the southern states, where many blacks also regarded the NAACP's approach to racial justice as militant. The NAACP's integrationist philosophy and program of aggressive litigation *was* rather "radical" in those times.

When white resistance prevented the kinds of sweeping changes that many blacks expected the Supreme Court's desegregation ruling to produce, the movement changed. So did the characteristics of what was called "militancy." Ideologically, the radicals of the late 1950s remained dedicated to racial integration and close to the spirit of U.S. political philosophy—i.e., they sought assimilation and reform, not "revolution." Tactically, however, they were very different. Organizations such as the Southern Christian Leadership Conference (SCLC) and the Congress of Racial Equality (CORE) called for nonviolent direct action—marches, picket lines, boycotts, and the like—to challenge discrimination. Ostensibly, nonviolent direct action worked by appealing to an opponent's latent sense of right and wrong. In practice, however, direct action was usually successful only when it created crises that the white community could not afford to ignore. Direct action was infrequent during the late 1950s but, beginning with the student sit-ins of 1960, it became a popular and widespread tactic in the first half of the 1960s. The Student Nonviolent Coordinating Committee (SNCC) joined the SCLC and CORE as major proponents of nonviolence. Then SNCC quickly drifted into militant voter registration and community organizing activities. These three organizations occupied positions on the radical end of the black political spectrum during the early 1960s. The NAACP and the Legal Defense and Educational Fund (LDEF), whose tactics continued to be limited largely to litigation, were by this time better classified as middle-of-the-road or moderate. The National Urban League was the most conservative of the national black organizations.

During the mid 1960s the predominance of nonviolent integrationism broke down, and militancy was transformed once again. As violence erupted in the black ghettos of northern cities and as many black activists began questioning the assimilationist orientation of the civil rights movement, leaders such as Martin Luther King and organizations such as the SCLC were increasingly defined as moderate or, at the very least, as "responsible" militants (Meier, 1965:55). *Real* militancy came to imply a separatist or nationalist outlook and an acceptance of retaliatory violence against an intransigent white power structure. One should not overgeneralize, for there were indeed several different types of black radicalism during the mid 1960s (Allen, 1969). Nevertheless, most black radicals rejected racial integration and strict nonviolence to some degree. Major proponents of the "new" black radicalism after 1966 were the Student Nonviolent Coordinating Committee, the Black Panther Party, the Revolutionary Action

Movement, the Republic of New Africa, and, to a far lesser extent, the Congress of Racial Equality.

While it is clear that black moderation and radicalism evolved during the 1950s and 1960s, students of black collective action are divided over its effects on the civil rights mainstream. Masotti *et al.* (1969:174), Muse (1968), and Powledge (1967), among others, contend that the escalation of black radicalism damaged the position of black moderates by strengthening white resistance to black claims and undermining black-white coalitions. Others have suggested that black radicalization not only failed to weaken moderates but actually enhanced the respectability of established leaders and organizations, thus increasing their ability to bargain for gradual reform (Elinson, 1966:371; Hough, 1968:224; Meier, 1965; Oberschall, 1973:230).

It is probably impossible to settle this debate in any conclusive manner; it relates to a multidimensional issue, and both positions undoubtedly contain at least a grain of truth. No scholar, however, has yet examined organizational funding patterns in light of radical flank effects.

The Importance of Outside Resources

Prior to the 1970s, most scholars tried to explain the emergence of collective action in terms of participants' motives. But as theoretical and empirical problems have emerged in such explanations (Gurney and Tierney, 1982; Jenkins and Perrow, 1977; McAdam, 1982), scholars began focusing on the organizational needs of social movements—especially the need to mobilize material and non-material resources (Jenkins and Perrow, 1977; Lipsky, 1968; McCarthy and Zald, 1973, 1977). Since many aggrieved populations lack the resources necessary to wage large-scale collective challenges, resources obtained from outside supporters are frequently essential. The utility of the resource mobilization perspective is still being debated (McAdam, 1982:23), but it has been rather firmly established that organized conflict cannot operate for long on shared discontent and moral commitment alone. Thus, an understanding of processes which affect a movement organization's ability to mobilize resources would be useful. Unfortunately, resource mobilization theorists have had rather little to say on this subject (McAdam, 1982:21).

Resources may include such material things as money, land, labor (Tilly, 1978:69), or facilities

(McCarthy and Zald, 1977:1220). But less concrete resources—including "authority, moral commitment, trust, friendship, skills, habits of industry" (Oberschall, 1973:28)—may also be valuable resources for collective action.

While it would be a mistake to equate resources solely with money, I believe money can serve as a convenient index of radical flank effects. I assume that outside supporters contribute money or other resources only to those movement organizations which they consider acceptable. Supporters need not totally approve of the organization to contribute to it. Rather, they need only have a perceived interest in supporting the cause and they need only define the movement organization as an acceptable beneficiary. I also assume that acceptability is a *relative* thing. A movement organization's acceptability may be largely a function of the relative acceptability/unacceptability of *other* movement organizations. I use the levels of outside financial support obtained by a given social movement organization as rough indicators of the organization's acceptability to financial supporters.

Bearing all of this in mind, one can conceive of several hypothetical effects of radical groups on resource mobilization by moderate groups. Each would be expected to produce a distinct pattern in outside contributions to moderate organizations. We would expect *negative* radical flank effects—backlashes caused by radicals—to produce *declines* in the outside incomes of moderate groups (or a leveling of prior patterns of increasing moderate incomes) following significant ideological or tactical escalations by more radical groups. We would expect *positive* radical flank effects, on the other hand, to produce *increases* in the outside incomes of moderate groups (or a leveling of prior patterns of decreasing moderate incomes) following such escalations. The absence of significant changes in the outside incomes of moderate organizations during periods of radical escalation would indicate an absence of radical flank effects or a balancing of positive and negative effects.[2]

There are two subtypes of positive radical flank effects. One of these occurs when the radicalization of an established organization—such as the Congress of Racial Equality or the Student Nonviolent Coordinating Committee—causes some of its outside supporters to defect to less extreme organizations. If this were to occur, increases in outside income to moderate groups would match decreases in outside income to radical groups. In other words, a fixed sum of total movement income would be redistributed. The second subtype, and the one which is more significant in theory, involves moderate income gains *in excess* of radical group losses. Here we have not merely a redistribution of a fixed sum of resources but also the infusion of new resources into moderate coffers in response to radicalization. My data indicate that this in fact occurred among civil rights organizations during the 1960s.

Data

To examine the relationship between radical flank effects and financial support, I set out to gather detailed information on resource mobilization by major black movement organizations during the 1950s and the 1960s. The ideal data would include total income broken down by its sources for each year and each organization. No such data have been compiled by students of the civil rights movement. The authors of organizational histories (Carson, 1981; Meier and Rudwick, 1973; Parris and Brooks, 1971; St. James, 1958) and of more general works on the movement (Brisbane, 1974; Muse, 1968) have provided limited information on the funding of particular organizations. None of these sources, however, contains data that are sufficiently systematic, detailed, and complete for an examination of radical flank effects.

I have used McAdam's (1980, 1982) data on movement income, which he compiled, not to study radical flank effects, but to determine the usefulness of resource mobilization theory as an explanation of the civil rights movement. McAdam was unable to obtain much information from primary sources such as organizational files and records. Consequently, he relied upon estimation and interpolation from incomplete secondary sources. In an effort to improve upon his data, I obtained financial information on major civil rights organizations during the period from 1952 through 1970, including two that he did not examine: the National Urban League and the Southern Regional Council.[3] I sought data for each of the following major black organizations active during the 1950s and the 1960s: Congress of Racial Equality (CORE); NAACP Legal Defense and Educational Fund, Inc. (LDEF); National Association for the Advancement of Colored People (NAACP); National Urban League (NUL); Southern Christian Leadership Conference (SCLC); Southern Regional Council (SRC); and Student Nonviolent Coordinating Committee (SNCC).

Table 1
Total Outside Income of Major Movement Organizations, 1952-1970

Year	NUL	NAACP	LDEF	SRC[a]	SCLC	CORE[k]	SNCC	Total Movement Income
1952	NA	NA	210,624[c]	27,495		4,604		
1953	NA	16,436	224,321[c]	35,735		5,989		
1954	NA	30,944	200,021	59,403		5,600		
1955	NA	40,606	NA	79,308		6,911		
1956	265,000[b]	NA	346,947	31,369		10,115[l]		
1957	265,000[b]	103,907	319,537	109,062	10,000[d]	15,506		
1958	265,000[b]	90,679	315,081	138,274	10,000[d]	15,506		823,012
1959	265,000[b]	93,703	357,988	162,285	25,000[e]	55,324		923,000
1960	265,000[b]	103,838	489,540	139,106	54,756	130,609	5,000[o]	1,187,849
1961	257,000	96,936	560,808	NA[f]	193,168	213,248	14,000[o]	1,475,160
1962	572,000	81,547	669,427	168,247	197,565	244,034	71,927[p]	2,004,747
1963	1,221,000	251,579	1,197,204	161,311	728,172	437,043	302,894	4,299,203
1964	1,539,000	292,579	1,425,321	180,005	578,787	694,588	631,439[q]	5,341,848
1965	1,824,000	388,077	1,661,793	101,105	1,643,000[g]	677,785	637,736[q]	6,933,496
1966	2,201,000	597,425	1,695,718	NA[r]	932,000	400,000[m]	397,237[s]	6,324,485
1967	2,812,000	1,294,909	2,046,356	138,670	932,000[h]	280,000[n]	250,000[o]	7,753,935
1968	3,921,000	1,904,512	2,535,430	269,112	1,000,000[i]	250,000[n]	150,000[o]	10,030,054
1969	8,619,000	2,418,000	2,811,825	204,591	500,000[j]	670,000[n]	50,000[o]	15,273,416
1970	14,542,000	2,665,373	2,980,998	174,321	400,000[j]	210,000[n]	25,000[o]	20,997,692

Notes:

a. Data on the Southern Regional Council relate to the organization's general fund only. Surviving financial reports prior to 1964 do not list information on special projects. I have excluded special projects income from the figures for 1964 through 1970 to permit trend analyses. It should be kept in mind that this seriously deflates SRC income during the mid and late 1960s.

b. I could not find any information for the National Urban League prior to 1961. According to Parris and Brooks (1971:394), NUL income during the mid- and late 1950s fluctuated between $209,000 and $315,000. In order to compute movement totals for those years, I have adopted the rather inelegant procedure of estimating yearly income midway between these two figures. The figure of $265,000 is a gross estimate only and should not be taken to mean that there were no changes in NUL income between 1956 and 1960.

c. This represents net income after fundraising expenses were deducted. LDEF financial reports for 1952 and 1953 do not list either fundraising expenses or gross income.

d. This is an impressionistic estimate of the SCLC's outside income derived from various primary and secondary materials.

e. This figure is an estimate based upon receipts for organizational contributions to the SCLC during 1959. The total rests upon my estimate that no more than $4,500 in individual contributions were received. During its early years, the SCLC received hundreds of individual contributions, most of which ranged from $2 to $5.

f. In order to derive a total movement income, I arbitrarily set SRC's outside income for 1961 at $140,000. This is probably somewhat lower than the actual figure, given the trend of previous years.

g. This figure is an estimate. The SCLC's income data for fiscal year 1964-1965 are available only for the first ten months (83.3 percent) of that year. I reduced the total income for the year as reported in the final audit by 9.8 percent, which was the proportion of the previous year's total income which came from outside sources. This yielded an amended fiscal year 1965 estimated income of $1,409,335.40. This figure, in turn, was increased by 16.6 percent (the estimated income for the two remaining months) to produce the estimated figure shown.

h. This figure is an estimate which was derived from various partial financial reports. It may exclude a limited amount of income from benefit concerts, etc.

i. This figure is an estimate.

j. SCLC income estimates for 1969 through 1970 are adapted from McAdam (1982), by permission of the author.

k. CORE's fiscal year ran from June 1 to May 31. My examination of monthly and quarterly CORE financial reports yielded no reliable manner in which to adjust these figures to a calendar year basis.

l. This figure is an estimate based upon a percentage of total CORE income for 1956 of $12,000 as reported by Meier and Rudwick (1973:78). The percentage, 82 percent, is taken from the internal/external ratio of the previous year.

m. See Meier and Rudwick (1973).

n. CORE income figures for 1967 through 1970 are based upon estimates by McAdam (1982). Each, however, includes foundation grants located in my search through *Foundation News* (Haines, 1983). Consequently, the numbers are somewhat higher than McAdam's estimates, especially for 1969.

o. McAdam (1982:253).

p. The SNCC income for 1962 is taken from Student Nonviolent Coordinating Committee (N. d.).

q. These figures are estimates. I divided external income for 10 months of each year (which is all that has survived) by 10 to yield a n estimated average monthly income. This is interpolated to yield the estimated yearly income.

r. SRC outside income for 1966 is missing. For purposes of producing a movement total, I arbitrarily set it at $101,105, the income of the previous year.

Table 2
Annual Rate of Growth in Outside Income, As a Percentage of Preceding Year[a]

Year	NUL	NAACP	LDEF	SRC[b]	SCLC	CORE	SNCC	Total Movement
1952								NA
1953	NA	NA	6.5	30.0		30.1		NA
1954	NA	88.2	NA	66.2		−6.5		NA
1955	NA	31.2	NA	33.5		23.4		NA
1956	NA	NA	NA	−60.5		46.4		NA
1957	NA	NA	−7.9	247.7	NA	53.3		NA
1958	NA	−12.7	−1.4	26.8	0.0	47.9		2.3
1959	NA	3.3	13.6	−8.7	150.0	141.2		9.7
1960	NA	10.8	36.7	10.2	119.0	136.1		28.7
1961	−3.0	−6.6	14.6	NA	252.8	63.3	180.0	24.2
1962	122.6	−15.9	19.4	NA	2.3	14.4	414.6	35.9
1963	113.5	208.5	78.8	−4.1	268.6	79.1	321.1	114.5
1964	26.0	16.4	19.1	11.6	−20.5	58.9	108.5	24.3
1965	18.5	32.6	16.6	−43.8	183.9	−2.4	1.0	29.8
1966	20.7	53.9	2.0	NA	0.0	−30.0	−37.1	−8.8
1967	27.8	116.7	20.8	NA	0.0	−30.0	−37.1	22.6
1968	39.4	47.0	23.9	94.1	7.3	−10.7	−40.0	29.4
1969	119.8	27.0	10.9	−24.0	−50.0	168.0	−66.7	52.3
1970	68.7	10.2	6.00	−14.8	−20.0	−68.7	−50.0	37.5

Notes:
a. Based on data in Table 1.
b. General fund only.

In 1981 I wrote to each of the organizations which still existed—all of them except SNCC, which had disappeared by 1972—requesting the necessary information. Only the National Urban and the Southern Regional Council provided the data. I subsequently examined the financial records of the NAACP and the Legal Defense and Educational Fund at their respective headquarters in New York City. I obtained partial funding data on the Southern Christian Leadership Conference, the Congress of Racial Equality, and the Student Nonviolent Coordinating Committee at the Martin Luther King Library and Archives in Atlanta, Georgia.

My attempt to improve upon McAdam's data yielded mixed results. I was unable to obtain even total outside income from some organizations during certain years—for the National Urban League before 1961, for the NAACP in 1956, for the Legal Defense and Educational Fund in 1955, and for the Southern Regional Council in 1966. The Southern Christian Leadership Conference and the Congress of Racial Equality refused to divulge their financial records, thus forcing me to rely upon sometimes incomplete archival material.[4] In general, I obtained the best data from those organizations most commonly designated as moderate: the NUL, the LDEF, the NAACP,

and the SRC. Fortunately, these are the organizations whose incomes comprise the dependent variants for this research.

Findings

Table 1 shows the total outside incomes of the major black organizations from 1952 to 1970.[5]

The organizations are arranged from left to right according to their moderation/militancy over the years; e.g., the National Urban League has long been the most moderate of the groups, while SNCC was the most militant. The Southern Christian Leadership Conference and SNCC were founded in 1957 and 1960, respectively. Data for the National Urban League (1952 through 1955) and the NAACP (1956) were not available. Therefore, I restrict my discussion and analysis to the years 1957 through 1970.

Two characteristics of the data in Table 1 deserve attention. First, the older, more established, and generally more moderate organizations —the National Urban League, the NAACP, and the Legal Defense and Educational Fund—received more outside income than other groups which were younger and more militant. Secondly, the incomes of the NUL, the NAACP, and the LDEF grew steadily during the 1960s. The incomes of the SCLC, CORE, and SNCC, on the other hand, grew rapidly during the early 1960s and then rapidly declined during the second half of the decade. Total movement income, however, increased steadily after 1957. (Combined totals for 1952 through 1956 are unavailable due to the lack of National Urban League figures for those years). With the exception of 1966, total movement income never failed to increase. During the 1950s, total income remained relatively constant.[6] During the early 1960s, and especially in 1963, it began to grow rapidly. Spectacular leaps occurred in 1963, 1969, and 1970.

Table 2 shows the relative magnitude of income growth for each of the seven organizations and for the movement as a whole. The greatest increase, 114.5 percent, occurred in 1963. Aside from that year, the greatest proportionate increases occurred at the end of the 1960s.

Table 3 shows the distribution of the total movement's outside income among the seven organizations. The National Urban League and the Legal Defense and Educational Fund received the largest shares of outside income during the late 1950s and the early 1960s. The LDEF received the most outside funding in 1957. By 1970, its share had declined considerably, but its raw income had not (Table 1). The NAACP's share of outside income declined during the late 1950s and early 1960s but recovered somewhat during the middle part of the 1960s. Most astonishing of all, however, is the National Urban League's staggering increase, especially during the late 1960s, when it

became the financial giant of black collective action. All of the more militant organizations—the Southern Christian Leadership Conference, the Congress of Racial Equality, and the Student Nonviolent Coordinating Committee—increased their shares of total movement income during the early 1960s, then entered a period of decline.

These changes in organizational shares of total movement income may be understood largely in terms of shifts in major sources of funding which took place during the 1960s. Unpublished analyses I have made of the data on which this paper is based (Haines, 1983, 1984) suggest that elite contributors became vastly more important money sources for moderate black organizations during the second half of the decade. Among these elite contributors were corporations, foundations, and the federal government.

Corporations were rather slow in becoming supporters of black collective action, but their involvement grew as the movement entered its nonviolent collective action phase around 1960. But business contributions became truly large only after successive summers of urban rioting (Colin, 1970). While several black organizations benefited from corporate donations after 1967 (Colin, 1970:73), the National Urban League provides perhaps the best illustration. In 1962, such contributions amounted to only $153,000. By 1970, they had risen to $1,973,000 (Haines, 1984a:18). Similarly, Cohn (1970) reports that the NAACP received considerable amounts from corporate

Table 3
Distribution of Outside Income as a Percentage of Total Movement Income[a]

Year	NUL	NAACP	LDEF	SRC	SCLC	CORE	SNCC	Total
1957	32.2	12.6	38.8	13.3	1.2	1.9		100
1958	31.5	10.8	37.4	16.4	1.2	2.7		100
1959	28.7	10.1	38.8	13.7	2.7	6.0		100
1960	22.3	8.7	41.2	11.7	4.6	11.0	0.4	100
1961	17.4	6.6	38.0	9.5[b]	13.1	14.5	.09	100
1962	28.5	4.1	33.4	8.4	9.9	12.2	3.6	100
1963	28.4	5.9	27.8	3.8	16.9	10.2	7.0	100
1964	28.8	5.5	26.7	3.4	10.8	13.0	11.8	100
1965	26.3	5.6	24.0	1.5	23.7	9.8	9.2	100
1966	34.8	9.4	26.8	1.6[b]	14.7	6.3	6.3	100
1967	36.3	16.7	26.4	1.8	12.0	3.6	3.2	100
1968	39.1	19.0	25.3	2.7	10.0	2.5	1.5	100
1969	56.4	15.8	18.4	1.3	3.3	4.4	0.3	100
1970	69.2	12.7	14.2	0.8	1.9	1.0	0.1	100

Notes:
a. Derived from the data in Table 1.
b. Based on estimated outside income

sources after 1967, but I can provide no independent verification of this due to the lack of such information in its Annual Reports.

Foundations also played an increased role in funding black organizations during the 1960s. As the black struggles of the 1960s progressed and as the militancy of the black population grew, foundation contributions became major sources of income for the National Urban league, the Southern Regional Council, and the Legal Defense and Educational Fund—all moderate organizations. In 1970, these three received an estimated total of $7,143,534 in foundation gifts, up from $1,461,264 in 1964 (Haines, 1984a:23). Not only was more money directed by foundations to moderate black groups as the decade wore on, but more foundations became involved and a much higher number of individual grants were made. On all of these dimensions, the increases in foundation involvement in funding black collective action and related activities far outpaced the *overall* expansion of foundation activity which occurred during the same time (Haines, 1984a:30-32).

One of the moderate organizations, the National Urban League, became the recipient of large amounts of federal government money during the late 1960s. While these funds were for NUL-run programs for the disadvantaged, not "contributions" in the conventional sense of the word, they were nevertheless unique among the seven major organizations and deserve to be mentioned. No federal money was channeled through the NUL until 1965. During that year, the League received $294,000 from the U.S. government. By 1970, the total had risen to $6,913,000, and it topped $13,000,000 in 1970.

Discussion

The most significant finding of the study is the dramatic increase in the level of outside funding for the civil rights movement as a whole during the 1960s (Table 1). Little increase in outside funding took place during the 1950s, when black radicalism was largely equated with litigation aimed at integration and when nonviolent protest was rare. But as nonviolent action became more frequent and intense during the early 1960s, outside funding accelerated. The year during which nonviolent direct action seems to have reached its dramatic zenith, 1963 (Burstein, 1979:169 Carson, 1981:90), was also the year of the steepest climb in outside income (Table 2). Outside supporters, it seems, were "discovering" civil rights. Income continued to climb until 1966, when it dropped for the first time. This was the year during which Stokely Carmichael of SNCC popularized the black power slogan. Ghetto rioting continued during the summer, drawing media attention. The income slump of 1966 probably reflected a decline in white support due to controversy surrounding the movement. It was, however, only a temporary setback for the movement as a whole. Total outside income resumed its upward spiral during the late 1960s. In fact, yearly proportionate increases for 1969 and 1970 surpassed all other years except 1963 (Table 2). In dollar amounts, these increases were unprecedented. Thus, it was clear that urban violence and black power did not have a negative radical flank effect, at least when measured by outside funding. On the contrary, the data suggest that there was a positive radical flank effect.

During the 1960s, and especially after 1966, three moderate organizations—the National Urban League, the Legal Defense and Educational Fund, and the NAACP—received increasingly greater shares of the movement's total outside funding. Not only did these three organizations suffer no financial backlash in the turbulent years of rioting and black nationalism, but their outside incomes rose more rapidly than ever before. The most moderate of the groups, the National Urban League, received a late-1960s windfall that was nothing less than astounding. Together, the NUL, the LDEF, and the NAACP accounted for all of the aggregate increases in combined movement income by the end of the 1960s. The radical organizations, on the other hand, received rapid increases in outside income during the early 1960s followed by equally rapid declines during the era of the new militancy.

McAdam (1982:208) argues that the level of outside funding for the civil rights movement depended heavily upon the relative acceptability of the organizations involved in the struggle. This, of course, is what I have suggested and is quite consistent with the notion of positive radical flank effects. McAdam suggests that, as movement goals and tactics became more radical around 1965 and 1966, outside support groups came to see the NAACP as virtually the only acceptable recipient of funding. Consequently, the NAACP's outside income rose rapidly. While my procedures for distinguishing between the NAACP's outside and internal income differ from those employed by

McAdam, my data bear out his conclusions about the NAACP's enhanced respectability. My data do suggest, however, that McAdam is wrong to conclude that the NAACP emerged from the fray of the mid 1960s as the *only* acceptable recipient of funding. To McAdam, the National Urban League did not qualify as a "civil rights organization" and consequently he did not examine its income trends. Regardless of how sociologists classify the NUL, it clearly fit the bill as well as or better than the NAACP did in the eyes of many outside donors.

The shift in outside funding from 1965 to 1970 was more than a zero-sum shift within the community of movement organizations, as McAdam's discussion (1982:208) might be taken to imply. That is, it was not merely a case of a fixed amount of outside money being reallocated among a fixed number of recipients. On the contrary, there was a vast increase in total outside funding as well as a greater concentration of resources in the coffers of two moderate organizations. This is vitally important. Had such moderate organizations as the National Urban League, the NAACP, and the LDEF done no more than pick up the funds that CORE and SNCC (and, to a lesser degree, the SCLC) had forfeited by virtue of their militancy, we would not have a true positive radical flank effect as I have conceived it. Rather, we would simply have a case of an intra-movement shuffling of resources, consistent with the fixed-total subtype. My data suggest that the radicalization of some factions of the civil rights movement increased the total amount of outside financial contributions in a variable-total manner. This is precisely what we would expect a positive radical flank effect to do to the financial support structure of a movement.

Conclusion

I have analyzed trends in resource mobilization by major civil rights organizations in order to test the hypothesis of radical flank effects. Admittedly, the approach which I have used lacks many of the essential characteristics of a controlled investigation. But rather than formally testing an hypothesis, I have sought to examine how the data fit the models of positive and negative radical flank effects. This analysis yields three findings:

1. The total amounts of money contributed to the seven organizations by outsiders increased dramatically during the late 1950s and the 1960s. It peaked during the turbulent late 1960s.

2. The increases in total movement income, especially during the late 1960s, primarily reflected vast increases in the incomes of moderate groups.

3. The increased income of the moderate groups did not result from a mere reallocation of a fixed sum of resources within the movement. Rather, it involved the injection of large amounts of new money into the moderate groups. Most of this new money came from elite white groups, which became increasingly important sponsors of moderate civil rights activity.

These findings suggest that positive radical flank effects contributed significantly to increases in the outside funding of moderate civil rights organizations in the 1960s. The increasing importance of corporations, foundations, and the federal government, moreover, suggests that a portion of the nation's corporate elite recognized that it had a crucial interest in pacifying the black population, particularly in the volatile cities, and in accommodating certain manageable black demands. It also suggests that many previously uninvolved groups were "enlightened" by the glow of burning cities, after years of indifference to nonviolent cajoling by the National Urban League and the NAACP. Some whites came to realize that the integration of blacks into the U.S. mainstream was not such a bad idea after all, that it was in their own best interests given the more radical alternatives, and that it was something they ought to be encouraging with their resources. The prime beneficiaries of such changes of heart were the big moderate groups, the very organizations that had become most concerned with an impending white backlash. Certainly, a white backlash did occur. But the data presented in this paper suggest that, beneath it all, there was occurring an important acceptance and facilitation of "reasonable" black activism and that the effort would not have been made without the progressive radicalization of large numbers of blacks in the United States.

This conclusion suggests a new question: are radical flank effects unique features of the black revolt, or might they be overlooked but critical factors in numerous social movements? I strongly suspect that they affected the course of the U.S. labor movement, and they may have been involved in the ill-fated campaign for the Equal

Rights Amendment. The difficulties in identifying positive and negative radical flank effects with confidence are considerable. Financial data, which serves as a measure of only one limited dimension, may be difficult to find for other movements. But these difficulties are not insurmountable, and if we are to understand collective action more completely, we need to carry on the search for evidence of radical flank effects.

Notes

1. Radical flank effects are relevant, for example, to the debate between the resource mobilization model of protest and that of Piven and Cloward (1977, 1978). The resource mobilization perspective stresses the dependence of protest groups on the resources available from third parties (Jenkins and Perrow, 1977; Lipsky, 1968). Implicit in this model is the notion that protest groups must refrain from tactics and statements which would alienate prospective supporters. Piven and Cloward, on the other hand, suggest that reliance on such resources only undermines protest goals and that protest groups can succeed by tactics of mass disruption. Positive radical flank effects in protest movements provide a link between the two; under certain circumstances, moderate groups might well be able to maintain good relations with supporting groups by distancing themselves from the disruptive activities of radicals while at the same time profiting from the crises that they create.

2. Obviously, radical flank effects are not the only factor which might affect rates of resource mobilization. Decisions to contribute funds for collective action are complex, and a more complicated multivariate research design would be necessary in order to make truly confident propositions about radical flank effects on resource mobilization. Factors such as the state of the economy and the competition from other movements also need to be considered.

3. For purposes extending beyond the topic of this paper, I also made a concerted effort to obtain figures that were broken down by the following donor categories: (1) government agencies; (2) corporations and other business firms; (3) charitable foundations; (4) labor organizations; (5) churches and religious organizations; (6) other types of organizations; (7) members, chapters, or branches (i.e., internal sources); and (8) nonmember individual contributors (Haines, 1983).

4. The otherwise excellent collections of original SCLC and SNCC materials which are maintained at the Martin Luther King Library and Archives contain only incomplete financial information. Surviving materials of the Congress of Racial Equality are somewhat better, but post-1967 information is missing. Even those existing organizations which have generally maintained the most complete and detailed financial records have lost older material. The National Urban League is unable to locate financial reports for years prior to 1961. The SRC, the NAACP, and the LDEF have also lost financial records for a few years of the 1950-1970 period.

5. I used different approaches to determining outside income for each organization. The *National Urban League* provided yearly income totals derived from several categories of donors, including "affiliate dues," "special events," and "other." I eliminated these three categories, leaving only income derived from strictly external sources. Income for the *Southern Regional Council* was taken directly from financial reports supplied by the SRC and the Atlanta University Archives. SRC figures appearing in Table 1 include "contributions from SRC members and friends" but do not include "members dues," fees, sales, subscriptions, and the like. Miscellaneous outside income, such as honoraria and overhead from grants, is included. In calculating the *NAACP*'s outside income, McAdam (1980:52) merely subtracted regular branch memberships from total organizational income. I used a more conservative approach, excluding all receipts from branches and miscellaneous income such as interest and dividends. For the *Legal Defense and Educational Fund*, I subtracted interest and dividends as well as the proceeds from the sale of securities. The *Southern Christian Leadership Conference* is not a membership organization, and from what little I could find out about the group's methods of fundraising, I think I can safely assume that little error results from treating all of its income as exogenous. I have done so for the most part, although funds of a clearly internal nature have been eliminated from the data when identified. The *Congress of Racial Equality*'s financial records make it difficult to distinguish accurately between income from internal and external sources. In most cases, for example, local CORE chapters were not set apart from other, non-CORE organizations, and their meager contributions to national CORE's coffers were simply lumped into the "organizations" category. Nevertheless, CORE chapters were notorious for their reluctance to contribute to the national office, so little is lost, I believe, in subtracting convention income, sales, and the like from outside income. *Student Nonviolent Coordinating Committee* records are even less specific than those of CORE, and I used a nearly identical procedure to determine SNCC's outside income.

6. The characterization of the 1950s trend as relatively constant suffers, of course, from my lack of an absolute baseline. While I lack estimates of the incomes of the National Urban League and the NAACP for 1952, I believe it is reasonable to estimate total movement outside income for that year is not more than $450,000 (Table 1). Assuming that this were true, the proportionate increase between 1952 and 1957 would have been nearly 83 percent. Such a growth rate over six years is not inconsiderable, yet the total amounts are so small in comparison to later years that the increases seem unspectacular. ✦

34

Factionalism, Group Defection, and Schism in the Hare Krishna Movement

E. Burke Rochford, Jr.

Introduction

Over the past two decades there has been an enormous amount of scholarly research addressing questions of recruitment and conversion to religious movements (Beckford & Richardson, 1983; Rambo, 1982; Snow & Machalek, 1984). Much of this research centers on the expansion efforts of a variety of new religious movements in America and worldwide (Barker, 1984; Beckford, 1985; Bromley & Shupe, 1979a; Downton, 1979; Rochford, 1985; Wallis, 1977). This outpouring of research has only recently been accompanied by investigations of the other side of the membership and conversion issue: how and why some previously committed adherents of new religions defect from their respective religious groups.

Studies of disengagement from new religions have largely turned traditional psychofunctional frameworks of recruitment and conversion on their heads.[1] Defection is treated as an individual experience involving a breakdown in the ideological and/or cognitive linkage between a convert's values and beliefs, and the religious doctrines and practices of the group. Defection is thus characterized as a process of falling from the faith" (Brinkerhoff & Burke, 1980; Bromley, 1988), or as an outcome of dissonance problems leading to deconversion" (Jacobs, 1984, 1987; Skonovd, 1983; Wright, 1983a, 1984).

In recent years, new religious groups have experienced organizational change involving institutionalization, on the one hand, and decline and failure, on the other (Bromley & Hammond, 1987; Robbins, 1988: 100-33). Internal conflict

and factionalism have also grown as members have sought to challenge policies and practices initiated by leaders (Balch & Cohig, 1985, cited in Wright, 1988; Ofshe, 1980; Rochford, 1985; Wallis, 1982; Wallis & Bruce, 1986). In turn, this conflict has produced more visible, if not new, forms of disengagement from new religions. On an individual level there are fringe members, dissidents, and apostates; on a group level, oppositional factions, schismatics, and ex-member support groups. Despite the existence of both individual and collective forms of disengagement from new religions, we know much less empirically and theoretically about the latter. For example, two recent classification schemes of disaffiliation by Richardson *et al.* (1986) and Robbins (1988: 88-99) do not consider collective forms of disengagement.

This paper attempts to further empirical and conceptual understanding of *collective* forms of disengagement from new religious movements. Following a number of recent calls for an integration of traditional and resource mobilization approaches (Ferree & Miller, 1985; Jenkins, 1983: Zurcher & Snow, 1981), I focus on the dual role of ideology and structure in the development of the Hare Krishna movement.[2] As we move empirically from individual to collective forms of disengagement, psychofunctional theories of defection need to be integrated with conceptual frameworks which bring structural and organizational factors to the forefront. While structural/organizational influences have been considered in some work on defection (Jacobs, 1984, 1987; Skonovd, 1981, 1983; Wright, 1983b), they have been largely reduced to factors promoting individual decisions to exit, such as the creation of dissonance problems for the convert.

This paper describes empirically the events and social forces giving rise to factionalism, group defection, and schism in the aftermath of the death of ISKCON's founding charismatic leader. My analysis of factionalism demonstrates how conflict emerged within the context of long-standing cleavages. My analysis of group defection and schism points to the influence of infrastructural supports and deficits (McCarthy, 1987; Zald & Berger, 1978) in determining modes of exit from exclusive and deviant religious organizations like ISKCON. This analysis also demonstrates the ways in which both structural and ideological concerns can interact to undermine

"Factionalism, Group Defection and Schism in the Hare Krishna Movement." *Journal for the Scientific Study of Religion* 28:162-179. Copyright © 1989 by the *Journal for the Scientific Study of Religion.* Reprinted with permission.

micromobilization in schismatic religious organizations, leaving them vulnerable to failure. In the broadest sense, this case study looks at the sources of insurgency and the fate of movements of exit" (Hirschman, 1970) as they seek to establish themselves as independent sectarian organizations.

After clarifying the setting and methods used for this research, I divide the remainder of the paper into three main sections. The first section discusses the succession crises arising within ISKCON's Los Angeles community following the death of the movement's founder, A. C. Bhaktivedanta Swami Prabhupada in 1977. The second details the developments which culminated in factionalism and group defection from the Los Angeles ISKCON community. The third section focuses on the emergence, mobilization efforts, and ultimate failure of the *kirtan* Hall, an incipient sectarian organization founded in Los Angeles by a group of ex-ISKCON members in 1979. The paper concludes with a number of theoretical implications suggested by this field study.

Setting and Method

Data for this paper were collected over a five-year period (1975-1981). While I have visited and conducted research in 10 ISKCON communities throughout the United States, the major part of my data comes from the Krishna community in Los Angeles. In conducting the research, I observed and participated in the Krishna lifestyle and religious practices, lived within the community for days at a time, and worked in the community's school as an assistant *gurukula* teacher.[3] (For a more detailed account of the methods used in this portion of the research see Rochford, 1985: 6-9, 21-42; 1988). Participant observation was also carried out with a group of former ISKCON members who defected in Los Angeles after the death of ISKCON's founding guru. It is this portion of the research which comprises the major data source for the present paper.

In June of 1980, I became reacquainted with a former ISKCON devotee whom I had known over a three-year period before his defection in 1978. He invited me to become a charter member of an organization which he and a handful of other ex-ISKCON members were starting in Los Angeles. The Kirtan Hall, he explained, would serve as an alternative organization, both for the growing number of ex-ISKCON members residing in Los

Angeles, and for others developing an interest in Krishna Consciousness.

I participated in the activities of the Kirtan Hall throughout the summer and autumn of 1980, attending virtually all of the group's twice-weekly meetings. During this period, I was able to interview formally and informally the leaders of the organization as well as most of its other members. All of the approximately 20 members of the group had been ISKCON adherents for six years or longer. Several had been involved in ISKCON as many as 10 or 12 years. One of the leaders was among the first 12 disciples initiated into Krishna Consciousness by Prabhupada in New York City. In the autumn of 1980, the Kirtan Hall disintegrated because of declining interest, an inability to recruit new members, and the move of one of the group's three founders to another state.

Prabhupada's Death: Crisis and Politicization

In November of 1977, ISKCON's founding guru died in Vrndavana, India, after a long illness. Prabhupada's death proved to be a major turning point in the development of ISKCON in America and worldwide. Just prior to his death, Prabhupada appointed 11 of his closest disciples to serve as gurus responsible for initiating new members into Krishna Consciousness and for helping to oversee the affairs of ISKCON's communities worldwide. Within months after ISKCON's spiritual and political reorganization, the movement began to experience the first of what would prove to be a series of succession problems culminating in factionalism, growing numbers of defections, and schism. Challenging groups, made up of former ISKCON members and dissident devotees who remained within ISKCON, combined against the new leaders. In 1980, four of ISKCON's new gurus were sanctioned by the movement's Governing Body Commission (GBC). One of the four broke with ISKCON, taking along as many as 100 of his disciples. By the end of 1980, ISKCON faced a level of internal conflict which threatened its viability as a movement-organization. (For more details on ISKCON's succession problems see Rochford, 1985: 221-55).[4]

The succession crises following Prabhupada's death were not uniformly felt throughout ISKCON (Shinn, 1987a: 129). Although all of ISKCON's communities were somewhat adversely affected, a handful (e.g., Los Angeles,

New York, Berkeley) experienced serious and on-going social conflict. As one of ISKCON's leaders from the east coast described it, the Los Angeles ISKCON community was at the center of the political controversy during the late 1970s.

> I remember devotees coming from LA and it was like Chicken Little, The sky is falling." We [devotees in the East] would say, Wait a minute, it's not that bad." They were surprised to find that things here were not that polarized. We came to think of that kind of talk as the LA doomsday philosophy. . . . LA had the most political reactions of anywhere in our whole society worldwide. (Philadelphia member, 1982)

The reason for the intensity of conflict in Los Angeles related most strongly to issues of power. Between 1978 and 1980, there was ongoing and sometimes bitter conflict between the local leadership and various factions of community members. The community witnessed numerous defections, and the purging of a number of devotees who refused to submit to the policies of the leadership, leading ultimately to the formation of conflict groups (Rochford, 1982, 1985). The depth of the anti-leadership feeling was expressed in a 1980 letter written by unidentified members of the Los Angeles community to Ramesvara Swami, the spiritual and administrative head of ISKCON's communities in the western United States.

> As you are well aware, a body of community members has been meeting for the past few weeks for the purposes of attempting to address some of the fundamental problems which face the New Dwarka community and the Movement in general. . . . We are very much desirous of seeing some of the long standing problems of the community solved through progressive dialogue. The breakdown in adequate communication is one of the principal difficulties. . . . If you do not take good advice on how to solve the problems of the community your opulence and reputation will decrease. Why? Because so many qualified men . . . will go away. After all, you have given so many invitations to good men from time to time to leave the community. Many more will gradually follow that path, feeling there is no scope for change here.
> . . .

As Stark and Bainbridge have noted, conflict resulting in factionalism and schism tends to occur in the context of subnetworks that existed prior to the outbreak of dispute" (1985: 101). Such was the case in the politicization of the Los Angeles ISKCON community following Prabhupada's death: Pre-existing interest groups mobilized in an effort to reform the community's economic infrastructure. At issue was ISKCON's long-standing practice of combining money-making with missionary work through the distribution of the movement's religious texts in public places, a process called *sankirtana*. By 1977, revenues from book distribution had begun to decline, while the public backlash against ISKCON's public-place strategies was peaking (Rochford, 1985: 171-89, 1987a, 1987b).

In the years preceding Prabhupada's death, some ISKCON members in Los Angeles sought to diversify the community's economic base in hopes of raising more revenue, on the one hand, and restoring sankirtana to its traditional missionary function, on the other. These efforts were largely unsuccessful, however, because Prabhupada steadfastly believed that book distribution would continue to provide for ISKCON's financial needs. In fact, Prabhupada actively discouraged efforts to develop business enterprises in Los Angeles because he thought they would undermine book distribution (Rochford, 1985: 295). With Prabhupada's death, deepening economic problems, and growing public opposition, two challenging groups in Los Angeles again mobilized to push for economic reform in 1978.

The Bhaktivedanta Fellowship comprised approximately 20 male businessmen. Several of the group's members were independent entrepreneurs, although the majority held management positions within ISKCON-owned businesses such as Spiritual Sky Scented Products and Bhaktivedanta Book Trust. The group was led by an ISKCON member who owned a successful travel agency. The fellowship became progressively political and strategically confrontational when its economic policy recommendations were rebuffed by the local ISKCON leadership. Within less than a year, the majority of the Fellowship's members abandoned ISKCON. Some defected, but most joined forces with the Fellowship's leader to begin an independent Krishna conscious community. Twenty to 25 families from the Los Angeles ISKCON community purchased 300 acres of land in the foothills of the Sierra Nevada in central California. The group lived in trailers, experimented with alternative forms of technology, and by all accounts continued to live a Krishna conscious lifestyle.[5]

The second challenging group was known as the Conch Club. This group was made up of eight to 10 male householders" (i.e., married devotees with families), most of whom had previously worked on the staff of ISKCON's *Back to Godhead* magazine. During the previous year, the president of the Conch Club, and one other member of the group, had been dismissed from the editorial staff of the magazine in the face of charges that their recent articles had treated the movement's theology in an overly liberal fashion. After their dismissal from the magazine's staff, neither was offered gainful employment within the community.

The Conch Club, like the Bhaktivedanta Fellowship, met with opposition from local leaders. Unlike the Fellowship, however, the Conch Club altered its initial objectives and began laying plans for defection. One year after their defection members of the Conch Club organized themselves and other ex-ISKCON members into an incipient sectarian organization. The remainder of the paper traces the development of the Conch Club, both within ISKCON and beyond, as its members sought to establish themselves in conventional society while still preserving portions of their Krishna beliefs and lifestyle. Studying the career of this group allows for understanding empirically and theoretically the processes promoting group defection and the problems faced by schismatics as they seek to build a sectarian organization.

Conflict Group Formation and Defection

The initial purpose of the Conch Club was to develop economic strategies to alleviate ISK-CON's deepening financial problems. Members shared the opinion that the financial future of ISK-CON rested on diversifying the movement's economic base. As the president of the Conch Club explained:

> So the [Conch] Club was developed out of people who had similar business interests. In the beginning it was a pretty straight kind of rotary club, very much in connection with ISKCON. We were *vaisnava* businessmen interested in helping the movement. (Los Angeles member, 1980)

Despite its initial alignment with ISKCON, the Conch Club soon came into conflict with the local ISKCON leadership. Ramesvara Swami, a long-time advocate of book distribution, continued to see ISKCON's financial future as directly tied to the distribution of Prabhupada's religious texts (Rochford, 1985: 225; Shinn, 1987 a: 111). These differences in economic policy placed the members of the Conch Club in political conflict with Rames-

vara Swami. Rather than push for its economic policies, the group chose instead to back away from its initial objectives. As the following statement by the Conch Club's founder suggests, the group's purpose changed rather dramatically.

> We got less and less concerned with our initial purpose and more and more concerned with just developing our psychological strength. . . . We just started to get together as friends. We went through a thing that I suppose a lot of devotees do when they first move out [defect from ISKCON]; they start remembering the old rock-and-roll. You know, we started in the '60s and took a month or two or three right up to the music of the present. Just feeding ourselves again with those lovely passionate sounds that meant so much to us and gave us so much energy and inspiration and was part of the development that brought us to Krishna Consciousness. . . . We started sitting down together playing chess and watching basketball on TV for hours on end. It was just a way of affirming once again a continuity in time, a continuity in history, a personal development which started long long ago was now continuing . . . . (Los Angeles member, 1980)

While the Conch Club served as a structure where members could bridge or reframe their cognitive orientations to their past lives in the conventional society (Goffman, 1974; Snow *et al.,* 1986),[6] the group also allowed its members an opportunity to discuss personal issues which cast doubt on ISK-CON, if not on Krishna Consciousness itself. One major issue had to do with ISKCON's strict prohibitions against sexual relations.

> [In the Conch Club] we could talk as friends talk. Not like devotees talk. There is a big difference between saying, Oh Prabhu, I have such sex desires. I am lower than the lowest. I'm a straw in the street." There is a big difference between that and saying, Oh man, look at that piece of ass. . . ." I mean you can't say that in the [ISKCON] community. You'll shock the *shikas* off the *bramacharies.* And you can't quite admit it to yourself either. . . . We learned an enormous amount about ourselves. . . . (Los Angeles member, 1980)

Members of the Conch Club also spoke at length about issues of independence and how their lives within ISKCON had not allowed for making individual judgments and decisions. ISKCON's exclusive structure and centralization of power had limited their ability to maintain a sense of control over their personal and spiritual lives. As the president of the Conch Club described it, it was this desire for personal independence which most concerned him and other members of the group.

I realized that my life within the *ashram* was of no more use to me spiritually. . . . It was very apparent that the further development of my spiritual life depended on my ability to choose my behavior. In order to have the ability, I had to gain economic independence from ISKCON. I knew that the kind of choices I wanted to make required making money, drawing a paycheck each week. I had to have money so I could have a car. . . . To live in an apartment I had to have money to pay for it. I wanted to work, to be responsible in terms of that work and my own life. So this was a big issue for all of us in the Conch Club. This was the only way we were going to gain independence from ISKCON, independence from the *swamis*. (Los Angeles member, 1980)

In sum, the Conch Club served as a mediating structure" (Robbins, 1981: 214-15) between ISKCON and the conventional secular society, allowing members to reconstruct their worldview in preparation for exiting. The group prepared its members ideologically for defection by bridging the two familiar, but previously unconnected and seemingly incongruent, frames.[7]

The Conch Club served its members socially, as well as ideologically, in their preparation for defecting from ISKCON. The social support provided by the group to each of its members is expressed in the following statement by a Conch Club member:

The Conch Club became an important source of support as each of us began to consider leaving ISKCON. We talked a lot about how it would be and what we would do. Let's face it, leaving [ISKCON] felt like a big risk to all of us. Many of us had been in the movement for many, many years. . . . In the end, we all left in roughly the same period. We started our own little community not far from the [ISKCON] Temple and we tried to help each other get over the whole ISKCON trip. (Los Angeles, 1980)

All the members of the Conch Club and their families defected from ISKCON within months of each other in the autumn and early winter of 1978. They established their own community in an apartment complex just a few blocks from the local ISKCON community. Three of the men found work together in a local publishing firm. Two others gained employment at a mortgage company. The women spent their days together tending to the needs of their children. Socially, their lives were tied to one another, and to a few other ex-ISKCON members who lived in the area near the ISKCON community. They often collectively attended the Sunday feast at the temple and could be found occasionally worshipping alongside committed ISKCON members during morning or evening services.

Although the members of the Conch Club and their families had defected from ISKCON, they continued to view themselves as Krishna devotees. Their reasons for leaving were motivated largely by political and economic concerns, rather than by serious spiritual misgivings or backsliding. In keeping with this desire to retain their devotee status, members of the Conch Club continued to use the Sanskrit names given them by their Spiritual Master and made reference to themselves as ex-CONS" rather than ex-devotees."

The Growth and Development of the Kirtan Hall

Within a year after leaving ISKCON, three of the original members of the Conch Club began planning what was to become the Kirtan Hall. Over a nine-month period in 1979 and 1980, they debated what the purpose, structure, and beliefs of the new organization would be. In the end they decided that the group should provide for the participation of a wide spectrum of people, whether former ISKCON members or other persons with emerging interests in Krishna Consciousness. As one of the founding trustees explained:

The idea [behind the Kirtan Hall] is to incorporate Americanism within spiritual life. We want people to stay within their daily lives. I mean the whole idea of people searching, like in the '60s, for a guru and some new lifestyle is dead. The guru concept is what is hurting ISKCON now. We want to create an organization where people can participate in a democratic way. . . . This is something ISKCON has gone away from with these gurus. (Los Angeles member, 1980)

The formal charter of the Kirtan Hall likewise emphasized the inclusive and denominational quality of the group:

(Purpose #1) To provide a friendly environment where peoplewhether the priestly type, those pursuing a professional career, or those simply earning an honest livingmay worship Krishna, the Supreme Personality of Godhead, by feasting, dancing, and chanting the Holy Name. (Charter for Lord Chaitanya's Kirtan Hall, 1980)

Originally a core group of 15 men and women met, along with their children, twice weekly in the home of one of the Kirtan Hall's founders. Attendance at the meetings tended to fluctuate between six and 30 adults. On average, a group of 10 adults and a half-dozen or more children would be present. Members collectively chanted, played music and danced, discussed the philosophy of Krishna Consciousness, and feasted on vegetarian foodstuffs.

The meetings in various ways mirrored ISKCON's beginnings in New York City in 1966 (see Goswami, 1980; Rochford, 1982: 402-03). Under the influence of one of Prabhupada's first disciples in the U.S., the *kirtans,* or chants, were simple, involving variations on the Hare Krishna mantra; the music was popular in character, and the discussions wide-ranging and accepting in tone rather than dogmatic. An excerpt from my field notes provides a flavor of the meetings and the group's accommodative style:

> Following Govinda's reading of Srila Prabhupada's purport from the *Bhagavad Gita* the discussion centered on the need for people to change their consciousness in order to be devotees of Krishna. As Rupa explained to the gathering: You can continue to engage the senses as long as you change the consciousness involved. Do what you must do in your life but do it for Krishna. You don't have to change your clothes, your job, nothing like that; just change your consciousness. God is merciful." (Los Angeles member, 1980)

During my months of participant observation, the Kirtan Hall gained only three new members who attended meetings on a regular basis. Without exception, those joining were former ISKCON members residing in the Los Angeles area. In the weeks prior to the demise of the Kirtan Hall, a feeble attempt was made to bring fresh blood" into the group. One of the leaders requested that for the next meeting everyone should bring a friend. Everyone nodded in agreement, but at the next meeting not even one new face was present. Nothing was said about the obvious failure and the meeting proceeded as usual.

The failure of the Kirtan Hall as an incipient sectarian organization was strongly influenced by its ineffective mobilization. Critical to successful adherent mobilization is the presence of lines of communication (Jackson *et al.,* 1960; Freeman, 1973) and cooptable networks (McCarthy, 1987; Snow *et al.,* 1980; Stark & Bainbridge, 1980) which link potential supporters to a movement's membership. Resource mobilization theorists refer to these dimensions of social structure as social infrastructural supports" (McCarthy, 1987; Tilly, 1978; Zald & McCarthy, 1987a). The presence or absence of infrastructural supports strongly influences the course and prospects of any social

movement organization (Zald & McCarthy, 1987b: 45; Jackson *et al,* 1960).

Stark (1987: 22-23) emphasizes that new religions can succeed only if they combine dense internal networks with open networks radiating outward into the surrounding society. A pattern of dense internal attachments provides the basis of group commitment and solidarity; open networks facilitate the work of recruitment. Successful religious groups are able to maintain the delicate balance . . . between internal and external attachments" (Stark, 1987: 23). Below, I consider the microstructural and ideological factors which constrained the Kirtan Hall's mobilization efforts, leaving it vulnerable to failure.

Microstructural Constraints on Recruitment

Members of the Kirtan Hall had strong ties with other ex-ISKCON devotees, and in some cases with still-committed ISKCON members, but had only weak" ties (Granovetter, 1973) with non-devotee acquaintances and co-workers. As I have already explained, their work lives and personal lives were entangled with one another as they sought to limit ties with others beyond their ex-member circle of friends. This process of differential association and differential identification" (Simmons, 1964: 254) effectively insulated them from at least some of the inevitable pulls" on their faith exerted by the conventional secular society. This pattern of relationships served, however, to limit their involvement to people who were largely unwilling or otherwise unavailable for membership in the Kirtan Hall.

Over the course of my research, only one young woman having no previous commitment to ISKCON attended group meetings. She was a co-worker of two of the Kirtan Hall's founders. She attended five meetings, asked many questions about Krishna Consciousness (for example, regarding its overly strict sexual proscriptions), but finally dropped out. She did report turning to vegetarianism during her period of involvement. Before actually departing from the group, she had suggested on several occasions that her husband was unhappy with her participation in the Kirtan Hall.

The Kirtan Hall's lack of success in mobilizing potential supporters through conventional interpersonal ties was also a function of having inherited ISKCON's public image as a peculiar and threatening cult. (See Liebman *et al.,* 1988: 344,

on how the development of a schismatic movement may be linked to the characteristics of its
parent religious group.) Members of the Kirtan
Hall consciously avoided telling others about
their prior involvement in ISKCON and about
their continuing interest in Krishna Consciousness. As one Kirtan Hall member stated, I just
can't risk telling people at work about Krishna; I
can talk about religious values and acting in a
Godly fashion but people would freak out if they
knew I was a devotee." As a result, network ties
in the workplace and beyond were only weakly
available for cooptation" (McCarthy, 1987: 59).

Fewer than one dozen still-committed ISK-
CON members attended a Kirtan Hall meeting,
each making only a single appearance. Although
I anticipated that at least a few of the ISKCON
members who attended would in time defect from
ISKCON and become involved in the Kirtan Hall,
none ever did. Despite the fact that several were
outspoken critics of ISKCON's spiritual and political reorganization, nevertheless they chose to
remain within the local ISKCON community. My
interviews and conversations with five of them revealed a degree of optimism that ISKCON's internal political problems were being resolved. All
explained that, while they had a number of good
friends who were members of the Kirtan Hall,
they would not risk being ostracized from the local ISKCON community by being aligned with
the new group.

Another factor which limited the appeal of the
Kirtan Hall to dissident ISKCON members was
the absence of a central charismatic figure to lead
the group. The Kirtan Hall prided itself on its
democratic governing structure, but without charismatic leadership the group lacked the principal
form of authority legitimating schism" (Wallis,
1979: 186). As a result, the group had no claim to
supernatural legitimation.

The ex-ISKCON members who attended the
Kirtan Hall tended to display two patterns of involvement: Most attended one or two meetings
before dropping out; others attended meetings
sporadically, expressing little or no interest in becoming formal members. The latter cited their desire to take part in the *kirtan* as the sole basis for
their occasional attendance.

When asked why they chose not to join the
Kirtan Hall, all of the ex-ISKCON members interviewed cited one of two reasons. About one-
third (N = 4) of the 15 interviewed reported that

they still held out some hope that ISKCON would
right itself spiritually and politically, making it
possible for them to return as ISKCON members.

> Radha reported that her husband did not want her
> to attend any more of the Kirtan Hall meetings.
> 'He said that it wasn't all over with ISKCON. We
> had to think about how devotees in the [ISKCON]
> community would feel. [He told me] if I want to
> worship, go to the Temple.' (Los Angeles mem-
> ber, 1980)

The majority (N = 11) of the ex-ISKCON members who chose not to continue their participation
in the Kirtan Hall expressed a general resistance to
joining another religious organization. One night
after a lecture the following rather heated exchange
took place between one of the leaders of the Kirtan
Hall and an ex-ISKCON member who had attended
meetings on two other occasions.

> As the meeting was nearing an end Jaya leaned
> over and suggested to Prabhu that he look over the
> Kirtan Hall charter. Prabhu responded with some
> feeling, No. I'm not interested in any charter. I
> didn't come here to join. I heard from Bhakta [an-
> other ex-ISKCON member] that there was going
> to be a *kirtan* here tonight. I love the *kirtan* but I
> don't want to join anything. After ISKCON I have
> had enough." (Los Angeles member, 1980)

Frame Maintenance and Ideological Work

While the Kirtan Hall suffered from ineffective mobilization because its members lacked access to cooptable networks, it also failed at recruitment because of ideological considerations. By
turning inward to assure the continuation of their
own faith, members of the Kirtan Hall effectively
abandoned recruitment as an organizational objective. The practical and ongoing focus of members centered largely on problems of internal
frame maintenance (Snow *et al.*, 1986: 478). Ultimately, the group spent the majority of its time
and energies involved in what Bennett Berger
(1981) calls ideological work."

Although the ex-ISKCON members of Kirtan Hall had attained some measure of insulation
from the larger secular culture, through what
might be called circumstantial work," or the creation of a social environment consistent with individual and group beliefs, they still faced the reality
of having to adapt to some of the demands of living and working in the conventional world. Moreover, many members of the Kirtan Hall did not desire to forsake all aspects of the material society.
Most members occasionally attended the cinema,
some consumed drugs and alcohol, and most

seemed willing to abandon what they saw as the unrealistic" sexual proscriptions to which they had previously adhered.

Bennett Berger (1981: 20-21) argues that apparent contradictions between behavior or lifestyle and ideology are threatening to the believer. While the believer can sell out" and accommodate his or her unconventional beliefs to the dominant worldviews most defectors from new religions in time do other adaptations are possible. As Berger describes them, these latter solutions involve ideological work on the part of individuals or groups.

> . . . a group may struggle against oppressive circumstances to make its beliefs more probably realizable; in this case ideological work is likely to attempt to mobilize the energies of believers in behalf of the struggle. Or . . . a group may accommodate its beliefs to the circumstances it cannot alter, while manipulating those it can to achieve the best bargain it can get. . . . All of these solutions require ideological work. (1981: 21)[8]

Many Kirtan Hall meetings involved discussion about what members called dovetailing." Dovetailing is a form of ideological work in which individuals and groups attempt to provide a sense of coherence and continuity" between everyday activity and belief (Berger, 1988: 37). The term was often used by Prabhupada as he instructed his followers that the material world should not be rejected but rather used in Krishna's service (Goswami, 1980: 82-86). In other words, a devotee of Krishna can be involved in material, secular activities as long as these pursuits are for Godly purposes. As a leader of the Kirtan Hall explained to the gathering one evening:

> Devotees appear, to the uninformed, to be involved in material activity but, in fact, they are liberated. Their activities are not generating *karma* because they have accepted Krishna, they are Krishna conscious. . . . Of course, we all must find a way to escape the material world, that is for sure. But there are liberal and conservative styles of getting out. So one should not just think that [being saved from the material world] requires renunciation. Because another way of getting out is to engage positively the objects and energy of the material nature in Krishna's service. By so doing one transforms matter into spirit. (Los Angeles member, 1980)

Following the formal presentation of Prabhupada's commentaries on the *Bhagavad Gita,* it was normal for those present to discuss the problems they encountered in dovetailing their ongoing life activities with their Krishna beliefs. One evening, a member of the Kirtan Hall raised these concerns:

> I find it more difficult to dovetail now that I am away from the Temple. It's harder to know if you're really dovetailing. Before, I could just go to the Temple President with my ideas and check them out. I can't be sure now that I am on my own. [With] Prabhupada's disappearance [death], how can you tell if you're dovetailing or just desiring too much? It seems like I am continually making decisions, but I don't know if I am dovetailing or fooling myself. Rupa: That's what we have the Kirtan Hall for. You have people here that you can check things out with. (Los Angeles member, 1980)

On other occasions, the question of what should be the appropriate limits of an individual's ideological work became a central issue of group discussion. One member, for example, talked about trying to dovetail an expensive automobile:

> Everytime I see a 450 Mercedes my desire is very strong. I once tried to dovetail a 450. It kind of worked, but it didn't really. But that is part of the fight; to go out there [in the conventional world] yet be internally Krishna conscious. That's our success. Jiva: Yes, but the important thing is to be sure you are not doing the other thing that doves do with their tail! [laughter by all present]. (Los Angeles member, 1980)

Implications

This study of factionalism, group defection, and schism has described and analyzed the relation among organizational change, structure, and ideology in the career of the Hare Krishna movement. The ethnographic data and analysis presented raise three additional issues concerning collective forms of disengagement and the development of religious movements and organizations:

(1) Zald and Ash argue that the inclusive organization retains its factions while the exclusive organization spews them forth" (1966: 337). The question remains: In what form do these factions go forth? The literature suggests that factions splinter from religious organizations as schisms, or sects, in Stark and Bainbridge (1985) terms. The case of the Conch Club suggests another alternative: Insurgent groups may also defect. Given these possible options, it becomes theoretically useful to account for why some dissident groups defect, while others splinter from their parent religious organizations as sectarian movements. Why, for example, did the Bhaktivedanta

Fellowship disengage from ISKCON as a schismatic group, while members of the Conch Club collectively defected, only later to build a sectarian organization?

It is a truism that religious organizations require resources such as money, people, leadership, and power to sustain their efforts; but resource accumulation is particularly problematic for insurgent groups seeking to exit highly centralized, totalistic, and deviant religious organizations like ISKCON. On the one hand, insurgents normally find it difficult to appropriate resources from within (Zald & Berger, 1978), and on the other, they may find it equally problematic to mobilize resources from the conventional society, given the movement's controversial public definition. Under such conditions, insurgent groups are hard pressed to accumulate the resources necessary to begin a schismatic organization, requiring them either to defect from the organization or to lower their political voice and accommodate rather than fight (Hirschman, 1970; Zald & Berger, 1978).

The ability of the Bhaktivedanta Fellowship to splinter from ISKCON was largely a function of having the independent financial resources of some of its members at its disposal to underwrite a new sectarian enterprise. Most other ISKCON members in Los Angeles and elsewhere lacked such discretionary resources. Few had individual bank accounts and almost all received financial assistance from their ISKCON community as their sole means of support. Like most other ISKCON devotees, members of the Conch Club lacked independent financial resources. Moreover, none had jobs outside ISKCON, and their employment possibilities were uncertain at best. In sum, the Bhaktivedanta Fellowship possessed the requisite infrastructural supports to break from ISKCON and begin an alternative Krishna Consciousness community. The Conch Club, by contrast, lacked such an option because it was resource-deficient. Its members were left to defect. Only after a period of resource accumulation (e.g., money gained from employment, housing) were they able to begin the task of building a sectarian organization.[10]

Thus, insurgent groups lacking in discretionary resources will have their exit options limited to individual or collective forms of defection, while dissidents who possess resources, or are able to appeal to resources controlled by external

groups (Zald & McCarthy, 1987a: 85), are likely to splinter from their parent religious organization as a schismatic group.[11]

(2) Defection from greedy" (Coser, 1974) and world-transforming religious movements (Bromley & Shupe, 1979a), such as ISKCON, is fundamentally a transition involving a change in status from member to ex-member, and perhaps to re-membering with the conventional society. This change may or may not involve a shift in cognitive orientation implied by concepts such as deconversion" (Jacobs, 1984, 1987) or desocialization and resocialization" (Lewis, 1986; Wright, 1983b). Many, if not most, ex-members of new religions do undergo changes in worldview following defection, re-establishing themselves as members of the dominant society. Other defectors, especially those who have discontinued their involvement for political or organizational reasons, may self-consciously seek to maintain their unconventional religious beliefs.

Members of the Conch Club, while questioning aspects of their Krishna conscious beliefs, remained converts as they sought to re-establish themselves marginally within the larger society. In rejecting ISKCON as unworthy of their membership, they had not abandoned their Krishna beliefs and way of life. Defection did not involve a process of resocialization leading Conch Club members to become recruited back into conventional social networks" (Lewis & Bromley, 1987: 511) and ultimately to the dominant worldview. Members sought, instead, to retain their identity as Krishna devotees. Through strategies of circumstantial and ideological work, members of the Kirtan Hall constructed a social world which supported their unconventional religious beliefs.

The theoretical implications of this study emphasize that leaving a religious organization by no means assures that the meaning systems" (Berger, 1963) of former members undergo a transformation toward a conventional worldview; some ex-members actively seek to retain their religious worldview and identity following defection. The Kirtan Hall represents one example of how this might be accomplished. Other strategies have been noted in the literature.

Several investigators of new religious movements have presented evidence that it is not uncommon for voluntary defectors later to become members of other new religions (Jacobs, 1987; Wright, 1983b). Richardson (1978, 1980) describes this process as a conversion career." Wright (1983b) reports that 78% of the voluntary defectors he studied joined another new religion after leaving their previous one. Jacobs (1987) found that 50% of the defectors in her sample had become affiliated with a different religious group. Although these researchers view such changes in membership as evidence of reconversion," I would argue that only the specific content of the defectors' meaning system underwent change. Their primary religious framework remained in place, despite a shift in organizational affiliation. Thus, joining another religious organization can be viewed as a strategy to avoid reconverting to the conventional secular worldview.

(3) A related issue concerns movement success and failure. Researchers of social movements often assume that defection and schism rob a movement of its energy and vitality (but see Gerlach & Hine, 1970: 63-78). Gamson goes so far as to argue that factionalism is the major cause of movement failure (1975: 101-03). This view of failure confuses the conceptual difference between movement-organizations and movements, and offers what Gusfield suggests is a linear image of social movements. He proposed that the focus on organizations in the study of social movements has essentially made movement-organizations synonymous with the Movement" (1981b: 320). If we view movements as the fortunes of movement-organizations, defection and factionalism easily become signs of failure; but if we take what Gusfield calls a fluid" perspective of social movements, we become less concerned about the boundaries of organizations and more alive to the larger contexts of change" in which those organizations exist (1981b: 323). When people defect from religious or secular movement-organizations for political rather than ideological reasons, they *remain members of the movement*. The members of the Kirtan Hall clearly remained largely committed to the practices and beliefs of Krishna Consciousness despite their decision to defect from ISKCON. ISKCON may have suffered factionalism, a loss of members, and decline by the end of the 1970s, but the larger movement lived on and continued to exert its influence in American society, though in perhaps less obvious ways.

Notes

1. There are exceptions in the literature. Role theory, for example, does not posit a direct or necessary congruence between an individual's pre-existing beliefs and values, and the doctrines of a particular religious group, as the basis for joining (Bromley & Shupe, 1979b, 1986). Lofland's and Stark's (1965) model of conversion blends both individual predispositions and structural factors to account for choices to become a religious adherent. Lofland's and Skonovd's (1981) treatment of conversion motifs suggests how a variety of social psychological and structural factors influence different types of conversion.

2. Throughout the paper I intend to distinguish between the Hare Krishna movement and the International Society for Krishna Consciousness (ISKCON). Until the death of the movement's founding guru in 1977, the Hare Krishna movement and ISKCON could reasonably be considered one and the same. As described here and elsewhere (Rochford, 1985), ISKCON faced factionalism and schism in the late 1970s, resulting in the emergence of a number of social movement organizations within the broader Hare Krishna movement. The analytic importance of this distinction will become apparent later in the paper.

3. Sanskrit words and ISKCON terms appearing in the paper are defined in the Appendix.

4. It should be noted that ISKCON's succession problems continue. Since 1986, four more appointed gurus have left ISKCON. Of the 11 originally appointed to serve as guru, six have either exited ISKCON voluntarily or been excommunicated (Rochford, forthcoming). In a recently publicized case, an ISKCON guru in West Virginia was excommunicated because of various legal problems involving members of his community (Gruson, 1986, 1987a, 1987b; Hubner & Gruson, 1987). Although it is still too early to predict the likely course of events, there are already initial signs of conflict between ISKCON and the excommunicated leader and his followers: Upon his excommunication, Kirtanananda Bhaktipada threatened legal action against ISKCON.

5. I know very little about the fate of the Bhaktivedanta Fellowship after its break from ISKCON.

6. Goffman defines a primary framework as a schemata of interpretation" (1974: 21) which renders aspects of the social world understandable and meaningful. By providing the basis of meaning, frames organize experience and guide action, whether individual or collective" (Snow *et al.,* 1986: 464). As others have noted (Gonos, 1977), Goffman's analysis of frames" and framework" represents a structuralist approach to microsociology. Goffman's frame analytic approach thus lends itself to linking traditional and resource mobilization perspectives to the study of movement participation. For an application of Goffman's frame analytic approach to the issue of movement participation, see Snow *et al.* (1986).

7. My use of the concept frame bridging" differs from the way Snow *et al.* (1986) have defined the term. They refer to frame bridging as the linkage of two or more ideologically congruent but structurally unconnected frames regarding a particular issue or prob-

lem" (1986: 467). By contrast, the cognitive bridge-work" of Conch Club members involved the attempt to graft at least portions of their pre-ISKCON interpretive frame onto their Krishna conscious worldview, without a resulting transformation of frame. (See Snow *et al.,* 1986: 473-76, on domain-specific and global transformations of frame.) The Conch Club, therefore, served a different function from other forms of re-evaluation therapy, exit counseling, and deprogramming which seek deconversion" as their objective. The next section will cover the strategies employed by Conch Club members to bridge their Krishna beliefs with the conventional worldview, and the overall problematics of this task.

8. In Goffman's terms, ideological work" is the cognitive work undertaken by individuals and groups to deal with the problematics of internal frame maintenance. (For an application to ISKCON of Berger's approach, see Rochford, 1985: 192-214.)

9. The Kirtan Hall formally disbanded in October, 1980. During the weeks just prior to its demise, the group failed to meet on a regular basis, and when it did there were often no more than three or four adults present. The final blow came when one of the leaders, in whose house the Kirtan Hall's meetings were held, relocated to the southeastern United States. I should add, however, that it was just after the group folded when I discontinued my field work and lost touch with members of the Kirtan Hall. It is possible that the group reformed sometime after my departure from the field.

10. Of course, what becomes of group defectors remains empirically problematic. If they are absorbed into conventional society and/or become members of new movements, they retain their status as defectors. Should they collectively unite to build a sectarian organization, they become schismatics. Group defection, as we see in the development of the Kirtan Hall, may represent a stage or way-station in the direction of sectarian schism, rather than a theoretically distinct phenomenon or process.

11. One schismatic group which broke from ISKCON was able to mobilize the support of a Prabhupada Godbrother" in India. In 1983, Dheera Krishna, the former president of the Los Angeles ISKCON community, was reinitiated by Sridara Maharaja. He returned to the United States and founded the Chaitanya Saraswat Mandal in San Jose, California (Rochford, 1985: 248-49; Shinn, 1987b: 130). Another group which splintered from ISKCON on the east coast of the U.S., the Sri Nitai Gaura Association, was also supported by Sridara Maharaja in the early 1980s (Shinn, 1987b: 130).

Appendix

*Ashram*in the present context, a place of communal residence.

*Bhaktivedanta*the name bestowed on Prabhupada by his spiritual master's Gaudiya Vaisnava Society in India in 1947, in honor of his philosophical learning and devotion.

*Bramacharie*a single male devotee.

*Conch*in the *Bhagavad Gita,* Krishna and Arjuna sound their conch shells indicating victory on the battlefield of Kuruksetra. Conch shells are sounded at the end of religious ceremonies held in ISKCON temples.

*Guru*a spiritual master, or teacher, who initiated disciples into spiritual life.

*Gurukula*a school dedicated to Vedic learning for boys and girls five years and over. The school is under the direction of the spiritual master.

*Karma*everyday material activities yielding good or bad reactions.

*Kirtan*collective chanting and singing of the holy names of God.

*Sankirtana*involves three types of activities in public places: Book distribution is the practice whereby devotees venture into airports and other public places to distribute religious texts for money; *Hare Nam* usually involves a group of ISKCON members going into public locations to chant and preach (may or may not involve literature distribution); *Picking* is a form of public solicitation which involves selling nonreligious products (e.g., candles, record albums, prints of art work) or seeking straight donations on behalf of worthy causes (e.g., to feed needy people).

*Shika*clump of hair which remains on the back of men's heads after they have otherwise shaved their heads.

*Swami*title for a devotee who is in the renounced order of life (i.e., has given up work and family obligations to commit himself fully to spiritual life).

*Vaisnava*a devotee of Krishna. ◆

Part 11

Outcomes and Consequences of Social Movement Participation and Activity

In this final part we take up the issue of movement impacts. Presumably the ultimate justification for studying social movements lies in their potential capacity to bring about various kinds of social change. Those involved in social movements certainly assume the efficacy of social movements as vehicles for social change. Movement scholars do as well. It is surprising, then, that the impact of social movements has been the subject of so little systematic scholarship.

Part of the problem stems from the difficulties inherent in measuring the impact of social movements. Take the case of the contemporary women's movement. One could easily generate a list of recent changes in American society that could plausibly be attributed to the women's movement. Examples include the expansion of abortion rights occasioned by *Roe v. Wade*; the increase in female elected officials; higher rates of conviction and stiffer sentences for rape; the spread of gender-neutral language. But generating such a list is far easier than systematically proving the connection between the movement and any given change.

To move beyond the realm of the plausible, the researcher must confront two daunting methodological challenges. First, one must show that the relationship between the movement and the presumed outcome is not *spurious*. A spurious relationship occurs when two phenomena are themselves a product of a third prior phenomenon. Let us illustrate the concept with an interesting historical example. Roughly 100 years ago, public

officials began to pave the major roads in and around London. The paving companies preferred to do this work when it was especially hot, as it was easier to melt and work with the tar on hot days than cool ones. But during this period, an intense heat wave brought emotional charges that the paving was causing prickly rash, stroke, and a variety of other maladies. The controversy resulted in a suspension of paving activities. But, of course, it was not the paving which caused the medical maladies; instead, both the paving and the maladies were byproducts of the hot weather.

The same might well be argued for any number of specific changes attributed to a given social movement. That is, the relationship between the movement and the changes could be spurious, with both resulting from some prior set of change processes. Let us return to our earlier example. Throughout the twentieth century, but especially since the onset of World War II, women have been entering the paid labor force in ever increasing numbers. Might it not be possible that many of the changes attributed to the women's movement—and indeed the movement itself—are really a result of this more general trend and the greater independence and societal integration which it has afforded women? We would be inclined to reject this latter view, but we offer it as a plausible alternative to an explanation that would look exclusively at the women's movement as the primary causal force behind the various changes noted earlier. At the very least, anyone who asserts a strong movement-centered view of social change will have to take seriously the issue of spuriousness.

Even if we could empirically rule out other prior causes, we would still have to contend with the matter of *mechanisms*. By mechanisms we mean those specific processes or dynamics that account for the causal force of social movements. We return again to our earlier example of the women's movement. Take any given change plausibly attributed to the movement and ask yourself the "mechanisms question." Can we specify the means by which the movement achieved this outcome? In some cases, such as the passage of a bill advocated by feminists, the means or mechanism may be clear. In this case the assertion of a tight causal link between the movement and a specific outcome would seem to be justified. But in other cases—a rise in the divorce rate, for instance—it would be a good bit harder to specify, let alone test for, the specific mechanisms linking the movement to the change in question. In such cases, any final judgement regarding the impact of the movement may prove elusive. As you read these selections, you might wish to reflect on these tough conceptual and methodological issues, asking yourself how well the author(s) has handled them.

Setting aside these issues, we conclude this introduction by distinguishing between various general categories of outcomes that might be reasonably ascribed to a given movement. We begin with a simple but important observation. While movements are typically associated with fairly specific goals, the impacts they ultimately have may be much broader and quite often unintended. Consider the American civil rights movement. At the most specific and obvious level, the movement was responsible for a great deal of consequential *state action*. This would include such landmark federal legislation as the Civil Rights Acts of 1964 and 1968 as well as countless executive, legislative, and judicial decisions at the federal, state, and local levels.

Of more general political significance were the *redistributions of political power* that resulted from the movement. Three such redistributions can be attributed to the civil rights/black power movement. First, the establishment of voting rights for African Americans in the South paved the way for greater black electoral representation in the region. Second, blacks took advantage of the momentum generated by the movement to become a major force in urban politics throughout the country. Finally, by breaking the electoral monopoly enjoyed by Democrats in the South, the movement ironically paved the way for Republican gains not only regionally, but nationally as well. Presidents Nixon, Reagan, and Bush all benefitted from sizeable electoral majorities in a region once controlled by Democrats.

Leaving the realm of institutionalized politics, the civil rights/black power movement may also be plausibly implicated in any number of broad *changes in public opinion and behavior* over the past quarter of a century. The striking gains in public support for integration and non-discriminatory practices is but one example. Another is the general visibility of African Americans on television. Blacks were all but invisible on network television well into the 1960s.

It would be hard to ignore the black struggle's crucial *impact on other movements*. As countless studies have shown, the other major American movements of the 1960s and 1970s were largely set in motion by the ideological, organizational, and tactical inspiration afforded them by the civil rights movement (Evans 1980; McAdam 1988).

Finally, movements also have powerful *biographical consequences* for those who commit themselves to the struggle. As researchers such as Fendrich (1977), McAdam (1989, 1988) and Whalen and Flacks (1989) have shown, the occupational, family, and political histories of activists often diverge markedly from those of their age peers. Movements are, thus, vehicles for personal as well as broad political and social changes.

The following readings illustrate the wide range of outcomes that may be associated with a given movement. The first selection, by Verta Taylor and Nicole Raeburn, underscores the personal impact of activism discussed above. Using survey and interview data, the authors document "five career consequences suffered by gay, lesbian, and bisexual sociologists who engage in various forms of personalized political resistance: 1) discrimination in hiring; 2) bias in tenure and promotion; 3) exclusion from social and professional networks; 4) devaluation of scholarly work . . . and 5) harassment and intimidation."

In the next selection, David Meyer and Nancy Whittier illustrate another of the general movement impacts discussed above: the role an earlier movement may play in influencing the timing, character, or specific features of later struggles. Using a variety of methods, the authors document the myriad ways in which the women's movement influenced the organizational, tactical, and ideological practices of the 1980s U.S. peace movement.

Finally, in the concluding selection Edwin Amenta, Bruce Carruthers, and Yvonne Zylan turn to a critical moment in the evolution of the U.S. welfare state to analyze the role that the Townsend Movement—a large and influential movement of the elderly—had in shaping federal policy toward the aged in the 1930s. Their article brings this survey of movement outcomes full circle. It is probably fair to say that we are motivated to study social movements principally because we regard them as powerful forces for institutionalized political change. The Townsend Movement proved to be just that.

References

Evans, Sara. 1980. *Personal Politics.* New York: Vintage Books.

Fendrich, James M. 1977. "Keeping the Faith or Pursuing the Good Life: A Study of Participation in the Civil Rights Movement." *American Sociological Review* 42: 144-57.

McAdam, Doug. 1989. "The Biographical Consequences of Activism." *American Sociological Review* 54: 744-60.

——. 1988. *Freedom Summer.* New York: Oxford University Press.

Whalen, Jack and Richard Flacks. 1989. *Beyond the Barricades: The Sixties Generation Grows Up.* Philadelphia: Temple University Press. ✦

35

Identity Politics as High-Risk Activism: Career Consequences for Lesbian, Gay, and Bisexual Sociologists

Verta Taylor
Nicole C. Raeburn

The gay, lesbian, and bisexual movement flourishes in the 1990s in part because of the formidable infrastructural base of cultural, political, social, educational, and professional organizations built by activists in the preceding decade (Morris 1984; Knopp 1987; Adam 1995). Throughout the 1980s, workplace organizing in the form of professional caucuses, corporate employee groups, and university associations of students and/or faculty and staff developed as gay men and lesbians joined forces in the struggle to win state and city executive orders banning job discrimination, health care and other employee benefits for domestic partners, the inclusion of sexual orientation in college and university affirmative action policies, and the incorporation of gay and lesbian studies into college and university curricula. While most analysts acknowledge that political activism in the work place has been critical to the growth and success of the gay, lesbian, and bisexual movement (D'Emilio 1992; Kopkind 1993), studies are generally silent about its impact on the lives of individual activists.

The social movement literature suggests that participation in protest can have substantial short- and long-term effects on the personal lives and work histories of activists (McAdam 1986, 1989; Whalen and Flacks 1989; Whittier 1991). In the case of the gay and lesbian movement, the risks of participation may be compounded by the fact that, as several studies have shown, disclosing one's sexual identity in the work place can result

in bias, discrimination, and job loss (Weinberg and Williams 1974; Blumstein and Schwartz 1983; Levine and Leonard 1984; Schneider 1986; Levine 1992; Badgett 1993a, b; Woods 1993; Sherrill 1994). Our goal is to examine the imprint that political participation, rather than simply coming out on the job, leaves on the lives and careers of individuals who identify as gay, lesbian, or bisexual.

The study is based on the Sociologists' Lesbian and Gay Caucus (SLGC), which mobilized in the early 1970s to promote the rights of lesbians and gay men in the profession of sociology and to demand their full inclusion in the larger society. A 1981 survey of members of the Lesbian and Gay Caucus concluded that those who are "known as homosexuals or, even more so, as activists, run considerable risk . . . of experiencing discrimination in being hired or promoted in a sociology department" (Gagnon et al. 1982:165). In this paper, we document sociologists' struggle to obtain equal rights for gay men and lesbians in academic life and assess the extent to which individuals' experiences and perceptions of discrimination in the profession are linked to activist participation.

We conceptualize the SLGC's strategies as a type of identity politics, described by new social movement theorists, that has dominated the political landscape in the United States and Western Europe since the mid-1970s (Cohen 1985b; Melucci 1989). The merits of identity politics for the lesbian, gay, and bisexual movement have been debated widely by scholars of gay and lesbian studies. At issue is the tendency to treat homosexuality as a stable, unified, and identifiable essence that both ignores the fluidity, instability, and multiple nature of most identities and reinforces the binary divide of homosexuality and heterosexuality that regulates sexual desires, actions, and social relations (Phelan 1989; Butler 1990; Fuss 1991, Weeks 1991; Plummer 1992). In this paper we do not focus on these criticisms but on the charge that identity politics represents a retreat from political and institutional change. The theoretical argument that drives our analysis is that virtually all forms of identity politics, because they take the individual to be the site of political activity, can be understood as what McAdam (1986) has termed high-risk activism. After a discussion of the data and methods, we describe the formation and evolution of the Sociologists' Lesbian and Gay Caucus, demonstrate how participation in the caucus facilitates individuals' awareness of the collective nature of their professional experiences, and distinguish two ideal types of identity expression practiced by caucus members: *coming out* or public disclosure motivated primarily by personal and individual considerations, and *personalized political resistance* exercised to promote public recognition of gays and lesbians, challenge institutionalized heterosexuality, and promote the collective interests of gays and lesbians in sociology and higher education.

We use longitudinal survey data to compare changes in the overall rates of work place and professional discrimination reported by gay, lesbian, and bisexual sociologists in 1981 and 1992. We draw from in-depth interviews to determine whether gay activism, rather than the simple disclosure of sexual identity, appears to be linked to the higher rates of discrimination reported in 1992 as well as to illustrate concretely the way that activism influences the academic careers and lives of gay, lesbian, and bisexual sociologists. We conclude by considering the implications of our theoretical argument that identity politics is high-risk activism for understanding the social processes that account for the enduring impact of social movement participation.

Identity Politics as a Form of High-Risk Activism

An analysis of the impact of activism on the careers of gay, lesbian, and bisexual sociologists requires a model of social movements that recognizes the distinctive personalized political strategies practiced by many grassroots movements since the 1960s (Barkan 1979; Epstein 1988; Echols 1989; Whalen and Flacks 1989; Taylor and Rupp 1993; Lichterman 1995). In contrast to resource mobilization theories, which treat social movement organizations as the principal carriers of political protest (Gamson 1975; McCarthy and Zald 1977; Morris 1984; Staggenborg 1991), new social movement perspectives propose the concept of collective identity to highlight the fact that people frequently enact their social and political commitments more as empowered individuals than as members of formal groups (Cohen 1985b; Melucci 1985, 1989; Offe 1985; Touraine 1985; Habermas 1987; Klandermans and Tarrow 1988; Giddens 1991).

We adapt Taylor and Whittier's (Taylor 1989b; Taylor and Whittier 1992a; Whittier 1995)

social constructionist perspective on collective identity, which draws from new social movement characterizations, to describe how gay, lesbian, and bisexual sociologists have negotiated a gay and lesbian presence in sociology to challenge the specific disadvantages they confront in academic life. Our approach examines the formation of oppositional collective identities as the consequence of three interrelated processes. The first is the creation of a *submerged network of activists.* The Sociologists' Lesbian and Gay Caucus represents the type of network of loosely connected individuals held together by common personal attributes, interaction, a shared discourse, and everyday resistance described by Melucci (1985, 1989) and other proponents of new social movement theory. The second process that underlies the emergence of collective identity is a sense of "we" or group consciousness that derives from activists' ongoing attempts to negotiate new *collective self-understandings* that specify their distinct and common experiences of inequality and reframe their individual biographies in more favorable collective and structural terms (Giddens 1991; Friedman and McAdam 1992; Gamson 1992a; Morris 1992; Hunt, Benford, and Snow 1994; Whittier 1995). This dimension focuses our attention on the way that participation in the SLGC shapes individuals' understanding of what it means to be a gay sociologist, imparts recognition of their shared interests, and contributes to their politicization. The third process of collective identity construction is activists' preference for *personalized political resistance,* which participants use in their daily lives as a means of challenging group invisibility and dominant representations of themselves, affirming new politicized identities, and contesting traditional distinctions between the political and the personal (Gamson 1989; Melucci 1989; Epstein 1990; Taylor and Whittier 1992a; Lichterman 1995).

It is the emphasis that proponents of identity politics place on individual political expression, or "the personal as political," that leads us to suspect that this may be a particularly risky form of political participation. To emphasize that not all forms of protest are equal in terms of their costs to participants, McAdam (1986) distinguishes between "high-risk activism" or actions anticipated to incur substantial legal, financial, social, or physical costs, and "low-risk" or relatively safer forms of political expression, such as signing a petition, expressing support for an issue, writing leaflets, or donating money. Critics of identity politics have suggested that, by highlighting the political implications of everything from one's personal relationships, consumptive preferences, and occupational choices to the structure of organizational decision making, recent movements have retreated from the public world of politics and promoting institutional change into the presumably safer private spaces of self, lifestyle, and culture (Bellah et al. 1985; Kauffman 1990; Echols 1989; Seidman 1993). We take issue with this view by arguing that, to the contrary, what Giddens (1991) terms "life politics" is a strategy of challenging dominant relations of power that has relatively high long-term costs for participants. The fact that in identity politics, individuals' personal lives, work, and activism all become sites of political expression means that activists who engage in this style of movement participation literally "put their bodies on the line for the cause." As a result, they become easy targets of stigma, harassment, retaliation, and even more extreme sanctions such as loss of a job, injury, or death—effects that have been shown to weigh heavily on individuals' decisions to become involved in unpopular causes (McAdam 1989; Opp 1989a; Wiltfang and McAdam 1991). In seeking to assess the risks of participating in gay activism in the work place, it would seem especially critical to examine career outcomes as possible effects.

Data and Methods

This research began as a replication of the 1981 study conducted by the American Sociological Association's Task Group on Homosexuality to investigate whether there have been changes in the barriers to hiring and promotion of gay, lesbian, and bisexual sociologists during the past decade (Gagnon et al. 1982). We used the methods of the earlier study by mailing questionnaires to the approximately 160 members of the Sociologists' Lesbian and Gay Caucus and to another half dozen lesbian, gay, and bisexual sociologists who responded to a request for volunteers published in the April 1992 issue of *Footnotes*. The instrument included both closed- and open-ended questions about individuals' sexual identification, disclosure of sexual orientation in the work place, history of activism, and professional experiences related to hiring and promotion, teaching and conducting research on gay, lesbian, and bisexual top-

ics, and any other areas of unequal treatment noted by respondents. There were 97 questionnaires returned, which represents approximately 60 percent of those mailed, almost twice the number (52) returned in 1981. Initially we planned to duplicate a second component of the 1981 study, a survey of heads of sociology departments. However, the ASA's Committee on Research on the Profession was unwilling to include items in their survey of department chairs that asked respondents to report, even anonymously, the sexual identities of faculty members.

Preliminary analysis of the 1992 survey revealed an unexpected finding that altered our research questions and pointed inductively to the theoretical concerns from social movement theory that guide our analysis. Despite several attempts to reach sociologists who might not be publicly known as gay, lesbian, or bisexual, only six individuals who were not members of the Sociologists' Lesbian and Gay Caucus requested and completed questionnaires. As might be expected, our sampling techniques failed to tap women and men who have chosen not to disclose their sexuality in the work context. In 1981, 32 percent of the sociology faculty and graduate students surveyed indicated that their sexual orientation was publicly known by most of their colleagues (see Table 1). By 1992, that figure had climbed to 54 percent, and, when asked if their department chair were aware of their sexual identity, the overwhelming majority (84 percent) responded affirmatively. Furthermore, slightly more than half of the sociology faculty answering the 1992 survey described themselves as activists engaged in varying degrees in research, advising, teaching, and community and professional service on gay, lesbian, or bisexual issues. In response, we recast our study as an analysis of the formation, strategies, and outcomes of activism. To gain insight into the political strategies used by sociologists and the consequences of those strategies, we conducted 16 in-depth interviews with gay, lesbian, and bisexual faculty who are members of the SLGC. We interviewed nine women and seven men; two interviewees were African American, and the rest did not identify as members of racial or ethnic minorities. Of 97 total surveys returned, 53 were completed by faculty, 30 were returned by graduate students, and 14 by non-academic sociologists. This analysis is based on the 53 questionnaires completed by sociologists who hold

Table 1
Disclosure of Sexual Orientation to Colleagues for Lesbian and Gay Sociologists in 1981 and 1992

	Out to Most				Out to Some				Out to None			
	1981		1992		1981		1992		1981		1992	
	n	%	n	%	n	%	n	%	n	%	n	%
Women	2	13%	23	44%	11	73%	27	52%	2	13%	2	4%
Men	15	41%	29	64%	17	46%	14	31%	5	14%	2	4%
Total	17	32%	52	54%	28	54%	41	42%	7	13%	4	4%
Total Percent Change from 1981-1992		+69%		−22%							−69%	

Note: Total N for 1981 = 52 (15 women and 37 men); total N for 1992 = 97 (52 women and 45 men).

faculty positions. Table 2 describes the age, sex, racial-ethnic composition, institutional employment, and tenure status of the 53 faculty respondents.

We use the survey and interview data to present empirical evidence of the mobilization of gay, lesbian, and bisexual sociologists, to document the collective strategies of resistance used in the struggle for equal treatment of gays in higher education, and to assess the extent to which the professional discrimination reported by gay, lesbian, and bisexual sociologists is a consequence of activist participation. Although almost all of the respondents belonged to the SLGC, about half of the caucus has been "paper" members who have remained more marginal to the SLGC and have not participated in gay activism in the profession. Our analysis of the impact of political participation on individuals' careers therefore compares the experiences of activists and non-activists and uses a chi-square test of significance.

The Sociologists' Lesbian and Gay Caucus: Negotiating a Gay and Lesbian Presence in Sociology

The Sociologists' Lesbian and Gay Caucus reflects the emphasis on community-building, identity formation, interest-group politics, assimilationist strategies, and personalized protest that

Table 2
Demographic Characteristics of Lesbian and Gay Faculty in 1992

	Women		Men		Total	
	n	%	n	%	n	%
Age						
Under 30	2	7%	0	0%	2	4%
30-39	10	37%	8	31%	18	34%
40 or over	15	56%	18	69%	33	62%
Race/Ethnicity						
White	26	96%	24	92%	50	94%
African-American	0	0%	1	4%	1	2%
Latino/a	1	4%	1	4%	2	4%
Institution						
State University	15	56%	14	54%	29	55%
State/Community College	2	7%	1	4%	3	6%
Private Religious	3	11%	5	19%	8	15%
Private Other	5	19%	5	19%	10	19%
Other	2	7%	1	4%	3	6%
Tenure Status						
Tenured	9	33%	15	58%	24	45%
Tenure-Track	10	37%	6	23%	16	30%
Non-Tenure-Track	6	22%	4	15%	10	19%
Other	2	7%	1	4%	3	6%

Note: Data are from the 1992 survey of 53 (27 women and 26 men) lesbian, gay, and bisexual faciilty.

were especially critical in gay politics from the mid-1970s, when the caucus formed, through the mid-1980s (Marotta 1981; Seidman 1993; Adam 1995). We use the collective identity scheme described earlier to document the way that gay, lesbian, and bisexual sociologists have forged a visible presence in sociology and to demonstrate how participation in the caucus has shaped members' understanding of what it means to be a gay sociologist, made them conscious of the political significance of sexual identity, and led to the adoption of personalized resistance strategies centering on identity to win acceptance in the discipline. Even though our emphasis here is on faculty members' political participation in the profession and on their campuses, for the majority of activists the SLGC is not the sole site of protest. Most are involved in the larger gay, lesbian, and bisexual movement in their communities.

The Formation of a Submerged Network

The Sociologists' Lesbian and Gay Caucus (originally named the Sociologists' Gay Caucus) formed at the 1974 Annual Meetings of the American Sociological Association in Montreal. From the outset, the overwhelming majority of caucus members have identified as gay, lesbian, or in a small number of cases bisexual, although the membership list includes some heterosexual scholars whose research focuses on gay and lesbian topics. Founders of the caucus set out to build an island of resistance and support for gay and lesbian sociologists and graduate students by sponsoring a series of sessions outside the formal meeting program of the American Sociological Association. Organizing activities at the annual meeting, which are announced in the caucus' newsletter published at least twice a year, continues to be a major project. The agenda includes social events, panels and paper sessions, a business meeting, and roundtable discussions to facilitate interaction among scholars doing research on gay and lesbian topics. Business meetings focus on monitoring the discipline for homophobic content and discriminatory practices and discussing larger national political issues confronting lesbians and gay men. In the early years, sessions were held on coming out in the classroom and the profession and more recently on teaching gay and lesbian studies and confronting homophobia. Only recently has the formal ASA program listed caucus events and locations.

Over the years the caucus' patterns of growth and changing sex composition have been consistent with those of the larger gay and lesbian movement, as well as with changes in patterns of attendance at annual ASA meetings. The organization started out small but militant. About twelve people, mostly men, attended the first meeting in 1974, and the caucus' first steering committee was made up of five men. In 1980, the year that the ASA Task Group on Homosexuality began its work, caucus membership had increased to close to 100, although attendance at the business meeting held during the annual ASA meetings was often less than two dozen. By 1992, the size of the caucus had grown to approximately 160 members, slightly more than one-third women, and business meetings attracted upwards of 50 people. And in 1994 around 50 people showed up at the caucus' informal networking dinner, an event that ordinarily had attracted only a handful of people.

Although several interviewees initially saw the caucus as providing a means to "survive feeling alone and isolated at ASA meetings," its significance extended beyond the meeting. Today several activists describe the SLGC as an "alternative institution" within the ASA that not only serves social and professional functions during the annual meeting but nurtures and ties together lesbian, gay, and bisexual sociologists throughout the academic year.

Collective Self-Understandings

From the start, documenting structural patterns of discrimination by tying individuals' personal experiences to systemic causes was the *reason d'être* of the SLGC. Like other new social movements that took hold in higher education in the period, cultural struggle has been as pivotal as contesting institutional practices. The stigmatization of gays and lesbians in social scientific and other public discourses served as an initial rallying point. One of its first successes was getting the ASA to pass a resolution condemning the sociological data used by the Anita Bryant campaign against gay civil rights in Dade County, Florida, in the late 1970s. The caucus also pressured the ASA to sponsor a sociological study of biases in the coverage of gay men and lesbians in introductory sociology textbooks and fought to win a session on gay and lesbian research on the program of the annual meeting.

The SLGC is more, however, than simply a watchdog over the ASA. Core members view the caucus as a means to politicize gay, lesbian, and bisexual sociologists by encouraging them to recognize the link between their own professional setbacks and the anti-gay content and practices of the discipline, higher education, and society in general. Two tactics used by the caucus, which are part of what Tilly (1978) would term its larger "repertoire of collective action," have been used to raise the political consciousness of gay, lesbian, and bisexual sociologists: *self-study* and *personal testimony*.

First, through self-study, the caucus has produced a formal body of research spelling out the common obstacles that gay and lesbian sociologists face in building academic careers. When the caucus formed, there was a paucity of research on lesbian, gay, and bisexual topics. The 1981 survey explained why: Half of the members of the Sociologists' Lesbian and Gay Caucus interested in writing dissertations on lesbian, gay, or bisexual concerns reported that they had been discouraged from doing so because of stigmatization, especially the tendency for others to assume that those who studied homosexuality were themselves lesbian or gay. Skeptical about the knowledge on gays and lesbians propagated by the discipline, caucus members found it necessary to draw from their own experiences to conduct a self-study that substantiated claims of discrimination in hiring, promotion, and research funding. Activists' struggle to document unequal treatment climaxed in 1979 when the SLGC convinced the ASA to appoint a Task Group on Homosexuality to "review existing knowledge in the sociology of homosexuality, identify topics in this field which demanded research, and submit its report to Council" (Gagnon et al. 1982:165). The Task Group, comprised of three members of the Sociologists' Gay Caucus and three persons who were not caucus members, issued its report in December 1981, along with recommendations that the ASA ensure the report's publication in an outlet with high visibility and create a permanent Committee on the Status of Homosexuals in Sociology to monitor the treatment of lesbians and gays in the profession. The results of the survey confirmed that gay and lesbian sociologists who made their sexual identity publicly known to others suffered discrimination in hiring and promotion in sociology departments, which had inhibited the majority from coming out and conducting research, advising, and teaching on gay and lesbian topics. It is perhaps understandable, in light of these risks, that one member of the Task Group, when discussing the results of the study at a regional professional meeting several years later, began with the statement, "I'm not a lesbian, even though I study lesbians."

The data used for this article were collected as part of the caucus' continuing self-study efforts to assess patterns of discrimination in the discipline. The interviews we conducted with caucus members document that the research promoted by the caucus has made many individuals aware of the collective significance of the problems they have faced in their own careers. Even though the majority of caucus members have participated in other gay, lesbian, and bisexual organizations that have played a part in their politicization, many activists view the caucus as critical to their understanding of what it means to be a gay or lesbian sociologist. A letter written to us by one of the women interviewed for this study illustrates the transformative potential of the caucus' activities. A lesbian feminist scholar who has published widely but not been able to obtain a regular faculty position, she found that our interview moved her to rethink the obstacles that have set back her own career:

> I have learned to think of my hurt in the academic system as very much related to the nature of my work . . . [and] to the larger economic circumstance that has existed since the time I completed the degree. . . . What I almost never see is that my choice to be a lesbian is significant in all of this. I can see that being a lesbian is an element in the whole deviant bundle that is me, but it is hard for me to feel that this lesbian element is more important, say, than my refusal to move anywhere for a job. However, I now think I must take into account how I felt in the interview . . . how great my fear was, how strong my denial, how shocked even I was by my own constant dismissal of the facts of my past and present. By the end of the interview, I was sweaty and tired and I wanted to stop early. "These are things I do not like to think about," I kept telling the interviewer. "These are things I do not want to know," and yet I know them.

The caucus has used a second strategy that goes beyond simply making gay, lesbian, and bisexual sociologists aware of their shared disadvantage to impart new expectations of equitable and fair treatment. At the annual ASA meetings, informal panels are held in which individuals give personal testimony to the negative and positive ways that their professional careers and lives have been influenced by being openly gay, lesbian, or bisexual. Several of our interviewers described these sessions as personally, socially, and politically enabling. One woman equated a particular session given by someone whose scholarly research and activism she had long admired to "a conversion experience." Despite the fact that the interviewee had made her career studying feminist topics and was a visible and politically active feminist, she described the speaker's courage, accomplishments, and success in a major department as "inspiring," and she claims she left the annual meetings determined to get involved in gay and lesbian activism on her own campus.

The tactics used by the caucus to impart collective consciousness and mobilize resistance are characteristic of the repertoires of action used by new social movements mobilized around identity (Seidman 1993). Critical of systems of knowledge that have represented gays and lesbians as socially pathological, deviant, and abnormal, the caucus advocates self-study to generate a new body of information that links individual gay, lesbian, and bisexual sociologists' experiences to institutionalized oppression (Giddens 1991). Groups that mobilize around identity also construct new oppositional identities through the kinds of survivor narratives used by the SLGC to illustrate both the everyday manifestations of heterosexual domination and the transformative potential of individual politics (Frank 1993).

Personalized Political Resistance

The self-reflexive tactics used by SLGC to direct attention to the specific forms of bias encountered by gay, lesbian, and bisexual sociologists imply strategies of change that emphasize the political expression of individuals as much as of organizations. Caucus members have drawn upon two different styles of identity expression to oppose and redefine the representation and position of gay men and lesbians in the discipline and the society at large: *coming out* and *personalized political resistance*. The difference between these two ideal typical styles, according to our interviews, is that coming out or the public disclosure of sexual identity, even though it may have unintended political consequences, is generally motivated by personal and individual considerations. In contrast we found that the various forms of personalized resistance used by core members of the

caucus—researching, publishing, teaching, and speaking in public forums about lesbian, gay, and bisexual topics, mentoring and advising lesbian, gay, and bisexual students, and advocating equal rights for gays in the profession and on their campuses—are more likely to be practiced for explicitly political and collective reasons. They can be viewed as examples of what Lichterman (1995) terms personalized political strategies in that they can be and are practiced in everyday life by individuals rather than by organizations, and their enactment as well as their consequences may not be confined simply to one area of an individual's life.

From the period when the caucus first formed until the mid-1980s, coming out, or publicly embracing a gay, lesbian, or bisexual identity, was treated in the movement as the quintessential expression of the insight that the "personal is political" (D'Emilio 1992). During the early years of the caucus, a core of members emphasized personal identity strategies to create a visible gay and lesbian presence in sociology, challenge dominant conceptions of homosexuality as deviance, and force public acceptance. The majority of caucus members, however, remained "closeted" in their professional lives: In the 1981 study fewer than one-third of those surveyed indicated that they had come out to most of their colleagues. Initially, men were somewhat more likely to come out than women. But even for men, fear of being publicly identified as homosexual was so great that, according to the 1981 report, it seems to have prevented the majority of gay and lesbian sociologists from engaging in a range of professional activities to promote their collective interests in the discipline, including coming out in job interviews, listing gay and lesbian publications and presentations on curriculum vitae, researching, publishing, and teaching about lesbian, gay, and bisexual topics, and mentoring lesbian, gay, and bisexual students. The recollections of a woman whose association with the caucus only began within the past five years, even though she has identified as a lesbian for more than 20 years, illustrate:

> I remember seeing the caucus' display in the registration area at the annual meetings for several years and wanting to go over to the table but having this incredible apprehension. I guess I was worried that if I went to any of the caucus' sessions or social events I would lose control over my identity as a lesbian. Even though most of the people in my department suspected it—and I had told lots

of people myself—I was afraid that coming out at the ASA would mean that my work would never be taken seriously or that I might never get a job if I decided to leave this one.

Because most gay, lesbian, and bisexual sociologists found it too risky to come out during the early years of the caucus, those who affirmed a public gay or lesbian identity tended for the most part to be political activists. Many were graduate students with connections to the larger gay and lesbian movement, and they worked in concert with a handful of heterosexual sociologists to carve out a place for gay scholarship, interaction, and political participation in sociology.

By 1992, the picture had changed sharply. Coming out had become the norm for caucus members. Although male faculty are still more likely than females to come out to most colleagues (58 percent versus 33 percent, respectively), almost half (45 percent) of faculty surveyed have come out to most of their colleagues, more than half (51 percent) have come out to some colleagues, and even a larger number (64 percent) reported that their chair is aware of their sexual identity. While a fair number of faculty continue to engage in partial disclosure, it is significant that only 4 percent reported that they have come out to none of their colleagues. Gay, lesbian, and bisexual faculty surveyed remain nevertheless cognizant of the risks they take by disclosing their sexual identity. The overwhelming majority (88 percent) believe that coming out in job interviews will hurt their chances of being hired, and most (57 percent) anticipate that conducting research on lesbian, gay, and bisexual topics will adversely affect their careers.

What has changed, according to our interviewees, is that simply disclosing one's sexual identity no longer carries the same intrinsic political significance that it did in the late 1970s and early 1980s when the ethnic-identity model dominated the gay and lesbian movement (Epstein 1987; Seidman 1993). Increasingly for many gay, lesbian, and bisexual sociologists, coming out may be motivated by personal and individual considerations rather than by political and collective aims. One man explained that for him coming out means "not having to compartmentalize my life radically between work and home because other people don't have to do it." A lesbian faculty member recounted coming out to "twenty white men [that she didn't even know] on a committee"

because she was charged with having a conflict of interest chairing the committee that was overseeing the program in which her partner taught. Another woman who gave up an academic career for full-time research because she "didn't want to work in a closeted environment" explained that coming out allowed her to experience her own life "in an authentic way" and gave her insight into other social issues. Some came out for the first time to colleagues when they were dealing with a partner's illness; for others, coming out coincided with a job search and the need to find a position for a partner, or adopting or giving birth to a child.

In contrast to individuals whose affirmation of gay identity is more personal, more than half (53 percent) of the faculty members of the SLGC in our 1992 survey are political activists. Caucus members use the term "activism" to refer to a range of personalized political strategies that promote the collective interests of gays and lesbians in the discipline, on their own campuses, and in the society at large. These include teaching courses that affirm gay, lesbian, and bisexual identities, conducting and publishing research that challenges dominant representations of homosexuality as deviance, and pushing for gay-affirmative change on their own campuses and in higher education. In 1992, a majority of faculty reported that their scholarship and teaching address gay and lesbian issues. An early caucus member described his own trajectory as typical: "A lot of people who got into the caucus like myself weren't doing any gay research, and all of a sudden we were because of the caucus, and now there's a group in the caucus that I think has had a very major impact on gay and lesbian studies." That the SLGC has played a critical role in encouraging sociologists to become activists is also illustrated by the story told by a faculty member in her mid-forties. She remembered: "I was dragged out of probably the last vestiges of my closet when asked by a caucus member whom I admired a great deal to participate on a panel discussing my professional career as an out lesbian sociologist. Even though I assumed that most people knew I was a lesbian, I had never been listed on the caucus' program." Another member also cited the caucus: "It was wandering into the caucus that helped provide some kind of support for me to be more out than I was. And I think it has made a difference to me in understanding my social location within sociology. . . . That sort of support both at the meetings but also through the year, in whatever way it comes, is very sustaining." Like other caucus members whose political participation reaches into their everyday lives, she has worked on behalf of gay and lesbian partnership benefits at her university and promoted the careers of gay and lesbian graduate students who are themselves activists in the profession.

The SLGC formed as a haven of support in a hostile political climate. By raising the political awareness of gay, lesbian, and bisexual sociologists, the activities of the caucus from its early coming out workshops and consciousness raising activities to the support provided those isolated on smaller campuses—greatly expanded the number of activist scholars in sociology. Most have found participation in the caucus rewarding because it has enhanced their solidarity with and support from other gay, lesbian, and bisexual sociologists and promoted a sense of pride and greater self-acceptance. Political participation, however, as we are about to discover, also has taken its toll on the careers and lives of these men and women.

The High Costs of Activism: Career Consequences

As more lesbian, gay, and bisexual sociologists have been mobilized to promote their collective interests, and gay men and lesbians have become more visible on their own campuses and in the profession at large, they have become easier targets of discrimination. In 1981, 27 percent of the gay, lesbian, and bisexual sociologists sur-veyed reported some form of professional bias related to sexual identity. By 1992, this figure had increased to 43 percent. Because we only had access to the aggregate data from the 1981 study, which combined the experiences of graduate students, faculty, and sociologists employed outside of academic settings, we have made a rough estimate of longitudinal changes between 1981 and 1992 by using the total number of respondents for both years.

Profiling the types of bias described by faculty in 1992, Table 3 shows the higher reported rates of discrimination for activists than non-activists. We use the shorthand notation "activists" and "non-activists" here to distinguish between sociologists engaged in various forms of political resistance on their campuses and in the profession and those who may have come out at work but do not have a history of political action. Consistent with our expectation that gender influences activist experience (McAdam 1992), we found that more men than women were gay activists (62 percent versus 44 percent, respectively). This is not surprising since, in the 1970s and '80s, women's social movement participation was more likely to have been channeled through feminist and lesbian feminist organizations while men took center stage in the struggle for gay rights (Taylor and Rupp 1993). Within both activist and nonactivist categories, however, men and women reported similar overall rates of career consequences.

Drawing from the interview data as well as the closed- and open-ended survey items, we turn now to a qualitative analysis of five types of con-

Table 3
Types of Career Consequences Reported by Activist and Non-Activist Faculty in 1992

| | Activists | | | | | | Non-Activists | | | | | |
| | Women | | Men | | Total | | Women | | Men | | Total | |
	n	%	n	%	n	%	n	%	n	%	n	%
Bias in Hiring	4	33%	3	19%	7	25%	1	7%	0	0%	1	4%
Bias in Tenure & Promotion	3	25%	4	25%	7	25%	2	13%	2	20%	4	16%
Exclusion from Networks	4	33%	5	31%	9	32%	1	7%	1	10%	2	8%
Scholarly Devaluation	5	42%	8	50%	13	46%	2	13%	2	20%	4	16%
Harassment & Intimidation	3	25%	1	6%	4	14%	1	7%	0	0%	1	4%
Discrimination in Any of the Above	8	67%	12	75%	20	71%	6	40%	3	30%	9	36%

Note: Data are from the 1992 survey of 53 lesbian, gay, and bisexual faculty: 28 activists (12 women and 16 men) and 25 non-activists (15 women and 10 men).

sequences experienced by gay, lesbian, and bisexual faculty: 1) discrimination in hiring; 2) bias in tenure and promotion; 3) exclusion from social and professional networks; 4) devaluation of scholarly work on gay and lesbian topics; and 5) harassment and intimidation.

Discrimination in Hiring

Gay, lesbian, and bisexual sociologists who participated in activism, according to the results of our survey, were more likely to encounter difficulties in obtaining academic positions than non-activists, with 25 percent of the former (7 out of 28) as compared to only 4 percent of the latter (1 out of 25) reporting discrimination in hiring (X^2 = 4.58, p<.05). These figures may even understate the difference since many individuals did not come out or get involved in gay and lesbian activism until after they were hired. As a result, their later decisions to engage in research and teaching on lesbian and gay topics, advise gay and lesbian students or gay student organizations, and/or actively push for gay-affirmative change on their campuses and in their wider communities did not come into play in their original job searches. Further, our data collection methods ruled out those who never found jobs in sociology. Finally, since sexual identity is neither essential nor fixed (Connell 1992; Rust 1993), some individuals in our sample did not identify as gay, lesbian, or bisexual when they were hired.

Because so few individuals come out directly in job interviews, conducting research on gay and lesbian topics is the form of activism most likely to influence hiring. The experiences of interviewees who, before going on the job market, had published in the area point to the risks. One woman who had published on lesbian and gay issues found it very difficult to obtain a tenure-track position. Several of her heterosexual feminist friends were being interviewed more often than she, despite the fact that her record was considerably stronger. One of these friends later informed her that after a job talk several people made remarks in private such as "Oh, thank God. . . . We were concerned that you were a lesbian." Another woman who had been shortlisted for a position specifically designated for someone in the area of sexuality learned that the job had been offered to someone who had done no work in the field. An insider later told her that the chair of the search committee explicitly stated, "We cannot bring in a lesbian."

Another woman, a scholar whose research focuses in part on lesbian feminism, was interviewed for a position as director of women's studies. At a social dinner the night before her interview, she learned that some of the faculty considered her work "dangerous." Further, she added, "an influential senior faculty member made it clear that, if I were offered the position, she would obstruct any attempts to hire my partner, who is a full professor in another discipline." The senior faculty member did manage to block the appointment after convincing others that because critics of women's studies associate lesbianism with feminism "it would not be a good idea to have an open lesbian as head of women's studies." Another interviewee who holds an administrative position at a major research university confirmed that she has found it "very difficult, [even] in fields like theater and women's studies where the climate should be more affirming, to bring lesbian and gay candidates to campus for an interview, let alone to make those kinds of joint appointments." Even more difficult, she said, are efforts to hire scholars of lesbian and gay studies, which she described as an impossibility at her university. Thus, from gatekeepers' decisions whether to bring in candidates to the final selections, the hiring process works against gay, lesbian, and bisexual candidates whose research focuses on lesbian or gay topics. The support of a senior openly gay man or lesbian in a department, sometimes in the position of chair, was cited by some of our interviewees as the factor most likely to explain their having landed an academic position despite a record of gay and lesbian scholarship.

Bias in Tenure and Promotion

Activists were also more likely than non-activists to report bias in the tenure and promotion process: 25 percent of activists (7 out of 28) versus 16 percent of non-activists (4 out of 25) reported problems that they linked to sexual orientation. That the level of discrimination reported by non-activists is greater than in the hiring process reflects the tendency to come out by the time of the tenure decision. Even though many of the activists limited their public association with the gay and lesbian movement before gaining tenure to publishing on lesbian or gay topics, they were still more likely to experience bias. Fearful of the risks associated with being too visible on a campus with no other "out and public" gay or lesbian faculty, one woman who had published on lesbian topics and was a leader in the lesbian and gay community outside the university decided that she would do "no public speaking as a lesbian before tenure." Likewise, a man who had been active in the gay and lesbian movement before moving into academia discussed how, before securing tenure, he chose less visible means of participating. "As soon as I got tenure, I started going back on television again," he noted.

The experiences of interviewees who engaged in other kinds of collective resistance besides publishing on lesbian or gay topics before gaining tenure or promotion point to the risks. One woman who was a visible gay activist both in and outside of the profession and faculty advisor to a gay student union was denied tenure in the mid-'80s, despite the fact that she had published in the major women's studies journals and "networked with all the major scholars in gay and lesbian studies." As a result, she ended up leaving the profession. Reflecting on the experience, she described how being "a heavy-duty gay activist" and advisor to the gay student union "made [her] chairperson frantic" and emphasized the role that her research on lesbian topics must have played in the evaluation:

> Why on earth did I think a bunch of white men at —— was going to give me tenure when in fact the words heterosexism, patriarchy, capitalism, feminism, lesbian . . . [were] in every single title?

Another woman whose research centered on lesbian topics was denied tenure in the early '80s by a high-level administrator despite the fact that her department, the dean, and an ad hoc review committee recommended her unanimously. The year that she went up for tenure, she was the only openly gay person on her West Coast campus where, she reports, she was "perceived as one of the campus radicals both politically, socially, from a feminist perspective, and as a lesbian." Only after a five-year battle did she finally win reinstatement with back pay, an experience that made her leery of going up for full professor. Similarly, another woman who has been in rank as an associate professor at a major research university for more than ten years admitted that she is afraid to put herself up for full professor because she expects her colleagues to discount her research on lesbian topics. Moreover, sympa-

thetic insiders have informed her that many senior faculty view her mentoring of students whose work focuses on gay or lesbian topics, her visibility via media interviews and public speeches on lesbian issues, and her active involvement in the gay and lesbian faculty organization as "evidence of [her] unwillingness to play the game their way."

Another case illustrates the widely shared perception among our interviewees that discrimination is often cloaked in unconvincing disguises. A gay man who specialized in research on homosexuality, taught courses on sexuality, and fought strenuously for gay-affirmative change within the profession recounted how "completely uncomfortable" his chair was with him. Not more than two weeks after finding out that the faculty member was HIV positive, the chair attempted to sabotage his access to a senior position by raising a minor technicality. On his vita, the faculty member had listed the Ph.D. completion date as the year that he defended his dissertation rather than the year the degree was awarded. Despite a letter from the American Sociological Association confirming the acceptability of this practice, the chair formed a committee to investigate. Shortly afterwards, the chair and university administration tried to make the faculty member sign a terminal contract. An insider on the committee reported that "in the deliberations they were clearly trying to get rid of [him] because [he] was gay and HIV positive." Our data suggest, then, that even though coming out for personal reasons can lead to difficulties in obtaining tenure and promotion, gay, lesbian, and bisexual sociologists known as activists are more likely to encounter bias.

Exclusion From Social and Professional Networks

Although simply coming out to colleagues can result in exclusion from social and professional networks, participating in gay activism places lesbian, gay, and bisexual sociologists at greater risk of encountering such segregation. Survey data show that while 32 percent of activists (9 out of 28) reported exclusion, only 8 percent (2 out of 25) of non-activists suffered these consequences ($X^2 = 4.65$, p<.05). Some interviewees sensed that they were shut out not so much because they were gay but because their activism made them, as one respondent put it, "very visibly gay." One woman, reflecting on her own isolation from social and professional circles, explored the distinction:

> It's not just that I'm out—there are a lot of out faculty on our campus now. It's that, to a lot of faculty and students, I have a . . . role as a kind of leader in terms of lesbian and gay issues, especially in dealing with university administration and system-wide change.

At times gay men and lesbians may not even know that they are being ostracized. Most interviewees mentioned that they had only become aware of their exclusion from colleagues who were included in these networks. One tenured faculty woman who is an activist on her campus emphasized that most discrimination takes place without awareness on the part of lesbians and gay men:

> I suffered horrible ridicule and discrimination in the department but usually didn't know about it until after it occurred. You see, I was so far outside the networks that no one even told me about all of the events I was missing.

A bisexual woman who previously identified as lesbian but recently married reported:

> When I really saw the homophobia was when I got involved with my husband and realized the extent to which I hadn't been invited to things when I identified as a lesbian. Because all of a sudden I was invited to stuff I'd never been invited to before.

Previous studies reveal that gay men and lesbians who work in traditional settings are likely to have fewer social contacts with co-workers than do their heterosexual peers (Humphreys 1972; Levine 1979; Lewis 1979; Schneider 1984, 1986, 1988). The vast majority of interviewees reported isolation not only from informal social circles but also from more formal and professional departmental, campus, and national networks. Sometimes the social segregation is voluntary. Several of the gay men and lesbians we interviewed explained that they are not always eager to socialize with heterosexual colleagues who insist that sexual orientation is exclusively a "private matter." The problem is that, in addition to being important sources of interpersonal support, social networks have been shown by previous studies to be linked to hiring and upward mobility (Jacobs 1986; Landino and Welch 1990; Reskin and Roos 1990).

Among those who failed to earn tenure, exclusion from both informal and formal networks was cited as a major factor. One woman who was recommended by her department for tenure but was denied at higher levels explained:

> I definitely feel [being excluded] very much had an effect on my tenure review. . . . They didn't invite me either as an individual or as a member of a couple to most things. And I think it made a big difference because when the higher-up committees review you, how strongly they support you and whether you're known to the top administrators or not makes a difference. I wasn't known to the top administrators except by my documents.

In the few instances in which interviewees were fully integrated into departmental and campus networks, respondents went out of their way to explain why: Either their campuses were situated in gay-affirmative regions of the country on the East or West Coast, or the composition of their departments had changed dramatically in recent years. An openly gay man who was recently asked to chair his department attributed the offer in part to the fact that several older and more conservative faculty members had retired, leaving the department socially and politically more progressive and making him one of the most senior faculty members.

Devaluation of Scholarly Work on Lesbian and Gay Topics

Since 1981, little has changed for those who have what several of our respondents called "lavender vitae," a record of scholarly publication on gay and lesbian topics. Even among the non-activist faculty in our sample, whose research focused on more mainstream subjects, 16 percent (4 out of 25) noted that they had been dissuaded from their initial intentions to do gay or lesbian research. Forty-six percent of activists (13 out of 28) reported being strongly discouraged by graduate advisors, mentors, and even supportive colleagues from beginning or continuing such work (X^2=5.61, p.<05). Those who defied the warning described systematic and continuing patterns of bias that included difficulties finding faculty willing to serve on their doctoral dissertation committees, obtaining research support in the form of grants and fellowships, getting their work fairly reviewed, and publishing in the top journals.

One woman who failed to land a permanent faculty position at an institution where she was already teaching was told that it was because her extensive list of publications focused on lesbians. After the hiring meeting, she was informed that "the faculty, all men but one, did not find [her] work interesting or exciting." A senior woman said that she had been advised recently by an ally "not to give a job talk focused on [her] work on lesbians." An associate professor looking toward promotion reported that none of her departmental colleagues has expressed an interest in her work in lesbian studies, even though she is frequently invited to speak on other campuses. Moreover, she added, there is "no recognition that my publication pattern—that is, chapters in edited volumes and articles in feminist journals—has been influenced by the nature of my work." Several respondents echoed her concerns, noting that they had been discouraged from seeking promotion to full professor because senior professors wanted them to have "a more traditional file." The overwhelming majority of those we interviewed interpreted both subtle and obvious admonitions to do "more mainstream work" as directives to do "straight work." Many also emphasized that their research on gay or lesbian topics is not only marginalized but often characterized as mere activism rather than serious scholarship. One man whose work focuses on the status of gays in the work place noted that his colleagues have referred to him as a "professional homosexual." Another common way of discrediting gay and lesbian studies is by questioning its content on scientific grounds:

> People [assume] you are doing it only as a political matter and not for intellectual reasons. . . . And then at the intellectual level, there are a lot of questions about whether or not anything said about us is generalizable, and consequently an unwillingness to see that what can be said about lesbians and gay men has any kind of universal significance.

Overall, the experiences described by these lesbian and gay sociologists in getting their work funded, published, and acknowledged are similar to those documented by early scholars of women's studies and black or African-American studies (Spender 1981; Lorde 1984; D'Emilio 1992). The ultimate impact of having one's research constantly underrated and questioned as to its relevance to the "central concerns of the discipline" can be seen in one of our interviewees' decision to leave the profession, an experience that he described as "the loss of a dream." This is not, however, an isolated incident, in addition to the four persons included in the interview sample who gave up academic careers because they encountered discrimination, our respondents named at least a dozen other gay and lesbian sociologists who have left academia voluntarily or as a result of being denied tenure. If there is

a single finding that best reflects the significance for one's career of concentrating on gay and lesbian subjects, it is that the fewest difficulties in hiring and in tenure and promotion were described by individuals whose research focuses on mainstream specialties. One respondent captured this point best when he remarked, "I think it's definitely considered more acceptable to *be* gay than it is to *write* about it."

Harassment and Intimidation

Activists were also somewhat more likely than non-activists to report being the target of harassment or intimidation, with 14 percent of the former (4 out of 28) as compared to 4 percent of the latter (1 out of 25) reporting such bias. That these figures are lower than the 27 percent rate of work place harassment documented in Comstock's (1991) study lends some credence to the general perception that college and university campuses are more tolerant of diversity than nonacademic settings. Nevertheless, interviewees' accounts validate the fear expressed by many respondents that visibility as an activist can lead to retaliation: "everything from students not taking your course to personal intimidation."

Several interviewees reported that students regularly voice homophobic reactions and/or write negative comments in evaluations. For instance, one man who was at the forefront of a struggle to create a more gay-friendly environment on his campus recalled that in the middle of a large introductory sociology class, a fraternity member who was not enrolled in the course barged into the room and called him "faggot." A lesbian known for her participation in the local lesbian, gay, and bisexual movement and her inclusion of gay and lesbian experiences in her teaching recounted some of the comments she has received on student evaluations:

> I don't think the university should allow dykes or homos to teach this course.

> I think it is sick that a lesbian fish-eater could be allowed to teach America's youth. Her anti-white male approach to teaching is disgusting and a cancer to American society today. My last words are down with Professor ——.

A number of the faculty we interviewed also encountered students who took their complaints outside the classroom. One woman reported that she "got turned in to the state legislature" for having her women's studies students write hypothetical coming out letters as part of an exercise on identity politics, and others also had their women's studies courses criticized in national publications for their lesbian content.

Some interviewees also reported incidents of blatant homophobia from colleagues and administrators. One man's department chair had a reputation for telling homophobic jokes. A woman who advises several lesbian graduate students quoted a male colleague who described her women students as arriving with long hair, nice clothes, and boyfriends, "and then after a few months in the department they shave off all their hair and get girlfriends." She said that other colleagues have told her that her own identity as a lesbian is the reason that there are "too many lesbian graduate students in the department."

In addition to the face-to-face homophobic incidents that gay and lesbian sociologists report, some of our interviewees indicate they have been subjected to anonymous harassment and intimidation. One woman repeated a message she received on her answering machine during the Senate committee deliberations on Clarence Thomas: "I'm surprised you're not at home gloating over this, you dyke." She was also sent a copy of a newspaper article about a study that she was conducting on women's economic status. The sender had defaced her picture and written a homophobic letter that asked: "What would a dyke know about single women raising kids on their own?" Placing her experiences in context, she explained: "A lot of times it's my visibility [as a lesbian] in the community and the university. I give talks, I'm quoted in the papers, and I'm on TV and radio . . . so I'm easily a target for that kind of stuff."

The dangers for lesbian and gay activists extend, then, outside the walls of the academy and can even include the types of hate-motivated violence analyzed by Jenness (1995). Women faculty were especially likely to describe this type of anonymous harassment and intimidation. When one woman was teaching a gender course in which conflict had erupted between male and female students, she reported that someone drove up to her house and left a note on the door reading: "Next time, we'll kill you, dyke." The cars of another woman and her partner were repeatedly vandalized or stolen following a widely publicized confrontation she had with a male graduate student who was "opposed to studying women." One of our interviewees reported being raped on a re-

search site visit, with the rapist repeatedly calling her a lesbian during the attack. Her experience is not unique in light of Schneider's (1991) finding that 20 percent of lesbians are sexually assaulted in the work place. That women in our survey sample were more likely than men to be subjected to harassment and intimidation illustrates the multiplicative effects of gender and sexual orientation as interlocking systems of oppression (Collins 1990).

We have assessed the risks of gay activism by looking at five different ways that political participation affects the careers of gay, lesbian, and bisexual sociologists. A few words are in order about the combined effects of the various obstacles described here on the careers of the men and women who participated in this study. Although 55 percent of the faculty surveyed (29 out of 53) reported some form of professional discrimination linked to sexual orientation, the disparity between the rates of discrimination for gay, lesbian, and bisexual sociologists who have a history of activist participation and those who do not is striking. Seventy-one percent of activists (20 out of 28) indicated that their careers have been negatively affected by their political activities, but only 36 percent (9 out of 25) of gay, lesbian, and bisexual sociologists who have come out but are not politically active reported career discrimination ($X^2 = 6.72$, $p < .01$). The paradox is that the same strategies of resistance that have opened the door for more lesbian, gay, and bisexual sociologists to come out in academia have also made the pioneers of the movement easy targets of retaliation and discrimination.

Conclusions

The Sociologists' Lesbian and Gay Caucus emerged and took shape in the 1970s and mid-1980s when identity-based organizing, ethnic-essentialist ideas, and assimilationist strategies dominated gay and lesbian politics and other cultural political struggles in the United States. In this article, we present data that challenge those who criticize identity-based strategies as a retreat from a politics into lifestyle, the self, and representation. We argue that the deployment of identity for the purposes of contesting stigmatized group representations and achieving institutional change is, instead, a form of high-risk political activism. We have arrived at this explanation by analyzing the professional and personal repercussions suffered by gay, lesbian, and bisexual sociologists who have promoted equality for gays in higher education. Although we have found the costs of activism to be substantial, it is clear that two decades of political struggle have opened the discipline to a certain degree by enhancing the opportunities for lesbian, gay, and bisexual sociologists to come out. There were, after all, almost twice the number of sociologists in academic positions willing to participate in our survey in 1992 than in 1981, and the majority of lesbian, gay, and bisexual sociologists are more open about their sexual identities today than they were a decade ago. Our findings do nevertheless provide support for the apprehension, still expressed by most gay academics, that coming out to colleagues and students, teaching and publishing on gay and lesbian topics, and promoting equality for lesbians, gays, and bisexuals in the academic workplace can have significant professional and personal costs. In light of the predictions of social movement theory, we are not surprised to discover that gay sociologists who are the most visible and politically active on their campuses are more likely to be the targets of discrimination. But our analysis also acknowledges that even those lesbian and gay sociologists who avoid activism and treat coming out as a personal choice face on-the-job discrimination, disadvantages, and harassment.

To return to the theoretical questions raised at the outset of this article, this study is one of few empirical examinations of the formation, use, and impact of identity politics that draws upon recent social constructionist models of collective identity in social movement theory (Cohen 1985b; Melucci 1985, 1989; Taylor 1989b; Taylor and Whittier 1992a; Whittier 1995). We conclude, therefore, by relating our findings to the larger body of literature on social movements. Our analysis illustrates, first, how personalized political strategies are used to contest oppressive identity models of dominated groups and derive from the concrete institutional and cultural practices that sustain a group's social position. The collective identity framework responds to the call of sociological post-modern and queer theorists (Seidman 1993; Gamson 1994; Stein and Plummer 1994) who emphasize the need to connect cultural representation and identity to the forms and sites of protest used by a particular challenging group and the unique structural disadvantages experienced by that group. The Sociologists' Lesbian and Gay Caucus mobilized to counter stigmatizing scientific and medical constructions of same-sex desire and to win acceptance of gays in the discipline and on their campuses. To the extent that these goals are tied to the discourses and institutional practices of higher education, they require individual strategies such as coming out, conducting research on and teaching about lesbian and gay lives, advising gay and lesbian students and/or student organizations, and actively pushing for gay-affirmative change on campus and in the wider community that have political as well as personal consequences. In an ideal world, the work of gay scholars and teachers would be seen as no more or less political than the work of any other academic. Because, however, the process of negotiating what it means to be a gay sociologist makes individuals a site of political activity, it not only alters the meaning of individuals' scholarship and teaching, but it increases their probability of experiencing discrimination and the likelihood that they will recognize it.

Second, by linking the two separate concepts of identity politics and high-risk activism, this study calls attention to another set of social processes that helps to explain the long-term implications of social movement participation. Scholars who have addressed the impact of what we have conceptualized as personalized political strategies widely agree that participation in the grassroots feminist, civil rights, student, anti-war, and sanctuary movements has stamped a lasting imprint on the occupations, incomes, marriage patterns, and personal lives of activists (McAdam 1986, 1988a, 1989, Marwell, Aiken, and Demerath 1987; Flacks 1988; Whalen and Flacks 1989; Wilitfang and McAdam 1991; Whittier 1991). Concentrated in certain "helping" or activist occupations, they earn significantly lower incomes than non-activists. Studies generally attribute these effects to ideology, specifically the fact that the movements under consideration made members' entire lives a political project and advocated the subordination of career to politics. Our theoretical argument posits that the negative effects of identity politics also may result from the repression, intimidation, and reprisals exercised by dominant groups. By highlighting the external processes that account for the transformative potential of protest on individual lives, our analysis sheds light on a set of factors that has been largely overlooked by the previous literature on social movements. Because identity politics can be both enabling and constraining, the same personalized political strategies that have opened the door for some gay, lesbian, and bisexual sociologists have made activist pioneers easy targets of exclusionary practices and discrimination that have altered the course of their academic careers.

Rather than close on such a pessimistic note, we should emphasize that our findings are based on the long-term experiences of the first generation of openly gay and lesbian sociologists. Certainly it cannot be denied that things have progressed since the late 1950s and early 1960s, when any sign of homosexuality by a college pro-

fessor was enough to warrant a visit from a legislative investigative committee (*Advocate* 1993). For a few gay, lesbian, and bisexual sociologists, activism has resulted in professional visibility, recognition, and other opportunities as the political climate in recent years has grown slightly more favorable and the field of gay and lesbian studies takes shape. Our study therefore suggests the need for greater attention by movement analysts to the positive as well as the negative individual outcomes of protest as well as to variations in the cost of political activism during different points in a movement's history. ✦

36

Social Movement Spillover

David S. Meyer
Nancy Whittier

In the early 1980s, antinuclear weapons activists and politicians courting their support actively sought the endorsement of the so-called "mothers" of the nuclear freeze, Helen Caldicott, perhaps its most prolific and polemical advocate, and Randall Forsberg, who drafted the initial proposal and political strategy. The visibility of these women reflected not only the perceived strength of the freeze movement, but also the less direct influence of an earlier movement—the second wave of feminist mobilization begun in the late 1960s. The notion of two women legitimately claiming leadership of a movement concerned with military and foreign policy is inconceivable without the influence of the women's movement.

Social movements are not self-contained and narrowly focused unitary actors, but rather are a collection of formal organizations, informal networks, and unaffiliated individuals engaged in a more or less coherent struggle for change (Buechler 1990; McCarthy and Zald 1977; Morris 1984; Staggenborg 1989). Because social movements aspire to change not only specific policies, but also broad cultural and institutional structures, they have effects far beyond their explicitly articulated goals. The ideas, tactics, style, participants, and organizations of one movement often *spill over* its boundaries to affect other social movements.

Scholars have found mutual influence among social movements in numerous empirical studies—the impact of the civil rights movements on the student and antiwar movements (McAdam 1988a), of civil rights and the New Left on the women's movement (Evans 1979), and of the struggle for the abolition of slavery on the woman suffrage movement (DuBois 1978)—yet this sub-

ject has received little theoretical attention. McCarthy and Zald's (1977) resource mobilization perspective points to competition among social movement organizations within a social movement industry or the broader social movement sector, but it conceptualizes inter-organizational relations relatively narrowly in terms of contemporaneous competition for resources and adherents. Subsequent studies have examined competition and interaction among organizations within *one* movement, while the social movement sector contains all social movements, including opponents as well as allies. Neither concept taps the interactions among allied, but separate, challenges, and neither calls attention to cooperation and mutual influence as well as competition. Subsequent studies have examined competition and interaction among organizations within the same movement or between movement and countermovement organizations (e.g., Gitlin 1987; Miller 1987; Staggenborg 1991), but they have not examined *how* different social movements affect one another or developed a systematic way to study these effects.

In this paper we explore the nature of movement-movement influence through a case study of the women's movement impact on peace protest in the 1980s. Historians and analysts have convincingly shown that the radical women's movement[1] of the 1960s and 1970s emerged from earlier civil rights, student, and anti-war movements, but scholars have conceptualized feminism primarily as influenced *by* other movements rather than as exerting an influence on them (Echols 1989; Evans 1979; Freeman 1975; Hole and Levine 1971). We argue here that the peace protest of the early 1980s was profoundly influenced by the women's movement. We use this case to begin building a theory of movement outcomes that considers a wide range of potential effects, including not only explicitly articulated goals, but also *spillover effects* on subsequent challenging movements.

Recognizing the phenomenon of social movement spillover adds to our understanding of social movement outcomes and the continuity of challenges over time. We begin by discussing the theoretical underpinnings of this work, drawing from both collective identity (Cohen 1985b; Melucci 1985, 1989; Taylor 1989b) and political process (McAdam 1982; Tarrow 1991; Tilly 1978, 1983) approaches to the study of social movements. We

"Social Movement Spillover." *Social Problems* 41:277-298. Copyright © 1994 by the Society for the Study of Social Problems. Reprinted with permission.

then examine the case of the peace movement, which historically has featured extensive participation by women, and trace the development of the "second wave" of feminist activism in the late 1960s, noting its roots in the peace and antiwar movements. We briefly describe the re-emergence of a broadbased peace movement in the early 1980s in the form of a nuclear freeze campaign and show that the women's movement influenced the ideological frames, tactics, leadership, and organizational structure of the freeze. We identify four specific routes of movement-movement transmission: organizational coalitions, overlapping social movement communities, shared personnel, and changes in the external environment achieved by one movement that then shape subsequent movements. We conclude with a discussion of the significance and implications of social movement spillover.

Conceptualizing Social Movement Outcomes

Although social movements struggle for a set of explicitly-articulated goals, including changes in state policy, the private sector, and cultural norms, they also influence indirect targets. These indirect targets include the practices, perspectives, and outcomes of other collective actors, as well as the lives of participants. There is virtually no theoretical literature that specifically addresses the influence of one challenging social movement on another (but see Giugni 1992b; Rucht and McAdam 1992). We draw on two distinct sets of literature to conceptualize social movement spillover effects: a political process approach that focuses on the effects of movements; and work drawing on new social movement theory that focuses on the continuity of collective challenges.

The *political process* approach defines a social movement as a sustained challenge to state policy that has observable origins, peaks, and declines in activity, and uses a combination of conventional and non-conventional collective action (e.g., McAdam 1982; Tarrow 1991; Tilly 1978, 1983). In this view, social movements are visible through their public actions, and their effects include state and organizational responses as well as *successor* effects on subsequent challenges to the state. Movements can affect one another by passing information about state responses to collective action, identifying potential strengths and vulnerabilities in the political structure, or affect-

ing changes in the external environment that restructure political opportunities (Gamson and Meyer 1992). As states alter the costs and benefits of collective action and develop new techniques for controlling collective action, they allow, encourage, or discourage movements to adopt particular strategies of influence. Clusters of social movements then flourish and decline in cycles as states respond to movement challenges and alter the opportunities available to contemporary and subsequent movements (Meyer 1993c; Tarrow 1991).

Others see social movements as more than just visible political challenges to the state, noting that movements often survive the low points of protest cycles and continue even when not staging direct political challenges to the state or public policy (Morris 1984; Taylor 1989b). By emphasizing the relationship between group consciousness and collective action, this work dovetails with new social movement theory, which argues that contemporary social movements are distinctive because they organize around a common identity and seek to challenge dominant meaning systems and definitions of their group as much as they seek changes in the state (Cohen 1985b; Melucci 1985, 1989; Touraine 1985; Pizzorno 1978). Scholars looking at social movement continuity point to the importance of oppositional culture and the collective identity of participants in sustaining a challenge over the long haul (Taylor 1989b). In this view, movements do not simply die or emerge from nowhere, but adopt a variety of forms and strategies in order to adapt to changing external and internal conditions (Rupp and Taylor 1987; Zald and Ash 1966).

Challenges take two main courses in their endurance over time. First, a number of studies point to the persistence of ideology, organizations, and strategies used by one constituency to address one set of issues. These include Isserman's (1987) analysis of the links between the Old Left and the New Left, Staggenborg's (1991) account of the changing structure and level of pro-choice activism over twenty years, Rupp and Taylor's (1987) documentation of the endurance of the women's movement in the 1940s and 1950s, Morris's (1984) examination of the civil rights movement's origins in the 1950s, and Whittier's (1994b) analysis of the long-term activism of participants in the radical feminist movement of the 1960s and 1970s. During the low points of protest cycles, movements survive in a variety of what Taylor (1989b) describes as "abeyance" structures, that is, organizational forms that preserve movement culture and values.

Second, and more important for our purposes, as a movement shifts into abeyance on one set of issues, its personnel and organizations may switch the grounds of the challenge to another set of issues. Rosenthal et al. (1985), for example, note the dense network among women's rights activists in New York state at the turn of the century, even as so-called "women's issues" were rarely their central explicit concern. Other scholars have identified the women's movement's origins in the civil rights and New Left movements (Evans 1979), the Communist Party's connections with women's liberation (Weigand 1993), and the roots of the 1960s student movements in the civil rights struggles commenced earlier (McAdam 1988a; Miller 1987). We thus see effects of social movements on other subsequent movements in response to changing political opportunities.

The effects of one wave of activism then include subsequent waves of activism. As a result, the questions of social movement continuity and social movement outcomes are inherently tied together. Challenges initiated by an oppositional group at one time are sustained in subsequent decades both through abeyance structures that maintain the identity and claims of the challenge, and through the transformation and migration of the movement into other related challenges. Social movement abeyance then is not necessarily a retreat from political mobilization, but may also include mobilization on different, more promising—or urgent—political issues. Social movement spillover is a product of both contemporaneous and successor effects, as movements influence each other directly, alter successive challenges, and affect the larger terrain on which they struggle. In order to understand the shift from issue to issue, we need to examine both changes in political opportunity structures and changes in activists' collective identities. We can examine movement outcomes on three interdependent levels: public policy, culture, and movement participants. Each of these is important not just for its impact on the larger society, but for its direct and indirect effects on other social movements. We focus here on allied movements of the left, but changes in policy, culture, and participants affect opposing movements as well.

Policy

Numerous studies of social movement effects deal explicitly with public policy. In most cases' scholars have focused on the relative success or failure of challenges. Gamson's (1990) influential work conceptualizes two components of success: a challenging group can win recognition as a legitimate actor in politics, and/or gain new advantages for itself or its beneficiary constituency. Broadly speaking, these dimensions refer to the substance (new advantages) and process (recognition and participation) of public policy. Subsequent scholars assessed outcomes differently but accepted this general definition of success (Piven and Cloward 1971, 1979; Button 1978).

Public policy includes both substantive and symbolic components. Policymakers often make symbolic concessions in an attempt to avoid granting the aggrieved group's substantive demands or giving it new power. In domestic policy, elected officials offer combinations of rhetorical concessions or attacks, in conjunction with symbolic policy changes, to respond to or preempt political challenges (Edelman 1971). In a particularly garish example, President Reagan attempted to obviate criticism of his education policies by enlisting a teacher in the space shuttle program. In foreign policy, the government may pursue arms control negotiations or softer or harder rhetorical lines in response to domestic pressures (Miller 1985). Both symbolic and substantive concessions in response to pressure from one social movement change the context in which other challengers operate. They may open or close avenues of influence, augment or diminish the pressure a movement can bring to bear, or raise or lower the costs of mobilization.

Culture

Social movements struggle on a broad cultural plane, of which state policy is only one parameter (Fantasia 1988; Gusfield 1981b; Taylor and Whittier 1994). Wuthnow (1989) suggests that contemporary social movements are a primary agent of cultural change and, in fact, collective actors often explicitly seek to alter the dominant culture. Campaigns may focus on changing discourse about a particular topic, challenging the symbolic meaning of objects, or overturning behavioral norms. The women's movement sought to change expectations about women's career and family positions, criticized language that relegated women to a subordinate position, and argued against standards of feminine appearance requiring women to wear make-up and restrictive clothing (Taylor and Whittier 1993). Social movement strategies draw on the dominant culture as well as incorporate new symbols, reconstruct discourse, and display alternative norms (Swidler 1986). Movements produce culture, and cultural changes are an important product of collective action.

In addition to their direct impact on social life, cultural norms and symbols constrain government policy. For example, military women's participation in combat roles, inconceivable two decades ago, is now a contested mainstream political issue. A number of scholars have argued that the cultural effects of movements, though often neglected by analysts, frequently last longer and have greater influence than more narrow, short-term policy victories and defeats (Breines 1982; Gusfield 1981b; Rochon 1992). Indeed, in the absence of concrete policy successes, movements are likely to find culture a more accessible venue in which to struggle. In the late 1970s and 1980s, Eastern European dissidents chose explicitly "antipolitical" strategies of participation, in a deliberate attempt to create a "civil society," that is, a set of social networks and relationships independent of the state (Havel 1985). This battle, in the least promising of circumstances, proved to be critical in precipitating and shaping the end of the cold war (Meyer and Marullo 1992).

The cultural changes promoted by a social movement affect not only the external environment but also other social movements. As sexism and racism became less acceptable in U.S. society, for example, they became less accepted in social movement organizations as well. Further, as Freeman (1983b) argues, the social movements of the 1960s encouraged activists to take up a broad variety of issues in extra-institutional challenges by demonstrating political efficacy, expanding tactical repertoires, and legitimating protest. Essentially, they helped create a civic culture of political activism in which lobbying, protest, and organizing were socially acceptable parts of everyday life. Importantly, these broad cultural changes influenced the development of movements on the left and the right.

Participants

Finally, social movements influence the people who participate in them. Through movement participation, individuals construct new politicized perspectives on the world and their own identities (Ferree and Miller 1985). Conscious of this, organizers seeking to mobilize protest explicitly try to change the "frames" through which activists view the world (Snow et al. 1986). Participants construct and internalize oppositional collective identities in the process of collective action (Morris 1992). That is, activists come to see themselves as members of a group that is differentiated from outsiders, interpret their experiences in political terms, and politicize their actions in social movement contexts and in everyday life (Melucci 1989; Taylor and Whittier 1992). Collective identities constructed during periods of peak mobilization endure even as protest dies down. One-time movement participants continue to see themselves as progressive activists even as organized collective action decreases, and they make personal and political decisions in light of this identity (Fendrich and Lovoy 1988; McAdam 1988a, 1989; Whalen and Flacks 1987; Whittier 1994b). By changing the way individuals live, movements affect longer term changes in the society.

In summary, movements can influence not only the terrain upon which subsequent challengers struggle, but also the resources available to the challengers and the general atmosphere surrounding the struggle. In changing policy and the policymaking process, movements can alter the structure of political opportunity new challengers face (Gamson and Meyer 1992). By affecting changes in culture, movements can change the values and symbols with which both mainstream and dissident actors operate (Edelman 1971; Gusfield 1981b). They can expand the tactical repertoire available to new movements (Meyer 1992; Tarrow 1993; Tilly 1992). By changing participants' lives, movements alter the personnel available for subsequent challenges. Taken together, *one movement can influence subsequent movements both from outside and from within: by altering the political and cultural conditions it confronts in the external environment, and by changing the individuals, groups, and norms within the movement itself.* Movement-movement influence is not a one-way street; rather, social movements may have a mu-

Figure 1

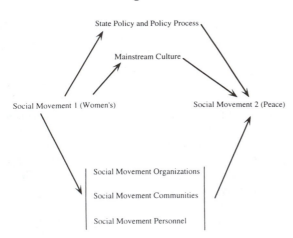

tual and reciprocal impact, as did the women's and peace movements.

The women's movement of the 1960s and 1970s produced far-reaching changes in policy, culture, and participants. It sought both concrete changes in government and corporate policy, and changes in popular attitudes and expectations about women's roles in politics and social life. In policy, the effects of the movement included formal prohibitions on sex discrimination, recognition of women's rights as protected by the government, and the legalization of abortion (Ferree and Hess 1985; Freeman 1975; Gelb and Palley 1987; Mansbridge 1986). Women became more visible in the policy process both inside and outside of government, winning greater access to formal political institutions and leadership positions in a broad variety of public policy advocacy organizations (Boles 1991; Freeman 1987; Klein 1984; Mueller 1987). Well after the peak of extra-institutional activity, women continued to enter mainstream political institutions, changed by their experience in the women's movement, ultimately altering even institutions as apparently intractable as the military and the Catholic Church (Katzenstein 1990).

The influence of the feminist challenge on mainstream culture was profound, as the movement expanded the range of employment and family options open to women and introduced concepts such as "male chauvinism," "sexism," and "sexual harassment" into popular parlance. By the late 1980s, polls showed widespread support among both women and men for such feminist

tenets as women's access to the professions, equal pay for equal work, and opposition to sexual harassment (Boles 1991). It is not surprising then, that the women's movement, based around a fundamental social cleavage, would affect other social movements.

Data and Methods

In order to discover the effects and routes of social movement spillover, we employ an inductive two-way process-tracing approach. By looking at the peace movement of the 1980s and comparing it with earlier peace movement campaigns, we can identify distinct differences in such variables as organizational structure, leadership, and values, and trace the roots of these changes back to the women's movement of the 1970s. We ask the counterfactual question: Would these historical departures be possible without the women's movement? We report only elements that cannot be explained credibly without reference to the women's movement. We also process-trace forward, examining the development of the women's movement by tracing the activities of key leaders and organizations to new issues and activities through time. We identify phenomena that can be explained most parsimoniously by spillover and provide historical evidence of how this took place in order to develop a robust and credible theoretical model.

This analysis draws on research conducted on the peace movement and on the women's movement during the 1970s and 1980s. The peace movement data include primary historical research and is supplemented by secondary sources (Kleidman 1993; Lofland and Marullo 1990; McCrae and Markle 1989; Meyer 1990, 1993a,b,c; Solo 1988; Waller 1987). Data on the women's movement include organizational documents and in-depth interviews with 44 core leaders in a cluster of feminist organizations in Columbus, Ohio, a mid-sized city centered around a university and state government, that typifies the local settings central to both the women's movement and the freeze.[2] These are supplemented by data on the women's movement at the national level from other studies (Echols 1989; Mansbridge 1986; Ryan 1992; Staggenborg 1991; Buechler 1990; Ferree and Hess 1985; Taylor and Whittier 1992).

The nuclear freeze movement was striking in its combination of national coordination and visibility with widespread grassroots organizing. The present study's combination of national-level and local-level data makes it possible to examine the impact of the women's movement on the peace movement both at the level of national policy and media visibility, and in the micro-mobilization contexts at the grassroots level that shape the participation of most activists (McAdam, McCarthy, and Zald 1988).

The Peace Movement and the Women's Movement

The peace movement and the women's movement have long and linked histories. The peace movement is comprised generally of two broad wings that have waxed and waned in concert (Wittner 1984). One, based primarily in pacifist and religious groups, has espoused a broad critique of U.S. foreign policy, and called for far-reaching transformation of governmental and social institutions. Activists within this wing emphasize expressive rather than instrumental activities and frequently engage in dramatic direct action and civil disobedience campaigns at military sites. A second wing, comprised primarily of liberal-internationalist groups, has advocated the management of international conflict and nuclear weapons through multinational agreements and arms control. Its activity has been largely based in Washington, D.C., and its partisans have worked primarily through institutional politics. Periodically, both wings have united to stage broad protest campaigns that have reached the political mainstream (Meyer 1991, 1993b,c).

Women participated extensively in both wings of the movement, but in different ways. Women have been extremely visible and active in the direct action wing of the movement, founding separate women's organizations such as the Women's International League for Peace and Freedom (WILPF, 1915) and Women Strike for Peace (WSP, 1960), and taking leadership roles in mixed-sex groups such as the American Friends Service Committee (AFSC). In this regard, women have been at the forefront of making morality-based claims against war in general, specific wars, and the nuclear arms race. They have emphasized images of women as mothers of prospective soldiers or as protectors of the home, often similar to conventional notions of women's difference. Within the institutionally oriented wing of the movement, men filled virtually all leadership roles in major organizations (e.g.,

Committee for a Sane Nuclear Policy [SANE], Federation of American Scientists, Council for a Livable World, Union of Concerned Scientists) before the 1980s. Women were far less visible, although they were active as participants and working in the rank-and-file of organizations.

In summary, women's participation in the peace movement was two-tiered before the feminist resurgence of the 1960s and 1970s. Women led or participated visibly in organizations that used traditional feminine roles to make moral claims against war and nuclear weapons, and they generally worked outside institutional politics. In the institutional wing of the peace movement, women were relegated to supporting roles. Claims of policy expertise and discussion of negotiations, compromises, and partial solutions remained the province of men.

Indeed, the subordinate role women were forced into in the campaign against the Vietnam War was one of the sparks for the resurgence of the feminist movement's second wave. Women who participated in the civil rights, student, and anti-Vietnam War movements rebelled against their second-class position and the trivialization of their concerns. Beginning in 1967, these women formed the initial socialist feminist and radical feminist groups (Echols 1989; Evans 1979; Freeman 1975). Early radical and socialist feminist organizations such as the Chicago Women's Liberation Union, Bread and Roses, New York Radical Women, and Columbus Ohio Women's Liberation remained closely linked to the New Left and peace groups from which they emerged. For example, Columbus Ohio Women's Liberation worked in coalition with anti-war and civil rights groups to organize a student strike at the Ohio State University in the wake of the Kent State shootings. Feminist groups that maintained close ties with the New Left and saw themselves as part of a broader movement to transform society along socialist lines were termed "politico" to distinguish them from emerging feminist groups with fewer ties to the male-dominated Left (Echols 1989).

In the early 1970s, however, radical feminist groups around the country distanced themselves further from the male Left and emphasized the separateness of the women's movement. By the mid-1970s an extensive and largely autonomous feminist community had emerged in most major cities (Buechler 1990; Echols 1989; Taylor and

Whittier 1992; Whittier 1994a). Feminist service organizations such as rape crisis centers and battered women's shelters combined with feminist businesses such as bookstores, music production companies, and women's theater groups to form a dense and wide-reaching network with a distinct culture. Although the radical feminist organizations that initially grew from the New Left were key to this community, organizations that emerged separately in the liberal wing of the women's movement were also connected, and feminists with varying outlooks cooperated on common issues, such as ratifying the Equal Rights Amendment (ERA).

The women's movement of the late 1960s and 1970s developed ideological frames, tactics, organizational structures, and culture that shaped later movements. Feminist organizations emphasized the politics of process, in an effort to allow all members to have an equal voice in making decisions about their actions. The New Left movements of the 1960s had claimed a commitment to "participatory democracy," but it was the women's movement that consistently attempted to implement a non-hierarchical structure through such practices as consensus decision making and rotation of leadership positions (Breines 1982; Epstein 1991; Pateman 1970). Because the feminist movement drew explicit connections between personal and political lives and between local and national politics, it sought social change from the bottom up as well as substantive policy changes from above. The slogan "the personal is political" came to mean that meaningful political change required change in the way people lived, and that the problems individuals experienced in organizing their own lives often reflected broader social injustices, and were therefore matters of legitimate political action. When the peace movement re-emerged in the early 1980s, its form and content reflected the wide-reaching impact of feminism.

Peace Protest of the 1980s: The Nuclear Freeze

The year 1980 was a watershed for peace activists and feminists alike. Ronald Reagan's election to the presidency was a major gain for the New Right, and activists on the left viewed it as signaling the beginning of increased anti-feminism and militarism. The administration's cuts in social programs decimated many social movement organizations (Imig 1992); at the same time the attack galvanized activists. For the women's movement, although the final push to ratify the ERA by 1982 was unsuccessful, it led to mobilization on a variety of other issues (Costain 1992; Mansbridge 1986; Ryan 1992; Staggenborg 1991). Yet an anti-feminist countermovement had gained sufficient strength and institutional support by 1980 to block most feminist challenges. Failure to pass the ERA led feminists to look for more promising issues for political action (Gelb and Palley 1987).

Coalitions between feminist and peace organizations increased in the face of what both viewed as a hostile political environment; peace and women's groups co-sponsored such events as a national march in 1981, a series of Mother's Day demonstrations for peace, and a demonstration of one million people in New York City in June 1982. At the local level, feminist groups in Columbus sponsored anti-nuclear weapons rallies, such as one in 1981 called "A Feminist Celebration for Life," vigils and protests against U.S. intervention in El Salvador and Nicaragua, and joined a coalition called the Federation for Progress that sought to bring together diverse progressive groups for political action.[3]

The nuclear freeze movement was arguably the largest and most visible of the challenges to conservative federal policies in the early 1980s, and it reflected the profound influence of the women's movement. Beginning in 1980, antinuclear weapons activists mobilized a broad-based peace campaign around a proposal that called for a "bilateral freeze on the testing, production, and deployment of nuclear weapons," generating the highest levels of antinuclear activism in the postwar United States (Meyer 1993b,c). A product of changes in the structure of political opportunity represented by a new bellicose foreign policy posture, and activist efforts from the grassroots, the nuclear freeze made its effects visible throughout U.S. politics and society. We can see its faces in both institutional and advocacy politics, in broad extra-institutional politics, and in mainstream political culture.

Institutionally, the larger peace movement's efforts centered on securing passage of a freeze resolution and endorsements of nuclear free zones or peaceful conversion programs in government venues. Beginning with a grassroots ballot effort in western Massachusetts in the fall of 1980, activists managed the passage of freeze referenda in nine states and won endorsement of the resolution in many other government institutions, ranging from hundreds of town meetings in New England in 1982 to the House of Representatives in 1983. Freeze campaigns generated dozens of proposals and efforts to revive and manage arms control, cancel dozens of weapons systems, and mandate lower military spending. Freeze-related organizations and political action committees (PACs) endorsed candidates in local and national elections, contributed volunteers and large sums of money, and claimed influence in dozens of electoral races. In 1984, the Democratic Party nominated for president one of six aspirants who claimed to support the nuclear freeze, and a freeze resolution was a visible plank in the national Democratic Party's platform. The freeze also buoyed support for moderation and arms control within mainstream political institutions (Meyer 1990). Freeze advocates testified before Congress, which considered dozens of movement sponsored resolutions, amendments, and bills.

The nuclear freeze campaign revived several existing arms control organizations, and also won support from Washington-based groups that focused on different issues, such as the National Council of Black Mayors, Common Cause, Greenpeace, and numerous trade unions. It also spawned scores of new groups at local and national levels, often organized along professional lines (see Conetta 1988). Virtually every mainstream religious organization in the United States endorsed the nuclear freeze proposal in statements such as the Catholic Bishop's Pastoral Letter on Nuclear Armaments (1983).

The movement was also visible in its extra-institutional political efforts. The nuclear freeze coordinated the largest demonstration in U.S. history, as one million people marched in New York City on June 12, 1982 under the twin slogans "Freeze and Reverse the Arms Race," and "Fund Human Needs." Local, often less visible, civil disobedience campaigns and demonstrations emerged across the country. These ranged from quiet and regularly scheduled peace vigils commemorating the bombing of Hiroshima, to direct action efforts to stop the transport of nuclear weapons. Militant direct action began in November 1980, when eight Catholic activists broke into a General Electric plant in King of Prussia, Pennsylvania to damage nuclear warheads with hammers, and eventually included more than two dozen similar "Plowshares" actions.

Activists also organized "peace camps" outside several military installations.

The movement also reached deeply into mainstream popular culture, serving as the catalyst for television news specials, for several movies, including the much publicized and controversial 1983 account of nuclear war in Kansas, *The Day After,* and for episodes on television serials such as *Lou Grant* and *Family Ties.* The movement was everywhere for awhile, dominating mainstream culture and media, and drawing unprecedented public scrutiny to United States nuclear weapons policy.

Women's Movement Influence

The forms and strength of peace protest in the 1980s were inextricably linked to the women's movement. The nuclear freeze emerged as a highly visible issue from a cluster of progressive social movements, all of which affected each other to some degree. The women's movement influenced both the direct action and institutionally oriented wings of the peace movement in four areas: ideological frames, tactical repertoires, organizational structure, and leadership.

Frame Alignment

The moral claims/direct action wing of the antinuclear weapons movement in the early 1980s was broader, larger, and more militant than ever before. Women leaders and activists remained prominent in the historically female direct action wing, which in the 1980s consisted both of new women's peace organizations (such as Women's Action for Nuclear Disarmament), revitalized women's peace groups (such as the Women's International League for Peace and Freedom), mixed-sex organizations (such as Educators for Social Responsibility and Physicians for Social Responsibility), and broader feminist groups (such as the National Organization for Women and assorted local organizations that addressed peace issues).

The direct action wing framed the issue of nuclear disarmament by drawing on both traditional and feminist views of gender. Snow et al. (1986) propose that social movements must bring their politicized interpretations of events, or frames, into alignment with potential recruits' pre-existing frames. When social movements can link their perspectives to widely-resonant beliefs or concerns they are likely to be more successful at gaining support (Snow and Benford 1992). We think that the notion of frame alignment is useful for understanding how the ideology of one movement spreads to another. Peace activists successfully linked peace and feminist frames.

On the one hand, the ideology of the direct action wing built in part on traditional notions of gender, emphasizing that women's special concerns as mothers led them to support peace. For example, Helen Caldicott was the most quoted speaker among dozens at the 1982 New York City demonstration, particularly for her remark that "there are no Communist babies; there are no capitalist babies. A baby is a baby is a baby" (Meyer 1990:129). The organization she founded, Women's Action for Nuclear Disarmament (WAND), coined slogans such as "you can't hug a child with nuclear arms." WAND and similar organizations also promoted an analysis of militarism rooted in a feminist critique of patriarchy. Caldicott (1984), for example, claimed that the arms race was the product of masculine competitiveness and could be managed by "tak(ing) the toys away from the boys." Other writers and activists equated nuclear missiles with the phallus, viewing nuclear proliferation as a sort of contest between male heads of state attempting to prove that "mine is bigger than yours" (Russell 1989). Books promoting these analyses sported titles such as *Nuclear Phallacies, Does Khaki Become You?* (Enloe 1988); and Caldicott's (1984) own *Missile Envy*. In essence, the long-lived *peace frame* that emphasized militarism and women's special caring for life was linked with a *feminist frame* that attributed the arms race to patriarchy. This proved a potent combination that successfully recruited both feminist and non-feminist women as activists for the freeze.

Tactical Repertoires

Successful tactical innovations developed by one social movement become part of a collective action repertoire upon which subsequent social movements draw (Tarrow 1993; Tilly 1978, 1992). For example, the civil rights movement adapted non-violent tactics such as sit-ins, passive resistance, and mass marches; these tactics spread to the student and anti-war protests that followed (McAdam 1988a). Similarly, the women's movement's tactical innovations influenced nuclear freeze campaigns.

Many actions by women's peace groups drew on a feminist tradition of theatrical tactics dramatizing the feminist frame linking militarism to patriarchy. For example, in 1981 and 1982 the Women's Pentagon Action staged large demonstrations and civil disobedience actions outside the Pentagon, linking the nuclear arms race to broader social injustices, including violence against women, poverty, and other violations of human rights (Cloud 1981; Epstein 1991). The Pentagon actions included expressions of mourning for societal injustice, anger at the perpetrators of injustice, and ended with participants symbolically "exorcising" the evil spirits of the Pentagon by weaving a "web of life" around the building, simultaneously trying to shut the building down. These symbols reprised decades-old self-consciously dramatic tactics. Activists combined direct political action with spiritual rituals they claimed drew on the strength of goddesses and other sources of women's power (Spretnak 1982). The effects of these events spread beyond the hundreds of women who participated, as the activists took the tactics and inspiration back to local communities where they organized a wide variety of campaigns.

Women organized "peace camps" outside military bases near the Puget Sound and in Seneca Falls in central New York (Krasniewicz 1992). Modeled after similar camps in Europe, the camps coordinated ongoing opposition to the transport of nuclear weapons. Activists lived in tents by the military bases for days, weeks, or even years, and engaged in public education, direct action, and civil disobedience campaigns. While European peace camps included women's, mixed-sex, and family camps, in the United States only women's camps developed. They built on the radical feminist practice of establishing "women-only space" in the belief that women were better able to act independently and strongly in the absence of men. The peace camps were one explicit way activists linked personal and political concerns, as women left home and family to live ongoing antinuclear protest. Activists tried to organize the camps in accordance with feminist ideals of egalitarianism. Organizations sponsoring more moderate activities tried to make the same connection between personal and political. In 1985, for example, a number of groups coordinated a "peace ribbon" campaign in which local activists and organizations made quilted squares depicting scenes of things they would miss in the event of a nuclear war. They sewed these segments together, creating a single ribbon that reached more than 10 miles. In a colorful demonstration, activists wrapped the ribbon around the Washington Monument.

Leadership

Women in the 1960s New Left criticized their exclusion from leadership positions (Echols 1989; Evans 1979). During the intervening years, feminist critiques of this exclusion from decision-making roles in government, business, education, and other arenas gained some ground (Boles 1991; Mueller 1987). As exclusively-male leadership became less common in some mainstream social institutions, it became largely unacceptable in ostensibly "progressive" organizations. One of the most striking changes in the peace movement was the visibility of women, most explicit feminists, in leadership positions in both wings of the movement.

In the direct action wing, Helen Caldicott's visibility as a national leader and spokesperson for the nuclear freeze clearly drew on the increasing credibility that the women's movement gained for women in the public arena. In the institutional wing, women won new credence for their expertise and political power. Members of Congress such as Democrats Patricia Schroeder and Barbara Boxer and Republican Nancy Kassebaum, elected in part because of the influence of the women's movement, were active freeze supporters and persistent advocates of arms control and military restraint. The earliest freeze organizers were disproportionately women, including Jan Orr-Herter, Wendy Mogey, and Sister Judith Schecket. Pam Solo, first strategy coordinator of the nuclear freeze campaign, organized the civil disobedience campaigns at the Rocky Flats nuclear plant in Colorado and later managed one of Schroeder's Congressional campaigns. Randall Forsberg, founder of the institute for Defense and Disarmament Studies (IDDS), was the intellectual architect of the freeze. Many women leaders entered the institutional wing of the peace movement bringing skills and perspectives directly from the feminist movement. Karen Mulhauser, for example, formerly director of the National Abortion Rights Action League (NARAL), became executive director of the Washington-based United States Citizens Against Nuclear War (US-CANW) (Staggenborg 1988).

Caldicott and Forsberg personified conflicting views in the women's movement about the nature of gender discrimination. Caldicott argued that women's attitudes and approaches to life were naturally different from those of men and that women needed to bring their distinct and caring perspective to their professions and to political life. Although being a physician enhanced her credibility, her rhetoric was based on moral outrage and emotional appeals, and emphasized her personal concerns as a woman and mother. Forsberg, in contrast, who drew credibility from her extensive training as an arms control analyst, argued that women could be as expert and detailed in their analyses of arms control as men, and contended that a nuclear freeze was a "rational and verifiable" first step toward disarmament anyone would support, regardless of gender. She based her appeals on rationality, detailed information, and technical analyses (e.g., Forsberg 1982). Regardless of their differences, Caldicott, Forsberg, and numerous other less well-known women owed their leadership roles to the gains of the women's movement.

Organizational Structure

Finally, the feminist movement influenced organizational structure of both wings of the movement. The women's movement consistently sought to put an ideal of collective structure into practice (Breines 1989; Epstein 1991). The direct action wing of the nuclear freeze movement established decentralized organizational structures that sought to avoid all hierarchy and used what activists termed "feminist process." Partisans argued for the necessity of egalitarian participation by all group members, consensus decision making, rotation of key tasks and roles among members, and attention to the emotions and interactions of participants in addition to the pursuit of instrumental goals (Epstein 1991).

A concern with non-hierarchical organizational structure shaped organizations in the institutional wing as well. For example, the Nuclear Weapons Freeze Clearinghouse (NWFC) served as a national coordinator for local and national groups. Its charter emphasized the need to promote "local self-determination" and allow for a diversity of analyses and tactical approaches. In keeping with organizers' aversion to hierarchy, the NWFC's top position was "coordinator," rather than "president" or "executive director." The first coordinator, Randy Kehler, adopted a leadership style in which he emphasized consensus politics, attention to democratic processes, and avoiding conflict, all hallmarks of feminist organizing in the 1970s.[4]

It is important to note that the women's movement was changed by the peace movement as well; social movement mutual influence is not a one-way street. A full discussion of the effects of the peace movement on the women's movement is beyond the scope of this paper (but see Whittier 1994b). In brief, as a result of contact with the peace movement, many women's organizations broadened the scope of issues they addressed to include nuclear disarmament, and were more likely to work in coalition with organizations that included men; perhaps they also became more tolerant to rhetoric based in "essential" differences between men and women, such as the capacity to give birth. Participants disagreed over whether freeze activism was integral to, or a distraction from, the feminist cause. Yet by responding to more favorable mobilization opportunities, the peace movement provided feminist activists with an opportunity and an outlet for directing challenges to the state.

Mechanisms of Transmission

In the section above, we outlined the *types* of effects that the feminist movement had on peace movement activity in the 1980s. We now turn to a discussion of the *processes* by which the women's movement influenced the nuclear freeze, in order to develop a model of movement spillover. We suggest four distinct routes of influence: organizational coalitions; overlapping social movement community; shared personnel; and broader changes in the external environment.

Coalitions

Social movements are comprised of multiple organizations working in coalition (McCarthy and Zald 1977; Staggenborg 1986; Zald and McCarthy 1987c). One of the hallmarks of left protest in the United States since the 1960s has been frequent large demonstrations sponsored by multiple organizations that address a "laundry list" of demands. Broad issues such as opposition to Presidents Reagan and Bush, opposition to the Persian Gulf War, the 1984 presidential candidacy

of the Reverend Jesse Jackson, and the confirmation hearings of Supreme Court nominees Robert Bork and Clarence Thomas, have pulled together groups from diverse movements including the peace, women's, anti-intervention, gay and lesbian, and AIDS movements. A bellwether issue, generally representing what activists view as either the most threatening and urgent problem or the most promising vehicle for action, comes to unify a broad spectrum of groups that share similar or related concerns. Ryan (1992) terms such causes "unifying issues" and argues that they are important less for the concrete improvements their success would bring than for their value as symbols that spur mobilization.

The nuclear freeze was such a unifying issue, drawing support from multiple movements. Participating and endorsing organizations included several explicitly feminist groups, such as the National Organization for Women. National coalitions such as the Monday Lobby Group (Hathaway and Meyer 1994) brought feminist organizations that endorsed the freeze together with peace groups that were not explicitly feminist. In addition to women's movement organizations that endorsed the freeze, many feminist groups formed to focus specifically on peace issues. Women's Action for Nuclear Disarmament (WAND), the Women's Pentagon Actions, women's peace camps, and a host of local groups were influential in the broader peace movement. Such groups often grew out of more general feminist organizing and served as a route for the transmission of feminist collective identity and organizational structure into the mixed-sex peace movement (Epstein 1991). In the process, activists drew explicit connections between their issues, noting, for example, that the Reagan administration cut social welfare spending to fund increases in military spending.

In short, coalitions are structuring mechanisms that bring a broad spectrum of otherwise distinct organizations into contact, spreading interpretive frames, organizational structures, political analysis, and tactics. Feminist analyses and processes, carried by participating groups, influenced the way coalition work proceeded, and as a result, percolated into peace organizations. The extent to which social movement organizations work in coalition rather than on single issues is one variable that may affect the degree of diffusion between movements. Because broad-based coalitions flowered in the 1980s and early 1990s, it is likely that mutual influence among social movements was particularly extensive.

Social Movement Community

Social movements are more than the sum of participating formal organizations (Oliver 1989). Challenges grow from what Buechler (1990:42) terms "social movement communities," or "informal networks of politicized individuals" who share a commitment to common goals of social change. Buechler conceptualizes social movement communities as associated with a single movement, but we suggest that a range of movements participants termed "progressive" (including the feminist and peace movements) have overlapping social movement communities that promoted the diffusion of feminism into the freeze campaign.

The women's movement community included by the late 1970s well-established cultural institutions as well as more informal overlapping friendship networks (Taylor and Whittier 1992). Much of this feminist community was autonomous, but parts overlapped with other movements, forming a larger "progressive social movement community." Because many women's movement community institutions produced texts, art, or events that were publicly available, activists in the peace movement could read, observe, and participate in feminist writings, cultural events, and conferences. Cultural organizations such as Syracuse Cultural Workers, founded by feminist musician Holly Near to produce and distribute art promoting social change, feminist bookstores that stock alternative peace-oriented publications, and performers such as the group Bright Morning Star, who sing folk music with peace and feminist themes, drew together participants in the two movements.

As a result of such overlap, feminist culture, including the avoidance of sexist language, norms for presentation of self (such as women not shaving their legs), and norms of interpersonal interaction (such as the value placed on open emotional expression) entered peace movement culture (Epstein 1991). As once marginal and challenging norms become institutionalized in a broader social movement community, they shift the boundaries of legitimate conduct and discourse within that community. Subsequent explicit political challenges on other issues then carry these norms. The social movement commu-

nity provides a route by which the innovations of one movement may diffuse into others. Structural characteristics of social movement communities and their contact with each other, such as the extensiveness of community institutions and the degree to which a social movement community is permeable to outsiders, vary for different movements and at different times, influencing the degree of diffusion.

Personnel

While social movements are often explicitly identified with only one issue or set of issues, activists rarely are. Protesting and organizing for a variety of related social changes over several decades is the rule rather than the exception for individual activists, as studies of participants in the civil rights, student, and women's movements show (Fendrich and Lovoy 1988; McAdam 1989; Whalen and Flacks 1987). Activists can shift goals and groups in response to the changing political environment, responding to proximate threats and opportunities, while maintaining an essentially consistent political worldview (Meyer 1993b,c). Participants in the women's movement developed enduring commitments to a broad set of goals aimed at transforming the existing social system (Echols 1989; Ferree and Hess 1985; Freeman 1975). It is not surprising therefore that many feminist activists joined and led nuclear freeze campaigns.

Veterans of the women's movement brought their feminist experiences and values with them when they entered peace movement organizations. Specifically, debates over non-hierarchical leadership structure, interpretative frames linking militarism to patriarchy, and the expectation that leaders would include women were all part of the legacy feminist activists brought (see Marullo 1992). In addition, extensive participant networks in the 1970s women's movement helped to draw in more feminist supporters of the nuclear freeze, and they promoted the coalitions and overlapping social movement communities discussed above. While it is a truism among activists that the same group of people show up at demonstration after demonstration, scholars have been slower to recognize the extent to which related movements share personnel.

Such shared personnel are an important route for inter-movement influence. Migration of personnel between issues and organizations is bounded by cultural and ideological constraints. We would expect this kind of spillover to be common among various causes within the progressive social movement community, but unlikely to occur between oppositional movement communities. In contrast, broader cultural changes would be reflected back and expressed through all sorts of challenging movements across the ideological spectrum.

Political Opportunity Structure

The 1970s women's movement affected the larger politics and society of the United States and as a result shaped social movements that grew out of that society. In particular, changes in norms regarding gender, and shifts in the political opportunity structure were important. Feminist activists won relaxation of both formal and informal restrictions on women's entrance into professional, scientific, and technical careers, and this allowed women to become recognized experts in nuclear weapons issues, arms control, or Washington politics. At the same time as it became legitimate for women to possess expert knowledge, it also became legitimate for men to confess fear about the nuclear arms race. Further, the feminist movement instituted gender balancing norms within the broader society that encouraged media and organizations to seek statements from women experts and activists as well as men. This gave women leaders more credibility and influence within the mixed-sex peace movement.[5] Finally, because the women's movement criticized largely-male leadership in most social institutions, it became more difficult for peace groups to continue the exclusion of women from leadership positions.

More broadly, the women's movement helped shape the political opportunity structure that the freeze campaign confronted. Veterans of the women's movement who had moved into government, social service, or foundation employment helped garner institutional resources and support for the freeze (Whittier 1994b). The extensive communications network of the women's movement was also an important resource for disseminating information about nuclear arms and antinuclear activity. Although the women's movement remains far from achieving its transformative goals, feminism has changed the face of politics in the United States, and subsequent movements are heirs to its legacy. Protest movements alter the structure of political opportunity, and thus the shape and potential efficacy of subsequent movements.

Conclusion

In this article, we have argued that the feminist movement led the 1980s peace movement to differ in several important ways from earlier waves of peace activism. Ideological frames linked militarism to patriarchy and urged women to agitate for peace not only because of their concerns as mothers but also because of their desire to eliminate sexism. Some of the most dramatic and innovative tactics illustrated these ideological frames, linked the personal and the political, and drew on women's separate efforts such as peace camps. Organizational structures reflect the concerns with process, consensus, and avoidance of hierarchy that activists emphasized in the women's movement. Finally, the emergence of visible women leaders in both wings of the movement reflect the influence of feminism on the peace movement and on expanded social roles for women in general. We have argued that the women's movement affected the peace movement through organizational coalitions, an overlapping social movement community, shared personnel, and effects on the external environment. At the same time, the peace mobilization of the 1980s afforded feminist activists the opportunity to stage political challenges in the absence of favorable opportunities for feminist mobilization.

This case highlights spillover effects during a period when mass protest was relatively infrequent, the overall social movement sector was relatively inactive, and the larger environment was hostile to challenges from the left. Such times provide special impetus for movement-movement linkages as beleagured activists and organizations pool their strength against powerful opponents. But social movement spillover also nourishes during periods of widespread upheaval, such as the late 1960s, when highly mobilized challenges feed off each other and the boundaries between social movements blur (Breines 1982; McAdam 1988a; Miller 1987). Although spillover effects help shape protest cycles, they are not limited to any one phase of the cycle.

The consideration of social movement spillover suggests the need for a broad approach to assessing movement outcomes. We have shown in this case that the effects of one movement have gone beyond its expressly articulated goals to shape the larger social movement sector. The longer term achievements of the feminist movement include the presence of influential women activists concerned with broad social and political issues defined in feminist terms; these women have won public support, media attention, and perhaps policy reform. In order to understand fully a movement's outcomes, we must examine its indirect routes of influence, such as through other movements, as well as its direct effects. A comparable assessment of the peace movement of the 1980s, while beyond the scope of this paper (but see Meyer and Marullo 1992; Rochon 1992), would similarly need to address not only policy changes, but also spillover effects.

Finally, recognizing social movement spillover adds to our understanding of the continuity of challenges over time. As social movement scholars increasingly recognize, movements do not necessarily end with policy victories or defeats or with the demise of particular movement organizations (McAdam 1988a; Rupp and Taylor 1987; Taylor 1989b; Whalen and Flacks 1987). Later movements may express predecessors' concerns and absorb their activists; movements seemingly in decline may be reflected and transformed in ongoing social and political struggles. For scholars spillover effects are cause for greater analytical inclusivity of interactions among movements and for research determining: what factors make one set of issues most promising for political action at a given time; and what variables shape the degree of inter-movement influence. For activists, spillover effects are cause for greater optimism about movement survival and the scope of social movement influence.

Notes

1. We follow the widespread distinction between two wings of the women's movement: one, termed radical, younger, or collectivist, which emerged from the student movements of the 1960s; and another, termed liberal, older, or bureaucratic, which grew out of the President's Commission on the Status of Women and the organizing efforts of professional women's interest groups (Ferree and Hess 1985; Freeman 1975; Taylor and Whittier 1993).

2. Respondents are a non-random sample of core leaders in radical feminist, university-affiliated, and liberal feminist organizations between 1969 and 1991. Core leaders were defined as those who held a formal leadership position, consistently initiated organizational decisions, or were mentioned by several other respondents as leaders. Interviews were in-depth and open-ended, and focused on the effects of respondents' feminist participation on their later political participation and on the evolution of women's movement organizations.

3. *WAC Newsletter*, May 1981; *WAC Newsletter*, June 1981.

4. It's not clear that this form of organization best served the movement's instrumental goals—especially in the short term. Activists on the left of the nuclear freeze consistently criticized the Nuclear Weapons Freeze Clearinghouse (NWFC) for being unduly concerned with avoiding potentially controversial or divisive issues. Such issues included military intervention in Central America or the Middle East, or even particular weapons systems, and more aggressive tactics. The NWFC, with Kehler at the helm, emphasized moderate politics and tactics, perhaps squandering the movement's strength (see Solo 1988).

5. Even President Reagan sought to legitimate his foreign policies by appointing a conservative woman to a visible position, Jeanne Kirkpatrick, as ambassador to the United Nations. ✦

37

A Hero for the Aged? The Townsend Movement, the Political Mediation Model, and U.S. Old-Age Policy, 1934-1950

Edwin Amenta
Bruce G. Carruthers
Yvonne Zylan

Perhaps more than any other social protest movement of the Great Depression, the insurgency of the aged led by Francis E. Townsend has been credited with transforming public social provision in the United States. Its opponents such as Frances Perkins (1946) and Arthur Altmeyer (1966) have attested to its importance, as have social scientists ranging from Piven and Cloward (1971), to Quadagno (1988), to Weir, Orloff, and Skocpol (1988, p. 23). Yet such claims are paradoxical. The "Townsend plan"—$200 per month for those 60 years old or older who agreed not to work and to spend the money—failed, and President Franklin D. Roosevelt refused to meet Townsend. Holtzman's (1963) study dismisses the movement of the Townsendites (as its partisans often called themselves) as a failure. The question remains: Was Townsend a hero for the aged?

This dispute is paralleled by social science debates about the outcomes of mobilizations and what constitutes "success" for them (e.g., Gamson 1990, app. A; McAdam 1982; Jasper, Nelkin, and Poulsen 1990). Some researchers (e.g., Gamson 1990) discount the macrosociological context, assuming that resource mobilization or collective action will achieve results; others (e.g., Kitschelt 1986) argue that the political context will decide both the move-

ment's form and the response to it. Yet they ignore an important question: Under what conditions do movements win benefits for constituents and recognition for the organization?

Our goal is to uncover the determinants of successes and failures. To do this we will first explore the Townsend movement's influence on the historical trajectories of old-age policy at the national level, examining the Social Security Act, the amendments to it in 1939 and 1950, and the wartime hiatus on social spending. Next we will use multiple regression techniques to analyze old-age assistance or "pensions" at the state level and we will analyze state "memorials" asking the national government to enact the Townsend plan—a form of acceptance. To examine the *conditions* under which the movement succeeded or failed we will employ Boolean qualitative comparative analysis (QCA), which locates combinations of conditions leading to qualitative outcomes (see Ragin 1987)—winning recognition, new advantages, and combinations of such victories and failures.

We argue that the political context mediates the impact of movement organization and action on its goals and sets the range of possible outcomes. Structural characteristics such as undemocratic political systems and patronage-based, traditional parties can deflect movement efforts. Middle-range influences of state bureaucracies and short-term political coalitions can intensify the impact of movements. To take advantage of openings, movements must back political action with organizational strength. We find that the movement helped the aged, but mainly through old-age assistance, on which the views of the Roosevelt administration and the Townsendites were not greatly in conflict. In some states the movement achieved high pensions and recognition, becoming in effect a "member" of the polity, to use Tilly's (1978) terminology. Strength in organization and standard political action—in favorable political party and state climates—led to success. By contrast, the movement had only a minor effect at the national level in improving old-age assistance. Even this gain would have been unlikely without the existence of a moderately strong pro-spending coalition.

Toward a Political Mediation Model of Protest Movement Outcomes

Analyses of movement outcomes are hampered by two key problems. First, what is meant

"A Hero for the Aged? The Townsend Movement, the Political Mediation Model, and U.S. Old-Age Policy, 1934-1950." *American Journal of Sociology* 98:308-339. Copyright © 1992 by the University of Chicago Press. Reprinted by permission.

by success is rarely well defined and varies from analysis to analysis. Movement organizations usually attempt to influence the policies of the state to aid their members, but there is no standard way to assess benefits gained through these policies. Second, research on movement outcomes often does not take into account the causes of mobilization that might also influence outcomes (cf. Snyder and Kelly 1979; Isaac and Kelly 1981; Burstein 1981). This is a problem because movements often hope to effect changes in public spending policies, and the determinants of such policies are often similar to those of social-movement formation (see Skocpol and Amenta 1986; McAdam, McCarthy, and Zald 1988). Thus, analyses may exaggerate the effect of the movement on policy outcomes. To sustain a claim that a movement's actions are effective, a researcher must show that their influences are in addition to other causes of changes in policies.

Success and the Social Movement

There are three levels of success for movements. The lowest is for the organization to achieve recognition from opponents or the state. Following Gamson (1990), we call recognition that does not win benefits "co-optation." At the highest level the challenger transforms itself into a member of the polity; that is, processes of government or interactions with opponents routinely favor the group (see fig. 1). A challenger's interests may be achieved through laws, state bureaus to enforce them, and the removal of the issue, favorably resolved, from the political agenda.[1]

At the middle level are gains in policies that aid the group. At this level, the movement organization can, at minimum, influence the thinking of the public or policymakers (Gusfield 1981a). In the best case, the organization may have its own program enshrined in legislation. Many cases fall in the middle: the movement's activity may keep its issue on the political agenda, but without its opponents recognizing the movement organization. Sometimes new spending legislation benefiting the group results from such activity—what Gamson calls "preemption." We refer to these gains as "concessions," because the organization has aided the group and will seek to gain credit for it. Laws establishing group-based rights with bureaucratic and fiscal reinforcement move a group closer to polity membership than do short-term and discretionary spending laws.

Theories of Movement Outcomes and Theories of Public Policy

Typically, theorists of movement outcomes focus on the structure and activity of movement organizations (e.g., Gamson 1990). Disputes center on the relative effectiveness of noninstitutional (Piven and Cloward 1971) and "assimilationist" (Lipsky 1968) means and on the optimal characteristics of the movement organization (Gamson 1990). Most agree that the movement's features matter most and that large movements engaged in coherent programs of collective action without displacement goals will typically succeed.

Others have argued that movements arise from individual responses to strains in the social fabric and are mainly ineffective (e.g., Smelser 1962). In this view, strains breed grievances, which lead to aggression, expressed partly in collective behavior. The goals of such movements are often labeled utopian. This view sees movements as correlating with policy change, but not causing it; instead, political institutions confront the strains that drive collective behavior. By resolving these strains—perhaps by enacting public spending to address social needs—these institutions subdue the grievances uniting the movement.

Some economic theories of public spending have much in common with this grievance view of movements (see Skocpol and Amenta 1986, pp. 133-36; Quadagno 1987, pp. 111-17). One economic theory holds that industrialization causes social dislocations—such as destruction of the ex-

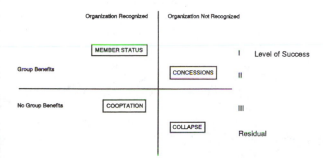

FIG. 1.—Levels of success for social movements

tended families who then no longer care for the aging population—that force political regimes to engage in public spending—such as old-age pensions. Some theories of capitalism argue that economic declines such as the Depression require public spending to legitimate the system. In both cases, economic conditions are the fundamental causes of both movements and public spending, and so movements have no independent effect.

Theories focusing on "political opportunity structures" (e.g., Kitschelt 1986) have similar implications for the outcomes of protest movements. In the strongest form of this argument, opportunity structures determine both movement formation and what may be perceived as gains won by the movement. A member of the polity may aid a movement in order to add to its coalition—perhaps by introducing a spending program favoring the challenger; the movement is an epiphenomenon—a sign that policies are changing, but not the cause of changes.

Some perspectives, focusing on party partisanship, the strength of organized labor, or on the state and political institutions, suggest that political conditions that influence spending policies may also spur movements. One view is that public spending programs are boosted when left or center political parties come into power (Shaley 1983; Myles 1984) or when labor movements are strong. These parties or the labor movement may also aid the mobilization of new groups. Others argue that state actors have distinct interests (Orloff and Skocpol 1984; Carruthers 1991) and may find it advantageous to encourage like-minded movements. Similarly, the policy framework of a polity may influence further innovations—and also movements (McCarthy, Britt, and Wolfson 1991).

The Political Mediation Model of Movement Outcomes

We take theories of public spending policies into account by arguing that the outcomes of movement organization and action are mediated by the political context. Figure 2 highlights the differences between our political mediation perspective and other points of view. Unlike those using the standard social-movements models (arrows labeled "II"), we argue that mobilization and collective action are usually insufficient for policy changes; under some circumstances, however, mobilization and collective action may bring

about changes. We avoid the strong view that the economy (arrows marked "I") or political opportunity structures (arrows marked "III") determine both movement formation and policy outcomes; we argue that movements can also influence outcomes, though no specific type of collective action is deemed the most efficacious. The political context mediates the relationship between action and outcomes (arrow IV).

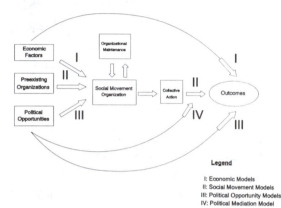

Fig. 2.—Models of social movement formation and outcomes. Legend: "I" represents economic models; "II" represents social movement models; "III" represents political opportunity models; "IV" represents political mediation models.

Two key long-term aspects of the political context are the political system and the party systems. First, an undemocratic political system—indicated by restricted voting rights and a lack of choice between parties—discourages both social movements and public spending policies. Even where movements coalesce in such polities, they are unlikely to achieve their goals, symbolic or substantive.[2] Second, traditional or patronage-oriented parties regard movements as menaces and programmatic spending policies as threats to the individualistic rewards on which such parties thrive. If movements contend in such polities, traditional patronage parties are more likely to give *symbolic* benefits than to pass programmatic spending policies because discretionary and individualistic policies are the lifeblood of these parties. We expect that these structural blocks will also thwart the efforts of state actors and insurgents in the party system to enhance programmatic public spending.[3]

We also anticipate more than one political path to changes in public spending policies. Favorable middle-range and short-term party and state conditions can produce social-spending gains for many disadvantaged groups. Left-center parties and state-building officials can be forces behind public spending. However, movements can fill voids where such actors are insufficiently powerful. If the structure of a political system is conducive—a democratic polity with an open party system—and a movement is strong in organization and in standard politics, it can be successful even if it lacks state or party allies.

Moreover, for issue-oriented movements such as the Townsend movement, the existing policy framework is also important in accounting for the possibilities of success and failure. A movement devoted to a policy at odds with the established framework is unlikely to be recognized (see fig. 1). When the policy orientation of a movement conflicts with established policy frameworks and the plans of both the regime in power and state bureaucrats, a movement is unlikely to achieve full success (right side of fig. 1). The best possible outcome is to win concessions, the worst is to "collapse," because the movement is expected to go unrecognized. Polity members may attempt to woo away the organization's supporters by amending current programs benefiting the group, but without transforming the policy framework. When the plans of the movement and the policy framework of polity members do not conflict, the movement can achieve recognition, but must avoid co-optation, a level of success lower in our scheme than concessions (left side of fig. 1). The organization has a chance to win polity membership by possibly securing policies to aid its constituents. These chances depend not only on its collective action and organizational strength, but also on conducive state or party circumstances.

The Failure of the Townsend Plan and the Rise of Old-Age Spending Programs

The Townsend movement was inspired by Townsend's September 1933 proposal: that all Americans over 60 years old be given $200 at the beginning of every month; everyone accepting this pension had to be retired and had to spend the sum by the end of the month. What was soon labeled the Townsend plan led in January 1934 to the not-for-profit "Old Age Revolving Pensions, Ltd." (OARP). The plan would end the economic woes of old age and solve unemployment, as the elderly would not compete with the young for

jobs, and new spending would stimulate the economy; the mandatory spending provision would make old-age pensions change hands or "revolve" faster than other money. Also, the plan would not aggravate the deficit; it was to be funded by a "transactions tax," a multiple sales tax.

The plan, however, was criticized heavily. The political Left argued that the transactions tax was regressive. The Right feared that the tax would cut profits and the spending would undermine the incentive to work. Scholars and policy experts also disapproved. The tax was set at a seemingly low rate, but it implied much higher levies on finished goods. Many thought it unworkable to register farmers for the tax. Economists estimated that a 2% tax would have amassed only $4-$9 billion yearly (Twentieth-Century Fund Committee on Old Age Security 1936; National Industrial Conference Board 1936). No economist felt that the aged would spend faster than those taxed. Soon the Social Security Board (SSB) was orchestrating this criticism (Cates 1983, pp. 52-33).

Yet the plan was no utopian scheme. The aged would have the right to a large national pension, whose size would be determined by revenues from an earmarked tax. Such pensions would have been simpler to administer than the two-part system that won out. Even if the tax had netted only $6 billion per year, that would have meant pensions of approximately $50 per month, much higher than assistance. A national sales tax would have been regressive, but so was the tax on the payroll for social insurance.

In January 1935 a Townsend bill was introduced in Congress, and in April it was followed by an amended bill, taking into account many criticisms. But this bill was rejected handily in the House, in a standing vote mainly along partisan lines with Democrats in opposition, 206-56. The totals were low because many members, especially Western ones, wanted neither to support the bill nor to go on record as opposed. In 1939, another Townsend proposal passed through the Ways and Means Committee, but only because the movement's congressional supporters were joined by adversaries, who hoped to discredit the movement with a lopsided roll-call vote. The 1939 rejection, 302-95, was decisive—fewer members feared to go on record, with only 55 Republicans and 40 Democrats in favor. Although the movement remained active in the 1940s, no

Townsend bill was ever again discharged from committee. The movement went unrecognized by its national-level opponents, and the plan failed to convince policymakers or the public.[4]

Despite these failures, innovations in old-age spending flourished. There were five main stages (see table 1). First, in the early 1930s states passed old-age pensions, and Congress promoted plans to aid these means-tested programs. Second, the administration saw through to enactment of the old-age insurance and assistance titles of the 1935 Social Security Act. Third, assistance and insurance were advanced in 1939. Fourth, these programs suffered setbacks during wartime. Finally, at the end of the decade, old-age insurance was upgraded.

By 1934, 23 states had adopted old-age pension programs. Efforts by the national government followed. The Dill-Connery Bill, which called for national matching funds for pension programs, passed the House in 1933 and 1934 (Epstein [1938] 1968). Roosevelt's appointment of the Economic Security Committee in June 1934 led to the omnibus Economic Security Act (bill) of January 1935. This bill included old-age "assistance" providing matching payments of up to $15 per person per month for state-level, old-age pensions. It also included old-age insurance, a national program that provided benefits for those 65 years old and older who had qualified by paying a payroll tax levied on wage earners and employers on earnings up to $3000. This tax was to take effect in 1937; no benefits were to be paid until 1942. The bill became the Social Security Act in August 1935. In 1939 Congress expanded old-age spending. It added insurance for dependents and survivors, revised the formula to ensure larger payments at the beginning of the term, advanced the starting point for benefits to 1940 instead of 1942 and slowed scheduled increases in the payroll tax. Congress also increased the maximum benefits under old-age assistance to $20, allowing the states to increase them to a maximum of $40.

The next decade saw more downs than ups for old-age spending. In 1942, Congress froze pre-

Period	Social Policy Developments
Recovery: The early depression and the first New Deal, 1936-35	California adopts first compulsory old-age pensions legislation (1929).
	Dill-Connery bill (1933-34) to give federal support to state-level old-age pensions debated in Congress.
	Twenty-three states adopt compulsory old-age pensions by the end of 1934.
The "reform" era and the second New Deal, 1935-37	Economic Security bill released, January 1935. The bill includes federal matching aid for old-age pensions, up to $15 per person. The bill also includes federal old-age benefits. A separate title includes a payroll tax; employers and employees each pay 1% of payrolls up to $3,000. The tax is scheduled to go into effect in 1937.
The late New Deal, 1937-40	1939 Social Security Act amendments provide insurance benefits for dependents and survivors, revise the benefit formula, advance benefits to begin in 1940, and hold employer/employee contribution rates to 1% through 1942. Matching payments for old-age assistance are increased to $20.
The prelude to war and the war years, 1940-45	Proposed increases in employer/employee contribution rate denied by conservative Congress seven times. The payroll tax rate is frozen until 1950.
The immediate post-war period, 1946-51	1948 Social Security Act amendments narrow coverage by redefining "employee" and excluding certain quasi-self-employed occupational categories.
	The Social Security Act amendments survive Republican opposition in the House in 1949 and are passed by the Senate in August 1950. New standards extend old-age and survivors' coverage to new groups, liberalize eligibility requirements, increase benefits overall, and extend federal matching provisions for medical care for the aged. Payroll tax rates are scheduled to increase to 2.0% by 1953.

Table 1
U.S. Social Spending Policies for the Aged, 1930-50

Sources: Altmeyer (1966) and Amenta (1989).

viously legislated increases in the payroll tax (Leff 1988), and the middle war years were harsh for social spending generally (Amenta and Skocpol 1988). Moreover, Congress rejected President Harry S. Truman's bid to enact health insurance in 1946, and old-age insurance was amended in 1948 to exclude many previously covered workers. After the election of Truman and a Democratic Congress in 1948, however, a victorious bid to improve old-age and survivors' insurance began, culminating in August 1950. These amendments extended old-age and survivors' coverage to new groups, increased the level of benefits by about 67%, lowered eligibility requirements, and provided federal matching funds for care of the aged at medical institutions. The payroll tax was legislated to increase to 1.5% in 1950, and 2.0% in 1953 (Cohen and Myers 1950).

The Impact of the Townsend Movement at the National Level: Comparisons Over Time

Were these old-age spending policies influenced by the Townsend movement? To answer this we analyze successful and unsuccessful episodes of national old-age policy-making and compare them with predictions based on the models. As noted above, national old-age laws were

passed in 1935, 1939, and 1950, and failed during the war years. We contrast old-age assistance and old-age insurance and analyze roll-call votes. These four cases provide evidence that the movement had its greatest impact in 1939, when it was strong both in mobilization and in political action-and when the pro-social spending coalition was moderately large.

With 450,000 members in February 1935, the movement had made a great leap forward in the second half of 1935, as can be seen through its dues-based finances (see table 2). In the first three quarters of 1935, OARP had gathered about $555,000, but in the last quarter alone brought in about $350,000, an unprecedented sum. That summer OARP also spread beyond the West. The movement peaked in membership near the start of 1936. Membership probably reached about 1.5 million (Holtzman 1963)—more than 18% of all those 65 years old and older. In the spring of 1936, membership slumped, dropping to 613,000 in 1938—7.2% of the aged. Yet the movement showed a resurgence of strength in 1939, embracing about 8.7% of those 65 years old and older. Membership declined during the war, leveling off at about 2.5% of the aged. Afterwards it degenerated; by 1949 it had dropped to less than 0.5% of

---

Table 2
Townsend Membership, Receipts, Endorsements, and the Strength of the Democratic Party Pro-spending Coalition, 1934-49

Year	Paid Membership (in Thousands)	Gross Receipts (in Thousands of $)	Membership as % of Persons 65 and Over	Townsend-backed House Members Elected, in Actual Nos. and (% of Those Endorsed)	Democratic House Majority and Rating
1934	N.A.	84	N.A.	N.A.	216, strong
1935	N.A.	905	N.A.		
1936	N.A.	562	N.A.	72 (28.8)	242, strong
1937	N.A.	369	N.A.		
1938	612.5	453	7.20	147 (55.7)	97, medium
1939	761.6	622	8.69		
1940	646.9	689	7.16	132 (58.1)	106, medium
1941	468.7	636	5.05		
1942	297.6	486	3.11	172 (60.3)	10, weak
1943	271.8	424	2.75		
1944	269.6	628	2.66	172 (75.1)	52, medium/weak
1945	234.8	512	2.23		
1946	173.6	519	1.60	182 (66.2)	-57, weak
1947	134.3	418	1.20		
1948	92.7	353	.80	135 (65.5)	92, medium
1949	52.8	328	.44		

Sources: Holtzman (1963, pp. 48-49, 172), U.S. Bureau of the Census (1975, p. 10), *Congressional Quarterly* (1985), U.S. Congress, House of Representatives (1936), and Amenta (1989).

those 65 years old and older (see Amenta and Zylan 1991).

The movement's political action campaign lagged well behind the mobilization of members. Its political activity centered on endorsing candidates for Congress—Republicans and Democrats—who were in favor of the plan.[5] Chosen by the movement's national leadership, the selections were publicized in the *Townsend National Weekly* (1938-50) and backed in rallies held by local clubs. Although the movement failed to endorse one-half of those voting for the plan in 1935 and running for reelection in 1936, in 1938 the endorsement policy worked, with 147 of its candidates winning. This was more than twice the number elected in 1936 and OARP's success rate had doubled to about 56%. The number of Townsend-endorsed House members averaged more than 150 in the 1940s, reaching a peak in the middle of the decade.

Other factors, however, especially the left-wing Democratic party coalition that took power in the 1930s, may have aided social spending. This pro-spending coalition is defined by the election of a president allied with the labor movement and other insurgent forces and a Democratic majority in Congress large enough to overwhelm Republicans and representatives of undemocratic regimes, who opposed spending (Amenta 1989). From 1933 to 1953, the White House was held by a reformist, labor-supported Democrat, and so the coalition depended on the size of the Democratic majority in Congress (see table 2). The largest pro-spending coalitions were in power from 1935 to 1939. From 1939 to 1943, the strength of the coalition was medium. From 1943 to 1945, the coalition was weak and did not regain its prewar level of health until 1949.

The political mediation model would expect that the movement would be most influential when it was strong in both membership and endorsements. Yet its influence would be magnified by a moderately strong Democratic coalition. We would expect that a very strong Democratic coalition by itself—as in the years from 1935 to 1938—would lead to widespread social-spending gains, including gains for the aged. A very weak coalition—as during the war period—would make any spending innovations impossible. For these reasons, we expect that the movement had its greatest impact in the late 1930s—when the movement was effective in both mobilizing mem-bership and electing members of Congress and the Democratic coalition was moderately strong. The comparison of the legislative episodes of 1939 and 1949-50 is instructive because, although the Democratic margin was similar, the movement was stronger in 1939. In addition, we expect that the movement's endorsements would be more likely to convert Republicans than Southern Democrats because the latter were from nondemocratic political systems.[6]

The Townsend movement had nothing to do with the earliest bids to enact old-age pensions in the states and little to do with the Social Security Act. As the Committee on Economic Security was constructing its proposals, the movement formed a political backdrop, putting pressure on the administration to propose something and on Congress to vote for something for the aged, accounting for some of the popularity of federal funds for old-age pensions. But the committee had planned at the outset to address economic insecurity due to old age, and the House had already passed matching funds for old-age pensions in 1933 and 1934. The movement was harmed by its incompetence in conventional politics. The first Townsend bill was poorly drawn up and amending the Economic Security bill was beyond its powers. The movement's regional isolation meant that only western representatives feared voting against it. The old-age spending programs that passed corresponded only marginally to the Townsend plan. Old-age assistance went only to the needy, and Congress, led by the Southern delegation, watered down the language concerning the adequacy of benefits (Quadango 1988). Old-age insurance began by collecting taxes without paying benefits. By contrast, the Townsend plan meant immediate, generous, and equal pensions to all of the aged as a right, in a pay-as-you-go manner. Old-age assistance was means tested and stingy; old-age insurance was to be given only to qualified recipients on the basis of previous wages. The movement opposed the insurance program—the administration's long-term solution—but could ally with those in favor of improving *assistance*—as the movement and the administration saw assistance as a short-term solution to poverty in old age.

One key circumstance was different during 1939. The movement had endorsed 147 winning House members including three on the important Ways and Means Committee (U.S. Congress, House of Representatives 1939). That year the

SSB and the Advisory Council (U.S. Congress, House of Representatives 1939, pp. 3-43) proposed "variable grants" for old-age assistance, a program designed to appease southern Democrats that would keep pensions low in the South, place the fiscal burden on the federal government, and lower federal spending elsewhere (U.S. Congress, Senate 1939, pp. 95, 180). Instead, however, the maximum federal matching payments for old-age assistance were increased from $15 per person to $20, and thus the issue was resolved in favor of the Townsend movement. Its influence was noted by Abraham Epstein: "If you keep the change to raise the Federal grant to $20 . . . you will merely inform all and sundry that all you have to do is to organize another crackpot group and Congress will raise it to $50, or $60, or $70, or $80. When are you going to stop this thing? Well, they will say 'It is Dr. Townsend that did the job,' and the Dr. Townsend movement will grow" (U.S. Congress, Senate 1939, p. 188).

In the wake of Townsend victories in the 1938 elections, Congress was anxious to give *something* to Townsend supporters. Because the Townsend plan and social insurance conflicted dramatically and the movement could not overwhelm administration forces, concessions were all the movement could hope to achieve.[7]

The war period, a third episode, demonstrates that a moderate level of movement strength in membership and political action was not enough to cause changes in spending, because when the political alignment in Congress is unfavorable, spending innovations and improvements are impossible. The Townsend movement kept its issue before Congress, in hearings led by Senator Sheridan Downey of California. Against its inclinations, the SSB drew up plans for a "double-decker" social insurance program, with each aged person receiving a flat amount while those who qualified received additional money according to previous earnings (Cates 1983, chap. 3). But the hearings were interrupted by the news from Pearl Harbor, and little was left of the pro-spending coalition by 1943. Old-age and survivors' insurance had its payroll tax cut instead.

In 1949, a Democratic coalition similar in size to that of 1939 came to power, and once again moderate changes in social spending occurred, though only in old-age insurance. Even with the collapse of its membership, the movement may have helped to elect representatives favorable not only to the Townsend plan, but to other old-age spending proposals. To determine the Townsend influence we analyze three key roll-call votes in the House. Our model expects two things: for the Townsend movement to influence the vote of members of Congress from states with voting rights, and for the movement to have only a marginal effect, as its membership had dropped severely by this point.

The pro-spending forces won two victories on rules forbidding floor amendments to the proposed bill. Republicans and conservative Democrats opposed the rule, which was intended to prevent crippling amendments. On both votes, Townsend-endorsed Republicans were more likely to cross their party's line, while Townsend-endorsed Democrats were slightly less likely to cross theirs. On the second gag rule vote the differences were substantial—among Republicans. Townsend Republicans were six times as likely to defect from the party-line position as their party colleagues. On a third vote, to recommit the bill in favor of a weaker Republican substitute (the Mason amendment), the House voted the measure down, mainly along party lines. Townsend Republicans were nearly four times as likely to vote against their party as their colleagues. By contrast, the Townsend endorsement did not persuade Democrats from the South to vote for social spending. On the first two votes, Townsend Southern Democrats were actually more likely than their nonendorsed counterparts to vote against progressive social security measures. Only on the third vote, to decide on the adoption of the gag rule, were Townsend-supported Southern Democrats less likely than other Southern Democrats to cross over (8%-17%). The movement aided the cause, but did not have as strong an impact as in 1939.[8]

Overall, these episodes of national policymaking support our model. A lack of congressional support and feeble lobbying efforts during the deliberations over the Social Security Act minimized the influence of the movement. The movement had its greatest impact in 1939 when it was strong in both membership and political action. Yet the movement's influence required a specific political condition: a medium-sized, social-spending coalition. Although the movement was relatively strong in its endorsements during the war period, it was not enough to overcome a Congress opposed to social spending. The movement had some impact in 1950 through the long-term effects of the endorsement policy. But the lack of membership support meant that endorsed representatives who voted against old-age spending did not fear electoral reprisals. How endorsed members voted also provides support for our perspective. Townsend-endorsed Southern Democrats, who came from undemocratic political systems, were much less likely to dissent from the antispending line than Townsend Republicans. Moreover, the movement had its greatest success in old-age assistance, rather than old-age insurance. In assistance, the plans of the movement and those of the administration were not contradictory. Both groups could agree on the need for pensions. At the national level, however, the movement gained only a few new old-age benefits and was never fully accepted as a legitimate representative of the aged.

The Impact of the Townsend Movement in the States: Multiple-Regression Analyses

Gauging the influence of the movement at the state level requires a focus on old-age assistance. By the end of 1938 each state had passed a program, but eligibility restrictions and benefit levels varied substantially (Amenta and Carruthers 1988). For instance, California was paying approximately $32 per month per person and Arkansas approximately $6—a disparity unwarranted by differences in incomes or costs of living.

Within the states the Townsend movement was at first concerned chiefly with the promotion of its national goals. Lobbying in state capitals often focused on passing legislative memorials to Congress entreating it to enact the Townsend plan. Many states passed such memorials, signaling that the movement was a force in state politics, but opening the way to the co-optation of the movement because memorials only gave recognition to the aged, but no advantages. The Townsend movement also pushed for improvements in old-age assistance (see, e.g., Putnam 1970, p. 122). In these bids the movement was able to coordinate with groups that opposed the national Townsend plan and wanted to work within the system defined by the Social Security Act. We first model the determinants of the *average old-age pension* per month at the end of 1940 (U.S. Social Security Administration 1950), a measure indicating generosity in old-age assistance. This measure was

regressed against measures associated with socioeconomic and political theories of public spending policies. Many of these variables may have influenced the movement as well as policies, and so we control for these influences.

To capture socioeconomic approaches, the first measure is the percentage of *aged* people, those over 65 years old (U.S. Bureau of the Census 1935, pp. 36-37; 1941, pp. 5, 43). Also examined is the influence of the Depression. The measure *depression on manufacturing* operationalizes the degree of economic decline in industry and incorporates wage-earner employment in manufacturing at the Depression's low point in 1933 as a proportion of employment in 1929 (U.S. Bureau of Census 1938, pp. 65-69) and rate of unemployment from 1930 to 1933 (U.S. Social Security Board 1937, pp. 58-59) in a standardized index, which scores negatively for severe depressions; this figure is multiplied by a categorical variable for 20 industrialized states (Amenta and Carruthers 1988). Similarly, the measure *farming depression* is the average of gross farm income in 1932, 1933, and 1934 divided by average gross farm income from 1924 through 1928 (U.S. Bureau of the Census 1932, p. 608; 1935, p. 589).

Our first political measures concern longterm features of state and party systems. *Voting rights* is the natural logarithm of the percentage of eligible voters voting in the 1932 presidential election (U.S. Bureau of the Census 1975, pp. 1071-72). Moreover, in the 1930s many states were dominated by traditional, patronage parties (Shefter 1983). *Traditional* party organization strength ranges from a high of five in states where such organizations predominated to a low of one (Mayhew 1986, p. 196). To measure *administrative strength,* a middle-range characteristic, we score one for each year until 1929 that the labor commissioner had rulemaking authority in the administration of safety laws (Brandeis 1935, p. 654). We expect that states with bureaus exercising such administrative powers would promote spending programs. In the shorter run, spending may have been encouraged where *Democrats in democratic political and open party systems* controlled the governments in the 1930s; such regimes would be likely to follow the lead of the national party. States with competitive parties, without dominant traditional party organizations, and with Democratic control of the government for four years or more during the 1930s are scored one; others zero (see Hansen 1983, p. 158). We also measure the timing of the *adoption of old-age pension* legislation, which scores states from one to 10 according to the number of years by 1939 that a state had passed a compulsory law (Epstein 1968, pp. 534-35; U.S. Social Security Board 1937, pp. 161-62; 1938), assuming that the earlier the program the greater the spending on it.

Movements, especially labor, and other organized groups may have also influenced pensions. *Union density* takes union members in 1939 as a percentage of the non-agricultural employed in 1940 (Troy and Sheflin 1985, p. 7-3; U.S. Bureau of Census 1948, pp. 194, 196). Next, we consider the per capita membership of the *Fraternal Order of Eagles* (1927, 1928, 1929, 1930), which began lobbying for old-age pensions in the 1920s. We calculated two measures of the strength of the Townsend movement and its collective action. *Townsend clubs* is the per capita number of clubs 1934-50 (Holtzman 1963, pp. 50-51). The overwhelming majority of these clubs were in existence by 1940, when the second wave of mobilization peaked. Examining the direct influence of clubs captures potential for disruptive activity and for sustaining other collective action, such as election endorsements. *Townsend-endorsed House*

members is the percentage of a state's delegation won by Townsend candidates in the breakthrough election of 1938. This measure is an indirect gauge of influence on state-level elections: working for congressional candidates doubtless affected state politicians from overlapping districts. Two measures are closely correlated (.73), and we enter the two measures separately in the models below.

We employed regression analysis separately on each of three theoretical groups: movements and interest groups; socioeconomic conditions; and political structures and circumstances. Using the results of this first round, we estimated models with indicators from all groups and then eliminated measures that proved insignificant. In each model we used as a control measure *per capita income*, initially computed for 1929 (U.S. Bureau of the Census 1975, pp. 243-45). Most measures of social spending "efforts" take into account the income level of the state or country. Thus, we expect a strong and positive effect of this measure, but do not otherwise interpret it. The preliminary regressions (results not shown, but available on request) indicate that social-movement factors potentially had a great influence on old-age assistance. Yet standard socioeconomic and, espe-

Table 3
Four Full Models of the Size of Old-Age Pensions, 1940 and 1946-48

Independent Measures	1940		1946-8	
	Model 1	Model2	Model 3	Model 4
Movement model:				
Townsend-endorsed House members, 1938	.146**	. . .	.252**	. . .
	(1.68)		(2.20)	
Per capita Townsend clubs, 1940	. . .	.112	. . .	.183*
		(1.01)		(1.49)
Political (opportunity) model:				
Voting rights	.237**	.218**	.199*	.251**
	(2.32)	(1.86)	(1.55)	(1.94)
Traditional party organization	-.225***	-.231**	-.190*	-.197*
	(-2.20)	(-2.08)	(1.63)	(1.66)
Administrative powers	.213**	.216**	.174**	.182**
	(2.38)	(2.36)	(1.87)	(1.91)
Democratic control in open, competitive system	.095	.086	.169**	.164*
	(1.07)	(0.95)	(1.77)	(1.67)
Control variable:				
Per capita income	.557***	.576***	.456***	.433***
	(4.86)	(4.95)	(4.01)	(3.72)
F	22.76	21.56	18.53	17.08
Adjusted R^2	.735	.724	.691	.672

Note: Coefficients are standardized and *t*-statistics are in parentheses. For definitions of measures, see text. $N = 48$.
* $P < .10$. ** $P < .05$. *** $P < .01$.

models also do well in explaining average pensions. Are the effects of Townsend movement measures due to the relationship between socioeconomic and political conditions and group mobilizations?

To test this we estimated a model including the Townsend measures and socioeconomic and political factors. Even when we control for economic and political explanations of social spending, the Townsend movement has an independent influence (see table 3). In model 1, we used a stepwise procedure to eliminate the measures from initial regressions that did not aid the explanation. This model, which, with adjustments, explains about 74% of the variance, includes the control measure and measures of voting rights, patronage-party organization, administrative strength, open Democratic party rule, and the Townsend political action measure, which was significant at the .05 level. Model 2, which is similar but includes the measure of Townsend clubs, performed almost as well, explaining 72% of the variance, with adjustments. Here the Townsend indicator was not significant, however, at the .10 level.[9]

In the 1940s the movement continued to elect members to Congress and to pressure state governments, which had two new incentives to raise assistance: the 1939 amendments, which increased the matching payments, and inflation due to war. To gauge the movement's influence we re-

gressed the average monthly old-age pensions in 1946, 1947, and 1948 against indicators from the best-fitting models from previous trials. Because the measure of Townsend clubs gauges the movement *in 1940* its disruptive and other effects may not have registered by then. The movement also refined its endorsement policy, and we use the average Townsend-endorsed share of the House delegation in elections from 1938 through 1946. The results indicate that the movement had an effect independent of other factors. Model 3, which is similar to model 1, explains 69% of the variance, and the endorsements measure is significant at the .05 level. In model 4, which is similar to model 2, all measures are significant at the .10 level or better—including the measure of Townsend clubs—and the model explains about 67% of the variance.[10]

All in all, the movement and its political activities had a consistently positive effect on pensions in the 1930s and 1940s, despite strong influences of party and state. The findings also suggest that the political activity of the movement had a major impact on the initial size of pensions in 1940, but less of an effect in the next decade. By contrast the organizational strength of the movement had little impact on initial legislation, but was key to the improvement of old-age assistance in the 1940s. Organizational might and political

Table 4
Four Models of Townsend Memorials

Independent Measures	1939		1945	
	Model 1	Model 2	Model 3	Model 4
Movement model:				
Townsend-endorsed House members	...	...	.442*** (3.51)	...
Per capita Townsend clubs, 1940	...	.525*** (4.38)	...	.469* (3.66)
Political model:				
Voting rights	.249** (1.94)	...	...	...
Traditional party organization	-.415*** (-3.36)	-.151* (-1.32)	-.203* (1.68)	-.167* (1.36)
Administrative powers	.306**	.255**	.252**	.245**
F	8.68	16.22	11.86	12.34
Adjusted R²	.329	.493	.409	.420

Note: Coefficients are standardized and *t*-statistics are in parentheses. For definitions of measures, see text. *N* = 48.
* *P* < .10. ** *P* < .05. *** *P* < .01.

action boosted óld-age assistance, but in an uneven and historically contingent way.

Was the movement heard as a legitimate voice for the aged? To answer this, we employ the measure *Townsend memorials*—a sum of state resolutions demanding the national adoption of the Townsend plan (Holtzman 1963, p. 192)—as the best indicator of how politicians viewed the movement.[11] States with unresponsive political parties and systems might discourage memorials, although not as vehemently as they did pensions; state and party champions of high spending might not be as supportive of bids to validate the Townsend plan. We employ the same political model as before, analyzing memorials passed through 1939 and through 1945. The results (in table 4) indicate that the movement was crucial to the passage of memorials. The club measure predicts memorials in both periods. Traditional party organization has a consistently negative effect and administrative powers a positive one.

Success and the Townsend Movement: A Qualitative Comparative Analysis

We want to know not only the determinants of pensions and the passage of memorials separately, but also combinations of these outcomes. In some states the movement approached membership in the polity: high old-age pensions and the acceptance of the movement; elsewhere it was rejected, and old-age assistance remained stingy. Some states gave concessions, as was true at the national level—at the state level, there were instances of co-optation—the movement was recognized, but pensions were low. In appraising combinational arguments, multiple regression can be marred by multicollinearity and the exhaustion of degrees of freedom (Ragin 1987, p. 162).

To address these issues, we employ qualitative comparative analysis (QCA). This examines many combinations of potential causes and generates the simplest combination of them leading to outcomes of interest (Ragin and Drass 1988). We argue that there is more than one path to public spending and that QCA can locate these paths. Yet QCA can employ only a limited number of (categorical) measures. One guide is to use measures from multiple-regression analyses (Griffin et al. 1991). We employ the two movement measures and the political measures of voting rights, traditional parties, administrative capacities, and Democratic party rule. Although these measures imply 64 combinations, many did not exist. For instance, no state lacking voting rights had patronage parties or administrative powers or Townsend clubs. We assume that nonexistent combinations would not have resulted in high pensions or memorials because this would mean that all *logical* possibilities were *socially* possible—too strong an assumption.

To determine which states had high pensions, we take the standardized residuals from the regression of old-age pensions on per capita income, the control measure. Those states with large, positive residuals had the strongest programs because, relative to the state's income level, pensioners were doing better; we do not discount the possibility of poor states having generous old-age assistance. We categorize 17 states as having "high" pensions.[12]

One also must decide how to evaluate "contradictory" cases—a combination of potential causes that sometimes leads to the outcome in question, sometimes not. To code these contradictions as "positive" outcomes is to examine the conditions under which the outcome at hand was *possible*. To consider contradictions as "negative" instances is to locate combinations that *always* led to the outcome. We rely on a third procedure: recoding contradictions by their main tendencies, counting them as positive if more than half of the instances lead to the outcome, negative otherwise, and then reanalyzing the data (see Ragin 1987, pp. 113-18).

Although the mediation model predicts more than one route to high pensions, it also anticipates roadblocks: a lack of voting rights or the presence of traditional parties will prevent high pensions. One route implies social movements; in states with voting rights and open parties—where the movement was strong in both organization and political action—pensions should also be strong. Generous pensions are also implied by states with open and democratic politics and either Democratic party rule or administrative powers, or both.

The initial analyses locate three possible roads to high pensions (see chart 1). As expected voting rights and open parties were necessary for high pensions; alternatively, a nondemocratic political or a traditional party system prevented high pensions. Otherwise, one of the routes to high pensions is suggested by political models—a combination of administrative capacities and

Chart 1
Paths to High Old-Age Pensions, 1946-48, QCA Analyses

Step 1. An Analysis of Cases in which High Old-Age Pensions Were Possible
VOTING RIGHTS*traditional parties*DEM RULE*endorsements +

Positive	*TT* Terms:	3	33%	Raw Terms:	3	13%
Contradictory	*TT* Terms:	1	11%	Raw Terms:	2	9%

VOTING RIGHTS*traditional parties*ADMINISTRATIVE POWERS*DEM RULE +

Positive	*TT* Terms:	3	33%	Raw Terms:	3	13%
Contradictory	*TT* Terms:	1	11%	Raw Terms:	3	13%

VOTING RIGHTS*traditional parties*ENDORSEMENTS*CLUBS

Positive	*TT* Terms:	0	0%	Raw Terms:	0	0%
Contradictory	*TT* Terms:	4	44%	Raw Terms:	17	74%

Step 2. An Analysis of Cases in which High Old-Age Pensions Were Certain
VOTING RIGHTS*traditional parties*DEM RULE*endorsements*CLUBS +

Positive	*TT* Terms:	2	50%	Raw Terms:	2	50%

VOTING RIGHTS*traditional parties*ADMINISTRATIVE POWERS*DEM RULE*clubs

Positive	*TT* Terms:	2	50%	Raw Terms:	2	50%

Step 3. Three Routes to High Old-Age Pensions, with Contradictions Resolved
VOTING RIGHTS*traditional parties*ADMINISTRATIVE POWERS*DEM RULE +

Positive	*TT* Terms:	4	50%	Raw Terms:	5	31%

VOTING RIGHTS*traditional parties*DEM RULE*CLUBS +

Positive	*TT* Terms:	4	50%	Raw Terms:	8	50%

VOTING RIGHTS*traditional parties*ENDORSEMENTS*CLUBS

Positive	*TT* Terms:	4	50%	Raw Terms:	12	75%

Note: A measure in all capital letters indicates its presence; a measure in lower case indicates its absence. "*TT*" refers to "truth table"; "Raw" refers to the number of actual cases adhering to the combination; DEM RULE refers to Democratic party control. An asterisk * indicates *and* in Boolean analysis; a plus sign (+) indicates *or* in Boolean analysis.

Democratic party rule. A second is expected by the social-movement model—the presence of organizational strength of the movement and success in endorsements.

When the contradictions are recoded, the mediation model is greatly supported. The analysis indicates three routes, each requiring voting rights and an open party system. First there is a "standard political" route through Democratic party rule in the context of administrative powers. Next there is a "movement model" in which both the movement's organizational strength and successful endorsements are required for high pensions. Finally, there is the combination of Democratic party rule and the presence of Townsend clubs.

Although they might discourage the passage of memorials, traditional parties are not expected to preclude them by their presence. After all, memorials cost nothing and might appease the movement. There are three main routes to memorials when contradictions are replaced by main tendencies and only voting rights is necessary in each (results not shown). The first route requires strength in Townsend clubs and endorsements and also Democratic party control and a lack of administrative capacities. The other two require open-party systems and administrative capacities; in one of these, Townsend club strength is also required, indicating that this influenced memorials more than endorsements did.

In the best case for the Townsend movement, a state would have high old-age pensions and would have recognized the movement through the passage of memorials—this was as close as the movement came to becoming a member of the polity. The case of concessions would include a strong assistance program but no memorials. The case of co-optation is the opposite; the movement was recognized through memorials, but assistance was not generous. Finally, in some states the movement failed to be recognized, and pensions were low. "New benefits" means being categorized as having high pensions, and "recognizing" the movement means passing one or more memorials. All told, the movement achieved something like membership in the polity in 12 states (see chart 2). In five states the movement won concessions, while 10 states were cases of co-optation, and in 21 states the movement failed completely. Movement strength in organization and endorsements correlates with the level of success achieved, but does not entirely explain it.

Chart 2
Townsend Membership in the Polity, Concessions, Co-optation, Collapse

Level 1: Twelve States Where the Townsend Movement Approached Polity Membership

1. Colorado*	5. North Dakota*	9. Massachusetts
2. Washington*	6. Idaho	10. Minnesota*
3. Oklahoma	7. Wyoming	11. Oregon*
4. Arizona*	8. California*	12. South Dakota*

Level 2: Five States Where the Townsend Movement Received Concessions

1. Utah	3. Kansas*	5. New Mexico
2. Nebraska*	4. Iowa*	

Level 3: Ten States Where the Townsend Movement Was Co-opted

1. Florida*	5. Nevada	9. Arkansas
2. Montana*	6. Michigan	10. Georgia
3. New Hampshire	7. Illinois	
4. Wisconsin*	8. Indiana*	

Residual: Twenty-one States Where the Townsend Movement's Prospects Collapsed

1. Louisiana	8. Texas	15. South Carolina
2. New York	9. Vermont*	16. Maryland
3. Ohio	10. Pennsylvania	17. North Carolina
4. Maine*	11. New Jersey	18. West Virginia
5. Missouri	12. Tennessee	19. Kentucky
6. Connecticut	13. Mississippi	20. Virginia
7. Rhode Island	14. Alabama	21. Delaware

Note: For definitions of the three levels of success, see text.
*States where the movement scored high on both membership and endorsements.

In the analysis of membership, when the contradictions are replaced with their main propensities, QCA supports the mediation model (see chart 3). Polity membership results from movement power in both dimensions, in the context of favorable political conditions. Two paths, which include the bulk of the cases, require both aspects of movement strength, organizationally and through political action. Yet movement strength is not sufficient; one route requires administrative capacities and the second requires Democratic party control. The third path is through Democratic party control and administrative powers, but without Townsend endorsements. A movement can appear to succeed without having put out much effort—the case suggested by the strong form of the opportunity model.

We expect concessions, the more favorable of the partially successful outcomes, to occur where generous pensions do not derive from movement strength in both dimensions, and this is what we find. The two paths to concessions work through democratic political systems, without traditional parties—and both imply Democratic party control. However, the influence of the movement is only partial in each case. One route requires success in endorsements, but weakness in organization; the other, the opposite. Partial movement strength under favorable political conditions brought benefits but not recognition.

By contrast, we expect that, in the context of favorable circumstances, movement strength in organization only might lead to co-optation. A context of traditional political parties, regardless of movement efforts, can also lead to this minimal level of success. This point of view is supported (see chart 3). One route works through traditional parties and movement strength in both dimensions. Under pressure, patronage parties recognized the movement, but did not pass high pensions. A second route works through strong movement organization, in an open party system with voting rights, but without Democratic party rule or administrative capacities. Although the third route—administrative powers in the context of a democratic political and open party system—is difficult to appraise, overall the analysis of co-optation provides support for the mediation model. The causes of movement collapse mainly parallel those of membership. The QCA locates two routes through traditional parties and a failure of endorsements. The third route involves the absence of voting rights, traditional parties, administrative capacities, both movement dimensions, and the presence of Democratic party rule—the typical Southern state.

Chart 3
Paths to "Membership," "Concessions," "Co-optation," and "Collapse"

Three Routes to Polity Membership for the Townsend Movement
VOTING RIGHTS*trad parties*ADMIN POWERS*ENDORSEMENTS*CLUBS +

Positive	*TT* Terms:	2	40%	Raw Terms:	5	50%

VOTING RIGHTS*trad parties*DEM RULE*ENDORSEMENTS*CLUBS +

Positive	*TT* Terms:	2	40%	Raw Terms:	5	50%

VOTING RIGHTS*trad parties*ADMIN POWERS*DEM RULE*endorsements

Positive	*TT* Terms:	2	40%	Raw Terms:	2	20%

Two Routes Leading to Concessions for the Townsend Movement
VOTING RIGHTS*trad parties*admin powers*DEM RULE*endorsements*CLUBS +

Positive	*TT* Terms:	1	50%	Raw Terms:	1	50%

VOTING RIGHTS*trad parties*ADMIN POWERS*DEM RULE*ENDORSEMENTS*clubs

Positive	*TT* Terms:	1	50%	Raw Terms:	1	50%

Three Routes Leading to the Co-optation of the Townsend Movement
VOTING RIGHTS*TRAD PARTIES*admin powers*DEM RULE*ENDORSEMENTS*CLUBS +

Positive	*TT* Terms:	1	25%	Raw Terms:	1	25%

VOTING RIGHTS*trad parties*ADMIN POWERS*dem rule*endorsements +

Positive	*TT* Terms:	2	50%	Raw Terms:	2	50%

VOTING RIGHTS*trad parties*dem rule*endorsements*CLUBS +

Positive	*TT* Terms:	2	50%	Raw Terms:	2	50%

Three Routes Leading to the Collapse of the Townsend Movement
voting rights*trad parties*admin powers*DEM RULE*endorsements*clubs +

Positive	*TT* Terms:	1	20%	Raw Terms:	7	39%

VOTING RIGHTS*TRAD PARTIES*admin powers*endorsements*clubs +

Positive	*TT* Terms:	2	40%	Raw Terms:	8	44%

VOTING RIGHTS*TRAD PARTIES*ADMIN POWERS*dem rule*endorsements

Positive	*TT* Terms:	2	40%	Raw Terms:	3	17%

Note: All results are with contradictions resolved into their main tendencies (see text). A measure in all capital letters indicates its presence; a measure in lower case indicates its absence.
"*TT*" refers to "truth table"; "Raw" refers to the number of actual cases adhering to the combination; DEM RULE refers to Democratic party control. An asterisk (*) indicates *and* in Boolean analysis; a plus sign (+) indicates *or* in Boolean analysis.

Discussion and Conclusion

Using several comparative strategies can help to make theoretical sense of a case study (Amenta 1991). Comparisons over time and across policies and states helped to answer different questions about the influence of the movement. Our approach also suggests that studies of the influence of movements need to take into account the determinants of movements as well as their organization and actions. These determinants may influence what seem to be successes won by the movement. More than that, however, studies of the development of public spending policies need to pay attention to the different routes to them (Therborn 1989). States could reach high old-age spending not only by standard statist and party ways, but also through routes paved by the Townsend movement.

For state bureaucracies and left-center parties to aid a movement, its constituency needs to be electorally desirable, and the movement cannot have "displacement" goals (Gamson 1990, app. A). The aged were a desirable constituency, but the Townsend plan sought to displace the administration's programs, limiting its influence. Although the movement made some notable gains, it never won membership in the polity and did not survive postwar prosperity. Old-age insurance, the program that preempted the name "social security," has perhaps raised the aged to a status where legislation and bureaucratic and fiscal practices combine to enforce their interests, but different forces won these victories (Derthick 1979). The movement aided those outside the system—those in the generation of the movement's activists—by upgrading old-age *assistance*, the main form of public social provision for the aged until 1950.

Analyzing the causes of social-spending policies, we find some support for economic, political, and movement models. Our analyses also indicate that the American experience can be examined with models based on European cases. With respect to social movements, this article provides evidence that movements need to be strong both organizationally and in standard politics to gain recognition and benefits for their supporters. Endorsements need organizational backing to make them effective, and organizations without political support are vulnerable. Strategic and tactical diversity can only aid a movement.

Yet the impact of social movements is mediated strongly by political conditions. Nowhere was the movement able to achieve both new benefits and recognition without favorable conditions in the polity. Among long-term political circumstances, democratic rights and open parties had gatekeeping roles. The key middle-range condition concerned state bureaus promoting public protection, and the main short-term condition concerned the rule of a Democratic party that in the 1930s and 1940s was almost a functional equivalent of a labor party on the European model (Greenstone 1969). Both facilitated movement gains. In states where the political or party system thwarted the goals of the movement, people contributing to the movement got little for their dues. By contrast, in states where politics were democratic, parties were open, and state or party sponsors were available, the movement did win advantages. Townsend was a hero for the aged but only on some issues, and his movement required help.

The results also question the degree to which the American political system has been "open" to the influence of social movements (Kitschelt 1986). As a system, it was simultaneously open and closed. Some parts of the system encouraged movements and helped them to succeed. Other parts—those without voting rights and open party systems—discouraged movements and prevented them from succeeding. Representatives of national-level nondemocratic political systems and traditional party systems made it difficult for movements to achieve more than partial victories. Multiple points of entry into the system make it seem more open to influence than it has been. The extension of voting rights throughout the nation and the decline of the traditional party organizations have opened the system more. Yet the expanding role of campaign money in American politics in the past two decades may have a similar discouraging and dampening effect on the efforts of movements (Edsall 1984).

Notes

1. A revised version of Gamson's (1990, p. 29) typology, this figure is a static representation of outcomes: protest movements may move into different categories over time.

2. Referees argued that the model does not seem to fit the civil rights movement, which was based in the nondemocratic South. We disagree because the model of movement emergence is multicausal and does not rule out the possibility of movements arising in nondemocratic polities. Our model also implies that full success would be unlikely in nondemocratic polities. We believe this fits the case, as the civil rights movement won its victories mainly through the actions of the federal government, whose officials were concerned with the voting behavior of African-Americans in the North, to bring recalcitrant Southern state legislatures in line (see McAdam 1982).

3. Both conditions have mattered in American history (Amenta and Skocpol 1989). The democratization of the polity was early—there was almost universal white male suffrage by the 1830s—but uneven—the South constricted voting rights from the turn of the century until the 1960s. Traditional parties took hold in the 19th century and only gradually lost their grip on politics.

4. In January 1939, an American Institute of Public Opinion poll found that, of those familiar with the Townsend plan, 35% were in favor and 53% opposed, the rest having no opinion. In July 1941, only 19% were in favor and 39% opposed, with 42% having no opinion (Cantril and Strunk 1951, p. 542).

5. In 1938, 169 Republicans and 77 Democrats were endorsed. In 1942, 1946, 1950, and 1952, more Democrats than Republicans were supported. Endorsements ranged from 206 to 285 in biannual elections from 1936 to 1952.

6. Examined separately, the movement's membership and its political action do not correspond to the ups and downs of public-spending policies in the 1930s and 1940s. The movement came too late to influence the drive for old-age pensions and the Economic Security Bill, taking off *after* the Social Security Act. Although the movement reached a recorded maximum of members in 1939, a year that old-age programs were upgraded, membership stabilized during the war, a poor period for social spending, and was minimal by 1950, when amendments passed. As for the political action, the movement did not make widespread endorsements until 1936, after the 1935 Economic Security bill. Moreover, the endorsement policy was successful during the war years—a dismal time for public spending.

7. Old-age insurance was amended to resemble more closely the Townsend plan's pay-as-you-go basis. These changes were proposed by the SSB and supported by administration Keynesians and business groups favoring reduced taxes (Leff 1988).

8. On none of the votes did Townsend support tip the balance. On the first vote, Townsend influence was minimal, not enough to account for the 19-vote margin of victory. Although the Townsend influence was greater on the second vote, that one ran almost strictly according to party lines. The Mason amendment was defeated handily. For details, see the *Congressional Record,* 1949, vol. 95. pt. 10, pp. 13818-819, and pt. 11, pp. 13972-973.

9. A referee suggested that we examine the issue of spatial autocorrelation (see Anselin 1988; Doreian 1980, 1981). If this were a problem, it would make our OLS estimates less efficient. Because of the political autonomy of the U.S. states and mass media, we do not think there are strong theoretical grounds for it. However, we explored the issue, constructing a contiguity matrix with ones for states that spatially adjoin and zeros otherwise. We employed both "spatial effects" and "spatial disturbances" specifications (Doreian 1980), using the SPACESTAT statistical package (Anselin 1990). The OLS residuals for the models presented showed some evidence of spatial autocorrelation, but the substantive results changed very little when the spatial autocorrelation models were fitted (results not shown, but are available). The regression coefficients never changed sign, and significance levels changed only slightly. In no case did a coefficient for Townsend movement measure become less significant than in the OLS specification. Thus, the OLS results are not misleading.

10. In these models, the measures of voting rights and per capita income are also updated to 1940. When a lagged dependent measure is introduced, results indicate that the endorsement and club measures have effects on *changes* in pension levels from 1940 to the end of the decade (not shown, but available from authors).

11. Our measure of recognition is a middle-level one, standing somewhere between "consultation" and "inclusion." Memorials validated the Townsend plan and the Townsend movement as a representative of the aged, but did not ensure full inclusion of the movement on all old-age policies. Thus, nowhere did the movement become a full member of the polity. Full membership would have entailed the passage of a state-level Townsend plan, with the movement involved in its implementation.

12. Our decisions in constructing the six independent measures were determined mainly by theoretical considerations, partly by breaks in the data. For voting rights we took a strong view, discounting only the lowest nine states—all former states of the Confederacy. We counted a state as having traditional parties if it scored three, four, or five on Mayhew's (1986) five-point scale, 13 states qualifying. The 15 states whose labor commissions won rule-making authority before 1920 were scored as having administrative powers. We used a relatively inclusive strategy for the movement: for organization (clubs), the cutoff was 10 clubs for 10,000 persons, with 23 states qualifying. For Townsend-backed House members (endorsements), the standard was 53% of the delegation, a natural break in the data that included 19 states. ✦

REFERENCES
and
INDEX

References

Aaron, Daniel. 1992. *Cincinnati, Queen City of the West, 1819-1838.* Columbus: Ohio State University Press.

Aberle, David. 1966. *The Peyote Religion Among the Navaho.* Chicago: Aldine.

———. 1965. "A note on relative deprivation theory as applied to Millenarian and other cult movements." Pp. 537-41 in W. Lessa and E. Vogt (eds.), *Reader in Comparative Religion: An Anthropological Approach.* New York: Harper and Row.

Abrahamian, Ervand. 1982. *Iran Between Two Revolutions.* Princeton, NJ: Princeton University Press.

Abrahamian, E. 1980. "Structural Causes of the Iran Revolution." *MERIP Reports* 87:21-26.

Abrams, Philip and Andrew McCulloch. 1976. *Communes, Sociology and Society.* Cambridge: Cambridge University Press.

Adam, Barry D. 1995. *The Rise of a Gay and Lesbian Movement,* Second Edition. Boston: Twayne.

Adorno, T.W., E. Frenkel-Brunswick, D.J. Levinson, and R.N. Sanford. 1950. *The Authoritarian Personality.* New York: Harper & Brothers.

Advocate (Los Angeles). "Florida's shame." August 10:15.

Afkhami, Gholam. 1985. *The Iranian Revolution: Thanatos on a National Scale.* Washington, DC: Middle East Institute.

Agosín, Marjorie. 1987. *Scraps of Life.* Trenton, NJ: Red Sea Press.

Âhanchîân, Jalâl. 1982. *Tarh-i Suqût-i Yik Pâdishâh* (The Plot to Topple a King). Self-published. Mill Valley, CA.

Ahlbrandt, Roger S., Jr., and James V. Cunningham. 1979. *A New Public Policy for Neighborhood Preservation.* New York: Praeger.

Ajzen, Icek and Martin Fishbein. 1980. *Understanding Attitudes and Predicting Social Behavior.* Englewood Cliffs, NJ: Prentice-Hall.

Albuquerque Journal. 1985. "Debate: building the road to change." February 3, Section B, p. 4.

Alexander, Jeffrey C. 1992. "Citizen and Enemy as Symbolic Classification: On the Polarizing Discourse of Civil Society." Pp. 289-308 in *Cultivating Differences: Symbolic Boundaries and the Making of Inequality,* edited by Michèle Lamont and Marcel Fournier. Chicago: University of Chicago Press.

———. 1982. *Theoretical Logic in Sociology, vol. 1. Positivism, Presuppositions, and Current Controversies.* Berkeley: University of California Press.

Allardt, Erik. 1981. "Ethnic Mobilization and Minority Resources." *Zeitschrift für Soziologie* 10:427-37.

Allen, Robert L. 1969. *Black Awakening in Capitalist America: An Analytic History.* Garden City, NY: Anchor Books.

Allison, Paul D. 1984. *Event History Analysis: Regression for Longitudinal Event Data.* Beverly Hills, CA: Sage.

Allport, Gordon. 1958. *The Nature of Prejudice.* New York: Doubleday Anchor.

Altmeyer, Arthur. 1966. *The Formative Years of Social Security.* Madison: University of Wisconsin Press.

Alvarez, Sonia. 1990. *Engendering Democracy in Brazil: Women's Movements in Transition Politics.* Princeton, NJ: Princeton University Press.

Amenta, Edwin. 1991. "Making the Most of a Case Study: Theories of the Welfare State and the American Experience." *International Journal of Comparative Sociology* 32:172-94.

———. 1989. *Lost Ground: American Social Spending and Taxation Policies in Depression and War.* Ph.D. dissertation. University of Chicago, Department of Sociology.

Amenta, Edwin, and Bruce G. Carruthers. 1988. "The Formative Years of U.S. Social Spending Policies: Theories of the Welfare State and the American States during the Great Depression." *American Sociological Review* 53:661-78.

Amenta, Edwin, and Theda Skocpol. 1989. "Taking Exception: Explaining the Distinctiveness of American Public Policies in the Last Century." Pp. 292-.333 in *The Comparative History of Public Policy*, edited by Francis G. Castles. Cambridge: Polity Press.

———. 1988. "Redefining the New Deal: World War II and the Development of Social Provision in the United States." Pp. 81-122 in *The Politics of Social Policy in the United States,* edited by Margaret Weir, Ann Shola Orloff, and Theda Skocpol. Princeton. N.J.: Princeton University Press.

Amenta, Edwin, and Yvonne Zylan. 1991. "It Happened Here: Political Opportunity, the New Institutionalism, and the Townsend Movement." *American Sociological Review* 56:250-65.

American Anti-Slavery Society. 1837. *Fourth Annual Report.* New York: American Anti-Slavery Society.

Archer, Margaret R. 1988. *Culture and Agency: The Place of Culture in Social Theory.* Cambridge: Cambridge University Press.

American Anti-Slavery Society. 1836. *Third Annual Report.* New York: American Anti-Slavery Society.

Andreas, Carol. 1976. *Nothing Is As It Should Be.* Cambridge, MA: Schenkman Publishing Co.

Anglin, Robert A. 1949. *A Sociological Analysis of a Pressure Group.* Ph.D. dissertation, Indiana University.

Anselin, Luc. 1990. *SPACESTAT. A Program for the Statistical Analysis of Spatial Data.* University of California, Santa Barbara, Department of Geography.

———. 1988. *Spatial Econometrics.* Dordrecht: Kluwer Academic.

Appert, Félix Antoine. 1875. *Rapport d'ensemble de M. le Général Appert sur les opérations de la justice militaire relatives à l'insurrection de 1871 (Summary Report of General Appert on the Military Justice Proceedings Regarding the Insurrection of 1871).* Paris: Imprimerie Nationale.

Archives Historiques de l'Armée de Terre. (Historical Archives of the Army). Vincennes, France.

Arjomand, Said Amir. 1988. *The Turban for the Crown: The Islamic Revolution in Iran.* New York: Oxford University Press.

Aron, Raymond. 1968. *La revolution introuvable: Reflexions sur la revolution de mai.* Paris: Fayard.

Arriagada Herrera, Genaro. 1991. *Pinochet: The Politics of Power.* Boulder, CO: Westview Press.

Ash, Roberta. 1972. *Social Movements in America.* Chicago: Markham.

Ashraf, Ahmad and Ali Banuazizi. 1985. "The State, Classes, and Modes of Mobilization in the Iranian Revolution." *State, Culture, and Society* 1:3-40.

Ashworth, John. 1987. *"Agrarians" and "Aristocrats": Party Political Ideology in the United States, 1837-1846.* Cambridge: Cambridge University Press.

Asnâd-i Lânih-yi Jâsûsî (Spy Nest Documents). 1980-1991. 77 Volumes. Tehran, Iran: Dânish-jûyân-i Musalmân-i Payrû-i Khat-i Imâm.

Atwood, Rufus. 1962. "The Origin and Development of the Negro Public College with Special Reference to the Land-grant College." *Journal of Negro Education* 31 (no. 3): 240-50.

Avorn, Jerry. 1968. *Up Against the Ivy Wall: A History of the Columbia Crisis.* New York: Columbia Spectator Board of Associates.

Axelrod, Saul, and Jack Apsche (eds.). 1983. *The Effects of Punishment on Human Behavior.* New York: Academic.

Babbie, Earl R. 1965. "The third civilization: An examination of Sokagakkai." *Review of Religious Research* 7:101-121.

Badger, Henry G. 1951. *Statistics of Negro Colleges and Universities: Students, Staff, and Finances, 1900-1950.* Circular no. 293 (April). Washington, D.C.: Office of Education, Federal Security Agency.

Badgett, M.V. Lee. 1993a. "Employment and sexual orientation: Disclosure and discrimination in the workplace." Unpublished manuscript.

——. 1993b "Economic evidence of sexual orientation discrimination." Unpublished manuscript.

Badie, B. and P. Birnbaum. 1979. *Sociologie de l'Etat.* Paris: Grasset.

Bailey, Kenneth D. 1973. "Monothetic and Polythetic Typologies and their Relation to Conceptualization, Measurement and Scaling." *American Sociological Review* 38:18-33.

Baker, Ella. 1979. Interview. New York, New York.

Balbus, Isaac. 1973. *The Dialectics of Legal Repression.* New York: Sage.

Balch, R. and J. Cohig. 1985. "The magic kingdom: A story of Armageddon in utopia." Presented at the annual meetings of the Society for the Scientific Study of Religion, Savannah, GA.

Balch, Robert W. and David Taylor. 1978. "Seekers and saucers: The role of the cultic milieu in joining a UFO cult." Pp. 43-65 in J. Richardson (ed.), *Conversion Careers.* Beverly Hills, Calif.: Sage.

Balser, Diane. 1987. *Sisterhood and Solidarity: Feminism and Labor in Modern Times.* Boston: South End.

Balta, Paul and Claudine Ruileau. 1979. *L'Iran Insurge* (Iran Rebels). Paris, France: Sindbad.

Bandura, Albert. 1986. *Social Foundations of Thought and Action: A Social Cognitive Theory.* New York: Prentice Hall.

Barkan, Steven E. 1984. "Legal Control of the Southern Civil Rights Movement." *American Sociological Review* 49:552-65.

——. 1980a. "Criminal courts and political protest: Mobilization and control in the Southern civil rights and Vietnam antiwar movements." Unpublished Ph.D. dissertation, Department of Sociology, State University of New York at Stony Brook.

——. 1980b. "Criminal prosecutions in the Southern civil rights and Vietnam antiwar movements: Repression and dissent in political trials." Pp. 279-99 in Steven Spitzer (ed.), *Research in Law and Sociology,* Volume 3. New York: JAI Press.

——. 1980c. "Political Trials and Resource Mobilization: Towards an Understanding of Social Movement Litigation." *Social Forces* 58-.944-61.

——. 1979. "Strategic, Tactical and Organizational Dilemmas of the Protest Movement against Nuclear Power." *Social Problems* 27:19-37.

Barker, E. 1984. *The Making of a Moonie.* New York: Basil Blackwell.

Barnes, Samuel H. and Max Kaase. 1979. *Political Action: Mass Participation in Five Western Democracies.* London, England: Sage.

Barr, Evan T. 1985. "Sour Grapes." *The New Republic* 193:20-23.

Barth, Ernest A.T. and Donald L. Noel. 1972. "Conceptual Frameworks for the Analysis of Race Relations: An Evaluation." *Social Forces* 50:333-48.

Barth, Fredrik, ed. 1969. *Ethnic Groups and Boundaries: The Social Organization of Culture Difference.* Boston: Little, Brown.

Barthes, Roland. 1986. *The Rustle of Language.* New York: Hill & Wang.

——. 1972. *Mythologies.* London: Jonathan Cape.

Bartley, Numan. 1969. *The Rise of Massive Resistance: Race and Politics in the South During the 1950s.* Baton Rouge: Louisiana State University Press.

Bashiriyeh, Hossein. 1984. *State and Revolution in Iran, 1962-1982.* New York: St. Martin's Press.

Bateson, Gregory. 1972. *Steps to an Ecology of the Mind.* New York: Ballantine Books.

Bauer, Janet. 1983. "Poor Women and Social Consciousness in Revolutionary Iran." Pp. 141-69 in *Women and Revolution in Iran,* edited by G. Nashat. Boulder, CO: Westview.

Baumgartner, M. P. 1984. "Social control from below." Pp. 303-45 in Donald Black (ed.), *Toward a General Theory of Social Control.* Volume 1: Fundamentals. New York: Academic Press.

Bay Area Friends of SNCC. 1963. Leaflet. No specified. date. In files of Meiklejohn Civil Liberties Institute. Berkeley, California.

Bayat, Assef. 1987. *Workers and Revolution in Iran.* London, England: Zed.

Beccalli [Salvati], Bianca. 1971. "Scioperi e organizzazione sindacate: Milano 1950-1970." *Rassegna Italiana di sociologia* 12: 83-120.

Becker, Howard S. 1963. *Outsiders: Studies in the Sociology of Deviance.* New Tork: Macmillan.

——. 1960. "Notes on the concept of commitment." *American Journal of Sociology* 66 (July): 32-40.

——. 1953. "Becoming a marihuana user." *American Journal of Sociology* 59: 235242.

Becker, Susan. 1981. *The Origins of the Equal Rights Amendment: American Feminism between the Wars.* Westport, CT: Greenwood.

Beckford, J. 1985. *Cult Controversies: The Societal Response to New Religious Movements.* New York: Tavistock.

Beckford, J. and J. Richardson. 1983. "A bibliography of social scientific studies of new religious movements." *Social Compass* 30: 111-35.

Beer, William R. 1980. *The Unexpected Rebellion: Ethnic Activism in Contemporary France*. New York: New York University Press.

Beery, Thomas, Sr. 1943. *Western Prices before 1861: A Study of the Cincinnati Market*. Cambridge, Mass.: Harvard University Press.

Beisel, Nicola. 1993. "Morals versus Art: Censorship, the Politics of Interpretation, and the Victorian Nude." *American Sociological Review* 58:145-62.

Bélanger, Sarah. 1988. *The Ethnic Competition Theory Revisited: The Case of Québec*. M.A. Thesis. Department of Sociology, McGill University, Montréal, Québec.

Belfrage, Sally. 1963. "Danville on trial." The New Republic (November 2):11-12.

Belknap, Michal. 1978. *Cold War Political Justice: The Smith Act, the CIA, and American Civil Liberties*. New York: Greenwood Press.

Bell, Derrick A., Jr. 1973. *Race, Racism. and American Law*. Boston: Little, Brown.

Bell, W. and M. T. Force. 1956. Urban neighborhood types and participation in formal associations." *American Sociological Review* 21:25-34.

Bellah, Robert N., Richard Madison, William M. Sullivan, Anne Swidler, and Steven M. Tipton. 1985. *Habits of the Heart*. Berkeley: University of California Press.

Bem, Daryl J. 1970. *Beliefs, Attitudes, and Human Affairs*, Belmont, CA: Brooks/Cole Publishing.

Benford, Robert D. 1993a. "Frame Disputes within the Nuclear Disarmament Movement." *Social Forces* 71:677-701.

——. 1993b. "You Could Be the Hundredth Monkey: Collective Action Frames and Vocabularies of Motive within the Nuclear Disarmament Movement." *Sociological Quarterly* 34:195-216.

——. 1992. "Social Movements." Pp. 1880-1887 in E. Borgatta and M. Borgatta (eds.), *Encyclopedia of Sociology*, Vol. 4. New York: Macmillan Publishing Company.

——. 1984. *The Interorganizational Dynamics of the Austin Peace Movement*. Unpublished M.A. Thesis, Department of Sociology, University of Texas at Austin.

Benford, Robert D., and Scott A. Hunt. 1992. "Dramaturgy and Social Movements: The Social Construction and Communication of Power." *Sociological Inquiry* 62: 36-55.

Berger, Bennet M. 1988. "Utopia and its environment." *Society* 25: 37-41.

——. 1981. *The Survival of a Counterculture*. Berkeley: University of California Press.

Berger, Morroe. 1950. *Equality by Statute*. New York: Columbia University Press.

Berger, Peter L. 1963. *Invitation to Sociology*. Garden City, N.Y.: Anchor Books.

Berger, Peter L. and Thomas Luckmann. 1966. *The Social Construction of Reality*. Garden City, NY: Doubleday.

Berger, Samuel. 1971. *Dollar Harvest: The Story of the Farm Bureau*. Lexington, Ma.: Heath.

Best, Joel. 1990. *Threatened Children: Rhetoric and Concern about Child-Victims*. Chicago: University of Chicago Press.

Bevel, Diane Nash. 1979. Interview . Chicago, Illinois. December 14.

Bevel, James. 1978 Interview. New York, New York. December 27.

Bibby, Reginald W. and Merlin B. Brinkerhoff. 1974. "When proselytizing fails: An organizational analysis." *Sociological Analysis* 35:189-200.

Bill, James A. 1988. *The Eagle and the Lion: The Tragedy of American-Iranian Relations*. New Haven, CT: Yale University Press.

——. 1972. *The Politics of Iran*. Columbus, OH: Charles E. Merrill.

Billington, Ray Allen. *The Protestant Crusade, 1800-1860*. Gloucester, Mass.: P. Smith, 1963.

Bird, Caroline. 1969. *Born Female*. New York: Pocket Books.

Bird, Frederick and Bill Reimer. 1982. "Participation rates in New Religious and Para-Religious Movements." *Journal for the Scientific Study of Religion* 21: 1-14.

Black, Donald. 1984. "Crime as social control." Pp. 1-27 in Donald Black (ed.), *Toward a General Theory of Social Control*. Volume 2: Selected Problems. New York: Academic Press.

Bleiweiss, Robert M. 1969. *Marching to Freedom: The Life of Martin Luther King, Jr.* New York: New American Library.

Blum, Alan F. and Peter McHugh. 1971. "The social ascription of motives." *American Sociological Review* 46:98-109.

Blumer, Herbert. 1969a. *Symbolic Interactionism*. Englewood Cliffs, NJ: Prentice-Hall.

——. [1946, 1951] 1969b. "Collective behavior." Pp. 165-221 in A. M. Lee (ed.), *Principles of Sociology*. New York: Barnes and Noble.

Blumstein, Philip, and Pepper Schwartz. 1983. *American Couples*. New York: William Morrow.

Bolduc, Vincent L. 1980. "Representation and legitimacy in neighborhood organizations: A case study." *Journal of Voluntary Action Research* 9:165-78.

Boles, Janet. 1991. "Form follows function: The evolution of feminist strategies." *Annals of the American Academy of Political Science* 515:38-49.

Bolton, Charles D. 1972. "Alienation and Action: A Study of Peace Group Members." *American Journal of Sociology* 78:537-61.

Bonacich, Edna. 1972. "A Theory of Ethnic Antagonism: The Split Labour Market" *American Sociological Review* 37:547-59.

Bond, Julian. 1980. Interview. Ann Arbor, Michigan. October 19.

Bonder, Gloria. 1983. "The study of politics from the standpoint of women." *International Social Science Journal* 35:569-584.

Bookin, H. 1972-1976. Private notes and personal communications.

Bookman, Ann and Sandra Morgen, eds. 1988. *Women and the Politics of Empowerment*. Philadelphia, PA: Temple University Press.

Boor, Myron. 1981. "Effects of United States presidential elections on suicide and other causes of death." *American Sociological Review* 46:616-618.

Bordogna, Lorenzo, and Giancarlo Provasi. 1979. "Il movimento degli scioperi in Italia, 1881-1973," in Gian Primo Cella (ed.) *Il movimento degli scioperi nel XX secolo*. Bologna: Il Mulino: 169-304.

Borhek, James T. and Richard F. Curtis. 1975. A *Sociology of Belief*. New York: Wiley.

Bourdieu, Pierre. 1991. *Language and Symbolic Power.* Cambridge, Mass.: Harvard University Press.

——. 1984. *Distinction: A Social Critique of the Judgement of Taste.* Cambridge, Mass.: Harvard University Press.

Brand, Enno. 1990. *Staatsgewalt: Politische Unterdrückung und innere Sicherheit in der Bundesrepublik* (State Violence: Political Repression and Internal Security in the Federal Republic of Germany). Göttingen, Germany: Verlag Die Werkstatt.

Brand, L.W. 1985. "Vergleichendes Resümee," pp. 306-334, in K.W. Brand (ed.), *Neue soziale Bewegungen in Westeuropa und den USA.* Frankfurt: Campus.

Brandeis, Elizabeth. 1935. "Labor Legislation." Pp. 399-700 in *History of Labor in the United States, 1896-1932.* Vol. 3, edited by John R. Commons. New York: Macmillan.

Brass, Paul R. 1985. "Ethnic Groups and the State." Pp. 1-58 in *Ethnic Groups and the State,* edited by P. Brass. London: Croom Helm.

Breines, Wini. 1989. *Community and Organization in the New Left, 1962-68.* New Brunswick, N.J.: Rutgers.

——. 1985. "Domineering others in the 1950s: Image and Reality." *Women's Studies International Forum* 8:601-8.

Breton, Raymond. 1988. "French-English Relations." Pp. 557-85 in *Understanding Canadian Society,* edited by J. Curtis and L. Tepperman. Toronto: McGraw-Hill Ryerson.

Breton, Raymond and Daiva Stasiulis. 1980. "Linguistic Boundaries and the Cohesion of Canada," Pp. 137-323 in *Cultural Boundaries and the Cohesion of Canada,* edited by R. Breton, J. G. Reitz and V. Valentine. Montréal: The Institute for Research on Public Policy.

Brière, Claire, and Pierre Blanchet. 1979. *L'Iran: La Revolution au Nom de Dieu* (The Revolution in the Name of God). Paris, France: Seuil.

Briët, Martien, Bert Klandermans, and Frederike Kroon. 1987. "How Women Become Involved in the Women's Movement of the Netherlands." In *The Women's Movements of the United States and Western Europe: Consciousness, Political Opportunities, and Public Policy,* edited by Mary Fainsod Katzenstein and Carol McClurg Mueller. Philadelphia: Temple University Press.

Brinkerhoff, M. and K. Burke. 1980. "Disaffiliation: Some notes on 'failing from the faith'." *Sociological Analysis* 41: 41-54.

Brinton, Crane. 1959. *The Anatomy of Revolution.* New York: Vintage Books.

Brisbane, Robert H. 1974. *Black Activism: Racial Revolution in the United States, 1954-1970.* Valley Forge, PA: Judson Press.

Brockett, Charles D. 1991. "The Structure of Political Opportunities and Peasant Mobilization in Central America." *Comparative Politics* 253-274.

Bromley, D. (Ed.) 1988. *Falling from the Faith, Causes and Consequences of religious Apostasy.* Newbury Park, CA: Sage.

Bromley, D. and P. Hammond (Eds.). 1987. *The Future of new Religious Movements.* Macon, GA: Mercer University Press.

Bromley, David A. and Anson D. Shupe, Jr. 1986. "Affiliation and disaffiliation: A role theory interpretation of joining and leaving new religious movements." Pre-

sented at the annual meetings of the Association for the Study of Religion, San Antonio, TX.

——. 1979a. *"Moonies" in America.* Beverly Hills: Sage.

——. 1979b. "Just a few years seem like a lifetime: A role theory approach to participation in religious movements." Pp. 159-85 in L. Kriesberg (Ed.), *Research in Social Movements, Conflict, and Change.* Greenwich: JAI Press.

Brooks, Thomas R. 1974. *Walls Come Tumbling Down: A History of the Civil Rights Movement, 1940-1970.* Englewood Cliffs. NJ: Prentice-Hall.

Brown, Barbara A., Thomas I. Emerson, Gail Falk, and Ann E. Freedman. 1971. "The Equal Rights Amendment: A Constitutional Basis of Equal Rights for Women." *Yale Law Journal* 80:955-62.

Brubaker. E. R. 1975. " Free ride, free revolution, or golden rule?" *Journal of Law and Economics* 18:147-61.

Bryan, Marguente. 1979. "Social psychology of riot participation." *Research in Race and Ethnic Relations* 1:169-87.

Brzezinski, Zbigniew. 1983. *Power and Principle: Memoirs of the National Security Advisor, 1977-1981.* New York: Farrar, Straus, Giroux.

Buechler, Steven M. 1990. *Women's Movements in the United States.* New Brunswick, N.J.: Rutgers.

——. 1986. *The Transformation of the Woman Suffrage Movement: The Case of Illinois, 1850-1920.* New Brunswick, NJ: Rutgers University Press.

Buerklin, Wilhelm. 1987. "Why study political cycles: An introduction." *European Journal of Political Research* 15: 131-43.

Bullock, Henry Allen. 1971. "Urbanism and Race Relations." Pp. 207229 in Rupert B. Vance and Nicholas J. Demerath (eds.), *The Urban South.* Freeport, NY: Books for Libraries Press.

——. 1970. "Education: parallel inequality." Pp. 269-79 in Allen Weinstein and Frank Otto Gatell (eds.), *The Segregation Era 1863-1954.* New York: Oxford University Press.

——. 1967. *A History of Negro Education in the South.* Cambridge: Harvard University Press.

Bunis, William K. 1993. *Social Movement Activity and Institutionalized Politics: A Study of the Relationship Between Political Party Strength and Social Movement Activity in the United States.* Unpublished dissertation, University of Arizona.

Bunster Burotto, Ximena. 1988. "Watch out for the little Nazi man that all of us have inside: The mobilization and demobilization of women in militarized Chile." *Women's Studies International Forum* 11:485-491.

——. 1986. "Surviving beyond fear: Women and torture in Latin America." Pp. 297-325 in June Nash and Helen I. Safa (eds.), *Women and Change in Latin America.* South Hadley, MA: Bergin and Garvey.

Burgess, M. Elaine. 1965. "Race Relations and Social Change." Pp. 337-358 in John C. McKinney and Edgar T. Thompson, eds., *The South in Continuity and Change.* Durham, N.C.: Duke University Press.

Burke, Kenneth. 1969a. *A Grammar of Motives.* Berkeley: University of California Press.

——. 1969b. A Rhetoric of Motives. Berkeley: University of California Press.

——. 1965. *Permanence and Change.* Indianapolis: Bobbs-Merrill.

Burstein, Paul. 1981. "The Sociology of Democratic Politics and Government." *Annual Review of Sociology* 6:291-319.

———. 1979. "Public opinion, demonstrations, and the passage of anti-discrimination legislation." *Public Opinion Quarterly* 43(2):157-162.

Butler, Judith. 1990. *Gender Trouble: Feminism and the Subversion of Identity.* New York: Routledge.

Button, James W. 1978. *Black Violence.* Princeton, NJ: Princeton University Press.

Cable, Sherry. 1984. "Professionalization in Social Movement Organization: A Case Study of Pennsylvanians for Biblical Morality." *Sociological Focus* 17:287-304.

Cable, Sherry, Edward J. Walsh. and Rex H. Warland. 1988. "Differential Paths to Political Activism: Comparisons of Four Mobilization Processes after the Three Mile Island Accident." *Social Forces* 66:951-69.

Caldicott, Helen. 1984. *Missile Envy: The Arms Race and Nuclear War.* New York: William Morrow.

Cameron, Samuel. 1988. "The Economics of Crime Deterrence: A Survey of Theory and Evidence." *Kyklos* 41:301-23.

Campbell, Donald T. and Julian C. Stanley. 1963. *Experimental and Quasi-Experimental Designs for Research.* Chicago, IL: Rand McNally.

Campbell, Stanley W. 1970. *The Slave Catchers: Enforcement of the Fugitive Slave Law, 1850-1860.* Chapel Hill: University of North Carolina Press.

Cancian, Francesca M., and Bonnie L. Ross. 1981. "Mass Media and the Women's Movement: 1900-1977." *Journal of Applied Behavioral Science* 17:9-26.

Cantril, Hadley. 1965. *The Pattern of Human Concerns.* New Brunswick, N.J.: Rutgers University Press.

———. 1941. *The Psychology of Social Movements.* New York: Wiley.

Cantril, Hadley, and Mildred Strunk. 1951. *Public Opinion, 1935-1946.* Princeton, N.J.: Princeton University Press.

Caplan, Nathan S., and Jeffrey M. Paige. 1968. "A study of ghetto rioters." *Scientific American* 219:15-20.

Carden, Maren Lockwood. 1974. *The New Feminist Movement.* New York: Russell Sage Foundation.

Carey, Gordon. 1978 Interview. Soul City, North Carolina, November 19 (Follow-up telephone interview November 1, 1979).

———. 1959. Report to CORE National Council. February 21-22.

Carlson, Oliver and Ernest S. Bates. *Hearst, Lord of San Simeon.* New York: Viking Press, 1936.

Carmen, Arlene and Howard Moody. 1973. *Abortion Counseling and Social Change.* Valley Forge, PA: Judson Press.

Carmichael, Stokely and Charles V. Hamilton. 1967. *Black Power: The Politics of Liberation in America.* New York: Vintage Books.

Carroll, Glenn R., ed. 1988. *Ecological Models of Organizations.* Cambridge, MA: Ballinger.

Carruthers, Bruce G. 1991. "What Causes State Autonomy? Organization Theory and the Political Sociology of the State." Revision of a paper presented at the annual meeting of the American Sociological Association, San Francisco, 1989.

Carson, Clayborne. 1981. *In Struggle: SNCC and the Black Awakening of the 1960s.* Cambridge: Harvard University Press.

Carter, Jimmy. 1982. *Keeping Faith: Memoirs of a President.* New York: Bantam Books.

———. 1978. *Public Papers of the Presidents: Jimmy Carter, 1977.* Washington. DC: U.S. Government Printing Office.

Cassell, Joan. 1977. *A Group Called Women.* New York: David McKay.

Cates, Jerry R. 1983. *Insuring Inequality.* Ann Arbor: University of Michigan Press.

Cave, George. n.d. "Born to Be Wild . . . but Enslaved at NYU." Brochure, Trans-Species Unlimited.

Centro de Comunicacíon y Participación de la Mujer. 1989. *Mujer, Participación Social y Política.* La Paz, Bolivia: Fundación San Gabriel.

Chafe, William H. 1972. *The American Woman: Her Changing Social, Economic, and Political Roles, 1920-1970.* New York: Oxford University Press.

Chafee, Zechariah, Jr. 1941. *Free Speech in the United States.* Cambridge: Harvard University Press.

Chafetz, Janet Saltzman and Anthony Dworkin. 1987. "Action and Reaction: An Integrated, Comparative Perspective on Feminist and Antifeminist Movements." Paper presented at the annual meeting of the American Sociological Association, Aug., Chicago, IL.

———. 1986. *Female Revolt: Women's Movements in World and Historical Perspective.* Totowa, NJ: Rowan and Allanheld.

Chambers, Clarke. 1952. *California Farm Organizations.* Berkeley, Cal.: University of California Press.

Chaney, Elsa. 1979. *Supermadre: Women in Politics in Latin America.* Austin: University of Texas Press.

Change International Reports. 1981. *Military Ideology and the Dissolution of Democracy: Women in Chile.* London: Change.

Chase, Stuart. 1962. *American Credos.* New York: Harper and Row.

Chavez, Cesar. 1966. "The organizer's tale." Pp. 138-47 in Staughton Lynd (ed.). *American Labor Radicalism.* New York: Wiley.

Chorley, Katharine C. [1943] 1973. *Armies and the Art of Revolution.* Boston, MA: Beacon Press.

Chuchryk, Patricia. 1991. "Feminist anti-authoritarian politics: The role of women's organizations in the Chilean transition to democracy." In Jane Jaquette (ed.), *The Women's Movement in Latin America: Feminism and the Transition to Democracy:* 149-184. Boulder, CO: Westview Press.

———. 1989 "Subversive mothers: The women's opposition to the military regime in Chile." In Sue Ellen Charlton, Jana Everett, and Kathleen Staudt (eds.), *Women, the State, and Development:* 130-151. Albany: SUNY Press.

———. 1984. *Politics, protest, and personal life.* Unpublished dissertation, York University, Canada.

Cincinnati Directory for the Years 1836/37. 1836. Cincinnati: E. Deming.

Cist, Charles. 1841. *Cincinnati in 1841: Early Annals and Future Prospects.* Cincinnati: E. Morgan & Co. Power Press.

Clark, B.D. 1972. *Iran: Changing Population Patterns In Populations of the Middle East and North Africa: A Geographical Approach,* edited by J.I. Clark and W.B. Fisher, 68-96. London: University of London Press.

Cleghorn, Reese. 1970 "Crowned with crises." Pp. 113-27 in C. Eric Lincoln (ed.), *Martin Luther King, Jr.: A Profile.* New York: Hill & Wang.

——. 1963. "Epilogue in Albany: were the mass marches worthwhile?" *The New Republic* (July 20):15-18.

Clifford. Dale L. 1975. *Aux Armes Citoyens! The National Guard in the Paris Commune of 1871.* Ph.D dissertation, Department of History, University of Tennessee, Knoxville.

Clift, Virgil A. 1966. "Educating the American Negro. In John P. Davis, ed., *The American Negro Reference Book:* 360-95. Englewood Cliffs, N.J.: Prentice-Hall.

Cloud, Kate. 1981. "Report on the Women's Pentagon Action." *Peacework.* December.

Cloward, Richard A. and Frances Fox Piven. 1984. "Disruption and organization: a rejoinder." *Theory and Society* 13:587-99.

Coast, L. 1974. *Greedy Institutions.* New York: Free Press.

Cohen, Jean L., ed. 1985a. "Social Movements." *Social Research* 52 (Winter).

——. 1985b. "Strategy or Identity: New Theoretical Paradigms and Contemporary Social Movements." *Social Research* 52:663-716.

Cohen, Wilbur J., and Robert J. Myers. 1950. "Social Security Act Amendments of 1950: A Summary and Legislative History." *Social Security Bulletin* 13 (October): 3-14.

Cohn, Jules. 1970. "Is business meeting the challenge of urban affairs?" *Harvard Business Review* 48(2):68-82.

Cohn, Norman. 1961. *The Pursuit of the Millennium.* New York: Harper and Row.

Coleman, James S. 1986. "Social Theory, Social Research, and a Theory of Action." *American Journal of Sociology* 91:1309-35.

——. 1957. *Community Conflict.* New York: Free Press.

Coleman, James S., Eliher Katz, and Herbert Menzel. 1957. "The diffusion of an innovation among physicians." *Sociometry* 20:253-70.

Collins, Patricia Hill. 1990. *Black Feminist Thought: Knowledge, Consciousness, and the Politics of Empowerment.* Boston: Unwin Hyman.

Collins, Randall. 1986. "Is 1980s Sociology in the Doldrums?" *American Journal of Sociology* 91:1336-55.

Colson, Charles W. 1976. *Born Again.* New York: Bantam Books.

Colvin, Mark. 1982. "The 1980 New Mexico riot." *Social Problems* 29:449-63.

Commons, John R. et al. *History of Labor in the United States,* Vol. II. New York: A. M. Kelley, 1966.

Comstock, Gary David. 1991. *Violence Against Lesbians and Gay Men.* New York: Columbia University Press.

Condit, Celeste Michelle. 1990. *Decoding Abortion Rhetoric: Communicating Social Change.* Chicago: University of Illinois Press.

Conetta, Carl, ed. 1988. *Peace Resource Book.* Cambridge, Mass.: Ballinger.

Congressional Quarterly. 1985. *Guide to U.S. Elections,* 2d ed. Washington: Congressional Quarterly.

Congressional Record. 1949. Proceedings of the 81st Congress. Vol. 95, pts. 9, 10. Washington, D.C.: Government Printing Office.

Connell, R.W. 1992. "A very straight gay: Masculinity, homosexual experience, and gender." *American Sociological Review* 57:735-51.

Conover, Pamela Johnston and Virginia Cray. 1983. *Feminism and the New Right. The Conflict Over the American Family.* New York: Praeger.

Conway, Flo and Jim Siegelman. 1978. *Snapping: America's Epidemic of Sudden Personality Change.* New York: Lippincott.

Copeland, Miles. 1989. *The Game Player: Confessions of the CIA's Original Political Operative.* London, England: Aurum Press.

Coser, Lewis A. 1974. *Greedy Institutions.* New York: Free Press.

——. 1969. "The Visibility of Evil." *Journal of Social Issues* 25:101-109.

——. 1967a. *Continuities in the Study of Social Conflict.* New York: Free Press.

——. 1967b. "Greedy organizations." *Archives Européennes De Sociologie* 8:196-215.

——. 1956. *The Functions of Social Conflict.* New York: Free Press.

Costain, Anne N. 1992. *Inviting Women's Rebellion: A Political Process Interpretation of the Women's Movement.* Baltimore: Johns Hopkins University Press.

——. 1988. "Women's Claims as a Special Interest." In *The Politics of the Gender Gap,* edited by Carol M. Mueller, pp. 150-72. Beverly Hills: Sage.

Costain, Anne N., and Douglas Costain. 1987. Unpublished calculations on feminist memberships made available to the author. Department of Political Science, University of Colorado, Boulder.

Cott, Nancy F. 1987. *The Grounding of Modem Feminism.* New Haven: Yale University Press.

Cottam, Richard W. 1980. "The Imperial Regime of Iran: Why It Collapsed." Pp. 9-24 in *L 'Iran d'Hier et de Demain* (Iran of Yesterday and Tomorrow). Québec, Canada: Collection Choix.

Craig, Richard C. 1971. The *Bracero* Program. Austin, Tx.: University of Texas Press.

Craig, Steven. 1979. "Efficacy, Trust and Political Behavior." *American Politics Quarterly* 7(2):225-39.

Cramer, J. 1989. *De Groene Golf. Geschiedenis en Toekomst van de Milieubeweging.* Utrecht: Jan van Arkel.

Craven, Paul and Barry Wellman. 1974a. "The network city." Pp. 57-88 in M. Effrat (ed.), *The Community: Approaches and Applications.* New York: Free Press.

——. 1974b. "Social movements: an analytical exploration of organizational forms." *Social Problems* 21:356-70.

——. 1973. "Stable resources of protest movements: the multi-organizational field." *Social Forces* 52:53-61.

Cressey, D. R. 1972. *Other People's Money.* Belmont, CA: Wadsworth.

Crittenden, Kathleen S. 1983. "Sociological Aspects of Attribution." *Annual Review of Sociology* 9:425-46.

Cronin, James E. 1989. "Strikes and Power in Britain." Pp. 79-100 in *Strikes, Wars, and Revolutions in an International Perspective: Strike Waves in the Late Nineteenth and Early Twentieth Centuries,* edited by L. H. Haimson and C. Tilly. Cambridge, England: Cambridge University Press.

Cross, Ira B. *A History of the Labor Movement in California.* Berkeley, California: University of California Press, 1935.

Crummett, Maria de los Angeles. 1977. "El Poder Femenino: the mobilization of women against socialism in Chile." *Latin American Perspectives* 4:103113.

Curtis, Louis A. Zurcher, Jr. 1973. "Stable Resources of Protest Movement: The Multi-organizational Field." *Social Forces* 52:53-60.

Curtis, Russell L., Jr. and Louis A. Zurcher, Jr. 1974. "Social Movements: An Analytical Exploration of Organizational Forms." *Social Problems* 21: 356-370.

D'Anieri, Paul, Claire Ernst, and Elizabeth Kier. 1990. "New Social Movements in Historical Perspective." *Comparative Politics* 22:445-58.

D'Emilio, John. 1992. *Making Trouble: Essays on Gay History, Politics, and the Universities*. New York: Routledge.

——. 1983. *Sexual Politics, Sexual Communities*. Chicago: University of Chicago Press.

Dabrowski, Irene. 1979. "Working-class women, paid work and volunteer work." Ph.D. dissertation, Department of Sociology, Washington University.

Dahl, Robert. 1967. *Pluralist Democracy in the United States*. Chicago: Rand McNally.

Dalfiume, Richard M. 1970. "Stirrings of Revolt." In Allen Weinstein and Frank Otto Gatell, eds., *The Segregation Era, 1863-1954*: 235-47. New York: Oxford University Press.

Dalton, Russell J. and Manfred Kuechler, eds. 1990. *Challenging the Political Order: New Social and Political Movements in Western Democracies*. Cambridge, England: Polity Press.

Daner, F. J. 1976. *The American Children of Krishna: A Study of the Hare Krishna Movement*. New York: Holt, Rinehart and Winston.

Danigelis, Nicholas L. 1978. "Black political participation in the United States: some recent evidence." *American Sociological Review* 43:756-71.

Danzger, M. Herbert. 1975. "Validating Conflict Data." *American Sociological Review* 40: (no. 5): 570-844.

Darley, John M. and C. Daniel Batson. 1973. "From Jerusalem to Jericho: A study of situational and dispositional variables in helping behavior." *Journal of Personality and Social Psychology* 27:100-8.

Dator, James. 1969. *Soka Gakkai: Builders of the Third Civilization*. Seattle: University of Washington Press.

Davies, James C. (ed.) 1971. *When Men Revolt and Why*. New York: Free Press.

——. 1969. "The J-curve of rising and declining satisfactions as a cause of some great revolutions and a contained rebellion." Pp. 671-709 in Hugh Davis Graham and Ted Robert Gurr (eds.), *Violence in America: Historical and Comparative Perspectives*. New York: Signet Books.

——. 1962. "Toward a theory of revolution." *American Sociological Review* 27:5-19.

Deckard, Barbara Sinclair. 1975. *The Women's Movement*. New York: Harper and Row.

Deere, Carmen Diana. 1986. "Rural women and agrarian reform in Peru, Chile, and Cuba." In June Nash and Helen I. Safa (eds.), *Women and Change in Latin America*: 189-207. South Hadley, MA: Bergin and Garvey.

Degler, Carl. 1967. "Revolution without Ideology: The Changing Place of Women in America." *The Woman in America,* edited by Robert Jay Lifton, pp. 193-210. Boston: Beacon Press.

Delgado, Gary. 1986. *Organizing the Movement: The Roots and Growth of ACORN*. Philadelphia: Temple University Press.

Della Porta, Donatella. 1991. *Il terrorismo di sinistra in Italia*. Bologna: Il Mulino.

Della Porta, Donatella and Dieter Rucht. 1991. "Left-Libertarian Movements in Context: A Comparison of Italy and West Germany, 1965-1990" (Discussion paper No. FS III 91-102). Science Center Berlin, Berlin, Germany.

Della Porta, Donatella and Sidney Tarrow. 1986. "Unwanted Children: Political Violence and the Cycle of Protest in Italy: 1966-1973." *European Journal of Political Research* 14:607-32.

DeNardo, James. 1985. *Power in Numbers: The Political Strategy of Protest and Rebellion*. Princeton, NJ: Princeton University Press.

Derthick, Martha. 1979. *Policymaking for Social Security*. Washington, D.C.: Brookings.

Donati, Paolo R. 1992. "Political discourse analysis." In Mario Diani and Ron Eyerman (eds.), *Studying Collective Action*: 136-167. London: Sage.

Doreian, Patrick. 1981. "Estimating Linear Models with Spatially Distributed Data." Pp. 359-88 in *Sociological Methodology,* edited by Samuel Leinhardt. San Francisco: Jossey-Bass.

——. 1980. "Linear Models with Spatially Distributed Data." *Sociological Methods and Research* 9:29-60.

Downes, Bryan T. 1970. "A critical reexamination of social and political characteristics of riot cities." *Social Science Quarterly* 51:349-60.

Downton, J. 1979. *Sacred Journeys: The Conversion of Young People to Divine Light Mission*. New York: Columbia University Press.

DuBois, Ellen. 1978. *Feminism and Suffrage*. Ithaca: Cornell.

Dubois, Pierre. 1978. "New forms of industrial conflict, 1960-74," in Colin Crouch and Alessandro Pizzorno (eds.) *The Resurgence of Class Conflict in Europe since 1968,* Vol. 2: 1-34. London: Macmillan.

Duff, Robert W. and William T. Liu. 1972 ."The strength in weak ties." *Public Opinion Quarterly* 36:361-66.

Dumond, Dwight. 1961. *Antislavery: The Crusade for Freedom in America*. New York: Norton.

Dunne, John Gregory. 1967. *Delano*. New York: Farrar, Straus and Giroux.

Durkheim, Émile. [1893] 1933. *On the Division of Labor in Society*. Tr. George Simpson. New York: Macmillan.

——. [1895]. *The Rules of Sociological Method*. Eighth 1966 edition. Translated by Sarah A. Solovay and John H. Mueller. New York: Free Press

Duyvendak, Jan Willem. 1992. *The Power of Politics: New Social Movements in an Old Polity. France 1965-1989*. Ph.D. Dissertation, Department of Political Science, University of Amsterdam, Amsterdam, the Netherlands.

——. 1990a. The development of the French gay movement, 1975-89. Unpublished paper, Universiteit van Amsterdam.

——. 1990b. Profiles and trajectories of five social movements. Unpubl. paper. University of Amsterdam: PdIS.

Duyvendak, J.W. and R. Koopmans. 1989. "Structures politiques, processus interactifs et le développement des mouvements écologiques." Paper presented at the symposion on Political ecologism: its constants and differences in Europe, ECPR-joint workshops, Paris, 10-15 April, 1989.

Duyvendak, Jan Willem, Hein-Anton van der Heijden, Ruud Koopmans, and Luuk Wijmans, eds. 1992. *Tussen verbeelding en macht: 25 jaar nieuwe sociale bewegingen in Nederland* (Between Imagination and Power: 25 Years of New Social Movements in the Netherlands). Amsterdam, the Netherlands: SUA.

Echols, Alice. 1989. *Daring to Be Bad: Radical Feminism in America 1967-1975.* Minneapolis: University of Minnesota.

Edelman, Murray. 1988. *Constructing the Political Spectacle.* Chicago: University of Chicago Press.

———. 1971. *Politics as Symbolic Action: Mass Arousal and Quiescence.* New York: Academic Press.

Edsall, Thomas Byrne. 1984. *The New Politics of Inequality.* New York: Norton.

Edwards, Lyford P. 1965. *The Natural History of Revolution.* New York: Russell and Russell.

Edwards, John N. 1977. "Age and social involvement." *Journal of Voluntary Action Research* 6:127-32.

Edwards, Stewart. 1971. *The Paris Commune 1871.* London: Eyre and Spottiswoode.

Ehlers, Tracy Bachrach. 1991. "Debunking marianismo: Economic vulnerability and survival strategies among Guatemalan wives." *Ethnology* 15:1-16.

Ehmke, Wolfgang, ed. 1987. *Zwischenschritte: Die Anti-Atomkraft-Bewegung zwischen Gorleben und Wackersdorf* (Way Stations: The Anti Nuclear Power Movement Between Gorleben and Wackersdorf). Cologne, Germany: Kölner Volksblatt Verlag.

Eisenger, Peter K. 1973. "The conditions of protest behavior in American cities." *American Political Science Review* 67:11-68.

Elinson, Howard. 1966. "Radicalism and the Negro movement." Pp. 355-375 in Raymond J. Murphy and Howard Elinson (eds.), *Problems and Prospects of the Negro Movement.* Belmont, CA: Wadsworth.

Emerson, Robert M. and Sheldon L. Messinger. 1977. "The micro-politics of trouble." *Social Problems* 25:121-134.

Enloe, Cynthia. 1988. *Does Khaki Become You?: The Militarization of Women's Lives.* London and Winchester, Mass.: Pandora Press.

Ennis, James G. and Richard Schreuer. 1987. "Mobilizing Weak Support for Social Movements: The Role of Grievance, Efficacy and Cost." *Social Forces* 66:390-409.

Enroth, Ronald. 1977. *Youth, Brainwashing, and the Extremist Cults.* Grand Rapids, Mich.: Zondervan.

Epple, R. 1988. *Friedensbewegung und direkte Demokratie in der Schweiz.* Frankfurt: Haag und Herchen.

Epstein, Abraham. (1938) 1968. *Insecurity: A Challenge to America.* New York: Agathon.

Epstein, Barbara. 1991. *Political Protest and Cultural Revolution.* Berkeley: University of California Press.

———. 1990. "Rethinking social movement theory." *Socialist Review* 20:35-66.

———. 1988. "The politics of prefigurative community: The non-violent direct action movement." In *Reshaping the U.S. Left: Popular Struggles In the 1980s,* eds. Mike Davis and Michael Sprinker, 63-92. London: Verso.

Epstein, Steven. 1987. "Gay politics, ethnic identity: The limits of social constructionism." *Socialist Review* 17:9-54.

Erbring, Lutz and Alice A. Young. 1979. "Individuals and Social Structure: Contextual Effects as Endogenous Feedback." *Sociological Methods and Research* 7:396-430.

Erskine, Hazel. 1971. "The Polls: Women's Role." *Public Opinion Quarterly* 35:282-87.

Escobar, Arturo and Sonia E. Alvarez, eds. 1992. *The Making of Social Movements in Latin America: Identity, Strategy, and Democracy.* Boulder, CO: Westview Press.

Etzioni, Amitai. 1975. *A Comparative Analysis of Complex Organizations.* New York: Free Press.

———. 1961. *A Comparative Analysis of Complex Organizations.* New York: Free Press.

Evans, Glenn V. 1977. Interview with Glenn V. Evans. Pp. 187-96 in Howell Raines (ed.), *My Soul is Rested.* New York: Bantam.

Evans, Sara. 1980. *Personal Politics.* New York: Vintage Books.

———. 1979. *Personal Politics: The Roots of Women's Liberation in the Civil Rights Movement and the New Left.* New York: Knopf.

Ewen, Stuart. 1976. *Captains of Consciousness: Advertising and the Social Roots of the Consumer Culture.* New York: McGraw-Hill.

Fanon, Franz. 1967. *Black Skin, White Masks.* New York: Grove Press.

Fantasia, Rick. 1988. *Cultures of Solidarity: Consciousness, Action, and Contemporary American Workers.* Berkeley: University of California Press.

Farazmand, Ali. 1989. *The State, Bureaucracy, and Revolution in Modern Iran: Agrarian Reforms and Regime Politics.* New York: Praeger.

Farmer, James. 1965. *Freedom—When?* New York: Random House.

Fatemi, Khosrow. 1982. "Leadership by Distrust: The Shah's Modus Operandi." *Middle East Journal* 36:48-61.

Faure, Christine. 1991. *Democracy Without Women: Feminism and the Rise of Liberal Individualism in France.* Bloomington: Indiana University Press.

Feagin, Joe R. and Harlan Hahn. 1973. *Ghetto Revolts: The Politics of Violence in American Cities.* New York: MacMillan.

Feijoó, Maria del Carmen. 1991. "The challenge of constructing civilian peace: Women and democracy in Argentina." In Jane Jaquette (ed.), *The Women's Movement in Latin America: Feminism and the Transition to Democracy:* 72-94. Boulder, CO: Westview Press.

Feldberg, Michael. 1980. *The Turbulent Era: Riot and Disorder in Jacksonian America.* New York: Oxford University Press.

Felsenthal, Carol. 1982. "What went wrong in the ERA fight." Kansas City Star. July 4: sec. A, pp. 29, 32.

Fendrich, James M. 1977. "Keeping the Faith or Pursuing the Good Life: A Study of Participation in the Civil Rights Movement." *American Sociological Review* 42:144-57.

Fendrich, James, and Kenneth L. Lovoy. 1988. "Back to the future: Adult political behavior of former student activists." *American Sociological Review* 53:780-784.

Fernandez, Roberto, and Doug McAdam. 1989. "Multiorganizational Fields and Recruitment to Social Movements." Pp. 315-43 in *Organizing for Change: Social Movement Organizations in Europe and the United States,* edited by Bert Klandermans. Greenwich, Conn.: JAI.

——. 1988. "Social Networks and Social Movements: Multiorganizational Fields and Recruitment to Mississippi Freedom Summer." *Sociological Forum* 3:357-82.

Ferree, Myra Marx. 1992. "The Political Context of Rationality: Rational Choice Theory and Resource Mobilization." Pp. 29-52 in *Frontiers in Social Movement Theory,* edited by A. Morris and C. Mueller. New Haven, CT: Yale University Press.

Ferree, Myra Marx, and Beth B. Hess. 1985. *Controversy and Coalition: The New Feminist Movement.* Boston: Twayne.

Ferree, Myra Marx and Frederick D. Miller. 1985. "Mobilization and Meaning: Toward an Integration of Social Psychological and Resource Perspectives on Social Movements." *Sociological Inquiry* 55: 36-61.

Fichter, Tilman and Siegward Lönnendonker. 1977. *Kleine Geschichte des SDS: Der Sozialistische Deutsche Studentenbund von 1946 bis zur Selbstauflösung* (A Small History of the SDS: The Socialist German Student League from 1946 to its Dissolution). Berlin, Germany: Rotbuch Verlag.

Finked, Steven. 1985. "Reciprocal Effects of Participation and Political Efficacy: A Panel Analysis." *American Journal of Political Science* 29 (4): 891-913.

Fireman, Bruce and William Gamson. 1979. "Utilitarian logic in the resource mobilization perspective." Pp. 8-44 in Mayer Zald and John D. McCarthy (eds.), *The Dynamics of Social Movements.* Cambridge, MA: Winthrop.

Fisher, Jo. 1989. *Mothers of the Disappeared.* Boston, MA: South End Press.

Fisher, Lloyd. 1953. *The Harvest Labor Market in California.* Cambridge, Ma.: Harvard University Press.

Fitzpatrick, Sheila. 1982. *The Russian Revolution.* New York: Oxford University Press.

Fitzsimmons-LeCavalier, Patricia and Guy LeCavalier, 1989. "Fight, Flight or Accommodate? Québec's Nonfrancophones' Response to Language Conflict." Paper presented at the annual meeting of the American Sociological Association, 9- 13 Aug., San Francisco.

Flacks, Richard. 1988. *Making History: The Radical Tradition in American Life.* New York: Columbia University Press.

——. 1971. *Youth and Social Change.* Chicago: Markham.

Flexner, Eleanor. 1959. *Century of Struggle.* Cambridge: Harvard University Press.

Flynn, Cynthia. 1979. Three Mile Island Telephone Survey: Preliminary Report on Procedures and Findings. Report submitted to the U.S. Nuclear Regulatory Commission. Seattle: Social Impact Research.

Flynn, John P. and Gene E. Webb. 1975. "Women's incentives for community participation in policy issues." *Journal of Voluntary Action Research* 4:137-46.

Fogelson, Robert M. 1971. *Violence as Protest.* Garden City, NY: Doubleday.

Folk, Patrick A. 1978. *The Queen City of Mobs: Riots and Community Reactions in Cincinnati, 1788-1848.* Ph.D. dissertation, University of Toledo.

Foran, John. 1993a. *Fragile Resistance: Social Transformation in Iran from 1500 to the Revolution.* Boulder, CO: Westview Press.

Foran, John. 1993b. "Theories of Revolution Revisited: Toward a Fourth Generation?" *Sociological Theory* 11: 1-20.

Forman, James. 1973. *The Making of Black Revolutionaries.* New York: Macmillan.

Forsberg, Randall. 1982. "A bilateral nuclear weapons freeze." *Scientific American* 247:52-62.

Forward, John R. and Jay R. Williams. 1970. "Internal-external Control and Black Militancy." *Journal of Social Issues* 25:75-92.

Foucault, Michel. 1980. *The History of Sexuality. Vol. 1: An Introduction.* New York: Vintage.

——. 1965. *Madness and Civilization: A History of Insanity in the Age of Reason.* New York: Random House.

Foundation for Iranian Studies. 1991. *The Oral History Collection of the Foundation for Iranian Studies.* Index and Transcripts. Washington, DC: Foundation for Iranian Studies.

Frank, Arthur W. 1993. "The rhetoric of self-change: Illness experience as narrative." *The Sociological Quarterly* 34:39-52.

Frankfurter, Felix and Nathan Greene. 1930. *The Labor Injunction.* New York: Macmillan.

Franklin, Ben A. 1963. "Danville method studied in South." The New York Times (August 11):71.

Franklin, John Hope. 1969. *From Slavery to Freedom: A History of Black Americans.* Third edition. New York: Vintage.

Franzosi, Roberto. 1981. "Strikes in Italy in the postwar period." Unpublished Ph.D. dissertation, Johns Hopkins University.

Frazier, E. Franklin. 1963. *The Negro Church in America.* New York: Schocken Books.

Freedman, Estelle. 1979. "Separatism as Strategy: Female Institution Building and American Feminism, 1870-1930." *Feminist Studies, 5:* 512-29.

Freeman, Jo. 1987. "Whom You Know versus Whom You Represent: Feminist Influence in the Democratic and Republican Parties." Pp. 215-44 in *The Women's Movements Of the United States and Western Europe,* edited by M. Katzenstein and C. Mueller. Philadelphia: Temple University Press.

——. 1983a. *Social Movements of the Sixties and Seventies,* New York: Longman.

——. 1983b. "Introduction." In *Social Movements of the Sixties and Seventies,* ed. Jo Freeman, 1-5. New York: Longman.

——. 1979a. "The Women's Liberation Movement: Its Origins, Organizations, Activities, and Ideas." In *Women: A Feminist Perspective,* edited by Jo Freeman, 2d ed., pp. 557-74. Palo Alto, Calif.: Mayfield.

——. 1979b. "Resource Mobilization and Strategy: A Model for Analyzing Social Movement Organization Actions." Pp. 167-89 in *The Dynamics of Social Movements: Resource Mobilization, Social Control, and Tactics,* edited by M. N. Zald and J. D. McCarthy. Cambridge, MA: Winthrop Publishers.

——. 1975. *The Politics of Women's Liberation.* New York: David McKay.

——. 1973a. "The origins of the women's liberation movement." *American Journal of Sociology* 78:792-811.

——. 1973b. "The Tyranny of Structurelessness." *Ms.* 2:76-78, 86-89.

Frei Montalva, Eduardo. 1966. "Second State of the Nation Address." May 21. Santiago: Ministerio de Relaciones Exteriores.

Freudenberg, William R. 1993. "Risk and recreancy: Weber, the division of labor, and the rationality of risk perceptions." *Social Forces* 71:909-932.

Frey, J. H. 1983. *Survey Research by Telephone.* London. England: Sage.

Friedan, Betty. 1976. *It Changed My Life.* New York: Dell.

——. 1963. *The Feminine Mystique.* New York: Dell.

Friedman, Leon. 1965. *Southern Justice.* New York: Pantheon.

Friedman, Debra; and Doug McAdam. 1992. "Collective identity and activism: Networks, choices and the life of a social movement." In *Frontiers In Social Movement Theory,* eds. Aldon D. Morris and Carol McClurg Mueller, 156-173. New Haven, Conn.: Yale University Press.

Frisbee, Parker. 1975. "Illegal migration from Mexico to the United States: a longitudinal analysis." *International Migration Review* 9:3-14.

Fromm, Erich. 1950. *Psychoanalysis and Religion.* New Haven: Yale University Press.

Fuller, Varden. 1967. "A new era for farm labor?" *Industrial Relations* 6:285-302.

Fuss, Diana. 1991. *Inside/Out: Lesbian Theories, Gay Theories.* New York: Routledge.

Gagnon, John, Suzanne Keller, Ronald Lawson, Patricia Miller, William Simon, and Joan Huber. 1982. "Report of the American Sociological Association's Task Group on Homosexuality." *The American Sociologist* 17:164-180.

Galarza, Ernesto. 1970. *Spiders in the House and Workers in the Field.* London: University of Notre Dame Press.

——. 1964. Merchants of Labor: The Mexican *Bracero* Story. San Jose, Ca.: Rosicrucian Press.

Gallie, D. 1983. *Social Inequality and Class Radicalism in France and Britain.* Cambridge University Press.

Gallup, George H. 1978. *The Gallup Poll: Public Opinion 1972-1977.* Wilmington, Del.: Scholarly Resources.

Galphin, Bruce. 1963 "When a Negro is on trial in the South." The New York Times Magazine (December 15):17ff.

Gamble, Douglas. 1977. "Garrison Abolitionists is the West: Some Suggestions for Further Study." *Civil War History* 23:52-68.

Gamson, William A. 1992a. "The Social Psychology of Collective Action." Pp. 53-76 in *Frontiers of Social Movement Theory,* edited by Aldon D. Morris and Carol McClurg Mueller. New Haven, Conn.: Yale University Press.

——. 1992b. *Talking Politics.* New York: Cambridge University Press.

——. [1975] 1990. *The Strategy of Social Protest.* Homewood, Illinois: Dorsey Press.

——. 1988. "Political Discourse and Collective Action." Pp. 219-44 in *International Social Movement Research,* vol. 1. Edited by Bert Klandermans, Hanspeter Kriesi, and Sidney Tarrow. Greenwich, Conn.: JAI Press.

——. 1980 "Understanding the careers of challenging groups: a commentary on Goldstone." *American Journal of Sociology* 85:1043-60.

——. 1968a. *Power and Discontent.* Homewood, IL: Dorsey.

——. 1968b. "Stable unrepresentation in American society." *American Behavioral Scientist* 12:15-21.

Gamson, William A., Bruce Fireman, and Steven Rytina. 1982. *Encounters With Unjust Authority.* Homewood, Ill.: Dorsey Press.

Gamson, William A., and David S. Meyer. 1992. "Framing political opportunity." Paper delivered at the annual meetings of the American Sociological Association. Pittsburgh.

Gamson, William A., and Andre Modigliani. 1989. "Media Discourse and Public Opinion on Nuclear Power: A Constructionist Approach." *American Journal of Sociology* 95:1-37.

Gamson, William A. and Emilie Schmeidler. 1984. "Organizing the poor: an argument with Francis Fox Piven and Richard A. Cloward. Poor People's Movements: Why They Succeed, How They Fail." *Theory and Society* 13:567-85.

Gamson, Josh. 1994. "Must identity movements self destruct?: A queer dilemma." Paper presented at the Annual Meeting of the American Sociological Association, August, Los Angeles, Calif.

——. 1989. "Silence, death, and the invisible enemy: AIDS activism and social movement 'newness.' " *Social Problems* 36:351-367.

Garfinkel, Herbert. 1969. *When Negroes March.* New York: Atheneum.

Garrow, David J. 1978. *Protest at Selma: Martin Luther King, Jr., and the Voting Rights Act of 1965.* New Haven: Yale University Press.

Gaviola Artigas, Edda, Ximena Jiles Moreno, Lorella Lopresti Martinez, and Claudia Rojas Mira. 1986. Queremos Votar en Las Proximas Elecciones. Santiago: Centro de Análisis y Difusión de la Condición de la Mujer.

Gelb, Joyce, and Marian Lief Palley. [1982] 1987. *Women and Public Policies* (2nd ed.) Princeton, N.J.: Princeton University Press.

Gellner, E. 1983. *Nations and Nationalism.* Oxford: Basil Blackwell.

Gerhards, Jürgen, and Dieter Rucht. 1992. "Mesomobilization: Organizing and Framing in Two Protest Campaigns in West Germany." *American Journal of Sociology* 98:555-96.

Gerlach, Luther P., and Virginia H. Hine. 1970. *People, Power, and Change: Movements of Social Transformation.* Indianapolis: Bobbs-Merrill.

Gharabaghi, Abbas. 1985. *Vérités sur la Crise Iranienne* (Truths About the Iranian Crisis). Paris, France: La Pensée Universelle.

Giddens, Anthony. 1991. *Modernity and Self-Identity: Self and Society in the Late Modern Age.* Stanford, Calif.: Stanford University Press.

Giddings, Paula. 1984. *When and Where I Enter: The Impact of Black Women on Race and Sex in America.* New York: Bantam.

Gilje, Paul A. 1987. *The Road to Mobocracy: Popular Disorder in New York City, 1763-1834.* Chapel Hill: University of North Carolina Press.

Gitlin, Todd. 1987. *The Sixties: Years of Hope, Days of Rage.* New York: Bantam.

——. 1980. *The Whole World Is Watching: Mass Media in the Making and the Unmaking of the New Left.* Berkeley: University of California Press.

Giugni, Marco G. 1992a. *Entre stratégie et opportunité: Les nouveaux mouvements sociaux en Suisse* (Between Strategy and Opportunity: New Social Movements in

Switzerland). Ph.D. Dissertation, Department of Political Science, University of Geneva, Geneva, Switzerland.

——. 1992b. "The role of diffusion processes in new social movements: Some conceptual clarifications.' New School for Social Research, Center for Studies of Social Change Working Paper (No. 143), July.

Giugni, M.G. and H. Kriesi. 1990. "Nouveaux mouvements sociaux dans les années 80: évolution et perspectives." *Annuaire Suisse de Science Politique 30.*

Glaser, Barney G. and Anselm L. Strauss. 1967. *The Discovery of Grounded Theory.* Chicago: Aldine.

Glazer, Walter S. 1968. *Cincinnati in 1840: A Community Profile.* Ph.D. dissertation, University of Michigan.

Glock, Charles Y. 1964. "The role of deprivation in the origin and evolution of religious groups." Pp. 24-36 in R. Lee and M. Marty (eds.), *Religion and Social Conflict.* New York: Oxford University Press.

Goffman, Erving. 1974. *Frame Analysis,* Cambridge: Harvard University Press.

——. 1963. *Behavior in Public Places.* New York: Free Press.

Golden, Miriam. 1988. *Labor Divided: Austerity and Working-Class Politics in Contemporary Italy.* Ithaca, NY: Cornell University Press.

——. 1986. "Interest representation, party systems, and the State." *Comparative Politics* April: 279-302.

Goldenberg, Edie. 1975. *Making the News.* Lexington, Ma.: Lexington Books.

Goldstone, Jack A. 1994. "Is Revolution Really Rational?" *Rationality and Society* 6:139-66.

——. 1991a. "Ideology, Cultural Frameworks, and the Process of Revolution." *Theory and Society* 20:405-53.

——. 1991b. *Revolution and Rebellion in the Early Modern World.* Berkeley, CA: University of California Press.

——. 1980. "The weakness of organization: A new look at Gamson's *The Strategy of Social Protest."* American Journal of Sociology 85(5):1017-1060.

Gonos, G. 1977. "'Situation' versus 'frame': The 'interactionist' and the 'structuralist' analyses of everyday life." *American Sociological Review*42: 854-67.

Goodwyn, Larry. 1965 "Anarchy in St. Augustine." *Harper's* (January):78-81.

Goswami, S. Dasa. 1980. *Planting the Seed.* Los Angeles: Bhaktivedanta Book Trust.

Gould, Roger V. 1993. "Collective Action and Network Structure." *American Sociological Review* 58:182-96.

——. 1991. "Multiple Networks and Mobilization in the Paris Commune, 1871." *American Sociological Review* 56:716-29.

——. 1990. *Social Structure and Insurgency in the Paris Commune, 1871.* Ph.D. dissertation. Harvard University, Department of Sociology.

Graham, Robert. 1980. *Iran: The Illusion of Power.* Rev. ed. New York: St. Martin's Press.

Gramsci, Antonio. 1971. *Selections From the Prison Notebooks.* Translated by Q. Hoare and G. N. Smith. New York: International Publishers.

Granberg, Donald and Sören Holmberg. 1988. *The Political System Matters: Social Psychology and Voting Behavior in Sweden and the United States.* Cambridge, England: Cambridge University Press.

Granovetter, Mark. 1982. "The strength of weak ties: a network theory revisited." Pp. 105-30 in Peter V. Marsden and Nan Lin (eds.), *Social Structure and Network Analysis.* Beverly Hills, CA: Sage.

——. 1978. "Threshold Models of Collective Behavior." *American Journal of Sociology* 83:1420-43.

——. 1973. "The Strength of Weak Ties." *American Journal of Sociology* 78:1360-80.

Green, Gerson. 1979. "Who's organizing the neighborhood? Community organizations: A report on their structure, finance, personnel, issues and strategies." Office of Community Anti-Crime Programs, Law Enforcement Assistance Administration. Superintendent of Documents stock no. 027-000-00783-0.

Green, J.D. 1986. "Counter-mobilization in the Iranian Revolution." In *Revolutions: Theoretical, Comparative, and Historical Studies,* edited by J.A. Goldstone, 127-138. San Diego: Harcourt Brace Jovanovich.

Greenberg, Louis. 1973. *Sisters of Liberty: Paris, Marseille, Toulouse and the Reaction to the Centralized State.* Cambridge: Harvard University Press.

Greenstone, J. David. 1969. *Labor in American Politics.* New York: Knopf.

Greenwood, Davydd J. 1977. "Continuity in Change: Spanish Basque Ethnicity as a Historical Process." Pp. 81-102 in *Ethnic Conflict in the Western World,* edited by M. J. Esman. Ithaca: Cornell University Press.

Griffin, Larry J., Christopher Botsko, Ana-Maria Wahl, and Larry W. Isaac. 1991. "Theoretical Generality, Case Particularity: Qualitative Comparative Analysis of Trade Union Growth and Decline." *International Journal of Comparative Sociology* 32:110-36.

Grimstead, David. 1972. "Rioting in Its Jacksonian Setting." *American Historical Review* 77:361-97.

Griswold, Wendy. 1987. "A Methodological Framework for the Sociology of Culture." *Sociological Methodology* 17:1-35.

Gruson, L. 1987a. "2 Hare Krishna aides accused of child molesting." *The New York Times* February 18.

——. 1987b. "Hare Krishna leader reported linked to slaying." *The New York Times* June 17.

——. 1986. "Web of inquiries in dissident's death reflects strife among Hare Krishnas." *The New York Times* August 19.

Gurin, G., J. Veroff and S. Feld. 1960. *Americans View Their Mental Health.* New York: Basic Books.

Gurin, Patricia, Gerald Gurin, Rosina Lao, and Muriel Beattie. 1969. "Internal-External Control in the Motivational Dynamics of Negro Youth." *Journal of Social Issues* 25:29-54.

Gurney, Joan M., and Kathleen J. Tierney. 1982. "Relative deprivation and social movements: A critical look at twenty years of theory and research." *The Sociological Quarterly* 23(1):33-47.

Gurr, Ted Robert. 1976. *Rogues, Rebels, and Reformers: A Political History of Urban Crime and Conflict.* Beverly Hills: Sage

——. 1970. *Why Men Rebel.* Princeton, NJ: Princeton University Press.

——. 1969. "A Comparative Study of Civil Strife." Pp. 572-632 in *The History of Violence in America,* edited by Hugh D. Graham and Ted R. Gurr. Praeger.

Gurr, Ted Robert, Peter N. Grabosky, and Richard C. Hula. 1977. *The Politics of Crime and Conflict: A Comparative History of Four Cities.* Beverly Hills: Sage.

Gusfield, Joseph R. 1981a. *The Culture of Public Problems: Drinking-Driving and the Symbolic Order.* Chicago: University of Chicago Press.

———. 1981b. "Social movements and social change: Perspectives of linearity and fluidity." Pp. 317-39 in L. Kriesberg (Ed.), *Research in Social Movements, Conflict and Change.* Greenwich: JAI Press.

———. 1970. *Protest, Reform, and Revolt.* New York: Wiley.

———. 1968. "The study of social movements" Pp. 445-52 in David Sills (ed.), *International Encyclopedia of the Social Sciences,* Volume 14. New York: Macmillan.

Guzman, Jessie P., ed. 1952. *1952 Negro Yearbook.* New York: William H. Wise.

Haas, David. 1982. "Survey Sampling and the Logic of Inference in Sociology." *The American Sociologist* 17:103-11.

Haber, Robert A. 1966 "From protest to radicalism: an appraisal of the student struggle 1960." Pp. 41-9 in Mitchell Cohen and Dennis Hale (eds.), *The New Student Left.* Boston: Dorsey.

Habermas, Jürgen. 1987. *Theory of Communicative Action,* Vol. 2. Boston: Beacon.

Hacker, Helen Mayer. (1951) 1979. "Women as a Minority Group." In *Women: A Feminist Perspective,* edited by Jo Freeman, 2d ed., pp. 505-20. Originally published in *Social Forces* 30 (1951): 60-69.

Haimson, Leopold H. and Eric Brian. 1989. "Introduction to Part II." Pp. 35-46 in *Strikes, Wars, and Revolutions in an International Perspective: Strike Waves in the Late Nineteenth and Early Twentieth Centuries,* edited by L.H. Haimson and C. Tilly. Cambridge, England: Cambridge University Press.

Haimson, Leopold H. and Charles Tilly, eds. 1989. *Strikes, Wars, and Revolutions in an International Perspective: Strike Waves in the Late Nineteenth and Early Twentieth Centuries.* Cambridge, England: Cambridge University Press.

Haines, Herbert H. 1984a. "Crisis and elite support of social movements: The case of civil rights." Paper presented at the annual meetings of the Midwest Sociological Society, Chicago, Illinois, April 18.

———. 1984b. "Black Radicalization and the Funding of Civil Rights: 1957-1970." *Social Problems* 32:31-43.

———. 1983. "Radical flank effects and black collective action, 1954-1970." Unpublished Ph.D. dissertation, University of Kansas, Lawrence.

Hall, John R. 1988. *"KANTER, SPSSX, A1,"* Reanalysis of *Rosabeth Moss Kanter Study of Commitment Mechanisms in Nineteenth Century Communal Groups* [MRDF]. Columbia, MO: John R. Hall [producer]. Columbia, MO: SPSS-X Public Disk, University of Missouri Computing Services [distributor].

———. 1987. *Gone From the Promised Land: Jonestown in American Cultural History.* New Brunswick, NJ: Transaction Books.

———. 1984a. "The Problem of Epistemology in the Social Action Perspective." Pp. 253-89 in *Sociological Theory 1984,* edited by Randall Collins. San Francisco: Jossey-Bass.

———. 1984b. "Temporality, Social Action, and the Problem of Quantification in Historical Analysis." *Historical Methods* 17:206-18.

———. 1978. *The Ways Out: Utopian Communal Groups in an Age of Babylon.* Boston: Routledge and Kegan Paul.

Hall, Stuart. 1982. "The Rediscovery of Ideology: Return of the Repressed in Media Studies." Pp. 56-90 in *Culture, Society, and the Media,* edited by M. Guervitch, T. Bennett, J. Curon, and J. Woolacott. New York: Methuen.

Hamilton, C. Horace. 1964. "The Negro leaves the South." *Demography* 1:273-95.

Hammett, Theodore M. 1976. "Two Mobs of Jacksonian Boston: Ideology and Interests." *Journal of American History* 12:845-68.

Hannan, Michael T. 1979. "The Dynamics of Ethnic Boundaries in Modern States." Pp. 253-75 in *National Development and the World System: Educational, Economic and Political Change, 1950-1970,* edited by John W. Meyer and Michael T. Hannan. Chicago: The University of Chicago Press.

Hannan, Michael T. and John Freeman. 1987. "The Ecology of Organizational Founding: American Labor Unions, 1836-1985." *American Journal of Sociology* 92:910-43.

Hansen, Susan B. 1983. *The Politics of Taxation: Revenue without Representation.* New York: Praeger.

Hardin, Russell. 1982. *Collective Action.* Baltimore, MD: Johns Hopkins University Press.

Harrell, Frank. 1990. "The logist procedure." Pp. 83-102 in *SAS Supplemental Library User's Guide,* 1980 Edition. Cary, NC: SAS Institute.

Harrison, Cynthia. 1988. *On Account of Sex.* Berkeley: University of California Press.

Harrison, Michael L. 1974. "Sources of recruitment to Catholic Pentecostalism." *Journal for the Scientific Study of Religion* 13:49-64.

Harvard Iranian Oral History Collection. 1987. *Alphabetical Folders and Reference Guide.* Cambridge, MA: Harvard University Center for Middle Eastern Studies.

Hathaway, Will, and David S. Meyer. 1994. "Competition and cooperation in social movement coalitions: Lobbying for peace in the 1980s." *Berkeley Journal of Sociology* 38.

Havel, Vaclav. 1985. "The power of the powerless." In *The Power of the Powerless,* eds. Havel et al., 23-86. Armonk, N.Y.: M.E. Sharpe.

Hawley, Ellis W. 1966. "The politics of the Mexican labor issue." *Agricultural History* 40, 3 (July): 157-76.

Hayden, Tom. 1988. *Reunion.* New York: Random House.

Hechter, Michael. 1987. *Principles of Group Solidarity.* Berkeley: University of California Press.

———. 1983. "A Theory of Group Solidarity." Pp. 16-57 in *The Micro-Foundations of Macro-Sociology,* edited by Michael Hechter. Philadelphia: Temple University Press.

———. 1978. "Group Formation and the Cultural Division of Labor." *American Journal of Sociology* 84:293-318.

———. 1975. *Internal Colonialism: The Celtic Fringe in British National Development, 1536-1966.* Berkeley: University of California Press.

Heckler, Margaret. 1977. Talk at Wellesley College. Wellesley, Mass.

Hegland, Mary Elaine. 1986. *Imam Khomaini's Village: Recruitment to Revolution.* Ph.D. dissertation. Department of Anthropology, State University of New York, Binghamton, NY.

———. 1983. "Two Images of Husain." Pp. 218-35 in *Religion and Politics in Iran,* edited by N. R. Keddie. New Haven, CT: Yale University Press.

Heirich, Max. 1977. "Changes of Heart: A Test of Some Widely Held Theories of Religious Conversion." *American Journal of Sociology* 83:653-80.

———. 1970. *The Spiral of Conflict: Berkeley 1964.* New York: Columbia University Press.

Henig, Gerald S. 1969. "The Jacksonian Attitude toward Abolitionism in the 1830s." *Tennessee Historical Quarterly* 28:42-56.

Henig, Jeffrey R. 1982a. *Neighborhood Mobilization, Redevelopment and Response.* New Brunswick, NJ: Rutgers University Press.

———. 1982b. "Neighborhood response to gentrification: conditions of mobilization." *Urban Affairs Quarterly* 17:343-58.

Hibbs, Douglas A., Jr. 1973. *Mass Political Violence: A Cross-National Causal Analysis.* New York: Wiley.

Higgs, Robert. 1977. *Competition and Coercion.* Cambridge: Cambridge University Press.

Hilgartner, Stephen and Charles L. Bosk. 1988. "The Rise and Fall of Social Problems: A Public Arenas Model." *American Journal of Sociology* 94:53-78.

Hillman, Robert G. 1981. "The psychopathology of being held hostage." *American Journal of Psychiatry* 138:1193-97.

Hilton, Bruce. 1969. *The Delta Migrant Ministry.* New York: Macmillan.

Himmelheber, M. and K. Philipp, eds. 1982. *Startbahn 18 West, Bilder einer Räumung* (Runway 18 West, Images of an Eviction). Darmstadt, Germany: Minotaurus Projekt.

Hirsch, Eric I,. 1990. "Sacrifice for the Cause: The Impact of Group Processes on Recruitment and Commitment in Protest Movements." *American Sociological Review* 55:243-55.

———. 1989. *Urban Revolt: Ethnic Politics in the Nineteenth Century Chicago Labor Movement.* Berkeley, Cal.: University of California Press.

———. 1986. "The Creation of Political Solidarity in Social Movement Organizations." *The Sociological Quarterly* 27:373-87.

Hirschman, Albert O. 1970. *Exit, Voice, and Loyalty: Responses to Decline in Firms, Organizations, and States.* Cambridge: Harvard University Press.

Hobsbawm, Eric. 1978. "The left and the crisis of organization." *New Society* 44 (13 April): 63-66.

Hoffer, Eric. 1951. *The True Believer: Thoughts on the Nature of Mass Movements.* New York: The New American Library.

Hole, Judith, and Ellen Levine. 1971. *Rebirth of Feminism.* New York: Quadrangle.

Hollander, Edwin P. 1958. "Conformity, Status, and Idiosyncracy Credit." *Psychological Review* 65:117-27.

Holley, J.W. and J.P Guilford. 1964. "A Note on the G Index of Agreement." *Educational and Psychological Measurement* 24:749-53.

Holmes, Dwight. 1969. *The Evolution of the Negro College.* New York: Arno Press and the New York Times.

Holmes, Sandra. 1979. "Middle-class women, paid work and volunteer work." Unpublished manuscript, Department of Sociology, Washington University.

Holstein, James A., and Gale Miller. 1990. "Rethinking Victimization: An Interactional Approach to Victimology." *Symbolic Interaction* 13:103-22.

Holt, Len. 1965a. *The Summer That Didn't End.* New York: Morrow.

———. 1965b. *An Act of Conscience.* Boston: Beacon.

Holtzman, Abraham. 1963. *The Townsend Movement: A Political Study.* New York: Bookman.

Home, Alistair. 1965. *The Fall of Paris: The Siege and the Commune 1870-1.* London: Macmillan.

Hooks, Bell. 1981. *Ain't I a Woman?* Boston: South End Press.

Hooper, Osman Castle. 1933. *The History of Ohio Journalism, 1793-1933.* Columbus, Ohio: Spahr & Glenn.

Horn, Alistair. 1965. *The Fall of Paris: The Siege and the Commune 1870–1.* London: Macmillan.

Horn, Nancy and Charles Tilly. 1986. "Catalogs of contention in Britain, 1758-1834." Center for the Study of Social Change Working Paper No. 32, New School for Social Research.

Horowitz, Donald. 1985. *Ethnic Groups in Conflict.* Berkeley: University of California Press.

Horst, Paul. 1955. "The prediction of personal adjustment and individual cases." Pp. 173-74 in Paul F. Lazarsfeld and Morris Rosenberg (eds.), *The Language of Social Research.* New York: Free Press.

Hough, J.C. 1968. *Black Power and White Protestants: A Christian Response to the New Negro Pluralism.* New York: Oxford.

Hougland, James G., Jr. and James R. Ward. 1980. "Control in Organizations and the Commitment of Members." *Social Forces* 59:85-105.

Howe, Daniel Walker. 1979. *The Political Culture of the American Whigs.* Chicago: University of Chicago Press.

Hubbard, Howard. 1968. "Five long hot summers and how they grew." *Public Interest* 12 (Summer):3-24.

Huber, Joan. 1976. "Toward a Socio-Technological Theory of the Women's Movement." *Social Problems* 23:371-88.

Hubner, J. and L. Gruson. 1987. "Dial Om for murder." *Rolling Stone* April 9.

Hughes, Langston. 1962. *Fight for Freedom, the Story of the NAACP.* New York: W. W. Norton.

Humphreys, Laud. 1972. *Out of the Closets: The Sociology of Homosexual Liberation.* Englewood Cliffs, N.J.: Prentice-Hall, Inc.

Hunt, Lynn Avery. 1992. *The Family Romance of the French Revolution.* Berkeley: University of California Press.

———. 1984. *Politics, Culture, and Class in the French Revolution.* Berkeley and Los Angeles: University of California Press.

Hunt, Scott A. 1992. "Critical Dramaturgy and Collective Action Rhetoric: Cognitive and Moral Order in the Communist Manifesto." *Perspectives on Social Problems* 3:1-18,

Hunt, Scott, Robert D. Benford, and David A. Snow. 1994. "Identity Fields: Framing Processes and the Social Construction of Movement Identities." Pp. 185-208 in E. Larana, H. Johnson, and J. R. Gusfield (eds.), *New Social Movements: From Ideology to Identity.* Philadelphia: Temple University Press.

Huyser, Gen. Robert E. 1986. *Mission to Tehran.* New York: Harper and Row.

Imig, Douglas Rowley. 1992. "Resource mobilization and survival tactics of poverty advocacy groups." *Western Political Quarterly* 45:501-520.

Inglehart, Ronald. 1977. *The Silent Revolution: Changing Values and Political Styles Among Western Publics.* Princeton: Princeton University Press.

Institute for Social Research. 1979. "Americans Seek Self-Development, Suffer Anxiety from Changing Roles." *ISR Newsletter.* University of Michigan, Winter: 4-5.

Irwin, J. 1970. *The Felon.* Englewood Cliffs, NJ: Prentice-Hall.

Isaac, Larry, and William R. Kelly. 1981. "Racial Insurgency, the State, and Welfare Expansion: Local and National Evidence from the Postwar United States." *American Journal of Sociology* 86:1348-86.

Isaac, Larry, Elizabeth Mutran, and Sheldon Stryker. 1980. "Political Protest Orientations Among Black and White Adults." *American Sociological Review* 45:191-213.

Isserman, Maurice. 1987. *If I Had a Hammer: The Death of the Old Left and the Birth of the New Left.* New York: Basic.

Jackson, Maurice, Eleanora Peterson, James Bull, Sverre Monson, and Patricia Richmond. 1960. "Failure of an Incipient Social Movement." *Pacific Sociological Review* 31:35-40.

Jacobs, Jerry A. 1987. "Deconversion from religious movements: An analysis of charismatic bonding and spiritual commitment." *Journal for the Scientific Study of Religion* 26: 294-308.

———. 1986. "Trends in workplace contact between men and women, 1971-1981." *Sociology and Social Research* 70:202-205.

———. 1984. "The economy of love in religious commitment: The deconversion of women from nontraditional religious movements." *Journal for the Scientific Study of Religion* 23: 155-71.

Jacobs, Paul. 1963. *The State of the Unions.* New York: Atheneum.

Jaggar, Alison. 1983. Feminist Politics and Human Nature. Sussex: Harvester.

James, William. 1958. *The Varieties of Religious Experience.* New York: The New American Library.

———. 1950 (1890). "The Perception of Reality." Pp. 283-324 in *Principles of Psychology,* Vol. 2. New York: Dover Publications.

Jaquette, Jane, ed. 1991. *The Women's Movement in Latin America: Feminism and the Transition to Democracy.* Boulder, CO: Westview Press.

Jasper, James M. 1990. *Nuclear Politics: Energy and the State in the United States, Sweden, and France.* Princeton, NJ: Princeton University Press.

———. 1988. "The political life cycle of technological controversies." *Social Forces* 67:357-377.

Jasper, James M. and Dorothy Nelkin. 1992. *The Animal Rights Crusade: The Growth of a Moral Protest.* New York: The Free Press.

Jasper, James M., Dorothy Nelkin. and Jane Poulsen. 1990. "When Do Movements Succeed? Three Campaigns against Animal Experiments." Paper presented at the annual meeting of the American Sociological Association, Washington, D.C.

Jasper, James M. and Jane Poulsen. 1989. "Animal rights and anti-nuclear protest: Condensing symbols and the critique of instrumental reason." Paper presented at the American Sociological Association annual meetings, San Francisco.

Jemison, Rev. T. J. 1978 Interview. Baton Rouge, Louisiana. October 16.

Jenkins, J. Craig. 1987. "Interpreting the Stormy 1960s: Three Theories in Search of a Political Age." *Research in Political Sociology* 3:269-303.

———. 1985a. *The Politics of Insurgency: The Farm Worker Movement in the 1960s.* New York: Columbia University Press.

———. 1985b. "Foundation Funding of Progressive Social Movements." Pp. 7-17 in *Grant Seekers Guide: Funding Sourcebook,* edited by Jill R. Shellow. Mt. Kisco, NY: Moyer Bell Ltd.

———. 1983. "Resource Mobilization Theory and the Study of Social Movements." *Annual Review of Sociology* 9:527-53.

———. 1981. "Sociopolitical movements." Pp. 81-153 in Samuel Long (ed.), *Handbook of Political Behavior,* Volume 4. New York: Plenum.

———. 1975. Farm Workers and the Powers: Farm Worker Insurgency (1946-1972). Unpublished Ph.D. dissertation. Department of Sociology, State University of New York, Stony Brook.

Jenkins, J. Craig, and Craig Eckert. 1986. "Channeling black insurgency: Elite patronage and professional social movement organization in the development of the black movement." *American Sociological Review* 51: 812-29.

Jenkins, J. Craig and Augustine J. Kposowa. 1990. "Explaining Military Coups d'État: Black Africa, 1957-1984." *American Sociological Review* 55:861-75.

Jenkins, J. Craig and Charles Perrow. 1977. "Insurgency of the powerless: Farm worker movements (1946-1972)." *American Sociological Review* 42:249-268

Jenness, Valerie. 1995. "Social Movement Growth, Domain Expansion, and Framing Processes: The Gay/Lesbian Movement and Violence Against Gays and Lesbians as a Social Problem." *Social Problems* 42: 145-170.

Johnson, Charles S. 1930. *The Negro in American Civilization.* New York: Henry Holt.

Johnson, D.G., and R.D. Lee, (eds.) 1987. *Population Growth and Economic Development: Issues and Evidence.* Madison: University of Wisconsin Press.

Johnston, Hank. 1991a. "Movements, Methods, and Melucci." Paper presented at the annual meeting of the Pacific Sociological Association, Irvine, California, April 14-17.

———. 1991b. *Tales of Nationalism: Catalonia, 1939-1979.* New Brunswick, N.J.: Rutgers University Press.

Johnston, Ruby F. 1956. *The Religion of Negro Protestants.* New York: Philosophical Library.

———. 1954. *The Development of Negro Religion.* New York: Philosophical Library.

Jones, Edward E. and Richard E. Nisbet. 1971. *The Actor and the Observer: Divergent Perspectives on the Causes of Behavior.* Morristown, NJ: General Learning Press.

Judah, J. Stillson. 1974. *Hare Krishna and the Counterculture.* New York: Wiley.

Kafka, Franz. 1937. *Parables and Paradoxes,* translated by Ernst Kaiser et al. New York: Schocken.

Kalter, Joanmarie. 1985. "Abortion Bias: How Network Coverage Has Tilted to the Pro-Lifers." *TV Guide* 33:7-17.

Kamalî, 'Alî. 1979. *Inqilâb* (Revolution). Tehran, Iran: Massoud Publishing House.

Kamrava, Mehran. 1990. *Revolution in Iran: The Roots of Turmoil.* London, England: Routledge.

Kane, Anne. 1991. "Cultural Analysis in Historical Sociology: The Analytic and Concrete Forms of the Autonomy of Culture." *Sociological Theory* 9:53-69.

Kanter, Rosabeth M. 1973. *Communes: Creating and Managing the Collective Life*. New York: Harper and Row.

——. 1972. *Commitment and Community: Communes and Utopias in Sociological Perspective*. Cambridge, Mass.: Harvard University Press.

——. 1968. "Commitment and Social Organization: A Study of Commitment Mechanisms in Utopian Communities." *American Sociological Review* 33:499-517.

Kaplowitz, Stan. 1973. "An Experimental Test of a Rationalistic Theory of Deterrence." *Journal of Conflict Resolution,* September, 17:535-72.

Karstedt-Henke, Sabine. 1980. "Theorien zur Erkldrung terroristischer Bewegungen" (Theories for the Explanation of Terrorist Movements). Pp. 198-234 in *Politik der inneren Sicherheit* (The Politics of Internal Security), edited by E. Blankenberg. Frankfurt, Germany: Suhrkamp.

Katz, Alfred H. 1981. "Self-Help and Mutual Aid: An Emerging Social Movement." *Annual Review of Sociology* 7:129-55.

Katzenstein, Mary Fainsod. 1990. "Feminism within American institutions: Unobtrusive mobilization in the 1980s." *Signs* 16:27-54.

Katzenstein, P.J. 1987. *Policy and Politics in West Germany: The Growth of a Semisovereign State*. Philadelphia: Temple University Press.

Kauffman, L.A. 1990. "The anti-politics of identity." *Socialist Review* 20:67-80.

Kautilîya. 1972. *The Kautilîya Arthaâstra*. Pt. 2, 2d ed. Edited by R. P. Kangle. Bombay, India: University of Bombay.

Kazemi, Farhad. 1980. *Poverty and Revolution in Iran*. New York: New York University Press.

Keddie, Nikki R. 1981. *Roots of Revolution: An Interpretive History of Modern Iran*. New Haven, CT: Yale University Press.

Kelley, Harold H. 1972. *Causal Schemata and the Attribution Process*. Morristown, NJ: General Learning Press.

Kendall, Patricia L. and Katherine M. Wolf. 1941. "The two purposes of deviant case analysis." Pp. 167-70 in Paul F. Lazarsfeld and Morris Rosenberg (eds.), *The Language of Social Research*. New York: Free Press.

Kennedy, David M. 1970. *Birth Control in America*. New Haven: Yale University Press, 1970.

Kerr, N. L. and S, E. Brunn. 1983. "Dispensability of member effort and group motivation losses: free-rider effects." *Journal of Personality and Social Psychology* 44:78-94.

Khalîlî, Akbar. 1981. *Gâm bih Gâm bâ Inqilâb* (Step by Step with the Revolution). Tehran, Iran: Surûsh.

Killian, Lewis M. 1984. "Organization, Rationality and Spontaneity in the Civil Rights Movement." *American Sociological Review* 49:770-83.

——. 1972. "The significance of extremism in the black revolution." *Social Problems* 20(1):41-48.

——. 1968. *The Impossible Revolution: Black Power and the American Dream*. New York: Random House.

——. 1964. "Social movements." Pp. 426-55 in Robert E. L. Faris (ed.), *Handbook of Modern Sociology*. Chicago: Rand McNally.

Kimmel, Michael. 1984. Review of *Regulating Society,* by Ephraim H. Mizruchi. *Society,* July/August:90-92.

King, Martin Luther, Jr. 1963. *Why We Can't Wait*. New York: Harper & Row.

Kirchheimer, Otto. 1961. *Political Justice: The Use of Legal Procedure for Political Ends*. Princeton: Princeton University Press.

Kirkwood, Julieta. 1986. *Ser Politica en Chile: Las Feministas y Los Partidos*. Santiago: FLASCO.

——. 1983a. "Women and politics in Chile." *International Social Science Journal* 35:625-637.

——. 1983b. "El Feminismo Como Negación del Autoritarismo." Santiago: Programa FLACSO, Materia de Discusión, No. 52.

Kitschelt, Herbert P. 1988. "Left-libertarian parties: Explaining innovation in comparative party systems." *World Politics* 40: 194-234.

——. 1986. "Political Opportunity Structures and Political Protest: Anti-Nuclear Movements in Four Democracies." *British Journal of Political Science* 16:57-85.

Klandermans, Bert. 1992. "The Social Construction of Protest and Multiorganizational Fields." Pp. 77-103 in *Frontiers of Social Movement Theory,* edited by Aldon D. Morris and Carol McClurg Mueller. New Haven, Conn.: Yale University Press.

——. 1990a. "Linking the 'old' and the 'new': Movement networks in the Netherlands," in Russell Dalton and Manfred Kuechler (eds.) *Challenging the Political Order*. New York: Oxford University Press: 123-36.

——. 1990b. *New Social Movements and Resource Mobilization: The European and the American Approach Revisited*. Department of Social Psychology. Vrije Universiteit, Amsterdam.

——. 1989. "Interorganizational Networks." Pp. 301-15 in *International Social Movement Research. Vol.2: Organizing for Change: Social Movement Organizations in Europe and the United States,* edited by B. Klandermans. Greenwich, CT: JAI.

——. 1988a. "The Formation and Mobilization of Consensus." Pp. 173-96 in *International Social Movement Research*, vol. 1. Edited by Bert Klandermans, Hanspeter Kriesi, and Sidney Tarrow. Greenwich, Conn.: JAI Press.

——. 1988b. "Union Action and the Free Rider Dilemma." Pp. 77-92 in *Research in Social Movements, Conflict and Change*. Vol. 10: *Social Movements as a Factor of Change in the Contemporary World,* edited by L. Kriesberg and B. Misztal. Greenwich, CT: JAI.

——. 1986. "New Social Movements and Resource Mobilization: The European and the American Approach. " *International Journal of Mass Emergencies and Disasters* 4:13-39.

——. 1984a. "Mobilization and Participation: Social Psychological Expansions of Resource Mobilization Theory." *American Sociological Review*, 49:583-600.

——. 1984b. "Social-Psychological Expansion of Resource Mobilization Theory." *American Sociological Review* 49:583-600.

——. 1983. "The Expected Number of Participants, the Effectiveness of Collective Action, and the Willingness to Participate: The Free-Riders Dilemma Reconsidered." Paper presented at the meetings of the American Sociological Association, Detroit.

Klandermans, Bert, Hanspeter Kriesi, and Sidney Tarrow, eds. 1988. *International Social Movement Research.* Vol. 1. Greenwich, CT: JAI Press.

Klandermans, Bert, and Dirk Oegema. 1987. "Potentials, Networks, Motivations, and Barriers: Steps towards Participation in Social Movements." *American Sociological Review* 52:519-31.

Klandermans, Bert, and Sidney Tarrow. 1988. "Mobilization into Social Movements:Synthesizing European and American Approaches." In *From Structure to Action: Comparing Social Movement Research across Cultures,* edited by Bert Klandermans, Hanspeter Kriesi, and Sidney Tarrow, pp. 1-38. Vol. I of *International Social Movement Research.* Greenwich, Conn.: JAI Press.

Klapp, Orrin. 1969. *Collective Search for Identity.* New York: Holt, Rinehart and Winston.

Kleidman, Robert. 1993. *Organizing for Peace: Neutrality, the Test Ban, and the Freeze.* Syracuse: Syracuse University Press.

———. 1986. "Opposing 'The Good War': Mobilization and Professionalization in the Emergency Peace Campaign." *Research in Social Movements, Conflicts and Change* 9:177-200.

Klein, Ethel. 1984. *Gender Politics: From Consciousness to Mass Politics.* Cambridge: Harvard University Press.

Knoke, David. 1981. "Commitment and Detachment in Voluntary Associations." *American Sociological Review* 46:141-58.

Knoke, David and Peter J. Burke. 1980. Log-Linear Models. Sage University Paper Series on Quantitative Applications in the Social Sciences, Series No. 07-020. Beverly Hills: Sage.

Knopp, Lawrence. 1987. "Social theory, social movements and public policy: Recent accomplishments of the gay and lesbian movements in Minneapolis, Minnesota." *International Journal of Urban and Regional Research* 11:243-261.

Koopmans, Ruud. 1995. *Democracy From Below and the Political Systems in West Germany.* Boulder, CO: Westview.

———. 1992a. "Van Provo tot RARA. Golfbewegingen in het politiek protest in Nederland" (From Provo to RARA: Waves of Political Protest in the Netherlands). Pp. 59-76 in *Tussen verbeelding en macht: 25 jaar nieuwe sociale bewegingen in Nederland* (Between Imagination and Power: 25 Years New Social Movements in the Netherlands), edited by J. W. Duyvendak, H. A. van der Heijden, R. Koopmans, and L. Wijmans. Amsterdam, the Netherlands: SUA.

———. 1992b. "Patterns of Unruliness: The Interactive Dynamics of Protest Waves." Paper presented at the annual meeting of the American Sociological Association, 20-24 Aug., Pittsburgh, PA.

———. 1992c. *Democracy from Below. New Social Movements and the Political System in West Germany.* Ph.D. Dissertation, Department of Political Science, University of Amsterdam, Amsterdam, the Netherlands.

———. 1991. "Demokratie von unten: Neue soziale Bewegungen und politisches System in der Bundesrepublik Deutschland im internationalen Vergleich." In R. Roth und Rucht D. (eds.), *Neue soziale Bewegungen in der Bundesrepublik Deutschland,* 2nd edition. Bonn: Bundeszentrale für politische Bildung.

———a. "Bridging the Gap: The Missing Link Between Political Opportunity Structure and Movement Action." Paper presented at the ISA Congress, Jul. 7-10, Madrid, Spain.

———b. "Patterns of unruliness: The interactive dynamics of protest waves." Unpublished paper, University of Amsterdam: PDIS.

Kopkind, Andrew. 1993. "The gay moment." *The Nation,* May 3:577, 590-602.

Kornhauser, William. 1962. "Social Bases of Political Commitment: A Study of Liberals and Radicals." Pp. 321-39 in *Human Behavior and Social Processes. An Interactionist Approach,* edited by Arnold Rose. Houghton-Mifflin.

———. 1959. *The Politics of Mass Society.* New York: Free Press.

Kraft, Joseph. 1978. "Letter From Iran." *The New Yorker,* vol. 54, December 18, pp. 134-68.

Krasniewicz, Louise. 1992. *Nuclear Summer: The Clash of Communities at the Seneca Women's Peace Encampment.* Ithaca: Cornell University Press.

Kriesberg, Louis. 1973. *The Sociology of Social Conflicts.* Englewood Cliffs: Prentice-Hall.

Kriesi, Hanspeter. 1993. *Political Mobilization and Social Change: The Dutch Case in Comparative Perspective.* Aldershot, England: Avebury.

———. 1991. *The Political Opportunity Structure of New Social Movements: Its Impact on Their Mobilization.* Wissenschaftszentrum Berlin für Sozialforschung, FS III 91-103.

———. "Federalism and pillarization: the Netherlands and Switzerland compared." *Acta Politica* 25: 433-450.

———. 1989a. Politische Randbedingungen der Entwicklung neuer sozialer Bewegungen, pp. 104-121, in R. Kleinfeld und W. Luthardt (eds.), *Westliche Demokratien und Interessenvermittlung. Beiträge zur aktuellen Entwicklung nationaler Parteien-und Verbandssysteme.* Hagen: Fernuniversität-Gesamthochschule.

———. 1989b. "The Political opportunity structure of the Dutch peace movement." *West European Politics* 12: 295-312.

———. 1989c. "New Social Movements and the New Class in the Netherlands." *American Journal of Sociology* 94:1078-1116.

———. 1984. *Die Zürcher Bewegung: Bilder, Interaktiotien, Zusammenhänge.* Frankfurt: Campus.

Kriesi, Hanspeter, Ruud Koopmans, Jan Willem Duyvendak, and Marco G. Giugni. 1992. "New Social Movements and Political Opportunities in Western Europe." *European Journal of Political Research* 22:219-44.

Kriesi, H., R. Levy, G. Ganguillet, and H. Zwicky. 1981. *Politische Aktivierung in der Schweiz. 1945-1978.* Diessenhofen: Ruagger.

Kriesi, Hanspeter and Philip Van Prang, Jr. 1988. "De beweging en haar campagne" (The Movement and Its Campaign). Pp. 13-53 in *Tekenen voor de vrede. Portret van een campagne* (Signing for Peace. Portrait of a Campaign), edited by B. Klandermans. Assen, Netherlands: Van Gorcum.

———. 1987. "Old and new politics: The Dutch peace movement and the traditional political organizations." *European Journal of Political Science* 15: 319-346.

Kritzer, Herbert M. 1977. "Political Protest and Political Violence: A Nonrecursive Causal Model." *Social Forces* 55:630-40.

Kuhn, Philip S. 1971. *Rebellion and its Enemies in Late Imperial China: Militarization and Social Structure.* Cambridge: Harvard University Press.

Kunstler, William M. 1966. *Deep in My Heart.* New York: William Morrow.

Kuran, Timur. 1989. "Sparks and Prairie Fires: A Theory of Unanticipated Political Revolution." *Public Choice* 61:41-74.

Kurzman, Charles. 1994. "A Dynamic View of Resources: Evidence from the Iranian Revolution." *Research in Social Movements, Conflict and Change* 17:53-84.

——. 1992. *Structure and Agency in the Iranian Revolution of 1979.* Ph.D. dissertation. Department of Sociology, University of California, Berkeley, CA.

Kushner, Sam. 1975. *Long Road to Delano.* New York: International Publishers.

Lachman, Sheldon J. and Benjamin Singer. 1968. *The Detroit Riot: 1967.* Detroit: Behavior Research Institute.

Laczko, Leslie S. 1986. "On the Dynamics of Linguistic Cleavage in Québec: A Test of Alternative Hypotheses." *International Journal of Sociology and Social Policy* 6:39-60.

Lader, Lawrence. 1973. *Abortion II: Making the Revolution.* Boston: Beacon Press

——. 1966. *Abortion.* Boston: Beacon Press.

Ladrech, R. 1989. "Social movements and party systems: The French Socialist Party and new social movements." *West European Politics* 12: 262-279.

Lakatos, Imre. 1978. *The Methodology of Scientific Research Programmes.* Cambridge, England: Cambridge University Press.

Lâlih'hâ-yi Inqilâb: Yâd-nâmih-yi Shuhaâ (The Tulips of the Revolution: Memorial for the Martyrs). Circa 1980. Tehran, Iran: Inti-shârât-i Anjuman-i Khidmât-i Islâmî.

Land, Kenneth C. 1969. "Principles of Path Analysis." Pp. 3-37 in *Sociological Methodology 1969,* edited by E. F. Borgatta. San Francisco: Jossey-Bass.

Landino, Rita. and Lynne B. Welch. 1990. "Supporting women in the university environment through collaboration and networking." In *Women and Higher Education: Changes and Challenges,* ed. Lynne B. Welch, 12-19. New York: Praeger Publishers.

Lane, Robert E. 1964. *Political Life.* New York: Free Press.

Lang, Kurt and Gladys E. Lang. 1961. *Collective Dynamics.* New York: Thomas Y. Crowell.

Lapham, Sandra C., Sandra F. Weber, Michael J. Burkhart, Richard E. Hoffman, and Kathleen Kreiss. 1984. "Risk factors for victimization during the 1980 riot at the Penitentiary of New Mexico." *American Journal of Epidemiology* 119:218-26.

Laue, James H. 1971. "A model for civil rights change through conflict." Pp. 256-62 in Gary T. Marx (ed.), *Racial Conflict.* Boston: Little, Brown.

Law, Kim S. and Edward J. Walsh. 1983. "The interaction of grievances and structure in social movement analysis: the case of JUST." *The Sociological Quarterly* 24:123-36.

Lawson, James. 1978. Interview. Los Angeles, California. October 2 and 6.

Lawson, Steven F. 1976. *Black Ballots: Voting Rights in the South, 1944-1969.* New York: Columbia University Press.

Lazarsfeld, Paul F., Bernard B. Berelson, and Hazel Gaudet. 1948. *The People's Choice.* New York: Columbia University Press.

Leahy, Peter J. 1975. *The anti-abortion movement: testing a theory of the rise and fail of social movements.* Ph.D. dissertation. Department of Sociology, Syracuse University.

Lears, T. J. Jackson. 1985. "The Concept of Hegemony: Problems and Possibilities." *American Historical Review* 85:567-93.

LeBon, Gustave. 1960. *The Crowd.* New York: Viking.

Lechner, Norbert and Susana Levy. 1984. *Notas Sobre La Vida Cotidiana III: El Disciplinamiento De La Mujer.* Santiago: FLACSO.

Lee, Robert. 1967. *Stranger in the Land.* London: Lutterworth.

Lefebvre, Henri. 1965. *La Proclamation de la Commune, 26 mars 1871.* Paris: Gallimard.

Leff, Mark H. 1988. "Speculating in Social Security Futures: The Perils of Payroll Tax Financing, 1939-1950." Pp. 243-78 in *Social Security: The First Half-Century,* edited by Gerald D. Nash, Noel H. Pugach, and Richard F. Tomasson. Albuquerque: University of New Mexico Press.

Leites, Nathan and Charles Wolf, Jr. 1970. *Rebellion and Authority.* Chicago: Markham Publishing Company.

Lemberg Center for the Study of Violence. 1968 "April aftermath of the King Assassination." *Riot Data Review* 2 (August). Waltham, MA: Lemberg Center for the Study of Violence, Brandeis University.

Lemert, Edwin M. 1951. *Social Pathology.* McGraw-Hill.

Lemons, J. Staniev. 1973. *The Woman Citizen: Social Feminism in the 1920s.* Urbana: University of Illinois Press.

Lenin, V. I. 1970. "What Is to be Done?" Pp. 458-72 in *Protest, Reform, and Revolt,* edited by Joseph R. Gusfield. New York: Wiley.

——. 1929. *What Is To Be Done? Burning Questions of Our Movement.* New York: International Publishers.

Levine, Martin P.. 1992. "The status of gay men In the workplace." In *Men's Lives,* eds. Michael S. Kimmel and A. Messner, 251-166. New York: Macmillan Publishing.

——. 1979. "Employment discrimination against gay men." *International Review of Modern Sociology* 9:151-163.

Levine, Martin P., and Robin Leonard. 1984. "Discrimination against lesbians in the work force." *Signs* 9:700-710.

Lewis, S.C. and S. Sferza. 1987. "Les socialistes français entre l'Etat et la Société: de la construction du parti à la conquête du pouvoir," pp. 132-51, in S. Hoffmann and G. Ross (eds.), *L'Expérience Mitterrand.* Paris: PUF.

Lewis, Steven H. and Robert E. Kraut. 1972. "Correlates of student political activism and ideology." *Journal of Social Issues* 28:131-49.

Lewis, Anthony, and writers for The New York Times. 1966. *The Second American Revolution: A First-Hand Account of the Struggle for Civil Rights.* London: Faber & Faber.

Lewis, Chester. 1981. Interview. Wichita, Kansas. February 3.

Lewis, David. 1970. *King: A Critical Biography.* New York: Praeger.

Lewis, J. 1986. "Reconstructing the cult experience: Post-involvement attitudes as a function of mode of exit and post-involvement socialization." *Sociological Analysis* 47: 151-59.

Lewis, J.and D. Bromley. 1987. "The cult withdrawal syndrome: A case of misattribution of cause." *Journal for the Scientific Study of Religion* 26: 508-22.

Lewis, John. 1979. Interview. Washington, D.C. November 9.

Lewis, Sasha Gregory. 1979. *Sunday's Women: A Report on Lesbian Life Today.* Boston: Beacon Press.

Lichbach, Mark I. 1994. "Rethinking Rationality and Rebellion: Theories of Collective Action and Problems of Collective Dissent." *Rationality and Society* 6:8-39.

Lichterman, Paul. 1995. *The Search for Political Solidarity: Culture and Commitment in Grassroots Social Movements since the 1960s.* New York: Cambridge University Press.

Lieberson, Stanley. 1970. *Language and Ethnic Relations in Canada.* New York: Wiley.

Liebman, Robert C. 1983. "Mobilizing the Moral Majority." Pp. 49-73 in *The New Christian Right: Mobilization and Legitimation,* edited by Robert C. Liebman and Robert Wuthnow. New York: Aldine Publishing Co.

Liebman, R., J. Sutton, and R. Wuthnow. 1988. "Exploring the social sources of denominationalism: Schisms in American Protestant denominations, 1890-1980." *American Sociological Review* 53: 343-52.

Lieske, Joel A. 1978. "The conditions of racial violence in American cities: a developmental synthesis." *American Political Science Review* 72:1324-40.

Lifton, Robert J., ed. 1967. *The Woman in America.* Boston: Beacon Press. Originally published as a special issue of *Daedalus: The Journal of the American Academy of Arts and Sciences* (Spring 1964).

Lijphart, Arend. 1977. *Democracy in Plural Societies: A Comparative Exploration.* New Haven: Yale University Press.

Linz, Juan J. 1978. "Crisis, breakdown, and reequilibration." Pp. 1-124 in Juan J. Linz and Alfred Stepan (eds.), *The Breakdown of Democratic Regimes.* Baltimore: Johns Hopkins University Press.

———. 1973. "Early State-Building and Late Peripheral Nationalism Against the State: The Case of Spain." Pp. 32-116 in *Building States and Nations,* vol. 2, edited by S.N. Eisenstadt and S. Rokkan. Beverly Hills: Sage.

Lionberger, H. F. 1960. *Adoption of New Ideas and Practices.* Ames: The Iowa State University Press.

Lipset, S. M. 1960. *Political Man.* New York: Doubleday and Company.

Lipset, S. M. and Earl Raab. 1973. *The Politics of Unreason: Right-Wing Extremism in America, 1790-1970.* New York: Harper and Row.

Lipset, S.M. and S. Rokkan. 1967. "Cleavage structures, party systems, and voter alignments." Reprinted in S.M. Lipset (ed.), *Consensus and Conflict: Essays in Political Sociology.* New Brunswick: Transaction Books, 1985: 113-185.

Lipset, Seymour Martin and Sheldon S. Wolin. 1965. *The Berkeley Student Revolt.* Garden City, New York: Doubleday.

Lipsky, Michael. 1970. *Protest in City Politics.* Chicago: Rand McNally.

———. 1968. "Protest as a political resource." *American Political Science Review* 62:1144-58.

Lissagaray, Prosper-Oliver. [1876] 1969. *Histoire de la Commune de 1871* (History of the Commune of 1871). 2 vols. Paris: Maspero.

Liu, Michael Tien-Lung. 1988. "States and Urban Revolutions: Explaining the Revolutionary Outcomes in Iran and Poland." *Theory and Society* 17:179-209.

Lodhi, Abdul Qaiyum, and Charles Tilly. 1973. "Urbanization, crime and collective violence in 19th century France." *American Journal of Sociology* 79:296-318.

Lofland, John. 1985a. *Protest: Studies of Collective Behavior and Social Movements.* New Brunswick: Transaction Books.

———. 1985b. "Social Movement Culture." Pp. 219-39 in *Protest: Studies of Collective Behavior and Social Movements,* edited by John Lofland. New Brunswick, NJ: Transaction.

———. 1978. "Becoming a world-saver revisited." Pp. 10-23 in J. Richardson (ed.), *Conversion Careers.* Beverly Hills, Calif.: Sage.

———. 1977a. *Doomsday Cult.* Enlarged Edition. New York: Irvington Publishers.

———. 1977b. "Becoming a world-saver revisited." *American Behavioral Scientist* 20:805-19.

———. 1977c. *The boom and bust of a millenarian movement: doomsday cult revisited.* Preface to the Irvington edition of J. Lofland, Doomsday Cult. New York: Irvington.

———. 1976. *Doing Social Life: The Qualitative Study of Human Interaction in Natural Settings.* New York: John Wiley.

———, with the assistance of L. H. Lofland. 1969. *Deviance and Identity.* Englewood Cliffs, NJ: Prentice-Hall.

———. 1966. *Doomsday Cult: A Study of Conversion, Proselytization, and Maintenance of Faith.* Englewood Cliffs, NJ: Prentice-Hall.

Lofland, John and Michael Jamison. 1984. "Social Movement Locals: Modal Member Structures." *Sociological Analysis* 45:115-29.

Lofland, John, and Sam Marullo, eds. 1990. *Peace Action in the 1980s.* New Brunswick, N.J.: Rutgers.

Lofland, J. and L. N. Skonovd. 1981. "Conversion motifs." *Journal for the Scientific Study of Religion* 20: 373-85.

Lofland, J. and R. Stark. 1965. "Becoming a world saver: A theory of conversion to a deviant perspective." *American Sociological Review* 30: 862-74.

Lomax, Louis E. 1962. *The Negro Revolt.* New York: New American Library.

London, Bruce and John Hearn. 1977. "Ethnic community theory of black social and political participation: Additional support." *Social Science Quarterly* 57:883-91.

London, Jaan and Henry Anderson. 1970. *So Shall Ye Reap.* New York: Crowell.

Lorde, Audre. 1984. *Sister Outsider.* Trumansburg, N.Y.: Crossing Press.

Lorwin, Val R. 1973. "Belgium: Religion, Class and Language in National Politics." Pp. 147-87 in *Political Oppositions in Western Democracies*, edited by R.A. Dahl. New Haven: Yale University Press.

Loua, Toussaint. 1873. *Atlas statistique de la population de Paris* (Statistical Atlas of the Population of Paris). Paris: J. Dejey.

Lumley, Bob. 1990. *States of Emergency: Cultures of Revolt in Italy from 1968 to 1978.* London: Verso.

———. 1983. "Social movements in Italy, 1968-78." Unpublished Ph.D. dissertation, University of Birmingham, Centre for Contemporary Cultural Studies.

Lunardini, Christine A. 1986. *From Equal Suffrage to Equal Rights.* New York: New York University Press.

Lundberg, Ferdinand and Marynia F. Farnham. 1947. *Modern Woman: The Lost Sex*. New York: Harper.

Luper, Clara. 1980 Interview. Oklahoma City, Oklahoma. (Follow-up interview, January 1981).

——. 1979. *Behold the Walls*. Jim Wire.

Lusky, Louis. 1964. "Justice with a southern accent." *Harper's* (March):62ff.

Lutz, Alma. 1968. *Crusade for Freedom—Women of the Antislavery Movement*. Boston: Beacon Press.

Lutz, James M. 1980. "Welsh Political Mobilization: A Comment and a Note." *American Sociological Review* 45:1028-31.

Lyman, Stanford M. and Marvin B. Scott. 1967. "Territoriality: a neglected sociological dimension." *Social Problems* 15:236-48.

Machalek, Richard and David A. Snow. 1993. "Conversion to New Religious Movements." Pp. 53-74 in *Religion and The Social Order: The Handbook on Cults and Sects in America,* Volume 3B. Greenwich, CT: JAI Press.

Machiavelli, Niccolò. 1980. *The Prince*. New York: New American Library.

Macpherson, W. J. 1987. *The Economic Development of Japan, C. 1868-1914*. New York: Macmillan.

Magendzo, Salomon, G. López, C. Larraín, and M. Pascal. 1985. Y Asi Fue Creciendo: La Vida de La Mujer Pobladora. Santiago: Programa Interdisciplinario de Investigaciones en Educacion Academio de Humanismo Cristiano.

Maguire, Diarmuid. 1990. "Parties into movements." Unpublished Ph.D thesis, Cornell University.

Mamonova, Tatyana, ed. 1984. *Women and Russia: Feminist Writings from the Soviet Union*. Boston, MA: Beacon Press.

Mansbridge, Jane. 1986. *Why We Lost the ERA*. Chicago: University of Chicago Press.

Marchant-Shapiro, Andrew. 1990. "Rehabilitating Kornhauser? Mass Society, Networks, and Social Movements." Unpublished paper. Union College. Department of Sociology.

Marcus, Alan I. 1991. *Plague of Strangers: Social Groups and the Origins of City Services in Cincinnati, 1819-1870*. Columbus: Ohio State University Press.

Marenches, Count Alexander de. 1988. *The Evil Empire: The Third World War Now*. Translated by S. Lee and J. Marks. London, England: Sidgwick and Jackson.

Marotta, Toby. 1981. *The Politics of Homosexuality*. Boston: Houghton-Mifflin.

Martin, Yancey. 1977. Interview with Yancey Martin. Pp. 52-56 in Howell Raines (ed.). *My Soul is Rested*. New York: Bantam.

Marullo, Sam. 1992. "Gender differences in peace movement participation." *Research in Social Movements, Conflicts and Change* 13:135-152.

Marwell, Gerald, Michael Alken, and N.J. Demerath. 1997. "The persistence of political attitudes among 1960s activists." *Public Opinion Quarterly* 51:359-375.

Marwell, Gerald and Ruth E. Ames. 1980. "Experiments on the provision of public goods. II. Provision points, stakes, experience, and the free-rider problem." *American Journal of Sociology* 85:926-37.

——. 1979. "Experiments on the provision of public goods. I. Resources, interest, group size, and the free-rider problem." *American Journal of Sociology* 84:1335-60.

Marwell, Gerald and Pamela Oliver. 1993. *The Critical Mass In Collective Action: A Micro-Social Theory*. Cambridge, England: Cambridge University Press.

Marwell, Gerald, Pamela E. Oliver, and Ralph Prahl. 1988. "Social Networks and Collective Action: A Theory of the Critical Mass. III." *American Journal of Sociology* 94:502-34.

Marx, Gary T. 1979. "External efforts to damage or facilitate social movements: some patterns, explanations, outcomes. and complications." Pp. 94-125 in Mayer N. Zald and John D. McCarthy (eds.). *The Dynamics of Social Movements: Resource Mobilization, Social Control, and Tactics*. Cambridge: Winthrop.

——. 1969. *Protest and Prejudice*. New York: Harper and Row.

Marx, Gary T. and Michael Useem. 1971. "Majority involvement in minority movements: civil rights, abolition, untouchability." *Journal of Social Issues* 27:81-104.

Marx, Gary T., and James L. Wood. 1975. "Strands of theory and research in collective behavior." Pp. 363-428 in Alex Inkeles, James S. Coleman and Neil Smelser (eds.), *Annual Review of Sociology*. Palo Alto: Annual Review.

Marx, Karl. [1871] 1940. *The Civil War in France*. New York: International Publishers.

Masotti, Louis H., Jeffrey K. Hadden, Kenneth F Seminatore, and Jerome R. Corsi. 1969. *A Time to Burn? An Evaluation of the Present Crisis in Race Relations*. Chicago: Rand-McNally.

Masters, G. N. 1982. "A Rasch Model for Partial Credit Scoring." *Psychometrika* 47: 149-74.

Mattelart, Michele. 1975. "Chile: The feminine side of the military coup or when bourgeois women take to the streets." *NACLA's Latin America and Empire Report* 9:14-25.

Matthews, Donald R., and James W. Prothro. 1966. *Negroes and the New Southern Politics*. New York: Harcourt, Brace and World.

Matthiessen, Peter. 1969. *Sal Si Puedes: Cesar Chavez and the New American Revolution*. New York: Random House.

May, Elaine Tyler. 1988. *Homeward Bound: American Families in the Cold War Era*. New York: Basic.

Mayhew, David R. 1986. *Placing Parties in American Politics*. Princeton, N.J.: Princeton University Press.

Mays, Benjamin, and Joseph W. Nicholson. [1933] 1969. *The Negro's Church*. New York: Arno Press and the New York Times.

McAdam, Doug. 1994. "Culture and Social Movements." Pp. 36-57 in *New Social Movements: From Ideology to Identity,* edited by Enrique Laraña, Hank Johnston, and Joseph R. Gusfield. Philadelphia: Temple University Press.

——. 1992. "Gender as a mediator of the activist experience: The case of Freedom Summer." *American Journal of Sociology* 97:1211-1240.

——. 1989. "The Biographical Consequences of Activism." *American Sociological Review* 54: 744-60.

——. 1988a. *Freedom Summer*. New York: Oxford University Press.

——. 1988b. "Micromobilization Contexts and Recruitment to Activism." *International Social Movement Research* 1: 125-54.

———. 1986. "Recruitment to High Risk Activism. The Case of Freedom Summer." *American Journal of Sociology* 92: 64-90.

———. 1984. "Structural Versus Attitudinal Factors in Movement Recruitment." Paper presented at the meetings of the American Sociological Association, San Antonio.

———. 1983. "Tactical Innovation and the Pace of Insurgency." *American Sociological Review* 48:735-54.

———. 1982. *Political Process and the Development of Black Insurgency, 1930-1970.* Chicago, IL: University of Chicago Press.

———. 1980. "The generation of insurgency and the black movement." Paper presented at the annual meetings of the American Sociological Association, New York, August.

———. 1979. *Political process and the civil rights movement 1948-1962.* Ph.D. dissertation, Department of Sociology, State University of New York at Stony Brook.

McAdam Doug, John D. McCarthy, and Mayer N. Zald. 1988. "Social Movements." Pp. 695-737 in *Handbook of Sociology,* edited by N. Smelser. Beverly Hills, CA: Sage.

McCain, James. 1978. Interview. Sumter, South Carolina. November 18.

McCall, G. J., and J. L. Simmons. 1978. *Identities and Interactions,* 2d ed. New York: Free Press.

McCarthy, John D. 1987. "Pro-Life and Pro-Choice Mobilization: Infrastructure Deficits and New Technologies." Pp. 49-66 in *Social Movements in an Organizational Society,* edited by Mayer N. Zald and John D. McCarthy. New Brunswick, N.J.: Transaction.

McCarthy, John D., David W. Britt, and Mark Wolfson. 1991. "The Institutional Channeling of Social Movements by the State in the United States." *Research in Social Movements, Conflict and Change* 14:45-76.

McCarthy, John D. and Mark Wolfson. 1988. "Exploring Sources of Rapid Social Movement Growth: The Role of Organizational Form, Consensus Support. and Elements of the American State." Paper presented at the Workshop on Frontiers in Social Movement Theory, June 1988, Ann Arbor, MI.

McCarthy, John D. and Mayer N. Zald. 1976. "Resource Mobilization and Social Movements: A Partial Theory." *American Journal of Sociology* 82:1212-41.

———. 1973. *The Trend of Social Movements in America: Professionalization and Resource Mobilization.* Morristown, NJ: General Learning Press.

McCollom, Rev. Matthew. 1979. Interview. Orangeburg, South Carolina. October 31.

McConnell, Grant. 1953. *The Decline of American Democracy.* New York: Atheneum.

McCourt, Kathleen. 1977. *Working Class Women and Grass Roots Politics.* Bloomington: Indiana University Press.

McCrea, Frances B., and Gerald E. Markle. 1989. *Minutes to Midnight.* Newbury Park, Calif.: Sage.

McDaniel, Tim. 1991. *Autocracy, Modernization, and Revolution in Russia and Iran.* Princeton, NJ: Princeton University Press.

McFarland, Andrew S. 1984. *Common Cause.* Chatham, NJ: Chatham House.

McGee, Michael. 1976. "Meher Baba—The sociology of religious conversion." *Graduate Journal* 9:43-71.

McHugh, Peter. 1968. *Defining the Situation: the Organization of Meaning in Social Interaction.* Indianapolis: Bobbs-Merrill.

McKenzie, Richard B., and Gordon Tullock. 1978. *The New World of Economics.* Homewood, IL: Irwin.

McKenzie, W. M. 1981. "Citizen participation: What motivates it." *Australian Journal of Social Issues* 16:67-79.

McKissick, Floyd. 1978. Interview. Soul City, North Carolina. November 18 (Follow-up telephone interview November 2, 1979).

McLendon, Irmgard. 1963. "Pritchett plan succeeds." *Atlanta Journal and Constitution* (July 18):14.

McMillen, Neil R. 1971. *The Citizens' Council, Organized Resistance to the Second Reconstruction, 1954-1964.* Urbana: University of Illinois Press.

McPhail, Clark. 1971. "Civil Disorder Participation: A Critical Examination of Recent Research." *American Sociological Review* 36:1058-73.

McPhail, Clark and David Miller. 1973. "The assembling process: A theoretical and empirical examination." *American Sociological Review* 38:721-35.

McPherson, J. Miller and William G. Lockwood. 1980. "The longitudinal study of voluntary association memberships: a multivariate analysis." *Journal of Voluntary Action Research* 9:74-84.

McRae, Kenneth D. 1986. *Conflict and Compromise in Multilingual Societies: Belgium.* Waterloo, Ontario: Wilfrid Laurier University Press.

———. 1983. *Conflict and Compromise in Multilingual Societies: Switzerland.* Waterloo, Ontario: Wilfrid Laurier University Press.

———. 1974. "Consociationalism and the Canadian Political System." Pp. 238-61 in *Consociational Democracy: Political Accommodation in Segmented Societies,* edited by K.D. McRae. Toronto: McClelland and Stewart.

McWilliams, Carey. 1942. *Ill Fares the Land.* Boston: Little, Brown.

———. 1939. *Factories in the Fields.* Boston: Little, Brown.

Mead, George Herbert. 1938. *The Philosophy of the Act.* (C. Morris, ed.) Chicago: University of Chicago Press.

———. 1936. *Movements of Thought in the Nineteenth Century.* (M. Moore, ed.) Chicago: University of Chicago Press.

———. 1934. *Mind, Self and Society.* (C. Morris, ed.) Chicago: University of Chicago Press.

———. 1932. *The Philosophy of the Present.* (A. Murphy, ed.) La Salle, Ill.: Open Court.

Meier, August. 1965. "On the role of Martin Luther King." *New Politics* 4 (Winter):52-59.

Meier, August and Elliot Rudwick. 1976. *Along the Color Line.* University of Illinois Press.

———. 1973. *CORE: A Study in the Civil Rights Movement, 1942-1968.* New York: Oxford University Press.

———. 1966. *From Plantation to Ghetto.* New York: Hill and Wang.

Melson, Robert and Howard Wolpe. 1970. "Modernization and the Politics of Communalism: A Theoretical Perspective." *The American Political Science Review* 64:1112-30.

Melucci, Alberto. 1989. *Nomads of the Present: Social Movements and Individual Needs in Contemporary Society.* London: Hutchinson Radius.

———. 1988. "Getting Involved: Identity and Mobilization in Social Movements." In *From Structure to Action: Comparing Social Movement Research across Cultures,* edited by Bert Klandermans, Hanspeter Kriesi, and Sidney Tarrow, pp. 329-48. Vol. 1 of *International Social Movement Research*. Greenwich, Conn.: JAI Press.

———. 1985. "The Symbolic Challenge of Contemporary Movements." *Social Research* 52:789-816.

———. 1980. "The New Social Movements: A Theoretical Approach." *Social Science Information* 19:199-226.

Messinger, Sheldon L. 1955. "Organizational transformation: a case study of a declining social movement." *American Sociological Review* 20:3-10.

Meyer, David S. 1993a. "Institutionalizing dissent: The United States structure of political opportunity and the end of the nuclear freeze movement." Sociological Forum 8:152-179.

———. 1993b. "Peace protest and policy: Explaining the rise and decline of antinuclear movements in postwar America." *Policy Studies Journal* 21:35-51.

———. 1993c. "Protest cycles and political process." *Political Research Quarterly* 46:451-479.

———. 1992. "Clashing laws: Civil disobedience and protest movements." Presented at the annual meeting of the American Political Science Association. Chicago.

———. 1991. "Peace movements and United States national security policy." *Peace and Change* 16:131-61.

—. *A Winter of Discontent: The Nuclear Freeze and American Politics*. New York: Praeger.

Meyer, David S., and Sam Marullo. 1992. "Grassroots mobilization and international change." *Research in Social Movements* 14:99-140.

Michels, Robert [1915] 1962. *Political Parties*. New York: Collier.

———. 1949. *Political Parties: A Sociological Study of the Oligarchical Tendencies of Modern Democracy*. Glencoe, IL: Free Press.

Migdal, Joel. 1988. *Strong Societies and Weak States*. Princeton, NJ: Princeton University Press.

Milani, Mohsen. 1988. *The Making of Iran's Islamic Revolution: From Monarchy to Islamic Republic*. Boulder, CO: Westview Press.

Millar, James, ed. 1987. *Politics, Work, and Daily Life in the Soviet Union*. Cambridge, England: Cambridge University Press.

Miller, Abraham H., Louis Bolce, and Mark R. Hallgan. 1976. "The new urban blacks." *Ethnicity* 3:338-67.

Miller, Barbara. 1981. "Women and revolutions: The brigadas femininas and the Mexican Cristero rebellion, 1926-29." In Sandra F. McGee (ed.), *Women and Politics in Twentieth Century Latin America*: 57-66. Wiliamsburg, VA: Studies in Third World Societies.

Miller, David L. 1985. *Introduction to Collective Behavior*. Belmont, CA: Wadsworth.

Miller, Francesca. 1991. *Latin American Women and the Search for Social Justice*. Hanover, NH: University Press of New England.

Miller, James. 1987. *Democracy Is in the Streets*. New York: Simon and Schuster.

Miller, Steven E. 1985. "The viability of nuclear arms control: U.S. domestic and bilateral factors." *Bulletin of Peace Proposals* 16:519-539.

Miller, William R. 1968. *Martin Luther King, Jr.: His Life, Martyrdom and Meaning for the World*. New York: Avon.

Mills, C. Wright. 1940. "Situated Actions and Vocabularies of Motive." *American Sociological Review* 5:404-13.

Ministerio de Relaciones Exteriores. 1968. *The Progress in Chile, 1965-1968*. Santiago: Ministerio de Relaciones Exteriores.

Mirfakhraei, Hooshmand. 1984. *The Imperial Iranian Armed Forces and the Revolution of 1978-1979*. Ph.D. dissertation. Department of Political Science, State University of New York. Buffalo, NY.

Misl-i Barf Âb Khwâhîm Shud: Muzâkirât-i Shûrâ-yi Farmândihân-i Artish (Dey-Bahman 1357) (We Will Melt Like Snow: Conversations of the Council of the Army Commanders [January 1979]). 1987. 3d printing. Tehran, Iran: Nashr-i Ney.

Mitchell, Robert C. 1979. "National Environmental Lobbies and the Apparent Illogic of Collective Action." Pp. 87-136 in *Collective Decision Making: Applications from Public Choice Theory*, edited by Clifford S. Russell. Johns Hopkins University Press.

Mizruchi, Ephraim H. 1983. *Regulating Society*. New York: Free Press.

Moaddel, Mansour. 1993. *Class, Politics, and Ideology in the Iranian Revolution*. New York: Columbia University Press.

Moe, Terry M. 1980. *The Organization of Interests*. Chicago: University of Chicago Press.

Moinat, Sheryl, W. Raine, S. Burbeck and K. Davison. 1972. "Black ghetto residents as rioters." *Journal of Social Issues* 28:45-62.

Molina, Natacha. 1990 "El estado y las mujeres: Una relacion dificil." *Transiciones: Mujeres en Los Procesos Democraticos*. Santiago: ISIS international, Ediciones de las Mujeres, No. 13.

Molotch, Harvey. 1970. "Oil in Santa Barbara and power in America." *Sociological Inquiry* 40:131-44.

Molyneux, Maxine. 1985. "Mobilization without emancipation? Women's interests, state and revolution in Nicaragua." *Feminist Studies* 11:227-254.

Moore, Barrington. 1978. *Injustice: The Social Bases of Obedience and Revolt*. White Plains, NY: Sharpe.

Moore, Douglas. 1978. Interview. Washington, D.C. November 1.

———. 1960. *Journal and Guide*. Vol. LX, March 5, 1960.

Morin, Edgar, Claude Lefort, and Jean-Marc Coudray. 1968. *La Brèche: Premières réflexions sur les événements*. Paris: Fayard.

Morris, Aldon. Forthcoming. *Origins of the Civil Rights Movement*. New York: Free Press.

———. 1992. "Political consciousness and collective action." *In Frontiers In Social Movement Theory*, eds. Aldon D. Morris and Carol McClurg Mueller, 351-373. New Haven, Conn.: Yale University Press.

———. 1984. *The Origins to the Civil Rights Movement*. New York: Free Press.

———. 1981. "Black Southern Student Sit-In Movements: An Analysis of Internal Organization." *American Sociological Review* 45:744-67.

———. 1980. *The origins of the civil rights movement: An indigenous perspective*. Ph.D. dissertation, Department of Sociology, State University of New York at Stony Brook.

Morris, Aldon D. and Carol McClurg Mueller, eds. 1992. *Frontiers in Social Movement Theory*. New Haven, CT: Yale University Press.

Morris, J.H. and R.M. Steers. 1980. "Structural Influences on Organizational Commitment." *Journal of Vocational Behavior* 17:50-7.

Morris, Roger. 1983. *The Devil's Butcher Shop: The New Mexico Prison Uprising.* New York: Franklin Watts.

Moshiri, Farrokh. 1991. "Iran: Islamic Revolution Against Westernization." Pp. 116-35 in *Revolutions of the Late Twentieth Century,* edited by J. A. Goldstone, T. R. Gurr, and F. Moshiri. Boulder, CO: Westview Press.

Moss, Bernard. 1976. *The Origins of the French Labor Movement: The Socialism of Skilled Workers.* Berkeley: University of California Press.

Mottl, Tahi L. 1980. "The analysis of countermovements." *Social Problems* 27:620-635.

Mueller, Carol McClurg. 1992. *Building social movement theory.* In Frontiers of Social Movement Theory, eds. Aldon Morris and Carol McClurg Mueller, 3-25. New Haven: Yale.

———. 1987a. "Collective Consciousness, Identity Transformation, and the Rise of Women in Public Office in the United States." In *The Women's Movements of the United States and Western Europe,* edited by Mary Fainsod Katzenstein and Carol McClurg Mueller, pp. 89-108. Philadelphia: Temple University Press.

———. 1987b. "The Life Cycle of Equal Rights Feminism: Resource Mobilization, Political Process, and Dramaturgical Explanations." Paper presented at the 1987 Annual Meetings of the American Sociological Association, Chicago.

Mueller, Edward N. 1980. "The Psychology of Political Protest and Violence." In *Handbook of Political Conflict,* edited by Ted Robert Gurr. New York: Free Press.

Mueller, Edward N. and Karl-Dieter Opp. 1986. "Rational Choice and Rebellious Collective Action." *American Political Science Review* 80: 471-564.

Mulhak, Renate. 1983. "Der Instandbesetzungskonflikt in Berlin" (The Squatting Conflict in Berlin). Pp. 205-52 in *Großstadt und neue soziale Bewegungen* (Large Cities and New Social Movements), edited by P. Grottian and W. Nelles. Basel, Switzerland: Birkhäuser.

Muller, Edward N. 1985. "Income Inequality, Regime Repressiveness, and Political Violence." *American Sociological Review* 50:47-61.

———. 1980. "The Psychology of Political Protest and Violence." in Ted Robert Gurr (ed.) *Handbook of Political Conflict.* New York: Free Press.

———. 1979. *Aggressive Political Participation.* Princeton University Press.

Muller, Edward N., Henry A. Dietz, and Steven E. Finkel. 1991. "Discontent and the Expected Utility of Rebellion: The Case of Peru." *American Political Science Review* 85:1261-82.

Muller, Edward N., and Karl-Dieter Opp. 1986. "Rational Choice and Rebellious Collective Action." *American Political Science Review* 80:471-88.

Muller, Edward N., and Mitchell A. Seligson. 1987. "Inequality and Insurgency." *American Political Science Review* 81:425-51

Müller-Rommel, F. (ed.). 1989. *New Politics in Western Europe: The Rise and Success of Green Parties and Alternative Lists.* London: Westview Press.

———. 1985. "New social movements and smaller parties: A comparative perspective." *West European Politics* 8: 41-54.

Muñoz Dálboro, Adriana. 1987. Fuerza Feminista y Democracia. Santiago: VECTOR Centro de Estudios Económicos y Sociales.

Murata, Kiyoaki. 1969. *Japan's New Buddhism: An Objective Account of Soka Gakkai.* New York: John Weatherbill.

Murphy, G.G.S. and M.G. Mueller. 1967. "On Making Historical Techniques More Specific: 'Real Types' Constructed With a Computer." *History and Theory* 6:14-32.

Murray, Florence. 1947. *The Negro Handbook, 1946-1947.* New York: Current Books, A. A. Wyn, Publisher.

———, ed. 1942. *The Negro Handbook.* New York: Wendell Malliet.

Muse, Benjamin. 1968. *The American Negro Revolution: From Nonviolence to Black Power.* Bloomington: Indiana University Press.

Myles, John. 1984. *Old Age in the Welfare State.* Boston: Little Brown.

Myrdal, Gunnar. 1944. *An American Dilemma.* New York: Harper & Row.

Nagel, Joane. 1984. "The Ethnic Revolution: The Emergence of Ethnic Nationalism in Modern States." *Sociology and Social Research* 68:417-34.

Nagel, Joane and Susan Olzak. 1982. "Ethnic Mobilization in New and Old States: An Extension of the Competition Model." *Social Problems* 30:127-43.

Nall, J. O. *The Tobacco Night Riders of Kentucky and Tennessee, 1905-1909.* Louisville, Ky.: Standard Press, 1942.

Nanetti, Raffaella Y. 1980. "From the top down: government promoted citizen participation." *Journal of Voluntary Action Research* 9:149-64.

Naraghi, Ehsan. 1994. *From Palace to Prison: Inside the Iranian Revolution.* Translated by N. Mobasser. Chicago, IL: Ivan R. Dee.

NARAL of Illinois papers. Manuscripts Department, University of Illinois, Chicago, library.

Narrative of the Late Riotous Proceedings against the Liberty of the Press, in Cincinnati. 1936. Cincinnati: Ohio Anti-Slavery Society.

Nash, June. 1990. "Latin American women in the world capitalist crisis," *Gender & Society* 4:354-369.

Nash, June and Helen I. Safa, eds. 1986. *Women and Change in Latin America.* South Hadley, MA: Bergin and Garvey.

National Advisory Commission on Civil Disorders. 1968. Report of the National Advisory Commission on Civil Disorders. New York: Bantam Books.

National Association for the Advancement of Colored People. 1930–70. *Annual Report of the National Association of Colored People.* New York: NAACP.

National Commission on Neighborhoods. 1979. People Building Neighborhoods. Final Report. Case Study Appendix. Superintendent of Documents stock no. 052-003-00616-2.

National Conference of Catholic Bishops. 1983. *The Challenge of Peace.* Washington, D.C.: U.S. Catholic Conference.

National Industrial Conference Board. 1936. *The Townsend Scheme.* New York: National Industrial Conference Board.

National Security Archive. 1989. *Iran: The Making of U.S. Policy, 1977-1980.* Microfiche Collection, Index, and Guide. Alexandria, VA: Chadwyck-Healey.

Neal, Arthur G., and Melvin Seeman. 1964. "Organizations and Powerlessness: A Test of the Mediation Hypothesis." *American Sociological Review* 29:216-26.

Nerlove, Marc and S. James Press. 1973. Univariate and Multivariate Log-linear and Logistic Models. Rand Report R-1300-EDA/NIH (December), Santa Monica, California.

Nerone, John. 1989. *The Culture of the Press in the Early Republic: Cincinnati, 1793-1848.* New York: Garland.

New Mexican. 1985 "Memories are 'tattooed' on minds of guards held hostage." February 3. Section E, p. 4.

New York Times. 1955-1971. *The New York Times Index.* New York: New York Times.

——. 1945-1974. *The New York Times Index.* New York: New York Times.

New South. 1963. "Civil disobedience and the law." 18 (October-November):24-28.

Nie, Norman, C., Hadlai Hull, Jean J. Jenkins, Karin Steinbrenner, and Dale H. Brent. 1975. *Statistical Package for the Social Sciences,* 2nd ed. New York: McGraw-Hill.

Nielsen, François. 1986. "Structural Conduciveness and Ethnic Mobilization: The Flemish Movement in Belgium." Pp. 173-98 in *Competitive Ethnic Relations*, edited by S. Olzak and J. Nagel. Orlando, Florida: Academic Press.

Nishikawa, S. 1986. "Grain Consumption: The Case of Choshu." In *Japan in Transition: From Tokugawa to Meiji,* edited by M.B. Jansen and G. Rozman, 421-466. Princeton, N.J.: Princeton University Press.

——. 1980. "The Flemish Movement in Belgium after World War II: A Dynamic Analysis." *American Sociological Review* 45:76-94.

Nizam al-Mulk. 1960. *The Book of Government.* London, England: Routledge and Kegan Paul.

Nye, Russel B. 1963. *Fettered Freedom: Civil liberties and the Slavery Question, 1830-1860.* Lansing: Michigan State University Press.

O'Brien, David J. 1975. *Neighborhood organization and Interest-Group Processes.* Princeton: Princeton University Press.

——. 1974. "Public goods dilemma and apathy of poor toward neighborhood organization." *Social Service Review* 48:229-44.

O'Donnell, Guillermo, Philippe C. Schmitter, and Laurence Whitehead. 1988. *Transitions From Authoritarian Rule.* Baltimore, MD: Johns Hopkins University Press.

OASS (Ohio Anti-Slavery Society). 1843. *Eighth Annual Report.* Cincinnati.

——. 1842. *Seventh Annual Report.* Cincinnati.

——. 1841. *Sixth Annual Report.* Cincinnati.

——. 1837. *Second Annual Report.* Cincinnati.

——. 1836. *First Annual Report.* New York: Beaumont & Wallack.

Obear, Frederick W. 1970. "Student activism in the sixties." Pp. 11-26 in Julian Foster and Durward Long (eds.), *Protest: Student Activism in America 1970.* New York: William Morrow.

Oberschall, Anthony R. 1994. "Rational Choice in Collective Protests." *Rationalization and Society* 6:79-100.

——. 1980. "Loosely Structured Collective Conflicts. A Theory and an Application." Pp. 45-88 in *Research in Social Movements, Conflict and Change,* Vol. 3. Edited by Louis Kreisberg. Greenwich, CT: JAI Press.

——. 1979. "Protracted Conflict." Pp. 45-70 in *The Dynamics of Social Movements: Resource Mobilization, Social Control, and Tactics,* edited by M. N. Zald and J. D. McCarthy. Cambridge, MA: Winthrop Publishers.

——. 1978a. "The Decline of the 1960s Social Movements." Pp. 257-89 in *Research in Social Movements, Conflicts and Change,* vol. 1, edited by L. Kriesberg. Greenwich, CT: JAI.

——. 1978b. "Theories of social conflict." Pp. 291-315 in Ralph Turner, James Coleman, and Renee C. Fox (eds.), *Annual Review of Sociology.* Palo Alto: Annual Review.

Oberschall, Anthony. 1973. *Social Conflict and Social Movements.* Englewood Cliffs, N.J.: Prentice-Hall.

Odland, John. 1988. *Spatial Autocorrelation.* Newbury Park, CA: Sage Publications.

Oegema, Dirk. 1991. "The Dutch Peace Movement, 1977 to 1987." Pp. 93-142 in *International Social Movement Research.* Vol. 3: *Peace Movements in Western Europe and the United States,* edited by B. Klandermans. Greenwich, CT: JAI.

Oegema, Dirk and Bert Klandermans. 1992. "The Erosion of Support: Perceived Political Changes and Participation in the Peace Movement in the Netherlands." Paper presented the First European Conference on Social Movements, 29 Oct.-1 Nov., Berlin, Germany.

Offe, Claus. 1985. "New Social Movements: Challenging the Boundaries of Institutional Politics." *Social Research* 59:817-68.

Office of the Attorney General of the State of New Mexico (OAGSNM). 1980. Report of the Attorney General on the February 2 and 3, 1980 Riot at the Penitentiary of New Mexico. Santa Fe: Office of the Attorney General of the State of New Mexico.

Oficina de Planificación Nacional. 1981. Programa Socio-Economico 1981-1989. Santiago: Ministerio del Interior.

Ofshe, R. 1980. "The social development of the Synanon cult." *Sociological Analysis* 41 (2): 109-27.

Oliver, Pamela. 1989. "Bringing the crowd back in: The nonorganizational elements of social movements." *Research in Social Movements* 11:1-30.

——. 1985. "Bringing the Crowd Back In: The Non-organizational Elements of Social Movements." Paper presented at the meetings of the American Sociological Association at Washington, D.C.

——. 1984. "'If You Don't Do It, Nobody Else Will': Active and Token Contributions to Local Collective Action." *American Sociological Review* 49:601-10.

——. 1983. "The Mobilization of Paid and Volunteer Activists in the Neighborhood Movement." Pp. 133-70 in *Research in Social Movements, Conflict and Change.* Vol. 5. Greenwich, CT: JAI Press.

——. 1980a. "Rewards and punishments as selective incentives for collective action: theoretical investigations." *American Journal of Sociology* 85:1356-75.

——. 1980b. "Summary of data collected at 1979 convention of National Association of Neighborhoods." Unpublished manuscript, Department of Sociology, University of Wisconsin.

Oliver, Pamela E. and Gerald Marwell. 1992. "Mobilizing Technologies for Collective Action." Pp. 251-73 in *Frontiers in Social Movement Theory,* edited by Aldon Morris and Carol McClurg Mueller. New Haven, CT: Yale University Press.

Oliver, Pamela E. and Gerald Marwell. 1988. "The Paradox of Group Size in Collective Action: A Theory of the Critical Mass. II." *American Sociological Review* 53:1-8.

Oliver, Pamela, Gerald Marwell and Ruy Teixeira. 1985. "A Theory of the Critical Mass, I: Interdependence, Group Heterogeneity, and the Production of Collective Action." *American Journal of Sociology* 91:522-556.

Olson, Mancur. 1979. Published letter. Pp. 149-50 in Louis Kriesberg (ed.), *Research in Social Movements, Conflicts and Change* Vol. 2. Greenwich, CT: JAI Press.

———. [1965] 1968. *The Logic of Collective Action.* New York: Schocken.

Olzak, Susan. 1992. *The Dynamics of Ethnic Competition and Conflict.* Stanford, CA: Stanford University Press.

———. 1989a. Analysis of events in the study of collective action, *Annual Review of Sociology* 15: 119-41.

———. 1989b. "Labour Unrest, Immigration, and Ethnic Conflict in Urban America, 1880-1914." *American Journal of Sociology* 94:1303-33.

———. 1986. "A Competition Model of Ethnic Collective Action in American Cities, 1877-1889." Pp. 17-46 in *Competitive Ethnic Relations*, edited by S. Olzak and J. Nagel. Orlando: Academic Press.

———. 1985. "Ethnicity and Theories of Ethnic Collective Behaviour." Pp. 65-85 in *Research in Social Movements, Conflicts and Change,* vol. 8, edited by Louis Kriesberg. Greenwich, CT: JAI Press.

———. 1982. "Ethnic Mobilization in Québec." *Ethnic and Racial Studies* 5:253-75.

Olzak, Susan and Joane Nagel. 1986. "Competitive Ethnic Relations: An Overview." Pp. 1-14 in *Competitive Ethnic Relations,* edited by S. Olzak and J. Nagel. Orlando: Academic Press.

Opp, Karl-Dieter. 1994. "Repression and Revolutionary Action: East Germany in 1989." *Rationality and Society* 6:101-38.

———. 1989a. *The Rationality of Political Protest: A Comparative Analysis of Rational Choice Theory.* Boulder, Colo.: Westview.

———. 1989b. "Social Integration Into Voluntary Associations and Incentives for Legal and Illegal Protest." Pp. 345-63 in *International Social Movement Research.* Vol. 2: *Organizing for Change: Social Movement Organizations in Europe and the United States,* edited by B. Klandermans. Greenwich, CT: JAI.

———. 1988a. "Community Integration and Incentives for Political Protest." Pp. 83-101 in *From Structure to Action: Comparing Movement Participation Across Cultures,* edited by B. Klandermans, H. Kriesi, and S. Tarrow. Greenwich, CT: JAI.

———. 1988b. "Grievances and Participation in Social Movements." *American Sociological Review* 53:853-64.

———. 1986. "Soft Incentives and Collective Action Participation in the Anti-Nuclear Movement." *British Journal of Political Research* 16:87-112.

Opp, Karl-Dieter, Käte Burow-Auffarth, Peter Hartmann, Thomazine von Witzleben, Volker Pöhls, and Thomas Spitzley. 1984. *Soziale Probleme und Protestverhalten. Eine empirische Konfrontierung des Modells rationalen Verhaltens mit soziologischen Hypothesen am Beispiel von Atomkraftgegnern.* Westdeutscher Verlag.

Opp, Karl-Dieter, and Christiane Gern. 1993. "Dissident Groups, Personal Networks, and Spontaneous Cooperation: The East German Revolution of 1989." *American Sociological Review* 58:659-80.

Opp, Karl-Dieter, and Wolfgang Ruehl. 1990a. "Repression, Micromobilization, and Political Protest." *Social Forces* 69:521-47.

———b. *Der Tschernobyl-Effekt. Eine Untersuchung über die Ursachen Politischen Protests.* Westdeutscher Verlag.

Oppeln, S. von. 1989. *Die Linke im Kernenergiekonflikt: Deutschland und Frankreich im Vergleich.* Frankfurt: Campus.

Oppenheimer, Martin. 1989. *The Sit-in Movement of 1960.* Brooklyn, N.Y.: Carlson.

———. 1968. "The student movement as a response to alienation." *Journal of Human Relations* 16:1-16.

———. 1964. "The southern student movement: year 1." *Journal of Negro Education* 33:396-403.

———. 1963. The Genesis of the Southern Negro Student Movement (Sit-In Movement): A Study in Contemporary Negro Protest. Unpublished Ph.D. dissertation. University of Pennsylvania.

Orloff, Ann Shola. 1992. "Gender and social citizenship in the welfare state." Paper presented at Indiana University's Political Economy Workshop, Bloomington, IN.

Orloff, Ann Shola, and Theda Skocpol. 1984. "Why Not Equal Protection? Explaining the Politics of Public Social Spending in Britain, 1900-1911, and the United States, 1880s-1920." *American Sociological Review* 49:726-50.

Ortoleva, Peppino. 1988. *Saggio sui movimenti del 1968 in Europa e in America.* Rome: Editori Riuniti.

Orum, Anthony. 1972. Black Students in Protest: A Study of the Origins of the Black Student Movement. Washington, D.C.: American Sociological Association, Arnold M. and Caroline Rose Monograph Series.

Otto, Karl A. 1977. *Vom Ostermarsch zur APO. Geschichte der außerparlamentarischen.Opposition in der Bundesrepublik 1960-70* (From Easter March to APO: A History of the Extraparliamentary Opposition in the Federal Republic of Germany 1960-70). Frankfurt, Germany: Campus.

Overbeek, J. 1974. *History of Population Theories.* Rotterdam: Rotterdam University Press.

Pahlavi, Mohammad Reza. 1980. *Answer to History.* New York: Stein and Day.

Paige, Jeffrey M. 1971. "Political Orientation and Riot Participation." *American Sociological Review* 36:810-20.

Palmer, Bryan. 1990. *Descent into Discourse: The Reification of Language and the Writing of Social History.* Philadelphia: Temple University Press.

Park, Robert Ezra. 1950. *Race and Culture.* Glencoe, IL: The Free Press

Parks, Rosa. 1977 Interview with Rosa Parks. Pp. 31-33 in Howell Raines (ed.), *My Soul is Rested.* New York: Bantam.

Parkum, Kurt H. and Virginia Cohn Parkum. 1980. "Citizen participation in community planning and decision making." Pp. 153-67 in David Horton Smith, Jacqueline Macaulay and Associates (eds.), *Participation in Social and Political Activities.* San Francisco: Jossey-Bass.

Parris, Guichard, and Lester Brooks. 1971. *Blacks in the City: A History of the National Urban League.* Boston: Little, Brown.

Parsa, Misagh. 1989. *The Social Origins of the Iranian Revolution.* New Brunswick, NJ: Rutgers University Press.

Parsons, Anthony. 1984. *The Pride and the Fall: Iran, 1974-1979.* London, England: Jonathan Cape.

Parsons, Talcott. 1951. *The Social System*. New York: Free Press.

——. *The Structure of Social Action*. 2 vols. New York: Free Press.

Parsons, Talcott and Edward A. Shils. [1951] 1962. *Toward a General Theory of Action*. New York: Harper and Row.

Pateman, Carole. 1970. *Participation and Democratic Theory*. Cambridge: Cambridge University Press.

Patrick, Ted. 1976. *Let Our Children Go*. New York: Ballantine.

——. 1974. "Ideological support for the marginal middle class. Faith healing and glossolalia." Pp. 418-455 in T. I. Zaretsky and M. P. Leone (eds.), *Religious Movements in Contemporary America*. Princeton, N.J.: Princeton University Press.

Pattison, E.M. 1974. "Ideological support for the marginal middle class. Faith healing and glossolalia." Pp. 418-455 in T.I. Zaretsky and M.P. Leone (eds.), *Religious Movements in Contemporary America*. Princeton, N.J.: Princeton University Press.

Paulsen, Ronnelle D. 1991. "Education, Social Class, and Participation in Collective Action." *Sociology of Education 64* (2): 96-110.

——. *Class and Collective Action: Variation* in *the Participation of Voting Adults in Non-Institutionalized Politics*. PhD. dissertation. University of Arizona, Department of Sociology.

Pearce, Jone L. 1980. "Apathy or self interest? The volunteer's avoidance of leadership roles." *Journal of Voluntary Action Research* 9:85-94.

Peltason, J. W. 1961. *Fifty-Eight Lonely Men: Southern Federal Judges and School Desegregation*. Urbana: University of Illinois Press.

Perkins, Frances. 1946. *The Roosevelt I Knew*. New York: Harper & Row.

Perlmutter, Edward. 1988. "Intellectuals and urban protest: Extraparliamentary politics in Turin." Unpublished paper.

——. 1987. "Modeling the polity: Autoriduzione in Turin." Unpublished paper.

Perrow, Charles. 1979. "The Sixties Observed." Pp. 192-211 in Mayer N. Zald and John D. McCarthy (eds.), *The Dynamics of Social Movements: Resource Mobilization, Social Control, and Tactics*. Cambridge: Winthrop.

——. 1972. *The Radical Attack on Business*. New York: McGraw-Hill.

Peterson, Donald W. and Armand L. Mauss. 1973. "The cross and the commune: An interpretation of the Jesus people." Pp. 261-279 in C. Glock (ed.), *Religion in Sociological Perspective*. Belmont, Calif.: Wadsworth.

Peterson, Horace C. and Gilbert C. Fite. 1957. *Opponents of War, 1917-1918*. Madison: University of Wisconsin Press.

Petras, James and Maurice Zeitlin. 1967. "Miners and agrarian radicalism." *American Sociological Review* 32:578-86.

Pettigrew, Thomas F. 1971. *Racially Separate or Together?* New York: McGraw Hill.

Petty, R. E., and J. T. Cacioppo. 1981. *Attitudes and Attitude Change: The Social Judgement-Involvement Approach*. Dubuque, Iowa: W. C. Brown.

Phelan, Shane. 1989. *Identity Politics: Lesbian Feminism and the Limits of Community*. Philadelphia: Temple University Press.

Phillips, Anne. 1991. *Engendering Democracy*. University Park: Pennsylvania State University Press.

Phillips, W. M., Jr. 1975. "Educational policy, community participation, and race." *Journal of Negro Education* 44:257-67.

Pih, Richard W. 1969. "Negro Self-Improvement Efforts in Ante-Bellum Cincinnati, 1836-1850." *Ohio History* 78:179-87.

Pinard, Maurice. 1987. "When does Ethnic Competition Lead to Ethnic Conflict?" *Contemporary Sociology* 16:771-72.

——. 1983. "From deprivation to mobilization: I. the role of some internal motives reexamined." Presented at the Meetings of the American Sociological Association. September, 1983.

——. 1975. "La dualité des loyautés et les options constitutionnelles des Québécois francophones." Pp. 63-91 in *Le nationalisme québécois la croisée des chemins*, Centre québécois de relations internationales. Québec: Université Laval.

——. 1971. *The Rise of a Third Party: A Study in Crisis Politics*. Englewood Cliffs, N.J.: Prentice-Hall.

Pinard, Maurice and Richard Hamilton. 1989. "Intellectuals and the Leadership of Social Movements: Some Comparative Perspectives." Pp. 73-107 in *Research in Social Movements. Conflicts and Change*, vol, 11, edited by Louis Kriesberg. Greenwich, CT: JAI Press.

——. 1988. "Intellectuals and the Leadership of Social Movements: Some Comparative Perspectives." *McGill Working Papers on Social Behavior*.

——. 1986. "Motivational Dimensions in the Québec Independence Movement: A Test of a New Model." Pp. 225-80 in *Research in Social Movements, Conflict and Change*, vol. 9, edited by Louis Kriesberg. Greenwich, CT: JAI Press.

——. 1981. "Le reférendum québécois." *Policy Options* 2(No. 4):39-44.

——. 1978. "The Parti Québécois Comes to Power. An Analysis of the 1976 Québec Election." *Canadian Journal of Political Science* 11:739-75.

——. 1977. "The Independence Issue and the Polarization of the Electorate: The 1973 Québec Election." *Canadian Journal of Political Science* 10: 215-59.

Pishtâzân-i Shahâdat dar Inqilâb-i Sivvum (The Front Ranks of Martyrdom in the Third Revolution). 1981. Qum, Iran: Daftar-i Intishârât-i Islâmî.

Piven, Frances Fox and Richard A. Cloward. 1979. *Poor People's Movements: Why They Succeed, How They Fail*. New York: Vintage.

——. 1978. "Social movements and societal conditions: A response to Roach and Roach." *Social Problems* 26(2):172-178.

——. 1971. *Regulating the Poor: The Functions of Public Welfare*. New York: Pantheon.

Pizzorno, Allesandro. 1978. "Political Exchange and Collective Identity in Industrial Conflict." Pp. 277-98 in *The Resurgence of Class Conflict in Western Europe since 1968*, Vol. II. Edited by Colin Crouch and Allesandro Pizzorno. London: Macmillan.

Ploski, Harry A., and Warren Marr II, eds. 1976. *The Afro American*. New York: The Bellwether Company.

Plummer, Ken. 1992. "Speaking Its name: Inventing lesbian and gay studies." In *Modern Homosexualities: Fragments of Lesbian and Gay Experience,* ed. Ken Plummer, 3-25. New York: Routledge.

Porter, Bruce and Marvin Dunn. 1984. *The Miami Riot of 1980: Crossing the Bounds.* Lexington, MA: D.C. Heath.

Portes, Alejandro. 1984. "The Rise of Ethnicity: Determinants of Ethnic Perceptions among Cuban Exiles in Miami." *American Sociological Review* 49:383-97.

——. 1971a. "On the logic of Post-Factum Explanations: The Hypothesis of Lower-Class Frustration as the Cause of Leftist Radicalism." *Social Forces* 50:26-44.

——. 1971b. "Political Primitivism, Differential Socialization, and Lower-Class Leftist Radicalism." *American Sociological Review* 36:820-35.

Powledge, Fred. 1967. *Black Power, White Resistance: Notes on the New Civil War.* Cleveland: World.

Praag Jr., P. van, and K. Brants. 1980. "Depillarization and Factionalism: The case of the Dutch labour party." Paper presented at the ECPR workshop on Factionalism and the Political Parties in Western Europe, Florence, March 1980.

Pratt, Henry J. 1972. *The Liberalization of American Protestantism.* Detroit, Mi.: Wayne State University Press.

Pred, Allan R. 1973. *Urban Growth and the Circulation of Information: The United States System of Cities, 1790-1840.* Cambridge, Mass.: Harvard University Press.

Price, Daniel O. 1969. *Changing Characteristics of the Negro Population.* Washington, D.C.: U.S. Government Printing Office.

Prins, Peter, 1990. "Actie Potentiaal: Ra, Ra?!" (Action Potential: Rah-Rah?!). Masters thesis, Department of Social Psychology, Free University, Amsterdam, the Netherlands.

Pritchett, Laurie. 1977. "Interview with Laurie Pritchett." Pp. 398-404 in Howell Raines (ed.), *My Soul is Rested.* New York: Bantam.

Project on Social Protest and Policy Innovation. 1985. Project Manual. Ithaca, NY: Cornell University.

Putnam, Jackson K. 1970. *Old-Age Politics in California: From Richardson to Reagan.* Stanford, Calif.: Stanford University Press.

Quadagno, Jill S. 1988. *The Transformation of Old-Age Security: Class in Politics in the American Welfare State.* Chicago: University of Chicago Press.

——. 1987. "Theories of the Welfare State." *Annual Review of Sociology* 13:109-28.

Ragin, Charles C. 1987. *The Comparative Method.* Berkeley: University of California Press.

——. 1980. "Aggregation Gain and Loss in Electoral Research (A Response to Lutz's Comment)." *American Sociological Review* 45:1031-36.

——. 1979. "Ethnic Political Mobilization:The Welsh Case." *American Sociological Review* 44:619-35.

Ragin, Charles, and Kriss Drass. 1988. "Qualitative Comparative Analysis, 2.02." Software. Northwestern University, Department of Sociology.

Raines, Howell (ed.). 1977. *My Soul is Rested.* New York: Bantam.

Rambo, L. 1982. "Bibliography: Current research on religious conversion." *Religious Studies Review* 8: 146-59.

Ramirez, Bruno. 1978. *When Workers Fight: The Politics of Industrial Relations in the Progressive Era, 1898-1916.* Westport, CT: Greenwood.

Randolph, Homer. 1981. Interview. East St. Louis, Illinois.

Ransford, H. Edward. 1968. "Isolation, powerlessness and violence: a study of attitudes and participation in the Watts riot." *American Journal of Sociology* 73:581-91.

Rauber, Paul. 1986. "With Friends Like These. . ." *Mother Jones* 11:35

Rayback, Joseph G. 1958. *The National Association for the Advancement of Colored People: A Case Study in Pressure Groups.* New York: Exposition Press.

Rayback, Joseph G. 1966. *A History of American Labor.* New York: Free Press. St. James, Warren D.

Reed, Merl E. 1966. *New Orleans and the Railroad: The Struggle for Commercial Empire, 1830-1860.* Baton Rouge: Louisiana State University Press.

Reeves, Minou. 1986. *Behind the Peacock Throne.* London, England: Sidgwick and Jackson.

Regalia, Ida. 1979. "Delgati e consigli di fabbrica nelle ricerche degli anni Settanta," in *Annali della Fondazione Luigi Einaudi,* vol. 13. Turin: Fondazione Einaudi.

Regalia, Ida. 1985. *Eletti e abbandonati: Modelli e stili di rappresentanza in fabbrica.* Bologna: Il Mulino.

Reinarman, Craig. 1985. "Social Movements and Social Problems: 'Mothers Against Drunk Drivers,' Restrictive Alcohol Laws and Social Control in the 1980s." Paper presented at the Annual Meeting of the Society for the Study of Social Problems, Washington, DC, Aug. 23-26.

Reisman, David. 1964. "Two Generations." In *The Woman in America,* edited by Robert Jay Lifton, pp. 72-97. Boston: Beacon Press.

Remmer, Karen. 1991. *Military Rule in Latin America.* Boulder, CO: Westview Press.

Reskin, Barbara, and Pat Roos. 1990. *Job Queues, Gender Queues.* Philadelphia: Temple University Press.

Rich, Richard C. 1980a. "A political-economy approach to the study of neighborhood organizations." *American Journal of Political Science* 24:559-92.

——. 1980b. "The dynamics of leadership in neighborhood organizations." *Social Science Quarterly* 60:570-87.

Richards, Leonard L. 1970. *"Gentlemen of Property and Standing:" Anti-Abolition Mobs in Jacksonian America.* New York: Oxford University Press.

Richardson, J., ed. 1978. *Conversion Careers: In and Out of the New Religions.* Beverly Hills: Sage.

——. 1980. "Conversion careers." *Society* 17: 47-50.

Richardson, James T. and Mary Stewart. 1978. "Conversion process models and the Jesus movement." Pp. 24-42 in J. Richardson (ed.), *Conversion Careers.* Beverly Hills, Calif.: Sage.

Richardson, James T., Mary W. Stewart and Robert B. Simmonds. 1978. "Conversion to fundamentalism." *Society* 15:46-52.

Richardson, J., J. van der Lans and F. Derks. 1986. "Leaving and labelling: Voluntary and coerced disaffiliation from religious social movements." Pp. 97-126 in L. Kriesberg (Ed.), *Research in Social Movements, Conflict and Change.* Greenwich: JAI Press.

Rieder, Jonathan. 1984. "The social organization of vengeance." Pp. 131-62 in Donald Black (ed.), *Toward a General Theory of Social Control. Volume 1: Fundamentals.* New York: Academic Press.

Robbins, T. 1988. *Cults, Converts, and Charisma.* Newbury Park, CA: Sage.

——. 1981. "Church, state, cult." *Sociological Analysis* 42: 209-26.

Robbins, Thomas and Dick Anthony. 1979. "The sociology of contemporary religious movements." Pp. 75-89 in Alex Inkeles (ed.), *Annual Review of Sociology,* Vol. 5. Palo Alto, Calif.: Annual Reviews.

Roberts, Dennis. 1965. Diary kept while working as legal assistant to C. B. King, civil rights attorney, in Albany, Georgia. 1963-1965. In files of Meiklejohn Civil Liberties Institute, Berkeley, California.

Roche, John P. and Stephen Sachs. 1965. "The Bureaucrat and the Enthusiast: An Exploration of the Leadership of Social Movements." *Western Political Quarterly* 8:248-61.

Rochford, E. B., Jr. Forthcoming. "Hare Krishna." *The New Catholic Encyclopedia,* vol. 18.

——. 1988. "The politics of member validation: Taking findings back to Hare Krishna." Presented at the annual meetings of the Society for the Scientific Study of Religion, Chicago.

——. 1987a. "Shifting public definitions of Hare Krishna." Pp. 258-60 in R. Turner and L. Killian, *Collective Behavior,* Third Edition. Englewood Cliffs, NJ: Prentice-Hall.

——. 1987b. "Dialectical processes in the development of Hare Krishna: Tension, public definition, and strategy." Pp. 109-22 in D. Bromley and P. Hammond (Eds.), *The Future of New Religious Movements.* Macon, GA: Mercer University Press.

——. 1985. *Hare Krishna in America.* New Brunswick, NJ: Rutgers University Press.

——. 1982. "Recruitment Strategies, Ideology, and Organization in the Hare Krishna Movement." *Social Problems* 29:399-410.

Rochon, Thomas R. 1992. "Three faces of the nuclear freeze." Claremont Graduate School.

——. "The West European Peace Movement and the Theory of New Social Movements." Pp. 105-21 in *Challenging the Political Order: New Social and Political Movements in Western Democracies,* edited by R. J. Dalton and M. Kuechler. Cambridge, England: Polity Press.

——. 1988. *Mobilizing for Peace: The Antinuclear Movements in Western Europe.* Princeton, NJ: Princeton University Press.

Roeser, Thomas F. 1983. "The Pro-life Movement's Holy Terror." *Chicago Reader* 12(44): 1, 14-24.

Rogers, Everett M. 1962. Diffusion of Innovations. New York: The Free Press of Glencoe.

Rogers, Everett M. and F. Floyd Shoemaker. 1971. *Communication of Innovations.* New York: Free Press.

Rogin, Michael Paul. 1987. *Ronald Reagan, the Movie: And Other Episodes in Political Demonology.* Berkeley and Los Angeles: University of California Press.

Rokeach, Milton. 1973. *The Nature of Human Values,* New York: Free Press.

——. 1968. *Beliefs, Attitudes, and Values.* San Francisco: Jossey-Bass.

Rose, Arnold. 1967. *The Power Structure.* New York: Oxford University Press.

Rose, Richard. 1971. *Governing Without Consensus: An Irish Perspective.* Boston: Beacon Press.

Rosenberg, Morris. 1979. *Conceiving the Self.* New York: Basic.

Rosenthal, Naomi, Meryl Fingrutd, Michele Ethier, Roberta Karant, and David McDonald. 1985. "Social Movements and Network Analysis: A Case Study of Nineteenth-Century Women's Reform in New York State." *American Journal of Sociology* 90:1022-55.

Rosenthal, Naomi and Michael Schwartz. Forthcoming. "Spontaneity and Democracy in Social Protest." In *Organizing for Change: Social Movement Organizations in Europe and the U.S. Vol. 5.* Greenwich, CT: JAI Press.

Ross, A. 1975-1976. Private notes and personal communications.

Ross, J. 1972. "Toward a reconstruction of voluntary association theory." *American Sociological Review* 22:315-26.

Rossi, Alice. 1967. "Equality between the Sexes: An Immodest Proposal." In *The Woman in America,* edited by Robert Jay Lifton, pp. 98-143. Boston: Beacon Press.

Roth, Guenther. 1971. "Sociological Typology and Historical Explanation." Pp. 109-28 in *Scholarship and Partisanship,* edited by Reinhard Bendix and Guenther Roth. Berkeley: University of California Press.

Roth, Julius A. 1962. "Comments on secret observation." *Social Problems* 9:283-84.

Rothschild-Whitt, Joyce. 1979. "The Collectivist Organization: An Alternative to Rational-Bureaucratic Models." *American Sociological Review* 44:509-27.

Rougerie, Jacques. 1971. *Paris Libre 1871* (Free Paris 1871). Paris: Editions du Seuil.

Rowan, Richard W. *Secret Agents against America.* New York: Doubleday, Doran, 1939.

Rucht, Dieter. 1992. "The impact of national contexts on social movement structure: A cross movement and cross-national comparison." Paper presented at the Conference on European/American Perspectives on the Dynamics of Social Movements, Washington DC.

——. "The Strategies and Action Repertoires of New Movements." Pp. 156-175 in *Challenging the Political Order: New Social and Political Movements in Western Democracies,* edited by R. J. Dalton and M. Kueehler. Cambridge, England: Polity Press.

——. 1989. Vorschläge zur Konzeptualisierung von Kontextstrukturen sozialer Bewegungen, Beitrag zum Workshop Vergleichende Analysen sozialer Bewegungen, WZB-Berlin, 21-22. Oktober 1989.

——, ed. 1984. *Flughafenprojekte als Politikum: Die Konflikte in Stuttgart, München und Frankfurt* (Airport Projects as a Political Issue: The Conflicts in Stuttgart, Munich, and Frankfurt). Frankfurt, Germany: Campus.

Rucht, Dieter and Donatella Della Porta. Forthcoming. "Left-Libertarian Movements in Context: A Comparison of Italy and West Germany, 1965-1990." In *The Politics of Social Protest: Comparative Perspectives on States and Social Movements,* edited by J. C. Jenkins and B. Klandermans. Minneapolis, MN: University of Minnesota Press.

Rucht, Dieter, and Doug McAdam. 1992. "Cross-national diffusion of frames and strategies." Paper presented at the 87th Annual Meeting of the American Sociological Association, August 20-24, Pittsburgh.

Rudé, George. 1964. *The Crowd in History: A Study of Popular Disturbances in France and England, 1730-1848.* New York: Wiley.

Rule, James and Charles Tilly. 1972. "1830 and the Unnatural History of Revolution." *Journal of Social Issues* 28:49-76.

Rummel, R.J. 1976. *Applied Factor Analysis*. Evanston, IL: Northwestern University Press.

Rupp, Leila J. 1985. "The Women's Community in the National Woman's Party, 1945 to the 1960's." *Signs* 10:715-40.

——. 1982. "The Survival of American Feminism." Pp. 33-65 in *Reshaping America*, edited by R.H. Bremner and G.W. Reichard. Columbus: Ohio State University Press.

Rupp, Leila J., and Verta Taylor. 1987. *Survival in the Doldrums: The American Women's Rights Movement, 1945 to the 1960s*. New York: Oxford University Press.

Russell, Diana, ed. 1989. *Exposing Nuclear Phallacies*. New York: Pergamon Press,

——. 1974. *Rebellion, Revolution, and Armed Force*. New York: Academic Press.

Rust, Paula. 1993. " 'Coming out' in the age of social constructionism: Sexual identity formation among lesbian and bisexual women." *Gender & Society* 7:50-77.

Ryan, Barbara. 1992. *Feminism and the Women's Movement*. New York: Routledge.

Sahlins, Marshall. 1991. "The Return of the Event, Again: With Reflections on the Beginnings of the Great Fijian War of 1843 to 1855 between the Kingdoms of Bau and Rewa." Pp. 37-100 in *Clio in Oceania: Toward a Historical Anthropology*, edited by Aletta Biersack. Washington, D.C.: Smithsonian.

——. 1985. *Islands of History*. Chicago: University of Chicago Press.

——. 1981. *Historical Metaphors and Mythical Realities: Structure in the Early History of the Sandwich Islands Kingdoms*. Ann Arbor: University of Michigan Press.

Saint-James, Fred. 1983. *Au Nom de Dieu Clément et Miséricordeux* (In the Name of God, Merciful and Compassionate). Paris, France: Mercure de France.

Sale, Kirkpatrick. 1973. *SDS*. New York: Vintage.

Salehi-Isfahani, Djavad. 1989. "The Political Economy of Credit Subsidy in Iran, 1973-1978." *International Journal of Middle East Studies* 21:359-79.

Salem, G. W. 1978. "Maintaining participation in community organizations." *Journal of Voluntary Action Research* 7:18-27.

Samuelson, P. A. 1954. "The pure theory of public expenditure." *Review of Economics and Statistics* 36:387-90.

Santa Cruz, Adriana. 1985. "Mujer." Editorial in Special Issue: *Mujer y Democracia*. Santiago: ILET.

Savage, W. Sherman. 1938. *The Controversy over the Distribution of Abolition Literature, 1830-1860*. Washington, D.C.: Association for the Study of Negro Life and History.

Sayre, Cynthia Woolever. 1980. "The Impact of Voluntary Association Involvement on Social-Psychological Attitudes." Paper presented at the annual meetings of the American Sociological Association, New York City, August.

Scharpf, F.W. 1984. "Economic and institutional constraints of full employment strategies: Sweden, Austria and West-Germany, 1973-82," pp. 257-90 in J. H. Goldthorpe (ed.), *Order and Conflict in Contemporary Capitalism: Studies in the Political Economy of West European Nations*. Oxford University Press.

Schelling, Thomas C. 1978. *Micromotives and Macrobehavior*. New York: Norton.

Schmid, Carol L. 1981. *Conflict and Consensus in Switzerland*. Berkeley: University of California Press.

Schneider, Beth E. 1991. "Put up and shut up: Workplace sexual assaults." *Gender & Society* 5:533-548.

——. 1988. "Invisible and Independent: Lesbians' experiences In the workplace." In *Women Working*, eds. A. Stromberg and S. Harkess, 273-296. Palo, Alto, Calif.: Mayfield Publishing Company.

——. 1986. "Coming out at work: Bridging the private/public gap." *Work and Occupations* 13: 463-487.

——. 1984. "Peril and promise: Lesbians' workplace participation." In *Women-Identified Women*, eds. Trudy Darty and Sandee Potter, 211-230. Palo Alto, Calif.: Mayfield Publishing Company.

Schoenberg, Sandra Perlman. 1980. "Some trends in the community participation of women in their neighborhoods." *Signs* 5:261-68.

Schoenberg, Sandra Perlman and Patricia Rosenbaum. 1979. "Prerequisites to participation by the poor in an urban neighborhood." Paper presented at annual meeting of American Sociological Association.

Schram, Sanford F. and J. Patrick Turbett. 1983. "Civil disorder and the welfare explosion." *American Sociological Review* 48:408-414.

Schutz, Alfred. [1932] 1967. *The Phenomenology of the Social World*. Evanston, IL: Northwestern University Press.

——. 1962. "On Multiple Realities." Pp. 207-59 in *Collected Papers*. Vol. 1. The Hague: Martinus Nijhoff.

Schwartz, Michael. 1976. *Radical Protest and Social Structure: The Southern Farmers' Alliance and Cotton Tenancy, 1880-1890*. Chicago: University of Chicago.

Schwartz, Michael and Shuva Paul. 1992. "Resource Mobilization Versus the Mobilization of People: Why Consensus Movements Cannot Be Instruments of Social Change." Pp. 205-24 in *Frontiers in Social Movement Theory*, edited by A. Morris and C. Mueller. New Haven, CT: Yale University Press.

Scott, James C. 1985. *Weapons of the Weak: Everyday Forms of Resistance*. New Haven: Yale University Press.

Scott, Marvin and Stanford M. Lyman. 1968 "Accounts." *American Sociological Review* 33:46-62.

Sears, David O., and John B. McConahay. 1973. *The Politics of Violence: The New Urban Blacks and the Watts Riot*. Boston: Houghton Mifflin.

See, Katherine O'Sullivan. 1986. *First World Nationalisms: Class and Ethnic Politics in Northern Ireland and Québec*. Chicago: University of Chicago Press.

Seeman, Melvin. 1975. "Alienation Studies." *Annual Review of Sociology* 1:91-123.

Seggar, John and Philip Kunz. 1972. "Conversion: Evaluation of a step-like process for problem-solving." *Review of Religious Research* 13:8-184.

Seidman, Steven. 1993. "Identity and politics in a 'postmortem' gay culture: Some historical and conceptual notes." In *Fear of a Queer Planet: Queer Politics and Social Theory*, ed. Michael Warner, 105-142. Minneapolis: University of Minnesota Press.

Serman, William. 1986. *La Commune de Paris (1871)* (The Commune of Paris [1871]). Paris: Fayard.

Serrill, Michael S., and Peter Katel. 1980. "New Mexico: the anatomy of a riot." *Corrections Magazine* 6(2):7-16, 20-24.

Sewell, William H., Jr. 1996. "Three Temporalities: Toward an Eventful Sociology." In *The Historic Turn in* the Human Sciences, edited by Terrence J. McDonald. Ann Arbor: University of Michigan Press. In press.

——. 1992. "A Theory of Structure: Duality, Agency, and Transformation." American Journal of Sociology 98:1-29.

——. 1980. Work and Revolution in France: The Language of Labor from the Old Regime to 1848. New York: Cambridge University Press.

Shaley, Michael 1983. "The Social Democratic Model and Beyond: Two Generations of Comparative Research on the Welfare State." Comparative Social Research 6:315-51.

Sharp, Elaine. 1978. "Citizen organizations in policing issues and crime prevention: incentives for participation." Journal of Voluntary Action Research 7:45-58.

Shefter, Martin. 1983. "Regional Receptivity to Reform: The Legacy of the Progressive Era." Political Science Quarterly 98:459-83.

Sherif, Muzafer, O.J. Harvey, B. Jack White, William R. Hood, Carolyn W. Sherif. 1988. The Robbers Cave Experiment: Intergroup Conflict and Cooperation. Middletown, Connecticut: Wesleyan University.

Sherrill, Kenneth. 1994. "Presentation of findings of committee on the status of lesbians and gays in the profession." Paper presented at the Annual Meeting of the American Political Science Association, September, New York City.

Shibutani, Tamotsu. 1970. "On the Personification of Adversaries." Pp. in 223-33 in Human Nature and Collective Behavior: Papers in Honor of Herbert Blumer, edited by Tamotsu Shibutani. Englewood Cliffs, NJ: Prentice-Hall.

——. 1961. Society and Personality. Englewood Cliffs, N.J.: Prentice-Hall.

Shinn, L. 1987a. The Dark Lord: Cult Images and the Hare Krishnas in America. Philadelphia: Westminster Press.

——. 1987b. "The future of an old man's vision: ISKCON in the twenty-first century." Pp. 123-40 in D. Bromley and P. Hammond (Eds.), The Future of New Religious Movements. Macon, GA: Mercer University Press.

Shorter, Edward, and Charles Tilly. 1974. Strikes in France. Cambridge, MA: Harvard University Press.

Shupe, Anson D., Roger Spielmann and Sam Stigall. 1978. "Deprogramming: The new exorcism." Pp. 145-160 in J. Richardson (ed.), Conversion Careers. Beverly Hills, Calif.: Sage.

Shuttlesworth, Rev. Fred. 1978. Interview. Cincinnati, Ohio. September 12.

——. 1977. Interview with Fred Shuttlesworth. Pp. 166-76 in Howell Raines (ed.), My Soul is Rested. New York: Bantam.

Sick, Gary. 1985. All Fall Down: America's Tragic Encounter With Iran. New York: Random House.

Sigmund, Paul E. 1984. "Chile: Free-market authoritarianism." In Robert Wesson (ed.), Politics, Policies, and Economic Development in Latin America: 1-13. Stanford, CA: Hoover Institution Press.

Silbey, Joel H. 1985. The Partisan Imperative: The Dynamics of American Politics before the Civil War. New York: Oxford University Press.

Sills, Davis L. 1957. The Volunteers. Glencoe, Ill.: Free Press.

Simmel, Georg. 1955. Conflict and the Web of Group Affiliations. New York: Free Press.

——. [1912] 1950. The Sociology of Georg Simmel. New York: Free Press.

Simmons, J. 1964. "On maintaining deviant belief systems." Social Problems XI: 250-56.

Simpson, John. 1988. Behind Iranian Lines. London, England: Robson Books.

Simpson, Richard L., and David R. Norsworthy. 1965. "The Changing Occupational Structure of the South." In John C. McKinney and Edgar T. Thompson, eds., The South in Continuity and Change. Durham, N.C.: Duke University Press, 198-224.

Sitton, Claude. 1963. "The 'movement' in Albany, Ga." The New York Times (July 11):24.

——. 1962. "When a southern Negro goes to court." The New York Times Magazine (January 7): 10ff.

Skidmore, Thomas and Peter H. Smith. 1989. Modern Latin America. New York: Oxford University Press.

Skocpol, Theda. 1982. "Rentier State and Shi'a Islam in the Iranian Revolution." Theory and Society 11:265-83.

——. 1979. States and Social Revolutions: A Comparative Analysis of France, Russia, and China. Cambridge: Cambridge University Press.

Skocpol, Theda, and Edwin Amenta. 1986. "States and Social Policies." Annual Review of Sociology 12:131-57.

Skolnick, Jerome H. 1969. The Politics of Protest. New York: Simon & Schuster.

Skonovd, L. N. 1983. "Leaving the cultic religious milieu." Pp. 91-103 in D. Bromley and J. Richardson (Eds.), The Brainwashing/ Deprogramming Controversy: Sociological, Psychological, Legal and Historical Perspectives. New York: Edwin Mellen.

——. 1981. Apostasy: The Process of Defection from Religious Totalism. Ph.D. dissertation, Ann Arbor, MI: University Microfilms International.

Smelser, Neil. 1962. Theory of Collective Behavior. New York: Free Press.

Smith, Charles V. and Lewis M. Killian. 1958. The Tallahassee Bus Protest. New York: Anti-Defamation League of B'nai B'rith.

Smith, Christian. 1991. The Emergence of Liberation Theology. Chicago: University of Chicago Press.

Smith, Constance and Anne Freedman. 1972. Voluntary Associations: Perspectives on the Literature. Cambridge, MA: Harvard University Press.

Smith, David Horton. 1981. "Altruism, volunteers, and volunteerism." Journal of Voluntary Action Research 10:21-36.

Smith, Michael G. 1969. "Some Developments in the Analytic Framework of Pluralism." Pp.415-58 in Pluralism in Africa. edited by L. Kuper and M. G. Smith. Berkeley: University of California Press.

Smith, Rev. Kelly Miller. 1978. Interview. Nashville, Tennessee. October 13.

Snow, David A. 1986. "Organization, Ideology and Mobilization: The Case of Nichiren Shoshu of America." In The Future of New Religious Movements, edited by David G. Bromley and Phillip E. Hammond. Macon, GA: Mercer University Press.

——. 1979. "A Dramaturgical Analysis of Movement Accommodation: Building Idiosyncrasy Credit as a Movement Mobilization Strategy." Symbolic Interaction 2:23-44.

——. 1976. The Nichiren Shoshu Buddhist Movement in America: A Sociological Examination of Its Value Ori-

entation, Recruitment Efforts, and Spread. Ann Arbor, Mich.: University Microfilms.

Snow, David A., and Robert D. Benford. 1992. "Master Frames and Cycles of Protest." Pp.133-55 in *Frontiers of Social Movement Theory,* edited by Aldon D. Morris and Carol McClurg Mueller. New Haven, Conn.: Yale University Press.

——. 1988. "Ideology, Frame Resonance and Participant Mobilization." In *From Structure to Action: Social Movement Participation across Cultures,* edited by Bert Klandermans, Hanspeter Kriesi, and Sidney Tarrow. Greenwich, Conn.: JAI.

Snow, David and Richard Machalek. 1984. "The sociology of conversion." Pp. 167-90 in R. Turner and J. Short (Eds.), *Annual Review of Sociology.* Palo Alto, CA: Annual Reviews Inc.

——. 1983. "The Convert as a Social Type." Pp. 259-89 in *Sociological Theory,* edited by Randall Collins. San Francisco: Jossey-Bass.

Snow, David A., and Susan Marshall. 1984. "Cultural Imperialism, Social Movements, and the Islamic Revival." Pp. 131-52 in *Social Movements, Conflicts, and Change.* V.7. Edited by Louis Kriesberg. Greenwich, CT: JAI Press.

Snow, David A. And Pamela Oliver. 1995. "Social Movements and Collective Behavior: Social Psychological Dimensions and Considerations." Pp. 571-599 in K. Cook, G. Fine, and J. House (eds.), *Sociological Perspectives on Social Psychology.* Boston: Allyn and Bacon.

Snow, David A. and Cynthia L. Phillips. 1980. "The Lofland-Stark conversion model: a critical reassessment." *Social Problems* 27:430-47.

Snow, David A., and E. Burke Rochford, Jr. 1983. "Structural Availability, the Alignment Process and Movement Recruitment." Paper presented at the annual meetings of the American Sociological Association, Detroit, August.

Snow, David A., E. Burke Rochford Jr., Steven K. Worden, and Robert D. Benford. 1986. "Frame Alignment Processes, Micromobilization, and Movement Participation." *American Sociological Review* 51: 464-81.

Snow, David A., Louis A. Zurcher, and Sheldon Ekland-Olson. 1980. "Social Networks and Social Movements: A Microstructural Approach to Differential Recruitment." *American Sociological Review* 45:787-801.

Snyder, David and William R. Kelly. 1979. "Strategies for investigating violence and social change: illustrations from analyses of racial disorders and implications for mobilization research." Pp. 212-37 in Mayer N. Zald and John D. McCarthy (eds.), *The Dynamics of Social Movements.* Cambridge, MA: Winthrop.

——. 1977. "Conflict intensity, media sensitivity and the validity of newspaper data." *American Sociological Review* 42:105-23.

Snyder, David and Charles Tilly. 1972. "Hardship and collective violence in France, 1830-1960." *American Sociological Review* 37:520-32.

Solo, Pam. 1988. *From Protest to Policy.* Cambridge, Mass.: Ballinger.

Sorin, Gerald. 1972. *Abolitionism: A New Perspective.* New York: Praeger.

Southern Regional Council. 1961. The Student Protest Movement: A Recapitulation. Atlanta: Southern Regional Council.

Southern Regional Council. 1960. "The student protest movement, winter 1960." *SRC-13,* April 1.

Southern Patriot. 1963. "Albany: an end and a beginning." (October): 1.

Spender, Dale. 1981. "The gatekeepers: A feminist critique of academic publishing." In *Doing Feminist Research,* ed. Helen Roberts, 186-202. London: Routledge & Kegan Paul.

Spengler, Joseph J. 1963. "Demographic and Economic Change in the South." In Allan P. Sindler, ed., *Change in the Contemporary South.* Durham, N.C.: Duke University Press, 26-63.

Spilerman, Seymour. 1976. "Structural characteristics of cities and the severity of racial disorders." *American Sociological Review* 41:771-93.

——. 1970. "The causes of racial disturbances: a comparison of alternative explanations." *American Sociological Review* 35:627-49.

Spira, Henry. 1985. "Fighting to win." In Peter Singer (ed.), *In Defense of Animals:* 194-208. New York: Harper & Row.

Spretnak, Charlene, ed. 1982. *The Politics of Women's Spirituality: Essays on the Rise of Spiritual Power Within the Feminist Movement.* New York: Anchor.

Sreberny-Mohammadi, Annabelle. 1990. "Small Media for a Big Revolution." *International Journal of Politics, Culture, and Society* 3: 341-71.

St. James, Warren D. 1958. *The National Association for the Advancement of Colored People: A Case Study in Pressure Groups.* New York: Exposition Press.

Staggenborg, Suzanne. 1991. *The Pro-Choice Movement: Organization and Activism In the Abortion Conflict.* New York: Oxford University Press.

——. 1989. "Stability and Innovation in the Women's Movement: A Comparison of Two Movement Organizations." *Social Problems* 36:75-92.

——. 1988. "Consequences of Professionalization and Formalization in the Pro-Choice Movement." *American Sociological Review* 53:585-606.

——. 1986. "Coalition Work in the Pro-Choice Movement: Organizational and Environmental Opportunities and Obstacles." *Social Problems* 33:374-90.

——. 1985. *Patterns of Collective Action in the Abortion Conflict: An Organizational Analysis of the Pro-Choice Movement.* Ph.D. diss., Northwestern University.

Stark, R. 1987. "How new religions succeed: A theoretical model." Pp. 11-29 in D. Bromley and P. Hammond (Eds.), *The Future of New Religious Movements.* Macon, GA: Mercer University Press.

Stark, R. and W. Bainbridge. 1985. *The Future of Religion: Secularization, Revival and Cult Formation.* Berkeley: University of California Press.

——. 1980. "Networks of Faith: Interpersonal Bonds and Recruitment to Cults and Sects." *American Journal of Sociology* 85:1376-85.

Stedman-Jones, Gareth. 1983. "Rethinking Chartism." Pp. 90-178 in *Languages of Class: Studies in English Working Class History.* Cambridge: Cambridge University Press.

Stegner, Wallace. 1949. "The Radio Priest and His Flock." In Isabell Leighton (ed.), *The Aspirin Age, 1919-1941.* New York: Simon and Schuster.

Stein, Arlene, and Ken Plummer. 1994. " 'I can't even think straight': 'Queer' theory and the missing sexual revolution in sociology." *Sociological Theory* 12:178-187.

Stempel, John D. 1981. *Inside the Iranian Revolution.* Bloomington, IN: Indiana University Press.

Stepan, Alfred. 1985. "State power and the strength of civil society in the southern cone of Latin America." In Peter Evans, Dietrich Rueschemeyer, and Theda Skocpol (eds.), *Bringing the State Back In:* 317-343. Cambridge: Cambridge University Press.

Stephan, Karen H. and G. Edward Stephan. 1973. "Religion and the Survival of Utopian Communities." *Journal for the Scientific Study of Religion* 12:89-100.

Stinchcombe, Arthur L. 1987. "Review of the Contentious French." *American Journal of Sociology* 93: 1248-49.

——. 1986. "Milieu and structure updated." *Theory and Society* 15: 901-13.

——. 1968. *Constructing Social Theories.* New York: Harcourt, Brace and World.

Stinson, Thomas F. and Jerome M. Stam. 1976. "Toward an economic model of volunteerism: the case of participation in local government." *Journal of Voluntary Action Research* 5:52-60.

Stokes, Randall and John P. Hewitt. 1976. "Aligning Actions." *American Sociological Review* 41:839-49.

Stone, L. 1972. *The Causes of the English Revolution, 1529-1642.* New York: Harper and Row.

Stone, W. G. 1982. *The Hate Factory.* Agoura, CA: Paisano.

Stouffer, Samuel A. 1955. *Communism, Conformity, and Civil Liberties.* New York: Wiley.

Stover, John F. 1961. *American Railroads.* Chicago: University of Chicago Press.

Straus, R. 1976. "Changing oneself: Seekers and the creative transformation of life experience." Pp. 252-272 in J. Lofland, *Doing Social Life.* New York: John Wiley.

Stryker, Sheldon. 1981. "Symbolic Interactionism: Themes and Variations." Pp. 3-29 in *Social Psychology: Sociological Perspectives,* edited by Morris Rosenberg and Ralph H. Turner. New York: Basic.

——. 1968. "Identity Salience and Role Performance: The Relevance of Symbolic Interaction Theory for Family Research." *Journal of Marriage and the Family* 30:558-64.

Stryker, Sheldon and Avi Gottlieb. 1981. "Attribution Theory and Symbolic Interactionism: A Comparison." Pp. 425-58 in *New Directions in Attribution Research,* Vol. 3. Edited by John H. Harvey, William Ickes, and Robert F. Kidd. Hillsdale, NJ: Erlbaum.

Student Nonviolent Coordinating Committee. 1960. *The Student Voice.* August.

——. N.d. "You can help support programs for SNCC." Mimeographed pamphlet. Martin Luther King Library and Archives, Atlanta, GA.

Studlar, Donley T. and I. McAllister. 1988. "Nationalism in Scotland and Wales: A Post-Industrial Phenomenon?" *Ethnic and Racial Studies* 11:4862.

Sullivan, William. 1981. *Mission to Iran.* New York: W.W. Norton.

Sutherland, S. L. 1981. *Patterns in Belief and Action: Measurement of Student Political Activism.* Toronto: University of Toronto Press.

Swafford, Michael. 1980 "Three parametric techniques for contingency table analysis: a nontechnical commentary." *American Sociological Review* 45:664-90.

Swidler, Ann. 1986. "Culture in Action: Symbols and Strategies." *American Sociological Review* 51:273-86.

Sykes, Gresham. 1958. *The Society of Captives: A Study of a Maximum Security Prison.* Princeton: Princeton University Press.

Tarde, Gabriel. 1969. *On Communication and Social Influence.* Chicago: Phoenix Books.

Tarrow, Sidney. 1994. *Power in Movement: Social Movements, Collective Action and Politics.* Cambridge, England: Cambridge University Press.

——. 1993. "Modular collective action and the rise of the social movement: Why the French Revolution was not enough." *Politics and Society* 21:69-90.

——. 1992. "Mentalities, Political Cultures, and Collective Action Frames: Constructing Meaning through Action." Pp. 174-202 in *Frontiers of Social Movement* Theory, edited by Aldon D. Morris and Carol McClurg Mueller. New Haven, Conn.: Yale University Press.

——. 1991a. "Kollektives handeln und politische gelegenheitsstruktur." *Kölner Zeitschrift für Soziologie und Sozialpsychologie* 43: 647-70.

——. 1991b. "Struggle, Politics and Reform: Collective Action, Social Movements and Cycles of Protest." Ithaca, NY: Western Societies Occasional Paper no. 21.

——. "The Phantom at the Opera: Political Parties and Social Movements of the 1960s and 1970s in Italy." Pp. 251-73 in *Challenging the Political Order: New Social and Political Movements in Western Democracies,* edited by R. J. Dalton and M. Kuechler. Cambridge, England: Polity Press.

——. 1989a. "Struggle, Politics and Reform: Collective Action, Social Movements and Cycles of Protest." Ithaca, NY: Western Societies Occasional Paper no. 21.

——. 1989b. *Democracy and Disorder: Protest and Politics in Italy 1965-1975.* Oxford, England: Clarendon Press.

——. 1988. "National Politics and Collective Action: Recent Theory and Research in Western Europe and the United States." *Annual Review of Sociology* 14:421-40.

——. 1983a. *Struggling to Reform: Social Movements and Policy Change during Cycles of Protest.* Ithaca, NY: Western Societies Occasional Paper no. 15.

——. 1983b. "Resource Mobilization and Cycles of Protest: Theoretical Reflections and Comparative Illustrations." Paper presented at the meetings of the American Sociological Association, Detroit.

——. 1978. *From Mobilization to Revolution.* Reading: Addison-Wesley.

Tarrow, S., L. Tilly, and R. Tilly. 1975. *The Rebellious Century: 1830-1930.* Cambridge, Mass.: Harvard University Press.

Taylor, D. 1975-1976. Private notes and personal communications.

Taylor, Ronald B. 1975. *Chavez and the Farm Workers.* Boston: Beacon.

Taylor, Verta. 1989a. "The Future of Feminism: A Social Movement Analysis." Pp. 473-90 in *Feminist Frontiers II,* edited by Laurel Richardson and Verta Taylor. New York: Random House.

——. 1989b. "Social Movement Continuity." *American Sociological Review* 54:761-75.

Taylor, Verta, and Leila J. Rupp. 1993. "Women's culture and lesbian feminist activism: A reconsideration of cultural feminism." *Signs* 19:32-61.

Taylor, Verta, and Nancy Whittier. 1994. "Cultures in conflict: Conceptualizing the cultural dimensions of political protest." In *Culture and Social Movements,* eds. Hank Johnston and Bert Klandermans.

——. 1993. "The New Feminist Movement." In *Feminist Frontiers III,* eds. Verta Taylor and Laurel Richardson. New York: McGraw Hill.

——. 1992a. "Collective Identity in Social Movement Communities: Lesbian Feminist Mobilization." In *Frontiers in Social Movement Theory*, edited by Aldon D. Morris and Carol McClurg Mueller, pp. 104-29. New Haven: Yale University Press.

——. 1992b. "Theoretical approaches to social movement culture: The culture of the women's movement." Paper presented at the Workshop on Culture and Social Movements, San Diego, CA.

Terdiman, Richard. 1985. *Discourse/Counter-Discourse: The Theory and Practice of Symbolic Resistance in Nineteenth-Century France.* Ithaca, N.Y.: Cornell University Press.

Therborn, Goran. 1989. " 'Pillarization' and 'Popular Movements,' Two Variants of Welfare State Capitalism: The Netherlands and Sweden." Pp. 192-241 in *The Comparative History of Public Policy,* edited by Francis G. Castles. Cambridge: Polity.

Thompson, Charles H. 1960. "The Present Status of the Negro Private and Church-related College." *Journal of Negro Education* 29 (no. 3): 227-43.

Thompson, John B. 1990. *Ideology and Modern Culture.* Stanford, Calif.: Stanford University Press.

Thompson, Lorin A. 1971. "Urbanization, Occupational Shift and Economic Progress." In Rupert B. Vance and Nicholas J. Demerath, eds., *The Urban South.* Freeport, N.Y.: Books for Libraries Press, 38-53.

Thornton, Russell. 1981. "Demographic Antecedents of a Revitalization Movement: Population Change, Population Size, and the 1980 Ghost Dance." *American Sociological Review* 46: 88-96.

Thursz, Daniel. 1972. "Community participation: should past be prologue?" *American Behavioral Scientist* 15:733-48.

Tillock, H. and Denton E. Morrison. 1979. "Group size and contributions to collective action: an examination of Mancur Olson's theory using data from Zero Population Growth, Inc." Pp. 131-158 in Louis Kriesberg (ed.), *Research in Social Movements, Conflict and Change.* Vol. 4. Greenwich, CT: JAI Press.

Tilly, Charles. 1992. "Contentious repertoires in Great Britain, 1758-1834." New School for Social Research, Center for Studies of Social Change Working Paper (No. 141), June.

——. 1986a. *The Contentious French: Four Centuries of Popular Struggle.* Cambridge, MA: The Belknap Press of Harvard University Press.

——. 1986b. "European violence and collective action since 1700." *Social Research* 53:159-184.

——. 1983. "Speaking your mind without elections, surveys, or social movements." *Public Opinion Quarterly* 47:461-78.

——. 1979. "Repertoires of Contention in America and Britain, 1750-1830." Pp. 126-55 in *The Dynamics of Social Movements,* edited by M. Zald and J. McCarthy. Cambridge, MA: Winthrop.

——. 1978. *From Mobilization to Revolution.* New York: Random House.

——. 1977. "Getting It Together in Burgundy." *Theory and Society* 4: 479-504.

——. 1975. "Revolutions and collective violence." In F. I. Greenstein and N. Polsky (eds.), *Handbook of Political Science.* Reading, Ma.: Addison-Wesley.

——. 1964. *The Vendée.* Cambridge, Mass.: Harvard University Press.

Tilly, Charles, Louise Tilly, and Richard Tilly. 1975. *The Rebellious Century: 1830-1930.* Cambridge, Massachusetts: Harvard University Press.

Toch, Hans. 1965. *The Social Psychology of Social Movements.* Indianapolis, Ind.: Bobbs-Merrill.

Tocqueville, Alexis de. 1955. *The Old Regime and the French Revolution.* Translated by S. Gilbert. Garden City, NY: Doubleday Anchor.

——. 1942. *Souvenirs de Alexis de Tocqueville.* Paris: Gallimard.

Tombs, Robert. 1981. *The War Against Paris, 1871.* London: Cambridge University Press.

Tomlinson, T. M. 1970. "Ideological foundations for Negro action: a comparative analysis of militant and non-militant views of the Los Angeles riot." *Journal of Social Issues* 26:93-119.

Touraine, Alain. 1985. "An introduction to the study of social movements." *Social Research* 52:749-787.

——. 1981. *The Voice and the Eye: An Analysis of Social Movements.* Cambridge, MA: Cambridge University Press.

——. 1978. *La voix et le regard* (The Voice and the Eye). Paris, France: Seuil.

——. *The Post-Industrial Society.* New York: Random House.

Townsend National Weekly. 1938-1950. Chicago: Townsend National Weekly, Inc.

Traugott, Mark. 1985. *Armies of the Poor: Determinants of Political Orientation in the Parisian Insurrection of June 1848.* Princeton: Princeton University Press.

Travers, Eva. F. 1982. "Ideology and Political Participation among High School Students: Changes from 1970 to 1979." *Youth and Society* 13 (3): 327-52.

Travisano, Richard V. 1970. "Alternation and conversion as qualitatively different transformations." Pp. 594-606 in G. P. Stone and H. A. Farberman (eds.), *Social Psychology Through Symbolic Interaction.* Waltham, Mass.: Ginn-Blaisdell.

Trent, William J., Jr. 1960. "The Relative Adequacy of Sources of Income of Negro Church-related Schools." *Journal of Negro Education* 29 (no. 3): 356-67.

——. 1959. "Private Negro Colleges Since the Gaines Decision." *Journal of Eduational Sociology* 32 (February): 267-74.

Troeltsch, Ernst. 1932. *The Social Teachings of the Christian Churches.* 2 vols. New York: Macmillan.

Trotsky, Leon. 1959 (1932). *The History of the Russian Revolution,* edited by F. W. Dupre. New York: Doubleday.

Troy, Leo and Neil Sheflin. 1985. *U.S. Union Sourcebook.* West Orange, N.J.: Industrial Relations Data and Information Services.

Troyer, Ronald J. and Gerald E. Markle. 1983. *Cigarettes: The Battle over Smoking.* New Brunswick, NJ: Rutgers University Press.

Truman, David. 1951. *The Governmental Process.* New York; Knopf.

Tsebelis, George, and John Sprague. 1989. "Coercion and revolution: Variations on a predator-prey model." *Mathematical Computer Modeling* 12: 547-59.

Tucker, David M. 1975. *Black Pastors and Leaders, Memphis, 1819-1972*. Memphis: Memphis University Press.

Tucker, Kenneth H. 1991. "How New Are the New Social Movements?" *Theory, Culture and Society* 8:75-98.

Tull, Charles J. 1965. *Father Coughlin and the New Deal*. Syracuse, N.Y.: Syracuse University Press.

Tullock, Gordon. 1971. "The Paradox of Revolution." *Public Choice* 11:89-99.

Turk, Herman. 1970. "Interorganizational networks in urban society: initial perspectives and comparative research." *American Sociological Review* 35:1-20.

Turner, Ralph H. 1983. "Figure and Ground in the Analysis of Social Movements." *Symbolic Interaction* 6:175-81.

——. 1981. "Collective behavior and resource mobilization as approaches to social movements: Issues and continuities." Pp. 1-24 in Louis Kriesberg (ed.), *Research in Social Movements, Conflict and Change*. Vol. 4. Greenwich, CT: JAI Press.

——. 1970. "Determinants of social movement strategies." Pp. 145-64 in Tamotsu Shibutani (ed.), *Human Nature and Collective Behavior: Essays in Honor of Herbert Blumer*. Englewood Cliffs, NJ: PrenticeHall.

——. 1969a. "The public perception of protest." *American Sociological Review* 34:815-31.

——. 1969b. "The Theme of Contemporary Social Movements." *British Journal of Sociology* 20:390-405.

——. 1953. "The quest for universals in sociological research." *American Journal of Sociology* 18: 604-611.

Turner, Ralph H. and Lewis M. Killian. 1957, 1972, 1987. *Collective Behavior*. Englewood Cliffs, NJ: Prentice-Hall.

Twentieth-Century Fund Committee on Old Age Security. 1936. *The Townsend Crusade: An Impartial Review of the Townsend Movement and the Probable Effects of the Townsend Plan*. New York: Twentieth Century Fund.

Tygart, Clarence E. and Norman Holt. 1972. "Examining the Weinberg and Walker typology of student activists." *American Journal of Sociology* 77:957-66.

U.S. Bureau of the Census. 1975. *Historical Statistics of the United States: From Colonial Times to 1970*. Washington, D.C.: Government Printing Office.

——. 1962a. *Census of the Agriculture, 1959*. "Color, Race and Tenure of Farm Operator." Vol. 2, chapter 10. Washington, D.C.: U.S. Government Printing Office.

——. 1962b. *Current Population Reports,* Series P-25, no. 247 (April). Washington, D.C.: U.S. Government Printing Office.

——. 1961. *Census of the Population, 1960. General Population Characteristics, U.S. Summary*. Final Report PC (1)-1B. Washington, D.C.: U.S. Government Printing Office.

——. 1952. *Census of the Population, 1950*. Vol. 2. Washington, D.C.: U.S. Government Printing Office.

——. 1949. *Statistical Abstract of the United States, 1948*. Washington, D. C.: Government Printing Office.

——. 1948. *Statistical Abstract of the United States, 1947*. Washington, D. C.: Government Printing Office.

——. 1941. *Statistical Abstract of the United States, 1940*. Washington, D. C.: Government Printing Office.

——. 1938. *Statistical Abstract of the United States, 1937*. Washington, D. C.: Government Printing Office.

——. 1935. *Statistical Abstract of the United States, 1934*. Washington, D. C.: Government Printing Office.

——. 1932. *Statistical Abstract of the United States, 1931*. Washington, D. C.: Government Printing Office.

——. 1925. *Statistical Abstract of the United States, 1924*. Washington, D.C.: Government Printing Office.

U.S. Commission on Civil Rights. 1977. *Reviewing a Decade of School Desegregation 1966-1975*. Washington, D.C.: U.S. Government Printing Office.

U.S. Congress, House of Representatives. 1939. *Hearings Relative to the Social Security Act Amendments of 1939*, vols. 1-3. 76th Cong., 1st sess. Washington, D.C.: Government Printing Office.

——. 1936. *Hearings before the Select Committee Investigating Old-Age Pension Organizations*. 74th Cong., 2d sess., vols. 1 and 2. Washington, D.C.: Government Printing Office.

U.S. Congress, Senate. 1941. *Hearings before the Special Committee to Investigate the Old-Age Pension System*. 77th Cong., 1st sess. Washington, D.C.: Government Printing Office.

——. 1939. *Hearings before the Committee on Finance on H.R. 6635*. 76th Cong., 1st sess. Washington, D.C.: Government Printing Office.

U.S. Social Security Administration. 1950. "Old-Age Assistance." *Social Security Bulletin* 13 (November): 12.

——. 1938. "Social Types of Public Assistance." *Social Security Bulletin* 1 (March): 44-50.

——. 1937. *Social Security in America: The Factual Background of the Social Security Act as Summarized from Staff Reports to the Committee on Economic Security*. Washington, D.C.: Government Printing Office.

Urwin, Derek W. 1982. "Territorial Structures and Political Development in the United Kingdom." Pp. 19-73 in *The Politics of Territorial Identity: Studies in European Regionalism*, edited by S. Rokkan and D.W. Urwin. London: Sage.

Useem, Bert. 1980. "Solidarity model, breakdown model, and the Boston anti-busing movement." *American Sociological Review* 45:357-69.

Useem, Bert and Peter A. Kimball. 1987. "A theory of prison riots." *Theory of Society* 16:87-122.

Useem, Bert and Mayer N. Zald. 1982. "From Pressure Group to Social Movement: Organizational Dilemmas of the Effort to Promote Nuclear Power." *Social Problems* 30:144-56.

Useem, Michael. 1975. *Protest Movements in America*. Indianapolis: Bobbs-Merrill.

Uzzell, David L. 1980. "Conflicting explanations of participatory group membership." *Journal of Voluntary Action Research* 9:203-210.

Valenzuela, Maria Elena. 1987. *La Mujer en Chile Militar: Todas Ibamos a Ser Reinas*. Santiago: Ediciónes Chile y America.

Valocchi, Steve. 1990. "The Unemployed Workers Movement of the 1930s: A Reexamination of the Piven and Cloward Thesis." *Social Problems* 37:191-205.

van den Berghe, Pierre L. 1981. *The Ethnic Phenomenon*. New York: Elsevier.

——. 1967. *Race and Racism: A Comparative Perspective*. New York: Wiley.

Vander Zanden, James W. 1961. *Race Relations in Transition: The Segregation Crisis in the South*. New York: Random House.

Vedlitz, Arnold and Eric P. Veblen. 1980. "Voting and contacting: two forms of political participation in a suburban community." *Urban Affairs Quarterly* 16:31-48.

Verba, Sidney and Norman M. Nie. 1972. *Participation in America: Political Democracy and Social Equality.* New York: Harper.

Viguerie, Richard A. 1980. *The New Right: We Are Ready to Lead.* Falls Church, VA: The Viguerie Company.

Ville de Paris. 1872. *Bulletin de statistique municipale, 1871* (Bulletin of Municipal Statistics, 1871). Paris: Imprimerie Municipale.

Volosinov, V. N. 1986. *Marxism and the Philosophy of Language,* trans. Ladislav Matejka and R. Titunik. Cambridge, Mass.: Harvard University Press.

Volpe, Vernon L. 1990. *Forlorn Hope of Freedom: The Liberty Party in the Old Northwest, 1838-1848.* Kent, Ohio: Kent State University Press.

Von Eschen, Donald, Jerome Kirk, and Maurice Pinard. 1971. "The Organizational Substructure of Disorderly Politics." *Social Forces* 49:529-44.

——. 1969. "The disintegration of the Negro nonviolent movement." *Journal of Peace Research* 3:216-34.

Wade, Richard C. 1954. "The Negro in Cincinnati, 1800-1830." *Journal of Negro History* 39:43-57.

Wade, Nicholas. 1976. "Animal rights: NIH cat sex study brings grief to New York museum." *Science* 194:162-166.

Wagner-Pacifici, Robin. 1986. *The Moro Morality Play: Terrorism as Social Drama.* Chicago: University of Chicago Press.

Walker, Rev. Waytt Tee. 1978. Interview. New York City, New York. September 29.

——. 1963. "Albany: failure or first step?" *New South* 18 (June):3-8.

Wallace, Michael and J. Craig Jenkins. 1995. "The New Class and the Ideological Bases of Political Protest: A Comparison of Eight Western Democracies." In *The Politics of Social Protest: Comparative Perspectives on States and Social Movements,* edited by J. C. Jenkins and B. Klandermans. Minneapolis, MN: University of Minnesota Press.

Waller, Douglas. 1987. *Congress and the Nuclear Freeze.* Amherst: University of Massachusetts Press.

Wallis, Roy. 1984. *The Elementary Forms of the New Religious Life.* London: Routledge & Kegan Paul.

——. 1982. *Millennialism and Charisma.* Belfast: The Queen's University.

——. 1979. *Salvation and Protest.* London: Francis Pinter.

——. 1977. *The Road to Total Freedom.* New York: Columbia University Press.

Wallis, R. and S. Bruce. 1986. *Sociological Theory, Religion and Collective Action.* Belfast: The Queen's University.

——. 1982. "Networks and Clockwork." *Sociology* 16:102-107.

Walsh, Edward J. 1989. *Democracy in the Shadows: Citizen Mobilization in the Wake of the Accident at Three Mile Island.* Westport, CT: Greenwood.

——. 1986. "The role of target vulnerabilities in high-technology protest movements: The nuclear establishment at Three Mile Island." *Sociological Forum* 1:199-218.

——. 1983. "Three Mile Island: meltdown of democracy?" *Bulletin of the Atomic Scientists* 39:57-60.

——. 1981. "Resource mobilization and citizen protest in communities around Three Mile Island." *Social Problems* 29:1-21.

——. 1978. "Mobilization theory vis-a-vis a mobilization process: the case of the United Farm Workers' movement." Pp. 155-77 in Louis Kriesberg (ed.), *Research in Social Movements, Conflicts and Change.* Vol. 1. Greenwich, CT: JAI Press.

Walsh, Edward J. and Rex H. Warland. 1983. "Social Movement Involvement in the Wake of a Nuclear Accident: Activists and Free Riders in the TMI Area." *American Sociological Review* 48: 764-80.

Walton, John and Charles Ragin. 1990. "Global and national sources of political protest: Third world responses to the debt crisis." *American Sociological Review* 55:876-890.

Walton, Norman W. 1956. "The walking city. a history of the Montgomery boycott." *The Negro History Bulletin* 20 (October, November):17-20.

Walzer, Michael. 1980. *Radical Principles: Reflections of an Unreconstructed Democrat.* New York: Basic Books.

Wandersman, Abraham. 1981. "A framework of participation in community organizations." *Journal of Applied Behavioral Science* 17:27-58.

Ward, Kathryn B. and Rachel A. Rosenfeld. 1987. "The Contemporary Women's Movement: An Empirical Test of Competition Theory." Unpublished revision of a paper presented at the 1986 annual meeting of the American Sociological Association, 30 Aug.-3 Sept., New York.

Warren, Donald I. 1975. *Black Neighborhoods: An Assessment of Community Power.* Ann Arbor: The University of Michigan Press.

——. 1974. "The linkage between neighborhood and voluntary association patterns: A comparison of black and white urban populations." *Journal of Voluntary Action Research* 3:1-17.

Warren, Rachelle B. and Donald I. Warren. 1977. *The Neighborhood Organizer's Handbook.* Notre Dame, IN: The University of Notre Dame Press.

Washburn, Philo. 1982 *Political Sociology: Approaches, Concepts, Hypotheses.* Englewood Cliffs, NJ: Prentice-Hall.

Washington, Joseph R., Jr. 1964. *Black Religion, the Negro and Christianity in the United States.* Boston: Beacon Press.

Watters, Pat. 1971. Down to Now: Reflections on the Southern Civil Rights Movement. New York: Pantheon.

Weber, Max. [1922] 1977. *Economy and Society,* edited by Guenther Roth and Claus Wittich. Berkeley: University of California Press.

Wechsler, James A. 1935. *Revolt on the Campus.* New York: Covici, Friede.

Weede, Erich. 1987. "Some New Evidence on Correlates of Political Violence: Income Inequality, Regime Repressiveness, and Economic Development." *European Sociological Review* 3:97-108.

——. 1977. *Hypothesen, Gleichungen und Daten.* Athenäum-Verlag.

Weeks, Jeffrey. 1991. *Against Nature: Essays on History, Sexuality and Identity.* London: Rivers Oram Press.

Wehr, Paul. 1986. "Nuclear Pacifism as Collective Action." *Journal of Peace Research* 22:103-13.

Weigand, Kate. 1993. "Vanguards of women's liberation: The Old Left and the continuity of the women's movement in the U.S., 1945-1970." Paper presented at "Toward a History of the 1960s" conference, State Historical Society of Wisconsin, Madison, April 29.

Weinbaum, Paul O. 1979. *Mobs and Demagogues: The New York Response to Collective Violence in the Early Nineteenth Century.* Ann Arbor, Mich.: UMI Research Press.

Weinberg, Martin S., and Colin J. Williams. 1974. *Male Homosexuals: Their Problems and Adaptations.* New York: Penguin.

Weir, Margaret, Ann Shola Orloff, and Theda Skocpol. 1988. "Introduction: Understanding American Social Politics." Pp. 3-29 in *The Politics of Social Policy in the United States,* edited by M. Weir, A. Orloff, and T. Skocpol. Princeton. N.J.: Princeton University Press.

Weisenburger, Francis Phelps. 1934. "A Life of Charles Hammond: The First Great Journalist of the Old Northwest." *Ohio Archeological and Historical Quarterly* 43:337-427.

Westby, David L. 1976. *The Clouded Vision: The Student Movement in the United States in the 1960s.* London: Associated University Press.

Whalen, Jack and Richard Flacks. 1989. *Beyond the Barricades: The Sixties Generation Grows Up.* Philadelphia: Temple University Press.

——. 1987. *Beyond the Barricades.* Philadelphia: Temple.

White, Harrison C., Scott A. Boorman. and Ronald L. Breiger. 1976. "Social Structure from Multiple Networks. 1. Blockmodels of Roles and Positions." *American Journal of Sociology* 81:730-80.

White, James W. 1970. *The Sokagakkai and Mass Society.* Stanford: Stanford University Press.

White, Robert W. 1989. "From Peaceful Protest to Guerilla War: Micromobilization of the Provisional Irish Republican Army." *American Journal of Sociology* 94:1277-1302.

White, Robert. 1988. "Commitment. Efficacy, and Personal Sacrifice Among Irish Republicans." *Journal of Political and Military Sociology* 16:77-90.

Whittier, Nancy E. 1995. *Feminist Generations: The Persistence of the Radical Women's Movement.* Philadelphia: Temple University Press.

——. 1994a. "Turning it over: Personnel change in the Columbus, Ohio women's movement, 1969-1984." In *Feminist Organizations: Harvest of the New Women's Movement,* eds. Myra Marx Ferree and Patricia Yancey Martin.

——. 1994b. *Feminist Generations: The Persistence of the Radical Women's Movement.* Philadelphia: Temple.

——. 1991. *Feminists in the post-feminist age: Collective identity and the persistence of the women's movement.* Ph.D. dissertation, Ohio State University.

Whyte, Martin. 1983. "On Studying China at a Distance." Pp. 63-80 in *The Social Sciences and Fieldwork in China,* edited by A. Thurston and B. Pasternak. Boulder, CO: Westview.

Wicker, Allan. 1969. "Attitudes vs. Action: The Relationship of Verbal and Overt Behavioral Responses to Attitude Objects." *Journal of Social Issues* 25:41-78.

Williams, Hosea. 1978. Interview. Atlanta, Georgia. September 22.

Williams, Robin M. 1970. *American Society: A Sociological Interpretation.* New York: Alfred A. Knopf.

Wilson, F.L. 1987. *Interest-group Politics in France.* Cambridge University Press.

Wilson, James Q. 1973. *Political Organizations.* New York: Basic.

——. 1961. "The strategy of protest: problems of Negro civil action." *Journal of Conflict Resolution* 5:291-303.

Wilson, John. 1978. *Religion in American Society.* Englewood Cliffs, N.J.: Prentice-Hall.

——. 1976 "Mobilizing people for collective political action." *Journal of Political and Military Sociology* 4:187-202.

——. 1973. *Introduction to Social Movements.* New York: Basic Books.

Wilson, Kenneth L. and Anthony M. Orum. 1976. "Mobilizing people for collective political action." *Journal of Political and Military Sociology* 4:187-202.

Wilson, William Julius. 1980. *The Declining Significance of Race: Blacks and Changing American Institutions.* 2d ed. Chicago: The University of Chicago Press.

Wiltfang, Greg, and Doug McAdam. 1991. "Distinguishing Cost and Risk in Sanctuary Activism." *Social Forces* 69:987-1010.

Winn, Peter. 1986. *Weavers of Revolution.* Oxford: Oxford University Press.

Wittner, Lawrence. 1984. *Rebels Against War: The American Peace Movement, 1933-83.* Philadelphia: Temple.

Woelfel, Joseph, John Woelfel, James Gillham and Thomas McPhail. 1974. "Political radicalization as a communication process." *Communication Research* 1:243-63.

Wolfe, T. 1976. *Mauve Gloves & Madmen, Clutter & Vine.* New York: Farrar, Straus & Giroux.

Wolff, Miles. 1970. *Lunch at the Five and Ten.* New York: Stien and Day.

Wolters, Raymond. 1970. *Negroes and the Great Depression.* Westport, Conn.: Greenwood.

Wood, James L., and Maurice Jackson. 1982. *Social Movements: Development, Participation, and Dynamics.* Belmont, CA: Wadsworth.

Wood, Michael and Michael Hughes. 1984. "The Moral Basis of Moral Reform: Status Discontent vs. Culture and Socialization as Explanations of Anti-Pornography Social Movement Adherence." *American Sociological Review* 49:86-99.

Woods, James. 1993. *The Corporate Closet: The Professional Lives of Gay Men In America.* New York: Free Press.

Woodson, Carter G. 1916. "The Negroes of Cincinnati prior to the Civil War." *Journal of Negro History* 1:122.

Wriggins, W. Howard. 1969. *The Ruler's Imperative.* New York: Columbia University Press.

Wright, C. R. and H. Hyman. 1958. "Voluntary association memberships of American adults: evidence from national sample surveys." *American Sociological Review* 23:284-94.

Wright, Stephen J. 1960. "The Negro College in America." *Harvard Educational Review* 30 (Summer): 280-97.

Wright, S. 1988. "Leaving new religious movements: Issues, theory, and research." Pp. 143-65 in D. Bromley (Ed.), *Falling from the Faith, Causes and Consequences of Religious Apostasy.* Newbury Park, CA: Sage.

——. 1984. "Post involvement attitudes of voluntary defectors from controversial new religious movements." *Journal for the Scientific Study of Religion* 23: 172-82.

——. 1983a. "Defection from new religious movements: A test of some theoretical propositions." Pp. 106-21 in D.

Bromley and J. Richardson (Eds.), *The Brainwashing/Deprogramming Controversy: Sociological, Psychological, Legal and Historical Perspectives.* New York: Edwin Mellen.

——. 1983b. *A Sociological Study of Defection from Controversial New Religious Movements.* Ph.D. dissertation, Ann Arbor, MI: University Microfilms International.

Wrong, Dennis. 1961. "The oversocialized conception of man in modern sociology." *American Sociological Review* 26:183-93.

Wuthnow, Robert, ed. 1992. *Vocabularies of Public Life: Empirical Essays in Symbolic Structure.* New York: Routledge.

——. 1989. *Communities of Discourse: Ideology and Social Structure in the Reformation, the Enlightenment, and European Socialism.* Cambridge, Mass.: Harvard University Press.

——. 1987. *Meaning and Moral Order.* Berkeley: University of California.

Wyatt-Brown, Bertram. 1965. "The Abolitionists' Postal Campaign of 1835." *Journal of Negro History* 50:227-38.

Wynia, Gary W. 1990. *The Politics of Latin American Development.* Cambridge: Cambridge University Press.

Yazdî, Ibrâhîm. 1984. *Âkharîn Talâsh'hâ dar Âkharîn Rûz'hâ* (The Final Efforts in the Final Days). Tehran, Iran: Intishârât-i Qalam.

Young, Andrew. 1977. Interview with Andrew Young. Pp. 472-80 in Howell Raines (ed.), *My Soul is Rested.* New York: Bantam.

Young, Ruth C. 1988. "Is Population Ecology a Useful Paradigm for the Study of Organizations?" *American Journal of Sociology* 94:1-24.

Zabih, Sepehr. 1988. *The Iranian Military in Revolution and War.* New York: Routledge.

Zablocki, Benjamin. 1980. *Alienation and Charisma: A Study of Contemporary American Communes.* New York: Free Press.

——. 1971. *The Joyful Community.* Baltimore, Maryland: Penguin Books.

Zald, Mayer N. and Roberta Ash. 1966. "Social Movement Organizations: Growth, Decay and Change." *Social Forces* 44:327-41.

Zald, Mayer N., and Michael A. Berger. 1978. "Social movements in organizations: coup d'etat, insurgency, and mass movements." American Journal of Sociology *83:823-61.*

——. 1987a. "Religious groups as crucibles of social movements." Pp. 67-95 in M. Zald and J. McCarthy (Eds.), *Social Movements in an Organizational Society.* New Brunswick, NJ: Transaction Books.

——. 1987b. "Introduction, the infrastructure of movements." Pp. 45-47 in M. Zald and J. McCarthy (Eds.), *Social Movements in an Organizational Society.* New Brunswick, NJ: Transaction Books.

——. 1987c. "Social movement industries: Conflict and cooperation among SMOs." In *Social Movements in an Organizational Society,* eds. Mayer N. Zald and John D. McCarthy, 161-180. New Brunswick, N.J.: Transaction.

——. 1980. "Social Movement Industries: Cooperation and Conflict Amongst Social Movement Organizations." *Research in Social Movements, Conflict and Change* 3:1-20.

—— (eds.). 1979. *The Dynamics of Social Movements: Resource Mobilization, Social Control, and Tactics.* Cambridge, Mass.: Winthrop Publishers.

Zald, Mayer N. and Bert Useem. 1987. "Movement and countermovement interaction: Mobilization, tactics, and state involvement." In Mayer N. Zald and John D. McCarthy (eds.), *Social Movements in an Organizational Society:* 247-272. New Brunswick, NJ: Transaction Books.

——. 1982. "Movement and countermovement: loosely coupled interaction." Paper presented at Annual Meetings of the American Sociological Association, San Francisco, CA, September 8, 1982.

Zeitlin, Maurice. 1966. "Economic Insecurity and the Political Attitudes of Cuban Workers." *American Sociological Review* 31:35-50.

Zetterberg, Hans L. 1965. *On Theory and Verification in Sociology* (2nd ed.). Bedminster.

Zijderveld, Anton C. 1979. *On Cliches: The Supersedure of Meaning by Function in Modernity.* London: Routledge and Kegan Paul.

Zinn, Howard. 1965. *SNCC: The New Abolitionists.* Boston: Beacon Press.

——. 1962. *Albany, a study in national responsibility.* Atlanta: Southern Regional Council.

Zolberg, Aristide R. 1972. "Moments of madness." *Politics and Society* (Winter): 183-207.

Zurcher, Louis A. 1977. *The Mutable Self.* Beverly Hills, Calif.: Sage.

Zurcher, Louis A., Jr., and R. George Kirkpatrick. 1976. *Citizens for Decency: Antipornography Crusades as Status Defense.* Austin: University of Texas Press.

Zurcher, Louis A. and David A. Snow. 1981. "Collective Behavior: Social Movements." Pp. 447-82 in *Social Psychology, Social Perspectives,* edited by Morris Rosenberg and Ralph H. Turner. New York: Basic Books.

Zygmunt, Joseph. 1972. "Movements and Motives: Some Unresolved Issues in the Psychology of Social Movements." *Human Relations* 25:449-67.

Zysman, J. 1983. *Governments, Markets, and Growth.* Ithaca NY: Cornell University Press. ✦

Index